第十一届中国城市住宅研讨会论文集

Proceedings of The 11th China Urban Housing Conference

绿色·低碳：
新型城镇化下的可持续人居环境建设

GREEN · LOW CARBON :
THE SUSTAINABLE LIVING ENVIRONMENT AND
CONSTRUCTION IN MODERN URBANIZATION

主　编：邹经宇　李秉仁　许溶烈
　　　　李　迅　林　拓

Chief Editor: Tsou Jin-Yeu, Li Bingren, Xu Ronglie,
Li Xun, Lin Tuo

中国建筑工业出版社
CHINA ARCHITECTURE & BUILDING PRESS

图书在版编目(CIP)数据

第十一届中国城市住宅研讨会论文集　绿色·低碳：新型城镇化下的可持续人居环境建设/邹经宇等主编.
北京：中国建筑工业出版社，2015.7
ISBN 978-7-112-18253-4

Ⅰ.①第…　Ⅱ.①邹…　Ⅲ.①城市-住宅建设-中国-学术会议-文集　Ⅳ.①F299.233.5-53

中国版本图书馆 CIP 数据核字(2015)第 141463 号

责任编辑：王莉慧　白玉美　率　琦
责任校对：姜小莲　党　蕾

第十一届中国城市住宅研讨会论文集
绿色·低碳：新型城镇化下的可持续人居环境建设
主编：邹经宇　李秉仁　许溶烈　李　迅　林　拓
*
中国建筑工业出版社出版、发行(北京西郊百万庄)
各地新华书店、建筑书店经销
北 京 红 光 制 版 公 司 制 版
北京市密东印刷有限公司印刷
*
开本：880×1230 毫米　1/16　印张：48¼　字数：1459 千字
2015 年 7 月第一版　　2015 年 7 月第一次印刷
定价：200.00 元
ISBN 978-7-112-18253-4
　　　　(27509)

Ms. Liang Yuchi   Research Assistant, Center for Housing Innovations, Chinese University of Hong Kong

主办单位　Organizer

香港中文大学中国城市住宅研究中心
Center for Housing Innovations, Chinese University of Hong Kong

支持单位　Supporting Organizers

中华人民共和国住房和城乡建设部专家委员会
Committee of Experts, Ministry of Housing and Urban-Rural Development, PRC

中华人民共和国住房和城乡建设部科学技术委员会
Committee of Science and Technology, Ministry of Housing and Urban-Rural Development, PRC

承办单位　Executive Organizer

青岛市城乡建设委员会
Qingdao Municipal Commission of Urban-Rural Development, the People's Government of Qingdao, PRC

当地支持单位　Local Supporting Organizer

青岛市科学技术协会
Qingdao Association for Science and Technology

中国城市住宅研讨会论文评审办法

Paper Review Method of the 11th China Urban Housing Conference

1. 邀请国内外城市规划、城市设计、建筑设计，建筑技术、房地产、城乡发展政策、空间规划等领域的知名学者，具有长期实践经验的产业界专家，担任本届中国城市住宅研讨会论文评审委员会委员。

2. 所有作者要求在截止日期前，于线上论文提交系统提交800～1000字的摘要，并另附一份参考文献列表。由中国城市住宅研讨会秘书处将所有摘要及相应的参考文献列表，按研究领域与方向进行分类，再以匿名方式发送给三位（或以上）论文评审委员，进行评审。

3. 论文评审委员需在截止日期前返回填妥的中国城市住宅研讨会论文评分表，并根据论文的贡献性、接纳性，分别给出0～10之间的某一数字作为该论文摘要的贡献评分、接纳评分，并且给予必要的评语。所有提交的论文摘要，将获得3位以上论文评审委员的评分及批语。

4. 中国城市住宅研讨会秘书处在收齐所有论文摘要评审结果后，将每篇论文的所有分数加以统计，并分别取贡献评分、接纳评分的平均值作为贡献评分结果、接纳评分结果，进行由高到低排序。完成初步评分统计后，上报中国城市住宅研讨会学术委员会。

5. 中国城市住宅研讨会学术委员会在综合考虑贡献评分结果、接纳评分结果、评委评语及评分详情基础上，确认获得录取的中国城市住宅研讨会论文集的论文摘要。

6. 中国城市住宅研讨会秘书处根据中国城市住宅研讨会学术委员会有关论文摘要录取决议，以电子邮件形式向被录取摘要的论文作者发出录取通知，邀请撰写论文全文，并于论文全文提交截止日期前提交于线上系统。最后将被录取的论文摘要标题、论文编号公布于本届研讨会网站。

第十一届中国城市住宅研讨会论文评审委员会

Review Panel of the 11th China Urban Housing Conference

（以英文姓氏排序 In alphabetical order of last name）

鲍莉　教授　　　　　　　　东南大学建筑学院
Prof. Bao Li　　　　　　　School of Architecture, Southeast University

Henco Bekkering　教授　　代尔夫特理工大学
Prof. Henco Bekkering　　Delft University of Technology

CAIRNS Stephen　教授　　新加坡-苏黎世联邦理工学院未来城市实验室
Prof. Stephen Cairns　　　Singapore-ETH Centre, Future Cities Laboratory

陈振康　先生　　　　　　　香港中文大学中国城市住宅研究中心
Mr. Chan Chun Hong, Felix　Center for Housing Innovations, Chinese University of Hong Kong

郑炳鸿　教授　　　　　　　香港中文大学建筑学院
Prof. Chang Ping Hung Wallace　School of Architecture, Chinese University of Hong Kong

车伍　教授　　　　　　　　北京建筑大学
Prof. Che Wu　　　　　　　Beijing University of Civil Engineering and Architecture

陈彦仲　教授　　　　　　　成功大学都市计划学系
Prof. Chen Yen-Jong　　　Department of Urban Planning, Cheng Kung University

周家明　教授　　　　　　　香港中文大学中国城市住宅研究中心
Prof. Chow Ka Ming, Benny　Center for Housing Innovations, Chinese University of Hong Kong

丁沃沃　教授　　　　　　　南京大学建筑与城市规划学院
Prof. Ding Wowo　　　　　School of Architecture and Urban Planning, Nanjing University

Dokonal Wolfgang　教授　　格拉兹技术大学城市规划学系
Prof. Wolfgang Dokonal　　Department for Urbanism, Graz University of Technolgy

Joachim Eble　教授　　　　Joachim Eble 建筑师事务所
Prof. Joachim Eble　　　　Joachim Eble Architektur

福田知弘　教授　　　　　　大阪大学
Prof. Fukuda Tomohiro　　　Osaka University

冯宜萱　女士　　　　　　　香港房屋委员会
Ms. Fung Yin Suen，Ada　　Hong Kong Housing Authority

王才强　教授　　　　　　　新加坡国立大学设计与环境学院
Prof. Heng Chye Kiang　　　School of Design and Environment，National University of Singapore

谢尚贤　教授　　　　　　　台湾大学土木工程学系
Prof. Hsieh Shang-Hsien　　Department of Civil Engineering，Taiwan University

黄一如　教授　　　　　　　同济大学建筑与城市规划学院
Prof. Huang Yiru　　　　　College of Architecture and Urban Planning，Tongji University

贾倍思　教授　　　　　　　香港大学建筑系
Prof. Jia Beisi　　　　　　Department of Architecture，Hong Kong University

姜中桥　女士　　　　　　　中华人民共和国住房和城乡建设部科技与产业化发展中心
Ms. Jiang Zhongqiao　　　　Center of Science and Technology of Construction Ministry of Housing and Urban-Rural Development. P. R. China

许麟济　先生　　　　　　　新加坡建设局国际开发署
Mr. Koh Linji　　　　　　Building and Construction Authority，Singapore

邝君尚　教授　　　　　　　香港科技大学土木及环境工程学系
Prof. Kuang Junshang　　　Department of Civil and Environmental Engineering，Hong Kong University of Science and Technology

刘少瑜　教授　　　　　　　新加坡国立大学设计与环境学院建筑系
Prof. Lau Siu Yu，Stephen　Department of Architecture，School of Design and Environment，National University of Singapore

李灿辉　教授　　　　　　　麻省理工学院城市研究与规划系
Prof. Lee Tunney F.　　　　Department of Urban Studies and Planning，MIT

梁以德　教授　　　　　　　中国绿色建筑与节能（香港）委员会
Prof. Leung Yee Tak，Andrew　China Green Building（Hong Kong）Council

李迅　教授
Prof. Li Xun

中国城市科学研究会
Chinese Society for Urban Studies

李彦颐　教授
Prof. Li Yen-Yi

台湾树德科技大学建筑与环境设计研究所
Graduate Institute of Architecture and Environmental
Design，Shu-te University

李振宇　教授
Prof. Li Zhenyu

同济大学建筑与城市规划学院
College of Architecture and Urban Planning，Tongji U-
niversity

林峰田　教授
Prof. Lin Feng-Tyan

成功大学城市规划学系
Department of Urban Planning，Cheng Kung University

郝琳　教授
Prof. Hao Lin

香港中文大学中国城市住宅研究中心
Center for Housing Innovations，Chinese University of
Hong Kong

林拓　教授
Prof. Lin Tuo

华东师范大学
East China Normal University

刘育东　教授
Prof. Liu Yu-Tung

亚洲大学
Asia University

马欣伯　博士
Dr. Ma Xinbo

中华人民共和国住房和城乡建设部科技与产业化发展中
心绿色建筑发展处
Section of Green Building Development，Center of Science and Technology of Construction Ministry of Housing and Urban-Rural Development. P. R. China

孟玟廷　教授
Prof. Maing Minjung

香港中文大学建筑学院
School of Architecture，Chinese University of Hong
Kong

毛其智　教授
Prof. Mao Qizhi

清华大学建筑学院
School of Architecture，Tsinghua University

Martin Waston　教授
Prof. Martin Waston

香港中文大学中国城市住宅研究中心
Center for Housing Innovations，Chinese University of
Hong Kong

Navvab Mojtaba　教授
Prof. Mojtaba Navvab

密歇根大学
University of Michigan

饶戎　教授　　　　　　　　　清华大学建筑学院
Prof. Rao Rong　　　　　　　School of Architecture，Tsinghua University

Riewe Roger　教授　　　　　　格拉兹技术大学建筑技术研究所
Prof. Roger Riewe　　　　　　Institute of Architecture Technology，Graz University of Technology，Austria

Jurgen Rosemann　教授　　　　新加坡国立大学
Prof. Jurgen Rosemann　　　　National University of Singapore

Gerhard Schmitt　教授　　　　苏黎世联邦理工学院
Prof. Gerhard Schmitt　　　　ETH Zürich

沈建法　教授　　　　　　　　香港中文大学地理与资源管理学系
Prof. Shen Jianfa　　　　　　Department of Geography and Resource Management，Chinese University of Hong Kong

沈杰　教授　　　　　　　　　浙江大学建筑学系
Prof. Shen Jie　　　　　　　Department of Architecture，Zhejiang University

宋凌　女士　　　　　　　　　中华人民共和国住房和城乡建设部科技与产业化发展中心绿色建筑发展处
Ms. Song Ling　　　　　　　Section of Green Building Development，Center of Science and Technology of Construction Ministry of Housing and Urban-Rural Development. P. R. China

苏瑛敏　教授　　　　　　　　台北科技大学建筑系
Prof. Su Ying-Min　　　　　　Department of Architecture，Taipei University of Technology

孙澄　教授　　　　　　　　　哈尔滨工业大学建筑学院
Prof. Sun Cheng　　　　　　School of Architecture，Harbin Institute of Technology

汤羽扬　教授　　　　　　　　北京建筑大学建筑遗产研究院
Prof. Tang Yuyang　　　　　　Academy of Architecture Heritage，Beijing University of Civil Engineering and Architecture

田恒德　教授　　　　　　　　香港中文大学建筑学院
Prof. Tieben Hendrik　　　　　School of Architecture，Chinese University of Hong Kong

邹经宇　教授　　　　　　　　香港中文大学中国城市住宅研究中心
Prof. Tsou Jin-Yeu　　　　　　Center for Housing Innovations，Chinese University of Hong Kong

邹克万　教授 　　　　　成功大学都市计划学系
Prof. Tsou Ko-Wan 　　 Department of Urban Planning, Cheng Kung University

吴光庭　教授 　　　　　成功大学建筑系
Prof. Wu Kwang-Tyng 　Department of Architecture, Cheng Kung University

吴志强　教授 　　　　　同济大学建筑与城市规划学院
Prof. Wu Zhiqiang 　　　College of Architecture and Urban Planning, Tongji University

徐腾芳　博士 　　　　　香港中文大学中国城市住宅研究中心
Dr. Xu Tengfang 　　　 Center for Housing Innovations, Chinese University of Hong Kong

杨建荣　教授 　　　　　上海市建科院（集团）有限公司建筑新技术研究所
Prof. Yang Jianrong 　　 Department of Building Innovation Technology, Shanghai Research Institute of Building Sciences (Group) Co., Ltd.

叶青　教授 　　　　　　深圳市建筑科学研究院股份有限公司
Prof. Ye Qing 　　　　 Shenzhen Institute of Building Research Co., Ltd

严汝州　先生 　　　　　香港房屋委员会
Mr. Yim Yuchau Stephen 　Hong Kong Housing Authority

于一凡　教授 　　　　　同济大学建筑与城市规划学院
Prof. Yu Yifan 　　　　 College of Architecture and Urban Planning, Tongji University

曾捷　教授 　　　　　　中国建筑科学研究院建筑设计院
Prof. Zeng Jie 　　　　 Architectural Design Institute, China Academy of Building Research

曾卫　教授 　　　　　　重庆大学建筑城规学院
Prof. Zeng Wei 　　　　 College of Architecture and Urban Planning, Chongqing University

詹庆明　教授 　　　　　武汉大学城市设计学院
Prof. Zhan Qingming 　　School of Urban Design at Wuhan University

张路峰　教授 　　　　　中国科学院大学建筑研究与设计中心
Prof. Zhang Lufeng 　　 Center of Architecture Research and Design, University of Chinese Academy of Science

张玉坤　教授 　　　　　天津大学建筑学院
Prof. Zhang Yukun 　　　School of Architecture, Tianjin University

序　言
Preface

　　中国是一个幅员辽阔、地大物博的国家。它无论从东西走向，还是南北走向来讲，都跨越了不同的地形地貌。这些自然地理特征不仅形成了资源禀赋的差异，也导致了建筑气候区的形成。同时，不同地域文化在历史进程中繁衍生息所形成的一些习俗、传统，也会对该地区的房屋形态有深远影响。基于这样的背景，导致了中国住房问题的复杂性和差异性，需要因地制宜地解决。因此，对于中国城市住房的研究，必须通过研讨交流的模式，集思广益，并借鉴国内外住房研究、科研及建设的成果和经验，结合地域自然、经济和人文特色，提出解决问题的办法。

　　也正因此，中国城市住宅研讨会每两年会在不同的城市举办，并以当时最具代表性的住房议题为主题，广开言路，集合海内外专家学者的智慧，推动中国住房的进步。学术会议不仅是引导专业领域学术研究方向的重要活动，更是被国际上广泛采用的一种重要的研究方法。通过这样一个平台，使业内人士可以了解当前专业领域的最新成果，同时还为与会学者、专业人士间交流以及学者间的合作创造机遇。中国城市住宅研讨会正是借鉴国际学术会议的经验，同时将与会团体扩展到产业界，致力于推动中国住房的研究和问题解决。然而不同于其他同领域国际学术会议所探讨的题目，具有普及性，中国住房问题有其时代性和地域性，这导致了此研究领域中的内容，必须进行具体问题具体分析，同时与时俱进，继而探索出适宜于特定环境、气候下住房问题的解决办法。

　　中国城市住宅研究中心（下文简称"住宅中心"）在原国家建设部（现为国家住房和城乡建设部）的支持下于1998年12月在部主楼301会议室成立，设于香港中文大学，并且同期举办了第一届中国城市住宅研讨会，由时任建设部部长的俞正声先生亲自主持，获得了许溶烈院士在内的多位专家亲临指导和支持。历届研讨会均遵循严格的匿名评审方式，由中国城市住宅研讨会论文评审委员会执行，确保每篇论文至少获得三位以上的评委打分，最终由中国城市住宅研讨会学术委员会讨论决定入选的论文名单。时至今日，研讨会已成功举办十届，获得了国内外专家学者的大力支持和热情参与，逐步成为住房领域的重要学术盛会之一，实为幸事。

　　于创办之日同时，中国城市住宅研究中心便以增进海峡两岸的交流合作为使命之一。风雨数载，住宅中心一直秉承此理念，通过每年于大陆及台湾举办建筑与城市规划领域的学术交流活动，增进海峡两岸学者、学生及专业人士的了解和合作契机。中国城市住宅研讨会作为住宅中心最重要的学术交流活动之一，也将永远是促进海峡两岸相关专业领域合作交流的平台，为推动中国住房的发展不懈努力。

　　当前中国的住宅产业发展日新月异，然而对住房建设的科学性、社会性和相关领域学科作交叉与综合探索的专门团队是相对稀少的。住房研究是从楼宇到社区，再到城市、社会的结合，资源分配的计划。本届中国城市住宅研讨会共收录了100余篇优秀的论文，涉及城市规划与设计、住房政策与发展、建筑技术与信息科技、住宅产业化、高密度人居环境建设、保障性住房建设、适老性人居环境建设等当前住房领域最重要的研究主题。从整体上看，围绕住房展开的社会、环境、人文及社区等相关跨学科研究的论文，所占比例超过了从建筑学角度探讨住房问题的论文。从此可看出，城市住房问题之复杂性与多元性已日益凸显，对于中国城市住房的研究，已不单单从住房建筑本身出发，而逐渐将其放置于更大的社会环境、文化环境和城市环境中，从不同的角度去审视。于此书出版发行之际，特为之撰序，希望各界专家不吝赐教，多多指点批评。

邹经宇

2015 年 6 月 23 日于香港

目　录
Table of Contents

包容性人居环境建设 ·················· 257
Inclusive Living Environment Development

专题一：社会与空间融合
Special Topic 1：Social and Spatial Integration

社会住宅与保障性住房建设 ································ 383
Social Housing and Affordable Housing Construction

城市与建筑：设计、更新及改造 ·········· 481
City and Building: Design, Renew and Reconstruction

专题一：城市更新与建筑改造
Special Topic 1: Urban Renew and Building Reconstruction

绿色建筑与建筑技术 ·················· 587

Green Building and Building Technologies

专题一：绿色建筑与建筑节能
Special Topic 1: Green Building and Energy Conservation

住宅产业化 ·· 711
Housing Industrialization

特 邀 论 文
Invited Paper

Quality Transcends Time:
Decoding of 21ST Century Public Housing Development in Hong Kong

Fung Yin suen, Ada JP
[Hong Kong Housing Authority, Deputy Director of
Housing (Development & Construction)]

Abstract: Hong Kong Housing Authority (HA) has been providing affordable, safe and comfortable public rental housing in meeting the needs of the low-income families.

HA cares for people, as well as the environment, and makes the best and sustainable use of tight resources on all fronts. We introduce the Performance Assessment Scoring System to measure contractors' performance more objectively and with transparency. Embracing a caring attitude to foster social, economic and environmental sustainability, we adopt passive design to create quality homes for our residents in a green and healthy living environment. We establish the Modular Flat Design which has been optimized to strike a better balance amongst various factors including valuable land resources, buildability, cost effectiveness, user-friendliness, safe and healthy living for people. HA has taken proactive move in applying Building Information Modeling (BIM) to improve design quality, production efficiency and sustainability in design and construction. To enhance social sustainability, we adopt people-oriented design approach and organize post completion review workshop. We also conduct resident survey for all newly completed projects to gauge residents' satisfaction level on the design and provisions of the estates in which they live. This paper highlights our key features essential in the delivery of quality public housing in the 21st century.

Keywords: Quality public housing, Modular flat design, Performance assessment scoring system, Building information modeling, Resident survey

1 Introduction

The Hong Kong Housing Authority (HA) develops and implements one of the world's largest public housing programme to help low-income families with housing needs gain access to affordable housing[1]. With this mission, we plan, build, manage and maintain different types of public housing to meet the needs of our customers in a proactive and caring manner, ensure cost-effective and rational use of public resources in service delivery and allocation of housing assistance in an open and equitable manner, and maintain a competent, dedicated and performance-oriented team. In addition to the vision and mission, we also insist on our four core values (4C), those are - Caring, Customer-focused, Creative and Committed.

2 Quality Management and Performance Assessment

HA has been operating as a value and quality driven organization underpinned by the core value of 4C.

2.1 Quality Management

HA has established, documented, implemented and maintained a quality management system and continually improves its effectiveness in accordance with the ISO 9001: 2008 Standard. All

3

processes of new works development are monitored, measured, and analyzed to demonstrate conformity of the services provided with the Quality Management System.

2. 2 Performance Assessment Scoring System (PASS)

Performance Assessment Scoring System (PASS) was first introduced in 1990 for applying in-
1) List management to assess the qualification and standard of contractors;
2) Tendering process for selection of tenderers and tender assessment;
3) Performance monitoring to ensure a smooth construction process and building quality; and
4) Review the effectiveness of the system.

We design the PASS to measure contractors' performance more objectively and with transparency. Better performers will have more chances to bid than poor performers.

2. 2. 1 PASS Principle and Assessment Items

The principle of PASS is *"What gets measured, gets done"*. It is adopted to-
1) measure contractor's performance objectively against a set of defined standards; and
2) provide a consistent means of comparing performance of individual contractors on individual projects.

The assessment is based on the quality of those items or sub-items of work that have been "done" at the time of assessment, but not necessarily on the final product nor after rectification of any defects or any incidental damages. Checks / inspections are on "the standards of finishes in progress and the quality of the materials on-site." Based on a "first-time-right" principle, i. e. work remedied after assessment will not be considered retrospectively as evidence of compliance.

2. 2. 2 Score Trend and Effect on Quality

Over the past years, the average Contractors score of New Works building contractors maintains from 78 marks in 1996 to 83 marks in 2014.

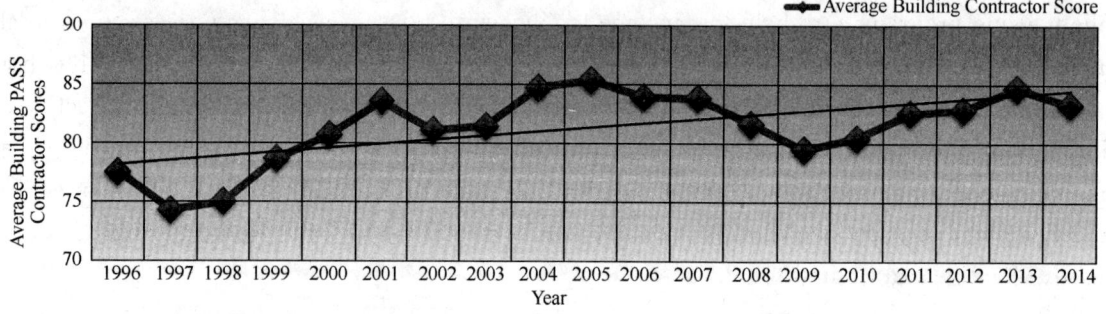

Figure 1　Average building PASS contractor score trend (1996-2014)
(Source: Hong Kong Housing Authority)

For Output Score, i. e. direct measurement of compliance of contract requirements / standards on workmanship / quality of completed works, it increased from 84 marks in 2002 to 91 marks up to first quarter of 2015.

2. 2. 3 PASS Family

The system has been developed to monitor performance of contractors of different

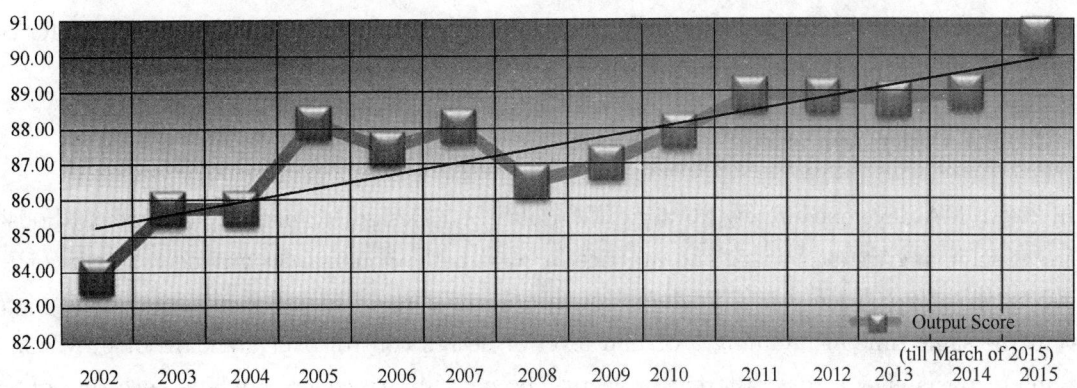

Figure 2   Annual output score trend (2002-2015)

(Source: Hong Kong Housing Authority)

works category-

(1) Performance Assessment Scoring System (PASS)

(2) Maintenance Assessment Scoring System (MASS)

(3) Building Services Performance Assessment Scoring System (BSPASS)

(4) Laboratory Assessment Scoring System (LASS)

(5) Piling Performance Assessment Scoring System (Piling PASS)

(6) Demolition Performance Assessment Scoring System (Demolition PASS)

(7) Soft Landscape Assessment Scoring System (SL PASS)

(8) Ground Investigation Assessment Scoring System (GI PASS)

3   Design and Innovation

Quality means fitness for purpose with value for money and sustainability in mind.

3.1   Microclimate Studies

Since 2004, we have been applying the micro-climate studies in all public housing projects during the early planning and design stages, to create quality living environment and improve the environmental performance of the projects. With the use of computerized simulation models, the local climate can be optimized to enhance wind environment of the site, natural ventilation, daylight and solar heat gain for the domestic flats.

3.2   Healthy Living Initiatives and Better Hygiene

We learnt from the outbreak of Severe Acute Respiratory Syndrome (SARS) in 2003 and developed the common w-trap system in 2006. Waste water from basins and showers is used to replenish the water seal. Normally, water supply would be suspended for about 4 hours in every quarter for the cleansing process and often caused disturbance to residents. In 2008, we pioneered the twin-tank system, with the water tank divided into two compartments, to provide an 'alternative operating' approach ensuring continual uninterrupted water supply to tenants when one of compartments is being cleaned. Less water wastage is assured under well-planned cleansing cycle for all the major water tanks, as well as providing convenience and better hygiene condition. Besides, to prevent Legionnaires' Disease, all new piping systems and associated fresh water storage tanks for cold water supply systems will be flushed clean and disinfected upon commissioning in accordance with Water Services Department's prevailing requirement before use by our tenants.

3.3 Modular Design Approach

In 2008, HA developed a new library of Modular Flat Design for use in public rental housing. We aim at achieving the best value and practice in sustainable housing design and construction, and striving for greater efficiency and productivity through wider use of mechanized building process, whilst at the same time maintaining a certain level of design control over standard of provision and maintaining consistency across different projects. The new library covers a whole spectrum of small modular flats and family modular flats. Individual designers are to articulate these standard modular flats in designing site specific domestic buildings to suit individual site configuration.

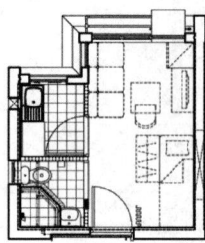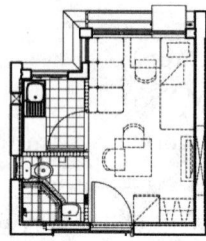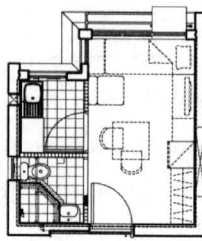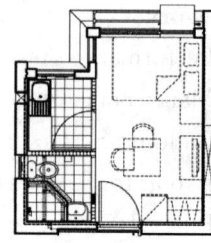

Figure 3　Furniture layout options for 1/2 person flats (illustration in plans)
(Source: Hong Kong Housing Authority)

Figure 4　Furniture layout illustrated in sketches
(Source: Hong Kong Housing Authority)

3.4　'Caring Design'

We provide Ideal Route Home for residents with proximity to public transport terminus and major estate facilities linked up with covered walkways and lift towers. Mitigation measures are adopted to protect residents from noise at source with specific road surfacing and enclosure; at noise propagation path with barrier or buffering building; and at the receiver end through building setback, flat configuration and disposition, acoustic balcony and acoustic windows. Social cohesion is enhanced with the provision of seats at communal areas and free WiFi at ground floor lobby. Through community engagement in the project planning and design stage, specific local issues are addressed and concerns of stakeholders are aligned and eventually no unresolved dispute has arisen.

4　Construction

We take proactive move in applying Building Information Modeling for demolition, site formation, piling, site works planning and costing. We also care for the safety and health of our stakeholders throughout the whole life cycle of housing development.

4.1 Building Information Modeling (BIM)

Since 2006, HA has adopted Building Information Modelling (BIM) to improve design quality, production efficiency and sustainability in design and construction. BIM is the process of developing and using 3-D digital representation of building data throughout its life cycle.

4.1.1 4D BIM for Demolition

In Lower Ngau Tau Kok Estate, the existing blocks were mainly constructed with pre-stressed precast reinforced concrete components. Such kind of demolition was of high risk and un-precedent in HA. Strategic aspects, like removal sequence and safe manoeuver zones for working plants were visualized and assessed by all relevant parties, including machineries operators. The demolition was a success resulted in zero accident and zero complaint on noise and dust from its neighbourhood.

4.1.2 BIM for Site Formation

Tung Tau Cottage Area Eastwas the first pilot project using BIM from design to completion stages. The complex site rendered the traditional 2D drawings insufficient in communicating any design proposals suitably. 3D BIM came in to play to show different design options in context, rotated and reviewed on computer screen.

4.1.3 BIM for Piling

The Wang Yip Street West site is located in the geologically complicated "Scheduled Area No. 2" region characterized by highly varying embedded marble cavities. Its development potential relies on a viable foundation design. The initial proposal included a 35-storey block supported on piles and a 9-storey block on shallow foundation. The site geology 3D BIM model was subsequently updated after detail ground investigation. By navigating such BIM model, the sub-soil stratum profile, the scattered marble cavities and the steep bedrock profile across the whole site were clearly visualized. A revised scheme was quickly arrived showing twin-tower domestic blocks supported on buoyancy raft, maximizing the development potential of the site.

4.1.4 BIM for Site Works Planning

In Sheung Lok Street project, large portion of existing retaining/soil-nailed walls have to be removed. To shorten the construction programme, the removal of soil-nailed wall, site formation, foundation and super-structural works have to be carried out concurrently. The work sequence and intricate interface planning were enabled by 4D BIM simulation.

4.1.5 5D BIM Pilots for Costing

HA has started studying 5D BIM for quantity takeoff since 2012. In pilot projects, material quantities were taken off directly from BIM models for project estimation and tendering process. The actual expense can be easily compared against estimates and useful for interim payment. BIM is now evolving from design to a project management tool.

Figure 5   Dimension accuracy is demanding in congested site
(Source: Hong Kong Housing Authority)

4.2   Safety, Health and Environment

4.2.1   Initiatives in Planning and Construction of New Housing Estates

We incorporate the concept of sustainability and follow the hierarchy of risk control strategy and endeavour to plan and design for safety. Site safety is always one of our key concerns and we set our safety goal at zero fatal accident and no more than 12 accidents per 1000 workers.

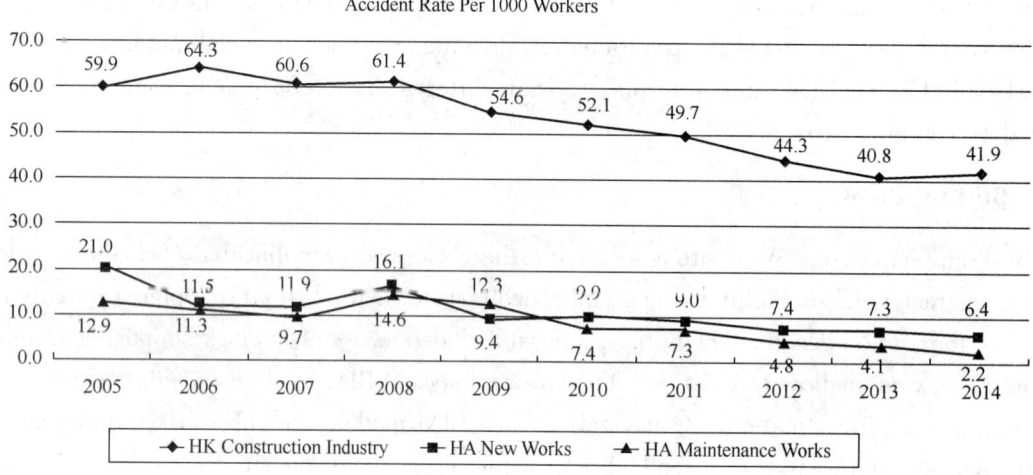

Figure 6   Accident rate per 1000 workers
(Source: Hong Kong Housing Authority)

Three-pronged approach of site safety and health management-

(1) Procurement strategy and performance monitoring with incentives and sanctions

We procure competent works contractors and monitor their performance for improvement:

①Requiring safety pledge and compliance with OHSAS 18001 through contractors' listing;

②Conducting Performance Assessment Scoring System (PASS), Housing Authority Safety Auditing System (HASAS), Housing Authority Lift and Escalator Nominated Sub-contracts Safety Auditing System and Surprise Safety Inspection Programme (SSIP);

③Adopting preferential tender award system (PTAS) for tender assessment. PASS, HASAS and SSIP scores, safety convictions and serious site accidents will affect PTAS score;

④Quarantine a tenderer involved in serious site accident to examine its competency;

⑤Taking regulatory action against a contractor involved in serious site accident.

(2) Contract requirements and administration

We procure competent works contractors and monitor their performance for improvement:

①hard paving, prefabrication, precast element, mechanization and large metal form work;

②implementation of safety guidelines published by Construction Industry Council;

③subletting up to 2 tiers for specific trades and prohibit subletting of site management;

④application of Integrated Pay for Safety, Environment and Hygiene Scheme;

⑤linkage of both HASAS and SSIP performances to pay for safety;

⑥caring for workers who are new to construction industry or a site;

⑦aligning training requirement of site staff of contractors.

(3) Partnership through research, promotion and training

We engage our stakeholders to enhance safety awareness and promote good practices –

①issuing best practice circulars to contractors, service providers and frontline staff;

②examining building information modeling and radio frequency identification for vehicle and workers' position tracking;

③developing mobile applications on smartphone for inspection and reporting by site staff;

④developing web system for capturing accident data for conducting statistical analysis.

4.2.2　Initiatives in Existing Housing Estates

We adopt measures to ensure the safety of our tenants, management and maintenance staff –

①providing fire drills for residents and launching Lift and Escalator Safety Campaign;

②implementing the OHSAS 18001 for maintenance works;

③updating Pay for Safety items and HASAS for maintenance contracts

④applying PTAS for our Building Maintenance District Term Contracts;

⑤taking regulatory measure for maintenance contractors for failures in safety audit;

⑥adopting Maintenance Assessment Scoring System (MASS) in maintenance contracts;

⑦organizing seminars to promote safety awareness among frontline line workers.

5　Environmental Considerations

To enhance the environmental sustainability, we optimize the greening ratio, specify green building materials, conduct carbon emission estimation to compare different design options and put waste management in action.

5.1　Greening

Greening purifies air and avoids urban heat island effect, aside from ecological and amenity value. We are committed to maximizing greening in the design of our new estates. We provide an overall greening area of at least 20% of the total site area, and up to 30% for larger sites over two hectares. Indigenous plants would be selected to maintain ecological balance.

5.2　Green Building Materials

We specify the use of timber from sustainable forest for our building components. Besides, recycled marine mud for backfills, recycled glass for eco-paving blocks, Ground Granulated Blast Furnace Slag (GGBS) to partially replace cement are being adopted in our projects.

5.3 Carbon Emission Reduction

Other environmental initiatives are also adopted to reduce carbon emission. For example, use of high efficiency T5 Fluorescent Tube and Electronic Ballast LED lighting at some communal areas, application of Photocell Sensor to control lighting on/off, setting timer according to season to control lighting on/off, and modernizing lifts with advanced VVVF control system, installation of Polycrystalline silicone and Amorphous silicone Photovoltaic (PV) panels of domestic tower roofs.

5.4 Waste Management

Our modular design enables massive precasting and prefabrication of building components in our building work. This generates 30% less construction waste, not merely 50% less cost comparing with similar building in the private sector and 75% less accident rate than the norm in Hong Kong. The built-in refuse disposal facilities also foster separation of domestic waste at source and the recycling of aluminium, waste paper, plastic bottles, glass bottles and even food waste.

6 Post-Occupancy Considerations

To enhance social sustainability, we adopt people-oriented design approach, organize post completion review workshop and conduct resident survey for all new building projects.

6.1 People-oriented Design Approach

Our adoption of passive design with provision of various communal facilities e. g. outdoor sitting area for tenants of all ages and abilities win high satisfaction rating. In macro measures we provide a green and healthy living habitat with effective estate management system and Total Maintenance Scheme through professional services for cost effectiveness, flexibility and efficiency. In micro terms we deliver useful guides and manual for reference by tenants. Intake Ambassadors are deployed to facilitate tenants' move-in.

6.2 Post Completion Review Workshop

A post-completion review workshop, among the project team, contractor's representatives and building manager was arranged to gauge feedback and review the handover and maintenance services and overall customer satisfaction. This serves as a partnering and a knowledge sharing platform amongst various stakeholders with an aim for continuous improvement.

6.3 Residents Survey

We treasure the views of our residents and conduct independent Residents Surveys for all newly completed estates since 2004. The major objective of the Residents surveys is to gauge residents' satisfaction level on the design and provisions of the estates in which they live, as well as to collect opinion on hypothetical design and provision scenarios that we would like to explore. Satisfaction level on "estate as a whole" from each Residents Survey conducted within a year will be aggregated to compile the Customer Satisfaction Index for that financial year. At the onset, our Key Performance

Indicator was pitched at 70%. In light of the consistently high satisfaction obtained from these surveys over the years, the Key Performance Indicator has been uplifted to 80% from 2011/12 onwards. With engagement of the residents in the planning and design of our estates, the Customer Satisfaction Index is continuously on the rising trend, reaching 95.56% in 2014/15.

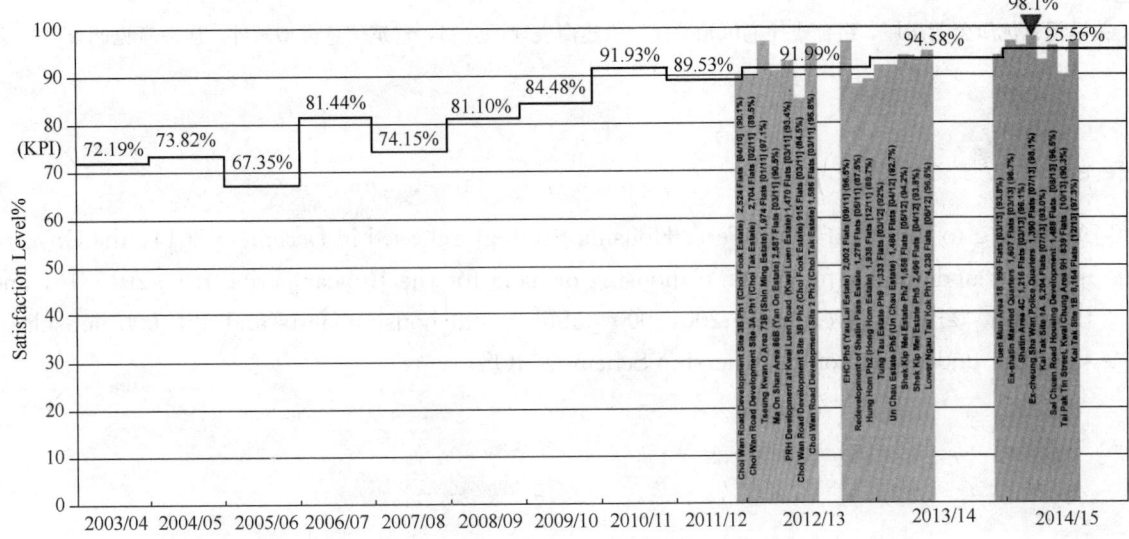

Figure 7   Customer satisfaction index from year 2003/04 to 2014/15
(Source: Hong Kong Housing Authority)

7   Conclusion and Way Forward

As the main provider of affordable public housing in Hong Kong, we take great pride in meeting the housing need of the people and at the same time providing good quality, harmonies and environmental-friendly homes. We apply sustainable planning principle to foster a Quality Living Environment of Public Housing. We build green and friendly "home" with sustainable initiatives to meet the rising expectation of the community. Our public housing programme has been the keystone to the stability and prosperity of Hong Kong and an anchor of our public administration for more than half a century. We will continue to provide quality communities and neighborhood that our residents will treasure and be happy to call them "home".

优质创新、持续发展：解构 21 世纪香港公营房屋

冯宜萱
[香港房屋委员会-房屋署副署长（发展及建筑）]

摘要：香港房屋委员会（房委会）一直致力提供可负担、安全及舒适的公营房屋，以满足低收入家庭住屋的需要。

房委会关怀市民，爱护环境，于各方面在可持续发展的前提下有效地运用紧绌的资源。我们引入承建商表现评分制，以客观和透明度衡量承建商的表现。持着关爱的态度，房委会采用顺应自然的设计模式，为居民创建优质家园以及绿色健康的生活环境，从而促进社会、经济和环境的可持续发展。房委会建立了组合式单元设计并持续为其

优化，在珍贵的土地资源，可建造性，成本效益，迎合使用者需要和为居民提供安全和健康生活等各方面，取得理想的平衡。房委会更积极地应用建筑信息模型软件以提高设计质量、生产效率、可持续性设计和施工。另外，为了促进社会的可持续发展，房委会的建筑项目采用以人为本的设计，在工程完成后会检查工作坊。我们也会对所有新建项目进行居民意见调查以了解他们对所住屋苑的满意程度。本文重点介绍房委会21世纪优质公共房屋的主要特色。

关键词：优质公营房屋，组合式住宅单元设计，承建商表现评分制，建筑信息模型软件，居民意见调查

References：

[1] According to the latest Long Term Housing Strategy released in December 2014，the Government has updated the projection of housing demand for the 10-year period from 2015/16，and the public target will comprise 200，000 public rental housing units and 80，000 subsidized sale flats under the Home Ownership Scheme（HOS）.

从环境变迁探讨台湾智能绿色建筑推动策略与未来展望

何明锦

（台湾科技大学建筑研究所）

摘要：面对全球气候变迁及通信技术进步，推动有助于永续发展、环境共生及应用 ICT 技术提升居住环境品质的智能绿色建筑，为当前全球建筑发展重点。台湾面对的自然及社会环境挑战尤为严峻，所以智能绿色建筑亦为台湾重要之建设发展策略。台湾智能绿色建筑之发展历程，以绿色建筑相关研究最早进行，随后智能建筑、绿色建材等亦渐次研究发展，并先后完成各项标准及评估方法与技术规范之制定，以及推动方案与相关法令之研订，智能绿色建筑产业已成为台湾建筑产业最重要的发展策略之一。本文针对台湾绿色建筑、绿色建材及智能建筑之发展脉络，说明相关标准之指标评估系统沿革及推动策略，并介绍室内环境品质之管制及既有建筑物节能与智能化改善等示范作为。而台湾智能绿色建筑在各界共同努力下已显现可观之成效，唯单一建筑毕竟影响空间有限，如能将此理念扩展到社区，甚至到城市范围，才能真正发挥安全、健康、节能、永续与舒适、便利的整体效益。建构可持续的智能的绿色社区与城市，不但关系居住环境与生活品质的提升，亦攸关台湾传统营建与通信产业的转型发展，其推动落实当非一蹴可及，必须循序渐进，本文特提出短中长期发展策略，作为后续推动之参考。

关键词：环境变迁，绿色建筑，绿色建材，智能建筑，既有建筑改善

1 环境变迁下的建筑新思维

1.1 环境变迁与极端气候的冲击

近数十年来，全球各地几乎都曾因为气候变迁、过度开发、治理失当等因素，而遭遇各种灾害不同程度的冲击，尤其是与气候有关的大型天然灾害，包括风灾、水灾及极端气候，不但发生频率增加，且灾害规模及造成的损害也增加。依据联合国 1980～2012 年的灾害统计显示，全球大型天然灾害发生的案例数从 20 世纪 80 年代每年约 400 件，已经跃升到近 5 年每年约 800 件（图 1），几乎是过去的两倍；而灾害规模及造成的损失也大幅提升，此外，根据联合国最新发布的"亚太地区的自然灾害：2014 年回顾"，报告显示，2014 年全球自然灾害中，几乎有一半发生在亚太地区，且全球气候变迁将使相关风灾与水灾发生频率持续增加。

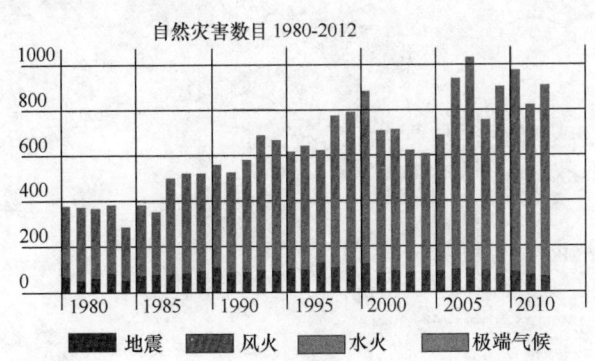
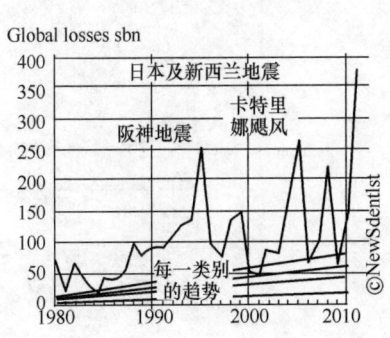

图 1 全球 1980～2012 大型天然灾害发生数及损失统计

（资料来源：http://reliefweb.int/map/world/natural-catastrophes-world-map-2012）

人类对于自然环境的破坏及资源的消耗同时引发严重的环境生态问题，并已扩大到全球尺度的规模，包括气候异常、海平面上升、臭氧层破坏、能源耗竭及粮食危机等，甚至直接威胁人类的健

康与生存，除了气候与生态系统的冲击之外，人类社会还面临了人口结构恶化、高龄人口比率急遽增加、城市人口集中及照顾需求增加等问题，因此，如何降低建筑开发对环境的冲击、减少能源消耗、减少温室气体排放量，并利用新科技设备以因应高龄社会，提升人类福祉，为全球当前各国皆须面对的迫切课题。

台湾地区由于地狭人稠、天然资源有限，且高龄人口数量及比例急剧上升，相较于世界其他地区，全球暖化、极端气候与资源枯竭对台湾造成的冲击将更为显著，台湾所面临的严峻挑战包括：

（1）根据气象局统计资料显示，台湾在过去100年的平均温度较过去上升约1～1.34℃，相较于全球平均的0.7℃，台湾升温幅度明显超过全球平均升温。

（2）台湾由于天然资源匮乏，台湾的能源97%以上皆依赖进口，全球能源及原物料短缺或价格的剧烈波动都将冲击经济与社会发展。

（3）台湾地处亚热带，并位于环太平洋地震带上，故每年都遭受台风、暴雨、干旱、寒流及地震等天然灾害侵袭。根据历年资料统计，平均每年约有3～4个台风侵袭台湾，而发生规模大于5级的地震为平均24.4次。就气象灾害而言，台湾因灾害性天气所造成的直接财物损失，每年平均约高达新台币150亿元（间接的损失更难以估计）。

（4）依据相关研究显示，台湾未来的降雨形态将逐渐变成降雨延时缩短、降雨集中、强度增强，且瞬间暴雨量增大之极端降雨形态，对于防洪减灾将造成莫大的压力，而另一方面，中南部发生干旱的几率也会逐年增加。

（5）台湾地形狭长，每年平均降雨量虽达2500mm，但因地质条件不佳且河川短窄流急，坡度大，容易造成各类的坡地及淹水灾害，却留不住宝贵的水资源，中南部发生干旱的几率也会随气候变迁而逐年增加。

（6）人口结构越趋恶化，一方面，高龄人口数量及比率急剧增加，依发展委员会之推估（如图2），台湾65岁以上老年人口比例在2018年将达到高龄社会的14.6%，并在2026年达到20.6%，成为超高龄社会，老年人口超过492万人，至2045年台湾的老年人口比例将超过3成以上；另一方面，过去60年来，台湾妇女生育率快速下降，已成为世界育龄妇女总生育率最低的地区之一。因此，相较于世界各地虽多同样面临高龄化社会问题，唯台湾社会老化的速度几乎为世界之冠，未来高龄化与少子化考验将更趋严峻，势必因此冲击劳动就业市场及加剧老人抚养负担与照护需求。

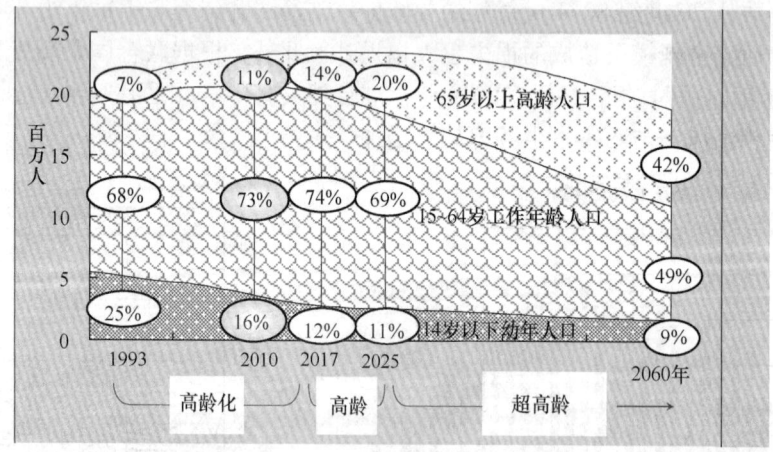

图2　台湾人口结构老化示意图

（资料来源：台湾发展委员会，2014）

1.2 建筑部门的永续发展策略

全球暖化与气候变迁的议题持续受到关注，从2011年12月在南非德班（Durban）召开的联合国气候变化纲要公约（UNFCCC）第17次缔约国会议（COP17）、2012年12月在卡达尔多哈开的

UNFCCC COP18 会议，到 2013 年 11 月在波兰华沙召开的 UNFCCC COP19 会议，均确认了全球必须努力把温度上升控制在 1.5～2℃ 的范围以内，但由于全球经济面临成长衰退的隐忧，各国的减碳承诺与减碳路线开始产生动摇，国际间许多需要仰赖大量资金投入的绿能产业与减碳措施，受到金融不确定性因素的影响，面临被迫暂停或缩小规模的窘境。国际间许多国家政府不得不开始思考如何在产业发展和促进环境永续之间找到一个平衡点，并且寻找新的科技与生活形态来支撑相关永续政策的推动，以建筑部门而言，"Green by ICT" 及 "ICT for Green" 的概念，已被视为兼顾带动产业发展及确保环境永续的发展策略，在此背景下，全球主要国家对于"绿色建筑"与"智能建筑"所能发挥的减碳效益与产业推升效益，均予高度重视，并催化了智能绿色建筑的快速发展。

面对气候变迁的严肃课题，20 世纪末全球发展出新的"永续发展"（Sustainable Development）思维，已成为人类最重要的课题，国际上不论地区国家，都必须加强对当地的环境努力及强化国际间相互的合作，以谋求人类最大的福祉。世界各国（包括美国、欧盟、日本等国际组织及国家）皆积极倡导环境保护，发展节能减碳的绿色建筑，期降低对环境的冲击。"绿色建筑"在欧洲称为"永续建筑"（Sustainable Building）、日本称为环境共生建筑（Symbiosis Housing），美国、加拿大都称为"绿色建筑"（Green Building），除名称差异外，其基本理念大致相同。目前全球已经有 26 个国家和地区建立了绿色建筑规章制度，台湾地区从 1991 年左右，即体认建筑开发与使用对生态环境、资源与能源耗用等议题之重要，积极致力于绿色建筑、绿色建材与永续环境技术的研究发展，并在 1999 年底建立绿色建筑标章评估制度，为全球第 4 个实施具科学量化的绿色建筑评估系统，也是第一个适用于热带及亚热带的评估系统，推动以来深获各界的肯定与支持，成效极为显著。

除绿色建筑规划设计技术外，随着计算机与电信技术发展，尤其是网路的普及应用，将 ICT 技术应用于节能领域，发展 "Green by ICT" 之概念，为联合国环境规划署（UNEP）、世界经济论坛（WHF）及各国认为极具发展潜力的做法。另外，利用网路整合提升建筑内部空间各项系统，并借助外界服务支援满足使用者需求，以提升居住环境之安全及加强对高龄者之照护，亦为因应高龄社会的重要方法之一，因此结合绿色建筑技术与 ICT 设备、系统以达到节能永续、安全舒适、健康便利的智能绿色建筑，已成为当前全球建筑发展的趋势，为了推动台湾智能绿色建筑的应用与发展，台湾于 2004 年即建立"智能建筑评估系统"，借助规章制度引导台湾建筑产业逐步朝向智能化方向发展；此外，政府亦于 2010 年核定"智能绿色建筑推动方案"，积极展开绿色建筑与智能建筑的整合与推动工作，以智能绿色建筑为发展基础，应用各项 ICT 技术提供服务，包含 IOT 物联网、云端应用服务、大数据及开放资料（Open Data）模式等，借助智能科技系统设施相助实施包括城市治理、居住安全安心、节能管理、交通运输、产业创新等应用服务，有效提供城市居民在生活、工作、交通、教育、医疗、照护、休闲等服务，建置更安全便利、健康舒适且节能永续的居住环境，未来并逐步由建筑扩大到社区、城市等，以建设节能永续的智能新台湾。

2 台湾绿色建筑推动策略与现况

2.1 绿色建筑内涵及评估指标

依据台湾"绿色建筑评估系统"对绿色建筑的定义为：在建筑生命周期中，消耗较少资源，使用较少能源、产生较少废弃物以及兼顾健康舒适之建筑物。绿色建筑在建筑类之评估内容系以基本型为基础，其他厂房类及住宿类则依据其建筑使用特色，酌予调整其评估内容，如厂房强调性能验证、住宿类则加强其自然通风等。至于基本型之评估内容，主要考虑台湾亚热带气候特性及掌握本土建筑特色，依生态（Ecology）、节能（Energy Saving）、减排（Waste Reduction）及健康（Health）四大指标体系，再细分为 9 项指标，包括生物多样性、绿化量、基地保水、水资源、日常节能、室内环境、CO_2 减排、废弃物减排、污水垃圾改善等，以量化之标准作为评估依据，构成完整的"绿色建筑评估系统"基础（如表 1）。至于旧建筑改善，则是考虑台湾目前旧建筑比例约占97％，且多数旧建筑于设计时并未将绿色建筑纳入规划，这些建筑多存在极大改善潜力，为鼓励这些建筑物进行改善，特别以其改善前后之性能比较作为评估依据，只要进步在 5％以上即可达到合格级，20％以上即达到钻石级。而社区类则是将原先的建筑物扩大，期望由点到面，形成更完整的区域，评估内容主要包括社区生态、机能、治安等以符合社区使用机能为主要评估要项。

EEWH 评估内容概要　　　　　　　　　　　　　　　表 1

大指标群	指标内容	
	指标名称	评估要项
生态	1. 生物多样性指标	生态绿网、小生物栖地、植物多样化、土壤生态
	2. 绿化量指标	绿化量、CO_2 固定量
	3. 基地保水指标	保水、储留渗透、软性防洪
节能	4. 日常节能指标（必要）	外壳、空调、照明节能
减排	5. CO_2 减排指标	建材 CO_2 排放量
	6. 废弃物减排指标	土方平衡、废弃物减排
健康	7. 室内环境指标	隔声、采光、通风、建材
	8. 水资源指标（必要）	节水器具、雨水、中水再利用
	9. 污水垃圾改善指标	雨水污水分流、垃圾分类处理、堆肥

（资料来源：台港两地绿色建筑的发展，2014）

2.2　绿色建筑推动策略

台湾于 1999 年完成"绿色建筑评估系统"，并自同年 9 月开始推动实施，制度推动初期，因属自愿性质，成效有限，为扩大绿色建筑政策，政府于 2001 年核定实施"绿色建筑推动方案"，规定公有建筑物总工程造价在 5000 万新台币以上者，需强制申请绿色建筑认证，由政府带头推动绿色建筑，自然形成绿色建筑产业之市场机制及环境。绿色建筑评估制度订定之初并未分级，唯为鼓励设计者追求较佳之绿色建筑设计，2007 年制定分级制度，绿色建筑评估依其得分高低，分为合格、铜、银、黄金及钻石五个等级，如此可有效区分判别绿色建筑的高下优劣，以利提升更优良的绿色建筑技术工法研发，自 2007 年实施以来，许多申请案例为达到较佳的分级等第，争相办理绿色建筑设计改善，以提升企业的形象与荣耀，充分达到"政府"、"民间"及"环境永续"三赢之局面。另为鼓励其他亦能符合绿色建筑精神之建筑技术与创意，台湾现行之绿色建筑评估系统，对于与绿色建筑生态、节能、减排、健康四大范畴有密切关系而不能量化、不能计算的巧思，或一些合乎环境美学、健康舒适、环境调和、自然生态的建筑设计，已订有加分升级的相关规定，借以广纳并表彰其特殊的绿色建筑设计创意。此外，为进一步提升台湾绿色建筑技术，参酌美、日、英等国家之绿色建筑评估制度，将原有一体适用的绿色建筑评估通用版本，于 2012 年完成《绿建筑评估手册——基本型》（EEWH-BC）、《绿建筑评估手册——住宿类》（EEWH-RS）及《绿建筑评估手册——厂房类》（EEWH-GF）等 3 类不同建筑类型分类之专用绿色建筑评估手册修订，同时针对台湾目前比例占比较多之既有建筑及社区，分别订有《绿建筑评估手册——社区类》（EEWH-EC）及《绿建筑评估手册——旧建筑改善类》（EEWH-RN）（如图 3）之专用绿色建筑评估手册，其中旧建筑改善及社区类于 2012 年 7 月 1 日开始实施，其他 3 类则于 2013 年 1 月 1 日开始实施，使台湾正式迈入绿色建筑分类评估时代。

图 3 EEWH 家族评估体系适用范围
（资料来源：绿建筑评估手册，2015）

2.3 绿色建筑标章推动现况

台湾"绿色建筑评估系统"是针对热带及亚热带气候条件所建立之"绿色建筑九大评估指标系统"（EEWH）进行评估，评估重点为建筑设计规划上强调简洁的造型，避免滥用建材资源、过量设计，鼓励借由适当建筑坐向、开窗面积、场地绿化及场地保水等设计手法，以达到建筑物节能减排与健康舒适要求，同时具有调节气候、增加大地蓄水能力、增进土壤生态等缓和城市热岛效应及减少城市洪水发生率等功能，进而提供一个健康舒适并兼顾永续发展的居住环境。由于绿色建筑强调减量设计，一般而言，相较于一般建筑，兴建绿色建筑费用并不会提高，但是在部分建蔽率较高之建筑物，由于在绿化量、场地保水等项目不易得分，所以可能采用设置太阳能电板或使用 Low-E 玻璃等做法，则可能会造成费用提高。至于实施绿色建筑后，相较于一般建筑物可达到之效益主要有以下几项：

（1）降低建筑开发对环境之冲击，善尽世界公民责任，并达到降低城市热岛效应等。

（2）节约资源，平均节约用电量 20%，用水量 30%。

（3）创造健康室内环境，增进居住环境品质。

（4）促进建材及节能技术研发，推动绿色产业发展，促使传统产业转型，提升产业竞争力。

绿色建筑达标评估制度包括针对完工建筑物颁发之"绿色建筑规章"，以及针对完成规划设计依据书图评定通过的"候选绿色建筑证书"两项，主要是希望借由候选证书的评定，提供事先评估并调整不适当设计的机会，减少建筑物完成后无法修改或必须耗费更大成本改正的状况。截至 2015 年 4 月底止，已有 5091 座公私有建筑物取得达标或候选证书之评定（如图 4），总楼地板面积约 65.88×10^6 m²，不只案例数量逐年增加，民间自发性申请达标之比例，更从早期的 6% 逐年提升，到 2014 年已达到 35%（如图 5）。获得绿色建筑达标认证的建筑物，无论

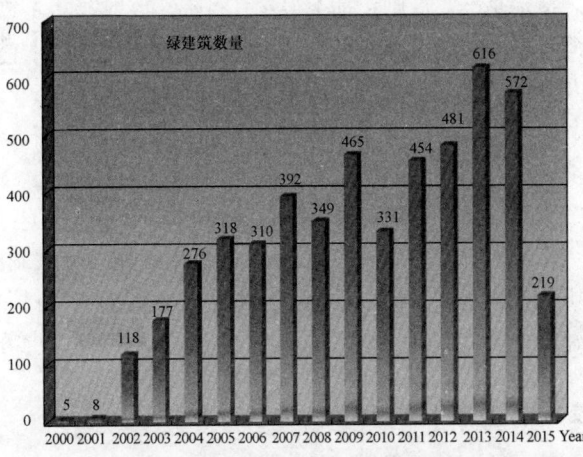

图 4 绿色建筑规章核发数统计图
（资料来源：台港两地绿色建筑的发展，2014）

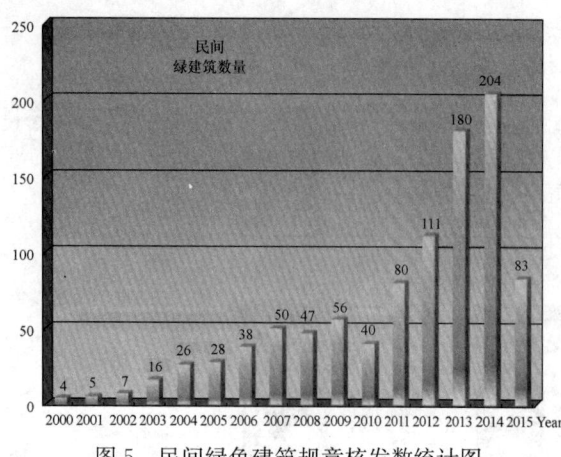

图 5　民间绿色建筑规章核发数统计图

（资料来源：建筑研究所）

是在节电、节水或降低 CO_2 排放等方面，均较一般建筑物有更好的成效。整体而言，总计这些绿色建筑完工启用后，在未来长达 40 年的生命周期中，估算每年约可省电 15.75 亿度，省水 74.36×10^6 t（相当于 29746 座国际标准游泳池的容量）。若按 t 水需耗 1 度电计算（含城市供水、扬水及净水处理），则两者合计减少之 CO_2 排放量约为 89.43×10^4 t，其减碳效益相当于 6×10^4 hm^2 人造林（约等于 2299 个台北大安森林公园面积）所吸收的 CO_2 量，其于使用阶段每年为业主节省之水电费计约新台币 35.9 亿元。

3　台湾绿色建材推动策略与现况

3.1　绿色建材内涵及评估指标

随着建筑物逐渐朝向密闭化、空调化发展，室内环境品质逐渐受到重视。依据统计，人的一生在室内的时间约为 90%，所以室内环境品质之优劣影响健康至巨，为提升室内环境之健康性及舒适性、降低建材制程中对环境造成之冲击，并带动传统建材产业升级，台湾继绿色建筑达标制度后，随即建立"绿色建材达标制度"。而"绿色建材达标制度"的推动，便是基于源头管制的概念，希望透过优质建材的选用，降低潜藏在室内环境中的危害因子、提高居住环境的舒适度，同时也兼顾环境友善、资源再利用等面向。此外，近年来国际上逐渐兴起绿色贸易及绿色经济的风潮，许多国家都把环境保护产品与绿色采购制度联结，建材产品若想要进入国际绿色贸易市场，必须积极进行产业升级与转型，并设法符合相关绿色规范。

绿色建材达标是基于"人本健康、地球永续"精神，依据建材生命周期，制定 4 大分类：生态、健康、高性能及再生绿色建材（如图 6）进行评定，4 个分类之绿色建材均需为合法之市售建材，且须符合绿色建材之通则要求及各个分类之特定基准，通则包括不得含有石棉、放射线、台湾环境保护署公告之毒性化学物质、无机卤化物及其他蒙特利尔公约管制化学品，且于原料取得、生产制造、成品运输及使用等阶段皆不造成环境污染，并符合品质及安全性之相关法规规定。

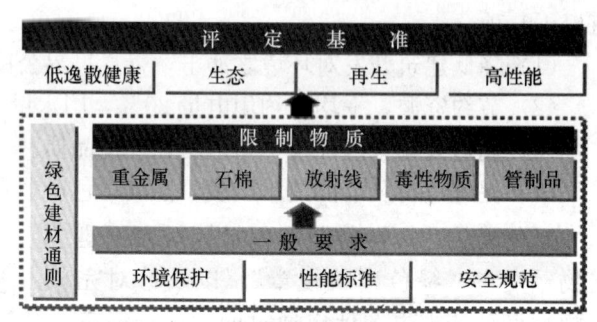

图 6　绿色建材达标四大分类及通则

（资料来源：绿建材解说与评估手册，2011）

各个分类之基准则规范各类绿色建材特殊之性能，其中："生态绿色建材"是指使用无匮乏危机之天然材料（例如竹材、再生林木材等），以低人工处理方式制成之建材；"健康绿色建材"是指低甲醛及挥发性有机化合物（TVOC）逸散之建材；"高性能绿色建材"则包括在隔声、透水、节能等性能上有高度表现之建材；"再生绿色建材"是指将本土废弃物依一定掺配比例再利用制成之建材。

3.2　绿色建材推动策略

绿色建材达标制度系参酌国际间相关建材达标精神、检测程序及评定基准，并依本土气候环境、产业现况，拟定相关制度，提出评定项目及评定基准，并自 2004 年 7 月开始受理绿色建材达标申请。绿色建材达标初期属推广及自愿申请性质，唯为加强推广应用，自 2006 年 7 月起，于"建筑技术规则"明确规定供公众使用之建筑物室内装修应采用 5% 以上的绿色建材，2009 年修正提高其使用率为 30%，2012 年 7 月开始，更将使用率提升至 45%，并增列户外铺面部分需使用 10% 以上的绿色建材，其规定内容为："建筑物室内装修材料、楼地板面材料及窗，其绿色建材使用率应达总面积 45% 以上，建筑物户外地面扣除车道、汽车出入缓冲空间、消防车辆救灾活动空间及无须铺设地面材料部分，其地面材料之绿色建材使用率应达 10% 以上"，在建筑法令的强制规定下，带动了台湾绿色建材的生产及消费风潮。

另外，为协助台湾建材业者进一步提升建材商品之国际竞争力，以争取国际绿色采购商机，本所近年来积极推动绿色建材达标国际接轨，已在 2013 年 10 月份辅导台湾绿色建材达标评定专业机构（财团法人台湾建筑中心）与韩国环保规章评定机构"环境产业技术院"（Korea Environmental Industry & Technology Institute，KEITEI）及泰国环保规章评定机构"泰国环境研究院"（Thailand Environment Institute，TEI）共同签署合作协议，并于 2014 年 10 月进一步与菲律宾环保达标评定机构"环保与永续发展中心"（The Philippine Center for Environmental Protection and Sustainable Development，Inc.，PCEPSDI）签署相关协议，相关协议可简化台湾厂商申请韩国、泰国与菲律宾达标之程序，双方之评定机构将相互承认对方认可之检测结果与制程查核结果，扩大推动绿色建材之国际接轨，协助台湾绿色建材业者逐步将产品行销至国际市场。

3.3　绿色建材规章推动现况

自 2004 年推动绿色建材达标制度以来，每年核发之达标数持续成长，截至 2015 年 4 月底，累计评定通过 1295 件达标，产品包括涂料、顶棚材料、地板材料、隔间墙材料、吸声材、磁砖、透水砖、高压混凝土地砖、填缝剂、胶粘剂、节能玻璃、隔声门窗等共 9401 种产品。2014 年单一年度评定通过件数达 255 件，此数量不仅较 2013 年评定通过件数（203 件）大幅成长 25.6%，也是历年评定通过件数最高的一年。绿色建材达标推动 10 年来，核发的标章件数持续显著成长，民众可选购之绿色建材产品趋于丰富多元，由此可见，达标制度确实带动了台湾绿色建材的产制及消费风潮，民间业界更因绿色建材产业的蓬勃发展，自发性地成立"台湾绿色建材产业发展协会"，共同推动绿色建材产业。

4　台湾智能建筑推动策略与现况

4.1　智能建筑内涵及评估指标

随着行动装置的普及及物联网技术的逐渐成熟，将通信设备与技术导入建筑，以提升居住环境品质并提高能源使用效率，已成为国际间建筑发展的主流趋势，在此背景下，世界各国包括美国、英国，日本、韩国及中国等皆积极推动"智能建筑"，智能建筑的发展概念是借由通信设备联结主动感知与控制系统，结合智能型高科技技术、材料、产品之应用，使建筑物更加安全、节能、健康、舒适、便利。依据台湾"智能建筑评估系统"，对智能建筑之定义为：建筑物导入节能概念与智能化相关产业技术，建构主动感知，及满足使用者需求之建筑空间；故以台湾本土生活习惯及民众生活需求为基础，提出 8 项评估指标，作为"智能建筑达标"之评估依据。评估内容分成两大群组，包括"基础设施"及"功能设施"，8 项评估指标包括综合布线、资讯通信、系统整合、设施管理、安全防灾、健康舒适、贴心便利及节能永续（详表 2）；并参考绿色建筑采分级制度，依建筑物之智能程度分成五个等级，即合格、铜、银、黄金及钻石级（详图 7）。此外，考量智能科技技术及系统设备进步快速，且为利于智能建筑认证制度及达标评估审查作业之推行，以达进一步加强普及智能建筑之目的，本所目前正进行智能建筑评估手册内容之修订，已经多次会议讨论后完成初步草案，并为使修正内容更为完备，特别再举办说明会进行意见征询，预定 2015 年 9 月完成 2016 年版之评估内容，并将自 2016 年 1 月 1 日正式推行实施。

智能建筑达标评估内容   表 2

大指标群	指标名称	评估要项
基础指标	1. 综合布线指标	布线系统规划设计、可支援之服务、导入时机与流程管制等
	2. 资讯通信指标	广域网路之接取、数位式（含 IP）电话交换、公众行动通信涵盖（含共构）等
	3. 系统整合指标	系统整合程度、整合方式、管理方式、整合平台等
	4. 设施管理指标	使用管理、建筑设备维护管理等
功能指标	5. 安全防灾指标	建物防灾、人身安全等
	6. 健康舒适指标	空间环境、视环境、温热环境、空气环境、水环境等
	7. 贴心便利指标	空间辅助系统、资讯服务系统、生活服务系统等
	8. 节能管理指标	能源监视系统、能源管理系统、设备效率、节能技术等

资料来源：建筑研究所，智慧建筑解说与评估手册 2011 年版。

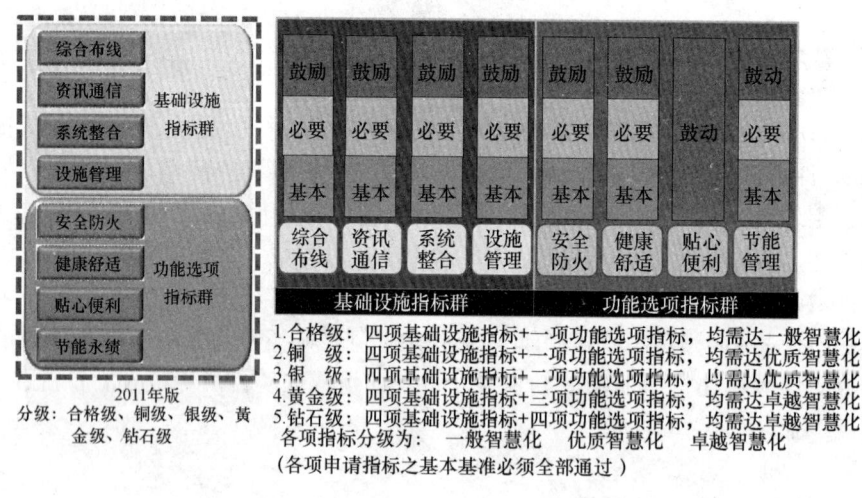

图 7　智能建筑评估系统内涵示意图
（资料来源：智慧建筑解说与评估手册 2011）

4.2　智能建筑推动策略

　　台湾的 ICT 产业在世界具领先之地位，同时又面对能源短缺、高龄人口急剧增加及民众对多元服务之需求提高等问题，以智能建筑为基础，配合数位汇流、云端运算、智能生活等发展，建设资讯化、人性化又兼顾永续化的生活空间与环境，乃当前重要议题。台湾于 1992 年开始进行相关研究，并于 2002 年完成智能建筑评估系统研订，2004 年开始推动"智能建筑评估"制度，2011 年因应世界发展趋势及科技之演进，汇整执行智能建筑相关业务的经验与问题，更新评估系统内容，以使智能建筑之评估得以更加完备，并符合科技之发展趋势与使用者需求。智能建筑标章评估系统，在制度设计上亦比照绿色建筑标章，分为"智能建筑达标"及"候选智能建筑证书"。相较于绿色建筑达标，显然智能建筑有待加强推动落实，所以参考绿色建筑以公有建筑作为领头羊之做法，智能绿色建筑推动方案于 2013 年修正，规定自 2013 年 7 月 1 日起总工程造价达新台币 2 亿以上之公有办公厅舍等特定类别建筑，须取得智能建筑候选证书与标章。

4.3 智能建筑达标推动现况

"智能建筑评估系统"之重点，主要着重在建筑物规划设计时导入智能化相关技术及应用，透过资讯通信之传递、综合布线及系统整合达到建筑物智能化的基本效能，亦借助智能化技术提升建筑物整体安全防灾功能，并以设备连动监控技术达成建筑节能、提升室内外环境品质之目标，同时再借助优良之设施管理，以维持导入之智能化功能都能发挥应有之功能效益，以提升建筑物品质。

由于智能建筑须增设部分设备、系统，相较于一般建筑，智能建筑须增加部分费用，其费用比例依智能化程度不同约在 2％～10％间。获得智能建筑达标之建筑物，具有以下较佳之性能与效益：

(1) 具整合性之建筑使用管理功能，可节省管理维护费用约 10％～20％。

(2) 借由主动感知与控制及能源管理系统，在相同空调环境下，可节省 10％的能源耗用。

(3) 具扩充性及系统性之资讯通信设备与网路系统，利于建筑物未来因应科技进步之提升弹性

(4) 借由主动感知监控之设备与网路，可有效加强防盗及防止与降低灾害意外等，提升居住环境安全性。

智能建筑标章自 2003 年推出正式受理，采取自愿申请方式，至 2015 年 4 月底止，计有 98 件获得智能建筑达标或候选智能建筑证书，申请案件以办公服务类及住宿类建筑为大宗，其中公有建筑物以办公服务类为最多，学校类次之；而民间建筑物则以住宿类最多，办公类次之。此外，为推动高贵不贵的智能绿色建筑，政府跨部门间也进行相关整合，共同推动合宜住宅及公营住宅将智能绿色建筑纳入规划，目前已有 1 万余户将智能绿色建筑纳入规划设计，其中部分已取得候选证书，完工后可让全民皆可共享智能永续生活环境，更能普及落实推动成效。

5 既有建筑节能与智能化改善

除新建建筑物外，由于既有建筑物约占建筑物总量 97％，这些建筑物普遍存在耗能、设备老旧、不符生态环境等问题，若不改善将造成能源浪费与温室气体排放等现象；此外，应用智能设备系统更可促进建筑安全、舒适健康及增进管理效率等，达到提升居住环境品质之目的。为鼓励既有建筑物进行改善，台湾自 2003 年开始进行既有建筑物节能及绿厅舍改善示范计划，并于 2008 年开始进行既有建筑物智能化改善奖补助计划，已完成数百案，对于建筑节能减碳、降低城市热岛效应及提升居住环境品质等，均有显著效益。

5.1 既有建筑节能与绿厅舍改善

建筑节能及绿厅舍改善计划是针对政府机构及大专院校选择具改善潜力之既有建筑物，进行绿色建筑改善及节能改造的示范计划，期能借助相关示范及推广，引导建筑物进行节能改善，以提高既有建筑物能源使用效率及减缓城市热岛效应，同时达到带动台湾相关绿能产业发展之目标。本项示范计划采用工期短、成本低、改善成效佳，且对于增进节约能源及减少 CO_2 排放量较有贡献之改善策略，包括空调系统节能、热水系统能源效率提升、老旧空调主机性能提升或更换、建置或升级建筑能源管理系统（BEMS）、进行测试调整平衡程序（TAB）、室内照明改善、外遮阳改善及屋顶隔热改善等 8 个项目作为补助改善之主轴，以降低建筑物耗能，俾提升建筑节能及经济效益。2003～2014 年期间总计已完成绿厅舍类改善 212 案、建筑节能类改善 297 案，对于场地保水、绿化、生态环境改善及节能等均有很大效益，也对减缓全球暖化及城市热岛效应有所贡献，可说是既有建筑改善之先驱及典范。其相关成效说明如下：

（1）实质节能效益：经统计上述投入改善工程之总金额约为新台币 11.7 亿元新台币，经推估具体量化每年之节电度数（kWh）及 CO_2 减排值，换算为每年节省金额约为 2.7 亿元新台币，推估回收年限约为 4.33 年，节能成效极佳。

（2）推广示范效益：所完成示范改善之 297 案例遍布全台湾北、中、南、东及离岛等地区，达到推广宣导效益，且为加强节能技术应用，已于 2012 年完成"既有建筑空调节能改善汇编"，并放置于本所网站（http：//www. abri. gov. tw）及绿色建筑资讯网（http：//green. abri. gov. tw）供免费下载，以提供各界参考应用，扩大建筑节能改善效益。

（3）带动节能产业与人才培训：执行本计划已带动台湾空调与动力系统等产业之发展，例如本计划大量而系统化进行空调工程改善，带动台湾许多大型中央空调主机制造厂获得大笔订单，总计空调吨数超过 10000 RT 以上，并因此促进其投入研发，提升技术，生产高能源效率之机型，促进台湾空调工程主机制造工业之发展。

5.2　既有建筑智能化改善

既有建筑物智能化改善之目标，为期望经由改善，达到提升建筑物安全、节省能源、节约管理人力、降低建物营运费用及延长建物之寿命等目标，并借助公有及民间既有建筑物智能化设计及改善示范工作，推广普及智能设备系统之应用，以期全面建构智能化居住空间。台湾自 2008 年起陆续执行相关奖补助工作，以现行智能建筑评估基准为基础，针对安全防灾监控及系统整合应用等改善重点，提供既有建筑物智能化改善之奖补助经费。既有建筑物智能化改善奖补助案主要改善手法包括：整合建筑能源管理系统并进行空调、照明设备连动管控、建置建筑物门禁管理系统、校园安全监控系统、建筑物室内空气品质改善、健康照护管理系统、个人生理资讯测量系统等，奖补助地点遍布全台湾及外岛地区。2008 ～ 2014 年间总计已完成公有建筑物改善 79 案、民间建筑物改善 111 案，透过上述奖补助案件，不但协助这些建筑物提升安全、节能、舒适及管理效率等，更达到促进智能化相关产业与技术发展，提升产业竞争力之目标。

既有建筑物智能化改善工作之改善项目，可区分为安全防灾监控、健康照护管理、便利舒适服务、系统整合应用等四大类型，经统计各类型改善项目之改善效益分别为：

（1）安全防灾监控：既有建筑透过安全监控设施设备布建计划，导入整合建筑防灾机能与人身安全监控于统一的管理系统平台，在实际营运管理与危机处理上有效缩短应变时程及降低意外事件发生率。

（2）健康照护管理：健康照护管理的导入，主要是为了减少人工测量及资料录入与管理时程，或减少紧急事件的应变与处理时间，依据调查结果显示，改善后能有效的缩减紧急事件应变作业时程。

（3）便利舒适服务：便利舒适服务项目主要的效益在于设施设备营运管理上，软体界面操作容易性、逻辑适宜性是否有效地展现信赖度，以及硬件运转动作上是否能减少甚至快速排除问题，经统计建筑物导入智能化管理服务，约可节省 50％ 系统设备应变处理时间。

（4）系统整合应用：既有建筑物导入系统整合应用项目，透过营运管理所节省之用电度数进行计算，智能化后可有效节省用电约 4％ 以上。

6　提升室内环境品质作为

由于人的一生约有 90％ 的时间处于广义的室内空间，因此，建筑室内空间的环境品质不仅与我们的工作效率息息相关，也与人体健康有着密切的关系。例如：在室内环境品质不良的"病态建筑"生活或工作，容易引发"病态建筑症候群"，症状包括喉咙干燥、眼睛及鼻子过敏、头痛、容易疲倦、咳嗽、气喘、皮肤红斑、发痒等。从室内环境的观点来看，建筑物之室内环境中的确潜藏着许多危害因子，增加居住者的健康风险，而大众对此议题的认知仍有不足之处，因此，政府部门及学术界必须对民众宣导健康室内环境的相关知识，并且积极研究相关诊断与改善技术，以确保居住者免于受到室内环境品质不良的慢性伤害。

6.1 室内环境品质诊断与改善

台湾自 2003 年执行"绿色建筑推动方案"起，即长期致力于改善室内环境品质相关研究，期望能从新建建筑物设计、旧建筑物的改善及建材源头管制三个方向来全面提升室内环境品质，并且推动相关政策与措施。2002～2007 年间推动办理"室内环境品质改善计划"，完成 18 处政府机构或大专院校之室内环境品质改善示范案例，并于 2008 年汇编出版《室内环境品质简易自评手册》，提供民众参考；基于"预防设计"与"诊断改善"的观念，2008～2011 年并持续办理"健康室内环境诊断咨询服务计划"，从以往着重于工程改善，转型为室内环境品质诊断与咨询服务，期间累计完成 44 案诊断咨询服务（托儿所 15 案、老人安养中心 11 案、住宅 10 案、小学 8 案），并于 2012 年出版《室内环境品质诊断及改善技术指引》，期能借助此技术指引将室内环境品质的观念推广至产、官、学界及一般民众。

6.2 "室内空气品质管理法"完成立法

室内空气品质对居住者的健康有着不可忽视的影响，尤其台湾的建筑逐渐朝向高层化发展，室内通风几乎全仰赖机械空调系统，且民众的居住空间普遍有过度装修的现象，而装修建材及家具中可能含有超量的甲醛（Formaldehyde）及总挥发性有机化合物（Total Volatile Organic Compounds，TVOC）等有害物质，再加上台湾的亚热带海岛型气候形态，年平均相对湿度高达 70% 以上，易孳生生物性污染物，使得建筑室内环境污染问题更加严重，在此背景下，台湾在 2011 年完成了"室内空气品质管理法"的立法程序，将过去以室外大气管制为主的空气污染防治概念，延伸到公共场所室内空气品质的管理，具体展现重视民众室内生活环境的决心。"室内空气品质管理法"定义之室内空气污染物包括：二氧化碳、一氧化碳、甲醛、总挥发性有机化合物、细菌、真菌、粒径小于等于 $10\mu m$ 之悬浮微粒（PM10）、粒径小于等于 $2.5\mu m$ 之悬浮微粒（PM2.5）、臭氧。

6.3 室内空气污染物之源头管制策略

室内空气污染物中的甲醛及 TVOC 中的苯（Benzene）已被联合国辖下的国际癌症研究署（International Agency for Research on Cancer）评估为第一级（Group 1）人类致癌物，其主要来源为室内装修建材及家具，例如：涂料、胶粘剂、填缝剂、木质板材、合成板材、地毯等，为了从源头管制室内空气污染物，绿色建材标章制度之推动过程中，将低甲醛、低 TVOC 逸散的"健康绿色建材"列为最优先推动且最早受理评定之类别，目前健康绿色建材标章评定项目包括地板类、墙壁类、天花板类、填缝剂与油灰类、涂料类、胶粘剂类及门窗类等 7 项，已将室内具甲醛及 TVOC 逸散之虞的建材完整纳入评估范围，且因甲醛及 TVOC 为建材中常见且健康危害程度较大之有害物质，故健康绿色建材评定基准系规范甲醛逸散速率须小于 0.05mg/（m²·h），TVOC 逸散速率须小于 0.19mg/（m²·h）。唯随着建材产制技术的提升与民众对于健康性能之要求日益提高，于 2011 年起将健康绿色建材评定基准进一步提升，依据甲醛及 TVOC 逸散速率，将建材分为 E1、E2、E 3 等 3 个等级（详表 3），其中 E 3 逸散等级门槛为原来之基准，E1、E2 逸散等级则为逸散速率更低之等级；相关分级制度有助于消费者识别及比较建材之逸散等级，并借助市场良性竞争，引导厂商持续研发逸散速率更低之建材，进一步降低室内空气污染源。

健康绿色建材标章逸散等级表 表3

逸散分级	TVOC 及甲醛逸散速率
E1 逸散	TVOC 及甲醛均≤0.005(mg/(m² · h))
E2 逸散	0.005＜TVOC≤0.06(mg/(m² · h))或 0.005＜甲醛≤0.02(mg/(m² · h))
E3 逸散	0.06＜TVOC≤0.19(mg/(m² · h))且 0.02＜甲醛≤0.05(mg/(m² · h))

此外，基于源头管制之精神，台湾"绿色建材达标制度"在"室内空气品质管理法"制定前即已将挥发性有机化合物（TVOC）及甲醛逸散速率纳入健康绿色建材评定基准，原 TVOC 管制项目包括苯、甲苯、对二甲苯、间二甲苯、邻二甲苯、乙苯等 6 项。至 2012 年实施"室内空气品质标准"，该标准定义之 TVOC 包括：苯（Benzene）、四氯化碳（Carbon tetrachloride）、氯仿（三氯甲烷）（Chloroform）、1，2-二氯苯（1，2-Dichlorobenzene）、1，4-二氯苯（1，4-Dichloro benzene）、二氯甲烷（Dichloromethane）、乙苯（Ethyl Benzene）、苯乙烯（Styrene）、四氯乙烯（Tetrachloroethylene）、三氯乙烯（Trichloroethylene）、甲苯（Toluene）及二甲苯（对、间、邻）（Xylenes）等 12 项化合物，为从源头加强管制建材之挥发性有机化合物，并与"室内空气品质管理法"及"室内空气品质标准"定义之 TVOC 管制项目一致，特于 2015 年将"健康绿色建材"评定基准中之 TVOC 管制项目扩增为 12 种，未来申请健康绿色建材评定，均需针对前揭 12 项化合物进行检测，以确保建材不致造成室内空气品质污染。

7 台湾智能绿色建筑推动策略与现况

由于世界各国均面临了环境变迁与人口高龄少子化的挑战，因此各主要城市正致力于智能科技的突破与创新运用，由于绿色建筑主要系以减量施作的被动（passive）技术手法，追求节能减碳、环境永续发展为主要目标，而智能建筑则希望借由科技主动（active）感知与主动控制之设备技术，达到兼顾节能减碳与人本关怀，促进环境永续与改善生活品质并重的目标。经过近几年来的推动与发展，台湾已经成为全球绿色建筑密度最高的地区之一，绿色建筑的设计水准与营建技术也不断提升。台湾的资讯通信技术与智能型穿戴装置相关产业，具有强大的国际竞争力，智能建筑的推动也让许多主动感知设备、通信设备、网路技术具体的导入了建筑场域。由于绿色建筑与智能建筑的发展已趋于成熟，台湾于 2010 年由政府核定推动"智能绿色建筑推动方案"，期望能整合绿色建筑的设计概念与智能建筑的系统设备，积极推动"智能绿色建筑"，由政府部门领头推动，将智能建筑与绿色建筑结合成为智能绿色建筑，并将其列为政府重要施政政策之一，刻正全力发展此一智能型新兴产业，以达到提升居住环境品质、促进节能减碳及带动产业发展三赢的目标。

7.1 智能绿色建筑定义及相关产业

比较绿色建筑与智能建筑之差异，绿色建筑主要系以被动的技术手法，追求节能减碳、环境永续发展的目标，智能建筑则借由科技主动感知之设备技术，达到提升生活环境品质并兼顾节能永续的目标，而"智能绿色建筑"则是整合绿色建筑与智能建筑之技术与设备特色，使其发挥更大效益。所以"智能绿色建筑"系指以建筑为载体，导入绿色建筑设计及智能型高科技技术、材料产品之应用，使建筑物更安全健康、舒适便利、节能减碳又环保。至于推动方式则考量现行法令制度与技术发展等因素，采用"绿色建筑达标"及"智能建筑达标"并行推动之方式（如图8）。

由于智能绿色建筑系结合绿色建筑设计及智能建筑技术，并借由网路结合各类支援服务，达到提升居住环境品质之目的，因此涉及之产业相当广泛（如图9），主要可分为以下两大类型：

（1）建筑本体相关产业：建筑设计、施工营造、绿色建材、能源管理设备系统、安全监控设备系统、节能家电设备系统、自动控制设备系统、空调节能设备系统、室内环境品质设备系统、节水设备系统、照明节能设备系统等。

图 8　智能绿色建筑推动示意图

（资料来源：智慧绿建筑推动方案，2010）

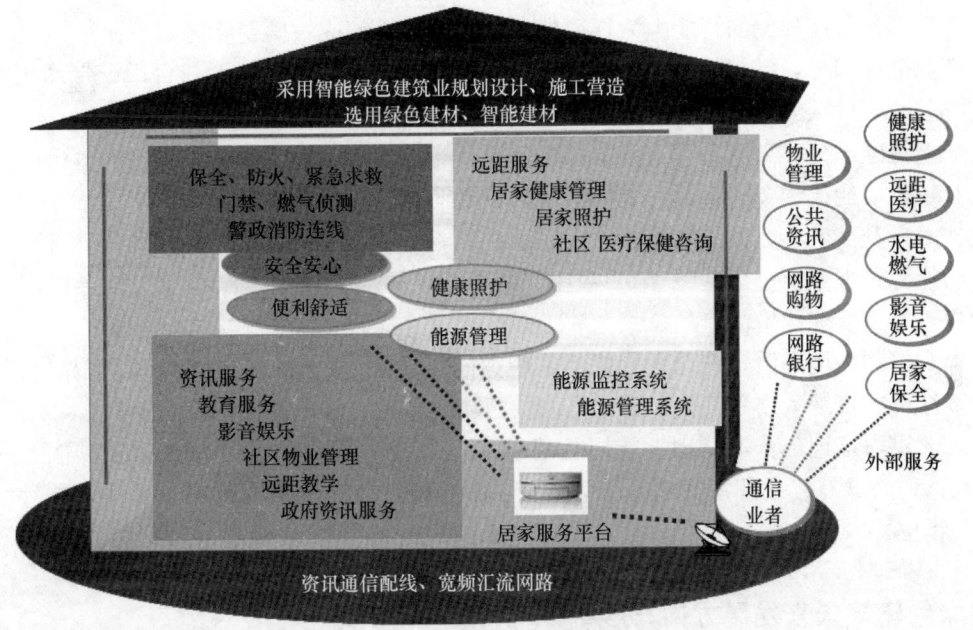

图 9　智能绿色建筑关联产业范畴示意图

（资料来源：智慧绿城市远景与推动发展方向规划研究报告，2013）

　　（2）外部支援服务相关产业：公共服务、资讯通信、物业管理、健康照护、远距医疗、居家保全、影音娱乐等。

7.2　智能绿色建筑推动策略

　　台湾目前智能绿色建筑之推动虽然在既有发展基础上，已有相当不错的成效，唯在整体发展上，仍存在产品及系统整合问题，世界各个地区抑或多或少都遭遇此一课题。而在台湾，因 ICT 产业发展虽在世界居领先地位，但是过去多着重于生产及代工，对于产品及系统间之整合问题较不重视，且对于不同设备间亦缺乏共通通讯协定，仅能依照产品业者之要求或采用国际标准建置，再加上建筑产业与资讯通信产业属跨领域产业，不同领域往往会产生沟通协调及整合问题，也因此成为造成现阶段推动智能绿色建筑面临课题之一。因此，台湾推动智能绿色建筑发展，正借助整合各部会资源积极推动，主要对策如下：

　　（1）加强研发能量：进行智能化之创新技术及相关产品研发，并研拟制订相关系统及设施标准与规格，以强化产业界研发能量，协助推动普及智能绿色建筑，满足市场需求。

　　（2）健全法制规范：检讨评估相关法制、规范、机制及措施内容，并制定管制及奖励措施，以健全推展智能绿色建筑产业之法制规范。

（3）培训专业人才：借助讲习培训、产业技术应用辅导及产学研合作等，并建立资讯交流平台，加强建筑师与电机技师等业界对于相关资讯技术之了解与应用，促使相关专业人员学得专业知识与技能，以满足产业发展所需。

（4）办理示范应用推广：透过建置展示场所，并配合优良案例，办理相关说明及研讨会议，以加强推广应用，以普及智能绿色建筑，满足智能生活需求，进而带动产业发展。

7.3 智能绿色建筑推动现况

台湾制定智能绿色建筑推动方案主要是以政策推展目标为导向，并期望能够开创资讯通信产业运用于智能绿色生活之新契机，以及对建构智能绿色建筑产业链基础能力上能有莫大助益为出发。智能绿色建筑推动方案自 2010 年推动迄今，在各相关部会积极全力推动发展下，除持续建构安全健康、舒适便利、节能环保的智能生活环境外，相关重大推动成效摘要陈述如下：

（1）产业推动部分，已超越计划目标值，共促进产业投资近 623 亿元新台币、带动相关产业产值达 8223 亿元新台币、创造约 26.4 万个就业机会。

（5）节能减碳部分，完成台湾 1 万余家绿色便利商店分级认证、核发绿色建筑达标及证书 5091 余件、既有建筑节能改善 209 案及三个科学园区节电辅导等，计减碳约 433×10^4 t。

（6）技术提升部分，完成能源效率分级标示、节能达标认证及省水达标认证等达 29194 余项产品、量贩店能源管理系统示范建置 1592 余座、既有建筑智能化改善 136 案及另辅导民间厂商如友讯及华硕投入开发智能化生活产品。

（7）提升居住环境品质，推动平价住宅采用智能绿色建筑部分，包括合宜住宅及公营住宅等，均已将智能绿色建筑纳入规划设计，部分案件并已陆续完工，总户数达 10000 余户。

（8）人才讲习培训部分，办理智能绿色建筑参访及技术推广讲习活动共 866 场次、参加者达 36000 余人次，除既有之北部智能化居住空间展示中心外，并建置中南部展示场所，总计参访人次达 110000 余人次。

8 智能绿色建筑未来发展方向与展望

8.1 从智能绿色建筑迈向智能城市

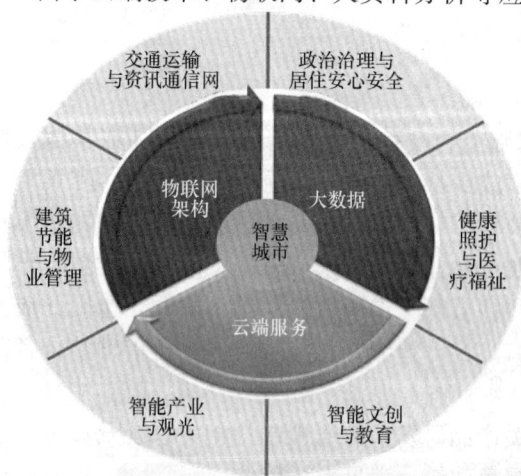

由于云端技术、物联网、大资料分析等应用趋于普及，世界各国尤其是先进国家如美国、日本、欧盟、韩国等均积极应用这些科技于日常生活服务，以居民需求观点思考城市生活，并将智能化生活的概念从建筑本体延伸到社区、城市，其推展智能社区及智能城市，主要聚焦于将资讯通信科技运用在建筑、节能、商业、医疗照护、交通、观光、安全及防灾等应用项目（详图10），以有效提高社会基础设施及运作能量，并期提升民众生活品质，同时达到促进能源效率及降低温室气体排放与废弃物量之成效，进而发展为永续成长的社区与城市。此外，智能社区及智能城市，其市场潜在规模可能高达千兆新台币规模，因此国际均已竞相展开相关推动工作。

图 10　智能城市三大核心与重要应用面向
（资料来源：智慧绿城市远景与推动发展
方向规划研究报告，2013）

未来台湾将在智能绿色建筑的既有基础上，

扩大层面，以社区与城市为对象，选择适当场域进行实证计划，而智能绿色社区与城市推动执行的重点，基于环境永续发展之考虑，低碳节能与绿化将作为必要之基本项目，至于其他服务应用如智能交通运输、智能学习、远距医疗照护、智能安全防灾、智能生活服务、智能联网等跨领域整合应用，则将于选定实证场域，再依据选定场域之使用者需求与智能治理等考虑，利用网路、云端科技与物联网等提供完整的服务。此外，由于台湾地区人口持续往都会区集中，造成城市人口密集、缺乏绿地、热岛效应等，同时乡村年轻人口外流，造成高龄人口比例偏高、医疗及各项生活服务不足等问题，因此，未来在推动智能社区及城市的实证计划，将分别选择城市及乡村地区，于城市中加强生态绿化，并利用网路、物联网等技术提供智能节能、智能交通、安全管理等，在乡村则利用网路、云端等技术引进远距医疗、智能教育及加强生活服务等，透过定制化之做法，考虑实证计划场域使用者实际需求，利用资讯通信科技及云端技术等，提供符合该地民众需求的优质服务，让使用者可实际体会到智能科技带来之安全、便利与舒适，创造有幸福感的生活。

8.2 短中长期发展策略

面对21世纪资讯化现代社会的生活需求，目前台湾所推动智能绿色建筑就是要让建筑成为科技的载体，并且能符合简易、模组化、人性化的应用，使居住环境可以更安全健康、便利舒适，并符合节能及永续发展的要求。为深化智能绿色建筑推动效益，并将既有发展成果与经验，扩大应用至智能城市的推动，可规划出短、中、长期的推动策略：

（1）后续推动重点

智能绿色建筑目前推动尚称顺利，短期内建议以延续计划推动，加强推广落实，并就目前可改善方式，做小幅度调整，以加强推动效益为目标。

（a）持续推动达标制度：持续加强深化推动智能建筑、绿色建筑，与绿色建材达标制度；并扩大绿色建材国际接轨，以协助产业拓展外销商机。

（b）加强普及智能绿色建筑理念，持续办理示范基地参访活动，并借助北中南智能展示场所，及相关宣导短片与讲习推广等，扩大宣导推广。

（c）推动"高贵不贵"智能住宅，部分合宜住宅及公营住宅已采用智能建筑设计并取得认证，未来将持续考虑住宅居住者特性与负担能力，引入适当智能化设备，以提升一般住宅品质以符合未来生活需求。

（d）加强办理既有建筑物改善，既有建筑物占比极高，多数均有耗能、安全或维护管理等问题，本所将持续办理能源效率提升及智能化改善示范计划，以提升建筑环境品质及使用效能，并借助庞大改善市场带动绿色及智能产业发展。另外，既有社区建筑智能化改善，尤其在安全监控及节能管理部分具有极大之发展空间，本部分除加强技术应用推广宣导外，并将探讨配套的奖补助措施之可行性。

（2）中期发展策略

经分析台湾建筑发展现况及参考国际发展趋势，未来智能绿色建筑的发展势必更为蓬勃，台湾如何在现有情况下，应用ICT产业研发优势，扭转台湾欠缺统整系统的劣势，掌握先机，是未来发展的重点。此外，"节能、创能、储能"为目前各国在推动节能减碳的三大重点策略，台湾在相关技术领域仍需积极进行研发，并引进新技术，未来可采取以下做法：

（a）节能技术及配套措施：利用能源可视化促进节能效益，除让使用者了解电力使用状况，做更好的控管之外，同时探讨配合差异电价，降低尖峰时间之用电量，使节电发挥最大之经济效益。

（b）加强再生能源应用：除加强太阳能发电及风力发电外，可进一步研发结合太阳能电板应用于建筑构件（Building Integrated Photo－Voltage）技术，并配合研修法规，以促进市电并连，推广再生能源应用。

（c）加强既有建筑节能改善：既有建筑约占97％，数量极为庞大，且既有建筑改善将可达到实质节能减碳效益并提升居住环境品质，国外多由政府提供补助或对改善支出提供抵减税等，台湾可参考其作法，以加速既有建筑节能改善。

（3）长期发展策略

参考国外做法，长期发展应着重于以人为本，探讨满足使用者需求，建立具备地方或族群文化厚度的智能创新科技与服务产业，并且参考日韩等国家之做法，从建筑个体扩展到社区甚至城市等范畴，使绿色建筑的生态环保、智能建筑的网路、云端等应用，均能发挥更大的整体效益，所以建议长期发展应朝以下方向努力。

（a）推动智能绿色建筑及智能绿色城市产学研合作机制，加强智能绿色建筑研发，尤其着重于人们使用需求、本土环境、文化及生活等，以使智能绿色建筑更符合人本及具备创新意义。

（b）推动智能绿色社区及城市实证计划，选择适当地点，结合政府、产、学、研各界，尤其是相关厂商的异业合作，进行实证性计划，以确实检讨各项做法之效益，并探讨可能的商业运作模式，以作为后续推动之智能社区、城市及模式行销海外之基础。

9 结语

台湾面对 21 世纪各种环境变迁与社会转型的冲击与挑战，除了必须善用网路与资讯通信技术，积极推动智能绿色建筑，使居住环境可以更安全健康、便利舒适，并符合节能及永续发展要求外，后续更需加强跨域整合，建构符合未来生活需求之智能绿色社区与城市环境，促进环境永续发展、提升民众生活幸福、平衡城乡发展及带动产业升级，而智能城市涉及的专业领域极为广泛，包括建筑、建材、ICT 产业、云端技术及系统设备等，甚至必须包括外围各项支援性服务，方能真正发挥智能生活之综合效益，且数位化的智能城市将大胆地跨越了人类既有的生活模式与城市治理经验，未来必须在产业与城市发展的过程中反复进行实证实验，以逐步缩小创新科技与普通百姓生活之间的距离，并试图描绘出智能城市前所未有的发展蓝图。

Policy and Future Development of Intelligent Green Building in Taiwan from the View of Environmental Change

Ho Ming-Chin

(Institute of Architecture，Taiwan University of Science and Technology)

Abstract：Due to the global climate change and the progress of ICT science and technology, the current global architecture development priority has moved to sustainability and environmental symbiosis of intelligent green building to enhance living environment. Considering the challenges of natural and social environment in Taiwan, intelligent green building is also Taiwan's major construction development strategy. This paper presents the development process and policy of intelligent green building in Taiwan. The promotion program of intelligent green building in Taiwan includes the research of green building, intelligent building, green building material, and their assessment tools, labeling systems, green building legalization, renovation of existing building and control of interior environment quality. Hereby the short and long—term development strategies to promote the intelligent green building in Taiwan are introduced. Additionally, enlarging intelligent green building to intelligent community and sustainable intelligent city for upgrading living environmental quality and initiating the opportunities for developing innovative ICT industry is planned in the coming future.

Keywords：Environmental change，Green building，Green building material，Intelligent building，Renovation of existing building

参考文献：

[1]　绿建筑评估手册[M]．台湾，2015．
[2]　何明锦，台港两地绿色建筑的发展，第三届[台港两地绿色经济比较研讨会][D]．2014．
[3]　绿建材解说与评估手册[M]．台湾，2011．
[4]　智慧建筑解说与评估手册[M]．台湾，2011．
[5]　智慧绿建筑推动方案[M]，台湾，2010．
[6]　智慧绿城市远景与推动发展方向规划研究报告[R]．台湾，2013．
[7]　ReliefWeb．Natural Catastrophes World Map 2012.
　　　http：//reliefweb．int/map/world/natural-catastrophes-world-map-2012.

Driving Innovation on Green Infrastructure Components for Sustainable Public Housing in Hong Kong

Yim Yuchau Stephen

(Hong Kong Housing Authority)

Abstract: Hong Kong Housing Authority has been providing sustainable public housing through mass production to help all families in need. Since 2010, we have been conducting research on "Green Infrastructure Components", including slope and roof greening, vertical greening, water saving irrigation system and management, as well as plant selection, to enhance human comfort and mitigate urban heat island effect.

To improve the sustainability of our green infrastructure components, another major aspect of our research was on water management. We have recently conducted innovative studies for Root Zone Irrigation System, Zero Irrigation Planting System (ZIPS) and Bio-retention System as water treatment. The trial results for the above systems were promising and fruitful on savings of water consumption.

Root Zone Irrigation System supplies water directly to plant roots so that evaporation of water can be minimized to reduce the water consumption for irrigation. The system achieves water saving up to 38% in the trial. The system provides an effective and low maintenance water saving mechanism for greening in the estate.

For the Zero Irrigation Planting System (ZIPS), we pioneered to apply sub-irrigation method to achieve "Zero irrigation" in Hong Kong, i. e. zero portable water consumption for planting. The system collects and upkeep storm water for irrigation through sub-irrigation mechanism; it reduces water consumption and provides a sustainable urban drainage system by reducing the volume of storm water entering the sewer system and to restore the natural hydrologic cycle. No manual watering has been applied to the trial scheme for 12 months with dry and wet season.

The Bio-filtration System collects rain water from roofs, covered walkways and planters etc., and passes through the bio-retention system for filtration and cleansing process; the filtered water is then re-used for irrigation purpose.

This paper shares our advancement on greening and water management, with focus on the above innovative systems, to promote a better and more sustainable greening environment.

Keywords: Green infrastructure components, Root zone irrigation system, Zero irrigation planting system, Bio-retention system, Sustainable greening environment

1 Introduction

Hong Kong Housing Authority aims to provide affordable quality housing in a proactive and caring manner, by using public resources effectively. Over 30% of Hong Kong population reside in public rental housing and the Government targets to build about 20, 000 new rental flats per year to meet the increasing needs.

The greening mission is to achieve an overall target of 30% green coverage for new development projects with site area not less than 2 hectares and target to achieve a sustainable urban environment. To drive innovations for green infrastructure components, we pioneer in researching "Green Infrastructure Components", and conducting greening studies since 2008. Major studies in recent years included slope greening, green roof and vertical greening researches. In 2008, the first light weight extensive low maintenance green roof was constructed at Fanling Ching Ho Estate (Figure 1).

From 2012 onwards, we focused on water conservation researches for landscape irrigation,

Figure 1　Green roofs at Ching Ho Estate
(Source: Hong Kong Housing Authority)

which included root zone irrigation system, zero irrigation planting system and bio-retention system. The trial results for the above systems were promising and fruitful on savings of water consumption and storm water management.

2　Study on Root Zone Irrigation System[2]

Root zone irrigation system achieves water saving up to 38% in the pilot scheme of a public housing project in Kai Tak area.

2.1　Basics of Root Zone Irrigation System

The root zone irrigation system consists of polyethylene dripping tubes wrapped with specially designed fleece, which is sewed into two further layers of non-woven fabric to form the Root Zone Irrigation Mat.

The function of the drip pipes is to fill the mat with water. The mat secures an even distribution of water as well as preventing sand and other materials from clogging the drip pipes. Irrigation is then performed by the water saturation effect of the mat and resulting capillary action, guiding the water towards the drier part of the soil. The roots of most plants can grow through the mats without changing the irrigation performance of the mat. The irrigation mats are usually installed about 10 to 20 cm below soil surface and can irrigate lawn areas, flower beds and small shrubs. The expected service life is about 15 to 20 years.

Figure 2　Installation of root zone irrigation system[2]

2.2　The trial at Public Housing Estate at Kai Tak

A trial system was set up at Kai Tak public housing site and the objectives were to compare the performance of conventional irrigation method (sprinkler system) with that of the root zone irrigation system in terms of water consumption and the healthiness / appearance of the plants.

Two planter areas of similar sizes were constructed. Six types of vegetation which were commonly adopted in HA's projects were planted. The conditions of the two planter pots at around the beginning and end of the study are shown in Figure 3 and 4 respectively. Planter pot No. 1 (on left side) was irrigated by the root zone system while planter pot No. 2 (on right side) served as the control was irrigated manually via a sprinkler system.

Figure 3　Photo of mock up planter pots 〔taken on 2 Februry 2011 (planting pot with irrigation mat on left side)[2]〕

Figure 4　Photo of mock up planter pots (taken on 5 June 2012[2])

Water / energy consumption of the two irrigation methods were logged on a weekly basis from March 2011 to March 2012. The healthiness of the plant species was also checked monthly by comparing the conditions of the root growth of the plants in the two pots.

2. 3　Findings

2. 3. 1　Growth and Appearance of Plants

A comparison of water consumption and the growth performance of the plant species were monitored as in Figure 5. No significant difference on the growth performance of the plant species in both the control and mockup planter pots was observed.

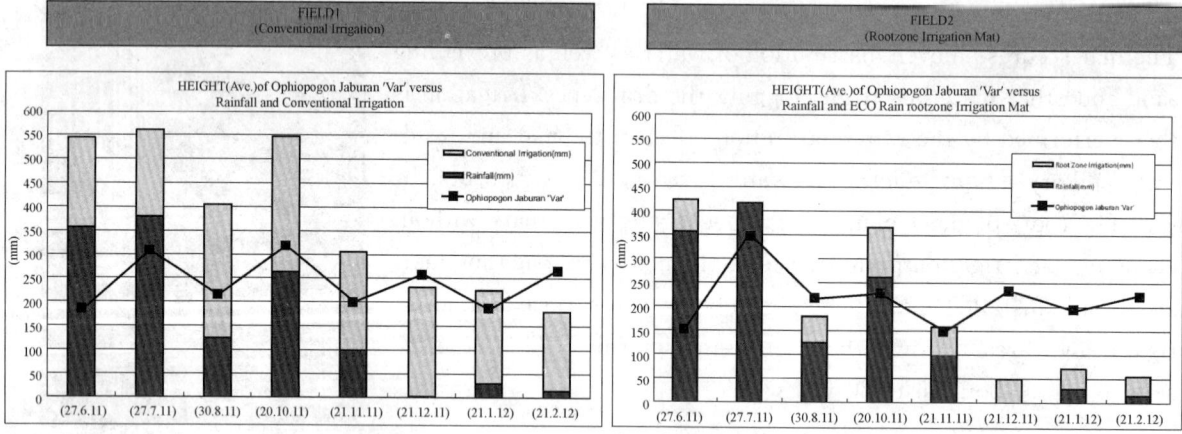

Figure 5　Plant growth monitoring graph[2]

2. 3. 2　Irrigation Water Consumption

The average water consumption rates of the pots provided with irrigation mat and manual irrigation from 12 May 2011 to 31 March 2012 were 1. 54 and 5. 7L/m² /day respectively. By adopting HKHA's latest standard manual irrigation rate of 2. 5L/m²/day, it can still maintain the plant growth to the same extent and the water saving potential was approximately 38%.

2.4 Benefits and limitations of the study

As the water is stored at the roots zone and there is no exposure of the irrigation water to the wind, it achieves considerable water savings when compared to conventional irrigation system.

However, the system also has several limitations. Firstly, the system is only suitable for lawn, turf, shrubs and small woody plants since the mat should be installed not deeper than 400 mm below soil surface. Secondly, in case of repair, excavation and backfilling are required as the irrigation mat and drip pipes are installed under soil.

3 Study on Zero Irrigation Planting System (ZIPS)[3]

Another pioneering study on sub-irrigation method was the Zero Irrigation Planting System (ZIPS) which can achieve "Zero irrigation" in Hong Kong, i. e. 100% water saving with zero portable water consumption for planting. The pilot project was at Lung Yat Estate, Tuen Mun executed in 2013.

3.1 Basics of Zero Irrigation Planting System (ZIPS)

There are two major design objectives of this research study. First, it aims to minimize the manual irrigation operation and maintenance cost. Second, it reduces the storm water runoff and ground water recharge. The Zero Irrigation Planting System (ZIPS) consists of two major components (Figure 6).

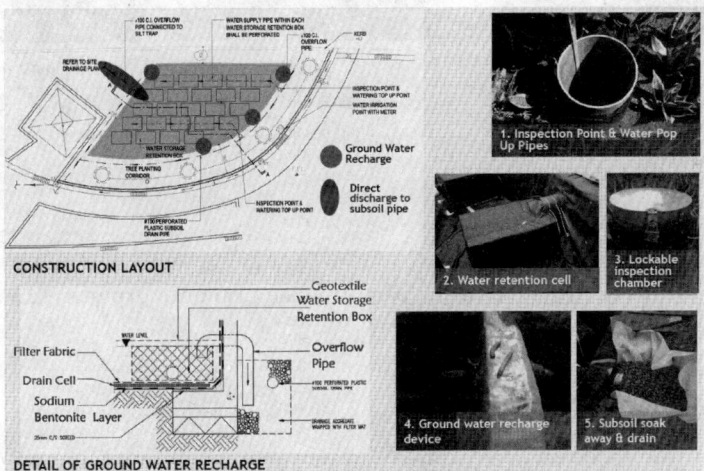

Figure 6　Major components of ZIPS[3]

3.1.1 Sustainable Urban Drainage System (SUDS)

(1) Decentralized network of site-specific storm water management techniques

(2) To reduce / defer the volume of storm water runoff entering the sewer system

3.1.2 Sub-irrigation Planting System

(1) The sub-irrigation system comprises a wicking bed mechanism which is a self-sustained and passive design to deliver the storm water stored in water retention cells to the vegetation and to min-

imize topsoil evaporation through capillary action.

(2) As the system collects and up keeps storm water for irrigation through sub-irrigation mechanism, it reduces water consumption and provides a sustainable urban drainage system by reducing the volume of storm water entering the sewer system and to restore the natural hydrologic cycle.

3. 2 The trial study at Public Housing Estate at Tuen Mun

The construction of the system was carried out from June to November 2013, from sub-base preparation to completion of planting works. The trial system was then monitored for more than 9 months since November 2013. The construction of ZIPS was illustrated in Figure 7.

Figure 7 Construction of ZIPS at trial planter[3]

3. 3 Findings

The monitoring is mainly focused on the performance of plants growth, the effectiveness of capillary action and water consumption.

3. 3. 1 Performance of plants growth

In regards of the consideration of plant species selection for this trial includes condition of drought tolerance, easy maintenance and aesthetics. Six species of plants were selected and well established in the controlled planter (Figure 8). During the monitoring period, only general horticultural maintenance was carried out, no manual watering was applied and no die-back or replacement was recorded.

3. 3. 2 Irrigation Water Consumption

After an initial infill of water to the system, no further manual watering was applied since 11/2013. The system collects, stores rainwater and delivers the water by itself. The lowest water depth during the driest period was about half of the maximum holding capacity. No manual watering was required throughout the whole study period. The sub-irrigation system reduced the evaporation rate

Figure 8   Plant species selected for trial of ZIPS[3]

and was self-sustained on irrigation water for the plants.

3. 4   Benefits and limitations

The system was an effective self-sustained sub-irrigation planting system which no manual watering was required to supplement the water stored in the retention cells. The water retention cells could also effectively serve as a rainwater buffer zone and no flooding under black rainstorm warning was observed. The water consumption and rainfall records indicated the system performed satisfactorily under both wet and dry seasons.

However, as the sub-irrigation planting system has a soil depth limitation of 600 mm, tree planting and podium application to be further studied.

4   Study on Water harvesting with bio-retention for water reuse[4]

Another recent study by Housing Authority was the application of the water harvesting with bio-filtration system which collects rain water from roofs, covered walkways and planters, then passes through the bio-retention system for filtration and cleansing process and the filtered water then re-use for irrigation.

4. 1   Basics of Water harvesting with bio-retention for water reuse

The main goal of the study is rainwater harvesting for landscape irrigation by collecting and treating rainwater to an acceptable quality, and storing on-site. This requires treatment systems that are capable of carrying out secondary treatment. Therefore, bio-retention treatment measures were selected as they can provide physical (sedimentation and filtration) and biological (pollutant degradation) treatment, whilst being largely self-sufficient and requiring low maintenance. The illustration of bio-retention treatment pond is at Figure 9.

4. 2   The trial study at Public Housing Estate at Shui Chuen O

The objectives of the study were to demonstrate the effectiveness of bio-rainwater harvesting

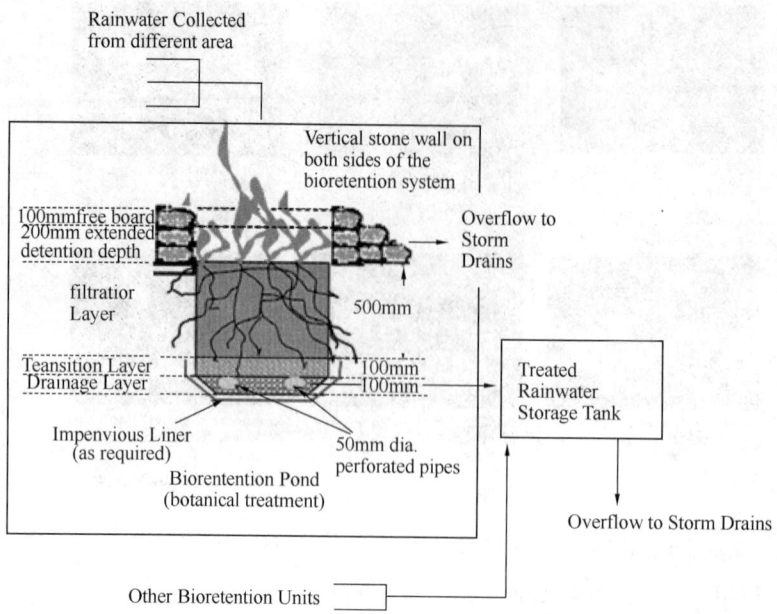

Figure 9   Bio-retention pond[4]

system and to ascertain the system could be operated in the housing estate in an effective way. The mock up of the system was constructed (Figure 10) and monitored from November 2012 to August 2013 to study the performance of selected plant species for bio-retention mock up system.

Figure 10   The mock up system[4]

4.3   Findings

The monitoring is mainly focused on the study the performance of bio-retention plants and compares the performance of chlorinator and UV lamp in terms of disinfection capability and energy efficiency.

4.3.1   Performance of plants growth

In regards of the consideration of plant species selection for this trial includes condition of inundation and drought tolerance, perennial and species without extensive root systems. Six species of plants were selected in the controlled planter (Figure 11) . All the species except Purple Heart are performing well and suitable for bio-retention.

Chinese pennlsetum狼尾草
(*Pennlsetu Alopecuroldes*)

Puple Heart 紫鸭 蹠草
(Setcreasea Purpurea)

Paper Reed纸莎草
(Cuperus Papyrus)

Chinese sivergrass细叶芒
(*Miscanthus Sinensis*)

水竹草

凤尾草

Figure 11   Plants species for bio-filtration[4]

4. 3. 2   Water treatment performance

Water passing through the bio-filtration and physical filtration generally had good water quality, complying with the majority of proposed Hong Kong Water Services Department (WSD) standard. However, the turbidity and colour results did not meet the WSD standard. For E. coli removal efficiency, the mock up showed efficient removal rate above 97%.

4. 4   Benefits and limitations

The system was an effective self-sustained bio-filtration system for recycling rainwater forirrigation use. However, further study is required to ensure the quality of filtered water to meet the irrigation water standard stipulated by WSD.

5   Way forward

Driving the green infrastructure component not only enhances the connectivity of green spaces in the public housing estates and bring along biodiversity, it can also improve the reuse of storm water and restore natural hydrology, reducing the volume of surface run-off and prevent flooding.

Among the various innovative studies, Zero Irrigation Planting System is the most effective sub-irrigation system for water saving and storm water management. More improvements are underway to improve its flexibility on tree planting and podium planting applications.

All these promising results of the pilot studies on green and water management provide a firm keystone for us to plan the green infrastructure and to provide a better and a more sustainable greening environment.

创建可持续香港公营房屋园境设计的绿色基建构件

严汝州
（香港房屋委员会）

摘要：香港房屋委员会一直通过大规模建造公屋来满足有需要的家庭。2010 年以来，我们致力研究"绿色基建构件"，包括坡度和屋顶绿化、垂直绿化、节水灌溉系统与管理，以及植物选择的研究，以提高人体舒适度和缓解城市热岛效应。

为了提高我们的绿色基础设施组件的可持续性，我们研究的另一个重要方面是对水资源的管理。最近，我们对根部灌溉系统，零灌溉种植系统（ZIPS）和作为污水处理的生物滞留系统进行创新研究。上述系统的试行结果十分理想，能有效减少灌溉用水量，成效令人鼓舞。

根部灌溉系统直接把水灌溉到植物的根部，减少水的蒸发以达到减少灌溉用水的目的。在实验中，该种系统能节约 38% 的灌溉用水。这种系统为楼宇绿化提供了一种高效的、低维护成本的节水方式。

对于零灌溉种植系统（ZIPS），在香港我们率先应用地下灌溉的方法来实现"零灌溉"，即无需使用食水灌溉植物。该系统收集和储存雨水，再透过下层土壤以毛细管提供水分进行灌溉，从而减低用水量。系统亦可减少雨水进入污水渠系统和恢复天然水循环，以提供可持续的市区排水系统。在雨季和旱季里，无人灌溉已在实验计划中应用长达 12 个月。

生物过滤系统从屋顶、人行道和花槽等收集雨水，并通过生物保留系统达到过滤和净化的作用。过滤净化后的雨水将用于绿化灌溉。

本文重点阐述以上各个创新系统，旨在分享我们在绿化和水资源管理方面取得的进展，借以推广更优质和更能持续的绿化环境。

关键词：绿色基建构件，根部灌溉系统，零灌溉种植系统，生物滞留系统，可持续绿化的绿化环境

References：

[1] Green infrastructure in Hong Kong Government greening website[OL] http：//www. greening. gov. hk/en/new _ trend/green _ infrastructure. html.

[2] Study Report of Water Reclaim cumRoot Zone Irrigation Systemat Kai Tak Site 1B by Hong Kong Housing Authority[R].

[3] Study Report of Zero Irrigation Planting System (ZIPS) submission by Hong Kong Housing Authority[R].

[4] Mock-up of bio-retention Rainwater Harvesting System in Shui Chuen O Phase 1 – Summary report for Hong Kong Housing Authority，by AECOM

Preparing BIM and COBie for AMIS Integration

Chau Sai wai[1], Leung Wing tai[1], Tam Siu ming[1], Leung Chi chung[1],
Chan Chun hong[2], Lee Tsz hang[2], Gao Chaohengfeng[2]
[1. Water Supplies Department, Hong Kong;
2. Summit Technology (Hong Kong) Limited]

Abstract: Today, operation and maintenance staff often spend an unnecessary amount of time looking for right information in order to fix a maintenance problem, where this information may be hard to obtain or outdated. Also, scattered and unstructured asset information handed over from construction stage would cost the maintenance team significant amount of time and resource to reorganize the information. Since Building Information Modelling (BIM) is very powerful tools for 3D visualization, inventory management and collaboration, it is also an excellent platform for asset lifecycle management. In order to take advantage of BIM platform, the authors participated in a pilot project that integrated the BIM model of existing installations with the Asset Management Information System (AMIS). Currently, there is no simple interface between BIM platform and AMIS. In this pilot project, a 3D BIM model was imported into the AMIS and Construction Operation Building Information Exchange (COBie) was tested for capturing useful asset information together with its geometric data stored in BIM platform to AMIS. This article reviewed and discussed on the implementation process of BIM and COBie for AMIS Integration. Though there are significant benefits come from this integration, however, the best practices and potential effectiveness need further study.

Keywords: BIM, COBie, AMIS, Asset management

1 Introduction

Building Information Modeling (BIM) is a platform to enable consistent and unified lifecycle information flow from the design stage, through the construction stage, to the operation and maintenance stage. As asset data is the key to success for the engineering and maintenance departments, asset managers are increasingly seeking methods to take advantages of the latest BIM technology. However, data mapping process between the capital project phase and operation and maintenance phase is not plain sailing. In order to smoothen the data mapping process, Construction Operation Building Information Exchange (COBie) is considered as one of the major candidates for information exchange between project phase and operation and maintenance phase. Instead of managing geometric information, COBie is an open-exchange standard focusing on delivering useful asset information for operation and maintenance phase. COBie is an important step for integrated BIM solution towards total asset life cycle management. As a globally recognized information exchange standard, its application standards were documented in BS1192-4: 2014.

Asset management information system (AMIS) can assist in asset management to organize and manage information more systematically and efficiently. Typically, this type of system is capable of tracking the asset conditions and associated location data throughout the whole asset lifecycle. These condition based maintenance capabilities enable proactive, rather than reactive, maintenance, which can help utility maximize productivity, reducing unplanned downtime, and extending asset life, all of which can contribute to reduced cost and improved service quality[1].

Through a pilot project, this article aims to find answers to the following questions:

- How to prepare BIM Model and COBie for integration?
- What are the merits of BIM integration with AMIS?

2 Background

Traditionally, the asset register stored in the AMIS can only be viewed in textual data format or in the form of asset hierachy tree structure. Engineers or asset managers cannot access the appearance of the object and its geometric environment through textual data. Even for small scale infrastructure project, data structure of the asset register can be quite complex and often, data need to be broken down into smaller asset groups and stored in multiple layers for implementation. Despite the complex data input structure, commissioning work constantly suffers from the data lost from previous lifecycle stages (Figure 1).

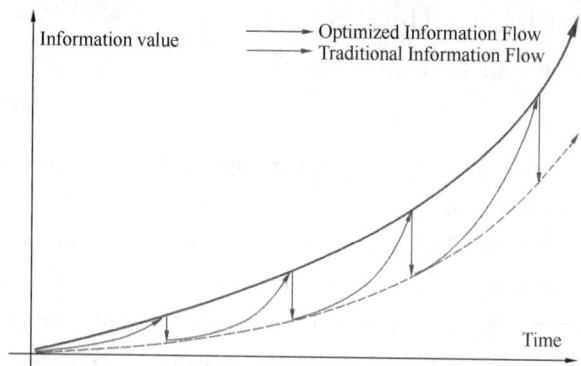

Figure 1   Information value is lost in the transition between building project work stages[2]

What's more, scattered and missing information from previous capital project phase would consume maintenance team months of time to reorganize and identify the useful data for asset management. Therefore, there are needs to adopt advanced implementation method with traditional AMIS.

3 Methodology

The authors recently participated in a project held by the Water Supplies Department (WSD), Government of Hong Kong Special Administrative Region to develop an achievable method to integrate BIM with AMIS. In order to take advantage of BIM as an asset lifecycle data platform, and as IFC model-based transformation is still under development, the authors resolved to prepare BIM with COBie for the integration.

3.1 Project Information

Basic project information   Table 1

Site Name	Tai Po Salt Water Pumping Station	Telegraph Bay Salt Water Pumping Station
BIM Model		

continued

Site Name	Tai Po Salt Water Pumping Station	Telegraph Bay Salt Water Pumping Station
Location	Tai Po	Telegraph Bay
Current Stage of Development	Existing installation	Existing installation
Usage	Supply of salt water for flushing	Supply of salt water for flushing
Capacity	50. 28 MLD	29. 8 MLD
Service Time	18 years	1 year
Owner	Water Supplies Department, Government of Hong Kong Special Administrative Region	Water Supplies Department, Government of Hong Kong Special Administrative Region

Project Objectives:

- Develop BIM Models, BIM Standards, and COBie deliverables.
- Integration of BIM and AMIS through COBie.

Before implementation, there are three different maintenance systems that are operating simultaneously to conduct regular maintenance jobs.

- Maintenance Work Management System (MWMS): manage regular maintenance order and data;
- Integrated Materials and Job Record Management System (IMJRMS): streamline waterworks inventory operations, enhance efficiency of inventory distribution and provide management information; and
- Supervisory Control and Data Acquisition (SCADA): provide remote monitoring and control of equipment.

3. 2　Project Implementation Process

As the project scope has been established, BIM development team began collecting information to prepare BIM model. Geometric and installation information of both pumping stations were obtained from as-built drawings, laser scan, and site visits. In order to prepare Level of Development (LOD) 500 BIM models for asset management, WSD asset management team extracted the operation and maintenance data from existing Maintenance Works Management System (i. e. works order system) and Integrated Materials and Job Records Management System (i. e. planned maintenance system) for input into the BIM models. In the process of creating COBie sheet for next implementation in AMIS, multiple coordination meetings were held between asset management team, civil, mechanical and electrical engineers, BIM consultant and AMIS consultant. In essence, all stakeholders were fully participated in the project from project inception. Based on the expert knowledge and experience from various stakeholders, the BIM development team managed to export suitable COBie sheets from BIM model. Effective communication was proven to be one of the key factors leading to the success of this project.

Subsequently, the new AMIS successfully imported the information from a COBie file, and integrated with BIM model through a 3D viewer, which allows the asset management team to access both geometric model and asset related information. After the implementation process, a BIM standard was prepared for WSD for future implementation of BIM for AM purpose. During the implementation, information stored in MWMS, IMJRMS, and SCADA was transferred into new AMIS (Figure 2).

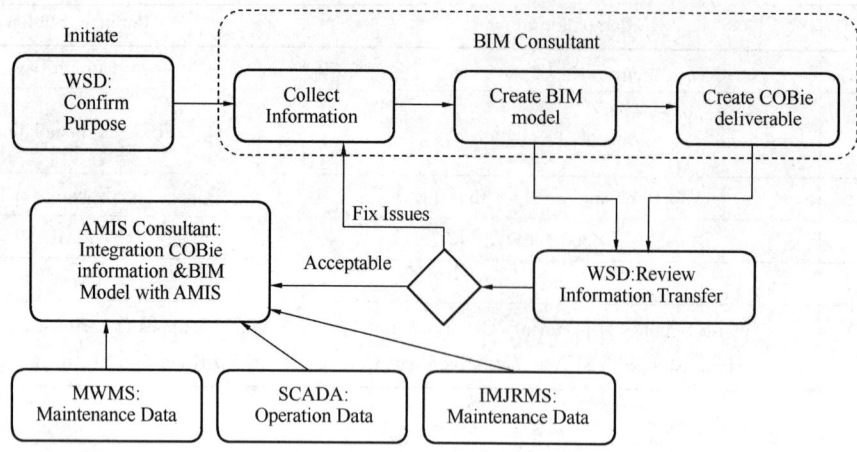

Figure 2 Overall project implementation process

4 Preparing BIM Model and COBie for Integration

Acritical requirement to produce suitable BIM model is to understand the building data structure and user requirements. The purpose of this integration project is to provide better asset management solution for owner. Therefore, Employers Information Requirements (EIR) on asset management had high priority for consideration. Owner's asset management team should participate in defining the requirement at initial stage of project implementation, while BIM development team has to understand the EIR and how to use BIM data structure to generate suitable COBie for information handover. During this project, significant amount of researches and discussions were held within the project team members. Regular exchange of findings and suggestions among project team members was proven to be a key factor to successfully capture the right information from the BIM model.

4.1 Asset Model Preparation

First of all, the geometric appearance and level of details of the BIM model has to meet the as-built requirement, which represents the accuracy in terms of quantity, size, shape, orientation and interfaces with other building systems. One of the challenges occurred in the early stage of the project is some of the as-built drawings were missing and the drawings were only available in paper format for model building. To implement the BIM model for AM, the BIM model needed to be realistic and matched with the actual working environment so that operation and maintenance staff can use the built-in BIM model features in AMIS to create and manage their works order effectively. Therefore, the right level of details and accuracy of geometric data for displaying the actual asset location is critical to the implementation of BIM for AM.

As both pumping stations are existing installations, "Scan to BIM" method was conducted to provide point cloud as supplementary information for modelling. Point cloud allowed BIM development team to visualize the actual physical environments of the pumping station without travelling to the site. Also, with the help of point cloud, BIM development team can examine areas such as confined space where the staff may have difficulty in accessing this type of areas (Figure 3). The

Point Cloud Model   BIM Model

Figure 3   Comparison between point cloud model with BIM model

graphical representation of the BIM model may be changed to suit users' need; however, BIM development team has to identify suitable color coding list, which include object name and corresponding RGB code for unification.

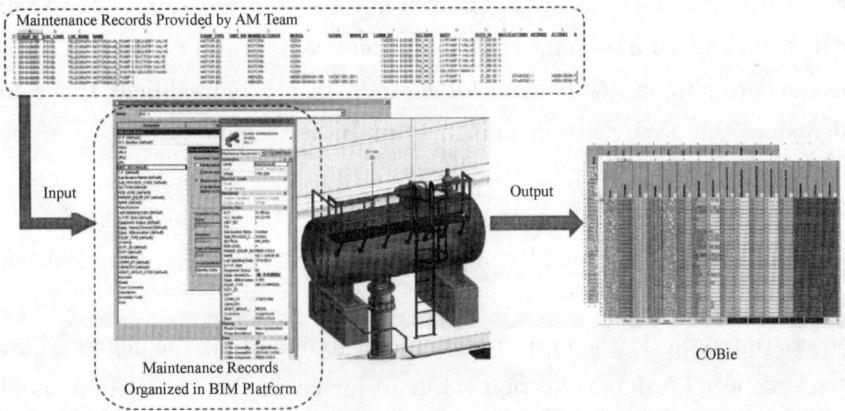

Figure 4   Data input & output in BIM platform

In consideration of creating LOD500 asset model, BIM development team has to define extra parameters to cater for asset management data. Assets that selected for planned maintenance would be assigned a unique number, which is used to track the assets in AMIS. This unique number must correctly mapped to the corresponding asset created in BIM model, and this number must be ensured to be included in the COBie spreadsheet for information exchange.

For existinginstallation, all textual information inputted into the BIM model and COBie worksheet should originate from the handing-over notes including information in the Operation & Maintenance Manual (O&M manual) and other related documents. The handing-over notes should be used to provide basic information such as dimensions, manufacturers and model number for the equipment of the project. The handing over notes is crucial for newly or existing installation in order to meet the requirement for implementing AMIS. The asset information in BIM models and COBie worksheets should be aligned with the data structure of AMIS.

Maintenance parameters and their values are standardized by the asset management team, then BIM development team created the corresponding parameter field in Revit. Since a comprehensive maintenance records contain great amount of parameters, to avoid repetitive creation, BIM development team took advantage of the shared instance parameter (figure 4). Shared parameters are stored in a text file independent of any family file or Revit project, which allows user to access the file and add any parameter contained to different families or projects.

4.2 COBie Preparation

The BIM model contains the asset location and its proximity surrounding areas and COBie defines the data structure that required for AMIS. It is crucial to understand BIM and AMIS data structure in order to generate appropriate COBie spreadsheet for smooth transition. The detail AMIS data structure may vary depending on the nature of the asset, but the logic of the asset registry and data hierarchy structure should be similar.

COBie was used bridge the gaps between BIM and AMIS. There is commercially available plug-in for BIM platform to generate a COBie spreadsheet directly from the BIM model. As required asset information has been well structured and organized in BIM model, users only have to adjust few instruction settings, and the plug-in will generate the COBie automatically. However, for assets with complex hierarchy structure the standard plug-in is not 100% compatible with AMIS. Therefore, BIM development team created a customized Application Program Interface (API) to remedy the inadequacy of the standard plug-in. Although COBie can be manually modified, this course of action is not recommended since the occurrence of human errors is unacceptably high even when processing small scale model.

There are two commonly used international standard for COBie namely Omniclass and Uniclass. The decision on using either COBie standard may be based on regional requirement and/or software environment.

For new or existing project, the project team ought to determine the degree of information needed for COBie spreadsheet. A data collection standard for particular installation should be prepared and listed in EIR. COBie data drop process shall be adopted, and stakeholders, including design and construction firm, need to participate in the data collection process to ensure accuracy and sufficiency of information across the building lifecycle.

5 Merits of Integrating BIM with AMIS

A well-implemented BIM could lead to better structured drawings that reflect the actual building environment. Engineers and asset managers can remotely examine the installations without physically access to the equipment (Figure 5).

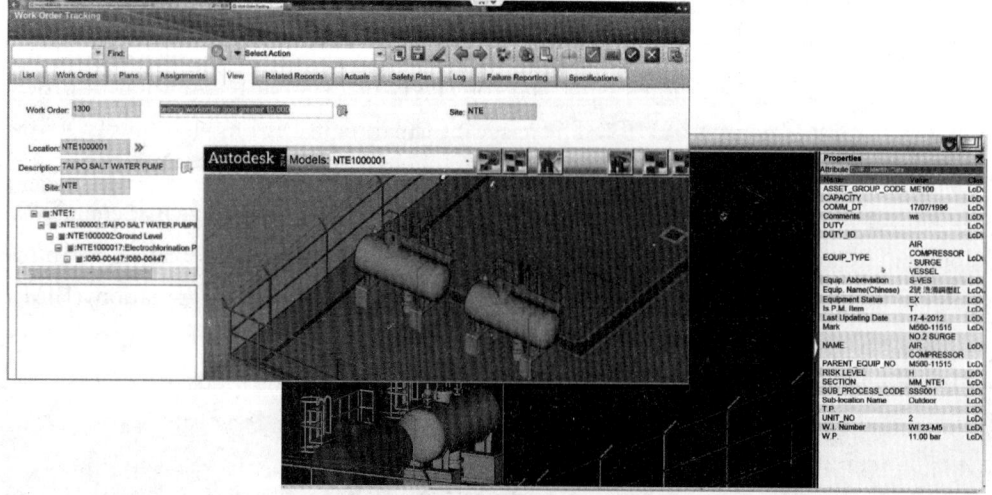

Figure 5　Access work order and equipment information from AMIS

A number of the key merits of BIM for AM are listed below：

• Easier to find building components，which eases the operation and maintenance of the building，through more structured storage of useful documents.

• BIM helps to identify visual and graphical information to aid in the display of knowledge that improves the usefulness.

• Better decision basis with more trustworthy calculations and a better understanding between designers and end-users.

• Better documentation in the project transition phase，which simplifies the handing over process and improve overall information flow. The integration between BIM and AMIS also allows user to retrieve useful information quicker，more efficient，and precise.

6　Conclusion

Authors conducted a pilot study which successfully integrated BIM with AMIS. The authors have better insight that the BIM/AM integration had enabled greater interaction between various stake holders for the asset management. It can also streamline the information flow between different engineering disciplines for better information exchange and sharing. More importantly，the BIM/AM integration service can reduce the data losses and duplication of data entry efforts and greatly improved data quality，time management and overall asset performance. While carrying out a standalone project does not guarantee success for future BIM/AM integration，it has nonetheless proved to be a topic of value and is well worth additional research on the topic.

Acknowledgements

The authors would like to express their gratitude to Water Supplies Department and its staff for their support in writing this paper. This project and this paper would not have been possible without their patronage and thrive for improvement. The authors would also like to acknowledge the staff of Summit Technology and Sino-iTech in their roles in developing the aforementioned project and providing the basis of this paper.

<h1 style="text-align:center">如何妥善处理 BIM 与 COBie 以便与资产管理系统整合</h1>

周世威[1]　梁颖泰[1]　谭少明[1]　梁志聪[1]　陈振康[2]　李子铿[2]　高超程丰[2]

（1. 香港水务署；2. 云峰科技香港有限公司）

摘要：现今运营和维修人员常常在搜索资料的过程中花费大量的时间精力，但有时搜索到的资料手册不一定符合环境。错误的资料可能会导致错误的维修决定，进而导致不必要的浪费甚至引起更严重的后果。资料对于资产管理的重要性毋庸置疑，然而资产管理人员在建造工程完成后所接收的资料通常杂乱并且有所遗失。重新输入储存这些资料对于资产管理人员来说也是一个耗时耗力的过程。BIM 作为一个良好的工具和分享平台，可以有效整理资料，应该在建筑生命周期内扮演重要角色。作者参与了一先导项目，项目团队利用 BIM 为运营中的抽水站建立包含运维资料的 BIM 模型，然后以 COBie 做为信息传递载体，实现 BIM 模型以及信息在资产管理系统中的整合。实践证明 BIM 在资产管理领域具有相当的价值，然而良好的作业方案及潜在效益仍需要更多的研究。本文基于作者参与的项目，讨论如何准备 BIM 模型和 COBie 以便于与资产管理系统整合。

关键词：BIM，COBie，资产管理系统，资产管理

References：

[1] Chang C Y，Tsai M D. Knowledge-based navigation system for building health diagnosis[J]. Advanced Engineering Informatics，2013，27：246-60.

[2] Nashwan N Dawood，Mohamad Kassem，Vladimir Vukovic. 2015. Whole Lifecycle Information Flow Underpinned by BIM：Technology，Processes，Policy and People[C]. Tokyo：IC-CBEI，2015.

[3] Chen H M，Hou C C，Wang Y H. A 3D visualized expert system for maintenance and management of existing building facilities using reliability-based method[J]. Expert Systems with Applications，2013，40：287-99.

[4] Farr E R P，Piroozfar P A E，Robinson D. BIM as a generic configurator for facilitation of customisation in the AEC industry[J]. Automation in Construction，2014，45：119-125.

[5] Kans M. An approach for determining the requirements of computerised maintenance management systems[J]. Computers in Industry，2008，59：32-40.

[6] Motamedi A，Hammad A，Asen Y. Knowledge-assisted BIM-based visual analytics foe failure root cause detection in facilities management[J]. Automation in Construction，2014，43：73-83.

[7] Nik-Mat N E M，Kamaruzzaman S N，Pitt M. Assessing the maintenance aspect of facilities management through a performance measurement system：a Malaysian case study. Procedia Engineering，2011，20：329-338.

[8] Lai J H K，Yik F W H. Hotel engineering facilities：a case study of maintenance performance. International Journal of Hospitality Management，2012，31：229-235.

[9] Love P E D，Matthews J，Simpson I，et al O A. A benefits realization management building information modeling framework for asset owners. Automation in Construction，2014，37：1-10.

安老空间·人文环境

郑炳鸿　董国华　许张敏

（香港中文大学建筑学院）

摘要：香港地区将会进入一个"长者社群"急速增长的阶段。当中的迫切性，大抵要在人口机会窗口（demographic window）关闭前，我们必须寻找到结构性的解答方案。为了正视这项人口老化导致长者"抚养率"上升的社会问题，从建筑研究的角度，又可否提供一些端倪，从而指向社会发展的创新思维呢？本文将以"活老"（active ageing）为出发点，从室内空间的改造、建筑设计及城市规划这3个建筑研究的主要层面来探讨及回应"安老空间"这迫切的社会课题，并建议如何透过"安老空间"方案来达致"老有所养"、"老有所依"及"老有所成"的人文关怀。

关键词：活老，安老空间，家居安老，长者价值

1 引言

香港在可见的未来将会进入一个"长者社群"急速增长的阶段，联合国经济和社会事务部预计香港将于2050年成为全球人口年龄最老地区的第四位。[1]当中的迫切性大约要在人口机会窗口（demographic window）关闭前，即老年人口超过15％之前（即是在2015～2019年其间），我们必须就人口老化寻找到结构性的解答方案。为了正视这项人口老化导致长者"抚养率"上升的社会问题，在城市设计、建筑及或空间改造的角度，又可否提供一些端倪，从而指向社会发展的创新思维呢？

2 "安老空间"

当"安老空间"的概念在2015年初由笔者通过"宣言"形式作起步的倡议后，在香港不同的层面引发多方的讨论及探求：首先不少学者及社会人士关注的"全民退休保障"而延伸的议题——"安老空间与福利社会"的矛盾与误解，是需要正视及梳理的，当中空间及建筑元素是否可以进行改造及更新而不必依赖福利制度的支持呢？从这条思路开始，"建筑师"作为"社会改革者"（social reformer）的角色，应该在此时此地可以发挥其整合及创新的专长。

对不少人来说，因为香港狭隘的生活空间及紧迫的城市环境，要达到"家居安老"（ageing in place）的理想，似乎是遥不可及。在此背景下，在考虑及研究"安老空间"这课题时，笔者认为其总体概念应以"活老"（active ageing）为出发点——即透过提升及改善长者的健康、群体参与和生活保障，从而提高他们或她们的生活质量（参照世界卫生组织的定义[2]）。由此角度思考，笔者建议"安老空间"的探讨及推展可以集中在4个互相关联的重点之上：（1）安老空间与社福基建；（2）安老空间与医护网络；（3）安老空间与住房设计；（4）安老空间与创新产业

要完善"安老空间"的概念，当中最关切的问题是，在现有的社福基建框架下，我们如何从创新产业的角度去诠释及改造不同规模的长者"安老空间"，满足他们或她们的医护需求，达到"家居安老"的目标，并且进一步建立具"长者价值"的家庭及社区关系网。要达到这个目标，我们必须以创新思维结合社区的特质，以先导计划而加以实践。在这基础上，本文将从室内空间的改造、建筑设计及城市规划这3个建筑研究的主要层面，就"安老空间"这一长者居住议题作进一步的探讨。

3 室内空间的改造

香港长者宿位严重不足,现时仍有大量需要照顾的长者未能入住院舍。据审计署发表的报告,截至 2014 年 8 月底,本港约有 3.1 万名长者仍在中央轮候册上轮候资助护理安老院或护养院宿位,平均轮候时间约为 3 年。2013~2014 年度,有 5700 名长者轮候至离世仍未获分配宿位,较 2010 年之前的每年 4000 至 4500 人严重。[3]截至 2015 年 1 月 31 日,共有 31655 位长者正在轮候护理老安院或护养院,而该年轮候期间死亡人数升至 5000 多人。因为每年轮候册的长者人数居高不下,即表示每年同时有数千宗新的申请[4],可见情况严重。翻查过往 10 年的资助宿位的数量,截至 2000 年 3 月底有 21600 个宿位,直到 2014 年 3 月,宿位却只有 26000 个,宿位数目在这 14 年间只增加了 20%。此外,香港房屋协会提供的"长者租住公屋单位"因空间狭小及设计简陋,被指责为非人性的居住空间(因此被称为"公屋劏房"),一直不受长者欢迎而入住率低,解决不到长者(尤其是基层长者)的居住问题。故此,有不少团体认为政府一直欠缺长者安老的长远规划,现有的社福制度未能达到"老有所养、老有所依、老有所为"的目标。

在此背景下,笔者认为除了继续争取增加长者宿位及租住单位外,我们亦应考虑"家居安老"的可能性。"家居安老"涉及两大元素:第一是软件支援,透过不同的资讯服务平台,支援长者的起居生活,便利他们或她们在家中安老;第二是硬件空间设计,从功能技术层面改善长者现有的生活空间,协助长者建立无障碍的家居。这种为长者而设的软硬件配合必然可以改善长者居住空间的质素(图 1),增加"家居安老"的可能,从而减少长者院舍的需求,舒缓长期紧张的长者宿位问题。

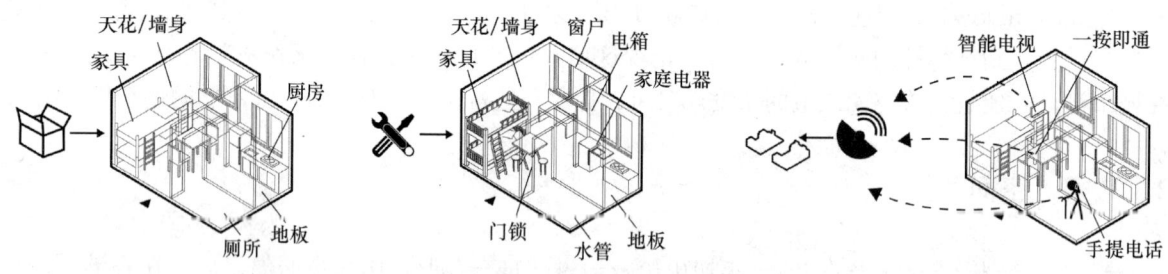

图 1 "家居安老"的软硬件配合
(资料来源:作者自绘)

就软件而言,根据世界卫生组织的"长者友好城市的基本特征清单"(Checklist of Essential Features of Age-friendly Cities),长者的起居生活支援主要涉及"定期广播与长者兴趣有关的资讯"、"以口头谈话的形式作为与长者沟通的主要方式"及"(长者)可以从可信任的人获得一对一的信息"。[5]长者安居协会自 1996 年开始提供"平安钟"、"管家易"等支援长者起居生活的资讯服务平台(包括呼援、关怀热线、护理及家务助理等服务),是这方面值得参考的先例。[6]在这基础上,笔者建议长者的生活支援可跳出语音系统的层次,以创新产业的方向发展。透过安装视像系统,长者生活支援可以突破更多空间上的阻隔,长者在家中能更有效地接收更多样化的有用资讯和处理生活上的种种事务。长者可以将不能理解的文字或图像,如说明书、公函等,透过视像系统来询问远在服务中心的人员。此外,一些难以透过静态图像形式来询问及解答的生活问题,如电器操作等,亦可以透过视像平台更有效地处理,变相为长者提供一个"虚拟"的"家务助理"。

就硬件而言,根据"长者友好城市的基本特征清单",长者住屋的最基本条件是其所有空间及通道的地面应为同一高度,以便长者能不受阻碍地行动。[7]香港房屋协会于 2013 年开始推行的"长者住安心"计划是这方面值得参考的先例。[8]该计划主要为长者提供专业的家居评估,就不同长者的身体状况,就家居的"硬件"作出设计方案,例如安装防滑地砖、使用免钻墙浴室扶手、拆除原有的门槛（以方便轮椅出入）等，以改善长者的生活空间。在这基础上，笔者就长者室内空间改造或设计提出以下两大设计原则：

（1）安全可达——因应长者的活动范围，我们必须考虑他们或她们肢体可达的高度和深度，按日常使用的便捷程度而作出适当安排。设计要避免难以触摸的储存空间和不必要的转折部位。整体而言，设计应参照如香港政府的《设计手册：畅通无阻的通道 2008》的标准规格，并应以务实简单的整体空间设计为依据。

（2）简约鲜明——考虑到长者视听及行动机能的退化，空间及设施的设计必须具较强的可依赖性；除了明确的指示外，一般设计应强调鲜明轮廓及色彩，以增强其识别性及分区功能。空间应避免重复的设计形态及幽暗角落。

此外，诚如不少学者指出，建筑本身涉及功能（utilitas）及美学（venusta）的考虑。[9]因此，除了功能上的考虑外，为长者而设的居住空间不能略过空间美学的关注（例如建筑符号、建筑风格等）、不能忽略建筑体验对长者日常生活的正面影响。一般而言，长者较接受平和、温暖及具家庭的感觉的居住环境，我们可以透过摆放绿意央然的植物、采用自然物料和暖色调墙面、规划宜室宜家的家具配置等来达到这美学上的目的。此外，为增加长者的认同和归属感，我们可以摆放具年代价值的物件、采用具吉祥意义的建筑装饰，或为空间设计注入传统中国建筑风格的元素。

4　建筑设计

世界卫生组织对"活老"有如此理解：

老年化发生于朋友、工作同事、邻居和家庭成员的场景之内。这解释了为什么相互依存（interdependence）及跨代间的团结（intergenerational solidarity）是"活老"的重要原则。[10]

由此可见，"安老空间"涉及如何在"建筑设计"及"城市规划"的层面上协助长者与家人及社区建立健康的关系，以满足强调关系性的"活老"的重要原则。下文我们会先从"建筑设计"的角度讨论长者与家人的关系。周永新教授在"香港退休保障的未来发展研究报告"指出长者居住状况因香港的家庭体制改变而急速变化，香港的独居长者比例不断上升（2001 年为 11.3%；2006 年为 11.6%；2011 年为 12.7%）；仅与配偶同住的长者比例同样不断上升（2001 年为 18.4%；2006 年为 21.2%；2011 年为 23.6%）。[11]分支家庭与父母分散，以至家庭过往对长者在身心上的支持功能逐步下降，值得社会关注。按一般观察，香港年青一代大都不愿意继续与父母同住。除了住屋空间的因素外，这与年青一代重视私隐独立有关。但由于受到中国传统价值观影响，大部分年轻人都愿意在婚后或独立后与父母保持接触及照顾对方。这与周教授在一个焦点研究小组所得的结果相近：

……在我们的焦点小组，除一人之外，所有参与者均表示他们或她们不希望与父母或配偶的父母同住……大多数与会者表示他们希望在自己的住所有更多的隐私。此外，他们或她们还分享了与父母或配偶的父母同住所产生的家庭矛盾的经验。焦点小组的参与者提出的理想安排是这样：父母或配偶的父母与自己住在同一地区或同一屋邨，以致可以经常探访他们或她们……[12]①

笔者相信这种在居住上的"关系—隐私"的张力可以透过合适的"建筑设计"解决。香港房屋协会策划的乐融轩是值得参考的先例。乐融轩是一个将私人住宅与长者住屋混合发展的建筑设计，其总体概念为长幼共融。当中的 60 个单位（6 至 11 楼）为长者租住房屋（设有为长者而设的家居设备），其余的 214 个单位（12 至 42 楼）为出售住宅。出售单位的业主可同时租用长者租住单位，以便照顾年长亲人。[13]设计能在尊重各人私隐的前提下，透过混合发展的住屋空间安排，促进建立家人与长者的健康关系，在一定程度之下满足上述的"活老"原则。然而，值得一提的是，不少人

---

① 值得注意的是，有焦点小组的参与者认为为了保护自己的隐私，父母或配偶的父母不应住在自己的隔壁甚或同一大厦内。但笔者认为这并非大多数人的意见。

指出乐融轩的长者租住单位租金太高（305～504 英尺的长者租住单位租金为 11300 至 18300 港元），以致反应未如理想，间接推翻了长幼共融的建筑设计。笔者认为在推动"活老"的前提下，政府可考虑以长者福利的形式资助同类长幼共融居住的安排，以鼓励子女与父母在邻近地方居住，重塑家庭过往对长者在身心上的支援功能。长远而言，政府就此的福利开支必会得到更大的社会回报。

此外，根据"香港统计年刊 2014"，香港私营工厂大厦的空置量约为 989000m²（2013 年），若包括小量公营工厂大厦的空置量，总空置量约为 1000000m²。若我们能因应各区的实际情况，有策略地透过改变空间用途释放这些空置单位，保守估计，这可供应数千甚至万多个长者宿位及租住单位，能直接回应上述长者安老宿位短缺的问题。空置的单位可根据上述的室内空间改造原则及其他相关的条例改造成有质素的住屋，供当区的长者安老。在政府政策的配合下，空置的空间可被活化善用。经改造后的长者单位，业主可以高于工厦的英尺价、但低于住宅的租金英尺价出租予长者，是为双赢的局面。在此之外，政府亦可考虑就改建及长者租金作出不同形式的资助计划。当然，计划的关键在于能以便利长者的通道连接改建的长者住所及区内的主要住宅区，以便长者能与同区居住的子女保持紧密的交往。此外，在这以社区为本位的基础上，我们更可以在长者可达的范围内，以点状的形式将长者支持站分布于社区内，在上述长者家居的软件支援之上，进一步提供有系统的社区医护网络。

5 城市规划

戴维·哈维（David Harvey）对城市规划有以下见解：

……在一个健康的城市环境中，我们会发现一个有组织的复杂系统，而不是一个杂乱无章的系统，这是社会互动（social interaction）的活力和能量，它关键地依赖于多样性、复杂性以及以受限制的创意方法去处理突发事情的能力。"当一个人想着城市的进程，跟着这个人必须考虑这些进程的催化剂，这也就是本质。"……有一些市场的进程正在工作，往往去对抗人类喜爱多样性的"自然"倾向，并产生令人窒息的划一土地用途。这个问题被严重地恶化，因为城市规划者宣称自己是多样性的敌人、担心混乱和复杂性。他们有这一个取向是因为他们认为这是混乱的、丑陋的和无可救药地不合理的。[14]

戴维·哈维所谈及的是一个城市环境应有的多元形态。香港的城市规划长期以约化多元空间用途的分区计划大纲图为主导，所产生的结果正是戴维·哈维所否定的欠缺互动的划一城市空间。由于香港的家庭及社会条件不断改变，预计将会有更多的"活老"社群出现。这些社群会通过不同的选择及取向形成多元的社区形态。戴维·哈维所指的"社会互动"对多元的"活老"社群尤为重要。在现有的城市里，我们要创造能引发互动进程的"催化剂"，将划一的空间转化为"有组织的复杂系统"，从而使"活老"社群在其中得到支援及发展。

自 2007 年起，香港中文大学建筑系的"社区营造学社"一直探究如何从人文景观（human landscape）的角度为香港城市发展贡献新的思维。"启德河绿廊·社区教育计划"成功地透过"绿廊"的概念将社区内零散的文化枢纽（cultural hubs）联结、将堵塞了的公共空间打通。透过教育、社区活动和空间使用的实例示范，凝聚黄大仙区内的持份者（community stakeholders），对"启德明渠"有了崭新的构想，重新诠释了"人"与"地"应有的关系。研究结果更推动了政府各部门关注启德河的发展。在这探索"人"与"地"关系的基础上，笔者在"安老空间"宣言中指出，形象化的社区长者平台"E—站"可作为塑造多元社区的"催化剂"。这社区设施可以作为可见的先导计划。计划以长者半小时的步行脚程为依据，按选定地区的条件，策略性地建设"E—站"。透过"E—站"，我们鼓励长者在可达的情况下接触区内不同年龄、背景和文化的社群，引发多元的社会互动，缔造相互依存及跨代间的团结。这除了可以为长者提供适量的运动外，他/她们因此亦可与其他人分享人生经验（例如技能分享及故事述说等形式）。正如启德河"绿廊"的概念，我们可透过

"E—站"等设施，打通不同地区被堵塞了的公共空间，有条理地编织一个盛载多元文化历史的社区网络。这种社区互动能积极地建立"长者价值"，促进"老有所成"。

除此之外，我们亦可参考外国经验，透过长者的参与将异质的绿色文化带入社区网络，作为对现代化的城市空间的一种抗衡。笔者认为若长者文化及绿色文化创新及有机地结合，便能为社区创造新的机遇。在"活老"社群的带领下，这亦为全民参与、缔造社区绿色文化踏出重要的第一步。这种长者主动参与的形式不单积极回应了"活老"的概念，更可创造新型的老人就业机会，减低社会及政府的财务负担。

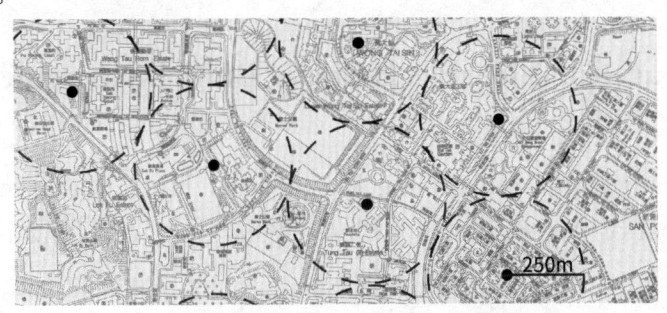

图 2　社区网络（长者半小时步行圈）

（资料来源：作者自绘）

透过与"E—站"相关的活动及工作坊，我们可以搜集城市肌理、文化数据、城市空间应用（spatial practice）、空间计划（spatial programme）和口述历史记录等重要的地区资料。只要加以叠加、整合，我们便能制作当区的文化地图（cultural mapping）。"文化地图"是以具象方式将"人文景观"刻画成图表。一些不易辨明的地区文化数据，如社会和文化的缺口、地面的可通行性、基建问题及空间应用也能够在图上反映。因此，文化地图是跨学科研究的重要基础，亦能为政策制定者和城市规划师提供重要的参考数据。值得一提的是，与其他的年龄组别比较，长者是可量性较高及属性较稳定的市区持份者，不单可作为一个含义更广的文化指标（cultural indicator），更可扮演合适的目标社群来研究文化区生成的限制。在地区文化的研究上，我们能将长者移动力较弱的不利因素转化成特定条件，借此透过他们揭示城市规划在培育文化上的缺口。

除此之外，就文化地图与城市空间的关系而言，我们希望指出，香港的城市肌理与大多数的西方社会有所差异。香港是以立体化城市的模式（volumetric city）发展。巴里·谢尔顿（Barrie Shelton），尤斯蒂娜·卡拉奇威茨（Justyna Karakiewicz）和托马斯·柯万（Thomas Kvan）合着的"香港造城记：从垂直之城到立体之城"（The Making of Hong Kong：From Vertical to Volumetric）就这方面有深入的讲解。[15]基于这城市发展模式的差异，我们必须寻求更能配合本土特色的绘图技巧（mapping technique），方可让"文化地图"这西方概念得以扎根于"地"，使之能应用在发展香港本土文化和推动营造长者友好的社区之上。

6　总结

上述的讨论由微观的长者生活空间为起始点，通过研究式的室内空间改造，在不同的新建及旧有住房进行策略性渗透，照顾到长者的生活细节，拓展出多层次的起居保障，此为人性化的家居改善，达致"老有所养"的目标。"活老"的概念延伸至建筑设计及社区安老设施的兴建，在其中，长者与家人联结，使他们或她们"老有所依"。在进一步的发展中，通过城市规划及社区营造的手段，我们可以将"活老"的概念有机地与社区融合为积极的催化剂，借此引发社区的互动，改变现时社会与长者隐而不见、老死不相往来的状况。最后，"安老空间"要突破空间制约、固有思维及社福框架，就必须因地制宜地配合香港独特的条件，结合创新技术，将"活老"的概念提升至创新产业的层面（例如"E—站"），在其中使"活老"社群得以参与及发挥，使他们或她们"老有所成"。以上由"活老"所引申出的"老有所养"、"老有所依"及"老有所成"的人文关怀应该成为我们社会的共同愿景。这共同愿景必须建基于社会共识。从建筑空间的角度,最有效凝聚共识的方法是由可见的社区设施开始,让市民能主动参与及亲身体验,这样便有利在"安老空间"的议题上,缔造一个由民间倡导、由下而上的健康社区发展模式。

Space for Elderly. Humane Built Environment

Chang Ping hung, Tung Kwok wah, Hui Cheung man

(School of Architecture, Chinese University of Hong Kong)

Abstract: In the foreseeable future, Hong Kong will enter a stage that the "elderly community" is rapidly growing. In view of it, it is urgent for us to find out the systematic solution before the end of the demographic window. In tackling the social issue of high "dependency ratio" caused by the ageing population, from the perspective of architectural study, are there some clues, which could direct us to an innovative approach to social development? This paper bases its study upon 'active ageing', discussing the pressing social issue of "space for elderly" from the 3 main layers of architectural study: interior spatial transformation, architectural design and urban planning. This paper suggests how the humanistic concern of providing our elderly with a sense of security, belonging and worthiness can be achieved by the implementation of "space for elderly".

Keywords: Space for elderly, Ageing in place, Elderly value, Active ageing

参考文献:

[1] United Nation, Department of Economic and Social Affairs. World Population Prospects, The 2012 Revision, Highlights and Advance Table[M]. New York: United Nations, 2013: 69.

[2] World Health Organization. What is 'Active Ageing'? [EB/OL] [2015-5-8]. http://www. who. int/ageing/active_ageing/en/#.

[3] 智经研究中心.「共居」新时代 长者「爱·回家」. [EB/OL]. [2015-5-8]. http://www. bauhinia. org/analyses_content. php? id=277;审计署. 审计署署长报告书(第六十三号报告). [EB/OL]. [2015-5-8]. http://www. aud. gov. hk/chi/pubpr_arpt/rpt_63. htm.

[4] 香港社区组织协会. 回应「长者院舍住宿照顾服务券」可行性研究(立法会 CB(2)1062/14-15 (02)号文件 LC Paper No. CB(2)1062/14-15(02)). [EB/OL]. [2015-5-8]. http://www. legco. gov. hk/yr14-15/chinese/panels/ws/papers/ws20150323cb2-1062-2-c. pdf.

[5] 长者安居协会. 协会服务. [EB/OL]. [2015-5-8]. http://www. schsa. org. hk/tc/services/index. html.

[6] World Health Organization. Checklist of Essential Features of Age-friendly Cities. [EB/OL]. [2015-5-8], http://www. who. int/ageing/publications/Age_friendly_cities_checklist. pdf.

[7] World Health Organization. Checklist of Essential Features of Age-friendly Cities. [EB/OL]. [2015-5-8]. http://www. who. int/ageing/publications/Age_friendly_cities_

checklist. pdf.

[8] 黄俊锋. 房协助长者建「无障碍」家. 明报. [EB/OL]. [2015-5-8]. http：//property. mpfi-nance. com/cfm/pa3. cfm? File＝20141227/paa01/ygha1h. txt.

[9] Roger Scruton. The Aesthetics of Architecture[M]. Princeton，N. J.：Princeton University Press，1980：223.

[10] World Health Organization. What is "Active Ageing"? [EB/OL]. [2015-5-8]. http：// www. who. int/ageing/active_ageing/en/♯.

[11] 香港大学社会工作及社会行政学系. 香港退休保障的未来发展研究报告[R]. 香港：中央政策组，2014：19-23.

[12] C. f. Chow NWS & Lum TYS. Trends in family attitudes and values in Hong Kong[Z]. Hong Kong：Central Policy Unit，2008：28.

[13] 香港房屋协会. 长幼共融，相邻乐聚[EB/OL]. [2015-5-8]. http：//harmonyplace. com. hk/tc/index. php? s＝about.

[14] David Harvey. The Condition of Postmodernity：an Enquiry into the Origins of Cultural Change[M]. Oxford：Blackwell，1989：73-74.

[15] Barrie Shelton, Justyna Karakiewicz, and Thomas Kvan. The Making of Hong Kong：From Vertical to Volumetric[M]. New York：Routledge，2011：161-162.

居住功能介入下的棕地保护更新可行性研究——以上海中心城区为例

李振宇　孙　淼

（同济大学建筑与城市规划学院）

摘要： 本文基于上海进入"存量规划"的大背景，分析中心城区棕地保护更新现状，提出居住功能介入下的城市棕地保护更新应是上海城镇化具有可行性的理想模式之一。通过对三个不同国外居住介入下的更新案例进行分析，从政治、行政、经济和技术四方面研究居住介入下的上海中心城区棕地保护更新的可行性并提出建议。最终运用类型学方法对既有居住现象进行分类，探讨未来综合性保护更新模式的适应性方针。

关键词： 居住，棕地，保护更新，上海中心城区，可行性研究

1　引言

棕地（Brownfield Site）一词，最早出现在 1980 年美国国会通过的《环境应对、赔偿和责任综合法》中。1994 年，美国环保局对其定义："棕地是被遗弃、闲置或不再使用的前工业和商业用地及设施，这些地区的扩展或再开发会受到环境污染的影响，也因此变得复杂。"在中国，棕地缺乏明确的定义，但往往被认为是有污染的、现已被废弃或将要废弃的城市工业用地。

"棕地保护"源自"工业遗产保护"。受城市保护主义思想影响，西方自 20 世纪 60 年代开始从单体建筑保护转向整体城区保护。2003 年，第 12 届国际产业遗产保护联合会（TICCIH）发表了《下塔吉尔宪章》，对工业遗产进行了完整定义：具有历史价值、技术价值、社会意义、建筑或科研价值的工业文化遗存，包括建筑物和机械、车间、磨坊、工厂、矿山以及相关的加工提炼场地、仓库和店铺，生产、传输和使用能源的场所，交通基础设施；除此之外，还有与工业生产相关的其他社会活动场所，如住房供给、宗教崇拜或者教育。从而对工业遗产的地域属性和社会属性进行了明确。

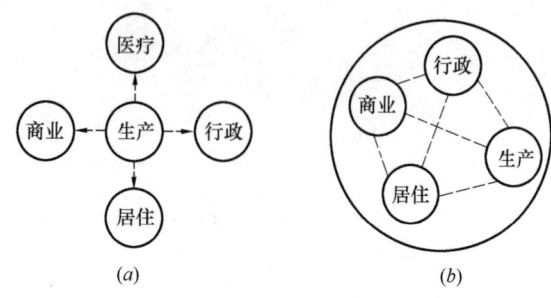

图 1　计划经济时代工业城区结构形式
（*a*）城市边缘"向心式"大型工业城；
（*b*）内城"交叉式"混合工业区

"棕地保护更新"是指相比文物古迹，工业遗产具有"低龄化"特征，在生产退出后依然有"再利用"价值。从资源节约的角度出发，走"发展里求保护，保护中为更新"的路线，选择性地保留和拆除，而非采用"要么保，要么拆"的极端做法，从而在保护的同时促进城市更新的可持续发展。

因此，城市棕地保护更新，应被认为是对有工业文化遗产属性的城市工业用地、仓储用地、交通用地，以及相关的居住、公共管理、商业服务、公用设施及绿化用地的整体保护，并基于可持续发展原则，在经济、社会、环境和城市文脉层面进行开发再利用的城市建设的综合性策略。

2　上海中心城区棕地保护更新背景

上海中心城区，指的是上海外环线以内区域，面积约 660km²。1843 年上海开埠成为国际航运码头，20 世纪初转型为远东金融贸易中心。新中国成立后，上海被定位为工业中心，城镇化进程全面以工业发展为依托，生产功能强势介入城市形态的发展。改革开放以来，随着产业转移和"退二

进三",中心城区大量工业停产或转移,大片棕地被废弃,成为进一步城镇化的障碍。上海现有工业用地占总建设用地的 29%,远高于伦敦 3.9% 的比例。究其原因有 4 点:1. 工业占据内城大量土地,并形成服务业城区中的飞地,严重隔断了城市空间和功能的延续性;2. 部分老工业城区由于宜居性较差,逐渐呈现高密度、低收入和犯罪率较高的社会特征;3. 大规模拆迁成本不断攀升,容易引发社会冲突;4. 老工业区往往拥有大量遗产建筑,具有区域的历史特殊性,模式化的开发较为困难。

3　上海中心城区棕地保护更新现状

上海中心城区的棕地保护更新,早期是"保护为主,更新为辅;建筑为主,城区为辅";2000年后,逐渐出现小规模厂区更新形成的创意产业园;而 2010 世博会则开始了成规模棕地更新的新阶段。通过对 46 处相关案例(图 2)的综合分析,得出上海中心城区棕地保护更新的 6 点特征:(1)自下而上:如早期的登琨艳工作室,缺乏政府层面的认可,完全为艺术家自发入驻再利用。(2)文化创意:废旧厂区空间大、租金低,适合小规模文创公司的发展。以上海市经济委员会推出的第一批 18 家创意产业园为例,其中 16家是由旧厂区改造而成。(3)更新成本高:老城区寸土寸金,人口密度高,搬迁难度大,还可能涉及遗产建筑的保护和修缮。(4)点状开发:以第一批 16 家创意产业园为例,建筑规模多在10000~20000m² ,很难形成片区。(5)离散分布:计划经济时代的"生产性城区"在城镇化进程中,生活部分的扩张将生产部分逐渐相互隔离,并形成一个个孤岛,以八号桥附近 5 个创意产业园为例,相距均在 1km 左右。(6)区位优先:由于商业主导开发,选址往往以区位优势为首

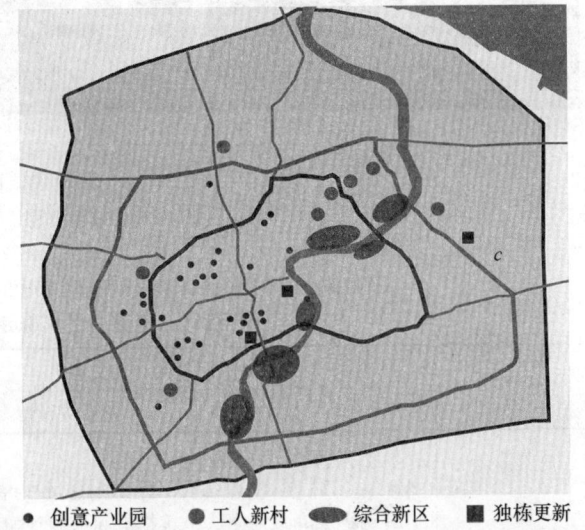

● 创意产业园　● 工人新村　⬭ 综合新区　■ 独栋更新

图 2　本文研究范围:上海中心城区 46 处棕地更新案例

要标准。早期创意产业园选址基本均在核心城区(内环内),近期规模性更新则多依托黄浦滨江岸线的优势。因此,传统保护更新过多强调商业效益,破坏了城市空间和社会结构的稳定,摒弃了原住民参与所引发的社会正效应。在这种背景下,基于城市的可持续发展原则和国外先进经验,本文提出:"成规模、以居住功能介入的城市棕地保护更新"应是上海城镇化具有可行性的理想模式。

居住功能介入的模式,涉及各种资源的合理分配和各方利益的有效平衡,并最终以公共政策的形式对建设活动产生影响。其可行性存在的核心是:政治家和公务员们在各种需求和压力下设计能得到住房金融家、建设者和消费者响应的住房计划。具体体现为政治可行性(某项住房计划获得政府通过)、行政可行性(政策贯彻中组织上的有序)、经济可行性(资源的合理配置,并使住房计划与国家经济和住房消费能力相适应)、技术可行性(规划设计策略、建设手段等)。

4　国外居住功能介入下的棕地保护更新案例

居住功能介入的模式,在欧美发达国家已成为城市棕地更新的常态。按照推动方向的不同,分为"自下而上"、"自上而下"、"混合并行"三种模式。如纽约苏荷区,早期的艺术家作为"开拓者",结合自身利益"自下而上"的推动苏荷区保护更新,并形成"艺术家租户联合会"和各方利益团体抗争,从而倒逼政府和社会一步步推动区域保护复兴;相比较而言,伦敦道克兰码头区改造则

是典型的"自上而下":通过政府设立伦敦道克兰城市开发区(UDA)和官方性质的伦敦道克兰开发公司(LDDC),并颁布一系列政策吸引大量资金、人才迅速进入区域,从而形成以居住、办公、旅游等功能混合的更新城区;而阿姆斯特丹东港则一开始就选择了政府主导、全民参与的"混合并行"模式:一方面政府成立"新增住房管理委员会"主持更新,一方面倡导"公私合营"的开发,并通过和原住民(多是年轻人、海员和外籍移民)协商,努力实现本地安置,建立社会住宅和商品住宅混合的社区,从而避免更新过程中出现中产阶层迁入、低收入阶层迁出的"绅士化"现象。

(a)　　　　　　　　　(b)　　　　　　　　　(c)

图3　工业建筑改造居住建筑

(a) 纽约苏荷区;(b) 伦敦道克兰码头区;(c) 阿姆斯特丹东港区

[资料来源:(a) http://news.hexun.com/2011-08-08/132209288.html;(c) 程晓曦.
阿姆斯特丹东港码头改造——城市复兴中的多重平衡 [J]. 世界建筑,2011,(4)]

苏荷区、道克兰区和东港区的可行性比较研究　　　　　　　　　表1

	可行性分析			
	政治可行性	行政可行性	经济可行性	技术可行性
美国纽约 SOHO区	1)早期:市政府立法禁止工业厂房改作他用。 2)中后期:在"艺术家租户联合会"申请下对工业厂房的居住功能转变进行合法化。 3)在遗产保护部门的支持下将SOHO区列为纽约的"历史文化保护区"	1)政府通过严格的政策指引和限制(如地面零售不得超过1万平方英尺,艺术家的LOFT不得小于1200平方英尺等),保障了LOFT模式在SOHO区的可持续发展,防止过度商业化带来的居住功能流失。 2)政府始终没有直接介入城区复兴,而是通过市场来引导	1)早期缺乏资金投入。 2)80年代起,政府逐渐放宽地产开发、银行贷款、商业入驻等限制。 3)市场条件下的居住功能导向:艺术家由于高昂的租金开始搬离,律师、医生、银行家等开始入住,艺术导向性功能逐渐被居住、商业所代替	1)早期居住更多体现艺术需求,类型多样,主要根据租金和个人承受能力进行选择。 2)80年代起,居住开始体现中高收入人群需求。建筑多为进深小、面宽大、框架结构的仓库,而原来一些的大体量厂房,部分被改造成商业办公,部分被拆除后重建。 3)80年代起新建大量建筑,解决商业、配套、停车等问题
英国伦敦道克兰码头区	1)1980年,通过《英国地方政府规划与土地法》,授权国家环境部长建立城市开发公司来负责城市开发区的工作。 2)成立伦敦道克兰城市开发区(UDA)和半官方性质的伦敦道克兰开发公司(LDDC),直属于中央政府	1)道克兰开发公司全权负责区域的规则,向中央政府和国家议会负责。 2)可从公共权力部门快速获得土地,并通过特殊议会授予程序获得"更新"的权力。 3)作为一个独立发展控制规划的部门,发展公司可以为投资者、发展者提供永久性服务。 4)具有推销宣传道克兰的权力	1)中央财政每年通过环境部门拨款6000~7000万英镑。 2)采取"公私合营"模式,按公私1:4的总量进行投资。 3)公有资金主要投入交通核基础设施建设,私有资金主要投入居住和商业设施建设。 4)商业化运作导致居住成本的攀升,绅士化现象严重	1)改善区域公共交通状况,解决地铁和公共汽车的可达性。 2)分片区采用不同手段进行更新,部分改造、部分拆除新建。 3)通过对传统街道空间的恢复及居住建筑的风貌化,将开放式居住社区打造成伦敦重要旅游景点。 4)通过插建、改造、挖建、贴建、加建等设计手法,对老仓储区进行居住功能导向的改造

续表

	可行性分析			
	政治可行性	行政可行性	经济可行性	技术可行性
阿姆斯特丹东港区	1) 1973年第三次物质空间规划将老城区复兴列入重点建设计划中。 2) 1985年6月12日，议会颁布了阿姆斯特丹东港改造基本原则政策文件。 3) 成立"新增住房管理委员会"参与整个东港区复兴计划	1) 国家以土地所有人的身份对开发项目进行规划、审批和监督控制，防止投机倾向。 2) 政府对开发进程提供全面的官方服务，并与建筑师、承建商和开发人员共同配合项目组完成整个复兴计划	1) 以租赁合同的方式规定土地的使用年限和使用性质，并租给私人开发商。 2) 采取"公私合营"的模式，政府和私人投资者共同成立了港区董事会负责管理和监督港区的规划与建设工作。 3) 政府自有资金主要进入公共住宅的建设	1) 强制设定社会住宅在混居社区中的比例，从30%~60%不等。 2) 大量的保留原有码头区建筑，通过邀请大量建筑师，进行居住性改造，避免模式复制下的浪费。 3) 编辑住宅图集，收录满足城市各类人群需求的住宅平面。 4) 对密度、高度、面宽、层数、街区尺度等方面做出严格设定

　　比较三种模式，"自下而上"的原始动力较弱、更新周期较长，但有利于城市形态的整体保护和对原住民的社会关怀，如早期苏荷区居民自发的对既有厂房进行修缮、分隔、装修，形成类型多样的"下层工作、上层生活"的LOFT居住模式，大拆大建现象鲜有发生，基本保留了老铸铁厂的原始风貌。但效率的低下，缺乏政治、行政和经济的支持，造成区域内火灾频发、治安混乱、乱搭乱建等社会问题，以及由于基础设施缺乏、生活配套无法跟上、来往卡车制造巨大的噪声和灰尘所形成恶劣的居住环境，这都使苏荷区在相当长时间里被称为曼哈顿岛上的"地狱中的一百英亩地"。

　　与之相反，"自上而下"着重于统筹管理、效率至上。相比苏荷区（0.44km²）前后近30年的更新历程，道克兰地区（8.5km²）更新在17年间即完成。其中泰晤士南岸居住导向的棕地更新，通过基础设施先行、并有效利用原有建筑物，从而创建一个极具吸引力的环境，确保优质的住房和设施以鼓励人们在此居住。然而在完全市场驱动下进行更新，使得道克兰的居住形态逐渐走向豪华式住宅，土地私有化拉大了贫富分化，原住民的流失率和失业率不断上升。此外，由于行政意志主导，更新目的性过于明确，很多不符合标准居住模式的厂房被拆除，部分区域城市形态遭到较大破坏。

　　"混合并行"模式强调不同阶层的居住利益平衡，因此操作最为繁杂，必须依托于一个高效的管理模式和合理的规划理念，从而达到对城市形态、经济成本、相关人群利益综合平衡的目的。阿姆斯特丹东港居住更新基于土地租赁和公私合营，在"政府主导、全民参与"模式下推动社区的阶层、功能和形态的多重混合，避免出现严重的"绅士化"现象。规划上推行低层高密度、保留原有城市形态、并充分利用滨水区建设公共空间，形成良好的城市交往环境，提升区域整体的居住质量。

5　上海居住功能介入的棕地保护更新可行性研究

5.1　政治可行性

　　针对土地资源愈加匮乏的现状，2014年上海市规土局制订的《关于本市盘活存量工业用地的实施办法（试行）》中提到，上海对存量工业用地将主要采取区域整体转型、土地收储后出让和有条件零星开发等实施路径。2015年5月1日正式实施的《上海市城市更新实施办法》中明确提到，上海已进入存量开发为主的内涵增长、创新发展阶段，城市更新将成为资源紧约束条件下上海城市可持续发展的主要方式。从而将棕地更新的迫切性上升到城市战略高度。相比西方国家，上海最大的政治困难在于土地性质的变更，由于居住用地在出让规模、规划指标等方面都和棕地现状有较大差异，求得保护和更新的一致尤为困难。因此，城市政府部门应对棕地保护更新整体立项，并制定不同于普通居住区的专项法规，允许棕地在一定标准的保护条件下进行土地转性。同时成立政府背景的开发公司，而将政府职能从直接参与转为宏观调控引导，从而保证开发过程中效率和公平并行。

5.2　行政可行性

上海在过去的棕地更新中，体现出较为粗放的行政介入方式，即保护和更新分离、居住和非居住分离、产权和使用权分离，再加上和户籍等社会因素的挂钩，直接导致了老厂房改造住宅现象鲜为发生。因此，应确立适宜性的行政介入模式，形成一整套针对棕地保护更新计划的社会政策，如教育、医疗、社会保障等，从而避免住户成为社会弱势群体。同时赋予开发公司以行政主导权，保证其可以快速获得各类许可，避免多个部门步调不一致形成的无谓消耗。如瞿溪路原上海豆制品厂改造廉租房项目，尽管已有居民入住，但审批依然迟迟无法完成，让便民项目成了尴尬角色。此外，在自上而下推行保护更新的同时，建立和建筑师、承建商、居民等沟通的长效机制，自觉接受各个相关团体的监督，促进自下而上力量的运行，避免出现因严重的"绅士化"现象带来的社会动荡。

5.3　经济可行性

经济层面的可行性在当今上海已凸显优势。于城市整体层面，中心城区棕地成规模的更新，能有效控制居住功能过度扩散所带来的城市运营成本，如基础设施、交通、环境等费用的增加。于开发方，居住主导的棕地更新对于区位要求不如商业主导的高，从而大大降低土地出让费用。但涉及保护的问题依然存在：长期以来，历史建筑保护资金主要依赖房屋所有者，政府财政补贴也仅限于列入文物保护单位的少数损坏严重的建筑。这远远无法满足大规模城市棕地更新中遗产保护对于资金的需求，从而造成被保护的成为"死"的遗产，而大多数则是直接被拆除。因此，通过市场和行政并轨的方式，将市场化经济引入，鼓励各类企业和个体参与更新过程，通过合适的比例共同投资，如政府主导基础设施和保障住房的建设，社会资金主导商品住房建设和遗产保护修缮，从而形成经济上的共赢局面，这方面阿姆斯特丹东港和伦敦道克兰码头区都是很好的范例。此外，通过专项资金的投入，在棕地上通过旧厂房改建或空地插建，为中低收入、特别是原住民建设保障性住房，并努力实现本地就业，从而保护中低收入人群的利益。住宅类型上，采用满足不同社会阶层的混合模式，通过价格的差异实现高收入人群对低收入人群的补偿，在经济和社会总成本上达成平衡。

5.4　技术可行性

棕地保护更新在发展的大前提下，最为重要的就是风貌的保护和历史建筑的再利用。30 余年的城镇化使得上海建设技术体系非常成熟。需要提升的是规划和设计技术体系。传统的功能分区、封闭社区、车行交通主导的理念需要打破：符合老工业区特色的低层高密街区、局部周边式的城市空间形态、宜于人行、小尺度、开放的混合型居住社区、结合厂房改造的多样化住宅，如 Loft、Soho 模式，都是棕地保护更新中应当出现的新可能。同时应关注社会问题，如邻里关系和社会交往的改善、通过设计减轻居住在老厂房里居民心理和生理上的不适，如通过建筑内部的现代化装饰，以及鲜亮色彩的介入来降低工业厂区的压抑感。此外，停车也是棕地保护更新所面临的困局，由于保护建筑地基和地下车库地基在深度、强度等方面存在矛盾，大规模挖掘地下空间成本较高。上海现有棕地保护更新的案例，无一例外呈现出停车的混乱。因此，可参考德国经验，将不宜改造居住的厂房更新为停车楼，一方面降低停车成本，另一方面也通过统一管理缓解车辆给社区带来的交通混乱。

图 4 棕地保护的三种居住模式
(a) 模式一：曹杨新村；*(b)* 模式二：田子坊；*(c)* 模式三：瞿溪路廉租房

6 上海棕地保护更新的现有居住模式

由于在政治和行政可行性上存在较大制约，上海中心城区既有棕地保护更新中的居住形态相对单一，根据居住功能介入的不同形式，将研究对象分为外部影响、间接依附、内部介入三类模式：1. 外部影响：即对传统工人住宅进行大规模修缮维护，如代表"一五"期间上海工业居住文化的"曹杨新村"，2009~2011 年间共进行了 3 次大修，通过电线重排、外墙粉刷、屋顶防漏、管道更新以及对室外公共空间和绿化设施的美化，让社区生活氛围重新焕发，并适应现代居住方式。作为一种政治认可度较高、行政操作简单、保护成本较低、保护技术成熟的棕地保护更新模式，在上海中心城区八大工人新村中均得到推广使用。2. 间接依附：即通过其他功能介入棕地保护更新，居住功能则依附其形成。如卢湾区田子坊，作为里弄工厂和民宅混合区，其延续老上海城市空间的设计方法和依托于视觉艺术和工艺美术的运营模式非常成功，并带动了日月光中心等项目的开发，在保护棕地遗产和新地产开发中取得各方利益的平衡。如今，如依托文创产业的徐汇滨江保护更新亦是这种模式。3. 内部介入：即直接对棕地及其附属建筑进行居住功能介入，如 M50 里的艺术家工坊，是集办公、交易、展示、居住为一体的更新方式。但由于缺乏法律上的认可，以及无法按照住宅标准进行建造（如采光、卫生、煤气等），此类居住形态多体现出临时性、随意性和混乱性的特征，居住环境恶劣，不易被社会所接受。近年来，随着租金攀升和行政介入，这种模式在不断淡出，取而代之是政府参与的厂房改造保障性住房，正逐渐成为上海中心城区居住介入工业建筑改造的新方向。

7 结论

因此，上海中心城区以居住功能介入的棕地保护更新应在政治、行政、经济、技术四方面形成统一的综合运作体系，通过政府支持、行政协调、市场运作、全民参与的"混合并行"模式，采用多样化的更新手段针对不同的居住介入方式，探索居住功能介入下的城市棕地保护更新的适应性路径，从而保证历史记忆的留存、提升废弃工业用地的整体价值、保障低收入人群的居住权利、促进社区邻里关系的优化。在城市"存量规划"发展的年代，让上海曾经的工业文化得到新的价值诠释。

致谢

本篇论文的写作得到国家自然科学基金项目《当代中国住宅建筑的类型学特征研究》的资助（编号：51278337），在此表示衷心的感谢！

Feasibility Study of the Conservation and Renovation on the Brownfield under the Residential Intervention—Case of the Central City in Shanghai

Li Zhenyu，Sun Miao

（College of Architecture and Urban Planning，Tongji University）

Abstract：This Paper is based on the background of the "Stock planning" in Shanghai. The paper analyses the status of the conservation and renovation in the central city, and proposes " Conservation and renovation on the urban Brownfield under the residential intervention" will be one of the feasible ideal modes in the urbanization. Through the analysis of the residential intervention in three different foreign cases, study the feasibility of conservation and renovation on the urban Brownfield under the residential intervention from politics, administration, economics and technique, and put forward the suggestions. Finally, use the typological method to classify the existing residential phenomenon, discuss the feasibility of the comprehensive conservation and renovation mode in the future.

Keywords：Living，Brownfield，Conservation and renovation，Central city of Shanghai，Feasibility study

参考文献：

[1] 王建国等. 后工业时代产业建筑遗产保护更新 [M]. 北京：中国建筑工业出版社，2008.

[2] 刘伯英，冯钟平. 城市工业用地更新与工业遗产保护 [M]. 北京：中国建筑工业出版社，2009.

[3] 田东海. 住房政策：国际经验借鉴和中国现实选择 [M]. 北京：清华大学出版社，1998.

[4] 李振宇，常琦. 十年之变 [J]. 城市建筑. 2014，10：7-9.

[5] 张松. 上海产业遗产的保护与适当再利用 [J]. 建筑学报. 2006，8：16-20.

[6] 程晓曦. 阿姆斯特丹东港码头改造——城市复兴中的多重平衡 [J]. 世界建筑. 2011，4：102-106.

[7] 孙群郎，黄臻. 纽约苏荷区(SOHO)的绅士化及其影响 [J]. 史林. 2013，2：1-7.

[8] 王欣. 伦敦道克兰城市更新实践 [J]. 城市问题. 2004，5：72-79.

[9] Feilden B. M. Conservation of Historic Buildings [M]. Burlington：Architectural Press，2003.

高雄厝设计准则应用于都会型建筑设计策略之实践

张博硕[1] 苏志勋[2] 李彦颐[3]
(1. 台湾弘宪联合建筑师事务所/树德科技大学室内设计系；
2. 台湾高雄市政府工务局/树德科技大学室内设计系；
3. 台湾树德科技大学建筑研究所)

摘要：高雄厝计划为近年来高雄市政府对于市民居住健康与舒适度的重视与期望，无论在于居住的质与量之上以高标准的审议外，更期望依照高雄特殊的环境条件各自发展出不同风貌之高雄厝（厝—房屋，下同—编者注）。而位于高度城市化发展下的高雄厝，又该具备何种特质与风貌，更是本研究积极推展都会型高雄厝研究的动机。以高雄厝五大核心价值："生态、经济、宜居、创意、国际"，以丰富的当地建筑与历史文化搭配前瞻的绿色建筑技术，作为建筑设计发想基础之外。将整合外部气候环境因子与检讨建筑物各项组件均以符合"高雄市高雄厝设计及鼓励回馈办法"之前提下发展，由外而内逐项检讨，景观规划、建筑主体、机能设备、绿源系统、环控机制等项目进行整体性规划设计，此外更反应所在位置之特有人文特色与城市纹理，以发展成能与亲和环境景观之"宜居"建筑。"全面采光"、"精简"平立面设计，机能分区平面配置可兼顾动静之居住需求及良好的家庭互动，景观阳台侧背向建筑凹角留设工作阳台之绝佳配置，融入现代设计法且引进自然光及风之对流维持良好室内环境质量。依空间量体的视觉比例配合室内采光需求，设计适合的开口比例主体重点加强主体列柱之垂直线条及天际线发展，能与城市天际线契合。以柱梁外露成遮檐来降低热能来源，达到减少空调使用的目的，符合现代人对健康建筑、居所宜居、低碳节能的需求。

关键词：高雄厝设计及鼓励办法，绿色建筑，宜居

1 计划缘起

由于高雄市参与联合国环境规划署与国际公园协会联合主办的国际宜居城市奖，是全球唯一涵盖城市景观、小区环境管理、生态建设、资源利用、人与自然及环境永续发展等重要议题的国际竞赛。借由此契机高雄市民逐渐重视环境与建筑之间的关联。历年来的高雄市硬件建设成果备受肯定，在各地方政府也积极制定地方绿色建筑自治条例或鼓励法令规范，在此风气与范畴之下，于2013国际宜居城市奖揭晓，更上一层楼，11项入围的城市建设，不仅是台湾得奖最多城市，更是全球得奖第一名的城市（图1）。

因应大高雄县市合并以及更具代表高雄地理特色的建筑风貌再造，高雄市政府提出高雄厝计划，同时配合推动高雄厝建筑走向符合国际趋势标准，营造永续生态城市。因此对于未来"高雄厝"的思考方向，除了将建筑元素融入地方特色与人文景观之外，更应该反映在以"永续"、"健康"、"节能"、"舒适"为要求之上，为此如何实时因应建筑室内环境变化，同时评估光电系统建筑之特性、设计具有智能之遮阳方式、自然换气甚至于开启相关建筑设备等对策成为"智慧绿能高雄厝"，使"高雄厝"室内外环境成为宜居城市的典范，为本计划最主要之起源。

高雄规划发展宜居城市朝向各种领域，以公共设施、景观工程、民生居住、城乡平衡等面向发展，"旗津海岸线保护工程"是透过海岸线保护的手段，以土地保育绿色海岸经营之理念，达成海岸自然生态、土地防灾安全、适意优美景观、休闲乐活游憩，以及寻求平衡之海岸土地利用与发展。鼓山区（鼓山绿邑-乐活新城）、大树区（走逛美丽新田园）两项获得铜牌的项目，都是以地方文化、历史保存为基础的区域性发展计划，涵盖了地方物产、休憩、文化保存及生活等面向，大树区—走逛美丽新田园有旧铁桥湿地的保存、三和瓦窑的产业新创及当地的玉荷包产业，鼓山绿邑有美术馆园区、中都湿地和铁道文化园区等亮点。

图1　高雄市宜居城市获奖案例

　　未来进行规划设计与建筑营造时，更需要加入健康宜居、低碳永续、历史人文的纹理进行设计，除了建筑本身不再是冰冷的硬件，在更多细节与细部空间能嗅到尊重地方风俗与人文纹理，在整体规划上更容易与地方纹理达成一致性。

2　工作内容计划说明

　　本文探讨之建筑物依循"高雄厝设计及鼓励回馈办法"以及"高雄市绿建筑自治条例"进行设计发想阶段的根本，以建构更舒适、更贴合环境之和善建筑，作为高雄市区为推动生态城市，营造绿色建筑环境，创造健康生活质量，促进绿色经济产业，并达到减碳减灾目标以成为环热带圈城市典范。

　　本规划案邻接计划道路部分建筑物有退缩，4m、7.8m及21.3m开放空间减缓对道路之压迫感，并外放提供较大之绿地空间，外观采取极简主义造型，塑造典雅清新市容，本案外墙以瓷砖作为主要材料，借助造型垂直带与水平带的变化，以及浅米色系与绿微反玻璃的陪衬下，塑造简捷的造型语汇，并在南台湾特有的湛蓝天空衬托下，反映出单纯清爽的视觉感受（图2）。

图2　建案场地与外观仿真示意图

2.1 外观建筑造型风格

◆ 立面设计

依空间体量的视觉比例配合室内采光需求，设计适合的开口比例，主体重点加强主体列柱之垂直线条收头及天际线之弧型框架造型之"都会简约风格"（图3）。

图3 建案外观采用浅色系列，并于北侧立面留设较大开窗部争取室内采光

◆ 绿色建筑、健康建筑的观念

以柱梁外露成遮檐来降低热能来源，达到减少空调使用的目的，以符合现代人对健康建筑的需求。

2.2 绿化-友善城市环境

将开放空间外放成为居住单位与街道等公共空间领域的中介，它是居民与居民或市民产生互动的空间，借助景观塑造，街道行人得以通视开放空间。从城市的角度，充满变化与趣味的景致可以被视为城市景观系统的一部分，能有效提供居民多元化户外休憩空间，创造优良居住环境（图4、图5）。

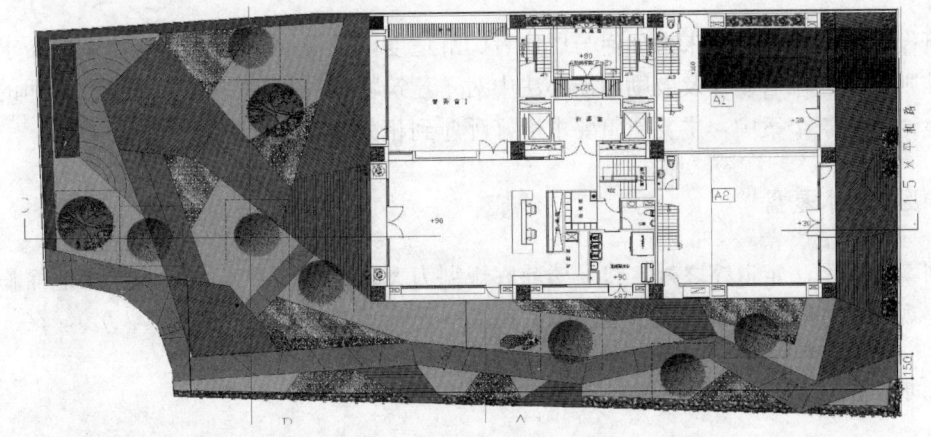

图4 规划案一楼绿化以及退缩建地改建为公园绿地营造"埕"空间

（1）本案之顶盖型沿街式开放空间与绿带及周边街道相衔接，小区居民使用可及性高；顶盖型

沿街式开放空间内设置水池、绿地及休憩平台，不仅提供居民平日休憩聊天场所，水池又可发挥阴离子水疗养生效果。

（2）沿街步道式开放空间种植林荫乔木及复层灌木，对小区可有效发挥节能减碳之功效。构筑为一健康环保的优良环境

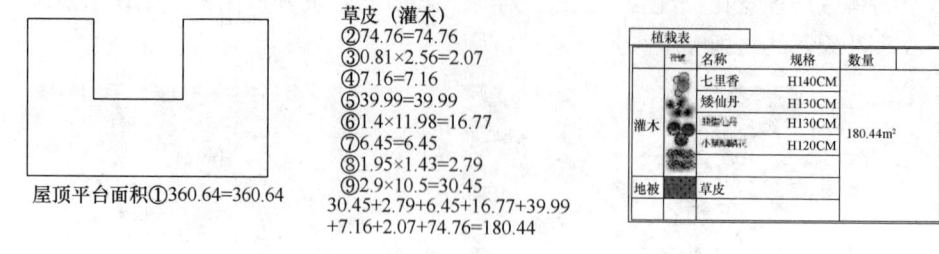

草皮（灌木）
②74.76=74.76
③0.81×2.56=2.07
④7.16=7.16
⑤39.99=39.99
⑥1.4×11.98=16.77
⑦6.45=6.45
⑧1.95×1.43=2.79
⑨2.9×10.5=30.45
30.45+2.79+6.45+16.77+39.99
+7.16+2.07+74.76=180.44

屋顶平台面积①360.64=360.64

植栽表			
	名称	规格	数量
灌木	七里香	H140CM	180.44m²
	矮仙丹	H130CM	
	黄金榕	H130CM	
	小叶黄扬	H120CM	
地被	草皮		

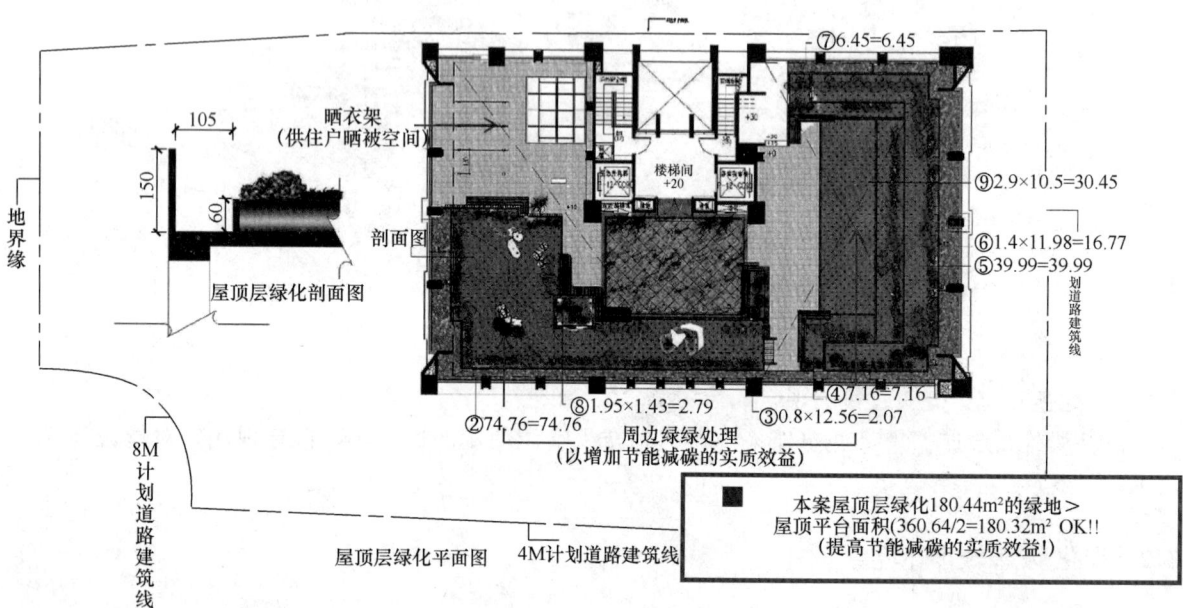

图5　建案屋顶设计为花园绿地，进而达成节能减碳也降低了建筑的受热

3　设计方案法规检讨

于建筑设计时间已考虑到未来如何与居住者的舒适度以及健康能有所呼应，借此需求将高雄厝十大设计准则以及高雄厝设计及鼓励回馈办法中对于建筑物相关规范进行规划设计时间的微调，且针对本文检讨之建筑个案中，主要建筑要求恰好呼应到相关法令。

3.1　会呼吸的透水基盘

本规划案中除了法定退缩之外，将一楼前庭规划为大绿地公园广场，以增加绿地面积除了美化整体建筑美观与增加建筑面积内透水铺面的面积。

3.2　埕空间营造

以高雄厝设计准则中，保留一空旷面积作为活动空间之外，更能借此空间元素转化为高雄各族群之中常出现之"埕"空间，在农业时期常作为建筑聚落中社交与农产品加工之场域，对于居民常有着深刻之生活体验印象（图6）。

图 6   建案绿地埕空间营造

3.3   开口部深采光设计

因本建筑案例四周并无明显遮蔽物，因此除了北侧之外其他三侧均有直接日照导致建筑物受热时数过长以及室内采光因直接日射导致居民不舒适以及室内采光均齐度不佳与眩光等疑虑，故此本设计将部分采光面改为深采光与设置深阳台设计排除相关室内光环境不良问题（图 7）。

图 7   采光面以深采光方式设计

3.4   遮阳景观阳台设计

景观阳台应以植栽及覆土方式设置绿化设施，且面积应达三分之一以上；其植栽栽种面积基准及覆土深度等设计并应符合建筑场地绿化设计技术规范规定。每层景观阳台面积之和，不得逾建筑面积八分之一；其面积未达 10m² 者，得建筑 10m²。

3.5   屋顶绿化与建筑减热设计

降低建筑物受热最积极的作为除了于屋顶设计有效遮阳设计之外，还能选择于屋顶空间设计空中花园或设置绿屋顶，根据研究屋顶绿化能有效减少 60%～70% 的建筑物得热。一方面降低建筑物受热减少建筑物室内使用空调系统的能耗之外，也提升了居民的整体生活质量（图 8、表 1）。

符合满足高雄厝设计准则相关项目 表 1

项次	设计准则	内 容
1	会呼吸的透水基盘	透过草坪与透水性的设计，让建筑物与土地联结与触动
2	有效的深遮阳	经由挑檐或遮阳或阳台等设计，对应出四个区域不同的方位与特性，能带来凉爽的遮阳，使其凸显出高雄市气候环境的性格

项次	设计准则	内　容
3	绿能屋顶的设计	将目前高雄地区屋顶层的现况，重新整合为具有自然生态风貌的特色，并搭配间接减低直达热负荷，与塑造出开放性的逃生平台
4	埕空间的创造	多元的族群文化建构了高雄市不同的聚落风貌，而河洛、客家、原住民族等所共通的集会场所氛围，更是当地文化中不可或缺的象征，故由天井、露台、阳台等小空间来重新诠释
5	创造有效通风的开口	经由开口部之设计，使空气自然对流，达成室内自然通风之均匀性，降低室内二氧化碳，并改善室内空气温湿度

图 8　建案顶楼屋顶绿化

4　年度研究成果与后续应用

本文研究建筑案例运用高雄市规范之自治条例，其中针对建筑设计与周边环境因子条件的呼应，一方面营造出舒适空间与能营造出宜居之亲善住宅，并且因应高雄市高温、高湿、长日照的特性反映在建筑物之立面、开口、周边环境，以调整微气候条件改造室内人居环境。同时透过绿色建筑自治条例与高雄厝奖励标章，对于建筑物质量更是一种肯定，相关研究也反映了获得高雄厝奖章之建筑案例，在高雄建筑市场中均能获得高度评价与高于市场价格接受度。

The Design Strategy of Kaohsiung Urban Residential Building for Kaohsiung LOHAS Architecture Design Guide Line

Chang[1] Po-Shuo，Su Chihshun[2]，Li Yen-Yi [3]
（1. Shu-Te University architecture and interior design Dept；
2. Public Works Bureau of Kaohsiung City Govemment；
3. Shu-Te University architecture and interior design Dept）

Abstract：The reason for the beginning of Kaohsiung LOHAS House Plan is that the Kaohsiung City Government is highly concerned about residential housing quality to live healthy and comfortable in recent years. The consideration of a high standard review are using on the quality and quantity of living environment. Thus，Kaohsiung LOHAS House

Plan are expecting to create different type of housing projects according to each special local environmental conditions. The motivation of this research is to create different types of Kaohsiung LOHAS House stereotypes according to different local characteristics within highly urbanized environmental condition. There are five core values as major concepts of Kaohsiung LOHAS House Plan：Ecology, economy, Livability, creativity, Internationalization". The major concepts of Kaohsiung LOHAS House Plan is to enrich the ground with a forward-looking building technology integrated with architecture. history and culture. Besides，the integration of external climatic factors and to review the structure of the building elements is under the control of Kaohsiung LOHAS House design guideline and incentives. The goal of Kaohsiung LOHAS House Plan is to help designers from the outside itemized review their design projects in order to develop the buildings become a Livable Architecture style.

Keywords：Kaohsiung LOHAS house design guideline and incentives，Green architecture，Livable architecture

参考文献：

[1] 高雄市建筑物屋顶设置太阳光电设施办法令[S]. 高雄市政府工务局，2012.

[2] 高雄市绿建筑自治条例[S]. 高雄市政府工务局，2012.

[3] 高雄市政府工务局 2012 年度补助建筑物设置太阳光电发电系统实施计划[R]. 高雄市政府工务局，2012.

[4] 高雄市政府绿建筑技术审议会设置要点[R]. 高雄市政府工务局，2012.

[5] 高雄厝设计及鼓励回馈办法[R]. 高雄市政府工务局，2014.

Can Inclusionary Housing Achieve Social and Spatial Inclusion in Chinese Cities?

Huang Youqin

(Department of Geography and Planning, University
at Albany, State University of New York)

Abstract: Faced with skyrocketing housing prices and the lack of affordable housing in Chinese cities, the Chinese central government has set up ambitious quotas for low-income housing for local governments, who in turn have embraced inclusionary housing as a new strategy to achieve housing affordability and social and spatial inclusion. Yet, inclusionary housing in China is complicated by the strong role of the central government in housing policy, the state ownership of urban land and local governments' right to lease land, and a private sector that historically had little role in the provision of low income housing. This paper evaluates inclusionary housing in the Chinese context, asking: 1) Has inclusionary housing achieved social and spatial inclusion? 2) If not, how can inclusionary housing in China be reformed to achieve social and spatial inclusion? Field work in Beijing shows while inclusionary housing in China is producing a large number of new units, it does not really result in social and spatial inclusion of the poor.

Keywords: Inclusionary housing, Low-income housing, China, Social inclusion, Spatial inclusion

1　Introduction

The neck breaking economic growth in China in recent decades is accompanied by spectacular achievements in housing consumption, with the rate of homeownership increasing from 20 to 70 percent, and per capita living space increasing from 4 m² to 29 m² during 1980 – 2010 in Chinese cities[1,2]. Yet, these dazzling improvements have not been enjoyed by all social groups, and those at the bottom of the social hierarchy have basically been excluded from this success story. In 2010, there were still more than 9% of households living with less than 8 m² per capita floor space. Meanwhile the unprecedented housing and land reform in Chinese cities have resulted in skyrocketing housing prices and severe shortage of affordable housing. Despite decades of massive provision of subsidized rental housing in the socialist era, the Chinese government has failed to provide adequate housing for the poor in recent decades[1].

Faced with intensified public discontent, the central government made a significant shift in housing policy in 2010 by moving away from stimulating economic growth to achieving social goals. The central government set up ambitious goals for subsidized housing (with 5. 84 million additional units of subsidized housing in 2010 alone, and another 36 million units for the period of 2011-2015), set quotas for local governments to develop subsidized housing, and included subsidized housing in the performance evaluation system for officials[3,4]①. The goal is to cover 20% of all urban households with subsidized housing and low-income households should enjoy 13 m² per capita by 2015. Even though the government reports that it has fulfilled and even surpassed annual targets, the actual performance is hard to evaluate as local governments often use various types of housing

---

① These targets include low-income housing as well as resettlement housing for urban renewal and shanty area redevelopment and housing with controlled prices (xian jia fang), subsidized housing for middle-income households.

development such as resettlement housing and housing developed by work units to meet their numerical targets. Yet, there is no doubt that China has since entered a new era of low-income housing.

Faced with state mandate for subsidized housing and severe budgetary pressures, local governments have explored different strategies to fulfill the quotas and to provide subsidized housing beyond traditional concentrated, large-scale projects by the government. A new strategy is called "pei tao jian she" (in short "pei jian"), which requires developers to provide a certain number of subsidized housing in their private housing development. "pei jian" is equivalent to inclusionary housing in the West. Inclusionary housing is defined as "a means of using the planning system to create affordable housing and foster social inclusion by capturing resources created through the marketplace," providing "incentives to private developers to incorporate affordable or social housing as a part of market-driven developments···."[5] This strategy is primarily used to meet goals of housing affordability and social inclusion, often targeting economic integration and poverty alleviation as well. In the U. S. and Europe, inclusionary housing was introduced and grew in popularity during the 1970s and 1980s, when existing social housing built through earlier government programs were being restructured and new programs were rolled out to encourage more private market responsibility for low-income housing provision.

Unlike the U. S. and Europe, private developers have played a very limited role in providing subsidized housing in China, since the government has been the main provider. Traditionally, subsidized housing in China has been developed in concentrated, large-scale projects containing only units for low-income households. They may be built by developers per government's request, but are managed by government agencies. As local governments provide urban land with no charge for subsidized housing, these concentrated subsidized housing projects tend to be located at urban fringe, with poor access to public services and economic opportunities [6,7]. This leads to the social and spatial marginalization of the poor, in addition to other social problems related to large projects of subsidized housing.

Given the huge demand for subsidized housing during rapid urbanization, and the rapidly rising housing inequality and residential segregation [8,10], inclusionary housing can potentially offer an important new strategy for China to meet its massive need for low-income housing, and at the same time reduce social and spatial segregation. In this paper, I aim to answer the following questions: How successful has inclusionary housing been in China? In addition to increasing the supply of subsidized housing, has it achieved social and spatial inclusion?

In China, there are three types of low-income housing: Cheap Rental Housing (CRH, lian zu fang), Public Rental Housing (PRH, gonggong zulin zhufang), Economic and Comfortable Housing (ECH, jingji shiyong fang) . PRH did not start until 2010; yet, PRH is becoming the focus of the low-income housing program, and CRH has been combined into PRH since 2014. While China has experienced an unprecedented housing construction boom with 33. 2 million units of residential housing completed during 1999 – 2008[11], the provision of low-income housing has been very limited. By 2007, the rate of coverage was at most 18 per cent. Because of local governments' dependence on land-related revenues, not surprisingly, low-income housing has been developed mostly at marginalized location at urban fringe [12]. The lack of accessibility, services and employment opportunities has created "spatial mismatch" in the suburbs in Chinese cities. For the same reason, many low-income households give up the right to rent/purchase low-income housing at marginalized locations, leaving many low-income housing vacant. For example, in Inner Mongolia province, less than 39%

of all subsidized housing built since 2008 are occupied [13]. The low occupancy rate among already limited low-income housing further compounds problems in low-income housing.

2 Inclusionary Housing as a New Strategy

To mitigate some of the problems in low-income housing, many local governments have experimented the practice of inclusionary housing. In 2007, State Council required that new CRH and ECH should be provided mainly through inclusionary housing in private housing projects, supplemented by concentrated development [14,15]. With this national embracement of inclusionary housing, it is clear that central government is interested in reducing increasing housing inequality and residential segregation, avoiding social problems associated with large scale low-income housing projects, and easing intensified public discontent due to skyrocketing housing prices and severe shortage of low-income housing. In particular, the central government established ambitious goals for low-income housing since 2010, and allocated quotas among local governments. This new mandate further compounds budgetary problems local governments facing since the fiscal reform in 1994 when local governments receive an increasingly smaller share of local revenues while shoulder an increasing larger share of public service provision[16,17]. As a result, local governments have adopted inclusionary housing with great enthusiasm to alleviate their financial and political pressures. For example, in Beijing, since 2010 all housing projects except high end commodity housing have to include subsidized housing, and the share of subsidized housing has been increased to at least 30%.

Since urban land in Chinese cities is owned by the state and local municipal governments are the sole providers of land lease-rights on the primary land market, municipal governments have monopoly of land supply. In addition to generating massive land conveyance fees, local governments are using their monopoly of the land supply to channel private investment into low-income housing development. To fulfill their quota for low-income housing, municipal governments set up annual target for inclusionary housing, and allocate low-income housing among appropriate residential land parcels that they are going to put up for leasing. While not every parcel of land is for inclusionary housing, developers have to comply with the requirements in order to access urban land for housing development as urban land is in short supply. The percentages required for low-income housing vary significantly between projects, locations, and cities, ranging from 5% to 30%.

As developer can access urban land only through the government on the primary market, they often have no option but to adopt inclusionary housing due to their need for urban land. Thus there is no doubt that developers have supplied required amount of low-income housing in their market housing developments. However, the amount of low-income housing provided through inclusionary housing is still relatively small given the fact that only appropriate new housing developments will comply with inclusionary housing, and the percentage of inclusionary housing units is relatively low. Furthermore, in the model of "controlling land price, bidding for inclusionary housing units" when the government does not set up the percentages for inclusionary housing, there are cases that developers were able to access urban land with as little as 100 m² of low-income housing units in their private housing projects [18]. There are also many "aborted biddings" ("liu pai") for land requiring inclusionary housing as developers avoid bidding for land with inclusionary housing requirement. Thus overall low-income housing provided through inclusionary housing is relatively small. The actual scale of inclusionary housing at national level is hard to estimate as housing statistics are compiled by type of housing instead of provision mode. In Guangzhou, among its 85, 000 units of low-income housing planned for 2012, only 8.2% of them are inclusionary housing units in private development by developers and another 9.6% in housing development by work units, while the majority will have to be provided by the government [19].

3 Problems in Inclusionary Housing

In addition to increasing the provision of low-income housing, inclusionary housing potentially can bring many benefits to residents, developers and the government. U. S. -based studies show that low-income residents may access improved social networks, higher levels of informal social control, higher rates of employment, enhanced respect for property, and improved access to services and infrastructure [20,21]. Meanwhile, private developers are able to develop at an increased density and enjoying faster-track permit processing and tax/fee waivers, and local governments might benefit politically and economically by successfully providing diverse housing options for the local labor force[22]. However, inclusionary housing in China so far is a government-driven campaign, mainly aiming to meet low-income housing targets set by the central government. Thus there are many problems and challenges in inclusionary housing.

First of all, while inclusionary housing may have fulfilled the numerical targets, it has not achieved the goal of social and spatial inclusion. The guiding principle of "being scattered on a large scale, being concentrated on a small scale" aims to avoid large concentration of low-income housing at the city level; yet it does not really target social and spatial inclusion at neighborhood level. The concept of "small scale" is very vague, which makes operation difficulty. In Beijing local planners and officials aim to have low-income housing in every residential area of about 30, 000 people, which is still a very large spatial scale for social inclusion. Not surprisingly, low-income housing provided through inclusionary housing is marginalized at both city and neighborhood level. Since municipal governments are under fiscal pressures to maximize land-related revenues while fulfill mandates on low-income housing, they usually designate cheaper land on the urban fringe for inclusionary housing projects rather than prime, central locations where higher fees can be demanded. At the neighborhood level, since developers have complete control over the location of low-income housing within their developments, it is common for them to build low income housing building/units at marginal, less desirable locations on the project. In fact, the concentration of low-income housing on a small scale is required to "facilitate management". In cities such as Panzhihua and Zhengzhou, the government requires developers to put low-income housing in their inclusionary housing projects in separate buildings from market rate housing; if not possible, in the same building but separate wings in the building to facilitate management [23]. Thus inclusionary housing in China is spatially marginalized both within a city, within a single development, and within a single building.

For example, Ocean Vista is the first inclusionary housing project with PRH in Beijing, which was built in 2011 and has served as a showcase project due to its relative good location and quality. Yet it is located between the Fourth and Fifth Ring Roads. Its 550 units of PRH are all concentrated in one 24-story building (denser and higher than the other buildings), at the corner of the project facing noisy high-speed railway and a major throughway. Residents of PRH complain that it is too noisy for them to open windows. Even though the government forbids developers to physically separate low-income housing from private housing [24], it is common to see various types of physical barriers between the two ranging from barricades, different entrances, different zones, green spaces, to fences, and walls. Thus despite good infrastructures in private housing projects, residents in inclusionary housing usually cannot access them.

Furthermore, the government requires "separatedmanagement" (fenkai guanli) of low-income housing from private housing in inclusionary housing projects, which further exacerbates social exclusion. Low-income housing in inclusionary housing projects are managed by municipal Affordable Housing Center, a government agency that often has an office on-site to take care of the rental business of low-income housing and serve low-income households. In comparison, private housing in the same project is sold by developers and managed by a private Property Management Company (PMC). The PMC is supposed to provide the same property services to low-income households in inclusionary housing as well; yet, the government pays a much lower property management fee for low-income households than homeowners pay out of their pockets[①]. Thus naturally the services they receive are different. The separation in management reinforces the two separate social groups.

Secondly, inclusionary housing fails to include and integrate migrants in Chinese cities. Due to the persistence of the Household Registration System (hukou) which ties territorial welfare goods to hukou status, migrants have conventionally been excluded from low-income housing in cities. In 2010 when PRH was first established, "qualified migrants" are part of its target population. State Council also required prefecture and higher level cities to include qualified migrants with stable jobs into the urban low-income housing program by the end of 2013[25]. Meanwhile other low-income housing such as ECH and CRH remain inaccessible to migrants. Thus PRH, especially those provided through inclusionary housing, offers a unique opportunity to integrate migrants into the mainstream urban society. Yet, with the exception of cities such as Chongqing, in most cities migrants' access to PRH remains a policy on the paper, and few migrants have actually benefited from it. For example, in Beijing, all districts and counties are required to incorporate qualified migrants into their PRH program before the end of 2013. Yet, only Shijingshan District has a real policy on migrants and there have been only 118 migrant households who have accessed PRH, while there are over 7 million long-term migrants in Beijing in 2010. According to an official in Beijing, the Beijing Municipal Government is trying to upgrade its economy and wants to drive out "low-end" population. Thus there is really no real intension to offer low-income housing to migrants, while population control remains a goal in large cities.

Third, currently the government is the main beneficiary of inclusionary housing, while both developers and residents are not benefiting much, which threatens the success and sustainability of inclusionary housing. The central government benefit politically by meeting its ambitious low-income housing target, while local governments benefit by meeting central government quotas and increasing the provision of low-income housing. Local governments are also somewhat relieved from the financial pressure to develop low-income housing by channeling private investment in low-income housing provision, although they do sacrifice some land conveyance fees and taxes and other fees.

In contrast, developers do not benefit much from inclusionary housing except land access. With higher profit margins in the high-end housing submarket and in the ownership sector, few developers have invested in rental and low-end ownership housing. Their recent participation in inclusionary

---

① For example, in Beijing, property management fee for low-income housing is usually less than 2.5 yuan/m², while for private commodity housing it is often 3-5 yuan/m².

housing is more a forced behavior than a self motivated action. Developers suffer various risks by a-dopting inclusionary housing. For example, the presence of low-income housing in their develop-ments may jeopardize their development's brand, lower the perceived quality of market-rate hous-ing, and thus negatively affects their sales and their profits. In other words, even though they may benefit from a lower land conveyance fee and enjoy tax/fee waivers, they may still suffer financially from the lower prices for their market-rate housing and the difficulty in housing sale. They also have to pay for low-income housing development in their projects upfront, and sell to the government lat-er at a predetermined price. The transfer of low-income housing to the government can be a lengthy bureaucratic process, and prices for building materials may increase, thus it takes a long time for de-velopers to recover their cost for housing development. In some cases, developers have to transfer low-income housing to local governments for free, thus they cannot even recover their costs, let a-lone profits. In addition, the presence of two vastly different socioeconomic groups in the same devel-opment imposes big challenges for property management. Therefore, for both financial and manage-ment reasons, developers are hesitant to invest in projects with inclusionary housing.

Similarly, low-income households are not enjoying additional benefits from inclusionary hous-ing. Since low-income housing quotas are set by the central government, inclusionary housing only changes the share of low-income housing by the government versus by private developers. Thus it does not really affect their chances to access low-income housing. Furthermore, rents/prices for low-income housing are regulated by local governments, thus low-income households pay similar rents/prices for their housing regardless whether it is in inclusionary housing projects or concentrat-ed low-income housing projects. In other words, economically residents do not really benefit from in-clusionary housing policy. Yet private housing projects may be better located than concentrated low-income housing projects, and may provide better access to public services and job opportunities. But as discussed earlier, inclusionary housing in current form does not necessarily lead to social inclusion thus they may not benefit from living in mixed-income community and enjoy improved social capital and economic opportunities. On the contrary, to cut costs, developers often build poor quality hous-ing for low-income households and situate their buildings at marginal locations with poor orienta-tion. Thus in some aspects, low-income households in inclusionary housing are in a worse position than those in concentrated development by the government.

中国城市住房配建可以实现社会和空间融合吗？

黄友琴

（纽约州立大学阿尔巴尼分校地理和规划系）

摘要：自中央政府提出保障性住房的目标后，地方政府积极采用配套建设以实现住房可支付性和社会融合。本文研究中国的包容性住房，试图回答以下问题：1）配套建设是否实现了社会和空间融合？2）如果没有，中国的配建要如何改革才能实现社会和空间融合？基于对北京的研究，显示中国的配建提供了一些低收入住房，但是没有实现低收入人群的社会和空间融合。

关键词：包容性住房，低收入住房，中国，社会融合，空间融合

References:

[1] Huang Youqin, William A. V. Clark. Housing tenure choice in transitional urban China: a multilevel analysis[J]. Urban Studies 2002. 39(1): 7-32.

[2] Yi Chengdong, Huang Youqin. Housing Consumption and Housing Inequality in Chinese Cities during the First Decade of the 21st Century[J]. Housing Studies, 2014. 29 (2): 1-22.

[3] State Council. 2010, (10). Guo Wu yuan guan yu jianjue e zhi bu fen cheng shi Fang jia guo kuai shang zhang de tong zhi (A notice to control decisively the overly rapid increase of housing prices in some cities.

[4] State Council. 2011. (1). Guowuyuan bangongting guanyu jinyibu zuohao fangdichan shichang tiaokong gongzuo youguan wentide tongzhi (A notice from State Council about issues related to further regulating the real estate market). These targets include low-income housing as well as resettlement housing for urban renewal and shanty area redevelopment and housing with controlled prices (xian jia fang), subsidized housing for middle-income households.

[5] Calavita, Nico, Alan Mallach, eds. Inclusionary Housing in International Perspective: Affordable Housing, Social Inclusion, and Land Value Recapture[M]. Cambridge, MA: Lincoln Institute of Land Policy 2010.

[6] Qian, Yingying, An Analysis on Low-income Housing Policy in China: Economic and Comfortable Housing and Cheap Rental Housing[J]. Zhongguo fangdichan (Real Estate in China), 2003, (8): 57-60.

[7] Li Pei, Zhongguo jingji shiyong fang zhence zhiding de yanbian yu quji chayi (The Evolution of and Regional Variation in Economic and Comfortable Housing Policy Design in China)[J]. Chengshi yu quyu guihua yanjiu (Urban and Regional Planning Research), 2009, 2(2): 68-86.

[8] Sato, Hiroshi Housing inequality and housing poverty in urban China in the late 1990s[J]. China Economic Review, 2006, 17(1): 37-50.

[9] Huang Youqin, Jiang Leiwen, Housing Inequality in Transitional Beijing[J]. International Journal of Urban and Regional Research, 2009, 33(4): 936-956.

[10] Huang Youqin. "From Work-unit Compounds to Gated Communities: Housing Inequality and Residential Segregation in Transitional Beijing" in Restructuring the Chinese Cities: Changing Society, Economy and Space[M]. edited by Laurence J.C. Ma and Fulong Wu. London and New York: Routledge, 2005: 192-221

[11] NBSC. Zhongguo tongji nianjian 2009 (China Statistical Yearbook 2009)[M]. Beijing: China Statistics Press, 2009.

[12] Dang Yunxiao, Liu Zhilin, Zhang Wenzhong. Land-Based Interests and the Spatial Distribution of Affordable Housing Development: The Case of Beijing, China[M]. Habitat International 44, 2014: 137-145.

[13] Inner Mongolian Bureau of Housing and Urban Rural Development. Report for National Subsidized Housing workshop, A Collection from the Subsidized Housing Workshop, Beijing. Internal document, 2014.

[14] State Council, 2007, No. 24; Ministry of Housing and Urban Rural Development (MOHURD), 2007, No. 162, lianzu zhufang baozhang banfa (Regulation on CRH).

[15] MOHURD, 2007, No. 258, Jingji shiyong zhufang guanli banfa (Management Regulation on

ECH).

[16] Tao Ran, Wang Hui. Incomplete and Transitional Land Reform in China: Challenges and Solutions)[J]. Guoji jingji pinglun (International Economic Review), 2010, 85(2): 93-123.

[17] Tsui, kai-yuen, Wang Youqiang, Between Separate Stoves and A Single Menu: Fiscal Decentralization in China[J]. The China Quarterly, 2004, 177: 71-90.

[18] Qi Lin. Beijing Bureau of Land Increases Threshold for Inclusionary Housing for Land Conveyance[M], 2012. http: //www. gtzyb. com/dichandizhen/20120920_20980. html.

[19] Guangzhou office of Housing Indemnity, 2012, Work plan for Housing Indemnity in 2011 in Cuangzhou, (Guangzhou Shi 2011 Nian zhn Fang Bao zhang Gong zuo Fang an) http: // www. cnki. net.

[20] Joseph, Mark. Is Mixed-Income Development an Antidote to Urban Poverty[J]? Housing Policy Debate, 2006, 17 (2): 209-234.

[21] Ellickson, Robert C. The False Promise of the Mixed-Income Housing Project[J]. UCLA Law Review, 2010, 983: 983-1021.

[22] Pendall, Rolf. From Hurdles to Bridges: Local Land-Use Regulations and the Pursuit of Affordable Rental Housing[M]. In Revisiting Rental Housing: Policies, Programs, and Priorities//edited by N. P. Retsinas and E. S. Belsky. Washington, D.C. : Brookings Institution Press and Joint Center for Housing Studies, 2008.

[23] Panzhihua Municipal Government. A Temporary Management Regulation about Affordable Housing in Inclusionary Housing Projects[OL]. www. panzhihua. gov. cn. [2012-05-31]

[24] Beijing Bureau of Housing and Urban Rural Development[EB], A Temporary Regulation on the Management of Public Rental Housing in Beijing, 2013, (15).

[25] State Council. Notice about Continuing Adjusting and Controlling the Real Estate Market [EB], 2013, No. 17.

新型城镇化与低碳城市
New Type Urbanization and Low-Carbon City

基于混合线性城市发展模式，郑州城市区可持续发展策略研究

李晨阳[1]　张敏建[2]

（1. 河南省城乡规划设计研究总院有限公司；2. 湖南大学建筑学院）

摘要： 近年来，我国各城市轨道交通迅速发展，人们的出行和生活方式也将随之得到极大的转变。由于多数城市的地铁建设仍处于初级阶段，因此各城市如何及时地改变发展策略以应对此种转变变得十分重要。实际上，针对以交通为导向的城市发展模式的研究在学术界已经取得了显著的成果，并形成了数种著名理论，如线性城市理论、交通导向发展模式理论（TOD）等。本次研究通过对国内外相关理论研究的梳理，基于现有线形城市发展模式理论和交通导向发展模式理论，以可持续发展为前提，提出了名为"混合线性城市发展模式"的尝试，并以郑州城市区为例，对郑州地铁一号线运用该城市发展模式进行可持续发展的规划策略分析。此种城市发展模式将上述两种城市发展理论（线性城市理论和交通导向发展理论）融合，以地下轨道交通系统为骨架，以串联各种城市功能为形式，将人们的生活与城市轨道交通系统相联系。模式的核心在于依据科学分析和统筹规划，将地铁沿线车站及其周边区域划分为住宅功能区、商业功能区等以及现有交通导向发展模式下的混合功能区，各功能区在交通、经济、城市结构、居民生活等方面相互影响。本次研究从宏观、中观和微观三个层次对案例进行分析。在宏观的区域发展层面，针对中原经济区的规划策略和混合线性城市发展模式的意义进行了研究；在中观的郑州地铁一号线沿线发展层面，对沿线 20 个地铁站点进行了具体的定位分析；在微观的各站点发展层面，选取三个重点车站进行详细分析和初步概念设计。最后，将几个层次中混合线性城市发展模式的运用情况做出分析归纳，为当代城市发展提供了启示和建议。

关键词： 混合线性城市模式，可持续发展，郑州地铁一号线，中原经济区（CPER）

1 引言

20 世纪 80 年代以来，中国开始实施改革开放的发展政策，并由此在经济发展方面创造了巨大成就。然而，由于经济的蓬勃发展以及其他政治和社会问题，自 1990 年以来一些负面的情况开始在中国显现，如资源枯竭和环境污染。自 1994 年可持续发展被提升到国家战略层面以来[3]，它始终被普遍看作一个适合中国国情的发展方式。可持续发展即既满足当代人的发展需求，又不损害后代人满足其发展需求的能力的发展模式。笔者认为，可持续发展的核心在于每一代人的需求管理。在技术层面，这种管理在经济、社会和环境三个方面可以通过控制需求和资源高效利用这两种方式来实现。进入 21 世纪头十年代，郑州市在实施中原经济区发展战略的同时，轨道交通系统也在迅速建立并完善，随之而来的是民众的出行和生活方式的极大转变。因此，在中原经济区战略规划大背景下，选择正确的发展模式以应对新的城市形态和社会问题，是郑州市坚持走可持续发展道路的关键所在。

2 混合线性城市发展模式

2.1 研究先例

2.1.1 经典线性城市理论

西班牙规划师 Arturo Soria y Mata（1844～1920）为了寻找适合马德里的自然友好型的城市发展模式，于 1882 年首次提出了线性城市规划设计方案，这是首个以线性城市理论为指导的城市规

划方案。方案中城市模型有以下特征：（1）由一条城市干道或者其他交通方式作为线性城市系统的核心；（2）城市核心交通干道与其他区域之间由绿化带或者缓冲区隔离；（3）公共区、教育区、居住区和公园区等城市各功能区沿核心干道平行布置。

就目前来看，虽然线性城市理论在实际操作中存在一定限制因素，但它相对于其他城市发展模式仍具有以下优势：（1）城市运行逻辑简洁、高效（2）城市系统是开放的、弹性的（3）公共交通在城市发展中处于主导地位。

2.1.2 公共交通导向发展理论（TOD）

20 世纪 60 年代以来，由于城市的扩张，公共交通导向理论已经被广泛应用于世界各国。与线性城市发展模式类似，TOD 理论同样是以公共交通作为核心的。在 TOD 理论中，城市建设在以公共交通站点为中心、半径为 400～800m 的区域内由内向外从高密度向低密度过渡。并且与线性城市理论中各城市单一功能区对应的是，TOD 理论中每个功能区均为具有特定发展主题的混合用地。

2.2 混合线性城市发展模式

Prof. Alfred Yeung 在 the Linear City Research under Linear City：sustainable land use and mass transit planning[4] 研究中发现，在可持续发展方面线性城市理论和 TOD 理论均有显著的优势：（1）在经济方面，提倡公共交通可以减少个人出行费用，缩短成本回收期，降低开发商的资金风险（2）在社会方面，这两种发展模式均能提高民众的出行便捷性和生活质量（3）在环境方面，公共交通可以降低能源消耗，改善交通状况。同时，这两种也有各自的不足之处：线性城市发展模式对于土地利用效率方面考虑较少，而 TOD 理论则缺乏对实施过程中可持续性的重视。

如果将传统线性城市发展模式比作"珍珠项链"（图 1a），将传统 TOD 模式比作"玛瑙项链"（图 1b），那么本次研究所要探讨的混合线性城市发展模式则更类似与上述两种传统模式融合成的"翡翠项链"（图 1c），新的模式延续了传统线性城市中城市功能区沿干路交通平行布置的布局模式，并将单一的"线性"城市形态拓扑为与城市公共交通系统根伟契合的"网状"城市形态。同时，新的模式引入 TOD 理论中的混合用地和主导功能区埋念，将传统线性城市的单一功能区调整为具有特定主导功能的混合功能区。这种新的城市发展模式在强化传统线性城市在可持续发展方面优势的同时，通过用地的混合利用来避免土地的低效利用和低便利性。

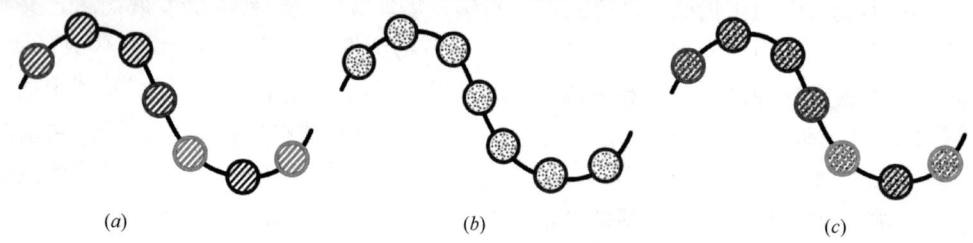

图 1　概念模型

（a）传统线性城市；（b）传统 TOD 模式；（c）混合线性城市发展模式

3　郑州地铁一号线发展概况

由于近些年的蓬勃发展，郑州的经济、社会条件都已经达到了《国务院办公厅关于加强城市快速轨道交通建设管理的通知》（国办发〔2003〕81 号）中的基本要求。此外，郑州的市内交通如今也面临着巨大的压力，并已经影响到了郑州的可持续发展。同时京广铁路和陇海铁路将整个城市分为西南和东北两个板块，极大地阻碍了郑州的地上交通联系。而城市的主要公共交通走廊上公交车长时间满负荷运行这一状况也表明目前城市公共交通系统（公交车和出租车）已经无法满足市民的日常出行需求。综上所述，郑州为了保证城市的正常运行，满足人民的基本生活需求，继续走可持续发展道路，必须建立并完善城市轨道交通系统。

2009年2月12日，国家发改委向河南省发展改革委下发《印发国家发展改革委关于审批郑州市城市快速轨道交通近期建设规划（2008～2015）的请示的通知》（发改基础［2009］369号）。四个月后，郑州地铁一号线开工建设。郑州市轨道交通系统（URTS）由总长度为202.53km的6条地铁线路组成。建设过程分为初期阶段（2009～2015）、发展阶段（2016～2020）和成熟阶段（2020年以后）三个阶段。

4 基于混合线性城市理论的郑州地铁一号线分析

4.1 轨道交通系统对郑州城市区发展的影响

作为中原经济区内最大的城市，在区域战略发展规划背景下，恰逢轨道交通系统的逐步建立，郑州市的发展将迎来新的历史阶段。如何解决交通问题是一个城市的发展是否可持续的关键之一。郑州市的公共交通供给量仅占城市交通总需求量的20%[5]，与香港的公共铁路系统和地下铁路系统共承担了城市交通总需求量的40%[6]相比，还存在很大差距。

地铁运营前后郑州市道路负荷强度模拟　　　　　　　　　　　　　　表1

轨道数目	道路负荷强度为 0～0.5 的道路占比	道路负荷强度为 0.5～0.7 的道路占比	道路负荷强度 0.7～0.9 的道路占比	道路负荷强度 0.9 以上的道路占比
无轨道	39.5%	27.0%	23.7%	9.8%
2 条轨道	45.2%	26.6%	21.8%	6.4%
5 条轨道	54.8%	25.6%	16.8%	2.8%

作为城市公共交通系统的一种，拥有巨大客运量的地铁系统将成为改善郑州交通状况的关键。本次研究模拟了地铁运营前后郑州市的交通状况（表1）。实验结果显示，在交通符合较轻时，ZML1和ZML2运营与否几乎没有差异；然而在交通量较大时，地铁的运营将大幅改善部分道路交通拥堵的状况。可以预见，地下轨道交通系统的建立对于郑州城市区的发展将产生极大的影响。

4.2 郑州地铁一号线运营概况

2013年年底，ZML1正式开始运营。起始运营前三周的运营数据显示，日总客运量最低为120999人，最高为292718人。各车站中二七广场站始终是日客运量最大的车站，紫金山站在大多数情况下是日客运量第二大车站，而排行第三的车站则在西流湖站、桐柏路站和郑州火车站之间变化。

4.3 特定车站的具体分析和概念设计

根据混合线性城市理论，本次研究的研究区域为ZML1一期线路500m范围内的一些区域以及几个典型功能区（绿地—西流湖公园、住宅区—国棉三厂、商业区—郑州CBD），总计26.3km²，人口20万人，如图2。以下是对三个典型功能区的具体分析和概念设计。

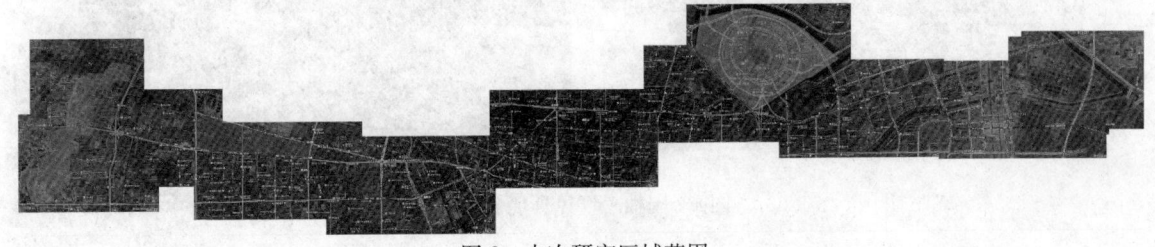

图2　本次研究区域范围

4.3.1 西流湖生态公园

西流湖公园共面积为 274hm² （其中水域面积 120hm²），人口约 9.6 万人。本次研究中西流湖公园被定位为绿地。基于对郑州生活方式的研究和对场地的地形分析，建议此处规划一个 3.2km² 的生态公园和一个 6000m 长的自行车慢行系统。另外，园区内还应设置一处游览服务中心、6 个自行车休息处和相应的隧道、天桥（图 3）。

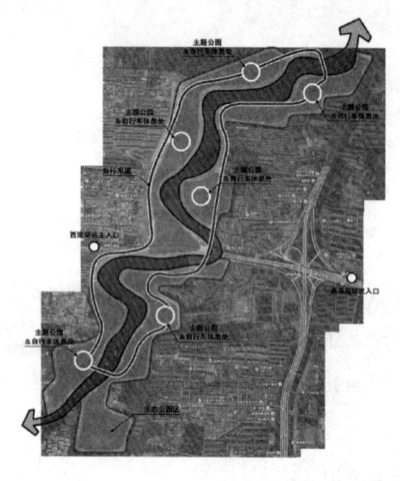

图 3　西流湖生态公园概念设计

现场勘查后发现，场地已经具有形成生态公园的初步自然条件，但湖水水量不足且水质较差，认为的环境破坏现象时有发生，同时区域内缺乏相关的配套设施。因此，目前的当务之急是遏制环境的进一步破坏，保证水源并改善水质状况，同时尽快完善相关配套设施。

4.3.2 国棉三厂城市更新区

国棉三厂现状分布着大量的低密度住宅楼，居住尺度和邻里交通比较便利，但缺乏商店、医院等公共服务设施，并且区内道路狭窄细长、仅容人行通过。

根据本次研究，国棉三厂被定位为住宅区。由上文调研结果可知，目前区内社区氛围较好，存在的问题在于环境状况和公共服务设施状况。笔者通过使用 Fluent 14.0 对场地进行分析得出在夏季盛行风情况下的现状场地空气流通评估报告（图 4）。结果显示狭窄的街道和长距离的平行于道路的建筑物墙面阻碍了风进入场地内部区域，这将导致小气候的失衡，并对区域内部风环境和空气质量造成负面影响。因此，进一步的详细空间设计中应对此问题进行针对性解决，从而改善社区环境状况。

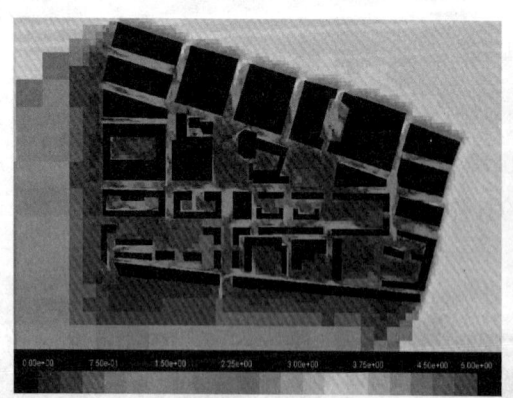

图 4　国棉三厂风环境分析图

4.3.3 郑州 CBD 商务核心区

会展中心位于郑东新区的核心位置，总面积 3.45km^2。区域内环分布着几栋 80m 左右的高层建筑，外环则散布着一些高度超过 120m 的高层建筑。

根据本次研究，会展中心被定为商业区。为保证场地的交通流通，研究建议建立一个环境友好型的交通连接系统。系统将连接内、外环交通，形成包括地铁、公交和私人小汽车在内的完善的公共交通系统。

5 结论

5.1 研究局限性

为了方便研究，本文对于概念分析和学术讨论做出如下假设：（1）忽略已经审批通过的法定规划中的相关政策和管理措施；（2）根据经验对于成本和资金问题进行估值。

因此，由于假设和理论缺陷存在，本次研究具有以下局限性：（1）研究中的混合线性城市发展模式仍是处于总体规划层面的发展策略，在详细规划层面还需进一步理论研究；（2）由于时间限制，本次研究仅对三个代表性区域进行分析，且由于调研数据不足，仅对代表性区域进行简要的分析和概念设计。

5.2 总结

本次研究在可持续发展中经济、社会和环境三个方面对混合线性城市发展模式进行介绍，并在中原经济区战略背景下对郑州城市区发展和郑州地铁一号线进行分析。实际上，这种理念是受到了 Alfred Yeung 教授的线性城市研究：可持续土地利用和交通规划的启发。根据基于混合线性城市发展模式对案例进行的一系列分析，总结出以下结论：（1）模式将有助于可持续城市空间的形成；（2）模式可以有效地连接每个城市功能区；（3）模式将有助于形成综合城市公共交通系统。

5.3 研究前景

目前，郑州地铁系统仅有一号线郑州运营。到 2020 年后，整个城市地铁系统将有六条线路同时运营，因此，混合线性城市发展模式将是一个极具潜力的研究领域。

致谢

首先感谢香港中文大学中国城市住宅研究中心邹经宇教授提供的研究机会和杨光辉教授的热切悉心指导。对于河南省城乡规划设计研究总院有限公司和湖南大学提供的技术帮助一并致谢。

Based on "Mixed Linear City Research", Sustainable Development Strategy Study of Zhengzhou Urban Area

Li Chenyang[1], Zhang Minjian[2]

(1. Henan Urban Plan & Design Institute; 2. Hunan University)

Abstract: In this paper, under the background of Central Plains Economic Region (CPER), based on existing linear city theory and Transit Oriented Development (TOD) theory, a comprehensive Linear City Development (LCD) is proposed to achieve sustainable development of Zhengzhou Urban Area by a case study of Zhengzhou Metro Line 1 (ZML1). In this case, detail analysis on each station of ZML1 and brief concept design of 3 typical functional area (green land area, residential area and commercial area with corresponding to environmental, social and economic aspect of sustainable development) is processed. Tersely, a Bicycle Slow Traffic System is suggested in Xiliuhu (Xiliuhu station of ZML 1) area for green land function, an Air Ventilation Assessment is conducted in Guomian-3 (Tongbai Road station of ZML 1) area for residential function and an Environmentally Friendly Linkage System (EFLS) is designed in Zhengzhou CBD (Exhibition Centre station of ZML 1) for commercial function.

Keywords: Linear city development (LCD), Sustainable development, Zhengzhou metro line 1 (ZML1), Central plains economic region (CPER)

参考文献：

[1] U. S. Energy Information Administration. International Energy Statistics and Short-term Energy Outlook. 2012

[2] China Water Risk. 2011 [2015-4-5][1]. http://chinawaterrisk. org/big-picture/china-water-crisis/.

[3] 国家发展和改革委员会,中华人民共和国科学技术部. 中国 21 世纪议程——中国 21 世纪人口、环境与发展白皮书[R]. 1994.

[4] Alfred YEUNG. Linear City: sustainable land use and mass transit planning, 2011.

[5] 郑州市统计局. 郑州统计年鉴 2012[J]. 北京:中国统计出版社, 2012.

[6] MTR. 2012 Sustainability Report, Hong Kong, 2013.

---

① 方括号内标注最近浏览该网页的日期。

以科学风水为思维的生态城市规划方法
——以台北淡海新市镇第二期计划为例

李子耀[1]　陈懿欣[2]　谢维展[1]
（1. 勃翔股份有限公司；2. 境群国际规划设计顾问股份有限公司）

摘要：本研究试图提出不同于传统城市规划思维，强调科学风水，打破规划范围的疆界，重视城乡环境所具备的空间连续性；分别从 GIS 建立国土安全格局、以景观格局分析生态底图、以生物气候地图检讨宜居环境等三大步骤，提出适地适性的生态城市规划方案，完成城乡共生底图，绘制成长管理边界，同时提出生态城市设计原则，作为新市镇土地使用划分及管理依据，借此改变传统城市规划设计观念与方法。

关键词：生态城市规划，区域空间规划，景观格局分析，生物气候环境，科学风水

1　着重科学风水的生态城市规划方法学

1.1　以生物区域思维建构城乡共生布局

为应对气候变迁风险，近年来全球城市规划思潮转向生态城市（Ecocity）理念发展，Ecocity Builders 网站①用以下四点对生态城市进行定义：（1）与自然生态系统紧密相关，具备自给自足能力的人居聚落；（2）包含城市居民及其生态冲击影响的实体存在；（3）自然生态系统之下的子系统，水流域及生物区域（Bioregion）的一部分；（4）世界、国家以及区域性经济体系之下的子系统。即是将人类居住的城市、周边的乡村、农田及森林，在生态面、文化面及经济面均视为一个完整的生物区域单元，自然森林提供人类身心休闲的场所以及从事生产所需资材；乡村及农田生产的食物供应城市居民；而城市则制造能源与经济成长供应乡村需求。这些城市、乡村及自然间的物质与能量流动循环（flows inward and outward），使得城镇所在的生物区域能够完整而持续运作。[1]

在城市扩张过程中，势必改变或建立起新的物质与能量流动关系，新建城区的土地利用及绿地系统等空间布局，将大幅决定该生物区域未来的运作方式。[1,2]生态城市的关键即在于整体环境系统运作，包括城市基础设施系统（如水资源、能源、粮食、下水道、废弃物等）及生态环境系统（如微气候环境、动植物栖息、景观价值）；两者间若能够建立有效的能量、物质交换与循环关系，始能达到城市与生态兼容的可持续发展。因此，隐藏在土地利用分区背后的空气、水、营养等看不见的流域循环，才是新型城镇化与城乡规划管理亟须关注的设计重点。[3]

1.2　研究目标

台湾传统的城市规划模式强调由上而下、整体重划、整体开发的方式，往往忽略新开发地区原有的地形地貌、水文、农业生产、景观格局、生物气候等环境纹理，未能充分反映当地环境特质，并切断了原有物质及能量的流动循环。以台北淡海新市镇计划为例，这个 1994 年开始，占地 1749hm²，预期引入 30 万人口的新市镇开发计划，目前已完成的第一阶段建设（约 446hm²），然其方格状道路划分无视原始地貌变化，进行大规模地整地开发，并规划高强度建筑的体量兴建，明显地阻断其与周边山脉、水系及聚落纹理的空间连续性，从而衍生冲突性景观、生物多样性降低、热岛效应等等课题。

---

① http：// www. ecocitybuilders. org/ why-ecocities/ecocity-definition/

在本次研究中，作者试图提出不同于传统城市规划思维，关注科学风水，打破规划范围的疆界，重视城乡环境所具备的空间连续性，并以台北淡海新市镇第二期计划区（以下简称淡海二期区）为实际操作对象；分别从 GIS 建立土地安全格局、以景观格局方法分析共生底图、以生物气候地图绘制成长管理边界等三大步骤（如图 1），提出适地适性的生态城市规划方案，并提议以此操作流程作为未来城市规划设计方法之借鉴。

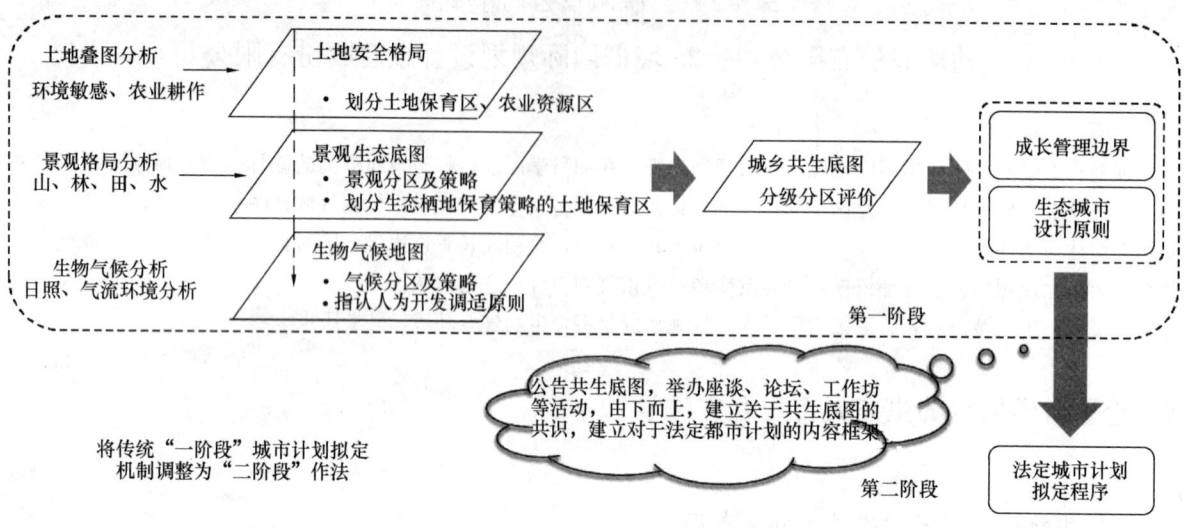

图 1　生态城市规划框架

2　城乡共生布局的关键步骤

2.1　以 GIS 建立土地安全格局

土地安全格局系指土地规划管理在应对全球气候变迁、粮食安全、土地保育及生态栖地维护等全球性或当地性之环境议题，为确保土地有序利用而建构之空间布局框架及土地使用原则。2014 年台湾修订的土地计划法草案已明确规范土地应依其环境特性、资源条件及发展需要，依序划定"土地保育地区"、"海洋资源地区"、"农业发展地区"及"城乡发展地区"等四种土地功能分区；而区域计划修正案（草案）则进一步提出环境敏感地区与农地需求总量等土地保育及利用之管制规范，两者皆是要建立完整的空间管理体系，确保土地使用基本原则。

2.1.1　建立分区分级体系

本研究延续土地计划法草案及区域计划修正案（草案）之精神，参考相关研究计划之成果[4,5]，首先建立土地保育地区及农业资源地区之分区分级原则，另考虑农田、水与林地斑块所构成之空间连续性及生态多样性，赋予农田除了人为耕作生产功能外，同时能够作为生物栖息与活动之场所，因此将林-田-水景观镶嵌之生态意义纳入农业资源地区分级划分（表 1）。

土地保育地区及农业资源地区分级原则表　　　　　　　　　　　　表 1

分区分级		分区分级目的与定义	生态意义	使用及管制方向
土地保育地区	保一	环境敏感程度较高，应保护、保育优良原生生态系统及涵养水源[4]	原生生态	确保区域内原生自然状态，禁止任何改变或破坏其原有自然状态之行为
	保二	环境敏感程度较低之地区，维持现有自然资源与生态系统[3]	生态保育	维护区内自然生态资源。区内任何兴建设施计划，均应征得主管机关同意
	保三	复育受损栖地环境，作为自然与人为开发区域的缓冲过渡区[3]	生态复育	在维持既存自然环境及生态栖地前提下，以开发许可管制，容许相关利用

分区分级		分区分级目的与定义	生态意义	使用及管制方向
农业资源地区	农一	具备优良农业生产环境、维持粮食安全功能之土地。[5] 具备良好、稳定、镶嵌度高之林-田-水生态体系之农业使用土地	生态复育	保全农业生产环境完整，并维持田-林生态体系之稳定，适宜推广农林混植型态之粮食生产模式。应禁止变更为其他使用分区
	农二	良好农业生产环境，在促进农业发展多元化之目标下，亦具粮食生产功能。[5] 具备林-田-水生态系统，但镶嵌度中等的农业使用土地	生态协调	使用上仍以农业生产为主，但放宽土地使用可使其多元发展复合农业，如休闲农业、循环农业、智能农业等
	农三	具有粮食生产功能，但生产环境受外在因素干扰之农业地区。[5] 受人为开发干扰，林-田-水生态系统呈现破碎化倾向之农业土地	生态协调	在不违反粮食安全的前提下，可允许其弹性使用及农地转用之开发许可申请，亦作为城市扩张的缓冲地区
	农四	位于坡地但具粮食生产功能之农地；此类农地水土及生态环境较为敏感[5]	生态复育	在不破坏水土保持及坡地生态多样性情，得进行低强度的土地开发利用

2.1.2 绘制土地安全格局底图

接着透过地理信息系统（GIS）工具之辅助，自土地测绘中心、农委会、灾害防救科技中心及当地社群团体搜集汇整研究区周边之地形测量图、土地利用现况、农田土地生产力、农田水利灌区、环境敏感地区等基础图资进行叠合分析，指认区域内环境基质，并依表1所制定之原则，绘制淡海二期区土地保育地区与农业发展地区之空间布局，建立土地安全格局底图。

在图资叠合分析过程，若遭遇分区重叠情形，采用"重叠分区，从严划设"之划分原则，采用保育层级较高的分区。例如，若一块土地同时符合农二及保三之划设条件，则应采用保三为最终划设之分区分级。然而若为既有聚落，则应以居住权益为优先，保持该土地为城乡发展分区。

2.2 以景观格局分析生态底图

景观格局方法着重于利用数学分析、指标量化等方式，解读景观组成及变迁趋势，透过此一方法，规划者可以掌握规划场地内的景观结构、斑块组成、斑块边界密度及连接度等其空间关系，从而推断解读其中生物物种、生态过程及人类经济活动分布与其背后的能源与物质流动关系。[6,7]

2.2.1 景观格局指标分析

本研究以土地测绘中心2013年土地利用状况调查成果图资为基础，利用FRAGSTATS软件进行景观格局指标分析，结果显示淡海二期区内景观变化相当多元，主要由少数极大面积的斑块以及大量的小面积斑块所构成。其中又以农田及林地斑块为面积最大的景观斑块，且两者相邻边界长度比例为全局最高，显示彼此镶嵌程度较高、关系密切，再次验证淡海二期区内，林-田-水等斑块组合构成重要的生态景观关系。

2.2.2 景观斑块空间布局分析

在景观斑块之空间分布方面，面积较大的林地斑块大致与北向坡地重叠，少部分位于南北走向的台地边坡地区。农田斑块主要分布于地势较平坦的河谷地区及台地之上，或是以梯田形式存在于南向坡地。聚落则集中于台地尾端，主要道路的两侧。整体而言，区内林地、农田及溪流等景观斑块，大致呈现顺应地形地势的东西向空间分布。

2.2.3 指认景观生态网络架构

引用景观生态学理论中对于良好的生态栖地斑块、生态跳岛及生态廊岛之定义[8]，进一步解析区内林、田、水等景观斑块的生态意义及生态价值，以指认区内重要且应当被保护的生态斑块，其中在林地斑块方面，作者指认出重要栖地斑块、东西向栖地走廊、边坡林地、河岸植生带，以及重要生态跳岛等具备健全区域生态网络机能之斑块，并提出划设为土地保育地区第三级作为生态维护之管理手段。

农田斑块部分，则综合比较景观格局分析斑块形状指标、斑块面积及邻近土地利用等条件，指认各农田斑块之生态价值，并依表1所提列之分区分级原则，纳入农业资源土地之分级划设。此外，考虑生态网络的完整性，对于东西向生态廊道的缺口，则提出框架性景观策略，未来应纳入生态城市设计原则中加以规范，逐步建构区内完整的生态网络。

2.3 以生物气候地图检讨宜居环境

城市化过程所带来的地貌改变，势必影响城市内外的微气候环境，"气候设计"即是要透过适当的规划设计方法，改善城市气候环境，而其核心理念即是强调"城市建设应该尊崇其所处的自然气候"。[10]目前世界各国已开始利用城市环境气候图（Urban Climatic Map）分析城市气候（包含温度、日照、湿度、风环境等因子）与城市形态间的交互影响，并提出相关的城市规划指引。[8,9]

2.3.1 气候统计资料分析

作者首先搜集气象局统计数据库中淡水测站（离淡海二期区最接近之测站）过去30年的观测数据进行分析，目标在建立区内的年度气候环境变化模式，其中包含气温、湿度、日照变化、降雨模式，并依季节及日夜差异，归纳整理区内风场环境变动趋势。

透过统计资料分析，可得知淡海二期区在夏季（6～8月）时最高温超过30℃，日间吹拂西北风（海风），夜间吹拂东南风（陆风）平均风速为2m/s；冬季（12～3月）时最低温则不到15℃，全日风速皆为北北东风（季风），风速较强，约为2.2～2.4m/s。

2.3.2 生物气候环境模拟

考虑透过单一测站的观测数据所建立的气候变动模式，仍无法完整反映出在空间上由地形地貌变化所引起的气候环境变化，故本研究进一步利用GIS与BIM软件整合地形高程模型，同时将气候观测数据输入Ecotect、Phoenics等环境分析软件，进行日射量、风向及风速环境模拟分析，另一方面亦配合利用美国地质调查局所Landsat计划所释出的卫星影像进行地表温度估算[10]，试图归纳区内因地形地貌所造成的生物气候环境变动趋势。

2.3.3 结合生物气候影响与景观生态格局的因子分析

在综合比较分析淡海二期区内地形地貌、景观格局、风场环境及地表温度等仿真成果后，可初步归纳出地形地貌与生物气候环境的交互影响关系。整体而言，区内气候环境受到地形影响最大，其次为地貌景观，再次为风的影响，例如，北向坡在夏初（5～8月）时因日照直射关系，而有较高的地表温度；而位于北向坡地的聚落，则又比同样位于北向坡的林地温度更高，水体温度则为最低。因而推论，在考虑过地形条件后，生态城市设计应首先利用地貌（土地使用分区）布局安排，以及通风廊道的留设，调控城市气候环境如热岛效应的影响。

2.4 绘制城乡共生底图

土地安全格局底图制订了地形地貌及环境敏感地区等物理环境的限制框架，景观生态底图则将土地使用的生态含义导入连续空间尺度中，两者彼此叠合，再依重叠分区从严划设的原则进行修编绘制，即完成淡海二期区的城乡共生底图，作为本区未来推动二阶段城市规划的重要参考基础(图2)。

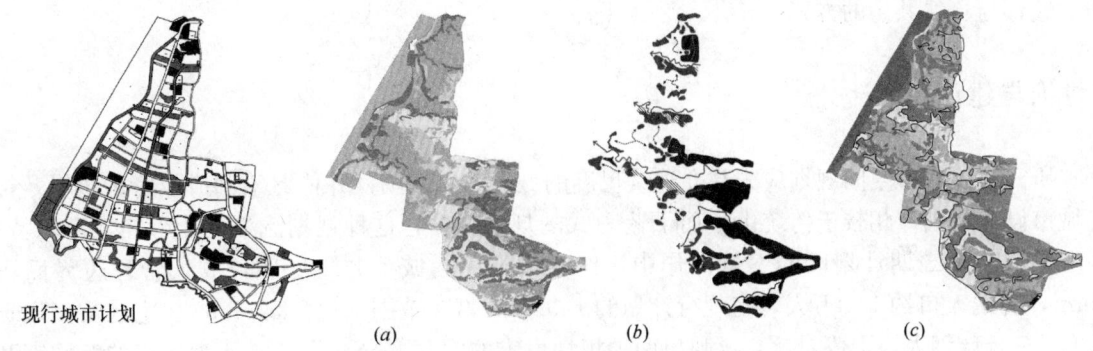

现行城市计划   *(a)*   *(b)*   *(c)*

图 2　淡海新市镇第二期计划区现行计划与城乡共生底图比较
(a) 土地安全格局；*(b)* 景观生态地图；*(c)* 城乡共生底图与成长管理边界

2.4.1　绘制成长管理边界

生态城市的重要理念之一，即是人类活动的成长应受到土地环境承载量的限制，在土地功能分区分级的土地管理架构中，土地保育地区及农三以外的农业资源地区，皆是架构在土地安全及景观格局之下，应作一定程度以上的生态保育及生态维持工作。

农三用地部分，则是在达到生态协调功能情况下，容许人为开发利用的范围，即为成长管理边界。第二阶段的城市计划拟定工作，应是以此为范围，及其衍生的人口承载量为基础，依城市发展定位及产业方向作城乡发展区分级（城一至城五），并进行城市设计及土地使用分区划分。在这次的研究案例中，成长管理范围约292hm²，以台湾平均城市居住人口密度（约3900人/km²）换算，约可容纳1.1万人，与淡海二期区现行计划所规划之17万人口形成强烈对比。

然未来若经由下而上社会参与讨论认为，人口承载量应再往上提高时，仍需尊重社会意向，适度地利用保三或农二用地作为城市开发地区，势必应提出最大容忍值的成长管理边界，制订更严格的生态城市设计原则，容许"城"与"农"、"保"共生的城市发展。

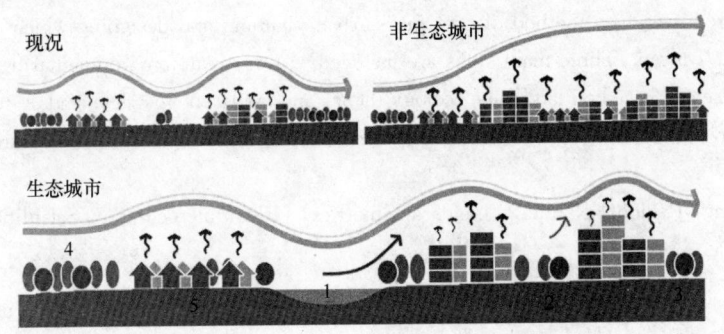

1. 新旧城区交接入，设置大面积景观生态水体，减缓热岛
2. 设置东西向开放绿带增加通风
3. 东南侧降低开发密度或留设开放空间，帮助夜间通风排热
4. 北侧保留或加强植生绿带，降低冬季东北季风冲击
5. 提高铺面透水率与绿覆率，加强场地保水

图 3　生态城市设计原则剖面示意图

2.4.2　拟定生态城市设计原则

生态城市设计原则的目的，在于响应各成长管理地区（城乡发展区）生物气候环境的人为开发调适对策，避免城市发展过度冲击周边环境，以及营造好的城市生活环境。本研究经过生物气候地图及影响因子分析，试图理解各城市成长地区的地形及地貌等条件，从而提出各区生态城市设计原则，以作为未来城市计划拟定及城市设计之指引（Design Guidelines）。图3为本研所针对淡海二期区内其中一个成长管理区域所绘制的生态城市设计剖面示意图，并与不适当的城市成长方式作比较，以说明生态设计的差异性，其中包含针对夏季缓解热岛效应之措施（如留设冷岛水体、设置通

风廊道等），以及调适冬季东北季风冲击之策略（如设置北侧挡风绿带等），未来城市计划拟定，规划者应将此原则纳入环境基础设施（Environmental Infrastructure）规划中整合考虑，以引导城市适地适性，与自然共生的方式成长。

3 讨论与建议

本研究提议城市空间规划应先建立连续尺度的城乡共生底图，并依此绘制成长管理边界及拟定生态城市设计原则；相较于传统由上而下蓝图式的规划程序，这种规划流程更能够当地环境特质。在淡海新市镇第二期计划区的案例操作中，作者提出一套城乡共生底图，成长管理边界面积约292hm²，容纳人口约1.1万人，与现行计划的1302hm²城市范围（包含526hm²住宅区及81hm²商业区）、17万计划人口形成对比，反映出两种规划思维的明显差异。作者并认为未来的新城镇开发计划，应建立二阶段的拟定程序，第一阶段为纳入科学风水思维，顺应当地风土及自然环境，绘制城乡共生底图及成长管理边界，并提出适宜当地特性的生态城市设计原则。其中城乡共生底图的绘制，即是一种城市空间设计过程，应同时考虑城市空间运用的合理性，应是后续研究所需注意的。第二阶段则再针对成长管理范围，由政府、专业者与小区进行从下而上的各使用分区开发内容的制定，建立起兼顾环境永续性与当地人文的规划操作系统。

Scientific Feng Shui Thinking in Ecological Urban Planning Method-A Case Study of the Second Stage Area of Danhai New Town Project

Lee Tzu yao[1], Chen I hsin[2], Hsieh Weichan[1]

（1. Artsome Eco-Tech Trade Co. ；2. EDS International，Inc.）

Abstract：This research tends to propose a new method of ecological urban planning and designing-which differs from the traditional top-down method in Taiwan. Three main steps are included：1）to create environmental basemap through GIS tools；2）to analyze the basemap based on landscape ecology theory and landscape metrics；and 3）to estimate living environment through urban climate diagnosis. The method is eventually advised as a new angle to transform those traditional planning methods.

Keywords：Ecological urban planning，Regional planning，Landscape metrics，Urban microclimate，Scientific feng shui

参考文献：

[1] Forman, Richard T. T. Urban Regions：Ecology and Planning Beyond the City. Cambridge：Cambridge University Press，2008.

[2] 朱伟兴，邬建国，张利权. 城市生态学：一个面临新挑战的生态学领域// 邬建国，韩兴国 黄建辉（编），现代生态学讲座（第二卷）：基础研究与环境问题[M]. 北京：中国科学技术出版社，2002 [2015-3-18]. http：//leml. asu. edu/ISOMES/2ndisome. htm.

[3] 境群国际规划设计顾问股份有限公司，生态城市设计方法-重建人与环境的共生关系. 未出版.

[4] 境群国际规划设计顾问股份有限公司，宜兰县区域计划规划期末报告[R]. 2013 [2015-5-7].

http：// www. cpami. gov. tw/chinese/index. php? option ＝ com ＿ content&view ＝ article&id＝18258&Itemid＝53.

[5]　农委会. 2014 年度宜兰县农业发展地区分类分级划设成果报告[R]. 台北：农委会，2014.

[6]　Dramstad，Wenche E. ，Olson，James D. and Forman，Richard T. T. Landscape Ecology Principles in Landscape Architecture and Land-use Planning. Washington，DC：Harvard University Graduate School of Design，Island Press and the America Society of Landscape Architects，1996.

[7]　角媛梅. 哈尼梯田自然与文化景观生态研究[M]. 北京：中国环境科学出版社，2009.

[8]　任超，吴恩融. 城市环境气候图[M]. 北京：中国建筑工业出版社，2012.

[9]　Verband Region Stuttgart. Klimaatlas Region Stuttgart. Stuttgart：Verband Region Stuttgart，2008.

[10]　Weng Qihao，Lu Dengsheng，Schubring J. Estimation of land surface temperature-vegetation abundance relationship for urban heat island studies. Remote Sensing of Environment，2004，89：467-483.

低碳智能城市评估指针系统之建构与分析

沈育生[1]　刘小兰[2]

（1. 政治大学地政学系；2. 政治大学地政学系）

摘要： 低碳智能城市系指结合科技、数字信息与低碳发展之永续城市，其发展除强调高科技应用与数字信息整合外，更为了降低碳排放量，以及解决过去城市发展所衍生的环境生态与社会发展之问题。低碳智能城市有效地衡量与评估，是低碳智能城市发展与建设的首要工作，因其可呈现城市发展的现况、与发展目标间的差距、引导城市朝向低碳智能化目标迈进，并可观测规划政策及措施执行的效度，以及监控低碳智能城市的发展状态，并加以调整。而要能有效地衡量与评估低碳智能城市的发展状态，需透过评估指针系统方可达成，但目前台湾甚少关于此议题之研究，也正突显本文之重要。因此，本文依据低碳智能城市的发展内涵、理念与目标，以台湾为实证案例，透过相关分析与因子分析定权法建构适宜之评估指针系统，并借此评估台湾各县市之低碳智能度发展状态。根据分析结果显示，适宜的低碳智能城市评估指针系统，应包括"经济及科技发展"、"资源消耗"、"环境保育及健康发展"、"地区发展"、"社会状态"等5构面，共21个指标。而台湾各县市在低碳智能发展的综合表现上，以台北市状态最佳。

关键词： 低碳智能城市，指标系统，因子分析定权法

1　前言

低碳智能城市系指结合科技、数字信息与低碳发展之永续城市，其发展除强调高科技应用与数字信息整合外，更为了降低碳排放量，以及解决过去城市发展所衍生的环境生态与社会发展的种种问题。故低碳智能城市系为在发展低碳经济的同时，从能源及生态角度，运用低碳技术、低碳政策，达到生产方式、消费方式、基础设施的低碳化，最大幅度减少温室气体排放量，建立高效率、高智能化、永续发展的宜居环境，亦即高智能化、高效率、高质量、高安全性、低能耗、低排放、低污染的城市发展形态。其内涵隐含了永续发展中的环境、社会、经济三面向，除融入生态、循环代谢城市等概念外，更强调信息技术、能源与碳排放的重要性，也因此，低碳智能城市倡导和实践低碳智能生活，最终实现城市社会-经济-环境复合生态系统的整体和谐与永续发展。[1~9]

低碳智能城市有效地衡量与评估，是低碳智能城市发展与建设的首要工作，因其可呈现城市发展的现况与发展目标间的差距，引导城市朝向低碳智能化目标迈进，并可观测规划政策及措施执行的力度，以及监控低碳智能城市的发展状态，并加以调整。而为能有效地衡量与评估低碳智能城市的发展状态，需透过评估指针系统之建构方可达成，但审视全球各城市政府，虽相继以低碳智能城市作为发展诉求，但不少的城市政府，却缺乏相对应适合该城市特性之评估指针系统，而台湾亦不例外。另外，上述指标的相关研究，多以概念或学理推演说明，仅部分研究进行实际的评估与分析。故本文依据低碳智能城市的发展内涵、理念与目标，以台湾为实证案例，透过相关分析与因子分析定权法建构适宜之评估指针系统①，并借此评估台湾各县市之低碳智能度发展状态，而其成果可供作未来低碳智能城市规划与政策研究拟定之参考。

2　研究设计

2.1　分析架构

本章针对低碳智能城市评估指针系统，建立一具体可操作之分析架构（图1）。该架构中包括：

---

① 本文所称的指标，系指未含规范性指标值之指标，亦可称为准则。

（1）界定低碳智慧城市内涵、范畴与空间范围：针对主题，确定研究范畴，并决定欲进行分析之空间范围；（2）综合整理相关文献：透过文献回顾，综合整理可用于建构低碳智能城市指针系统之相关学理与衡量指标；（3）研究设计：通过研究，提出低碳智能城市指针系统之建构原则与分析方法；（4）搜集整理样本数据：根据上述之基础，以改制前的台湾本岛 22 县市为例，搜集实证所需的样本数据；（5）建构评估指针系统：先透过相关分析，初步筛选与低碳智能城市概念相关之指标，并以所筛选之指针为输入变量，利用因子分析定权法，进一步地筛选代表性指标，并产生各指标的相对权重，据此建立低碳智能城市评估指针系统；（6）评估分析各县市状态：根据上述实证所建构之指针系统，评估台湾各县市之低碳智能发展状态；（7）结论及建议：根据上述评估结果，提出本章的结论及建议。

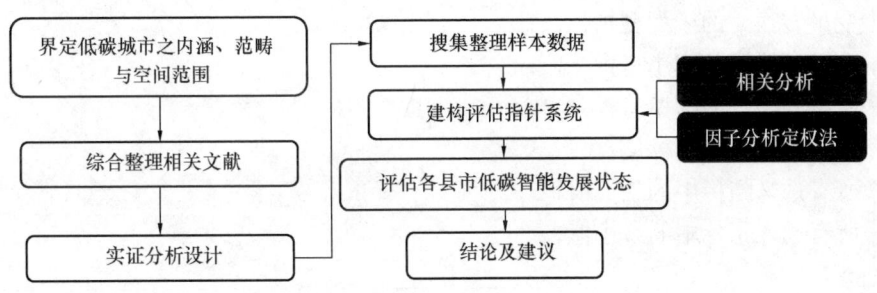

图 1　低碳智能城市评估指针系统之分析架构图

（资料来源：作者自绘）

2.2　分析方法及权重计算

过去在指标选取上，多是恣意且主观，而本章为避免指标选择的主观性，采用相关分析及因子分析定权法之方式。相关分析是测量各指标与低碳智能城市概念（即碳排放量、信息建设经费）之相关性，并据此初步筛选出与低碳智能城市概念相关之指标；而因子分析定权法之方式，亦即利用因子分析结果，进一步地选取出影响力强且具代表性的指标，并决定各构面与指标之相对权重，借此确立各构面与指标的相对重要性。而所建构评估指针系统中的权重，包括构面权重与指标权重。前者系由各构面可解释变异量占所选出构面的总解释变异量之比例计算而得，如式（1）；后者系依各构面内各指针因子负荷量所占比例，与构面权重相乘而得，如式（2）。

$$A_i = a_i / \sum_{i=1}^{n} a_i \tag{1}$$

$$B_{ij} = A_i \times (\mid b_{ij} \mid / \sum_{j=1}^{m} \mid b_{ij} \mid) \tag{2}$$

式中　A_i——构面权重；

a_i——各构面可解释变异量；

B_{ij}——构面所涵指标的权重；

b_{ij}——各指针因子负荷量；

i——构面；

j——构面所涵括的指标。

此外，在因子分析的实证操作上，本文以主轴因素法（Principal-axis Factoring Analysis）作为因子萃取（Extraction）的方式；而因子转轴方式，则采用构面间相互独立的直交转轴法（Orthogonal rotation）中之最大变异旋转法（Varimax）。

2.3　指标变项之界定

低碳智能城市包括了低碳发展及智能城市之概念，因此，在界定其评估指标时，将综合整理上述二类概念之相关指标与研究成果。[1~9]另外，为避免受到主观评价的影响，以及为使评估结果，具备客观性、可比较性与可验证性，故以量性指标为主。综合整理相关研究，归纳出 63 个量性指标作为输入变项。此外，在相关分析中，以碳排放量、信息建设经费作为衡量低碳智能城市概念之变项。

由于上述各指针/变项之原始数据、类型、方向与单位不尽相同，且指标数值间相差悬殊，故透过式（3）、式（4）进行变换处理。其中，若指标为望大型指标（数值愈大愈好），采用式（3）进行转换；若指标属望小型指标（数值愈小愈好），则采用式（4）进行转换。

$$x_l^c = (x_l - x_{\min})/(x_{\max} - x_{\min}) \tag{3}$$

$$x_k^c = (x_{\max} - x_k)/(x_{\max} - x_{\min}) \tag{4}$$

式中　x_l^c——变量转换后的望大型指标值；

　　　x_k^c——变量转换后的望小型指标值；

　　　x_l——原始的望大型指标值；

　　　x_k——原始的望小型指标值；

　　　$x_{\max}$——所有选入指标中的最大值；

　　　$x_{\min}$——所有选入指标中的最小值。

3　样本数据说明

在进行实证分析时，考虑数据的一致性、分析的精确性与连贯性，故实证之案例地区，以改制前的台湾本岛 22 县市为主。另外，本文所分析的各个指标及变项，皆为数值形态；而其数据来源，皆取自于城市及区域发展统计汇编，以及"主计处"与各县市的统计数据库。但因局限于政府所建置的数据内容，故进行相关分析及因子分析时，所采用的样本为 2006~2010 年 22 县市资料；而进行县市低碳智能性评估时，则以 2010 年 22 县市的数据为主。

4　低碳智能城市指标体系之建构与评估

4.1　低碳智能城市指针系统之建立

4.1.1　基于相关分析之低碳智能城市指标筛选

本文透过相关分析，测量各评估指标与低碳智能城市概念（即碳排放量、信息建设经费）之相关性，并据此初步筛选出与低碳智能概念相关之指标。根据分析结果，本文采用相关系数显著之 31 个指标；另外，基于低碳智能城市之发展理念及内涵（如居民健康及生活质量之维护、低碳产业转型等），故纳入部分不显著之指标，如 Gini 系数、台湾低碳低污染产业产值比例、病床数、医疗保健支出、公共设施面积、地区失业人口等指标项。因此，共计有 37 个指标，作为下述因子分析定权法之输入变项。

4.1.2　基于因子分析定权法之低碳智能城市指标体系建构

本文透过因子分析，建构适宜的低碳智能城市指标。在进行因子分析前，须检测数据是否能进行因子分析，其可借由 Bartlett 的球形检定、KMO 值进行判断，其中 Kaiser 曾提出，KMO 值小于 0.5 时不适合进行因子分析，而 KMO 值大于 0.8 时是非常适合分析的。透过检定，KMO 值为 0.817，且 Bartlett 球型检定的卡方值为 25524.295，P 值（0.000）达显着，故显示数据适合进行因子分析。

另外，在因子/构面萃取时，须符合 3 项原则，分别是：（1）Kaiser 标准－取特征值（eigen value）大于 1 者；（2）Cattell 标准[①]－由陡坡图陡阶的陡缓变化决定之；（3）累积解释变异量不得少于 75％。而根据本文因子分析的实证结果（见表 1），5 个因子/构面个数为较佳之萃取个数，而 5 个因子之累积解释变异程度高达 79.23％，且各因子的特征值皆大于 1，显示皆符合因子萃取原则。

此外，在合适度检定上，须透过残差分析来进行。其分析的原理，当再制相关矩阵与原相关矩阵越接近时，残差矩阵的数值越小，表示模式拟合越佳。而本文求算残差矩阵之结果，其最大残差值为 0.089（小于 0.1），表示模式合适度佳。

因子分析结果表 表 1

低碳智能城市评估构面	构面 1—经济及科技发展	构面 2—资源消耗	构面 3—环境保育及健康发展	构面 4—地区发展	构面 5—社会状态
特征值	38.64	11.36	5.43	3.73	2.62
解释变异量（％）	49.54	14.56	6.96	4.78	3.35
累积解释变异量（％）	49.54	64.11	71.08	75.87	79.23

根据因子分析结果，所选取用以评估低碳智能城市的指针系统，包括了"经济及科技发展"、"资源消耗"、"环境保育及健康发展"、"地区发展"、"社会状态"等 5 构面，共 22 个指标。而上述的构面及指标，进一步透过式（1）与式（2）的计算，可求算出其相对权重值，结果如表 2 所示。

根据表 2，"经济及科技发展"的相对权重最大，其值为 0.6，是最重要的评估构面。而其所涵盖的指标，包括：国内低碳低污染产业产值比例、低碳低污染产业的就业人数比例、网络用户数量、网络硬件建设量，亦为重要的评估指标，并反映出城市的经济及科技发展水平为低碳智能发展之基础。而"资源消耗"与"环境保育及健康发展"分别是第二及第三重要的影响构面，其相对权重值分别为 0.18 与 0.09，而其所涵盖的各种能源与土地的消耗量，以及各类污染排放等指标，皆为低碳智能城市发展上须关注的环境、资源、健康课题。此外，"地区发展"与"社会状态"等两个构面，以及其所涵盖的指标，亦具有一定程度的重要性和影响力。

低碳智能城市评估指针系统 表 2

指标架构	指标内容	属性	构面权重	评估指标权重
F1：经济及科技发展				
台湾低碳低污染产业产值比例	三级产业产值占总产值比例	望大型		0.162
低碳低污染产业的就业人数比例	三级产业就业人数占总就业人数比例	望大型	0.6	0.156
网络用户数量	装设网络之用户数	望大型		0.144
网络硬件建设量	网络硬件建设长度	望大型		0.138
F2：资源消耗				
石化能源消耗量	生活与各类生产活动所消耗石化能源量	望小型		0.0324
电力消耗量	生活与各类生产活动所消耗电力	望小型	0.18	0.0306
再生能源使用量	生活与各类生产活动所消耗再生能源量	望大型		0.0288
水资源消耗量	生活与各类生产活动所消耗水资源量	望小型		0.0306
F3：环境保育及健康发展				
PSI＞100 日数比率	PSI 大于 100 的日数占观测总日数比例	望小型	0.09	0.0189
污水排放量	生活与各类生产活动所排放的污水总量	望小型		0.018

---

① Cattell 标准又称为陡坡图检验（scree test）。

续表

指标架构	指标内容	属性	构面权重	评估指标权重
垃圾产生量	生活与各类生产活动所产生的废弃物总量	望小型		0.018
病床数	医疗机构之病床总数	望大型		0.0162
医疗保健支出	县市内居民医疗保健的总负担金额	望小型		0.0189
F4：地区发展				
节能绿色建筑数量	节能及绿色建筑物之数量	望大型		0.0096
公共设施面积	公共设施用地之土地面积	望大型	0.06	0.0070
森林覆盖面积	森林所涵盖之土地面积	望大型		0.0091
城市紧密度	城市计划区面积占县市土地总面积的比例	望大型		0.0078
F5：社会状态				
地区失业人口	无就业的劳动人口	望小型		0.0064
Gini 系数	判断收入分配公平程度的指标	望小型	0.04	0.0068
汽机车持有数	领有牌照之汽机车数量	望小型		0.0064
资源回收量	各组织单位及小区之资源回收总量	望大型		0.0068

注：1. PSI 系综合悬浮微粒、二氧化硫、一氧化碳、臭氧及二氧化氮等 5 种空气污染物浓度值换算而得的空气污染指标值；
    2. 指标为望大型，系指标值愈大愈具有低碳智能特性；而指标为望小型，系指标值愈小愈具有低碳智能特性。

4.2 各县市低碳智能发展状态之评估

本文利用表 2 所建构的低碳智能城市指针系统，进行台湾各县市低碳智能发展状态之评估。以个别县市低碳发展状态的评估结果而言，各县市中表现最佳者为台北市，其总评分达 0.7647，且在"经济及科技发展"、"地区发展"、"社会状态"等构面上皆表现不俗，若该城市欲提升其低碳智能发展程度，可从"资源消耗"与"环境保育及健康发展"两构面进行改善。反之，表现最差者为彰化县，其总评分仅达 0.2624，故在改善上，需优先改善"经济及科技发展"此面向。

另外，借由总评分四分位数的分析，可知排序较前的县市（如台北市）多为社经文化与城市发展程度高，且已将低碳智能设为城市发展目标者；反之，排序较后的县市（如彰化县），其环境发展多遭受危害，且社经与城市发展程度不高者。因此，社经文化与城市发展程度、环境保育，以及县市所设定发展目标与政策，皆会影响县市低碳智能度的状态。

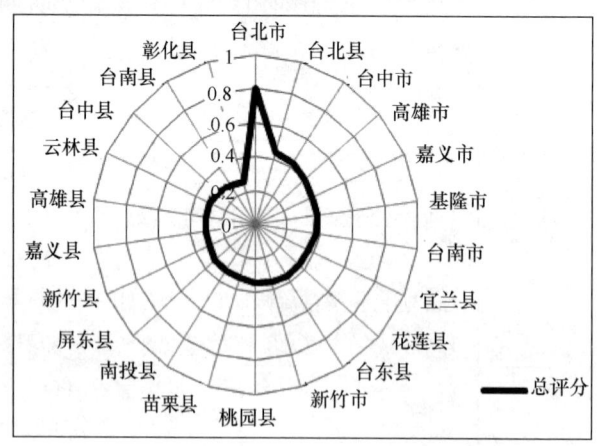

图 2　各县市低碳智能发展状态（评分）图
（资料来源：作者自绘）

5　结论与建议

近年来，气候暖化、永续与智能化议题备受全球重视，致使低碳及智能成为城市规划所重视的发展目标。虽各国相继以低碳智能城市作为发展诉求，但不少城市政府，却缺乏相对应适合该城市特性之评估指针系统。因此，本文透过相关分析与因子分析定权法，建构适宜台湾之评估指针系统，并借此评估台湾各县市之低碳智能度发展状态，而其成果可供作未来低碳智能城市规划与政策研究拟定之参考。根据本文的实证结果显示，低碳智能城市评估指针系统，包括"经济及科技发展"、"资源消耗"、"环境保育及健康发展"、"地区发展"、"社会状态"等5个方面，共21个指标。而台湾各县市在低碳发展的综合表现上，以台北市的状态最佳，而以彰化县表现最差。最后，在低碳智能城市评估指标的应用上，由于须因地制宜，故在不同地区应用时，可斟酌当地风土民情作调整；此外，也须因时制宜，故该指标应随时势的发展而调整之。

Development of Low-Carbon and Intelligent City Indicator System

Shen Yu-Sheng [1], Liu Hsiao-Lan [2]

(1. Department of Land Economics, Chengchi University;

2. Department of Land Economics, Chengchi University)

Abstract: The low-carbon and intelligent city is the city combines the technology, digital information, low-carbon, and sustainable development together. The development of low-carbon and intelligent city not only can integrate the digital information and apply high technology, but also can solve the environmental problems and carbon emissions of urbanization. Effective evaluation on the status of low-carbon and intelligent city is the most important tasks. In order to evaluate the status of low-carbon and intelligent city effectively, city governments need to go through with the indicator system. However, most city governments lack the suitable indicator system of low-carbon and intelligent city. Therefore, this paper is to establish the appropriate indicator system of low-carbon and intelligent city by correlation analysis and factor analysis rating method, and evaluate the status of low-carbon and intelligent cities within the Taiwan domain. According to the empirical results, there are five evaluative aspects for the low-carbon and intelligent city: 1) economic and technological development, 2) consumption of energy and resource, 3) health and environmental conservation, 4) local development, 5) social status. Based on the comprehensive performance of the low-carbon and intelligent city indicator system, Taipei City shows the best performance, whereas Changhua County shows the worst performance.

Keywords: Low-carbon and intelligent city, Indicator system, Factor analysis rating method

参考文献：

[1] Chan H W, Choy H T, Yung H K. Current research on low-carbon cities and institutional responses. Habitat International, 2013, 37: 1-3.

[2] Chen F, Zhu D. Theoretical research on low-carbon city and empirical study of Shanghai. Habitat International, 2013, 37: 33-42.

[3] Baeumler A, Ijjasz-Vasquez E, Mehndiratta S. Sustainable Low-Carbon City Development in China. New York: World Bank Publications, 2012.

［4］ Deakin，M. Creating Smart-er Cities. New York：Taylor & Francis，2012.

［5］ Deakin，M. Smart Cities：Governing，Modelling and Analysing the Transition. New York：Taylor & Francis，2013.

［6］ Deakin，M. From Intelligent to Smart Cities. New York：Taylor & Francis，2014.

［7］ 仇保兴．兼顾理想与现实—中国低碳生态城市指标体系构建与实践示范初探［M］．北京：中国建筑工业出版社，2012.

［8］ 沈清基、安超、刘昌寿．低碳生态城市理论与实践［M］．北京：中国城市出版社，2012.

［9］ 顾朝林．气候变化与低碳城市规划(第 2 版)［M］．江苏：东南大学出版社，2013.

园宅——新型城镇化住宅概念探讨

李映彤

（湖北工业大学艺术设计学院环境系）

摘要："园宅"的理念源自中国传统古典私园。它通过对自然式景观居住思想的传承，重新审视新型城镇家庭结构的居住方式和审美文化，对中国古典私园的造园要素进行解构重组，并以之置换现代建筑顶界面、底界面、侧界面、楼道、构件以及设备，打造出全新的，拥有合宜尺度和美学意味的住宅。从"古典私园"到"园宅"，其根本变化是将"古典私园"的"园"纳入"宅"中，保留古典私园的审美意境，不再是走出建筑去体验风景，而是居住在内外空间交融的住宅环境之中，这样不仅可以更有效地利用城镇土地资源，让人更好地享受绿色，享受生态，减少能源消耗，还能以中国古典私园深厚的文化底蕴再树中华民族自信心，提升中国新型城镇住宅的文化品位，为世界住宅产品增添一种新的范式。

关键词：园宅，古典私园，城镇化，重构

1　引言

在城镇化过程中，城市地产业的大肆扩张，崇"洋"求"新"的建筑审美心理，既割裂了建筑与自然的关系，也切断了建筑与历史的纽带（图1）。

承载着中国古代景观居住美学思想的古典私园早已失去居住功能，成为旅游景点；代表当今成功人士身份的欧式别墅，充斥着城镇的每一个角落。它们都无法成为新时代城镇化住宅形态可资借鉴的样板，因为古典园林失去了当下的现实性，欧式别墅则与自然毫无关系。因此，如何在尊重自然和历史的基础上推进城镇化，重构新的城镇住宅形态和空间环境，走可持续发展的城镇化之路成为城镇化建设中亟待解决的现实问题。"园宅"就是针对这一需求而提出的概念。

图1　"洋楼"与"别墅"

（资料来源：出自百度图片）

2　中国古典私园中的自然式景观居住文化

古典私园是中国古代的先人寄情山水，追求与自然相融的诗意生活境界的充分体现，两千多年来，代表中国传统思想的文士阶层的价值观念、社会思想、道德规范、生活追求和审美趣味深深地影响了中国古典私园的造园艺术。文人追求田园之乐，并以此成就了中国古典私园的灵魂。

中国古典私园不满足于物质与技巧的华美，更注重自然属性，主张在特定环境中建造人性化的自然风景，以自由的方式造就建筑与山水花木动态交融的景观环境，体现生机盎然的自然之乐和人类精神，从而使人类精神与自然交融共生。

体现城市生活居住文化的古典私园，其使用空间是有限的，园林意境创造则需在有限中感受无限。因此，必须对其整体空间进行精心布局，以使空间层次丰富、变幻不定、妙趣横生，增强其意境之美，其手段之一即为空间的划分。

在私园的空间构成方式中，庭院是造园的最小单位，若干个庭院构成小园，若干个小园构成大园，将场地的中心位置留给山、水、植物等自然要素，利用长廊、小桥或墙垣划分、组织成多样化景区，是造园的传统手法。建筑和自然要素相互对比，极大地丰富了空间的视觉观感，是营造古典私园自然意境的重要手段。

山、水在古典私园中不仅被塑造、欣赏，在欣赏山水的过程中人与自然相化而相忘成为寄情避世的山水自然。《园冶》说："因借无由，触情俱是。"古典私园中的山水，不仅师法自然，兼备自然山石的形神之外，还具有传情的作用，咫尺之间借一番山林野趣，是园林意境创造的重要方式。

花木种植是古典私园不可或缺的部分，景观的形成大多与花木相关联，甚至直接以花木作为主题，或是用于观赏，或是间接地抒发某种意境和情趣。春夏秋冬，雨雪阴晴的变化，改变着人们的感官，从而改变着空间境界，深深影响人的感受。通过花木的掩映分隔构筑空间，渗透景观的层次，引发超然的精神境界和幽微的心理情趣。

匾额、楹联直接以诗词艺术的形式参与园林意境的构成，以其点睛之笔概括出空间特色，或景观特征，含蓄蕴厚，以其言简意赅的文字沟通观者的视觉、听觉、嗅觉等与园的联系，从而在人心目中产生高于实景的深远境界，在其片言只语中把人们对人生、宇宙的种种感悟与周围景观融成一体，使景中生情，因此是古典私园中调动主观想象力，深化空间意境的重要因素（图2）。

图 2　古典私园印象
（资料来源：出自百度图片）

然而，在当下，城市居住用地的使用空间更加有限，古典私园形式还适合于当今的住宅形式吗？在城市空间之中再造古典私园仍然具有其存在的价值吗？如何审视中国古典私园，体悟其文化的精髓，在追求人类生活与自然和谐的生存发展中，发扬古典私园生活的文化精神，创造出适宜于当下的居住空间，传承自然式景观居住文化，是"园宅"这一建筑形式有待研讨的命题。

3　园宅与中国古典私园的异质同构

"园宅"和古典私园在居住文化的审美上具有共通性，都是对自然式景观居住观念的传承，在建造理念上是同构的。

从"古典私园"到"园宅"，其根本变化是将"古典私园"的"园"纳入"宅"中，正如古典私园将大自然的道纳入园中一样，园宅更是把古典私园的道纳入其中，这种住宅建筑形式，环境优美，宜人乐居，冬季能保持温暖，夏季能保持凉爽，充分利用纳入宅内的自然能源，如太阳能、风能，减少能源的消耗，同时，又能使居住者在自信、满足的景观居住心态中更好地享受绿色，享受生活，对环境、社会和经济要素产生最小的负面影响。

就具体空间形式而言，从"古典私园"到"园宅"演变存在具体设计要素上的异同：

空间功能不同，古典私园的居住形式是以中国传统族居的生活方式为前提的，无论从人员结构还是家国礼仪上，都呈现出一定的规制，在多元文化背景下的现代社会，"园宅"秉承自然式住宅文化思想，重新审视现代家庭结构的居住方式，相对自由的特征给园宅的设计提供了宽广的空间。

场地不同，园宅的场地从选址上不可能像古典私园那样到自然界里"相地合宜"，去获得一大片含有丰富景观元素的区域，个体现代人一方面不具备这种能力，另一方面，现代生活也离不开城市区域的范围，城市土地的属性和价格都决定了"园宅"场地面积的有限性。

建筑结构、形式不同，传统古典私园的建筑多半是木构架结构，随着现代建筑材料、建筑施工工艺发展，古典私园的造园要素得以解构重组，置换以现代建筑顶界面、底界面、侧界面、楼道、构件以及设备，给园宅的结构和形式带来充分的可变因素，打造出全新的，拥有合宜尺度和美学意味的住宅。

造景细节不同，传统宅园的造景要素因当时的条件，主要以自然界存在的"叠山、理水和花木"为主，现代科学技术的发展，除了给"叠山、理水和花木"的营造带来了新的手段和形式之外，更加植入了诸如以计算机及互联网技术为前提的数字化虚拟景观成像等条件，为园宅的造景提供了丰富的可行性。

尽管在设计要素上存在诸多的异同，但"园宅"在建造理念上是对自然式景观居住观的传承，在审美标准上是一致的，和传统古典私园在本质上是共通的，所以，无论"园宅"出现何种样式，它和中国古典私园应该是异质同构的（图3）。

图3　门窗同构

（资料来源：出自百度图片）

4　园宅存在于当下的现实性

景观作为现代居住空间中重要的构成部分，已经渐渐成为人们选择居住空间不可或缺的因素。然而，当将景观与居住联系在一起的时候，人们要么是记起中国古代的园林，要么就是联想到拥有院落的别墅，从而进行仿制，这样的建筑再现与当下的社会性和地域性是严重脱节的。

古典园林的布局是把空间的主要部分让给山、水、植物等自然要素，因此占地面积极大，据记载，白居易的"履道坊宅园"是最小的私园，其水域面积也超过了5亩。

别墅"Cottage"一词是舶来的，指在风景区或在郊外建造的供休养的住所。国内通常把一户一栋的住宅称为别墅，这样的独立住宅在国外叫"house"，一般在城市边缘或远郊都有数平方公里范围这样的"house"社区。

以上两者居住建筑空间和景观要素也是基本割裂的，都是走出建筑进入自然环境，而"园宅"目标是将"古典私园"的"园"纳入"宅"中，打造出一种新的建筑形式，真正地实现居住在景观之中。

在国外还有一种被称为"villa"或者"Luxury house"的顶级豪宅，如"流水别墅"，设计师是现代建筑运动中的"有机建筑"流派的代表——赖特，他主张"设计每一个建筑，都应该根据各自特有的客观条件，形成一个理念，把这个理念由内到外，贯穿于建筑的每一个局部，使每一个局部都互相关联，成为整体不可分割的组成部分"，这样的独立式景观住宅设计思想和手法，才与"园宅"有接近的含义，如果用中国景观居住的审美思想去构建和体味，其中国名字应译为"园宅"（图4）。

图4 纳园入宅
（资料来源：出自百度图片）

首先，"园宅"的审美标准和古典私园一致，古典私园这种建筑形式在中国古代的消费对象就是"达官贵人"，他们在个人财富极大丰富的时候，将住宅的功能引向了户外，去享受一种"悠然见南山"的高品质生活，既是自身文化品位的体现，又是社会贤达身份的象征，"园宅"传承了古典私园的这种建造理念，是对中国传统文化的继承和发展，同时也符合一部分先富起来的人群的消费心理。

其次，"园宅"将古典私园引向户外的功能回归到建筑本身，消耗更少的城市居住用地，土地成本的极大降低，使得建造的可能性大大地提高。

第三，"园宅"空间行为注重与自然的互动，阳光、空气、水和植物这些自然要素通过合理的规划，与现代新材料、新工艺相结合，使此种住宅能够最大限度地亲近自然，对环境、社会和经济要素产生最小的负面影响。

环境保护是当今世界具有共识性的话题，就低碳建筑而言，我们可以从技术、经济、地域、伦理等各方面进行探讨，产生各种各样的住宅形式。住宅，是居民的生活在文化品位和社会地位上的表现。然而，营造什么样的住宅才是人们应该去追求的目标呢？答案是很难统一的。

中国古语讲："三分匠人七分主人"，住宅的拥有者才是真正的主导，要达成低碳的目标，最为直接的方法就是锁定社会经济的主导消费人群，开发出既能引导他们健康的审美观和消费观，并彰显他们社会身份，又低消耗的住宅产品。"园宅"就是一种值得探索的低碳住宅形式。

5 总结

"园宅"继承了以自然为审美标准的中国传统文化；遵循并发展了中国古典私园的布局方法；是用当代建筑的新功能、新结构、新形式等建筑语汇构成的情景交融的高品质住宅建筑产品。它既能满足社会经济的主导消费人群的居住需求，又符合低碳环保的现代建筑理念，能够引领景观居住建筑可持续发展的未来，是中国古典私园的当代表象。

致谢

感谢第十一届中国城市住宅研讨会组委会对我申报选题的认可，"园宅"是一个崭新名称，组委会能够接纳这一命题，体现了本论坛对学术探讨极为勇敢的探索精神，也是对研究者莫大的鼓励！在"园宅"研究的过程中，得到我老师陈望衡先生的首肯，并为我的同名著作作序，范明华先生为我的文字提出宝贵意见，深表感激！我的妻子陆焰和家人给我提供研究的时间和空间，是我的幸运！我的朋友和学生以及湖北工业大学艺术设计学院给我提供思考和研究的土壤，在此表达我深深的谢意！

（本论文是 2013 年度湖北省教育厅艺术学研究项目"中国古代景观居住思想在湖北山水民居中的当代表象研究"（项目编号 13g236）的阶段性成果。）

Yuanzhai—The Investigation about the New Urbanization Residential Concept

Li Yingtong

(Department of Environmental Design，School of Arts and Design，Hubei University of Technology)

Abstract：The concept of "Yuanzhai" is stem from the Chinese conventional and classical private garden. By inheriting the natural landscape living thought and inspecting the resident manner and aesthetic culture of the new urban family structure，it can deconstruct and regroup the elements of Chinese classical private garden. At the same time, the top, bottom, side interface, corridor, components and equipments are replaced. Thus, we can create a brand new house provided with the appropriate scale and aesthetic meaning. From classical private garden'to "Yuanzhai", The radical change of this process is that putting the concept—"Yuan" of Chinese private garden into living space and reserving the aesthetic and artistic conception of private garden. That is to say, we are no longer out of the building to experience the scenery, but living in the residential environment of inside and outside space blending. Not only can we more etlectinely use urban land resources, make people better enjoy the green and ecological, and reduce consumptions, but also build Chinese national self-confidence and improe Chinese new urban residential culture grade with the profound cultural background of Chinese private garden，adding a new paradigm for the housing products.

Keywords：Yuanzhai ，Classical private garden，Urbanization，Deconstruct

参考文献：

［1］ 计成. 园冶——中国古代园林、别墅营造珍本［M］. 胡天寿译. 重庆：重庆出版社，2009.

［2］ 弗里德曼·A. 住宅的可持续发展绿色社区的规划与设计［M］. 刘星译. 辽宁：辽宁科学技术出版社，2010.

［3］ C·亚历山大 . 俄勒冈实验［M］. 赵冰，刘小虎译. 北京：知识产权出版社，2001.

［4］ 阿诺德·伯林特. 环境美学［M］. 张敏，周雨译. 湖南：湖南科学技术出版社，2006.

［5］ 戴维·索特. 景观建筑学［M］. 王玲，孟祥庄译. 北京：中国林业出版社，2008.

［6］ 陈望衡. 环境美学［M］. 湖北：武汉大学出版社，2007.

［7］ 埃比尼泽·霍华德. 明日的田园城市［M］. 金经元译. 北京：商务印书馆，2000.

［8］ 荆其敏，张丽安. 生态的城市与建筑［M］. 北京：中国建筑工业出版社，2005.

宜昌秭归地区夯土房保护与功能再造——以界垭村扶贫项目为例

李映彤　闫永祥　张　群

（湖北工业大学艺术设计学院）

摘要：宜昌秭归地区原生态的夯土房，黄泥、细沙、木构、厚墙体，接地气，冬暖夏凉，和自然同频，有着不可磨灭的地方形象印记。通过研究它的功能、结构和美学形式，将夯土房与现代建筑元素相结合，把现代材料和建造工艺融入夯土房原始形态的加固中，同时拓展出新的功能空间，合理规划化其内部功能分区，使居住、接待与农产品种植、养殖、储存等功能区域形成实用而有序的空间形式，既传承夯土房原有形式美，也使其在衍生新功能的状态下仍然与环境相互协调，设计出具备新形势下功能需求，同时传承原建筑形式美感的、生态的住宅空间环境。宜昌秭归地区界垭村夯土房保护与功能再造是新农村、新城镇建设和政府扶贫工作的现实体现。通过寻找该住宅形式在新形势下与文化、自然、生活相结合方法，让具有地方特色的建筑在新农村、新城镇建设的过程中获得重生，为中国的美丽农村建设提供一条充满着阳光和希望的新路径，这既是一个事关农村稳定与发展的重大课题，也是一个事关城镇化未来走向的大问题。

关键词：夯土房，城镇化，保护，功能再造

1　引言

在我国几千年的农耕文明中，由民居构成的村落，记录着人们的生产生活方式。然而，在急剧的社会变迁和城镇化过程中，传统民居构成的村落正在凋零、消失。由政府主导的许多"新"农村建设和小城镇建设，虽然设施现代、功能齐全，但建筑风格整齐划一，因袭雷同，与传统农村特有的自然环境、历史环境和生活习俗常常是互相抵牾，格格不入。因此，如何在尊重自然和当地历史的基础上再造富有当地建筑特色的新农村，推进城镇化，重构新的聚落形态和空间环境，走可持续发展的城镇化之路，便成为农村建设和城镇化建设中亟待解决的现实问题。

本文通过对界垭村一处农户夯土房改建的调查、分析和设计研究，探索艺术设计在"老房子接出一块新空间"[①]的理念下，能够作出的可行性思考。

2　夯土房普遍存在的优劣问题

随着能源危机、气候变暖、环境污染等威胁人类聚居环境的一系列问题的日益加剧，可持续发展已成为当前人居环境建设的必由之路。夯土建筑作为生土建筑的主要结构形式之一，其建筑材料主要为生土，可再生并且能循环利用，是名副其实的生态建筑，其建设主要以村民为主体，自我设计、选购材料并实施建造，存在一定的优势和问题。

2.1　接地气的建筑

生于自然：夯土建筑贴近自然，夯土房屋及其组成的村落多依当地地形而建，村落布局顺应当地的地势起伏，与当地的自然景观自然结合，是建筑与自然环境有机融合的典范（图1）。

材料生态：夯土房屋采用的主要建筑材料是生土和木材，取材方便，生土材料可以有效地平衡室内湿度和温度，能很好地隔绝夏天室外热量，也能有效地抵御冬天室外寒气入侵，有冬暖夏凉的

---

① 高建平. 生态、城市与救赎. 美学的当代转型：文化、城市、艺术 [M]. 河北：河北大学出版社，2013：104.

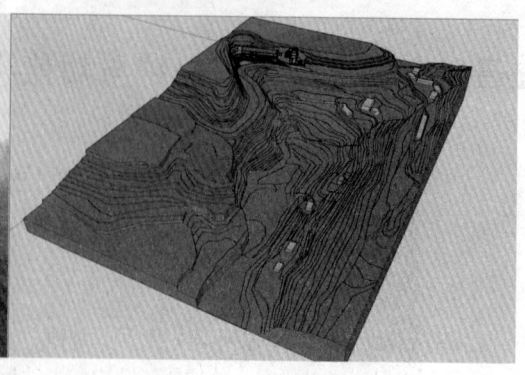

图 1　界垭村全景

（资料来源：笔者现场拍摄及表现图）

特点，以确保室内舒适度，生土还是非常理想的防火材料，另外生土可以对其内部的木材等有机材料起到防虫、放腐蚀的保护作用，夯土墙体可以吸收内部空间中的污染物，具有吸声降噪的作用，可塑性强，易于进行建筑形体的设计；房屋的檩条和屋架采用的木材，多取材于村庄周围的山林；工艺简单，以木制或石制杵、锤等工具，将原状生土逐层夯实形成承重墙体，技术难度不高，造价低廉，住户可以进行自建。

这种因地制宜、就地取材的性质，决定了夯土建筑在其生命周期内的耗能非常低，此外，夯土房屋拆除后的建筑废料可以直接回归农田，以此实现循环利用和生态平衡，更有利于促进本土传统文化的发展和延续，是一种非常接地气的环保建筑。

2.2　显而易见的问题

结构设计有待提升：农村地区的大部分夯土房屋没有正规的建筑标准，只是根据当地经验随意地建造房屋，在房屋的选址、材料的选取、建筑层数、高度、结构体系、平立面的布置等方面都缺乏正规设计，造成夯土房屋功能空间形式单一；

材料强度有限：夯土墙是由颗粒状的原状土夯实而形成强度，本身强度有限，如果夯筑的质量得不到保证或者未采取有效的构造措施，结构的整体性和安全性难以得到保障；

通风和采光条件差：由于夯土墙强度低的缺点，决定了其作为受力构件的截面尺寸较大，尺寸增大后墙体的自重明显增加，墙开门、开窗受到极大的制约，严重影响了建筑内部空间的通风和采光；

耐久性差：由于夯土墙体密实度差，造成墙体防水抗渗性能较弱，受到雨水侵蚀后，墙身表面容易剥落，墙根易碱蚀腐烂，秭归地区气候环境潮湿，这一现象极为明显（图 2）。

图 2　室内与外观

（资料来源：笔者现场拍摄）

利用科学的建造方法提高传统夯土建筑的质量和抵御自然灾害的能力，把现代材料和建造工艺融入夯土房原始形态的加固中，通过合理的建筑平面布局和规划，提高居民的居住环境质量，传承传统民居文化，对新农村建设的可持续发展有着非常重要的意义。

3 保护的内在与表象

建筑的生命可以从两个方向进行思考，一是建筑本身，按照修旧如旧的原则对建筑的形式进行修复和加固，保留建筑的"形式态"，这是文物保护的做法；二是根据人生活过程中的行为特点，对建筑所围合的功能空间进行合理规划和重组，这是对传统"生活态"的尊重。

3.1 老房子的维护

在夯土建筑本身的保护方面可以根据空间围合的界面结合夯土房特有的属性进行逐项思考：

底界面基础部分，选址尽可能避让山体滑坡及洪水等自然灾害的路径，地基与基础应引起足够重视，采用砖、石材料砌筑墙根，并应采取有效的防水排潮措施；

侧界面主要包含横墙（山墙）和纵墙，在夯土中可以加入适量的纤维有助于墙体的塑性，使房屋具有更好的坚固性能；墙体结构方面，在夯土墙体中设置木柱和圈梁提升整体刚性；在夯土墙的纵横墙交接处设置竹片、荆条或树条等编织而成的拉结网片对墙体转角处和内外墙交接处墙体进行加强，对该部位墙体起到约束作用，提高房屋的整体性。夯土材料强度有限，改良夯土墙的材料，提高墙身的承载力与耐久性，通过必要的构造措施，保证房屋结构的整体性与安全性。

顶界面主要是屋顶，最好采用双坡屋面，用轻质屋面材料，屋顶草泥厚度不宜大于120mm，屋盖与墙体之间应采取可靠的构造措施连接，屋盖的檩条、木屋架如果直接搁置在山墙上，檩条将荷载直接传递至土墙上，檩条下部墙体在应力作用下会发生局部受压破坏，使墙体形成较大竖向裂缝，可以通过在檩条与夯土墙接触部位加设垫块，增大檩条与墙体之间的接触面积缓解檩条下夯土墙承受的集中应力。

门、窗关系到通风和采光，用方木或原木过梁可以减小门窗上角的应力，增加门窗同墙体接触的紧密度，尽可能扩大开窗面积，使室内获得更多的光线。

以上这些措施，简单便于操作，而且重要的是，对于造价增加很少。

3.2 尊重生活态

夯土结构房屋在保护时更要尊重传统风俗，延续老百姓的生活态，才能延续建筑的内在生命力，现有村镇住宅，有的已经存在和发展了数十年甚至上百年，由于农村居民习惯了农业耕作，适应了大自然变化的规律，在勤劳工作之余自然地享受着天地的馈赠，因此他们的居住环境是和谐而生动的，是朴素而美好的。

然而，在当下多元文化的社会背景下，如何从环境美学的层面分析居住美的本质，探讨"宜居—利居—乐居"的内在关系，论证家的幸福感首先是对生活的爱和对自然美的心灵观照，由此引导人们尊重生命、关爱环境的审美情怀，才是提升生活品位，促进新农村建设健康发展的内在动力和源泉。

在此基础上，尊重民众的创造性，发现传统农宅的布局优点，与周边建筑和自然环境相互协调，尊重农村百姓的生活与生产习惯，满足居住生活与农副业生产的双重功能；提炼、保留传统住宅的审美观及建筑符号，沿袭传统坡屋顶的建筑形式，继续使用夯土墙，充分利用其良好的保温隔热性能及可呼吸性能，通过调整开天窗方式和布局，最大限度地改善室内通风、采光环境，提升室内环境舒适度，既做到人畜共院，又做到人畜隔离，改善庭院卫生条件，提高居住的品质，将保护与再造两者结合起来，这样的村镇住宅才是真正有特色、有生命的住宅，才能促进我国村镇住宅建设全面、健康、生态地发展。

4 功能再造、接出新空间

对界垭村黄家的设计思考就是从住户的特殊家庭情况出发进行的实践：

住户是一对 50 岁左右的中年夫妇，丈夫 2013 年查出患上了脑瘫，接着，儿子也查出患有同样的疾病，孙子 4 岁，随儿媳妇去了娘家，一家人就靠女主人种两三亩山地，打点临工贴补买药、过生活⋯⋯

两间夯土房位于山谷的中段，离九畹溪公路步行 15 分钟左右的路程，与资助改建的茶场遥相呼应，建筑虽然老旧，但是农事井井有条，鸡场、猪圈安排在房前空地的南北两头，空地前的堡坎下是一排高高的乔木迎着山谷的风摇曳（图 3）。

图 3 现场环境

（资料来源：笔者现场拍摄）

设计根据老夯土房的普遍问题提出了加固和改善措施，在加固的结构件上，顺应坡屋顶角度延伸出屋顶天窗，协调了建筑形体，既解决了内部空间的通风和采光问题，也把蓝天、星空这些大自然的因素带入到了室内。

平面规划体现功能，其思考主要是围绕空间设计如何帮助没有特殊谋生技能的女主人增加收入展开的，希望在尊重他们正常的生活前提下，接出一块新的功能空间，达成设计目标，实际操作是：根据场地错落有致的地形特征，以堡坎下迎风摇曳的那排乔木作为景观亮点，从堡坎上的平台悬挑一块茶廊底界面，让出乔木自然生长空间，在规整的茶廊平面中增加精致的曲折，从而获得更丰富的景深；营造出与山谷可以对话的、半开敞的品茶空间。从设计师自身出发，体味该功能空间被消费的心理可能性。

平台南边的鸡场予以保留，只是按照茶廊的边界形式进行了隔离和规整；考虑风向和气味的原因，平台北边的猪被移至东北角，增加一个新猪圈，并将公厕的功能并入，原有砖泥砌筑的猪圈改造为游客一个标准客房，可以满足需要留宿客人的要求。

特别值得一提的是，在设计进展的过程中，考虑到业主没有进行过专业的服务培训，难以提供高品质的服务，设计利用原有猪圈的门洞和宽敞屋檐，在客房外立面设立了一套简单易行的自助泡茶界面，让游客能够根据自己的选择自主操作、自行投币，让游客能够充分地融入自然（图 4）。

空间是用来容纳生活的，而生活是多姿多彩的，每一个家都有自己的故事，同样的条件，不必产生同样的住宅，除了地形特征、文化根源的影响之外，还有设计师的人文关怀，按这样的理念进行设计，新农村就不会、也不应该出现"千村一面"的现象。

图4 设计方案
（资料来源：笔者设计方案表现图）

5 总结

新农村建设是目前国家关注的重大问题，城镇化不能以破坏大自然的生态环境为代价，人居环境设计的原动力在于尊重生活现象的真实存在，在人与自然环境间建立长效性的亲和关系。在保持自然环境的前提下，提升景观居住审美意识，提升人居生活品质，针对性地解决农民生活中的现实问题。

希望通过对界垭村夯土住宅的调查、分析和设计经验，实现城镇化不是城市对农村的消灭，而是城市与农村两者的互动与相互影响，城市也好，农村也好，都应该以生活为主题，以谋求幸福和与大自然和谐共生为最高追求，这才符合自然之道，才能创造高质量的人居环境和最美、最宜人的景观形象。

致谢

本文的撰写基于湖北三峡世家农业开发有限公司田开宇先生投资的界垭村茶农扶贫项目，感谢他们对我设计理念的认可，并邀请我担当此项目的设计主持，才有机会实践我的设计思想，从而完成此文章。在项目的研究过程中，我的研究生张群、曹晓霓收集了大量有关夯土房的珍贵资料，闫永祥协助了整个项目的设计，在此一并表示感谢！同时对湖北工业大学艺术设计学院以及我的家人、同事和朋友们给予我各方面的支持表达衷心谢意！最后，感谢第十一届中国城市住宅研讨会组委会对我申报选题的认可，感谢组委会能够接纳这一命题，是对我莫大的鼓励！

（本论文是2013年度湖北省教育厅艺术学研究项目"中国古代景观居住思想在湖北山水民居中的当代表象研究"（项目编号13g236）的阶段性成果。）

Rammed Earth House Protection and Function Reconstruction in Zigui，Yichang：The Case of Poverty Alleviation in Jieya

Li Yingtong，Yan Yongxiang，Zhang Qun
(School of Arts and Design，Hubei University of Technology)

Abstract：The rammed earth house in Zigui，Yichang city is originally made of yellow mud and raw sand, which is of thick wall and down to earth，As a place where local people lives, it is warm in winter and cool in summer，Furthermore，we are deeply impressed by the harmony between its existence and nature. Through the research on its function，structure and aesthetic form，by combining with rammed earth house and modern architect element，we can integrate modern materials and technology with original form，developing the new functional space at the same time，and programming its internal functional partition reasonably. so that the living，reception and agricultural products planting，breeding，storage area to contrast practical and orderly space form，it can not only inherits the original beauty in form of rammed earth construction，but also coordinate with the environment in the derivation of new functions of the state. So as to design functional requirements under the new situation，at the same time，inherit the residential aesthetic form of space and environment. Zigui area of Yichang rammed earth house protection and function reconstruction is the embodiment of the new countryside，new urban construction，cultural heritage protection and inheritance work. By looking for the method of combining the residential form in the new situation with culture，nature and life，let the construction with local characteristics reborn in the process of the new rural development，then providing a new path full of sunshine and hope to build beautiful countryside of China. This is a matter of the rural stability and development major issue，and also a big problem concerning the future of urbanization.

Keywords：Rammed earth house，Urbanization，Protection，Function reconstruction

参考文献：

［1］ 住房城乡建设部村镇建设司. 抗震夯土农宅建造图册［M］. 北京：中国建筑工业出版社，2009.

［2］ 高建平. 美学的当代转型：文化、城市、艺术［M］. 河北：河北大学出版社，2013.

［3］ ［日］隈研吾. 自然的建筑（第2版）［M］. 陈菁译. 山东：山东人民出版社，2012.

［4］ 荆其敏，张丽安. 城市母语——漫谈城市建筑与环境（第2版）［M］. 天津：百花文艺出版社，2004.

［5］ ［日］芦原义信. 外部空间设计［M］. 尹培桐译. 北京：中国建筑工业出版社，1985.

［6］ 2015年中央一号文件. 关于加大改革创新力度加快农业现代化建设的若干意见.

"新常态"下自下而上的城市设计及管控模式研究

陈 鑫

（东南大学建筑学院）

摘要： 城市设计在我国经过了二十几年的实践，业已成为城市空间环境控制的重要环节，然而却依然存在着些许不足，这从一定程度上反映了我国一贯"自上而下"的线型城市设计体制的弊端。本文从问题着眼，基于城市、建筑联动机制提出一种"自下而上"的城市设计策略和管控手段，从具体的建筑设计入手，寻求对城市的合理锲入，通过城市建筑的网络化关联，实现一种城市总体秩序下的动态平衡，以适应"新常态"下我国城市设计的全新要求。

关键词： "新常态"，城市设计，建筑设计，自下而上，联动机制

1 我国城市设计发展现状

"城市设计"作为一种中观层面的城市形态管控手段，是介于城市规划和建筑设计之间的中间环节，在西方有着长足的发展。作为一门系统的学科，城市设计从 20 世纪 80 年代传入我国，便与我国城市规划、建筑设计等多项专业结合，并具有了中国化的诠释，根据《中国大百科全书》定义，城市设计则为："是对城市体型环境所进行的设计，一般是指在城市总体规划指导下，为近期开发地段的建设项目而进行的详细规划和具体设计"。从字面中不难发现，我国的城市设计带有一种明显的"自上而下"的线型管控特征，即通过预设的总体规划或上位规划的限定与严格管控，从上至下的贯彻和执行具体的设计活动。总体来说，这种传统的、建立在"精英管控"下的线性机制可以通过权威性的强制管控在一定程度上实现城市空间、形态的管理，能够以高效的运作适应我国快速城镇化的进程。然而，这种自上而下的城市管控机制却因为忽略了微观的建筑设计的能动作用，一定程度上造成了城市设计与建筑设计的脱轨，建筑设计往往以一种"试错"的方法被动的附和上位规划思想，使城市设计凸显出一定的缺陷和弊端，主要体现在以下几个方面：

1.1 政府职能的泛化

政府部门作为城市建设的主管机构，也是城市设计工作的管理者。而在我国，政府也往往充当业主的身份参与设计任务的制定，其扮演着评价、管理、业主、监督等多种身份[1]。这就意味着政府在管控的同时往往将个人的喜好强加于设计之中，甚至对具体建筑的设计细节过度干涉，这种自上而下的植入式倾向导致城市设计被简化成一组具体的概念性建筑设计组合，从而丧失了城市设计宏观管控的真正意图。

1.2 市场调节机制被弱化

城市运作由两个根本动力来源：权利与市场。自上而下的权力宏观调控和自下而上的市场调节相互作用才能保障城市运作的顺利进行。而在我国城市设计之初就为强大的权力机构所左右，权力层没有充分意识到市场机制对资源的有效配置作用。在这种"自上而下"的权利导向下，市场机制只能被动的迎合，不能良好的发挥自我调节作用，以造成私人利益的受损和公共利益得不到优化配置。

1.3 行业壁垒的普遍存在

城市设计由于牵扯到的业主及各种利益集团较多，因此其运作过程并非直线流程，而是一个较

111

长的循环过程。由于我国长期以来各部门之间的职责独立和权责划分，往往因为某个环节的权责与利益矛盾而阻碍设计、管理和运行的持续进展，从而使建筑与城市系统之间难以形成连续的空间架构和功能网络，造成城市系统运作效率低下和经济投入上的重复与浪费。例如城市中心商业区地下立体化步行交通系统，由于地下联系通道属市政部门管辖，地铁线路与站场隶属地铁运管部门，不同职能部门有着各自的利益和管理需求，最终使地下空间不能得到最高效、经济的配置，造成空间资源的浪费和人们生活的不便。[2]

由此看来，我国传统城市设计理念中这种自上而下的逐级渗透模式虽然对城市空间的整体管控具有一定的实效性，但容易造成某种主观效应，同时资源配置效率不高，可持续性较弱，因此，一种新型的城市设计理念亟待出现。

2 "新常态"对城市设计与管控的诉求

城市设计的核心任务是城市空间优化与再生产，通过行政手段、程序机制、政策管理以及反馈机制对城市形态、空间进行动态调整，实现宏观环境与微观环境的良好过渡与接洽。因此，城市设计已经不仅仅是简单的自上而下的"单线管控"模式，而是趋向一种城市设计与建筑设计相互协同的"双向限定"。[3] 如果说我国以往的城市建设遵循由"总体规划—分区规划—详细规划—项目设计"的纵向流程，那么这种纵向结构正趋向扁平，城市设计与建筑设计不再是传统的前后关系，而是彼此渗透和交融，体现为城市设计与建筑设计的一体化联动机制。

首先，在城镇化快速发展的"新常态"下，城市系统越来越复杂，建筑界面在这种交叠的系统中变得越发衰弱和消解，必须融入城市环境的整体，成为城市中各种关系的网络节点，建筑单体

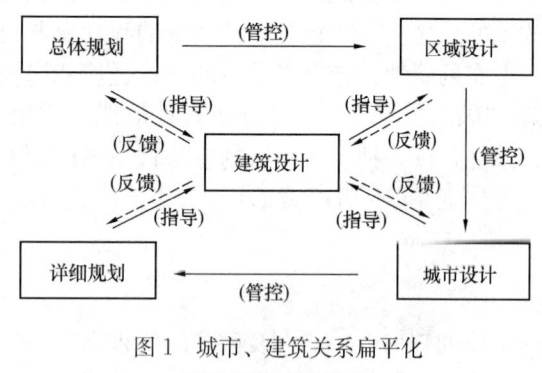

图1 城市、建筑关系扁平化
（图片来源：作者自绘）

（节点）通过这种网络化的结构向城市辐射、反馈与互动，继而实现自我的意义与价值。其次，当代社会中，城市不再由单一主体所主宰，而是全民参与、全民共享和全民共治，体现出强烈的民主意识[4]。因此，线型单一的强制手段已经不能满足城市发展和多样化的社会需求。在这种"新常态"下，笔者发现建筑单体设计能动性对城市系统的关联作用越发明显，城市的运转和城市空间形成很大程度上已经打破了一种自上而下的"生产关系"，而是"自下而上"的建筑、城市一体化的联动机制（图1）。

3 "自下而上"的新型城市设计与管控模式

所谓"自下而上"，即一切的设计运行并非简单的由上位限定和管控，而是充分发挥建筑设计的能动性，提升建筑师的主导作用，在建筑与城市之间建立一种网络化的互动关联系统，系统中有整体对局部的统摄，更有局部对整体的反馈，建筑设计可以通过其空间创造主动地回应和反馈城市空间的演变。一定程度上消解了上位的过度管控后，建筑创作的自由度也将大大提升，多元的适应性在不违背城市整体空间形态的前提下能够充分发挥市场机制的调节作用，自发的整合各项资源，使公共资源得到更大程度上的合理配置。

从具体的设计来看，"自下而上"的联动机制就是通过对场地的解读，提出有效的应答和介入，通过对上位规划的研读和吸收，在交通流线、空间形态以及功能设置等方面给予自下而上的回应。具体的规划和建筑设计能够通过互动和反馈机制能动的在现实性和可操作层面对之前的上位的城市设计进行二次论证和修订，通过动态的循环往复过程，使资源得到切实合理的配置。在网络城市中，建筑与城市的关系犹如"针灸"和"机体"的关联作用，建筑设计通过自身的调整，具有强化

或削弱对城市系统的作用能力，如同针灸的补、泻，采用不同的设计策略，寻求对城市的合理锲入，通过城市建筑的网络化关系，实现一种城市总体秩序下的动态平衡[4]。

"自下而上"的城市设计与管控是一个循环往复的过程，建筑师将上位规划的指导思想自上而下的延续，并将公众的信息反馈自下而上的汇聚，才能对城市设计做出正确的应答和及时的修正，因此对政府、建筑师和公众均提出新的要求。

3.1 政府的弹性控制与引导

政府应在一定程度上完成角色的转变，削弱其作为业主的主观意识，充分发挥其引导职能，通过一种"弹性"的控制实现"设计城市而不是设计具体建筑"的初衷。明确自己的权责范围，在宏观层面和外部空间规定城市形态的量化标准。对于非规定性的导则，则可以用"应"、"宜"、"可"等描述性语言进行不同程度的表达。[5]而无论规定型或是非规定性，均不应含有对具体的空间审美形态进行判断，以保证建筑师兼顾城市整体空间利益的同时具有相对的创作自由。好的建筑设计往往会综合平衡局部空间与整体空间的利益，做出应对于具体场地特征的设计解答，进而成就一个良好的城市设计。

3.2 以设计为主导的管控

城市的生长发展具有恒持性和历时性，在不断演进中实现城市空间的生产与增值，以往的管控手段以静态的终极目标为宗旨其实忽略了城市发展的变调性和动态性，设计成果往往还未来得及实施，城市形态业已发生转变，造成城市空间管控的失效。"自下而上"的管控就是看到了城市空间的自组织性和微观城市元素之间的关联互动性，以渐进式、阶段性和局部性的空间协调进一步对宏观城市空间进行整合，通过建筑设计为主导的管控，从小到大对城市空间进行动态微调。[5]相对于行政管控而言，设计管控更为柔性，通过在方案阶段对设计要点的制定以及后期审查的把握（尤其在易于出现行业壁垒的环节给予高度重视），在城市主管部门的统一协调下对各种设计资源进行前瞻性的统筹与规划，权衡各部门利益进行空间调整，从设计的角度对城市设计进行管控，使公共资源得到合理配置。

3.3 加强民主的公共参与和反馈机制

"自下而上"的城市设计与管控需要基层信息的即时反馈，继而对城市空间形态做出及时调整和优化。公共参与可分为三种方式进行：其一是在设计前期调研阶段通过发放问卷和民意调查收集公众的切实诉求和真实想法，并作为设计的依据；其二是在设计过程中通过成果公式广泛汲取公众意见，以便对接下来的设计任务和目标做出及时调整；其三，在项目建成后广泛收取民众对城市和建筑空间的使用感受，以便总结归纳。[6]公共参与和信息反馈是通过自下而上的途径，使城市设计者、市民和政府之间达成共识，促使城市、建筑一体化。

3.4 建立以建筑师为主导的联动设计平台

"自下而上"的模式将建筑师的作用凸显了出来，在这个庞杂的网络化城市系统中，建筑师之间必须建立起一种有效的协同机制才能对项目进行有效而合理的管控。这里可参照国外先进的建筑师协调机制，以期为联动模式的城市设计提供可操作的办法借鉴。

3.4.1 "协商控制区规划"制度（Z. A. C）

"协商控制线区规划"简称（Z. A. C）是法国城市规划中的一种常用手段，通过对私空间的限制继而实现公共空间的平衡。Z. A. C 的管理机构一般由地方政府或民间组织构成，通过委托建筑师来进行总体设计。建筑师需要对地块中包括入口道路、建筑布局、地块衔接、土地利用、立面控制、分类规划等各项内容进行深入的调研分析，从整体着眼，局部入手进行设计。[7] "协调建筑师"

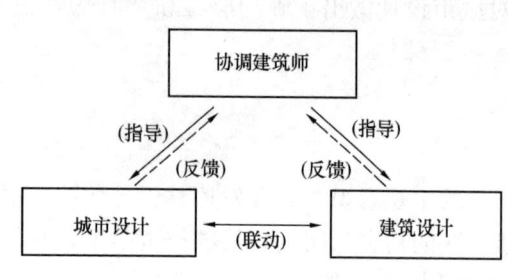

图2 "协调建筑师"制度关系图
（资料来源：作者自绘）

被赋予技术层面上的话语权和决策权，一旦某项设计超出了预设控制点，协调建筑师有权对方案进行修改，直至回到预定的设计目标。由于决策层有了专业人士的话语地位，在一定程度上减少了设计的随意性，并且建筑师之间通过 Z. A. C 搭建了一个信息互通的平台，使建筑整体风格、外立面形式等得到相互调节。Z. A. C 制度如同在城市规划和建筑设计之间增加了一个环节，通过即时评估和规范管控保障了设计成果的有效落实，避免了城市设计中预设的成果与实际成果的偏差与背离（图2）。

3.4.2 "协商建筑师"制度（MA-BA）

"协商建筑师"制度简称（MA-BA），是一种建筑师之间的合作机制。MA 是 "master architect（总建筑师）" 的缩写，BA 是 "block architect（地块建筑师）" 的缩写，MA-BA 制度的确立就是强调在城市总建筑师的引导下，通过地块建筑师的通力合作，使局部的能动性加以整合，从而达到建筑、城市联动的目标。[8] 在 MA-BA 制度中，总建筑师被赋予一定的技术和行政权力，并施行设计指导和协调工作。由于总建筑师的存在，各个地块建筑师通过信息互通实现了每一个地块之间建筑形态的整体协调。地块建筑师往往根据实际情况，对整体项目的运行提供有益的建议，对整体项目的运行进行即时调整，以实现地块建筑和区域城市的联动与契合，实现局部利益和整体利益之间新的平衡。最终协同控制城市设计和大型项目的有序进行（图3）。

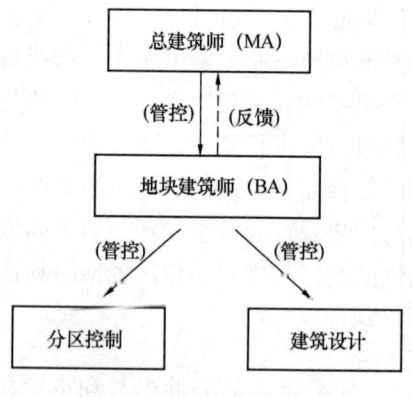

图3 "MA-BA 制度"关系图
（资料来源：作者自绘）

无论是 "Z. A. C" 模式还是 "MA-BA" 模式，其强调的都是通过 "自下而上" 的方式实现建筑设计与城市设计的互动。通过个体的管控对整体操作层面进行反馈和自适性调整，通过局部调整实现整体和谐，为当代快速城镇化背景下的城市设计和运作提供实施途径。

4 结语

总之，"自下而上" 的城市设计与管控手段实现的是城市、建筑的联动，城市设计与管控模式能够从微观的调控实现对宏观的协调。在当代中国快速城市化的 "新常态" 下，这种新型的联动设计与管控模式能够将建筑有效地纳入城市系统的整体框架中去，通过更时效、更可控和更民主的方式实现城市资源的优化配置和利益的平衡，最终实现城市设计的可持续发展。

Research on Urban Design and Management from Below Under the "New Normal"

Chen Xin

(School of Architectur，Southeast University)

Abstract：Urban Design contributes to appearance of urban space after twenty years of practicing in our country. Nonetheless，deficiencies are still there，which reflect problems in our "top-down" urban design system. In this paper，an urban design and control strategy is proposed，starting with the specific architectural design，better integrating into the urban design，coming into the network of urban architecture，ultimately，a dynamic balance can be build. This balance will help to a better adapting to the new requirements of urban design under the "new normal" in China.

Keywords：The "new normal"，Urban design，Architecture design，"Top-down" urban design system，The network of urban architecture

参考文献：

[1] 韩冬青，冯金龙. 城市 . 建筑一体化设计[M]. 第 1 版. 江苏：东南大学出版社，1999：57-96.

[2] 海沃德. 城市设计与城市更新[M]. 第 1 版. 北京：建筑工业出版社，2009：216-221.

[3] 张勇强. 城市空间发展自组织与城市规划[M]. 第 1 版. 江苏：东南大学出版社，2006：145-148.

[4] 王建国. 现代城市设计理论与方法[M]. 第 1 版. 江苏：东南大学出版社，1991：85-126.

[5] 唐斌. 本体之外——基于 CA 理论与神经网络学说的建筑城市性研究[J]. 建筑学报，2013，1：96-99.

[6] 赵亮. 从"失效"到"实效"——快速城镇化背景下的我国城市设计体系研究[J]. 城市规划，2011，12：91-96.

[7] 李少云. 探索务实的城市设计运作体系[J]. 建筑师，2012，6：10-13.

[8] Krier Rob. Urban Space，Christine Gzechowski，George black[M]. NY：Rizzoli International Publications，Inc. ，1991.

基于 S.E.T. 模式的中小城镇规划研究
——以黑龙江省绥化市西部新区为例

邢 军 陈 宇 陆 明

（哈尔滨工业大学）

摘要： 运用单一发展模式进行城镇开发的片面性、发展不平衡性的弊端日渐凸显。针对这一问题，很多城镇和地区都运用了 S.E.T. 模式（S.E.T.＝SOD＋EOD＋TOD）进行规划。本文将 S.E.T. 模式应用于绥化市西部新区的城市规划中，通过对规划后绥化市西部新区用地指标、空间结构、功能结构等方面的定性和定量分析，综合评价了 S.E.T. 模式的优势与不足，对其可行性及适用范围进行了验证，对指导今后中小城镇规划的实践具有一定的意义。

关键词： S.E.T. 模式，中小城镇规划，绥化市西部新区，多要素综合导向

1 引言

中小城镇的规划建设日益受到各地方政府及城市规划工作者的重视。许多中小城镇借此机遇开始快速发展，城镇用地也不断扩张，形成一个个以新型住区或工业新区为主要功能的城镇新区。这些城镇新区的建设需要通过不同的城市规划手段，满足其不同的发展需求。近年来，运用单一发展模式进行城镇开发的片面性、发展不平衡性的弊端日渐凸显[1]。

针对这一问题，很多城镇和地区都运用了 S.E.T. 模式（S.E.T.＝SOD＋EOD＋TOD）进行规划。但是，S.E.T. 模式也并不适用于所有的中小城镇，具有一定的适用范围，而针对 S.E.T. 模式科学性、适用范围的科学研究及应用到实际项目中的后续评价研究尚不完善。

本文以黑龙江省绥化市西部新区规划为例，应用了 S.E.T. 模式进行规划。通过对规划后绥化市西部新区用地指标、空间结构、功能结构等方面的定性和定量分析，综合评价了 S.E.T. 模式的优势与不足，对其可行性及适用范围进行了验证，形成了科学、完善的理论方法。

2 S.E.T. 模式解析

S.E.T. 模式是针对运用单一模式进行城镇开发，导致城镇发展片面性、发展不平衡等问题提出的城镇发展模式。近年来，国内很多城镇和地区都运用了这种模式进行规划。S.E.T. 模式的核心是将城镇空间结构划分为公共服务设施系统、生态绿地系统和道路交通系统，针对各个系统分别采用 SOD、EOD、TOD 理论为指导，并将各个系统相叠加，各要素综合组织的综合性规划(图1)。

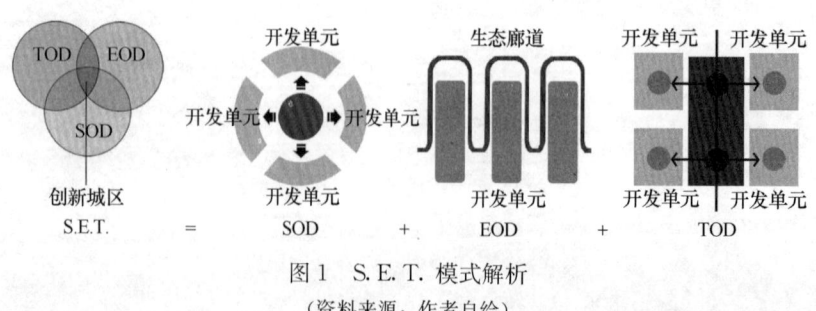

图 1 S.E.T. 模式解析

（资料来源：作者自绘）

2.1　SOD 的内涵

SOD（Service-Oriented Development），即大型公共设施导向开发模式。其实质是通过大型公共设施的完善，以点带面，提升新区功能，激发新区活力，进而影响城市整体的发展。[3]

中小城镇城市新区的建设，其最重要的功能之一就是承载旧城区人口的疏散，因而通常会建设比例较高的居住用地。采用 SOD 模式进行开发建设，为城市新区规划相应数量与规模的公共服务设施，一方面可以作为城市新区的触媒，吸引人口向新区疏散；另一方面也可以为城市新区的居民提供相应的生活服务。

2.2　EOD 的内涵

EOD（Ecology-Oriented Development），即生态环境导向开发模式。其实质是通过生态绿地系统的规划建设，改善城镇的生活环境。[7]

中小城镇的建设，不仅要注重城镇的经济发展，更应注重生态环境的保护与优化。采用 EOD 模式进行城镇规划，建设完整的生态绿地系统，主要包括四类绿地系统的建设：通过城镇公园绿地、街头绿地、防护绿地等多种绿地的规划，形成城镇绿地网络系统；通过滨水绿地的规划，形成城镇带状绿地系统和滨水景观廊道；通过种植行道树、居住组团绿地和广场景观绿化，形成城镇微型绿色斑块；通过城镇边缘区的农田、林地的保护，形成城镇外围绿地系统。通过城镇各类绿地系统的综合，既可以为城镇居民提供游憩空间，又能够优化城镇的生态环境。

2.3　TOD 的内涵

TOD（Transit-Oriented Development），即公共交通导向开发模式。其实质是通过公共交通网络的建设，对公共交通节点和中央商务区为核心的土地进行混合开发建设，使城镇各功能区具有更好的交通便利可达性。

中小城镇由于城市用地规模较小，城镇居民更适合采用步行或公共交通为主要出行方式。采用 TOD 模式进行城镇规划，建设完善的公共交通系统，一方面可以使居民更方便地到达城镇各功能区；另一方面可以将公共交通节点与公共服务设施节点综合建设，强化节点功能，促进土地高效利用，降低基础设施投资成本。

2.4　S. E. T. 模式综合实施

S. E. T. 模式的综合实施过程主要包括三个步骤。首先，分别采用 SOD 模式进行城镇公共服务设施规划、采用 EOD 模式进行城镇绿地系统规划、采用 TOD 模式进行城镇公共交通系统规划，分别形成满足城镇发展需要的城镇公共服务设施网络、绿地景观网络系统和公共交通网络体系。然后，将采用不同模式规划的公共服务设施网络、绿地景观网络和公共交通网络进行叠加，形成复合性城镇空间规划结构。最后，将各网络系统进行综合，这是 S. E. T. 模式综合实施的关键，其方法主要包括以下几个方面：

（1）对不同网络系统在城镇空间上相邻近的节点进行综合规划。例如，在 TOD 模式中对公共交通节点进行混合开发建设，可以与节点附近的大型公共服务设施相结合，形成综合性城镇节点，既能够节约城镇用地，又能够强化节点的作用，提升节点等级。对于与城镇绿地节点相结合的综合性节点，应更加重视，使节点的建设既满足居民使用的功能性需求，又保持良好的生态环境，形成富有层次性的景观效果。

（2）对不同网络系统在土地利用上的冲突进行权衡。例如，在 EOD 模式中规划的某处公共绿地,同时在 SOD 模式中规划的公共服务设施用地。针对这种潜在冲突,要根据实际情况进行权衡,原则上低等级的一般性功能应避让高等级的节点性功能,散点性功能应避让连续性功能,小众性功能应避让大众性功能。例如,某处城镇用地在城市 EOD 规划过程中被划定为公园绿地,在 SOD 规划过程中被划定为娱乐用地,则该用地应规划为公园绿地。

(3)对做出避让的功能进行补偿。在土地利用冲突中,被舍弃的功能,应在其他用地进行功能补偿。例如,在上述假设中,用地被划定为公园绿地,舍弃了其在 SOD 规划中的娱乐功能,故在其他适宜用地应规划一处相应的娱乐用地。对于不同的功能,其补偿方式和补偿程度应有所区分。对于公益性质的用地,如公共绿地、城市广场等应严格补偿,补偿比例应大于 1,且补偿用地质量应不低于原有用地;对于公共服务性质的用地,如学校、医院等应进行同等补偿,补偿比例应等于 1,且补偿用地质量应与原有用地近似;对于其他营利性质的用地,如酒吧、KTV 等,补偿比例可根据实际情况进行缩减。

(4)对综合后的用地进行整体调整。经过不同网络系统的综合,城镇用地的总体结构已有所改变。因此,对综合后的用地应重新审视,进行整体调整。

3 绥化市西部新区概况

绥化市域位于黑龙江省中南部,松嫩平原的呼兰河流域,东西宽 305km,南北长 308km。绥化市区地处松嫩平原城镇密集区,以哈大齐工业走廊为中心,受工业中心直接辐射影响,是哈尔滨都市经济圈副中心城市和黑龙江省中部地区中心城市,绥化市的发展对于带动黑龙江省北部地区的经济发展具有十分重要的作用。

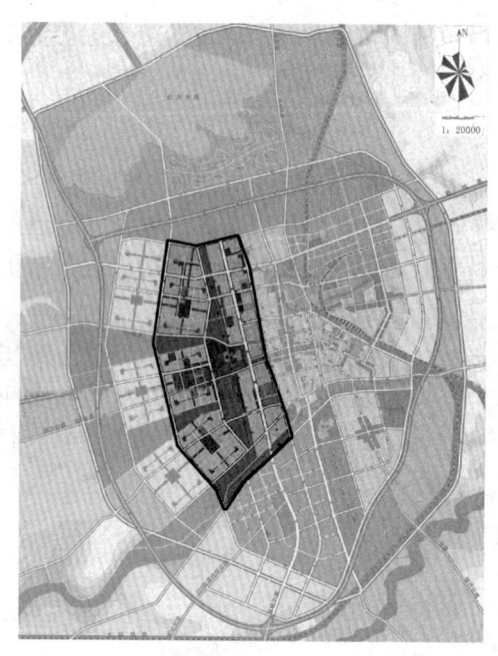

图 2　绥化市西部新区在绥化市区位
(资料来源:上海同济城市规划设计研究院.
绥化市城市总体规划(2012-2030),2012.)

绥化市西部新区位于绥化市城市规划区康庄路以西,是绥化市重点发展区域(图 2)。绥化西部新区内部主要道路结构为两横一纵,由东西走向的 S304、S305 省道和南北走向的康庄路组成。沿康庄路现有居住小区若干,建筑形式较为统一。其余片区存在部分村落和未建设用地及部分农田。

绥化市西部新区现状内部道路网结构不完善,无法满足城市发展需求;土地开发利用率低,西部有大量土地闲置,未得到合理开发利用;新区现状的公共服务设施无法满足新区居住区的发展需求;消防、给排水、电力、通讯等基础设施建设虽然已经达到一定规模,但标准较低;城市缺乏特色风貌,对特色资源整体保护与利用不足,城市环境景观形象杂乱,城市出入口景观急需改造,缺少具有标志性的景观节点。

4　S.E.T. 模式引导下的绥化西部新区规划

采用了 S.E.T. 模式对绥化市西部新区进行规划。规划的过程根据 S.E.T. 模式的综合实施方法分三个步骤进行。

4.1 系统划分

在规划的第一阶段，分别采用 SOD 模式、EOD 模式和 TOD 模式对绥化西部新区的公共服务设施网络、绿地景观网络系统和公共交通网络体系进行规划（图 3）。

将绥化市西部新区根据用地性质和空间结构划分为文化休闲片区、商业金融片区、滨水宜居片区、行政办公片区、现状保留片区、教育培训片区六个片区。以行政中心、商业服务中心及科研培训等大型公共设施的建设作为增长点，结合会展中心、历史遗址展示、医疗服务、博览中心等次级公共设施，带动绥化市西部新区土地高效有序开发。在片区组团层面，将各片区内的学校、医院、活动中心、幼托等设施集中布置，建设社区综合服务中心，激发社区活力，带动各个社区高效发展。

在进行绿地系统规划过程中，发挥绥化市西部新区现有生态环境优势，充分保护绥胜干渠，由红星水库引入人工河，提升绥化市西部新区的人居环境和生活质量。在绥化市西部新区宏观层面的空间布局上，采用组团式布局结构，利用楔形绿地和中央绿轴将新区划分为多个居住组团，提高新区城市居民的生活环境品质。在各居住区内部微观层面的空间布局上，采用圈层布局结构。主核心是居住区中心绿地，次核心由商业服务设施构成，外层为居住组团，利用环形道路组织居住区的交通，结合十字形绿色廊道，形成符合圈层结构的空间布局。

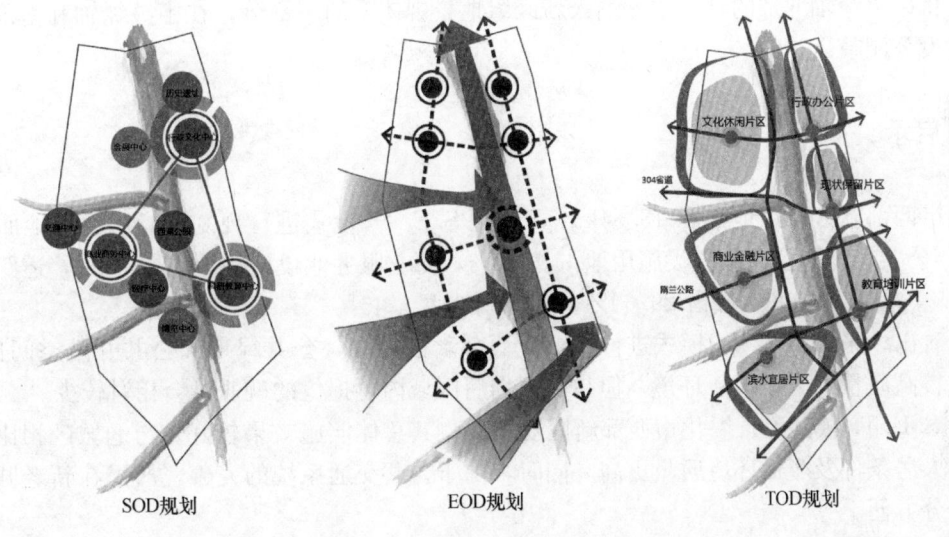

| SOD规划 | EOD规划 | TOD规划 |

图 3 S.E.T. 各系统规划

（资料来源：作者自绘）

运用 TOD 模式，以高密度组团的集中模式实现用地集约性与环境生态性的平衡。在各组团的核心区域设置快速公交站点，围绕站点布置行政、商业、文化、教育等多种功能，支持并带动区域的整体发展。

4.2 系统叠加

在分别采用不同模式对绥化市西部新区的公共服务设施网络、绿地景观网络系统和公共交通网络体系规划完成后，将各个系统进行叠加，形成复合性空间规划结构。通过系统的叠加，基本形成绥化市西部新区的总体规划结构：六区、四心、一轴、三带、多节点。

六区是指由中央绿轴和楔形绿带划分的文化休闲片区、商业金融片区、滨水宜居片区、行政办公片区、现状保留片区、教育培训片区。

四心是指采用 SOD 模式规划的行政文化中心、商业服务中心、科研培训中心，加上以西湖公园为核心的生态景观中心。

一轴是指贯通新区南北的中央滨水景观轴。

三带是指划分各居住组团的两条楔形绿带和南部绥胜干渠滨水景观带。

多节点包括各个区域内部的次级公共服务设施节点、各区域组团内的绿地景观节点，以及各公交站点为核心的混合功能节点。

4.3　系统综合

在进行系统叠加后，对各系统进行综合调整。

将各区域内的大型公共服务设施核心与片区内的各个公共服务设施节点、片区组团中心绿地集中布置在各居住区核心位置，综合布局，强化核心的功能和服务等级。

通过权衡公共交通网络系统和大型公共服务设施核心的节点规划，将新区西部公交干线沿中央绿轴西侧布置，避免穿入居住组团，并确保各公交站点距离组团核心在五分钟步行范围内。

在公共服务设施与组团中心绿地综合布置时，会对中心绿地进行占用，在规划时对绿地进行补偿。其补偿方式为，通过组团内道旁绿地的规划，形成贯穿各组团的环形绿带网络，使绿地渗透入各个微型居住组团。

最后根据各片区现状和实际需要，保留和建设一处飞机堡遗址、一处市民文化娱乐广场和一处体育馆。将中央绿轴北部的红兴水库纳入新区绿地景观体系的一部分，在中央绿轴和南部绥胜干渠交界处建设公园节点。

5　规划启示

绥化市西部新区总用地面积 15.54km²，运用 S.E.T. 模式进行规划后，居住用地面积比例为 37.90%，公共管理与公共服务设施用地占 9.35%，商业服务业设施用地占 4.31%，道路交通用地占 17.39%，公共绿地和水域占 29.60%，其他用地占 1.45%。

可以看出，采用 S.E.T. 模式进行的绥化西部新区规划，公共绿地和公共开敞空间比例较高，能够形成较高质量的人居生活坏境。但是，规划后区域内可提供的就业机会相对较少。

采用 S.E.T. 模式进行绥化市西部新区规划后，其总体实施效果较好。与老城区相比，新区居民的总体人居条件及生活环境质量更高。同时，由于公共交通系统的完善，居民在新老城区直接的出行也十分方便。

在就业方面，新区楔形绿地的外端保留现状的一般农田，部分居民仍从事农业活动，作为经济收入的一部分。新区内还有大部分居民保持其在老城区的工作，通过公共交通作为日常通勤交通方式。新区内建设了一定数量的公共服务设施和商业服务设施，也有部分居民进入这些商场、学校、会展中心等从事相应的工作。

根据规划的结果及实际实施效果分析，可以看出：采用 S.E.T. 模式进行中小城镇规划，可以对城镇的公共服务设施进行合理布局，促进城镇的均衡发展；还可以为居民提供高质量的人居条件和生活环境；同时可以为居民提供与城镇其他地区之间便利的公共交通条件。但是，采用 S.E.T. 模式进行规划，对居民的就业考虑不足，会导致居民的就业问题，且无法快速拉动城镇的经济增长。

因此，S.E.T. 模式更适用于经济发展已基本达到稳定，人们更注重人居条件和生活环境的中小城镇。同时，由于 S.E.T. 模式对城镇用地的布局结构要求较高，因此更适用于已开发程度较小的城镇新区。针对 S.E.T. 模式中考虑较少的就业问题，可以通过适当增加无污染产业区、开发城镇农田、增加通勤公共交通等手段加以改进。

The Study of Small Town Planning Based on S. E. T. Model——The West District of Suihua City, Heilongjiang Province as An Example

Xing Jun, Chen Yu, Lu Ming

(Harbin Institute of Technology)

Abstract: The disadvantage of imbalance while using a single mode for the development of urban is becoming highlighted. In order to solve this problem, a lot of towns have used the S. E. T. mode (S. E. T. =SOD+EOD+TOD) planning. In this paper, the S. E. T. mode was used in the planning of the New West District of Suihua. By the analysis of the land use, the spatial structure and the function structure, we made an evaluation of the advantages and disadvantages of the S. E. T. , and verified its feasibility and scope of application. And it would be significant to small town planning in the future.

Keywords: S. E. T. mode, Small town planning, The new west district of Suihua, Multi-factor-oriented

参考文献：

[1] 贺海龙. 新型城镇导向下中小城镇规划建设存在的问题及对策[J]. 现代农业科技, 2014, 15：349-351.

[2] T. A. A, A. W. J. B, H. J. P. T. The Integration Of Expert Knowledge In Decision Support Systems For Facility Location Planning[J]. Computers, Environment and Urban Systems, 1995, 19(4)：227-247.

[3] 王青. 以大型公共设施为导向的城市新区开发模式探讨[J]. 现代城市研究, 2008, 11：47-53.

[4] Nasri A, Zhang L. The analysis of transit-oriented development (TOD) in Washington, D. C. and Baltimore metropolitan areas[J]. Transport Policy, 2014, 32(1)：172-179.

[5] 万婷, 王莹. 城乡统筹发展空间布局模式研究——以哈尔滨东部地区为例[J]. 四川建筑科学研究, 2014, 05：286-289.

[6] 李浩. 基于"生态城市"理念的城市规划工作改进研究[D]. 北京：中国城市规划设计研究院, 2012.

[7] 陈海涛. 生态导向发展模式(EOD)下的城市绿地系统规划应对策略研究[D]. 湖北：华中科技大学, 2012.

光电系统之隔热效应对于顶楼居住环境的影响评估

程达隆[1]　李彦颐[2]　林嘉雄[3]　吴奎宪[4]　李韦葶[5]

（1. 台湾树德科技大学计算机与通讯系；2. 台湾树德科技大学建筑研究所；
3. 台湾树德科技大学室内设计系；4. 台湾树德科技大学计算机与通讯系；
5. 台湾树德科技大学环境美学研究室）

摘要：高雄市，一个兼具海洋与工业为发展背景的亚热带城市，除了既定的高温炎热的刻板印象外，地形地貌更包含沿海、平原、丘陵、高山等四种地形。在发展地方建筑风貌再造的原则之下，高雄市政府大力推动具有光电系统之阳光建筑作为城市发展的愿景，同时配合推动高雄厝建筑走向符合国际趋势标准，营造永续生态城市。

健康建筑，其定义为："一种体验建筑室内环境的方式，不仅包含物理测量值，如温湿度、通风换气效率、噪声、光、空气质量等，尚须包含主观性心理因素。一栋健康建筑必须包含以上所有"。在此前提下，如何有效降低屋顶层的自然光源直接得热，以及有效降低室内温度。在气候剧烈异变下，许多建筑物绿化的相关研究，均证实建筑物绿化能有效降低建筑物的温度，但甚少提及屋顶太阳光电设施对于室内温度的改善研究。

本研究主要针对：（1）温度；（2）相对湿度；（3）噪声；（4）二氧化碳为主要研究因素。基于高雄厝与光电系统设置的基础前提下，分析撷取屋顶架设光电系统上方、屋顶层、室内层各楼层温度差异，并提供市民架设光电系统后耗能效应作为比较差异值。本研究建立监测数据库并应用于高雄厝，将微气候因素图表分析与可视化图像建立评估数据，结合现有光电系统与室内降温、通风换气，经过计算后评估是否能达到舒适范围。透过网络搜集环境数据，提供给住户或研究人员使用。

关键词：隔热，光电系统，温热环境，节能减碳

1　计划缘起

因应大高雄县市合并以及更具代表高雄地理特色的建筑风貌再造，陈菊市长提出高雄厝计划，同时配合推动高雄厝建筑走向符合国际趋势标准，营造永续生态城市，市府大力推动具有光电系统之阳光建筑。因此对于未来"高雄厝"的思考方向，除了将建筑元素融入地方特色与人文景观之外，更应该反映在以"永续"、"健康"、"节能"、"舒适"为要求之上，为此如何实时因应建筑室内环境变化，同时评估光电系统建筑之特性、设计具有智能之遮阳方式、自然换气甚至于开启相关建筑设备等对策成为"智慧绿能高雄厝"，使"高雄厝"室内外环境成为宜居城市的典范，为本计划最主要之起源（图1）。

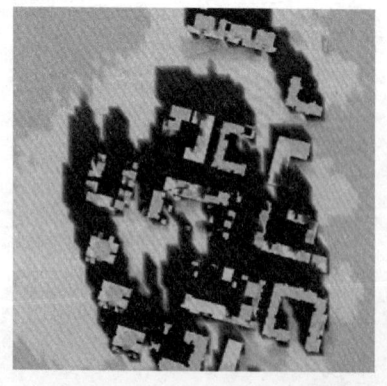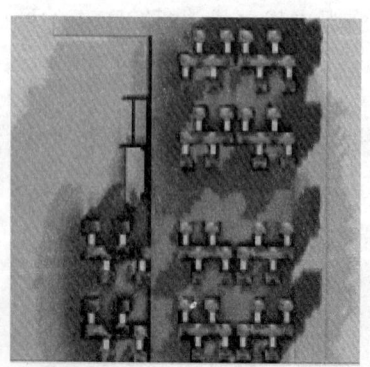

图 1　运用光源仿真软件计算建筑受热时数

2 工作内容计划说明

以高雄市区内透天厝住家已完成架设太阳光电系统者为优先测量对象，延续去年研究成果，今年朝向实际建构完成之透天厝进行测量室外屋顶与室内温度、湿度之差异比较。运用 2013 年研究成果所整合的远程监控系统与现场实测双重检验下，同步进行比较有无光电板对于室内建筑温度与湿度的变化差异（图2）。

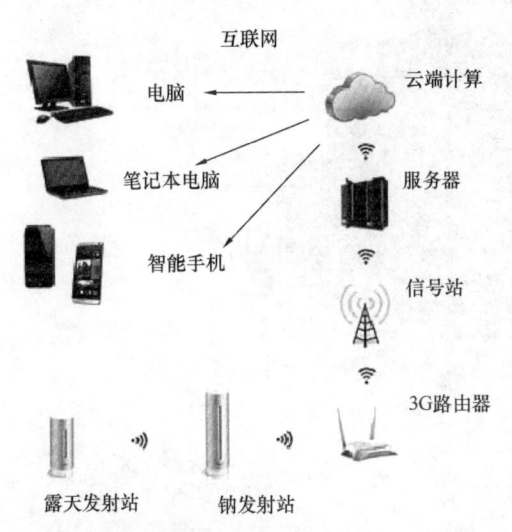

图2　监测系统与当地气象站

2.1 微环境检测

◆测量时间条件

基础要求实测日期，必须为夏季晴天且温度须高于 30℃，长期监测需进行约 4～5 天，并进行气象分析与气象站比对。并针对变化较剧烈之气候状态提出相关佐证数据与背景信息。

◆测量时段

期望采样数值于日间及夜间，得以解析一天当中不同时段之夏至微气候差异，因此于设定日间上午（AM08：00～AM10：30）、中午（PM12：00～PM14：30）及晚上（PM18：00～PM20：30）时段针对上述量测项目进行微气候环境因子采样。各时段采样时间预计于 3h 内完成全部采样点之数据收集，将时间延迟误差率降低（图3）。

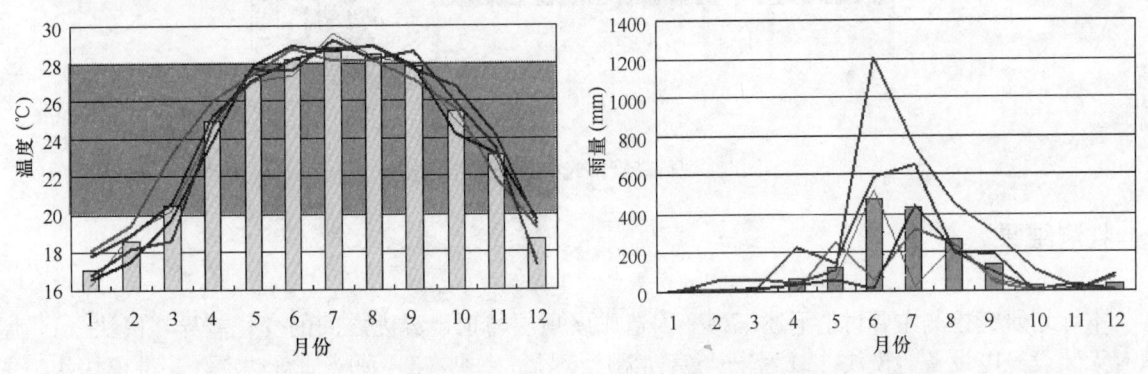

图3　月平均温度变化分析（左）、月平均湿度变化分析

2.2 历史资料汇整

参考高雄市政府在市区中设置之气象站作为基础数据进行分析，同时针对高湿高温区段进行对策研究拟定，依照不同面向之气候数据进行交叉比对，以高雄市气候特征进行评估与解析（图4）。

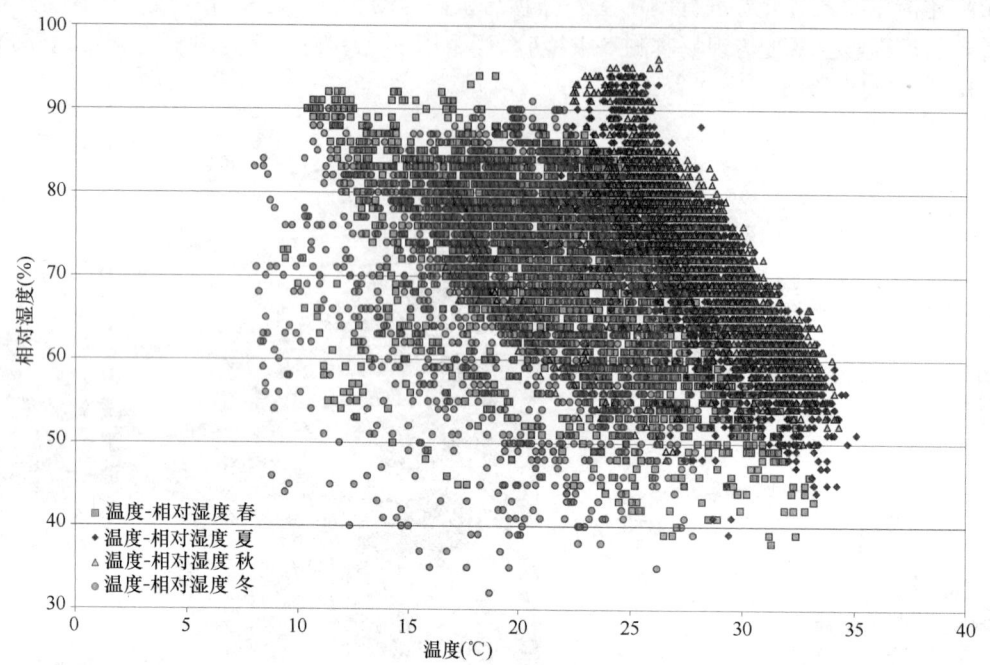

图4 高雄市年平均温度与湿度交叉比对

2.3 比较屋顶设置不同隔热工法差异

因建筑物之屋顶构架系统不同，可概括分为有无违章建造屋顶的案例，因此对应在不同目标上，并非每种建筑类型与业主需要的都是增高性做法，本研究将针对不同属性之团队结合实测分析评估不同屋顶之光电系统设置，影响范围为何？有效降温数值最高与最低可差异几度，进而评估何种屋顶工法在高雄屋顶施作，能达到优化的隔热效果（图5）。

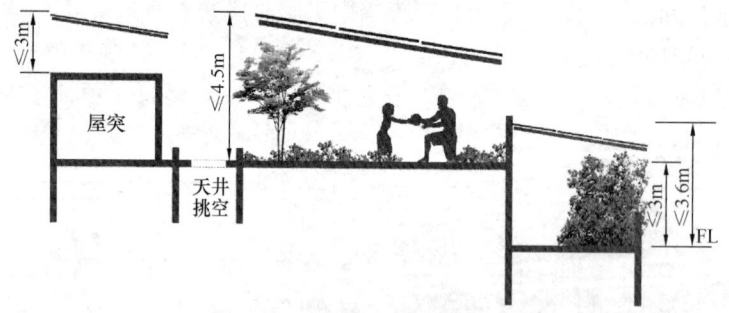

图5 现行高雄市光电设施作示意图

3 监测结果

本计划研究检测主要讨论下述三种变因造成屋顶层与顶楼温度之间的变化差异：模块（1）屋顶有无装设光电设备、模块（2）室外与室内温度变异、模块（3）顶楼加盖铁皮，三种模块作为主要讨论的面向，而从中检讨降温效益与节约用电以及衍生出来比较铁皮屋顶与光电系统相关营造经费与经济效应（图6、图7及表1、表2）。

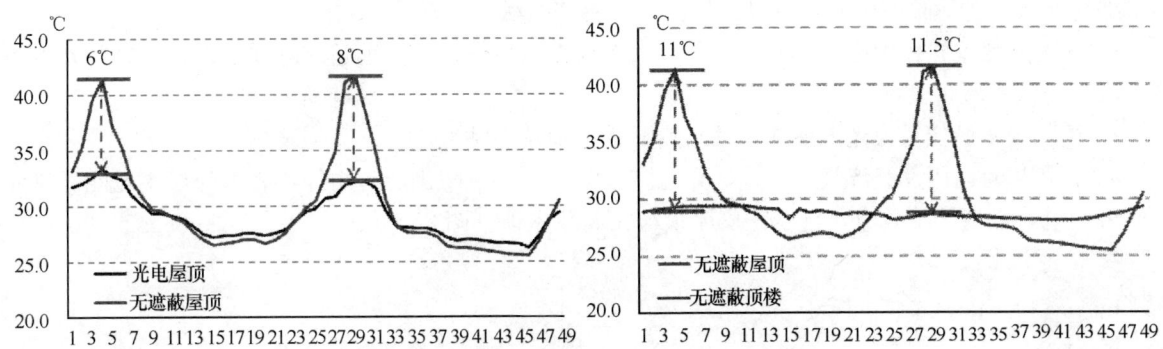

图 6　三种屋顶层现况温度分析

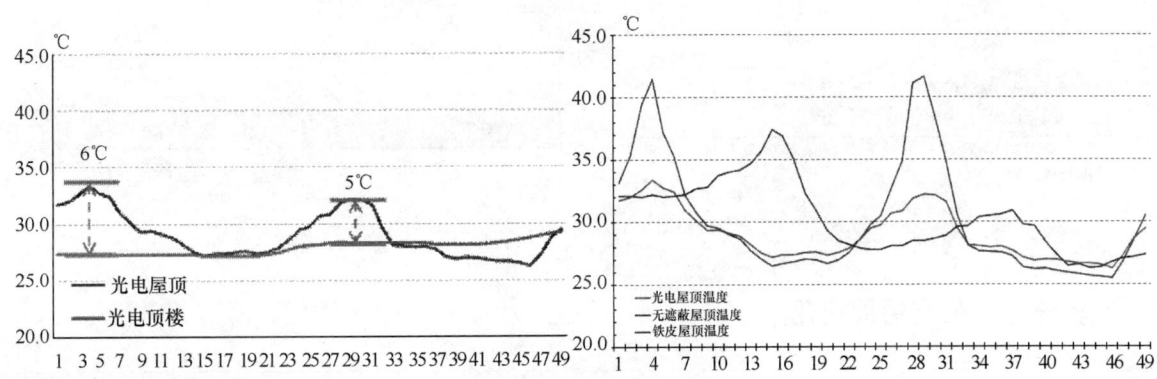

图 7　三种屋顶层总综合比较图

总综合比较分析表　　　　　　　　　　　　　　　　　　　　　表 1

模块 \ 时段		早上	中午	下午	午夜
无遮蔽屋顶	屋顶	33.2℃	40.6℃	27.6℃	28.3℃
	顶楼	29.6℃	29.8℃	28.6℃	27.2℃
温差		3.6℃	10.8℃	1℃	1.1℃
光电屋顶	屋顶	30.1℃	35.1℃	30.6℃	27.2℃
	顶楼	27.5℃	28.8℃	28.1℃	26.8℃
温差		2.6℃	6.3℃	2.5℃	0.4℃
铁皮屋顶	屋顶	33.2℃	37.4℃	29.6℃	27.3℃
	顶楼	31.6℃	32.6℃	28.6℃	27.2℃
温差		1.6℃	4.8℃	1℃	1.1℃

三模块经济效益比较表　　　　　　　　　　　　　　　　　　　表 2

模块 \ 项目	建置成本（新台币）	年维护费用（新台币）	年收益（新台币）	屋顶	顶楼	顶楼冷气使用时数
				温差		
无遮蔽屋顶	0 元	7500 元（防水工程）	0 元	40.6℃	29.8℃	6～12h
				10.8℃		
光电屋顶	500000 元	0 元（不计天灾毁损）	81650 元	35.1℃	28.8℃	约 4h
				6.3℃		
铁皮屋顶	135000 元	0 元（不计天灾毁损）	0 元	37.4℃	32.6℃	约 10h
				4.8℃		

综合比较三种屋顶模块时，可以比较出几个特殊的状态：

1. 室内温度差异作为比较，变化差异最大者为无遮蔽屋顶，但远超过舒适范围；次之为光电屋顶；末之为铁皮屋顶。

2. 降温效率最佳者为光电屋顶，且与热舒适范围较为贴近。

3. 未来空间运用及经济效益衡量，光电屋顶除了下方空间仍能运用外，有另外产生电能提供屋主回售台电，创造经济效应，优于铁皮屋顶与无遮蔽屋顶（图8）。

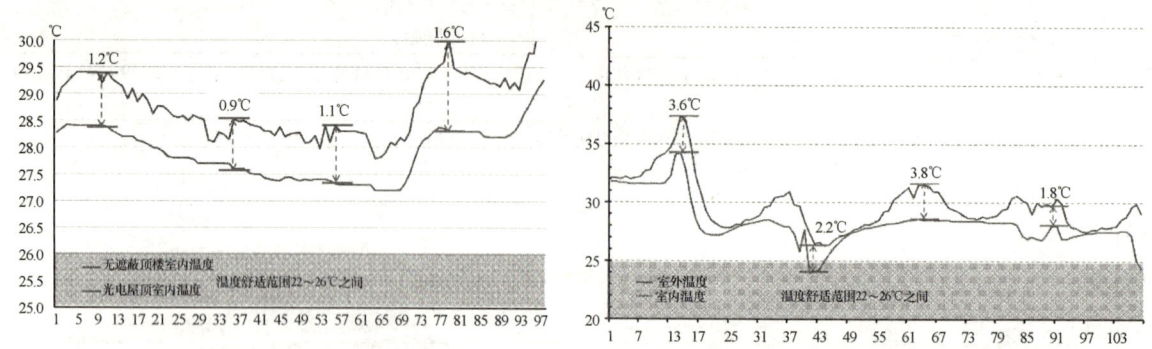

图 8　顶楼层室内外温度与环境舒适范围比较

4　年度研究成果与后续应用

本研究针对目前高雄市长日照时数以及高温的环境下，提供市民、从业建筑设计与营造工程等专业从业人员一个实地监测的数据，依据高雄市相关太阳光电补助及奖励办法，鼓励市民思考未来对于住宅的环境以及建筑物的隔热、节能、减碳等，由每一位市民住宅改造着手，借助太阳光电系统的建置，除了降低顶楼空间的温度，减少冷气空调的使用时间之外，更能借助由太阳光电板所产生之电能透过回售电能降低自家经济上的负担。

本文研究针对屋顶无遮蔽、装设太阳光电板、铁皮屋顶三种形态进行比较，从综合比较表可明显看出：整体而言，降温效果优劣比较依序为光电屋顶＞铁皮屋顶＞无遮蔽设施，其中无遮蔽设施室内外温差最大可达到10.8℃，虽然铁皮屋顶温度差异最小但室内外屋温度达到32.6/37.4℃。

已装设太阳光电屋顶的案例，一日之中室内外的温度差异发生在午夜最小0.4℃，最大发生在中午温差约6.3℃，且在顶楼室内温度与人体舒适温度22～26℃差异最小，为三个模块之中最佳的一组案例。理想的建筑物顶楼绿化与发展绿能系统设计草图如图9所示。

图 9　建筑物顶楼绿化与发展绿能系统设计草图

Influence of Thermal Insulation Effect of Photovoltaic System on Attic Living Environment

Cheng Da-Long[1]，Li Yen-Yi[2]，Lin Chia-Hsiung[3]，Wu Kuei-Sian[4]　Li Chun-Ting[5]

（1. Shu-Te University Department of Computer and Communication；
2. Shu-Te University architecture and interior design Dept；3. Shu-Te University Department of Interior Design；4. Shu-Te University Department of Computer and Communication；5. Shu-Te University Department of Interior Design）

Abstract：Kaohsiung city，a subtropical city with both marine and industrial development background. In addition to the established stereotype of high temperature hot outside，kaohsiung also includes the coastal terrain，plains，hills，mountains and other four terrain. Under the principle of developing local architectural style transformation，Kaohsiung City Government is actively promoting a sunny building photovoltaic systems of vision as the urban development.

The study focuses on，1. temperature，2. relative humidity，3. noise，4. carbon dioxide as the main research factor. Kaohsiung based on the following basic premise house with photovoltaic systems set up to analyze the erection capture roof top photovoltaic systems，the temperature difference between each floor attic，interior layer，and provide the public after the erection of photovoltaic systems as an energy effect difference value.

This study was set up to monitor the database and applied Kaohsiung LOHAS house plan，the micro-climate factors Chart establish and evaluate data visualization，combined with existing photovoltaic systems and indoor cooling，ventilation，assess after calculating whether to reach a comfortable range. Collect environmental data through the internet，available to households or researchers.

Keywords：Insulation，Photovoltaic systems，Warm environment，Energy saving & carbon reduction

参考文献：

[1] 江哲铭、林俊兴等. 住居空间物理环境基准之研究—室内环境质量量测法初探[G]. 台湾建筑学会第四届建筑学术研究发表会论文集. 1991.

[2] 林宪德. 绿建筑解说与评估手册[M]. 台湾建筑研究所. 2007.

[3] 刘国轩. 卧室空间热舒适性之实测与改善策略模拟研究——以开口部变化与多层次外墙为变因[D]. 台北科技大学建筑与都市设计研究所，2006.

[4] 林宪德. 建筑耗能调查分类与住宅类耗能调查之研究[M]. 台湾建筑研究所，2005.

[5] 周伯丞，李彦颐，朱元祥，江哲铭. 工作空间空气与温热环境之研究[G]. 台湾建筑学会第十三届建筑研究成果发表会论文集. 2001.

Beyond Low Carbon: A Comparative Case Study of Long-Lasting Housing Performance in Pearl River Delta Area, China

Wang Qing, Jia Beisi

(The University of Hong Kong)

Abstract: Green building and low carbon building concepts become important research issues in Pearl River Delta where the social and economic transformation towards post-industrialization era takes place, and a knowledge-based economy confronts with short life span of housing. However, green building concept and practice are often misunderstood and constantly accompanied with ignorance of time, and people in different levels of built environment. This study therefore introduces Open Building concept aiming to increasing the life span of urban housing in this region. The paper firstly reviews studies of essential qualitative principles providing the conditions of long lasting building. Based on the adaptive housing evaluation system, one historical building and one contemporary building, are selected, evaluated and compared in four spatial levels. The decision making process are analyzed as well. The paper concludes that, in order to increase life span of housing in this region, low carbon green building design needs to consider the whole life span and interaction with people in different spatial levels. It further verifies that the traditional buildings overtake the new buildings in several key characters of long lasting building, such as the representative outdoor space, strategically located structure and consistent interactive with the people, while new strategically design have advantages like flexibility, technology and construction integration.

Keywords: Green building, Long lasting building, Open building, Levels

1 Introduction

Green building and low carbon building concepts become important research issues in Pearl River Delta where the social and economic transformation towards post-industrialization era takes place, and a knowledge based economy confronts with short life span of housing. Theoretically, in order to explain the sustainable development issue comprehensively, there are many definitions including the landmark one which was first coined in 1987, i. e. "Development that meets the needs of the present without compromising the ability of future generations to meet their own needs" (WCED, 1987). According to Williams (2007), the three spheres of sustainability (i. e., social, environmental, and economical) must be solved simultaneously. However, there is no common position on the nature of this change or how it is to be achieved. In the field of architecture, studies on green building and the recent hot issue: low-carbon building are mainly focused on physical environmental concerns and are likely to result in a purely scientific way of architectural design, construction, and usage. Under this scenario, the sustainability of green building becomes questionable.

2 Current problems of green building and pearl river delta area, China

General speaking, green building concept and practice are often misunderstood and constantly accompanied with ignorance of time, and people in different levels of built environment.

2.1 Ignorance of time, people and levels

Most of green building theories and practices try to deal with urgent contemporary environmental issues and their future impacts, but ignore the long-lasting issue of buildings especially houses. This lack of focus on longevity results in the need to consider aspects beyond natural environment, such as society, economy, and other issues. On the other hand, architecture is accused of producing an academic result that is estranged from the everyday world. The demands placed on architecture have become increasingly complex, while critical points have become more significant as a result of differing interests. Besides, there is a rising fierce debate between technologically sustainable development and ecologically sustainable development. Technology is one of the architecture conditions, and the condition implementation with people involvement is a cultural issue rather than a technical one. Furthermore, most ideas of existing green building or evaluation systems only cover the adjustment at design stage and the control over construction stage. These ideas lack systematic solutions in accordance with the sequence of physical built environment. Level refers to not only green technologies, but also to the decision making process in different layers and their interrelation.

2.2 Sustainable problems of Pearl River Delta area, China

As one of the most important economic zones and highly developed urbanization areas in China, the Pearl River Delta region is treated as a pioneer and experimental area that has faced social and economic transformation from the industrialization to the post-industrialization era and has become a knowledge-based city. The National Development and Reform Commission intends for the Pearl River Delta region to move up the value chain by 2020, to foster advanced manufacturing and high-technology industries, to develop globally advanced capabilities in scientific innovation, and to build strong modern service sectors (Enright, Scott, & Petty, 2010). Besides, housing with a short life span is typical in this region and as a common phenomenon in the entire country. An economical and suitable method for sustainable and long-lasting housing construction is thus urgently necessary.

3 Theoretical Framework

3.1 Open building concept and level strategy

In this context, open building (OB) theory can be seen as an architectural solution for the new society and its continuity, as well as a tool for evolving green building practices under complicated situations. OB theory was proposed by N. J. Habraken in the 1960s that aims at adapting to the diverse requirements of residents and long-term uncertainty. It is an innovative approach to design and construction that enhances the efficiency of the building process, while increasing the variety, flexibility and quality of the product. In the OB perspective, the building is viewed as a well-organized combination of systems and sub-systems, each of which can be carefully coordinated to ensure an effective process and product for the homeowner and a parallel positive outcome for the building professionals. Habraken later divided a residential building into "support" and "detachable unit", and eventually proposed the "level" concept, which tries to distinguish the selection, control, and responsibility from construction to the usage stage. In general, the best buildings are those most able to provide capacity to changing functions, standards of use and life-style, and improved parts over time (Kendall, n. d.)

3.2 Other level concept and long lasting issue studies

Some other scholars like Stewart Brand has similar concept that divide the building into several sharing layers of change, based on the fact that different rates of change of its components (Figure 1). He further pointed out that a 'learning' building would affect all of a building's basics - its design process, budget, technology, overall shape, space plan, materials, and structure.

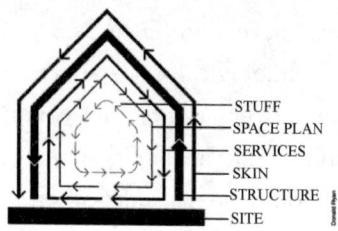

Figure 1 Sharing layers of change
[Source: Brand S (How Buildings Learn: What Happens After They're Built). Oxford: Oxford University Press, 1987]

In addition, according to Eberle, another successful architect from Europe for promoting long lasting housing, "Architecture is based on three things: social and cultural understanding of our society, technology and its background, science, and an ability to make a formal decision. If we understand this, then it is clear to me that design is not about creating new things, but rather about creating a building, which will last at least 200 years." (Dietmar Eberle: Lecture delivered at HKU on the 24th October, 2003)

3.3 Long lasting practical attempts in Japan

Practically, SI housing and KSI housing concept initially emerged in Japan is proposed in order to achieve 100 years or even 200 years housing. They have clear purpose, rules and designcriteria, as well as supported industry system. Among the essential technologies complying with the concept of KSI housing, UDC has specified the following most important design criteria as essential requirements. (1) Structure life of 100 years; (2) One large floor slab without unevenness and sub-beams; (3) Vertical drain pipes installed in the common area; (4) Electrical wiring should be separated from the structure. (Satoshi, & Masami, 2000)

4 Evaluation Method

On the other hand, some Chinese researchers not only simply follow western and Japan's theoretical experiences but also started developing their own evaluation system under domestic condition, especially flexibility and adaptability, which normal Green Building Concept and evaluation system have ignored. Among those researches, one outstanding case is that Ouyang wen and her students have developed an adaptive evaluation system for medium and small scale housing. The principle and method mainly include subjective and objective weighting methods, subjective way refers to experts consultant while subjective way refers to frequency analysis and theory analysis. Scoring is divided into general items and awarded item and final score is summation (Ouyang W et al, 2011).

However, according to above discussion, comprehensively, this evaluation is still lacking of level strategically concerns and people participation consideration. Therefore, evaluation method of this paper firstly will divide the build environment into four levels, and reorganized the items of "Evaluation System of the Adaptive Design of Medium and Small Scale Housing". Result revels it only covers level two to level four that author will discussed evaluated projects in level one from social, environmental and economical aspects, as well as people participation (Figure 2).

Levels	Evaluation Items	Evaluation Way	People Participation
Level One Infrastructure and Other Public Elements	Social and Cultural, Environmental, Economical	Discussion and Summary	Discussion and Summary
Level Two(44 points) The Load Bearing Structure& Staircase	1.1 Spatial Structure, 3.1 Durability(3.1.1), 3.2 Safety, 6.2 Design Standardization, 7.1 Structure and Wall	Scoring and Discussion	
Level Three(42 points) Facade & Service Core	2.2 Spatial Quality, 3.1 Durability(3.1.3), 4.1 Pipeline Arrangement(4.1.1), 4.2Pipeline Overhaul, 4.3 Pipeline & Equipment Replacement, 7.3 Equipment and Pipeline	Scoring and Discussion	
Level Four(114 points) Function Layout and Interior	1.2 Spatial Division, 1.3 Spatial Usage, 2.1 Barrier free Design, 3.1 Durability(3.1.2), 4.1 Pipeline Arrangement(4.1.2) 5 Interior Decoration, 6.3 Component Usage, 7.2 Decoration	Scoring and Discussion	

Figure 2   Evaluation method

5   Comparative case studies

Based on the developed adaptive design evaluation system, one historical building within historical area: Renewal for Jiefangzhong road in Guangzhou, and one new design building within the same area, are selected, evaluated and compared in four spatial levels respectively.

5.1   Level one: infrastructure and other public elements

Comb pattern, the major urban pattern in Guangdong cultural area, has been approved that is a successful model integrated with traditional culture, climate adaptability and life style (Lu, 2008). Renewal for Jiefangzhong road in Guangzhou (JFZ) is located in the most traditional district of Guangzhou city, which can be seen as a reconstruction practice of cities in Lingnan/Guangdong for the new mode of development. Its initial design attempt is to consider three sustainable aspects in level one: social and cultural, economical and environmental (Chen, He, & Zhang, 2010)

Since it is with most typical old Guangzhou urban fabric structure and commercial-living pattern, most valuable historical buildings are preserved by government. And it is regarded as a political experimental project, which will be applied in the future renewal actions for the entire city. Different from real estate led model, the major developer of this project is government and its cooperation with residents. Long term value is priority and the residents return is voluntary, density controls as well as low cost and high quality construction are major challenges. Building density, arrangement, orientation and greenery design are key issues for constructing a micro climate friendly environment (Figure 3).

	Social & Cultural	Economical	Environmental
Renewal of Jiefangzhong road (JFZ) in Guangzhou	-Restructure public space -Remain traditional dimension and density -Strategically located structure(traffic) -Consistent interactive with the people	-Government led model, -Cooperation with residents, -Functional mixed	-Building density control -Building arrangement and orientation -Greenery design

Figure 3   Design considerations of three aspects in level one

5. 2 Level two comparison: the load bearing structure and staircase

The score of two cases in this level are more or less the same except design standardization is missing in historical building (Old). In the new designed volume (New), thanks to the reinforced concrete frame, location and typology of structure and beam are with strategic consideration for responding surrounding older structure dimension and enhancing adaptability, as well as better ventilation. It can be assumed that outcome of plan possibilities is far beyond the historical ones vertically and horizontally (Figure 6).

5. 3 Level three comparison: facade and service core

The score of new design is significant higher than that of historical ones, the differences mainly lie on the service core and pipeline system design (Figure 5). Service core and pipeline system are strategically designed in the new ones (location, dimension and industrial integration) that facilitate the replacement and renovation activities, light facade material also enables the easy movable action from residents and is suitable for subtropical weather of Guangzhou (Figure 4).

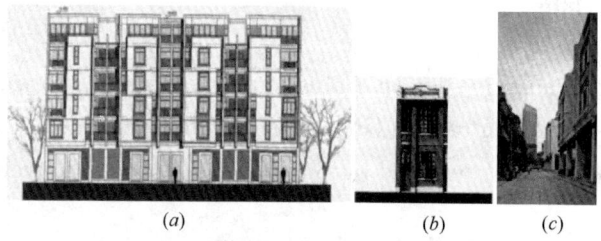

(a)   (b)   (c)

Figure 4 Facade of two cases

(a) New building elevation; (b) Renewal building elevation; (c) Space between new and old

[Source: Chen X H, He Z Q, and Zhang Z H (New Expedition of Old City Renewal for Jiefangzhong Road, Yuexiu District, Guangzhou). Architectural Creation, 2010, 12: 186-193]

Index			New	Score	Old	Score
1. Spatial Flexibility	1.1 Spatial Structure	1.1.1 Structure Selection	Reinforced concrete frame	22		19
		1.1.2 Floor high (H) 2.5< H<3.3	Satisfied	3	Satisfied	3
3. Durability	3.1 Durability	3.1.1 Structure	Design life > 50 yrs	1	Design life > 100 yrs	4
	3.2 Safety		Satisfied Regulation	2	N/A	0
6. Component & Standardization	6.2 Design Standardization		Module Design	2	N/A	0
7. Technology Integration	7.1 Structure and Wall		N/A	0	N/A	0
Total Score			44		30	26

(a)

Index				New	Score	Old	Score
2. Spatial Adaptability	2.2 Spatial Quality (Interior physical environment)	2.2.1 Sound		Satisfied	1	Satisfied	1
		2.2.2 Ventilation	General requirement	Satisfied	2	Satisfied	2
			natural ventilation priority, with air condition system as a supplementary	Satisfied	1	Satisfied	1
		2.2.3 Lighting	General requirement	Satisfied	2	Satisfied	2
		2.2.4 Thermal	General requirement	Satisfied	1	Satisfied	1
3. Durability	3.1 Durability	3.1.3 Service pipeline	Pipeline design life	Satisfied regulation	1	Satisfied regulation	1
4. Service Pipeline Integration	4.1 Pipeline Arrangement	4.1.1 Public	General requirement	Satisfied	2	Satisfied	2
			Other requirement	N/A	0	N/A	0
	4.2 Pipeline Overhaul	4.2.1 Access opening position	General requirement	Satisfied	2	Satisfied	2
			Separated opening in units	Satisfied	1	N/A	0
		4.2.2 Access opening dimension	General requirement	Satisfied	2	Unsatisfied	0
	4.3 Pipeline & Equipment Replacement		Replacement not destroy structure	Satisfied	2	Satisfied	0
			Replacement not destroy interior	Satisfied	2	N/A	0
			Replacement not influence other resident units	Satisfied	2	N/A	0
			Other method	N/A	0	N/A	0
7. Technology Integration	7.3 Equipment and Pipeline		Same floor drainage, centralized water supply	Satisfied	2	N/A	0
Total Score				42		23	12

(b)

Figure 5 Evaluation result in level two and three

(a) Evaluation result of level two; (b) Evaluation result of level three

5.4 Level four comparison: function layout and interior

Score in this level is similar with level three, new design solution perform better. Spatial flexibility and decoration convenience are major reasons (Figure 6). Furthermore, a fact not revealed in the evaluation table is that despite the ownership of those cases are both belongs to the residents (more than 80% of original residents returned to live in this district), the low income level majority as well as low component replacement convenience limited their changeability behavior.

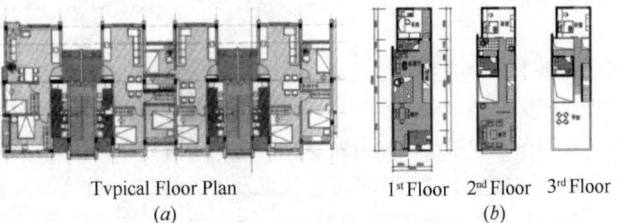

Typical Floor Plan
(a)

1st Floor   2nd Floor   3rd Floor
(b)

Figure 6   Function layout of two cases
(a) New building typical floor plan; (b) Renewal building floor plan
[Source: Chen X H, He Z Q, and Zhang Z H (New Expedition of Old City Renewal for Jiefangzhong Road,
Yuexiu District, Guangzhou). Architectural Creation, 2010, 12: 186-193]

6 Conclusion

In order to achieve 100 years building or more, green building or low carbon building is not sufficient and comprehensive enough as an ideal solution, long lasting building is also the high quality building bound by the specific social, cultural and technological conditions, it is a process rather than an outcome, it is a cooperation rather than a simple decision making. Therefore, Open Building theory and its 'Level' strategy is introduced. By developed evaluation system, two selected cases are more specifically evaluate and easier compared.

Renewal of Jiefangzhong road is with high evaluation outcome in level one since its strategically located structure with mature local cultural atmosphere and traffic convenience, as well as consistent interactive with the people by enhancing quality of public space. Although the structure selection is different, historical building and new design have similar performance in level two since their similar dimension and durability, which brings a human friendly environment physically and psychologically. In the facade and service core level, new design has better performance mainly because its independent service core and integrated facade design system, the advantages not only reflect in flexible usage, maintenance and replacement, but also better indoor and outdoor environment performance. In the level four, new design still performs well as a result of better consideration in higher level that the decoration activity has little influence to the structure, facade and service core area. Government dominant leading model bring more harmony cooperation with residents, the way is consultant mainly. Spatial quality and interior spatial division is the result of discussion. Despite some reasons limit owners changeability activity at this moment, they has more passion, power and capability to control and rearrange these units in the future.

低碳住宅的反思：珠江三角洲地区住宅的长效性案例比较分析

王　擎　贾倍思

（香港大学）

摘要： 绿色建筑和低碳建筑概念在中国及其最发达的地区之一珠江三角洲正变得非常流行，而这一地区却经历着社会和经济从工业化到后工业化的转型，以及知识型经济冲击下住宅寿命短的严峻挑战。但是绿色建筑的概念和实践通常忽略了时间的轴线、人的参与和层次的划分策略。因此，本研究介绍了开放建筑的概念和"层次"策略，并总结了国外和国内关于长效住宅研究的基本原则和特征。根据发展了的"中小住宅适应性评价体系"，本文选择了广州历史城城区的一栋历史建筑和一栋以历史建筑为原型设计的新建筑进行四个层次的分析和比较。结论表明，为了提高住宅的寿命，低碳建筑或绿色建筑需要考虑全寿命周期以及建筑和参与者之间在各个层级的关系。另外，历史建筑在高质量的外部开放空间和人性化的结构尺度等方面优于新建的建筑，而新建住宅在灵活性和建造技术集成度等方面则优于历史建筑。

关键词： 绿色建筑，长效建筑，开放建筑，层次

References and bibliographies：

[1] Chen X H, He Z Q, and Zhang Z H, New Expedition of Old City Renewal for Jiefangzhong Road, Yuexiu District, Guangzhou. Architectural Creation, 2010, 12：186-193.

[2] Brand S, How Buildings Learn：What Happens After They're Built. Oxford：Oxford University Press, 1987.

[3] Eberle D. Notes of speeches at University Hong Kong. Hong Kong：(unpublished), 24 October 2003.

[4] Enright M J, Scott E E, and Petty R, The Greater Pearl River Delta 6th Edition. Invest Hong Kong, 2010.

[5] Habraken N J, The Structure of the Ordinary：Form and Control in the Built Environment. Cambridge and London：The MIT Press, 1998.

[6] Kendall S, and Teicher J, Residential Open Building. New York：Taylor & Francis, 2000.

[7] Lu Q, Guang Dong Vernacular Dwellings. Beijing：China Architecture & Building Press, 2008.

[8] Ouyang W, Meng X, Jiao Y, et al. Evaluation System of Adaptive Design of Medium and Small-scale Houses. New Architecture, 6：39-42.

[9] Satoshi I, and Masami A, KSI Experimental Housing Project - Pilot project of Kodan Skeleton Infill Housing. Proceedings of Continuous Customizing in Housing, 2000, 55-62.

[10] WCED, Our Common Future. Penguin Books；Reprint edition, 1994.

[11] Williams D. (2007), Sustainable Design. New Jersey：John Wiley & Sons, 2007.

新型城镇化背景下回迁房设计研究

胡文荟　高　瑞　赵欣悦　林宏达

（大连理工大学建筑与艺术学院）

摘要： 在新型城镇化飞速发展的背景下，农村的集约建设问题越来越受到重视。本文对该背景下农村集约建设中回迁房的设计进行了探讨。介绍了该区域回迁民生活方式的特殊性及对居住空间的特殊要求，从住宅精细化、可持续性及院落空间的延续三个方面对回迁房进行了探讨，以设计出宜居、节能的回迁房为目的，为新型城镇化的发展的质量提供保障。

关键词： 新型城镇化，回迁房，精细化设计，多样性，节能

1 引言

城镇化是现代化的必由之路。面对当前严峻的"农业、农村、农民"三农问题和全面建设小康社会，推进新型城镇化建设是解决该问题的重要途径，对加快社会主义现代化建设有深远影响。随着现代经济的不断发展和社会生活水平的不断进步，全国各地的城镇化水平进一步提高，城镇化率大幅提升。在积极发展的同时也出现了消极的一面，如传统村落的消失、本土文化的失落、城镇面貌千篇一律、生态景观遭到严重破坏等，这些问题都严重影响我国新型城镇化的发展质量。

与城镇化相比，新型城镇化是坚持以人为本的城镇化，是以节约集集约、生态宜居为基本特征的城镇化，在推进新型城镇化的过程中必须从实际出发来提高我国的城镇建设水平。在此背景下农村的集约建设作为现代化进程的一部分具有重要意义。

回迁房项目很好的集约了居住空间，集约了农村土地用地，在新型城镇化的农村集约建设中占有重要比重。

回迁房指开发商征收土地时，赔给回迁民的房子。本文指农村集约过程中建设的将农民集中安置于原地的集合住宅。由于回迁房属于安置项目，产生的经济效益较小，在实地调研中发现农民的回迁房常以低品质的商品房形象出现，照搬大城市的住宅模式，忽视本身的特殊性：回迁房的居住对象为城镇的农民或个体户，多以自给自足经济链条存在，回迁后生活习惯鲜有改变，生存空间却大大压缩。照搬城市住宅模式的后果是出现了户型单一、套型基本空间不完备、空间利用率较低、储物空间不够、能源浪费等情况。这些问题与新型城镇化提倡的宜居相违背，成为当前城镇化发展的弊端。

本论文就上述出现的问题对新型城镇化背景下回迁房设计进行论述，从建筑本身进行探讨。

2 住宅精细化设计

住宅空间包括入口门厅、起居室、卧室、厨房、卫生间、储藏空间等。居民回迁前多以农耕、个体经营为主，居住在拥有宽敞庭院的低矮住宅中，回迁后被安置在面积狭小的高楼上，应根据他们的实际需求对各功能空间进行优化设计。

门厅。门厅作为住宅的入口，承接着室内外空间的连接作用，成为从公共空间向私密空间过渡的缓冲区域。在回迁房设计中，户型面积允许时，应当预留适当的门厅空间来满足功能需要：随身物品的搁置，包括手机、钥匙、背包、雨伞；更衣整装；迎送亲朋等。由于难以割舍原有的习惯，回迁民会寻找机会开辟土壤种植果蔬，因此，入户后农具的存放问题尤为突出。此外，门厅应避免与客厅直视，设置一定的分隔以保证私密性。

起居室。起居室是一个家庭的公共空间，承担着休闲、会客、文娱等功能，是一个家庭的核心部分。对大多数人来说，起居室是对环境要求最高的一个功能空间，应有良好的通风及采光条件（以南向采光为宜），面积不应小于 $12m^2$，同时要合理的组织交通，以便家庭成员间的有效活动及沟通。起居室面宽不宜小于 3.6m，往往和用餐空间相连，由于回迁房套型面积较小，两者还可能是相互重叠的空间；起居室可以和阳台同步设置，以保持整个空间的延续性，设计时要注意起居室至阳台的家具布置，减少交通流线，保证空间的完整性。受原有生活习惯影响，起居室应有足够的储藏空间来实现原有庭院的贮藏功能。

卧室。卧室是家庭中私密性最强的部分之一。回迁房设计中由于面积限制，除休息外，卧室还可能承担着书房、化妆、更衣甚至起居室的功能。尺度上，双人间面积最小为 $10m^2$，单人间不得小于 $6m^2$。

厨房。厨房是多数回迁家庭解决一日三餐的地方，对其平面布置、形状和大小有一定要求，同时由于面积的限制，与起居室、餐厅的关系处理，考虑日后的扩展的可能性也成为一个设计要点。厨房应配置服务阳台，以便放置燃气热水器、洗衣机生活物品等；尽量靠近餐厅，距离入口不能太远，过长的流线会影响洁污分区。布置形式上 L 型厨房操作面更为连续，转角处的利用提高了使用率，但就与服务阳台的结合方面，应优先考虑一字形和 U 形布置方式。

阳台。阳台分服务阳台与生活阳台两种。由于回迁民以农民为主，原来的农具存放成为回迁后的一大问题。服务阳台的设计为其提供了安置的场所。服务阳台常与厨房结合，满足存储、洗衣、摘菜等功能。生活阳台应避免设在主卧，以免因晾晒休闲等行为经过卧室，打扰家人休息。其可与客厅结合，冬季阳台封闭做成落地玻璃窗，形成阳光间利用太阳能采暖，实现保温节能的效果。由于回迁房面积有限，阳台宽设为 1.2m 即可满足日常晾晒衣物的基本使用要求，保证更多的面积留给室内空间。

卫生间。调研发现，回迁房设计中卫生间常出现视线干扰，门的位置影响其他使用功能，储藏柜空间不足，数量安排不合理等问题。与厨房相似，卫生间也是设备管道集中的地方，与厨房相邻，不仅有利于管线布置更有利于干湿分区。设计时除要直接采光通风，满足洗手、如厕、洗澡等基本功能外，在回迁房中尽量使淋浴空间位于角落，湿区在内，干区在外，如果可能将洗衣机放置临近卫生间的外部。由于卫生间要放置各种卫生纸、巾、盆、拖把等零碎物品，对其中的储藏功能，台面宽度要求较高。另外，亦可将盥洗盆放在过道，如厕盥洗互不干扰。

值得一提的是回迁房设计中储藏空间的设计。回迁前居民生活在拥有大庭院大面积的住所里，回迁后生活空间压缩，农具、被褥衣物的存放对橱柜、储藏空间的要求高于普通商品房住宅，在设计时应有所顾虑；门厅作为室内外空间的过渡，驻足、更衣换鞋、零时物品的储藏、存放空间成为必须；客厅由于其多功能性导致客厅内物品种类复杂，零散物品层出不穷，除要有足够的墙面放置家具外，还要有专门的地方保存零碎物品；厨房虽然功能较为简单，但操作的高效、便利离不开足够存储柴米油盐、锅碗瓢盆等物品的空间以及良好便利的相应存储位置。便利整洁的储藏空间设计不仅给回迁民带来便利的生活，还为实现一个舒适、赏心悦目的家提供坚实的基础。

3 可持续性设计

随着生活水平的提高，人民生活方式的不断改变，对住宅的要求也相应提高。在追求可持续发展的现今，住宅的可持续性设计也成为大家关注的对象之一。本文从住宅的多样性和节能两个方面对回迁房的可持续性进行探讨。

3.1 多样性设计

不同对象的生活方式及社会结构不同，其对生活空间的需求也有很大差异。与商品房设计之初就有明确目标人群不同，回迁房的目标对象是原住于城镇的农民，家庭结构构成复杂，既有新婚的一代居，也有父母两代共同生活的二代居，甚至三代同堂的三代居。不同的家庭结构对居住空间要求不同，家庭结构的改变也使得居住空间做出相应的变化。

所以，在户型设计中应当考虑各种家庭的使用情况，设计时应该采取一定的方式使回迁居民在后期的使用过程中可以按自己的需求对空间进行灵活的调整和改造。

（1）灵活墙的运用。在回迁房设计中，用灵活墙适当的替换部分非承重墙是提高空间适应性最重要的手段之一。灵活墙是指可以更换位置的非承重墙，由轻质材料构成，存在于在地板与承重墙之间，可以在不改变整体结构的居住空间中添加或删除。

居民回迁后的居住时间里，家庭会出现生长发展的过程，对套内空间的要求相应产生变化。通过灵活墙的适用，在对住宅改造最小的前提下实现大小空间的分割与合并，以满足不同时期的使用需求。如将空间较大的起居室或卧室划分出一间卧室、儿童房或书房等，或不需要时将其还原为一个统一的大空间。同时，灵活墙还可以结合壁柜形成储藏空间，充分提高空间的使用效率。

（2）采用门式隔断等对家具进行处理。回迁房设计中可采用推拉门、折叠对开门对过渡空间进行分隔，如把其将餐厅与起居室、餐厅与厨房、门厅与起居室相连接，实现空间的分割与合并。同时，在储藏空间合理的基础上将室内家具与墙体整合或成为墙体的一部分以简化室内布置，从心理上扩大空间，实现空间的多样性。

（3）运用空间回路手法。空间回路原指"在建筑空间中可以循环地行走及观看，体验步移景异的感受"[1]。在回迁房设计中可以将阳台与客厅、卧室相连接，或阳台与主次卧相连接，形成回路，营造出多样化的室内行为动线；也可以在非承重墙上增设洞口，在视觉上形成空间回游，为父母在忙于家务的过程中照看孩子提供可能。空间回路的设计不仅摆脱了原先单调反复的路径，提供了多条动线，增加了室内通风采光（图1），还加强了家庭成员间的交流。同时，多选择的路径和窗洞的开设给住户带来多角度的体验和丰富的空间层次感。

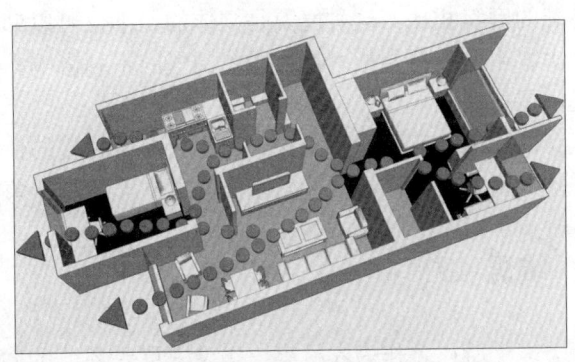

图1　空间回路下的室内通风
（资料来源：笔者自绘）

3.2　节能设计

回迁后居民原有的经济链条被打破，不仅要缴水电费，还增加了物业、暖气等费用，这对于多年来处于烧炕取暖，自给自足的农民来说是一笔不小的支出。因此，对回迁房进行节能设计，降低取暖费用，减少居民回迁前后生活支出差距不容忽视。

（1）太阳能的利用。北方住宅冬季采暖是最需要解决的问题。平面上，建筑南向布置阳光间，冬季白天蓄热夜间释放热量给房间供暖，结合空间回路手法实现热气流通，构造简单，造价低廉。同时在屋顶和阳台安置太阳能集热板，主被动式太阳能相结合，不仅能提高回迁房的舒适度，更能实现建筑节能，降低农民居住成本的效果。

（2）合理控制住宅的体形系数。建筑的体形系数与建筑外表面积有关，体形系数越大，从墙体散失的热量越多。在保证回迁房南向采光采暖合理的同时，减少立面凹凸，把体型系数控制在有效范围是减少建筑散热的有效措施。

此外，注意墙体保温、合理确定窗墙面积、门窗比、屋顶的保温等措施在回迁房节能设计中也至关重要。

4 传统院落空间的延续

院落式住宅是中国传统的经典住宅形式，院落作为一种空间组织手法，具有活动交叉、功能模糊以及景观渗透三重属性，这些空间属性能很好的促进家庭成员间的交流、邻里间的交往，感受自然。回迁后居民被安置在封闭狭小的楼上，生活环境发生了很大改变。院落的丧失使居民不仅缺少了邻里间的人文关怀，更缺少了感受自然的精神体验。对传统院落生活的延续也成为高质量回迁房设计的一个重点。

（1）阳台在实用功能和与自然的联系方面与传统院落相似，在回迁房设计中，适当的扩大阳台、露台空间，使其与客厅融为一体，有利于扩大室内空间的生活状态，是延续院落空间常用的手法。

（2）宅前花园。在每栋楼前设置一个入户花园，以楼栋为单位，回迁民入户前经过一个自有空间，形成室外公共空间和家庭生活空间的过渡，增强回迁民从开放到私密过程的心里体验。由于该入户花园可以进行驻足、交往，进行邻里间的互动，与传统院落中"前院"相似，成为延续院落空间的另一种手法。

（3）对局部楼层进行开敞设计。通过侧面开敞，引入自然，形成回迁楼中公共的空间庭院。与传统的庭院相比，这种庭院是立体的，不仅可以仰望天空，还可鸟瞰地面景观，增加了竖向的空间层次。由于上覆楼板，还摆脱了天气的不利影响，虽然会牺牲一定的面积，但为回迁民之间的交往提供了更多的机会。

通过以上三种设计手法，努力在高楼林立的住宅中营造一片绿地，一片宁静的交往空间，寻回失落的庭院文化，还原礼乐相成、共享天伦的景象。

5 结语

综上所述，作为农村集约建设中重要环节的回迁房，设计时应该注重对其自身特殊性的分析，了解各功能空间的特点，有针对性地进行解决。同时，考虑家庭的生长发展周期，采用低技术低成本实现建筑的多样性和节能，达到住宅的可持续性设计，并对注重院落空间的延续。通过对以上三方面问题的分析对回迁房进行设计，在当前新型城镇化大力发展的背景下，不仅有利于保证住宅的质量，保证新型城镇化的质量，更有利于推动我国现代化的发展。

Research on Affordable Housing Under the Background of the New Urbanization

Hu Wenhui, Gao Rui, Zhao Xinyue, Lin Hongda
(School of Architecture and Fine Art, Dalian University of Technology)

Abstract: Under the background of the new type of rapid development of urbanization, the intensive construction in rural areas is becoming more and more important. In this paper, we discussed the affordable housing under the background of intensive construction in rural areas. We introduced the particularity of lifestyle of the residents and their special requirements for living space. Three aspects of the affordable housing design were discussed, including residential fine, sustainability and the continuation of the courtyard space. Our purpose was to design a habitable, energy-efficient

138

housing，which guarantees the quality of the development of new type of urbanization.

Keywords：New type of urbanization，Affordable housing，Fine design，Diversity，Energy saving

参考文献：

[1]　周燕珉. 住宅精细化设计[M]. 北京：中国建筑工业出版社，2008.

[2]　吕忠正. 集合住宅地域性与生态性整合设计策略研究[D]. 辽宁：大连理工大学，2010.

[3]　王玮龙. 中小户型居住空间弹性设计研究[D]. 辽宁：大连理工大学，2013.

[4]　姜涌，段勇. 集合住宅储藏空间设计[J]. 华中建筑，2009，03：51-56.

[5]　范恩闯. 商品房工程中回迁房项目设计研究[D]. 北京：北京建筑大学，2014.

[6]　GB 50096—2011. 住宅设计规范[S]. 北京：中国建筑工业出版社，2011.

[7]　GB 50016—2014. 建筑设计防火规范[S]. 北京：中国计划出版社，2015.

[8]　GB 50352—2005. 民用建筑设计通则[S]. 北京：中国建筑工业出版社，2005.

浙江中部地区城乡新社区集聚背景下人居环境重构的设计策略研究

李 乘 沈 杰

（浙江大学建筑工程学院）

摘要：本文从目前全国新型城镇化发展进程的区域性产业集聚特征分布考虑，选择了极具代表性的且对城乡传统人居环境冲击相对比较剧烈的浙江省中部发达地区城乡新社区集聚区建设作为主要研究对象。从城乡人居环境学所关注的人文关怀视角出发，通过浙江省义乌市新社区各镇街新社区集聚区的各类别集聚建设项目的调研、策划、设计和施工等的全建设周期的参与实践，分步骤完成各阶段实施过程中的"动态人居环境信息处理及反馈设计模块数据库"的建设。为国内现阶段针对沿海省份产业发达地区大规模城乡集聚战略推行和与之对应的新社区人居环境建设保障，提供更翔实的具有社会学意义的城乡建筑规划学设计基础。使之成为全国新型城镇化战略下，各种类别产业集聚模式和与之相对应的城乡人居环境重构体系的系统性设计方法提供系列创新的可能。

关键词：城乡新社区集聚区建设，人居环境重构，产业/居住集聚，动态人居环境信息处理系统的设计模块数据库，数字化信息收集处理分析平台，基于体验式周期性反馈的创新设计方法

1 引言

浙江产业集群的发展是浙江经济发展的一大特色和优势。浙江省产业集群是由市场选择、当地特定经济条件和社会文化背景决定的，在一定地域空间集聚而形成具有比较优势、能带动当地经济和社会发展的特色产业及其组织形式，其中相当一部分是当地产业和专业性商品市场互为依托、联动发展的一镇一品、一县一业的"区域块状经济"；有的是在特定条件下（如有利的区位、特殊的人缘关系、传统的能工巧匠）从家庭到工业、合伙企业或乡村集体企业起步，形成具有比较优势的小企业集群和专业化产业区[1]（浙江省委政策研究室，2002）。

作为"中国小商品城"之称的义乌市，在围绕小商品大市场已形成服装、针织、饰品、拉链、玩具、小五金、印刷与毛纺八大优势制造业集群的基础上，在产业集群经济效应与政策的引导下，制造业迅速向义乌经济技术开发区、五个工业园区与七个特色工业园区集聚，进一步形成以园区为载体的新型制造业集聚中心。产业集聚在空间布局上日趋完善，工业园区有效地提升了农村工业化的质量。更重要的是，在产业集群经济促进下，交通运输业、电信服务业、旅游餐饮业、房地产业与各种服务业迅速发展，2003 年第三产业在 GDP 的比重达 43.7％，而工业、各种服务业的迅速发展产生的就业乘数效应促进了农村劳动力的转移，自 20 世纪 80 年代初以来，义乌市 31.6 万农村劳动力中，就有 22 万人转向了第二、第三产业，实质性地推动了城镇化进程，城镇化水平从 1978 年的 8％提高到 2003 年 55 ％。显而易见，义乌产业集群与工业化、城镇化互动发展成功模式就表现在农村工业—产业集群（围绕小商品市场）—工业园区—产业劳动力结构升级—就业乘数效应—城镇化进程这种互促共进的良性循环关系上[2]（徐剑锋，2002；笔者整理）。

2 浙江中部地域产业分布特征和城乡新社区集聚的动态发展关系

在以义乌为典型的浙江中部商品经济发达地区，凡是具有良好集聚效应的工业园区作为地方工业生产活动的主要空间载体，在带动地方经济结构与产业空间组织调整的同时势必连锁性地引发就业结构的变化，并从多方面、全方位地驱动城市空间结构演进。（1）工业园区内的产业集聚成长、发展对用工的需求，其本身如同一个巨大的劳动力吸纳市场，在给城镇人口提供就业机会的同时，也吸收了大量农村人口，并通过劳动力的转移实现人口城镇化；（2）工业园区建设发展所催化、引

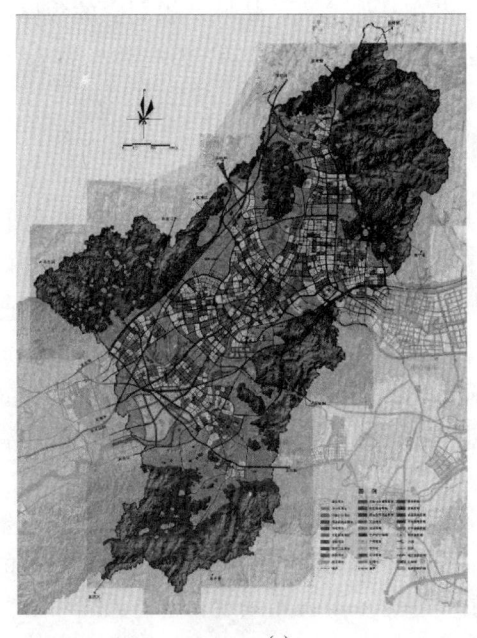

(a) (b)

图1 义乌市域总体规划图

(a)《义乌市域总体规划（2006—2020）》；(b)《义乌市域总体规划（2006—2020）》
［资料来源：(a) 浙江省城乡规划设计研究院，义乌市建设局2006；
(b) 中国城市规划设计研究院，义乌市规划设计研究院，2015年3月］

发的城市新区建成、经济活动的空间重组、人口的迁移流动及社会的阶层分化与空间隔离化，也影响和改变着城市各个区段之间的关系，从而带动城市地域功能的分化演替，最终改变城市功能格局及城市整体的地域结构特征；（3）依托城市所具有的功能，为工业园区内从事生产、服务的人群提供必需的居住、教育等服务，反过来促进了工业园区及其产业集群的进一步发展[3]（王慧，2003；笔者整理）。

凡是能够满足市场需求（与国内、国际市场接轨），围绕产业链（或者价值链）有效地进行分工、合作的企业群落，基于竞争能力地提升（交易成本的下降、产品的多样性、差异性、知识学习），则在特定的区域就会衍生出新的产业区（产业集群区），而产业集群区的一系列乘数效应则自然而然地迸发出劳动力（人口）集中、生产性服务业的发展、技术水平的提升，使得产业集群区的本身成了一个生产、服务和被服务的中心，促进了人口的非农化和第三产业的发展；同时，产业集群使得地方经济得以发展，无论在产业集群区就业的劳动力、还是从事相关服务业的劳动力的收入水平提高，使得其对城市文明生活的向往逐步得以实现，所有这些环环相扣的环节，在促进工业化、城镇化过程中发挥着不可低估的作用；另一方面，城镇所具有的一些功能性服务，如技术培训、人力资源、基础设施、生活配套性服务等又为产业集群区的进一步发展提供了支撑；而城镇人口规模的逐步扩大又为产业的发展提供了更为强劲的消费市场（消费容量和消费能力），进一步促进了与市场接轨的产业集群发展，从而形成地方产业集群与工业化、城镇化互促共进良性循环。[4]

在此次调研中，笔者参与的建筑设计团队——浙江省建工建筑设计院有限公司隶属于浙江省建设投资集团有限公司。作为三家与义乌市政府战略协议的代建总承包单位之一（另外两家单位分别是绿城房产建设管理有限公司以及中国联合工程公司）。作为建筑设计师的我很荣幸地参与了义乌市城乡新社区集聚项目的大量建筑规划和实践活动，当面对汹涌而至的城镇化浪潮之下，各种集聚项目蜂拥而至，笔者不禁犹豫再三，传统设计理念和方法能否适应新时代城乡产业集聚的总体要求。也正是通过这一系列充分的大型工程实践过程的反复思考，笔者逐渐开始思考如何合理的处理好在新型城镇化进程中，新社区建设中充分考虑被安置居民的新城市生活；如何在近乎一朝一夕之间，尽量弱化空间居住环境聚变所产生的社会问题和潜在其他危机。从城乡规划学的角度出发却又不同于传统建筑规划设计的手段来实现上述目标的达成。

3　集聚民的心理特征和行为模式的考察调研

首先，我们将被安置居民群体在面对其人居环境变化的心理感受和行为模式作为核心线索展开：选取居住区集聚和产业集聚推行分别对应形成了被安置人群各自的全新的城市新社区的生活空间组团和工作空间组团的各自行为特征模式。[5]用社会行为对城市居住和工作空间的变化产生的反应状况建立行为模式监控模拟的人居环境学的解析体系。以特定时间段的居住期作为维度进行问卷式的调研互动，以求得各种特定新社区集聚安置模式下，不同村落构成新居住组团的特有状态和情况。这种调研的方式往往渗透在整个城乡产业规划过程中，在不同的项目推进阶段，需要有不同侧重的且与之匹配的人居环境的考虑。

乡村和城市生活空间特征的转换，不仅仅是在房屋户型和造型上的改动，而是其基本生活资料的变化。行为模式，不再由自然村落的体系来界定，而是开始在城市的维度进行，大规模的乡村扁平化的水平乡野流线，由高层的居住社区取代。阡陌交通的乡野自然景观，也有人工小区的集中绿化组团所取代。这一系列集聚民众的心理特征模拟和行为模式变化，需要由两部分的设计考虑，第一部分，是前期的规划设计中，充分考虑到原有村落各自的风貌文化特质和生活元素构成，这一系列的建筑规划空间特质和景观要素，虽然已经天壤之别，但是还是可以通过一系列的建筑构成和景观重塑给予必要的优化和重新构成。[6]比如在设计中，不用过分欧式的建筑元素和园林构成手法转而细分和追本溯源原先各个村落的形态文化要素，将各自高层组团和次级构成和原有村落拆迁构成的自然村做整合性重新设计。一定程度重塑家族系下的村落形态特质，将新的现代居住区组团和原有村落构成体系进行优化对比，而不是割裂和放弃。[7]第二部分则是通过充分考虑的设计以后，在入住阶段后持续跟踪走访得到的新的资讯信息，建立相关的人居环境持续数字化信息收集处理分析平台来弥补后期项目中所缺失的居民生活要素的考虑和不足。这一数据库的设置和运行将可以为以后类似项目的设计关注点做更为全面的分析和设计规划支持。

4　居住区集聚民的普遍问题和挑战

其次，被安置居民在居住区集聚中所不可避免地产生两大方面的问题：（1）对传统人居环境居住空间上的巨大冲击和缺失。从传统乡居文化特质的生活模式剥离到了新城市社区的日常生活行为模式的转变，政府在新社区集聚政策推行的力度与居住人群快速城镇化过程中的适应能力，在很大程度上无法实现匹配。[8]导致了城市新社区在空间秩序上城镇化的成功和居民个体行为模式的市民化不适应之间产生了巨大的鸿沟。从产业结构特征上说，手工艺加工为基础的产业模式一定程度上脱离了农业生产资料的掣肘，但是依然无法改变生活方式等方面和城市的区别。[9]（2）与此同时，基于新兴产业导向为基础的产业和工业集聚，又使得居民们产生工作场所和工作性质上相对之前传统工艺方法和流程的差异性。这种双向反差不可避免的导致昨天的农民面临一朝变市民的尴尬境地。[10]尤其是针对部分下山农业户籍为主的拆迁安置居民，更为明显地感受到生产生活上的城乡巨大差异性。

5　系统性解决方案的提出

基于此，作者希望提出建立以城市新社区的居民实现集聚过程中，将集聚区的居住空间组团和工作空间组团中行为模式和心理状态的模拟和调研，借助数字化信息收集处理分析为平台的体验式周期性反馈的创新设计方法。尽力在空间构成方法和材质运用等建筑学手法最大化弱化现代高层居住集聚区和集中式产业集聚区对新社区居民由于环境巨变所产生的消极影响[11]。将城镇化政策背景下的社会人关怀通过人居环境的要素重新构建的方法和策略，实现城市新社区在动态集聚后，社会文化稳定和产业效应的继续繁荣。

6 产业集聚区和居住区集聚区建设的实施进程以及其突出问题

特别选择《义乌市城乡新社区集聚建设实施办法（试行）》以及基于特定建筑规划设计项目为基础的实际案例来遴选分析，针对义乌这样典型的小商品发达的城乡地区，在推行城乡新社区集聚建设的过程中，都遇到了哪一些问题，又该如何来解决和处理上述问题。办法中提到："……所称城乡新社区集聚建设是指按照价值置换方式，实行多村集中联建，采用高层公寓加产业用房、商业用房、商务楼宇、货币等多种形式置换，推动农村向社区转变，农民向市民转变。"其中的多村集中联建，表明了多数农民离开了其之前数代所居住的乡村，利用市场价值置换的方式，居住到一个新的城乡结合的新社区。这一新社区的设计和规划则大多数由现代建筑市场化产物的地产设计手段来进行。总平面布置形态均采用了现代居住区规划设计的手法，以下就是我院设计的义乌苏溪第一集聚区新院区块规划建筑设计方案总平面图以及分期开发设计规划：

项目由附近的几大村落构成，安置居住民分别来原先自然形态的村落。相互之间本来的邻里关系被忽然拉近，加之原先的低层居住建筑被高层所取代。我们在方案设计过程中，按照居住区级组团和邻里组团两大居住单元体系构成，统一层面的规划设计和各分区融合原始地缘村落相结合的手法和方式来进行，并且充分考虑了其分期开发居住拆迁的可能性。

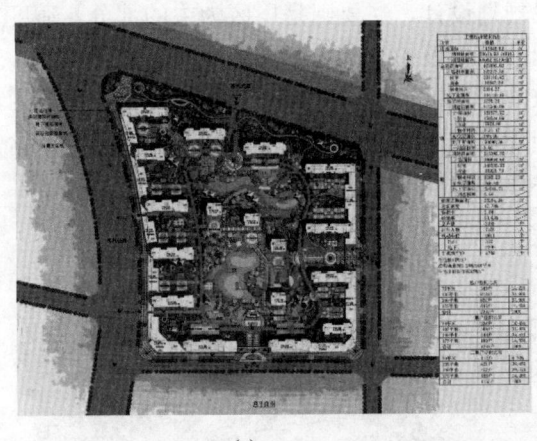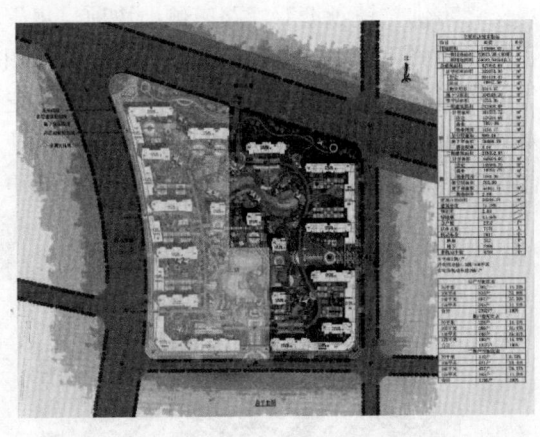

(a)   *(b)*

图 2　义乌苏溪第一集聚区新院区块规划建筑设计方案总平面图

(a) 项目规划设计总平面图；*(b)* 项目分期实施总平面图

（资料来源：浙江省建设投资集团有限公司，浙江省建工建筑设计院有限公司，2013 年 12 月）

7 产业集聚项目实践和分析

产业集聚项目分布于义乌各个区域，其中选取了稠州街道的产业集聚区项目以及佛堂镇的项目作为例子来进行说明。产业集聚需要解决的问题更多是为了新的新社区集聚居民的工作生活之用[12]。义乌主要民间作坊形式生产的主要有针织类、小商品类等，普遍面积不大，因而其柱网分割方式更趋向规整且有利于分割分配。

8　实际产业集聚项目分析

义乌市稠江街道产业集聚用房，主要分为厂区部分以及其宿舍区和办公区等。基本的总图构图采用的是规整的方式，产业组团间以连廊相连，方便货梯的运输和交通的便利性。办公和宿舍组团相对独立于厂区设计，并且有相对独立的出入口。

(a)　　　　　　　　　　　　　(b)

图3　义乌市稠江街道产业集聚用房建筑规划设计方案

(a) 项目规划街角鸟瞰图；(b) 项目规划设计总平面图

（资料来源：浙江省建设投资集团有限公司，浙江省建工建筑设计院有限公司，2014年5月）

义乌市佛堂镇盘塘双峰路南侧地块项目集聚建设规划设计，主要则是厂区为主的部分，适度布置了部分办公用房和辅助用房。基本的总图构图采用的是规整的方式，产业组团间以连廊相连，方便货梯的运输和交通的便利性。整体布局都缺乏细致的规划景观要素的重组和构成，相对比较简单粗暴地处理了工作环境的变迁和安置的新型工业工作环境对安置民众的变迁意义所在。这方面给予的创作空间和余地很小，我们也依然在尝试着更为合适和合理的手法。

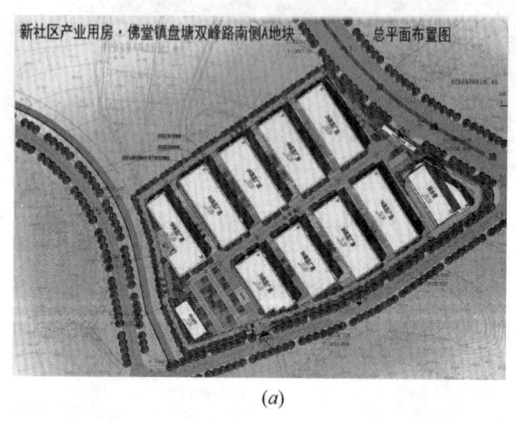
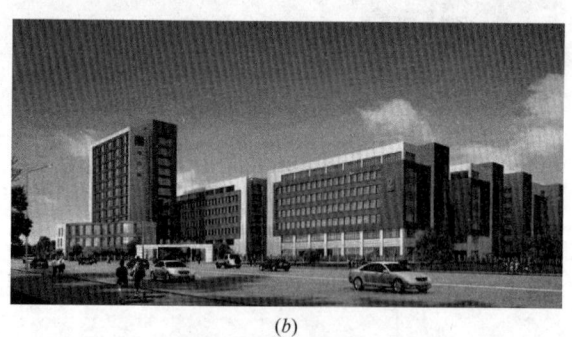

(a)　　　　　　　　　　　　　(b)

图4　义乌市佛堂镇盘塘双峰路南侧A地块集聚建设建筑规划设计方案

(a) 项目规划设计总平面图；(b) 项目街角透视图

（资料来源：浙江省建设投资集团有限公司，浙江省建工建筑设计院有限公司，2014年8月）

致谢

非常感谢浙江大学建筑工程学院博士生导师沈杰教授长期以来的悉心指导和帮助，感谢浙江省建设投资集团有限公司和浙江省建工建筑设计院有限公司的长期培养和项目支持，特别是庄月金院长的倾力帮助才使得此次研究能够充分展开。

The Integrated Design Strategies Research for Reconfiguration of Human Settlements Environment under the New Community Agglomeration Process in the Middle Area of Zhejiang Province

Li Cheng，Shen Jie

(College of Civil Engineering and Architecture，Zhejiang Universtiy)

Abstract：This article starts to oversee the features and effects of regional industrial agglomeration distribution under the national level new urban development process today，and choose the typical but the most challenged to the traditional human settlement district—the very well economic developed middle part of Zhejiang Province，as the research target. With the perspective from the human caring point from the discipline of urban and rural human settlement，through a serials of architecture design and construction projects for Zhejiang Yiwu New Community Industrial and Residential Agglomeration in different towns and streets，we started to finish all the phrases step by step towards building up the Data-based Modular Design Strategies for the Dynamic Information Processing System regarding Human Settlement. This particular design system will be extremely effective to provide the profound significance for the urban and rural architecture planning research foundation during national industrial/residential agglomeration strategies of the well-developed district on the east coast of China and their residential agglomeration process accordingly. For the purpose of creating an possible systematic and effective design approach for diverse industrial agglomeration and their reconstruction of living residential human settlement under the general national new urban planning strategies.

Keywords：The construction of urban and rural new community，The reconstruction of human settlement，Industrial/residential agglomeration，The data-based modular design strategies for the dynamic information processing system regarding human settlement，The platform for information collection and analysis with digital techniques，The daily living experience based periodical design information feedback loops as An innovative strategies.

参考文献：

[1] 徐维祥. 产业集群与城镇化互动发展机制及运作模式研究[M]. 北京：经济科学出版社，2009.

[2] 徐剑锋. 发达地区县域城市化特征及其存在的问题——以浙江省义乌市为例[J]. 上海经济研究，2002，12：54-62.

[3] 王慧. 开发区与城市相互关系的内在肌理及空间效应[J]. 城市(6)徐维祥，唐根年，陈秀君：产业集群与工业化、城镇化互动发展模式研究 871 规划，2003，3：20 -25.

[4] 徐维祥，唐根年. 基于产业集群成长的浙江省农村劳动力转移实证研究[J]. 中国农村经济，2004，6：70 -76.

[5] 李丽萍. 城市人居环境[M]. 北京：中国轻工业出版社，2001.

[6] 李王鸣，叶信岳，孙于. 城市人居环境评价——以杭州城市为例[J]. 经济地理，1999，19.

[7] 苏雪串. 城市化进程中的要素集聚、产业集群和城市群发展[J]. 中央财经大学学报，2004，

1：49 -52.

[8]　郭克莎. 工业化与城市化关系的经济学分析[J]. 中国社会科学，2002，2：44 -55.

[9]　吴良镛. 关于人居环境科学[J]. 城市发展研究，1996(1).

[10]　仇保兴. 新型工业化、城镇化与企业集群[J]. 现代城市研究，2004，1：17-23.

[11]　张智，魏忠庆. 城市人居环境评价体系的研究及应用[J]. 生态环境 2006，15(1)：198-201.

[12]　王玲慧. 大城市边缘地区空间整合与社区发展[M]. 北京：中国建筑工业出版社，2008.

以农业种植为导向的北京地区集合住宅室内热环境研究

刘 烨[1] 张 睿[2]

（1 北京建筑大学；2 天津大学）

摘要： 粮食安全和食物里程问题促使人们转向城市、城郊等传统意义上的非农业地区寻找可耕种土地。近年来，居民在建筑室内或阳台的种植实践屡见不鲜。然而，由于城市建筑空间环境并不适合农业种植，这种方式不仅收益有限，也不利于建筑空间和城市景观的塑造。本研究以北京地区城市集合住宅为对象，对封闭阳台和室内空间进行热环境测量试验。旨在表明，在冬季和春季，部分集合住宅测点温度环境条件适合农作物种植；夏季，所有测点的温度环境条件都不适宜种植。

关键词： 垂直农业，建筑-农业一体化，室内种植，集合住宅，热环境测量

1 引言

粮食安全和食物里程问题数十年来备受关注。一方面，随着人口增加和耕地减少，全球范围的粮食安全问题日益严重。为了应对全球饥饿问题，人们不得不将寻找可耕种土地的目光转向城市、城郊这些传统意义上的非农业地区。[1,2]另一方面，基于全球化经济，运输业的技术进步和产业发展，蔬菜、水果等农产品的"食物里程"不断提高。而中国由于人均耕地面积远低于世界平均水平，且城镇化进程推进快速，食品窘境更为突出。为解决上述问题，城市农业和基于建筑的垂直农业逐渐为人们所关注。在实践方面，近年来，城市居民的室内种植、屋顶农园或阳台农园实践屡见不鲜。

在理论层面，造成农产品生产和运输消耗资源大的原因有两个：温室大棚、智能温室为代表的设施农业生产能耗，而远途运输农产品的高"食物里程"。二者产生的根本原因都是当地气候和天气条件不适宜进行露天农业生产。[3,4]相对于当地自然环境一年四季的剧烈变化，农作物生长和人日常生活、工作活动，对温度和光照的需求相对集中，适宜温度和舒适温度的较大范围可以确定在 10～30℃。[5,6]实际生活中，黄河以北的城市建筑冬季供暖、夏季空调降温，具有一定的温度环境调节控制资源。而北京地区集合住宅的封闭阳台、室内窗台和地面空间，都可以进行农业种植，城市建筑具有农业种植的潜力。城市集合住宅中进行农业种植生产确有存在土壤。然而，城市建筑的空间环境并不适合农业种植，这种室内活动与空间环境的"不配套"不仅影响了农作物种植收益，也不利于建筑空间环境和城市整体景观的塑造。

2 现状及实验目的

通过对种植活动参与者及组织者的访谈，结合自身的种植活动经验，取得了种植活动的基本年度周期表，并提出假设：在集合住宅主要居室冬季供暖，春、夏两季正常使用的前提下，北京地区封闭阳台和室内靠窗区域冬季适宜农业种植，春季随着太阳光照强度增加、日照时间延长，某一时段起不再适宜种植，夏季室内环境则不适宜农业种植。实验旨在明确北京地区集合住宅是否满足农作物种植温度需求，总结这类空间环境特点，并尝试基于现有集合住宅提出改进策略。

3 热环境实验

北京的平原地区年平均气温为 11～13℃，1 月平均温度为 -4～-5℃，7 月平均温度约为

26℃^[7]，温度差异大，在中国建筑气候分区中，属寒冷地区。该地区建筑以防寒保温为主，兼顾防热。热环境实验以北京地区城市集合住宅为对象，针对建筑室内和封闭阳台内部，选取冬季大寒日前后，春季集中供暖结束后，夏季大暑节气前后，进行实验（图1）。

阳台测点（如②-a、③-a、⑤-a、⑥-a）位于阳台的几何中心，距地面100cm；室内测点（如①-a）距南向采光面75cm正中，距地面100cm。①

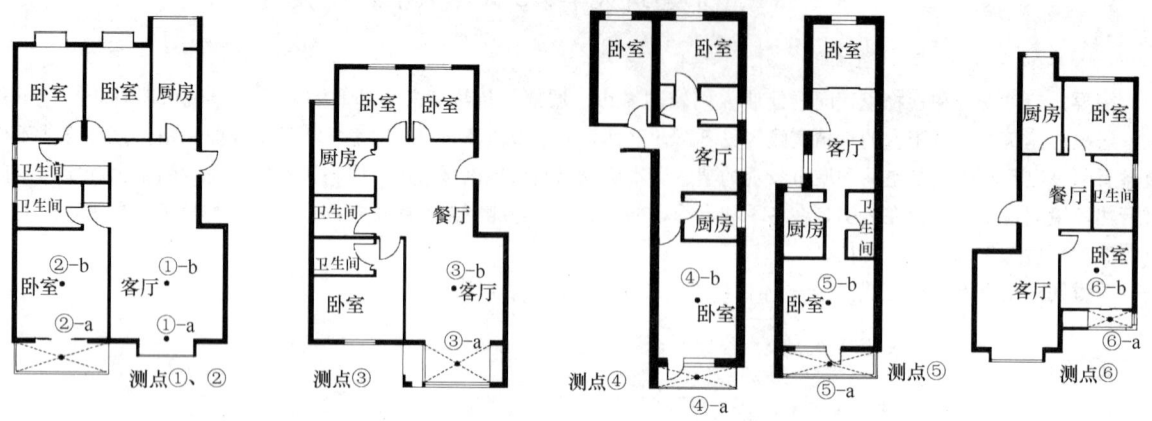

图1　测点区域分布图

数据分析时，采用两种方式判断该点是否满足农作物温度需求：（1）明确极限温度值和基本温度范围，将测点的日最高、最低和平均温度，与室外环境和其他测点比较。（2）农作物生长适宜的日夜温度不同。实验选取对温度和光照要求较低的白菜和绿叶菜类，以日间20～30℃（20～25℃最佳）、夜间10～20℃（10～15℃最佳）为标准，计算测量当天日夜满足要求的时间总长，并进行比较。

3.1　冬季实验

冬季测量实验时间为2013年1月9日～17日。实验目的：（1）基本测点温度环境是否满足农作物需求。（2）总结满足温度需求的空间特点。

3.1.1　日最高温度、最低温度与日较差

测量时段中，室内各测点与室外环境温度有显著差异。1月9日～17日，室外日平均温度始终低于0℃，室内和阳台内测点受供暖的影响，日平均温度分布在7.89～24.32℃之间，明显高于室外。室内外日平均温度差最大可达30.02℃，出现在9日的测点①-a（表1）。

建筑室内和阳台空间测点温度变化幅度达，测量中温度极端最大值为36.56℃（17日的④-a），极端最小值为6.19℃（14日的⑥-a）。其中，测点①-a除16日外，日最低温度高于20℃，②-a、③-a和⑤-a的日最低温度处于15～20℃，测点④-a的日最低温度范围为10～15℃之间，测点⑥-a多日日最低温度低于10℃。测点⑥-a的低温温度过低，测点④-a的低温温度较低，不满足农作物生长需求。在高温方面，除测点②-a（改点测量时段短）外，其余测点的日最高温度都曾超过30℃，其中⑤-a日最高温度达36.56℃（17日）。由于高温过高可能引发农作物徒长或其他病虫害，所以该环境并不适宜种植。不同天气条件下，各个测点的日最低温度较为稳定，日最高温度具较大差异。晴天的日最高温度远高于雾霾天。其中，测点⑥-a在测量时段中不同天气的日最高温度差异最

---

①　实验选取BES-01温度自记仪，分辨率为0.01℃，测量精度±0.5℃，测量范围-30℃～+50℃，测量时间4次/s，记录时段为10min一次。

大，达到20.25℃。

测点①～⑥日最高温度、最低温度、日较差和日平均温度（单位：℃）　　　表1

位置	①-a	②-a	③-a	④-a	⑤-a	⑥-a
测量时段最大值	34.13	27.69	30.69	33.88	36.56	31.38
测量时段最小值	19.56	15.25	18.81	13.13	16.88	6.19
位置	①-a	②-a	③-a	④-a	⑤-a	⑥-a
1.9 / 晴 / −5.7　日最高温度	34.13	27.69				
日最低温度	20.31	16.13				
日平均温度	24.32	19.98				
1.10 / 阴雾 / −6.7　日最高温度	24.94	21.38				
日最低温度	20.63	15.25				
日平均温度	21.92	17.54				
1.13 / 阴雾 / −4.0　日最高温度	24.00		21.31	16.38	20.13	11.13
日最低温度	20.13		18.88	13.19	17.31	6.69
日平均温度	21.07		19.68	13.75	17.78	7.89
1.14 / 阴雾 / −5.8　日最高温度	26.00		23.38	19.75	23.13	23.75
日最低温度	20.44		18.81	13.13	16.88	6.19
日平均温度	21.61		20.01	14.29	18.36	11.92
1.15 / 间晴 / −4.4　日最高温度	27.88		25.13	20.25	24.44	21.25
日最低温度	20.44		18.81	13.13	17.13	6.75
日平均温度	21.98		20.29	14.52	18.44	10.29
1.16 / 晴 / −5.7　日最高温度	29.44		26.44	25.25	26.19	26.06
日最低温度	19.56		19.06	13.31	17.06	6.81
日平均温度	22.88		20.97	15.09	19.33	11.26
1.17 / 晴 / −4.8　日最高温度			30.69	33.88	36.56	31.38
日最低温度			19.25	13.38	17.31	7.19
日平均温度			22.41	16.19	21.52	12.43

3.1.2　符合农作物需温度需求的时长

测点的日间温度处于20～30℃、夜间温度处于10～20℃时，较适于农业种植。[①]测量时段的日间：测点④-a和⑥-a的日间温度长时间低于20℃或高于30℃，不满足农作物的温度需求。①-a，③-a和⑤-a较长时间处于20℃至30℃之间，满足需求。此外，晴天和雾霾天，测点日间温度差异很大。晴天时，①-a处于适宜温度范围内时间仅有5.17小时，阴霾时则始终处于适宜温度范围内。测量时段的夜间：测点①-a夜间温度始终大于20℃，不满足农业种植需求。③-a夜间大部分温度处于15～20℃，短时高于20℃，接近农作物夜间温度需求。②-a、⑤-a夜间温度始终处于15～20℃，符合农作物需求。④-a的夜间温度处于10～15℃，整体较低；⑥-a夜间温度始终低于15℃，且大部时间低于10℃，不满足农作物需求（表2、表3）。

---

① 时长计算以10min为基本单位，四舍五入日出、日落的时间。1月9～10日间时长9.67h，夜间14.33h。13～14日间时长9.67h，夜间14.33h。15～17日间时长10h，夜间14h。在天气方面，13～14日的日照时间为0h，15～17日则分别为2.7h、6.1h和8.0h。

9 日~10 日，测点①-a 和②-a 满足农作物日夜温度需求时间表（单位：h） 表2

测点 温度范围	1.9		1.10	
	测点①-a	测点②-a	测点①-a	测点②-a
日间 20～30℃	5.17 (2.67)	7.83 (5)	9.67	4.67
夜间 10～20℃	0	14.33	0	14.33

13 日~17 日，测点①、③、④、⑤和⑥满足农作物日夜需求时间表（单位：h） 表3

测量日期	测点 温度范围	测点①-a	测点③-a	测点④-a	测点⑤-a	测点⑥-a
1.13	日间 20～30℃	9.67	5.5	0	0.5	0
	夜间 10～20℃	0	14.34	14.34 (14.34)	14.33	0
1.14	日间 20～30℃	9.67 (1.5)	7	0	4.83	5.67
	夜间 10～20℃	0	13.33	14.34 (14.34)	14.33	1.67 (1.67)
1.15	日间 20～30℃	9 (2.67)	7.5 (0.67)	0	4	1.83
	夜间 10～20℃	0	13.5	14 (14)	14	0
1.16	日间 20～30℃	10 (5.67)	8 (3)	2.67	9.33 (3.67)	3 (1.17)
	夜间 10～20℃	0	9.83	14 (14)	14	0
1.17	日间 20～30℃		9.17 (4.33)	3 (1)	4.33 (2)	2.83 (2.33)
	夜间 10～20℃		7.5	14 (14)	14	1.5 (1.5)

注：1. 日间温度中（n）表示总时中 25～30℃的时长；
2. 夜间温度中（n）表示总时中 10～15℃的时长。

测量时段中，部分测点满足农作物的温度需求。其中，测点③-a 和⑤-a 最接近农作物种植的温度需求，符合农作物夜间温度需求，且在日间较长时间满足要求。其余各点中，测点①-a 夜间温度过高，测点④-a 和⑥-a 则夜间温度及阴霾天气时日间温度过低，均不适宜农作物种植。

3.2 春季测量实验

春季测量实验仅选取测点①和②，时间为 2013 年 4 月 2 日~5 月 1 日。日常使用时，①和②仅在正午及下午时段短暂通风。②的阳台门日间开启宽度大于夜间。实验目的为确定停止供暖后，建筑室内和阳台空间温度环境是否满足农作物需求。

测量中，室外的日最低温度在 0.5℃（6 日）~13.3℃（9 日）之间，4 月 20 日前始终低于 10℃。室外日最高温度在 9.2℃（19 日）~28.6℃（29 日）之间，仅有 10 个测量日的日最高温度高于 20℃，环境不适宜露天种植。室内测点除 2 日的测点②（14.38℃）外，日最低温度均大于 15℃，除 4 日的测点②外，日最高温度均大于 20℃，相对而言，适宜农业种植。然而，27 日以后，两测点夜间温度都高于 20℃，不再适宜种植。此外，测量时段中，①日间温度在 20～30℃时长为 329.83h，②则为 279.50h。①①夜间温度处于 10～20℃的时长 142.33h，②则为 242.67h（表4）。三个不同时段中，测点①日间温度达到 20℃的时间长，夜间在 20℃以下时间短，环境整体温度高。结果表明，4 月 24 日前，室外不具备农作物种植的温度条件，室内温度环境满足基本需求。4 月 25 日~5 月 1 日，室外温度逐步上升，适宜露天种植。同时段，测点①、②温度整体较高，不再适宜种植。

---

① 测量时段长 30 天，计 720h，日间时长 399h，夜间时长 321h。

4月2日～5月1日，测点①、②满足农作物温度需求的时段（单位：h）   表 4

测点与时间 温度范围	测点①				测点②			
	4.2～4.11	4.12～4.21	4.22～5.1	4.2～5.1	4.2～4.11	4.12～4.21	4.22～5.1	4.2～5.1
日间 20～30℃	78.28	121.39	130.16	329.83	71.32	97.58	110.49	279.5
夜间 10～20℃	90.17	29.83	22.32	142.32	111.17	89.83	41.67	242.67

3.3 夏季测量实验

夏季测量实验时间为 2013 年 7 月 22 日～8 月 1 日，包括阴天、多云和晴天多种天气，测点包括①～④。实验旨在确定夏季最热时段内，室内和阳台空间环境是否满足农作物种植的温度需求。测量时段中，各个测点的温度均超过 20℃。其中，温度处于 20～30℃ 时间最长的是测点②和③。夜间温度在 20～30℃ 时间最长的是测点④，日间温度在 20～30℃ 时间最长的是测点③。总体而言，各个测点中，测点③的温度环境条件最接近农作物的温度需求（表 5）。集合住宅建筑日常使用、日间不开启空调时，建筑室内和阳台空间的温度环境很难满足农作物需求。

测点①-a～④-a 满足农作物日夜需求的时间表（单位：h）   表 5

项目 测点	日间累计小时数		夜间累计小时数	
	20～30℃	30℃及以上	20～30℃	30℃及以上
测点①	70.67	75.00	79.5	14.83
测点②	86.33	59.33	82.5	11.83
测点③	89.5	56.17	84.17	10.17
测点④	75	70.67	90.33	4

3.4 阳台与室内测点温度比较

测量时段中，测点温度受室内供暖、围合面散热、通风换热能力和温室效应积聚热量等几方面影响。其中，日最低温度主要受到建筑室内供暖、通风换热能力和围合面散热影响，不同天气条件下差异不大。日最高温度差异则由该区域积聚热量的能力决定，由太阳光辐射决定。冬季测量实验中，阳台测点③、⑤和①适宜农业种植的时间长度优于其他测点。它们的夜间温度一般低于 20℃，日间温度上升迅速，较长时间停留在 20～30℃ 内，与室内测点相比，夜间温度较低，更适宜农业种植。然而，最不适宜农业种植测点⑥也位于阳台。它夜间温度和阴霾天气的日间温度过低。实验结果表明，如果阳台与室内隔断门隔热效果良好，冬季不开启，则可能引发阳台夜间温度过低。日间，受温室效应的影响，温度上升快，但高温停留时间短，昼夜温差极大，并在晴、雨、阴霾天气时温度差异大。春季测量实验中，虽然难以从测量结果直接比较室内和阳台温度差异，但是阳台测点低温较低，高温可以凭借通风调节。夏季测量实验中，各测点温度均不满足农业种植需求，但具有多个采光通风面的阳台测点，更为接近农作物种植要求。

4 实验结果与空间环境特点分析

首先，满足农作物温度需求的室内和阳台空间都充分利用了建筑供暖资源，能够借助温室效应积聚热量，并充分通风。冬季，建筑供暖是温度环境的重要保障，适宜建筑室内与测量空间热交换能够保障夜间的温度需求，而过度的热交换，可能导致夜间温度过高（测点①），热交换不足则不能达到温度需求（测点⑥）。春季，停止供暖后，温室效应积聚的热量是主要环境温度热量来源，有效减少散热是关键，春季后期，充分通风则是温度环境保障关键。就目前使用条件，夏季较难达

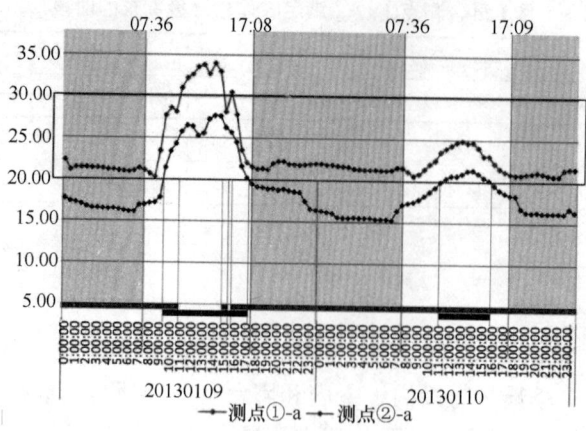

图2 1月9日～10日，测点①、②满足温度需求时间段
（灰色部分为夜间，白色为日间）

到农作物温度环境需求，通风能够在一定程度上提高适宜性。为了提出满足农作物种植的温度和光照环境条件，遮阳网和保温措施是集合住宅室内和阳台空间种植的必备设施。

致谢

国家自然科学基金项目《基于低影响策略的合作型城市农业住区系统构筑及评价》（51208339）

The Study on Agricultural Planting-Oriented Indoor Thermal Environment of Collective Dwellings in Beijing

Liu Ye[1], Zhang Rui[2]
(1. Beijing University of Civil Engineering and Architecture; 2. Tianjin University)

Abstract：Problems of food security and food miles urge people to look for the arable land within urban and suburban areas. Recently, practices of indoor or balcony cultivation are increasingly prevalent. However, most of urban architectural space environment is not suitable for farming, which's limited the profit of planting, as well as the quality of architectural space and city landscape. The study will be focused on city collective dwellings in Beijing area, with thermal environment measurements of enclosure balconies and interior space. The results show that, in winter and spring, part of the measuring location's temperature environment are suitable for crops; in summer, the temperature conditions are not suitable for planting.

Keywords：Vertical farming, Building-integrated agriculture, Indoor planting, Collective dwellings, Thermal environmental surveys

参考文献:

〔1〕 D. Despommier. The Vertical Farm-Feeding the World in the 21st Century. New York：Thomas Dunne Books，2010.

〔2〕 V. Puri and T. Caplow. How to Grow Food in the 100% Renewable City：Building-Integrated Agriculture. Peter Droege. 100% Renewable：Energy Autonomy in Action. London：Earthscan Ltd，2009. 229-241.

[3] A. Viljoen，K. Bohn. Continuous Productive Urban Landscapes：Designing Urban Agriculture for Sustainable Cities. Oxford：Architectural Press，2005.

[4] 申黎明等编著. 人体工程学·人—家具—室内. 第1版[M]. 北京：中国林业出版社，2010.

[5] 程智慧主编. 蔬菜栽培学总论. 第1版[M]. 北京：科学出版社，2010.

[6] 张玉玺. 北京市蔬菜价格波动的特点、原因及对策[J]. 蔬菜，2011，7：4-5.

[7] 中国气象网. [2013-06-01]. http：//www. weather. com. cn.

[8] 孙艺冰，张玉坤. 都市农业在国外建筑和规划领域的研究及应用[J]. 新建筑，2013，4：51-56.

新型城镇化视角下西南乡村建筑创作探讨
——以四川省汉源县九襄镇石牌坊社区为例

曾　卫　尹艺霖

（重庆大学建筑城规学院）

摘要： 随着我国新型城镇化建设的不断推进，乡村聚落也在不断更新和发展。乡村建筑作为乡村特色延续的重要因子，它的更新与发展对乡村而言至关重要。本文从新型城镇化的视角出发，以四川省汉源县九襄镇石牌坊社区为例，通过空间布局、场所重塑、适宜技术等方面的分析，针对当代西南乡村建筑创作的趋势，为改善乡村环境，恢复乡村特色，加强居民对家园的认同，以及保障乡村可持续发展提供一个新的思考角度，同时对我国新城镇化建设下的乡村发展建设具有一定的借鉴意义。

关键词： 新型城镇化，西南地区，乡村，建筑创作

1 引言

乡村是人类聚集的初级体现，乡村以它适宜的尺度、丰富的建筑和空间形式，以及与自然的和谐相处的方式体现着它的优越性。瑞士农业科学家和心理分析学家特奥多尔·阿伯特在《不丧失灵魂的进步》一书中认为，乡村为我们提供接近自然和生态的居住场所，易于把握和识别的社区环境，人们在其中较易实现自我价值。乡村还具有它不可替代的特征和价值，如果我们的乡村和城市一样，将会导致人类精神生活的失调。[1]因此，乡村应该区别于城市拥有属于它自己的美丽。然而，30年的快速城镇化的过程在给乡村带来了经济发展、劳动力解放的同时也给乡村带来了许多负面的问题，例如，人口的缺失，"城乡二元"加剧，土地资源的浪费，生态环境的恶化等，种种原因导致乡村的美丽正在一步步消失。2014年3月中央公布了《国家新型城镇化规划》（2014～2020年），旨在强调以可持续发展为导向的具有中国特色的城镇化建设，优化人居环境，改变人们对乡村的认知。本文以新型城镇化为视角，对汉源县九襄镇石牌坊社区进行分析，力图理清西南传统乡村建设的文化内涵，以及如何在当下的城镇化建设中实现其特有的空间魅力，探索传统乡村聚落保护与更新的新线索。

2 从新型城镇化视角看西南乡村建筑创作

西南地区由于其独特的自然环境、气候、地形、人文、材料、技术等因素，迥异于其他地区，形成自己独特的地域特色。西南乡村的建筑创作是在充分考虑其自然环境、建造材料、建造技艺等方面并结合当地地域文化特点而进行的。城镇化是人类社会发展、进步、繁荣、文明的历史过程。发达国家都经历过城镇化速度上升的过程，我国自改革开放以来城镇化经历了一个速度快、持续推进的发展过程。30多年的快速城镇化，积累了一些经验，也出现一些突出的矛盾和难题。2014年3月中央公布了《国家新型城镇化规划》（2014～2020年），这是一个战略性的规划，它对以后的规划设计及建筑设计领域产生很大影响，同时也能引起人们对城乡特色的保护和反思。[2]

2.1 新型城镇化视角的引入

新型城镇化是以促进农村转移人口的全面发展为根本目的，与工业化、现代化协调发展，不以牺牲农村发展利益为代价，以城市群为推进新型城镇化的主体形态，形成合理的城镇规模等级体

系，并走集约、高效的可持续发展道路的过程。[3]城镇化是乡村发展的必然结果，而传统城镇化建设只重视经济发展和物质空间建设，却忽略了对传统乡村聚落内涵的关注和保护，导致乡村景观的丢失。因此本文希望以新型城镇化的视角作为切入点，审视我国西南地区传统乡村的保护与更新。

2.2 作为城镇化建设中的乡村建筑

乡村建筑是乡村居民组织家庭生活、开展公共活动、从事农、工、副业生产等的场所。乡村建筑不仅要满足居民居住、工作、娱乐等物质需求，同时也要满足居民审美、归属感等心理需求。由于时代的不同，人们生活方式的转变，传统乡村建筑已不能满足使用者的使用要求，因此，在新型城镇化视角下，乡村建筑作为人们生活的必需空间同时也是体现乡村地域特色的重要因子，它的更新创作应该立足于当下乡村的现实情况，考虑居民的物质需求和精神需求，充分尊重乡村的历史文脉和景观环境，最终成为人类生存空间与自然空间相互作用具体形式。

2.3 新型城镇化下的西南乡村建筑创作

西南地区自古以来，其自然地理和人文历史独树一帜，孕育出独特的乡村建筑。在当下新型城镇化建设中的乡村建筑应学习和借鉴传统乡村民居的经验，并将相关建造理念和方法运用到实际的创作中来。如传统造房中人与自然和谐的建造思想，依山就势的自由建筑布局，灵巧通透的建筑形式，地方建筑材料的使用，适宜的建造工艺，丰富的建筑空间等。而且在当今生活方式的推动下，有些传统空间被赋予不同的意义。例如，传统坡屋顶空间起着防潮通风的作用，而如今可演变为阁楼空间或者晒台空间，吊脚楼下部空间转变为停车空间或者绿化景观空间等。在当下西南乡村建筑的创作过程中，应当在考虑居民使用功能的基础上，既采用现代建筑的设计策略与工艺，又恰当运用传统建造技术和地方材料，尽可能减少对自然环境的破坏，有意识将传统空间和生活环境与现代生活方式相结合，既延续传统文脉又反映当代乡村建筑发展历程及时代特点，赋予乡村建筑新的活力。

3 新型城镇化视角下九襄镇石牌坊社区解析

对于传统的乡村聚落而言，乡村的建筑的发展应该建立在对其传统空间审美的认同和深入的文化认知上。因为对传统空间内在的共鸣是乡村建筑保护和发展的前提，特别是在当下新型城镇化的大环境下，这种理解和认同更是显得十分必要。本文以新型城镇化为理论视角，以汉源县九襄镇石牌坊社区为例，希望通过对其设计策略剖析，从建筑对话、场所重塑、风貌延续、居住环境、适宜技术等多个角度展示在当今社会下西南乡村建筑创作的人居理念、文化内涵与工艺手法，以此作为延续传统乡村聚落空间的第一步。

3.1 空间格局中的建筑对话：尊重历史的建筑布局

在原来粗放式城镇建设的背景下，多数有文化价值的乡村都面临历史文化遗产破碎化的问题，面对这一窘境，新型城镇化的乡村建设应从乡村聚落演化的过程中总结时间与空间的相互作用关系。并梳理历史与现代的脉络关系，为整合碎片化的空间格局提供线索。

空间格局直接反映乡村建筑的内在本质。在传统乡村聚落中，新建筑与历史建筑如何对话能反映设计者对聚落历史的认知，同时也能反映乡村文脉的延续情况。

九襄镇位于四川省雅安市汉源县北部（图1），气候温和、历史悠久、物产丰富，是汉源县北部区域的经济文化中心。九襄石牌坊社区位于镇区南部，北邻九襄古街，东邻石牌坊广场，用地约3.33hm²，南北长约299m，东西最宽约116m。社区毗邻历史街区和文化古迹，具有良好的区位优势和历史景观（图2）。在这样富有地域文化特色的环境下，利用相似或同类的建筑形象容易得到和谐的整合环境，同时同类因素的存在能够弱化因视觉反应而引起的紧张感。因此运用相似的坡屋顶形式，组群式布局，适宜尺度等手法处理新旧建筑之间的关系，同时在建筑形式和材质上力图真实展示现代建筑的时代性。由此既能强调石牌坊社区延续已久的文化脉络，又能在通过现代建筑自身的特点与传统建筑产生对比，形成新旧建筑的对话，达到真正的和谐。

图1　九襄整体风貌　　　　　　　　　图2　周边现状

（资料来源：作者自绘）

3.2　场所精神的重塑：传统空间的延续

场所精神一词源于拉丁语，是古代人类文明的一种观念，被认为是人类在场所中的守护神。挪威学者诺伯舒兹在《场所精神》中提到两种场所精神：定向感和认同感。前者是人类辨识空间的能力，知道自己的位置，后者是对场所的认同感。不论哪种场所精神都是场所的灵魂，它能使人区别场所之间的差异性，同时唤醒人们对一个地方的记忆。[4]

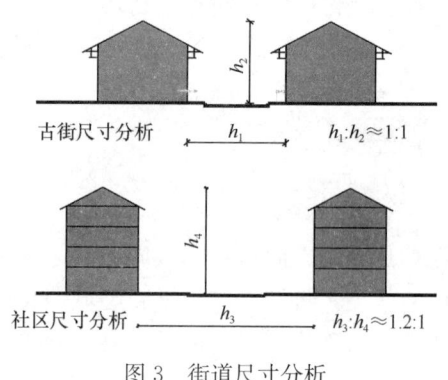

图3　街道尺寸分析

（资料来源：作者自绘）

石牌坊社区的空间构成遵循着九襄古街的空间秩序进行，而九襄古街的空间模式可以简化为街巷空间和建筑空间，即公共空间和私密空间的划分（图3）。他们之间仅以狭小的檐下空间作为过渡。虽然在使用功能上石牌坊社区作为新型的现代居住小区与老街完全不同，但是作为老街历史空间的延伸，石牌坊社区应该既与历史街区相协调，又能为居民提供优质的现代社区环境。因此石牌坊社区在生活空间、建筑形式、街道尺寸、居住环境等方面都予以充分思考并对周边环境进行相应处理，从而真正达到当下时代环境下的场所精神重塑的设计思想。

3.3　适宜技术的运用

西南乡村的传统建造技术是在漫长的造房过程中对自然地理、气候环境、文化习俗、地方材料等的综合反馈，在上述诸多因素的影响之下，西南乡村的传统建筑有强烈的地域性特色，随之而来也产生了具有地方性的适宜建造技术。适宜技术是一种"合理的技术"，是根据当地实际情况，侧重建筑技术的适宜性、高效性，通过普遍的建筑设计手法，提高对能源和资源的利用效率。

石牌坊社区用地南低北高，在整体布局方面，结合地形，将带有商业性质的居住单元，沿周边布置，既能减少用地的剩余边角又能得到易于管理和使用的中央空地，同时有效减少外部环境对内的干扰。在地势处理方面，由于用地内坡度较小，对自然基面进行充填整平，减少工程量，同时也减少对自然地貌的破坏。在建筑形态方面，沿用地坡度方向，建筑依次跌落，在有效解决地势高差

图4 沿街透视效果

（资料来源：作者自绘）

问题的同时，在建筑形态上得到丰富的造型（图4）。在建筑景观方面，社区将中央空地加以绿化，并布置生态景观，以求达到与传统民居中庭院相同的空间效果。

4 结语

乡村作为人类聚落的一种重要形式，随着社会经济的发展，产业结构的变化，乡村聚落也在不断更新和发展。新型城镇化建设不断深入，乡村建筑创作已逐渐从只关注现代化和物质化空间的议题转向一种统筹兼顾、延续特色、面向未来的综合创作。这一转变使得我们重新审视西南地区乡村保护与更新的方法和体系，并能启发我们解决关于乡村特色延续的难题。

基于以往的西南地区的乡村建设的认识，对乡村地域性的认知程度直接影响乡村建筑创作的走向，在新型城镇化视角下西南乡村建筑创作不仅应将真实的现代生活模式，当下审美需求，适宜建筑技术作为一种空间、形式生成方法运用于建筑创作当中，同时也要兼顾考虑乡村特有的自然环境和历史文脉，将两者与乡村的更新有机结合起来，在历史与当下、场所与功能、延续与展望之间寻求平衡。

Analysis of the Architectural Creation of the Southwest Rural Based on the New Urbanization Perspective—A Case Study of Community of Shipaifang, Hanyuan in Sichuan Province

Zeng Wei，Yin Yilin

(Faculty of architecture and urban planning，Chongqing University)

Abstract：With the advancement of new type of urbanization construction in China，rural settlements are also constantly updated and developed. As a continuation of the important factor of the rural characteristics，the renewal and development of rural construction is very crucial for country. Through the perspective of the new urbanization，this paper analyses the space layout，reshaping，the appropriate technologies of community of Shipaifang. In a bid to think about the architectural creation of the southwest rural. It's expected that it will provide a perspective for construction of rural development and recovery of rural characteristic.

Keywords：The new urbanization，The southwest，Rural，Architectural creation

参考文献：

[1] 王路. 农村建筑传统村落的保护与更新——德国村落更新规划的启示[N]. 建筑报，1991，11：16-21.

[2] 宋春华. 新型城镇化背景下的城市规划与建筑设计[J]. 建筑学报，2015，2：1-4.

［3］　徐选国，杨君. 人本视角下的新型城镇化建设：本质、特征及其可能路径［J］. 南京农业大学学报（社会科学版），2014. 14(2).

［4］　丁云，"场所精神"的再生——从大井巷看传统历史街区场所精神的承续［D］. 北京：中国美术学院. 2008.

［5］　单卓然，黄亚平. "新型城镇化"概念内涵、目标内容、规划策略及认知误区解析［J］. 城市规划学刊，2003，(2).

［6］　戴志中. 回归建筑本质的山地建筑创作［J］. 重庆建筑，2005，1：18-23.

［7］　曹珂，肖竞. 文化景观视角下历史名城保护规划研究——以河北明清大名府城保护规划为例［J］. 中国园林，2013，2：88-93.

［8］　王建国. 新型城镇化背景下中国建筑设计创作发展路径刍议［J］. 建筑学报，2015，2：9-12.

［9］　王家倩. 历史环境中的新旧建筑结合［D］. 重庆：重庆大学. 2002.

［10］　诸大建. 如何走向更好的城镇化［J］. 城市中国，2013，6：30-33.

［11］　余熙文，李晓琼. 新型城镇化视角下的地域建筑文化研究［J］. 云南民族大学报，2014，31(3)：61-64.

［12］　杨崴. 传统民居与当代建筑结合点的探求——中国新型地域性建筑创作研究［J］. 新建筑，2000，2：10-11.

［13］　刘先觉. 现代建筑理论［M］. 北京：中国建筑工业出版社. 2008.

可持续城市人居环境与海绵城市建设

李贞子[1]　车　伍[1]　刘　宇[1]　赵　杨[2]

（1. 北京建筑大学城市雨水系统与水环境省部共建教育部重点实验室；

2. 北京雨人润科生态技术有限责任公司）

摘要：水资源与环境系统决定自然环境与人居环境的健康与可持续发展，是我国生态文明建设的关键环节。由于城市化及气候变化的影响，洪涝、干旱、水资源短缺等雨水问题严重制约人居环境的可持续发展。海绵城市建设的实践对构建可持续城市人居环境起到有力的推动作用。本文从人居环境与海绵城市的内涵出发，阐述海绵城市与可持续城市人居环境的关系，分析在可持续城市人居环境下，海绵城市建设的关键性问题，并结合实际案例说明海绵城市建设的具体实践。

关键词：可持续人居环境，海绵城市，雨水管理

1　引言

2014 年，中国城镇化率已达 54.77%，毫无疑问，中国城镇化的高速发展为城镇带来更多的机遇和更好的生活品质。然而，由于人类活动的日益增强、城镇区域在自然场地上的高强度开发，对城镇的自然本底造成严重破坏。为扭转过去"粗暴"的发展模式，构建青山绿水式的可持续人居环境，生态文明建设已成为国家发展的战略目标，并纳入社会主义核心价值体系。《住建部 2014 年工作要点》及习总书记的讲话中均明确要求城市不能建成"水泥森林"，而应是建设"顺应自然，有自然积存、自然渗透及自然净化功能的'海绵城市'"，并指出"环境就是民生，青山就是美丽，蓝天也是幸福。要像保护眼睛一样保护生态环境，像对待生命一样对待生态环境"，更是道出了人居生活与生态环境的联系。2015 年 3 月的中央政治局会议《关于加快推进生态文明建设的意见》上首次将"绿色化"纳入"新型工业化、城镇化、信息化、农业现代化"的协同发展建设模式。可见，以生态文明建设推动可持续人居环境构建是我国长期的艰巨任务。

非可持续的城市化发展削弱城市抵御灾害的能力，受极端气候的影响，更是引发一系列生态环境问题，尤其是洪涝、径流污染、水资源短缺等雨水问题。以 2013 年为例，我国由于洪涝、干旱和水污染而造成的直接经济损失分别占全国 GDP 的 0.55%、0.22%、1.17%。人们对雨水的感情也从"润物细无声"的欣喜到"逢雨色变"的哀叹，不禁感叹："我们的城市怎么了？"严重影响可持续人居环境的目标实现。因此，建设海绵城市，是解决雨水问题、水生态问题、环境问题的有效途径，是实现"美丽中国"的有力支撑。

2　海绵城市与构建可持续城市人居环境的关系

1976 年人居大会首次提出全球范围的"人居环境（Human Settlements）"概念，旨在对人居环境前景发出警告，谋求人居环境的可持续发展自此成为世界性的热点议题。[1]1993 年吴良镛先生第一次正式提出建立"人居环境科学"，目的是要了解、掌握人类聚居发生、发展的客观规律，从而更好地建设符合于人类理想的聚居环境。人居环境是人类生存活动密切相关的空间，是在自然界中得以生存的人工环境基础。人居环境的核心是"人"，是以自然环境为背景的人类活动的反应，人创造人居环境，人居环境又对人的行为产生影响，是人类互动与自然环境相互作用的结果。可持续人居环境是在保障经济发展的同时，更关注生态环境的保护和生活品质的提升，强调用自然工法构建人居环境，尽量减少人类对自然的扰动，除此之外，强调文化发展的关键性。[2,3]

人居环境建设是人类在自然土地上的革命。但在这一过程中，也会有一些违背自然规律或对环境造成破坏的做法，尤其是最近几十年的发展。我国很长一段时间的城市土地规划特别注重土地的经济价值和资源高效利用，几乎是用工程学的方法对待土地，忽视土地的自然属性，将场地中的微地形统统扫平，城镇整体竖向关系被破坏，一条条自然曲折的河流也被无情地填埋与废弃，城镇原有蓄—排系统破坏严重。另一方面，水的社会循环与自然循环关系的弱化。现代雨水排放更多依靠管网，迅速收集径流，使径流难以在城镇区域留存，其保水量下降。其次，管网铺设是有覆土深度的要求，因此雨水管网的出水口大都距常水位很近，一旦发生暴雨，水位上涨，就会产生河道顶托现象，合流制溢流污染严重。这种传统的排水模式较为单一且工程化，对于随机性较强的降雨事件而言，并不能真正解决排水防涝问题，这就导致汛期雨水资源大量流失，旱季却无水可用。供水则更多依靠地下水源，地下水的过度开采导致地面沉降等现象，导致水的恶性循环。现实证明，雨水问题已成为制约可持续人居环境构建的重要因素之一。

我国人居环境的研究与实践走过 20 多年的发展历程，涉及领域从建筑学和城乡规划不断向地理学、社会学、生态学等其他学科渗透，形成综合性、多目标的方式解决人居环境问题。在历史城市保护、城市更新、旧城改造、新城建设都有大量的实践经验。然而，以生态理念为出发点的现代可持续雨水管理措施的实践应用相对匮乏。可持续城市人居环境的建设若不重视城市、自然、与水的和谐关系，那么由此引发的雨水问题将会为人居环境带来大量环境、经济损失，甚至是生命的代价。为解决这一突出问题，美国、澳大利亚、不丹等国家都将雨水管理纳入到可持续人居环境建设规划当中，作为非常重要的一个环节，如，不丹于 2013 年 6 月发布的《不丹城镇村落区域人居环境规划发展指南以削减环境影响》中提出采用 WSUD、SUDS、BMPs 的雨水管理模式改善住区排水系统，并达到削减径流污染、提高生物多样性等综合生态效益，以应对城市化和气候变化导致的雨水问题。[4]我国现代雨水管理体系和机制的逐步建立和完善，尤其是海绵城市建设的实践，为我国可持续城市人居环境提供新的建设思路。

海绵城市是以雨水管理为引导，通过绿色措施与灰色措施的结合、源头削减—中途转输—末端调蓄的结合、地上措施和地下措施的结合等综合管理模式和多层次手段，采用渗、滞、蓄、净、用、排多种技术措施，使城市在降雨时能够就地或者就近吸收、存蓄、渗透、净化雨水，补充地下水、调节水循环，在干旱缺水时将蓄存的水释放出来，并加以利用，从而让水在城市的迁移活动更加"自然"，旨在建设具有自然积存、自然渗透、自然净化功能的海绵型人居空间，使城市可以如海绵一样，在适应环境变化和应对自然灾害方面具有良好的"弹性"。[5,6]以解决排水防涝、污染控制、雨水资源化等水问题，综合达到水土保持、提高生物多样性、恢复自然水文循环等生态效益，及文化、社会和经济效益。图 1 所示为海绵城市与可持续城市人居环境建设关系示意图。

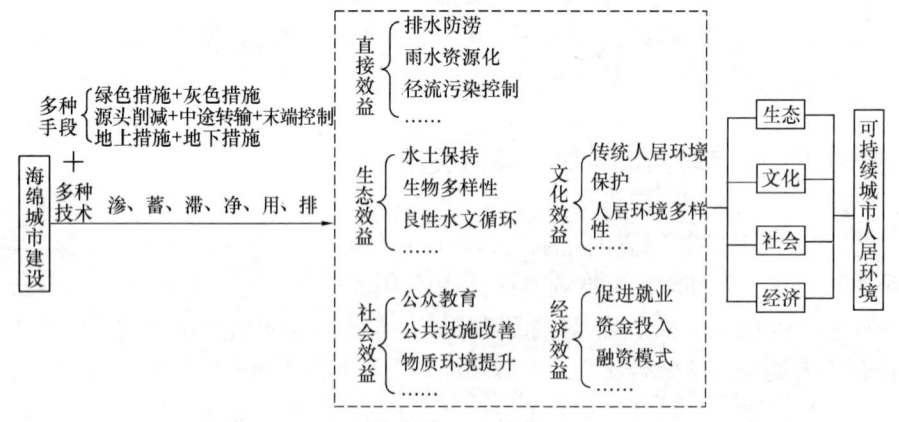

图 1　海绵城市与可持续城市人居环境关系示意图

很显然，中国现代雨水管理经过近 20 年的研究与实践已显现自己的体系特点，海绵城市即是在 LID，WSUD 等现代雨水管理体系的基础上，结合中国国情和城市发展特征而形成。[7]2015 年，是我国推行海绵城市建设的关键节点，国家审批通过 16 个城市的试点申报，同时，已有上百个城市结合自身特点制定了相应的海绵城市建设方案。海绵城市建设结合城市内涝防治规划、水系规划等，综合提出城市海绵化的实施方案，在部门合作、资金投入和运作模式及公众教育等方面都有很大的突破和进展。据相关调查显示，海绵城市建设将带来 6 万亿的资金投入。可见，国家对海绵城市建设的高度重视与实施力度。

3 可持续城市人居环境下海绵城市建设的关键问题

目前，海绵城市已成为全国范围内城市人居环境建设的热点，但越是在这样的情况下，越要冷静思考。在构建可持续人居环境下背景下，海绵城市建设的关键问题是什么？如何平衡海绵城市与其他城市规划的关系？如何更好地推行海绵城市建设？都是现在必须思考且亟待审视的问题。

3.1 整体系统性的管理思维与实践

不同于传统目标单一、工程化的雨水管理模式，海绵城市强调生态优先，保护优先原则，并与城市总体规划、其他专项规划等协同建设，这就要求具有整体系统性的管理模式，从三个方面充分做到整体系统性：（1）思想上的整体系统性。海绵城市建设采用尊重自然、顺应自然、让自然做功的方式处理人、水、自然的关系，这也正是中国古代自然哲学观的现代应用与诠释，即讲求人居环境的整体性和联动性，关注人类活动对水文的影响，将人与自然连为整体，在处理任何问题时，以整体性的思维方式来思考问题并解决问题；（2）人居环境营建上的整体系统性。海绵城市建设需统筹协调城市规划、道路交通、园林绿地等多个相关部门，且需要对场地的整体把握。因此，要将雨水管理纳入到整个人居环境的营建过程中。例如，在选址阶段，就要选择利于排水、便于用水之地。在城市规划建设时，其空间布局要考虑水的走向、排水渠道的设置及便于雨水资源利用的汇流方式。注重人居环境整体的竖向设计，便于对雨水径流的引导；（3）雨水管理上的整体系统性。综合水循环管理系统被视为是精明、综合、弹性的水管理系统，是人类宜居环境构建的必要保证[1,5,9]。处理雨水问题时，将整个区域的水系统统筹考虑，即统筹考虑防洪、引水、用水、蓄水、排水、景观用水、水质净化等，雨水则是其中一个重要的子系统。雨水管理是在整个水系管理大背景下进行。通过源头控制—中途转输—末端调控的全过程管理，且每一子系统都通过严格的布局和竖向调整保证措施的有效性。

海绵城市建设首先要从思想上转变对水的态度，从哲学层面来讲，这是一种思维方式的影响，进而影响人在应对问题时的具体方式，从整体的、系统的角度出发，并表征在具体的实践上。

3.2 海绵城市建设对土地利用结构更新的要求

经济发展、生态环境保护、生活舒适度提升等目标都需要通过土地利用结构的调整与更新得以实现[8]。海绵城市建设在很大程度上是要实现土地的海绵化，即：需要依托土地改造得以实现。发达国家已注意到土地利用同雨水管理的重要关系。如欧盟于 2011 年制定的《欧盟洪水指令手册》，土地开发前应依据洪涝风险图作为土地开发的重要依据，保留必要的泄洪通道和雨水调蓄绿地等生态空间，降低城市的洪涝灾害，奥克兰的大区规划亦有同样的规定。

我国现行土地管理制度和土地政策不利于土地海绵化的实现。一方面，城市"三规"和城市更新等规划阶段会对土地利用结构和模式进行分配和调整，也将土地归属到不同部门进行管理，如道路用地归道路交通部门、绿化用地归园林部门、河道及周边用地归水利部门或河道部门等。要实现土地海绵化就需要同众多部门协调合作，各部门应考虑其营建活动对场地水文状况的影响，并为雨水管理措施的实施预留部分用地，这也是为什么需要打破部门之间的障碍、实现多部门合作的重要原因之一。另一方面，土地利用规划、城市总体规划及部分城市制定的城市更新计划明确提出加强保护基础性生态用地和一定绿地率的要求，如绿色开放空间、水系等，但对雨水功能用地并没有进一步要求，相应管理部门甚至会认为其雨水功能性用地会破坏土地的原有功能而加以阻挠。因此，土地海绵化的实现同时也是土地"革命"，必须打破原有桎梏，在土地相关规划阶段预留雨水功能性用地。

3.3 海绵城市建设与传统人居环境保护协调

国家将旧城区作为海绵城市建设的重要试点，并制定相应的城市更新计划，也可看处对旧城区人居环境整治的决心。吴良镛院士认为"更新"包括改造、改建或再开发（redevelopment）、整治（rehabilitation）及保护（conservation）三方面内容。[9]城市更新是为提升环境质量对生存空间的改造，可以是空间开拓，增加新的内容，或是对现有空间的重新分配与再利用，但要注意保护现有的格局和形式。同时，我国许多城市的旧城区同时又是历史文化名城保护区，在该区域的任何营建活动都要正确处理好城市丰富的历史和文化遗产。海绵城市在旧城推行过程中受到文保部门的疑问与限制，措施的推行遇到重重困难。部分地区文保部门认为历史保护区内用地应受到严格限制，不能随意进行更改，要以保护历史风貌为前提，部分建设施工行为会破坏保护区内原有历史风貌。

其实，海绵城市与历史文化名城保护作为生态文明建设的重要组成部分，其最终目标都是可持续人居环境的构建，不应被割裂开来。如果历史城区难以避免洪涝灾害、水生态恶化，又何谈"可持续"？对历史城区的保护并不意味着人居环境品质的下降，也并不是完全脱离现代而保护，人居环境是最难能可贵的一个有机体，是时时被人们使用，并不是博物馆里的摆设。历史城区保护是对文明的保护，海绵城市建设则是对生存环境的改善，两者之间存在必然联系。历史保护最重要的是留下人类发展的文明印迹，而单一目标的保护并不能达到历史保护的真正内涵。另一方面，对历史遗产并没有充分的认识。古人很注重人居环境中的雨水管理，会通过城市布局、竖向设计、景观小品等来达到排水、蓄水的目的，如宏村的综合水系规划设计、赣州与水塘串联的福寿沟、收集屋檐雨水营造水景或利用等。[10]但保护者由于缺乏对传统雨水管理和水文化内涵的深层次认识而对原有措施造成一定程度破坏。在旧城中推行海绵城市，可以将古代经验与现代雨水管理融合，兼顾雨水管埋与历史保护，更有助于提升历史城区环境质量和文化景观的要求。

4 案例——以嘉兴市海绵城市试点建设为例

嘉兴市成功申报我国第一批"海绵城市"建设试点，示范区范围按照建设情况分为四类：旧城改造示范区域、南湖重点保护示范区域、已建新城改造示范区域、未建新城建设示范区域。

示范区内以老旧城区为主，雨污合流问题较多。由于过去对土地的不合理开发与利用，河道被大量填埋，并形成很多"断头浜"、"死水湧"，水系调蓄能力下降，连通性破坏，且雨水管道标准偏低。一方面雨季排水不畅，积潦之灾经常发生，另一方面，合流制溢流给河道造成严重污染较高的建筑密度、土地硬化面积及绿地空间不足，为海绵城市的落实加大挑战难度。

因此，面对上述问题和困境，嘉兴市采取一系列综合的管控方法，以达到海绵城市的建设目标。把海绵城市建设理念融入城市开发建设全过程，依托"五水共治"，坚持"人水和谐"的管理理念，遵循"渗、滞、蓄、净、用、排"的建设方针，优先对现有水系和绿地空间保护、生态修复、有机更新、LID建设等方面内容，以"节水优先、空间均衡、系统治理、两手发力"的治水思路，系统解决水安全、水资源、水环境问题。通过整体系统式的建设模式，构建源头、中途、末端各层级结合、绿色、灰色结合、大小排水系统结合的管理措施。其改造模块包括：公建与居住小区 LID 改造、城市道路改造、管网提标改造、地块有机更新改造、末端湿地、塘等调蓄控制设施、废弃人防改建延时调蓄隧道等，来达到年径流总量控制率 78％、径流削减不低于 40％（以 SS 计）等目标

（图2）。嘉兴市在海绵城市建设中，根据不同的建设区域制定相应的控制目标和管理措施，统筹协调土地、道路、园林等部门以保证措施的有效落实，不论是在技术措施还是管理理念，都充分体现系统管理思想。部分已建成示范项目已收到很好的雨水控制效果和生态景观效果（图3）。

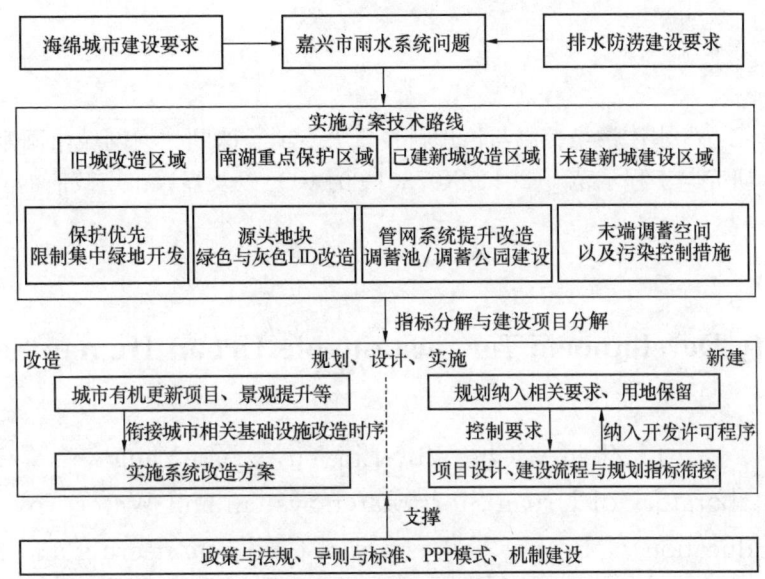

图2 嘉兴市海绵城市建设试点示范区技术路线

图3 嘉兴市部分海绵体实施后效果图

嘉兴作为历史文化名城，以水定城、因水兴城的水系与街道、建筑租住空间格局和水文化是其最大的文化遗产，在海绵城市建设中其历史性体现扔有不足之处，应尽力挖掘历史文化遗存，结合历史文化特征进行规划建设，增加人居环境的历史性、识别性、多样性及居民认同感，构建可持续人居环境。

5　结语

可持续人居环境绝不是仅靠"整洁"的河道、大面积的绿地和树木就可以实现。真正的可持续人居环境深入人心的，是看得见韵味的过去、望得见美好的未来，既有古典韵味的奢华，又有现代社会的明快，是从宏观层面对人居环境长期发展的一种深层考量，讲求空间与时间的合理配置。让理念和方法回归自然，保持对科学和自然的敬畏与尊重，这才是解决问题的根本之道。海绵城市建设是一个庞大、复杂的系统工程，解决的不仅是雨水问题，更是水生态、自然环境、人类生存的大问题，创建"望得见山，看得见水，记得住乡愁"的可持续人居环境，构建真正的"美丽中国"。

致谢

感谢国家"十二五"水体污染控制与治理科技重大专项子课题"河网城市雨水径流污染控制与生态利用关键技术研究与工程示范"（2011ZX07301-004-01）以及嘉兴市市政府的支持。

Sponge City Development for Sustainable Urban Human Settlements

Li Zhenzi，Che Wu，Liu Yu，Zhao Yang

（1. Key Laboratory of Urban Stormwater System and Water Environment
〈Ministry of Education〉，Beijing University of Civil Engineering and Architecture；
2. Beijing Yuren Rainwater Ecotechnology Co. Ltd）

Abstract：Water resources and environment system determines the healthy and sustainable development of the natural environment and human settlements，is a key link in the construction of ecological civilization in china. Due to the impact of climate change and urban sustainable development，flood，drought，water shortages and other problems seriously restrict the sustainable development of urban human settlements. The sponge city construction is a powerfully impetus to the construction of sustainable urban human settlements. This article from the concept of human settlements and sponge city，elaborate the relationship between the sustainable urban human settlements and sponge city. Analysis the key problems of sponge city construction in the background of the sustainable urban human settlements，combined with the actual case to explain the practice of sponge city construction.

Keywords：Sustainable human settlements，Sponge city，Stormwater management

参考文献：

［1］ 张云彬. 环境友好型城市人居环境规划与管理研究［M］. 上海：同济大学，2009.

［2］ 吴良镛. 从"广义建筑学"与"人居环境科学"起步［J］. 城市规划，2010，34（2）：9-12.

［3］ 吴良镛，人居环境科学研究进展（2002—2010）［M］. 北京：中国建筑工业出版社，2011：3-16.

［4］ Guidelines for Planning and Development of Human Settlements in Urban and Rural Areas of Bhutan to minimise environmental impacts［EB/OL］.［2013-7-18］. www. mowhs. gov. bt/wp-content/uploads/2010/11/final. pdf.

［5］ 住房城乡建设部. 海绵城市建设技术指南——低影响开发雨水系统构建［M］. 北京：中华人民共和国住房城乡建设部，2014.

［6］ 仇保兴. 海绵城市（LID）的内涵、途径和展望［J］. 城乡建设，2015，2：8-15.

［7］ 车伍，赵杨，李俊奇.《海绵城市建设技术指南》解读之一基本概念与综合目标［J］. 中国给水排水，2015（8）：1-5.

［8］ 黄晓燕，曹小曙. 转型期城市更新中土地再开发的模式与机制研究［J］. 城市观察，2011，2：15-22.

［9］ 吴良镛. 北京旧城与菊儿胡同［M］. 北京：中国建筑工业出版社，1994.

［10］ Che Wu，Qiao Mengxi，Wang Sisi. Enlightenments from ancient Chinese urban and rural stormwater managements practices［J］. Water Sci Technol，2013，67（7）：1474-1480.

［11］ 李贞子，车伍，王建龙，等. 中国古代雨水管理智慧对构建海绵城市的启示——以宏村为例［C］//第十一届国际绿色建筑与建筑节能大会论文集：城市发展研究增刊，2015（22）.

青岛西海岸新区启动区水敏性城市设计研究：
迈向弹性水系统的生态社区

王子鑫　干　靓

（同济大学）

摘要：水敏性城市设计，最早于 20 世纪 80 年代在澳大利亚提出。美国、英国、新西兰和日本等国先后提出了类似的水设计与水管理概念并进行了诸多探究。然而国内对于水敏性城市设计的探讨与实践相对较少。水敏性城市设计，是将整体水文循环与城市发展和再开发相结合的综合水设计与水管理措施，旨在通过低环境影响的处理手段来探索水和社会、生活之间的关系。青岛西海岸新区濒临黄海，海洋资源丰富却缺少淡水资源。随着该区升级为国家级新区，未来的发展对水资源的需求量逐渐增大，如何处理水城之间的关系是新区新一轮规划中的核心议题之一。本研究引入弹性水系统管理概念，将水循环与宜居性和活力性相结合，通过整合布局城市多源水系统和公共休闲、视觉景观等不同功能用地，提出对当地水生态环境低影响语境下的主要设计策略。

关键词：青岛西海岸新区启动区，水敏性城市设计，生态社区，弹性水系统，活力

1 引言

城市水系统的规划正在从单一的水文技术性手段过渡到综合各方面、多功能元素的哲学探索。[1]近年来，西方对于城市水系统提出的新型规划理论有美国的低影响开发（Low Impact Development）、绿色基础设施（Green infrastructure）、多目标洪泛区管理（Multi-objective flood plain management）、英国的可持续排水系统（SUDS）、新西兰的低影响城市设计与开发（LIUDD）等概念。

其中，水敏性城市设计（Water Sensitive Urban Design）于 20 世纪 80 年代末在澳大利亚首次提出。它通过将城市整体水文循环与城市的发展和建设过程相结合，旨在将城市发展对水文的负面环境影响减至最小，保护自然水系统，将雨水处理与景观相结合，保护水质，减少地表径流和洪峰流量，在增加水文价值的同时减少开发成本。[2]

水敏性城市设计是手段，水敏感城市是希望达到的预期结果。水敏感城市主要包括以下三个原则：（1）城市集水区：可以接触不同供给规模不同水源处的水；（2）城市生态系统服务：城市建成环境补充和支持自然环境功能；（3）城市水敏感社区：可持续的社会政治资本存在，公民的决策和行为具有水敏性。[3]

2 研究范围

本论文研究地块位于青岛西海岸新区启动区，面积 0.3km²。西海岸新区核心区面积 34km²，启动区的核心区面积 2.8 km²（图 1）。2014 年 6 月 10 日经国务院批复同意设立的青岛西海岸新区，是中国第九个国家级新区。作为国家级新区，青岛西海岸新区具有改革先行先试、新产业集聚等特征，便于开展创新性设计。而作为示范段率先启动的新区启动区，将重点打造成集生态、智能、海洋经济、升级版 CBD 于一体的核心。

2.1 水资源时空分布不均衡

新区降水受海洋和山峰影响，降水量年际变化较大。夏秋季大于冬春季、西部大于东部、南部

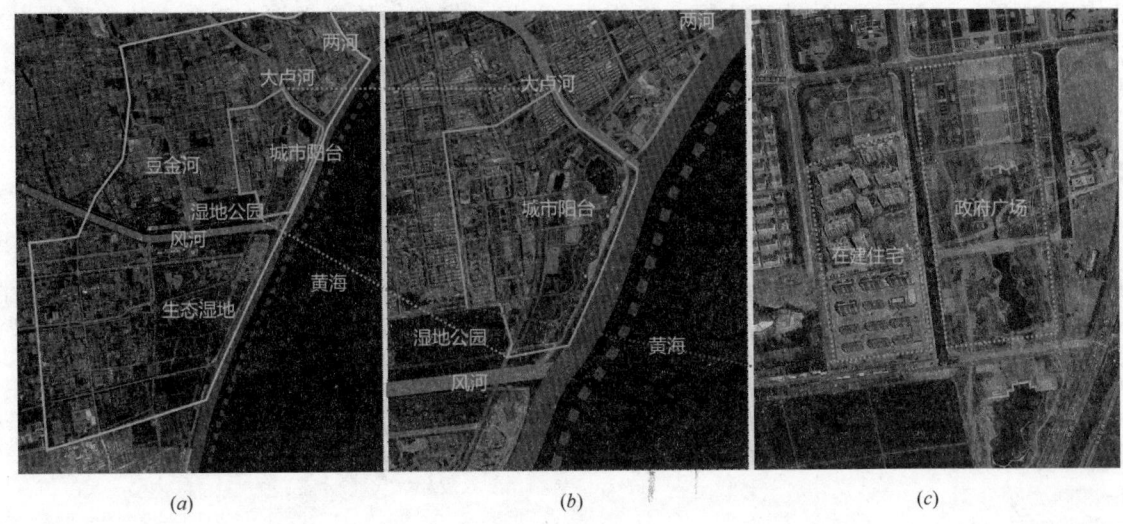

图1 研究地块示意图
（a）西海岸新区核心区；（b）西海岸新区核心区启动区；（c）生态居住示范区

大于北部。历年平均降水量865.2mm（2005～2013年）。近年来，西海岸新区全年平均降雨量逐渐下降。其中，汛期（6～9月）降雨量占全年降雨量比重较大。

蒸发量以春、夏两季最大。春季具有风干物燥、降雨少蒸发大的特点，多出现春旱。夏季湿热多雨，适宜作物生长，但由于降雨时空分布不均，易造成旱涝并存。历年平均蒸发量1312.4mm（2007～2014年）。平均蒸发量甚至超过降雨量。

青岛西海岸新区水文情况统计　　　　　　　　　　　　　　　　表1

时间	全年平均降雨量（ml）	全年平均蒸发量（ml）	6～9月份降雨量（ml）	6～9月占全年降雨比例	风河最大洪峰流量（m³/s）
2007	1457.2	1312.9	903.9	62%	394
2008	1006	1206.1	568.4	57%	423.0
2009	539.8	1380.2	313	58%	49.6
2010	783.6	1233.3	400.4	51%	143
2011	682.7	1331.8	438.8	64%	156
2012	1142.6	1292.6	448	39%	240
2013	743.3	1296.2	281.7	38%	43.5
2014	735.9	—	327.3	44%	—
平均	865.2	1312.4	452.7	52%	—

资料来源：青岛西海岸新区（黄岛区）气象局。

西海岸新区启动区内主要河流为风河、大卢河和两河。三者都为季风区雨源型河流，汛期河水暴涨暴落，汛后基本断流。流入黄海。

2.2 水资源短缺

2.2.1 可利用水源有限

青岛市区内，水资源主要来源为大气降水。水资源人均占有量313m³，仅为城市生产和人民生活需求量的1/3。2000年青岛市的水资源开发利用还是以地下水为主，达总供水量的一半多。2009

年青岛市对地下水的开发利用程度大幅度降低，转为以开发利用地表水作为青岛市的主要供水水源，对于其他水源的使用程度也有所提高。目前青岛市对于地下水的开采利用已无潜力，要想在未来解决青岛市的缺水问题，只能转向地表水的开发利用和外来水源的调度使用。[4]

2.2.2 水质性缺水

风河、大卢河和两河上游都建有工厂。工厂污水直排入河道内。风河水质达到Ⅲ类标准百分率为 66.67%，入海口断面为中度污染。2010 年在原胶南市全年共采集、检测水样 300 份，19 项检测结果全部达到《生活饮用水卫生标准》（GB 5749—2006）放宽限值要求的水样 165 份合格率为 54.3%。2011 年合格率为 46.0%。2012 年合格率为 74.1%。[5]

2.3 公共空间缺乏活力

城市建成环境质量不高。西海岸新区在胶南老城区的基础上发展起来。所研究地块内总面积 23hm²。已建成环境占 3/4。其中，政府广场面积为 11.5hm²，轴线长度 640m。采用传统现代城市大尺度、大轴线、大空间的政府广场做法，缺乏娱乐休闲的空间和综合功能的引入。地块整体尺度过大、硬化率过高。政府广场中虽然有水面存在，但水岸皆为硬化，水生态环境单一。

正在建设的海韵丽都住宅小区与经济开发区烟台前安置房建筑主体已基本完成。均为传统小高层和高层住宅建筑做法。小区内景观绿化尚未成型。

(a)   (b)   (c)

图 2　地块建成环境图片

(a) 政府前广场；(b) 海韵丽都住宅区；(c) 经济开发区安置区

（资料来源：青岛西海岸新区航拍图，2014；作者拍摄，2015）

3 设计策略

针对研究地块内有关水资源、水系统和水活力的种种问题，提出水敏性城市设计的设计策略（表2）。弹性水系统，包括以下几方面内容。

问题导向的设计策略分析　　　　　　　　　　　　　　　　　　　　　　表 2

问题 ＼ 策略	集水设施增加	水系统循环利用	河道自然化	生态净化植物群落	雨洪管理
水时空分布不均衡	●●●	●●	●●	●●	●●●
水资源缺乏	●●●	●●	●●	●●	●●●
缺少活力	●●	●●	●●	●●●	●●●
水生态脆弱	●	●	●●●	●●●	●

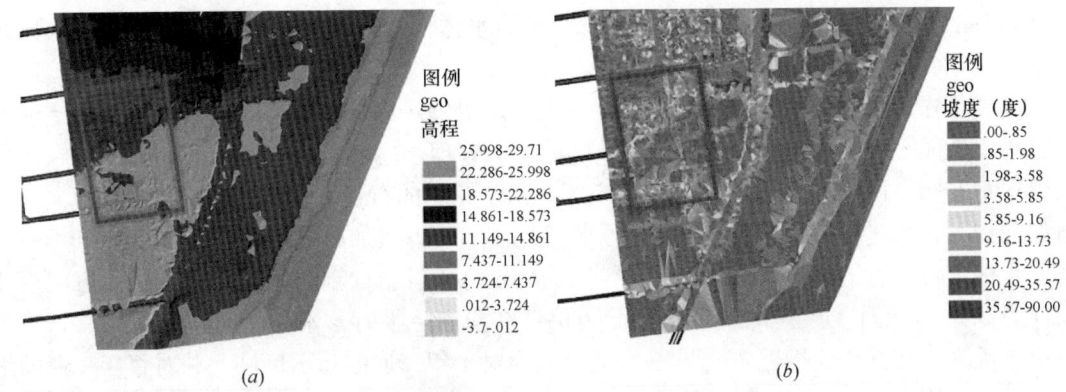

图 3　研究地块现状分析图

（a）高程分析图；（b）坡度分析图

（资料来源：作者自绘）

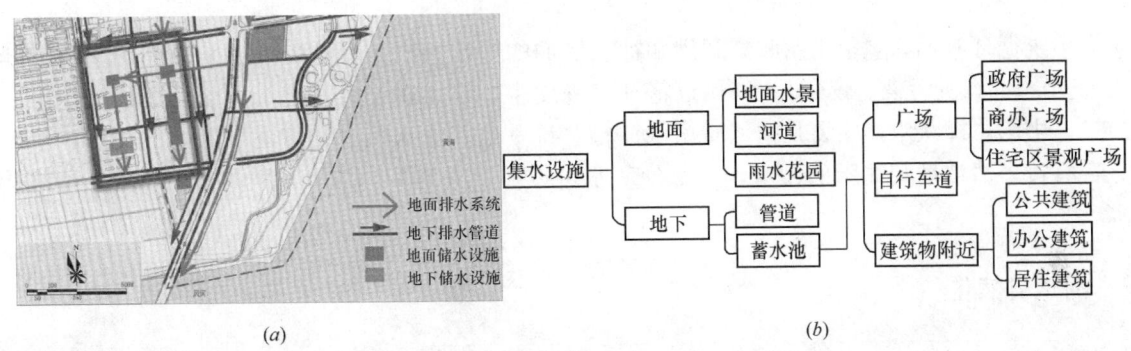

图 4　集水设施分析图

（a）排水系统规划图；（b）集水设施分类图

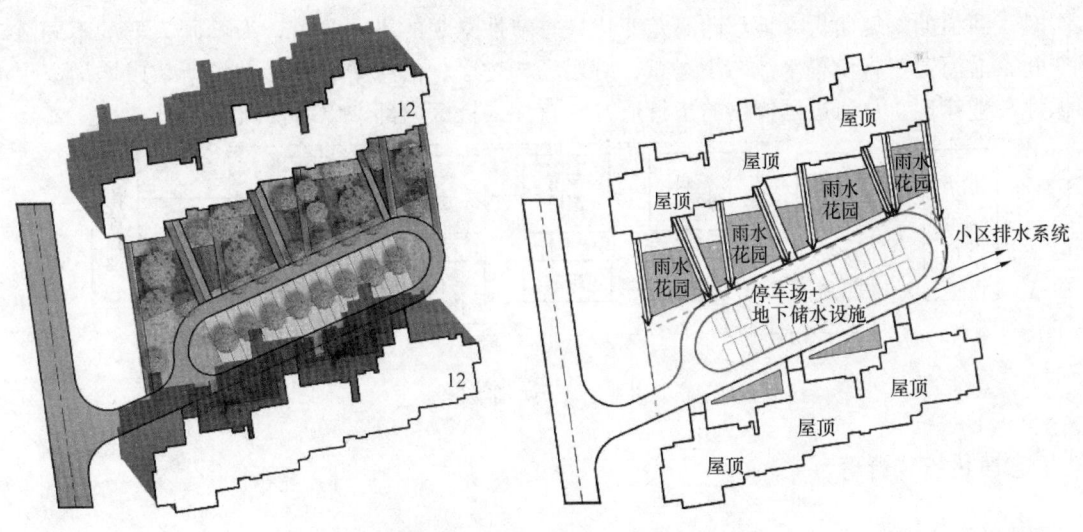

图 5　集水设施节点示意图

（资料来源：作者自绘）

3.1　集水设施增加

集水设施，包括地面和地下两部分。两者互相连通，共同打造综合水收集系统（图 4）。地面水体，主要依靠现有政府广场水景发展起来，以避免在缺水的现状条件下继续挖掘新的水体。

169

其余零散水体，则依靠各类广场中的水景建设。地面水体依据地块高程和坡度，主要排入地块南部湿地。

雨水花园将作为主要的地面储水设施大量引入。大型公共建筑、商务办公楼宇以及住宅建筑旁都将设置雨水花园来增加雨水渗透率。对于社区的雨水管理，一般采用集中处理的方式，在住宅楼之间设置雨水花园（图5）。对于街道等线性空间，雨水花园的布置沿线性展开。径流的流向在不影响交通的前提下，通过街道固有的坡度、雨水收集池闸口等方式加以引导。[6]

地下水体，分为管道和蓄水池两部分。管道为传统排水设施规划的管道系统。主要方向由北向南，坡度为2.5‰，经管线汇集后排入风河。为保证在暴雨降临时蓄水池能迅速蓄积雨水，将严格控制地块渗透率，使其达到接近80%。蓄水池可以应对十年一遇的暴雨事件，并对百年一遇的洪涝灾害起到缓冲作用。对于大型公共建筑和办公建筑，可以设置集中、大型的地下储水设施。对于社区住宅，则采用分布式雨水收集、储蓄装置，将储水过程分散到每栋建筑。

3.2 水系统循环利用

水系统循环利用，包括雨水收集利用和社区层面的中水回用。黄岛区雨水呈中性，pH值一般为5.5~8.0，有机污染物较少、DO接近饱和、硬度小、总体属于轻污染水。[7]具有较大的回收利用前景。中水，即灰水，主要是指从厨房洗涤槽、洗手盆、洗衣机水、淋浴水产生的污水。[8]除了部分含有过多清洁剂和油脂的污水，大部分灰水可以通过处理和回收，成为冲洗厕所和浇灌花园的水。

3.3 河道自然化

现状水体，仅为政府广场南部的水景。堤岸皆为硬化，水环境单一、水生态脆弱。希望通过模拟自然河道形态，增加水体的变化和趣味性。通过软化地面，减少硬地率。和缓的河岸坡道为暴雨来临时提供了充足的泄洪通道。当河道水位过高时，河岸两旁的自然式土地可以被淹没来缓解洪峰。同时，河道的蜿蜒曲折、地形的高差变化、季节性景观的不同等等，为不同人群的不同活动创造了空间。沿河道，将设置水池、小瀑布、游乐场、餐厅、信息中心等活动场所，以增加滨水活动的知识性和趣味性。从河道延伸出的步行道，一直深入社区内部，以增加社区活力。

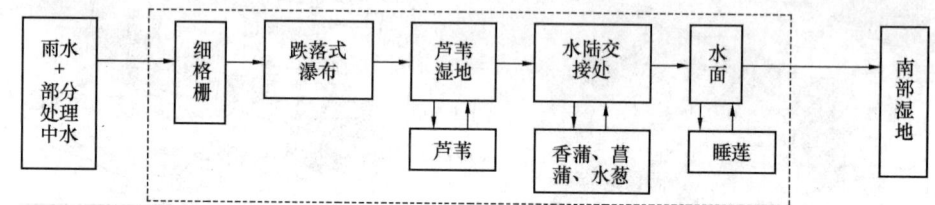

图6　植物净化过程

3.4 生态净化植物群落

从居住区、商务办公区收集处理的雨水、中水等，部分由地表径流流入河道中，最后汇入南部湿地。主要引入草丛湿地植被型植物群落。兼具耐湿和耐旱的特点。因为香蒲能耐高浓度的重金属而且适应能力强、生长快，富集能力强等，与水葱搭配有利于有效净化城市生活污水中的磷、氮等污染物质。芦苇的密植，可以减缓水流速度，使悬浮物沉降，与其共生的生物群落共同净化水质。睡莲夏季生长迅速，耐污能力强，对水质有净化作用的同时也起到景观美化作用。

4　小结

通过现状问题分析，提出针对性水敏性设计解决策略，在解决生态问题的同时为社区注入活力，是本论文希望达到的目的。希望它能够成为中国城市水系统创新的生态示范区。

The Research on the Water Sensitive Urban Design for the West Coast Core Area in Qingdao：The Transition Toward a More Water-Resilient Eco Community

Wang Zixin，Gan Jing

（Tongji University）

Abstract：The water sensitive urban design(WSUD) was first referred in Australia in 1980s. The USA，UK，New Zealand and Japan have already proposed some similar strategies of sustainable urban water system. However，in China，few studies are concerned about it. WSUD is an integrated method of management and technology which combines the urban water circulation with the urban (re)development. This paper focuses on one community in the west coast core area in Qingdao and aims to find an appropriate way to practice the method of WSUD in coastal area. The west coast core area in Qingdao is the ninth new national area and has a strategic position in the development of China. In that place，the seawater resource is abundant while the freshwater utilized is limited. The relationship between the water and the urban development would be significant to study. This paper recommends a method of resilient water system in this area and tries to combine the water circulation with the city's liveability and vitality under the target of providing multi-resource water and active public space for the citizens with low impact on the local environment.

Keywords：The west coast core area in Qingdao，Water sensitive urban design，Eco-community，Resilient water system，Vitality

参考文献：

[1]　Segaran R R，Lewis M，Ostendorf B. Stormwater quality improvement potential of an urbanised catchment using water sensitive retrofits into public parks[J]. Urban Forestry & Urban Greening，2014，13(2)：315-324.

[2]　Tony H F Wong，Urban Design-the Journey Thus Far[J]. Environment DesignGuide，2007，(8)：1-10.

[3]　Wong，T. H. F and Brown，R. R. The Water Sensitive City：Principles for Practice，water science and technology，60(3)：673-682.

[4]　王川子. 青岛市城市发展与水资源供给的矛盾及解决方案[D]. 北京：中国海洋大学，2011. DOI：10. 7666/d. d169771.

[5]　徐修臻. 黄岛区（原胶南市）城乡生活饮用水水质监测与分析[D]. 山东：山东大学，2014.

[6]　洪泉，唐慧超. 从美国风景园林师协会获奖项目看雨水花园在多种场地类型中的应用[J]. 风景园林，2012，1：109-112.

［7］ 李甲亮，肖新峰，程建光等．城市雨水处理与资源化利用研究［J］．山东科技大学学报（自然科学版），2009，28（2）：51-54. DOI：10. 3969/j. issn. 1672-3767. 2009. 02. 011.

［8］ Dolman，N，Savage，A，Ogunyoye，F（2013）Water-sensitive urban design：learning from experience. Proc Instit Civil Eng-Municipal Eng 166：pp. 86-97.

宜居城市与宜居语境下的水及水文化

周 勇 蔡有德

（台湾大学建筑与城乡研究所）

摘要：1516 年，托马斯提出理想国，向往半农半 X 的生活状态；1898 年，Howard 提出田园城市，批判城市扩张而产生的拥挤、环境问题。宜居城市的提出，逐渐成为提高市民效能、实现城市可持续发展的重要策略。近年来，宜居城市的评选成为大热，宜居城市指标也成为学术界研究的热点，本文通过文献回顾国内外对于宜居城市的影响因素及评价指标的研究，比较研究国外与国内的评价体系差异性，国内目前侧重硬件评价，国外偏重软件评价，但目前的评价体系及理论仍比较分散，存在多角度理解，由此导致每年例行各类城市评比会引起诸多争议。本文归纳宜居城市排名分析并论证，在区域宜居性上看，宜居城市的分布与水、水系发展具有高度的相关性，水是一切生命之源，水及水文化从原始社会到农业社会、工业社会，都发挥着极大的作用，在区域宜居性上看，水与宜居城市存在辩证的关系。接着，本文从城市规划层面分析城市宜居性，实地踏勘调研台北市，选取具有代表性的大安区调研研究：水与水文化而带来的气候湿润度和生活舒适度是他们选择台北市定居的重要因素，以及水岸农业带来的情感舒适度，其重要性堪比城市的就业机会的吸引力。最后提出，虽然宜居城市的内涵、定义、指标仍在初步摸索阶段，但我们仍可以友善、有序规划水资源，高效可持续利用水岸资源，发展水岸农业与城市农业，提升城市宜居性。

关键词：宜居城市，水文化，水

1 前言

城市作为人类社会的最伟大、最人性的发明，而水是生命之源，是城市发展的必需品。在不同时期，不论对于促进城市凝聚力或引起城市矛盾，水都被描述成城市中最重要的社会权力。水，作为人类发展的永恒议题，伴随农业社会到工业社会，再到后工业化社会，其作为一个新陈代谢的巨系统，在帮助城市蜕变与成长。但在过去两百年，科学与技术对于人类与城市社会深远的影响，以及其引发的环境革命，让人类克服诸多的自然限制，电力改变昼夜、空调改变温度，"环境是限制因素"的感觉在渐进消失。[1]Matthew Gandy 通过观察 19 世纪的工业城市的扩展来验证此一说法，水与城市的关系，并以细菌城市（bacteriological city）比喻来推广城市清洁形态模式，以建设城市基础设施并实现公民权利的建设。[2]但是，工业发展丰富人类物资生活的同时，也带来的系列环境发展的恶果，面对城市经济的不可持续发展以及城市人口扩张造成的问题，Howard 提出田园城市概念，旨在解决城市的拥堵与交通问题。[3]而后，陆续有学者加大对此的研究，David Smith 在《宜人与城市规划》一书中强调宜人的重要性，并明确其城市宜人的概念，并阐明宜人性包含公共卫生环境，生活环境，历史建筑三个方面的内容，Jane Jacbos 在《美国大城市的死与生》提倡保持城市的多样性，并尽可能支持错综复杂并且相互功能的多样性，以此满足人们的生活需求。[4]到 20 世纪 90 年代，联合国人居大会形成的《人居议程》，以及国际宜居城市研讨会（IMCL）都把将人类栖息地的改善当作联合国新时期的关键使命。

但是，在宜居城市建设以及评选过程中，则出现诸多争议，比如，今年亚洲幸福经济体评价中亚洲第一是泰国所引发的网络大争论。对此，本文采用类比分析的方法分别对 2015 年全球宜居城市排名、2015 年亚洲宜居城市排名以及 2015 年中国宜居城市排名进行聚类分析，从区域区位理论分析，得出：在地理分布上，全球宜居城市多集中在北半球，以发达国家居多；亚洲宜居城市以日本最多，东南亚地区为主；而中国宜居城市则集中在沿海地区与长江、黄河流域。从区域宜居性上看，宜居城市的分布与水、水系发展具有高度的相关性，这一切与水是一切生命之源，水及水文化从原始社会到农业社会的演变不谋而合。而宜居城市的评价指标中，很少直接说明，城市与水的关系。这或许与科学技术让人们忽略自然的感觉，也慢慢忘却聆听自然的声音，尊重自然的循环。水在城市生态系统扮演新陈代谢的功能，随着城市化的推进，也推进水的商品化过程，因而20世纪90年代开始，越来越多学者对于水资源整合管理作为可持续水资源管理战略被广泛研究，Meed（2008）证明水文循环的混合，并提议需要将更多关注放在区域、网络与流体之间的相互作用的可持续管理。[5] Linton 在《社会权利与水的都市化》（Social Power and The Urbanization of Water）更是发出："谁的水？谁的城市？谁的自然？"（whose water? whose city? whose nature?）的哲思，城市用水是组建城市功能的政治生态系统的重要组成部分，则讨论水与城市的关系，更多是讨论城市与人、人与人之间的城市社会关系。而一个理想的城市就需要融合自然、社会进城市之中，如果城市可持续发展，必须让发展回归城市，并让城市环境还给市民。[6]

丹麦未来学家沃尔夫·伦森指出：人类在经历狩猎社会、农业社会、工业社会和信息社会之后，将进入一个以关注梦想、历险、精神和情感生活为特征的梦想社会，人们消费的注意力将主要转移到精神需要。① 全球城市在追求生活品质的同时，也尝试以指标来呈现宜居程度，目前有许多国际组织定期对全球城市进行调查、评比宜居程度，作为各城市发展的参考。笔者以国际宜居城市台北市作为参考，研究台北宜居性的发展方向。从城市农业与田园城市的发展策略及对于水岸农业的推广的工作，发现城市越宜居，人的需求、活动需求越容易满足。台北，多元、自信、弹性的城市品质，正越来越影响其市民的活动，让城市的环境回归到市民的手中，让发展的效益回归到城市中。

2 国内外宜居城市理论研究

2.1 国外宜居城市研究

1516年 Thomas More 提出理想国（Utopia），批判16世纪的新政治与圈地运动，向往半农半X的生活状态。1898年，Edward Howard 提出田园城市（Garden City），批判城市扩张而产生的拥挤、环境问题，并针对城市—乡村二元分离提出，城市与乡村必须要有机结合[3]。

第二次世界大战后，宜居城市的概念被正式提出，1954年，出现以希腊学者 C. A. Doxiadis 为代表的研究宜居的学术团队。1963年，世界人居环境学会（World Society of Ekistics）成立，并于1976年召开首次人类住区大会，成立联合国人居中心（UNCHS）。20世纪80年代之后，永续发展成为人们的共识[4,7]，2010年，宜居城市的提出，逐渐成为提高市民效能、实现城市永续发展的重要策略之一。

2.2 国内宜居城市研究

自古以来，天人合一想法深入人心，苏州园林、园冶等，枯山水都可以看出，山水人相融的愿景，一直是中国人心中的向往之地。1993年，吴良镛院士等专家正式倡导人居环境科学，并开设人类环境科学概论课程，于2001年著有《人居环境科学导论》，在此背景下不少学者开始对人居环境问题进行研究，宁越敏等对人居环境的内涵、评价方法进行了理论上的探讨，构建人居环境评价指标体系[4,7]。在宜居城市研究方面，仍有众多学者，对就业岗位、生态、文化等方面展开研究，其中，袁锐（2005年）提出：宜居城市就是要适宜人类工作、生活、居住的城市，宜人性是对宜居城

---

① 第五产业，百度百科，网址：http://baike.baidu.com/link? url＝hkmUF8lx _ X3tOcQVN0fxjyKDHpzNr2JF _ 5zc3t1MGNHlCiEQVCpCrxzVG _ 5wt-flu7KqETnPKMebBionbzUmxK；摘自2015年5月8日。

市最基本的要求。[8]近年来,宜居城市的评选成为大热,宜居城市指标也成为学术界研究的热点,通过中国知网 CNKI 检索发现 2008 年至今"宜居城市"关键词的文献多达 3000 篇。研究多为,岑驰明提出绿色低碳城市构建宜居澳门[9];赵树枫在分析北京城市化与郊区化过程中建设宜居城市,必须要重视新农村建设,促进农村人员与城市人员的流动。[10]在城乡二元互动中,城市农业的发展,逐渐成为乡村与城市连接的一个较好的纽带。在此基础上,张文忠更是进一步阐明宜居城市与城市功能优化的关系,着重提出宜居城市的五个基本条件,即安全城市、健康城市、生活便利的城市、低碳出行绿色交通的城市,具有良好关系与社区互动的城市。[11,12]朱鹏则基于需求层次分析纳入宜居城市的建设,提出社交需求、尊重需求、自我实现需求与宜居城市的关系,而则进一步拉近了互动性活动在宜居性城市的重要性。[13]因而逐渐有研究新加坡的宜居城市的学者提出,其高效的水资源利用、绿色城市、城市农业(城市农夫、屋顶农业)的综合发展对于宜居城市的建设影响重大。

2.3 宜居城市评价体系争议性

目前城市的主要问题主要是人口膨胀、资源短缺、环境污染与社会问题[14],为了"城市让生活更美好"的目的,人们一直在探索城市发展的理想模式,宜居城市的概念提出到发展经过几十年(我国仅仅十几年),已经被认为是目前解决城市发展问题比较有效的途径之一。有学者提出,宜居城市应该是人与自然共同协调、永续发展的动态目标,但如何评价城市的宜居性,目前,有经济学人智库的世界最佳居住城市评选指标体系,大温哥华区宜居区域战略规划指针体系和我国的宜居城市科学评价指标体系。国外与国内的评价体系差异性,国内目前侧重硬件评价,而国外偏重软件评价,[14]但目前的评价体系及理论仍比较分散,存在多角度的理解,由此导致每年例行各类城市评比,往往会引起诸多争议,今年亚洲幸福经济体评价中泰国是亚洲首位所引发的网络大争论。

3 城市、水与宜居性

3.1 城市与城市的自然

古代城市,发源于河流湖泊,一是农业生产、货物运输的生产功能需求,二是安全防卫的需要。但广义的看,城市,兴起于环境,但也受制于环境(危害),城市易发生旱灾与火灾、地震及火山爆发。但工业革命、信息革命中的科学技术已经让人工力量渐渐突破环境的限制,城市回复力(Resilent City)越来越强,面对灾害时表现出希望与机会的力量。[1]城市作为人类文明的载体,积累、传承并创新人类生产与生活活动经验,传统韦伯(Webber)的城市观认为城市是一个共同体,必须具备如下基本条件:防御设施、市场、法律、团体性格、自律与自主性[15],城市历史的发展经验逐渐表明:城市的市场、团体性格、自主性与自律则被进一步放大,尤其是世界城市人口由 20世纪 50 年代的 30%,到 2014 年的 54%,预计到 2050 年城市人口将达到 66%①,其中,老龄人口与儿童的比重越来越大,按照城市生态学的观点,如果把城市比作是一个生态系统,一个交织社会过程与生物物理过程的生态系统,那如何实现从青壮年的城市变为老人的城市,则是颇为紧迫的议题。

同样,城市生态系统也可理解为一个能量流动的系统,其中,食物也是能量来源,将城市想象成食物的流动,强调城市与人类农业景观互动的方式,追溯城市居民的日常卡路里消耗,从零售店、批发商、到初级生产者,注重跨时空的连接网络,串接因城市居民不断变化的事物需求而改变

---

① 2014 年全球城市人口比例数据分析,中国报告大厅网,网址:http://www.chinabgao.com/stat/stats/39318.html,摘自 2015 年 5 月 9 日。

的农业实作。[1]在此循环过程中，碳循环、水循环则成为焦点。

3.2　城市与城市的水

城市是人工构造的景观，而水是城市的命脉与生机的源泉，水流也是城市界定方向与界线的重要标志。[1]罗兰·巴特曾说："在每个城市里，地方的体验式河流、运河或是水流，在道路和水流之间有某种关系……让居民在适应上遭遇困难的城市，正是没有水的城市，没有海岸、湖泊、河流、溪流，这些城市都有生活的困扰，有易读性的困境。"有水的城市，则多了一份神韵，城市的水具备新陈代谢的功能，在城市植物组群中现在除了反映传统生态因素，也会反映社会经济和文化因素，文化偏好与物理因素相互关联[1]，比如台北新市长推行的台北城市农园的新政方针，则具有明显的文化偏好。工业化、郊区化、逆城市化、绅士化，① 城市在不断扩张与变迁的过程中，也留下了自然植物的碎片，创造出新的生态，比如绿色空间的产生。可以说，城市化过程，是一个抛弃泥土、以不透水的表面取代可透水的土地的过程，但也是再次利用水资源、回归自然的过程。

3.3　城市的宜居性与城市的水及水的利用

水是城市生活的根本。水污染与净水供应一直是城市两个最主要的水议题。现代城市发展，一方面是城市安全运动的斗争史，将水资源的管理运用达到放大[17,18]，不论如何变化，水的命运与人类的命运息息相关[18]，以台北淡水河系为例，一万到五千年前，台北是个湖，先民在湖岸营生。清朝时，淡水河系有舟楫之利，可上溯到大溪以上，运送各种物资，便利茶的出口。随着河流淤积，日据时期已无航行之利，纵贯铁路与公路完成，取代了横向的沟通管道，市镇间的关系随之转变。迄今，淡水河系逐渐由一个边缘地带变为城市水岸农业景观地带。②

在考量宜居性的问题的时候，会思考人的天性是什么？喜欢充实的生活，从生活中获得满足感，在社会里找到自我价值。而符合人的本性的生活方式就越是适宜居住与生活，对我们大多数人来言，生活跟我们所居住的地点（城市）是联系在一起的，身体舒适度、社区互动程度、社会舒适度都直接影响着宜居性，进而影响人的身体、身心的健康。与此相似，健康城市（Health City）的提出与发展，则为宜居性的探索提供了一条新的发展道路，去建设更好的城市，通过对自然的再认识，对水的再利用，鼓励更多的植物生长。[19]换言之，城市农业的发展，有利于健康城市的建设。没了可持续的城市，就没有了可持续的世界。而发展农业生产，充分利用城市的水资源，以物构建社交网络。

4　台北经验：宜居建设与城市农业的发展

刘易斯·芒福德在《城市文化》一书中强调说，城市的生命力，重在储存文化、流转文化、创造文化。而台北市，作为全球最宜居城市之一，台北的宜居性，更多表现在台北个性，即市井文化、建筑文化、水文化，更重要的是台北所特有的城市街区缝隙空间及其衍生出来的城市农业、绿色植栽的社区行为，在一个个城市的缝隙空间中，产生无数社区的活动网络。

4.1　宜居台北、城市的水与城市农业

随机访谈居住与生活在台北的人，水与水文化而带来的气候湿润度和生活舒适度是他们选择台

---

① 对应英文为"gentrification"，又译士绅化、缙绅化、中产阶级化或贵族化。这是社会发展中的一种可能现象，指某旧区原本聚焦低收入人士，改建后地价、房价上升，导致高收入人士取代低收入人士。
② 自然的文化塑造，网址：http://www.slidefinder.net/-/17/20171548，摘自 2015 年 5 月 10 日。

北市定居的重要因素，以及水岸农业带来的情感舒适度，其重要性堪比城市的就业机会的吸引力。

在一个个热岛效应不断加剧的城市里，城市开放空间却越来越少并且趋于单调，快节奏的城市生活让城市居民几乎无法喘息。人们除了要忍受汽机车尾气所带来的空气污染，还要担忧状况频出的食品安全。但是翻开历史我们可以发现，一两百年前的台北盆地与我们目前所面对的状况是完全不同的：阡陌纵横的水圳与农田，再加上有机分布其间的同庄聚落，让当时生活在盆地里的人们不必面对我们现代人所无法逃避的种种城市生活困境。但是，随着时代的演进，城市步入了快速发展的阶段。只不过，潜藏在人们心里的农耕生活则一直未被遗忘。目前城市农耕在全球各地逐渐发展成熟，旨在让冰冷的钢筋混凝土城市成为一个宜居友善的农耕城市，以回归人们最初的生活景象。

4.2 台北城市农业

台北都会区有很多"城市园圃"的实际案例，各种类型的公共园圃已经在台湾北部地区蓬勃地发展起来了。比如，有结合既有公共设施而设立的农耕空间：台北市万华区龙山小学的药草；还有在公有建筑物的屋顶设立屋顶菜园：台北市大安区锦安图书馆的屋顶，给小区规划师与市民提供了体验农耕学习农耕的空间；也有为老人提供社交平台的屋顶菜园：大安老人服务中心银发农园；而最为难得的，则要数直接利用小区内的公有空地，由市民自力营造出来的多元绿化与农耕的"城市园圃"：位于松烟文创园区与台北机厂西边的松山区复健里巷弄内的"幸福农园"。

幸福农园，原本只是一处破旧的眷村，拆迁之后被小区居民开辟为城市农园。园圃里种满了各种时令果蔬，还开辟着园艺治疗作用的小花园，为小区居民创造更加宜人的公共空间，塑造更加贴近自然的邻里生活，让居民日常活动与农业耕作紧密结合在一起，进而打造出一种居于城市又超越城市的新城市生活形态。自"幸福农园"创办以来，举办了多次活动，从庆祝第一次收成的成果与栽种经验分享，到举办烹饪比赛，无形间凝聚了小区意识，打破在紧绷的城市生活下，人与人间的冷漠与疏离感，人们回复到了最初的生活愿景。原本只是一个带动小区绿化的小小念头，却衍生为效益更大，结合教育、运动、休闲、环保等多功能场域，揭开了城市生活的另一种样貌①。

台北新市长上任后，城市农耕的开展，为小区居民一起体验农作的生活成为常态创造了可能，而这不仅能够凝聚小区邻里的感情，还可以在日常生活中落实环境教育，创造可食地景，健全多样化的城市生态环境，由外而内地绿化城市空间，绿化每个城市农人的内心。

4.3 城市农业发展的共享愿景

据 NGO 城市农耕团体的调查，大台北地区目前还有许多的空地空间，尤其台北市仍有近 200 公顷的公有空地。而许多既有的公共建筑屋顶，校园空间，还有容积奖励的开放空间等等，都可以成为我们发展城市农耕的潜在空间。如果可以创造更多的城市农耕基地，然后用农耕实作的方式，用农业景观的呈现，来实实在在地改善我们这个城市的体质，那么也许我们已经又朝着宜居城市的方向迈进了一步。同样，因农业作为食材景观的特性，更有利于形成一种共享的社会网络，拉近人与人之间的社交距离，构建台北共享城市的新愿景。

5 总结与展望

虽然宜居城市的内涵、定义、指标仍在探索实践阶段，也学界也从主观因素、客观因素去完善指标，并深化客观因素的软件（文化）与硬件（基础设施）的建设与评价，总体上，目前宜居城市指数逐渐在（1）倾向于经济实力、政治文化影响力；（2）倾向于气候、生活舒适方面达到一种平

---

① 摘自台北都市农耕网，www.facebook.com/fun。

衡，两者之长兼具。而论城市与水、水系的关系论证，一方面从历史观考证水作为城市之源的作用，另一方面从生物物理角度看水循环的生态系统与城市生态系统的关系，但对于水循环的生态系统涉及水资源管理、水的技术管理（自然水系到人工的排水沟、地下水道、自来水管线的演变；自然水源到人工的稳定水源的转变并对城市的影响）的进一步研究。宜居城市的呈现的水系地理的分布集中的特征，水系从社会生产角度对于城市的形塑机制仍需要进一步研究。但是，在目前宜居城市语境下，提升城市内部宜居性水平，我们仍可以通过友善、有序规划水资源管理，高效、可持续利用水资源，通过发展水岸农业与城市农业发展水岸资源，通过在社区、街区缝隙空间发展食材景观（城市农业），从城市内部提升市民的生活舒适度、身体舒适度，以及社区网络交流互动。

致谢

在本文撰写过程中，感谢台湾大学建筑与城乡研究所黄丽玲老师的指导与帮助。

Water and Water Culture on the Context of Livable City

Zhou Yong，Cai You-De

（1 Institute of Building and Planning，TaiWan University）

Abstract：In 1516，Thomas More proposed 〈Utopia〉 for a dream about'Semi rural semi X'life. In 1898，Edward Howard proposed 〈Garden City〉 to criticize Traffic Congestion and Environmental Pollution. While the concept of Livable City was engendered，it became one of the most important strategies to improve public performance and achieved sustainable development. In recent years，the selections of Livable Cities have become popular，livable city indexes are also becoming hot spot of research. Firstly， this paper focuses on the review of theory of livable city， then compares with foreign and domestic rating system. Secondly，we analyse livable city rankings，in regional position，we reach the following conclusions：livable cities are mostly located in coastal areas，and the distributions of livable cities are highly correlated with water or water system. Water is the source of all life，water and water culture play a significant role in the agricultural community and industrial society. In addition，we analyze TaiPei，the best livable city in Asia，then we find that climate moisture and comfort of life accompanied by water and the water culture is an important factor promote them to settle in Taipei. What's more，the emotional comfort of living in waterfront is more important than the attraction of employment opportunities. Finally，even thought the connotation of a livable city is still preliminary in exploratory stage，but we can still plan the water resources friendly，also need to be efficient and sustainable to develop waterfront agriculture and urban agriculture，so that we can enhance the livability of the city from the inner city livability.

Keywords：Livable，Water，Water culture

参考文献：

[1] Benton-Short, Lisa, John Rennie Short. 城市与自然[M]. 徐苔玲、王志弘译. 台湾：群学，2008.

[2] Broich, J. London：Water and Making of the Modern City[M]. Pittsburgh：University of Pittsburgh Press，2013.

[3] （英）埃比尼泽·霍华德. 明日的田园城市[M]. 李经元译. 北京：商务印书馆，2000.

[4]　董晓峰，杨保军. 宜居城市研究进展[J]. 地理科学进展，2008，3：323-326.

[5]　Medd，Will Marvin，Simon. Making water work：intermediating between regional strategy and local practice[J]. Environment and Planning D：Society and Space，2008：280-299.

[6]　Linton，Jamie. What is Water? The History of a Modern Abstraction[M]. Vancouver：UBC Press，2010.

[7]　董晓峰，杨保军，等. 宜居城市评价与规划理论方法研究[M]. 北京：中国建筑工业出版社，2010.

[8]　袁锐. 试论宜居城市的判别标准[J]. 经济科学. 2006(4).

[9]　岑驰明. 我们与宜居城市何以渐行渐远？[J]. 澳门月刊，2014，7：10.

[10]　赵树枫. 乡村建设在宜居城市中的地位与动力机制[C]. 建设宜居城市研讨会，2005.

[11]　张文忠，尹卫红，张景秋，等. 中国宜居城市研究报告[M]. 北京：社会科学文献出版社. 2006.

[12]　张文忠. 城市内部居住环境评价的指标体系和方法[J]. 地理科学，2007，27(1)：17-23.

[13]　朱鹏. 基于人的"需求层次"理论的宜居：城市评价指标初探[J]. 河南科学，2006，2：134-137.

[14]　黄升旗. 我国城市化发展问题研究[M]. 长沙：湖南师范大学出版社，2010.

[15]　刘涛. 城市宜居性指标体系对比分析研究[D]. 北京：北京林业大学，2011.

[16]　何一民. 中国城市史[M]，湖北：武汉大学出版社. 2012.

[17]　Swyngedouw，Erik，The city in a glass of water：circulating water，circulating power，in Social Power and the Urbanization of Water[M]. Oxfor：Oxford University Press，2004：27-50.

[18]　Hallström，Jonas. Constructing a Pipe-Bound City：A History of Water Supply，Sewerage，and Excreta Removal[M]. Linköping：Linköping University Electronic Press，2002.

[19]　王俊雄，张枢. 台北，原来如此[M]. 台湾：台北市城市发展更新处，2013.

可持续高密度人居环境建设
Sustainable High-Density Living Environment Development

Exploration and Evaluation of Policy Options to Combat Unauthorized Building Works in Hong Kong

Yau Yung

(Department of Public Policy, City University of Hong Kong)

Abstract: Unauthorized building works (UBWs) have recently aroused wide public concern in China, particularly in those densely-developed cities like Hong Kong, Shanghai and Taipei. UBWs are building works carried out without any prior approval or consent by the public authority. On account of their unlawful nature, UBWs pose serious threats to the safety of the local communities by undermining structural stability and fire safety of the buildings. Yet, studies related to the formulation of policy for tackling UBW problem have been rare. To straddle the existing research gap, a policy Delphi study was carried out with an expert panel to identify and prioritize policy options for combating UBWs in Hong Kong. Policy Delphi was adopted because it allows a systematic approach to obtain, exchange and develop informed options on a particular policy issue. Hong Kong is a good laboratory for the study of UBW-related policy because there are over one million UBWs of different types throughout the territory. Besides, UBW issues have triggered various political crises and sagas in Hong Kong. More importantly, fires in buildings with illegal subdivisions of dwelling units have recently resulted in deaths and injuries. A three-round policy Delphi survey was conducted on 53 local building-related experts or professionals in late 2013. The first round of the survey aims to identify possible actions or policies that could be taken to cope with the UBW problem in Hong Kong's urban areas. 274 possible options were returned and they came under ten broad categories. In the second and third rounds of the survey, the ten option categories obtained from the first round were evaluated with reference to their desirability and feasibility. The results of the policy Delphi survey suggest that imposing heavier punishments against non-conforming owners was regarded as the top-priority option. On the other hand, options like simplification of building approval process and expedited implementation of mandatory building inspection are poorly-received. These findings have far-reaching implications on the formulation of government policies regarding building safety in Hong Kong.

Keywords: Building safety, Building illegality, Hong Kong, Policy Delphi, Unauthorized building works

1 Introduction

Besides poor design and workmanship, building illegality also contributes to an unsafe built environment. Building illegality can take many forms, including squatter settlements and unlawful additions, alterations and removals [1,2]. In particular, unauthorized building works (UBWs) proliferate in many Chinese cities such as Shanghai, Hong Kong and Taipei. Despite the growing volume of literature on building control, the main focus of previous research tends to be one-sided. Building control of new developments have predominated the literature while only little work has been dedicated to the control of existing buildings. To break such an imbalance of research focus between new and existing buildings, this study aims to identify and prioritize policy options for cracking down on the problem of unauthorized building works (UBWs) in urban areas of Hong Kong. Hong Kong is a good laboratory for the study of UBW-related policy because there are over one million UBWs in some 39, 000 private buildings throughout the territory. In light of the highly-compact development pattern in Hong Kong, the safety and health threats posed by the UBWs are extremely significant. More importantly, public concern over the UBW problems has been further amplified by the UBW-related scandals of political figures like top government officials and legislative councilors.

The issue of UBW triggered various political crises and sagas in the city. Although a handful of papers work on UWBs in Hong Kong [3~6], no previous attempt has been made to exploring workable solutions to the UBW problem in the city. To fill the research gap, we aim to look for some policy options for solving the UBW problem in Hong Kong with the application of policy Delphi.

2 UBW problem in Hong Kong

From the legal viewpoint, all building works in Hong Kong are subject to statutory control under the Buildings Ordinance and its subsidiary legislations. The Buildings Department executes and enforces these legislations. To make sure the design and carrying out of a building work are up to minimum acceptable standard, approval and consent must be obtained from the Building Authority (i. e. the Director of the Buildings Department) before the building work can commence, unless the work is exempted from this requirement by the ordinance [6]. Building works that contravene this stipulation are generally regarded as UBWs [5]. UBWs take different forms, including illegal flower racks, drying racks, air-conditioner supporting frames, metal cages, cocklofts, roof-top structures and dwelling subdivisions. In the past few decades, UBW proliferation led to many casualties in the city. For instance, at least 21 people were killed and 135 were injured in building-related accidents involving UBWs during the period between 1990 and 2002 [4]. The number of reports on UBWs received by the Buildings Department rose from 12, 427 in 1997 to 41, 403 in 2014 [9,10]. As estimated, there have been around one million UBWs of different types in Hong Kong [9,10]. UBW proliferation creates different safety and health hazards to the community. Since UBWs are undertaken without the scrutiny and approval of the public authority, their safety standards are not guaranteed. UBWs may be structurally unsafe and may impose excessive loads on the buildings in which they are erected, thereby jeopardizing the latter's structural stability [6]. In addition, UBWs endanger fire safety of a building. On the other hand, unauthorized structures protruding from external walls of buildings may adversely affect the natural lighting and ventilation for the occupants. Besides, UBWs can hinder the carrying out of repairs and maintenance for buildings [11]. From the economic viewpoint, the presence of UBWs suppresses the property value and building failures associated with UBWs can result in considerable compensations or damages for casualties and property losses [12].

In Hong Kong, the Building Authority is empowered by Section 24(1) of the Buildings Ordinance to serve statutory orders on building owners to remove any UBW within a specified period of time. The UBWs that should be removed are explicitly specified in the orders. Section 40(1BA) of the Buildings Ordinance stipulates that non-compliance with a statutory order served under Section 24(1) without any reasonable excuse is a criminal offence. The offenders are liable on conviction to a maximum fine of HK $ 200000 and to a maximum imprisonment of one year. In addition, defaulted owners may be subject to a further fine of HK $ 20000 for each day of continuation of the failure to comply with an order. To supplement the criminal punishment, the statutory orders issued are registered with the Land Registry against the titles of the properties concerned. Such a registration will only be discharged when the owners comply with the subject order to the satisfaction of the Building Authority. The Building Authority is authorized under the Buildings Ordnance to issue warning notices to owners of premises with UBWs, and to register the notices in the Land Registry if the UBWs are not removed within a specified period.

Nonetheless, enforcement against UBWs in Hong Kong is selective. Since 1975, the Buildings Department has implemented an enforcement policy to prioritize the enforcement actions against different types of UBW [13,14]. However, this enforcement policy has been regarded a "toleration policy" which cannot work effectively to reduce the number of UBWs in Hong Kong [13]. The Buildings Department has lacked the capacity to handle the tremendous amount of UBWs in the city even though a number of initiatives such as Mandatory Building Inspection Scheme (MBIS), Minor Works Control System (MWCS) and third-party risks insurance for buildings have been taken by the government [15]. In this light, it is crystal clear that a more effective policy is urgently needed to bring the UBW problem in Hong Kong to an end.

3 Research Design

For better-informed policy making, it is essential to be aware of all available options as well as views of experts. Therefore, policy Delphi is adopted to generate options and collate opinions from a panel of experts. It is a group-based idea-generating technique which is superior to its non-group counterparts in many aspects such as number of options produced and quality of ideas produced [16].

4 The policy Delphi technique

Policy Delphi was first introduced in 1969 [17]. Policy Delphi serves to offer the best possible information for the decision——or policy——makers and guarantee that all possible options are on the agenda [18]. It can also examine and estimate the acceptability of the options. Unlike conventional Delphi which was designed originally to seek a consensus among a group of experts on a particular topic, policy Delphi seeks to generate the opposing views on the potential solutions to a policy problem [18]. Policy Delphi rests on the premise that decision-makers do not necessarily want a group of experts to come up with a decision for them [17,18]. Rather, the decision-makers simply need a group of experts or informed advocates to suggest all possible options and justifications for their consideration. Therefore, by its nature, policy Delphi is a tool or technique that is suitable for policy analysis rather than achieving a decision [18]. Policy Delphi avoids the possibility of face-to-face debates which could happen in focus group interviews. This helps to eliminate undue influence of dominant personalities [19]. In general, a policy Delphi process includes several question-response rounds. In this study, the policy Delphi process includes five steps: 1) formulation of the issue; 2) exposing the options; 3) determining initial positions on the issue; 4) exploring and obtaining the reasons for disagreements; and 5) re-evaluating the options. For the current study, the policy issue is about resolving the problem of proliferation of UBWs in Hong Kong's urban areas.

5 Policy Delphi surveys and expert panel

For the purpose of this study, a three-round policy Delphi exercise was undertaken. A specific questionnaire was designed for each round of the survey. In the first-round survey, the panel members were asked to suggest possible actions or policies could be taken to cope with the UBW problem in Hong Kong's urban areas. Open-ended responses were used to formulate options. In the second round, the panel members were asked to evaluate the options suggested during the first round based on their desirability and feasibility. Desirability of a option concerns benefits or positive effects resulted from the option. It is gauged on a four-point scale (4=very desirable, 3=desirable, 2=undesirable and 1=very undesirable). Feasibility of a option concerns the practicality of the option, hindrance to implementation and acceptability to the public. Again, it is measured on a four-point scale (4=definitely feasible, 3=possibly feasible, 2=possibly unfeasible and 1=definitely unfeasible). Apart from the ratings, the panel members were asked for open-end responses for explaining their evaluation (e. g. why a low level of desirability was accorded to a specific option). In the third-round survey, the panel members were informed of the consolidated inputs from all respondents in the second round and they were then required to reassess their initial positions.

The design of the expert panel is vital in policy Delphi for ensuring that the options relevant to a particular issue or topic are thoroughly explored. In this study, the panel members were those people with committed interest in the quality of the urban built environment and in-depth knowledge of the UBW issues in Hong Kong. Purposive sampling, which is commonly used in other policy Delphi studies, was employed for the selection of panel members. 200 experts were invited to participate in the policy Delphi through e-mail in November and December 2013. These experts had varied backgrounds, and they included seven architects, eighteen building surveyors, four builders, eleven property and facility managers, five fire engineers and nine structural engineers. 53 of 200 invited experts (26. 5%) submitted responses to the first-round survey. Some of the responding experts dropped out after the first round such that the panel completing both second and third rounds consisted of 42 (79. 2%) of the first-round respondents. The second and third rounds were conducted in February 2014 and March 2014 respectively.

6 Results of the policy Delphi surveys and Discussion

In the first-round survey, 274 possible options to tackle the problem of UBW proliferation in Hong Kong's urban areas were returned. Many options were very similar or duplicated so all the options were reviewed and reduced to ten broad categories. These categories include "public education" (e. g. programs for educating the general public about UBWs), "financial assistance" (e. g. grants or loans for homeowners with financial difficulties for UBW removals), "market approach" (e. g. setting up a platform for informing the public about the seriousness of UBW proliferation in each building in the territory), "revamp or abolishment of enforcement policy", "validation of UB-Ws" (e. g. retrospective approval of certain types of UBW), "simplification of building approval process" (e. g. streamlining the building approval exercise and widening the scope of privately certifiable minor works under the MWCS), "tighter regulation of builders" (e. g. penalizing builders of UBWs with heavy fine, imprisonment and removal from register), "heavier sanctions against nonconforming owners", "facilitation of in-flat inspection" (e. g. simplifying the process of obtaining a warrant from the court for the entry of the public officials into premises for inspection) and "expedited Mandatory Building Inspection Scheme" (e. g. increasing the number of target buildings for the MBIS each year). In the second and third rounds, the panel members were directed to rate each of the ten option categories obtained from the first round with reference to its desirability and feasibility. Table 1 summarizes the panel members'desirability and feasibility ratings for each policy option category.

Statistics of the desirability and feasibility ratings obtained in the second and third rounds   Table 1

Option	Desirability				Feasibility			
	Second Round		Third Round		Second Round		Third Round	
	Mean	σ	Mean	σ	Mean	σ	Mean	σ
Public education	2.39	0.92	2.36	0.91	3.11	0.89	3.09	0.87
Financial assistance	2.58	0.87	2.57	0.88	2.98	0.83	3.01	0.84
Market approach	2.64	0.81	2.61	0.83	2.69	0.90	2.68	0.92
Revamp or abolishment of enforcement policy	2.88	0.90	2.85	0.91	1.99	0.88	1.94	0.89
Validation of UBWs	2.35	0.91	2.37	0.92	2.51	0.92	2.53	0.94
Simplification of building approval process	2.01	0.87	1.99	0.87	2.43	0.86	2.42	0.89
Tighter regulation of builders	2.97	0.87	2.95	0.89	2.39	0.86	2.33	0.88
Heavier sanctions against non-conforming owners	3.22	0.86	3.25	0.86	3.02	0.87	3.05	0.85
Facilitation of in-flat inspection	2.85	0.88	2.83	0.89	2.52	0.91	2.51	0.88
Expedited Mandatory Building Inspection Scheme	2.17	0.92	2.19	0.93	2.12	0.87	2.09	0.89

As shown in Table 1, the results obtained in the second and third rounds of the policy Delphi survey did not deviate significantly. Concerning the desirability criterion, "heavier sanctions against non-conforming owners" had the highest mean rating, followed by "tighter regulation of builders" and "revamp or abolishment of enforcement policy". These findings imply that deterrence was viewed as the most effective strategy in solving the UBW problem in Hong Kong. By imposing heavier punishments or penalties on the non-conformers, who can be owners or buildings of UBWs, the government could reduce the number of UBWs in the city. On the other hand, "simplification of building approval process" and "expedited MBIS" were rated as the least desirable options. Some of panel members expressed that simplified statutory procedures for obtaining building approval could hardly offer property owners incentives to follow the legislative requirements. They worried that the private certification under the minor works control system might result in poor-quality building works, undermining building safety in the end. As for increasing the annual number of target buildings under the MBIS, it was considered undesirable because the scheme covers private buildings aged 30 years or above. However, in reality, many UBWs are erected in younger buildings in Hong Kong. As for feasibility, "public education" was ranked the first, with "heavier sanctions against non-conforming owners" and "financial assistance" being the second and the third respectively. Conversely, "revamp or abolishment of enforcement policy" and "expedited MBIS" received the lowest feasibility ratings. As stated by some of the panel members, it would be impractical for the Buildings Department to shift away from its prevailing toleration policy because the department's manpower was far from enough to tackle the huge amount of UBWs in Hong Kong. These panel members did not expect the Hong Kong government would increase the resources for the Buildings Department appreciably in the near future. For the same reason, the Buildings Department was thought to have no spare capacity to handle more buildings under the MBIS.

Based on the desirability and feasibility ratings obtained in the third round, imposing heavier punishments against non-conforming owners was regarded as the top-priority option. Nevertheless, this option is not without criticism. Some panel members expected that local property owners might object the legislation amendments as they would worry about breaking the law unknowingly. In other words, it is necessary to help property owners fully understand what UBWs are and the proper procedures of obtaining building approval before revising the penalty levels. Other options like "facilitation of in-flat inspection" and "financial assistance" were generally considered desirable and feasible as well. In many occasions, identification of UBWs, particularly those constructed inside dwelling units like illegal subdivisions of housing unit, is particularly difficult. Therefore, many panel members welcomed the expedited process for the Buildings Department's officials to obtain a warrant for in-flat inspection. Besides, the panel members though that the government could serve as a facilitator for the market approach, providing building-based or even property-based information of UBW to the market. In the medium or long run, the market approach can help cultivate a culture of building safety within the local community.

On the other hand, options like simplification of building approval process and expedited implementation of mandatory building inspection are poorly-received. Besides, the survey findings show that the experts cast a doubt on the legalization of the existing UBWs. In this regard, the introduction of the Household Minor Works Validation Scheme (HMWVS) by the government in 2010, which allows retrospective approvals of UBWs by the Building Authority, is expected to be ineffective in solving the UBW problem.

7 Conclusion

In light of the proliferation of UBWs in Hong Kong, a policy Delphi study was carried out to identify and prioritize policy options for solving the problem of UBW proliferation in the city. 53 local building and property experts participated in a three-round policy Delphi survey. The survey findings suggested that imposing heavier punishments against non-conforming owners is the most preferable policy option. In fact, the policy options investigated in the study are not mutually exclusive. Some options can complement with each other. For example, imposition of heavier penalties against perpetrators and market approach can be supplemented by public education programmes in order to achieve better policy outcomes. Furthermore, this study offers the first illustration of how policy Delphi can be used as a technique for researching complex urban issues like building illegality. As demonstrated, policy Delphi can be used to develop a more realistic and implementable urban policy. Yet, stakeholders of the built environment such as property owners and insurance companies have been ignored in this study. Therefore, further research is warranted for studying the opinions of these stakeholders about the possible policy options to the UBW problem.

Acknowledgements

The work described in this paper was fully supported by a grant from City University of Hong Kong (Project No. 9610285).

探索及评估解决香港违章建筑的方案

邱 勇

（香港城市大学公共政策学系）

摘要：违章建筑最近在中国，特别是在那些人口稠密的经济发达城市如香港、上海和台北，引起了公众的广泛关注。违章建筑之泛指没有事先从政府机关得到批准或同意而进行的建筑工程。基于它们的非法性质，违章建筑危害建筑物的结构稳定性和消防安全，对社区安全构成严重威胁。然而，关于制订解决违章建筑问题政策的研究并不多见。为了跨越现有的研究空白，本研究成立了一个专家小组，采用了政策德尔菲法，探讨及按优先顺序列出打击香港违章建筑的政策方案。本研究采用政策德尔菲法，因为它为获取、交流和发展特定政策问题的明智方案，提供一个有系统的方法。香港是一个研究违章建筑相关政策的良好对象，因为那里有超过一百万不同类型的违章建筑。此外，违章建筑问题在香港引发的各种政治危机和一连串社会新闻。更重要的是，在住宅单位的"劏房"发生的火灾造成伤亡。在 2013 年下旬，本研究进行了三轮德尔菲政策调查，有 53 位本地在建筑方面的专家或专业人士参与其中。第一轮调查的目的是找出有可能解决香港的市区违章建筑问题的措施或政策，收到的方案有 274 个，而这些方案分为十大类别。第二轮和第三轮的调查主要评价从第一轮中得到的十个方案类别的可取性和可行性。政策德尔菲调查的结果表明，对违规业主从重处罚被视为最优先的方案。在另一方面，简化审批建筑工程的程序和加快强制验楼是认受性较差的方案。这些发现对香港政府制定有关楼宇安全的政策，产生深远的影响。

关键词：楼宇安全，建筑违法，香港，政策德尔菲，违章建筑

References：

[1] Smart A. Agents of eviction：the squatter control and clearance division of Hong Kong's Housing Department[J]. Singapore Journal of Tropical Geography, 2002, 23：333-347.

[2] Winayanti L, Lang H C. Provision of urban services in an informal settlement：a case study of Kampung Penas Tanggul, Jakarta[J]. Habitat International, 2004, 28：41-65.

[3] Ho D W C, Chau K W, Yau Y. Evaluating unauthorized appendages in private apartment buildings[J]. Building Research and Information, 2008, 36：568-579.

[4] Leung A Y T, Yiu C Y. A review of building conditions in Hong Kong. In Leung A Y T, Yiu C Y (ed.) Building Dilapidation and Rejuvenation in Hong Kong[M]. Hong Kong：CityU Press, 2004：11-34.

[5] Yiu C Y, Kitipornchai S, Sing C P. Review of the status of unauthorized building works in Hong Kong[J]. Journal of Building Surveying, 2004, 4：28-34.

[6] Yiu C Y, Yau Y. Exemption and illegality-the dividing line for building works in Hong Kong [J]. CIOB(HK) Quarterly Journal, 2005, 10：16-19.

[7] Buildings Department. Monthly digest：March 2001[M]. Hong Kong：Buildings Department, 2001.

[8] Buildings Department. Monthly digest：March 2014[M]. Hong Kong：Buildings Department, 2014.

[9] Planning and Lands Bureau. For a culture of building care：a comprehensive strategy for building safety and timely maintenance -implementation plan[M]. Hong Kong：Planning and

Lands Bureau, 2001.

[10] Policy 21 Limited. Report on survey on subdivided units in Hong Kong[M]. Hong Kong: Policy 21 Limited, 2013.

[11] Chan K J K. Maintenance of old buildings[J]. The Hong Kong Surveyors, 2000, 11: 4-7.

[12] Yau Y. The value of building safety: a hedonic price approach[J]. Urbani izziv, 2015, 26: 1-15.

[13] Lai L W C, Ho D C W. Planning buildings for a high-rise environment in Hong Kong: a review of building appeal decisions[M]. Hong Kong: Hong Kong University Press, 2000.

[14] Buildings Department. The Buildings Department's internal guidelines on prioritisation of 'actionable' unauthorised building works: a summary[M]. Hong Kong: Buildings Department, 2011.

[15] Audit Commission. Director of Audit's report no. 64[M]. Hong Kong: Audit Commission, 2015.

[16] Herbert T T, Yost E B. A comparison of decision quality under nominal and interacting consensus group formats: the case of the structured problem[J]. Decision Sciences, 1979, 10: 358-370.

[17] Turoff M. The design of a policy Delphi[J]. Technological Forecasting and Social Change, 1970, 2: 149-171.

[18] Turoff M. The policy Delphi. In Linstone H A, Turoff M (ed.) The Delphi method: techniques and applications. [M]. MA: Addison-Wesley, 1975: 84-100.

[19] Franklin K K, Hart J K. Idea generation and exploration: benefits and limitations of the policy Delphi research method[J]. Innovative Higher Education, 2007, 31: 237-246.

Designing the City of the Future

Stefan Schmitz

(RSAA | architecture and urban design)

Abstract: This paper summarizes the key factors which need to be taken into account for a successful sustainable urban development. 12 fields of actions which need to be taken into account right from the beginning were identified.

Keywords: Eco city, Smart city, Urban design, Sustainable city design, Green design

1 Introduction

"Better City - Better Life", the slogan of the world expo 2010 Shanghai [1] puts it in a nutshell: Cities play a key role for people's quality of life. A city cannot survive without a constant and reliable energy supply. Energy needs increase with rising living standards.

Considering the fact that traffic and buildings make up 70% of energy consumption, the need for sustainable urban development was globally recognized at government level and programs costing billions regarding measures of energy saving and the use of renewable energy were applied.

The People's Republic of China is a global leader in the planning and realization of new cities. China just reached an urbanization rate of 50% and another 310 million people are expected to migrate from rural to urban areas in the next two decades [2].

However, the opportunities to transform this growth into sustainable structures are hardly being perceived. Nowadays, a multitude of urban development projects are generated, bearing the attributes "ecological" and "sustainable", without actually deserving them. Even though many aspects of energy saving and environmental protection are taken into account, as long as the use of private cars has priority and the lack of sun protection is compensated by the use of energy-consuming air-conditioning systems, there can be no reference to sustainable urban development.

New city developments have to apply strategies and technologies for saving energy on a micro and macro level, in buildings, public spaces, traffic, waste management and industry. All resources of waste heat must be used for the generation of heat and electricity, in order to cover the energy needs of the urban population. We need new cities, in which energy, waste-water, solid waste, transport systems, public infrastructure, buildings, waste heat and local resources are planned and developed in a way that urban sectors can function as a power plant with a closed energy cycle.

Sustainable urban planning requires a holistic point of view, comprising all aspects of urban life and can only be met by a plan combining diverse expertise. It includes all stages, from location analysis, to urban conceptual design, all the way to planning of building facades. In doing so, it is important to develop coordinated and mutually reinforcing measures for energy saving, the use of renewable energy and environmental protection, with low needs of high maintenance technology.

2 Eco city Elements

From our professional experience, we identified 12 fields of actions that need to be taken into account right from the beginning:

2. 1　Polycentric structure

A modern city should be developed in polycentric instead of a monocentric city structure. This allows organizing the city growth step by step by implementing independent urban districts with individual characteristics which help people identify themselves with their living place. These polycentric city structures with good accessibility of basic facilities are a precondition for a city of short distances. The key target is to develop independent and self-sufficient urban entities. Employment decentralization helps improving the commuting patterns by shortening individual commuting distances. [3]

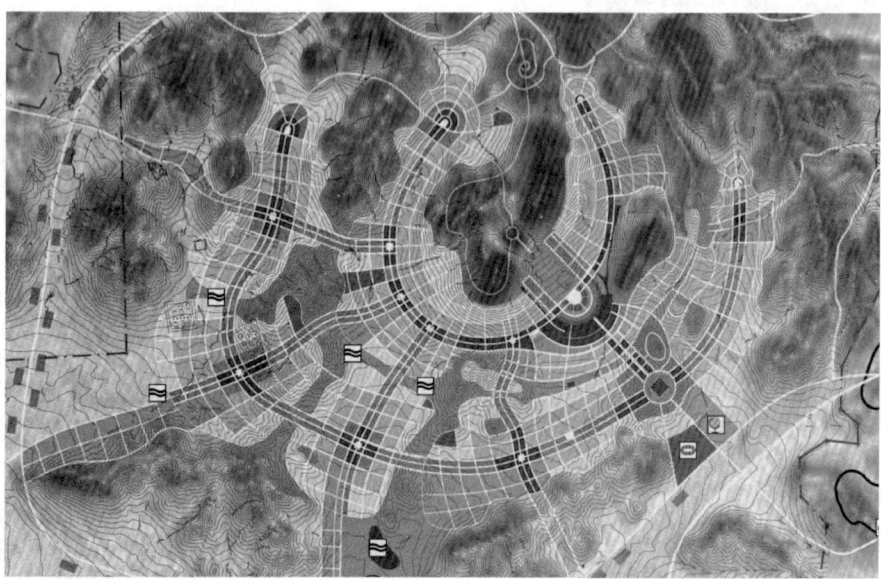

Figure 1　Land use plan of Maidar eco city, Mongolia (RSAA)

2. 2　Density Distribution

The development of the city districts need to define a suitable density target instead of fueling further urban sprawl. High density is a precondition for the economic use of the area, efficient use of infrastructure, an efficient public transportation system and a city of short distances. However, the density should be limited to still allow enough solar radiation, good natural lighting conditions, good natural ventilation and sufficient open space. The distribution of the density should follow the public transport system and concentrate the highest density around public transport spots.

2. 3　Mixed use

A functional and social mixture is a precondition for livable surroundings and solid urban structures. Diverse functions and a broad offer of services within walking distance are preconditions for a city of short distances. Innovative, small-scale structures create urban quarters with individual characteristics and identities and are a precondition for a local economic development. [4]

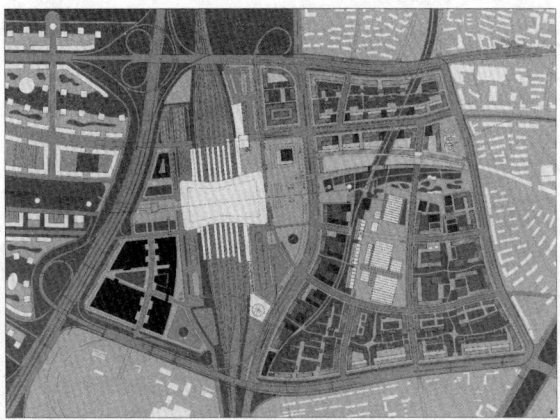

Figure 2　Building functions distribution plan of
Qingdao traffic business district (RSAA)

2. 4　Public Space

Ecological city development also means paying a great deal of attention to the design of the open public space. The quality of the outdoor space is a precondition for people to make green trips rather than taking the car. The creation of characteristic squares, streets and quarters create a distinctive city image. The use, re-use and revitalization of cultural heritage sites within the urban texture should be strongly promoted. These projects help the creation of sui genesis by using historical patterns for the scale and the design of buildings and public space. Another aspect that should be taken into account is the planning of multi-functional and alternative space for everyday life, such as public plazas for different activities, public parks or market halls.

2. 5　Urban Landscape

Existing natural elements should be integrated the urban tissue to minimize ecological footprints. Biodiversity and habitats for urban wildlife in the surrounding landscape should be preserved as much as possible. If there are no or not sufficient existing natural elements, landscape patterns for high social usability for sports / leisure should be created close to residential areas. Continuous green corridors as open space connections within the city should be developed together with the cyclist and pedestrian network already in an early stage of the design process. The green corridors also serve as natural ventilation corridors and can be used as storm water infiltration areas. Also in China, the urban gardening movement is growing in all major cities [5]. Thus the creation of sites for local production within the city and organization of direct marketing is another aspect of urban landscape design in eco cities.

2. 6　Mobility Concept

The Mobility Concept should give priority to public transportation as the most important element of sustainable individual trips and to pedestrians and cyclists paths as main framework for the traffic within urban quarters. A great deal of attention needs to be paid to the design of efficient connections between different traffic systems and the design of the public transportation hubs. The urban design and the traffic design concept should select strategic locations of parking areas to reduce the volume of individual motorized travel. The residential and commercial areas should be designed as car-free zones. E-Mobility and Car-sharing systems can help to further reduce the eco footprint of local traffic. In the Netherlands and in Germany, the concept of "shared space" promotes the equal right of use for the public space to all participants (cars, bikes, pedestrians)[6].

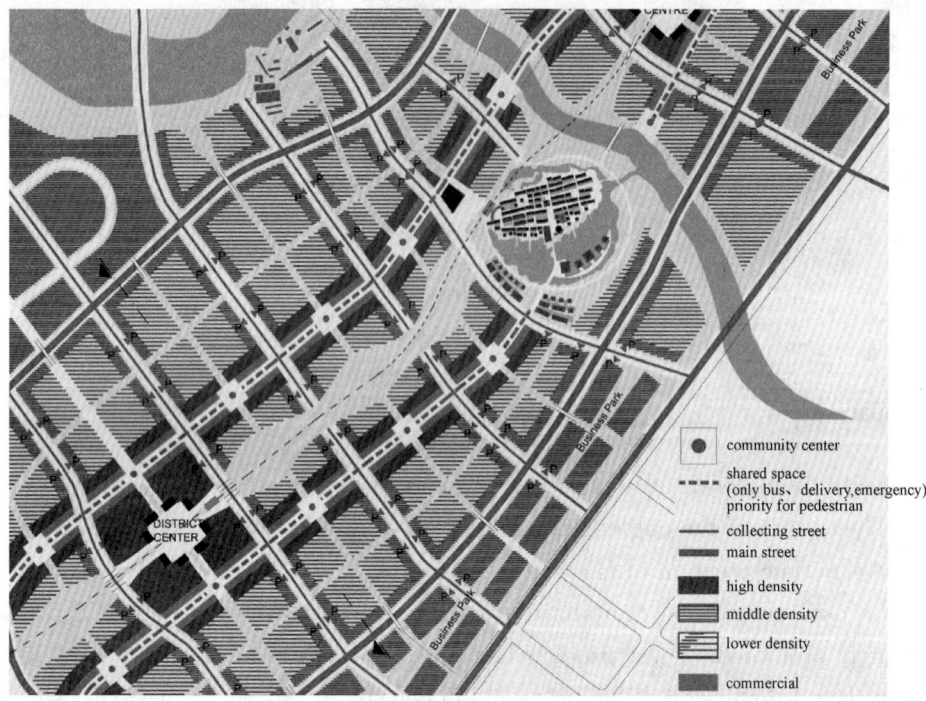

Figure 3　Traffic concept for Sino-Singapore eco city Tianjin (RSAA)

2.7　Public Infrastructure

The use of renewable energy demands for decentralization and multiplication of production units according to the regional sources. Energy efficiency should be maximized; the energy sources should be selected according to the local resources and conditions. We propose decentralized systems of waste-water treatment and electric energy production and the production of heating energy from centralized generation systems within neighborhood areas. If possible, the waste heat from industrial processes in surrounding areas should be utilized. With the increased availability of internet, the single elements of public infrastructure start to be connected to smart grids, or even smart cities.

2.8　Water System

Most of the urbanized coastal regions of china already undertake measures to avoid a potential water shortage. Main targets of any future urban development must be the collection and use of as much rainfall as possible, and the recycling and reuse of the wastewater. This should include concepts for natural storm water management, concepts for sustainable use of local water systems, subtraction of potable water by use of rainwater and grey water for toilets, gardens, car wash and washing machines, production of modern technologies with de-central systems for water supply and waste-water disposal, recycling of waste-water resources and composting systems for biological fraction.

194

2. 9   Waste Management

Waste is not waste but resource. According to the European Environment Agency, in 2010 35% of the European municipal waste was recycled, with Austria (63%), Germany (62%), Belgium (58%) and Netherlands (51%) already reaching the European target of 50% recycling rate for municipal waste by 2020[7]. Next to recycling, modern waste management strategies include waste to energy (incineration of waste), engineered landfills, hazardous waste treatment and handling, separation technology and bio-gas production from waste.

2. 10   Building Standard

According to the International Energy Agency (IEA) buildings represent 32% of total final energy consumption. In terms of primary energy consumption, buildings represent around 40% in most IEA countries [8]. Thus, implementing a low energy standard for buildings is one of the main points of action of any eco-city development. However, that must not automatically come along with only high-tech solutions. The first step should be the avoidance of energy use (e. g. intelligent design, flexible floorplans, low A/V ratio), the second the improvement of the efficiency of the energy use (e. g. insulation standard, heat exchange systems) and the third step should be the production of the needed energy (renewable energy sources). Other aspects that should be taken into account are the use of environmental friendly and healthy building materials and the eco footprint of the building materials (energy needed for production and transportation).

2. 11   Economic Indicators

Ecologic city projects are economic city projects. Already in an early design stage, the live cycle costs of buildings and infrastructure should be considered. In general, a higher urban density makes infrastructure facilities more efficient. The intelligent location of daily life needs can be a strategy to reduce traffic and traffic infrastructure.

2. 12   Design and Decision Making Process

All the above mentioned points have strong influence on each other and cannot be designed independently. The designers of the different mayors must work together as an integrated planning team already in the early conceptual phases. The process requires an intelligent management of planning and decision making as well as a professional mediation for balancing the different interests of relevant planning partners. Already in an early stage, the approval authorities, local experts and the local community should be involved in the process. It is also possible, to include external investment in these early phases and to set up the projects as public-private partnerships.

3   Conclusion

In order to design these new cities, we need a wide, interdisciplinary and inter-sectoral approach to develop an overall concept which will embrace all areas, from single buildings, to the neighborhood and the whole city, aiming at developing permanent and sustainable structures which offer citizens a high quality of life, contribute to protecting the environment and can prevail in the global competition among cities.

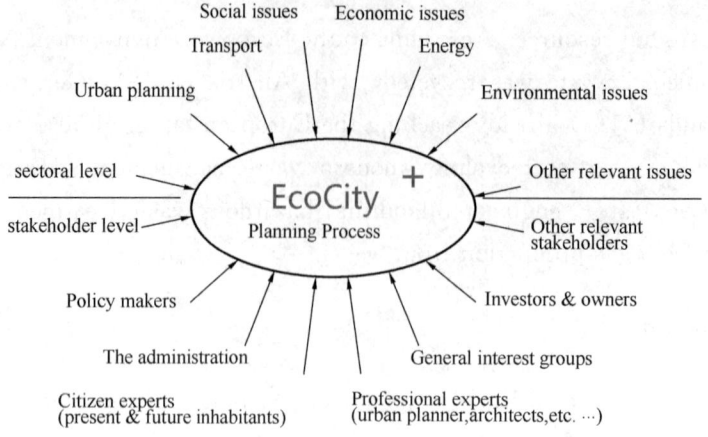

Figure 4   Ecocity plannung process

未来生态城市设计

Stefan Schmitz
（RSAA -建筑设计和城市规划）

摘要：本文以能源需求和城市可持续发展为背景，依据 RSAA 的专业经验，总结了一个成功的生态城需要考虑的关键要素。这 12 个关键要素需要在设计之初就加以思考。

关键词：生态城，智能城市，城市规划，可持续城市规划，绿色规划

References：

［1］ www. expo2010. cn.

［2］ United Nations Development Programme China National Human Development Report, 2013：4.

［3］ Dong Lin, Andrew Allan, Jianqiang Cui, Rlaph McLaughling. The effects of polycentric development on commuting patterns in metropolitan areas：9.

［4］ Deopletriented Cities：Mixed use Development creats social and Economic Benefits http://www. wri. org/blog/2014/07/people-oriented-cities-mixed-use-development-creates-social-and-economic-benefits.

［5］ echinacities, Creative Crops：Urban Farming in China http://www. echinacities. com/expat-corner/Creative-Crops-Urban-Farming-in-China.

［6］ http://www. netzwerk-sharedspace. de/.

［7］ http://www. eea. europa. eu/de/pressroom/newsreleases/hoechste-recyclingraten-in-oesterreich-und.

［8］ http://www. iea. org/aboutus/faqs/energyefficiency/.

新时代背景下多层高密度住宅的应用与发展

曾 皓 赵 祥

（西南科技大学土木工程与建筑学院）

摘要：在快速城市化过程中，我国城郊住区建设以高层住区为主。但高层住区的适应性差，难以应对多样的居住需求。新型城镇化着力于中心城区的人口疏解，城市人口分布及居住需求在未来将有较大变化。本文对多层高密度住宅和对高层住宅进行了对比分析，指出在城郊地区建设新型多层高密度住宅能够更合理地满足新的居住需求，应对居住形态的变迁，并以实例进行了说明。

关键词：多层高密度，住宅，新型城镇化，居住需求

1 引言

为快速提高城镇化水平，我国曾走过一段粗放型的城镇化发展道路。大城市在不断地吸纳农村人口和占用土地资源后却不能有效解决城市人口膨胀所导致的居住以及就业问题。为解决以上问题，政府提出了以人为本的新型城镇化发展模式。在此背景下，城市住宅建设方式也将随之改变。与大量在城市中心建设高层住宅相比，在郊区建设多层高密度住宅能更好地适应新的居住需求。

2 多层高密度住宅的概念

"多层高密度住宅"概念源于英国，在英国"多层"是指高度低于24.3m的民用建筑，在我国最新的防火规范（GB 50016—2014）中，多层建筑是指低于27m的民用建筑[1]；而"密度"则指选定区域范围内的建筑密度，这点有别于我国"建筑密度＝建筑覆盖率"的概念，暂且称其为"A型建筑密度"，其计算方式为：A型建筑密度＝建筑覆盖率×选定区域内房屋平均层数。"高密度"是一个相对概念，其衡量标准取决于选定用地在城市中所处区域的A型建筑密度平均值。[2]

20世纪下半页，随着高层住宅的大量修建，许多问题被揭露出来，诸如照顾儿童不便，工程造价高，能源消耗大，消防隐患多等。因此，英国政府在1975年颁布的《住房法》里禁止了以高层住宅为主的住区建造。[3]1972年，L. Martin和L. March在《Urban Space and Structures》中论证了在同一地块内考虑必要的日照、通风等条件下，高度只有塔式住宅1/3的庭院式住宅能提供与塔式住宅相等的居住面积（图1）。[4]在此背景下，"多层高密度住区"的设计理念便被提出。在过去的40年中，西方国家对多层高密度住宅进行了大量研究与实践论证，例如在《城市与形态》一书中，Serge Salat用多种数据证实了多层高密度住宅在解决居住舒适度，城市拥堵，社区配套等问题时比高层住宅具有更多优势。[5]实际案例中也可证实这一点，如阿姆斯特丹的Borneo-Sporenburg住宅区（图2），该项目在25hm²的半岛状用地上容纳了2500个住户，户均用地面积仅10m²，而其中最高的建筑也只有7层。

上述国外经验说明，城镇化发展到一定阶段后，在解决市民居住的问题上多层高密度住宅比高层住宅更加合理。中国目前正处于新型城镇化的快速发展阶段，人口分布与社会需求等方面的变化也会对住区建设提出新的挑战。

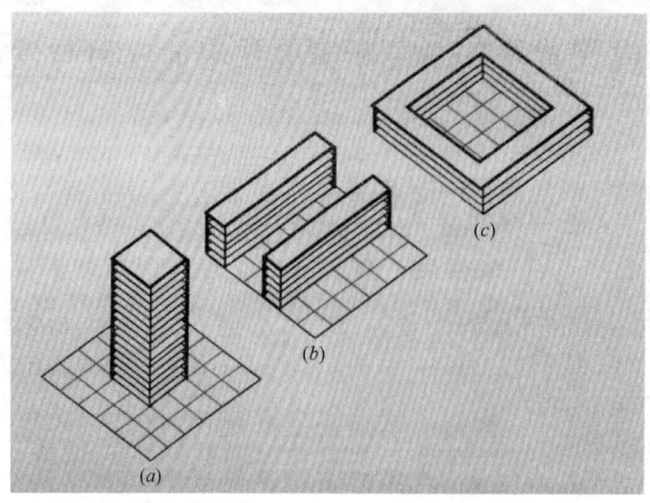

图 1 Urban Space and Structures 中展示的图例

图 2 Borneo-Sporenburg 住宅区
（资料来源：1. 格拉罕·陶尔 城市住宅设计. 江苏：江苏科学技术出版社，2007.
2. www. west8. nl/cn/projects/all/borneo _ sporenburg/)

3 中国社会变化对住宅建设的影响

3.1 人口分布与人口结构的变化

随着新型城镇化的加快，农村人口会更多地向市镇迁移，而城市公共交通的发展和卫星城镇的建设也使得城市居民向城郊迁移，未来城郊将成为城市的主要居住区域（图 3）。[6]2032 年中国人口总量将达到峰值 14.5 亿，随着出生于第一批婴儿潮时期的人相继死去，到 2050 年，人口总量又会回落到 13.2 亿[7]，即 20 年之内人口减少 1.3 亿。2013 年我国开始进入人口负债时代[1]，中国人口老龄化速度加快，据联合国预测，到 2030 年中国 60 岁以上的老年人口将占总人口数的 30％。人口的减少和老龄化不可避免地带来住房空置问题，住宅建设必须考虑控制规模，以避免住宅反复拆建造成不必要的经济浪费、环境污染和劳动力消耗。

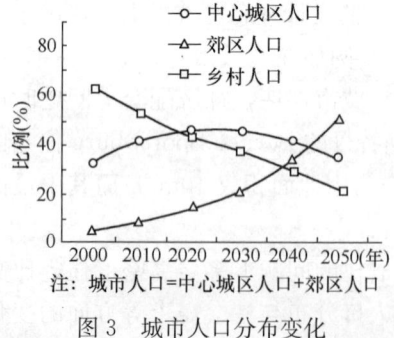

注：城市人口=中心城区人口+郊区人口

图 3 城市人口分布变化
（资料来源：笔者自绘）

3.2 居住需求的个性化

据国家统计局 2013 年的数据显示，中国的家庭人口平均数已从 1990 年的 3.96 人/户下降到 2013 年的 2.72 人/户，并在持续下降中。[8]随着家庭规模的缩小，居民对住宅空间提出了更强的个性化需求。作者通过对 18～65 岁之间的 260 位城市居民进行问卷调查后发现，其中 64.3% 的受访者表示当前市面上的户型不能完全满足居住需求，主要不足在于空间划分单一的 nLDK^2 模式不能满足居民对个性空间的需求，未来的住宅建设应更多考虑户型空间的个性化设计。

4 多层高密度住宅与高层住宅对比分析

在面对社会变化与个性化需求时，能容纳同样居民数量的多层高密度住区比高层住区的适应性更强，且前者能提供更优质的居住环境。

4.1 户型空间的灵活性

目前，市面上的住宅户型往往是普适性的，难以精准满足不同住户的个性需求，对居住空间进行"二次设计"是应对个性化需求的可行办法。由于受到结构和设备的严格限制，高层住宅的空间可变要素很少，所谓的个性化多止于装饰，不能灵活地进行空间组合。而在多层高密度住宅内，住宅以框架结构为主，空间布局灵活性远大于高层住宅，能更好地满足居民个性化的居住需求。

另外，在面对人口数量从增长到缩减的变化过程中，空间灵活性差，无法适应改造要求的高层住宅只能被闲置或拆除。而多层住宅墙体布置较为自由，对新的功能需求适应性好，能延长其使用寿命，避免不必要的资源浪费。工程实例如山本理显设计的东云集合住宅 a 区，设计中采用了家庭与小型办公相结合的 SOHO 模式（图 4），平面布局可根据使用者需要时调配住宅与办公的比例。[9]

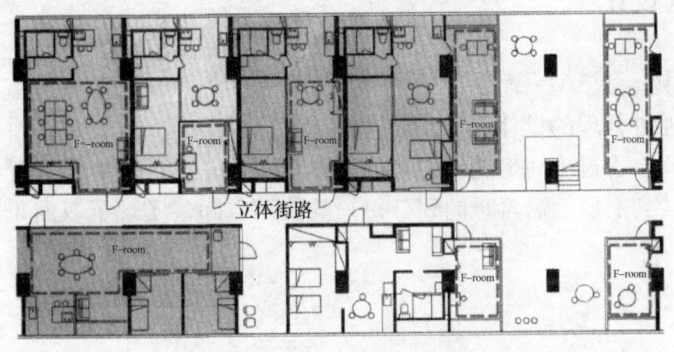

图 4   东云集合住宅部分平面图

[资料来源：[日]《新建筑》，第 75 卷 6 号，2000（05）]

4.2 住区的居住环境品质

通过对高层住宅、胡同、大杂院和庭院式多层住区的外部空间进行比较研究，发现人们在低层围合空间内心理上的归属感和认同感更好。[10]在多层高密度住宅内，住宅围合产生的庭院空间能供人们聚会和休闲；虽然高层住宅也有地面开放空间，但这些缺少围合的空间往往缺少社交氛围，经常沦为闲置绿化带或停车场（图 5）。[11]同时，多层高密度住宅可以利用高大的树木有效阻挡来自街道的噪声，而高层住宅大多则是暴露在街道的声场之中。[12]

图 5　上海与柏林住区卫星图对比

（资料来源：笔者自绘）

5　多层高密度住宅规划设计

以上对比研究表明，多层高密度住宅在提升居住环境和解决空间可变性的问题上，与高层住宅相比优势明显，具有广阔的应用前景，但其规划设计并非过去多层住宅的简单复制，而是需要精心设计，并力求通过低成本技术手段来提供高度的灵活性。

5.1　住宅户型空间设计

在多层住宅设计中，将户型平面设计成小面宽大进深的形状，可以有效节约用地，而内部房间采光不足的问题可以通过合理的设计进行改善。位于德国汉堡的 Baufeld 10 项目中（图 6），户型被设计为复式结构，入口层通过中间走道横向划分入户空间，并在这个楼层布置一些对采光要求弱的房间，而通过楼梯连接到上层之后再竖向划分每户的使用空间，实现了双向采光，解决了大进深下的采光问题。

5.2　公共空间设计

过去多层住宅以板式一梯两户的单元式住宅楼为主，公共空间只起交通作用，邻里交往没有依托。因此在新型多层高密度住宅设计中，各户之间的公共空间不能只是单纯的交通空间，而是能够发生"事件"的场所。Guallart Architects 在 Sharing Blocks 项目中正是运用了这样的设计思路，建筑师分析了 13 个居住基本功能，将其中可以共享和半共享的功能如吃饭、休息、洗衣、办公等纳入公共或半私密空间（图 7）。增加了住户在日常生活中互相接触的机会，提高了住户的归属感。

5.3　结构空间设计

为使户型在全生命周期中的适应性增大，其中结构框架的模数设计需要仔细考虑。例如 7m×6m 的柱网可以形成单位面积为 42m² 的空间，这样一个单位面积可作为廉租房或老年公寓，两个单位则可转变为 84m² 的经济适用房；而非承重墙体的运用也方便了住户对住宅进行改造。只要选取

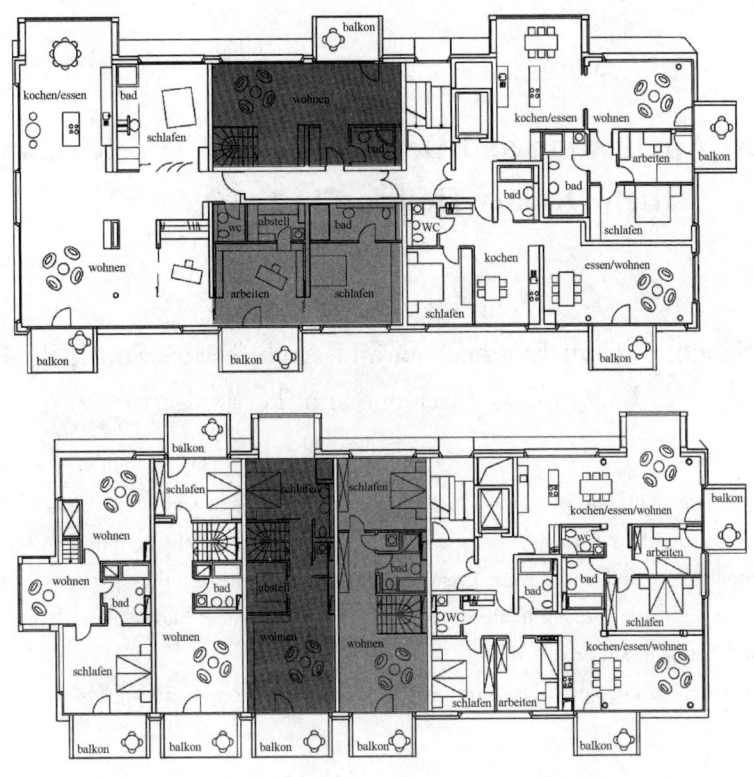

图 6　Baufeld 10 平面图

（资料来源：www.dezeen.com/2011/03/17/baufeld-10-by-love-architecture/）

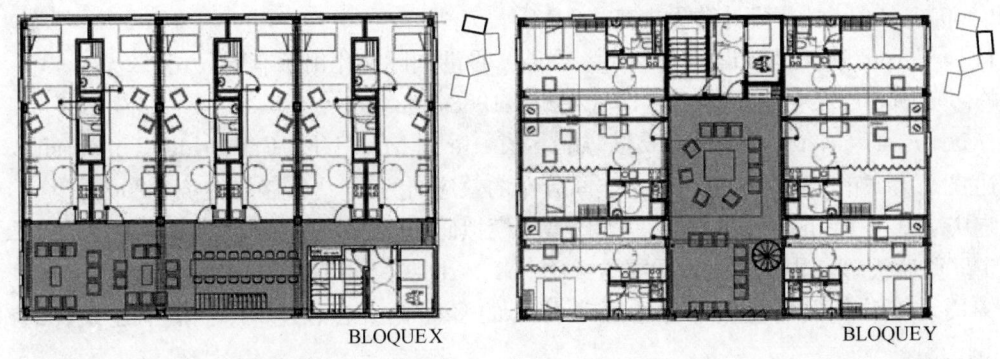

BLOQUE X　　　　　BLOQUE Y

图 7　Sharing Blocks 平面图

（资料来源：www.guallart.com/projects）

合理的柱网形式，多层板式住宅还可以在住宅需求减少的背景下将住区本身改造为活动中心、办公等其他用途，实现居住、工作的同区域。这不仅符合家庭办公一体化的趋势，也符合我国的可持续发展战略。

6　结论

西方发达国家城市建设的经验和中国的城市化现状说明，当城市化发展到一定阶段必然导致人口郊区化。多层高密度住宅无论是在功能适应性上，还是在全生命周期内的经济性上，居住环境品质与高层住宅相比都有很大优势。在国家努力实现新型城镇化的背景下，新型多层高密度住宅在中国仍处于探索阶段，但其前景广阔，应当大力推进研究与实践。

The Application and Development of Mid-Rise and High-Density Housing in the New Era

Zeng Hao，Zhao Xiang

(School of Civil Engineering and Architecture South West
University of Science and Technology)

Abstract：During the rapid urbanization the large number of high-rise residential district is difficult to meet the needs of people who live in suburban. The new urbanization focus eson easing urban population centers，the city population distribution and housing demand will have a greater change in the future. This paper compares the mid-rise and high-density housing with high-rise housing to figure out that the mid-rise and high-density housing model can adapt to the new housing demand better in suburban.

Keywords：Mid-rise and high-density，Housing，New urbanization，Residential needs

参考文献：

[1] GB 50016—2014 建筑设计防火规范，2014.

[2，5，11] Serge Salat. 城市与形态[M]. 香港：香港国际文化出版有限公司，2013.

[3] 吴峥. 英国高层住宅的兴衰[J]. 时代建筑，1988，02.

[4] L. Martin，L. March. Urban Space and Structures[M]. UK：Cambridge University，1972.

[6] 蒋讠夬强. 大城市人口郊区化与住宅空间分布的效应研究[J]. 人口与经济，2002，03.

[7] 韩晓庆. 基于 Leslie 模型中国未来人口策略模拟研究[D]. 辽宁：东北财经大学，2012.

[8] 谢宇，张晓波等. 中国民生发展报告 2013[M]. 北京：北京大学出版社，2013.

[9] 李锦霞，王洁. 以邻为鉴，打造匠心独具的多样化集合住宅[J]. 华中建筑，2004，04：62-64.

[10] 张双庆. 传统院落在现代高容积率住宅与居住环境中的沿革探索[D]. 四川：四川大学，2006.

[12] 谭明洋. 从环境心理学论当代居住区环境设计[D]. 陕西：西安美术学院，2013.

夹缝中的可生长性思维——高密度城市中心住区人居环境的改造策略

王 倩 戴 航 郭 苐

（南京东南大学）

摘要：在城市化不断快速发展的过程中，高密度城市中心区的一些老居住区正在经历着物质性老化和社会性衰败，并且也逐渐暴露出一系列不符合现代居住需求的人居环境问题；本文以南京某高密度城市中心住区为研究对象，以走访和问卷调查的方式阐述了其存在的人居环境问题；基于这些问题，本文就该住区的现有状况提出了一种可生长性思维下的改造策略，并结合国外案例以及多种可生长性技术方法对人居环境的改造改善策略进行了引荐式的探讨，阐释了可生长性思维在高密度城市中心住区人居环境改造中的长远意义兼具可持续性发展的价值。

关键词：高密度住区，人居环境，可生长性，改造策略

1 引言

20 世纪 70～90 年代，为了解决我国城市大规模化发展下的人口居住问题，国家兴建了一批数量庞大的居民新村或居住区，这一时期建设的住宅大部分以低标准住宅为主。在城市化不断快速发展的过程中，这部分住宅正在经历着物质性老化和社会性衰败，而城市中心区的居住者对住宅要求也发生了很大的变化，高密度性使得现代居民生活在类似"夹缝"般的环境中，这些包含了多元化时代印记的高密度住区也逐渐暴露出一系列问题：原有的低标准住宅及其高密度人居环境已经不能适应现代化居住者的要求，例如一家几代人在低标准住宅中的"蜗居"生活，居民自行加建乱建问题，停车区占用公共空间和道路等等各种问题导致公共空间急剧减少，这些问题使得其居住环境逐渐恶劣，对城市的影响也慢慢从为了解决人口居住问题转向了改善类似的人居环境问题。

2 "夹缝"中的人居环境问题调查：以南京某高密度市中心住区为例

以南京某高密度城市中心住区为例，该居住区用地面积 91070m²，容积率为 2.2，住宅建设从 1960 年到 1990 年并以 1980 年为主（图 1），土地权属也较为复杂。对该区居民主要以走访和问卷调查的方式从住宅基本情况，公共设施配置，住区环境，住宅内部情况以及居民对更新和改造意愿等方面进行了分组调研。调研数据结果表明该高密度住区公共居住环境质量对居民的日常生活具有重大影响，主要突出体现在几个方面见（图 2），首先是居住质量低下：该住区住宅人均住房面积严重不足，主要集中在 10～15m²，远低于南京全市人均住房面积且户型偏小，以低于 60m² 户型为主，导致居民的基本生活都存在问题；除此之外居住质量下降还体现在建筑物年久失修，建筑防水层渗漏，外墙，窗户和门难以保温隔热，能耗大等方面；其次是公共空间的丧失：由于中心区高密度的特征其本身的公共空间就呈现出稀缺的状态，随着机动车辆的增加而车位严重不足导致乱停车现象，寻找停车位的车辆在交通道路上和宅间空地上"见缝插针"，以及居民在公共空地乱加建违章建筑最终致使公共活动空间的严重丧失；生态环境恶化也直接导致了人居环境质量的下降：集中体现在绿化缺乏，乱加建违章建筑，杂物堆积以及；除此之外，公共基础设施不完备也在一定程度上体现了低质量人居环境的特征：严重缺乏室外休息与活动设施，尤其是对于整日居留的老年人更为明显；虽然人居环境日益恶劣，但是在调研中还发现，由于该居住区位于市中心区，交通便利且工作地点近等优势，居民对就地改善还是异地搬迁的态度更倾向于前者，希望能就地改善住宅条件，这也意味着在对待类似该高密度中心住区的基本问题，迫切需要一系列具有针对性的改造策略。

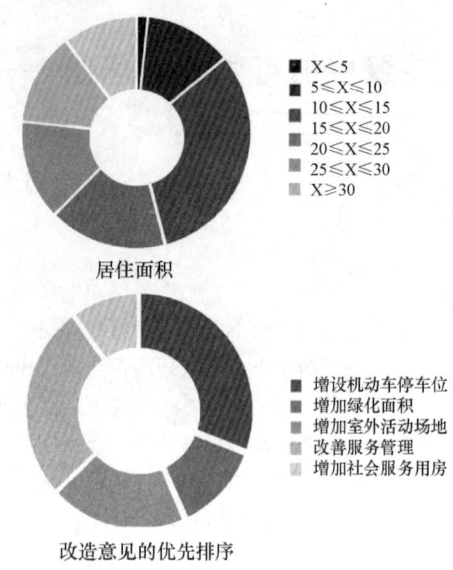

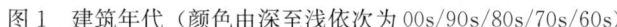

图1　建筑年代（颜色由深至浅依次为 00s/90s/80s/70s/60s)　　　　图2　部分调查结果

3　从传统的"推倒式"更新策略到"可生长性"改造思考

然而针对这种特殊"夹缝"中的人居环境问题，由于城市中心住区的高密度性，传统的"推倒式"大规模重建更新方式必定会面临一系列的现实问题：归属利益的平衡，大规模居民合理拆迁安置问题，住宅拆除和新建过程中对城市环境以及周边居民生活影响问题等等，尤其是近几年建筑现场作业中建筑垃圾产生的粉尘污染问题等等，因此传统的更新策略在一定层面上仍然无法在短期内使"夹缝"中的人居环境实现自下而上的切实改善以及有效提供远期发展下的人居环境保障。

那么在现有的建筑技术支撑下，并且针对这种特殊的夹缝式高密度住区，是否能够提供一种的"可生长性"的策略，即在保证居民正常生活的情况下，自然合理地改造原有正常使用的建筑和公共空间，具有弹性地改善室内外的人居环境，在改造和利用中犹如就地生长般地最小可能性的降低对居民正常生活的影响，并且在远期发展中不断提供再改造利用的可能性，能够可持续地生长更新，对城市和社会作出适应性地改变。

实现这种可生长性思维的建筑技术在国外住宅设计中已经发展地相当成熟，即高度的预制装配和独立单元模块，然而这些技术方法在国内高密度城市中心住区人居环境改造中的利用方面还是非常少的，并未发挥其可持续特性的最大优势。预制装配既是以工业化的生产方式，将预制的构件在工地装配而成；独立单元模块是具有独立性特征的建筑单元或结构单元模块，其标准化模块的实现方式是在工厂预制，运输至作业场地并通过预设方案进行组装拼插，并且能够满足拆卸变更要求，实现再利用的生长特质。

相对于传统的改造方法，以预制装配和单元模块为支撑的改造方式最大的优势是能够减小"夹缝式"居住环境中的改造负担，由于其现场作业的比例大大减少，并且为集成施工，自动化程度高，施工速度快，因此能够最大限度减少对正常居住生活的影响；由于施工现场主要由机械完成，因此也大大节约模板、脚手等，在施工作业中不仅使周围居民的安全性能够得到保证，也大大减少了废弃物的产生，粉尘和噪声等环境污染，其另一方面优势是在改造后能够为高密度中心住区提供"可逆性"改造的可能性，由于独立单元模块自身具有完整独立性而单元之间非传统的依附关系，因此可以实现拆卸再利用，在高密度的旧居住区改造中可以高度体现其绿色可持续性的价值。

4 可生长性技术支撑下的改造策略探索

基于这种生长性思维，结合国外经典案例，针对在南京某高密度城市中心住区的调研中发现的人居环境问题，主要可以从以下几个方面进行探索研究。

4.1 基于可扩容模块的功能性改造

可扩容的模块是利用独立支撑的高度预制化技术而实现功能性模块的增加，可以保证在装配使用中的独立性从而降低对原有建筑的影响。由 ISA 建筑工作室设计并由 2010 年建成的天普大学学生公寓，是由工厂预制的住宅模块装配而成（图 3），每个模块单元内包含卧室、厨房、卫生间和地面装修，运输到现场装配完毕后只需进行外立面和室内装修。功能性模块可以是为老龄化社区添加的电梯等交通空间模块，也可以根据多种户型满足不同规模家庭的使用需要而添加居住功能块单元，如厨房、阳台、甚至在竖向上添加整体住宅单元，这种改造方式直接以增加室内居住面积来提高居住质量，同时可以避免因居住面积过小而导致居民生活空间向外扩张占用公共空间的行为。

4.2 可逆式的公共空间模块

由于整个住区大多在 20 世纪 80 年代建成，公共配套设施以及场地非常缺乏，使得居住区建筑功能单一化，不能够刺激社区生活的产生与人际交往。针对高密度夹缝式的住区，除了利用集中式且便于管理的装配式立体停车方案还原原本就稀少但被车辆占用的大量公共场地外，还可以增设可自由拆卸组装且能循环利用的公共空间模块，这样不仅可以直接增加公共空间来解决居民公共活动问题，还能在远期提供根据需要而变的可能性，比较经典的案例为 2010 年上海世博会挪威馆，其展馆由 15 个木结构单元拼接而成（图 4），每一个单元都能自由拆卸组装，可以根据不同的功能如公共景观凉亭，社交聚集地等在其他场所进行重复利用，而将各个部件组装起来只需 6h。因此可以利用预制装配化的这种可逆特性在高密度居住区中发挥其最大的可持续优势。

图 3　天普大学住宅模块　　　　　　　图 4　上海世博会挪威馆单元模块

4.3 老住宅的一体化整体模块更新

对于年代久远不宜居住的小型住宅而言，由于建筑防水层渗漏，外墙、窗户和门难以保温隔热，建筑能耗大等方面已经不能适宜就地改造的方式，因此要快速更新不仅需要预制装配的方式，还需要进行一体化的整体设计，一体化系统需要将功能空间，结构，装饰，设备要素整合起来（图 5），比如在伦敦莫里街住宅的 8m×3.2m×3m 单元模块中，就将内部分隔墙、外墙内表面石膏板和外表面镀锌钢板以及其中间填充有保温隔热隔声材料进行一体化设计，并且在工厂预制成形进行现场整体模块的装配。这样即可以保证全装修住宅的建造能在工厂中一次性完成，也能有效地减少建造和装修的工期，保证原住户能够在短期内入住并且从时间上也降低地对周边居民正常生活的影响。

4.4 预制单元模块支撑下的立面改造

丰富多元的建筑造型不仅能为高密度建筑群体营造良好的居住氛围，并且可以得到居民对所属各个建筑体以及住区本身的认同感；预制装配式立面模块能在解决大规模立面改造问题中充分体现其设计优势，如 SHoP 建筑事务所在纽约 MULBERRY 公寓中的参数化立面设计（图 6），建筑表皮由 CNC（计算机数字数控）制造的砖板嵌入式单元模块装配而成，不仅呼应了城市规划要求对建筑立面"石早建筑"外墙的要求，并且以充满活力的现代性表皮为街区创造了一个动感的视觉印象。

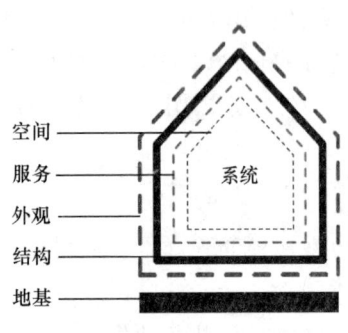

图 5　一体化设计建筑要素　　　　图 6　MULBERRY 公寓的参数化立面

5　总结

基于可生长性思维的改造方式种类繁多，针对高密度城市中心住区种种人居环境问题而言，无疑需要类似具有可持续特质的"可生长性"思维。其改造策略需要工业化的技术支撑，预制装配式住宅在国内经过 20 多年的发展，已经从实验性研究阶段走向了可行的工程实施阶段，而高度的预制装配技术在国外已经发展成熟也有不少的开发团队，但是由于国内在高度的预制装配方面的技术还未能达到能够普遍应用的程度，因此就南京某高密度中心住区而言，对预制化要求较高的一体化住宅更新可能尚未普及，但是对于可循环利用的可扩容单元模块、装配式立体停车等设施都已经可以投入市场，为高密度城市中心住区的人居环境改造方面做出积极的贡献。

Metabolic Strategy for Transformation of High-Density Residential Environment in Central City

Wang Qian，Dai Hang，Guo Di
(School of Architecture，Southeast University)

Abstract：Under the background that China urbanization develops rapidly, those old urban central residential areas which with high-density characteristic are undergoing physical aging and social decline, at the mean time, some residential environment problems that couldn't meet the urban living demand have been emerging. In a case study of Nanjing, a series of residential environment problems are revealed in this paper by means of visiting and investigation; Based on these results , a metabolic renovation strategy is suggested according to its quality of high-density; And combined with some successful cases, targeted measures that supported by existing architectural technologies are also offered in this paper, which aims to present the sustainability values of metabolic renovation strategy in residential environment development.

Keywords：High-density residential，Residential environment，Metabolic strategy，Renovation

参考文献：

[1] 吕俊华. 中国现代城市住宅：1840-2000[M]. 北京：清华大学出版社，2003.

[2] MIKN 设计事务所. 住区再生设计手册[M]. 范悦，周博译. 辽宁：大连理工大学出版社，2009.

[3] 王静茹. 可生长性结构思维下的建筑生成及结构表达[D]. 江苏：东南大学，2009.

[4] Ryan E Smith，Prefab Architecture. A Guide to Modular Design and Const[J]. Wiley，2010.

[5] Javier Mozas. HoCo：Density Housing Construction and Costs[J]. A＋T Ediciones，2009.

城市高层建筑集聚区域内开放空间的微气候环境研究

张馨元[1]　臧倩[1]　张逸凡[1]　于明霞[1]　童滋雨[1,2]
（1. 南京大学建筑与城市规划学院；2. 通讯作者）

摘要： 城市高层集聚区极易发生"热岛效应"、"干岛效应"，导致微气候环境的恶化。城市中心区内的开放空间常常陷入高层建筑的包围之中，其微气候环境由于受周边建筑和自身材质的影响，旋风或污染物沉积等不利因素都可能发生。因此认知此类型开放空间的微气候环境对城市的发展较为重要。选择南京商业中心新街口莱迪广场为研究对象，从实际调研出发，分析城市中心区高层聚集区域内以硬质铺地为主的开放空间的微气候环境质量，从而为探寻其与周边环境的关联关系奠定基础，并为开放空间的选址和设计提供参考依据。

关键词： 城市微气候，开放空间，高层集聚区

1 研究背景

城市中心区通常高层密集，既遮挡阳光，又影响空气流动，极易导致"热岛效应"、"干岛效应"的发生，导致微气候环境的恶化。以绿地为代表的城市开放空间对城市微气候具有明显的改善作用，包括通风、降温等。然而，城市中心区内的开放空间常常陷入高层建筑的包围之中，且硬铺地占到很大比例。在这种情况下，尽管开放空间仍能提供市民休憩活动的场所，但周边的高层建筑也常引发遮挡阳光和视线，影响空气流动，旋风与污染物沉积，对周边地块产生不利影响等问题。然而，目前对这种高层集聚区域内的以硬质铺地为主的开放空间的微气候状态尚缺乏明确的量化描述和认知，也缺乏周边高层建筑的分布对开放空间内微气候影响机制的研究。

国内外现有研究表明，城市开放空间形态对周边地块微气候存在影响。Sozer证明了高层聚集区的环境布局包括建筑面积和体积、街道的方向和宽度等，对实现开放空间更好的空气流动有影响。[1]次年，Shishegar对街道设计和城市微气候进行了研究，将重点放在了街道的几何形状（高宽比）、方位和空气流通以及日照辐射上。她认为街道将影响空气和气流，高宽比越低获得的阳光越多，街道的方位几乎不影响街道峡谷的太阳辐射数量。[2]国内方面，伊娜和冷红以哈尔滨高层区为例，调研得到各布局模式的综合舒适参考值，模拟所得的各布局微气候舒适程度依次为L围合式＞山墙错落式＞行列式＞规则围合式＞斜列式。[3]绿地因素也对城市开放空间微气候具有明显的改善作用，包括通风、降温等。佟华等人指出，植被可以降低当地和下风方向的空气温度，节约在炎热天气下制冷所需的能源，降低城市热岛强度。以绿地为中心的低温区域，成为人们户外休憩活动的最优良环境。[4]此外，周媛等人以沈阳市夏季为例，综合利用RS-GIS-CFD数值模拟法，从水平方向及垂直方向对城市风速、污染物、地表温度的空间扩散进行数值模拟分析，总结了气象要素及污染物扩散规律，并提出了基于气候环境特征的城市绿地景观格局优化的相关规划策略。[5]光照强度与开放空间微气候环境舒适度也存在关联性。王新军，秦佳等人提出，照度的分布与公共开放空间的功能与性质有关。而作为微气候的影响因素之一，较高的照度均匀度，适宜的水平照度和垂直照度，能使开放空间形成良好的光环境氛围。[6]

因此，通过对微气候各影响因素与开放空间空间形态的相关性关系研究，认知开放空间的微气候状态并探究相关规律，从而对开放空间进行更合理的设计，提高其使用效率和改善其使用体验。继而在后期结合绿地空间的微气候研究成果，通过添加乔、灌、草等不同植被，有针对性地改善开放空间中的微气候不利区域，进一步提高其微气候环境质量，以充分发挥城市开放空间的社会与环境价值，用以之后在此类型的城市设计中加以参考。

2 研究方法

本研究采用的研究方法包括对选择案例的现场实测、基于合理算法的插值计算以及数据统计和地理统计分析方法。

鉴于现状条件复杂，且受到人流车流以及临时性活动的影响，使用软件模拟的方法不能真实反映出实际状况，为了更准确地获取其微气候状况，本研究采用了密布观测点的方式。

尽管采用密布观测点的方式，但仍是散点式的观测结果，为了更全面地反映开放空间的微气候状况，本研究采用插值计算，生成覆盖整个开放空间的微气候场。常用的插值计算方式包括距离反比插值法、克里格插值法、样条函数插值法等。其中样条函数插值法被证明更有利于温度场的计算模拟[7]，故本研究采用该方式。

本研究将在两个方面通过统计分析微气候因素与开放空间环境的潜在规律和相互间的作用规律。一方面是微气候因素之间的相互影响，主要采用数据统计和回归分析的方法；另一方面是开放空间形态与周边环境对微气候状态的影响，主要采用地理统计和空间分析的方法。

3 案例研究

本研究通过实地取样观测了解场地性质，结合获取的调研数据进行数据分析，结合场地形态特征进行数据反馈，获得对于开放空间空间形态与微气候因素的关系的认知。

3.1 案例选择

南京莱迪广场地处南京第一商圈——新街口核心商业圈，位于新街口商业步行街和正洪街的交汇处，总面积约为5400m²。该广场周边密集分布着南京中心大厦和南京商贸世纪广场2幢超高层建筑，中央商务楼、文化宫综合楼和正洪大厦3幢高层建筑，以及一些多层建筑，地下为地铁通道和南京时尚莱迪购物中心，仅有东南角、西南角和西北角三个出入口。此外，南京时尚莱迪购物中心的出入口位于广场中央，上部覆盖白色张拉膜构筑物，占地面积约为700m²。广场周边多为商业性建筑，在10：00～21：30人流相对聚集。

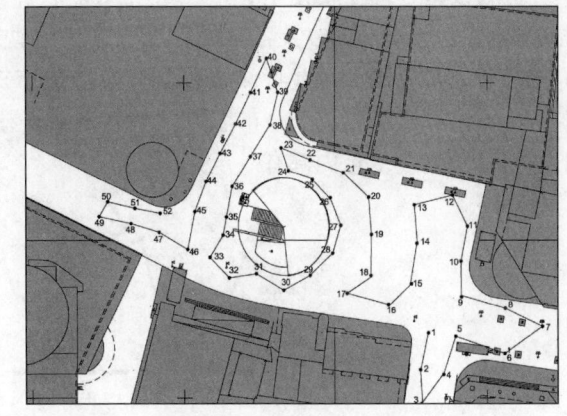

图1　南京莱迪广场52个采样点分布图

在观测点的选择上，由于研究数据需要全面而又准确地反映广场的特点，本研究于整个广场范围内均布52个采样点，采样点间距为10m左右，在转角、广场开口、建筑边界和常年阴影区等微气候因素变化显著的区域，适当增加采样点（图1）。

3.2 微气候因素选择与观测

微气候因素有很多种，如风速、温度、相对湿度、气压、光照、CO浓度、CO_2浓度、环境噪声强度等。人体所感受到外界环境的舒适度主要由环境中的温度、相对湿度、风速和光照决定。[8]由于对温度和相对湿度的测定需要在晴朗无风的天气条件下进行，因此，本研究不将风速作为研究对象。同时，由于调研地块位于高层密集的城市中心区，人流密集，旋风与污染物沉积问题时有发生，CO₂浓度、CO浓度也对该开放空间的微气候环境产生了不可小觑的影响。因此，本研究最终选择了温度、相对湿度、光照、气压、CO_2浓度与CO浓度六种因素作为主要研究对象。

在本次研究中，观测温度、湿度、气压、CO浓度、CO_2浓度因素的仪器为9565-P型温湿度测试仪。观测光照因素的仪器为TES照度计1332A。

在观测时间的选择上，由于微气候环境对人类交通休憩影响较大的时段为白天，而该广场在白天人群最为密集的时段为中午和下午，所以本研究的观测时间在11：00～17：00之间波动。

在观测高度的选择上，鉴于人类大部分户外活动是在离地2m的范围内进行，因而观测高度约为1.5～1.7m。

同时，由于高层建筑和硬质地面对微气候的影响是累加的，微气候的各个因素会有一定程度的波动，因此本研究将测量的时间控制在较短的时间内，并且通过三次测量取平均值的方式来提高测量准确度。

3.3 观测结果

本研究对新街口莱迪广场的52个观测点共进行了14次观测，时间从2014年9月～12月，历时3个月。测量完成后将获得的所有微气候因素数据汇总为表格，表格中每个观测点包括6种微气候因素（温度、相对湿度、光照、气压、CO_2浓度与CO浓度）的14次观测结果，分别以时间加微气候因素名的方式进行区分，以便后期进行数据的进一步整合模拟分析。

4 结果分析

4.1 微气候温度因素与城市平均温度比较

观测数据处理主要使用Microsoft Excel软件。根据观测数据计算各观测点的温度、湿度、光照强度、压强、CO_2、CO及各自的三次测量平均值并绘制52个观测点的分布折线图，分析每次微气候各因素分布规律，寻找特殊位置点。通过分布折线图将调研数据与全市气温的对比，我们发现，整个广场的温度明显高于全市温度，且各观测点差异较大（图2），说明了城市高层建筑集聚围合的开放空间积热较多且内部有一定差异。

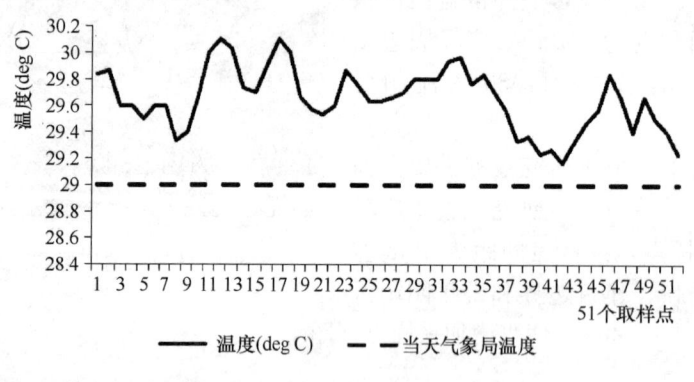

图2 观测温度与城市平均温度比较

4.2 微气候因素相关性分析

观测数据处理使用Microsoft Excel、IBM SPSS Statistics软件。导入每次调研掌握的52个取样点数据信息并选取其中两个因素（如温度T和湿度H）一个做自变量x，一个做因变量y，形成该次调研的因素关联折线图，并导入 SPSS 进行线性和非线性函数模拟并对 14 张图进行分析剔除和归纳。从因素关联折线图可以看出，14 次因素关联曲线走势基本一致，即多次调研的微气候因素关联趋势一致。通过 SPSS 完成的函数模拟证明，其他微气候因素均与温度存在一定关系。温度的高低影响着其他因素的变化指数。温度与 CO_2 呈正相关，即温度越高，CO_2 浓度越高（图 3a）；而温度与湿度、压强虽然不成线性关系，但呈负相关，即温度越高，相对湿度和压强越低（图 3b、3c）。这个现象可能是由于莱迪广场主要为硬质铺地，且植被较为缺乏，且被高层建筑包围，造成了干热的现象。

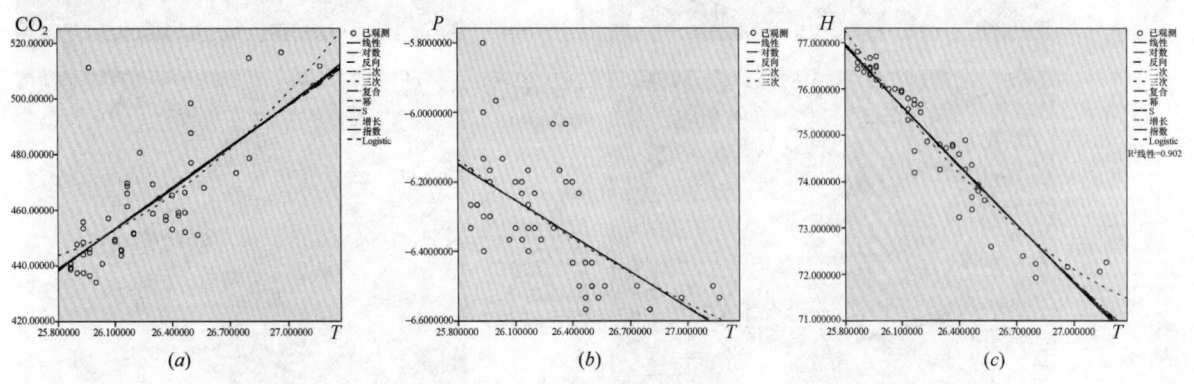

图 3　温度与 CO_2，压强，适度关系

(a) 温度与 CO_2 关系图；(b) 温度与压强关系图；(c) 温度与湿度关系图

4.3　微气候因素与开放空间形态分析

微气候因素与开放空间形态分析主要以 ArcGIS 软件为平台，将不同的微气候因素按时间序列导入并通过样条函数插值计算，得到覆盖整个开放空间的各微气候因素场域图。从 14 次调研的 6 个环境因素所生产的 84 张图中，经过同类因素图比较分析，挑选出特征明显图加以分析研究，发现温度因素、CO、CO_2 的特征较为明显。

从挑选出的温度场域图来看（图 4），新街口步行街南北贯通，通风较好，所以温度较周围要低 1～2℃。

然而，在 9 月 27 日、10 月 10 日、10 月 19 日、11 月 22 日等日期，因路口处布置了青奥会纪念品商店，通风条件受阻，导致 E 开口积热。此外，A 开口温度一直较高，原因可能是受阳光直射，没有遮挡物，通风条件较差，开口较小，贴建筑轮廓线太近，受建筑外表皮热辐射较多。与此同时，B 开口较广场中间温度更高，原因大致为距离 A 开口较近，虽然道路宽敞，但很少有自然风，阳光直射强。而 D 开口处有南京新百商场的出入口，在人流通过时室内冷气会外涌，又处于阴影区，所以温度较低。同时在靠近 C 开口处也有一处出入口，同上，温度会有所下降。

另外，广场中间莱迪广场的圆形顶配的背面，因人流量较大且没有遮蔽物，玻璃顶棚吸热辐射等原因，温度较周围更高。同时，临近建筑轮廓线的位置温度较高（部分门店出入口除外）。然而，广场偏东侧的大片空地上因经常布置临时展柜、特卖会等，温度变化幅度较大，不易观察。

从 CO、CO_2 场域图来看，高浓度区域多发生于 A、D 开口，以及中央广场出入口，莱迪地下商场出入口（图 5）。而广场内不允许机动车通行，故 CO、CO_2 与四周道路上运行机动车尾气的扩散并没有直接原因。因此我们推测 CO、CO_2 浓度与广场的通风条件与广场使用人群聚集程度有很大关系。

5　结论

本文围绕南京城市中心区域的一个高层密集，以硬质铺地为主的开放广场，在其中均布调研取

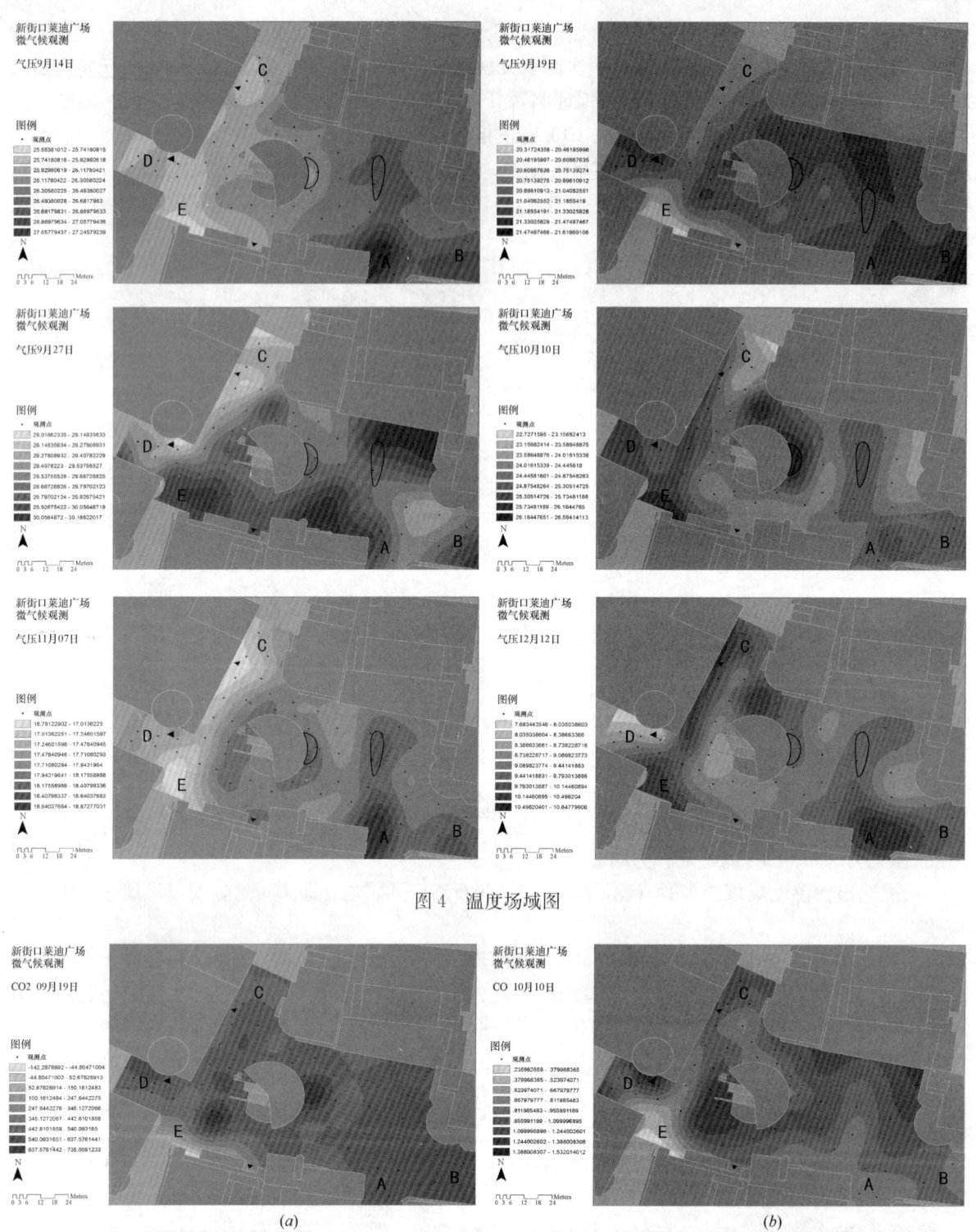

图4 温度场域图

图5
(a) CO₂ 场域图；(b) CO

样点，观测每个取样点的微气候要素数据，包括温度、湿度、光照强度、CO 浓度和 CO₂ 浓度等，将观测值导入 GIS 软件并通过插值计算得到覆盖整个开放空间的各要素场域图并运用 Excel 折线图进行特殊点筛选分析。通过比较这些微气候要素场域图与开放空间的形态特征，我们发现，当处于高层建筑的包围中时，以硬质铺地为主的开放空间的开口位置对微气候环境各因素有明显影响，各因素在广场边缘区域与中央区域有微小差异，各微气候因素之间关联性也较为明确。而且广场中央的地下空间出入口和遮蔽物对各因素也有一定影响。

城市高层建筑集聚域的开放空间微气候环境相对情况变化更复杂，波动较大，但也存在一些温度偏高，湿度气压异常的特点，因此针对此类在城市化进程中较为多见的开放空间，不能仅仅停留在满足人们交通与休憩的需求上，更应通过改良城市开放空间设计来改善城市微气候环境，提高人类的生存质量与生活品质，促进城市的经济发展，最大限度地发挥环境功效与社会价值。

致谢

本论文受到南京大学本科创新计划 G1410284060《基于微气候的城市开放空间设计策略研究——以南京为例》的资助。

Microclimate of Open Space Among the Zone of High-Rise Buildings

Zhang Xinyuan[1], Zang Qian[1], Zhang Yifan[1], Yu Mingxia[1], Tong Ziyu[1, 2]
(1. School of Architecture and Urban Planning,
Nanjing University; 2. Corresponding Author)

Abstract：The zone of high-rise buildings is extremely easy to lead to the "heat island effect" and "dry island effect", which could result in deterioration of microclimate environment. Open space in city center is often surrounded by high-rise buildings and the micro climate environment is affected by surrounding buildings and its material, in which place, whirlwind or deposition of pollutants and other unfavorable factors deteriorating the microclimate are more likely to occur. Therefore, it is important to recognize the microclimate of this type of opening space for the development of the city. This study selects the Leddy Plaza, the typical hard paving tile square in the central business district of Nanjing Xinjiekou, based on the long-term site research to analyze microclimate environment quality in the hard paving tile open space in the city center full of high-rise buildings. After the analysis, this study attempts to lay the foundation for exploring the relationship between microclimate environment and the surrounding environment and eventually provides references for the open space location choice and design strategy.

Keywords：Urban microclimate, Open space, Zone of high-rise buildings

参考文献：

[1] Sozer, H. 高层建筑发展项目对微气候的影响[C]. 世界高层都市建筑学会第九届全球会议论文集，2012：540-545.

[2] Shishegar N. Street design and urban microclimate: analyzing the effects of street geometry and orientation on airflow and solar access in urban canyons[J]. Journal of Clean Energy Technologies, 2013, l(1): 52-56.

[3] 伊娜，冷红. 基于关联分析的高层住区布局模式微气候评定——以哈尔滨高层住区为例[C]. 城乡治理与规划改革——2014 中国城市规划年会论文集，2014：25.

[4] 佟华，刘辉志，李延明，桑建国，胡非. 北京夏季城市热岛现状及楔形绿地规划对缓解城市热岛的作用[M]. 应用气象学报，2005，16(3)：257-366.

［5］ 周媛，石铁矛，胡远满，刘淼．基于城市气候环境特征的绿地景观格局优化研究［J］．城市规划，2014，5：83-89.

［6］ 王新军，秦佳，史洪，龚声明，张新荣，孙忠伟．城市公共开放空间光环境研究［J］．建筑电气，2013，5：31-35.

［7］ 陈思宁，郭军．不同空间插值方法在区域气温序列中的应用评估：以东北地区为例［J］．中国农业气象，2015，36(02)：234-241.

［8］ 戴亦欣．低碳技术推广促进过程中的公众认知模型构建［J］．现代城市研究，2011，11：31-38.

可持续发展指数——香港公营房屋的实战经验

陈少德[1]　卢颖妍[1]　黄盛[1]　沈小茵[2]

（1. 香港房屋委员会；2. 香港品质保证局）

摘要：香港房屋委员会（房委会）管理公共租住房屋（公屋）单位 74 万个，公屋大厦有不同的楼宇设计及楼龄。为提高现有公屋可持续性，房委会采纳一套以可持续发展为本的维修保养策略，并采用香港品质保证局"楼宇可持续发展指数"评定公屋大厦不同设计的可持续发展成效，其指数为一环保建筑评级系统，以了解其需要改善的地方，在订立长远维修保养和改善工程计划时制定先后次序。为取得最高成本效益，房委会把楼宇可持续发展指数的衡量准则，策略性地应用到若干选定的公共屋邨，涵盖主要款款设计的公屋大厦，从而得出现有公屋可持续发展的表现概况，并采用绿色建筑环境评价规划个别屋邨的具体改善项目。

关键词：可持续发展指数衡量准则，楼宇可持续发展指数，温室气体排放，绿建环评

1　引言

在香港，公共租住屋邨（下称"公共屋邨"）居民逾 200 万人，占人口三成左右。香港房屋委员会（下称"房委会"）为法定机构，负责研订并推行公营房屋计划，照顾低收入家庭的住屋需要。现时，房委会管理公共租住房屋（下称"公屋"）单位约 74 万个，遍布逾 200 个屋邨约 1200 幢多层大厦，楼宇设计、楼龄和楼宇状况都有所不同。为确保现有公屋长远可持续发展，又能应对社会不断变化的需要，房委会在经济、社会和环境三个范畴订立以可持续发展为本的维修保养策略，从而订定维修保养和改善工程计划实施蓝图（图1）。

要有效订立这样大量现有公屋的长远维修保养和改善工程计划，务必采取审慎做法，以楼宇可持续发展表现验证制度衡量辖下楼宇组合的可持续性表现。该组合主要涵盖过往数十年所推出逾 20 种标准大厦设计类型。此举有助于订立所需改善计划，以保持和提高其可持续性。本论文阐述房委会如何善用以可持续发展为本的维修保养策略和凭借可持续发展指数衡量准则验证制度，提高楼宇可持续性。

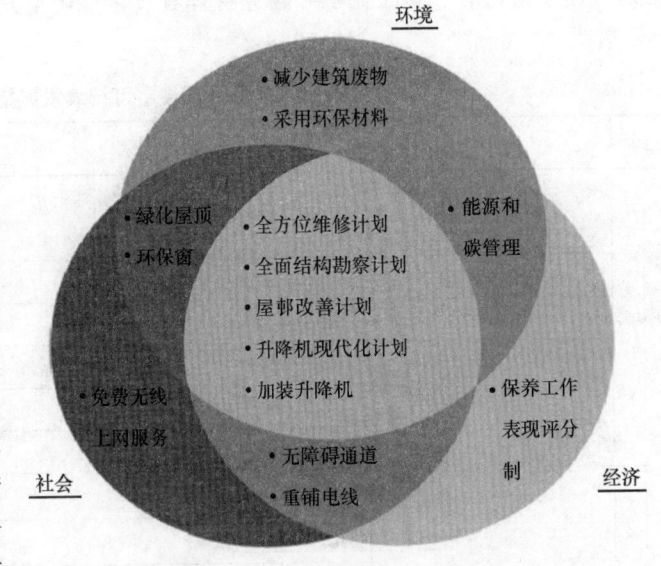

图 1　以可持续发展为本维修保养策略的三个范畴

2　可持续发展指数衡量准则

过往十年，不同环保建筑评审制度或认证计划面世，旨在提高楼宇可持续性表现。世界各地先后推出多种环保建筑评级制度或认证计划，例如英国的建筑研究院环境评审法、日本的建筑物综合环境性能评价体系，以及美国的能源和环境设计领先认证。在香港，愈来愈多新建筑项目采用绿色建筑环境评价，原因在于这成为建筑事务监督给予总楼面面积宽免的先决条件之一。2012 年底，香港品质保证局推出楼宇评审计划，名为香港品质保证局楼宇可持续发展指数，作为量度全港现有楼

宇环境、社会和经济表现的基准工具。

2.1 香港面对的可持续性挑战

香港乃全球人口最稠密的城市之一，经济体系以服务为本，没有大规模高耗能行业，故此所排放温室气体主要源于发电，占本地总排放量逾六成。在各种电力最终用途当中，楼宇耗电量最大，占全港耗电量约 89%。[1]香港正在面对楼宇老化问题，房委会也不例外。现时，约三成公屋楼龄达 30 年或以上。为释除公众对高龄楼宇安全和质量的疑虑，政府推行强制验楼计划和强制验窗计划，房委会也主动订定连串改善计划，照顾年事渐高租户和未来十年新一代租户的需要。

2.2 可持续性研究和香港品质保证局楼宇可持续发展指数

为向楼宇业主和物业管理公司提倡楼宇可持续性概念，香港品质保证局针对香港独特状况，并顾及香港法例、楼宇减碳、应课差饷租值的经济因素等本地背景，调研制订量化楼宇可持续发展指数，用以评审现有楼宇在环境、社会和经济范畴的表现。[2]香港品质保证局可持续发展指数衡量准则是基于联合国环境规划署可持续建筑促进会 2009 年财务及可持续发展评核报告[3]和国际标准化组织（下称"ISO"）几个关于楼宇可持续性的主要标准订定，要旨在于向持份者指出重要表现指标；掌握改进机会；划一表现指标，确定表现基准以作比较；以及处理香港关键可持续性问题。该评审制度不但实际，而且实施成本也不高。衡量准则包含 20 个表现指标，针对本地关键可持续性问题，促进持份者、楼宇业主和物业管理者按基准衡量其楼宇在社会、经济和环境三个范畴的表现（表1）。

香港品质保证局楼宇可持续发展指数衡量准则概要　　　　　　表1

范畴	问题	表现指标	衡量方法
环境	气候变化	温室气体排放量	按所占用室内楼面面积单位计算（单位计算）的温室气体排放量
	破坏臭氧	大气中消耗臭氧物质排放量	前述单位计算的消耗臭氧物质排放量
	生物多样性	楼宇内生态	采纳建议做法
	运用资源	耗费饮用水	前述单位计算的耗水量
		运用可借生物降解材料	采纳建议做法
		废物循环再造	前述单位计算的循环再造废物量
社会	楼宇保安和安全	楼宇坚固度和质量	遵从规管度和以外事项
		防火	遵从规管度和以外事项
		升降机和自动梯安全	遵从规管度和以外事项
		应急计划	采纳建议做法
		以设计防范犯罪	犯罪率
	用者健康和舒适度	用者舒适度——照明舒适度	楼宇用者满意度调查
		用者舒适度——气温舒适度	楼宇用者满意度调查
		用者舒适度——噪声控制	楼宇用者满意度调查
		室内空气质量	楼宇用者满意度调查
		饮水质量	采纳建议做法
	社会基建	运输设施、公共设施和无障碍设施的通达度	楼宇用者满意度调查
	睦邻关系	邻里满意度	邻里满意度调查

范畴	问题	表现指标	衡量方法
经济	楼宇资产值	楼宇应课差饷租值	应课差饷租值变化百分率
	楼宇维修保养	保持楼宇持续运作的维修保养开支	按前述单位计算的维修保养开支

3 公营房屋实践经验

3.1 先导计划

香港现有大量公屋单位，为有效订立长远的维修保养和改善工程计划，必须审慎衡量各种大厦设计类型的可持续性表现，以便推出所需改善项目，保持并提高其可持续性。房委会研究过楼宇可持续发展指数的应用和可能带来的效益后，于2012年推出先导计划，把可持续发展指数应用于若干选定屋邨，当中包含大多数公屋大厦的标准设计类型。先导计划的范畴不独涵盖登记、保持并改进选定公屋大厦的楼宇可持续性，而且还须培训管理和前线人员、编订自动化范本以便输入和分析数据、按20项表现指标收集楼宇信息、提交表现数据报告、验证报告，以及务求不断改进而检讨。在下文各段落，房委会就如何克服技术困难分享经验，并扼要讲述改进公共屋邨可持续性表现的方法。

3.1.1 环境范畴

房委会从先导计划找出温室气体排放量和废物回收是影响公屋环境可持续性表现的关键因素。

（1）减少温室气体排放量

事实上，房委会自2008年起为主要的公屋大厦设计类型订定温室气体排放量基线，并研订一套系统化的数据收集方法，以量度各主要大厦设计类型的温室气体排放量。据量度结果显示，在公共屋邨的公用设施当中，电力照明和升降机系统是排放温室气体的两大类装置。

为求减低电力照明装置的耗能量，我们实施了一系列节能措施，包括选用光感控制器和计时开关以尽量利用日照、采用T5光管，以及于2012年起推出为期42个月的计划，把所有现有屋邨照明装置的电磁镇流器更换为节能电子镇流器。

随着楼宇可持续发展指数的先导计划收集和分析更多数据，已登记屋邨的指数经过首次验证之后，发现节能计划有待完善的地方。我们注意到，有些屋邨大厦按实用楼面面积的单位计算，公用地方的温室气体排放量较高，所以应先行落实节能举措。为此，我们按照楼宇可持续发展指数表现指标的结果，重订在一些屋邨的优先次序，完善电子镇流器更换计划。

关于升降机服务方面，房委会自1989年起推行升降机现代化计划，当中包括更换老化升降机机箱、机械和控制系统，以提升效能和乘搭舒适度，并为较旧屋邨加建升降机层站，通达大厦每一层。现时，所有新的升降机系统都已改进舒适度、增加载客量和提高速度、增设层站和报层系统等。在节能方面，与旧升降机相比，这些新升降机耗能减少逾30%。

（2）废物回收

促进废物回收的有效方法，是在指定地点预留足够空间用于回收作业。为了让租户更积极参与废物回收，我们鼓励他们把可循环再造的家居废物拿到公共屋邨回收站，换取小礼品。房委会一直积极推展家居废物源头分类计划，2013～2014年度，回收的废纸、塑料樽、铝罐和旧衣物合共33618t。

为了尽量减少厨余，我们于2011年12月起推行厨余回收试验计划，在屋邨内设置堆肥机。计划逐步扩展至14个屋邨，不仅把邨内回收的厨余运往邨外循环再造，转化为鱼粮，又采用微生物处理方式把邨内回收的厨余就地循环再造，转化为堆肥。逾 3000 户已登记参与计划，每月平均收集的厨余约重 24590kg。为鼓励租户减少厨余，我们在所有屋邨举办一连串厨余有"宝"创意食谱比赛等运动，同时在房屋资讯台播放教育短片。

（3）其他结果

楼宇可持续发展指数也提供有用方法，可比对标准设计大厦类型按所占用室内楼面面积单位计算的公用食水耗用量。一些示例见于表 2。

三种大厦设计类型食水耗用量

表 2

大厦类型	每年每 1000m² 食水耗用量（m³）
A	130
B	63
C	46

据观察所得，A 类型设计大厦与其他两类标准设计大厦相比，耗水量较高。经过深入调查之后，我们发觉耗水量较高的原因是大厦范围覆盖的绿化带多达 40%。基于这个因素，我们会进一步研究节水措施，包括检视种植花木和灌溉模式、对植物的挑选和应用雨水收集系统。

3.1.2 社会范畴

房委会所采纳的维修保养策略以人为先、以可持续性为本，由于符合楼宇可持续发展指数社会范畴下的表现指标，所以先导计划结果进一步证实其成效。

关于楼宇保安和安全方面，房委会除了例行检查楼宇共用部分之外，还透过全方位维修计划把标准提高一些，该维修计划既积极主动，又以顾客为先，保持楼宇组成部分和装置的状况。房委会聘用训练有素的家居维修大使对楼龄逾 10 年的公屋大厦逐户勘查，视乎其楼龄，以五或十年为周期，务求为租户及早修葺，并及时指教导租户留意单位维修，以防小维修问题变成大。2011 年，第二个全方位维修计划开展，于 121 个屋邨推展室内勘察计划，其中 97 个屋邨于 2015 年 3 月完成。自推行全方位维修计划以来，租户满意度维持在八成左右。

在房委会工作表中，应急计划是重要的一项。除了手册订明的一系列紧急应变程序和定期演习之外，房委会自 2012 年起，已采纳 ISO 31000 风险管理框架的系统管理方法进行维修保养和改善工程。房委会在危害识别和风险评估的过程中，对外部和内部背景详加检讨。这个框架有利于对复杂风险的评估。

使高楼龄屋邨可持续发展而又切合租户的最新需要，是房委会所要面对的挑战。房委会屋邨改善计划下屋邨改善项目规划的一些主要考虑因素，为提升社会基建和公用设施、提供无障碍通道和改善行人流通。屋邨改善计划是专为高楼龄屋邨而设，经过全面结构勘察计划确定为结构安全，而且维修在经济上可行。某个屋邨租户的主要关注事项是借着意见调查和咨询收集得来。改善工程以人为本，切合不同年龄群组的需要，尤其是长者方面，而不是以设施为本。我们会在没有升降机设施的旧公屋大厦旁加建升降机塔，又会在有不同高低建筑平台的屋邨加建升降机塔。我们会更新公用设施和非住宅物业用途，以切合租户以至邻近地方的最新需要。举例来说，把长期空置率高的停车场大楼创新地改建为教育中心。我们又把康乐设施优化，以切合不同年龄群组的需要，以及重新塑造公共空间，以促进社交互动，包括安装长者健身器材和儿童游玩设备。为顾及长者和残疾租户的需要，把免受日晒雨淋的通道和无障碍通道融入整体行人网络中，以改善行人流通。

3.1.3 经济范畴

按所占用室内楼面面积单位计算的楼宇维修保养开支，是楼宇可持续发展指数下量度楼宇经济表现的关键。为了符合最大成本效益，房委会已研订一套维修保养和改善工程的成本指标，以控制并监察维修保养和改善工程的预算和开支。在推行全方位维修计划下以客为先的预防性维修保养时，公屋单位修葺率已受到控制，无须进行较昂贵的日常维修，从而减低相关开支。

随着推行各种节能举措，屋邨公众地方的耗电量已逐渐减少。2013～2014 年度，公屋大厦公众地方的耗电量为每月每个单位 56.5kW/h。[4]这个耗电量相当于五年间减少 15.7%（图 2）。在香港，为了提高节能效益及响应减碳，房委会分两期在全港辖下公共屋邨推行 ISO 50001 能源管理体系认证。第一期于 2013 年 10 月展开，所有现有屋邨于 2015 年 4 月获得全面认证。

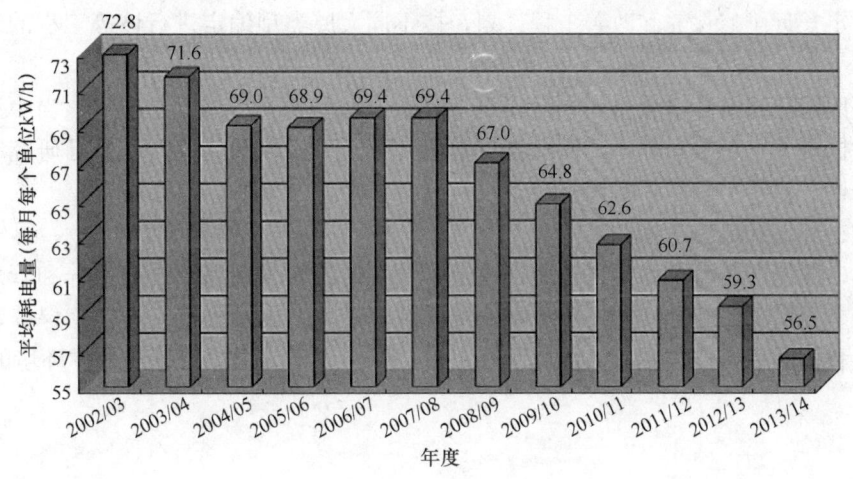

图 2　屋邨公众地方平均耗电量[4]

3.2　先导计划检讨

参加该计划可以得到其他无形裨益。举例来说，前线员工对于楼宇可持续性的意识有所提高。该计划推动他们更积极参与实行各项环境、社会和经济举措。楼宇可持续发展指数为楼宇可持续性提供既全面而又非常实用的订立基准机制。量化表现指标让参加者得以在相关范畴检查楼宇表现和方便日后自我对照。

据参加计划的结果显示，参加先导计划的所有公屋大厦的楼宇可持续性表现都较香港基准为高，并获颁香港品质保证局楼宇可持续发展指数验证标志。事实上，房委会是首家取得该验证标志的机构。截至 2015 年首季为止，参加楼宇可持续发展指数计划的公屋大厦约为数 80 幢。

楼宇可持续发展指数涵盖环境、社会和经济三个范畴的楼宇表现，而且可用性有所优化，同时能广泛审视庞大房屋组合而涵盖不同大厦类型设计的可持续性表现，借着表现指标所提供的量化参考数据显示有待改进的地方。

从楼宇可持续发展指数先导计划所汲取的经验，房委会在其环境管理体系下已经建立有系统的验证制度，而且在策略上选定一批代表主要大厦类型设计的公共屋邨参加该计划，有利长远维修保养和改善策略的部署，以提高现存公屋的可持续性表现。

另一方面，对于个别屋邨具体改善项目的设计规划，采纳绿色建筑环境评价评估方法可能很有用。绿色建筑环境评价评估方法是以环保取向和工程方式设计，提供详细的环保评级，借着设计、标准规格和测试作改善。[5]

房委会已把绿色建筑环境评价评估方法应用于葵盛西邨屋邨改善计划，该屋邨楼龄为 39 年，有公屋大厦 10 幢，单位逾 5200 个。规划、设计、建造、运作、管理设备涵盖地盘、材料、用水、室内环境质量、创新和加建等各方面，均已经过全面评估。继可行性研究完成之后，我们向香港绿色建筑议会申请葵盛西邨的绿色建筑环境评价认证，该屋邨于 2014 年 6 月绿色建筑环境评价初步评估中取得"铂金"评级，属首个住宅屋邨在既有建筑类别荣获绿色建筑环境评价初步评估的"铂金"评级。从这个项目汲取的经验，会应用于同一大厦类型设计的同类改善项目。

4 结语

为提高现有公屋可持续性，房委会采纳一套以可持续发展为本的维修保养策略，纳入社会、环境和经济各项举措，并结合楼宇可持续发展指数的有效楼宇表现验证系统。可计量表现指标提供重要资料，以便房委会审视辖下不同类型大厦的表现，并与香港基准水平比较，从而为其楼宇组合作全盘考虑，订定长远维修保养和改善工程计划，按不同大厦类型编定进行该等工程的先后次序，有效善用资源。

房委会利用绿色建筑环境评价（既有建筑）规划个别屋邨的具体改善项目，当中涉及精密设计工具、广泛数据收集、记录和环境范畴详细技术研究等。所汲取的经验，以及已研究制定绿色建筑环境评价的规格，对于个别屋邨的同类改善项目具有实际参考价值。

有了品质、环境和能源管理体系（已取得 ISO 9001、14001 和 50001 认证），再辅以楼宇可持续性评审工具，便能严密监察和检讨公屋楼宇组合的可持续性表现以及维修保养和管理实务，务求不断改进。房委会借着实施可持续发展为本的维修保养策略，以及推行长远维修保养和改善工程计划，有效保持和提高现有公共屋邨的可持续性，以达到为香港人提供可持续居住环境的目标。

Sustainability Metrics-A Hong Kong Public Housing Empirical Experience

Chan S. T.[1], Lo W. Y. Winnie[1], Wong S. Alan[1], Sham Connie[2]
(1. Hong Kong Housing Authority;
2. Hong Kong Quality Assurance Agency)

Abstract：The Hong Kong Housing Authority (HKHA) manages a housing stock of 740,000 public rental housing (PRH) units of different block type designs and ages. In driving sustainability of the existing PRH, HKHA adopts a set of sustainability-focused maintenance strategy. Sustainability performance of different housing block types is gauged by using the Hong Kong Quality Assurance Agency Sustainable Building Index (SBI), which is a green building rating system, to facilitate the identification of areas for improvement and setting of priorities in the formulation of long-term maintenance and improvement (M&I) programmes. To maximize cost effectiveness, HKHA applies SBI metrics strategically to a selective number of PRH estates which represent the majority of the block type designs to obtain an overview of sustainability performance of the existing housing stock and makes use of the Building Environmental Assessment Method (BEAM) Plus for planning of specific estate-based improvement project.

Keywords：Sustainability metrics，Sustainable building index，Greenhouse gas emission，BEAM plus

参考文献：

[1] Hong Kong Electrical and Mechanical Services Department，Hong Kong Environmental Protection Department Guidelines to Account for and Report on Greenhouse Gas Emissions and Removals for Buildings (Commercial，Residential or Institutional Purposes) in Hong Kong，Environmental Protection Department and Electrical and Mechanical Services

Department，2010.

[2] Hong Kong Quality Assurance Agency，Council for Sustainable Development HKQAA Sustainable Building Index（SBI）Metrics Handbook and Report Template，Version 1.3，the HKQAA，2013，10.

[3] Clare Lowe/ Alfonso Ponce，United Nations Environment Programme-Sustainable Buildings and Construction Initiative's（UNEP-FI/ SBCI's）Financial and Sustainability Metrics Report，2009.

[4] Sustainability Report. Quest for Excellence in Low Carbon Housing，HKHA，2012，13.

[5] BEAM Plus Existing Building，Version 1.1 April 2010，BEAM Society.

高密度环境下底层架空设计在旧工业区更新中的应用：以香港观塘区为例

刘思琪　王嘉毅

（香港中文大学）

摘要：香港是世界上城市建设和人口密度最高的城市之一。在这种极端的城市环境下，城市的空气质量和相关的城市问题需要得到更多的关注。观塘作为香港东九龙地区最大的工业区，正在经历着从简单制造业到商业、办公、仓储、工业制造和住宅的混合功能转变。观塘旧工业区由于原先的高密度建筑环境和现在巨大的人口流动、交通运输量，通风环境和停车位不足等问题变得尤为明显。本文提出底层架空的设计方法，结合观塘旧工业区现状，通过 CFD（Computational Fluid Dynamics）模拟证明底层架空设计对旧工业区更新的实际意义。

关键词：旧工业区，底层架空，公共停车，CFD，风环境

1　引言

香港是世界上高密度城市之一。高密度主要体现在两点：一是人口的高密度，香港的人口密度每年愈长，2011 年香港的官方数据表明，香港的人口密度达到了世界第三，直到 2014 年年末为止。香港的人口已经达到了 726 万人；二是指建筑的高密度，香港一共分为三大部分：香港岛，九龙半岛和新界，总共的陆地面积约 1100km²，但香港的主要地形为丘陵地形，使得香港的发展面积只有其总陆地面积的 25％。为了让香港承载 726 万人，香港的现代建筑以高层建筑为主，有大量的摩天大楼分布在维多利亚港两岸。据统计，香港的建筑中超过 90m 的建筑超过 3000 座，摩天大楼的数目居于世界首位。人口的上升和土地面积的局限直接造成了香港的高密度环境。在这种极端的城市环境下，城市的空气质量和土地使用规划变得尤为重要。

观塘位于香港的九龙半岛的东面，作为香港的首个卫星城，观塘是东九龙地区中最大的工业区。其中有许多工业大厦，同时也有住宅大厦，工业和住宅大厦的共存，使得观塘变成香港密度最高的地区之一。进入 20 世纪 90 年代后，香港制造业的衰退和逐渐转移到其他地方，使得观塘区出现大量空置的大厦，位于观塘地铁站附近的工业大厦被改建成商业大厦或用于货仓用途，部分大厦则被改建成写字楼，从此，观塘的老旧大厦兼具了商业、办公、工业和住宅的功能，本来高密度的设计，加上现在巨大人口流动，使得观塘成为了香港环境最差的地区之一，高密度设计的弊端和城市问题在该区域显得尤为突出。

底层架空设计作为一种地域性显著的设计方法，非常适用于南方亚热带、热带地区典型的湿热气候。在建筑技术方面，底层架空设计基本可以适用于所有现代建筑结构，而制约它的主要是人们的思想观念和底层空间所带来的商业价值。[1]本文主要探讨高密度城市环境下地面风环境的改善和大量的路边停车所造成的道路拥堵的解决方案。

2　现存问题

2.1　城市热岛效应和地面风环境

热岛效应是高密度城市设计最突出的问题之一。许多建筑拥有深色的表面使得地面吸收更多来自太阳的能量，使得区域内的空气温度明显升高。同时，高密度的建筑布局造成不理想的风环境，

减弱了区域内的空气的流动，不利于城市与周边环境的热交换。空气温度的上升使得该区域不适合行人行走，进一步削弱了区域的商业价值。

2.2 汽车尾气

作为工业区，观塘有大量的货车出入，货车尾气的污染严重，同时，高密度的城市布局，减弱了区域内的空气流动，使得货车尾气的排放物无法在短时间内离开该区域，进一步加剧了观塘的汽车尾气污染情况。尾气的污染不仅仅不利于行人行走，同时还会对周边居民的健康造成严重影响。

2.3 停车空间

由于过去观塘的大厦大部分都是用于工业用途，所以大部分的大厦都会有独立的停车场。但是，自从观塘转型以后，观塘的大厦综合了商业、办公、工业等功能，使得区域内的车流量增多，停车的需求也增加。过往的首层为停车场的设计不能再满足如今的停车的需求。大量的货车和其他种类车辆停在了道路两旁，不单单加重了道路的运输压力，还会减弱道路的安全性，使得在高密度环境下狭窄的道路变得等价狭窄。另一方面，原有建筑的底层大多为"私有"停车场，由于不同的"私有"停车场存在较大差异的使用量和闲置状况，同时停车管理缺乏联系和统一标准，间接地造成了道路交通拥堵的状况。

3 研究范围

本次研究选取观塘骏业街、鸿图道、开源道和巧明街围合的建筑群作为研究对象，总占地面积为 40896m²。通过实地勘察，发现该建筑群中大部分拥有独立的地面独立停车场（图1）。本研究希望通过数字建模，对该建筑群进行底层架空改造，CFD模拟后分析该种改造对通风环境及其他相关方面的影响和改善。

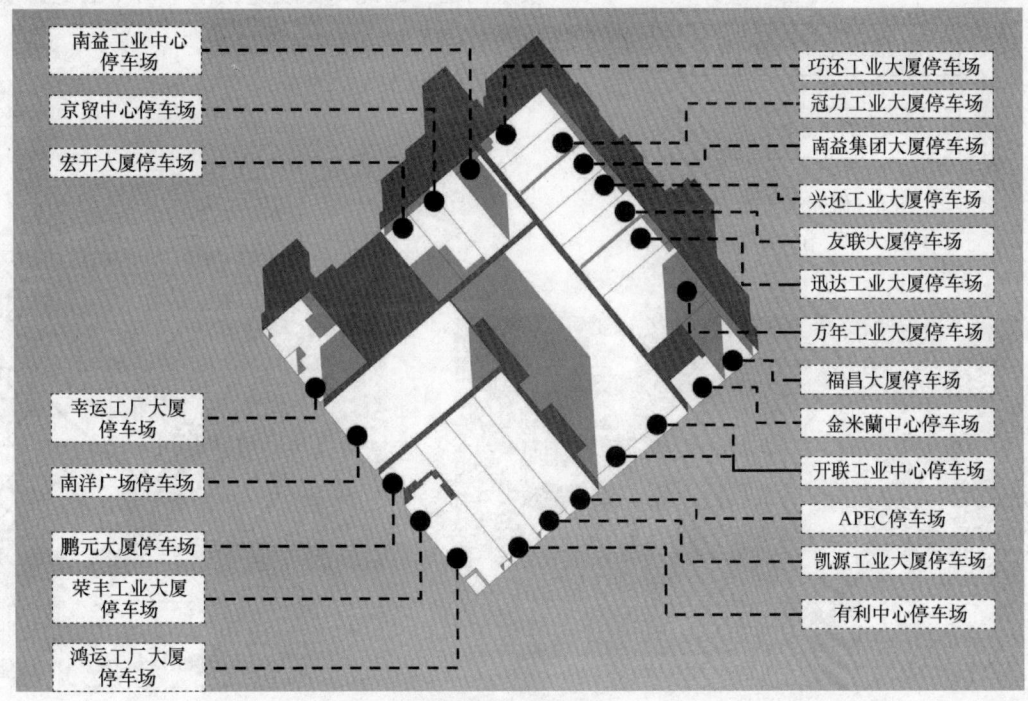

图 1　地面独立停车场示意

（图片来源：作者自绘）

4 研究流程

5 风环境模拟

5.1 模型建造

根据研究场地的建筑尺寸，利用 Sketch up pro 建立比例为 1∶1 的模型进行研究，为保证在模拟条件和真实的情况尽量相似，还建造研究场地周边的建筑群模型。研究场地改造的底层架空为6m。本研究会使用 Harpoon 对研究场地及其东侧周边建筑进行的模拟网格化，通过对地面以上 2m 高度的水平网格进行细化，可以获得较好的模拟效果，网格类型选择为 ANSYS 中的六面体构造。同时，本次的 CFD 模拟将使用 FLUENT 软件。

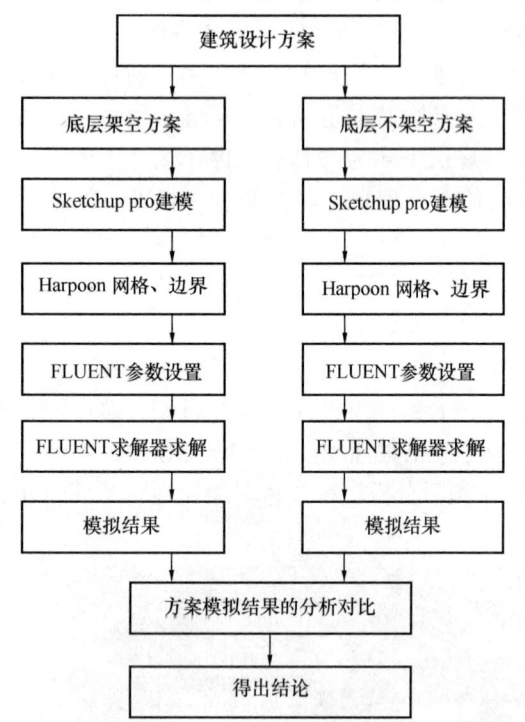

图 2 研究流程图
（图片来源：作者自绘）

5.2 更新改造

考虑到原有建筑内独立停车场位置和现有底层空间商业价值，对整个研究区域进行部分架空改造，释放底层空间。在调研中我们发现，研究场地存在很多巷道，多数巷道宽度小于 2.5m，这些巷道使用率偏低。行走于这些巷道内的人往往不会选择在其中停留过多时间，一方面是由于两侧高楼带来的压抑感，另一方面则是封闭环境下带来的空气质量问题。因此，在改造模型中对中心巷道实施了拓宽（图 2）。

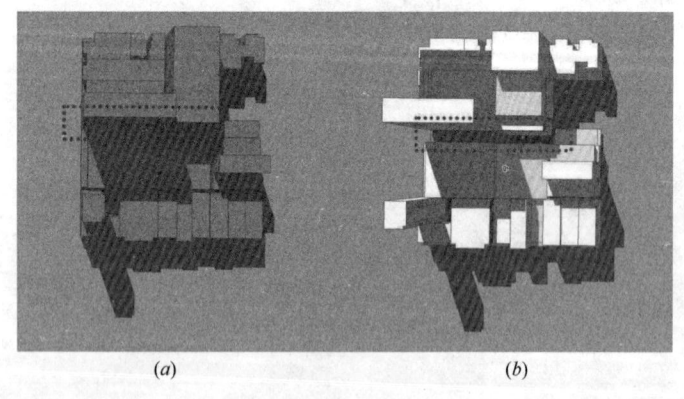

图 3 模型建立
(a) 原有建筑；(b) 改造后建筑
（图片来源：作者自绘）

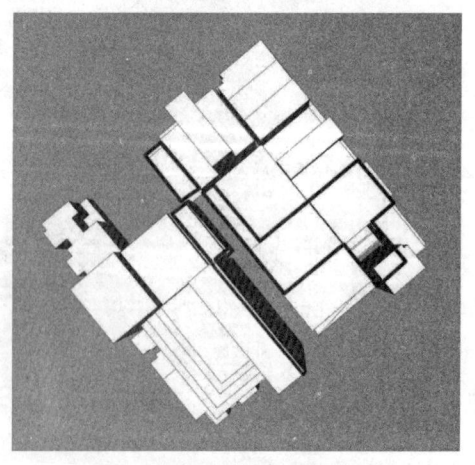

图 4 底层架空改造范围示意
（图片来源：作者自绘）

5.3 数据选择

在通风环境模拟中，通常会有 16 个方向的风测数据以供选择。[2] 由于研究区域内没有当地的测风站，风向数据会选用临近的香港启德测风站的数据（ABL-BC）。根据启德测风站的风玫瑰图，结合研究区域建筑主要朝向，在本次 CFD 的模拟中选用东风（BC-3x3-0.33-90.prof）和东南风（BC-3x3-0.33-135.prof）作为基本的风场数据，分别进行风速模拟。

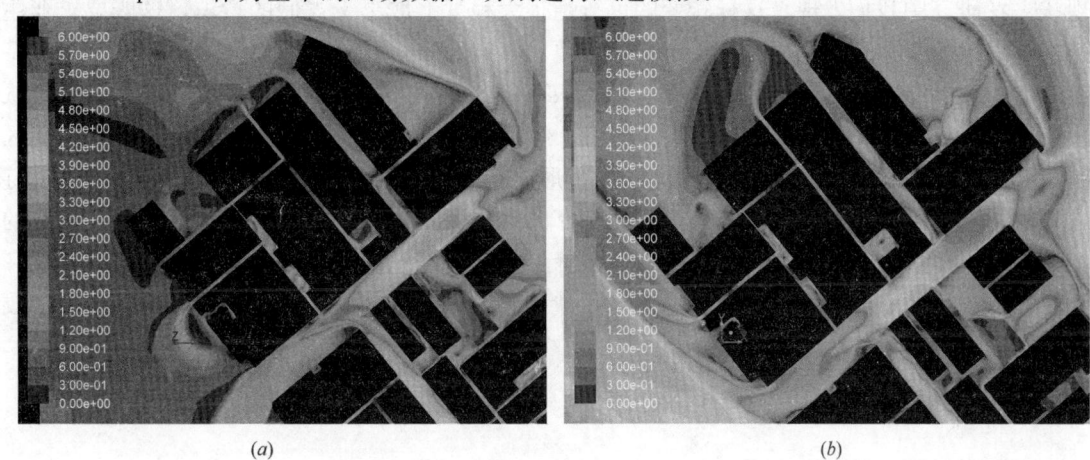

(a)　　　　　　　　　　　　　(b)

图 5　原有建筑未架空形式风速模拟
（a）模拟风向 90°；（b）模拟风向 135°
（图片来源：作者自绘）

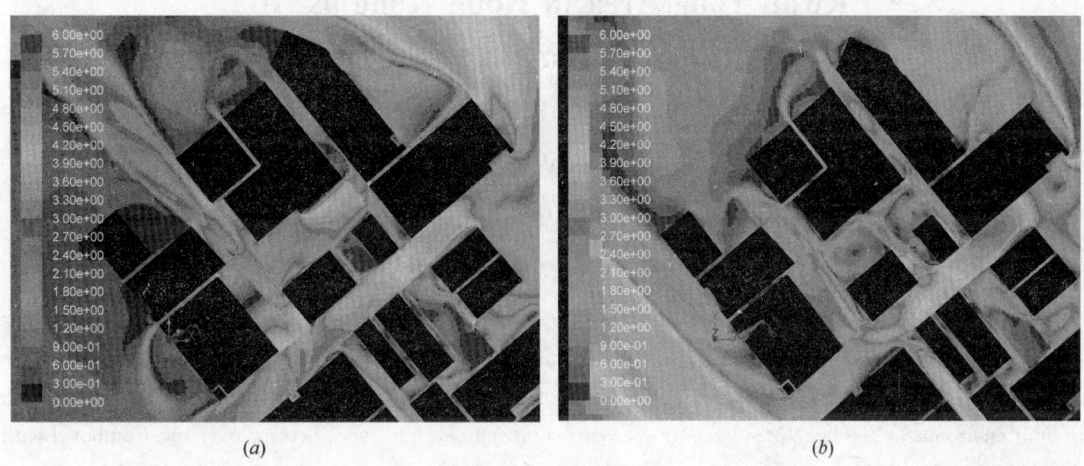

(a)　　　　　　　　　　　　　(b)

图 6　改造建筑架空形式风速模拟。
（a）模拟风向 90°；（b）模拟风向 135°
（图片来源：作者自绘）

5.4 结果分析对比

CFD 结果表明，原先建筑群相对封闭的外立面限制了内部的通风质量，部分区域平均风速小于 2m/s。通过改造后，建筑群内部的风环境得到了一定程度的改善。尤其是通过区域底层空间架空和拓宽主要内部巷道，整个区域变得相对开放和通透，有利于内部空气流动。

6　结论和启示

基于 CFD 模拟图像，我们建议将上述风环境较差（$V<2m/s$）[8] 的内部空间设置为公共停车场，这是一个由原本封闭的多个"私有"停车场转化而成的城市公共停车场，由于停车场统一化和系统化的处理使得停车在规模上有所增加；同时作为城市公共停车场将有效缓解路边停车和交通拥堵的现状。在研究中我们发现，这样转变的可行性很大程度上取决于人们的意识，这既要求业主放弃地面空间带来的商业利润，同时有更高的管理要求。

在改造的底层空间中，风环境较好（$V>2m/s$）[8] 的空间设置为公共半开敞空间。研究区域的道路普遍狭窄（$W<10m$）且车速较慢，结合图 3，图 4 的结果分析对比，架空空间的边缘区域（靠近邻近建筑墙体）具有较好的通风环境，可以形成良好的空气流动，适合设置为行人步行通道。

在香港，随处可见的架空设计让这个人口稠密的地区保持健康和生机。在香港其他工业区的调研中，如火炭工业区，已经有很多类似的架空设计用作公共停车空间。作为可以解决城市问题和提升工业区空气质量的有效途径，底层空间架空设计和改造将对新兴的工业区设计和老旧工业区改造产生一定的启示和借鉴作用。

Application and Enlightenment for Bottom Overhead in Old Industrial Area Regeneration-Taking Kwun Tong Area in Hong Kong as An Example

Liu Siqi，Wang Jiayi

（Chinese University of Hong Kong）

Abstract：Hong Kong is one of the most high-density cities around the world. People have paid more and more attentions on urban air quality and related social issues. As the biggest industrial area in east Kowloon, Kwun Tong is now experiencing a significant transformation, from manufacture to mixed functions and industries. Because of the high-density built environment and huge population flow, ventilation and parking issues become obvious. Combined with the present situation of Kwun Tong, the significance and performance of bottom overhead design in industrial area has been discussed through the method of CFD simulation.

Keywords：Old industrial area，Bottom overhead，Public parking system，CFD，Ventilation

参考文献：

[1]　叶伟华，王扬. 建筑底层架空式开放空间设计[J]. 新建筑，2001，6：56-58.

[2]　Edward Ng. Policies and technical guidelines for urban planning of high-density cities- air ventilation assessment（AVA）of Hong Kong. Building and Environment，2009，44：1478-1488.

[3]　李俊果，李朝阳，王新军. 香港大型公共建筑底层架空及启示[J]. 华中建筑，2009，12：25-29.

［4］ 崔霖．底层架空的哲学意义［J］．华中建筑，2001，1：71-73.

［5］ Jacob L. Vigdor（2010）．Is urban decay bad? Is urban revitalization bad too? ［J］Journal of Urban Economics，2010，68（3）：277-289

［6］ 谢浩．底层架空空间的优化设计［J］．建材发展导向，2001，3：41-44.

［7］ 张宾．建筑底层架空对风环境影响的研究［D］．河北：河北工程大学，2013.

［8］ Hong Kong Planning Department，（Department of Architecture，Chinese University of Hong Kong．）Final report-Feasibility study for establishment of air ventilation assessment system ［R］．2005．Ng Y Y，Tsou J Y．Feasibility study for establishment of air ventilation assessment system，Final report［R］．Hong Kong：Department of Architecture，Chinese University of Hong Kong．16，2005.

OPTIMIZED NATURAL VENTILATION: Development of Conceptual and Architectural Solutions to Optimize Natural Ventilation in High-Rise Apartment Buildings in Sub-Tropical Regions

Ferdinand Oswald[1], Roger Riewe[2]

(1. University Assistant Cand. Dr. Dipl. Ing. Arch. Institute of Architecture Technology, Leader of IAT-LAB Laboratory Section, Graz University of Technology, Austria; 2. University Professor Dipl. Ing. Architect and Head of Institute of Architecture Technology, Graz University of Technology, Austria)

Abstract: The content of this paper is the research project OPTIMIZED NATURAL VENTILATION, which like to show up conceptual and methodological principles to develop architectural concepts that are able to guarantee increased comfort by means of natural ventilation in residential buildings in sub-tropical regions. The paper intends to deliver underlying basic information that will also facilitate the subsequent development of specific apertures for large cities. In addition, criteria resulting from problems such as air pollution and noise emission also need to be fulfilled. In order to do that, it will be necessary to optimize and detect basic conditions needed for natural ventilation in this context, such as optimum aperture typology, and facade structure.

Keywords: Natural ventilation, Architectural solutions, Apertures, Wind blades, Facade structures

1 Introduction

Over recent decades, residents living in modern residential buildings in tropical metropolises are increasingly using split-system air conditioners. The use and energy consumption of such systems in those regions are enormous, and especially the latter is a serious disadvantage in operating air conditioning systems. It is assumed that the additional energy consumption of seven-million metropolis Hong Kong alone will rise to 6.8 GWh per annum due to the use of ventilation systems. The South Eastern Chinese coastal region with its 150 million inhabitants requires an energy quantity of 145 GWh per year to cool their apartments with air conditioners[1]. At the same time, these split-system air conditioners continue to heat up the urban environment with their warm exhaust air, discharging 40% of required cooling energy in the form of heat into the ambient air, thus also exacerbating negative effects of the urban heat island. According to statistical calculations, the worldwide urban population will almost double by 2020, increasing from 3.5 billion to 6.3 billion [2]. Subsequently, energy required for cooling will almost double by 2050 as well[3]. Given that the urban population cannot do without air conditioning, this forecasted growth is bound to pose a huge challenge to energy production and the carbon footprint. For future conurbations in sub-tropical regions, therefore, it will be of crucial importance to seek specific solutions for problems such as overburdened energy grids and local climate change. Reducing the use of split-system air conditioners is an urgent issue. It seems possible to increase comfort and reduce mechanical ventilation at the same time with the help of specifically natural ventilation systems for residential housing in tropical regions. Scientific research has shown that natural ventilation increases living comfort up to 85% [4]. Two architectural parameters that are of decisive significance for optimizing the effects of natural ventilation thus also reflect the current state of research as follows:

1. 1 Dimensions and positioning of the ventilation apertures

In the experimental procedure by Yin et al.[5], fully open apertures placed at different heights (top, bottom and centre) were compared to one another in order to analyse the effectiveness of different aperture positions and their airspeed. Test results show that it is vital to arrange the apertures in such a way that air movement actually reaches the residents in order to cool them. If apertures are near to the ceiling or floor, fresh air moving at maximum speed will only partly reach the people in the room.

1. 2 Wind blades

Vertical wall elements on the facade that influence the flow of wind into the building can also be referred to as wind blades. Literally translated from English, they could also be described as "wing walls", because they protrude from the facade like wings. Wind blades can have substantial influence and positive effects on the rate and speed of ventilation during cross ventilation within the residential unit. According to current scientific research, wind creates different pressure conditions that significantly influence the air change rate, depending on what direction it comes from [6]. These cantilevering wall elements (in vertical or horizontal positions) thus influence pressure conditions and direct air into the building. If such a vertically protruding wall element is located within an aperture, it divides it into two sections. The impact (positive and negative effects) such a wing wall on the facade's structure may have on airflow within the building has not yet been investigated.

2 Hypothesis

The aim of this research project OPTIMIZED NATURAL VENTILATION is to promote conceptual and methodological principles to develop architectural concepts that are able to guarantee increased comfort by means of natural ventilation in residential buildings, not just in sub-tropical regions. The research project intends to deliver underlying basic information that will also facilitate the subsequent development of specific apertures for large cities. In addition, criteria resulting from problems such as air pollution and noise emission will also be fulfilled. In order to do that, it will be necessary to optimize and detect basic conditions needed for natural ventilation in this context, such as optimum aperture typology and facade structure. This project aims to identify optimum airflow dynamics and the highest possible air change rate while also taking aperture, facade and floor plan sections of a residential building into account. Concepts will be assessed and results compared in wind tunnel experiments and using computational fluid dynamics, thus establishing the best combinatorial models.

3 Arguments

Due to high humidity and temperatures in Hong Kong (as in other sub-tropical and tropical climates), there is a very high potential of energy conversion efficiency to increase comfort by means of natural ventilation. Comfort is subjective. Nevertheless, Szokolay [7] has developed a mathematical relation to calculate comfort. His methods enable scientists to determine comfort in relation to temperature and wind speed.

This psychrometric chart of Hong Kong's comfort zone shows that comfort is dependent on all weather conditions such as solar incidence, cloud, precipitation, wind direction, air speed, temperature and humidity. Additional climate data over a one-year period is shown as points (days). The area within the pink line indicates how natural ventilation increases comfort days.

The chart in Fig. 1 shows that natural ventilation generates 30% more comfort in one year. However, this one-year period also includes the colder season in which natural ventilation is not necessarily required for comfort. In October, which is a hot month, natural ventilation can even provide residents with 85% more comfort during that period.

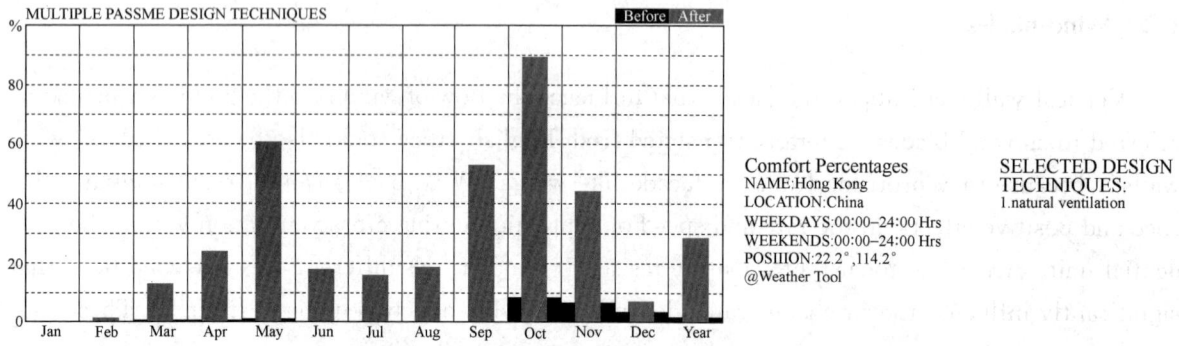

Figure 1 Percentage of comfort throughout the year and per month achieved through natural ventilation in Hong Kong, data from psychrometric chart[4]

4 Methodology

4.1 Theoretical

Optimized natural ventilation based on two architectural levels

In order to optimize airflow dynamics in terms of their even distribution and air change rate in the room, and thus increase living comfort, two architectural parameters described in more detail below are tested, compared and aligned with each other. This involves introducing ambient air into specified apertures within the building envelope. Natural ventilation occurs through apertures located on opposite sides. Taking external influential factors such as the direction and speed of the wind into account is a key criterion.

4.1.1 Aperture types: aperture typologies with equally sized cross sections

This experiment focuses on two different types of apertures with equally sized total cross sections and equally deep wall thicknesses (0.20m), where a fully open aperture and a perforated wall with several small openings are compared with each other. Figure 2 illustrates these two different wall

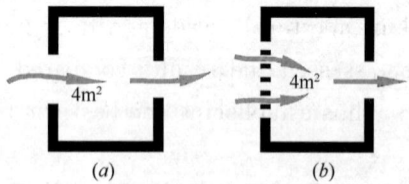

Figure 2 Comparison of two different aperture types with equally sized cross sections (4m²) represented as floor plans. (a) Single aperture; (b) Perforated wall with several small openings[16]

230

aperture typologies with identical cross sections as a floor plan.

When comparing both aperture types, it becomes immediately evident that the large wall aperture could also serve as a glazed window aperture. In comparison to a fully open aperture, the perforated wall (ventilation blocks) has numerous positive characteristics. It plays a decisive functional role in the history of architecture in tropical and sub-tropical regions. The name "ventilation blocks" stems from the production of these walls from many small single blocks, such as bricks or concrete slabs. "Ventilation blocks and their use in South East Asia" is the subject of a book of the same name [8]. The perforated shear wall facade has several advantages: it provides protection against burglary and overlooking (private sphere), and the effects of rain, sun and stormy weather. Another great advantage of this aperture typology compared to a large single opening is that people could do without protective elements against sunlight and overlooking. The advantages and characteristics of such "climate regulating envelopes in sub-tropical residential buildings" are described in detail in one of this book's chapters of the same name [9]. This aperture type has not yet been tried out in high-rise apartment blocks. This research project aims to undertake specific investigations in order to assess the basic efficiency of its implementation in high-rise apartment blocks.

4.1.2 Facade structures: vertical wind blades at or in front of apertures

On the windward side (a), vertical wind blades are placed one-sided adjacent to, centrally and at both sides of the apertures respectively. The impact of these structural facade elements on inflow and outflow on the leeward rear side (b) of the building are assessed in relation to the air change rate and speed of different wind directions and forces. Figure 3 (a) shows a floor plan with a vertical cantilevering wall element (wind blade) on the left side of the window opening (seen from inside the building). The wind direction is assumed to be between 45° and 90° in relation to the right-hand side. While a pocket of negative pressure develops on the side of the wind blade facing away from the window, positive pressure builds up in the bottleneck at the window opening. As a result, air is forced into the opening because of the increasing pressure difference between a and b.

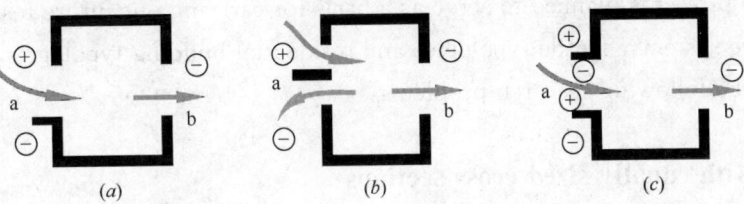

(a)　　　　　　　　(b)　　　　　　　　(c)

Figure 3　Air pressure levels at cantilevering wall elements represented as floor plans.
(a) One-sided; (b) In the centre of the wall opening; (c) On both sides of the wall opening[16]

If a vertical cantilevering wall element is fitted into an aperture (Figure 3 (b)), it divides that aperture into two sections. With a wind direction of 45° to 90° towards the right-hand side, positive pressure will again build up on the windward side, thus promoting inflow. Corresponding negative pressure on the rear side of the element may have the desired effect of causing an outward airflow at this point. While leeward outflow could affect the efficiency of cross-ventilation, a centrally positioned vertical wall element could deliver good cross-ventilation characteristics if different wind directions prevail (45° from left or right), without having to provide an additionally adjustable vertical element (shift).

If wind blades are attached to both sides of the aperture, two regions of positive and negative pressure develop at each element. The impact of this configuration on flow characteristics strongly depends on the wind direction and also needs investigating as described above (Figure 3 (c)) . Negative effects of this configuration on flow characteristics have not yet been verified.

4. 2 Experiments in wind tunnels

Experimental research to ascertain pressure distribution on the building's façadecan carried out in an atmospheric boundary layer wind tunnel at the Institute of Fluid Mechanics and Heat Transfer (ISW), Graz University of Technology. In this tunnel the atmospheric boundary layer can be simulated which strongly depends on the nature of the terrain.

After adaption of the round-rod grid to the velocity profile at the chosen location, height and density of suitable roughness elements (developed on a modular basis) are then ascertained in experiments. Numerical simulations to determine relevant data for ground roughness to suit the characteristic wind profile are described in [10]. For more details, please refer to the description of this tunnel [11] which is designed for aerodynamic experiments with uniform velocity and a low degree of turbulence in the jet. In previous experiments at the ISW, this had been effected by using pneumatically operated mechanisms [12a, 12b, 12c].

4. 3 Numerical flow simulations

Numerical flow simulation (Computational Fluid Dynamics, CFD) represents the numerical solution of Navier-Stokes equations which describe the motion of fluids subject to prevailing physical laws. Due to the availability of modern computer technology, scientists are now able, for example, to calculate wind flow through urban quarters with their complex geometry [13].

5 Conclusion /Expected results

This research project is planned to serve as a basis for carrying out future tests to experimentally develop aperture systems, facade typologies and residential building typologies, as well as to provide solutions to the following research problems:

Aperture types with equally sized cross sections:

Can a perforated wall deliver required air change rates despite the higher air drag due to its small openings? Can penetrating air be distributed more effectively in the room through many small openings than through a fully open aperture, thus providing more comfort? In order to answer these questions, the wind speed is to be measured and the distribution of the air flow within the residential unit is to be made visible. Will strong impinging eddies (caused by weather conditions) be filtered out by the perforated wall, thus preventing them from entering the interior? How are flow velocities distributed within the room and which air change rates will be achieved globally with these two different aperture types? So far, no proof has been presented as to the effectivity of the aforementioned perforated aperture typology. That question needs to be analysed in experiments and simulations, and since simple relations will not yield any constructive results in this case, only measurements will lead to assessable results.

Facade structures: vertical wind blades at or in front of apertures:

How can vertical facade elements optimize ventilation? With the configured facade structures described above, a procedure is employed which should yield optimal scenarios. Furthermore, vertical facade structures like that could become part of the supporting building structure and fulfil the task of shading building apertures at the same time [14]. As far as different requirements are concerned, the facade structure could therefore present a viable solution within an architectural building concept. This configuration of positioning elements in different places in front of the aperture, and the ventilation of the residential unit with all its consequences regarding air change rate and air speed has not yet been scientifically investigated in this form. Horizontal wall elements are not going to be tested in this project, because controlling thermally-caused vertical air motion under the influence of wind is of lesser importance and not subject of this research.

The results of this research are not intended to bring forth just one possible solution. On the contrary, it is hoped to gain a great deal of knowledge with respect to combinational models of different architectural parameters and particular wind characteristics, thus building a basis for further investigations. Basic research generates fundamental knowledge required to develop aperture systems, facades and residential building typologies within a broad spectrum. Essentially, this research project paves the way for the adaptation of experimental procedures, which will subsequently lead to feasible experimental developments.

6 Summary /Expected effects from the project results

As a basis for the development of new application-oriented approaches, the results of this research project are intended for long-term use in residential housing. This will not only apply to new buildings, but also include modification and renovation of existing residential buildings, hence their optimization by means of natural cross-ventilation.

Due to air pollution, opening up the facade to interior habitable space has become practically impossible in many urban areas, not only in China, but also in European cities. Air filtration as a measure to mitigate the impact of pollution, however, may lead to a reduction of fresh air inflow due to the drag caused by air filtration systems[15]. There is a subsequent risk that the air change rate will not suffice to guarantee comfort. As opposed to mechanical ventilation, airflow conditions during natural ventilation are solely influenced by architectural elements such as aperture types, facade structures and floor plan configurations. Numerous scientific papers have already stressed the necessity of these investigations; however, tangible results have yet to be presented [5].

Research results emerging from OPTIMIZED NATURAL VENTILATION will provide the basis for further research projects, thus helping future scientists to find answers to the following crucial questions:

How will such filters need to be designed in order to ensure vital air change despite their filter effect? Which aperture types best allow the integration of filtration systems (porous perforated walls or large openings)? How should the three architectural parameters be modified to make optimized air change with air filter applications really effective despite the larger drag?

Developing procedures will provide a basis for further experiments. Moreover, planners and architects will be able to use optimized results and expert knowledge gained from this project in the field of facade structures and aperture systems. Subsequently，European and Asian window and filter manufacturing companies could develop new aperture systems in co-operation with research institutions. Appropriate perspectives need to be in place to promote and facilitate realisation of such projects together with research institutions，to bring them into mass production and into markets in Europa as well as tropical and sub-tropical regions.

优化自然通风：发展概念和架构解决方案，优化亚热带地区高层公寓楼的自然通风

Ferdinand Oswald[1]，Roger Riewe[2]

（1. 奥地利格拉茨技术大学建筑技术研究所实验室；

2. 奥地利格拉茨技术大学建筑技术研究所）

摘要：本文的研究成果出自研究项目"优化自然通风"。该项目揭示了在亚热带地区，可以通过自然通风带来的提升舒适度的建筑概念之理念及方法论原理。本文旨在转达潜在的基本信息，以为大城市未来发展具体的"缺口"提供便利。此外，来自空气污染、噪声扩散等问题的标准仍需要被满足。为了实现这个目的，在最适宜孔径类型学、立面结构等领域下，优化及探测自然通风的基本条件是十分必要的。

关键词：自然通风，建筑解决方案，缺口，风力叶片，外观结构

References：

[1] Lang Siwei. Progress in energy-efficiency standards for residential buildings in China[J]. Energy and Buildings 36，12，2004：1191-1196.

[2] Population Development in Cities 2050. McKinsey，2013.

[3] National Bureau of Statistics of China. Office of Dissemination[M]. China Statistical Yearbook 2011. Beijing：China Statistics Press，2012：93.

[4] U.S. Department of Energy. Weather Tool 2001，© Autodesk，Inc. 2010；Weather data Download，report on the data (STAT) and ASHRAE Design Conditions Design Day Data file (DDY)[R].

[5] W. Yin, G. Zhang, W. Yang, X. Wang. Natural ventilation potential model considering solution multiplicity, window opening percentage, air velocity and humidity in China. Journal of Building and Environment[M]. 2010，45：338-344.

[6] G. Moeseke, E. Gratia, S. Reiter, A. D. Herde. Wind pressure distribution influence on natural ventilation for different incidences and environment densities[J]. Journal Buildings and Energy，2005，37：878-889.

[7] S. Szokolay. Introduction to Architectural Science[M]. The Basis of Sustainable Design. 2. Edition，2008：42.

[8] L. C. Kien. Ventilation Blocks and their use in southeast Asia[M]//F. Schätz, (Ed.). Casting Architecture-Ventilation Blocks. National University of Singapore，2013：22-27.

[9]   F. Oswald. Wall instead of Air Conditioning-Climate-Regulating Shells in Subtropical Residential Housing[M]/U. Hirschberg, D. Gethmann, R. Riewe, (Ed.). GAM 09 Architecture Magazin, Walls: Spatial Sequences, Springer Verlag Berlin -Vienna, 2013: 180-195.

[10] W. Meile, W. Gretler. Numerical simulation of flow in approach sections of boundary layer wind tunnels for aerodynamic structure investigations[J]. Research in engineering, 1991, 57 (6): 187-198.

[11] W. Gretler, W. Meile. The 2 m wind tunnel at the Institute of Fluid Mechanics and Gas. Dynamics at the Technical University of Graz[J], Austrian engineering and Architect Magazine, 1993, 138(3): 90-96.

[12a] Teppner, R. , Langensteiner, B. , Meile, W. , Brenn, G. , Kerschbaumer, S. Flow around and through a building storey with fully opened or tilted windows[M]. Proceedings of the 2nd Central European Symposium on Building Physics (CESBP 2013), Vienna, Austria, September 9-11, 2013: 717-724.

[12b] Teppner, R. , Langensteiner, B. , Meile, W. , Brenn, G. , Kerschbaumer, S. Air change rates driven by the flow around and through a building storey with fully open or tilted windows[G]. Proceedings of the ANSYS Conference & 9. CADFEM Austria Users' Meeting. Wien, Austria, 24-25. April. 2014.

[12c] Teppner, R. , Meile, W. , Langensteiner, B. , Kerschbaumer, S. Projektvorstellung "Native"-Analyse natürlicher Lüftungskonzepte für Wohngebäude durch Windkanal-experimente und numerische Strömungssimulationen[C]. ANSYS Conference & 7. CADFEM Austria Users' Meeting 2012, Wien, Austria, 2012: 26-04.

[13] J. Franke, C. Hirsch, A. G. Jensen, H. W. Krüss, M. Schatzmann, P. S. Westbury, S. D. Miles, J. A. Wisse, N. G. Wright. Recommendations on the use of CFD in wind engineering[C]. Proceedings of the International Conference on Urban Wind Engineering and Building Aerodynamics//van Beeck, J. P. A. J. (Ed.). COST Action C14, Impact of Wind and Storm on City Life Built Environment. Karman Institute, Rhode-St-Genèse, Belgium, 5 - 7 May, 2004.

[14] WOHA. The Met, Residential High-Rise in Bangkok. Selected Works Vol. 1. Patrik Bingham-Hall: Pesaro Publishing, 2011: 122.

[15] DIN EN 1822-1: 2011-01. High efficiency air filters (EPA, HEPA and ULPA) -Part 1: Classification, performance testing, marking. German version EN 1822-1: 2009, Berlin: Beuth Verlag GmbH, 2014.

[16] Copyright Ferdinand OSWALD. University Assistant Dipl. Ing. Arch. Institute of Architecture Technology. Austria: Graz University of Technology, 2015.

Interior Space Optimisation and Shared-Living Infrastructiure As Strategies for Domestic Space Reduction in Hong Kong

Ernst Alexander Dengg[1] , Dylan Mundy-Clowry[1] , Johannes Würzler[2]
(1. Graz University of Technology; 2. Graz University of Technology)

Abstract: This paper serves as a status of our current research in the field of space optimisation and collective living design in the context of Hong Kong's urban housing fabric. The approach to this research has been to analyse the space-use efficiency of an exemplary housing project. Together with observations on emerging trends in co-operative living environments, this research is intended as guideline for the potential development of optimum building typologies in China Urban Housing.

Keywords: Space optimisation, Housing efficiency, Sustainability, Shared economy, Collective Living

1 Introduction

The continuous growth of the global population and the resulting increase in urban migration leads to an increasing constructed landscape. Residential buildings cover the main part of this building volume and are a chief cause of CO_2 emission, waste of resources and energy consumption. Despite the tremendously great improvements in fields of energy and building technology, the field of space optimisation has much scope to innovate in order to contribute to a sustainable built environment for the future.

The numbers of households are continuously increasing and the trend toward larger homes is even exaggerating the global need of more housing space. According the data from the National Association of Home Builders, homes in the United States more than doubled in size between 1950 and 2002 (from 90m² to 210m²) . In China, houses tripled in size with per capita floor space increasing from 8. 1m² to 26. 5m² and from 6. 7m² to 22. 8m², in rural and urban China respectively, between 1978 and 2002[1]. It is clear that despite innovations in sustainable building practices combined with an enhanced environmental awareness, space optimisation plays a minor role in the sustainable agenda.

We recognise the challenge of an ever increasing urban population, the increase in single person households along with an ageing demographic. Therefore, we propose that the potential for the optimisation of private households, combined with increased emphasis on collective infrastructure, energy resources and social spaces, can finally be sincerely explored as a solution for relieving the strain on building demand and therefore reducing energy consumption and CO_2 production. We also propose that embracing such design principles and challenging the form of current urban housing would foster a vibrant urban living experience and maximise the spatial capacity of communal spaces.

2 Housing Size in Hong Kong

For the purpose of this paper we address our attention toHong Kong. The period of housing development in Hong Kong between the 1950's to the 1980's witnessed the construction of typologically and architecturally innovative structures[2]. Under specific political, social, climatic as well as spatial conditions, these building designs could be considered as a cross pollination of the modern European *Existenzminimum* design and traditional Chinese building typologies. A highly evolved and notably efficient transcultural hybrid, Hong Kong's urban housing models have been recognised and exported across the world[3]. With the key issues of mass housing provision in Hong Kong always depending on the balancing of efficiency versus liveability[4] we aim to address the conflict between the two, holistically.

Housing developments since the 50's in Hong Kong evolved out of sheer demand to provide, safe, fast and cost effective housing for the rapidly increasing population in the city. The result of ambitious building projects such as the Man Wai Lau were some of the most densely occupied settlements in the world. As one can expect, housing units were spatially restrictive with many unrelated families having to occupy the same residential unit. The space efficiency was of such high priority that little or no consideration was given to the social and cultural amenities of such housing complexes

"Such tiny flats have generated social repercussions. As a result of crowded conditions at home, the city's residents flee to streets and shopping malls that are enervated on Saturdays to the point of pedestrian gridlock. Although contributing to urban vitality, theHong Kong press has noted that the family home as a place to sleep only, combined with parents holding more than one job each, results in a lack of family life and cohesion critical to traditional Chinese culture. Unlike the minimum, monofunctional dwelling, the multi-generational, mixed-use traditional shophouse supported that culture." [3]

In our research we are addressing two contradicting challenges, the challenge of spatially optimising new residential units by reducinginefficient 'individual space', meanwhile actually increasing the quality of life for individuals in a collective environment.

3   Spatial Analysis of Living Space

Our Research assesses working patterns and lifestyles that are not conducive to the type of urban housing currently conceived in China. We maintain that the current spatial design of modern Hong Kong typologies do not adhere to emerging living and working practices, practices such as collective living and working. We recognise the shared economy as a growing trend in the economic development of urban centres. Space therefore could also be considered as potential shared commodity in the context of a culture of collaborative consumerism.

3. 1   Assessment of Spatial Efficiency

After analysing the amount of active space use of a typical apartment layout in Hong Kong, one can draw conclusions on the ultimate effectiveness of the time and space use of a particular living unit. This should tell us a number of things about the routine rhythm of space use of a particular unit, but also provide us with quantitate information with which to calculate what areas of a residential unit could be considered for sharing in a collective environment.

In 2004, Dobbelsteen and Wilde invented indices for quantifying space use in living room. They differentiate between two dimensional (use of one layer of floor or ground space), three dimensional (picture of all two-dimensional layers related to a reference layer), and four dimensional space use (time) . The latter needs to be observed over a period of time[5]. Our research does not use their conception and indices but we follow conduct as well a two dimensional, a three dimensional and a four dimensional analysis; considering as well the time as the fourth dimension.

3.2　Analysis of a Typical Residential Unit inHong Kong

The aim of our research is to improve housing efficiency through detecting unused spatial potential and reducing it to a minimum. This analysis involves looking at opportunities of reducing domestic private space that could otherwise be considered shared infrastructure between other private households in an urban context, particularly Hong Kong.

The floor plan we are looking at is located in Tseung Kwan O (New Territories, Hong Kong). The residential development of the MTR Corporation was formerly known as Dream city the LOHAS Park (LOHAS means lifestyle of health and sustainability). LOHAS Park would be recognised as an exemplary urban housing project in Hong Kong and for this purpose is a suitable subject for our research. For the research, two residents (a couple) were interviewed and their living habits were applied onto the space analysis.

3.2.1　Living Space Analysis

We firstly analysed the residential area in 2D. This is the way, most architects and planners understand the floorplan, even though it is very static and not yet a spatial research. Nevertheless, the top view of 2d space use delivers a very clear image of the floor plan and allows reading more into the design. Surprisingly, as figure 1 shows us that even in the 2D analysis, there are many redundant spaces, which means they may not necessarily be there. The figure is self-explanatory and should stimulate the thoughts about the resource space, but is has to be highlighted that we could detect 6.22m² (of 39.14m²) which are redundant spaces, which is very exactly twice the space of the bath room.

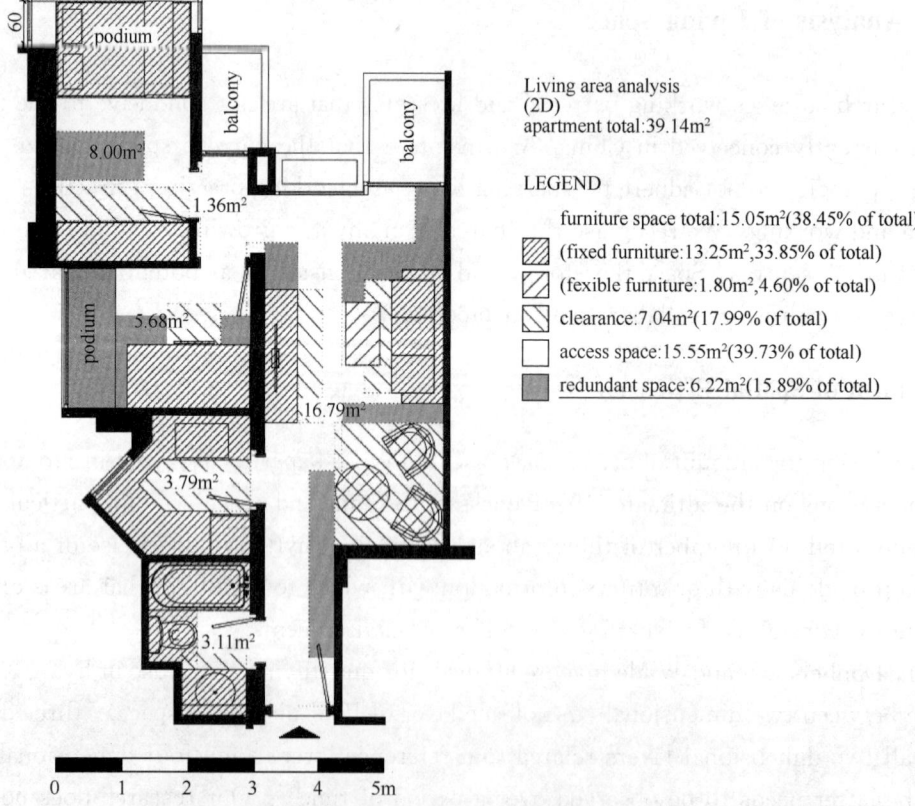

Figure 1　Living area analysis

In figure 2 we see the intensity of vertical space use. In reality nearly none of the existing furniture (except the cabinet in the bedroom) reaches room height. Here, we see that there is a huge potential of generating more space efficient solutions to storage and utilities.

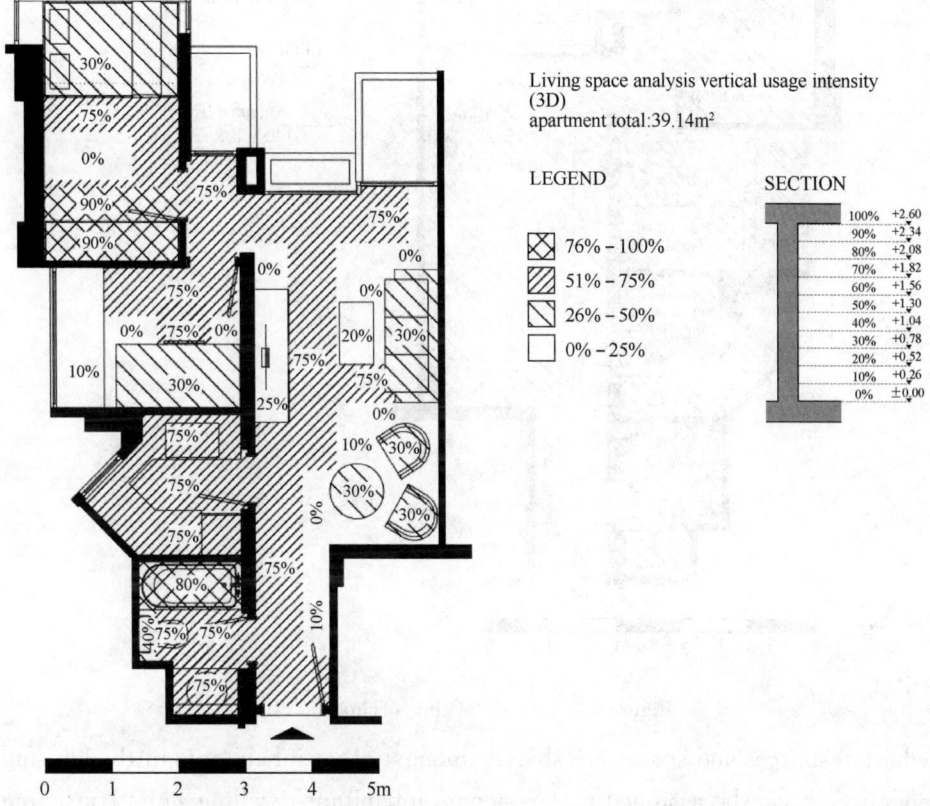

Figure 2　Living space analysis vertical usage intensity

For the analysis of time occupancy rate of living functions, figure 3 gives us deeper insights of the time expenditure of the residents in the apartment. Numbers are average value of both dwellers. As we can in the figure see, many of the living function were used very briefly. The kitchen for instance is used for 25 minutes per day per person in average.

3. 2. 2　Observation

Upon completion of our initial analysis, we observe that our findings can provide an insight into the spatial time use efficiency. This research should not be misunderstood that we are stating that certain usable space should be removed or reduced from the existing floorplan, but the its effectiveness should be reflected upon in terms of gross floor area made available to private households.

There is scope for improvement in achieving a truly optimised residential unit by reconsidering the volume space that is allocated towards private residential

It is obvious that the dedicated kitchen space is not sufficiently optimising the use of private residential space due to the amount of time it is being privately utilised.

4　The Potential for Implementing Individual and Collective Spaces in Urban Housing Design in China

"Shared living" and "Co-Living" are terms that illustrate a resurge in co-operative living envi-

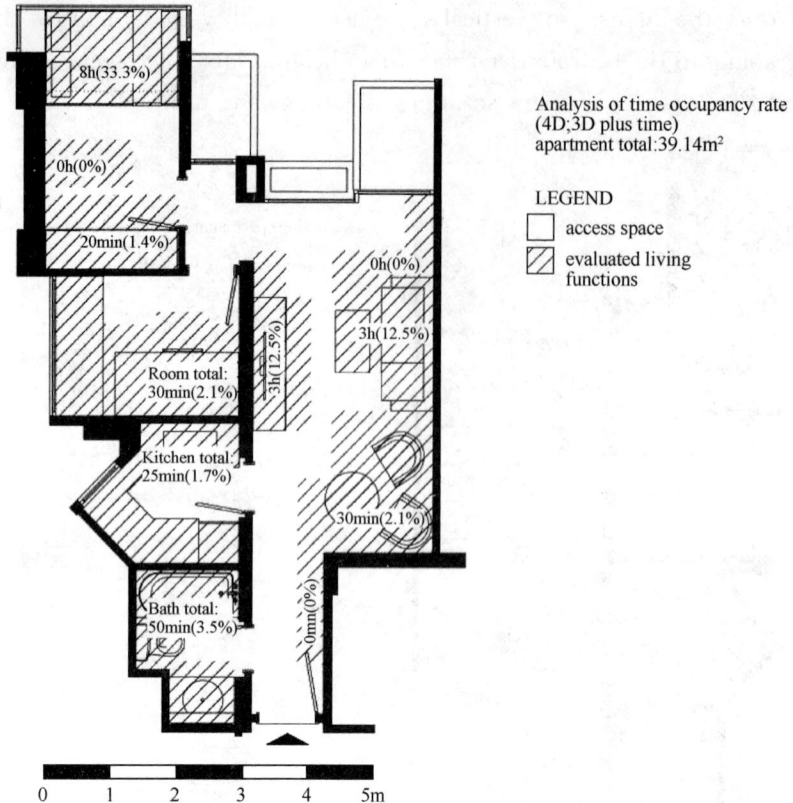

Figure 3 Analysis of time occupancy rate

ronments where resources and spaces are shared amongst other inhabitants in the housing accommodation. Generally, it can be assumed that residents inhabitant dwelling units consisting of private sleeping area while sanitary and social resources are shared. We aim to resolve issues of reduced gross floor area of private residential units with the improved quality of life of increased collective infrastructure and space Shared space should not be perceived as an invasion of privacy but quite the contrary, with the clear boundaries of "collective and individual spaces" [6] ones individual space should perceived as a clear solitary retreat. Meanwhile the collective spaces within itself should offer opportunities for the individual to engage in collective and individual routines, which would require a sensitive application of design.

5 Conclusion

The application of principles adopted from co living or shared living environments, along with the tools used to determine the ultimate efficiency of individual living spaces should relieve the pressure on the demand for urban housing resources and construction in spite of the projected increase in the urban population in china in the next 30 years. We intend to investigate the opportunities and potential for this research to inform new forms of urban housing that can address the challenges of emerging demographic, economic and cultural issues in china's urban regions. Future research will adopt methodology from the Field of VR technology in order to determine spatial perception of optimised and collective living scenarios. This research would provide the foundation for understanding how to manipulate housing design in an innovative, inclusive and effective manner.

优化室内空间及建设共享生活基础设施，
作为缩小香港处所空间的策略

Ernst Alexander Dengg[1]，Dylan Mundy-Clowry[1]，Johannes Würzler[2]
（1. 奥地利格拉兹技术大学；2. 奥地利格拉兹技术大学毕业生）

摘要：此文为本研究机构当前在空间优化及基于香港房屋结构肌理的集体生活设计研究成果。本文采用分析一个样例房屋的空间使用效率作为研究方法。结合对于合作生活环境这一新趋势的观察，本研究旨在提出一个最适宜的中国住房类型设计指导。

关键词：空间优化，房屋效率，可持续发展，共享经济，集体生活

References：

[1] Mason Bradbury，M. Nils Peterson，Jianguo Liu. Bradbury，M，Peterson，M N，Liu，J. Long-term dynamics of household size and their environmental implications[J]. Popul Environ，2014.

[2] Christ，E，Gantenbein，C. Hong Kong Typology：An architectural research on Hong Kong building types[M]，2011：24-24.

[3] Crisman P. Transcultural Hybrid：Emergence of a Hong Kong Housing Typology[M]. qoth ACSA Annnal Meeting Proceedings，Architecture in Communication，2002：529-535 Crisman P. Transcultural Hybrid：Emergence of a Hong Kong Housing Typology[M]，2002：2-4.

[4] Ng E，Wong K S. Efficiency & Livability：Towards Sustainable Habitation in Hong Kong[M]，Hong Kong Housing Authority Conference 2003，2003.

[5] Dobbelsteen A v d，Wilde S d. Space use optimisation and sustainability - environmental assessment of space use concepts[J]. Journal of Environmental Management，2004，73：81-89.

[6] Hertzberger H. Lessons for students in Architecture[M]，010 publishers，1991：12-12.

Sustainable Housing Developments in High Density Environment: A Comparative Study of Urban Environment within Low-Rise and High-Rise Clusters

Maing Minjang

(Chinese University of Hong Kong)

Abstract: This paper discusses findings on comparative analysis between low-rise and high-rise clusters within high-density environments and how these developments compare against sustainable parameters for urban planning. Parameters that affect urban environment are climate, street canyon geometry (measured through sky view factor, SVF), urban temperatures, orientation and building geometries. Case study of Hong Kong was selected due to its initiatives in sustainable high-rise affordable housing design and construction, taken by the city's largest developer, Hong Kong Housing Authority over the past few decades. Field measurements, observations and simulations were conducted at three adjacent sites of 3-story, 20+ story housing buildings to study changes in air temperatures, SVF and radiant heat. It was found that low-rise developments had higher fluctuations in temperature and also tended to have higher radiant heat flux compared with the high-rise developments.

Keywords: Sustainable developments, Low-rise high-rise, Density, Urban environment

1 Introduction

In high-density urban cities, sustainable housing developments need to confront complex challenges of environmental performance, social integration and economic cohesion, with heavy emphasis on healthy housing and better surrounding (adjacent) living urban environments - such as improving green spaces[1]. However, appreciable amounts of open green spaces are scarce within densely built-up areas and tend to be concentrated in parks or designated recreational areas. Limited space prompts for sustainable design strategies that compromise on better performance at the housing unit scale but put more focus on collective shared spaces in urban outdoor environment to improve quality of life. Application of green features on buildings, green walls or green roof, can decrease urban heat islands in street canyons [2]. Vegetation can have substantial affect on urban climate and studies have found that vegetation could be used to mitigate some of the anthropogenic effects generated by development of urban areas [3].

Case study of Hong Kong was selected due its high density and the government's initiatives to address pressing needs for sustainable development. High-rise towers and low-rise housing clusters with different layouts exist within the dense city, much like many cities undergoing rapid urbanization; Mongolia with ger districts and Indonesia with kampung districts. To compare how vertical and horizontal stacking of housing units and integration with vegetation affect the urban environment two housing development types of low-rise horizontal compactness and high-rise vertical compactness were considered. This paper will discuss context of low-rise and high-rise housing development in Hong Kong, field and simulations studies and form comparisons from the findings.

2 Sustainable DevelopmentAgenda

Sustainable development is defined as "development which meets the needs of current generations without compromising the ability of future generations to meet their own needs", as defined by the World Commission on Environment and Development in 1987. This would later became the theme of United Nations First Earth Summit at Rio de Janeiro, Brazil 1992[1] and become further defined into three categories referred to as the three pillars of sustainable development: economic, social and environment. When considering housing developments in high-density living environments, some common issues that arise are: mass housing demand, insufficient urban infrastructure, urban heat island, and social exclusion. In rapid urbanization, vast settlements form clusters of buildings of similar building types throughout the urban areas. In developing countries this is noted from vast periphery settlements around city centers where mainly migrant communities converge, making sustainable development a critical agenda to form healthy and diverse communities.

2.1 Hong Kong housing and urban villages

Hong Kong, although a developed country struggles with issues of rapid urbanization from influx of mainland Chinese migrants and increasing disparity of wealth in high density environment of 26km² built-up area for 7.24 million people (as of mid-2014). Housing affordability is having an impact on housing demand with the city having to address large demand for affordable housing - public housing. The Hong Kong Housing Authority (HKHA) has become the biggest developer for housing in the city and provides housing wholly and partially subsidized to almost half the city's population. HKHA is under much pressure to build public rental housing (PRH) units and in 2014 has set a target to build 200,000 new PRH units by 2025 [4]. High-rise developments seem to be the main solution and housing towers both public and private have been rapidly erected throughout the city.

Urban villages formed from high-rise towers being implanted neartransportation nodes in areas which once were rural farm villages comprising of mainly small 3-story houses. The change inland use creates the scenario of high density living with newer 20-40story housing towers alongside these low-rise village clusters (Figure 1). This paper will use this scenario to investigate how high-rise and low-rise housing developments are affected by the environment and how they respectively address the three pillars of sustainability, with more focus on the environmental sustainability aspects.

(a)   (b)

Figure 1

(a) Low-rise and High-rise housing clusters co-exist in case study location of Tai Wai, New Territories,

Hong Kong[5]; (b) The three test sites A, B and C representing different scale clusters.

[(Source of Image in Figure 1 (a) from: Zhang, L. (South China Morning Post) Photo by David Wong)]

3 Methodology

The investigation consisted ofsite selection and collection of field measured and simulated data.

Data collection was done in two parts: (Ⅰ) field observation and measurements; and (Ⅱ) computer simulations to make correlations with the field data analysis.

3.1 Selected Site Description

The selected test site for this investigation is Tai Wai [aerial photo of area in Figure 1 (*a*)], which is an area in the New Territories of Hong Kong that in recent years has undergone drastic changes in building types, particularly since the 1970s with the introduction of mass public housing. It falls within the boundary of the Sha Tin New Town Development, which is regarded as one of the most successful new town developments in Hong Kong. The area has several urban village clusters of low-rise 3-story buildings, in some cases almost walled in by high-rise housing blocks[5]. This stark contrast makes this an ideal test site comparison of the low-rise and high-rise urban environments under same climate conditions.

Three housing types were targeted: (A) side-by-side low-rise (3-story) housing buildings in the village; (B) relatively porous high-rise 30-story housing buildings, placed parallel to N-S axis; and (C) high-rise 20-23 story housing buildings placed in a circular almost-enclosed layout. The building locations and types can be further seen in Figure 1 (*b*). Site A is called Tin Sum Village and Sites B and C are within the public housing development, Sun Chui Estate.

3.2 Data Collection

In Part Ⅰ, 13 test locations within A, B, and C were marked to make field observations of space use and measurements of air temperature and solar radiation over two days, 29 April and 8 May 2015from 10:30 a.m. to 12 p.m. and 10 a.m. to 12:30 p.m. respectively. Air temperature was measured with temperature data loggers (HOBO) at each 13 locations and solar radiation was measured with a net radiometer at one location in each of the three sites as shown in Figure 2 (*a*). Nearest weather station data, referenced as HKO (Hong Kong Observatory) data was downloaded and used to compare with the field measurements. Fish-eye lens photos were taken at each testing location at 1.5m above the ground to determine the sky view factor (SVF) at each of the 13 test locations.

In Part Ⅱ, simulations were performed for the housing clusters to understand the shading profiles and solar radiation gradients for the block layouts and various heights. The three sites were studied for shading analysis and solar radiation using Autodesk ECOTECT analysis software using Hong Kong weather data provided by City U of Hong Kong. Results would be reviewed with the field measurement data to make comparison between predicted and empirical methods.

4 Discussions

4.1 Field Measurement

The measurement data was compared for the three sites to understand how the building masses, building heights and orientation layout affected the urban environment.

The recorded temperature readings were processed into half-hour averaged air temperatures which showed that in fact the low-rise housing development (urban village) had more air tempera-

244

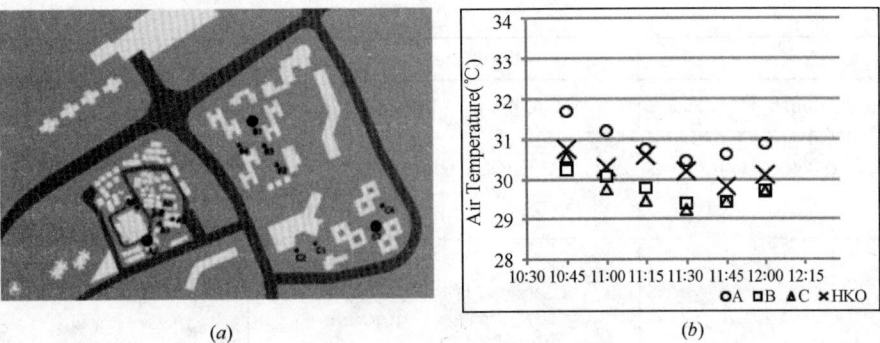

Figure 2

(*a*) 13 test locations marked as red dotes and solar radiation was measured in 3 locations marked with
larger circle (A2, B1 and C3) (*b*) Overall half-hour-averaged air temperature of 3 sites

ture fluctuations especially within the more open spaces and tended to be hotter than the local weather station data by up to 2 degrees C. The housing towers were comparatively cooler with Site B being slighter hotter than Site C. For Site B, where towers are oriented in N-S axis, the measured points in the open space (test locations B1, B2 and B3) were found to closely follow the HKO data. Site C, being an enclosed cluster of towers tended to be the coolest and as recorded in the observations thermally most pleasant of the three sites.

Overall, an average air temperature comparison of the three sites show that low-rise village development of Site A has the highest air temperature over the high rise housing blocks by about 1 degrees C and a higher deviation from the local weather data, HKO data, as shown in Figure 2b.

4.1.1 SVF comparison to air temperature

Further analysis of temperature data and measured SVF at the various test locations, showed that the lowest temperature reading within each of the3 sites had the lowest SVF and highest temperature in locations with highest SVF. SVF is a value between 0 (no visible sky) and 1 (no foliage/ obstructions visible) that gives a proportional measurement of the visible sky at a given point. High SVF are in open parks within villages and wide open spaces between housing towers (Table 1). SVF has been studied to have relatively strong relationships with air temperature to urban environments [6] and is a significant factor in its impact on radiant heat flux in urban areas.

Comparison of average, highest and lowest temperature readings at each site A, B and
C shown against the SVF values at the maximum (highest) and minimum (lowest) temperature curves
at same site. HKO data are instant air temperature from nearest weather station   Table 1

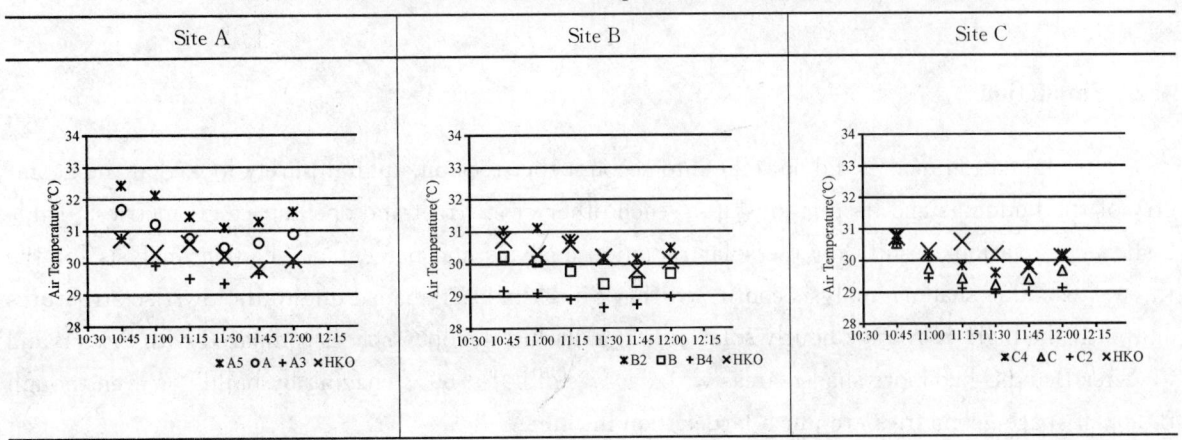

245

continued

Site A		Site B		Site C	
SVF in Site A ranges from 0.111 to 0.501		SVF in Site B ranges from 0.149 to 0.372		SVF in Site C ranges from 0.089 to 0.199	
Location A5 has highest Ta reading	Location A3 has lowest Ta reading	Location B2 has highest Ta reading	Location B4 has lowest Ta reading	Location C4 has highest Ta reading	Location C2 has lowest Ta reading
SVF=0.501	SVF=0.134	SVF=0.372	SVF=0.149	SVF=0.199	SVF=0.089

4.1.2 Radiation

The total radiation at each site was compared with the global radiation readings from the closest HKO station, in this case King's Park conservatory, as shown in Figure 3 Site C (high-rise towers in enclosed layout) had the biggest deviation from the global HKO data and was significantly lower at all times during the field measurement period. Sites A and B showed some fluctuation but in general closely followed the HKO data. This explains the significant difference noted in the observations that stated the open spaces between the Twin Tower blocks in Site C were thermally pleasant.

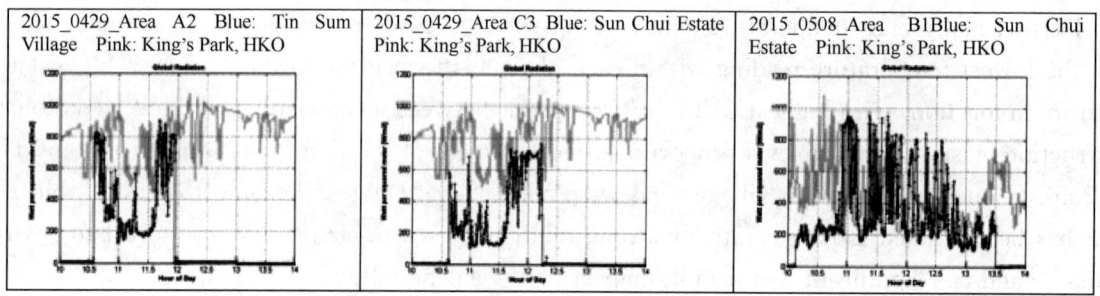

2015_0429_Area A2 Blue: Tin Sum Village Pink: King's Park, HKO	2015_0429_Area C3 Blue: Sun Chui Estate Pink: King's Park, HKO	2015_0508_Area B1Blue: Sun Chui Estate Pink: King's Park, HKO

Figure 3 Comparison of solar radiation readings at three sites plotted against
HKO global radiation of the measured day

4.2 Simulation

The simulation models did not take into account the trees on site but purely looked at the geometry of the buildings and its relationship to each other, the street and open space geometries. Table 2 shows the various results for the solar radiation analysis and percentage shading analysis for the three sites. The shading analysis confirmed that Site A is least shaded due to its low-rise structures and with the highest average hourly solar radiation within the open spaces compared with Sites B and C. Sites B and C had more shaded areas with average of 50%-60% shading by buildings even though the open space geometries are much larger than in Site A.

Simulated results of three sites		Table 2
Site A	Site B	Site C

Solar Radiation Analysis (Average Hourly)

| A2 radiation 342Wh | B1 radiation 156Wh | C5 radiation 223Wh |

Percentage Shading

| A2 is 0-10% shaded | B1 is 60% shaded | C5 is 50-60% shaded |

4.3　Social and economic conditions

The observations recorded significantly more social interactions in open areas where the air temperature recordings were comparatively low which was at location C2 From the three sites, the open spaces in Site C were the most densely populated with people of all ages and further enhanced with many seating areas, trees and located next to a neighborhood retail center. Open spaces in Site B, which had two badminton courts, open podium space and bicycle parking station, were the least used during the tested period with observations recorded as feeling uncomfortably hot. Open spaces in Site A were hardly used, except for few village residents and some customers using the retail spaces on first floor of the village houses. There was more social and economic diversity triggered by small businesses.

5　Conclusion

The low-rise 3-story village cluster has many positive attributes towards sustainable development, with financial opportunities and diversity in community of visitors, residents and age groups, however are more susceptible to temperature changes as shown by higher fluctuations of air temperature by more than 1-degree, compared to the adjacent high-rise 20- to 30-story housing towers. Even with trees within some parts of the pocket parks throughout the village the air temperature was generally higher than at the tested locations within the high-rise development. For the high-rise housing developments the enclosed cluster showed particularly low measured radiation levels meaning consistent shading within the open spaces had significant impact on measured and perceived radiation. The simulated data closely related to the measured data showing that due to the high-angle sun, the percentage exposed and solar radiation is highest at the low-rise clusters. Overall the field measure-

247

ments, observations and simulations provide a comprehensive account of environmental and community patterns within the low-rise and high-rise developments, with simulations providing rationale for the radiation patterns.

可持续的住房建设在高密度环境下：
城市环境的低层和高层集群内的比较研究

孟玟廷

（香港中文大学）

摘要：本文讨论了在高密度环境中高层集群和低层集群的比较以及如何将这些事态发展对可持续参数为城市规划之间的比较分析的结果。影响城市环境的参数是气候，街道峡谷几何，城市的温度，方位和建筑物的几何形状（通过天空视野因子，SVF 测量）。香港案例入选由于其在可持续发展高层保障性住房的设计和施工计划，采取全市最大的开发商，香港房屋委员会在过去的几十年。现场测量，观测和模拟，在 3 楼的三个相邻的部位进行的，故事 20＋住宅建筑研究改变空气温度，SVF 和辐射热。结果发现，低层发展了在温度较高的波动和也倾向于与高层的发展相比具有较高的温度的辐射热通量。

关键词：可持续发展，低层高层，密度，城市环境

References:

[1]　United Nations. Report of the United Nations Conference on Sustainable Development[R/OL]. Rio de Janeiro, Brazil, June 2012 http://www.uncsd2012.org/content/documents/814UNCSD%20REPORT%20final%20revs.pdf.

[2]　Alexandri, E, Jones, P. Temperature decreases in an urban canyon due to and green roofs in diverse climates[M]. Building and Environment. Elsevier, 2008: 480-493.

[3]　Avissar, R. Potential Effects of Vegetation on the Urban Thermal Environment[M]. Atmospheric Environment. UK, 1996: 437-448.

[4]　Transport and Housing Bureau, Hong Kong Housing Authority Housing Department. Planning, construction and redevelopment of Public rental housing flats[R/OL]. Hong Kong Audit Commission Report No. 62. Chapter 2, 4 April 2014. http://www.aud.gov.hk.

[5]　Zhang, Lilly. Tai Wai: Alarm bells ring in bicycle town[N]. South China Morning Post, 24 August 2012.

[6]　Svensson, M. Sky view factor analysis - implications for urban air temperature differences[J]. Meterol Appl, 2004, 11: 201-211.

垂直社区——香港单栋式高层住宅基本特征研究

周伊利　宋德萱

（同济大学建筑与城市规划学院；高密度人居环境生态与节能教育部重点实验室）

摘要：单栋式高层住宅是香港地区重要的城市住宅类型，也是香港高层住宅的原型。本文先对单栋式高层住宅进行定义，展现单栋式高层住宅"基座＋塔楼"的基本造型与功能承载。结合单栋式高层案例研究，本文还对单栋式高层进行高度分级，即通过庇护层的有无、庇护层的数量以及建筑总体高度等维度进行划分。在此基础上，探究城市土地、城市景观、项目场地、周边建筑等城市要素对单栋式高层住宅在总体布局、朝向、空间划分、交通核心位置等方面的影响，体现单栋式高层住宅在高层高密度城中"面向"城市的特点，既反映城市住宅的一般特征，也体现出亚洲高密度环境下城市住宅的独特性。

关键词：垂直社区，单栋式高层住宅，高密度城市，城市住宅

1　引言

伴随着城市化进程，国内大城市在发展中各种问题凸显，如住宅用地日趋紧张、城市规模不当、城市效率低下等，亟须借鉴外部有益经验，来促进可持续发展。香港是亚洲典型的高层高密度城市，人口密度大，高层住宅数量众多。香港的密集的高层住宅具有较突出的节地效果，充分体现高密度城市的土地价值，能发挥出各种城市要素的聚集效应。单栋式高层住宅是香港地区重要的城市住宅类型，其形成和发展都与香港的各种城市要素密切相关。

通过对单栋式高层住宅基本特征的研究，有助于明晰香港地区数量众多、类型多样的高层住宅形态的内部逻辑，窥"单栋式"之一斑可知高层住宅之全貌。探究单栋式高层住宅形成的外部因素，可挖掘城市要素与城市住宅的关联性，从而体现这类高层住宅独特的城市性。明晰香港的高层住宅基本特征无疑可为我国其他高密度城市的住宅建设提供有益的借鉴。

2　"单栋式高层住宅"解析

在香港地区，高层住宅的起点高度为30m。这里的"单栋式"，是指只有一栋建筑体的项目，而且建筑内部只含有一个交通核心或者若干个相互连通的交通核心。因此，单栋式高层住宅是指高度超过30m、只有一栋建筑体且含有一个交通核心或若干连通交通空间的住宅。

从整体形态来看，香港地区的高层住宅还有合栋式、多栋式等类型。合栋式是指项目含有两座以上的塔楼，它们合建成一栋高层建筑，每座塔楼具有各自的交通核心，水平方向不连通。多栋式，是指由两栋及两栋以上的塔楼住宅构成的形态，多栋式的塔楼又可分为单栋式和合栋式，这类住宅通常居住单位数量较多，建筑规模较大。单栋式高层住宅是合栋式和多栋式住宅的原型，合栋式和多栋式高层住宅中必然含有若干个"单栋式"单元，其特点也源自这些组成单元。

3　基本造型与功能承载

单栋式高层住宅所处场地通常较小，却要承载一个完整的住宅项目的各项功能。除主要的居住功能之外，单栋式高层住宅还要包括停车、会所、社区服务等现代城市住区的基本功能，形成"五脏俱全"的社区。单栋式高层住宅的形态特征明显，可概括为"基座＋塔楼"模式。单栋式高层住宅的内部空间在垂直方向高度集成，与基本造型高度匹配，反映出土地高效率使用和空间集约

程度。

3.1 "基座＋塔楼"的基本造型

"基座＋塔楼"模式是香港地区单栋高层住宅的基本造型，这类建筑形式是建筑师李景勋先生在 1962 年首次引入香港的，现已成为主导香港城市生活的一个要素。[①]

在一个住宅项目中，除去必要的规定退界，基座占地面积基本占满基地的绝大部分，以实现对有限土地的最大利用。基座的层数通常从 1～8 层不等，具体依功能空间和地形高差而定。1962 年的《建筑条例》允许住宅的底层全部作非居住用途，如商铺、停车场及其他，最初只允许适用一层楼面，后来很快增加到多层楼面。

塔楼是位于基座之上的部分，单层面积一般比基座小。塔楼部分的居住单位有视线距离、采光、通风、防火等多重限制条件，致使塔楼在建筑形态塑造受到较多约束，许多项目的塔楼单层面积很小，居住单位数量少，形成长细比较大的"筷子"楼，这也是高密度城市向空中要空间的重要例证。

塔楼部分的居住单位通常采用剪力墙结构，跨距较小，垂直支撑结构分布较密。而在基座部分，非居住用途需要较大的空间，垂直支撑结构尽量少而集中。因此，在塔楼和基座之间一般都存在结构转换层，实现不同形式结构的转换，使不同部分的结构类型匹配不同空间利用。

3.2 垂直分布的功能空间

为满足社区各项功能需求，单栋式高层住宅在水平方向严重受限的既成实事面前，不得不向空中要空间，将不同开放层级的空间根据一定的规则组织在一起，以获得最大的空间利用和土地价值。

3.2.1 面向城市的空间

香港不仅有较大的购物商场，也有到处可见的沿街商铺，商铺寸土寸金。在单栋式高层住宅的沿街基座部分，除必要的出入门及公共设施外，都尽可能开辟为商铺门面，将有限的沿街面形成面向城市生活的商业空间，既方便市民的日常生活又增加街道空间的活力，提高土地的经济价值，促进城市生活的多样性。

3.2.2 社区公共空间

社区公共空间主要包括停车场、会所、社区服务等，通常位于基座的较高层部分，一般对社区内部居民开放，是城市空间到居住空间的过渡。单栋式高层住宅由于基地所限，停车位较为紧张，在基座部分还要设置停车场，通过坡道或车辆升降机实现车辆的垂直交通，非如此无法容纳社区的停车需求。地下空间的建造成本较高，经常部分被用于停车空间，部分作商业等用途。

社区会所一般包含休憩、娱乐、健身等公共设施，是一个住宅项目的特色所在。单栋式高层住宅中，会所一般会进行分层设置，使不同年龄段的社区居民都能找到适合的活动场所，促进社区居民的交流，这也是社区活力的来源之一。在会所中，泳池是最常见的设施。在炎热的夏天，泳池是良好的致凉场所，为多数市民所喜欢。

3.2.3 居住单元空间

居住单元层是住宅的核心部分。与国内其他大城市相比，香港的住宅套型面积均偏小，70～

---

① Barrie Shelton, Justyna Karakiewicz, Thomas Kvan. 香港造城记——从垂直之城到立体之城 [M]. 胡大平、吴静译. 北京：电子工业出版社, 2013.

80m² 的三居室单位相当常见，卧室面宽不超过 3.0m 的比比皆是，甚至还有的为 2.1m。标准单位层外部造型呈现出重复、密集的构图。普遍存在的阳台空间增加了立面造型的层次性，雨棚、遮阳、窗间墙等构件则具有遮阳挡雨功用，还可以增加建筑立面的光影效果，在一定程度上减少了重复密集构图立面的单调感觉。

除标准单位层之外，单栋式高层住宅一般都有特色单位层。在标准层的基础上将相邻的若干单位水平打通，形成相连大户。还有上下层的居住单位垂直连通形成复式单元。特色单位通常位于建筑顶部，由于面积较大，就有一定的形体变化余地，这也正契合了顶部造型变化的需求。

4 高度级别

高度和层数是研究单栋式高层住宅特征的两个重要参数。住宅层数是高层住宅庇护层设置的主要依据。按香港地区的建筑物规定，层数超过 40 层的建筑必须设置庇护层，"当住用建筑物或综合用途建筑物高度在最低地面楼层以上逾 25 层，但又不多于 40 层时，屋顶应设计为庇护层（Refuge Floor，意义同的"隔火层"、"避难层"）"①，且隔火层与地面层（Ground Floor）之间、隔火层之间的层数不超过 24 层。当住宅超过 40 层时，主要屋面通常不做逃生层之用，一般会成为观景平台或者为天际屋居住单元所使用。顶层到最近庇护层不超过 25 层。因此，当建筑含有一层隔火层最高可设置在 26 层，层数达到极限为 50 层，具体高度还与住宅层高有关。依据以上规定，拥有两层隔火层的住宅，其最多楼层数可达到 75 层。

因此，根据庇护层的设置与否和数量，单栋式高层可分为三个级别（图1）：一类为单栋高层住宅，即 40 层以下的普通高层住宅，无须专门设置庇护层；二类为单栋超高层住宅，层数 41 层以上至 50 层，必须至少设置一层庇护层；三类为单栋摩天住宅，层数 51 层以上，必须至少设置两层庇护层。

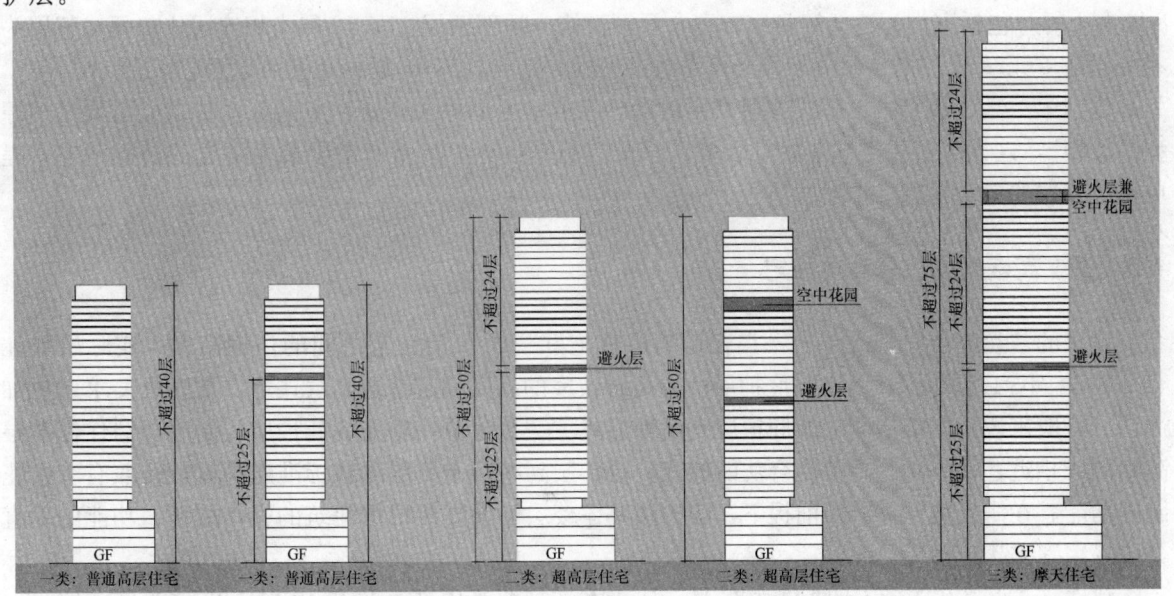

图1 三个高度级别的高层住宅层数示意图

需要指出的是，通透的庇护层减少了对空中气流的阻碍，降低了建筑的水平风压。兼做空中花园的庇护层还为住户提供了绝佳的观景平台，在较高的层面上获得良好登高、环顾的视野，这对身处高楼丛林的人们来说，在某种程度上不失为一种视觉的解放。为提倡空中花园的建设，管理部门对空中花园的面积进行有条件豁免。在满足净高不低于 4.8m，而且花园面积超过整层面积的一半

---

① 香港房屋署网站公开资料：1996 年提供火警逃生途径守则 21.2。

等条件前提下，空中花园的面积不计入容积率的计算。这样的豁免对"锱铢必较"的香港房地产开发商形成实实在在的利益引导。因此，在那些无须设置庇护层或只须设置一层庇护层的项目中，会出现超出规定数目的庇护层（有时兼做空中花园），这对改善城市的微气候无疑是有益的。

4.1 第一高度级别：普通高层住宅

普通高度级别的单栋高层住宅数量众多，是香港地区私人参建的单栋式商品住宅的主体。40层以下的高层住宅无须专门设置庇护层，由于没有通透庇护层的分段作用而呈现出较强的整体性。这类单栋式高层住宅结构体系复合程度较低，建设工期较短，建造成本较低，开发商的资金回收较快。由于建造量通常较小，在建造期间对城市环境、交通等影响都较小。这类高层住宅通常体型较小，能适应城市各种区域的住宅建设，体现出较强的灵活性。

加多利峰（KADOORIE LOOKOUT），位于亚皆老街和梭椏街转角地块，属于转角布房式平面，高28层，共55个居住单元。靠近亚皆老街的地面层、地下一层、地下二层都设为商铺之用。机动车出入口位于枣梨雅道，从入口层到3层均为停车空间，5层为住区会所，6层以上居住单元层，其中标准层共17层，顶部为4层复式居住单位层。顶部四层的立面比标准居住单元层有更大面积的玻璃幕墙、更完整的实体外墙、更规整的轮廓线，形成较大的差异。

有的40层以下的高层住宅项目出于增加活动空间、提高居住品质、增加物业的售价等考虑，也会设置庇护层，通常作空中花园，成为项目的一大特色。

维壹（Harbour One）位于香港岛石塘咀德辅道西458号，2012年入伙，实际共有38层，却在7层及32层设置了两层空中花园，兼顾了庇护层的功能。项目本身位置优越，可以远眺维多利亚港，又毗邻名校，所以成为该区域价格最高的物业之一。两个"额外"的空中花园无疑成为该物业的卖点之一，这也反映出高层居住者对空中花园的认可和对社区公共开放空间的期盼。该项目的8楼为会所，包括室内泳池、健身室、宴会厅等设施。顶部两层41、42层为相连居住单元，整层为一个居住单元，41层的单元由于部分外墙收进形成大平台，而42层的单元可以登临天台。

作为第一高度级别，单栋式普通高层住宅已经具备了单栋式高层住宅的基本特点，可谓是"原型的原型"，这类高层住宅具有数量众多、分布广泛等特点，也是城市中最为常见的高层住宅，是单栋式高层住宅"入门"类型。

4.2 第二高度级别：超高层住宅

这里的"超高层"特指介于一类普通高层住宅和三类摩天住宅之间的住宅高度，实际层数在41~50之间，必须至少设置一层庇护层。超高层住宅的高度超越普通高层住宅，在防火要求上更加严格。一般来说，超高层住宅的庇护层有两种方式。一种为单一功能的庇护层，层高与居住标准层高相同或相近；另一种为具备复合功能的庇护层，层高相当于两层居住标准层高度，还兼有空中花园的功能。在满足庇护需求的前提下，庇护层具体楼层位置则要根据建筑的整体造型、功能的垂直分段等因素来确定。

瀚然（AREZZO），位于西摩道33号，属于香港岛西半山区，共有48层，23层为庇护层。由于该项目地势较高，背山望海，既可远眺维多利亚港，又可观览中环都市景观。瀚然共有127个住宅单元，每个标准层有三个居住单元，49层三个居住单元整合成两个稍大单位，50、51层各为一个单元，51层可上天台，天台还有游泳池等设施。顶部的两层局部外墙形成退让，将顶部的与标准居住单元层区分开来。该项目虽然采用在交通核心单边布房的格局，但在面山一侧也布置了卧室等空间，这是对双面自然景观的响应。

有些单栋式超高层住宅不仅有一层必需的庇护层，还设有一个空中花园层兼有庇护层的功能。港图湾（BAYVIEW）就是个庇护层和空中花园分别设置的案例。港图湾位于香港九龙土瓜湾旭日街 9 号，拥有 175 个居住单元，最高楼层为 48 层，实际楼层数为 44 层，20 层为庇护层。1、2 层为停车空间，地面层与 1 层局部为商业空间，3、5 层为社区会所，32 层开辟为空中花园。该项目采用了双边布房的方式，标准层每层五个居住单元，其中三个面海，海景视野宽阔，海心公园及景云街游乐场也尽收眼底。位于 32 层的空中花园犹如社区的空中客厅，在通透、开敞的空中花园中，观者既可低伏园林花草，也可放目维港两岸，既可观城市之景，又可享处高之乐。

4.3　第三高度级别：摩天住宅

"摩天"是高度的一种形象说法，是指物体高度接近天空。按照上文的分类，51 层以上的高层住宅被视为摩天住宅，必须至少设置两层庇护层，建筑高度属于最高级别。这类摩天住宅最大的特征是高度远远超过周围建成环境。摩天住宅的发展是城市经济繁荣、社会信心增强的重要标志。摩天住宅具有高度奇高（通常是 180m 以上）、建筑造型别致、方位一般较独特等特点。

摩天住宅一般具有较强的标志性，能在整个城市或局部区域中形成方位指向、空间引导等作用。摩天住宅的标志性首先源自其出奇的高度。截至 2015 年 5 月[1]，香港地区高度超过 200m 的单栋式住宅项目有尖沙咀的名铸（261m，在所有住宅类型中高度排名第二，仅次于天玺）、跑马地的晓庐（252.4m）和御峰（219.8m）、荃湾的乐悠居（212m）等。有特色的建筑造型也是成就其标志性的重要因素。在高密度城市中，建筑所处方位也是直接影响视线的可达性，从而决定建筑的"被观"程度。

名铸（The Masterpiece）位于九龙尖沙咀，是河内道 18 号的重建项目，混合了商场、酒店、居住三种主要功能。该项目实际有 64 层，26 层为庇护层，47 层空中花园兼作庇护层，此外，9 层也设为空中花园。基座部分主要为 K11 商场、酒店大堂及后勤设施等功能，结构转换层之上的 8 层为会所，10～24 层为酒店客房区，27 层以上为住宅部分。住宅平面采用了内廊式布局：一个交通核心通过内廊连接所有居住单元。27～57 层为标准居住单元层，每层有 11 个居住单元；58～62 层为相连大户单元层，每层 6 个居住单元；63、65，66、67 为复式居住单元层，每两层有 9 个复式居住单元。居住单元的变化也同样反映在外立面上，尤其是在端部圆弧墙面和外窗的变化。庇护层和空中花园的分段有效减弱了建筑形体对周边环境的遮挡感觉。名铸与周边的建筑存在较大高度差，使得在港岛的上环至中环、金钟、铜锣湾等多数区域都能获得良好的视线可达性，周围的建筑都不能掩盖其高耸的形象。

5　单栋式高层住宅的城市影响要素

高层住宅是现代城市发展到一定阶段的产物，因此，城市要素是高层住宅的形态发展必然相关的。所谓城市要素，是能反映城市形成和发展独特形态的物质要素和非物质要素，通过高层住宅特征的研究也有反映出一个城市的独特性。香港单栋式高层住宅的发展是与香港这个国际大都市的形成和发展的独特要素密切相关联的，如特色的土地制度、建设用地的珍贵稀缺、街区地块的日益细分、城市土地的高效利用、房地产市场的高度发达和建筑技术的成熟发达等。

香港是世界上人口最稠密的城市之一，市区人口密度平均 2.1 万人/m²。土地对于香港城市发展来说是一种首要稀缺资源。从历史上看，香港城市的发展始终伴随着两种活动：填海和开山，其目的就是要争取更多的可用建设土地。高层住宅以其高容积率、节地等特点与香港城市建设土地日渐稀缺相匹配，因此，在过去将近半世纪的时间，香港始终坚持高层高密度的发展模式。城市街区的规模都较小，同时街区内部地块划分细密，使得成片土地开发的机会越来越小，促使了项目开发者采用了单栋式高层来满足居住单元数量和面积需求。单栋式高层住宅对于城市土地的具有较强敏

---

① 数据来源：skyscraperpage.com，数据统计是指一个住宅项目中的最高一座住宅楼。

感度，由于其容量相对较小，在城市开发中具有较强的灵活性，能够适应城市的变化。

香港曲折的海岸线为住宅提供了不可胜数的海景，最著名的是海景要数维多利亚港了。维多利亚港南北两侧各类建筑大多以朝向港湾作为主要居住空间的优先选择方向。在港岛的北区，海景朝向甚至超越南面朝阳方向，起居室、卧室等主要居住空间均朝向维多利亚港海面。

在高密度城市环境下，并非所有的住宅项目场地都能有幸获得自然景观的"垂青"，视觉距离是众多住宅项目朝向和布局的最主要限制因素之一，城市道路、公园、绿地等城市开放公共空间就成为住宅获得足够视距的空间类型。城市中公共活动发生的场所也成为"景观"之一，对周边的住宅朝向具有强烈的引导性。单栋式高层住宅由于其形体的屏风效应较弱，使周边的其他建筑也能获取相应的宝贵景观资源。

6 结语

单栋式高层住宅是香港地区重要的城市住宅类型，其形成和发展都与香港的各种城市要素密切相关。单栋式高层住宅是香港社会经济发展的必然产物，蕴含着国际大都市的居住文化，是对香港城市面貌的一种体现。

本文对单栋式高层住宅进行了定义：只含有一个交通核心或者若干个相互连通的交通核心高层住宅；提出"基座＋塔楼"的基本造型，分析了三个开放层级的空间，即面向城市的空间、社区公共空间、居住单元空间；还根据庇护层的数量、层数和高度对高层住宅进行高度分级，即一般高层住宅、超高层住宅和摩天住宅，结合高层住宅案例分析三个高度级别住宅的特征。单栋式高层住宅形成和发展受到特色的土地制度、建设用地的珍贵稀缺、街区地块的日益细分、城市土地的高效利用、房地产市场的高度发达和建筑技术的成熟发达等要素的影响。

致谢

本文所受资助：城镇群高密度空间效能优化关键技术研究，编号：2012BAJ15B03。

Vertical Community:
Essential Features of Single-Unit High-Rise Dwelling in Hongkong

Zhou Yili, Song Dexuan

(College of Architecture and Urban Planning, Tongji University; Key Laboratory of Ecology and Energy Saving Study of Dense Habitat, Ministry of Education)

Abstract: Single-unit high-rise dwelling is the prototype of all residential building in HK; other types are result from the variation, evolution and combination of this prototype. Concept of single-unit high-rise dwelling is defined in the paper; the differences are emphasized between single-unit residential, multi-unit building and multi-building residential community. Single-unit high-rise dwelling can apparently be divided into two parts: tower and base, both in shape and function. In this article, numerous single-unit cases are discussed and graded according to the overall height and number of refuge floor, with a goal of finding a hierarchical classification code. Furthermore, this paper also focuses on how land utilization, landscape, base condition, surrounding buildings and other urban elements affect single-unit dwelling in every way: the layout, orientation, space division, location of the core tube. And it also elaborates design code for the urban residential: In high-density environment, urban residential must "face" to the city, and respond to the urban surroundings, which reflects the uniqueness of the Asian high-density urban housing.

    Keywords: Vertical community, Single-unit high-rise residential building, High-density city, Urban housing

参考文献:

[1] Barrie Shelton, Justyna Karakiewicz, Thomas Kvan. 香港造城记——从垂直之城到立体之城 [M]. 胡大平、吴静译. 北京: 电子工业出版社, 2013.

[2] Skyscraper Source Media. 2001 [2015-5-9]. http: // skyscraperpage.com.

包容性人居环境建设
Inclusive Living Environment Development

专题一：社会与空间融合
Special Topic 1：Social and Spatial Integration

基于居民 SES 分异的滨水公共绿地游憩公平性研究：
以上海苏州河滨水绿地为例

董楠楠[1]　刘强[2]　张圣红[2]

（1. 同济大学；2. 上海怡仁景观规划设计有限公司）

摘要：上海快速更新改造的背景下，土地集约化利用和产业结构的调整升级导致中心城区居住空间形态多元并存的现象。滨水区作为城市极具活力的地区之一，容纳了城市改造过程中形成的不同经济水平、文化背景和社会特征的人群聚居功能及其游憩功能。在滨水区居住空间分异背景下滨水区新建绿地的公平性和使用效率是本研究关注的核心问题。尽管在空间距离的布局方面，社区与绿地之间的可达性在滨水区开发中被普遍关注，但是这些空间为导向的布局设想与人口入住后的实际使用效果往往呈现错位。其中公园服务覆盖的实际人口数及覆盖人群的社会经济地位（socio-economic status，简称 SES[①]）的差异，直接影响到这些绿地公园的游憩与实际使用特点。本研究结合问卷、访谈等社会学调研方法，通过统计分析总结归纳了样本滨水区中居民对公园绿地游憩使用需求，研究结果主要集中在 2 个方面：首先，居民 SES 层级与公园游憩需求层级相关，居民 SES 越高，对公园绿地特殊游憩需求越明显，SES 较低的社区居民则更加关注公园的基本游憩功能；其次，滨水公园内的游憩使用差异性程度与周边社会空间的 SES 分异程度相关，周边居民 SES 水平相差越大，公园内游憩使用的差异性越大。基于上述研究结果，本文进一步探讨了基于 SES 差异性的滨水居住区景观供给与外部公共绿地的社会性功能耦合策略，并从规划布局、空间设计、管理养护方面总结了结合社会人口 SES 属性的社会性滨水公园设计策略。以满足实际使用人群的需求，促进不同 SES 阶层人群的交流与融合，实现滨水区公园绿地供给的公平性。

关键词：居民 SES 分异，公共绿地，游憩，公平性

1 引言

城市滨水公共绿地是城市居民重要的游憩场所，城市滨水区复杂的社会空间界面背后隐藏着滨水区社会价值的差异，在这样的背景下，深入剖析滨水公共绿地使用状况的社会分异特征和原因，为实现滨水区公园绿地供给公平性具有重要的现实意义。本文的研究对象是上海苏州河滨水公共绿地，作为上海 9 个市辖区的区划边界的苏州河[1]，其周边居住空间社会分异现象突出，基于此现实基础，选取两个代表性的苏州河滨水公共绿地，即梦清园、蝴蝶湾绿地，探讨滨水区居住空间分异背景下公共绿地的游憩公平性。

2 苏州河滨水公共绿地与居住空间分布的关系

2.1 苏州河滨水公共绿地分布

本文所谈的苏州河滨水公共绿地是指直接与水相连的面向公众开放的、可供使用的绿地。苏州河沿岸的绿地类型较多，其中以居住绿地（G41）和带状滨水绿地（G14）为主。苏州河沿岸公共绿地岸界长 13.3km，占绿化岸线的 66.6%。将苏州河沿岸从外白渡桥到中环路之间的滨水公共绿地编号，共 18 块绿地分布（图 1）。

---

① 社会经济地位，简称 SES，是结合经济学和社会学关于某个人工作经历和个体或家庭基于收入、教育和职业等因素相对于其他人的经济和社会地位的总体衡量。

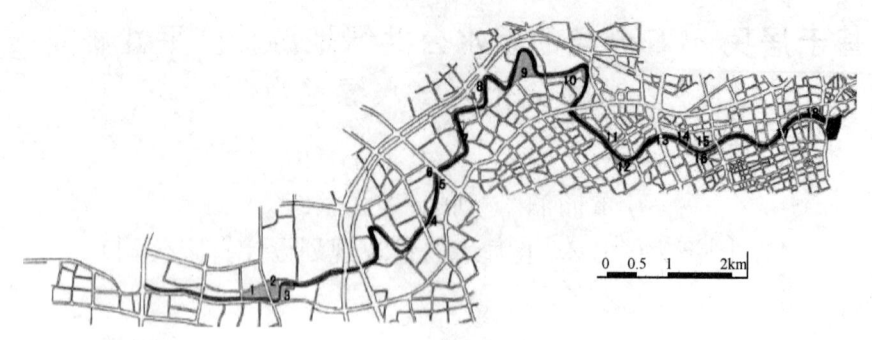

图 1　苏州河滨水公共绿地分布图

2.2　苏州河滨水居住空间社会分异特征

苏州河滨水居住空间的类型主要有三种：旧住区，工人新村，商品房住区。苏州河滨水的旧住区主要指建国初期建的棚户简屋及旧式里弄。新中国成立后到 20 世纪 80 年代，上海政府对苏州河沿岸旧住房进行了不同程度的改建，但由于拆迁成本很高，加上城市规划和城市土地出让的滞后，使得苏州河两岸仍遗留大量旧住区。工人新村主要是新中国成立以后政府或企事业单位给工人建设的住宅，80 年代末，苏州河沿岸涌现了大量如长白新村、武宁新村、长寿新村、长风新村等的工人新村。商品房主要是住房市场化后开发商通过购买土地、功能置换建设的住宅区。苏州河沿岸的商品房是拆除原来的棚户区后建设的新住区，如位于普陀区的中远两湾城，是原著名的棚户区"潭子湾"。苏州河滨水居住空间分布总体呈"圈层式"分布特征，局部为"交错式"布局特征[2]。苏州河东部区域（天目西路以东）居住空间主要为旧住区，有部分新楼盘的开发；中西部区域（天目西路以西）北岸以工人新村为主，南岸主要为商品房住宅区。从图 2 中可以看出，滨水公共绿地较多的区域往往是商品房集中的区域，而较大面积的滨水公共绿地往往被商品房包围，滨水公共绿地呈狭长带状分布的区域往往是旧住区或部分商品房集中的区域。

将图 2 中的 11 各区块内的各居住空间类型面积和各区块内的滨水公共绿地面积进行比较（图 3），发现滨水公共绿地面积较大的地块为商品房最为集中分布的区域，也是居住类型较为单一的区段（如 1、6、7 地块），换言之居住空间类型差异度较小的区域往往滨水公共绿地面积较大；滨水公共绿地较少的区域（如 8、9、10、11 号地）则为旧住区集中的区域。由此说明滨水公共绿地面积多少与商品房集中程度有关，商品房越集中，公共绿地面积越大；旧住区越集中，公共绿地面积越小，商品房住区居民享有更多的公共绿地。

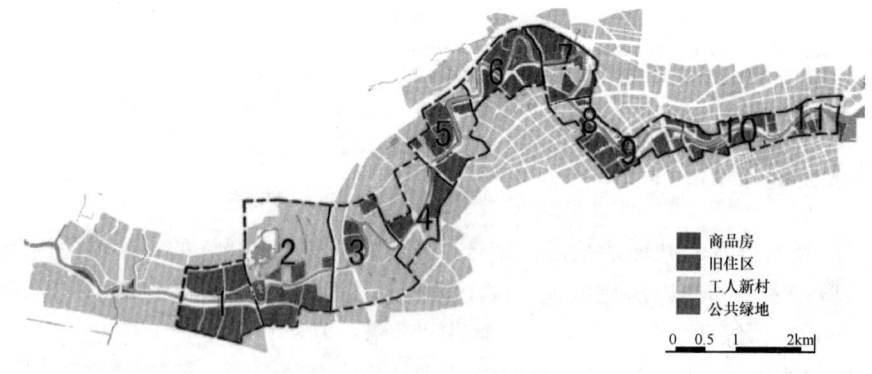

图 2　苏州河 1km 分段图

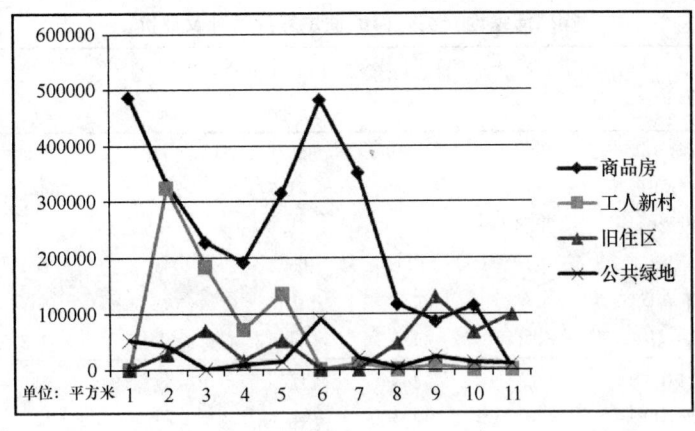

图 3　居住空间类型面积分布与公共绿地面积分布关系图

3　案例分析：基于居民 SES 分异的滨水公共绿地使用特征

3.1　研究样本与数据

本文选取最能够代表苏州河滨水公共绿地的两块公共绿地：梦清园和蝴蝶湾绿地，作为案例进行实证研究。梦清园是苏州河沿岸最大的滨水公共绿地，占地 8.6hm²，是拆迁旧厂房而建，其周围是商品房；蝴蝶湾绿地是苏州河沿岸较为特殊的小型滨水公共绿地，占地 1.6hm²，其周围以旧住区为主。本文主要通过实地发放调研问卷、访谈以及网上查阅等获取相关数据。共发放问卷 200份，回收有效问卷 183 份。其中，蝴蝶湾绿地 91 份，梦清园 92 份。发放时间分别为：2012 年7 月～10 月、2013 年 6 月～9 月，包含节假日和工作日。此外，亦有多次对苏州河沿岸滨水空间的走访考察。数据的处理方式采用 SPSS17.0 中的描述分析和 Excel 统计分析。

3.2　居民使用者 SES 分异与滨水绿地使用特征的关联性

本文通过分析被访者年龄、受教育程度、职业和收入等因素，将其划分为六类使用人群（表1），并调查总结这六类人群分别在蝴蝶湾绿地和梦清园中的游憩使用特征（表2、表3）。

使用人群分类表　　　　　　　　　　　　　　　　　　　　　　表 1

按收入分级	比例（%）	特　征　描　述
中老年低收入者	34.7	50 岁以上的退休或一般工薪阶层；高中及以下学历为主；月收入 3000 元以下
年轻低收入者	7.3	20～35 岁年轻打工或待业者；大专及以下学历为主；月收入 3000 元以下
年轻中等收入者	23.9	35 岁以下的打工和刚工作的毕业大学生；大专和本科学历为主；月收入 3000～5000 元之间
中青年高收入者	16.6	20～45 岁年轻的管理者或白领；本科及以上学历；月收入 5000～10000 元之间
中老年高收入者	6.3	45～55 岁高层管理者或白领；本科及以上学历；月收入 10000～30000 元之间
在校学生	6.2	以高中生为主

由表 2 可以看出，蝴蝶湾绿地的使用方式以运动健身、跳舞等主动休闲为主；使用频率较高；交通方式以步行为主，占 94%，这说明使用者大都来自周边社区，绿地服务半径不大；影响居民使用蝴蝶湾绿地的主要因素是"距离"和"活动设施"，分别占 42.4% 和 54.5%；被访者对于基本游憩设施的需求较高，对于特殊游憩设施的需求如健身设施需求较低。

蝴蝶湾绿地 6 类人群的使用差异特征及评价 表 2

使用特征指标			使用群体类别						总体
			1	2	3	4	5	6	
消使用评价	生活质量影响度（%）	非常积极	10.3	7.7	0.0	0.0	0.0	0.0	4.1
		比较积极	69	15.4	51.7	87.5	66.7	0.0	54.1
		没影响	20.7	76.9	48.3	12.5	33.3	100	41.8
	使用满意度（%）	满意	69	100	65.5	25	66.7	100	67.3
		不满意	6.9	0.0	0.0	0.0	0.0	0.0	2.0
		一般	24.1	0.0	34.5	75	33.3	0.0	30.7
使用行为	活动类型（%）	被动休闲	79.3	69.2	17.2	25	100	0.0	39.8
		主动休闲	20.7	30.8	82.8	75	0.0	100	60.2
	结伴模式（%）	单独	62.1	7.7	37.9	75.0	0.0	0.0	42.9
		家人	27.6	23.1	55.2	12.5	66.7	0.0	17.3
		朋友	10.3	69.2	6.9	12.5	33.3	100	39.8
	使用频率	一周几次	89.7	30.8	20.7	12.5	100	12.5	42.9
		一月几次	6.9	53.8	79.3	81.3	0.0	87.5	53.1
		很少	3.4	15.4	0.0	6.3	0.0	0.0	4.0
	交通方式（%）	步行率	100	76.9	93.1	100	100	87.5	93.9
		骑车率	0.0	15.4	3.4	0.0	0.0	12.5	4.1
		公交率	0.0	7.7	3.4	0.0	0.0	0.0	2.0
影响因素	距离因素（%）		41.4	15.4	41.4	76.5	100	0.0	42.4
	环境优美因素（%）		31.0	7.7	6.9	17.6	33.3	37.5	19.2
	活动设施因素（%）		13.8	69.2	82.8	70.5	0.0	62.5	54.5
	河边新鲜空气（%）		55.2	7.7	10.3	11.8	33.3	0.0	23.2
	其他（%）		3.4	0.0	3.4	0.0	0.0	0.0	2.0
使用需求	服务半径（%）	≤15	86.2	69.2	41.4	6.3	0.0	50	30.6
		≤30	13.8	30.8	58.6	93.7	100	50	69.4
	设施需求（%）	基本要求	37.9	76.9	58.7	18.7	0.0	87.5	48.9
		简单设施	41.4	7.7	3.4	18.8	33.3	0.0	18.4
		特殊设施	20.7	15.4	37.9	62.5	67.7	12.5	32.7

注：在社会群体类别中，1 代表中老年低收入者，2 代表年轻低收入者，3 代表年轻的中等收入者，4 代表中青年高收入者，5 代表中老年高收入者，6 代表在校学生。

根据表 3 可以看出，梦清园的被访者使用行为以散步、陪小孩等被动休闲为主，占 55.6%；绿地内的主园路使用率很高，主要用以散步和慢跑等。游憩使用频率以一周几次为主，占 46.5%；交通方式中通过骑车和公交方式到达公园的比例增加，这说明绿地的服务半径较大，具备良好的社会知名度；影响居民使用梦清园的主要因素是"环境优美"和"河边新鲜空气"，分别占被访者的 73.2% 和 53.5%。

梦清园 6 类人群的使用差异特征及评价 表 3

使用特征指标			使用群体类别						总体
			1	2	3	4	5	6	
使用评价	生活质量影响度（%）	非常积极	25.6	50.0	55.0	29.4	11.1	0.0	31.5
		比较积极	69.2	0.0	40.0	67.4	44.4	100	58.7
		没影响	5.1	50.0	5.0	5.9	44.4	0.0	9.8
	使用满意度（%）	满意	95.7	50.0	94.4	84.6	50.0	100	87.3
		不满意	0.0	50.0	0.0	0.0	0.0	0.0	1.6
		一般	4.3	0.0	5.6	15.4	50.0	0.0	11.1

使用特征指标		使用群体类别						总体
		1	2	3	4	5	6	
使用行为	活动类型（%） 被动休闲	64.1	50.0	65.0	64.7	88.9	0.0	65.2
	主动休闲	35.9	50.0	35.0	35.3	11.1	100	34.8
	结伴模式（%） 单独	41.0	50.0	30.0	23.5	11.1	50.0	33.7
	家人	46.2	50.0	50.0	70.6	66.7	50.0	53.3
	朋友	12.8	0.0	20.0	5.9	22.2	0.0	13.0
	使用频率 一周几次	69.2	0.0	40.0	35.3	11.1	75.0	50.0
	一月几次	10.2	0.0	35.0	11.8	33.3	25.0	18.5
	很少	20.5	100	25.0	52.9	55.6	0.0	31.5
	交通方式（%） 步行率	64.1	100	75.0	76.5	77.8	100	72.8
	骑车率	17.9	0.0	15.0	11.8	0.0	0.0	13.0
	公交率	17.9	0.0	0.0	11.9	22.2	0.0	14.2
影响因素	距离因素（%）	10.7	0.0	15.8	21.4	0.0	0..0	12.7
	环境优美因素（%）	60.7	50.0	94.7	71.4	71.4	100.	73.2
	活动设施因素（%）	3.5	0.0	21.1	28.6	0.0	0.0	12.7
	河边新鲜空气（%）	35.7	100	73.7	57.1	42.9	100	53.5
	陪小孩玩（%）	7.1	0.0	10.5	14.3	0.0	0.0	8.5
使用需求	服务半径（%） ≤15 分钟	33.3	50.0	83.3	75.0	100	50.0	61.9
	≤30 分钟	66.7	50.0	16.7	25.0		50.0	38.1
	设施需求（%） 基本要求	42.9	50.0	36.8	37.5	62.5	25.0	41.2
	简单设施	25.7	0.0	31.6	37.5	12.5	0.0	27.1
	特殊设施	31.4	50.0	31.6	25	25	75.0	31.7

注：在社会群体类别中，1 代表中老年低收入者，2 代表年轻低收入者，3 代表年轻的中等收入者，4 代表中青年高收入者，5 代表中老年高收入者，6 代表在校学生。

不同社会群体使用公共绿地的特征具有差异性，这种差异性与其自身的 SES 有关。同一 SES 层级的使用群体在不同公共绿地内的使用行为、需求以及影响使用因素也会有较大的差异，SES 越高的使用群体在不同公共绿地的使用差异性越大；使用群体的 SES 越低，在不同公共绿地的使用特征越相似。

3.3 公共绿地游憩使用差异与周边社会空间 SES 层级关系

蝴蝶湾绿地和梦清园在物质空间条件和周边社会空间结构上有明显的差异性，蝴蝶湾绿地是设施较为简单的滨水小型公共绿地，周边界面 2/3 以上被旧住区包围；梦清园是设施齐全的综合性主题公共绿地，完全被商品房包围。梦清园中的中老年高收入者数量远超过了蝴蝶湾绿地，而年轻低收入者的数量则低于蝴蝶湾绿地（图 4），说明梦清园被访者的 SES 水平高于蝴蝶湾绿地，这与公共绿地周边的社区状况相符合，梦清园周边是较高 SES 人群聚集的商品房住区，而蝴蝶湾绿地周边是较低 SES 人群聚集的旧住区。

通过比较分析这两个案例公园使用特征（表 4）可以看出周边社区居民的 SES 水平影响公共绿地的使用人群使用行为和要求：较高 SES 社区包围的公共绿地，SES 层级低的使用者对公共绿地的游憩要求反而较高，他们对景观美感要求较高，强调的是环境的感官体验；而较低 SES 社区包围的公共绿地，SES 层级低的使用者对绿地游憩要求较低，他们更关注的是肢体体验，如对于运动设施和距离的要求较高。

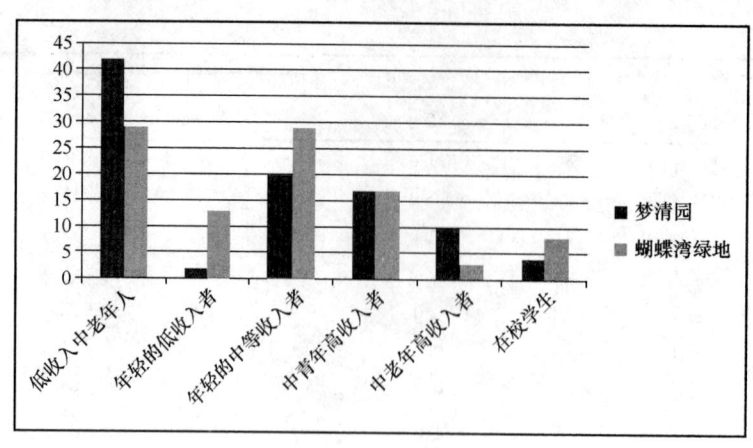

图 4　使用人群数量对比图

使用人群使用特征　　　　　　　　　　　　　　　　　　　　　　表 4

使用群体类别	使用类型	使用特征
中老年低收入者	H 低要求高频率安静经济型	以被动休闲为主、多单独使用、步行、使用满意度最高、较高环境品质需求、使用频率最高、对公共绿地复杂设施要求较低
	M 中要求高频率安静康乐型	以被动休闲为主、多与家人结伴、较多步行、最高满意度、最高使用频率、较高环境品质需求、对复杂设施要求较高
年轻低收入者	低要求低频率社交型	以被动休闲为主、多与朋友结伴、较多步行、使用满意度较高、公共绿地影响力较小、使用频率较低、对公共绿地设施要求较高
年轻中等收入者	H 低要求低频率运动经济型	以主动休闲为主、多与家人结伴、主要步行、受公共绿地活动设施影响最多、服务半径要求 30min 内较多、对复杂设施要求较低
	M 中要求高频率安静经济型	以被动休闲为主、多与家人为伴、主要步行、较高使用频率、最高满意度、服务半径要求在 15min 以内居多、对复杂设施要求较高
中青年高收入者	H 高要求低频率安静型	以主动休闲为主、最高单独使用、最高步行率、满意度最低、公共绿地影响力较大、使用频率较低、服务半径要求 30min 内、对公共绿地复杂设施要求较高
	M 低要求中频率康乐型	以被动休闲为主、多与家人为伴、主要步行、较高满意度、公共绿地影响力较大、使用频率居中、服务半径要求 15min 内居多、对公共绿地复杂设施要求居中
中老年高收入者	H 高要求便捷康乐型	以被动休闲为主、多与家人为伴、最高步行率、较高满意度、公共绿地影响力居中、最高使用频率、服务半径要求 30min 内居多、对公共绿地复杂设施要求较高
	M 低要求低频率安静康乐型	以被动休闲为主、多与家人为伴、较高步行率、满意度居中、公共绿地影响力居中、使用频率较低、服务半径要求 15min 内、对公共绿地复杂设施要求较高
在校学生	中要求中频率便捷社交型	以主动休闲为主、多与朋友为伴、较高步行率、最高满意度、最低公共绿地影响力、使用频率居中、对公共绿地复杂设施要求较高

注：M 代表梦清园，H 代表蝴蝶湾绿地。

4　基于 SES 分异的社会性滨水公园供给策略建议

快速城市化的背景下，城市滨水区出现了高强度、快速度的投资建设所带来的一系列滨水区开放空间的物质形态和社会空间问题。苏州河滨水公共绿地使用的社会分异正在逐步扩大，这种差异度将随着苏州河滨水物质空间的现代化建设逐步扩大。基于调查研究结果，本文进一步探讨基于

SES 差异性的滨水居住区景观供给与外部公共绿地的社会性功能耦合策略：首先，从规划层面，在规划滨水区公共绿地整体布局时，结合社会和人口 SES 属性规划相应的绿化设施与节点，不同 SES 阶层的人群对公共绿地设施的要求不同，如较高 SES 阶层对公共绿地的特殊设施需求较高，因此要考虑公共绿地设施的艺术性和文化性，合理的设施配备提高公共绿地的使用效率；其次，从空间设计层面，要考虑公共绿地的多元空间特征，即不同的公共绿地采取不同的设计手法、风格和主题，保证滨水公共绿地的丰富性和多样性；最后，从管理养护层面出发，可将动态的 SES 与物质规划后续使用结合起来，建立动态绿地系统指标数据库，调研滨水区相关社区人群的 SES 状况，了解滨水区的每年人群 SES 状况，根据实际使用人群 SES 的不同状况，形成合理的动态管理养护机制。促进不同 SES 阶层人群在公共绿地内相互交流与融合，实现滨水区公园绿地供给的公平性。

Study on Recreation Equity of Waterfront Park Based on Socio-Economic Status Differentiation: Cases Study of Waterfront Green Space of Suzhou River in Shanghai

Dong Nannan[1], Liu Qiang[2], Zhang Shenghong[2]

（1. Tongji University；2. ERA Landscape Planning and Design co. , ltd. ）

Abstract：Against a new tide of renovation, Shanghai has seen the intensive land use and restructuring of industry, which lead to a coexistence of different residential space forms in downtown areas. As an important area of vitality in a city, waterfronts attract people across different socio-economic levels, cultures for living and recreation purposes. This paper takes the equality and effectiveness of using new green areas under the condition of residential space differentiation as the core problem. Considering the arrangement of distance distribution, the actual use of green space for community residents always differs greatly from expectation, despite of an increasing attention to the green areas accessibility. The green areas and parks are affected by proportion of users and their socio-economic status (SES) in recreation and service. With research methods of questionnaires and interviews etc. , The results are summarized as two main aspects：1. The link between SES hierarchy and the hierarchy of park recreation needs. The specialized recreation needs increase with the higher SES residents; the low-level SES residents are otherwise basic needs oriented. 2. The recreation differentiation in waterfront parks is closely related with surrounding SES. The recreation functions differ much greater with the rising gap of residents' SES. The paper discusses about waterfront residential areas' landscape supply and the coupling strategy of social function of public green area based on SES differentiation. It gives a summary of waterfront parks' design strategies considering human SES properties from the aspects of internal functions, facility arrangement and site selection. It aims to encourage the exchange and mix of people across different SES, meeting the needs of park users and guarantee the equal use of waterfront parks.

Keywords：Socio-economic status differentiation, Public park, Recreation, Equality

参考文献：

[1] 董楠楠，刘强. 大城市中心区行政区划边界的景观风貌评价[A]//中国风景园林学会. 中国风景园林学会 2011 年会论文集(上册). 中国风景园林学会，2011：5.

[2] 王涵. 城市滨水区居住空间分异研究——以上海市苏州河滨水区为例[D]. 上海：华东师范大学，2008.

Social Inclusive Housing: Communal Living

Cheuk Ho Chuen Rex

(School of Architecture, Chinese University of Hong Kong)

Abstract: With the acceleration of urbanization, cities have been expanding, urban sprawl and so on, resulting in efficient land use, urban transport further deterioration of urban development should be compact urban containment blind expansion mode, play to the combined effect of urban space, urban development cost savings, and promote sustainable development of the city. In this context, we should take into account the needs of people humanities, dig, and design more suitable for people living in the urban space.

Keywords: Communal living, Compact city, Sustainable communities, Social inclusive design

1 Introduction

With the acceleration of urbanization, cities have been expanding, urban sprawl and so on, resulting in efficient land use, urban transport further deterioration of urban development should be compact urban containment blind expansion mode, play to the combined effect of urban space, urban development cost savings, promote sustainable development of the city. In this context, we should take into account the needs of people humanities, dig, and design more suitable for people living in the urban space.

After changing the aged older outdoor environment feel on a lot of investigation, and then discussed the various characteristics of existing outdoor environment is how to help or hinder the elderly to use and enjoy the outdoor environment. Also that I believe it should have six design principles "street life" model, and start on these six principles, in order to make the living environment more social inclusive. Also the social inclusive design should be one of the essential element for the future city and residential development.

Regardless of age, physical condition, people can easily understand and use in accordance with the "street life" design principles outdoor environment, which is what we have been committed to the pursuit of creating a truly inclusive community durability.

For the future city and housing planning and development, it should define in 4 different level:

1. Compact City
2. Sustainable Communities
3. Social Inclusive Design
4. Communal Living

1.1 Compact city

After the 1990s, the government put forward the "compact city" concept (that is, high-density, mixed-use city), carried out intensive development in existing urban land, including re-use of the brown area (industrial land), and do new development in high-density areas near transportation nodes, transport facilities. Compact city policy was later packed into "urban renaissance" concept, the government sought to slow the widely publicized anti-urbanization through urban regeneration policy trends in the brown area was redeveloped, the government encouraged people to return to the higher density of towns and city. Therefore, architects and planners of the mission is to create "sustainable settlements" and "sustainable communities" to encourage those designed to provide high quality of life for residents, so that people are willing to live permanently.

1.2 Sustainable Communities

Sustainable community for everyone to provide a good quality of life, and provides a safe comfortable environment for pedestrians and cyclists. Government highly acknowledged in the policy of high-quality design is an important part of sustainable settlements. What is a high quality design? The book presents seven design principles of high-quality design, including the "place self-characteristics", "public and private spaces clear separation" and "residential communities should be attractive with outdoor space", the designer should know What sustainable communities (for example, there is a convenient path, mixed-use, attractive, security, a sense of community and a healthy environment), the book also mentions about the design guidelines issues, some specific design guidelines can clearly to guide the design, but most guidelines is empty pan, difficult to apply in practice. High-density communities can take different forms design, not only to consider internal and external features, but also to consider the relationship with the surrounding environment, but also consider the architectural style and detail, as well as external sites, parking layout.

Figure 1　Idea of sustainable communities

1.3 Social Inclusive Design

Street life and the concept of inclusive design complement each other. Inclusive design means that no matter how the user's age and health, we design products, facilities and quality of service should be able to fit them to use.

1.4 Communal Living

"Communal living" concept, which aims to provide an inclusive design for people of different sectors, but also a natural extension of inclusive design concept can be expanded to the community scale, scope and even the village town. It is a sustainable policy. We continue to develop, under the public demand for sustainable communities growing environment made history

2　Type of Communal Living

There are two main types of Communal living:

1. When residents get older, it can very easily in this life is very pleasant, if they wish, they can continue to live at home.

2. It is inclusive of all community members, including Alzheimer's disease, including patients can be easy and pleasant to live here.

Communal living contributes to sustainable communities. An important aspect of social sustainability of social is cohesion and social inclusion. Sustainable neighborhoods should provide equality of chances and opportunities. Inclusive design means that no matter how the user's age and health, we design products, facilities and quality of service should be able to fit them to use.

2.1 How to design a Communal living with the local identity

1. Streets, open spaces and buildings are long-term, gradually built up.

2. Any changes are small, incremental.

3. The new planning, development should place the form, style, color and materials.

4. The street pattern should be rich layers, including Main Street, auxiliary street, alley and sidewalk?

5. sites and buildings should be easily understood in accordance with the principles of the elderly familiar understanding of design?

6. design principles buildings and street sketches should be understood in accordance with the elderly familiar with easily understood?

2.2 How to create space on the Communal with a legibility?

1. Appropriate scale neighborhoods based on blocks should be arranged in an irregular road network;

2. The district should adopt a smaller scale, scale control between 60-100m;

3. Communal interconnected good, short and narrow;

4. Functions and entrance places and buildings should be clearly visible, clear and unambiguous;

5. The flag should be realistic style of a large pattern and a large sign, with a clear color and background contrast;

6. Street sketches and other potential subtle clues should be set at the appropriate keys and visual terminals.

2.3 How to create a unique Communal space?

1. With localized features;

2. There are a variety of urban and architectural forms;

3. With a variety of small, informal, popular and easy to understand the local development of space, they shall be provided with a variety of activities in the functions and features;

4. A variety of development of space, such as public squares, village green and parks;

5. Use the different regional styles, colors and materials to form streets, places, buildings and structures;

6. with a variety of historic, urban nature, unique buildings and structures;

7. A variety of places full of interest and activities;

8. Aesthetic characteristics of the elements and the use of characteristic elements exist, such as trees and street comedy coexists.

2.4 How to create a safe Communal living?

1. Use a mix function;

2. The building's doors and windows facing the street;

3. By clearly marked bike lanes separated from the sidewalk;

4. Through the trees, pavement parking lot or bike lanes separated from pedestrians and motor vehicles;

5. Set at the crossroads at both ends with controlled lights visual and auditory signals, which travel time is set long enough to ensure passage of the frail elderly;

6. In the pedestrian road and crossroads in a fresh color and texture contrast to the measures set vehicle deceleration;

7. Set spacious sidewalks, and ensure their well-maintained, clean and clean;

8. Paving material should be smooth and no reflection, should adopt a clear color and texture to the wall, bike lanes and deceleration of the vehicle in marked contrast with the formation;

9. Pavement should be flat, smooth, non-slip;

10. Grille and gutter hole should be smaller than the size of the heel stick and prevent the fall;

11. The blade should be planted small trees, to prevent adhesions after rain soaked the leaves on the road caused by slippery roads, causing the elderly slide;

12. Architectural design and planning should avoid very dark on the sidewalk and an extremely bright contrast region;

13. Provide adequate street lighting for the visually impaired person.

3 Communal living-How is future?

Achieve "living street" ideal model is to create a whole new town and the settlements, but new communities in the planning and implementation of all small proportion; practice can be used in the reconstruction and regeneration of urban settlements in the design for strategy is actually very needs. According to the author the new urban residential areas or settlements "street life" There are 17 recommendations, which summarizes summarizes the important features for dementia patients living on the street. At the same authors also design these strategies can be applied which do distinguish between large housing development projects such as the new urban design, new urban expansion and sustainable settlements, private or community.

The early design phase to apply these design strategies, including those related to the overall planning of urban and street network shape design strategies can be applied only in the early stages, and the design strategies such as sidewalks and other road need to be considered in the detailed planning stage, involving street sketches and other finer level of design strategies can then consider the implementation of the construction design stage.

4 Evaluation of Communal living

Research on the elderly living on the street to understand the views of the outdoor environment and it can improve the lives of the elderly, which is the ultimate goal of research "Communal living" policy. It also enables the elderly to remain independent - "Living in place" under its guidance, residential new or renovated for the elderly to continue to go out, make use of local facilities, to communicate with people in a residential area inside provided possible. In the inclusive design, "street life" helped to create for the entire development environment. In building sustainable communities, street life beneficial aspects related to social sustainability, while supporting alternative vehicle with walking and cycling facilities, help achieve environmental sustainability. While the elderly do experience dementia research, people and the environment for further research methods, and finally the concept of street life to some extent adverse changes in the existing industrial design attitude, we should not hold so-called "modern architecture decisions On", the architects tried to shape and change the point of view of human behavior, but we should be to design a more user-friendly outdoor environment to adapt to people's living habits need, this is the inclusive urban design should do . Therefore, we should create a distinctive design approach - a full play to the designer's creativity and skill of methods analyze the situation while the previous successful and unsuccessful cases, according to the user's needs, then put concrete Solution strategy.

5　Communal space design feature

Successful Communal space also includes a three-dimensional characteristics of architecture, in the form of a two-dimensional plane and entities providing fun and focus. Traffic is the essence of the street, but it has more features, but these features emphasize speedy passage of the modern city has often been forgotten. Analysis of street space found two main types: curved (meander) and non curved (linear). Street - City Plaza is a traditional European city for the existence of space systems. Rob Krier in the preamble of the "urban space" in a book he describes a way of understanding the urban fabric - In traditional urban design, building facades momentum enclosed urban space is limited to a finite set of "empty", which also confirmed the plan of urban space is a continuous public domain, linked to each other inside and outside. This form of traditional urban space constitutes a great impact.

Figure 2　Idea of communal space

6　Conceptual space and intimate space

How to transform the city in a small abandoned lots into vibrant public space in midtown Manhattan Paley Park is a case worthy of recommendation. This lot with a relatively small budget into a shade in front waterfalls, white tables and chairs arranged in a simple activity but a decorative shop floor stage public events. Enter this oasis city noise drowned by water, air quality has improved significantly in the summer months to reduce the temperature of the plants and water, the park offers inexpensive food, the bustle of midtown Manhattan in play major social space the role of spatial scales and its facilities meet the requirements of users. Paley Parkis a favorite subject of space.

7　Spatial information exchange space

Another common problem is the impact of urban space in modern city signs flooding. Whether

East or West of the city, facilities dissemination of information often affects our perception of urban space, written information or advertising facilities to replace the role of space as the transmission of information, as defined architectural space boundary from the outset does not exist. Modern city needs is to clearly define the public domain, rather than relying on information dissemination systems and corporate advertising. The spread of cultural values should be space rather than those signs.

8   Conclusion

The main urban form is vertical rather than horizontal, such as when the modern landscape of tower blocks in common, Floor or skyscrapers, almost impossible to create a continuous urban space. This result is just the opposite with the Noli map, gives the impression of just individual buildings, neighborhoods and continuous form was gone. So, in order to build a form outdoor space, you must carefully handle the edge of space and neighborhoods, establishes one corner, recess, corner, corridor and other outdoor spaces.

社会包容性住房：小区生活

卓浩泉

（香港中文大学建筑学院）

摘要：随着城市化进程的加快，城市规模不断扩大，城市扩张等，致使土地的有效利用，城市交通是城市发展的进一步恶化，应该紧凑城市遏制盲目扩张模式。为了发挥城市空间的集聚效应，节约城市发展成本，促进城市的可持续发展，我们应该考虑到人们的人文需求，设计更适合居住的城市空间。

关键词：共同生活，紧凑型城市，可持续发展小区，社会包容性设计

Reference：

[1]   References Bramley, G. An Affordability Crisis in Britain: Dimension, Causes and Policy Impact[J]. Housing Studies, 1994, 9(1): 103-124.

[2]   Fallis, G. (1985) Housing Economics[M]. 1985, Butterworth, Co, Toronto, Boston. [3] Hancock, K (1993) Can Pay? Won't Pay? The Economic Principles of Affordability[J]. Urban Studies, 30(1), 127-145.

[3]   Hancock,K., Jones, C., Munro, M., Satsangi, M., Mcguckin, A. Housing Costs and Subsidies in Glasgow: The Impact of Housing Subsidies in the Glasgow Travel-to-workarea[M]. Joseph Rowntree Foundation, York, England, 1991.

[4]   Hong Kong Housing Authority (HKHA). Report of the Ad Hoc Committee to Review Domestic Rent Policy and Allocation Standards[R]. Hong Kong: HKHA, 1990, 12.

[5]   Hong Kong Housing Authority (1985, 1990, 1995, 1996, 1997) Housing in Figures[R], Hong Kong. Housing Authority, Hong Kong.

[6]　Hong Kong Housing Authority Report of the Committee on Housing Subsidy to Tenants of Public Housing，1986 Hong Kong Housing Authority，Hong Kong.

[7]　Hong Kong Housing Authority Consultation Document，Ad Hoc Committee to Review the Housing Subsidy Policy[R]，1992 Hong Kong Housing Authority，Hong Kong.

[8]　Hong Kong Housing Authority（1996）Safeguarding Rational Allocation of Public Housing Resources：Report on Final Recommendations，Hong Kong Housing Authority，Hong Kong.

[9]　Hong Kong Housing Authority（1999）Rental Housing Committee Paper No. RHC 12/99，Hong Kong Housing Authority，Hong Kong.

[10]　Hong Kong Housing Authority（2002）Hong Kong Housing Authority Corporate Plan 2002/03.

[11]　（Hong Kong）Housing Branch. Homes for Hong Kong People：The Way Forward-Long Term Housing Strategy Review Consultative Document[R]，Government Printer，Hong Kong，1997.

[12]　Hong Kong Housing Bureau Paper on Housing（Amendment）Ordinance prepared for the Provisional Legislative Council Panel on Housing. Hong Kong：Housing Bureau，1997.

[13]　Hui，E. C. M. Public Housing Rents in Hong Kong：A Supply Approach[J]. Housing Science，1999，23(3)：141-151.

[14]　Hulchansky. The Concept of Housing Affordability：Six Contemporary Uses of the Housing Expenditure-to-Income Ratio[J]. Housing Studies，1995，10(4)：471-491.

[15]　Lau，K. Y. Safeguarding the Rational Allocation of Public Housing Resources in Hong Kong：A Social Policy Discussion[J]. Asia Pacific Journal of Social Work，1997，7(2)：97-129.

[16]　Nelson，P. K. Housing Assistance Needs and the Housing Stock[J]. American Planning Association Journal，1992，58(1)：85-102.

[17]　Social Welfare Department. Support for Self-reliance：Report on Review of the Comprehensive Social Security Assistance Scheme[R]. Hong Kong：Social Welfare Department，1998.

[18]　Wong，H.，Chua，H. W. Research on Expenditure Pattern of Low Expenditure Households in Hong Kong[M]. Hong Kong：Hong Kong Council of Social Service，1996.

[19]　Whitehead，C. E. M. From Need to Affordability：An Analysis of UK Housing Policy[J]. Urban Studies，1991，28(6)：871-887.

基于自组织理论的城市边缘空间的交通系统研究——以浙江松阳老街为例

黄海静[1,2]   马   汀[1]

（1. 重庆大学建筑城规学院；2. 重庆大学山地城镇建设与新技术教育部重点实验室）

摘要：本文以浙江松阳老街交通系统改造为例，分析提出城市边缘空间交通系统发展需要解决的问题，包括交通拥堵、道路系统混乱、与城市车行交通系统无联系等问题。通过分析松阳老街的自组织演变形成与自组织形成过程与自组织退化过程，提出城市边缘空间交通系统发展停滞的关键原因是其自组织系统的开放性降低，系统自我发展的内力减少。并提出城市边缘空间交通系统的自组织更新需要根据自组织演变过程阶段性进行。最后提出通过合理引入车行交通系统，作为刺激老街交通系统的外部条件，并在系统自组织演变的各阶段进行评估与引导，推动系统自组织演变良性发展。

关键词：自组织，城市边缘空间，交通系统

1 引言

城市边缘空间是一种独特的城市建设与组织形式，作为城市交通系统的组成部分，城市边缘空间内建筑密度大，路面情况较差，行人较多，交通基础设施不完善，往往成为城市交通发展的阻碍。但城市边缘空间内的街巷连接便捷、灵活可达，是增加城市活力的重要因素。[1] 如何有效利用城市边缘空间的街巷特性和活力要素，对于改善城市交通组织十分关键。

在以往的城市边缘空间改造中，环境内的原有的交通系统被粗暴的破坏，城市边缘空间交通系统原有的运行机制与交通空间也随之消失。因此，研究城市边缘空间交通系统组织生成机制尤为必要。

2 相关概念

2.1 自组织理论

自组织理论以复杂系统的形成和发展为对象，研究复杂系统是如何在一定的条件下自行组织、自行创生、自行演化，由无序向有序、低级有序向高级有序发展的。[3]

自组织理论是一种理论集合，其核心理论是耗散结构理论与协同学理论，耗散结构理论是自组织理论的基本条件，探讨自组织出现的条件环境问题，研究一个系统如何开放，开放的程度，如何创造条件推动系统自组织等问题。协同学是自组织理论的基本动力，提出自组织演化中的基核、协同、序参量等重要概念，同时研究各概念之间相互作用的原理。[3,4]

2.2 城市边缘空间

城市边缘空间指在城市发展过程中，因发展滞后，没有明确规划与"正规"权利约束控制，被"正规"城市发展进程所边缘化，而由居民自发建设形成的城市空间。这样的城市空间通常是城市中心区内尚未更新改造的老旧街区，或是早先的城市边缘区由于城市化的快速发展而成为农业及外来人口的集聚点演变成的"城中村"，或是自行侵占土地而逐步形成的居民聚居点。[4,5]

城市边缘空间由于外界干预较少，同时具有一定的开放性和内部的协同机制，满足自组织系统形成的条件，城市空间内部往往以自行组织、自行创生、自行演化的模式"自然"发展着。[6]

2.3　交通系统

交通系统的含义范围较广，但城市边缘空间的交通空间系统范围较小，主要是指城市边缘空间内部与周边城市空间的交通，本文主要研究交通系统中的交通方式、街道形态与道路系统结构。

3　松阳老街的现状与问题

松阳位于浙江省丽水市，位于浙江省西南部（图 1a），松阳老街街区主要包括以现松阳县城中心"北直街——人民大街——南直街"为主要街道的城市空间，被当地人称为"老街"（图 1b）。

本研究选择老街中段，即由"太平坊路——新华路——长松路——紫荆路"划分的街区空间进行研究（图 1c）。街区多数清至民国初年建筑风格的两层式前店后宅楼房，内部为多为院落式传统民居。松阳老街内的交通方式长期以来以步行为主，近年来电动自行车作为一种交通方式出现，并逐渐成为空间内主要的交通方式。

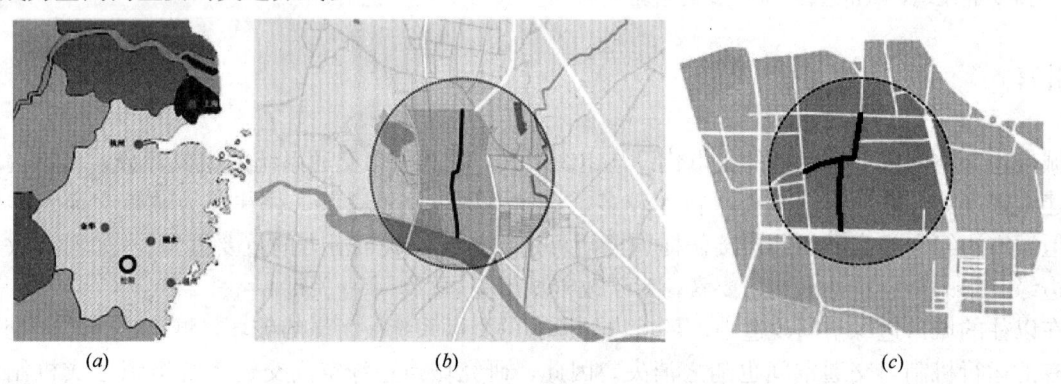

(a)　　　　　　　　　　(b)　　　　　　　　　　(c)

图 1　松阳老街区位
（a）松阳区位；（b）老街区位；（c）研究对象区位
（资料来源：作者自绘）

松阳老街在清朝初期开始形成，清朝中期由于县城南门松阴溪码头的修建，大大刺激街道周边的发展，在清末民初发展达到鼎盛，由 20 世纪 80 年代开始，发展逐渐停滞，老街交通系统受到现代城市交通系统的割裂与冲击，产生了诸多问题。

（1）交通混乱拥堵

老街的街道尺度是以适合步行的尺度形成的，可以承载的流量与流速都有限，当城市中的非机动车大量进入时，在与行人争夺道路空间的同时，车流由于街道尺度狭窄常形成拥堵。

（2）停车组织无序

老街在至今的发展之中未形成有效的非机动车停放组织方式，非机动车完全依照个人需要而无序停放，占据了街道与巷道空间。

（3）巷道系统破坏

无人管理的状况下，道路、广场、活动场地等交通空间被侵占，居民向周边索取生活空间，在巷道中自主建房，使巷道形成交通断点，原有巷道网络系统被破坏，干道之间的联系减弱甚至消失。

（4）交通节点稀缺

由于老街交通系统发展在原有的交通节点被逐渐侵占，新的节点还未形成的现状下，系统中鲜有反应信息聚集的交通节点。并且，老街中也缺乏与外部现代城市车行交通系统相连接的功能空间。

3.1 松阳老街自组织演变机制

外部环境变化产生了系统内部进行自组织演变的可能性，城市边缘空间交通系统与城市周边交通系统存在人口、资金、信息的交流，具有开放性。内部与外部的相互交流，使城市边缘空间交通系统发展呈现非平衡性和非线性。系统中各要素不断改变，联动整个系统状态的不断改变，从而形成涨落（图2）。[2]

松阳老街在历史发展的过程中，一直未有强力规划与权力约束，老街的发展实质上是一种自我组织、自我生长的状态，老街在发展形成过程中的存在明显的自组织发展与退化过程，这是研究老街交通系统自组织系统的重要依据。

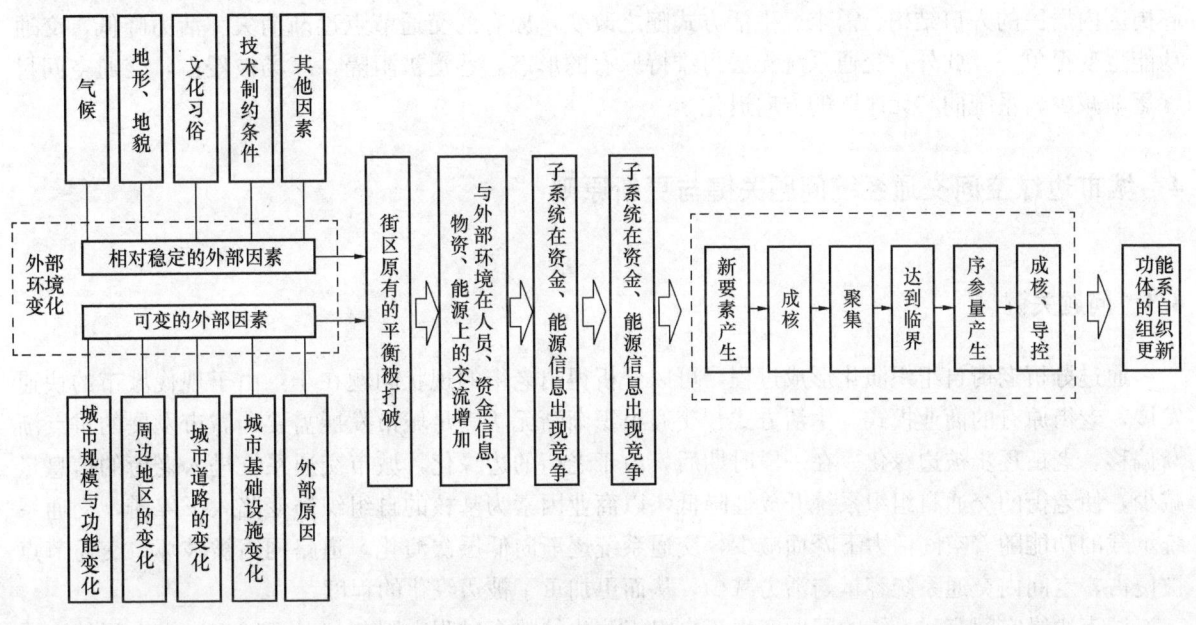

图2　自组织演化机制

（资料来源：作者自绘）

3.2 松阳老街交通系统的自组织形成

清朝松阳县城扩大，并在南门外的松阴溪修建码头，该码头成为了松阳县城的商业与交通的节点，由码头至县城中心的路径成为了县城主要的交通干道，道路周边的空间商业价值增加，主干街道两侧商铺随之逐渐增加，空间内的道路网络根据商业的价值，人流的流向，货物的运输方式产生了一定的秩序，最初的街道形态与尺度形成，完成了自组织演变中"无序到有序"的过程。

在商业发展过程中，空间内居民的人口结构、需求、生活方式也向适应商业发展的方向演变，产生了新的需求与活动，同时随着人口、资金、产品等信息的不断进入与聚集，空间内交通系统发展非平衡，某些地点产生了突变，成为了交通系统中的交通节点。完成了自组织演变中"自组织聚散"的过程。

随着空间不断发展单纯的线性街道无法承载不断涌入的信息量，开始向周边扩展，形成道路网络，并在新的道路系统中重复自组织过程，完成"自组织演化"的过程。

松阳老街交通系统在形成的自组织演变过程中对于商业利益竞争是交通系统自组织发展的内部动力，而商业经济活动、生活活动模式、传统宗族居住文化、建筑建造技术等要素作为自组织演变的序参量控制着系统的发展，使老街的交通系统呈现以步行为主要交通方式。商业街道为主干，院落间尺度较小的巷道辅助的形态。

3.3 松阳老街交通系统的自组织退化

20 世纪 80 年代，随着松阳县城的逐步发展，城市交通网络发生很大变化，码头的废弃使原先的商业路径消失，老街的商业价值大大降低。老街周边的道路进行了拓宽与整治，成为城市车行交通的主干道，老街的交通功能减弱。同时由于无法通车，老街的交通系统无法满足现代城市交通需要，城市发展的焦点从老街移开，老街自身又因为复杂的产权问题和尚存的商业价值未被拆除和规划，老街在这段历史时期成为了城市边缘空间。

由于交通系统的开放性降低，功能减弱，其自组织系统的演化产生了发展倒退的情况，周边道路的商业价值与活动减少，逐渐成为普通的居住街道，商业收缩至老街主干道。商业功能倒退又引起街区内居民的人口结构、需求、生活方式随之改变，原有的交通节点逐渐消失、活力降低，交通功能也变得单一。此外，交通系统无法再维持原有的形态，巷道被阻隔，广场被侵占，交通空间尺度逐渐减少，系统向"无序"的方向退化。

4 城市边缘空间交通系统问题关键与更新原则

4.1 问题关键

通过分析老街自组织演化形成过程，可以分析得出老街的现状问题在于：由于现代城市的快速发展，老街原有的商业模式、生活方式、交通组织渐渐无法满足城市发展需要，城市发展的重点渐渐偏移，老街逐步被边缘化。在一段时期后，由于老街的边缘化，城市交通系统进入老街的信息量减少，使老街的交通自组织系统开放性降低，以商业因素为基核的自组织演变陷入了停滞，交通系统承载的功能随着空间活力下降而减少，交通系统逐渐向低层次演化，道路网络被破坏，交通节点被侵占，空间内交通系统容量与活力减少，从而更加重了被边缘化的程度。

城市边缘空间交通系统的问题产生于自组织演化的整个过程，因此，对于城市边缘空间的交通系统的更新需要在系统的演化过程中逐步介入。

4.2 更新原则

（1）整体性原则

城市边缘空间交通系统更新应兼顾其交通系统所有组成因素的利益，而非仅仅强调其交通系统中的某一个要素。避免由于单一因素的加强，而导致城市边缘空间交通系统整体优势被破坏。

（2）地域性原则

城市边缘空间交通系统演变应尊重地域性。每一个城市边缘空间都有其特定环境文化，城市边缘空间交通系统更新应建立在普遍规律认知的基础上，深入研究形态系统的特殊性，并保护和创新这种特殊性，从而保证城市边缘空间的自我发展。

（3）诱发性原则

某些城市边缘空间形态构成要素的介入会给城市边缘空间交通系统形态系统带来"刺激点"，通过安排和设计这些要素，可以提升城市边缘空间交通系统的开放性，带动城市系统良性发展。

（4）阶段性原则

城市边缘空间的交通系统自组织演化过程具有阶段性，其更新手段应符合系统的演变阶段。在更新手段介入前应对系统的自组织演变做出评估，确定该阶段系统自组织演变的阶段、开放程度、竞争与协同的要素、导控因素等，才能确定适合的具体的更新策略。

5 自组织理论下的松阳老街交通系统更新研究

5.1 更新定位

从街区内居民与商户的生产生活角度出发，改善当前交通系统存在的拥堵、混乱现状，满足居民对于车行交通的需求，同时创造符合当前居民活动模式的交通节点，通过对不同的自组织演变阶段进行调研与评估，制定针对性的更新策略。

5.2 "无序到有序"阶段

增加老街交通系统的开放度是这一阶段的主要目标，通过增加老街交通系统内的新功能，提高人群的参与度来实现。老街的居民对于车行交通的需求强烈，可以此需求作为更新策略的突破点。

改造老街现有道路系统，建立初步老街的车行交通网络；评估改造发展的效应，逐步在街区周边建立机动车停车场，使街区内步行交通系统与周边城市空间的车行交通系统建立可能联系（图3a）。从而引导老街内无序的车行交通系统朝向有序状态发展。

5.3 "自组织聚散"阶段

利用老街内部的竞争与协同疏通交通作为该阶段的主要目标。增加老街开放性可能产生交通系统发展的不平衡，而不平衡带来的竞争与协同将会在老街"通行"与"居住"的冲突中体现。老街的某些地区因通行需求越来越大，道路通行不便的问题将会暴露出拓宽或改道的需求，阻碍通行的建筑也会凸显出来，根据交通系统暴露的问题进行整改（图3b），对这一阶段中老街自发形成的节点进行优化与引导是设计的重要任务。

5.4 "自组织演化"阶段

老街交通系统在前两个阶段的发挥中已经积累了大量信息要素并在某些地点产生了突变，承载新功能的交通系统已基本完成。在这一阶段中，老街新的交通系统能够良性的外延伸与发展（图3c），因而该阶段的主要任务是评估与指导老街交通系统发展的进程，并对外部环境的变化及时做出反应，防止自组织系统产生退化。

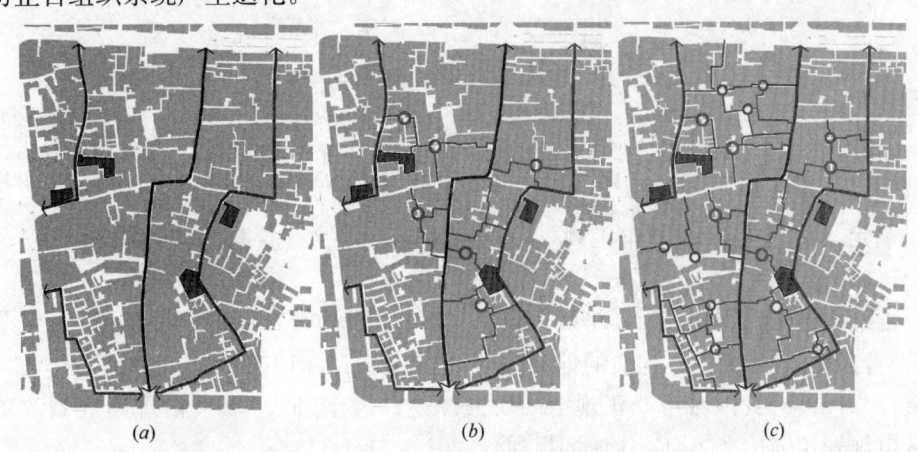

图3 自组织理论下的松阳老街交通系统更新
(a) 建立车行交通网络；(b) 节点自发形成；(c) 系统外延伸与发展
（资料来源：作者自绘）

6 结语

城市边缘空间交通系统由于矛盾集中、影响要素复杂，其发展与更新必须遵循系统要素的特征及关系，通过自组织理论的引入，更清晰地对其交通系统的演变与发展进行探讨，阐明宏观与微观、个体与群体、静止与变化之间的辩证关系。不断思考建造规律，善待各类影响因素，向场地学习，寻找真正适合城市边缘空间发展与更新的道路。

Strategy of Urban Marginalized Space Upgrading Based on Self-Organization Theory: Based on The Laojie Community of Songyang in Zhejiang

Huang Haijing[1,2], Ma Ting[1]

（1. Chongqing University School of Architecture and Urban Planning；

2. Key Laboratory of Mountain Town Construction and New Technology,

Ministry of Education，Chongqing University）

Abstract：Taking the upgrading on traffic system of Laojie community of Songyang as an example, we analyze its current characteristics and propose key problems in the urban marginalized space traffic system, including traffic congestion, the road system chaos, and no contact with city public traffic system. By analyzing the self-organization generation and degeneration of Laojie community, we propose the key problem on the stagnation of urban marginalized space traffic system is openness reduction. Besides, we propose the upgrading on the urban marginalized space traffic system should phase based on the stage of self-organization. Finally we propose introducing the city public traffic system into traffic system of Laojie community as the stimulation to the traffic system, estimate the system in each stages of self-organization, to make the self-organization system as a benign development.

Keywords：Self-organization, Urban marginal space, Traffic system

参考文献：

[1] 王晖. 城市的非正规性：我国旧城更新研究中的盲点[J]. 华中建筑, 2008, 3：152-155；159.

[2] 王晖，龙元. 第三世界城市非正规性研究与住房实践综述[J]. 国际城市规划, 2008, 6：65-69.

[3] 吴彤. 自组织方法论研究[M]. 北京：清华大学出版社, 2001：22.

[4] 卢健松. 自发性建造视野下建筑的地域性[J]. 建筑师, 2010(S2)：49-54.

[5] 宁一瑄，章征涛. 我国城市非正规空间研究综述和展望[R]. 城乡治理与规划改革——2014中国城市规划年会论文集(12-居住区规划), 2014：361-371.

[6] 李娜，杨俊雷，韩敏，等. 城市规划和公共政策视角下的非正规城市思考[C]. 云南：云南科技出版社, 2012：1-10.

中国社区规划师的角色建构

武明妍

（湖北省武汉市华中科技大学建筑与城市规划学院）

摘要：当代中国社区呈现多元模式，主要包括新开发的居住小区、历史形成的旧居住区及"城中村"社区等，并且各种形式常常混合分布在一片区域中。社区构成的复杂性意味着社区问题与社区需求的复杂性。而规划师和建筑师的视角更多的关注与城市大型广场、公园、商业中心，对于小尺度的、最贴近普通居民生活的社区空间却知之甚少，而这些空间恰恰承载了人们最真实的生活图景。同时，随着社会制度体制的改革和完善，政府更加注重听取来自最基层的声音。由于意见和想法受到前所未有的重视，居民也获得了满足感，表达自己需求的愿望也随之更加强烈。于是公共领域多元价值取向的协调问题也越来越得到社会的关注，公共参与成为社区规划中最顺理成章也是最为困难的环节。近年来，社区规划师制度渐渐兴起，被视为提升社区规划中公共参与度、平衡各方利益的有效途径。本文的第一部分重点分析社区规划师在中国开始兴起的缘由，认为在社区矛盾尖锐与居民公共参与意识提高两个因素的共同作用下社区规划师应运而生；第二部分简要介绍目前中国以政府主导自上而下设立的社区规划师的类型及工作内容，并以该制度建立较早的城市深圳为例，介绍了中国社区规划师代表政府与社区居民沟通协商、为社区规划提供技术支持、争取更多的利益等具体工作；第三部分研究目前中国社区规划师对于社区规划的积极作用和局限性，肯定了社区规划师为居民参与规划提供渠道、推动社区规划的科学性和可实施性、促进社区规划的可持续发展。同时提出目前社区规划师还存在一定的局限性，如未获得法定规划的地位、在市场利益驱动下缺乏宏观整体的思路以及制度推广难度大，获得社会认可尚需时日等；第四部分强调社区规划师可以作为"公众参与的倡导者"，更好地促进居民参与到社区规划中来，进而推进社区居民的自我治理。在与其他社会工作者一起为社区发展工作中，需承担鼓励多方参与、研究居民多元化、需求充分对话、友好协商、公平公正的社会责任，以推动包容性社区发展目标的实现。

关键词：社区规划师，中国特色国情，公众参与

1 社区规划师在中国兴起的缘由

1.1 多元模式发展下的社区问题日益尖锐

当代中国社区呈现多元模式，主要包括新开发的居住小区、历史形成的旧居住区及"城中村"社区等，并且各种形式常常混合分布在一片区域中。社区的复杂性意味着社区问题与社区需求的复杂性和多样性。2011年，中国城镇化率超过50%，建设用地规模迅速扩展，在严保全国18亿亩耕地红线面前，城市建设用地规模的进一步扩展受到国家政策的刚性约束，城市规划建设的重心将由增量建设逐渐转移到存量建设地的规划利用上。而社区是各种社会功能和角色汇聚的最小城市细胞，个人和社会的关系以日常生活的方式通过社区得以具体实现，逐渐成为人们思想、观念、意识交流和活动聚会的重要舞台。在过去城市规划建设过程中，规划师和建筑师的视角更多的关注与城市大型广场、公园、商业中心，对于小尺度的，最贴近普通居民生活的社区空间却知之甚少，而这些空间恰恰承载了人们最真实的生活图景。城市更新的脚步并没有转向社区，太多的经济空间的诞生意味着原来社区生活空间的消亡，原来积累与社区中社会、环境、人口的矛盾更加尖锐突出，亟待解决。

1.2 社区居民公共参与意识的增强

随着社会制度体制的改革和完善，政府更加注重听取来自最基层的声音，通过对居民声音的前

所未有的重视，居民也获得了满足感，表达自己需求的愿望也随之更加强烈。随着政府对更加广泛的信息来源、创造力来源以及解决方案来源的开发，居民更多的参与能够改进公共政策的质量；居民对政策过程的更多参与有助于政策的执行；对政府的公共信任度，能够为一些新型合作关系的产生创造更多的可能性。当然，在目前居民的参与社区建设中有存在着若干问题，如参与主体以老年人、妇女较多，更多的社会精英关注于自身的发展，对于社区的关注度很低；参与的形式表面化，只是"走过场，走形式"虽然也有听证制度，但并没有形成制度化的规定，而且参加听证会的代表往往也不具备足够的代表性；此外，参与的时序性较差，很难对于某个项目或制度进行较长时段的跟踪，起不到监督反馈的作用。

2 社区规划师的类型及工作内容

2.1 社区规划师的类型

笔者根据吴丹《深圳社区规划师制度的模式研究》一文，总结了四种社区规划师的类型，如表1所示：

不同类型规划师一览表   表 1

类型	主导力量	动因	专长	特征
行政力量担纲型	城市规划主导门	传统规划路径陷入困境	代表官方机构与社区居民沟通	吸纳社区居民诉求，提高决策的科学性
专业技术人员担纲型	行政系统委派技术人员	社区问题涉及规划、土地、产业、交通等多部门	侧重技术沟通与协调，推进政府各部门合作	尚处于探索阶段，未形成完整体系
社区主导型	社区聘请规划师	社区治理混乱，缺乏动力，需自主规划	规划师寻求现行政策、规划体系与社区发展思路之间的平衡	经济实力雄厚，社区领导人具有一定的发展眼光
城市更新的市场驱动型	原农村集体经济组织聘请	城市更新推动	为社区争取最大利益，提供类似控规的编制任务	市场化运作

注：表格内容由笔者整理。

2.2 社区规划师的工作内容

2.2.1 代表政府与社区居民沟通协商

通过行政系统委派的社区规划师，是对于传统的、自上而下的规划路径的一次完善和补充，吸收居民的利益诉求，在规划过程中考虑利益的平衡因素，促进规划的有效实施。在沟通过程中，也可促进官方规划管理与社区居民的沟通，使社区居民从不理解，排斥到渐渐理解和接受，使原来的"被规划"转变为主动参与规划。

2.2.2 为社区规划提供技术支持

社区的问题往往较为复杂，涉及土地、发改、交通、基础设施等多个环节，规划作为一个综合的技术部门，应对各项问题进行统筹，协调各部门关系。由于社区规划师有规划编制单位的技术人员构成，可以为社区的工作提供技术方面的支持。

2.2.3 为社区争取更多的利益

在上文提到的社区规划师的类型中，其中一类是由社区聘请规划师，这类规划师试图通过自下而上的社区规划影响规划的实施，从资源、片区功能和规划布局通盘考虑所服务社区的定位，致力于实现社区规划和其他相关专项规划的衔接和互动，保障该社区的利益。

3 社区规划师的积极作用和局限性

3.1 社区规划师的积极作用

3.1.1 为居民参与规划提供渠道

当下，居民的公共参与意识在普遍提高，规划师深入社区，一方面可以让居民了解规划的工作内容和流程，了解规划意义；另一方面，居民可将自己的诉求表达出来，能够一定程度上将自身的想法赋予到规划方案中。

3.1.2 增进规划的科学性和可实施性

多年来，我们的规划都是自上而下的，根据规划人员有限的知识和经验做判断，即便有前期调研，由于数据的时效性较短和统计的科学性不足，对于各类分析的指导作用也相对有限。而全方位的深入社区却能为前期的调研带来最直观可信的资料，提高之后规划策略的科学性。

3.1.3 增强规划的可持续进程

目前社区的规划项目的周期较短，规划师在完成一项社区规划工作后就会直接进行其他规划工作，而对于之前的规划不会持续关注，不会对出现的问题进行及时的调整和反馈，对规划应对不确定因素的能力较差，最后会出现规划失效的状况。

3.2 社区规划师的局限性

3.2.1 未获得法定规划的地位

社区规划尚未在城市规划体系中获得法定规划的地位。由于社区规划与现行的官方规划存在一定矛盾和冲突，所以社区规划师所做的决策在目前也仅仅是参考建议，并不一定具备法律效力和实施能力。

3.2.2 市场利益驱动下缺乏宏观整体的思路

社区规划师是为社区服务的，在一定程度上会以实现社区利益最大化为工作目标，在对于社区发展的思考中缺乏对于社区所在片区甚至更大范围的宏观考虑，对于社区的发展定位和策略会与整体发展思路有悖。

3.2.3 制度推广难度大，获得社会认可尚需时日

目前社区规划时制度尚在推广和试点阶段，广大居民对于社区规划师甚至规划这个行业都不甚了解，社区规划时真正能在社区发挥作用尚需时日；此外，许多规划专业的学生也未从传统的规划师的职业发展思路中跳出来，把社区规划时的工作与普通的社区居委会等管理部门的工作混为一

谈，并不能认识到社区规划师的巨大能量，对于这一发展方向的认可度不高。

4　当代中国社区规划师的责任

无论如何，应该说中国城市社区的发展迎来了最好时期，中央和地方政府大力的政策扶持和经济投入，以及普通百姓的积极关心，都为市民生活品质的进一步提升做好了诸多准备。社区，就像城市机体的千百个细胞，任何一个的病态都痛及乃至染疾全身。社区主义实际上蕴含着一种社会的系统观和全局观，一个社区乃是一个城市的缩影。社区的复杂性决定了社区规划师的多元构成和"服务型"角色。

4.1　综合的知识结构

除了一定的空间规划专业知识外，还需要对环境设施、建筑改造、土地经济、文化历史、心理、卫生、物业、税收及法律等知识有一定程度的掌握。此外还有对于国家政治、经济决策的宏观把握。同时，知识日新月异，规划技术已有翻天覆地的提升，规划师个体的持续学习、综合运用能力极为重要。

4.2　较强的沟通组织能力

社区问题琐碎，常常涉及个人利益与公共利益的矛盾与冲突，特别考验社区规划师的协调与应变能力以及"公"与"私"程度上的把握。社区规划师所要面对的主体是普通的社区居民，他们可能对于规划的认识存在偏差，急迫的维护自身利益，这更需要规划师的耐心的服务态度和平衡各方利益的能力。

4.3　本地化

社区规划师对于服务地区的了解程度是个非常重要的因素。一个社区规划师对本社区及更大区域的了解和感情是处理实际问题的有力保障。国外很多社区规划师就是本社区居民，甚至设计事务所就开设在社区内，可以对社区的日常问题给出具体策略和长远计划。反之，邀请不了解本地情况的规划师来服务本社区，短时间内必然会对与社区的认识有偏差，影响社区发展。

4.4　较长的服务时间

对一个社区而言，社区规划师应相对固定并服务社区 3~5 年甚至更长的时间，这样可以较长期地跟踪社区发展过程，将社区具体问题与长远规划进行统筹考虑。对于具体的项目实施可全程跟踪，及时对出现的问题进行调整。

致谢

本论文的完成，得益于潘宜教授在住区规划与社区发展这门课程上讲授的知识，引导我关注社区规划师，这一新兴制度的形成与发展，使本人有了完成此篇论文所要求的知识积累，更得益于导师耿虹教授从选题的确定、论文资料的收集、论文初稿与定稿中对字句的斟酌倾注的大量心血，在此对潘宜教授和我的导师耿虹教授表示感谢！

同时，在论文写作过程中，我还参考了有关的书籍和论文，在这里一并向有关的作者表示谢意。我还要感谢我的各位同学，在这段时间里，你们给了我很多的启发，提出了很多宝贵的意见，对于你们帮助和支持，在此我表示深深地感谢！

最后，感谢生我养我的父母。谢谢他们给了我无私的爱，为我求学所付出的巨大牺牲和努力。

Role Building of Community Planner in China

Wu Mingyan

(Architecture & Urban Planning College, Huazhong University of
Science and Technology)

Abstract：Nowadays, Chinese communities have multi-modes, including new built communities, old residence zones and some communities developed from village. In addition, all of them are often mixed in the same region. The complexity of community means the complexity and diversity of community issues and community demands. Planners and architects pay more attention to the large-scale civic square, park, commercial center, however, they lack of knowledge about small scale but most ordinary residents relevant living community space, the space which shows the most real picture of daily life. At the same time, with the reform and improvement of the social system, government pays more attention to the voices from the social basic units. Because the ideas and opinions are unprecedentedly heard, residents also acquire the satisfaction and desire to express their needs more intensively. Therefore, the coordination of diversity values in public has attracted more and more attention in our society. Public participation has become the most logical but also difficult problem in community planning. In recent years, the community planner system has been established, regarded as an effective way to improve public participation and balance the interests of all parties in community planning. In the first part, the paper presents the reason why community planner system has been established. It is showed that two factors, sharp contradictory in community and improvement of public participation, work together to start the community planner system. In the second part, the paper introduces what community planners need to do under Chinese national conditions, and uses Shenzhen, one of pilot cities in China, as a typical case. It describes that community planners represent the government to communicate with residents, to provide technical support and earn more interests for community planning. In the third part, the paper analyzes the current positive function and limitation of community planner system. One the one hand, it agrees with that community planners provide opportunity for residents to join in planning, improve the scientific and implementation of community planning, and promote sustainable development of community planning. On the other hand, currently, the system still has limitation, like no statutory planning status, lacking of macro integration under market interest drive, difficulty in extension, and need more time to acquire social recognition. In the last part, the paper emphasizes that community planners need to work as "advocates of public participation", leading residents into the community planning, which will promote "self-governance" of community residents. During cooperation with other social workers, community planners should encourage residents with different values to work together and solve problems through sufficient dialogues and discussions. They must undertake the responsibility of social equality and justice to achieve the goal of diversity community development.

Keywords：Community planners, Chinese national conditions, Public participation

参考文献：

［1］ 吴丹. 深圳社区规划师制度的模式研究[J]. 规划师，2013，9：36-40.

［2］ 赵蔚. 社区规划的制度基础及社区规划师角色探讨规划师[J]. 规划师，2013，9：17-21.

［3］ 许志坚，宋宝麒. 民众参与城市空间改造之机制——以台北市推动"地区环境改造计划"与"社

区规划师制度"为例[J]. 城市发展研究，2013，1：16-20.

[4] 王婷婷，张京祥. 略论基于国家—社会关系的中国社区规划师制度[J]. 上海城市规划，2010，5：4-8.

[5] 黄瓴，许剑峰. 城市社区规划师制度的价值基础和角色建构研究[J]. 规划师，2013，9：11-16.

[6] 邓昭华. 西方规划师职业素养的形成与启示[J]. 规划师，2014，11：127-131.

夹缝中的空间公平：重构旧居住区公共服务中心

孙弘捷

（江苏省南京市三江学院建筑学院）

摘要： 公共服务中心是城市基层服务设施的载体，本文从空间公平的视角出发，关注旧居住区集中的主城区，研究旧居住区公共服务中心建设所面临的多重问题。分析空间规划层面的设计策略，提出旧居住区在用地资源紧张的情况下，通过建立预先评估机制，对有限的可操作面积进行合理的配置和重构，达到延续社会结构，实现社会价值的目标。

关键词： 旧居住区，公共服务中心，空间公平，空间形态

1 引言

居住区公共服务中心是最接近民众生活的基层服务设施载体，反映了当代社会的人文活动和经济发展趋势。随着城市社区化进程的加快，公共服务中心经历了从无到有的发展过程，目前形成了以社区综合服务大楼、社区卫生服务中心两大基本主体组成的社区公共服务中心，以及由此衍生的配套教育、小型商业金融服务中心、休闲广场，甚至是辐射地区交通的公共枢纽中心。公共服务中心的多层次和复合化不断改变了原区域的空间格局，推动了区域经济发展。

然而，在人口规模饱和，社会结构趋于稳定的旧居住区，依照公共服务中心面积功能配比的模块化策略，或是按照人均占有率的量化测算所指导的规划设计只能解决空间标准的问题，而规避现实条件的复杂性。空间公平概念的介入有利于规划设计人员从社会公平这个全新的角度看待旧居住区更新发展过程中面临的各种问题，系统分析和解决矛盾。

我国对城市公共中心的研究从 20 世纪末开始，对空间公平的研究从 21 世纪初起步，主要集中在城市公共空间价值的探讨、人本主义城市公共空间发展、公共空间效率和公平的实现；在社区层面的探讨主要集中在社区体系的建设、空间发展模式、空间形态、公共服务设施可达性研究等层面。将社区发展与空间公平两者结合起来的研究还不多。社区中心作为居住核心区，不仅仅需要解决空间问题，还需要解决空间的价值和意义，与社会结构的匹配度，以及社会发展的深层次问题。

2 基于空间公平的讨论

2.1 旧居住区的空间公平

2.1.1 空间公平的概念

空间公平（spatial equality）是一个地缘概念，可以理解为地区发展的均衡性以及公共资源的合理分配。空间公平、空间正义是近几年多学科关注的热点，人文地理、城市规划、社会学经济等多个学科都在从不同的层面对这个领域开展研究。"空间公平是城市公共空间研究的根本议题。作为公共资源，公共空间分布直接影响公共福利分配，实现公共资源和服务分配的空间公平是规划从业人员的首要目标之一。"[1] 民众是空间体验的主体，空间公平性一方面依赖于技术层面的物化实现，另一方面依赖于民众对空间分配和空间归属的认可。此外，政策的影响、体制的变化、经济的发展、交通系统的更新、需求层次的变化又促使着新一轮公共服务空间的调整，空间公平的感知度

与需求度呈螺旋上升的发展趋势。

2.1.2　空间公平的实现和评价

空间公平在居住区规划的层面的物化体现一直停留在政府管理、规划单位配置的状态，政府和规划层面的从业人员主要关注指标的实现和规范的执行，实际情况是现在每个区域面临的具体问题往往具有共性也有个性：共性的问题是民众对空间公平的关注度更集中在生活基本服务设施、医疗资源、教育资源、交通可达等这些基本资源的空间分配尤其是社会公平层面的分配，这与每个家庭的生存发展息息相关。个性问题是由于各区域资源满足情况不同，带来的区域主体的资源诉求分异。由于地理位置的差异和资源配置的不均等性，空间公平不可能是均质发展的过程，这也决定了空间公平的实现不是绝对的。此外，空间公平的评价标准也很难界定，社会公共资源分配的均等化、均质化都不能简单地在定性定量的维度予以确定。更何况使用空间的社会群体构成本身就具有多样性，行为方式、价值取向都决定了对空间公平的评价需要在多个层面展开。因此，将空间公平的意愿简单物化、定量配置的做法是否真正发挥作用，是否产生效益，都是值得大家思考的问题。

2.2　旧居住区公共服务空间建设现状

2.2.1　旧居住区的空间公平的特殊性

城市的发展没有终点，只有空间的延续和消失。居住空间的形成有历史成因，也有场所价值的累积，是重叠发展的过程。作为城市肌理的重要组成部分，城市旧居住区往往是城市发展的成熟地区，甚至是中心地区，经过多年的积累，人文脉络清晰，社会结构相对稳定。但是随着居住环境的老化，高收入群体迁出原居住环境，选择居住条件更好的、配套服务更完整的地区居住。旧居住区越来越成为经济基础薄弱或不愿外迁的弱势群体的聚集地。原先的资源优势由于系统性的缺乏慢慢弱化，同时随着各种商业地产的开发，各种高等级的商业娱乐中心、健身中心、科教中心的建设冲击着旧居住区传统的公共设施，使得旧居住区公共中心的地位逐步弱化，与此同时，旧居住区新的居住行为对空间公平的诉求与现实的滞后也成为主要矛盾。

2.2.2　旧居住区公共服务空间面临的困境

针对旧居住区公共服务空间的更新发展，城市的决策者们和规划师通过物质补充的途径，更新配套旧居住区的公共服务设施，完善旧区域的机能，延续旧居住区的使用寿命。然而在建设的过程中，实际面临的问题和矛盾非常多，并且建成后也面临着运行管理和使用效率的困境。

2.2.2.1　建设用地资源紧张

居住区的主要用地构成以住宅、公建、道路、绿化四类用地为主，旧居住区的住房类型包括转型的传统单位大院、老私房、新建商品房，调整中的公共配套设施呈零散布置状态。用地情况呈现出复杂性和破碎性，能够调剂用作公共服务中心用地的资源紧张，夹缝空间屡屡出现。大部分公共服务空间的选址是通过土地置换，或直接通过其他公共建筑改扩建而成，随机性和非科学性等被动几率大大增加，也为后期的运营和使用效益的实现带来不稳定因素。

2.2.2.2　更新周期长，矛盾多

由于城市管理主体的多样化和更新速率的不同，各方矛盾的调和也是焦点问题。主要包括：拆迁与安置、升级与置换前期所涉及的与原用地权属单位的协调、原住居民的各项权益的保障；建设过程中，涉及市政基础设施的对接、交通系统的协调、更新时序的控制等层面，这些已经不是一个部门能解决的问题，需要多方面协调共同研讨，加强公众参与、信息公开、政策扶持等机制的保障。

2.2.2.3 运营及效益实现

建成后的公共服务中心按标准化配置各项服务设施，共性有余、特色不足，主要原因是缺少对社区阶层分层化分析和综合评价机制。现在大多数社区公共服务中心的核心使用群体，除处理社区业务的办事人员以外，多为中老年人和孩童，如果出行距离较远，使用效率将更加下降。服务中心本身也无更多的财政支出来维持社区公益项目的更新发展，这些原因导致综合服务能力下降，人们更愿意去等级更高，服务系统更周全的市区级中心活动，导致资源的闲置。虽然出于经济效益的需要，社区服务中心往往附带小型商业项目（多为兴趣班和培训机构），能够为社区运营解决一部分的经济效益问题，但从综合情况来看仍不容乐观。

3 旧居住区公共服务中心的空间形态

3.1 旧居住公共服务中心体系

根据用地规模职能设置的分级管理体制，居住区公共服务中心划分为区级、街道级、居委会三个等级，按照《城市居住区规划设计规范》GB 50180—93（2002 年版）的要求，目前主要按千人指标、服务半径确定配置数量和配置规模。南京主城四区是旧居住用地集中、类型多样、时间跨度完整的区域，同时也是各项公共设施发展较为完备的地区。目前，主城四区（鼓楼区、玄武区、建邺区、秦淮区）按照行政区划，辖 39 个街道，337 个社区，13 个行政村，各街道社区服务中心设置完备。

街道级社区服务中心由于政府干预，对标准的贯彻执行力度最优，用地规模和设施标准都比较完善。主要以行政区划内的居住区为载体，以政务服务、医疗卫生为主。服务范围大，与居民的日常生活紧密相关，使用频率高，力求"高效、集约"。

社区级以及居委会社区服务站作为上一级的补充，以居住小区或组团为载体，服务范围小。为居民提供较为综合、全面的基本日常生活服务项目。包括：社区管理、政务服务、文化娱乐、基层商业服务等设施，功能设置上与上一层拉开层次，力求"亲民化、均等化"，由于地理位置往往是深入街巷的夹缝空间，目前也是矛盾和问题最多的区域，是需要关注的重点。

3.2 旧居住区公共服务中心的基本空间形态

旧居住区的传统公共空间形态是以居住空间为主体，多层次服务设施为补充的状态。这也决定了旧居住区的公共服务中心空间格局上因区域条件限制而异，大多以：沿街线状公共服务空间、集中的面状公共服务空间、离散的点状公共服务空间这三种常见形式嵌入城市旧居住区的肌理中。通过对南京主城四区的 37 个街道社区、337 个社区及居委会抽样走访调研，总结这三种典型的空间格局对空间公平性实现的影响，分别从：空间与交通可达性，包括布点合理性和服务可获得性；空间与群体相关性、空间与社会相关性，包括空间渗透、功能共生三个层次五个方面进行比较分析。在可达性层面的基础上，增加了与空间公平相关的，关于城市空间与群体相关性以及与社会相关性的观察层面。

公共服务中心空间形态与空间公平　　　　　　　　　　　　　　表1

研究层面		沿街线状服务空间	面状服务空间	点状服务空间
空间与交通可达性	布点合理性	较优	优	一般
	服务可获得性	综合可获得性最佳	可获得性视通达情况定	可获得性优
空间与群体相关性	—	中青年群体为主	综合群体	老幼群体为主

研究层面		沿街线状服务空间	面状服务空间	点状服务空间
空间与社会相关性	空间渗透	外强内弱	一般	内强外弱
	功能共生	强	较弱	弱

注：1. 可获得性：指服务需求者可获得服务的性质和程度。

2. 空间渗透：基层服务空间与居住空间及社会空间的内外关联度。

通过表 1 的比较，无论是哪类的空间形态，对交通系统的依赖度都非常高。沿街展开的线状公共服务空间主要借助交通资源的优势，公共设施与道路相结合，开放性较好，资源配置高效，但区域感略弱，在资源分配上具备一定的均质优势，规模效应一般；集中的面状公共服务空间一般处于区域的核心位置，环境较优，容易产生规模效应，居民出行目标明确，效率实现度较好，但社区空间与社会的关联度较弱；离散的点状公共服务空间是基层社区常见的空间形态，有利于增大服务半径，但各区域互动性较弱，不利于产生集聚效应，区域识别性较差，出行方便，出行效率却降低。

4 旧居住区公共服务中心规划策略

通过上述分析，旧居住区公共服务中心所包含的三级体系的建设需要放到统筹整合的层面上进行梳理。服务中心不只是一个位置上的概念，更是一种社会结构的支撑。在规划设计的层面需要综合多学科研究成果，结合各方面的需求和现实状况，实现空间公平和资源优化。达到民众满意的生活质量标准，构建优质生活圈，这也是社会主义核心价值观在民众基本生活层面的体现。

4.1 建立旧居住区公共服务中心分级预评估机制

在旧居住区现有的用地和交通条件下，大部分公共服务空间的选址存在一定的政策因素或主观因素，缺少依据，所以建立完备的预评估体系非常重要。通过科学理性的判断和调研总结，能够从一定程度上减少客观因素带来的负面影响，建议包括的评估因素有：

现有用地条件评估：确定土地资源容量，开发强度。对现状用地可更新调整的可能性、新建区域发展的需要等进行综合评价，既需要保证土地合理开发，也需要保证新建或改建区域对土地资源的高效利用。

现行服务区间、服务强度评估：解决旧居住区同类设施布置过近，服务范围重叠的问题，避免重叠地区服务资源过剩所带来的资源浪费，实现区域资源共享，提高设施资源使用效率。

服务目标人群评估：对服务人群的社会身份、年龄构成、价值观、居住偏好、出行方式等进行评估，尤其是老人和孩童，确定服务主体的社区交往需求以及对应的不同基本生活场所需求。

交通系统评估：交通是加强空间与社会联系，体验和发生社会交往的重要途径，对研究区域步行交通，非机动交通，机动交通的可达性进行评估，确定分级交通控制下的服务中心可达性目标的实现，鼓励人行交通所带来的积极的社会交往空间的延续。

4.2 重构旧居住区公共服务中心体系

重构是城市社会空间衍化的趋势和规律，居住区的公共服务中心有独特的社会价值属性，无论是长期社会发展演变的成果还是规划设计构建的空间形态，都在为社会空间价值体系的持续发展提供支持。站在旧居住区空间延续的角度，需要在充分评估的基础上对所在区域的核心价值、与交通系统的关联度、空间秩序、功能优化等多个层面进行调整。

4.2.1 中心区域恢复城市语境，提升区域中心象征意义

对于每一个地域来说，每一个新的公共空间的重构都是新的生活机能的注入，民众是充满期待的。公共服务中心是缩小的城市机能的综合体，公共空间需要与城市互动，体现城市语境，提升区域的象征意义，发挥社区社会职能。在实践过程中，政府管理者或运营阶层在意识层面已经开始不断强化服务中心差异化的重构，在恢复区域的历史价值和人文特色方面做着努力，如：南京华侨路街道青岛路社区青年驿站、新街口街道北门桥社区邻里中心、挹江门街道鲁迅园社区都在根据区域自身的特点进行新的中心区域重构的尝试，在解读地段原始语境，提升区域价值的方面作出了可贵的探索。

4.2.2 交通系统局部优化调整

合理的交通系统规划可以提高安全性、趣味性和可达性。旧居住区有路网系统成熟，支路密集的资源优势，但是机动车交通出行的普及也给过窄的主干道带来承载压力过大的问题。居住区服务中心选址的关键是依附主要道路以获取足够的服务人口，但将支路系统城市化是对原居住区结构的破坏。因此，对交通系统的优化调整一方面需要借助密集支路构建人行和非机动交通体系，实现慢行交通的优先规划，对弱势群体的出行方式予以优先考虑；另一方面也要考虑公共交通出行和机动车出行的需求，为这部分的出行留出空间并限定范围。

4.2.3 有限集中与相对分散的空间秩序梳理

良好的空间秩序可以提升社区核心的空间价值。根据旧居住区公共服务空间布局的特点，公共资源分配模式采取有限集中和相对分散的空间布局。集中有利于控制规模尺度，节约土地资源，发挥规模效应；分散有利于空间多样化的形成，激发多重交往空间。因此，对旧居住区来说，将空间质量要求高，互补功能强的服务空间进行有限的集中；对空间尺度要求低、规模小、功能独立的空间采取相对分散的布局，是实现高效节约发展的有效途径。

4.2.4 功能置换与功能混合

功能调整是重构过程的必经之路。功能置换是根据评估情况，移除功能实现不足的服务空间；将零散近似的功能空间进行集聚处理，产生规模效应；对功能缺失的区域加强覆盖。功能混合是加强功能互补的服务空间的集聚，公共服务与其他产业的共生能够发挥良好的外部效应，为居住区的经济生活和人文生活注入活力，这也是目前新建服务中心的主流处理方式。旧居住区由于多方面因素的限制，小尺度的空间密集，而单一的功能体量没有生存空间，更需要我们在小而微的层面进行功能设计和统筹安排，增加功能服务的社会价值和经济价值。

5 总结

规划设计层面对空间处理的模式化使我们忽略了社区原本的公共属性和使用群体对社会公平价值实现的诉求。本文借助空间公平的社会视角，对旧居住区公共服务中心的建设现状和困境进行思考，提出预先评估是空间重构的先决条件，对土地资源、社会资源、交通资源、社会阶层等进行调研分析，规避不利因素，整合成熟资源。并对公共服务中心体系重构的方法进行了探索，提出：明确社区边界，整合功能资源，实现高效集约；确定服务区间和强度，合理配置服务中心规模；提升区域场所的空间识别性和社会价值的建议。借此文对城市空间公平，尤其是弱势群体的空间公平实现提请设计人员关注，作为城市的规划者，承担社会责任义不容辞。

Spatial Equality in the Crevice: Restructure the Public Service Center of the Old Residential

Sun Hongjie

(School of Architecture, Sanjiang University)

Abstract: The public service center, which is the carrier of the urban basic service facilities. This text focus on the old residential areas concentrated urban areas, research on the multiple construction problems of the construction of the service center in old residential, from the angel of spatial equality. Analysis the design strategy of spatial planning, proposed that in case of limited land resource, we should set up per evaluation mechanism, configure and reconstruct areas of limited to achieve the continuation of the social structure and realization of the social value.

Keywords: Old residential, Public service center, Spatial equality, Space form

参考文献：

[1] 徐宁. 基于效率与公平视角的城市公共空间研究综述[C]. 多元与包容——2012 中国城市规划年会论文集(04. 城市设计)，2012.

[2] 戴德胜，姚迪，段进. 比较与重构——中外典型社区中心空间发展模式的调查研究[J]. 城市规划学刊，2013.6

[3] 江海燕，周春山，高军波. 西方城市公共服务空间分布的公平性研究进展[J]. 城市规划，2011：35-37.

[4] 陈竹，叶珉. 西方城市公共空间理论——探索全面的公共空间理念[J]. 城市规划，2009：33-36

[5] 路郑冉，戴铜，孙伟斌. 论城市社区空间形态营造[J]. 华中建筑，2014，11：171-173.

[6] 胡畔，张建召. 规划整合中的公共服务中心体系优化方法研究——从集约到均等的实证定量分析[C]. 多元与包容——2012 中国城市规划年会论文集(13. 城市规划管理)，2012.

[7] 姜洪庆. 基于社会结构转型过程中的规划方法思考——社区空间研究初探[J]. 城市规划，2010. 11：9-13

[8] 魏皓严. 社区中心的建设[J]. 规划师，2000，16(2)：112-115

[9] 王立，王兴中. 城市生活空间之力观下的社区体系规划原理[J]. 现代城市研究，2011，9.

[10] Xu Xin, Yu Wenbo, Yang Yuren. A Discussion on the Phenomenon of Non-Dependency of Community Facilities and Its Planning Countermeasures[J]. China City Planning Review, 2011, 20(1).

移民聚居区对城市空间活力影响研究——以大连市东关街为例

栾一斐[1]　周　博[2]

（1. 大连民族大学建筑学院；2. 大连理工大学建筑与艺术学院）

摘要： 随着现代化建设对城市改革要求的深化，城市的高速发展加剧了空间发展的不平衡。这种不平衡具体表现为日渐衰落的棚户区与城市新型现代化建设区所带来的城市效应的差距。城市外来移民通常利用社会网络聚居在城市衰落的边缘地带，这些边缘地带随之作为城市中一种新型的城市"第三空间"——移民聚居区，在城市中异军突起，其发展潜力不容小视。随着现代化城市建设的不断深入，城市中这种新兴的移民聚居区与城市建设发展区域的问题日益尖锐并逐渐升级为一种动态的矛盾，针对这些问题的研究对于城市空间的平衡发展尤为重要。本文以城市"第三空间"的移民聚居区为研究对象，结合道格·桑德斯的《落脚城市》中所提出的"移民聚居区是移民在城市中生存、流动的必要的城市空间"的理论，对大连市东关街的街区尺度的及空间句法的研究，分析和总结移民聚居区及其特有空间尺度及肌理模式对于城市空间活力的影响。

关键词： 移民聚居区，棚户区改造，城市空间平衡发展，城市空间影响力

1　引言

中国经济的高速发展使城市建设有了翻天覆地的变化。我们在逐步加快城市化进程的同时，也同样感受到城市所面对的各种有形和无形的压力。当大批量外来人口涌向城市而城市空间无法承受更多的负载时，这种压力就会从边缘空间寻求突破。中国近几年来不断涌现出"城中村"这样的聚集地。"城中村"现象并没有随着时间的推移而得到应有的改善，反而呈现日益加深的发展态势，其最主要的表现就是原有城市棚户区与城市外来流动人口结合，不断发展为了城市中的外来人口聚集地，使静态矛盾升级为动态矛盾。无论城市发展如何繁荣，依然始终无法回避该问题的存在。

西方社会相对发展中国家更早的地面对了城市化发展矛盾，他们应对此类城市中的移民聚居区的方式也更为理性，其中许多理论可以为我们现阶段对"城中村"或"城市孤岛"问题的研究提供一定的借鉴和启发。近年来最值得关注的理论由英国记者道格·桑德斯提出，他在《落脚城市》中写道："人类所做一切的城市化努力最终会导致人类彻底从乡间的农业生活移入城市，而外来人口利用城市网络进入城市的过程绝对不是一蹴而就的。"道格·桑德斯以实地考察的方式再次印证的简·雅各布斯在《美国大城市的死与生》中城市多样性的理论。具体说，城市在短期内形成的城市空间压力总会以特殊的形式得以释放，移民聚居区是乡村走向城市的必然产物，而城市规划者应该以更为理性和宽容的态度面对城市中的移民聚居区的存在。

2　移民聚居区的本质

移民聚居区多数是以城市为基础而言的。在过去，社会上涌现出许多与之相近的名字，例如"贫民窟"、"棚户区"、"城市边缘区"、"城中村"、"城市孤岛"、"落脚城市"等。这些名字在给人直观的想象之外，并没有深度解释该类区域的本质含义。另外，随着时间的推移，许多此类城市区域的定位也存在着改变，例如原本的"棚户区"与"城市边缘区"往往是原有城市空间发展不利的产物，其所承载的人群主要来源于城市中的固有生活于社会底层的居民。但随着时间的推移和经济体制的改革，这些地区渐渐被城市外来流动人群占据，或者以固有底层居民与外来人群相结合的形式呈现。此时，无论是"棚户区"还是"城中村"都不能完全概括新型城市的下这一类特殊区域的发展状态。

移民聚居区指的是由相同的移民通过社会关系迁移、聚居而成并在移民的迁徙过程中提供落脚

功能的或者说过渡功能的地区。桑德斯引用了 R·斯凯尔登（Ronald Skeldon）和 C·蒂利（Charles Tilly）对移民迁移活动的研究结论来阐释这一含义："斯凯尔特①通过对秘鲁库斯科的移民的研究发现，最早的移民通常都会先定居在城市的中心地区，过了数年以后，他们一旦在城市里站稳脚步，就会外移到城市边缘的新兴区域并形成聚居地。这种聚居地一旦形成，新的移民通常就会借助于乡族网络直接落脚于这些聚居地。蒂利指出，在迁徙目的地，连锁式移民通常也能够造就持久的社会关系，由相同出身的人口造成。最极端的情况下，这类移民会组成都市村庄。"② 理性来说，移民聚居区一种概念，而并非是对一种新名词的定义。当该区域在我国城市中的发展矛盾日益显著而又往往被忽略的同时，在新环境下对其概念的明晰是必不可少的。

3 大连市移民聚居区的形成原因

本文以大连市东关街作为移民聚居区的主要研究对象，大连市东关街为历史遗留街区，现已成为城市中心区域的典型移民聚集地，如图 1 所示。大连市的建市历史并不长，在清末民初时期才形成一定的人口数量，且来往此地多为一水之隔的山东人，是典型的移民城市。局数据统计，截至2015 年为止，大连市人口总数约为 670 万，其中山东省后裔仍占据 76.24% 之多。大连人的本土文化也受外来文化的影响，诸如在语言、文化、生活、习俗等方面都带有外地城市的印记。因为大连市本地人的父辈多为漂洋过海来连闯荡的外地人，所以将这一类人群叫做"海南丢"，隐含被茫茫大海以南的山东故土抛弃之意。虽然随着时间的推移，大连市已经形成一定的人口规模和自身特色，但是从城市历史文化角度来说，根植于历史记忆中的"海南丢"文化却没有消失。

图 1　现存东关街区域鸟瞰图
（图片来源：作者自摄）

就东关街而言，在近代历史上，大连市的规划版图受外来殖民统治的影响，被沙俄欧罗巴市街、行政市街和中国人市街，而东关街正处于中国人市街的核心。1900 年左右，大连正值城市建设初期，各区域招募一定的劳力，大批量的外来务工人员涌入大连市区，由于沙俄统治的市街不能够容纳中国人，中国人市街成为这些劳动人员的主要生存之所。随着这一人口数量的增加，外来务工人员在不断供应国外殖民主义者的建设活动之外，自身也慢慢发展成为一个庞大的聚落并展开一系列积极活动。为了满足聚落本身的经济、生活、娱乐的需要，东关街作为民族资本的发源地渐渐变得发达起来，其中不乏文化与商贾名人。但随着改革开放的到来，民族资本在城市各区得以均衡发展，东关街的辉煌也随之暗淡。许多在建市初期，建筑风格和质量都不如东关街的街区因为时代的

---

① 引文如此。斯凯尔特按规定应译为斯凯尔登。

② 道格·桑德斯. 落脚城市——最后的人类大迁徙和我们的未来 [M]. 陈信宏译. 上海：上海译文出版社. 2012。

必然淘汰反而有了较为成熟的更新。相比之下，一直停留在过去辉煌中的东关街日渐衰败下去。现有东关街的建筑仍具有一定规模，但是建筑质量较差，现已成为市区内典型的移民聚居区。从建市初期以来，其外来流动人口数据也随着历史的变迁发生着的明显的变化，如表1所示。

1905 年～今东关街街区建筑使用人群及使用情况   表 1

时间	使用人群主要来源	使用人群主要身份	建筑使用功能	外来人口比例
改革开放以前 （1905～1949）	山东、河北省务工人员及城市固有居民	商人、工人	商业、娱乐、生产、居住、医疗	约 65.5%
改革开放以后 （1949～2005）	城市固有市民	普通居民	商业、生产、居住	约 34.3%
近 10 年 （2005～今）	黑龙江、吉林、山东、河南省务工人员及城市固有居民	工人、普通居民	居住	约 78.6%

表格来源：根据大连市西岗区人口普查表及东关街现场调查问卷总结绘制。

基于大连的人口发源特点，东关街形成移民聚居区的主要原因有以下三点：

（1）位置处于城市中心

"可达性"和"易达性"是移居区的形成原因之一，外来城市移民者的核心目标是深入城市完成个人能力的自我实现。此时其所居住的地点距离意向城市越近，就越有利于目标的实现。反之而言，城市中心区域的薄弱环节更有发展成为移民聚居区的可能性。如果移民者将暂居地选择在城市周边或者郊区，则无法有利实现的深入城市的目的，此时的聚落也未能完成"城市化"的逆转，依然处于"城市"与"郊区"之间的尴尬状态。大连市西岗区为大连市的中心区域，而东关街又处于西岗区的核心部位，接近大连市繁华区域。其西距大连市火车站约 800m，距离人民广场大连市政府约 1000m，距离希望广场与中山广场约 2000m，在交通上十分便利。这给予外来务工人员接近城市中心和本土社会的可能。

（2）"廉价住房"实现落脚的可能性

根据对各个城市的移民聚居区的研究，在工作之外，能够获得廉价住宅是使我们现在所分析的地区对贫困移民产生吸引力的另一个因素。正如就业与邻近经济中心相关联，住宅和经济因素与空间整合度相关。现有东关街的建筑质量较差、环境较为恶劣，其住房租金也随之降低。根据统计，该区域住户平均住房费用不足 500 元/月，约为该区域其

图 2　东关街在大连市的区位
（图片来源：作者根据百度地图截图绘制）

他居住小区的平均租房成本的 1/5。廉价的住房成本给予外来务工人群暂居的便利，使他们在适应城市节奏之后进行下一步的调整和改变。

4　大连市移民聚居区的特点

（1）"暂居性"

阿尔瓦·阿尔托在《鲑鱼与山川》一文中写道："就像是大鲑鱼或鳟鱼。它们并非生而成熟，它们甚至并非出生在其正常生存的海洋或水体，它们出生在日常生存环境的千里之外。那里没有大江，只有小溪和山间闪烁的水体。"[①] 鲑鱼在河中出生，却来到大海中长大，如同所有置身社会的人们。极端来说，所有生活在城市中的人都具有暂居性，差别只是程度上的区分。如今选择来到东关街居住的居民多数为外来务工人员，这与东关街形成初期的情况相似。但是值得注意的是，过去移

---

① 何潇 . 阿尔瓦·阿尔托：芬兰的两张面孔 [J]. 三联生活周刊，2014.43.

民至此的外来人员已经发展为本地市民，其户口和生活都得以一定的保证，所有生活链条都已经稳定地扎根于城市。而如今移居东关街的民众往往是外来城市生活底层的人群，他们希望通过城市中的某个落脚点为跳板，能够谋求生活上的改变。根据东关街过去的历史发展模式来说，虽然该区域的人口随时可能"洗牌"，但是该区域的人口来源与去向已经形成了固有的模式，从该区域的人口流动方式可以看出，移民聚居区的本质就是移民迁徙到城市过程中的过渡性的空间。

（2）外来人口的"内聚力"

聚居区的形成，是一个单向的"内聚"的过程，封闭是形成移民社区的既有特征的基本原因。根据斯凯尔登和蒂利对移民迁移活动的研究结论：移民聚居地一旦形成，新的移民通常就会借助于家族网络直接落脚于这些聚居地。这也就形成了蒂利所称的"连锁式移民迁移活动"。大连市东关街的现有移民同样具有"连锁式移民前迁移活动"特征，而这种连锁式移民聚居地铸就了持久的社会关系，据统计，现有东关街的人群来源主要为黑龙江省、吉林省、山东省及河南省务工人员，在近十年的时间中，东关街的固有居民有所变动，但是人口来源却鲜有变化。可以看出，外来人口在将东关街作为移民据点的同时，也将它作为了子辈或者种族同乡来到城市的落脚点。

5　移民聚居区对于城市空间活力影响

（1）移民聚居区的空间尺度对于城市空间多样性的影响

街区尺度是影响城市空间活力重要因素，芦原义信在《街道的美学》中对于街道宽高比的研究中，街道的宽高比于是衡量街道宽高比例的尺度准则。根据研究显示，当 $D/H>1$ 时，超过 2 时则产生宽阔之感；当 $D/H<1$ 时，随着比值的减小会产生接近之感。在东关街街道的尺度研究中可以发现，主要存在着 3 种街道 D/H 尺度：

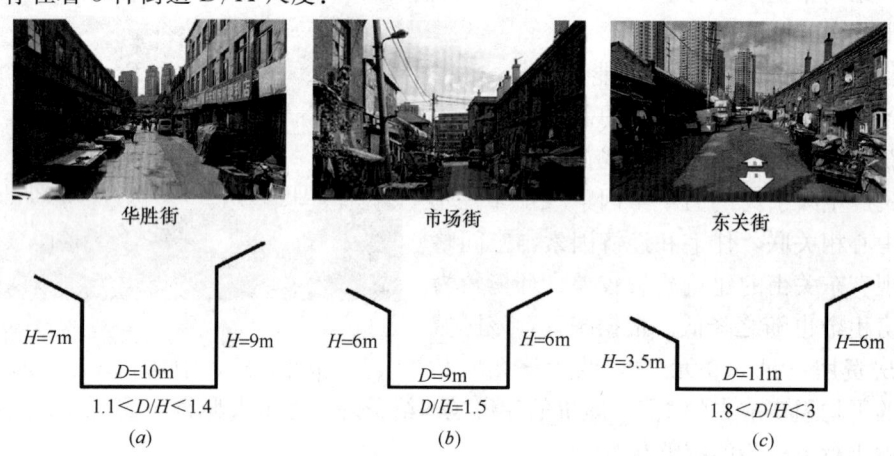

图 3　东关街街区空间的整合情况
（a）华胜街街道宽高比；（b）市场街街道宽高比；（c）东关街街街道宽高比
（图片来源：作者自摄、自绘）

东关街的街区 D/H 值多集中于 1.5 左右，相比城市的宽阔马路，这种街道尺度提供给人们一种难得的亲切感。在一种体系中，建筑是围绕街道服务的，街道不只是通行的道路，还是城市生活的场所，它具有围合性，实际上是属于室外的起居室。而另一个体系中，街道是为建筑服务的，是起串联作用的。街道的生活功能被弱化了，失去了人情，室外是一个空旷的，无限延伸的地方。越小型越弱级的街道恰恰是城市生活、城市文化最好的繁衍地。[①] 在这里，东关街的移民聚居区的空间尺度为城市空间多样性提供了更大的可能。

---

① 昝兒 . 街道生活［J］. 知乎周刊 . 总第 021 期 .

（2）移民聚居区空间整合度对于城市空间影响

劳拉·沃恩在《城市环境中物质隔离与社会边缘化的关系》一文中提到，"上层阶级位于整合度高于平均水平的街区，也就是街道体系中最容易到达的部分，而底层的人则居住在低于平均整合度的区域，也就是不那么容易到达的街道。空间句法以前的研究中发现了以下结论。整合度高的街道容易容纳城市中活跃的经济和社会活动如果认为主要街道构成了街区的全部空间结构，也就是空间句法的研究表明这些街道与城市的经济活跃区紧密相关。"① 通过对东关街的空间句法研究，同样可以得出相应的结论。东关街街区排布方式遵循建市初期俄国人对于中国街市做的总体规划，街区排列围合而完整，我们可以看到，即便经过百年的历史变迁，这种完整合度极高的街区形式并没有得到破坏。然而，这些围合完整的街区内部却存在着大批改建或者扩建的建筑，与其外部形成强烈的对比，如图 4 所示。

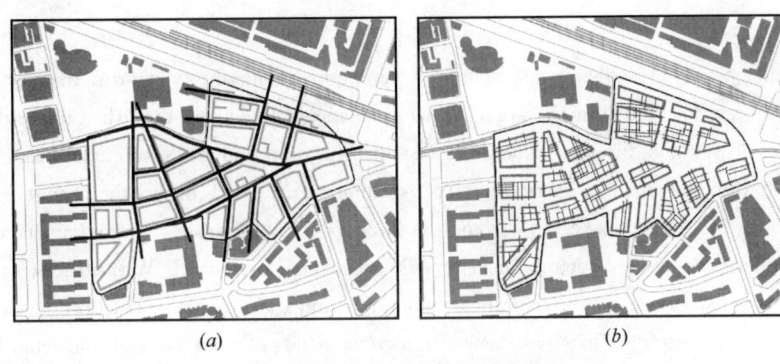

图 4　东关街街区空间的整合情况

（a）街区内部第一层级的整合度示意；（b）街区内部第二层级的整合度示意

（图片来源：作者自绘）

我们发现在整合度较高的外部街区，其建筑性质也更为开放和多样，建筑用途也不单单是居住，也有饭店、修缮、快递收发等多种对外用途。而在街区内部，则是形式复杂的住居，建筑肌理呈现自发增长的态势。对于街区肌理自发生长的模式并不是东关街独有，在哈尔滨道外靖宇街、武汉青山区工人村等多处都有存在。在过去，部分学者与政府规划部门对于这些区域呈"分坏而合好"的态度，即在不破坏总体整合度极高的街区之外，大肆掏空街区内部的增减建筑。我们可以发现的影响就是，如同大自然中的食物链一样，被清除的贫民窟周边地区在市场中显著贬值——空间变化引起连锁反应，而空间组织的改善并没有对下层阶级带来多大影响，他们还是会城市夹缝中得到生长，但是不同的是，再次生长带来了空间组织的分散，由于阶级等级的不同，分散的移民者势必与原有稳定的城市居民发生矛盾。这种矛盾从另外一个角度上可以说明，移民聚居区内部肌理增长在一定程度上对于城市中的高度稳定空间是有益的，然而这种增长规律和模式应该具有适度性。一旦在移民聚居区内部发生肌理的持续疯长，则依然会打破原有组织链条，而现实中则会增加一定的安全隐患。理性来说，城市规划者应该更为细致地引导移民聚居区内部的扩建行为，而不是大肆破坏和销毁内部建筑空间。

6　总结

本文以大连市东关街为例，系统说明了一个移民聚居区的形成原因、发展特点，并且通过大连市东关街的街区尺度的及空间句法的研究，总结了移民聚居区及其特有空间尺度及肌理模式对于城市空间活力的影响。文章最后总结得出，类聚以及相对完整的区域对于移民群体十分重要，这使他

---

① 劳拉·沃恩．城市环境中物质隔离与社会边缘化的关系 [J]．世界建筑，2005.11.

们能够有进一步在经济和社会上发展的可能，合理规划而非破坏聚居区的复杂肌理组织是必要的。

The Study of the Immigrants' District Effect on Urban Space Vitality Illustrated by the Case of Dalian Dongguan Block

Luan Yifei[1]，Zhou Bo[2]

（1. Dalian Nationality University；2. Dalian University of technology）

Abstract：As the deepening of modern construction on the requirements of city reform，the city's rapid update exacerbates the unbalanced development of urban space. This imbalance embodies in the urban effect differential brought by the declining shanty towns and the construction of new urbanization and modernization area. Urban immigrants through social networks often inhabit in the brink of city's declining area which brings the change from quantitative to qualitative in the city. As a result，these areas become the late-model "third space" -immigrant communities in urban city with unexpected emergency and its potential development cannot be overlooked. With the deepening of the modern city construction，the problem in the new immigrant communities and the urban construction development area is becoming sharper and gradually upgrading to a dynamic contradiction. Study of these issues is particularly important to the balanced development of urban space. This thesis focuses on the immigrants' district concentrated area as the research object，combined with Saunders D.'s theory that immigrants' concentrated community is the necessary urban space for their living and flowing in the city proposed in his Arrival City. Based on the research on block scale and space syntax of Dalian Dongguan Street，this thesis summarizes the effect of immigrants' concentrated community and its unique spacial scale and fabric on the city spacial vitality.

Keywords：Immigrants' district，Reconstruction of slum areas，Fair space in city，The influence of city space

参考文献：

[1]　道格·桑德斯. 落脚城市———最后的人类大迁徙与我们的未来[M]. 陈信宏译. 上海：上海译文出版社，2012.

[2]　尹海洁，高云红. 作为城市"第三空间"的移民聚居区———来自《落脚城市》的启示[J]. 理论月刊杂志，2015.02

[3]　劳拉·沃恩. 城市环境中物质隔离与社会边缘化的关系[J]. 世界建筑，2005.11

[4]　雅各布斯. 美国大城市的死与生[M]. 金衡山译. 江苏：译林出版社，2005.

[5]　Magnusson W. Seeing Like a State，Seeing Like a City. In Annual Meeting of the Canadian Political[M] Science Association，University of British Columbia，Vancouver. 2008.

[6]　黑川纪章. 城市革命[M]. 徐苏宁，吕飞译. 北京：中国建筑工业出版社，2011.

[7]　郭春林. 日本社区营造的启示[J]. 中州建设，2011.09

[8]　Colin Clark. The Conditions of Economic Progress. California：Mcmillan. 1957

[9]　西村幸夫. 再造魅力故乡日本传统街区重生故事[M]. 王惠君译. 北京：清华大学出版社，2007.

Housing Diversity in Transitional Suburban China: A Study of Songjiang, Shanghai

Sea Eun Cho[1], Saehoon Kim[2]

(1. Interdisciplinary Program in Landscape Architecture, Seoul National University; 2. Graduate School of Environmental Studies, Seoul National University)

Abstract: This study discusses the issues related to housing diversity, especially in the case of Songjiang, and illustrates the different levels of diversity of two study areas by using the entropy index. China presents an interesting case of discussion regarding both the suburbanisation process and urban diversity, which fundamentally differs from the Western discourse in terms of how it is manifested and its urban implications. In particular, housing diversity in China can be considered to be almost a laissez faire condition relevant to the rapid economic and housing reforms since 1980s. Hence, this study attempted to understand how in actuality housing diversity is evidenced in two areas of Songjiang, as the basis for further in-depth investigation of urban implications of diversity.

Keywords: Housing diversity, Diversity index, Chinese suburb, Urban characteristics

1 Introduction

The issue of urban diversity is a multi-faceted issue discussed in many academic fields, including social sciences, economics and urban planning. Naturally, for each of the different academic realms the issues and implications of diversity differ. In urban design and planning, the notion of diversity was first discussed by Jane Jacobs through her seminal work "The Death and Life of Great American Cities (1961)" whereby mixed land-use, building age, scale and building-use was attributed in creating urban vibrancy[1], which are argued to positively influence economic productivity and social diversity. Feinstein also concerned with the concept of a just city and social diversity, differentiated "urban diversity" in terms of the physical form/place aspect and the social aspect[2,3]. From this point of view, housing diversity is considered to be of a unique matter because it is closely related to social diversity whilst embodying inherently physical aspects, acting as a key element in describing a particular community or an area's diversity. Against this background, this study aims to discuss some of the issues surrounding housing diversity and through the illustration of two areas in Songjiang, Shanghai discuss the general attributes of different levels of housing diversity present in the study areas.

2 Literature Review

Insofar, the value of housing diversity or housing mix has been recognized as means to achieve social diversity, although the focus of research may vary according to different national contexts. Studies conducted in US mainly recognize social mix as a measure of socioeconomic diversity and relates this issue to racial integration, further supporting the idea of housing mix. In UK the notion of social exclusion is made prominent which is discussed as a negative consequence of neoliberalism, by which policy initiatives not only aim to overcome housing issues but also tackle other social concerns such as poverty, drug use and school drop-out rates[4]. In both cases, achieving social diversity is a core objective and within this framework housing mix or diversity is pursued.

Despite such propensity to link housing diversity to social diversity, there are only a small number of empirical studies that prove such relationship. More interestingly, discussions surrounding diversity is inherently associated with social values whichcomplicate this already multi-faceted notion, and although there have been studies that investigate urban and social diversity this topic is yet to be fully tackled by urban design researchers[5,6,7].

Housing diversification in China is of a different nature compared to that of the West. Housing diversity was not promoted to encourage social diversity *per se*, but social diversity occurred first as a consequence of economic and housing reforms which in turn caused housing diversification. A large number of cities in China have experienced an influx of migrants due to its thriving economy and had also undergone a process of neighborhood composition transition from 'danwei' to 'xiaoqu' where people started to choose and pay for where they live rather than being assigned to where they live[8]. Furthermore, the Chinese government also actively experimented with housing diversification in the 1980s and onwards to improve housing environments responding to the changed living standards and demands of the Chinese people[9]. Hence, different social strata abruptly emerged due to the modernizing process in China and in turn housing diversification followed.

Thus, a completely different nature and case of diversity exists in China. Taking into consideration that diversity needs to be understood in terms of specific institutional and local contexts, this study aims to focus on two areas in Songjiang, a suburban city located 40km away from Shanghai city, to understand the urban implications of what this type of diversity might represent. One way of achieving this may be through measuring different levels of diversity. For this study, the basic spatial unit of measurement is the individual residential complex or apartment complex, and the aspects to diversity measurement are year of build, total number of households, floor area ratio and green ratio.

The mix of old and new properties has been identified as being a key aspect of housing diversity in previous studies since it relates to the different levels of housing affordability. Thus, looking at the year of build of different properties is considered to be a good indication of diversity. The total number of households is a measure indicative of physical housing diversity, since a wide range of size and scale of residential complexes pose very different impacts on the urban environment. For instance, a complex that only accommodates for less than 100 households is evidently different from that which houses more than 3, 000 households. Similarly, the differences in the floor area ratio in conjunction with the green ratio indicate the varying degrees of density of the built environment.

3　Research Method

3.1　Study Area

Suburbs in Shanghai are unique in that it is physically and socially a heterogeneous environment, which is undeniably different from its Western counterparts. The suburbs in Shanghai are well connected through public transportation, have mid to high-rise residential buildings and various housing types, are built to relatively high densities and accommodate for people with diverse socioeconomic backgrounds. There are people with moderate income level, recent migrant workers from the surrounding rural areas and the more affluent white collar workers who commute to the city centre of Shanghai[10]. Such characteristics of the suburbs in Shanghai are in stark contrast to the often criticized monotonous, low-rise, low-density suburbs of the West.

The study areas of housing diversity are two districts in Songjiang, namely Jiuting and the oldcity centre which is part of the New City (xincheng) development. Songjiang xincheng is an area strategically developed through the '1966 Plan' of Shanghai which in effect is a suburban urbanization development strategy. Formerly, an agricultural county, Songjiang transformed into an industrial satellite town during the 1990s, and in the 2000s various projects were constructed including the Thames Town project and also the university city area where seven universities are located in pursuit of the "Advance the Nation through Science and Education, and Keep Pace with the Times" strategy[11].

Meanwhile, Jiuting zhen, which borders Minhang district and is closest to the Shanghai city centre, is an important area as it was the hottest real estate site since the 1990s due to the first wave of displaced inner-city residents entering the area[4]. Jiuting continues to be the preferred area of residence for those commuting to Shanghai today, and is the home for many young families and professionals. The locational advantages created by the No. 9 Metro line seems to be most apparent in Jiuting where significant population increase has been recorded. According to the Songjiang statistical yearbook, the number of residential groups administrated by these committees increased from 44 in 2003 to 1, 089 in 2013.

To summarise, both the old city centre encompassed in the xincheng development, and Jiuting are areas representative of "consumption-centered lifestyle" and are the results of the development styles of the 2000s[4]. This research focuses on the burgeoning area of Jiuting as a place where diverse socio-demographic characteristics are recognized, and the old city as a site where a mixture of original and new developments are present.

(a)　　　　　　　　　　　　　　　　　　　　(b)

Figure 1　Example of a large residential development in Jiuting

(a) The entrance to the development with guards; (b) Driveway through the development

3. 2　Measuring diversity

The data used to measure diversity for this study were collated from the Soufun website. This particular website was chosen based on the knowledge that Soufun is one of the main property information providers in China and is known for its extensive database. The research excluded any properties with incomplete information (i. e. , cases where any of the four diversity aspect information were missing) and collected in total, 67 cases for Jiuting and 35 cases for the old city centre of Songjiang. The relevant information then was sorted into the following categories shown in Table 1.

List of categories for each of the diversity aspect　　　　　　　　**Table 1**

Diversity aspect	Categories
Year of Build	Pre-2000/2000 – 2004/2005 – 2009/post-2010
Total number of households	Less than 500 households/500 – 999/1000 – 1499/1500 – 1999/2000 – 2499/More than 2500 households
Floor area ratio	Less than 0. 50/0. 50 – 1. 00/1. 00 – 1. 50/1. 50 – 2. 00/More than 2. 00
Green ratio	Less than 30%/30% – 35%/35 – 40%/45 – 50%/More than 50%

In order to measure diversity, the entropy index which is derived from information theory and frequently used in population segregation studies, was used as shown in Equation (1):

$$h_i = -\sum_{j=1}^{k} p_{ij} \ln(p_{ij}) \tag{1}$$

In which　k——number of groups;

p_{ij}——proportion of population of jth ethnicity in tract i;

n_{ij}——number of population jth ethnicity in tract i;

n_i——total number of population in tract i;

For this study, the standardized value of the entropy index was used as this allows for a more intuitive understanding of the values. This is because the maximum value of the entropy index depends on the number of categories and is calculated by taking the natural logarithm of the total number of categories.

The minimum standardized entropy index value of 0 indicates absolute homogeneity meaning that only one category exists. The maximum value indicates heterogeneity meaning that for all categories there is even distribution. For this study, the standardized entropy index value ranging from 0. 5 – 0. 75 is interpreted as showing average heterogeneity, and values higher than 0. 75 is considered as showing high levels of heterogeneity.

4　Results

4. 1　Basic description of data

In terms of year of build, properties built between 2005 and 2009 is most common in Jiuting which accounts for roughly 40% of total cases (n=27). In the old city centre, the post-2010 period represented the highest number of cases accounting for approximately 43% of total cases, which was followed by the 2000 – 2004 period. Hence, it can be presumed that the old city area went through high levels of development during the start of the 2000s, and this level of construction returned after 2010, whereas in Jiuting there was consistent level of development since the 2000s.

For the total number of households, both areas show very similar tendencies where residential complexes with less than 1, 000 households are dominant. In Jiuting, complexes with households less than 499 comprise the majority accounting for roughly 45% of total cases, which is then followed by the 500 – 1, 000 households category. This propensity is also apparent in the old city centre. However, the stark differences between these two areas are that Jiuting also has very large complexes, where there are 7 cases recorded for the more than 2, 500 household category. In the old city centre, there are generally not many cases above the 1, 000 household category.

When comparing the floor area ratio, in Jiuting approximately 31% of cases (n=21) are recorded for the 0.5-1.0 category. In fact, in Jiuting, residential complexes are relatively evenly distributed across all FAR categories higher than 0.5. In contrast to this, there are no cases with FAR less than 1.00 in the old city centre. The dominant category is 1.50-2.00 and there are 8 cases that record for FARs higher than 2.00, which is compellingly more than that of Jiuting (n=4).

In terms of green ratio, for Jiuting the highest numbes of cases belong to the category of more than 50%. This is then followed by the 40%-45% category which is only one case more than the 45%-50% category. Overall in Jiuting, the majority of properties have a green ratio that is higher than 40%. However, as for the old city area the 35%-40% category takes up almost 43% of cases, and is followed by the 30%-35% category showing generally low levels of green ratio in properties.

4.2 Diversity index results

Theresults of the entropy index and the standardized values are shown in Table 2. In this section, only the standardized entropy index value is discussed. Overall, both areas showed relatively high levels of diversity where Jiuting scored remarkably high in all four aspects, compared to that of the old city area. The lowest entropy index value in Jiuting was at 0.852 for the total number of households, which is still a considerably high value indicating high levels of heterogeneity. The highest entropy index score was 0.924 for the green ratio, whilst both the year of build and floor area ratio scored similarly at 0.906 and 0.903 respectively. Hence, based on this particular dataset, Jiuting represents an extremely heterogeneous housing environment.

For Songjiang old city, the floor area ratio shows the lowest entropy index value at 0.625, comparatively indicating a more homogeneous aspect. This particular diversity aspect is where the two study areas differ the most because Jiuting scored a very high value of 0.903. On the other hand, in the old city centre, the year of build scored highest at 0.879 indicating a high level of diversity, but this is in fact comparable to the lowest entropy index value of Jiuting (0.852, total number of households). This was closely followed by the green ratio (0.836), and then the total number of households (0.730).

Comparingacross the different diversity aspects, the biggest difference between the levels of diversity were shown by the FAR and the total number of households. This indicates that there are different characteristics to the urban density and size of residential complexes. Whilst the FAR is evenly distributed in Jiuting indicating a mix of both low and high densities, the residential complexes in the old city are concentrated in the higher FAR categories suggesting a more densely built-up area. It is also interesting that whilst from the basic data description, the overall tendency of the total number of households overlap, there are actually different levels of diversity for the two areas. Again, Jiuting seems to have a more even distribution among the different sizes of residential complexes, whereas the old city shows higher concentration of properties that accommodates for less than 1,000 households.

Diversity index values　　　　　　　　　　　　　　　　　　　**Table 2**

Diversity aspect	Jiuting		Songjiang old city	
	H (x)	H' (x)	H (x)	H' (x)
Year of Build	1.256	0.906	1.219	0.879
Total number of households	1.526	0.852	1.308	0.730
Floor area ratio	1.453	0.903	1.006	0.625
Green ratio	1.656	0.924	1.498	0.836

5 Conclusions

In conclusion, the two areasinterestingly differ on several points. First, it seems that the xincheng master plan and its construction in the early 2000s had sparked immediate development in the old city area which was resumed again after 2010. This may be due to a deliberate phased type of development employed by the urban government or it could also be that there were external conditions acting on the development process. Careful speculations can be made that because of the real-estate bubble anticipations, cautious behavior was taken from the supply side in this area. However, it seems that this was not the case in Jiuting where Year of Build showed very high levels of diversity indicating that housing development was consistent in all categories of period.

Another interesting point is that despite the preconceived notion that Jiuting, being a developer-led area with fewer constraints of land use, might suffer from hodgepodge development, this does not seem to be the case. In fact, the total number of households and the total area of site show very similar patterns with the old city.

However, Jiuting shows extremely high diversity index values for FAR, whereas the old city scores the lowest for this particular aspect. This probably indicates that thereis a higher mix of low-density properties in Jiuting, which may be in the form of apartment-villa mixed residential complexes or villa only complexes. These villa properties are indicative of upper middle-class residents and this probably contribute towards the high levels of diversity for green ratio in Jiuting as well. However, this is not to say that there aren't these type of properties also in the old city, but it seems that they are provided to lesser extents. It is unclear whether this is because the demand for these properties are less in the old city area, because from previous studies resident income levels for the two areas do not differ greatly, or if it is related to the government-led development mode.

As a conclusive comment, it needs to be said that although Soufun is considered to be one of the most comprehensive websites on properties' information in China, there are obvious possibilities of data error. Also, although this research searched through all the properties listing for the study areas from Soufun, there were limited number of cases that had all the relevant diversity aspect information resulting in a relatively small sample size. However, it needs to be stressed that these diversity measures were employed to "illustrate" an overview of the study areas, and to tentatively affirm the conceived characteristics of these areas.

In future, a more robust database could be constructed including an extensive list of diversity aspects-such as the number of different household layouts, the actual building block characteristics, and the comparison between residential complexes and the surrounding urban blocks-that may allow in-depth comparative investigations of these two areas. Based on a full understanding of the different aspects of housing diversity further research opportunities may arise such as investigating the relationship between socialand housing diversity. This may enable further understanding on why and to what extent urban diversity should be considered as a favorable condition.

Acknowledgements

This work was supportedby the BK21 Plus Project in 2015 (Seoul National University Interdisciplinary Program in Landscape Architecture, Global leadership program towards innovative green infrastructure).

关于中国居住区居住类型多样性的特性研究

Sea Eun Cho[1]，Saehoon Kim[2]

（1. 景观建筑跨学科项目，首尔国立大学；2. 环境科学研究生院，首尔国立大学）

摘要：本论文是针对上海松江的两个地区运用熵指数（entropy index）测定居住多样性的研究。中国区别于西方国家呈现郊外化现象和城市内多样性的发展，这在城市设计侧面来说是有趣味的事例。所以本论文在城市内的多样性中限定居住多样性根据建筑时期、社区人口、社区面积、容积率、绿化率来指标化多样性的程度来考察两个地区之间的特性。

关键词：居住类型多样性，多样性指数，中国郊区，城市特征

References：

[1] Jacobs J. The death and life of great American cities[M]. New York：Random House，1961.

[2] Fainstein S S. Cities and Diversity：Should We Want It? Can We Plan For It? [J]. Urban Affairs Review，2005，41(1)：3-19.

[3] Fainstein S S. The just city[M]. New York：Cornell University Press，2010.

[4] Shen J. Suburban Development in Shanghai：A Case of Songjiang [D]. Cardiff：Cardiff University，2011.

[5] Blanco H，Alberti M，Forsyth A，et al. Hot，congested，crowded and diverse：Emerging research agendas in planning[J]. Progress in Planning，2009，71(4)：153-205.

[6] Talen E. Design for diversity：evaluating the context of socially mixed neighbourhoods[J]. Journal of Urban Design，2006，11(1)：1-32.

[7] Talen E. Neighborhood-Level Social Diversity：Insights from Chicago[J]. Journal of the American Planning Association，2006，72(4)：431-446.

[8] Bray D. Social space and governance in urban China：The danwei system from origins to reform[M]. California：Stanford University Press，2005.

[9] Lü J，Rowe P G，Zhang J. Modern urban housing in China，1840-2000[M]. Munich：Prestel Pub，2001.

[10] Johnston C. Housing policy and social mix：an exploratory paper. Shelter NSW [DB/OL]. [2002]. http：// www. shelternsw. infoxchange. net. au/docs/ rpt02socialmix-sb. pdf.

[11] Tongji University. Survey of Songjiang and the Evolution of Songjiang New City Planning[2]. // Zhenliang Wang，Jiafeng Liu. A Classic Planning of New City in China. Shanghai：Tongji University，2003：1-19.

台北市安康公共出租住宅的参与式规划及其政策含义

慕思勉

（财团法人台湾大学建筑与城乡研究发展基金会）

摘要：近年持续高涨的房价使得台北市的公共出租住宅的供给浮现为最重要的住宅政策，为了解决过去低收入家户集中居住所造成的负面效果，新的公共住宅以高质量建设环境、周边小区共享的公共设施以及社会混居为主要目标。然而，社会混居的含义与做法尚有待探讨，本文以安康公共住宅的参与式规划为例，以低收入家户生活与空间需求之调查为主，经过居民、专家学者、公共部门等之参与讨论后，研究拟定五项社会混居主要议题，包括社会网络、公共空间与社会互动、弱势社群的生活支持、社会资本与社会企业、租户与第三部门参与的管理机制建立等。社会混居表达了对建立社会融合与包容的小区的期待，需要充分考虑住户特性与需求，发展多样社会计划，促进相互认识与认同的机会，考虑更多居民可积极参与以及第三部门投入管理机制的建立为主要政策建议方向。

关键词：台北市公共住宅，社会混居，小区营造，参与式规划

1 前言

台湾近几年房价持续高涨，年轻人越来越不容易在都会区购屋，许多社会团体组成社会住宅推动联盟，要求政府重视居住人权问题，并要求由公共部门供给足够数量之社会住宅。台北市公有住宅存量仅占全市住宅存量之 0.6%，低于临近日本（6.1%）、韩国（6.1%，含兴建中）、新加坡（3%）等国家和中国香港地区（30%）之平均水平。[1]政府响应民间的要求，2011 年制订《住宅法》，其中第三条关于社会住宅的定义为："指由政府兴办或奖励民间兴办，专供出租之用，并应提供至少百分之十以上比例出租予具特殊情形或身份者①之住宅"。台北市于 2010 年开始推动社会住宅，预定场地的周边居民普遍持反对意见，认为社会住宅将影响小区环境质量与治安恶化，导致房价下跌。市府以高规格工程质量与建筑意象，提供周边小区可共享的多元公共与商业设施，以及社会混居的原则作为响应。其中，社会混居即是将青年住户与弱势、低收入住户混合居住，青年住户指年龄满 20 岁未满 46 岁之市民，各类所得数据清单在 50% 分位点以下（2012 年度为家庭年收入在新台币 148 万元以下），弱势家户则指依住宅法或社会局认定之低收入家户。

然而，在社会混居原则下如何让不同的居民皆能安居，尚缺乏充足讨论与更细致的政策规划。社会混居仅是让低收入户不易被辨识，以减少歧视或被标签，抑或存在更积极的社会效果？社会混合是否即代表社会互动与融合的自然发生？不同收入、身份的居民是否存在潜在矛盾，使公共住宅成为冲突之地？更根本的，本文关注公共住宅仅是政府提供住宅单元由市民承租的空间单位，抑或是另一种类型的"小区"？本文以安康公共住宅计划为例，探讨上述问题，即混居模式公共住宅可能产生的问题以及解决问题之方法，作为社会混居政策研究拟定的实行参考。

2 文献探讨

社会混合（social mix）已成为许多国家与城市推动公共住宅的重要方向，主因在于过去低收入

---

① 依据第四条具特殊情形或身份乃指以下其中之一，包括低收入户、特殊境遇家庭、育有未成年子女三人以上、于安置教养机构或寄养家庭结束安置无法返家、未满二十五岁、六十五岁以上之老人、受家庭暴力或性侵害之受害者及其子女、身心障碍者、感染人类免疫缺乏病毒或罹患后天免疫缺乏症候群者、原住民、灾民、游民、其他经上级主管机关认定者等。

户集中小区所衍生之被标签、歧视、社会隔离等诸多问题。因此，社会混居作为社会融合政策的一环，期望城市或住宅开发过程中能够容纳多样所得家户共同居住。[2]社会混合的实质形式上，为在开发项目中将销售房与出租之公共住宅混合组成新的小区。其基本目标不仅在于提升实质环境质量，更期望促进社会互动，以维持良好的生活质量与小区运作。从形塑小区（community building）的观点，社会混合的公共住宅被赋予诸多期待，包括新颖的公共住宅建筑意象；借助与较高收入家户的互动，增加低收入家户的社会资本；改变低收入家户的行为模式；建立主流社会规范或以较高收入者作为学习对象；期待较高收入者联结外部政治资源与维系住宅市场价值等。[3]然而，这些期待未必皆能落实，有些研究认为社会混居仅是政策上的修辞，忽略了多样社会与族群组成所隐藏的小区张力。维系小区的规范经常以中产阶级的文化、社会价值与小区整合的逻辑，强加于低收入户身上以至于在管理制度、小区成员内部之间衍生新的标签化问题。[4]或者，社会混居稀释了低收入家户的文化认同，破坏了社会网络，削弱其潜在政治力量。[5]

为了营造社会混合的小区，需要在实质空间与设施、居民本身、管理制度等各方面的规划策略。社会混居最大的困难在于居民本身既存的偏见，如何改变居民的意识是关键，初期推动将出售住宅与公共出租住宅分开但邻近街廓配置为宜，政府必须投入资源于出租住宅的设施与管理，提供与邻近小区可共享的社会福利设施与儿童游戏空间等，待社会逐渐改变对出租住宅的印象后，再推动同一基地的社会混居。[2]在实质空间的设计上，外观上的一致性、可共享的公共空间或设施等户外空间以及小区活动中心等，以增加居民的非正式互动，并建立使用方式、目的以及管理的共识。另一策略为提供经济与生活适应自立的服务与支持，包括个案管理与咨询、财务能力与家务管理辅导、就业的教育与辅导等，其中包括年轻人的价值观、长远的学习与规划等。[3]管理上，透过正式住户管理公约与监督制度与非正式的工具，规范可接受的社会行为，以及在规划、决策与治理过程中建立居民参与机制。[3]管理上过去由政府主导，渐渐走向鼓励小区的参与，培养住户的房东意识。[6]以及第三部门的角色应受到重视，不论是在慈善、救济、发展、政治行动与特定利益辩护等可扮演重要角色，发展赋权的活化小区计划。[7]对低收入小区而言，借助与专业者的合作，组织自己的非营利团体，维持小区相近的收入，培植小区的政治基础，维持丰富且多样性的文化认同为社会住宅发展可发展的方向。[5]

以上经验研究脉络虽与台北市的政策未尽相同，但这些研究指出社会混合的理想小区假设，在实务中社会混合并非即代表社会融合或小区的自然发生，牵涉混居的方式与低收入家户社会网络、实质的空间设计、管理制度以及管理主体等之细致设计。

3　研究对象与研究方法

研究对象为台北市安康平宅改建为公共住宅计划，安康平宅兴建于1975年，为社会福利措施的一环，共计11栋四层建筑，分散在9个街廓，面积约3.52hm²。入住对象为社会局认定之低收入家户。现住户共771户，人口共2486人，老年人、幼儿、在校学生人口比例偏高。因建筑逐渐损坏，且存在住户缺乏脱贫动力、标签化、有些家户亲职功能不彰、青少年辍学吸毒等诸多问题，台北市乃计划拆除既有建筑，分期改建为公共出租住宅。计划特性包括：为了取得更多居住单元，将土地使用强度从原225%容积调升为450%，最高约28层楼高；其次是社会混居，未来计划容纳3300余家户，其中三分之二提供青年住户，另外三分之一则作为低收入住户，安康原住户优先入住。租金方面，青年住户的房价为附近房价的七折；低收入户的租金由社会局研究拟定，以低于市价四成方向规划中。租期方面，青年住户的租期最长可至五年。低收入户若持续具有社会局认定的低收入身份则可持续居住。

本文内容为安康平宅改建计划规划行动的一环①，透过社会参与式规划，将安康小区居民、非营利组织、公共部门、现有青年住户、专家等纳入在问题探究的过程，使用的研究工具包括：（1）小区工作站的建立，理解居民日常生活，建立讨论公共事务网络。（2）现有低收入住户空间使用状况的观察与访谈。（3）召开各类工作坊，邀请上述关系人的参与，建立对话平台，讨论关于居民互动与邻里空间、公共设施、社会混居、维护管理等各项议题。借助上述意见之收集以及与市府各部门政策衔接的行政座谈后，汇整出可行的政策与空间规划建议。

4　议题讨论

4.1　标签化、小区网络与社会混居

在调查期间发现外围居民对安康小区确实存在负面观感，包括"不太敢进入安康小区""贫民窟"、"影响房价"、"丐帮"等形容用语。在驻地工作站的小区日常观察中，亦发现有游民酒醉躺楼梯间、精神障碍者赤裸上身发病大叫、夜晚隐藏角落的吸毒者、少年犯罪与少女怀孕、夜晚青少年在篮球场聚集等诸多问题。有些孩童在学校被老师或同学歧视，有些人在职场被同事语言嘲讽等，显示安康居民普遍有被外部小区标签化、歧视的经验。歧视亦存在于小区内部，如对外籍配偶或原住民等弱势少数的歧视。育有子女的家长普遍存在不安全感，教导孩子不要与小区其他小孩互动或到公共空间玩耍。但小区并非都是负面的，亦有一般小区所不常见的邻里网络与互助情谊，如协助照顾邻居幼儿、帮忙安抚精神疾病发作欲轻生的住户、协助照顾因伤无法行动的独居长者等，弥补了正式社会福利输送所不及之处。

未来安康公共出租住宅的混居模式，采取随机抽签决定入住单元，将安康家户分散在更多的年轻家户之中，以改善上述问题。但在高楼化的居住模式下，上述小区网络不易维系。因此，规划策略建议混居采每一楼层配置多样化家户为基本原则，使得不同世代、不同家庭类型家户可以混居。较低楼层应优先考虑高龄者与身体障碍者的需求，家有精神障碍者的家户较倾向居住在较安静的区位，可考虑3楼以上至中楼层。年轻家户的移动能力相对较佳，对小区公共空间的依赖亦相对较低，可配置于较高楼层。

除了随机抽签的选择外，亦应细致考虑小区网络的形成。针对家户之间已建立的良好互助网络，若住户有意愿，应提供可共同抽签选择居住单元的机会。此外，应尝试新的居住文化形成的可能性，如组成不同的居住成员，发展"共居"文化，即将有意愿的单身长者、小家庭、身体障碍家户等组织在同一楼层，提供公共空间，鼓励自力维护环境质量、组织共食活动等，在逐渐少子化、高龄化社会趋势下，营造相互照顾包容的居住文化。

4.2　公共空间与社会互动

现有安康小区为低楼层小区，除了夜晚的后巷、篮球场成为吸毒、聚众喧哗等之外，一楼不同开放空间提供多样居民互动机会。未来公共住宅增加居住单元数量，朝向高层化发展。在高层化的环境中，儿童、老人、身体障碍者等，在心理上存在与地面活动的距离感。除了提供楼层的选择机会外，高层化环境中高低不一的户外平台空间，可作为住户晒棉被、散步、运动、乘凉、儿童游戏、大人种花种菜的多样化活动发生的空间，有助于身心健康与邻里互动的促进。但这类空间亦可能为视觉死角，需要加强管理以及居民参与管理的机制建立。此外，地面层的儿童游戏场、户外开放空间亦为促进住户自然接触互动的空间。

---

① 本研究为公营住宅小区社会参与式设计规划案的部分内容，由市政府委托，规划期间为2013年5月～2014年6月。

　　另一公共空间议题为既有建筑纹理是否需要全部拆除，平宅象征了20世纪70年代为了解决快速都市化衍生违建住房的福利政策施为。从建筑类型的角度，安康平宅建筑的配置特性为半室外直行楼梯与四户组成的4拼公寓住宅。一楼的梯间特性为穿透的通廊，联结两侧街道，因场地坡度，两侧通廊入口形成阶梯或平台空间。阶梯空间成为住户可驻足聊天的地方，平台空间则与行道树形成小型休憩空间，使用电动代步车的身障者亦可无障碍的通行。部分街廊的两栋间人行道的榕树下形成的聊天空间与平台上的聊天空间，形成特殊的巷弄质量。因此，局部保留场地的环境纹理并活化利用为新小区的公共空间，例如社会企业、青年微型创业、小区二手物资平台、长者聊天休息、青少年创意空间等复合性空间，成为公共住宅愿景的孵育基地。平宅的保留亦意味着承认安康小区为居住记忆的一部分，而非有待完全铲除的污名化地点。

4.3　弱势社群的生活支持与设施

　　如同前言所述，社会住宅的10%以上比例应出租予具特殊情形或身份者，社会团体则倡议公共住宅应至少提高至30%，以解决弱势者租屋不易的问题，但必须对弱势者特性规划配套机制。除了提供小区活动中心作为未来公营住宅与周边小区可共享的设施，以增加小区互动外，针对特定社群应考虑其生活特性与空间需求。在高层化居住环境与缺乏互动的环境中，老人或特别是单身、怀病老人容易感到孤寂，甚至发生轻生等现象，有赖小区组织接轨社会局政策，建立老人关怀据点，培训小区民众或长者担任志工，提供关怀访视、电话问安咨询、送餐、健康促进等各项服务，形成守护长者的安全小区。此外，低收入小区中精神障碍者比例偏高，社会混居后有可能形成冲突或误会的来源，引进专业社会团体建立会所（clubhouse）为可行做法之一，提供精障者生活训练、职业培训、生活重建等服务，协助精障者稳定生活，减少机构化安置的机会。

　　儿童、青少年为低收入家户希望所系，但安康小区中许多家户亲职功能不彰，子女若在学校受挫或受同侪影响，极易选择离开学校甚至落入帮派、染上药瘾等，最后难以脱离低收入家户身份。为了辅助这类高关怀家户，目前社会局委托社会团体，利用课辅班作为平台，以青少年为核心联结家长建立网络，结合教学、生活照顾、福利服务等，补充亲职功能不足，并培养青少年成长阶段的自信心与责任感。这类辅导机制应持续进驻未来的社会混居小区，提供学校正式课业之外的多样课程，不仅提供低收入户亦提供年轻家户的孩童使用。另外一项存在于安康小区中的问题即为吸毒者比例偏高，社会混居后亦并不意味会自然消失，甚至从目前从事辅导工作的社会团体的经验，认为有可能更加恶化，因此，亦需要提供专业民间团体进驻的空间。

4.4　社会资本与社会企业

　　社会混居的重要假设之一为透过住户间的互动增加低收入户的社会资本与扩展社会网络，这类提法忽略了低收入户本身拥有的资本。成为低收入户有许多不同的原因，如失去收入主要来源、负担家计者久病不愈、户内有身心障碍者等，但也有创业失败、具有才能或热心公共事务的居民。如在本计划之小区调查与工作坊中，发现许多妇女愿意积极投入公共事务，这些妇女有不同的生命故事，有一位曾经营餐厅的妇女即提出未来家户增加之后，可组织小区妇女共同经营小区厨房，提供独居老人或学童供餐服务。另外一位妇女年轻时亦曾任武术教练，亦乐意参与技艺传授的工作。这些个案显示低收户家户本身拥有的资本，有待发掘、组织与培植，发展为各类商业或具公益之活动，实现社会互助与建立小区的基础。

　　因此，公共住宅中可导入社会企业的观念与做法，社会企业为具社会责任、关注社会议题的产品或服务，兼顾社会公益与获利性的企业经营模式。例如本计划访谈胜利身心障碍潜能发展中心，该组织依身心障碍程度安排职能训练后，协助受训者进入职场或开创事业，目前已有经营便利商店、加油站等成功经验。借助多样化、个性化社会企业商店的进驻可营造别具一格的活力街道，不仅提供住户或身心障碍者就近就业，亦能引入社会教育活动，活络外围小区商业。这类社会企业的进驻需要在未来招标时采用方案评比方式，由承租意愿者提出服务计划书，说明弱势居民或居民就业回馈方案，经评选后让具社会企业精神之店铺优先进驻。

4.5　管理、租户角色与第三部门的参与

目前台北市各公营住宅委托民间物业公司管理，工作内容包括公共事务管理（带看房屋、入住作业、小区访视、退租作业、续约工作、缴款单投递、咨询服务及临时状况处理等）、机电设备保养、小区安全维护、小区清洁维护、室内检修服务等。住户管理方面，以租赁契约与住户公约等规范承租户，规约中分为绝对禁止事项及轻微违规事项，分别以终止租约及记点制来规范。租户有违规情形产生，物业管理公司先采劝导方式，劝导不成，报告市府，由市府记扣点，倘扣分累计达30分即终止租约。

针对目前管理制度，在主要以现居住在公共住宅的青年住户为主的工作坊中，普遍认为租户意见必须经由物业管理公司再转达市府，缺乏有效整合与反应管道。租户认为由租户组成管理委员会承担某部分公共事务或意见整合功能有其需求。针对公约与记点制，租户认为公约需要配套措施，例如公约不准在阳台晒棉被，屋顶又不开放使用的状况下，需要合理配套办法才能遵守。针对混居，青年住户意见不一，有些认为因生活习惯等不同，应将青年住户与低收入分开，有些则认为愿意发挥所长投入在课后辅导或独居老人的照顾等活动，但应配套延长租期等制度设计。在以物业管理公司为主的座谈会中，从管理效率的角度，亦认为空间配置上将低收入户集中居住，便于福利输送与管理等。此外，为了增加轮转，现有规定青年住户最长可居住五年，正在养育小孩的家长认为租期短，迁移的压力会让小孩学习不稳定，对小区的认同也很难培养。

整体而言，目前公营住宅之管理制度仅着重在硬件维护与记点制，亦即市府委托代理人扮演房东角色。但面对社会混居下多元组成的小区成员，市府应更着重于经营，亦即如何鼓励租户投入在公共事务的参与、第三部门或非营利组织的引入、冲突化解的机制建立、低收入住户的赋权计划等皆需要政府的资源投注与制度上的规划。

5　结论

透过安康公共住宅的参与式规划过程，不论安康居民、青年租户、专家学者、公共部门等参与者皆认为社会混居是应推动的方向，但到底青年住户与弱势住户之间以不同场地配置，抑或分栋或分层配置，其效果尚难以完全推论。目前的策略是为了避免被标签或被辨识采取随机抽签的单一做法，还有待检讨。以他国经验，在居民对弱势住户尚存在偏见或认识不够充足时，即存在潜在冲突的可能。在不被辨识的策略下，忽略了低收入或弱势住户之间的互助网络，为维系稳定生活的重要方式，需要较具弹性与可操作的混居原则。此外，针对单身老人、精神障碍者、青少年、吸毒者等弱势或特定需求者，需要硬件设施与社会团体软件的资源引入，稳定小区生活。低收入家户社会资本的拓展，不能仅期待自然的互动以达成，需要从其自身拥有的潜力或资本着眼，并协助开拓微型小区企业与协同网络的建立。空间上，各类公共空间与设施具有相互认识与促进互动的媒介作用，但亦需要妥善的管理支持。亦即，社会混居的公共住宅需要从租户的认识与需求中，找出可稳定生活且自我认同的基础条件，才能进一步思索公共住宅作为"小区"的可能。

在此目标下，政府不仅扮演居住单元的房东、管理者角色，亦应扮演促成社会融合的触媒。亦即，在物业的硬件管理与公约之外，需要更充足的社会营造计划以运作小区。委托具有小区营造专业的第三部门，不论是在促进家户相互认识、租户公共事务的参与、冲突的协商、低收入家户的扶助等皆可扮演重要角色。租户亦然，除了被管理的租户角色外，在租户意见的整合、冲突的协商、公共事务的管理等配合制度的设计，可扮演更积极的角色。

本文作为初步的探讨，指出社会混居的公共住宅具有高度理想化的、具社会融合与包容的小区期待，需要充分考虑住户特性与需求，发展多样社会计划，促进相互认识与认同的机会，考虑更多居民可积极参与的管理机制为主要政策方向的建议。近年台北市的公共住宅持续成为热门议题，新上任的市长柯文哲誓言推动兴建五万户公共住宅计划。在新建的捷运联合开发住宅与公共住宅共构项目中，购买户对未来公共住宅的疑虑引发社会广泛关注，显示社会混居方式存在意见歧异。除了量的供给，或者依赖良好的环境设计、新颖的外观设计、专业的物业管理等高质量意象建立外，公共住宅的社会设计有待充足的讨论与政策上的研究拟定，本研究与规划行动中所汇整的建议有其认识上的限制，有待进一步在可行的财务等条件下进行政策制定与后续实行上的检验。

致谢

特别感谢参与本规划项目之合作伙伴——专业城市改革组织的彭扬凯秘书长以及林于婷、陈涵光等在公共住宅与小区工作中的启发。

The Participatory Planning of the Ankang Public Housing Project and Its Policy Implications

Mu Szu-Mien

(Taiwan University Building and Planning Research Foundation)

Abstract：The AnKang Affordable Housing is the biggest low-income community in Taipei. The city government is promoting the new public rental housing policies to renew the community. The social mix strategies are adopted to expect a more healthy and cohesive community. By participatory research and planning methods, this project gathers various opinions, expectations and suggestions from the low-income residents, young tenures, NGOs, professionals, policy makers. The main conclusion is that social mix rental housing is not only units to accommodate renters, but a community. Then, the community building has to plan various social programs and spaces for empowering low-income households. Furthermore, The shaping of positive social interaction among diverse groups of residents and renter's participatory needs to fully integrated into the future housing management system.

Keywords：Public rental housing, Social mix, Community building, Participatory planning

参考文献：

[1]　台北市政府. 台北市出租住宅行动纲领[EB/OL]. 2013. http：//www. housing. gov. taipei/.

[2]　Park Kun-Suk. What is Problem in Housing Complex by Social Mix and How Change Direction of It[J]. Architecture，2010(7)，18-20.

[3]　Chaskin R. J. & Joseph M. L. Building "Community" in Mixed-Income Developments Assumptions，Approaches，and Early Experiences[J]. Urban Affairs Review，2010，45(3)，299-335.

[4]　McCormick N. J.，Joseph M. L. & Chaskin R. J. The New Stigma of Relocated Public Housing Residents：Challenges to Social Identity in Mixed-Income Developments. City & community，2012，11(3)，285-308.

[5]　Pyatok M. Mixed-Income Housing：Social Integration or Cultural Hegemony？ Proceedings of International Conference on Social Housing in Taiwan[M]. 2011，153-163.

[6] Kim S. H. Public Rental Housing in Korea[J]. Taiwan Architect，2014，469：78-83.

[7]　Ha S. K. Social housing estates and sustainable community development in South Korea[J]. Habitat International，2008，32(3)，349-363.

Toward an Urban Frontier and Inter-Linkage: The Taipei Metropolitan Resiliency

Ling Tzen-Ying Jeuuy

(Department of Architecture Tamkang University)

Abstract: The hybridization or cross breeding of the regional spatial transformation creates an urban frontier that expresses the tectonic shifts focusing on urban activities change and population migration. The scalar shift that spans across the regional scale brings what lacks within the inter-linkage of "city" and "world" and look beyond the territorial division at large. In Taipei, the phenomenon of geographic concentration of human activity in the metropolitan areas implies the underlying characteristic expounded beneath that can be utilized. Size and growth rate of urbanization thru the population concentration highlight the presence of an intense redistribution and the mean to do so, creating a frontier land in need of inter liking. The negative effects of isolation are magnified in locations with higher potential in other uses.. The empirical results highlight the need for improved connectivity between the northern and other regions in Taiwan and the need to address two major issues--the need re-examine the management policy for land and industry development and the need to provide the suitable public facilities and services for the changing population structure. Within this realm, we inquire the urban-landscape hybrids that will behave as a protector to preserve the ecologies and natural resources of the frontier as well as furthering the inter-linkage of the urban landscape. As this may become an ordering principle for a new economy, one must accept the new mechanism for organizing the patterns of human settlement as well as the economies of production and distribution. This paper contends the Taiwan experience provides a model for other developing cities and provides a reference in understanding the parameters and management policies.

Keywords: Inter-linkage, Resiliency, Frontier, Taipei metropolitan

1 Introduction

Urbanization begins from early trade based settlements that traded by water and land with agricultural hinterlands and other settlements (Jacobs, 1969); to industrial manufacturing centres with concentrations of factories, labour and rail and sea trade connections (Soja, 2000); finally to post-industrial cities where agglomerations of knowledge intensive services locate and electronic communication networks and flows of capital are central (Castells, 2000). The modern metropolis, in a significant sense, has become "unbound. "Just as the clear internal border between city and suburb has begun to disappear, the external boundary of the city region is becoming less confining, opening up the urban hinterland to ever larger regional scales(Soja, 2000). This calls for a shifting urban framework as inter-linkage becomes a factor of land use legacies, remnant configuration and local socio-economic and environmental concerns. The Megapolitan concept seems to have popularized the idea that the modern cities are better reviewed not in isolation, as centers of a restricted area only, but rather as parts of "cities systems," as participants in urban networks revolving in widening orbits (Gottmann, 1987: 52). Models of the good city-of the kind of urban order that might enhance the human experience-invariably tend to project from the circumstance of the times and as geographical entities, cities are hardly discernible places with distinct identities. Without clear boundaries and they have become sites of extraordinary circulation and translocal connectivity, linked to processes of spatial stretching and interdependence associated with globalization (Amin, 2006).

The shift within the Taiwanese urban order is parallel to this development. Over the last decades，Taiwan has developed its economy from a heavily agricultural economy into an industrialized e-conomy and dramatic changes have taken place in its urban landscape，reflecting a fact that the environment has been seriously transformed during the development process. Gathering on Taiwan urban literature（see Liu 1975，Tang 2003，Tsai 1985，Ling 2010）clearly notes the urbanization process that metropolitan developments in the northern，central and southern Taiwan emerged in the mid twenty century and extensively incorporated the major cities and their surrounding satellites into urban regions with industrial economies，employments and communications expanded beyond the city jurisdiction boundaries and driven the metropolitan areas into functional regions. Taipei TMA undertook such process as the socio-economic factors affected the urban land use and local environmental conditions. The first part of this paper develops a theoretical approach by reviewing literature which helps to identify the typology and the process of the urban morphology. The second part is a case study of Taipei Metropolitan area. It is mainly a study including relevant literature，reports，official documents and statistics. In order to clarify some implementation details，key actors who have participated or are participating in the design and implementation process of Taipei Metropolitan urban development and inter-linkage issues were reviewed.

2　Urban Form and Extending the Frontier

Polycentrism is a spatial reality（HALL and PAIN 2006）and is becoming a new referential for public policies（Gloersen，Lahteenmaki-Smith et al. 2007）. Hilberseimer's Decentralized City responded to the problems cause by the industrial age. Pollution，insalubrities，crime and traffic in city centres，addressing the fact that moving about the urban core is essentially a necessary issue to be addressed as it expands beyond the initial boundary. Complex processes of global urbanization are rendering cities into all-embracing social spaces as the world and its ways pours into them，such that they are increasingly read as emblems of the modern（Amin and Thrift，2005b）.

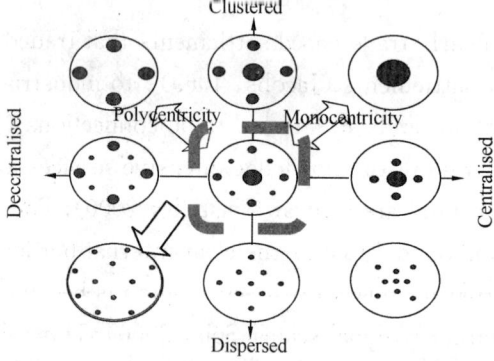

Figure 1　Urban core hierarchy patterns thru clustering and centralization

(Source：compiled by this study)

Jean Gottmann recognized the theoretical impacts of his work："the Megapolitan concept seems to have popularized the idea that the modern cities are better reviewed not in isolation，as centres of a restricted area only，but rather as parts of'city systems'，as participants in urban networks revolving in widening orbits. (1987：52)""Every city in this region spreads out far and wide around its original nucleus；it grows amidst an irregularly colloidal mixture of rural and suburban landscapes；it melts on broad fronts with other mixtures，of somewhat similar though different texture，belonging to the suburban neighbourhoods of other cities. (Gottmann，1987）""the Megapolitan concept seems to have popularized the idea that the modern cities are better reviewed not in isolation, as centers of a restricted area only, but rather as parts of 'city systems,' as participants in urban networks revolving in widening orbits." "We must abandon the idea of the city as a tightly settled and organized unit in which people, activities, and riches are crowded into a very small area clearly separated from its non-urban surroundings" (Gottmann, 1987: 52). Hashim Sarkis critiques the current discourse on the Urban Age and its over-concentration of effort on the Global City, asking, "Why the city should be considered the ultimate spatial manifestation of globalization?" This condition was observed as early as 1960's by Melvin Webber, who stated that the visual symbols of urbanization are to be marks of the important qualities of urban society.

···We have compared these symbols with our ideological precepts of order and found that they do not conform; And so we have mistaken for "urban chaos" what is more likely to be a newly emerging order whose signal qualities are complexity and diversity.

Interactions can be defined as linkages across space (such as flows of people, goods, money, information and wastes) and linkages between sectors (for example, between agriculture and services and manufacturing), including 'rural' activities taking place in urban centres (such as urban agriculture), or activities classified as 'urban' (such as manufacturing and services) taking place in rural settlements. Koolhaas (1994), on the other hand, stated that "if there is to be a 'new urbanism' it will not be based on the twin fantasies of order and omnipotence; it will be the staging of uncertainty; it will no longer be concerned with the arrangement of more or less permanent objects but with the irrigation of territories with potential", "a good deal of the land in the 'twilight areas' between the cities remains green, either still farmed or wooded, matters little to the continuity of Megalopolis" (GOTTMANN 1961: 42) Gottmann expressed that it was the economic activity and the transportation, commuting, and communication linkages within Megalopolis that mattered most. This constant shift of clustering and dispersion are expanding toward hinterland. Acknowledging that while, "a good deal of the land in the 'twilight areas' between the cities remains green, either still farmed or wooded, matters little to the continuity of Megalopolis (GOTTMANN 1961: 42)" The evolution of urban form can be viewed through the tension between forces of centralisation and forces of dispersion.

3 Inter-Linkage in Taipei Metropolitan Area

Taipei metropolitan area, comprising of Taipei city, New Taipei City and Keelung City, is the most densely populated and converged urban area in Taiwan and clearly formed a polycentric centre. There are many small towns scattered throughout the region, fewer medium cities, and only one or two very large urban centers. One reason for the hierarchical organization of cities in the landscape is the distribution of goods and services as described by Friedman (1973). This is certainly the state of Taipei Metropolitan Area (TMA). The city experienced decentralization after 1945 with the arrival of the KMT troop. The new settlement arrived and segregated the city centre and he periphery territory became even more apparent. With the implementation of the new land zoning law, certain production activities were expelled from the city centre. Before the 1960s, Taipei was a major distribution centre for agricultural products and the main consumption centre in Taiwan (Chou, 2002). In the late 1980s, Taiwan underwent a process of deindustrialization related to global and regional economic reorganization process. The number of financial, insurance, service industries in Taipei increased significantly, while most manufacturing industries moved out of Taipei to Southeast Asia and China (Ching, 1999).

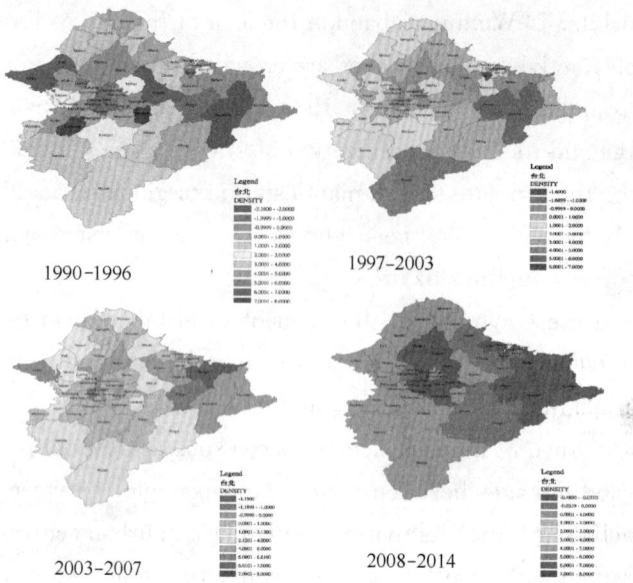

1990-1996   1997-2003

2003-2007   2008-2014

Figure 2   Taipei metropolitan population change 1990-2014
(Source: compiled and drawn by this study)

A few clustering factors should be mentioned: firstly, from 1985 on, after the martial law was lifted, the city underwent a rapid economy growth and urban agglomeration and development in the economic core reached saturation point by the late 1980s; there was not sufficient space to accommodate Taipei's new global activities. Two major consequences resulted. First, it fuelled a rampant development in land speculation, and real estate prices soared to a record level. Secondly, as the northern core dominates the economic and social activities at large, the territorial reorder deems necessary and important. The accelerated consumption of the regional infrastructure and resources demands an integration and reconfiguration of the urban planning and management system. The urban development expanded to eastern suburbs of Taipei, and lead to spatial shift of the urban economic core. Secondly, the export-based manufacturing headquarters, mostly acting as subcontractors of Japanese and Western trans-nationals, moved to Taipei, emerging certain clustering pattern of industries (Ling, 2010). From both its place within the global commodities trade and Taipei assumes the role of global city (Wang, 2003; Kwok, 2005).

We observe that Taipei attracted most of the service industries to migrate to the center and the labor force also shown a strong increase as well. Taipei along with New Taipei city exhibit an employment increase in 2014, exploits scale economies in production, retailing and public goods. The existence of specialized service sector employment in TaipeiTMA means that the employment structures of the centers appear to have formed a "divergence club" and becoming more unlike each other. Unlike industrial activities, services have few negative externalities and more modest space demands, thus are highly amenable to city centre environments. The international skilled workforce at the centre of these services is attracted to the "buzz" of city centre life. Below we find the sectoral composition for the 2014 as we see a high centralization of service sector and decentralization of manufacturing sector within the TMA.

Taipei metropolitan area is seen expanding in two distinct directions-from the eastern edge of Taipei City (Neihu and Nangang districts) toward Xizhi, Keelung and Ruifang, and from the south-

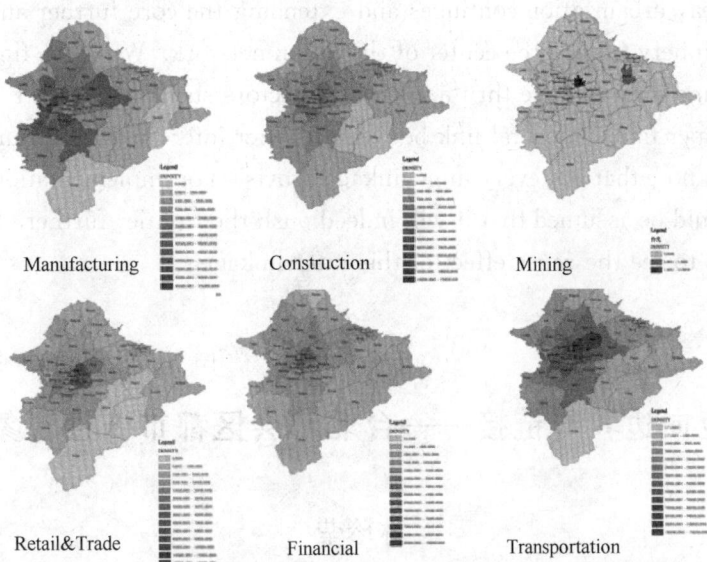

Figure3　Taipei metripolitan sectoral employment demarcation

(Source: compiled and drawn by this study)

ern edge (Wenshan District) southward toward Xindian. These areas are growing into high density living areas and buildings. The cause effect of this high-density development is due to the population increase rate in these areas and the easy access with the MRT. Additionally, land development is concentrated on remaining vacant land surrounding built districts or where the population density was high. The most prominent is the capital city of Taipei, where no single centrality is identified. The mixed urban activities are not coherent to the city plan. The population density has shown a decrease in growth rate, most notably in the core of Taipei city. One sees the extension of the metropolitan proper southward toward Taoyuan County, while the regional development always faces an important disparity (HOU, 2000) between north and south or between east and west.

4　Conclusions

The ordering principle for a new frontier in Taipei Metropolitan area assumes a mechanism for organizing the patterns of human settlement as well as the economies of production and distribution thru urban inter-linkage and easy access to and from the frontier. Taipei Metropolitan possesses the potential for an inter-linkage, even amidst the uneven geographic growth which accentuates the polar differences of "center" and the "periphery". The phenomenon of geographic concentration of specific sector and economic activity as well as population convergence in the metropolitan areas implies the underlying characteristic expounded beneath that can be utilized. Taipei Metropolitan exhibits the inter-linkage, even amidst the uneven geographic growth which accentuates the polar differences of "center" and the "periphery". This is accomplished thru the iner-linkage of the MRT service. This also provided the structure for resilience in the TMA.

Today, TMA's growth exhibits a loosening core and divergent expansion toward the peripheral area, pushingthe core frontier even further. Higher densities do facilitate the use of public transport, walking and cycling, making it more efficient to provide services and promote urban vitality. Size and growth rate of urbanization thru the population concentration highlight the presence of an intense redistribution, accentuating the need for inter-linkage in the frontier land of Keelung. Within the Metropolitan area，urbanization continues and extending the core further and strengthening the connection from periphery toward the center of the urban network. While we find a positive relation between clustering and inter-linkage thru network connectors such as the MRT service，the conclusive result in this paper finds a general link between frontier inter-linkage and urbanization，however，it is important to note that not every inter-linkage provision or implementation policy is suited for all locations nor should be assumed that it will indeed push the frontier further. Further detail study should be conducted to see the cause effect of this inter-linkage.

迈向边界与链接——台北都会区都市弹性现象

林珍莹

（淡江大学建筑系）

摘要：由于工业化与都市化造成大量人口密集迁居于各大都市与相邻区域，形成了所谓的都会区（metropolitan regions，或称为城市—区域 city—regions 等现象）。此现象与全球经济化的发展彻底地动摇了可辨识的空间领域；动摇了都市结构与其尺度，呈现出异质化的空间发展趋势，带动都市间的变迁与成长。故全球化的"全球思维、在地行动"的具体表征，可落实于地域产业分工之上及其连动联系之架构中。台北都会区的变化和都会人口迁移，目前呈现快速变化、发展与挤压，跨越了地理集中性，产生了蔓延与重新分配的驱动力，亦打破原治理的分界线。各种抢占区域发展的战略优势地位，迅速发展为具有弹性的地理链接的活动，创造了都市边疆弹性发展的链接性。本文通过 2001～2011 工商普查数据研究发现台北都会区在 10 年间，蔓延发展的情况显著，从都会空间结构变迁的分析可以发现 2001～2011 年的主要变迁多集中在都市周边地区。由空间分布情况来看，台北都会区蔓延发展的趋势主要分为两个路径方向，其一，由台北市东侧边缘的内湖区与南港区往东扩张，另一路径系自台北市南侧边缘的文山区往南扩张至新店市与树林镇的空间模式。服务业产业结构专业化与网络形成一种新的连结。本文依据台北都会区都市结构与专业化蔓延程度的分布，建议都市规划需讨论具都市周边地区环境变迁问题，以及供给服务、调节服务务和文化服务等功能的可能性。

关键词：连结，弹性化，都市边疆，台北都会区

References：

[1] 1986，1991，1996，2001 Industry，Commerce and Service Census［M］. 7th revised edition. Directorate General of Budget，Accounting and Statistics（DGBAS），Executive Yuan census and website：http：//eng. stat. gov. tw/.

[2] Amin，A. ，Thrift，N. Cities：Re-imagining the Urban［M］. Cambridge：Polity，2002.

[3] Acharya，S. R & Morichi S. Motorization and Role of Mass Rapid transit in East Asian Mega Cities［J］. IATSS Research，2007，31（2）：6-16.

[4] Ash A. and Thrift N. What's Left？Just The Future［J］. Antipode，2005，37（2）.

[5] Amin，A. . The Good City［J］，C Urban Studies，2006，43（5/6）. 1009-1023.

[6] Bernick，M. ，and Cervero，R. Transit villages in the 21st Century. 43（5/6）. New York，Mc Graw-Hill，1997.

[7] Cheng，L，a Hsia，CJ. Asian Economic Crisis，State Policy，and Urban Movements：A Taiwan Version［J］，Asian Geographer，2000，19（1-2）：63-73.

[8] Ching，C. H. Taipei Metropolitan Economic Structure and spatial distribution changes while

becoming a world city[J]. City and Planning, 1999, 28(4): 495-518.

[9]   Ching, C. H. . The Development of Economic Structure, Producer services and growth con-strains[M], (Ed. P, Globalization Taipei: Political Economy of Spatial Development, 35-54. London: Routledge In R. Kwork.

[10]   Chou, T. L. . Globalization, Territorial Strategy and Transformation in Taiwan's Urban System[J]. City and Planning, 2002, 29 (4): 491-512.

[11]   Friedman, J. . Urbanization, Planning and National Development. 1973, Sage, Beverly Hills, CA.

[12]   Gottmann, J. Megalopolis: The Urbanized Northeastern Seaboard of the United States. 1961, New York, Twentieth-Century Fund.

[13]   Gottmann, J.. Megalopolis Revisited: 25 Years Later. 1987, College Park, MD, The University of Maryland Institute for Urban Studies. .

[14]   Gløersen, E. , Lähteenmäki-Smith, K. &. Dubois A. Polycentricity in Transnational Planning Initiatives: ESDP applied or ESDP reinvented? 2007, Planning Practices &. Research, Vol. 22, No. 3, 395-415.

[15]   Greene and Pick, . Exploring the Urban Community: A GIS Approach, Transactions in GIS, 2006, Volume 10, Issue 3, 485-487

[16]   Hall P. . Why Some Cities Flourish while Others Languish. In: UN-Habitat (ed.) The State of the World's Cities Report, 2006/2007. (13). UN-Habitat/Earthscan: London.

[17]   Hall, P. and Pain, K. The Polycentric Metropolis. 2006, London, Earthscan

[18]   Hardt M. &. Negri A. . Empire, 2000, Cambridge, MA. Harvard Graduate School of Design Press.

[19]   Hilberseimer, L. The New City: Principles of Planning, 1944 (Chicago: Theobald, 1944); The Nature of Cities: Origin, Growth, and Decline, Pattern and Form, Planning Problems (Chicago: Theobald, 1955).

[20]   Hough M. . City Form and Natural Process. 1995, New York: Routledge.

[21]   Hou, J.. From Dual Disparities to Dual Squeeze: The Emerging Patterns of Regional Development in Taiwan. 2000, Berkeley Planning Journal 14: 4-22.

[22]   Jacobs, J. The Economy of Cities. 1969, New York: Random House.

[23]   K. C. Hsu, T. Y. Lai, and C. H. Lee. The Causes Which Influence the Change of Spatial Development Pattern in Taipei Metropolitan Area, 2014, International Journal of Engineering and Technology, Vol. 6, No. 6. 497-502.

[24]   Koolhass R. Delirious New York: A Retroactive Manifesto for Manhattan, 1994, The Monacelli Press.

[25]   Landes, D. S. The Unbound Prometheus. 1969, Cambridge: Cambridge University Press.

[26]   Ling, T. Y. Industry Spatial Clustering in Taiwan, 2010, The Journal of Asian Comparative Development. Volume 9, issue 1. 103-132.

[27]   Liu, K. C. et at, Urban Development in Taiwan: Retrospect and Prospect, 2001, Population Journal, 26, 1-25.

[28]   McKinney ML. Urbanization, biodiversity, and conservation. 2002, BioScience. 52: 883-890

[29]   Moriconi-Ebrard, . L'urbanisation du monde depuis 1950, 1993 (Collection Villes) (French Paperback)

[30]   O'Donoghue D. Some Evidence for the Convergence of Employment Structures in the British

Urban Systems from 1978 to 1991, 2000, Regional Studies, 34. 2, 159-167.

[31] Pendall, Martin, & Fulton. . Holding the line: Urban Containment in the United States. 2002, A discussion Paper prepared for Center on Urban Metropolitan Policy, Washington, DC. : The Brooking Institution.

[32] Sarkis H, . The World According to Architecture: Beyond Cosmopolis, 2010, Cambridge, MA. Harvard Graduate School of Design, 104.

[33] Soja, E. Postmetropolis: Critical Studies of Cities and Regions. 2000, Oxford and Malden, MA: Blackwell.

[34] Tang, C. P. . Democratizing urban politics and civic environmentalism in Taiwan. 2003, The China Quarterly, 162: 1029-1051.

[35] Velasquez MR, Barajas, D. . Hilberseimer: Radical Urbanism, 2008, 04 28th. http: // www. a-u-r-a. eu/upload/research _ radicalurbanism _ 100dpi _ 2. pdf? PHPSESSID = 1994337267bf5d06e80f6fdcf94c5471

[36] Webber M. Explorations into Urban Structure', 1964, [Publication in the City Planning Series] by Melvin M. Webber [editor], John W. Dyckman, Donald L. Foley, Albert Z. Guttenberg, William L. C. Wheaton, Catherine Bauer Wurster, published by University of Pennsylvania Press, Philadelphia.

[37] Yeh, J.-P. Train à grande vitesse et projet d'urbanisation : la mise en place de la ligne Taïpei Kaoshiung à Taiwan. 2007, Paris, Université Paris-Diderot. Doctorat de Dynamiques comparées des sociétés en développement.

[38] Zardini, M. Toward a sensorial urbanism, in Sense of the City: An Alternate Approach to Urbanism, 2005, Lars Muller Publishers

包容性人居环境建设
Inclusive Living Environment Development

专题二：适老性人居环境
Special Topic 2：Active Aging

藏区传统民居建筑空间更新研究：以老年居住建筑为例

潘　卉　焦自云

（南京三江学院建筑学院）

摘要：本文旨在探讨将传统藏式建筑和现代老年居住建筑功能相融合，以其生态的智慧和顺应当地气候特征的建筑设计方式，营造出迎合当地老年生活需求的居住类建筑。

关键词：西藏，传统民居，更新，老年居住建筑

1　引言

近年来，中国步入老龄化社会的浪潮已席卷全国。自 2010 年以来，地广人稀的西藏，其老龄人口已接近西藏总人口 10%，人口年龄结构正由成年型向老年型快速转变。我国当前对于老年居住建筑的研究往往聚焦于经济发达、人口稠密的中东部，研究成果也更适用于中东部的气候和人文环境。西藏地理位置和气候条件特殊，当地技术和经济条件相对落后。如何能合理应用藏区本土成熟的民居设计经验，将传统藏式建筑和现代老年居住建筑设计手法相融合，以其生态的智慧和顺应当地气候特征的建筑技术营造出迎合当地老年生活需求的居住类建筑，使传统藏区民居空间迸发出新的活力，是本文研究的重点。

2　选址

西藏地处高原，号称"世界第三极"，这里气候高寒缺氧，植被稀少，地形沟壑万千。气候特征为低温、干燥、多风，区域差异和垂直变化显著；太阳辐射强，温度年较差小而日较差大。这种独特的高原气候对于西藏地区居住建筑的影响非常明显。无论是寒冷的拉萨地区，还是气候相对温和的林芝地区，全区基本无采暖设施，大体上靠日照解决采暖问题。建筑南北向温差大，昼夜温差大，这都是建筑选址和布局要慎重考虑的环境条件。

藏区老年居住建筑的选址和总体布局，应做到以下几点：场地应选择在阳光充足、空气流通、场地干燥、排水通畅、地势较高的地段。选址应考虑临近城市社区中心或社会服务设施，以临近医院为佳。建筑布局应充分考虑日照、天然采光、自然通风的卫生条件。当选址位于有高差的地段尤其是山区内时，应选择南向山坡的中下部，以便冬季有防风保护，又尽可能的接受太阳辐射。

值得注意的是，出于宗教信仰的缘故，藏族人对于自然界和生存环境存在尊崇和敬畏心理，不允许破坏场地和基址的事情发生。因此藏区老年居住建筑的选址和布局应尽量顺应地势，对地形不做或少做改变；植物茂盛之处不要砍伐、神山圣地之所不要动土。

3　生态模式语言

3.1　保温、抗震的空间格局设计

虽然受到高原严酷的自然环境和匮乏的物质资源的限制，藏族人民仍然在民居建筑中积累了不少适应自然条件的生存智慧。寒冷的气候环境使藏式建筑的保暖性成为重中之重，这也是贯穿藏区城镇规划和住宅设计的一条主线。此外，青藏高原地处地质构造断裂带，是我国地震活动最强烈的

地区之一。

建筑材料的稀缺和运输的困难导致传统民居空间较为低矮，（一般净高为 2.2m），并且形成开间与进深相同的"方室"空间。这种低矮的层高助于减少建筑围护结构和外界的热交换，在冬季大风的环境中非常有助于建筑的防风。而方室空间有利于节约围护结构，获得最大使用面积。藏式建筑的平面多为规整对称的方形，如"回"、"曰"或"凹"字形等。传统民居立面也采取左右对称的布局（图1）。从建筑节能概念来讲，这种规整的方形体量有利于控制建筑的体型系数(指围合的建筑物室内单位体积所需围护结构的表面面积)；从抗震的角度而言，有利于控制重心和形心的统一，在最大程度减少建筑受到水平荷载变形的可能。

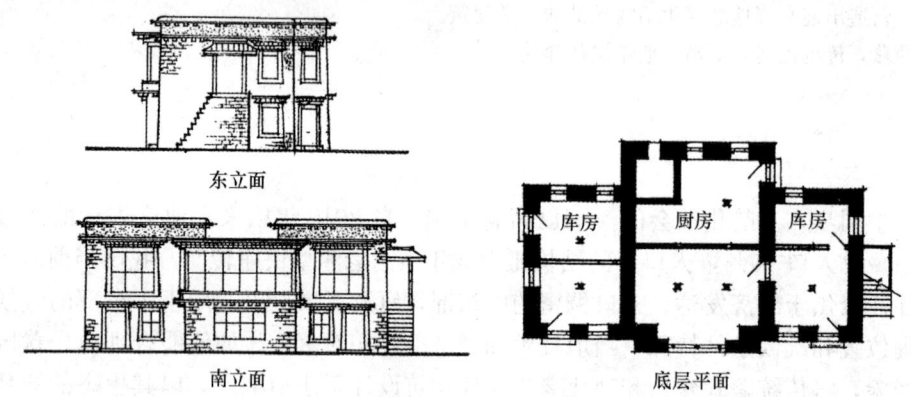

东立面

南立面

底层平面

库房　厨房　库房

图 1　典型传统藏民居平立面

3.2 "应时而迁"的空间环境设计

由于地处低纬度高海拔地区，西藏空气稀薄，太阳能资源极其丰富，气候日温差大而年温差小。这种气候特征对于藏族居住行为影响至深。当地人认为起居场所宜"应时而迁"：传统藏式民居的起居室，在冬天是设有火塘的厨房，夏天则是楼层靠上的房间，开大窗以便通风。这也提示我们，在进行老年居住建筑设计时，应考虑到不同季节气候对空间使用的影响并做出对策。为有效提升抗震效率并为绿色节能提供条件，老年居住建筑的平面布局宜规整，建筑体量宜简洁，建筑群组可结合庭院或中庭丰富空间。藏区人热爱大自然，只要天气适宜，即使是老年人也会尽可能利用户外空间活动。因此对于环境和空间场所的设计，应当具备丰富多样的形式以满足老年人在不同季节和气候的活动需求。传统藏式建筑中主屋的前廊、"凹"字形布局的半开敞庭院、屋顶平台等户外活动空间就是很好的选择。以前廊为例，它一般为一个柱距即 2m 宽，冬季太阳高度角较低，阳光可照射进前廊，温暖舒适，搬出室内的藏凳，就很适合老人逗留；夏季太阳辐射强烈，前廊上方挂上帘幕作为活动室的遮阳设施，即可抵挡烈日炙烤，成为老人纳凉休息的好去处。这种季节性悬挂的帘幕使建筑形态发生了动态的变化，一方面赋予了建筑造型和色彩以灵动的活力，一方面以较低的造价和简易的技术满足了老年人在不同气候条件下的空间使用要求。

3.3 依托日照的民居布局与家具布置

值得关注的是，西藏地区的最差朝向是北面，它与同时段南面温差可达 3℃，因此在进行建筑布局时，北向和东向应避免安置老年人的起居空间，可设置储藏和交通等辅助空间以便起到御寒缓冲的作用。"冬天阳光有主人"，这是对高原人喜欢晒太阳的生动写照。高原人离不开太阳，老年人更是对太阳有着特殊的依赖和感情。老年居住房间除尽量朝南外，层高可适量降低(净高以 2.2～2.5m 为宜)，房间面积以满足基本功能需求为宜，进深不应过大，以减少冬季热能耗；同时窗户可以适当降低窗台，扩大窗面积，以利于阳光照进房间。在布置家具时，可将床垫和坐具靠在南面窗边接受阳光照射，而把橱柜(藏语为"恰岗"，储存食物以及其他生活用品)放在房间北面，可以防止食物腐烂，这是老年人足不出户就可以晒太阳的最理想的房屋室内布局。对太阳能的利用是贯彻到藏式建筑的方方面面的，外墙上门窗的黑色边框、走廊栏杆下黑色的挡雨墙都和吸收太阳热量密不可分。这些实用性、装饰性和生态适应性原则的完美结合对于藏式老年居住建筑都具有重要的启发意义。

4 建筑布局和空间营造

在藏族先民的眼中，太阳是最为神圣庄严的天象。日出东方，因此东方成为吉祥的方位。温暖地区的住宅朝东就具有吉祥的寓意，即使在寒冷的地区，主屋朝南但院门也尽量朝东以迎接第一缕阳光。西藏老年居住建筑的平面布局和空间营造，应以获取最适应当地地理气候、具备良好功能与视觉感受，并顺应地方文脉特色的形式为主旨。就平面布局而言，可采用规整的方形、矩形以及其变体和组合。以当地典型的"凹"字形平面为例，建筑凹口面南，以利采纳阳光，并可围合出光照条件良好的院落空间。南向的居室采用大面积开窗，北面布置储藏室和次要房间，开窗少而小，东西面不开窗或少开窗，以避寒风，由此构成南面开敞、三面封闭的居住单元。这些居住单元一般为平房或二至三层楼房，至多不超过四层，底层是抬高基底的地垄墙或杂物库，二、三层安排老年人生活起居和辅助空间，可在三层设置佛堂，屋顶平台设置供老年人夏季乘凉或祈福的场所。

4.1 中柱横厅与方室

不同于汉族传统建筑，藏式建筑室内空间的中心往往是一根或若干根柱子，它代表来自"世界中心"的护佑，是藏式建筑室内空间的重要元素和特征。传统藏式民居的房间多为正方形和进深小、开间大的横厅平面模式，人们的日常行为和家具布置方式都与之适应。20世纪60～70年代，进深大、开间小的竖厅模式曾一度被内地技术工人带入该地区，但不久被淘汰，原因是房间的后部晒不到阳光，造成了面积和热量的浪费，在20世纪90年代又回归了传统"横厅"式布局。在电力供应尚且不足、城镇很多居民住宅仍在靠燃烧柴薪和牛粪取暖的今天，藏区老年建筑空间布局仍应以务实为重，居住单元宜沿用这种横厅式布局，为方便阳光直射，应把坐具和卧具尽量沿南墙摆放，以顺应藏族老人喝茶聊天晒太阳的生活愿望。

此外，普通藏式建筑的柱距和柱高基本相等，无论是外形简单的单层民居还是体量复杂的宫殿建筑，几乎都是由这种立方体反复叠加，形成一种朴素的模数概念。这种以柱为中心的单元模式空间延续至今，构成了藏族普遍认同和偏爱的室内空间模式。老年人随着生理机能的弱化，生活方式遵循从独立生活到需求介护，再到临终看护的规律，因此老年公寓的设计宜遵循可互换性规律，使房间根据老年人身体情况可进行功能布局和面积的调整，以避免老人因体质变化而不断搬迁。因此藏式建筑中的单元模式空间具有一定的借鉴价值。将空间布局建立在方格柱网的基础上，将楼梯、电梯井、通风井等竖向构件等距分散布置。梁柱作为结构套件采用统一的模式，保证了由内而外的不同构件的最大连续性和统一性(图2)。

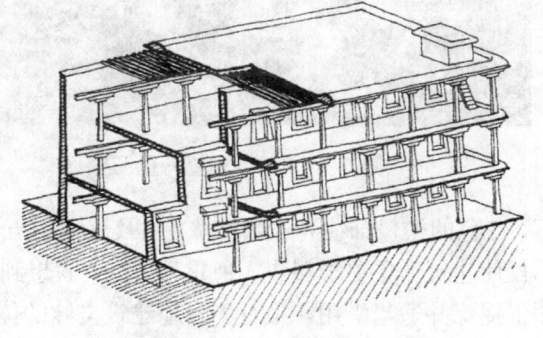

图2 中柱横厅与方室与空间可换性规律

4.2 多元公共活动空间

老年公寓或福利院里，缺乏行动力的老人大部分时光在室内度过，将孤独的老年人拉回有益的社交活动中使其重拾活力，是设计的重点，具体方法可以是为原本封闭内向的建筑赋予一些有利于交往和娱乐的开放式节点。藏区多山，山体建筑和平地建筑在布局上多有不同，公共活动空间的布置也有所区别。平地建筑采用院落式或者单排式，以凹形平面中间作为公共聚会场所，外围院落宽敞。山地建筑由底部的地垄墙抬起，和山体联结成为平面，可以将一到两间大堂替代院落或广场，作为公共活动的集会场所。

前文提到，藏式居住建筑室内的中柱蕴含着"世界中心"、"顶梁柱"的良好寓意。在设计老人之家的公共聚会区时，可以借此充分发挥梁柱结构的作用，突出其造型感和结构美。可以利用外露的主次梁和柱子界定聚会中庭的领域和空间的方向，利用成排等距的柱子确定空间的节奏，可以根据特定的要求用中柱将中庭分割为所需的空间大小和形状，根据不同的开场和封闭的情况给人以不同的空间体验。

除了常规的内聚性中庭空间，还可以利用屋顶平台、院落和前廊等建筑空间元素组成形式丰富的公共活动空间节点以满足不同时节不同活动的需求：由于干燥少雨，传统藏式民居多采用平屋顶形式，屋顶承担多重角色：晾晒粮食，转角处的桑墩用以祭祀祈福，还是藏民夏季纳凉之所。可以设置缓步楼梯或坡道通往屋顶，以供老人散步和消暑。南向的门廊或阳台，在炎热期配合以简便的活动遮阳设施即可凉爽宜人，在严寒期可以避开阴冷的北风和高原的风沙，享受温暖的日照。藏族人素来喜爱植物，在建筑围合出的院落内种植树木、养育花草，结合休憩小品可以营造出舒适宜人的微气候环境。这些都是老年人进行交流和公共活动的重要场所。

5 造型与装饰元素

高寒干燥的气候造就了藏式建筑方正平整的形体，其外观稳重敦实，内部院落灵活有机。老年居住建筑的造型设计，应以现代的技术和施工手段结合藏式建筑中经典的造型手法和装饰元素，以塑造出浓厚地域感和乡土气息，从而引发当地老年人的心理认同感。传统藏式建筑的造型特色具体

图 3　藏式建筑造型特色

总结如下（图 3）：外墙面自下而上有明显收分，一般墙体收分比例随层数增加而增大，在 2%～10%以内，这样既有利稳固，又节省材料，并产生稳定向上的视觉印象。在大面积的粗糙石材或夯土外墙面上嵌入细致的黑色窗套木构小窗，木窗下小上大。此外，用成堆捆扎好的边玛草（一种当地灌木）在椽盖之下压实堆放而成红色、黑色边玛墙屋檐，既可减轻自重，又是当地特有之装饰要素。屋面女儿墙四角半米高"L"形墙垛插立的树枝风马旗和五色经幡。藏族居住建筑多采用缤纷明亮的颜色，如白色外墙，黑色的门窗边

框，红色的檐口饰线和边玛草墙，以及屋顶的五色经幡，这些色彩的组合与宗教含义相吻合，它们不仅使建筑形象更加明快、稳重，更使人联想到生命的蕴意。对这些西藏传统建筑的典型形象进行加工提炼并适当沿用，是对于当地建筑文脉的体现，对于地域特色的表达，更是对老年人生活环境和归属感的尊重。

6 自然崇拜与宗教文化的影响

在藏族先民的眼中，太阳是最为神圣庄严的天象。日出东方，因此东方成为吉祥的方位。温暖地区的住宅朝东就具有吉祥的寓意，即使在寒冷的地区，主屋朝南但院门也尽量朝东以迎接第一缕

阳光。而藏民居院门上经常看到日月图案，就是为家庭带来好运的吉祥象征。

宗教渗入到西藏城市空间和建筑的每一个细胞。往往一个城市是以民居对某个寺庙的围合集聚而成。单体民居是遵循"三界"的空间秩序而构。即使步入暮年的老年藏民，也身体力行的将转经、供奉和朝拜嵌入到日常生活中。他们清晨第一件事，是到房屋最顶层或核心位置的经堂朝拜，身有余力的会前往寺庙、佛塔转经诵佛。屋顶作为最接近天界的地方，设有煨桑炉（"松科"）、女儿墙墙垛插有五色经幡。居住建筑的天花板、梁柱、廊道乃至灶房墙面上，通常都绘有宗教题材的装饰画，墙檐、院内矮墙、门窗的黑色边框、外墙转角的处理都和宗教有关。在藏区老年居住建筑的设计中，应当充分了解并尊重老年人宗教信仰和日常生活不可分割的生存状态。其中居住单元应留有凹室、壁龛或者独立的墙面以供摆放佛像。环境设计上应为老人每天清晨的转经活动提供合适的室外场所，转经场地形式不拘泥，大的可结合周边自然环境转山、转湖、转寺、转塔，小的可在建筑场地内设置"林卡"风格的庭院，道旁设置玛尼堆。高原上的人每天所见即高山、蓝天，养成奔放的性格。景观布置不用刻意叠山理水，可以用大尺度草坪密林烘托绿化，以自然景观为基调，使鲜花、丛林成为景观的主体。此外，应尊重藏民的宗教洁净观念、对朝向和方位、对颜色爱憎等有充分了解。

7 结语

西藏传统建筑作为我国地域建筑的经典代表，以其独特的形式忠实地体现了地方文化的特殊性。在银发时代来临的今天，我们只有在深层次的理解藏式建筑所蕴含的文化含义和精神实质的基础上，切实了解老年人的生理和心理特征、尊重其生活习惯，才能在老年居住建筑这个时新的建筑领域赋予传统藏式建筑以新的生命力。

致谢

国家自然科学基金资助（项目批准号：51408337）。

The Analysis of Renewal of the Traditional Tibetan Dwelling Space：Housing for the Elderly as An Example

Pan Hui，Jiao Ziyun

（School of Architecture，SanJiang University）

Abstract：The purpose of this paper aims at the combination of the traditional Tibetan architecture and modern architectural function of the housing for the elderly，and thus create the residential buildings suitable for the local elderly with its ecological wisdom and architectural methods adapt to the local climate characteristics.

Keywords：Tibetan，Traditional residential building，Renewal，House for the elderly

参考文献：

[1] 王娜 . 西藏人口老龄化现状、发展趋势及对策分析[J]. 西藏发展论坛，2013(4) .

[2] 周燕珉 . 城关区社会福利院，拉萨，西藏，中国[J]. 世界建筑，2014，(4).

[3] 木雅，曲吉建才．西藏民居[M]．北京：中国建筑工业出版社，2009.

[4] 何泉．藏族民居建筑文化研究[D]．西安：西安建筑科技大学，2009.

[5] 南文渊．藏族生态伦理[M]．北京：民族出版社，2007：10-11.

[6] （挪）KnudLarsen，Amundsinding-Larsen．拉萨历史城市地图集传统西藏建筑与城市景观[M]．李鸽，曲吉建才译．北京：中国建筑工业出版社，2005.

[7] 汪永平．拉萨建筑文化遗产[M]．南京：东南大学出版社，2005.

[8] 徐宗威．西藏传统建筑导则[M]．北京：中国建筑工业出版社，2006.

[9] 潘卉．从空间设计原则和细节谈老年居住建筑——赫曼·赫兹伯格的 De Drie Hoven "老年之家"作品解析[J]．华中建筑，2013，(5).

[10] 养老设施建筑设计规范 GB 50867—2013[S].

[11] 孙大章．中国民居研究[M]．北京：中国建筑工业出版社，2004.

[12] 焦自云．西藏庄园建筑初探[D]．南京：南京工业大学，2006.

积极老龄化下的空间规划与设计：新河养老社区设计探索

李 明[1] 张 玲[2]

（1. 中国矿业大学力学与建筑工程学院；2. 中国矿业大学艺术与设计学院）

摘要：当今我国养老问题日趋严重，如何为老年人提供健康、舒适的大环境，实现真正意义上的：老有所养，老有所为，老有所乐，老有所医？本文，正是针对这些问题，以新河养老社区设计为案例，探讨积极老龄化下的空间规划与设计。

关键词：积极老龄化，空间规划，场所意义，空间层级

1 引言

当今我国养老问题日趋严重，国家政府提出了多项措施，提出社会养老服务体系建设应以居家为基础、社区为依托、机构为支撑的模式建构。我国传统的养老设施与功能空间相对单一，仅能满足老年人生活的基本需要；但社会对养老空间的品质、价位有着多层次的需求，单一的类型是无法解决这一复杂的社会性的问题。

如何为老年人提供健康、舒适的大环境，实现真正意义上的：老有所养，老有所为，老有所乐，老有所医？因此，借鉴国外先进的产业发展模式，找出一条多元化空间发展的新途径，是保证我国养老产业发能够健康、可持续发展的重要任务。本文，正是针对这些问题，探讨积极老龄化下的空间规划与设计。

我国现在的老年居住方式，是以高比例的老年人口居住于现有住区为特色；然而，住区并不等同于社区。也不能因为被动性的老年群体的存在而成为有存在价值的养老社区。理想的，应该是一种复合型养老社区，是在传统养老模式的基础上产生的一种创新型的养老模式，它是依托大型中心城市的辐射而建成的具有卫星城性质的服务型养老社区，集养老、医疗、生活、娱乐等功能于一体。在居住环境中，居住主体的生活满意度与参与休闲活动两者关系密切，是其与周围空间环境互动的结果。如何设计一个可以赋予老人适宜的场所意象与家居感受的实质性空间？如何将空间规划与老人行为模式关系的研究用于创造老人理想的"家"空间？如何为老人提供具有可及性、私密性、舒适度、适应性、社交性的场所？本文的第一个部分，将通过影响老年人行为的五个基本性能指标：活力、感知、适合性、易达性、可控性，探讨规划空间层级的设计与场所理论的关联性；第二部分通过分析新河养老地产案例，从老人行为与空间层次、公共空间设计、多元化空间层级设计的关联性等方面，了解具体的案例是如何将理论研究的成果作用于空间设计，进而提升老人居住空间品质，达到真正意义上的积极老龄化下的空间规划与设计。

2 空间层级的设计与场所意义的关联性

探讨空间，也就是谈论与大小、比例、尺度、位置相关的内容；空间本身是中性的，是一种实质性的存在。但空间可以被赋予意义——当它与人的行为互动，给予使用者活力、感知性、适宜性、易达性、可控性①——这就是场所的意义。在积极老龄化下讨论空间，目的在于为身心机能弱化及脱离城市主流活动而在心理上产生边缘化和孤独感的老人，提供一个可以赋予这个特殊群体具

---

① 凯文·林奇在《城市形态》一书中，提出关于社区宜居品质（Settlement quality）的五个基本性能指标：活力、感知、适宜、可及、可控。

有场所意象与家的感受（sense of home）的实质空间，达到健康、参与、有保障①的社会生活状态。

养老社区作为老龄化社会城市的基本组成单元，应促使老年群体形成归属感，产生在宜人空间尺度范围内和在适宜的活动领域范围内的行为。多样的活动类型、空间场所能够在此功能目标下为老年人创造多层次的社会交往。正是这些活动与交往，促进老年人在社区中和社区间的活动，积极的空间营造。对老人来说，一个成功的居住空间不仅具有功能性，更应提供支持性：可以提供支持老人这个特定群体的特有行为的空间。这就要求在空间规划与设计中，探讨空间规划向度与老人行为向度的关联性，研究空间规划层级与老人休闲活动的关系。

3 新河养老社区空间设计探索

3.1 单元空间与易达性

建筑师首先要做的是设计促进老年人多层次交往，融入社会活动的空间，鼓励老人在适宜尺度下的积极的出行活动。影响老年人出行的因素，其一比较重要的是目的场所的易达性。由于老年人身体机能的弱化，空间设计要控制场所易达的区域范围，支持老年人日常出行意愿，社区的单元空间尺度相对要小，这是基本的空间条件。社区范围内老年人的出行类型主要包括基本的生活活动圈和扩大的邻里活动圈。基本活动圈是指老年人日常行为活动频率最高、逗留时间最长的场所．其活动半径为 180～220m，对于老年人来说，这是一个舒适的步行距离：符合老年人 5 分钟的持续步行行走能力。扩大邻里活动圈是指老年人住所周边熟悉的习惯性到达区域。其活动半径不大于 450m，这是基于低于老年人 10 分钟步行疲劳极限距离范围来考虑的。在老人的心理上，目的场所距离家的远近可以影响到其对领域感的可控性，距离短接近住所且便于到达，使老年人增加出行的意愿和频率，积极参与社会生活。要达到这一目的，在邻里单元空间的控制上就要有别于一般社区；单元空间的基本规模，就要和老年人的基本生活圈和邻里活动圈相关内容结合设计。限定活动的出行距离，是促进老年人积极出行的空间保障。

新河老年社区尺度建于主城区边界，距离主城新建三级综合医院 4km，2km 处为省级自然保护区，项目占地面积约 50hm²。基于促进老年人出行交往的目的，社区的设计里，5、6 栋老年居住建筑组成一个单元空间，单元的中心结合不同主题的庭院空间布置公共活动空间。设计的主要目的在于使巨大的空间尺度得到有机分解，使空间的距离感控制在老年人心理上可控的范围之内。中心活动空间包含小型诊所、辅助食堂、护理站、活动室等和老年人活动圈密切相关的公共活动配套设施。从最远的居住建筑到中心活动空间的直线距离控制在 220m 以内。社区内各单元空间以一系列步行为主的街巷空间联系（图 1），相关设计处理在交通空间的讲述中会谈及。这是出行距离控制

图 1 主街空间

① 积极老龄化是在 1999 年国际老人年，世界卫生组织提出的口号，政策框架要求在三个方面的基本支柱采取行动：健康·参与·保障。

和单元空间尺度设计相结合的设计实践，体现的是对老年人出行行为支持与关怀的人本设计。

3.2 空间尺度与可控性

在《美国大城市的死与生》中，简·雅各布斯谈到了柯布西埃的梦幻之城，认为其超大空间空旷冷漠缺乏人情味，使得场所与人产生心理距离。在城市建设中，用地日趋紧缺，建筑向高空发展，直接或间接损害外部空间的宜人尺度。活动场所的空间尺度对老年人的出行意愿有很大影响。超大空间缺少对行为活动的包裹感，削弱老年人出行到达的行动意愿。正是因其非近人尺度的空间体量，而并不利于鼓励社区内的交往和出行。小尺度空间让人体会温馨和亲切，鼓励到达和作为出行目的地。

同样在新河老年社区的设计中，考虑到老年人对于空间条件及尺度的感受。伴随着老年人身体机能衰退的是各种感官器官功能的下降，因此，他们对于不易把握、空旷的空间场所怀有较强的排他性和畏惧感。具有领地感的、便于认知和把控的小尺度的公共场所较易吸引老年人的出行。因而典型的外部空间特征是采用庭院元素，建筑围合而成庭院空间，形成单元空间；每个单元空间自成体系，而不同的单元空间又以庭院空间相连接（图 2）。以这种空间的联系，可以在场地空间内衍生，形成收放有致的小尺度的庭院空间。

图 2　庭院空间

3.3 空间层级与场所认知

场所除了本身所代表的空间的实质意义外，对于老年人来说，更重要的是心理层面的意义：如何使老人对所处的环境产生场所认同感和场所依赖感？这是老年人消除对环境空间的陌生感和抵触感，在主观上产生到达场所的意愿，融入社区社会生活的必备条件。一个方面，场所活动设施的配置需按老年人的需求，其目的除了餐饮、就医、咨询等生活必需外，还应设计场所空间，提供个体间社交互动，通过空间结构的分析，平面及空间组织旨在促进互动、促进老人的群聚活动。这就需要进行空间层级的设计，以设计提供支持和鼓励老人出行参与社会互动行为的场所空间。从环境心理学的角度来看，视觉、听觉、嗅觉、触觉等感知能力与交往活动密切相关，由此可以理解个体间直接交流的老年人对于场所空间的感受：多层次、小尺度的层级空间较易吸引老年人的出行。

新河养老社区针对中国的老年社区，结合中国国情及老年人需求而弹性设置相关设施。而场所空间上，则创造出多元的空间层级——将空间分为私密、半私密、半开放、开放四个层级，每一个层级的场所均有其独特的空间属性与边界性，由安全度高的私密空间到互动性强的开放空间，各层级空间具有空间上的变化，又有相互之间空间组织的连续性。居住单元空间无疑是最为隐秘的私人空间，因而设计上要具有鲜明的家的领域感而获得老年人对空间的认同感。第二个层级空间是家门口或后庭院处与外界接触的邻里空间。家门口的空间设计上产生一个后退的场所，与邻近居住空间共同围合出一个小的领域，这样的一个简单的节点设计，可以让邻里间共有一个短暂停留聊天的空间，提供私密空间向外的空间转换；后庭院空间以植被围合出小尺度空间，既有行动上的边界性又具有视线上的联系性。半开放空间层级，设计的出发点是一个多元化的空间，以建筑所围合的院落空间为基本单元，多个院落空间以路径、台阶等缓冲元素联系在一起，形成错落有致的完整的聚落空间。最后一个层级：开放空间，这是社区最重要的公共空间，是群体活动的场所。开放空间一般位于老年人易达的场所，同时在社区内多点分布。开放空间一般由于其过大的尺度缺少对行为活动的包裹感，形成空间压迫。设计上着力于符合老年人心理、行为的空间场所，需对其进行分解、限定、重组；或是在较大尺度空间周边布置小尺度的庭院、停留场所，大空间也可以有亲密性：透过其相邻的小空间塑造出来。对于身体日渐衰弱的老年人来说，由于较为不易适应环境的变化，不同空间大小层级可以整合出一个多元化的空间结构，这是不可或缺的；而其空间设计的成功与否，取决于能否增进老年居住者参与社交活动的意愿与其空间方便程度。

3.4 交通空间与活力

交通空间以动态流通的方式存在，更强调空间导向性。这种导向性客观地吸引人们的视线，给予恰当的心理暗示：老人在漫步过程中，因循引导暗示自觉向目标靠近，实现空间场所的移位和转换。新河养老社区，其规划、建筑、景观完全按照老年人的需求设计，住区规划实施严格的人车分流，不仅全面实现无障碍通行，这种环境下的出行对老年人来说是愉悦的和享受的，在居住区内的步行交通体系规划设计中应予以足够重视。

对于老年人来说，出行意愿更易受到心理距离的影响。单一线性的交通空间会给人以单调枯燥的感觉，增大心理的距离感。而交通空间的价值绝不仅仅在于其本身的交通性。基于交通空间自身特有的多义性，通过设计的手段，可以拓展其空间价值。交通空间作为一种中介空间，往往处于两处或多处空间场所的中间地带，必然具有过渡空间的特征。在居住区中、室内外空间之间、不同开放度空间之间、大小尺度空间之间、竖向标高变化空间之间、公共性层次差异空间之间等，一系列的空间过渡与衔接，需充分考虑人行为方式和心理感受的特殊性。同时，场所联系和空间组织，起关键性作用的恰恰是交通空间，它是形成空间秩序的结构框架与连接纽带。在交通空间网络体系里，每个线性的视觉端点都可以塑造成活动节点，每个动线的交接处，都可以创造成偶遇、问候、聊天的场所。设计中，可以在视觉的端点处、动线的交接处，创造一些"事件型空间"[①]。人们对空间场景变化的感知来自于历时性体验。穿行交通空间的过程，就是一种时间与空间的交融，空间因借于时间的推移而成就价值。在感知空间时，人们正是借助时间的延续而最终实现空间体验。交通空间作为典型的联系空间，同样具有场所感和空间体验的特征。如在主街的街角处搭建的戏台，结合临近的会所建筑，形成交通空间和开放空间及建筑空间的连接与转换（图3）。在交通空间中引入

图片3 事件空间

这些滞留性空间，让老人在出行的过程中，于无意间发生一些故事，增加了空间的趣味性，增加了行走的乐趣，无形中缩短了出行的心理距离感。

在交通空间网络体系里，每个线性的视觉端点都可以塑造成活动节点，每个动线的交接处，都可以创造成偶遇、问候、聊天的滞留性空间。人们对空间场景变化的感知来自于历时性体验。穿行交通空间的过程，就是一种时间交融的过程。在感知空间时，人们正是借助时间的延续而最终实现空间体验。交通空间作为典型的联系空间，同样具有场所感和空间体验的特征。这在老年人的日常出行交通空间里显得尤为突出。

---

① 事件空间通过反文脉、叠置（建筑蒙太奇）、波普化、反讽等的创作手法向传统提出挑战。重视与人的生活联系，重视人对建筑的主观体验和感受过程。使建筑创作真正从"结果"走向"过程"。与事件空间相关的建筑师彼得·埃森曼、伯纳得·屈米、丹尼尔·李伯斯金强调将"事件"带入建筑的观点，强调人在建筑空间中的各种主观体验活动和感受而形成事件的"过程"。

4 结语

本项目是对复合型养老社区营建的一次尝试，文章则是针对空间与老年人生活社交等活动的关系的研究。在宜人的空间场所内易于发生生动的事件，优质的空间品质提高老年人群的自发性活动频度；而随着自发性活动量的增加，社会交往活动几率也会相应增长。由此，探求创造一个能够符合老年人宜居的空间设计，使其能够提升老年人身心和社交上的能力，是十分重要的。逐步进入老龄化社会，如何设计一个可以提供全方位照顾与支持的空间环境，使老人可以健康、有保障的参与到社会生活中来，这在我国是一个当务之急的必要课题。

Spatial Planning and Design for Active Aging: Design Exploration of Xinhe Aging Community

Li Ming[1], Zhang Ling[2]

（1. School of Mechanics Qu Civil Engineering, China University of Mining and Technology; 2. School of Art and Design, China University of Mining and Technology）

Abstract: Due to the rising problem of aging, there has become a strong trend of aging community construction. How to provide healthy, comfortable environment for the elderly? To solve these problems, with the examples of Xinhe aging community, spatial planning and design for active aging are discussed.

Keywords: Active aging, Spatial planning and design, Place meaning, Hierarchy of space

参考文献：

[1] 周燕珉，程晓青，林菊英，等．老年住宅[M]．北京：中国建筑工业出版社，2011．

[2] FAY J. Aging in Community[M]. Cambridge: Massachusetts Institute Technology, 2008.

[3] 裘知，王竹，张红虎．杭州天目山"菜单自助式"复合型养老社区设计探索[J]．华中建筑，2014，8：74-78.

[4] 肖兰．我国社区复合型老年建筑空间构成研究[D]．北京：清华大学，2008.

[5] 外山义，等．组团护理单位[M]．东京：筒井书房，2000.

[6] 橘弘志，等．特别护理老年人设施的公共空间的半私密半公共领域的考察[R]．日本建筑学会计画系论文集，2002：157-164.

[7] 李斌，李庆丽．养老设施空间结构与生活行为扩展的比较研究[J]．建筑学报，2011，5：153-159.

[8] 张强．居家养老模式下老年人居住环境及生活行为的调查[D]．上海：同济大学，2007：49-54.

[9] （丹麦）杨·盖尔．交往与空间：国外城市设计丛书[M]．何可人译．北京：中国建筑工业出版社，2002.

[10] （美）布拉福德·珀金斯．老年居住建筑[M]．北京：中国建筑工业出版社，2008.

积极老龄化背景下老年住宅设计探讨

黄海静[1,2]　冉嘉诚[1]

（1. 重庆大学建筑城规学院；2. 重庆大学山地城镇建设与新技术教育部重点实验室）

摘要：人口老龄化是社会经济发展和科学技术进步背景下，人们物质生活、精神文化生活水平提高和医疗卫生条件改善的必然结果。老年人由于身体物理机能的退化，其家庭和社会地位发生变化而导致他们生理和心理状态的变化，加重了老人的孤独感、失落感。为了促进社会进步，保障老年人的权力，老龄化需要被"阳光"的对待。文章结合积极老龄化这一背景，基于老年人生理、心理、行为特征以及人体工程学，从总体布局、单元及套内空间三个方面研究老年住宅，并提出相应设计要点。

关键词：积极老龄化，生理心理特性，老年住宅设计

1 引言

依照世界卫生组织的标准，当一个国家或地域 60 周岁以上的老年人达到总人口的 10%，或者新标准 65 周岁以上的老年人达到总人口的 7%，称为"老龄化国家"；当 65 周岁以上的老龄人口超过 14% 时，称为"老龄国家"。[1]自 20 世纪 90 年代开始，各发达国家相继进入老年化社会。1996年世界卫生组织提出了积极老龄化，2002 年联合国第二届世界老龄大会将其写进了政治宣言。[2]积极老龄化是指为了提高老年人的生活质量，使健康、参与和保障的机会发挥到最大效益的过程。

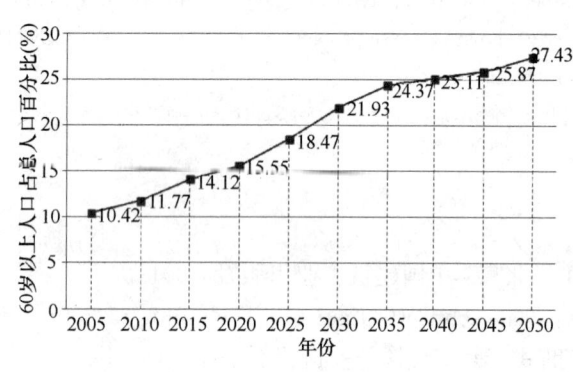

图 1　我国 60 岁以上人数占总人数百分比

（2005～2050）

（资料来源：根据资料整理自绘）

中国人口众多，老年人口基数庞大（图 1），作为最早进入老龄化社会的发展中国家之一，与许多发达国家不同的是我国老龄化属于未富先老，即我们经济发展程度与老龄化程度不平衡，这表明实行社会养老在我国还需要一段时间。另一方面，由于受我国传统文化思想影响，大量老年人更愿意在家中颐养天年，子女也希望父母在家中养老以报养育之恩，在相当长的时间内，住宅养老仍然是我国主要的养老方式。因此，结合老年人生理、心理、行为特征及人体工程学研究老年住宅设计，为老年人提供一个积极健康的居住环境对于实现积极老龄化意义重大。

2 老年人生理及行为心理特征

进入老年期后人的生理机能逐步衰退，其感知系统、神经系统、肌肉及骨骼系统退化，对环境的适应能力及抗病能力都减弱。老年人由于生理机能的退化身体各部分相对萎缩，导致他们人体尺度的变化；老年人退休后与社会发生脱离，其社会角色和家庭角色都发生了变化，导致了他们心理上的显著特征：他们时常会产生孤独感、失落感、抑郁感。

老年人的生理、心理特征也会影响其行为特征。由于运动机能退化，过量的运动对老年人来说比较困难，他们的活动范围因此缩小。其孤独、失落的情绪导致他们愿意和亲近熟悉的人待在一起。这也就造成了老年人对"家"的依赖。积极老年化强调健康、参与和安全保障。因此，老年住

宅设计必须从老年人的生理特征、心理特征、行为特征和人体尺度几方面进行分析（表1），才能真正满足老人的居住需求。

老年人生理、心理特征及需求　　　　　　　　　　　　表1

老年人生理特征	老年人生理需求	老年人心理特征	老年人心理需求
·神经系统功能退化 ·感觉机能退化 ·肌肉骨骼运动机能退化 ·呼吸系统退化 ·新陈代谢减慢 ·对环境适应能力减慢 ·免疫力退化	·对声环境的要求 ·对光环境的要求 ·对热环境的要求 ·对人体功效环境的要求 ·对无障碍环境的要求	·孤独 ·失落 ·抑郁 ·多疑、敏感 ·固执、偏激	·安全感 ·归属感 ·舒适感 ·私密感 ·家庭感 ·场所感 ·邻里交往

资料来源：根据资料整理自绘。

3　基于老年人生理心理特征的老年住宅设计要点

3.1　住宅总体布局设计要点

（1）选址布局要求

随着年龄增长老年人生理机能下降，其夜间睡眠质量下降。在老年住宅规划选址时，应选择相对安静的区域。同时，住宅布局应该保证规范要求的日照时间，并拥有良好的朝向及采光，因为自然光可促进钙质的吸收和产生维生素 D，有益于老年人身体健康。

（2）畅通环境空间

小区内部环境空间设计首先应该考虑无障碍要求，小区出入口应确保安全，宜采用平缓的坡道代替台阶，当确有较大高差时应设置自动扶梯或升降梯；并在入户单元处及各活动场地都设置无障碍坡道。其次，为了给老年人提供健康的生活环境，小区规划时应设置老年人活动空间，如健康休闲步道，每隔一定距离应设置供老年人休息停留的空间，这段距离应保持在180～220m，符合老年人5分钟舒适步行距离。[3]

（3）增设配套设施

老年人由于子女忙于自己的工作常常不能陪在身边，难免会产生孤独感。在住宅小区设计时，应增设便于老年人相互交流的活动用房，适当加大适宜老人公共活动的空间，并组织相应老年人活动，以增加其参与性和存在感。强调"医住一体化"，在小区还应配备一定的医疗服务设施，以方便老年人就医和保健，如设置小区诊所等。

（4）营造场所感

老年人的记忆力、认知力下降，迷路的情况时有发生，因此，老年人居住小区设计时应注意营造老人熟悉的场所感。老年人有自己的生活年代，通过研究他们的生活习惯和行为喜好，并考虑适宜老年人的人体尺度，在小区规划中植入相应的标识性符号，从而提高小区各场所的可识别性，便于老人的空间定位。

3.2　住宅单元及套型设计要点

（1）无障碍设计

住宅单元无障碍设计包括公共空间无障碍设计和套内空间无障碍设计。老年人的肌纤维随着年龄的增长变细、肌肉韧带萎缩，且骨骼老化，行动不便，容易疲劳。因此老年住宅的楼层不宜过高，或者合理设置担架电梯。老年人住宅公共空间应做无障碍扶手，公共楼梯休息平台应设计富足的空间供老年人停留休息。

同时，套内走道部分应考虑轮椅通行尺寸的要求，宽度达到 1100～1200mm。厕所、浴室应设安全扶手，方便老年人生活。老年人运动系统衰退，在厨房、厕所设计时应该注意地面防滑处理，应尽量避免室内高差。同时在老年住宅中应该安装紧急呼救按钮，以便发生意外情况时老年人能够及时呼救。

（2）套型位置模式

为避免老人的孤独感和失落感，套型组织时，老年人住户应尽量与一般住户混合居住。当老人独居时，老年住户可以与其他一般住户同层布置、垂直布置、混合布置。在垂直布置老年住户时要注意无障碍电梯的设置。

当老人和子女以两代居居住时，可采用三种模式：分居型——老年人和子女在一套住宅内共同使用住宅的一个部分或多个部分；邻居型——两个家庭相邻而居，或同住一层楼，或仅以一墙相隔，两代人生活完全独立；近居型——老年家庭与年轻家庭就近居住，比如位于同一小区（表2）。[4]

老年住宅套型布置方式　　　　　　　　　　　　　表2

独居型			两代居		
垂直布置	同层布置	混合布置	分居型	邻居型	近居型
■老年住户　　□其他住户			■老年住户　　□子女住户		

资料来源：根据资料整理自绘。

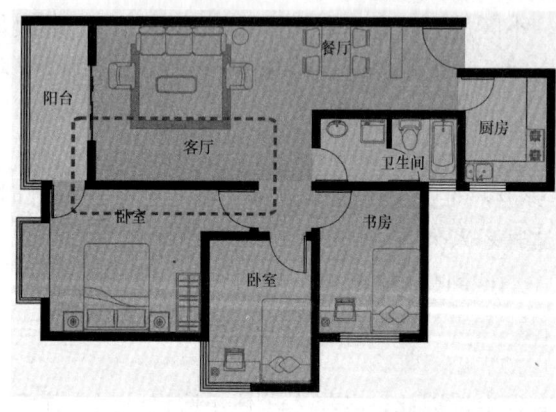

图2 卧室、客厅与阳台回游空间设计
（资料来源：根据资料整理自绘）

（3）套型空间设计

老年人由于生理机能下降其泌尿系统衰退，晚上起夜频繁。与家人同住的老人住宅设计时，宜在老人卧室入口处考虑设置老人专用的卫生间，或是将老人卧室布置在家庭卫生间附近，以方便老年人如厕，提高其睡眠质量。

为了方便行动不便的老年人在室内活动，宜适当加大住宅开间，增加开口位置，将老年人住宅室内设置成串联在一起的"回游空间"（图2）。这不仅可以扩大空间感，还增加各空间的可视性和开敞性，从而提高了老年人住宅的安全性。

3.3 住宅室内空间设计要点

（1）适宜的空间尺寸

老年人由于生理机能发生变化，人体尺度也发生了变化。研究表明：老年人70岁时身高比年轻时降低 2.5%～3%，老年女性的缩减有时最大可达6%。通过身高降低率可以近似推测出我国老年人大致人体尺度（表3），老年人由于行动不便，走路时会借助辅助工具如拐杖、轮椅等。因此，室内设计应根据老年人体尺度其活动范围确定空间尺寸、家具尺寸及布置方式。

老年人人体尺度测量 表3

测量姿势	测量项目	男（mm）	女（mm）
立姿	正立时举手高	2028	1877
	身高	1672	1549
	眼高	1560	1439
	肩高	1400	1282
	肩宽	404	357
	手臂长	708	658
	腿长	935	971
坐姿	正坐时举手高	1682	1634
	坐高	1307	1243
	眼高	1202	1137
	正坐时肩高	1033	977
	膝盖高	526	494
	正坐时前伸手臂长	799	748
	腿弯至臀部水平长	446	453

资料来源：根据资料整理自绘。

（2）舒适的物理环境

老年人睡眠质量不好，要保证室内门窗和墙体的隔声性能，为老年人提供一个安静的居住环境。同时可采用富含蓝绿色光成分的光源以较高的照度进行照明，这会对缓解失眠带来好处。[5] 老年人环境适应能力退化，免疫力下降，对环境温度、湿度变化非常敏感，在住宅设计时应保证通风良好，并注重建筑围护结构的热工性能，保证室内良好的热舒适环境。

（3）淡雅的室内色彩

老年人阅历丰富而追求宁静、平和，室内配色应根据房间功能，结合老人心理感受整体考虑。例如客厅是家庭群体生活的空间，除用于休息外，也是接待宾客和娱乐的场所，老年人在客厅空间逗留的时间相对较长，所以色调可以明快活泼些，但不宜用太强烈刺激的色彩，以免给老人造成烦躁的感觉。卧室是家居中私密性要求最高的场所，老人居住空间中卧室的色调选择应以私密和安静为前提，卧室中的色彩最好偏暖、柔和些，以利于老人的休息。书房是老人们用于阅读、书写和学习的一种静态工作空间，色彩配置上要求能够头脑冷静、注意力集中和安宁。室内色调必须以雅致、庄重、和谐为主色调，例如选用灰色、褐灰色、褐绿色、浅蓝色、浅绿色等最佳。[6]

4　结语

人口老龄化是我国发展不可回避的一个社会问题，贯彻积极老龄化理念对我国老年事业发展十分关键。本文基于老年人及行为生理、心理特征的分析，研究老年住宅总体布局、单元及套型、室内空间设计的要点，以期为老年人营造安全、舒适而健康的积极化的居住空间环境。

To Explore the Elderly Residential Design Under Active Aging Background

Huang[1,2] Haijing，Ran Jiacheng [1]

（1. Chongqing University School of Architecture and Urban Planning，Chongqing；2. Key Laboratory of Mountain Town Construction and New Technology，Ministry of Education，Chongqing University）

Abstract：Population aging is the inevitable result of the improvement of people's material life，spiritual and cultural living standards and health conditions in the context of the socio-economic development and scientific and technological progress. An aging population lead to the workforce reduction，the elderly dependency ratio rises，pension funds surge in spending and other issues. Meanwhile，The elderly due to physical deterioration of physical function，their families and social status changes which resulting in changes in their physical and mental state and increasing the loneliness and a sense of loss of the elderly. Therefore，no matter the country or individual，aging need to be "sunshine" treatment. Combining active aging against this background，studying elderly housing design point based on the elderly physiological，psychological，behavioral characteristics and ergonomics

Keywords：Active aging，Physiological and psychological characteristics，Elderly housing design

参考文献：

[1] 周燕珉，王富春．"居家养老为主"模式下的老年住宅设计[J]．现代城市研究，2011，10：68-69．

[2] 蒋子桓．积极老龄化理论及政策研究[D]．北京：清华大学，2009．

[3] 陈佳伟，翁彩虹，刘婷婷．基于美国经验谈混合养老社区中的老年人出行关怀[J]．城市建筑，2014，05：44-45．

[4] 乔会卿．老年人住宅户型设计研究[D]．四川：西南财经大学，2011．

[5] 翁季，陈仲林，胡英奎，等．光生物效应研究综述[J]．灯与照明，2007，01：2．

[6] 马亮．老年人住宅室内色彩设计[J]．艺术科技，2013，11：12．

少子化与房价因果关系之研究——以台湾六大城市区为例

林左裕　黄虹茌

（政治大学地政学系）

摘要：本研究综合人口、社会及经济的角度，运用共整合分析及 Granger 因果关系检定来检视台湾六大城市区（台北市、新北市、新竹市、台中市、台南市及高雄市）房价及少子化之关系。研究结果发现，六大城市中台北市、新北市、台南市、高雄市房价与少子化间存在关系。台北市与新北市是房价影响生育率，在房价长期不合理上涨趋势下，导致生育率下降；而台南市与高雄市是生育率影响房价，长期所得偏低且成长速度缓慢，民众选择以降低生育，减少家庭支出成本累积购屋资金，导致生育率下降，房价上升之现象。这些不同区域间房价与低生育率之相互关系，可提供政府未来制定政策时有效参考。

关键词：少子化，房价，共整合，因果关系

1　引言

近年来全球不论已发展与否，正经历重要的人口变迁问题。根据美国开发总署（United States Agency for International Development，USAID）统计数据①显示，全世界 1970 年、1990 年及 2013 年平均总生育率分别为 5.1、3.92 及 2.78，40 年期间全世界总生育率下降约 47%，其中，台湾的生育率更是低于 1.3，已进入所谓的超低生育率②之现象。不论于欧美地区或东亚地区，少子化现象已成为全球化的共同趋势之一。台湾之人口结构近年亦已逐渐转型为高龄化及少子化的社会，老年人口逐年递增，而幼年人口却逐年递减。1947 年时 65 岁以上人口比例为 2.53%，至 2011 年时已增加为 10.89%；而 0～14 岁之幼年人口则由 42.33% 减少至 15.08%，开始出现人口衰退的警讯。根据最新发布之 2014 年 10 月人口统计资料显示，0～14 岁人口占总人口比率 14.03%；15～64 岁人口占 74.07%；65 岁以上人口占 11.9%，由此可知老年人口比仍然逐渐增加，幼年人口比例也未见改善，而育龄妇女总生育率亦逐年递减，1951 年之总生育率高达 7，自 1954 年起皆低于 2，于 2010 年时已不足 1。

理论上，高房价对家庭生育行为有两种影响层面，分别是若房价过高以致无法负担的情况下，对于配偶的组成有负向影响因而减弱生育行为；或夫妻购置不动产后，却因高额的房屋贷款而对生育行为有资源排挤效果。实际上，影响房价的因素众多，为消除总体经济因素、税制政策、社会文化等干扰，本研究拟运用台湾六大城市区（台北市、新北市、新竹市、台中市、台南市及高雄市）的区域性追踪资料，以深入分析房价与少子化的关系。本研究期透过数据资料的实证结果，探讨房价与少子化间的关系，除填补文献对此重大议题探讨之不足外，提供政府于施政上之参考，进而改善生育率下滑现象。

2　理论基础

整理国内外相关文献，发现人口结构转变对房价的影响是显著的（Mulder and Billari, 2010, Levin 等，2009；Murphy 等，2008；Mulder, 2006；Krishnan and Krotki, 1993）。拥有房屋者与

---

① 2014 World Population Data Sheet of Population Reference Bureau.

② 超低生育率（thelowest-lowfertility）主要是指总生育率低于或小于 1.3，此现象肇始于 20 世纪 90 年代之欧洲，之后蔓延至亚洲国家。

无拥有房屋者，对房价变动产生的财富效果有不同的结果，房价上涨时，拥屋者会提高生育，无拥屋者会降低生育（Mulder and Billari，2010；Dettling and Kearney，2013）。有研究更进一步探讨自有住宅率与生育率之关系，房价与住宅自有率存在长期均衡关系，且房屋自有率较高的地区，生育率较低（Mulder and Lo，2012；Billari，2010；吴闵钰，2007）。另外，将房价纳入影响生育率的因素，研究发现房价与生育率存在长期均衡关系，且其关系为负向关系（简淑苹，2013；陈明吉等，2012；Yi and Zhang，2010）。如表 1 整理房价与生育率分析相关文献。

房价与生育率分析相关文献汇整表 表 1

作者	影响因素	研究方法	结果
Malmberg （2010）	总生育率、人口资料、家户所得、高等教育比率	追踪数据、固定效果模型	低生育率跟人口老化所产生的年龄结构变迁，将导致瑞典房价的缓滞成长
Yi and Zhang （2010）	生育率、房价指数、女性劳动参与率、女性与男性实质工资	Johansen 检验、共整合检定、ECM 模型	房价指数平均上涨 1%，总生育率下降 0.45%
Michael and Kevin （2013）	生育率、家户所得、房价	追踪数据、固定效果模型	房价与收入呈正向关系，收入与生育率呈负向关系，高房价的区域反而生育率较低
Dettling and Kearney （2013）	生育率、房价、所得、失业率、住宅自有率	追踪数据、固定效果模型	房价的上涨 10% 会替拥有房屋的人带来增加 4.5% 的生育率，无拥有房屋者，下降 1%
Lo（2012）	自有住宅率、总生育率	区域追踪数据、固定效果模型	台湾之生育率与住宅自有率有显著的负向关系
Hui 等 （2012）	生育率、房价、扶老比	共整合检定、向量自我回归模型（VAR）、向量误差修正模型（VECM）、Granger 因果关系检定	香港房价上涨 1%，老年人口及生育率分别降低 0.52% 及 1.65%，且长期而言，房价及扶老比皆会影响生育率
陈明吉等 （2012）	总生育率、房价所得比、女性劳动参与率、女性高等教育比、龙年效应、家庭计划转折期	共整合检定、向量自我回归模型（VAR）、向量误差修正模型（VECM）、Granger 因果关系检定	房价所得比为预测总生育率重要变量
彭建文、蔡怡纯 （2012）	总生育率、住宅自有率、家户可支配所得、有偶率、女性高等教育比	追踪数据共整合检定、向量误差修正模型（VECM）	生育率与住宅自有率具长期均衡关系，但短期可能因正负向关系互相抵消而不显著
简淑苹 （2013）	总生育率、房价指数、女性劳动参与率、失业率、家户所得年增率、物价指数年增率	共整合检定、向量自我回归模型（VAR）、向量误差修正模型（VECM）、Granger 因果关系检定	生育率与房价及家户所得年增率有长期共整合关系

数据来源：本研究整理。

　　本研究探讨的主题为少子化与房价之关系，根据相关文献回顾，以新家庭经济学理论作为基础（Wills，1973；Schultz，1985；becker1991），从生育的机会成本切入，再根据 Yi and Zhang（2010）的研究，房价上升使家庭于其他消费的可支配所得降低，因此产生负的收入效应，依据新家庭经济理论，假设孩子为正常财①，负的收入效应将降低生育的需求，据此本研究就台湾的房价对生育率的影响进行实证。根据过去实证女性劳动参与、女性高等教育比率、失业率、家户所得对生育率有显著影响（Bar and Leukhina，2010；Jones 等，2008；Schultz，2001；Narayan，2006；Hotz 等，1997；Schultz，

---

①　正常财：即正常商品，是经济学术语。需求量随消费者的实际收入上升而增加的商品被称为正常财。

1997；Becker，1991）可作为模型建立控制变量之参考。研究方法部分，国外的文献的研究方法大部分以追踪数据为主，运用区域型追踪减少总体因素的干扰，而国内的文献多半以共整合检定向量自我回归模型（VAR）、向量误差修正模型（VECM）、Granger 因果关系检定进行房价与生育率之因果关系的探讨（Malmberg，2010；Michael and Kevin，2013；彭建文等，2012）。

3 实证结果与分析

本研究根据相关文献与数据分析后，总体数据部分，被解释变量为育龄妇女总生育率，解释变量为房价指数、失业率、消费者物价指数、实质台湾生产毛额、女性高等教育比率和公民可支配所得年增率，以 1998 年第一季至 2013 年第四季为研究期间；个体数据部分，比对房价指数与其他变数之重叠时间范围后，决定采用以 2004 年第一季至 2013 第四季为研究期间；而空间范围为台北市、新北市、新竹市、台中市、台南市、高雄市之六大城市区，本研究以共整合检定及因果关系检定，分析台湾少子化现象与房价之间所存在之影响关系，以了解近 20 年内台湾人口政策之妥适性，并分析此波房价高涨与人口变动之间的关系。

3.1 单根检定

本研究依据选取之总体经济变量进行单根检定，ADF 检定与 PP 检定之结果有所不同，如表 2 所示，除了变量 GDP 和 CPI 能够拒绝有单根的虚无假设外为 I（0）定态序列，其余变量在取一阶差分后成为定态资料，故为 I（1）序列。

		总体经济变量单根检定表			表 2
检定统计量		ADF 检定		PP 检定	
		T-统计量	落后期	T-统计量	落后期
级别	TFR	−2.315429	5	−2.431232	4
	HPI	0.562665	1	0.475082	4
	UR	−2.706226	2	−2.043941	5
	CPI	−3.952738	3**	−3.770814	4**
	GDP	−4.318572	2***	−2.593030	2***
	EDU	1.098159	4	−0.021356	5
	IR	−2.044498	5	−1.880726	3
一阶差分	TFR	−5.353528	3*	−3.719707	2**
	HPI	−6.452871	0***	−6.375255	1***
	UR	−4246261	2**	−3.410251	1***
	EDU	−3.317367	3***	−9.238256	1***
	IR	−8.085690	3***	−4.529827	1***

注：＊和＊＊和＊＊＊表示在 1％、5％、10％的显著水平下，拒绝有单根的虚无假设。

3.2 共整合检定

本研究透过单根检定确定的形态后，接着对非定态的数据进行共整合检定，确定变量间是否存在长期趋势关系。如表 3～表 8，台北市、新北市、台中市、台南市、高雄市，房价与总生育率之间皆存在共整合现象，表示这些城市得房价与生育率存在长期趋势关系；而新竹市在本次检定中，并未出现共整合现象，表示新竹市的房价与生育率间没有明显的趋势关系。

台北市共整合检定表　　　　　　　　　　　　　　　　　表 3

Hypothesized No. of CE	Trace Statistic	0.05 临界值	P 值	Max-Eigen Statistic	0.05 临界值	P 值
None	5.019348	15.49471	0.0068***	4.477593	14.26460	0.0058***
At most 1	0.541755	3.841466	0.0617***	0.541755	3.841466	0.0617**

注：＊和＊＊和＊＊＊表示在1％、5％、10％的显著水平下，拒绝没有共整合虚无假设。

新北市共整合检定表　　　　　　　　　　　　　　　　　表 4

Hypothesized No. of CE	Trace Statistic	0.05 临界值	P 值	Max-Eigen Statistic	0.05 临界值	P 值
None	18.65831	15.49471	0.0161**	11.79246	14.26460	0.0983*
At most 1	6.865847	3.841466	0.0088***	6.865847	3.841466	0.0088***

注：＊和＊＊和＊＊＊表示在1％、5％、10％的显著水平下，拒绝没有共整合虚无假设。

新竹市共整合检定表　　　　　　　　　　　　　　　　　表 5

Hypothesized No. of CE	Trace Statistic	0.05 临界值	P 值	Max-Eigen Statistic	0.05 临界值	P 值
None	7.766414	15.49471	0.4907	5.920217	14.26460	0.6235
At most 1	1.846197	3.841466	0.1742	1.846197	3.841466	0.1742

注：＊和＊＊和＊＊＊表示在1％、5％、10％的显著水平下，拒绝没有共整合虚无假设。

台中市共整合检定表　　　　　　　　　　　　　　　　　表 6

Hypothesized No. of CE	Trace Statistic	0.05 临界值	P 值	Max-Eigen Statistic	0.05 临界值	P 值
None	21.60771	15.49471	0.0053***	15.89234	14.26460	0.0274**
At most 1	5.715377	3.841466	0.0168**	5.715377	3.841466	0.0168**

注：＊和＊＊和＊＊＊表示在1％、5％、10％的显著水平下，拒绝没有共整合虚无假设。

台南市共整合检定表　　　　　　　　　　　　　　　　　表 7

Hypothesized No. of CE	Trace Statistic	0.05 临界值	P 值	Max-Eigen Statistic	0.05 临界值	P 值
None	13.88653	15.49471	0.0861*	9.426948	14.26460	0.2523
At most 1	4.459579	3.841466	0.0347**	4.459579	3.841466	0.0347**

注：＊和＊＊和＊＊＊表示在1％、5％、10％的显著水平下，拒绝没有共整合虚无假设。

高雄市共整合检定表　　　　　　　　　　　　　　　　　表 8

Hypothesized No. of CE	Trace Statistic	0.05 临界值	P 值	Max-Eigen Statistic	0.05 临界值	P 值
None	27.93818	15.49471	0.0004***	22.09606	14.26460	0.0024***
At most 1	5.842118	3.841466	0.0156**	5.841466	3.841466	0.0156**

注：＊和＊＊和＊＊＊表示在1％、5％、10％的显著水平下，拒绝没有共整合虚无假设。

3.3　因果关系检定

研究结果显示六大城市的因果关系可分为三类，第一类为房价影响生育率，台北市与新北市存在此类型的因果关系，且台北市相对新北市更为显著，也就是说房价长期不合理上涨，在庞大的房贷压力下，导致生育率降低；第二类为房价与生育率之间无因果关系，新竹市与台中市在房价与总生育率之间，并不存在因果关系；第三类为生育率影响房价，台南市与高雄市存在此类型的因果关系，表示长期低生育率，导致房价的上涨，也就是说南部地区的家庭，因所得相较北部地区较低，在购屋与生育之间的决策，选择减少生育方式降低家庭开销，累积储蓄购买不动产，呈现生育率下降，房价出现上涨的趋势。

4　结论与建议

4.1　结论

本研究假设低生育率长期来看人口需求减少，应该会有抑制房价的效果，但有趣的是结果显示低生育率导致高房价，进一步观察两个变量的影响，出现当房价越高时，生育率越低的现象，显示房价高涨增加家庭的支出比例，降低生育的意愿，导致少子化的现象，此现象在台北市与新北市更为明显，依据此研究结果，政府欲提高生育率，除了刺激经济成长，提升国民所得外，更重要的是将房价控制在合理的范围，减轻家庭支出上的负担比重，以提升家庭生育的意愿，使人口结构回复到正常的机能；进一步观察六大城市状态，除新竹市外，其他五大城市房价与生育率皆存在长期趋势关系，且因果关系呈现不同的影响方向，北部区域市房价领先生育率，显示台北市与新北市房价上涨快速，加上所得提升的速度缓慢，家庭收入受到房价上涨的压缩，降低生育的意愿、中部区域因果关系不明显台中市的房价与总生育率存在长期趋势关系，但其因果关系并不显著，表示房价与生育率之间存在相同趋势变化，但相互没有影响、南部区域市生育率领先房价台南市与高雄市在购屋与生育之间的决策，以减少生育的方式，降低家庭支出，将所储蓄的资金投入不动产，使房价出现上涨的现象。

4.2　建议

依据研究结果，北部地区与南部地区存在不同的问题，台北市与新北市的房价影响生育率，在房价长期不合理上涨趋势下，导致生育率下降，因此为解决人口问题，政策上应着重在修正房价方向思考，运用调整税制结构、健全租屋市场等，使房价回归合理，并提供相关配套措施如租金补贴、社会住宅等，减轻年轻族群的负担，以提升生育诱因；台南市与高雄市则是生育率影响房价，相对北部地区而言南部地区的所得偏低且成长速度缓慢，民众在面临生育与购屋的抉择上，选择以降低生育，减少家庭支出成本方式累积购屋资金，导致生育率下降，房价上升之现象，因此在政策上的建议上，可朝向刺激地方产业发展，提升家户所得方向思考，或是强化社会福利如生育补贴、租屋补贴等，透过所得提升与健全社会福以增加育儿的诱因。

A Study of the Lead-Lag Relationship between Housing Price and Low Fertility Rate -The Case of Six Municipalities in Taiwan

Lin Tso-Yu Calvin　　Huang Hong-Ren

(Department of Land Economics, Chengchi University)

Abstract: This study therefore intends to integrate factors of demographics, sociology and economics to investigate the fertility rate by multiple regression analysis, and to explore the relationship of housing price and low fertility rate by cointegration and Granger Causality test. Finally, this study examines the relationship between the housing price and low fertility rate in 6 cities in Taiwan (Taipei City, New Taipei City, Hsinchu City, Taichung City, Tainan City, and Kaohsiung City). Results of this study found that the relationship between the housing price and low fertility rate in Taipei City, New Taipei City, Tainan City, and Kaohsiung City. Housing price affect fertility rate in Taipei City and New Taipei City. In the long run, the unreasonable trend in housing price leads to low fertility rate. Fertility rate affect housing price in Tainan City and Kaohsiung City. The income will be stagnated and economic growth will be slow. In order to reduce the household costs, households choose to reduce fertility to cope with the high housing prices. Results of this study provide precious implications for policy decision making in the future.

Keywords: Low fertility rate, Housing price, Cointegration, Granger causality

参考文献：

[1]　林左裕、简淑苹. 房价与少子化的关系[G]. 2012 住宅学会、都市计划学会、区域科学学会与地区发展学会联合年会暨论文研讨会，2012.

[2]　彭建文、蔡怡纯. 住宅自有率对生育率之长短期影响—追踪资料共整合分析应用[J]. 人口学刊，44：57-86.

[3]　黄智聪、黄修梅. 台湾地区妇女学历对生育率影响之再审视[G]. 台湾经济学会与北美华人经济学会 2005 年联合年会，2005.

[4]　Hui, E. C. M., Zheng, X. & Jiang H. (2012). "Housing price, elderly dependency and fertility behaviour." Habitat International; 36 (2): 304-311.

[5]　Levin, E., Montagnoli, A., & Wright, R. E. (2009). "Demographic change and the housing market: evidence from a comparison of Scotland and England." Urban Studies; 46(1): 27-43.

[6]　Mulder, C. H., & Billari, F. C. (2010). "Homeownership regimes and low fertility." Housing Studies; 25(4): 527-541.

[7]　Simon, C. J. & Tamura, Robert (2009). "Do higher rents discourage fertility? Evidence from U. S. cities, 1940-2000." Regional Science and Urban Economics; 39: 33-42.

[8]　Yi, Junjian & Zhang, Junsen(2010). "The effect of house price on fertility: evidence from Hong Kong." Economic Inquiry; 48(3) : p635-650.

"1＋1"社区养老模式探究

王立舟

（华中科技大学建筑与城市规划学院）

摘要：在城市人口老龄化的背景下，本文首先研究了国外养老型社区的四类运营模式：生活自理型社区、生活协助型社区、特殊护理社区，以及混合型的持续护理退休社区，提出对国内养老社区建设的实质性建议，并结合国内的相关成功案例，如北京的乐成养老恭和苑、浙江城乡社区的"星光老年之家"等，总结出目前我国养老体系的发展大致分成的三种模式：居家养老、社区养老、机构养老。通过对这三种模式的对比分析，立足于我国经济尚且不发达的基本国情，作者试图找出既适应我国当下现状，又可以持续长远发展下去的一种社区养老模式。为此，文章提出了这样一个观点：从城市公共服务设施配建的角度来架构社区养老服务体系，进而得出"1＋1"的社区养老模式，并讨论了这种模式分等级配置的运行方式和运用"BOT"方法的开发方式。

关键词：老龄化，社区养老模式，"老人之家"，"居家养老"，BOT

1　引言

2010 年第六次全国人口普查显示 60 岁及以上人口占总人口的 13.26％，相比较 2000 年第五次人口普查上升 2.93 个百分点，其中 65 岁及以上人口占 8.87％，比 2000 年人口普查上升 1.91 个百分点。按照人口老龄化的定义，60 岁以上的人口占总人口比例达到 10％，或 65 岁以上人口占总人口的比重达到 7％，则这个国家或地区开始进入老龄化社会。而来自联合国的一份报告显示，到 2049 年，中国 60 岁以上的老年人将占总人口的 31％，老龄化程度仅次于欧洲。这预示着，从现在开始到未来的 20～30 年间，中国将是世界上人口老龄化速度最快的国家之一。

老龄人口的增加和老龄化速度的不断加快，使养老成为我们国家的热点问题，从社会、经济、环境的各个角度，对养老制度以及养老模式提出新一轮的挑战。特别是针对老年人的生活照料、康复护理、医疗保健、精神文化的需求日益凸显，而"养老型社区"的建设在这些伴随着"老龄化"而来的问题中，显得极具必要性，拥有很强的发展潜力。

模式的选择探究是架构社区养老必须解答的关键问题之一，中国一直以来传统的家庭养老模式，与我国目前所处有关人口、经济、社会、文化等多方面的特殊国情两者之间的矛盾，在计划生育政策所导致的少子老龄化的背景下提前暴露出来。我国的经济水平尚不发达，与世界上的发达国家间存在着很大的差距，然而计划生育政策长期执行在减缓人口增长的同时，也使少子化速度加快，大量的独生子女家庭将迎来养老时代。在有限的经济条件下，家庭养老功能逐渐衰退，传统的独立家庭养老模式受到冲击，老龄化的问题开始影响和制约着我国养老及养老模式的选择。

2　国外社区养老模式借鉴

老龄化的现象在国际上是各国都在面临的课题，众多发达国家在很早以前就已经进入老龄化社会，人口老龄化对社会的各个方面都产生了深远的影响。

美国是发达国家中生育率最高和人口增长最快的国家之一，而早在 20 世纪 40 年代，美国就开始进入了人口老龄化社会，现 65 岁以上老龄人口占总人口的 17.4％，是典型的老龄化社会。与中国人口老龄化进程相比，美国人口老龄化具有以下特点：一是进入老年社会的时间长，美国步入老年国家之列已持续了 70 年，二是人口老龄化发展较慢，在西方发达国家中处于中等水平；三是高龄老年人口比重大。随着人口预期寿命的延长，美国老年人口比重还将不断提高。在人口老龄化程度不断加重的过程中，美国在应对人口老龄化方面积累了丰富的经验。美国的社区居家养老是"品质养老"的典范，它的社区具备了强大的助老功能，使得美国老年人能内安其心、外安其身，实现"安养—乐活—善终"的老年生活目标，所以多数美国老年人选择社区养老模式。

美国的养老社区一般分为四类：生活自理型社区、生活协助型社区、特殊护理社区，以及混合型的持续护理退休社区。第一类：生活自理型社区，主要面向年龄在 70～80 岁之间、生活能够自理的老年人；第二类：生活协助型社区，主要面向 80 岁以上、没有重大疾病，但生活需要照顾的老年人，社区提供包括餐饮、娱乐、保洁、维修、应急、短途交通、定期体检等基础服务，并可通过付费方式享受其他生活辅助服务，以及用药管理老年痴呆症的特殊护理；第三类：特殊护理型社区，主要面向有慢性疾病的老年人、术后恢复期及记忆功能障碍的老年人，社区内设有专业护士，提供各种护理和医疗服务；第四类：持续护理退休社区，面向那些退休不久、当前生活能够自理、但不想由于未来生活自理能力的下降而被迫频繁更换居所的老年人，为了实现对入住老年人的持续护理服务，此类社区一般是生活自理单元、生活协助单元与特殊护理单元的混合。

在这四大类养老社区中，居家养老服务的四种做法对国内相关方面建设具有实质性建议。一是全托制的"退休之家"，设施完备、服务周到。设施包括了医务室、图书室、计算机室、健身房、洗衣房、紧急呼叫系统等。服务包括了就餐、打扫房间、组织活动、出行安排等。二是日托制的"托老中心"，白天在中心活动，晚上回家休息。中心同样设施完备，并提供星级服务。起居室一人一床，一人一房。还有阅览室、保健室、活动室等。老年人除了不用为一日三餐操心外，还可以阅读、交往、制作手工艺品，安度晚年。三是组织"互助养老"。让老年人结伴认对、互助养老。四是提供上门服务。美国政府有一个福利性居家养老项目：由政府财政出钱，派家庭保健护士为有需要的老年人提供服务。家庭保健护士不同于保姆，她们不仅仅为老年人做饭、洗衣、打扫卫生，还得有护理知识。

3 我国社区养老模式探究

3.1 国内案例研究

在国内老龄化的进程中，有关养老型社区的建设方案，各地也都就当地的现实条件，做了一些探索实践。

如北京的乐成养老恭和苑，它从老年人的生理与心理需求两个方面双向出发，认为我国人口老龄化正呈加速发展态势，除了生理上的照料外，老年人更需要精神上的关怀。周边良好的医疗资源提供了安全感，交通便捷为亲友探望提供了便利，让老年人感觉没有被社会抛弃，这种理念和实践一直指导着乐成在养老型社区方面的建设。

贯彻这样的理念，恭和苑选址在城市核心地段而非青山绿水的郊区，它认为首先老年人越上年纪就越喜欢热闹，越怕被社会抛弃，在郊区其实会加重老年人的社会隔离感；再则优质的医疗资源通常分布在城市中心的大医院里，在郊区，万一遇到老年人紧急的医疗需求，可能耽误救治；最后，也是最重要的，核心市区交通环境较好，子女亲朋探视就更加方便。出自乐成养老的各个恭和苑都始终遵循"选址城市核心区"的不二法则，这不仅是乐成养老区别于其他养老机构的本质特点，更是恭和苑模式的核心所在。真正体现了养老社区为老年人而建的诚意与用心。

除了北京的乐成养老恭和苑，还有浙江城乡社区的"星光老年之家"，它倡导以养老服务志愿者为基础的居家养老服务体系；沈阳正在进行的由政府出面，购买公益岗位与发挥中介组织服务的居家养老服务模式；青岛的多样化养老服务模式；广州实行以居家养老为基础、社区服务为依托、机构养老为补充的养老模式。这一系列的实践探索，为奠定我国社区养老的完善理论提供了经验基础。

3.2 三大养老模式

通过对现有实践和国外建设经验的横向比较，不难得出，目前我国养老体系的发展大致可分为三种模式：居家养老、社区养老、机构养老。

3.2.1 居家养老模式

居家养老模式目前是我国最主要的养老模式，是中国社会养老服务体系的基础，也是体系的核心与重点。通过政府与社会各个阶层，为居家老人提供生活照料、家政、康复护理和精神慰藉等服务，让老年人既不脱离家庭，又能在家人与社会政府的共同努力下获得专业化的社会服务。居家养老模式是占用社会资源成本最低的模式，在我国经济尚且不发达的今天，它作为主流，存在于养老服务体系中。

3.2.2 社区养老模式

以社区为单位，根据社区的规模大小、诉求服务半径，建立不同等级规模的社区养老中心，即现在的"老人之家"。这类非营利性的机构类似于国外案例中的"退休之家"和"托老中心"，它具有完备的设施和周到的服务，包括了医务室、图书室、计算机室、健身房、洗衣房、紧急呼叫系统等，从活动到睡觉吃饭全方位为老年人提供服务，可满足无特殊要求老年人的生活需求，主要面向需要人员看护而家人又因各类问题难以实行完善照顾的老年人。此外，社区养老还可以提供居家养老所不能提供的服务，如"互助养老"，让老年人结伴认对，互助养老。

3.2.3 机构养老模式

这类模式包含了社会上的各类养老机构，与社区养老不同的是，养老机构为营利性单位，它对老年人实行的专业化照顾也更加全面，并配有专业的护士，提供各种护理和医务服务。往往面向有特殊照顾要求的老年人，如有慢性疾病的老年人、术后恢复期的老年人及记忆功能障碍的老年人，可作为居家养老与社区养老的补充，照料到后者无法顾及到的方面。

我国目前并存的这三大类社区养老模式，居家养老模式处于主流地位，他是我国社会养老服务体系的基础，亦是完善体系的核心与重点。社区养老服务则是居家养老服务的依托，是为了更好地实现居家养老服务的效果。机构养老服务是居家养老服务的支撑，是在当居家与社区养老服务根本无法实现养老服务基本需求时，由养老服务机构承担养老服务。这种以居家养老为主，社区养老、机构养老为辅的复合型模式构成了我国社区养老服务体系。

4 "1＋1"社区养老模式创新

以原有的社区养老服务体系为基础，结合我国重视居家养老的特点和经济条件尚不发达的基本国情，为了更好地确保老年人的生活质量，作者在这里设想了一种新的社区养老模式——"1＋1"模式。所谓"1＋1"，第一个"1"指的是以点状分布在各个社区之中的"老人之家"，第二个"1"指的是目前仍占主流发展的"居家养老"。但在新的模式中，"居家养老"并非居于主流地位，而是与"老人之家"相辅相成。

4.1 运营模式——从公共服务设施配置的角度出发

4.1.1 "老人之家"

"1＋1"社区养老模式中的"老人之家"作为公共服务设施的组成部分，它的用地布局按照"多中心分级配套"的总体布局模式分级配置，根据不同的服务工作类型和服务半径构筑市级、居住区级和居住小区级三级"老人之家"，形成等级完善、结构清晰的养老服务体系。

4.1.1.1 市级"老人之家"

市级"老人之家"负责下一级机构的布点规划、责任区划分、管理人员调度、物资流通，制定相关的服务政策、措施，以及从本市和本市以外区域向"老人之家"的物资输送、人才引进。市级"老人之家"作为市内最高等级的养老服务机构并不直接向需求人群提供服务，重在维持下层次机构的正常运行，为"1+1"模式中的行政管理中心。

4.1.1.2 居住区级"老人家"

这一级的"老人之家"同样不为需求人群直接提供服务，它负责接收上一级机构的物质输送，落实管理人员的调度和相关政策、措施的实施，同时又对下一级居住小区级"老人之家"负责：管理物资配置、征招管理人员和服务人员。居住区级"老人之家"在"1+1"模式中起到承上启下的作用，深化细化、落实上一级机构下发的指令，再具体分配给各个小区级"老人之家"。

4.1.1.3 小区级"老人之家"

小区级"老人之家"直接为老年人提供服务，接收上一级机构按需派发的各类物质资源和工作管理人员，同时可根据服务对象和相对工作量，自主向社会征召无偿或有偿的管理、服务人员。这一级"老人家"作为服务体系的最底层，也是"1+1"运营模式的基础，它直接面对需求人群，应加强内涵建设，实现基本现代化，不断提高服务能力。小区级"老人之家"由两个部分组成：非营利性部分和营利性部分。非营利性部分可满足无特殊要求老年人的需求，包括了医务室、图书室、计算机室、健身房、洗衣房、紧急呼叫系统等，从活动到睡觉吃饭全方位为老年人提供服务，参照以前的社区养老模式，还可发起"互助养老"等一系列活动。营利性部分则面对有特殊要求的老年人，有专业的医务人员配置，提供各类护理和医务服务，并向被服务人群索取一定得服务费，作为支撑医疗专业服务持续发展下去的资金来源。

三级"老人之家"各司其职，相互配合，作为"1+1"社区养老模式的重要组成部分，它支撑起整个服务体系的网络骨架，保证养老服务的运行和质量。

4.1.2 "居家养老"

"1+1"模式中的"居家养老"是由我国传统的居家养老模式与"老人之家"结合而来，它的主体仍然是以家庭照顾为主，然而当家人因为各类原因在老年人需要的时候无法做到全方位的照顾时，家人可向责任区内的小区级"老人之家"求助，由"老人之家"派遣护理人员到家中无偿地进行临时照料。将"居家养老"与"老人之家"的服务体系紧密结合，随着"1+1"模式的发展，最后达成将"居家养老"作为"老人之家"体系最基层的分支，融入大的服务体系，使老年人无论处在家中还是在当地的"老人之家"都可得到全方位的照料。

4.2 建设模式——"BOT"开发模式的运用

BOT(build—operate—transfer)即建设—经营—转让，它是用于基础设施建设的一种模式，是指政府通过契约授予私营企业(包括外国企业)以一定期限的特许专营权，许可其融资建设和经营特定的公用基础设施，并准许其通过向用户收取费用或出售产品以清偿贷款，回收投资并赚取利润；特许权期限届满时，该基础设施无偿移交给政府。

作者设想的"1+1"养老型社区的建设模式将"老人之家"作为遍布城市住区范围内的公共服务设施看待，它的体系化发展必然会给当地政府带来新的挑战，立足于我国基本国情，将"BOT"开发模式融入"老人之家"体系的建设，可缓解"1+1"模式起步阶段产生的资金压力，有利于此模式的持续发展。

根据"BOT"开发模式，将"老人之家"三级体系重新划分成两类：市级和居住区级为第一类、居住小区级为第二类。第一类由政府筹集资金建设管理，是体系的行政管理中心，第二类通过签署契约授予私营企业或国有企业一定期限的专营权，由这类企业筹集资金建设管理，特许期限届满时，居住小区级"老人之家"必须无偿移交给政府，由政府继续经营管理，以保证"1＋1"模式长期运行。小区级"老人之家"在由企业管理阶段时，仍然受到上一级机构的管制，资金周转、物质流通都会受到严格管控，体系化的建立为"老人之家"运营的公平公正，在市场经济的背景下，提供了强有力的保障。

5 总结

随着人口老龄化速度的加快，社区养老的发展会越来越强劲，社区养老服务设施的体系化建立是发展的必然趋势。文章中提到的"1＋1"社区养老模式是从公共服务设施配建的角度出发设想而来，是居住区的重要组成部分，此模式中所涉及的各个机构，以及它的等级制度、规模大小都应与居住区的建设紧密结合，为未来我国城市人口老龄化进程中社区规划的发展，添加浓墨重彩的一笔。

Research on the "1＋1" Model of Urban Community Providing for the Aged

Wang Lizhou

(School of Architecture and Urban Planning Huazhong University of Science and Technology)

Abstract: Under the background of the urban population aging, this paper studies the four categories of operation modes of foreign pension community which are independent-living community, assisted-living community, special-nursing, and the hybrid continuing care retirement community. Extraction of substantive suggestions on the construction of domestic pension community, and combined with the related domestic success stories, such as Beijing's nursing home, Zhejiang's "star old house" and so on, the article summarizes three endowment patterns of our country, which are family endowment, community endowment and institution endowment. Based on the basic national condition of less economically developing Status in China the author tries to find out a model of community provide for the aged which adapt to the present situation in our country, and can sustain long-term development, through comparative analysis of these three models. Therefore, this paper puts forward such a view: to construct community service pension system from the angle of the urban public service facilities and come to the "1＋1" model of community endowment. In this paper we also discuss the model of hierarchical configuration operation way and using "BOT" method of development way.

Keywords: Aging, Community pension mode, The old man's home, Family endowment, BOT

参考文献：

[1] 郑建娟. 我国社区养老的现状和发展思路[J]. 商业研究，2005，12.

[2] Cox CB. Community Care for an Aging Society[M]：Issues, policies and services[M]. Springer Publishins company，2004.

[3] 武丽. 我国城市社区养老发展可行性分析[D]. 四川：西南财经大学，2007.

［4］　宋言奇．城市老龄社区构建问题三议[J]．城市规划汇刊，2004，(05)．

［5］　苗瑞凤，孙钦荣．社区养老与城市社区组织结构重构[C]．中国老年学学会 2006 年老年学学术高峰论坛论文集．2006．

［6］　胡守强．中国 BOT 项目的主要风险和成功要素分析[D]．北京：对外经济贸易大学，2005．

城市社区配套设施的适老性规划设计研究

林婧怡

（清华大学建筑学院）

摘要： 随着城市老龄化率的不断增长，城市社区配套设施的使用主体将逐渐转向老年人群体。本文通过数据分析及案例调研的方法，研究了老年人对配套设施的使用需求及行为特征，探讨了配套设施功能构成、规划布局、规模及配建形式的适老性需求，并对老龄社会背景下社区配套设施的规划思路提出了建议。

关键词： 社区配套设施，适老性，规划设计，老年人需求

1 引言

中国城市正面临严峻的老龄化问题。近年来，城市老年人口比重在不断上升。以北京、上海为例，截至 2013 年底，其 60 岁及以上的户籍老年人口分别占到总人口的 20.3％和 27.1％。根据我国当前构建的社会养老服务体系可知，依托社区在宅养老是城市老年人的主要养老方式，因此城市社区应当更好地适应老年人的养老居住需求。然而长期以来，我国城市社区的规划建设并没有过多关注老年人群体。无论是老旧社区还是新建社区，在社区尺度、空间环境、配套设施等方面都还未能针对城市老龄化的快速发展做出充分的应对。本文将以社区配套设施为切入点，分析探讨老龄化背景下城市社区配套设施的规划建设需求。

2 老龄化背景下的城市社区配套设施规划研究进展

近年来，从老龄化视角探讨城市社区配套设施规划设计的相关研究主要表现在以下两个方面。

2.1 对配套设施规划指标的探讨

我国现行的指导社区配套设施规划的规范包括国家标准（如《城市居住区规划设计规范》），和地方标准（如《北京市居住公共服务设施规划设计指标》、《天津市居住区公共服务设施配置标准》、《上海市城市居住地区和居住区公共服务设施设置标准》等）。但这些标准在编制时对老龄化的需求考虑并不充分。例如 1993 年出台的《城市居住区规划设计规范》（GB 50180－93）中，各级公共服务设施对老年人的特殊需求未作过多考虑（李小云等，2011）。在 2002 年版修订的《城市居住区规划设计规范》中，虽然增加了对老年人设施相关要求，但却缺少从居住区配套设施整体层面对适老性的考虑（胡惠琴等，2014）。

在具体的规划指标要求上，武田艳等（2011）认为，现行规范中仅采用"千人指标"来推算配套设施规模的方法具有局限性，不能有效解决老龄化状况下社区配套设施的配置标准问题。陈喆（2013）认为应在规范中细化适老性配套设施指标，并强调了指标数据的制定需考虑老年人口的变化因素，给出弹性的规模参考标准。

2.2 对配套设施空间布局模式的研究

一些学者从社区配套设施的选址、规划布局方面进行了相应的研究。从空间可达性角度，陈小卉等（2013）指出与老人日常生活密切相关的社区配套设施（如商业设施和文化体育设施）应保证服务半径 300m 之内。从空间组织关系角度，周典等（2014）认为配套设施的布局模式与社区尺度和路网

结构紧密相关，配套设施应依托于更小规模的居住组团尺度和车流量较少的道路来建立，从而保证老人使用的便利性和安全性。

2.3　现有研究评述

由上可知，目前国内学者对城市社区配套设施的适老性研究主要集中在规划指标和空间布局模式两方面，可看作是以"设施规划主体"(胡畔等，2013)为视角的研究。而针对配套设施的研究还可从"设施使用主体"(胡畔等，2013)的角度来进行探索，即以使用者需求为导向来考虑配套设施的规划要求。然而从已有的研究文献来看，虽然已有部分学者针对社区配套设施的使用状况和居民需求展开了调研(胡惠琴，2014；任晋锋，2012)，但尚未形成能够直接指导具体规划设计的研究成果。

基于此，本研究将采用"使用主体"的视角，通过分析老年人的设施使用需求和日常行为模式，探索社区配套设施在类型配置、选址布局等方面的适老性需求，并尝试给出相应的规划配置指标及设计要求。

3　城市社区配套设施的适老性规划需求研究

从规划层面对社区配套设施的适老性需求研究主要应解决三个问题：一是"建什么"，即分析老人需要哪些社区服务，从而确定社区配套设施的类型和功能配置；二是"怎么建"，这包括确定设施的配建形式、选点布局等；三是"建多大"，即确定设施的用地需求及合理规模。本研究采用数据分析结合案例研究的方法，从适老性的角度分别针对上述三个问题进行探讨。

3.1　数据来源

本研究采用"2010年中国城乡老年人口状况追踪调查"(下简称"调查")的统计数据[①]，分析样本总量为10032个。

3.2　数据分析及其发现

3.2.1　社区配套设施的配置状况及老年人需求分析

根据调查问卷的问题设置情况，结合研究需求，本次选取"老年饭桌或送饭"、"日托站或托老所"、"康复治疗"、"上门护理"与"上门看病"5类社区服务或配套设施的供给状况和老年人实际需求进行分析，数据分析结果如图1。从图中可知：(1)在上述5类社区服务或配套设施中，老年人对于"老年饭桌或送饭"和"日托站或托老所"的需求比例是较高的，均超过三分之一；从社区实际的配置状况来看，这两类设施的配建比例也均超过半数。(2)每类社区服务或配套设施的提供或配置状况均要高于老年人所反映的需求，这说明老年人的需求应已得到满足。

然而，通过对社区配套设施的实际使用情况分析发现，老年人对于这些设施的利用状况并不理想。以日托站或托老所为例，在配置了这类设施的社区中，95.1%的老人表示从未使用过，3.5%的老人是偶尔使用，仅有1.4%的老人表示经常使用。

上述现象的产生可能有以下原因：(1)现行的社区配套设施规划指标不合理，适老设施的配建要求高于老年人的实际需求；(2)设施的选址位置或配建形式不合理，老人不方便到达和使用；(3)设施的服务内容和定位不准，从而导致老人的潜在需求没有显现。这些问题均可能造成设施供需不平衡，设施使用率较低，甚至出现空置等现象。

---

① 本研究所采用的基础数据由中国老龄科学研究中心提供。

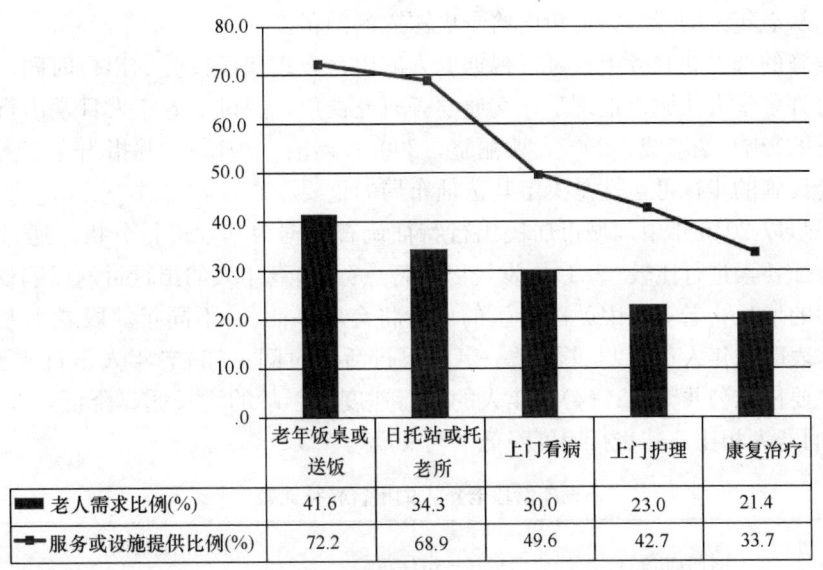

	老年饭桌或送饭	日托站或托老所	上门看病	上门护理	康复治疗
■ 老人需求比例(%)	41.6	34.3	30.0	23.0	21.4
■ 服务或设施提供比例(%)	72.2	68.9	49.6	42.7	33.7

图 1 社区服务或配套设施供给状况与老年人实际需求的比较

3.2.2 不同年龄段老年人对社区配套设施的需求特点分析

为了更细致地了解老年人的需求特点，本研究进一步分析了不同年龄段老年人对上述 5 类社区服务或配套设施的需求比例。从图 2 中可以看出，无论对于哪类设施，70～74 岁年龄段的老人都呈现出更明显的需求。而在这一年龄段前后，则分别呈现出线性增长和线性降低的趋势。

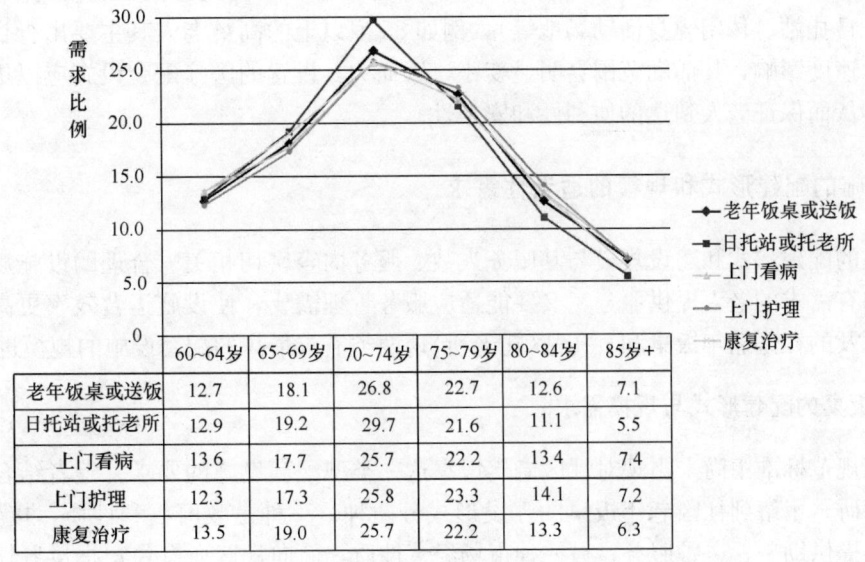

	60~64岁	65~69岁	70~74岁	75~79岁	80~84岁	85岁+
老年饭桌或送饭	12.7	18.1	26.8	22.7	12.6	7.1
日托站或托老所	12.9	19.2	29.7	21.6	11.1	5.5
上门看病	13.6	17.7	25.7	22.2	13.4	7.4
上门护理	12.3	17.3	25.8	23.3	14.1	7.2
康复治疗	13.5	19.0	25.7	22.2	13.3	6.3

图 2 按年龄段划分的老年人对社区配套设施的需求比例

综上所述，从配套设施的功能类型需求来看，"老年饭桌或送饭"和"日托站或托老所"是老年人最需要的两类设施；从需求人群来看，约半数的老年需求群体为 70～79 岁的老年人，设计时应重点考虑这一年龄段老年人的使用需求。

3.3 配套设施规划布局的适老性需求

社区配套设施规划布局的适老性需求主要体现在各类设施的布点位置及服务范围是否符合老年人的行为特点及使用规律。目前在规划设计时，对于配套设施服务半径和选址的要求主要依据规范标准要求，应当从老年人的行为特征角度给予更深入的阐释。

社区配套设施的选点和服务半径可以根据老人的出行方式和可接受的出行时间、距离来综合确定。近年来已有许多学者从城市地理学、交通学等研究视角，探讨了老年人日常出行模式对社区配套设施规划建设的影响（柴彦威，2005；曹丽晓，2006；周洁，2013），并指出老年人的主要出行方式为步行，配套设施的步行可达性是决定其选址布局的重要因素。

本研究进一步以2010年中国城市居民出行特征调查数据为基础进行分析，通过对不同年龄段老年人的出行特征要素进行比较（表1），发现以下特点：（1）老年人的出行目的以购物和休闲健身为主，而随着年龄的增长，老年人因就医产生的出行将会增多；（2）不同年龄段老年人的出行时间并无明显差异，这表明老年人都会尽量保证一定的出行活动时间；（3）老年人出行主要以步行为主，而长距离出行主要依靠公共交通；（4）老年人的步行速度随年龄的增长明显降低，85岁以上的老年人与65~75岁的老人相比，其步行速度降低了约90%。

不同年龄段老年人的出行特征比较①　　　　　表1

老年人分类	出行的主要目的	出行方式	平均出行时间 （min）	步行速度 （km/h）
65~75岁	上班，购物，接送孩子	步行、公交和自驾车	26	5.4
75~85岁	购物，休闲健身	以步行和公交为主	25	3.1
85岁以上	购物，休闲健身，就医	以步行为主	24	0.57

由上可知，社区配套设施的规划布局应根据老年人的适宜步行距离来确定选址及服务范围，对于不同类型的设施，由于老人使用频率的不同，或使用对象年龄的差异，也会影响其规划布局的特点。一些与老年人日常生活紧密相关、使用频率较高的配套设施应设置在更近便的步行范围内（例如老年饭桌、日托站、休闲健身活动场地等）。例如85岁以上的高龄老人其主要出行目的之一为就医，但受步行速度影响，其活动范围会明显变小，因而为其设置的医疗配套设施应以更小的服务半径进行布局，从而保证老人到达的便利性和安全性。

3.4 配套设施的配建形式和规模的适老性需求

配套设施的配建形式和建设规模与其服务人数、服务内容密切相关。合理的设施规模既应保证为一定范围内有需求的老人提供服务，又要能适应服务管理需要，使设施运营效率更高。本小节主要针对前文提及的社区老年饭桌和日托站（托老所）这两类需求最高的配套设施的规模进行探讨。

3.4.1 老年饭桌的配建形式与规模需求

目前国家规范标准中尚未出现对社区老年饭桌这一类型配套设施的要求。笔者结合对北京、上海等城市的调研，了解到社区老年饭桌的建设形式分两种：一种是政府福利性质，接受政策补助，专门为老年人提供助餐、送餐服务；另一种市场经营性质，面向社区所有住户提供餐饮服务，同时也可满足老年人就餐需求。对于政府福利性质的老年饭桌，其规模应满足各地方政府提出的最低服务人数要求，以便获得政策补助；例如服务于20人的社区助餐点，面积不小宜于50m²。而对于市场经营性质的社区饭桌，根据案例调研分析和对同类餐饮店规模的类比，其经营面积宜控制在150~450m²。

3.4.2 日托站的配建形式与规模需求

在《社区老年人日间照料中心建设标准》（建标143－2010）中，日托站（日间照料中心）的面积规

---

① 本表中相关数据由清华同衡规划设计研究院城市交通规划研究所提供。

模是按照居住区—居住小区—居住组团三个级别来进行确定，进而根据不同级别的服务人数总量来推算日托站的面积限值为 1600m² 、1085m² 和 750m² 。然而通过对全国多地的调研可知，日托站的配建形式并非与居住区级别和人口数量相对应，而是呈现出小型化、平均化的特点——大部分的日托站规模在 100～500m² 左右，服务人数为 20～30 人。这是因为老年人通常都以步行方式到达日托站，因此每个日托站的服务范围有限，不可能吸引过多的老年人；同时较小规模的日托站更利于服务管理。此外，考虑到运营效率问题，部分日托站可能会与养老院或老年综合服务中心合设，以实现空间的相互借用，提高设施利用效率。

4 老龄化背景下城市社区配套设施规划思路探讨

通过前文的分析研究可知，随着城市老龄化的快速发展，社区配套设施的使用主体将逐渐转向老年人群体，设施的类型、规模、布局会因老年人的使用特征而产生新的需求。而这些需求又会对今后的社区配套设施规划思路带来哪些改变？本文对此给出了进一步的探讨如下。

4.1 设施规划模式向扁平化、网络化发展

以往社区配套设施的规划建设是以"居住区—小区—组团"三级划分为基础，分别针对不同级别给出所对应的设施类型，并采用人口总量和千人指标对设施规模进行控制。而在老龄社会背景下，这样的规划模式和控制方法需要作出调整。正如前文在对日托站的需求分析中所指出的，社区日托站的配建模式并非要与居住区的三级空间结构相对应，而是应重点考虑在老年人合理的出行范围内近距离提供服务这一特点。对于社区卫生服务站、社区老年人活动场站、部分社区商业配套设施等老年人日常使用频率较高的设施也与此同理。然而，现状规划中这些设施大部分配置在居住小区级别，其所对应的居住空间规模尺度已超出老年人（特别是 70～79 岁的老年人这一主要需求群体）的出行能力；而现行规范上在居住组团级别规定配建的设施种类很少，并不能满足老人的需求。

因此本研究认为，考虑到老年人行动范围有限（比一般人减小），这些配套设施应优先置于组团级别的近家范围内，且应以更匀质的设施布局方式分散设于适宜居住规模单元中，保证老人到达的近便性。而在居住区和小区级别，则可减少或不进行配建相应设施。这种规划模式的特点在于减少了配套设施的配建层级，使与老年人日常生活密切相关的设施的空间分布密度加大，从而形成扁平化、网络化的布局，更加符合老年人的使用需求和出行特征。

4.2 设施功能趋于复合

当社区配套设施的布局向网络化均布发展后，其功能类型也将从单一型向复合型转变。这是因为当设施的分布密度增加后，每个设施对应的服务人数会相应减少，因而其面积规模不会过大。从规划角度讲，这几类设施均要考虑老人到达使用的便利性，很容易形成向最优选址集聚的趋势，而由于各类设施面积都很小，若在社区规划中为其一一划出单独的用地则会造成土地利用的极大浪费，而集中建设功能复合型设施的模式有助于节约用地。

更重要的是，从设施运营角度讲，复合型设施相比单一型设施更有利于降低运营风险。以前文调研的日托站和老年饭桌为例，两者的常见面积均在 100～200m² ，虽然设施规模小，但服务人员配置数量并不因此减少很多，而受其服务能力所限，在经营上会面临更大的风险。而功能复合型设施可使服务内容的多样化，例如同时开展老年饭桌、日间照料、医疗康复等多种服务，满足不同年龄层老年人的需求，扩大服务范围和服务能力，通过多种经营提高人员服务效率和空间使用率，从而降低运营风险。

4.3　设施布局与慢行、绿化体系的整体性设计

老年人的出行以步行为主，社区配套设施的规划布局应注重与以步行为主导的慢行系统相衔接，保证老人出行的安全性。同时，由于老人的活动时长和活动范围有限，应在选址规划时注意使配套设施与绿地、活动场地进行串联，使老人的购物、就医活动与锻炼、休闲活动通过慢行系统连接，为老人设计出合理的行动路径，以提高出行活动效率。

5　结语

城市社区配套设施的规划建设需要及时应对城市老龄化的快速发展。这不仅限于对现状配套设施规划指标和空间布局模式的探讨，还应从设施使用主体即老年人需求的角度展开研究。通过分析老年人的使用需求和日常出行特征可以看出，社区配套设施在功能类型上应更多适应于 70～79 岁的老年群体，在规划布局上须着重考虑老人步行到达的便利性和安全性，在配建形式和规模上应结合运营管理需求。本文最终提出，社区配套设施在规划建设上应向扁平化、网络化、复合化和整体化的发展思路。这些思路如何能更有效地落实在具体的规划指标及空间形态上，还需今后展开进一步的探讨。

The Adaptability for the Aged of Public Facilities in Urban Community Planning

Lin Jingyi

(School of Architecture, Tsinghua University)

Abstract：With the increasing of urban aging rate, the main user of the urban community facilities will gradually turn to the elderly group. Through data analysis and case research, this article analyzes the demand for the use of the community facilities and behavior characteristics of old people, and discusses the function, layout, size and construction form and size of the facilities, then gives some suggestions for the planning thought of community facilities under the background of aging society.

Keywords：Community facility, Adaptability for the aged, Planning and design, Demand of old people

参考文献：

[1]　李小云，田银生. 国内城市规划应对老龄化社会的相关研究综述[J]. 城市规划，2011，9：52-59.

[2]　胡惠琴，畅流. 北京市既有住区公共服务设施适老性问题及改造策略初探[J]. 住区，2014，4：136-141.

[3]　武田艳，何芳. 城市社区公共服务设施规划标准设置准则探讨[J]. 城市规划，2011，35（09）：13-18.

[4]　陈喆，胡惠琴. 老龄化社会建筑设计规划：社会养老与社区养老[M]. 北京：机械工业出版社，2013.

[5]　陈小卉，杨红平．老龄化背景下城乡规划应对研究——以江苏为例[J]．城市规划，2013，09：17-21．

[6]　周典，徐怡珊．老龄化社会城市社区居住空间的规划与指标控制[J]．建筑学报，2014，05：56-59．

[7]　胡畔，张建召．基本公共服务设施研究进展与理论框架初构——基于主体视角与复杂科学范式的递进审视[J]．城市规划，2012，12：84-90．

[8]　任晋锋，吕斌．北京核心城区社区公共服务设施问题及对策研究——以西城区调研为例[J]．现代城市研究，2012，2：53-59．

[9]　柴彦威，李昌霞．中国城市老年人日常购物行为的空间特征：以北京、深圳和上海为例[J]．地理学报，2005，3：401-408．

[10]　曹丽晓，柴彦威．上海城市老年人日常购物活动空间研究[J]．人文地理，2006，2：50-54．

[11]　周洁，柴彦威．中国老年人空间行为研究进展[J]．地理科学进展，2013，5：722-732．

小城镇老旧社区户外交往空间适老化改造策略研究

徐煜辉[1,2]　龚雪[1]

（1. 重庆大学建筑城规学院；2. 山地城镇建设与新技术教育部重点实验室）

摘要：随着老龄化趋势的加速，老年人已经成为了城市老旧社区的主要居住群体。社交是老年人实现其他需求的前提，而社区户外交往空间则是老年人社交需求的重要载体。对城市老旧社区进行改造时，应充分考虑其需求。通过对城市老旧社区户外交往空间的适老化改造研究，发现在城市规划领域缺乏单独以小城镇老年人需求为主的研究。基于此，论文选取重庆市梁平县梁山街道北池社区为例，通过对社区住宅入口交往空间、小区院落交往空间以及社区中心广场交往空间的调研，从人口老龄化的现实状况入手，以老年人的社交需求为切入点，借助社交心理学、城市规划学与行为心理学的研究成果，分析了社交需求对老年人的重要性以及老年人对社区户外交往空间的实际需求，提出对应的适老化改造对策，为其营造舒适、健康的户外交往环境。

关键词：小城镇，老旧社区，户外交往空间，适老化改造，梁平县梁山街道北池社区

1　引言

随着老龄化进程的加快，针对其发展现状而开展的老旧居住社区改造研究日益受到关注。老年人作为城镇老旧社区居住的主要群体，随着年龄变化，其需求特殊引起了城乡规划学的重视。诺伯格·舒尔茨指出，交往是空间性的，空间是表现我们"在世界中交往"的各种结构的重要方面之一。[1]社区户外交往空间作为老年人社交活动的主要场所，是他们社交需求得以落实的物质空间载体。对他们大部分人而言，也是其发挥"剩余价值"的重要舞台。

老年人退休后，由于社会角色的转换与生活时间的改变，其社交需求表现得尤为明显。研究发现，缺乏交往的鳏寡孤独老人患病率高于与之同样情况但有良好交往的老人的 1.6 倍，死亡的可能性高出后者两倍。[2]然而小城镇中可供老年人就近进行户外交往的空间资源较为稀缺，且老年人出于生理机能的减退，引发其感知能力、反映能力、认知能力与健康状况的下降，活动范围缩小，主要聚集在居住社区。目前众多学者的研究视角大多聚焦于大中城市老旧社区，忽略了小城镇。在此背景下，展开对小城镇老旧社区户外交往空间的适老化改造研究显得尤为迫切。

2　概念解析

2.1　老旧社区

"老旧社区"指老旧住宅单体及其居住环境在一定的自然地域空间、社会经济形态和使用时间区段的整体功能状态产生"综合性陈旧"过程的社区。[3]而文章中所研究的老旧社区，主要基于城乡规划视角，特指在城市更新与老龄化程度加剧的背景下，社区建筑质量良好且居住群体主要以老年人为主，但户外设施陈旧、空间环境品质较差的居住社区。

2.2　户外交往空间

户外交往空间是人们交往行为发生的载体，它包含两个因素：一是在具体的地点，有一定形式的物理空间；二是在这个空间环境中有交往行为发生。二者相辅相成、不可分割，行为受空间形态影响，合理的空间会促进交往活动的发生，反之会抑制；由于行为与空间的统一性，设计师有意识

的设计将促进交往空间的适应度与交往的发生率，从而有效改善交往状态。[4]本文研究的户外交往空间指社区室外环境中老年人交往频率较高的住宅入口空间、小区院落空间和社区中心广场空间。

2.3 适老化改造

受中国养老传统美德的影响，居家养老是目前我国主要的养老模式，适老化户外环境是老年人居家养老的重要基础。旧有社区环境有老年人多年形成的社会网络，更具有归属感，但随着人口老龄化加剧，其在一定程度上已不能满足老年人社交需求发展。因此，本文所提的"适老化改造"是指针对老年人特殊需求，本着以老年人为本的理念，在满足其心理和生理需求的前提下，为其营造一个轻松、自在的人性化交往空间，而对旧有社区户外环境进行改造的过程。

3 老年人社交活动对社区户外交往空间的需求

恩内斯特·贝克指出"现代生活的特征是对个人英雄主义的渴望，表现在城市中个体空间的强化和公共场所的丧失，而在个体进程中，孤独化现象又是生物本能最大的恐惧之一"。[5]交往活动作为老年人社交需求的外在表现，是其参与社会，排除孤独，实现自我满足、自我认识与自我完善功能的有效途径。熟悉老年人社交活动特征与空间需求原则，是空间适老化改造成功的重要因素之一。

3.1 社交活动特征

（1）集聚性。指在社交活动中，老年人因共同的兴趣爱好而互为吸引和共鸣引起的同龄、同性以及跨年龄集聚的现象。这要求空间设计必须注重功能的复合，满足老年人交往的社会性需求。

（2）随意性。社区中的交往活动具有较大随意性。这一特点要求交往空间必须是由不同空间联系、穿插、渗透而形成的网络，而不是一个孤立的空间，这也就决定了空间设计必须是从整体规划到局部处理的统一过程，不是单纯某一局部的设计或是在总体布局确定后才进行考虑的问题。[6]

（3）地域性。老年人习惯在特定的地区和专门的空间中进行活动。正如我们所知，老年人都十分"念旧"，一般不会轻易改变在所熟识的环境中活动的特征。

3.2 空间需求原则

（1）功能多样性原则。简·雅各布斯指出充满活力的街道和居住区都拥有丰富的多样性，而失败的城市地区多样性都明显匮乏。[7]因此，在对老旧社区户外交往空间进行改造时，应注重功能的多样性，满足不同老年人对空间的需求，增加其外出活动次数，提升社区活力。

（2）整体性原则。指对社区户外交往空间进行改造时，应融入当地特色，同时注重空间设计与社区内不同社交活动类型对应的空间层次和老年人需求（表1）相结合，从社区整体空间出发，合理进行功能分区，避免出现因考略局部而忽略整体，造成功能布局的重复与设施的浪费。

不同社交活动的空间设计要求　　　　　　　　　　　　　　　　　　　表1

空间要素	个体活动	小团体活动	群体活动
空间规模	单人规模的私密性空间	2～5人规模的半私密性空间	5人规模以上的开放性空间
老年人空间需求	私密性需求、安全需求	趣味性需求、社交需求	功能多样化需求、舒适性与可达性需求
对应的社区户外交往空间层次	社区住宅入口交往空间	小区院落交往空间、社区住宅入口交往空间	社区中心广场交往空间

续表

空间要素	个体活动	小团体活动	群体活动
老年人对空间设计的要求	私密性较强，具有明显的排他性，空间尺度较小，且空间围合度强却不封闭	私密性次之，是私密与公共空间的过渡，空间围合度适中，视线有一定的阻隔但不阻断	空间功能综合性较强，空间尺度较大，视线通透连续，且设有相应的配套设施

注：资料来源：作者自绘。

（3）可达性与舒适性原则。为使老年人方便到达不同层次的户外交往空间，应当注重空间的可达性与舒适性，合理地设计和安排户外空间，减小各项设施场地的服务半径，回避和减弱气候等不利因素，增加标识系统、感官刺激和环境感知，以帮助老人在户外明确方向和找到路线。

4 适老化对策的提出——以梁平县梁山街道北池社区为例

4.1 区位概况

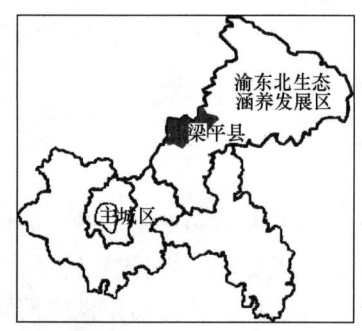

图 1　梁平县区位图
（资料来源：作者自绘）

梁平县位于渝东北生态涵养发展区（图 1），属于重庆直辖的县级农业型小城市，人口老龄化程度在渝东北城镇中位于前列（图 2）。依据第六次全国人口普查主要数据公报显示，全县常住人口为 68.75 万人，其中 65 岁及以上人口为 8.44 万，占总人口比重为 12.27%，同第五次相比上升了 5.17%。根据一般国际评判进入"老龄化社会"标准，梁平县已经迈入老龄化城市，且老龄化速度较快。

北池社区属于梁平县梁山街道管辖区域（图 3），地理位置比较特殊，既处于县城政治、商贸、文化中心，也属于城乡接合部。由于建设年代较早，辖区内建筑质量虽良好，但道路与环境品质较差，是梁平县旧城改造的重点对象。根据梁山街道北池社区便民服务中心提供的人口信息得知，目前社区内居住人口为 18316 人、6879 户，人口结构中老年人所占比重高于全县平均数值，达 13.06%。

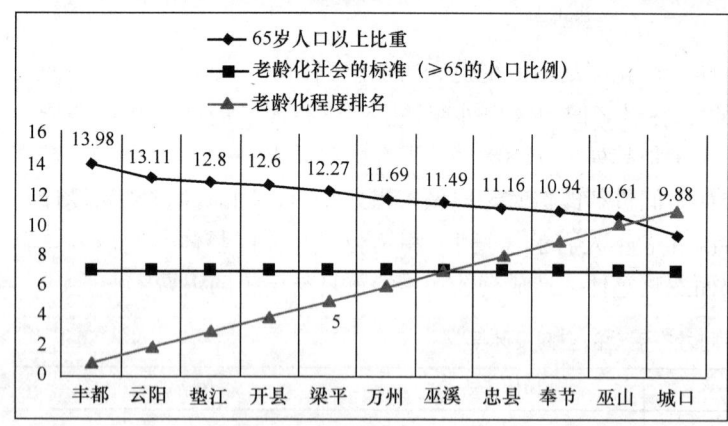

图 2　梁平县老龄化数据分析图
（资料来源：作者自绘）

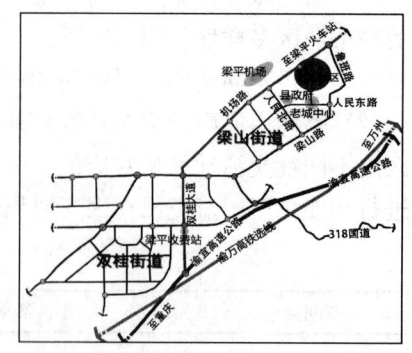

图 3　北池社区区位
（资料来源：作者自绘）

4.2 交往空间现状分析

对社区进行实地调研和访谈后，总结出北池社区户外交往空间与老年人社交需求间的矛盾主要体现在三个空间层次：社区住宅入口交往空间、小区院落交往空间和社区中心广场交往空间。

（1）社区住宅入口交往空间

住宅入口空间不仅为室内与室外的过渡，同时也控制着人们心理空间从"外"向"内"的转换，是一个充满感性的空间，老年人行为易受到空间形式的暗示。社区内部分老年人由于身体原因，喜欢在住宅入口区域进行小范围社交活动，但由于入口空间过于开敞且无支撑长时间驻足停留的因素，使得该空间只是交通性过道，无交往行为发生（图4）。这样的空间会影响老年人外出频率，减少其与他人交往的机会，不利于其身心健康发展。

过于开敞的入口空间　　　　　缺乏休息设施的入口空间　　　　　缺乏绿化的入口空间

图4　社区住宅入口交往空间现状图

（资料来源：作者自摄）

（2）小区院落交往空间

芦原义信在《外部空间设计》中提出外部空间模数为 20～25m，在此距离范围中人们可以看清对方的面部，因此有利于营造出舒适的交往空间环境。北池社区中住宅间距都处于这距离内，所以形成的院落空间有较强的围合感和领域感，且尺度宜人。但现场调研发现老年人很少在小区院落空间展开交往活动，主要因为：一是交往空间缺失，由于院落空间设计过渡注重景观设计忽略了人交往的需求，造成空间可供老年人活动的平台偏少，无法满足其在此交往的需求；二是部分院落空间封闭，缺乏外部呼应，虽领域感强，但让人感觉压抑，不利于老年人与他人进行愉快的交流（图5）。

无可供活动的场所空间　　　　　过于封闭的院落空间　　　　　无交往行为发生的院落空间

图5　小区院落交往空间现状图

（资料来源：作者自摄）

（3）社区中心广场交往空间

中心广场作为社区交往中的公共性空间，具有较强的开放性，同时也是社区老年人户外交往活动最为重要的空间之一。实地考察发现社区广场空间主要存在四方面的问题：一是空间完整性遭破坏，导致空间规模无法满足社区内老年人群体活动需求；二是广场空间功能单一，无法满足老年人群与其他年龄层次的人群进行交流；三是广场边缘空间处理不当，利用休息与健身设施作为广场空间与城市道路间的划分，给老年人与他人交流以及观赏时造成心理上的不安全感；四是广场空间公共性太强，缺乏私密与半私密空间，无法满足老年人个人以及小团体的社交活动私密性需求（图6）。

4.3　适老化改造思路

一是交往空间改造设计要符合老年人活动特征和空间需求原则。二是结合当地的地域特征与老年人的实际需求，对于不同的活动特征给予不同的空间设计解决对策。

空间完整性遭停车破坏　　　　　空间层次单一，缺乏多样性　　　　广场边缘空间设计呆板

图6　社区中心广场交往空间现状图

（资料来源：作者自摄）

4.3.1　社区住宅入口交往空间

（1）调整入口空间尺度。对原本过于开敞的入口空间，通过减少硬质铺地的面积，增加适当比例的软质面积（绿化），营造缓冲空间，以留出老年人从私密空间进入公共空间的心理转换时间，同时满足其就近交往需求。

（2）增加空间驻留性。通过休息设施配置与绿化空间相结合的形式，保持适当围合以增强空间领域感，提高老年人外出频率，促进交往发生（图7）。

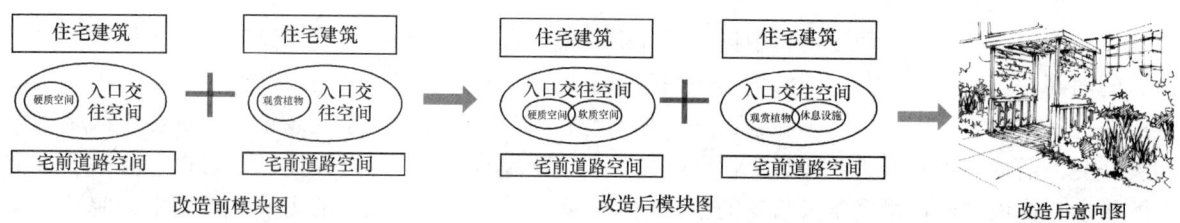

图7　社区住宅入口交往空间改造示意图

（资料来源：作者自绘）

4.3.2　小区院落交往空间

（1）增加交往活动空间，丰富院落空间层次。根据老年人在院落空间进行交往活动类型进行空间层次的调整，提供交往活动平台，满足景观空间与活动空间比例；

（2）进行空间开敞面的营造。格式塔心理学中的"图—底"关系分析表明，四面围合的空间封闭性极强，有强烈的向心性和领域感，会令老人感到压抑。所以在空间设计时应注意周边环境渗透与开敞面的营造，给老年人一个轻松、自在的交往空间（图8）。

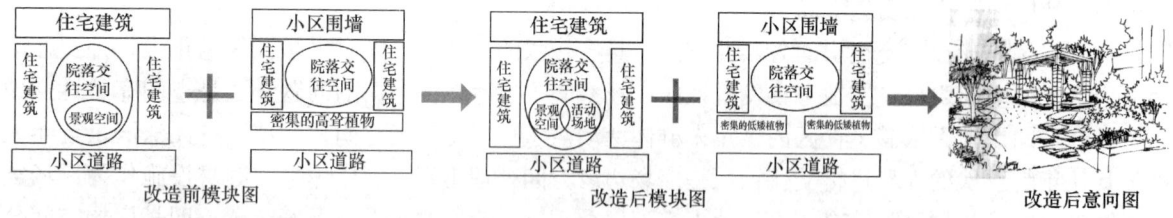

图8　小区院落交往空间改造示意图

（资料来源：作者自绘）

4.3.3　社区中心广场交往空间

（1）优化广场空间的功能布局。对空间破碎的广场进行功能布局的调整，将停车空间置换到广

场边缘的建筑物前或地下车库，还原空间的完整性，满足老年人群体活动的空间需求；

（2）丰富广场空间层次，增加空间功能多样性。对缺乏私密与半私密性空间的广场，通过增加绿化配置和活动配套设施的围合来营造出多层次的空间，支撑老年人个体与小团体以及群体活动的时空重叠性需求；对功能单一的广场空间进行局部功能的增设，满足老年与其他年龄层次的交往；

（3）重视边缘空间设计。C·亚历山大在《建筑模式语言》中总结了有关公共空间中边界效应和边界区域的经验。[8]所以对广场边缘空间改造时，可以利用边界线的凹入凸出，为需要逗留的老人提供适合滞留的小空间。

（4）注意细节把控。老年人随年龄的增大，视力、感知力等下降，导致空间方向感与识别能力减弱。因此应建立具有意向性的标志物，创造空间场所的特征，增强居民的地域认同感。比如：通过在社区广场空间中，增设醒目的雕塑来帮助对焦，增强老年人对空间距离的感知，同时在广场上有高差变化的地方采用不同色彩和材质，帮助老年人更好识别空间变化，提高安全保护等（图9）。

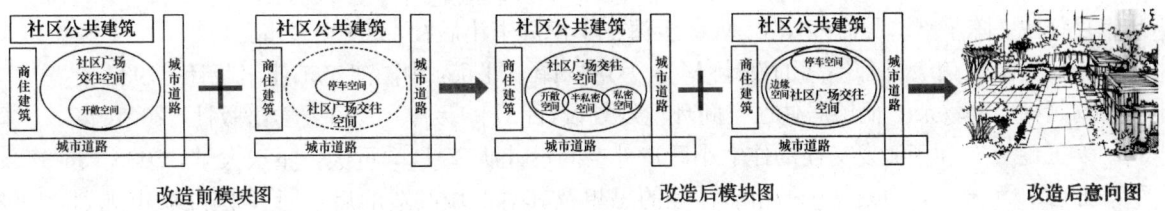

图9　社区中心广场交往空间改造示意图

（资料来源：作者自绘）

5　结语

老年是每个人都要经历的阶段，交往空间作为老年人精神养老的重要保障，因此每个人都将会是空间适老化的受益者。规划师是空间设计者，应充分研究老年人社交需求，探析促进老年人交往的老旧社区户外空间改造对策，让空间设计适应"老有所养，老有所依、老有所教、老有所乐、老有所为，老有所学"的要求，更好地应对人口老龄化带来的城市空间问题。

Analyze Strategies of How to Transform Deteriorating Neighborhoods'
Outdoor Communication Spaces into More Suitable
Neighborhoods for the Aging People in Small Towns

Xu Yuhui[1,2], Gong Xue[1]

（1. Chongqing Planning & Design Institute；2. Key Laboratory of New Technology for Construction of Cities in Mountain Area，Chongqing University）

Abstract：With the acceleration of aging trend，the elderly has become the main groups of the urban old community. Social networking is the precondition to implement their other demand，and to the elderly，community outdoor contact space is the important carrier of social demand. We should give full consideration to its needs in the reconstruction of old city community. There is no enough studies about elderly demand of small towns through searching for studies about old city community outdoor contact space of aging. Based on the above, taking Beichi street community in Chongqing Liangping，this paper analyzes the importance of social demand for the elderly and the actual needs of the elderly in community outdoor contact space to put forward the corresponding optimal aging reform countermeasures through the reseach about the residential entrance communication space，yard communication space and center square communication space with the help of research results of social psychology, urban planning and of behavioral psychology. So we can create a comfortable and healthy outdoor environment for the elderly.

Keywords：Small towns, Old community, Outdoor communication space, Elderly-adaptive, Beichi street community in Chongqing Liangping

参考文献：

[1]　李耀培．中国居住实态与小康住宅设计[M]．江苏：东南大学出版社，1999：143.

[2]　陈晓露．老年人的社会交往心理[M]．北京：中国社会出版社，2008：45.

[3]　夏征农，陈至立．辞海缩印本[M]．上海：上海辞书出版社，2010：498.

[4]　（日）芦原义信．外部空间的设计[M]．尹培桐译．北京：中国建筑工业出版社，1985.

[5]　刘延枫，肖敦余．低层居住区空间环境规划设计[M]．天津：天津大学出版社，2001.

[6]　姜玉艳．有利于激发交往的住宅小区户外空间设计研究[D]．重庆：重庆大学，2006：36-37.

[7]　方可．简·雅各布斯关于城市多样性的思想及其对旧城改造的启示[J]．国外城市规划，1998（1）：49.

[8]　向岚麟．园林中的边缘空间探析——以城市公共绿地为例[D]．四川：西南交通大学，2006.

[9]　Rutledge，Albert JA. Visual Approach to Park Design Rutledge[M]．New York：Gsrland STPM Press，1981.

重庆地区"倒按揭"养老模式的调查研究与政策建议

白 竞 潘雨红

（重庆交通大学管理学院）

摘要： 当前，我国社会老龄化和未富先老的现实问题已日益凸显，养老金短缺，养老保障体系不健全、养老模式单一等问题急需解决办法。本文以重庆市为研究对象，将本地区现有的养老模式与"倒按揭"养老模式作比较，通过对案例社区和敬老院的走访调研、面对面专家访谈，并结合当地人口结构等方面的资料进行研究，分析"倒按揭"养老模式在重庆地区的可行性，就存在的问题提出相关的建议。

关键词： 倒按揭，养老模式，重庆地区

1 引言

"倒按揭"养老模式也被称为"以房养老"或者"住房反向抵押贷款"养老模式，是指老人将自己所拥有的房产抵押给金融机构（如银行），从而可以以定期的方式获得金融机构给予的抵押资金。目前，这种养老模式在美国等一些国家取得了不错的成绩。我国的房地产市场起源于 20 世纪 90 年代末，并且在随后的 20 年内一直处于一个高速发展的状态，这就是使得很多城镇居民都拥有自己的一套或者是多套房产，这便为"倒按揭"养老模式提供了可能性。

"倒按揭"养老模式作为目前解决我国现有养老政策不足的一种重要补充，在我国即将到来的老龄化社会中可以扮演一个重要的角色。与目前我国传统的养老模式不同，"倒按揭"养老模式可以依托一些金融机构，以房养老，解决在现有养老模式中普遍存在的养老资金短缺问题。重庆市作为中国四大直辖市之一，也是中国西南地区经济重镇，其幅员辽阔，地势起伏较大，地形较为复杂多以山区和丘陵为主，这种显著的地理特征，造成重庆市主城面积小，人口密度大的特点，其人多地少的特点就制约着去建立大型的社区养老院，或者是政府养老院。随着老龄化问题的到来，更需要有经济实用性的养老体系，以解决目前在养老问题上普遍存在的资金短缺问题。"倒按揭"养老模式在解决养老问题上的资金短缺方面起到一种重要的补充作用，但是，与目前重庆市传统的养老模式相比，它有何具体优势，它在实际操作过程当中面临的问题是什么，以及该如何具体的实施，是现在当地政府和学者需要解决的问题。

2 国内外"倒按揭"养老模式的现状

2.1 国外"倒按揭"养老模式的现状

美国对于"倒按揭"养老模式的研究在世界各个国家中是起步比较早的国家，其起源于 1961 年。但是直到 1987 年美国联邦住房与城市发展部根据《国家住房法案》推出住房转换抵押贷款，美国政府才算是真正的开始接受并推行"倒按揭"养老机制（HECM）。而 HECM 在当时的美国社会仅仅是一个临时性的实验项目，由美国联邦住房管理局提供担保，当时的美国社会，很多金融无法真正的预测该业务的风险和营利，导致"倒按揭"养老模式的发展步履维艰。[1]美国国会在 1998 年将 HECM 计划的地位确定为永久性的，并对美国房管局的"倒按揭"业务进行了拓展即可以提供保险，这些变动为美国"倒按揭"市场带来了快速发展。如 2005 年，全美发放的 HECM 贷款同比增长了 77%，为 43131 笔，超过了这种模式推出后十年成交量的总和。但是美国这种"倒按揭"业务的快速发展完全

是房地产市场非理性繁荣的结果，在 2008 年发生的金融危机严重遏制了"倒按揭"养老模式在美国的发展，并且在之后的几年里，HECM 的签约量急剧减少。所以，作为这次金融危机的发源地，美国的次贷危机也间接地导致了美国倒按揭市场的由盛转衰。

2.2　国内"倒按揭"养老模式的现状

国内"倒按揭"养老模式与国外相比较起步比较晚，从 2003 年开始在我国受到了广泛的关注，上海住房公积金中心在 2007 年首先推出了使用房屋返租养老的模式，但是由于种种原因，这种政府政策并没有真正被过多的上海市民所了解并接受，接着在北京和南京也开始试行以房换养的养老模式，而且南京幸福人寿保险在 2010 年就开始为参保人员推行"倒按揭"养老产品，但是最后都没有取得预想的效果。

从"倒按揭"养老模式在美国的发展轨迹中，我们可以看出，HECM 的成交量与住房的价格是紧密相关的，而且美国过分的把"倒按揭"机制交给市场，没有一个很好地政府宏观调节机制，一旦当金融市场发生震荡时，就会不可避免地殃及"倒按揭"养老机制。然而美国的金融市场与我国的金融市场存在着本质上的差别，而且美国把"倒按揭"养老模式过分的市场化，这在我国也是不可取的。从我国已经开始试行倒按揭养老模式的地区，可以了解到，他们过分的追求倒按揭养老模式的优势及可能取得成效，并且在实施过程中使"倒按揭"养老模式过分的脱离现有的养老模式，所有很难取得预想的成效。我们在实施倒按揭养老模式的时候，要充分的结合我国的具体国情，从我国每个区域的实际情况出发，分析如何更好地实施"倒按揭"养老机制。

3　重庆市现有养老模式的调查分析

3.1　家庭式养老

家庭式养老是以家庭为单位的一种养老模式，这种养老模式是现在大多数家庭采取的一种养老模式。在中国始终贯彻着"百善孝为先"的思想，所以对于父母及家中老人的赡养是每一位年轻人和每一个家庭应尽的义务。并且随着中国老龄化社会的逐渐到来。这种以家庭为主要载体的养老模式，会在很大程度上分化社会责任，减轻社会上对于养老资金需求的负担。但是由于老年人和年轻人的生活习惯以及生活作息规律具有很大的差异，这会在是家庭成员中的两代人甚至是几代人之间产生很大的矛盾，导致家庭关系不和谐。并且，由于现在结婚的新婚夫妇很多都是双独，这样一对年轻人就要同时赡养四位老人，这就会导致家庭的财政开支出现危机。所以这种养老模式虽然是现在社会普遍采取的一种养老模式，但是其还是存在很大弊端。

3.2　社会式养老

社会式养老主要是指社会上开设的养老院以及其他机构，将社会上的一些老人聚集起来，进行集中服务的一种养老模式。在重庆市开设有多家公营及私营的养老院，本文笔者通过走访多家重庆市的养老机构发现，私营的养老机构，要比公营的养老机构设施齐全，以及获得服务标准也相对较高一些，很多私营的养老机构已经拥有，医疗护理、康复护理，以及善终等服务，当然其价格也相对比较高。与家庭式养老模式不同，这种养老模式主要是通过一些社会途径，以及政府提供的一些保障制度提供的养老的方式。笔着通过走访，发现这种养老模式的优势在于可以提供集中式养老服务，同时也可以为一些特殊老人提供一些特殊的服务，这种集中式的有利于资源的有效和优化配置，不至于产生社会资源的浪费，同时集中式养老可以使养老机构更加专注专业地为老人服务，并且在养老机构里，老人与老人之间可以相互做伴。但是其也存在着一些弊端，比如一些可以提供更好的服务的私营养老机构的收费普遍偏高，使得老人及其家庭难以承受，其次就是很多老人不愿意居住在养老机构里，因为在这里面他们会长时间的见不到自己的子女及亲人，最后就是很多性价比比较高的养老机构，以及可以提供特殊服务的养老机构的床位不足。

3.3 社区式养老

社区式养老是通过政府扶持、社会参与、市场运作，逐步建立以家庭养老为核心，社区服务为依托，专业化服务为依靠，向居家老人提供生活照料、医疗保健、精神慰藉、文化娱乐等为主要内容的服务。但是社区养老并不是单纯的家庭养老，同时与社会养老模式也有区别，他主要是是把机构养老中的服务引入到社区，实行社区的在家养老。他重点吸收了家庭养老和社会养老两种养老方式的优点和可操作性，把家庭养老和机构养老的最佳结合点集中在社区。也是对于我国社会即将面临的巨大老龄化问题多提出的一种新型养老模式。从重庆市民政，局获得的消息，截止到 2014 年 11 月，全市共建成运营各类社区养老服务中心 826 个，累计完成建设投资达 1.82 亿。作为一种处于起步阶段的养老模式，必然存在着一些弊端；第一，其资金紧靠政府扶持，资金构成过于单一，不利于其长远的发展；第二，管理的规范化有待于进一步的提高，由于其处于刚刚起步阶段，很多措施还是在处于试点时期，其建设、服务模式以及运营模式都不是很完善，有待于进一步提高。

本文对重庆市现有养老模式进行了实地调研，并对掌握的资料和数据进行了统计和整理，对每一种养老模式提出了自己的看法，并指出了其存在的一些问题，但是通过对上述三种模式的对比研究，不难看出它们存在的一个共同的问题，就是资金的短缺，换句话说，就是对于处于城市当中的老人在老年阶段也许会有一套或者多套房子居住，但是却没有足够的资金进行养老，这应该引起社会的普遍关注。

4 "倒按揭"模式在重庆市的调查研究

通过对重庆市现有养老模式进行充分调研之后，发现其主要问题即是老人晚年所获得的以及拥有的资金不足以支撑其晚年的生活。为了解决这个问题，可以引入"倒按揭"养老模式。

调研团队在重庆市选取了重庆市比较有代表性的南岸区、渝中区、沙坪坝区、江北区、巴南区五个区域，以这五个区域为主要研究对象，并在这五个区域的商业中心区域进行了走访调查和问卷调查的方式进行调研。此次问卷设计主要是由三个部分组成：第一部分主要是用来区分不同的调查对象，主要包括户籍、性别、年龄和学历等，通过这个部分，主要是想获取其不同的年龄结构的人群，以及不同的文化背景的人对于实施倒按揭养老模式感性认识上的看法；第二部分比较系统地分析了受访人员的职业，家庭成员的构成，拥有的房产数以及退休后可能拥有的可支配的资金数等一系列的问题，从受访人员对这些问题的回答中可以得出，他们对于实施倒按揭养老模式上理性的认识，从而可以得出一些比较可靠的信息；第三部分主要是通过调研工作人对受访者对"倒按揭"养老模式进行简单的讲解之后，他们对于这种养老模式的选择意愿。在本次调研中，调研团队共用了五天的时间，采用的是一对一现场填写，现场提问，现场讲解"倒按揭"养老模式的，并现场收集问卷的方式进行现场收集。

4.1 如何对房产做一个正确的评估

调研团队在进行调研的过程中发现，当很多人了解用自己的房子可以换取养老资金，从而为自己以后的养老提供资金保障的时候，他们有接受的意愿，可是他们不知道如何对自己的房产进行估价。在调研中我们的调研人员也发现，拥有房产的受访人员，他们拥有房产的地理位置，年代等存在着比较大的差异。是否能对房产做一个正确、公正的估价，在一定程度上制约着人们对于"倒按揭"养老模式的接受程度。

4.2 养老金如何发放

调研团队在进行调研的过程中发现，很多人比较关心，当他们所拥有的房产抵押给金融机构以后，自己将要获取的养老金会以何种方式发放。如何发放养老金，以怎样的方式发放，发放的时间点如何固定以及对于失独老人和失去自理能力且子女不在身边的老人，他们的养老金该由谁领取，这些都是"倒按揭"养老模式在推行过程中需要解决的问题。

4.3 "倒按揭"期限到期后，房产如何处理

调研团队在进行调研的过程中发现，很多人关心自己的房产在自己百年之后将如何处置，如果还想将房产留给自己的子女该如何做，以及如果中途想放弃"倒按揭"该如何做。这也是在推行"倒按揭"揭养老模式过程中需要思考的问题。

5 在重庆地区推行"倒按揭"养老模式的建议

在这次调研中，我们发现，重庆的消费水平偏高而市民的资金收入水平普遍偏低，并且重庆市人口年龄结构正在逐步进入老龄化，施行"倒按揭"养老模式作为现有养老机制的一种重要补充，可以解决重庆市现有养老机制中以资金不足为主的诸多问题。但是如何在重庆市推行"倒按揭"养老机制，本文给出以下的相关建议：

5.1 建立起一整套完整的评估体系

重庆市的房地产业是一个起步相对比较早的城市，其主城区的建设也有几十年之久，并且重庆市区的区域发展的成熟程度也存在着很大的差异。对于这种差异，可以根据重庆市现在的区域房产价格，以此为基础对房产的年代，户型，面积，地势等进行进一步评估。政府可以出台一套房产评估的具体实施标准，具体的评估工作可以由私营企业实施，但是评估结果要由政府把关，防止暗箱操作，欺骗房产拥有者的行为。这样就可以在社会上形成由金融机构牵头，评估公司实施，政府监督的立体评估体系，可以更好地实施房产评估工作。

5.2 多元化的资金发放方式，发放时间

由于每个人对于资金的发放方式的需求不同，金融机构可以针对不同的需求人群，设置多元化的养老金发放方式。比如，对于采取家庭养老方式的人员，他们更需要的是可自由支配的现金，对于采取社会养老方式的人群，由于他们的参与的社会活动比较少，他们更多的是需要支付给社会养老院的养老金。采取有弹性的养老金发放机制，发放的方式及时间可根据不同的人群自由决定。这样可以更大限度的让"倒按揭"养老模式的申请者获得更多的养老资金的支配权。

5.3 有效的房产处理方式

对于"倒按揭"养老模式的实施后，老人百年之后的房产处理上，也可以采取多种方式相结合的方法。首先，老人的家人可以对房产在一定的时间、权限之内拥有优先赎回权。其次，若在中途，"倒按揭"申请人放弃对于"倒按揭"养老的施行，让他们偿还已经发放的养老金，并且在赔付一定的违约金之后可以拿回房产。最后，如果老人在"倒按揭"养老模式实施过程中，意外去世，其余下的资金可由亲属继承，直到所有的养老资金发放完为止。通过这几点措施的实施，也可以最大限度避

免"倒按揭"养老模式在实施过程中申请人与金融机构之间的纠纷。

6 结语

重庆市在西南地区占据着一个举足轻重的地位,其各项措施的实施都可以为西南地区的其他区域提供一个重要参考,由于西南地区人口众多,并且该地区的经济处于一个起步阶段,现有的社会经济基础不足以应对即将面对的老龄化问题,而且现有的养老模式过于单一,各项基础设施也有待于进一步改善。如何解决养老问题上的资金问题就显得尤为重要,本文为此提供了一个切实可行的办法,但是任何一项措施的施行都是一个循序渐进的过程,并且要在其后期施行过程中不断的健全,完善。

致谢

对于论文的完成,导师给予了很大的支持,同时也付出了比较多的心血,在此对导师的帮助表示衷心的感谢!对于论文的写作也受到同学和朋友的帮助,值此也对他们表示衷心的感谢!论文最后的完成也离不开每一位受访者的鼎力配合,也为他们送上最衷心的感谢!最后,要感谢会议组委会提供的这次机会!

Research on Pension Model of "Reverse Mortgage"
——A Case Study of Chongqing

Bai Jing，Pan Yuhong

(School of Management，Chongqing Jiaotong University)

Abstract：at present，the aging society and "growing old before becoming rich" have been the practical problems of China. The problems of shortage of pension，unsound pension security system and the single endowment mode are badly in need of solutions. This paper taking Chongqing city as the research object，compare the local existing pension model with the "reverse montgage" pension model. Visiting investigation to the case-studied. communities，face-to-face interview with experts，and research integrated with materials of the local population structure were couducted. This paper analyze the feasibility of "reverse montgage" pension model in Chongqing and put forword relevant suggestions on existing problems.

Keywords：Reverse mortage，Pension model，Chongqing

参考文献:

[1] 侯世宇,孙洋．美国倒按揭市场的演化路径及启示[J]．金融发展评论,2012,11：84-91.

[2] 金晓彤,崔宏静．亚洲国家"以房养老"模式的经验与借鉴——以日本和新加坡反向住房抵押贷款为例[J]．亚太经济,2014(1)：11-15.

[3] 宋慧中．香港"倒按揭"业务实践[J]．全球瞭望,2013,17：79-81.

[4] 包林梅．住房逆抵押贷款定价分析[J]．经济与管理研究．2011,6：124-128.

[5] 赵立志,夏咏雪,马卓然,等．我国城市"以房养老"的问题与对策研究[J]．城市发展研究．

2014，11：16-19.

[6] 李晓东．个人存量房产养老倒按揭问题探讨[J]．地产经济，2011，10(4)：108-109.

[7] 张建伟，韩青．发展住房反向抵押养老保险的宏观策略分析[J]．城市发展研究，2014，21(6)：73-79.

[8] 田淑芳．"以房养老"意愿调查报告——基于合肥、安庆、淮南三城市的调查．辽宁医学院学报，2012，3：140-142.

[9] 王新．走出"以房养老"困局之对策[J]．现代经济探讨，2014，2：20-22.

[10] 吴玉韶．中国老龄事业发展报告[M]．北京：社会科学文献出版社，2013.

[11] 邱峰．"以房养老"：养老保障新模式探析[J]．中国房地产金融，2012，9：27-30.

[12] 崔兴岩，李芸，于涛．倒按揭：中国老龄化社会以房养老模式研究[J]．现代管理科学，2013，11：70-72.

[13] 李一，徐迪．倒按揭养老期权定价模型研究——以杭州为例[J]．财经论坛，2010，5：81-82.

[14] 周江雄．生命表的构造理论[M]．天津：南开大学出版社，2001.

健康老化背景下的城市农业空间规划设计研究：
以台湾大学的公馆菜园实践为例

周 勇

（台湾大学建筑与城乡研究所）

摘要： 当城市农业理念进入人们视野，成为城市可持续发展的策略之一。但是在规划设计及建筑设计领域，城市农业仍是一个新兴的理论。与此同时，人口老龄化是人类社会发展的必然趋势，老年问题也是一大挑战，但对于发达国家，年老的问题已经被重新定义，老化的含义已经超过生命价值，更延伸到社会价值、工作价值。本文从空间专业者的角度出发，梳理分析城市规划实务中空间设计与规划着重空间性而忽视社会性，强调工具理性而忽视公民参与，造成社会资源分配不均，社会关系疏离、环境品质恶化等问题。接着，以台湾大学公馆菜园为实践案例研究，即结合台湾社会人本理念与老龄化现状进行的都市农园与老人空间设计的探索实践案例，从社会的空间规划方面入手，构建起以人为本的物质空间，有效利用城市缝隙空间，建设城市菜园，从空间上保障老人的生命价值；从空间的社会规划方面，以城市农园和当地福利组织的方式，把城市农业的生产活动、社交活动根植定位在城市农园，将与农业产品的销售网络、城市农业的分享、公益教育搭建当地福利组织与 NGO、学生团体上，以让老人的工作价值再现，发挥老人健康老化的社会价值，进而实现健康老化的空间网络与分享、公益的社会网络两者并重。以此提出：以老人为主要劳动力的城市农业发展策略，使得城市农园不仅成为空间中承载老人、社区、福利机构、NGO 的社会关系网络的交流平台，在一定程度上纾解了城市空间的食品供应问题，更为重要的是，它为老人的健康老化的可持续化提供可能，其分享、服务、公益的社会价值与理念对社会的和谐发展有裨益。中国作为后发国家，在快速城镇化过程中，往往是规划的空间性与社会性两者并存，但是在实务规划中往往弱化空间的社会性部分，在以经济持续发展、环境友好保护、资源有效利用的新型城镇化背景下，城市农业与老龄化的规划实践，可作为新型城镇化策略之城市老人当地健康老化可行性路径。

关键词： 健康老化，城市农业，台北，空间设计

1 引言

当代城镇化的快速发展，使得人类遇到了两个极大的挑战，一个是城市/城镇的食物供应，社会各界积极探索解决方案，城市农业理念被引入城市研究领域时，纷纷被推崇成为城市可持续发展的策略之一，但是在实际设计及现实社会中，城市农业的推进仍处在新兴阶段，亚洲的日本、新加坡、韩国等国以及中国台湾地区实施较为卓越。城镇化发展的另一个挑战是人口老龄化，人口老龄化是人类社会发展的必然趋势，特别对于战后婴儿潮世代，据统计局资料显示，中国台湾地区老龄人口（≥65 岁）占总人口比例早在 1992～1993 年便从 6.8％上升至 7.09％超过联合国标准 7％，已迈入老龄化社会。2013 年城镇化率达到 85％。城镇化引起的老龄、食品供应问题也逐渐成为多学科的难题。

近年来，健康老化的议题逐渐成为社会工作者关注的焦点，年老在过去更多是被污名化，但目前社会逐渐形成共识：年老只是生命体征的一个阶段，年老的问题也已经被重新定义。同时，健康老化的含义已不仅仅是生命价值的健康老化，更延伸到社会价值、工作价值的实现。随着健康老化的内涵的丰富，结合城市农业的兴起，城市农业的空间实践逐渐成为政策管理者、城市规划者青睐的一项行动策略，但在实际操作中，不容忽略的一个难题是偏重物质空间的规划而忽略社会网络的构建，即社区人与人之间的交际网络，而这也是本文试图解决的要点之一。本文研究通过在台湾大学公馆菜园与大安老人服务中心的银发农园的实践参与，提出，以社会关系网络的构建为基础的城市农业的空间规划，是新型城镇化背景下的人口老龄化与粮食供应问题的有效途径之一，以此，更

有利于实现社会网络与空间网络并重，人与社会、社会与空间相协调。

2 国内外城市农业实践研究

城市农业最早出现日本学者青鹿四郎所发表的《农业经济地理》一书，1977 年农业经济学家艾伦·尼斯在《日本农业模式》一文中明确提出城市农业（urban agriculture）。随着工业化、城镇化的推进，食品的供应问题逐渐成为一个极大的挑战，此时，日本、新加坡等国家的城市农业的成功经验，迅速进入人们视野，城市农业也逐渐成为解决粮食危机、食品安全、城市可持续发展的一个可行策略之一。[1,2]

日本的城市农业主要集中在三大城市圈内，即东京城市圈、大阪城市圈、中京城市圈。[2]其主要特点是合理的政府政策引导，强力的地方农业合作社，有效的城市农夫，具体表现在城市农业以政府的城市规划、土地税收制度为上位指导进行合理布局，宏观的进行区域布置，差异化种植；高效的地方合作社开展园艺生产设施的普及、生产技术的培训，并搭建"农户＋公司"的物流渠道，一是保护农户利益和农产品价格，二是实现较高的农产业商品率；作为生产前线的城市农户，其高效、务实、集约实施的有机绿色农业，是产品的根本保证。[1,2]

新加坡贵为田园城市（Garden City），因自然资源匮乏，过去农产品主要依靠进口，李光耀执政后，主推以高科技、高产值的方针，通过高效集约的策略（淡化水、循环水、进口水等）填补水资源短缺的问题[3]，发展现代化集约的农业科技园，强调新农业技术开发的农业生物科技园，生态的海水养殖场，以此推动生态多样化和经济可持续性。新加坡的城市农业发展至今，已经出现很大比重的职业城市农户，即主动选择务农生活的城市农人，更多已经把传统的工作、休闲延伸到城市农业是一种生活方式，与高科技、军公教等职业一样，这种现象可以看出，过去农业是一种生存手段，转变为农业是一种休闲观光方式，再到如今，农业是一种生活方式、生活组合的选择。

目前，台湾城市农业实践多表现在设施农业、现代农业物流、种苗业、农业科技园区、循环农业、休闲观光农业、生态农业等方面，与城郊农业有些类似，但很少涉及社交网络的实践探索，这点与日本、新加坡相比仍有不小差距。[4]

3 健康老化背景下的城市农业与空间规划建设路径

3.1 老龄社会的健康老化

对于婴儿潮时代的人来说，年老的已被重新定义，他们更愿意用有活力、较不感到危险的、听起来年轻一点的字汇形容自己。年老，并不代表自己身体机能的丧失，年老只是生命状态的一个必须经历的过程，最多可称之为失能，而且更多失能的是环境而不是个人，没有与老人身体状况相匹配的环境（人行空间、绿色空间、无障碍空间环境），让其自然健康老人。[5,6]这时候，健康老化的概念就应运而生，即让老人的身体、心理及社会全面安适的状态，让其基本保持与他人的正向互动、有成长的机会、有目的感、独立和创造力等要求，实现他有生产力的老化。[5]健康老化，强调的是工作价值、社会价值、生命价值三者的实现，在工作价值要求上，年老的人越来越希望通过工作价值的实现来赢得社会的理解与支持，这样的个人意愿，通过劳动获取报酬，实现社会价值，更容易帮助他们保证自己活力与生活热情，也可带来更多成就感。

但是，必须考量的是工作价值、社会价值、福利价值都不能跟生命相比，年老的人的生命与身体考虑应该放在首要位置。这时候，我们就需要考虑到所发展的活动能否不碍于老人的生命价值。当我们在关切或照顾老人时，老人医疗、老人身体体征检查，变回面临如何兼具关爱与成本效益的问题[6]，当我们对老人没有责任但愿意提供关切与照顾的情形出现时，问题就是处在了钱非万能、但没钱却万万不能以及法律责任问题。

这时候老人照料者的定义就出现了多重变化，我们所需要的并不是一个固定的老人照顾者，而可能是基于社交网络的一个平台，在此背景下的城市农业就是可能的一个方向。

3.2　在农业生产下的城市，到在城市中的农业

亨利·勒菲弗①在《空间：社会产物与使用价值》(Space：social product and use value)中曾如是说："由空间中的生产转变为空间的生产，乃是源于生产力自身的成长，以及知识在物质生产的直接介入"。[7]这种知识最后会成为有关空间的知识，虽然我们已经有空间中的事物的生产转向空间本身的生产，但空间中的生产并未消失。我们生活中的能量流动、原料流动、劳动力流动，都可以在此理解的范畴。

从城市的发展史便可以判断出，农业生产造就人类文明，农业生产产生农业剩余后，产生城市，此时的农业只是一种生产手段，强调空间中的农业生产本身。但是，随着历史演进，尤其到18世纪开始，工业革命的发生，农业生产的角色渐渐在改变。到现代，已经完全发展到空间本身的生产，农业也不再仅仅是生产手段，比如观光农业等。但回到城市农业，以台湾的城市农业不同时代背景的农业与生活为例，即可以发现：(1)在1960年之前，包括日本殖民统治时期，台湾属于农业经济时代，农业发展，乃至于农业的现代化发展，农业都是作为一种生活方式，农民有一块自己的土地是自己最大的愿望。这在国民政府土地改革之后变为现实，而进一步推动农业生产。(2)20世纪60~80年代，工商经济兴起，农业资本转向商业资本，农业生产产值逐年降低，即使是农村的居民，也不再根植于农业生产，而是趋向于营利性更高的现代化农民，此时的农业逐渐变为一种生活手段。(3)近20年来，城市拥堵问题、环境问题、食品问题凸显，加之城市农业的生产功能的重要性渐渐被休闲、观光、教育功能所取代，城市农业再度成为一种生活方式。此时，所强调的不再是空间中农业本身的生产，而更多强调空间(绝对空间、关系空间即社会关系网络)的生产。[2]

3.3　"人、城市、农业、自然"＋"社会网络"＝四位一体

现象学与空间分析大师海德格尔(Heidegger)在《建造住宅思考》(Building dwelling thinking)提出，我们定居，只有通过建造，建造是以定居为目标的，此时便已实现三位一体，加入人的因素后便是四位一体，就如"桥，是一种物，它聚集四位一体，但它以这样一种方式聚集……但只存那些自己本身就是一种地点的东西，才能使一场地成为空间"。[8]社会网络的作用就如海德格尔所言的桥一样，在城市农业产生之前或之时，社会网络并不存在于城市农业中，它起初作为空间的一个生产手段而存在，但因为在生产与社会变迁过程中，社会网络随着城市农业的发展而发生变化，即在"建、居"之后有了"思"的再建构，此时的社会网络开始服务于老龄化社会中的老人，其目的也开始转向于健康老化，而这时的四位一体，更像是城市农业、城市老人、城市空间、自然的四位，构建起健康老化的社交网络这一整体梦想。

4　基于参与式规划的城市农业实践

4.1　都市规划的变革——参与式引导

参与式规划缘于20世纪60年代美国伯克利分校，经由对城市规划的反思而发起的规划运动，

---

① 指Henri Lefebvre(1901~1991年)，其译名还有昂利·列斐伏尔，昂希·列菲伏尔等，现代法国思想大师，生后留下60多部著作、300多篇论文，是区域社会学，特别是城市社会学理论的重要奠基人。——编者注

在 20 世纪 60～80 年代风靡全美。80 年代，台湾多名规划学者如夏铸九、刘可强等从伯克利分校到台湾大学，推动台湾的参与式规划运动，台北十四号公园、宝藏巖国际艺术村等都属于台大城乡所参与式规划的杰作。King Santley 认为参与式规划是一个含义较广的概念，它可以指任何尺度与类型的参与设计过程，区域规划、城市设计、乡镇规划、住宅社区设计等[9]，其强调空间专业者为了什么来参与，规划与社区居民相关系的并不是参与，而是居民的生活，以居民的生活方式与生活伦理回归到规划的空间策略上，这便是参与。而操作的方法随着信息技术的变革也越发多样，但最核心的因素，即沟通仍是最重要的手段。

4.2　都市农业兴起与发展：粮食安全的意象之外

都市农业在城市中渐渐脱离原有生产功能之后，被赋予了休闲观光、教育、研发方面的新的意义，都市农业更多成为都市人享受生活、体验农耕文化的一个手段。

4.3　台湾大学公馆菜园的规划实践

本文根据作者在台湾大学城乡所环境规划的实习课程，以营造与设计（building and plan）为理念，结合台湾社会人本理念与老龄化现状进行的城市农园与老人空间设计的探索实践，我们通过一群人在生活中运用学校的公共空间资源，与非校人员共同耕作与维护农作物，以此搭建社区的社交网络的更好形成。我们采取的研究方法：参与式规划、田野调研等方法。

4.3.1　公馆菜园的规划与设计策略

（1）基于空间网络的规划策略

从社会的空间规划方面入手，构建起以人为本的物质空间，有效利用城市缝隙空间，建设城市菜园，设计老人空间，从空间上保障老人的生命价值。

（2）基于社会网络的营造策略

从空间的社会规划方面，以城市农园和当地福利组织的方式，将城市农业的生产活动、社交活动根植定位在城市农园，将与农业产品的销售网络、城市农业的分享、公益教育搭建当地福利组织与 NGO、学生团体上，以让老人的工作价值再现，发挥老人健康老化的社会价值，进而实现健康老化的空间网络与分享、公益的社会网络两者并重。

（3）基于人、城市、自然、空间的四位一体的整体策略

构建起城市农业、城市老人、城市空间、自然的四位统一，整合成以健康老化为目的的社交网络，服务于社区中的老人。

4.3.2　公馆菜园的空间设计与营造

公馆菜园的场地建设分为三个部分：公馆屋顶（120m²）、公馆二楼阳台花园（约 60m²）、公馆一楼外围开放空间（约 50m²），并分别设置为生态环保蔬菜花卉园、育苗花园、社区公共菜园。即（1）屋顶生态环保蔬菜花卉园：屋顶空间充足、日照充分，采用区块划分的模式，直接分隔为 40 份，以期提供给 40 人，以种植可食用蔬菜以及可观赏的花卉为主。（2）公馆二楼阳台的育苗花园：因公馆二楼日照每日时间只有 2～3h，且较为潮湿，有利于育苗培育，远期也可以发展成为带有教育意义的社区农业技术中心。（3）公馆一楼的社区菜园：此部分因为一楼的可进入性、可接触性最高，也方便于年老的人参与互动，我们充分挖掘利用的缝隙空间，为相关的老人一个可耕种的空间。

总体上，结合城乡所公馆楼的场地，构建起以人为本的物质空间，有效利用城市缝隙空间，建设以老人为服务对象的城市菜园，从生产上保障老人的工作价值。

4.3.3　公馆菜园的社会网络构建与维系

空间的社会性方面，我们通过参与式、以点带动的方法，通过实习课学生的参与，与社区老人一起建设公馆一楼的菜园，并引入当地福利组织（台北慈济组织、大安老人服务中心），提供技术帮助。

我们设立品牌"abuleo"（西班牙语），旨在将城市农业的生产活动、社交活动根植定位在城市农园。通过慈济与大安老人服务中心，我们形成生产"abuleo"—代理（慈济等NGO）—销售终端客户，进而将与农业产品的销售网络、城市农业的分享、公益教育搭建当地福利组织与NGO、学生团体上，以让老人的工作价值再现，发挥老人健康老化的社会价值。

在推动农园建设过程中，我们会积极邀请参加周边社区的相关活动，比如大安老人服务中心银发农园的农耕工作交流坊活动，实现健康老化的空间网络与分享、公益的社会网络两者并重。

图1　有机菜的商标

4.3.4　公馆菜园的经验总结与展望

公馆菜园，其实只是台北，这一座城市中，新的空间使用的方式，它象征着一个食材景观（food landscape）的议题，是一个强调共享的生活理念，也是一个社区互动的公共治理的场域。通过经营公馆菜园，可以帮助社会理解食物与农耕；增强在地理解，强调空间资源与人的资源的整合使用；强化合作机制，共同协作，增加人与人的互动性，最终实现区域的可持续发展。

5　总结

本文提到的台湾大学城市菜园与台北大安区老人服务中心的银发农园，都是作为一种城市农业的形式存在大城市的中心区，承担着后工业化社会里市民户外休闲活动的一种选择，结合休闲、教育、生产等复合功能。城市农园的设计，主要以社区、近郊、街道缝隙空间，规划规定大小的农地提供种植花草、蔬菜，让城市人体会农耕与田园的乐趣。而以城市老人为主要服务对象的城市农园，更是实现老人的社会价值与工作价值，有利于老人的健康老化。

综上所述，以老人为主要劳动力的城市农业发展策略，使得城市农园不仅成为空间中承载老人、社区、福利机构、NGO的社会关系网络的交流平台，在一定程度上纾解了城市空间的食品供应问题，更为重要的是，它为老人的健康老化的可持续化提供可能，其分享、服务、公益的社会价值与理念对社会的和谐发展有裨益。中国作为后发国家，在快速城镇化过程中，往往是规划的空间性与社会性两者并存，但是在实务规划中往往弱化空间的社会性部分，在以经济持续发展、环境友好保护、资源有效利用的新型城镇化背景下，城市农业与老龄化的规划实践，可作为新型城镇化策略之都市老人当地健康老化可行性路径。

A Study of Spatial Planning and Design Based on the Healthy Aging: A Case of Mansion Garden in Taiwan University

Zhou Yong

(Institute of Building and Planning, Taiwan University)

Abstract: When the concept of urban agriculture into view, it has become one of the strategies of sustainable urban development. But in the planning and architectural design, urban agriculture is still an emerging theory. At the same time, population aging is an inevitable trend of development of human society, elderly issues are also big challenges. But for developed countries, the old problems have been redefined. The mean of aging has not only exceeded the value of life, but also extended to social values and work values. This paper, from space professional's point of view, sorts out the issues about Urban Planning and Space Design practice in terms of focusing on spatial planning while ignoring society, emphasizing the instrumental rationality and neglect citizen participation, resulting in uneven distribution of social resources, the deterioration of social alienation, environmental quality, etc. issues. Subsequently, This paper cited Taiwan University mansion garden as an example, in terms of the practice of the silver-haired farm case studies that explore the practice of combining Case Taiwanese society Humanism and the aging of the current situation of the city and the old farm space design. This study, starts from space planning for society with the community pronged approach, builds up a people-oriented material space, effectively taking the advantage of urban gap space to build up urban gardens, so as to protect the value of life of the elderly spatially. Meanwhile, this study also looks into the social planning for spaces, through urban farm and the way of local welfare organizations, rooted the city agricultural production activities and social events at the urban farms. This will work with agricultural products sales network, sharing of urban agriculture, public education welfare organizations to set up on the ground with the NGO, student groups, in order to reproduce the work value of senior group, develop the social value of healthily aging, so as to realize the mutual success of sharing and space network of healthy aging and the social network of public benefit. A strategy of urban farm development with senior people as the major labor force is proposed. The urban farm has not only become space carrying the elderly, communities, welfare organizations, NGO's social network platform, to a certain extent, to relieve the city space food supply, more importantly, it provides the possibility of sustainable aging for healthily aging. Its sharing of services, social values and the concept of public do interests to the harmonious development of society beneficial. Spatial planning and social often coexist in the rapid urbanization process of China, a developing country. But in practice, the social planning part of the space is often weakened in order to continue economic development. Under the environmental-friendly protection, effective use of resource of new urbanization background, urban agriculture and planning practices of aging, can be used as the new urbanization strategy of urban elderly and healthy aging in the feasibility of the route.

Keywords: Health aging, Urban agriculture, Taipei, Urban plan

参考文献：

[1] 吕宇弘. 都市农业与休闲农业发展之研究：以台中市为例[D]. 台湾：中兴大学，2006.

[2] 蔡正明，杨振山. 国际都市农业发展的经验及其借鉴[J]，地理研究，2008，3(27)：362-375.

[3] 郑钰琳. 种出绿色生活圈：志愿务农者的生活方式与农耕生活风格社群之形成[D]. 台湾：台湾大学，2007.

[4] 葛永红，王亮，我国都市农业的发展模式研究[J]. 经济纵横，2002，9：87-89.

[5] 梅陈玉婵，杨佩珊（著）. 台湾老人社会工作：理论与实务[M]. 台湾：双叶书廊有限公司出版，2006.

[6] 陈大卫. 台湾游民问题的结构分析[D]. 台湾：世新大学社会发展研究所，2000.

[7] Lefebvre，Henri. 空间：社会产物与使用价值，空间的文化形式与社会理论读本.[M]，王志弘译. 台湾：明文书局，1994.

[8] Heidegger，Martin. Building dwelling thinking, in David Farrell Krell(ed.), Martin Heidegger Writings. New York：Harper&Row，1977.

[9] Stanley King. Co-design：a process of design participation[M]. New York：Van Nostrand Reinhold，1989.

[10] 李小云，原居安老的城市老年友好社区规划策略研究[D]. 广东：华南理工大学，2012.

Living Arrangement: A New Definition for Empty-Nesters in Mainland China

Tsang Yimkwan, Ma Jianxing

(Chinese University of Hong Kong)

Abstract: Since China is prone to the problems of increasing number of Empty Nesters, the paper will demonstrate the proposed living arrangement to create a new definition of filial piety and identity for elderly people to alleviate the severity.

Keywords: Living arrangement, Empty nest, Filial piety, Wellbeing, Aging society

1 Introduction

Previous literatures have all suggested the importance of building designated facilities to meet the increasing number of senior population, but little have actually looked into their expectations and wellbeing in the future.

1.1 Current Situation

According to the Chinese Sixth National Population Census, the number of people that falls under the age group of 65 and above has increased from 6.96% to 8.87%[9]. In fact, the number of individuals that are 60 and above has also risen significantly from 10.33% to 13.26% in a decade. Both increasing trends have suggested the country is gradually marching to the universal phenomenon of "aging society," especially in the metropolitan cities of coastal areas where the communities are structurally aging[9]. The effects of aging baby boomers have already started to kick in within the last decades for the more developed countries (e.g., Japan & Germany)[1].

One of the most common consequences of the aging baby boomers across the globe is Empty-Nest (kong chao), suggesting the physical absence of the next generation to be living in the same household[6]. In the United States, people have often referred people facing Empty-Nest Syndrome as Empty Nesters. After having spent a significant amount of time as a parent, it is expectable to foresee the transition would be difficult for some parents. For those who have retired, the lost of both working and caretaking identities may require one's extra adjustment to create a better meaning of their later lives with independence[7]. Empty-Nest syndrome has been seen as the final stage of family life cycle development because it usually happens when children are all grown up and chose not live with their parents[6]. With the increasing life expectancy[1], it is even more essential to understand and make an effort seek ways to tackle the situation.

As a result, this paper aims to look into the possibility of creating a new meaning of filial piety and identity for the elderly by proposing a home-sharing program. The new identity of active aging would: 1) provide them independence when diminishing the society perception of viewing them as the unproductive burden of the family, 2) loosen the anxiety of caregivers with potential sacrificing values, 3) better social inclusion and integration with the society that hasmore companions and opportunity for higher level of wellbeing. The concept of home-sharing living arrangement was proposed in the 20th century that aimed to redistribute resources [18]. The arrangement would reduce the owner's expenses by sharing the dwelling and maintenance cost with the non-relative (s). However, such practice had gradually fallen out from favor due to the public concern with privacy and other emerging alternative living arrangement.

1.2 Potential Solution

However, the authors believed that in order to alleviate the sociocultural problems that associated with the current aging society in China, home-sharing program should be re-proposed again with applicable adjustments to meet the Chinese situation. For the purpose of this paper, Empty Nesters would also be divided into three categories: 1) Empty Nesters (EN), that are completely capable of an autonomous life, 2) Aging Empty Nesters (AEN), that might be seeking for interdependence and companionship, 3) Empty Nesters with Special Needs (ENSN), is the group of people with physical or cognitive disabilities. There are three levels of proposed living arrangement: 1) Home sharing, 2) Cohousing, 3) Congregate housing.

2 Home Sharing Arrangement

Home sharing is an intergenerational social housing program that attempts to create a shared area for the group of EN and temporary residents[2]. The relationship between them could range from a simple business deal (i. e. , lodger) to companionship (i. e. , caregiver). As EN is expected to consist of people whose children live away from home, the number of people that have not achieved "young-old" (65-74) [8] could be relatively high. Since the driving reinforced factors are finance (e. g. , increasing housing expense) and wellbeing (e. g. , deterioration in physical and mental health), the proposed living arrangement home sharing would be amended into three-pronged approach-housing-oriented, service-oriented and mixed-oriented. Housing-oriented is for the home seeker (s) to look for a relatively more affordable dwelling by utilizing the vacant space from an empty nester that wants extra money. Service-oriented is for the empty nester that has no financial concerns but in needs for service (e. g. , care & accompany) to have the home seeker (s) to provide such service. And mix-oriented is to allow home seeker to rent a room in the dwelling at a much lower rate with the compensation of care service. Therefore, a mutually agreed-upon understanding and ongoing communication are vital to recognize the expected roles. The fulfillment of norm of reciprocity is encouraged when dealing with the potential lifestyle conflicts with these temporary residents.

2.1 Matchmaking process

The matchmaking process can be classified into two formations upon on the intergenerational participants' choices: informal arrangement and formal arrangement.

Informal Arrangement

The arrangement is also known as "private arrangement" that negotiated by the unrelated people who want to share or seek for dwelling. Some common ways are included by not limited to word-of-mouth and advertisement. The entire process to draft the tern condition of the contact is completely personalized between the homeowner and home seeker (s) to meet their needs.

Formal Arrangement

An official and authorized third-party will be presented to assist the negotiation between the home owner and home seeker (s). Demands and restrictions on both parties will be drafted according to guidelines. It is expected that formal arrangement would be a prevailing trend among the elderlies because of the reassurance from the third-party.

The agency for providing service of home-sharing can be sponsored and developed by the government and variety of charitable organizations or even private sponsor. Residential committee in each housing community will be an ideal agency for assisting the home-sharing program. Independent organization plays a vital position in serving the community's residents, managing residential community and building social cohesion [16].

The following steps are modified by the Match-Up Home Sharing Program from the Livable New York Resource Manual to aim to achieve a successful match.

1. An application will be required for both parties to fill before the start of home-sharing program. Basic personal information, including living habitats, home characteristics and personal traits, will be collected to assist the preparation for potential match-up.

2. After that, participating dwelling (s) would be evaluated by the agency staff to measure and ensure the appropriateness for home-sharing during one or multiple home visit (s).

3. Next, the agency staff will conduct an in-person interview to further understand some more in-depth information (e. g., living habits, personal needs, physical conditions, and criminal background) of both parties.

4. An initial match-up will be proposed based on the gathered information. Computer software is expected to be able to apply to the match-up process as soon as the applicable algorithms are formed with the Big Data usage.

5. Reference will be made to allow both parties to understand the information of the opposing party.

6. In-person meeting and communication will then be arranged prior to the step of evaluating compatibility. Arrangement will be terminated as soon as either party was unsatisfied. After that,

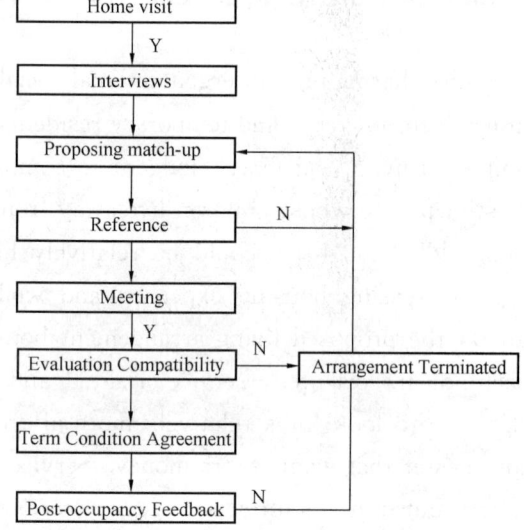

Figure 1　Flow chart of match-up process
(Source: Author)

both parties will go back to the proposing match-up stage for another. If both parties are satisfied with the arrangement, term condition agreement will be established.

7. Last but not the least, a post-occupancy feedback will be conducted to assure the appropriateness. Any dissatisfaction will result in the return to the proposing match-up stage.

2.2　Benefits and potential barrier (s)

The intergenerational home sharing program benefits will bring affordability for both parties and a certain level of companionship for the empty nesters. Senior empty nesters are experiencing the lack of a thoroughly established social security with insufficient income in China [17]. As most socially isolated elders would experience loneliness and some depressive symptoms [13], companionship and social interaction would be able to enhance their level of wellbeing. The existence of young-adults itself would be able to provide a further emotional security assurance for this vulnerable group of empty nesters. However, the lack of popularity at the beginning stage may lead to a major barrier to provide sufficient number of applicants to look for applicable candidates for a successful matchup. It would be a location-specific process as urban areas are more prone to the adverse effect (e. g. , rising price and large scale of population) from unaffordability and urbanization. Last but not least, stable and adequate funding is vital to guarantee the successful operating system.

Co Housing

With "aging in place" being a prevailing trend [1], cohousing is suggested for AEN. It is a type of intentional housing composed of private homes supplemented by shared facilities for several people that are unrelated but with common interests. It combines the advantages of autonomy from private dwellings and community living [3]. The dwelling is planned, owned, and managed by the residents who share activities (e. g. , cooking, dining, & child care). Common facilities may include a dining room, laundry area, guest rooms, and recreational features for both social and practical reasons. It is applicable to people of all ages with the needs of belongingness. It is the type of permanent housing that is able to grow old and continue to contribute productively. Visitors (e. g. , children & friends) could stay in the community's guestrooms.

Several residents would share a single dwelling in an agency-sponsored residential community. The agency will be responsible of the location, maintenance and management of the dwelling. Cohousing is believed to be able to create a positively meaningful and sustainable living relationship while preserving the traditionalhousing scheme. Cohousing living arrangement was originally stemmed from Denmark in 1960s when young families who brought adjacent properties to sharing the child minding work. Later development redefined the cohousing scheme to match the contemporary lifestyle for autonomy. Individuals would have their own spaces but shared public facilities with the group.

2. 3　Matchmaking process

In order to improve the problem of AEN in Mainland China, the new cohousing living arrangement is proposed to redesign to adopt the society situation.

1. Site visit is necessary to help them understand the future accommodations environment.

2. Reference to check the participants' background.

3. Contract should then be conducted to fit the participants' needs.

4. AEN can pay the living cost payment by retirement pension. Property mortgage from the government is also available with special conditions.

5. During the period of occupancy, housekeeping service such as cooking and cleaning and personal care service may be provided by agency.

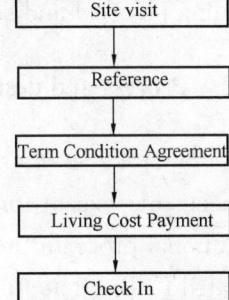

Figure 2　Flow chart of cohousing arrangement

2. 4　Benefits and potential barrier (s)

AEN do not have to worry the responsibility for seeking or interviewing housemates, and the number of vacant rooms in a dwelling will not fluctuate the living cost. A steady and expected terms can be anticipated when drafting/ renewing any new contracts despite of the composition of AEN. Privacy and independence can be maintained with a maximized degree of socialization. Since Chinese people have a tendency and culture to "buy" and "own" a home, it is believed to be difficult to convince AEN to pay for another place to live. It is uncertain whether AEN would be comfortable enough to face changes (i. e. , relocation and sharing spaces) at that age, assuming a great level of emotional attachment would have been formed.

3　Congregate Housing

Last but not the least, ENSN can live in the congregate housing that has private rooms arranged around shared living spaces with universal designs. This less demanding environment allows occupants to maintain an independent living while having a high level of supportive assistance for these vulnerable elderly occupants[4,5]. Along with the increasing needs of staff counseling and involvement, external supportive services (e. g. , skilled nurses) would also available to enhance the level of assistance.

With the group of ENSN, it is inevitable tomove into such setting with high level of monitoring. Home-delivered service is no longer sufficient to meet the needs because previous housing designs did not consider their needs. Based on the 2015-2020 China's Old-Age Industry Development Research Report, the amount of home nursing is not sufficient to meet the demands of the old people so that nearly 90 percent of the old people had to stay home and taken care by the relatives[14]. It is understandable to expect the lives for both ENSN and caregivers could turned to be quite miserable and undesirable.

The proposed congregated housing living arrangement is targeted specifically to create an assisted living environment while maximizing the level of independence. Different from the traditional nursing home, congregate housing arrangement should be able to provide a more satisfying and appealing physical and social environment.

3. 1　Process and design

The process of arranging the congregate housing program is similar to the cohousing living arrangement; except for the fact that this proposed congregate housing program is expected to receive additional program funding with the involvement of professional people from the gerontological and related fields. The fulfillment of universal design and high level of supportive assistance will be in exchange of a large funding which may not be provided by agency-sponsor but expected to receive from the government budget (e. g. , pension) .

3. 2　8Principles

There is a broad spectrum of universal design ranging from indoor space, neighborhood to outdoor landscape. 8 principles on identifying the home universal design and high level caregiving in congregated housing will be briefly discussed as follow:

1. Privacy: Auditory and visual privacy are significant parts in physical separation[15]

2. Social Interaction: Creates platform for social exchange to cope with isolation and loneliness

3. Security: Minimizes the risk of harm because of the gradually decrease of mobility in ENSN

4. Accessibility: Employs designs to reduce the complexity on the control of amenities

5. Familiarity: Enhances the comfort level and avoid big changes

6. Aesthetics: Employs human-oriented design to install appropriate items that signifies individual beauty and characteristics

7. Adaptability: Allows flexibility to fit the potential change of both people and environment

4 Conclusion

Current paper proposed a home sharing, cohousing, and congregate housing as the potential solution to alleviate the sociocultural problems in Mainland China. With the increasing number of empty nesters and drop in elderly support ratio, it is now reasonable to understand the importance of proposing the concept of active aging along with the new form of living arrangement that meet the emerging needs. Although the concept of home-sharing program has already existed for decades, it was never been hugely emphasized in China. With the ability to provide affordable housing and (or) companionship, it is believed to be very useful and practical for the intergenerational group of people. And for those who are looking for a stable, expectable place with autonomy, cohousing will be perfect for them to allow them to maintain a high degree of autonomy while being able to connect with people that shared the same interests. Congregate housing is designed specifically with the 8 principles to ensure their residents' living quality and wellbeing in different aspects. This proposed living arrangement is expected to be able to provide them the opportunity to have a fulfilling, glamorous life while possessing a high degree of autonomy.

居住安排：为中国内地的空巢者提供新定义

曾艳君　马健翔

（香港中文大学）

摘要： 针对中国所面临的空巢老人增长所带来的问题，此文提出了新的养老宜居方案旨在重新定义认识对老年人的孝道，从而缓解空巢老人增长所面临的问题。

关键词： 居住安排，空巢者，孝道，生活素质，老龄化社会

References：

[1] Brandon, Emily. 10 Rapidly Aging Countries[N]. US News RSS. June 16, 2014. Accessed March 28, 2015.

[2] Danigelis, Nicholas L. , Alfred P. Fengler. No Place like Home: Intergenerational Homesharing through Social Exchange[M]. New York: Columbia University Press, 1991.

[3] Durrett, Charles, William H. Thomas. Senior Cohousing Handbook a Community Approach to Independent Living[M]. 2nd ed. Gabriola Island, B. C. : New Society Publishers, 2009.

[4] Kaye, Lenard W. , Abraham Monk. Congregate Housing for the Elderly: Theoretical, Poli-

cy, and Programmatic Perspectives[M]. New York：Haworth Press，1991.

[5] Lemke，Sonne，Rudolf H. Moos. Personal and Environmental Determinants of Activity Involvement Among Elderly Residents of Congregate Facilities[M]. Journal of Gerontology，1989：139-148.

[6] Preedy，Victor R. Handbook of Disease Burdens and Quality of Life Measures[M]. New York，NY：Springer，2010.

[7] Saltz，Gail. Six Steps to Surviving an Empty Nest[J/OL]. TODAY. com. December 10，2003. Accessed March 23，2015. http：//www. today. com/id/3079353/ns/today-parenting _ and _ family/t/six-steps-surviving-empty-nest/#. VQuptzSUf _ t.

[8] Zizza，Claire A.，Kathy Jo Ellison，Catherine M. Wernette. Total Water Intakes of Community-Living Middle-Old and Oldest-Old Adults[J]. The Journals of Gerontology Series A：Biological Sciences and Medical Sciences，2009：481-86.

[9] National Bureau of Statistics of China. The Sixth National Population Census Database [ ]，2010.

[10] 孟丹丹. 空巢老人过亿 中国陷入"未富先老"困境[N]. 联合早报，2015-2-2.

[11] 穆光中（主编）. 挑战孤独-空巢家庭. 第1版. 石家庄市：河北人民出版社，2002.

[12] DiCarlo，Antonio Scotto. Match-Up Home Sharing Program[A/OL]. Livable New York Resource Manual. Accessed http：//www. aging. ny. gov/livableny/ResourceManual/Housing/III1g. pdf.

[13] Singh，Archana，Misra，Nishi. Loneliness, depression and sociability in old age[J]. Industrial Psychiatry Journal，2009，18(1)：51-55.

[14] 中国产业研究报告网. 2015—2020年中国养老产业行业分析及发展趋势研究报告[R]. 2015.

[15] Regnier，Victor，Jennifer Hamilton. Best Practices in Assisted Living：Innovations in Design，Management and Financing[M]. Los Angeles，CA：National Eldercare Institute on Housing & Supportive Services，Andrus Gerontology Center，University of Southern California，1991.

[16] 张良礼. 社区居委会在社区服务体系建设中的地位与作用[R/OL]. 中华人民共和国民政部 2008. http：//www. mca. gov. cn/article/mxht/llyj/200801/20080100009898. shtml.

[17] 姜向群. 养老补偿论：建立对城乡低收入老年人群体的公共资源补偿机制[J]. 人口研究，2008，4.

[18] Attias-Donfut，Claudine. Cultural and Economic Transfers Between Generations：One Aspect of Age Integration[J]. The Gerontologist，2000，40(3)：270-272.

社会住宅与保障性住房建设
Social Housing and Affordable Housing Construction

基于长效使用的保障性住宅冗余性设计的层次与内容

周 曦 张 芳

（苏州科技学院建筑与城市规划学院）

摘要： 住宅需求是个动态发展的过程，特别在近阶段大规模建设的保障性住宅中，低水平的建设标准与未来住宅需求的快速发展间存在很大的矛盾。冗余性设计可以解决住宅形制的稳定性与需求的易变性之间的矛盾，是实现住宅长效使用的一种有效方法。保障性住宅的冗余性设计分为三个层次：住宅套型内、住宅建筑公共空间、住区规划部分。在住宅套型设计中：改进最易发生变化的建筑空间的结构，采用一些新技术解决厨卫空间的变化，另外在装修和预埋管线中留有余地以适应改建；在住宅建筑的公共部分：通廊、电梯、设备平台、公共管井和住宅底层部分等预留设计余量，方便未来的增建或改建；在住区规划中：预留用地以备未来改造升级公共景观和活动空间，新增停车设施和设备机房，并视情况加建社区用房和配套商业，以满足住户不断发展的公共需求。

关键词： 保障性住宅，冗余性，长效使用，层次，设计

保障性住宅是指政府为中低收入住房困难家庭所提供的限定标准、限定价格或租金的住房，一般由廉租住房、经济适用住房和政策性租赁住房构成。我国近年来为了弥补之前保障性住宅的历史欠账，满足社会底层居民的住房需求，短时间内开发建设了大量保障性住宅。这些保障性住宅数量多、标准低、配套少，虽然短时期内满足了居民的基本居住需求，但是长期来看很容易随着社会经济发展而被迅速淘汰。因此，寻求在保障性住宅的建筑设计、规划设计、开发管理过程中预留一定发展余地，应能即契合当下需要又能适应未来发展，才能避免大拆大建达到长期使用的目标。

1 近阶段保障性住宅建设蕴藏的问题

保障性住宅一般由廉租住房、经济适用住房和政策性租赁住房构成。1998年房改后保障性住房建设长期滞后，总量小、比例低，国务院于2010年提出将在今后五年内计划兴建三千余万套保障性住房，力争使保障性住房在住宅中比例达到20%。[1]集中大片建设保障性住宅是目前保障性住宅建设的一大现象。受制于住宅设计和建设的特点，固定不变的住宅建筑和住区环境存在不少问题，体现在以下几个方面[2]：

1.1 难以适应服务对象的变化

随着国民经济发展，城市居民收入逐渐提高，城市中极端困难的居民比例必然会下降。而且未来外来长期务工人员、收入超过目前保障性住宅限定标准的"夹心层"居民也将纳入保障性住宅中来。目前困难居民对保障性住宅的要求仅限于"有、无"的问题，对住宅的空间、设备、装修、环境、配套等要求不高。但是当未来保障性住宅服务对象扩大到城市20%居民时，各种不同的需求将会体现，目前大量建设的雷同的保障性住宅能否适应多变的需求将打上一个问号。

1.2 难以适应未来居住标准的提高

保障性住房的建设标准是与当地人均住房面积挂钩制定的，一般以60%为标准，目前标准多为人均15～20m²。从历史的发展来看，改革开放以后我国城镇居民人均居住面积的增长速度是非常快的，相应的保障性住宅建设标准也不可能一成不变。从国外早先保障性住宅发展经验来看，建设标准也是随着时间推移、经济发展水涨船高。香港公共房屋1992年以来户型面积也呈现逐渐增大

的趋势，从 1992 年的人均 8.4m² 逐渐增大，到 2007 年已达 12.2m²。1992～1998 年人均居住面积 5.5m² 为主力套型，近年已经过渡到以 7m² 以上为主。住宅设计寿命达 50 年以上，新建数千万小套的保障性住宅，仅能满足基本的居住要求，还远没有达到舒适的标准。如果这批保障性住宅设计不能升级改造，将无法满足未来住户的需要。

1.3 形成居住隔离，造成新的社会阶层断裂。

这方面西方发达国家在过往的保障性住宅建设中是有过深刻教训的。如 20 世纪第二次世界大战后法国遭遇住宅危机，在 50 年代初期到 70 年代中期，以政府为主导短时间内在城市郊区，兴建了一大批大型"社会住宅区"。这批住宅区功能单一，区位偏远，建筑体量巨大，外形单调、景观乏味。很快遭遇中产阶层流失，迅速沦为低收入者和贫困人口的聚居地。社区治安和基础设施恶化，形成严重的社会问题。[3]这些相同的情况正在我国各城市交替上演，政府在城市郊区新建大片保障性住宅小区。单一的、低标准的保障性住区圈定了城市底层居民，居住隔离造成社会贫困的固化，对社会的发展与稳定是极为不利的。

2 保障性住宅长效使用的解决之道——冗余性设计

目前保障性住宅建设的特点是社会现状所决定的，首先需要解决的是大量城市底层居民住宅有无的需求问题，受制于目前有限的财政能力很难一步到位兴建高标准的保障性住宅，也违背了保障性住宅社会保障的基础目的。但是，世界各国特别是发达国家过往的发展经验告诉我们，保障性住宅如果不能与时俱进，不断更新改造，低标准的住宅和住区很难满足未来发展的需要，流失优质居民、固化贫困阶层，易于形成新的"贫民窟"。这是设计师和政府部门所不愿意看到的。

那么怎样才能解决这一两难的问题呢？其他设计领域中的"冗余性"设计提供了很好的借鉴思路。冗余性在各领域中有不同内容的阐述，主要的思想是设计中留有一定的余地，具备多种解决方法，如果其中某一部分、某一支系产生问题，可以以另一部分代替而不影响整体功能。目前住宅设计中，对这方面的考虑是很少的，没有冗余性的设计很难满足未来的需求。

住宅设计中，特别是低标准建设的大量保障性住宅中需要引入"冗余性"设计理念。设计应留有足够的发展余地，预留多渠道解决方案。当未来形势发生变化时，住宅和住区具备替代解决措施，这样才能达到长效使用的目标。[4]

3 住宅套型层次上的设计内容

3.1 结构限制与空间划分

目前住宅建筑几种结构形式中砖混结构和剪力墙结构应用最广，其房间四周墙体即结构，对套型内房间空间的重组限制很大。以日本为代表的 SI 住宅体系中，采用支撑结构 S（Skeleton）与填充部分 I（Infill）分离，即 SI 分离的设计方法。通过采用厚板及大跨度框架结构，套内可以形成任意自由分割的各种空间。其相应的结构技术代价是我国目前很难承受得起的。[5]

强调增加保障性住宅套内空间的冗余性，并不是强调实现类似 SI 住宅那种无限可变的套内空间。相比商品房住户多样化的个性需求，保障性住宅是以满足基本的居住要求为主要目的：首先需要厨房、卫生间必需的功能空间，其次做到家庭内每个代际（父母、子、女、祖父母等）拥有一个卧室空间、外加阳台、起居室、餐厅等辅助功能空间形成住宅套型。

家庭结构中代际数变化较大，特别在子女成长期和老年期有着不同的需要。如同一住宅套型在夫妻结婚时需要一个卧室就够了，生育子女后祖父母帮扶带孙辈，三代同堂时需要三室甚至四室；等子女长大后祖父母离开卧室数量可以减少；需要赡养祖父母时卧室数量又要增加。因此，卧室数量是保障性住宅中需要变化最大的部分。最简单的调剂方法是利用客厅的空间：需要增加卧室数量时削减客厅面积隔断成小房间，极端情况下取消客厅形成大卧室；当家庭代际数量减少，卧室需求下降时可以打通客厅相连卧室形成较大客厅空间，增加日常活动面积。这种空间调剂方式对建筑结构的影响很小，只需要局部增加过梁，改变剪力墙、框架柱位置即可实现。2011 年湖南省保障性住宅设计竞赛一等奖作品中针对不同的家庭结构和人员构成，设计的户型通过对客厅空间的调剂实现了多种分隔方式，可以满足三口之家、四口之家、五口之家及合租家庭的不同需求。[6]

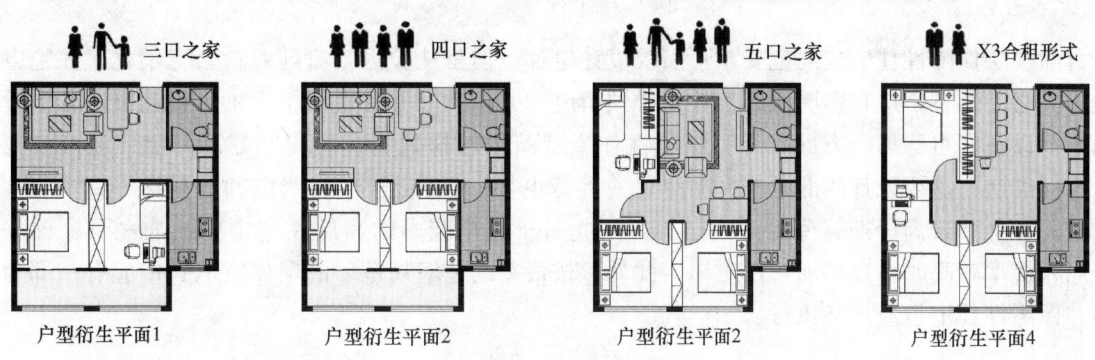

图 1 公租房户型衍生平面

（图片来源：根据 2011 年湖南省保障性住宅设计竞赛一等奖作品整理）

3.2 厨卫特殊功能空间的解决方法

厨房和卫生间作为住宅内的特殊功能空间与其他功能空间，如客厅、餐厅、卧室等存在较大不同。一是涉及防水防潮问题；二是厨房有通风和防爆要求，厨房必须具有直接对外通风，卫生间不能处在下层住宅厨房、餐厅的上空；三是房间大小面积与其他房间差异较大，很难相互转换。

目前保障性住宅中受到总面积的限制，厨房空间普遍过小，而随着生活水平提高，厨房电器设备（如烤箱、电蒸锅、洗碗机、消毒柜等）增多，需要更大的厨房空间。由于厨房的特殊性，向外扩张困难较大，也不能将其他房间改为厨房。可以参考欧美住宅中厨房结合家庭室的设计方法，将厨房面积扩大，餐厅并入厨房内，形成餐厨合一的房间。未来套内居住人口减少，将相连的卧室改为餐厅，现餐厨房间作为厨房使用，相应扩容了厨房面积。

3.3 管道线路的革新

套型中排水管线的改造难度最大，制约了卫生间位置和数量的调剂。应采用同层排水和管道墙等成熟技术。虽然需要增加一些造价，但是可以将排水管线对套型空间的影响减少到最小，灵活增减卫生间数量。

SI 住宅中采用架空地板或者吊顶预设线缆，这种设计代价很大。保障性住宅套型空间的调配集中在客厅改卧室、餐厨厅改厨房、卫生间增减等几个特定的方面，在可能需要改变的区域可以按两种空间布置多预设一些线缆接口。不需要使用时用白盒覆盖，需要改造时再打开改成插座接口，这种技术方法是最经济的一种冗余性设计措施。

3.4 装修构造的处理。

SI 住宅中可变部分的装修产品及构造措施已经十分成熟，目前缺少的主要是产品推广和客户认知。今后保障性住宅应提倡以装修房标准交付，一是节省了困难住户装修的费用；二是避免了装修扰民；最重要的一点是可以预置可变部分的装修构造，方便以后套型的升级改造。如在需要拆除的分隔墙底铺设与房间相同的地板或地砖，顶面完成粉刷装饰，这样移除隔墙后可以不需要二次补装；在需要增加卫生间的区域地面和墙体预先完成防水处理，增加卫生间时铺贴瓷砖饰面即可。

4 住宅公共空间

4.1 垂直交通中电梯冗余

目前多层保障性住宅按规范要求不需要设计电梯，但是从长远来看随着社会老龄化，住宅电梯是生活的必需装备，应在多层保障性住宅中预留电梯井位置，并在楼层平台上预设门洞，未来投资增加电梯设备即可。另一方面，部分保障性住宅建筑的电梯数量也存在问题。高层住宅按规范要求，每标准层只需要设计两部电梯。据测算人等待电梯的极限是 90s，当电梯数量达不到 60 户/部时，居民在上下班高峰期等待时间会过长。因此对于住户较多的高层住宅中应增加一个电梯井空位，当入住率较高时可以增加一部电梯。此外，按最新的住宅规范，高层住宅电梯中应有一部为担架梯，保障性住宅也应严格执行。

4.2 集中管道井冗余

目前住宅建筑中集中管井主要解决了强电、弱电、给水及北方采暖地区的热力管线。未来可能增加的管线有南方非采暖区的供热管线、中水管线及通信线缆。特别是多层住宅中，不强制要求集中管道井，导致公共管线占用楼道空间，对未来管线的增加是十分不利的。保障性住宅无论多层或高层都应预留足够的管道井，并适当加大空间以备未来增设管线。

4.3 太阳能集热装置预留空间

太阳能集热装置是绿色住宅中较为成熟的一项技术，但是对安装位置和管线预设有较高要求。目前多层和小高层住宅上部楼层住宅经常采用屋顶安装太阳能集热板，需要在给水井中设计冷水进水和热水出水管道。对于高层住宅和小高层住宅低层楼层住户可以采用阳台栏板式太阳能集热板，这需要在阳台外预留足够的安装位置，并在阳台内预留集热水罐安装位置，还需要设计冷水进水管和通往厨卫的热水出水管。

4.4 住宅底层公共空间冗余

随着生活水平提高，住户对社区公共服务的要求必然提高，需要能有足够的建筑空间容纳公共服务。除了住区社区服务中心外，每栋住宅需要分散的公共服务设施。按欧美发达国家经验，住宅楼底层可能需要公共餐厅、休闲游艺、网吧、书刊杂志阅览、酒吧/咖啡/茶室、总服务台、洗衣间等空间，按国内社区服务需要还要增设快件收发寄存、老年康复服务等。住宅建筑底层近期按住宅设计，结构设计考虑到改造为大空间的可能性，以便远期改造为公共服务空间。

5 住区规划设计

目前住区规划设计含保障性住宅项目往往采用高强度使用模式，规划用地内几乎没有预留发展空间。这种规划设计只能满足当下的居住及服务需求，对未来可能的新增建筑空间几无余地可以安插。按住区规划发展规律，保障性住区新增需求集中在以下几个方面。

5.1 景观及活动空间

住户对住区公共活动及景观的要求会随着社会发展迅速提高。法国近期开展的社会住宅区改造和新加坡 1989 年开始的"组屋更新计划"中常采用拆除部分住宅建筑加大绿化活动空间的方法，以及架空局部住宅低层，让各楼间绿化景观相互渗透。

5.2 停车设施

随着保障性住宅服务对象扩大，居民生活水平提高，未来私家车将成为生活必需品。目前低至 0.4 辆/户的停车标准显然不能满足未来停车需要。保障性住区停车设施可以考虑两步走的策略，在目前停车数量基础上预留一定的升级余量，日后可以扩容，达到户均车位 0.8~1 辆的标准。具体可以采取三种办法：（1）地下机动车库适当增加层高，停车区净高增加到 3.6m 以上，以后可以增设双层升降横移式机械车库，可以增加约 40% 的停车数量。（2）预留空地日后建设机械停车楼。这种方式是日本等发达国家在旧区改造中经常采用的方案。（3）将小区部分空地改为生态停车位。停车位下铺植草砖，上覆盖树木，中间以绿篱分隔，最大限度削弱停车位的负面效应。

5.3 设备机房

家庭用电负荷呈现不断增长趋势，此外未来发展纯电动或插电式混合动力新能源汽车，都需要增设充电桩，家庭直流充电桩常规充电模式下输入功率在 10~40kW，当住区内电动车达到 20%~30% 以上比例时，会对电网负荷产生影响，届时需要扩容变配电房机组数量，变配电房需要预留增建空间。此外，秦岭以南夏热冬冷地区现为非采暖区，日后需要考虑集中供暖，需要增建锅炉房的空地。其余电信、给水排水等设备增建所占空间较小，目前机房已足够容纳。

5.4 社区用房

目前保障性住区社区用房包括物业管理、文化娱乐、医疗保健等几个部分，一般面积为总规划建筑面积的 1%~3%。未来随着老龄化趋势，需要增加社区医疗、养老等服务用房；随着住户文化娱乐要求提高，还需要增加体育健身、社团活动、教育培训等社区用房。[7]规划中宜留出空地方便加建。

5.5 配套商业

保障性住区内部分住户为社会弱势群体，因文化、年龄、身体方面原因在就业方面存在困难。政府及社区管理单位应设置一部分商业用房优先供给就业困难的社区居民经营。另外可以筹建一些小型手工工场，供社区中年龄大、文化低的居民兼职工作，提高住户收入。这些经营性用房可以作为远期项目在规划中留足余地，未来视情况分批实施。

6 结语

近期我国集中大量建设保障性住宅有效地缓解了城市困难居民的住宅需求，但是以发展的眼光来看目前采取固定设计的保障性住宅不能满足不同人群、不同时间段、不同生活的需要，也就不能适应长期有效的使用。

研究中将冗余性设计理念引入到保障性住宅中，即在建筑设计和住区规划中预先留有一定变通的余地，具备多种解决问题的方法。根据保障性住宅设计内容分为三个层次，分别从住宅套型空间、住宅建筑公共空间以及住区规划从小到大不同层面上分析了设计问题，提出了一些解决方法。如果在保障性住宅建筑设计及规划中能够意识到，进而运用这些设计思想，将会极大地促进保障性住宅灵活适应未来发展需要，从而有效地延长保障性住宅的使用周期。

致谢

本课题受《基于可变适应性的保障性住宅设计策略研究》，住房和城乡建设部科学技术项目科研，项目编号 2013-R4-4 资助。

Level and Content of Redundant Design of Indemnificatory Housing—Based on Long-Term Use Technology

Zhou Xi，Zhang Fang

(Su zhou University of Scien ce and Technology)

Abstract：The demand for housing shows a dynamic process of development，especially in the recent stage of large-scale construction of Indemnificatory Housing. There is a big contradiction between the low level of construction standards and the rapid development of the future housing demand. The contradiction between the stability of housing pattern and the mutability of housing demand can be solved by redundancy design，which can achieve the long-term use of housing. The redundancy design of Indemnificatory Housing can be divided into three levels：the interior of the department，the public space of department，residential planning. Teasing out the area most liable to modification in the department，it can be adapted by improving the building structure and bringing in some new technology to solve the kitchen space and bathroom；furthermore，in the process of decoration and embedding the pipeline adequate leeway can be left for reconstruction. In the public space of department，such as corridors，elevators，equipment platform，public piping shafts，and the ground floor of the department，a part of space can be set aside for future promotion and reconstruction. In the residential planning，reserved land can be set aside for the future upgrading of public landscape and space，for parking space and equipment room，and for community housing and commerce，to fulfill the continuous development of the public needs.

Keywords：Indemnificatory housing，Redundancies，Long-term use，Level，Design

参考文献：

［1］ 生态文明视角下的城乡规划——2008 中国城市规划年会论文集［G］. 焦怡雪 . 关于保障性住房面积标准问题的探讨 . 2008：1-10.

［2］ 住宅和城乡建设部住宅产业化促进中心 . 公共租赁住房产业化实践——标准化套型设计和全装修指南［M］. 北京：中国建筑工业出版社，2011.

［3］ 索健，张挺，胡懿睿 . 当代欧盟住宅存量更新范例及其设计手法研究［J］. 建筑学报，2013，3：22-27.

［4］ 贾倍思 . 长效住宅——现代建宅新思维［M］. 江苏：东南大学出版社，1993.

［5］ 孙志坚 . 住宅设计的多样化对应手法——日本从住宅标准设计到支撑体住宅［J］. 工业建筑；

2007，9：48-51.

[6] 伍江军，王之旷，王小凡. 保障性住房设计初探——2011 年湖南省保障性住房设计竞赛一等奖获奖作品解析[J]. 中外建筑，2012，1：93-96.

[7] 张农科. 政府保障性住房物业管理模式探讨[J]. 中国物业管理，2011，10：6-9.

中国社会住宅现状特征及发展展望

甘振坤　王　珺

（北京建筑大学）

摘要：在中国，主导设计和建设的力量已经从完全政府行为发展成为政府、开发商以及建筑师三方共同协作的局面。随着我国内地商品房价格飞涨，计划生育政策带来的人口结构变化，解决中国中低收入人群的住房问题迫在眉睫。近几年来，随着一批有着设计理想的建筑师、开发商的介入，社会住宅的设计环节受到了特别关注，并由此产生了一系列实验性实践。随着设计解决社会问题开始进入人们的视野，建筑师在社会住宅的问题上越来越能发挥自己的专业优势，改善只重视数量不考虑质量的现状。社会住宅不再仅仅需要满足居住的基本要求，还应为居住着提供更高的居住尊严和生活品质。本文着重对比分析 2000 年之后中国社会住宅中出现的特色案例，结合针对社会居住问题的研究，从设计角度、用户需求和运行策略角度考虑，关注空间品质，提出适合中国当下国情的社会住宅设计模式语言应该具备经济集约、舒适美观、复合可变等特点，并对中国社会住宅的发展趋势进行展望。

关键词：特殊国情，高品质，经济集约，灵活，多变

1　中国社会住宅的发展现状

1.1　社会住宅定义

社会住宅泛指由政府或相关社会机构主持运营，通过租赁的方式提供给特定人群的住宅。特定人群通常是低收入人群或需要得到社会福利保障的弱势群体。房屋一般由政府出资或与其他社会机构共同出资主持建设，或直接收购改造现有房屋，其租金通常远低于市场价格。社会住宅并非一个统一名词，在不同国家或地区类似的住宅类型有各种不同的称谓。例如美国从经济角度出发称其为 Affordable Housing、日本称为公营住宅；强调经营机构的特殊性，中国香港称公共屋邨（简称公屋）、新加坡与马来西亚称组合房屋等。针对中国的特殊国情，本文所讨论的中国社会住宅，特指区别于传统意义商品房的；面向年轻人、企业职工、中低收入者等特殊人群提供的；具有很强社会性质的；以出租为主结合少量买卖的居住建筑。

1.2　中国社会住宅发展概述

目前中国的社会住宅类型构成主要有两部分：其一为由政府完全出资主持推行的社会保障性住宅；其二为社会、地方政府及开发商共同合作建设的面向更为广泛的低收入群体的居住建筑。后者由于专业经营者的介入而显示出更高的活力，为本文主要的研究对象。改革开放 30 多年来，中国经历了从公有分配到私有购买的一系列住房体制改革，期间取得了显著成绩。然而也存在一些发展不到位的方面，例如经济适用房和廉租房的数量、质量不能满足市场需要，商品房价格过高使购买者难以承受等。自新中国成立至今，中国保障性住房制度施行可大致分为以下三个时期：新中国成立后至改革开放前"福利住房制度"；改革开放后至 1998 年同时并存施行住宅私有化与福利分房两种住房制度；1998 年之后，初步建立现代社会保障性住房制度。

1.3　国家相关政策分析

2003 年 8 月 12 日国务院发布了《关于促进房地产市场持续健康发展的通知》，该通知中将经济适用房定义为具有保障性质的政策性商品住房，并且将房地产业作为国家发展的经济支柱产业之

一，自此开始，住房"商品化"愈走愈远，住房价格不断飞涨，以至于形成今日中国房产泡沫的问题。尽管从 2004 年开始国家意图通过央行调高存贷款利率、国务院相继出台老"国八条"和新"国八条"来调控住房市场，但都没有起到明显效果。国务院总理温家宝在 2008 年 10 月国务院常务会议上提出通过国家的投资建设，增加保障房数量，降温房地产业，使住房回归公共性。

1.4 社会住宅发展面临的问题

中国社会住宅体系的建立面临众多历史遗留问题。长久以来，中国的社会福利居住制度缺乏统一的组织管理机构，没有形成普遍、稳定的社会住宅体系。至 1998 年之前，社会住宅的建设工作均由各个工作单位负责，以家属院的形式向单位职工提供无偿或象征性收取费用的居住服务，并由单位进行管理。这种由单位集团承担向内部人员提供居住空间的义务，缺乏更高层面上统一监管的社会住宅体系，造成集团之间住房条件差异化的现象，并加重了集团在住宅建造和管理上的负担，导致大量拥挤居住及房屋老旧缺乏维修的现象出现。住房商品化改革策略的自身缺陷是社会住宅发展所面临的另一重要问题，过度依赖市场调控机制造成住房价格泡沫。住房的商品和投资属性被不断强化，而忽视了最为根本的社会属性，住房市场现状无法满足低收入阶层的基本住房诉求。

2 中国社会住宅特色案例分析

2.1 分析目标及分类原则

本文研究案例的目的在于寻找新时代适合中国年轻人的经济型住宅类型，案例主要来源于 2000 年以后国内的优秀项目。选取案例的类型主要有以下三类：独立设计建造的公寓、改造出租型公寓、万科系列研究。前两类研究针对的分别是新建住宅以及改造型住宅，它们基本可以涵盖中国现在具有社会性住宅的主要特征，是探索符合中国国情社会住宅的重要参考。万科系列研究是万科公司近些年来对社会住宅尤其是极小户型的丰富实践，是对开发商对于社会住宅最深刻的思考。

2.2 独立设计建造公寓

2.2.1 宁波市鄞州区人才公寓

人才公寓是一个人才保障房项目，由 DC 国际建筑设计事务所设计，地处宁波高教园区，主要为园区内各企业引进青年人才提供小型单身公寓而使用。"人才公寓"的设计理念是城市生活最大化，住区不再是内向的、封闭的，而应当承担一系列城市的基本功能，将居住与交往、休闲、运动、娱乐融为一体。为了达到这个目标，建筑师在东侧城市快速路边设置了 16 层的综合体，与 31 层的住宅建筑相呼应，将城市的活力与住区的功能交织在一起。建筑师为了更佳的采光，将建筑保持了正南北的朝向，场地布置则顺应周边城市肌理，与建筑产生 45° 的错角，带来了很强的视觉效果。不论是 70m² 的两居室还是 45m² 的一居室，都进行了跃层的设计，实现了每一户都能拥有南北朝向、自然通风，并且每户都是上下两层、独立起居室。

2.2.2 退台方院

退台方院是网龙公司的职工宿舍，位于福建省长乐市，由 OPEN Architecture 设计。由于场地所处的位置临近海边，周边没有明确的边界，建筑形式为内向型的方形合院。整个场地内一共有三栋朝向各不相同的退台建筑，目的在于营造独立而集中的内部空间，促进集体社区的强烈感受。不同朝向的退台为居住的职工提供了一系列朝四周自然景观开放的共享屋顶平台，让社区感与自然观感得到了良好的平衡。几何形起伏地面内部容纳了大量的配套设施，满足了景观与服务的双重需要。户型上，一共有三种不同的居住单元。单元 A 是一个 11.9m×4m×3m 的长方盒子，提供了拥有独立阳台的一居室空间；单元 B 基本可以看做两个单元 A 并置的体量，该户型提供了空间更加丰富的两居室空间；单元 C 是三种户型中面积最大的，主要的两个边长为 15.5m 和 9.7m。这个户型提供了三室一厅的居住空间，并且为每一个卧室设置了独立的阳台。单元 A、B 布置在方形建筑的四边上，C 单元布置在转交处。穿插联系这些居住空间的是走廊、楼梯间和公共客厅，这就使得不同职位的员工在这个社区中平等地居住在一个屋檐下，共享着公共资源，也体现了新时代的企业文化。

2.3 改造出租型公寓

2.3.1 YOU＋国际青年社区

YOU＋是目前最具年轻活力的青年公寓，从最初的广州高露洁牙膏厂厂房开始，YOU＋的通常会在公司集中或者交通便捷的产业园区租赁整栋旧楼，然后对其进行特色改造。在功能的整体布局上，YOU＋采用了 1＋n 的模式，即首层空间特别是一楼大厅及周边设置为公共的活动空间，楼上则是集中的青年公寓，属于私密空间。在首层的公共空间安排了咖啡厅、台球室、健身房会议室等设施，住户们的社交生活在此都能得到满足，促进了彼此之间的交流，这也是 YOU＋相较于传统的公寓，最突出的优势所在。居住单元的设计上，空间相对集约，因为社交活动已经从公寓提取到了首层，所以居住空间更多的是为生活起居服务的。管理模式上，YOU＋对入住的人群进行了详细的限定，年龄超过 45 岁或已婚人士就会被拒之门外。与其说是公寓设计，不如将其定位为一个产品比较贴切。

2.3.2 自如寓

自如寓也是针对年轻人使用的高品质社交公寓，多由旧办公楼等改造而成。在建筑格局上，亦使用了底层公共上层私密的布局，整楼实行统一的物业管理。与 YOU＋最大的不同，自如寓并没有对入住群体身份进行具体的限定，并且提供了更加丰富的户型设置。户型提供了从 15～67m² 不等的几种类型。最大的户型设置了步入式衣橱、开放式厨房及餐厅，适合多人合租居住。最小的户型可谓是麻雀虽小五脏俱全，适合经济相对紧张的单身年轻人居住。不论面积大小，所有户型均采用了简约的现代装修风格。纵观 YOU＋与自如寓，它们所倡导的社交型居住模式十分值得借鉴，集约的空间、丰富的内饰都迎合了年轻人对于个性生活的需要，但昂贵的租金会成为它服务更多青年人的阻碍，如果减去过度装饰、降低成本，让价格回归寻常，一定能创造更多的社会价值。

2.4 万科系列研究

2.4.1 土楼公社

2005 年，都市实践建筑事务所与万科开始探讨社会力量介入低收入住宅设计的可能性，这意味着中国企业关注低收入人群的社会意识开始觉醒。土楼公社选址在广佛高速公路旁，为附近工厂区的工人们提供住所。建筑设计为 e 形平面，外方内圆，打破了传统土楼完全封闭的格局，体量上成台阶式螺旋上升。方圆之间夹出几个弧形的中庭空间，配合开放式外廊和转角平台，为居民提供了大量的交往空间。土楼公社共有 282 间普通及集体宿舍，标准的居住单元面积在 30m² 左右。每种户型都包含客厅、卧室、开放式厨房以及独立的卫生间和阳台。土楼公社对居住群体做出了详细的要求，只要月收入在 2600 元以下且无房无车，就可以申请入住。土楼公社的管理是由租户自主组织进行的，公共服务可以根据自己情况着力参加，劳动所得可以补偿租金。

2.4.2 18m² 极小户型

2011 年，万科在西安长安区大学城推出了"18m² 极小户型"。这个项目是为了解决"85 后"城市青年的居住需求而产生的。万科整合了国内著名的建筑、家电、通讯等领域的专家，希望能探讨出一种极小空间居住多元化的可能性。万科首先分析了确定 18m² 的依据，即 18m² 是容纳满足起居、卧室、厨卫、书房等日常生活基本要求的最小复合单元。其次，需要明确年轻人群体对于住房的四种不同价值观：居所是独享空间，居所是社交与生活空间，居所是地位体现空间，居所是家人生活空间。这一系列的价值观就会转化成生活习惯，进而成为功能需求，对住宅内的格局产生最直接的影响。万科在设计具体户型之前，明确了年轻人在不同场所内的具体生活习惯，对客厅、卧室、书房、卫生间、收纳空间、餐厅和厨房进行了精细化设计。通过不同的家具组合和使用状态，改变空间属性，可以营造不同的情景感。

2.4.3 MI 公寓

MI 公寓的户型方正，拥有办公、聚会、休憩三种生活模式，在 25m² 内提供客厅、卧室、卫生间、厨房、书房等多种功能的复合空间，这里压缩了 90m² 居室内全部的设施，没有丝毫的空间浪费。不论是卫生间还是厨房，都严格按照人体工学尺寸设计，增加储物空间的同时也尽量保持整洁性。MI 公寓另一个最突出的特点是可以成为大学生的创业工作室，合理的价格良好的环境，丰富的使用模式，满足了青年创业者的主要需求，这里也可以成为企业投资留住顾客和人才的配套设施。从紧凑经济的面积到丰富多变的户型设计，从模式的应变转换到互联网销售的新颖火爆，MI 公寓的表现是可圈可点的，它的特点会成为未来中国社会住宅的重要参考。

2.5 案例横向比较

中国社会住宅案例评价表　　　　　　　　　　　　　表 1

	宁波人才公寓	退台方舍	自如寓	YOU+青年社区	土楼公社	18m² 极小户型	MI 公寓
经营层面							
出租／出售	两者都有	出租	出租	出租	出租	出售	出售
提供统一管理	✓	✓	✓	✓	✓	✓	✓
提供管家服务	✗	✗	✗	✓	✓	✓	✓
对住户有选择性	✓	✓	✓	✓	✓	✓	✗
销售模式	传统	传统	传统+线上	传统+线上	传统	传统+线上	传统+线上
住区规划层面							
新建／改建	新建	新建	改建	改建	新建	新建	新建
单体／群体	群体	群体	群体	群体	单体	群体	群体
开放的住区边界	✓	✓	✗	✗	✓	✓	✓
户外公共空间	✓	✓	✓	✗	✗	✗	✓
与城市重要功能区的位置关系	位于新城区高教园区	远离城市中心区	市中心、郊区均有分布	大多位于非城市中心区	远离城市中心区	位于大学城	位于青岛国家广告园
交通通达性	紧邻城市干道	临近城市次要道路	临近公共交通线路	临近公共交通线路	毗邻广佛高速	毗邻二环南路	毗邻城市干道

续表

	宁波人才公寓	退台方舍	自如寓	YOU+青年社区	土楼公社	18m² 极小户型	MI公寓
周边服务设施及商业	各项设施齐全	无	生活设施齐全，部分网点周边较差	生活设施齐全，部分临近学校	一公里半径内有商场和学校	自有 500000m² 商业配套	临近 3 个商圈，生活文卫设施齐全
足够的停车位	充足	仅自行车库	不充足	不充足	无	充足	不充足
建筑设计层面							
主要结构形式	框架	框架	多为框架	多为框架	框架	框架	框架
主要建筑平面形态	一字型、L型	回字形	多样	多样	圆形	长方形	长方形
良好居住朝向	东南、西北	南北	多样	多样	多样	不详	不详
主要户型种类及使用面积	70m² 左右的两房占总数 60%，45m² 左右的一房占 40%	47m²、95m²、150m²	30~70m² 之间，以 30m² 为主	户型种类不定，多在 30m² 左右	35m²、50m²	18m²	23~41m²，以 25m² 为主
户型组合可变性	×	×	×	×	√	×	×
私有户外空间	无	内院、屋顶平台	部分有	屋顶天台	无	无	无
公共起居室	×	√	√	√	×	×	×
内部服务设施及小型商业	商业、办公	商店、洗衣房	配有健身房、洗衣间、休息室等	健身房、游戏区、休息区等	商店、饭店	自有 510000 m² 商业配套	商店、饭店
室内装修层面							
室内初始装修程度	设施齐全；质量较差	不详	生活设施、家电齐全；质量较好	设施、家电齐全；鼓励改造	设施齐全，质量较好	设施、家电齐全；质量较好	精装修
空间功能的复合性	小户型内压缩进普通住宅的所有基本功能	将起居与卧室空间复合，保留阳台	起居与卧室空间复合	充分利用纵向空间，将起居与卧室复合	起居与卧室空间复合；阳台与洗漱空间复合	起居与卧室空间复合，压缩其余生活空间	小户型内压缩进普通住宅的所有基本功能

3　中国社会住宅发展展望

3.1　户型设计原则

第一，建筑面积不能过大。由于房价的上涨，住房的成本与户型建筑面积有着最直接的关系，为了降低年轻人的居住成本，新时代中国社会住宅首先要有经济合理的建筑面积，这一面积可以分为 25m²、45m²、65m² 等几级标准；第二，在设计户型时要考虑到使用面积必须尽量提升，提高空间利用率；第三，户型设计上要考虑到开放性的原则，平面布局可以根据使用需求发生变化，以应对不同情境下对于空间的使用需求；第四，使用的装饰装修材料应当价格经济、无污染、可回收。

3.2 住区及建筑设计原则

住区规划应当顺应场地，合理布局。对城市开放，在不阻断城市肌理的前提下实现人车分流，并合理布置停车空间。住区内提供完善的配套设施与相应的服务设施，回馈城市区域功能需求。有着丰富的植物配置，营造绿色生态环境，配套雨水回收体系并有着全年龄段无障碍通行系统。建筑布局应注重充足的采光与良好的组团空间。施工质量应达到高品质工业化百年住宅，与此同时尽可能地利用被动式节能技术，做到环境友好。建筑及住区需要充分考虑活动与社交空间，增强邻里间的交往与互动。

3.3 经营与管理模式原则

利用互联网更好地经营和管理社区，出售与出租结合，提供更加丰富的居住模式，为不同收入等级的年轻人创造对应的住房空间。与此同时，可以为低收入群体提供多样的服务创收岗位，形成社区由居民自己管理的模式，既减轻了低收入人群的居住负担，又加强了社区居民的交流联系。

4 结语

中国社会住宅只重视数量不考虑质量的现状急需改善，社会住宅不再仅仅需要满足居住的基本要求，还应为居住者提供更高的居住尊严和生活品质。政府、开发商以及建筑师三方应当加强协作，从设计角度、用户需求和运行策略角度考虑，关注弱势空间、提升建成环境的空间品质，中国的社会住宅还有很长的路要走。

致谢

十分感激马岩松先生在北京建筑大学 ADA 中心举办的社会住宅研究 studio，为笔者提供了一次研究中国社会住宅发展现状的契机，同时也对 studio 中国组团队成员们的辛勤合作表示感谢。

Developing Status and Prospects of Chinese Social Housing

Gan Zhenkun，，Wang Jun
(Beijing University of Civil Engineering and Architecture)

Abstract：The leading power of design and construction has evolved from a totally government action into a collaboration of government，developers and architects. The price of commercial residential building in Chinese mainland is skyrocketing. And the family planning policy also cause demographic changes. So it is high time to develop social housing in order to solve the housing problems of low-income groups in China. Social housing construction in China is still at the exploratory stage. In recent years，the design process of social housing received a particular attention as a number of aspiring architects and developers got involved. Series of experimental practice were born as a result. Social housing not only needs to meet the basic requirements of living，but also offer a better living life with dignity and quality. This article focuses on comparative analysis of characteristic cases of Chinese social housing after 2000. It considers design perspective，customer demands and operation strategy combining with research of social living problems. And finally the article puts forward a suitable social housing design pattern language based on Chinese social condition with characters of economical，compatible，humanized，beautiful，complex and variable.

Keywords：Special nation condition，High quality，Economical，Flexible，Variable

参考文献：

［1］ 马振伟．保障性住房设计研究初探［D］. 山东：山东建筑大学硕士学位论文，2011.

［2］ 席佳．极小型居住空间设计探讨［D］. 广东：华南理工大学硕士学位论文，2012.

［3］ 董屹，崔哲，平刚．宁波鄞州区人才公寓设计笔记［J］. 城市建筑，2011，11：41-46.

［4］ 曹勇．青年群体居住需求和住宅设计研究［D］. 陕西：西安建筑科技大学，2010.

［5］ 贾倍思．香港公屋本质、公屋设计和居住实态［J］. 时代建筑，1998，（3）：58-61.

［6］ 李勤．宜居背景下北京保障性住区营建模式研究［D］. 陕西：西安建筑科技大学 ，2013.

［7］ 李允．中国大都市保障性住房政策实施的困境与出路分析［D］. 吉林：吉林大学，2012.

我国公共租赁房中的适老性问题与设计策略[①]

王超[1]　宋昆[2]　王小荣[2]

（1. 北京市建筑设计研究院有限公司；2. 天津大学建筑学院）

摘要： 随着我国人口老龄化日益凸显，老年人的养老问题成为一个普遍性的社会问题，而住房问题是养老问题的关键所在。对于无力购买住房的老年人群，租住便成了住房困难者的最佳选择。因此，建设带有适老型住宅的公共租赁房小区是解决低收入老年人住房困难问题的最有效途径。本文在公共租赁房中适老型住宅建设比例分析的基础上，提出了保障性住房中适老型住宅的设计策略。

关键词： 保障性住房，公共租赁房，适老型住宅，适老性设计

世界范围的人口老龄化使得养老问题逐渐显现。我国是人口大国，加之计划生育政策的长期执行，人口老龄化发展很快，老年人的养老问题成了一个普遍性的社会问题。住房问题是养老问题的关键所在。在中低收入群体中，很大一部分也是老年人及老年家庭。老年人的住房保障是社会问题，政府应当对老年人居住的基本需求给予保障。要使困难老人能够老有所养、老有所依，解决他们的住房问题是最基本也是最必要的，是政府义不容辞的责任。

1 保障性住房中的适老型住宅建设需要

1.1 解决老年人住房问题的需要

研究老年人的住房保障，首先应当了解我国老年人的生活情况。据国家统计局第六次全国人口普查数据显示，我国 60 岁及以上人口占 13.26%，65 岁及以上人口占 8.87%。由于老龄人口的增加，老年人住房问题也逐渐凸显出来。

城市中的老年人无住房主要有两种情况：一是原有住房拆迁。由于老年人原住房面积很小，拆迁款远远不足以重新购买一套同地段适合居住的住房，有的甚至连城市周边的住房也无力购买；二是老年人或赡养老年人的困难家庭将原有住房变卖。这些家庭大都由于经济困难才将原有住房出售，出售房款也挪作他用，无力购买新住房。此外，还有很多老年人居住在棚户区，人均住房面积小，公共设施水平低，卫生条件差，老年人居住生活极不方便。因此，如何解决这些困难老年人及家庭的居住困难问题是使这些老年人老有所养的关键所在。

从全球的范围来看，选择居家养老的占老年人群体的绝大多数。为了满足老年人的养老需求，很多国家都建造了老年公寓、老年社区等老年设施齐全、服务周到的住所供老年人选择居住。

通过对各种老年人居住形式的对比分析，笔者提出了适老型住宅的概念，即进行了适老化设计，能够适应老年人及老年家庭使用的住宅。在空间上，适老型住宅经过适老化设计，无论是室内空间还是室外空间都能够满足老年人的居住需求；在使用人群上，适老型住宅适合老年人及家庭居住，同时也能够为有潜在需求的家庭提供适宜的可持续的生活空间。适老型住宅强调空间的适用性与可持续性，将普通使用功能的空间扩展为适宜老年人生活的使用空间，是具有可持续使用功能的居住场所。从整体角度讲，在保障房中建造一定数量的适老型住宅，能够迅速解决一部分生活特别

---

① 天津市应用基础与前沿技术研究计划（15JCYBJC22200）"基于居家养老体系的新型住环境构建理论与方法研究"。

困难的老年人和老年家庭的居住问题，也利于随着经济发展逐渐扩大保障范围。

1.2 解决低收入弱势群体住房困难的需要

1.2.1 公共租赁房中建设适老型住宅

我国的保障性住房为中低收入住房困难家庭提供，主要分为两大类：一类是半市场化的经济适用房和限价商品房；另一类是非市场化"只租不售"的廉租房和公共租赁房（图1）。

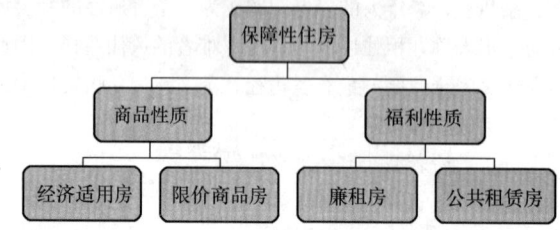

图1 保障性住房分类

在经济适用房和限价商品房的"买房"范畴内，中低收入群体想要拥有保障性住房产权必须借助于住房贷款。老年家庭或孤寡老人由于年龄和经济能力问题，很难得到银行的贷款，因此不具备购买保障房的客观条件，租住便成了住房困难又需要得到住房保障的老年人的最佳选择。结合我国经济发展状况与老年人住房的实际情况，建设带有适老型住宅的公共租赁房小区是解决老年人住房困难问题的最有效途径。主要原因有以下三个方面：

（1）公共租赁房只租不售，解决的是老年人"有房住"的现实问题，而不是"有住房"的产权问题；

（2）相对于其他类型的保障性住房，公共租赁房对收入、户籍的限制较少，准入条件较宽；

（3）我国政府大力发展建设公共租赁房，也为解决老年人住房困难问题提供了良好的条件。

1.2.2 公共租赁房中适老型住宅建设比例分析

适老型住宅需要满足老年人的各种必要的生活需求，在建设面积及成本上都会适当提高。因此，适老型住宅的建设量及比例应控制在一个合理的范围内，以保证其经济性与适用性。虽然老年人及老年家庭总数在不断变化，但其比例在一定时间内，相对处于动态平衡（表1）。

天津市有 60 岁及以上老年家庭户数统计　　　　　　　　　　　　　　　　　表1

级别分类	天津市各地区分类别 总户数（单位：户）	有 60 岁及以上老年人口 的家庭户数（单位：户）	所占本级别家庭 总户数的比例
总计	3661992	1104458	30.160%
城市	2501235	756074	30.228%
镇	374642	92507	24.692%
乡村	786115	255877	32.550%

资料来源：作者根据国家统计局第六次全国人口普查结果统计绘制。

由表1可以看出，天津市60岁以上老年家庭户数量已超过三成。此外，笔者收集到天津市具有公共租赁住房申请资格及已入住的家庭人员的年龄状况：截至2012年6月30日，天津市具有公共租赁房住房申请资格的共有29246人，11240户；已入住21273人，7904户。其中，60岁以上家庭共3423户，占总户数的25.61%（表2）。

	60-64	65-69	70-74	75-79	80-84	85-89	90 及以上	总计
家庭户数	1209	619	550	491	344	152	67	3432
所占比例	10.76%	5.51%	4.89%	4.37%	3.06%	1.35%	0.60%	25.61%

具有申请资格的全部家庭中各年龄段老年人家庭占总家庭数的数量及比例　表 2

资料来源：作者根据天津市国土资源与住房管理局提供数据绘制[①]。

从上表可以看出，具有申请资格的困难老年人家庭中，60～69 岁年龄段的老年人所占比例最大。这个年龄段的老年人大都能够自理或半自理，住宅的适老化设计无疑能够给其生活带来便利，延长老年人独立生活的时间，减少家庭和社会的抚养压力。综合表 1、表 2 的数据，在保障性住房中建设适老型住宅，要以满足现有的全市平均的老年家庭户比例 25%～30% 为宜。同时，这部分适老化的保障性住房，还包括病残家庭的需要。

1.2.3　已建成的公共租赁房小区现有的适老性问题

在天津已建成的保障性住房小区中，秋怡家园公共租赁房小区具有一定的代表性。秋怡家园作为天津市保障性住房建设的重点工程先后接受了胡锦涛、温家宝等国家领导人的考察，建设施工质量较高。因此，笔者以秋怡家园平面设计为例，研究我国保障性住房中所欠缺的适老性设计问题（图 2、图 3）。

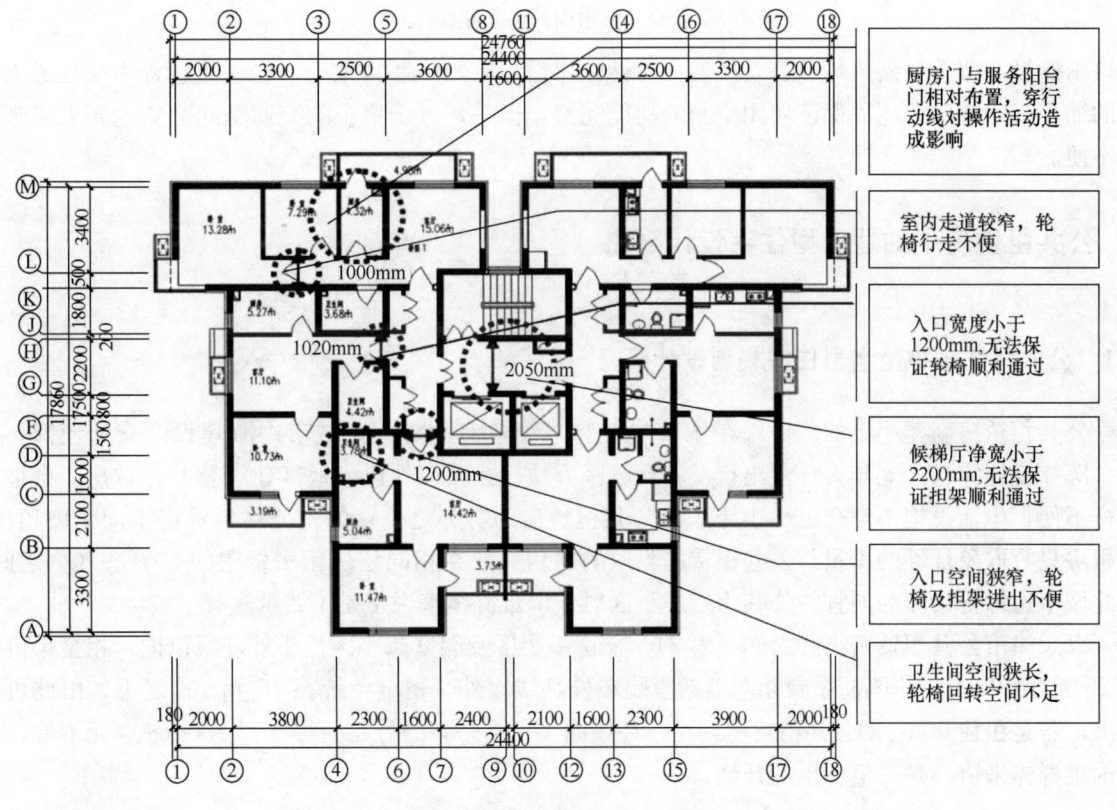

图 2　秋怡家园标准层平面适老性设计问题

通过对已建成保障性住房小区的调研，可以看出，保障性住房在设计中虽然考虑了无障碍设计，但是对老年人使用空间细节思考还是有所欠缺，例如厨房操作台下没有轮椅移动空间，单元门

---

① 数据计算方法：笔者根据天津市国土资源与住房管理局提供的具有申请资格的家庭数据，以家庭为单位，根据每个家庭成员的年龄，统计出具有申请资格的有老年人的家庭数量及比例。

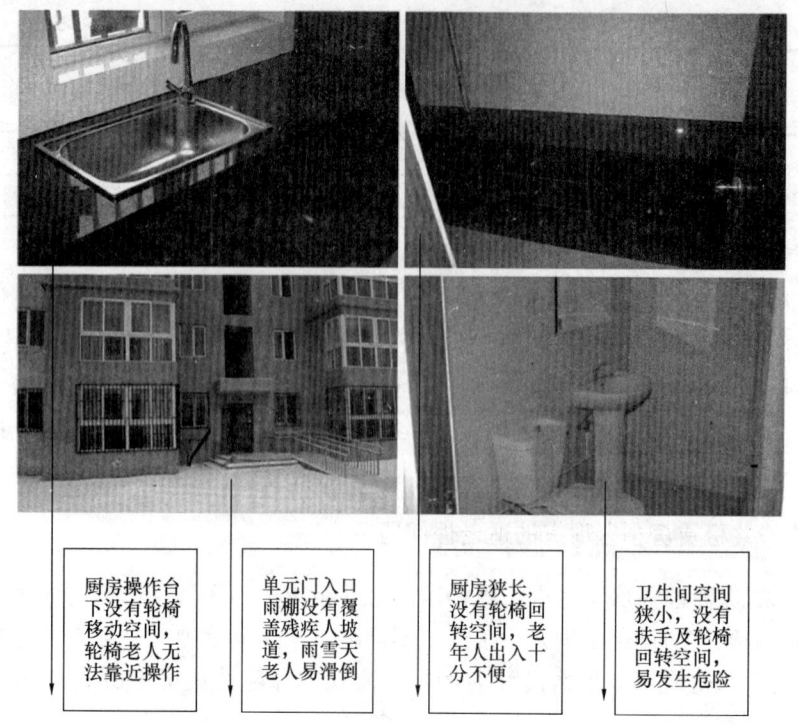

| 厨房操作台下没有轮椅移动空间，轮椅老人无法靠近操作 | 单元门入口雨棚没有覆盖残疾人坡道，雨雪天老人易滑倒 | 厨房狭长，没有轮椅回转空间，老年人出入十分不便 | 卫生间空间狭小，没有扶手及轮椅回转空间，易发生危险 |

图 3　秋怡家园室内外适老性设计问题

入口雨棚没有覆盖残疾人坡道等。虽然保障性住房设计以经济性为原则，在设计过程中往往最大限度的缩小交通空间，用以保证使用空间的功能完整，但是，过于狭小的交通空间会给老年人带来极大不便。

2　公共租赁房中的适老型住宅设计研究

2.1　公共租赁房中适老型住宅规划设计研究

公共租赁房新建小区的选址，在城市中心和边缘各有利弊。在城市中心建设，交通便捷，公共、医疗设施完备，老年人日常出行、看病就医方便。在城市外边缘地区建设公共租赁房，会造成出行不便，生活设施不健全也是边缘地区公共租赁房的劣势之一。但是公共租赁房不同于廉租房，廉租房只收取象征性的房租，公共租赁房收取的房租一般在相同住房租房费用的 50%～70% 之间。因此城市边缘价格较为便宜的公共租赁房小区对于困难群体来说也是不错的选择。

以天津市公共租赁房小区为例（表 3），福桥里小区及朗庭园小区位于外环线以内，租金单价都在 20 元/m² 以上；华明新家园和双港新家园在外环线以外，租金单价在 15 元/m² 以下。由此可以看出，若是租住 50m² 的公共租赁房，在外环线内要比在外环线外每月多支付 500～600 元不等，对于困难群体来讲，是一笔不小的开销。

天津市现出租的公共租赁房小区租金价格（2013 年）　　　　表 3

	福桥里小区	朗庭园小区	华明新家园	双港新家园
租金单价（元/5m²）	24	23	12	13
租金总价（元/50m²）	1200	1150	600	650

资料来源：笔者根据天津市保障性住房网资料绘制。

从老年人和年轻人生活的区别来看，老年人不需频繁的来往于工作场所与住所之间，因此，老年人可以选择离医院较近且房租低廉的边缘地区租住住房。综合现实问题的考虑以及资料查阅和实地调研，基于我国国情与公共租赁房小区的发展现状，同时考虑老年人的生活需求，笔者总结出建设带有适老型住宅的公共租赁房小区规划要点：

（1）适老型住宅比例准确：适老型住宅合理的规模测算可以保证困难老人及赡养老人的困难家庭按照预期规划顺利入住，及时的解决住房困难问题；也可以合理分配建设资金，减少不必要的损失，降低单位建造成本，加大建设量，快速有效地完成公共租赁房适老型住宅的建设。建议以满足现有的全市平均老年家庭户比例25％为起点，短期内控制在老年家庭比例上限30％以内。由于适老型住宅不同于一般意义上的老年住宅，同时受社会因素和经济因素的影响，因此，适老型住宅的比例应当随着社会经济的发展不断调整，以保证其准确性。

（2）容积率合理经济：公共租赁房要科学的计算出容积率的范围。适老型住宅的容积率应适当的满足老年人居住的日照需求，避免华而不实，把资金投入在满足弱势群体生活最必需的设施配备上，为所有居住者创造便利的生活条件。

（3）公共交通顺畅：公共租赁房应当在城市中心区和周边地区均匀分布，城市周边地区的公共租赁房小区更应当注重公共交通系统的完善，确保青年人出行顺畅，老年人出行方便。在公共租赁房片区的附近，必须有便利的交通系统与无障碍设施方便老年人到达各种公共场所。

（4）公共配套设施完善：公共租赁房的建设应当重视社区配套设施，应配备相应的养老机构、医疗所等，满足小区内老年人的日常需求。小区周边应当配建医院和适当的公共配套设施，并应与住宅建筑同步完成，确保公共租赁房小区居民的基本生活需求。

（5）设计规划适度超前：公共租赁房小区在建成后会延续使用很长一段时间，在这期间内，不仅经济、社会环境会有所变化，承租人群也会发生变化。因此，公共租赁房的设计既要结合当前的经济、社会形势，又要有一定的超前性和预期性。尤其是公共租赁房中的适老型住宅，要立足于我国人口老龄化的实际情况。

2.2 公共租赁房中适老型住宅建筑设计研究

公共租赁房中的适老型住宅是为解决老年人最基本的居住问题而建设的，需要满足老年人生活的最低需求，是一个居住的下限。因此，未必所有的功能性设计都能实现，而是以扩大保障范围，节约单位建设投资，扩大建设量为准则。通过相关资料查阅以及公共租赁房的实际建设情况调研，笔者将老年住宅的设计内容归类为两大类，即功能性设计及舒适性设计，去除老年住宅设计内容中的舒适性设计以及一部分暂时非必需的功能性设计，总结出新建公共租赁房小区适老型住宅设计要点如下：

（1）单元出入口坡道处设雨棚；当坡度＞1/8时，需设置醒目的指示牌，扶手保持连续、牢固安装；

（2）建筑内部交通空间净宽不应小于1200mm，以便老年人顺利通行；

（3）母子门门洞预留宽度1200～1600mm，可确保求助人员及担架通行顺畅；

（4）门厅需考虑担架出入所需的空间和乘坐轮椅老年人、借助拐杖行走老年人的使用要求；

（5）厨房操作台下宜局部留空，老年人既可以接近也可形成一定的回转空间；

（6）坐便器旁设置可变化扶手，辅助老人起坐等动作。卫生间最好有一面是隔墙，利于改造。

3 结语

随着老龄化大潮的到来，世界各国在老年人的住房问题上给予的关注越来越多。困难老人的住房问题是一个社会问题，需要社会各界，包括医疗、护理、交通各个相关部门相互合作，共同寻求一个经济、适用，符合我国国情的有效途径。相对于很多发达国家，我国的保障性住房对于老年人的居住使用要求考虑得较少，将要面临的问题相当严峻。通过在公共租赁房中建设一部分适老型住宅来解决困难老人及老年家庭的住房问题，需要各种相关政策的规范与监督。随着时间的推移，老年人口快速发展，现有的保障性住房在未来的几十年甚至更短的时间内，就无法满足逐渐老去的人们的需求。怎样去适应、应对人口老龄化，既是一个前瞻性的问题，又是无法回避的现实。这不单单是政府、建筑师的责任，而是整个社会义不容辞的责任与义务。

The Research of Public Housing in Elder-Suitable Residential Design Strategy of China

Wang Chao[1], Song Kun[2], Wang Xiaorong[2]

（1. Beijing Institute of Architectural Design；

2. School of Architecture，Tianjin University）

Abstract：Worldwide population aging makes the pension problem gradually revealed. Our country have an enormous population，and long-term birth control policy makes the aging population developed rapidly，therefore the elderly pension problem has become a universal social problem. Housing problem is the key to pension problem. In low income groups，a large portion of them is the elderly family. The elderly housing security is a social problem，the government should give protection to the basic needs of their live. To make the old people have a dependent live，solve their housing problem is the most basic and necessary way. it's the duty of the government.

Keywords：Public housing，Elder-suitable residential，Elder-suitable design，Renting public housing

参考文献：

[1] 王璐. 旧住宅的适老性改造[D]. 山东：山东建筑科技大学，2007.

[2] （美）珀金斯·J·戴维·霍格伦. 老年居住建筑[M]. 北京：中国建筑工业出版社，2008.

[3] 张佳佳. 廉租房住宅适应性与舒适性设计研究[D]. 陕西：西安建筑科技大学，2008.

[4] 陈理力，胡惠琴. 香港老年人租贷公房政策借鉴——以北京老年人住房政策为比较对象[J]. 中国住宅设施，2009(8).

[5] 周燕珉. 老年住宅[M]. 北京：中国建筑出版社，2011.

[6] 何青峰. 老龄化背景下城市"适老化"住宅建设研究：以浙江省为例[D]. 浙江：浙江大学，2012.

[7] 许婷. 社区居家养老模式与社区老人设施研究[D]. 天津：天津大学，2013.

[8] 王超. 保障性住房中的适老型住宅研究[D]. 天津：天津大学，2013.

南京高强度大型保障性住区适居性评价研究

汤楚荻　王承慧

（东南大学建筑学院城市规划系）

摘要：2010 年以来，某些大城市保障性住房建设量大、建设期短，政府基于质量保证、统筹融资、整合资源、平衡土地利益的考虑，大规模、集聚型、高强度的保障性住房建设成为选择。为警惕"建设质量、建筑形式和居住环境"的物质空间标签化伴生的空间分异和社会隔离，应启动跟踪研究。本文聚焦住区适居性，选择南京两个高强度大型保障性住区进行调查研究。适居性评价涵盖客观评估和居民满意度两方面，居民满意度突出保障性住房住区中家庭类型居住满意度的针对性分析。本文最后从保障性住房政策、规划设计、建成管理的角度，对不可避免的高强度开发提出整合性策略。

关键词：保障性住区，高强度，适居性，居住环境

欧美第二次世界大战后的公共住房和社会住房，其规模化集聚和社会负效应的关联值得中国警惕，特别是某些高强度公共住房和社会住房由于"建设质量、建筑形式和居住环境"与普通住房有明显差距，加剧了空间标签化，推动了消极的空间分异和社会隔离。但是他国经验也告诉我们，某些高强度公共住房和社会住房成为极具价值的可支付住房资源，最具代表性的案例就是美国纽约高层公共住房、新加坡高层组屋和香港高层公屋。因此，高强度本身不是问题，高强度的度、设计、建设以及管理是关键。中国近年各地不断涌现高强度大型保障性住区，保障性住房人群具有和国外差异极大的复杂性，亟须进行针对性的适居性研判。

1 南京高强度典型案例选择与研究思路

南京主城 1994 年以来保障性住房空间格局经历了"1997～2001 年主城内点状、小规模分散式建设；2000～2005 年主城外提速发展；2005～2010 年沿高速路、公路、铁路呈现团块集聚趋势；2010 年以来某些区域大规模集聚"态势。2010 年以来新建的保障性住房更是出现高强度的特征，住宅地块容积率出现超出 3.0 的趋势。其中，莲花村和丁家庄具有典型性。

这两个住区的相似之处在于，规划人口都达到 5 万人，用地规模分别达到 128hm² 和 85hm²，开发用地毛容积率都达到近 2.0，住宅地块净容积率普遍超过 3.5，甚至达到 4.2。

在建设机制上却有所不同，影响到规划设计理念的差异；前者为行政区组织开发，多家开发公司介入，有一定的统一规划，但整体性不强；后者为市级国资平台组织开发，规划控制更加强有力。

入住人群也有所不同。前者入住人群以集

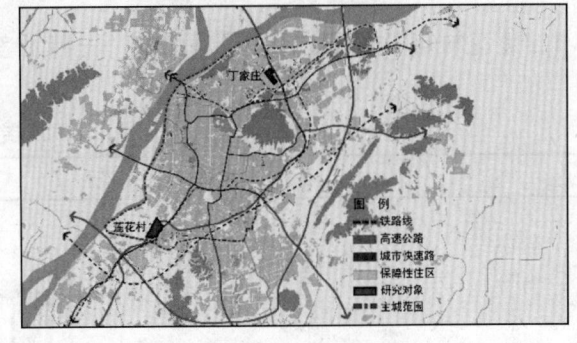

图 1　莲花村、丁家庄保障性住区区位图

体土地拆迁安置居民为主，还有大量租赁住房居民；后者目前入住人群除了拆迁安置居民外，还有大量廉租房、公租房以及双困户经济适用房居民。

本文研究思路突出保障性住房人群的适居性评价，通过住区实地考察和居民家庭抽样问卷调查，涵盖客观评估和居民满意度两方面。客观评估对象包括功能结构、交通组织、公共设施、建筑组群、开放空间；居民主观满意度包括对居住环境、公共设施、住房、出行的满意度评价（见表

1)。继而比较两个住区之间的满意度差异，以及不同人群居住满意度的差异，并分析原因。然后，结合两个保障性住房的规划理念、人口构成和建成管理，基于适居性评价结论探讨住房政策、规划设计、建成管理的策略。

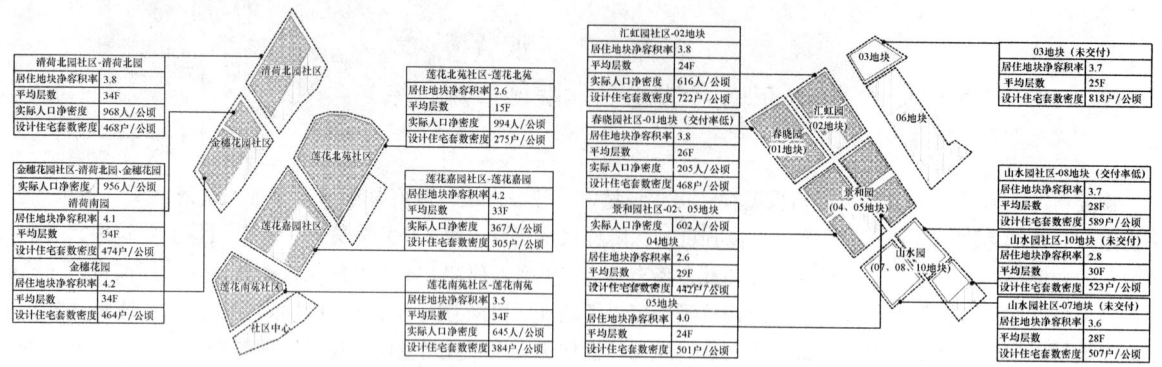

图2 莲花村、丁家庄空间组成与强度密度分布示意图

(注：①实际人口按已入住流动人口和常住人口的总和计算；②03、07、10
地块尚未交付，01、04、08地块尚未完全交付，08地块交付不足1%，不做计算；
③图中▨▨▨是居住地块，▥▥▥是公共服务设施独立用地，▭▭▭是独立用地边界)

客观居住环境特征					物质空间环境的居民主观满意度评价										
功能结构	交通组织	公共设施	建筑组群	开放空间	小区环境满意度				公共设施满意度			住房满意度			出行满意度		
					①楼间距视野	②室外活动场地	③景观绿化	④住宅建筑外观	①公共设施可达性	②公共设施拥挤度	③公共设施服务	①套型拥挤度	②房间功能使用	③住房质量	①步行友好性	②交通站点可达性	③乘车环境舒适度

图3 适居性比较评价体系图

2 莲花村与丁家庄的居住环境特征及客观评价

2.1 莲花村与丁家庄的居住环境比较——特征差别与原因

莲花村、丁家庄居住环境特征比较 表1

		莲花村	丁家庄
功能结构	图例： ● 轨道交通站点 Ⓜ 规划轨道交通站 ⓢ 社区巴士站 ━━ 城市快速道路 ━━ 城市道路 ━━ 居住区及组团道路 ▨ 公共服务及商业 ▤ 居住用地 ▦ 景观河流 ▨ 公共绿地及广场	大规模分隔型组团布局	小规模紧凑型街区布局

续表

		莲花村	丁家庄
公共设施布局	图例：	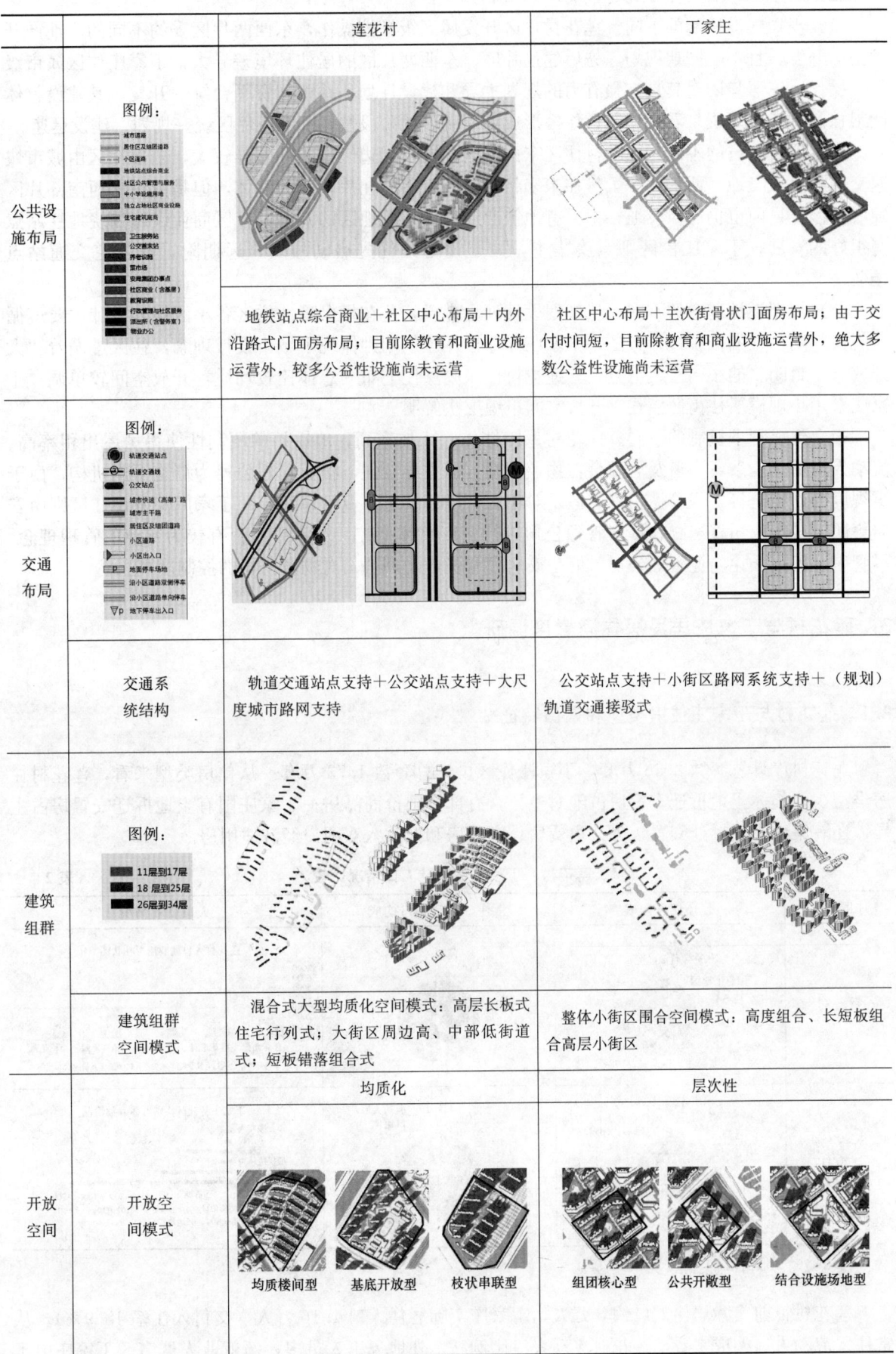	
		地铁站点综合商业＋社区中心布局＋内外沿路式门面房布局；目前除教育和商业设施运营外，较多公益性设施尚未运营	社区中心布局＋主次街骨状门面房布局；由于交付时间短，目前除教育和商业设施运营外，绝大多数公益性设施尚未运营
交通布局	图例：		
	交通系统结构	轨道交通站点支持＋公交站点支持＋大尺度城市路网支持	公交站点支持＋小街区路网系统支持＋（规划）轨道交通接驳式
建筑组群	图例： 11层到17层 18层到25层 26层到34层		
	建筑组群空间模式	混合式大型均质化空间模式：高层长板式住宅行列式；大街区周边高、中部低街道式；短板错落组合式	整体小街区围合空间模式：高度组合、长短板组合高层小街区
开放空间	开放空间模式	均质化	层次性
		均质楼间型　基底开放型　枝状串联型	组团核心型　公共开敞型　结合设施场地型

表1所呈现出的居住环境特征的原因机制如下：

（1）规划建设机制的不同。莲花村住区开发属区级管控操作，东西两片区委约不同的房地产开发公司开发，且不是同期规划，先后建设片区、东西两片区的居住环境差异大；丁家庄住区属市级管控操作，安居集团对其具有强有力的规划主导和建设计划，并由国资平台统一开发，其建设整体性很强。从建设历程来看，莲花村住区形成具有明显的阶段性，丁家庄住区统一规划、建设迅速。

（2）项目区位的不同。莲花村住区东西片区的城市周边区位条件差异较大，东部片区由城市快速交通隔离成飞地，西部片区虽然在未来将与河西南部居住片区成为整体，但是由于河西南部片区发展缓慢，目前也仍然似飞地；幸而有地铁通达提升了该地区的价值，社区商业设施围绕地铁站点有很好的发展；丁家庄住区则紧凑集中，处于该地区优先启动板块，远期附近有轨道交通站点接驳。

（3）规划设计理念的不同。从规划设计理念来说，莲花村保障性住区各小区规划设计主要遵循大规模封闭小区的传统设计方法；丁家庄保障性住区规划则体现了城市设计理念，住区遵循着"大开放、小封闭"的小街区组织方式。莲花村住区高层住宅布局总体比较均质，开放空间较单调；丁家庄采用小规模居住街区模式，开放空间组织层次鲜明。

（4）建成管理机制的不同。莲花村保障性住区入住率高，地铁站的便利性使得房屋出租率高、流动人口情况复杂，街道及居委会在物业管理方面主导性强，物业管理公司为街道下属机构，由于重视度高，安全等常规管控较好，但是对于资产经营缺乏专业管理经验；丁家庄保障性住区则由安居集团下属子公司安居颐和资产管理公司进行资产总体把控，对资产经营有较为专业的管理理念，尽管引进了市场化物业管理公司，但是安居颐和资产管理公司对物业公司的控制度高。

3 莲花村与丁家庄居民居住满意度调研

3.1 莲花村与丁家庄住房类型和人口特征

莲花村设计总套数2.36万套，丁家庄住区设计总套数1.73万套。从住房类型来看，莲花村住房类型少，集体土地拆迁安置房占绝对主导，有部分限价商品房；丁家庄国有土地拆迁安置房占主导，还有集体土地拆迁安置、公共租赁房、廉租房和低收入双困户经济适用房。

莲花村、丁家庄住房及人口情况比较 表2

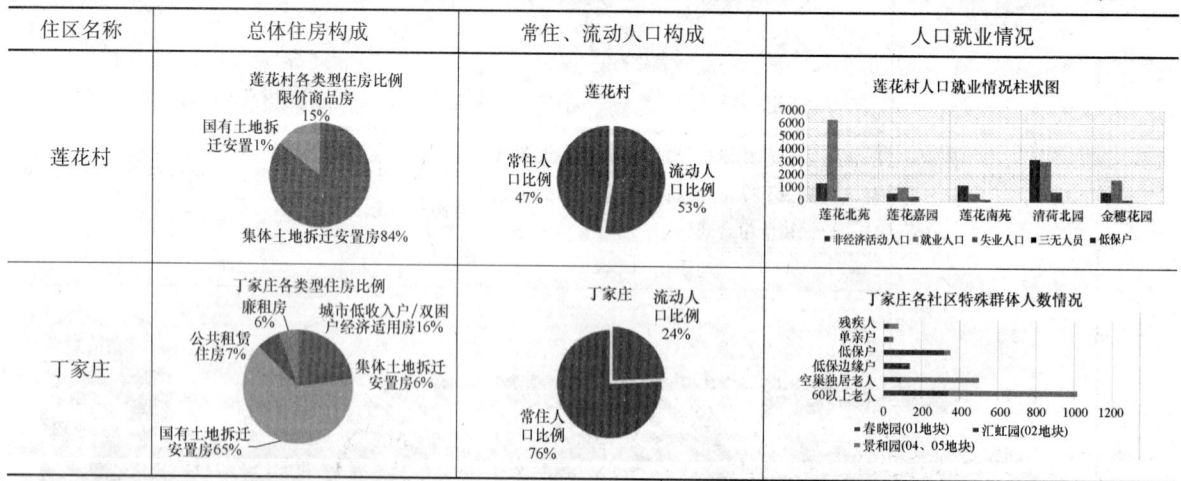

资料来源：笔者根据调研访谈资料整理自绘。

莲花村目前实际居住人口约5万人，丁家庄实际居住人口1.16万人（交付入住率48.9%）。从常住、流动人口构成来看，莲花村流动人口比例高，外地务工人员多，新就业人群多。丁家庄由于存在廉租房、公租房和双困户经济适用房，人口呈现出明显的高失业率，其低保户和低保边缘户数量大、占比高，产生了局部的贫困聚集。

本文通过抽样调查分别获取占总人口5%的家庭问卷数据，根据居民的住房类型、家庭结构、居民年龄三个因子对居民家庭进行聚类，得到莲花村有以下五类主要家庭：青年单身租户、拆迁安置传统三代户、青年夫妇租户、拆迁安置核心三人户、核心三口租户；丁家庄有以下四类家庭：拆迁安置传统三代户、拆迁安置成年三人户、老年夫妇廉租或公租户、核心三口租户。

3.2 莲花村与丁家庄总体居住满意度比较

由于莲花村规划设计质量以及建设把控远低于丁家庄，因此小区环境满意度大大落后于丁家庄，住房满意度也落后于丁家庄20%；公共设施由于两个片区的公益性设施都不够健全，因此满意度在60%左右趋近；莲花村由于地铁通达的缘故出行满意度高达92%，这一点远远超出丁家庄。

就居民居住总体满意度来看，莲花村和丁家庄满意度都超过了70%，丁家庄更是达到了92%，可见丁家庄良好的规划设计和建成管理的作用很大。对于莲花村，出行条件满意度对总体满意度贡献最大；对于丁家庄，住区环境满意度对于总体居住满意度贡献最大。

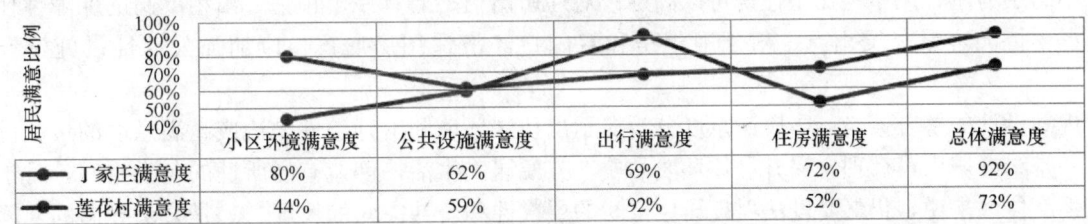

居民满意比例	小区环境满意度	公共设施满意度	出行满意度	住房满意度	总体满意度
丁家庄满意度	80%	62%	69%	72%	92%
莲花村满意度	44%	59%	92%	52%	73%

图4　莲花村、丁家庄保障性住区居民居住满意度比较

3.3 莲花村与丁家庄不同类型家庭的居住满意度比较

莲花村：不同类型家庭的居住满意度差异较大，租户的满意度高于拆迁安置户，其中青年单身租户的总体满意度最高，因为其最在意出行和商业性设施。集体土地拆迁安置传统三代户的总体满意度最低，因为其最需要公益性公共设施，也最在意小区环境，对住房也习惯于农村式住房。

丁家庄：不同类型家庭的居住满意度差异没有莲花村大。总体最满意的家庭类型也不是租户家庭，而是国有土地拆迁安置三代户和老年夫妇廉、公租房户，因为其搬迁前后居住环境得到很大提升。但是在住房满意度上差异较大，老年夫妇廉、公租房户最为满意，而国有土地拆迁安置三代户因为面积并没有太大改善，满意度最低。

两个住区中，同为拆迁安置户的居住满意度差异较大；同为外来核心三口租户，对两个住区的满意度是相似的，在86%~89%之间，因为其属于主动择居行为，总体满意度较高。

以上分析揭示，居民满意度除了与居住环境本身的客观条件有关外，还与居民人口和家庭属性、与其入住前的居住条件有很大关系，因为这些因素将影响其对于小区环境、公共设施、出行条件和住房的在意程度和满意基准点。

对于集体土地拆迁安置居民，对高层住房会有较大的抵触情绪，应该着意提高小区环境舒适度，快速跟进公益性公共设施；对于整租、群租户中特别是新就业年轻人，对高层住宅接受度高，应该着重增加轨道交通临近型的公共租赁住房资源，提高住房户型的灵活度；对于廉、公租房家庭，同时具有老龄化特征，应当着重促进居家和社区养老等公益性设施的优化布局。

4 基于适居性的高强度大型保障性住区规划整合性策略

住房政策的整合策略：结合保障性住房保障对象人群制定针对性的住房建设计划，对于之前没

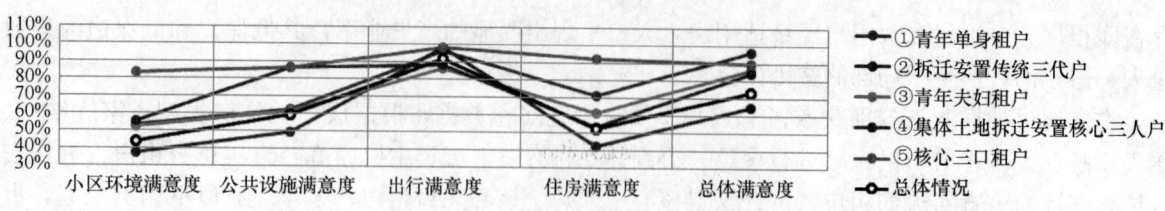

图 5 莲花村主要家庭类型的居住环境满意度比较

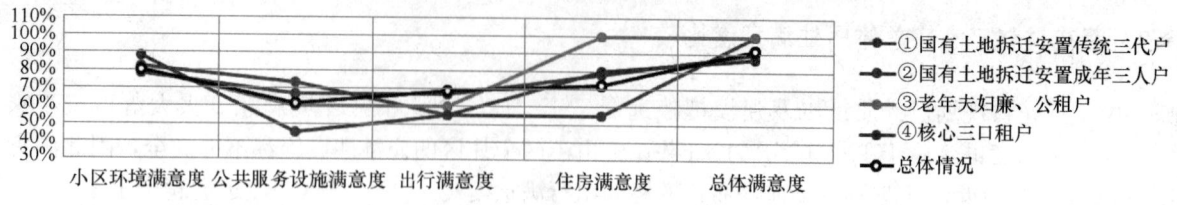

图 6 丁家庄主要家庭类型的居住环境满意度比较

有脱离农作生活的集体土地拆迁安置居民，适当控制开发强度，如果需要补偿多套住房，自住型住房以小高层为主，用于租赁型住房可以高层；对住房出租率要有一定预估，出租率高的保障性住房应重点支持大容量公交出行；对于廉租房和双困户经济适用房居民，应加强公益性设施建设和服务。

规划设计的整合策略：居民满意度分析揭示出住区环境和出行条件是达成高满意度的最关键条件。一是结合城市设计理念提升居住环境品质，方便居民生活，创造有场所性的各类空间，对于高层高强度住区来说，仍然要设法保证居住空间的层次性和公共空间的尺度。二是公交导向的空间布局，公共设施、道路网络和公交站点关系清晰，注重站点周边步行环境联系。

建成管理的整合策略：社区管理应按照人口特征调整居委会管理规模，低收入群体集中和流动人口多的社区管理难度大，应缩小社区居委会管理人口规模；物业管理则建立政府、政府机构和非政府机构（包括市场机构和非营利机构）的合约关系，进行相应制度设计，委托具有专业资产管理能力的机构进行建成后维护、管理和运营，盘活商业设施资产，适当补贴物业管理运营，长期保证物质空间品质。

致谢

本文受国家自然科学基金项目（51208091）资助。

Habitability Evaluation on High Density Large-Scale Affordable Housing in Nanjing

Tang Chudi，Wang Chenghui

（Architecture School，Southeast University）

Abstract：The 12th Five-Year Plan has opened an era of affordable housing construction. Since distinct building form, quality and residential environment may lead to social tagging, this paper focuses on habitability by tracking two typical cases in Nanking. Habitability evaluation contains objective assessment and residential satisfaction. Residential satisfaction aims at seeking differences between residence groups. Finally this paper proposes integration strategy for unavoidable high-density development of affordable housing estates from perspectives as policy mechanism, planning and management.

Keywords：Indemnificatory and affordable housing，High-density，Habitability，Residential environment

参考文献：

[1] 王承慧. 转型背景下城市新区居住空间规划研究[M]. 江苏：东南大学出版社，2011.

[2] 刘玉亭. 城市保障房住区建设及其居住环境研究评述[J]. 现代城市研究，2014，11：2-6；29.

[3] 谭艳慧. 住区容积率与居住形态的演变及相互关系研究[D]. 山东：山东建筑大学，2010.

[4] 蒙春运. 高容积率保障性住房规划设计研究[D]. 江苏：苏州科技学院，2011.

广州市低收入大学毕业生非正规群租现象研究

张梦竹[1]　王博祎[2]　麦夏彦[3]

（1. 北京大学城市与环境学院；2. 同济大学建筑与规划学院；
3. 伦敦政治经济学院）

摘要：本文基于对广州体育西地区大学毕业生非正规群租现象研究，以问卷调查、结构性访谈等方法分析低收入大学毕业生群租住客的社会经济特征及住房需求特点，并对比分析我国正规"商品房-保障房"住房体系、非正规城中村租赁房与该种非正规群租房与低收入大学毕业生住房需求的匹配程度。研究发现，在我国正规"商品房-保障房"二元住房体系供给不足背景下，以低收入大学毕业生为目标的非正规群租住房借助市中心二手房市场过滤机制形成，这是一种不同于城中村租赁房、符合毕业生住房需求、对我国当下"商品房-保障房"的二元住房体系的有重要补充的住房类型，可通过优化内部环境、规范管理等方式纳入我国保障住房体系，是解决我国低收入大学毕业生"住房难"问题的可行思路之一。

关键词：低收入大学毕业生，非正规住房，群租，保障房

1 引言

大城市"低收入大学毕业生住房难"是我国当前城市住房供给体制失灵背景下社会与学术界广为讨论的话题。由于被高房价的商品房住房体系以及高户籍要求的保障房体系双双排斥在外，低收入大学毕业生已成为我国二元住房体系中的"夹心层"。在此背景下，近年我国大城市出现了低收入大学毕业生非正规"聚居"、"群租"等现象。目前已有学者对北京、上海等低收入毕业生聚居现象进行了研究，归纳了这一群体的特点以及其聚居模式。学者们将收入低、聚居于城乡接合部或近郊、住房质量低的大学毕业生群体定义为"蚁族"[1]；"蚁族"聚居区在空间分布上主要集中在城乡接合部、近郊、城中村等房租便宜、交通相对便利的地方，且多居住在"群租房"内。[1~4]

目前国家和地方政府出台了多项法规明令禁止"群租"，使得这样的低收入大学毕业生"群租"处于非法、非正规的城市管理的灰色地带。但部分学者认为"低收入大学毕业生群租"是中国特色城镇化道路的一个环节，并从住房保障制度不健全、商品房户型需求与供给矛盾等层面解释了"蚁族"聚居区的形成原因。[1~5]近年来，广州中心区的商品房小区内出现了低收入大学毕业生群租现象。本文基于对广州体育西地区低收入大学毕业生群租现象的调研，分析低收入大学毕业生的住房需求特点，并将其住房需求与城市正规商品房、保障房、非正规城中村住房与商品房小区内的群租房等四种住房供给进行匹配分析，试图从城市住房供给体系视角探究低收入大学毕业生群租现象的成因，并进一步探究将国家禁止的低收入大学毕业生聚居的"群租房"进行规范、优化并纳入城市保障房体系的合理性和可行性，试图为解决我国低收入大学毕业生住房难问题提出有意义的思路。

2 低收入大学毕业生住房需求特点

本文选取广州市体育西地区作为研究对象。体育西地区位于广州市天河中心区，是广州最为繁华和重要的 CBD 区域，也是广州就业密度最高、房价最高的地区之一；同时也是广州"低收入大学毕业生非正规群租"现象最为明显的地区之一：在广州 96 家低收入大学毕业生群租的"青年公

寓型群租房"① 中，体育西地区的 6 个旧住宅小区内就分布有 48 家，近 600 名低收入大学毕业生聚居于此。值得指出的是，广州体育西大学毕业生聚居的"青年公寓"实际上属于政府禁止和严厉打击的"群租房"范畴内②，长期游走在城市相关管理法律法规边缘的"灰色地带"。

本次研究选取了位于体育西的六运小区、天荣小区、育蕾小区三个小区，对位于其中的 9 家低收入大学毕业生非正规群租的"青年公寓型群租房"进行了实地调查，对居住在"青年公寓型群租房"中的 175 名低收入大学毕业生进行了问卷调查、结构式访谈调查，并对 4 名"青年公寓"的投资者、2 名所在小区的物业公司负责人、2 名居委会管理人员进行了半结构式访谈调查。

2.1 社会经济特征

居住在"青年公寓型群租房"内的低收入大学毕业生均为非本地户籍（100%），年龄集中在 20~25 岁（82%），都有大专及其以上的学历（100%），毕业年限多在 2 年以内（82%），42% 的毕业生已就业但工作时间不足半年，45% 的人处于求职阶段，已就业的毕业生职业多为销售、文职等，毕业生（82%）月收入处于 2000~4000 元之间，人均月收入仅 2150 元，远低于 4977 元的广州社会平均工资水平。总体而言，这一群体有"刚离校、学历高、收入低"的基本特征。

2.2 住房需求特征

根据调查，低收入大学毕业生对住房的基本需求可以总结为"价格低、交通便、配套全、与同龄人合居"。这一群体在选择住房时考虑的因素按照重要性从高到低排序依次为价格便宜、交通便捷、周边配套完善、内部人群性质、内部格局舒适。

在住房价格上，低收入毕业生所能承担的房租支出为 400~600 元/月，毕业生阿峰说："我们刚毕业，睡上下铺床比较适应，但房租低比较重要。"在住房区位上，此群体期望能够在离工作地很近的城市中心区居住，期望的单程通勤时间为 20 分钟内。在周边配套上，此群体对住房周边的生活服务配套的依赖和需求很高。在室内设施配套上，此群体对室内设施的要求较为基础，但对电脑和网络的需求很高。在住房内部社会环境上，毕业生热爱交往且需要与同龄互帮互助，在"群租房"住了半年的毕业生阿华说，"这里跟以前在学校的时候很像，很有人情味，暂时没想着搬走。"

3 低收入大学毕业生住房需求匹配分析

3.1 商品房与低收入大学毕业生匹配分析

近年广州市区的商品房均价基本稳定在 15000~30000 元/m² 的高位水平，远远超出低收入大学毕业生的购买能力。而从房屋租赁市场来看，广州就业密集区及主要的通勤居住区的正规商品房单间住房的租赁价格为约为 1000~2000 元/月（表 1），而低收入大学毕业生的平均月收入仅为 2150 元/月，可接受的月房租支出仅为 400~600 元。这样的低收入水平和支付水平使得低收入大学毕业生基本无法在正规商品房租赁市场中得到合适的住房供给。

---

① 投资者购买或租赁小区内商品房并将其改建为适合多位大学毕业生同时居住的非正规"群租房"，并以床位为单位出租给大学毕业生，房东通常将其挂名为"XX 青年公寓"通过网络平台进行宣传和推广。
② 住建部于 2010 年出台的《商品房屋租赁管理办法》中第八条明文规定"出租住房应当以原设计的房间为最小出租单位，人均租住建筑面积不得低于当地人民政府规定的最低标准。同时，厨房、卫生间、阳台和地下储藏室不得出租供人员居住。"

广州天河区商品房出售和租赁信息比较 表1

小区	特点	售价（元/m²）	租赁（元/月）	毕业生支付水平
六运小区（体育西）	1.17～21 年房龄二手房 2. 旧式多层半开放小区 3. 配套完善，位于城市就业密集的中心区	15000～25000	整套：3000～4500 单间：1300～1700	平均月收入：2150 元/月
骏景花园（车陂）	1.5～10 年房龄二手房 2. 新式高层门禁小区 3. 配套一般，距离城市就业密集的中心区 5～6km	15000～26000	整套：3000～5000 单间：1000～1500	月均房租支出：400～600 元/月

3.2　保障房与低收入大学毕业生匹配分析

广州的保障性住房供给体系分为经济适用房和公租房两部分，通过低价出售和租赁住房给予城市住房困难人群住房保障。经适房不开放给单人申请，并严格要求申请人及家庭成员具有本市城镇户口；公租房可开放给单人申请，但严格要求申请人为年满30岁、具有本市城镇户口的市民。而低收入大学毕业生基本都为年龄在25岁以下的非本市户籍的单身青年，被完全排斥在广州的保障房体系之外（如表1）。此外，低收入大学毕业生的工作地和求职地区都位于城市就业密度的中心区，但广州经适房和公租房多建在远离市区的城市边缘地区，交通配套也较为缺失，难以满足低收入大学毕业生的工作和生活需求。

3.3　城中村住房与低收入大学毕业生匹配分析

城中村住房价格低廉、交通区位较好、周边往往有较好的生活服务设施，满足毕业生的住房支付水平、交通需求以及服务配套的需求，是一部分低收入大学毕业生的住房选择。以天河区棠东村为例，单间住房的月租金为400～800元/月，符合毕业生的低支付水平。但由于城中村内外部卫生条件较差、城中村内的流动人员（外来务工人员）多、居住安全保障低，大部分低收入大学毕业生不愿居住在较低租金的城中村住房中。此外城中村住房的内部配套设施也较不完备，毕业生阿东说："城中村很多都没网没热水。之前去过冼村的一家，周围环境也没现在这里（群租房）好"。

3.4　"青年公寓型群租房"与低收入大学毕业生匹配分析

3.4.1　住房成本匹配分析

"青年公寓型群租房"以床位为单位的出租模式极大地降低了单人房租支出水平，单个床位仅250～450元/月的租金水平在低收入大学毕业生400～600元/月的房租支付能力范围内，能够满足低收入毕业生的低房租支出的需求，而习惯大学宿舍居住形式的大学毕业生也对以床位为单位的居住形式有良好的适应性。

3.4.2　住房区位条件和交通设施配套匹配分析

"青年公寓型群租房"位于广州就业密集的中心区（体育西），能够很好满足低收入大学毕业的工作通勤等出行交通需求。根据调查，居住在"群租房"内的82%低收入大学毕业生就业地点在公寓集中地的2km范围内（图2），毕业生住客的平均单程通勤时间为18分钟，远低于46分钟和28

分钟的广州、全国平均水平；平均单程通勤距离仅为 1.76km，远低于 15.16km 和 9.75km 的广州、全国平均水平；平均交通费用仅为 145 元，仅占其月均收入的 4.54%，远低于 8.93% 的广州平均居民交通支出占收入比重。总体来看，87% 的毕业生住客对通勤时间和费用成本表示满意。此外，体育西与车陂片区周边公共交通服务完善，在体育西片区有 2 个地铁站和 9 个公交车站。72% 的毕业生住客通勤及外出活动不需换乘。仍四处求职的毕业生阿聪说："从公寓走两三分钟就到体育西路地铁站，到其他地方找工作很方便。这是当时选在这里住的主要原因。"

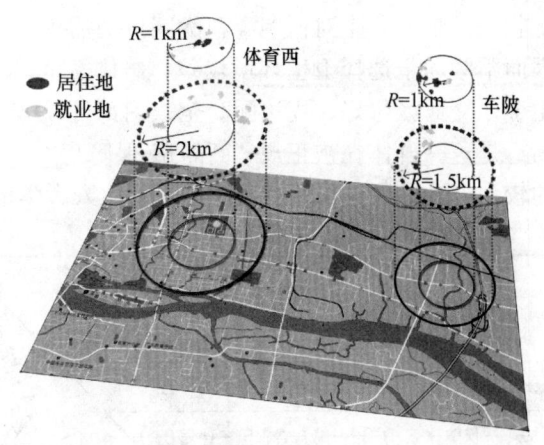

图 1　低收入大学毕业生住客的"居住-就业"空间分布
（资料来源：根据调查数据，作者整理绘制）

3.4.3　住房周边环境和生活配套设施匹配分析

"青年公寓型群租房"位于环境治安良好、生活配套完善的城市中心区旧商品房小区内，小区内及周边有大量沿街商铺，餐饮、购物、娱乐等设施一应俱全。根据调查，大部分低收入大学毕业生住客对小区内的餐饮店、便利店、洗衣店等生活服务设施的需求和使用程度高。此外，相比城中村，这些小区内部卫生环境较好、居民素质较高，并有物业和安保公司管理，能满足毕业生对居住环境的需求。总体上，居住在群租房内的 82% 低收入毕业生对住房周边配套及环境表示满意。

3.4.4　住房内部环境和室内配套设施匹配分析

首先，"青年公寓型群租房"设置的较高"准入门槛（只允许有大学毕业证或学生证的人员入住）"将背景复杂的社会人员排除在外，使得有较高素质、相似生活习惯的大学毕业生聚居在公寓内。而房东也要求至少入住一个月并交纳押金以降低内部住客的流动性，这都保障了毕业生的居住安全。同时，被调查的"群租房"内均形成了良好的交流氛围，与大学宿舍的生活与交流模式相似。

其次，群租房的低私人空间的群居模式在低收入大学毕业生的接受范围内。根据调查，一套群租房通常给 10～20 名毕业生同时居住，每间卧室通常有 4～6 个床位（上下铺床），76% 的被访毕业生住客表示对目前"四人间"、"六人间"群居形式的低居住空间满意。究其原因，一是这样低居住空间的"群居"方式和大学宿舍生活高度相似，大学毕业生能良好适应这种低居住空间的"群居"方式；二是在支付的租金远低于正规市场价格以及自身低收入的经济社会状态下，毕业生住客愿意通过压缩居住空间和降低居住质量来降低住房费用成本。

最后，群租房的室内设施配基本满足毕业生的生活需求，室内配备有桌椅、沙发、电视、空调、热水器、洗衣机、网络等基本生活设施。毕业生住客需求值高于 75% 的设施在被调查公寓中都有配备，82% 的被访住客也对室内设施配备表示满意。此外"青年公寓型群租房"对社区环境及生活并未带来负面影响。根据对小区居委会管理人员的访谈，居委会没有收到过关于毕业生"群租房"的投诉。相反低收入大学毕业住客潜在地促进了社区的文化娱乐消费等，让社区的文化氛围更显浓厚。

3.5　住房供给匹配分析结论

通过将低收入大学毕业生的住房需求与四种主要住房供给类型进行匹配分析发现：低收入大学毕业生被大城市高房价的商品房住房以及高户籍门槛的保障房双双排斥在外；城中村住房虽然满足

低收入大学毕业生对低租金和优区位的需求，但这一群体对居住环境卫生、居住安全等要求较高，因而不倾向于选择卫生环境较差、居住安全得不到保障的城中村住房。"青年公寓型群租房"因低租金、交通区位好、周边配套全、内部环境较为安全等与低收入大学毕业生的住房需求匹配度较高，是这一群体在被正规"商品房-保障房"二元体系排斥在外，在城市非正规住房市场中寻求到的较为合适的住房供给类型，也是低收入大学毕业生群租现象的重要成因。

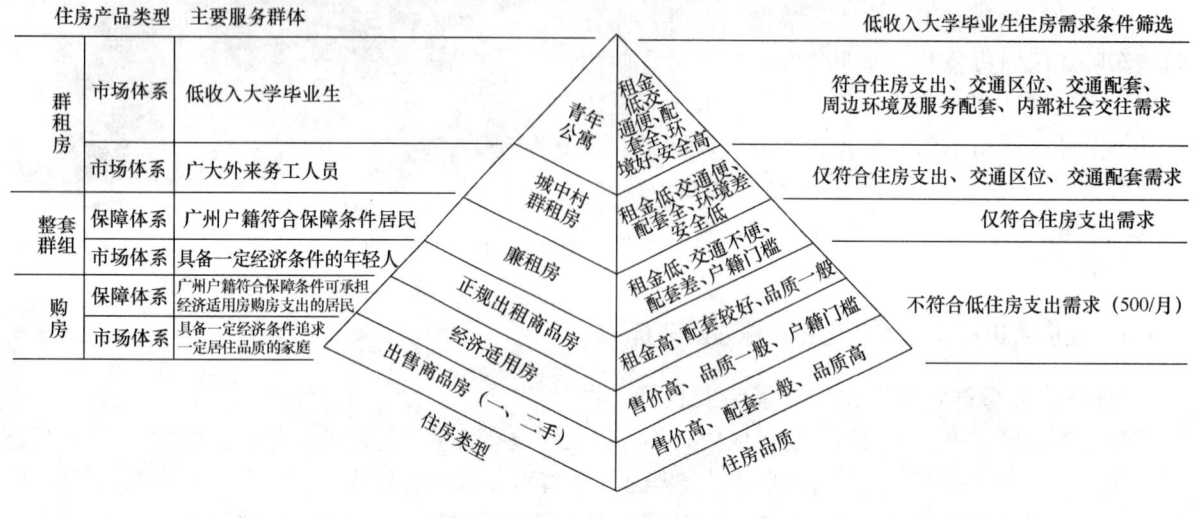

图2　我国住房供给机制分析

（资料来源：作者绘制）

4　"低收入大学毕业非正规群租"现象对我国保障房建设的启示

低收入大学毕业生涌入非正规群租房的现象暴露出我国在快速城镇化时期出现的城市住房供给失灵、非正规经济管治失效、大学毕业生住房难等多种问题。笔者认为在当前情况下，通过对我国保障性住房体系的改善和优化可能是在较快时间内帮助解决大学毕业生住房难的思路之一。

4.1　扩大住房保障体系的覆盖面，保障低收入大学生的基本住房需求

体育西地区"低收入大学毕业生非正规群租"现象反映了我国正规保障房体系的覆盖面较窄的问题。刚离校的大学毕业生往往被大城市高房价的商品房以及高户籍门槛的保障房双双排斥在外，由于对居住环境、安全的高要求也不倾向于选择能满足价格和区位需求的城中村非正规住房。"青年公寓型群租房"尽管能满足低收入大学毕业生的住房需求，但属于城市管理的"灰色地带"，其居住的稳定性和安全性难以得到法律法规的保障。在此背景下，着眼于解决城市弱势群体住房需求的国家保障性住房体系应当适当扩大其保障覆盖面，将非本地户籍、在当地就业的低收入大学毕业生纳入保障体系，给予一定的住房补助或提供类似"青年公寓"的学生宿舍型的基本保障性住房。

4.2　非正规住房供给的正规化，利用市场机制补充保障房体系

广州体育西"低收入大学毕业群租"现象中的"群租房"经营行为是我国二元住房体系供给不足所引发的"非正规经济"现象。目前在我国地方政府财政有限的情况下，对保障性住房的建设和供应远远满足不了城市弱势群体的住房需要。合理利用市场机制作用下产生的、有社会积极效应的非正规住房供给，无疑是解决我国快速城镇化时期对弱势群体住房供给不足问题的思路之一。从广州体育西地区出现的非正规"青年公寓型群租房"来看，其提供的住房与低收入大学毕业生的基本居住需求上具有良好的匹配性，有潜力通过一定手段进行优化管理、纳入到国家正规保障性住房供

给体系中，对我国低收入大学毕业生提供廉价、安全、满足基本居住需求的住房供给进行有机补充。

4.3　激活存量住房，实现灵活多样的保障房供给

保障住房发展应积极激活存量住房市场，扩大保障性住房的供给量。从国外保障房建设经验来看，灵活多样的住房供给是解决低收入人群住房问题的重要途径。英国的保障房建设更多是依靠市场、公私合营来进行大规模的开发和再利用[6]，而澳大利亚则逐渐采取依靠私有租赁市场提供保障房的方式进行住房供给。[7]国内学者也提出，除了积极发展保障性住房增量市场外还应重视存量住房市场。[8]一方面，政府可采购旧住宅以弥补保障性住房的供给不足；另一方面，旧住宅的良好区位可缓解新建保障性住房过于集中郊区的矛盾，有利于为被保障人群提供多种区位的住房选择。

Study on Informal Multiple-Occupancy Rental Housing of Low-Income Graduates in Guangzhou City

Zhang Mengzhu[1]，Wang Boyi[2]，Mai Xiayan[3]

（1. College of Urban and Environment Sciences，Peking University；

2. College of Architect and Urban Planning，Tongji University；

3. London School of Economics and Political Science）

Abstract：This paper based on in-depth field investigations of low-income graduates informal multiple-occupancy housing in Guangzhou City，analyzes the housing requests of low-income graduates and make a comparative study on how formal commercial housing，affordable housing，informal urban village housing and multiple-occupancy housing match the housing requests of low-income graduates. The findings indicate that without adequate formal housing provision for vulnerable low-income graduates in China，the multiple-occupancy housing emerging in Guangzhou housing market is an innovative supplement in the existing housing system with significant high match with the graduates' housing request. Based on these findings some suggestions are put forward that government should bring informal multiple-occupancy housing into affordable housing system to help solve the issue of housing provision scarcity for low-income graduates.

Keywords：Low-income graduates，Informal housing，Multiple-occupancy housing，Affordable housing

参考文献：

[1]　廉思. 蚁族：大学毕业生聚居村实录[M]. 西宁：广西师范大学出版社，2009.

[2]　韩晗. 京沪穗三城"蚁族"阅读调查[N]. 中国图书商报，2010：05-22.

[3]　吴双霞，祁新华，罗栋燊. 蚁族城市租住区位规律研究——以福州市为例[J]. 人文地理，2012，26(04)：59-62.

[4]　高源，吴晓庆，王雅妮，等."蜂族"群体住房调查及规划设计策略——以南京市宁康苑小区为例[J]. 规划师，2012，28(2)：94-99.

[5]　顾朝林，盛明洁. 北京低收入大学毕业生聚居体研究——唐家岭现象及其延续[J]. 人文地理，

2012，27(05)：20-24.

[6] Christine M E，Whitehead. Planning Policies and Affordable Housing：England as a Successful Case Study[J]. Housing Studies，2007(20)：25-44.

[7] Judith Yates，Maryann Wulff. Market Provision of Affordable Rental Housing：Lessons from Recent Trends in Australia.[J]. Urban Policy and Research，2005(15)：5-19.

[8] 宋英潇. 我国大学毕业生住房保障制度研究[J]. 建筑经济，2008(S2)：15-17.

东北地区保障性住房居民室内环境改造行为研究：以沈阳市为例

李翥彬[1]　范　悦[1]　刘文昭[2]

（1. 大连理工大学建筑与艺术学院；2. 辽宁省城乡建设规划设计研究院）

摘要： 本研究以保障性住房住户的居住环境改造行为为关注点，希望通过这一直接反应物质空间与居住需求错位的现象，探求住户多样化的居住需求，从而为保障性住房设计提供参考，丰富现有基础研究成果。本研究选取了建设于不同时期的沈阳市六个保障性住房小区作为研究对象，共实际走访调查 369 户，并对平面布置图进行了数据采集，结果显示共有 101 户居民对室内环境进行了不同程度的改造。本文基于改造目的将其分为三种类型，并深入探讨了住户的改造行为与家庭结构以及居住模式存在关联。这些改造行为也直接反映了现有保障性住户的多样化居住需求。现有的部分研究已经对这种多样化需求进行了一定程度的探索，但受制于建筑结构等多方面因素，很难满足如此多样的居住需求。如何回应这些多样化的居住需求应该是未来保障性住房设计研究的重要方面。

关键词： 保障性住房，室内，环境改造，东北地区

1 引言

自 1998 年中国住宅商品化改革以来，保障性住房的发展经历了不断发展变化的过程。从最初的大力发展经济适用房，到逐步弱化经济适用房在保障性住房中的地位，转而发展租赁型住房。作为"十二五"规划的收官之年，2015 年政府工作报告指出保障性安居工程的任务为 740 万套。如果此目标得以实现，那么"十二五"期间保障性住房的实际开工量将比预计任务增加 300 多万套。[1]政府在保障性住房上的投入依然很大。

作为政府公共政策的重要组成部分，保障性住房领域吸引了包括建筑学学者在内的多学科领域研究人员的关注。社会学者更加关注制度运行过程中出现的问题，例如土地供应，融资机制，法律法规建设等。[2,3]并对国际上相关国家的经验进行了系统化的总结，提出在中国发展保障性住房过程中值得借鉴的经验。[3]建筑学领域的学者则更加关注保障性住房终端产品的设计以及建造方式方法。采用工业化的建造方式成为在短时间内提供足量合格保障性住房产品的重要手段。相关领域的专家学者进行了深入而广泛的讨论[4]，并进行了一定数量的工程实践。[5]同时，设计研究人员针对不同的城市和地区均进行了保障性住房设计的相关研究。[6,7]这些相关的设计研究大都从规范和标准出发，旨在有限的面积内提供符合居住家庭基本生活需求的功能，并没有对居住者的实际使用需求给予充分的关注。李培在对北京经济适用房的居住满意度进行系统研究之后提出了理想的经济适用房的套型面积，以及项目选址、配套设施建设等多方面建议。[8]另外一些学者通过实际的走访调查总结归纳低收入人群的居住生活方式及居住需求，并在此基础之上讨论其对设计的启示[9,10]，进行了一定的设计实践探索[11]，取得了一定的成果。

众所周知，人的居住需求具有多样化的特点。这种多样化表现在不同家庭之间的需求差异，以及同一家庭不同时期的需求差异。目前，保障性住房的分配多采用摇号配租的方式进行，此种方式虽然尽可能保证了分配的公平性，也使居住者无法选择居住户型，进而导致在已经完成配租的保障性住房中，室内环境改造行为普遍存在。本文通过对沈阳市典型居住小区进行调研，以居民的室内环境改造行为为主要的研究对象，希望通过调查探明此种改造行为的比例，并对改造行为进行归纳分析，为将来保障性住房设计，尤其是公租房的设计提供参考。

2 调研概要

本研究选取东北中心城市沈阳作为调研对象，选取了六个保障性住房小区（图 1）。其中包括两

个廉租房小区，四个经济适用房小区（包含少量廉租房）。本次调研通过实际走访调查记录共搜集到平面图资料 369 份。目前沈阳市保障性住房设计由于并没有统一的设计导则或规范，仅仅规定了套型面积上限（廉租房 50m²，经济适用房 60m²），因此，搜集到的户型呈现多样化的特点。其中较为常见的户型以及户内空间利用情况如图 2 所示。总体来看，虽然面积有限，现有保障性住房设计依然在有限的空间内提供了基本的居住需求。通常户型内包括有独立的卧室以及卫生间，其中部分户型厨房与起居室没有进行明确划分，用餐及起居空间合并。由于中式烹饪特点，一般在相对封闭的空间进行，便于排烟，以减少对室内空气环境质量的影响。

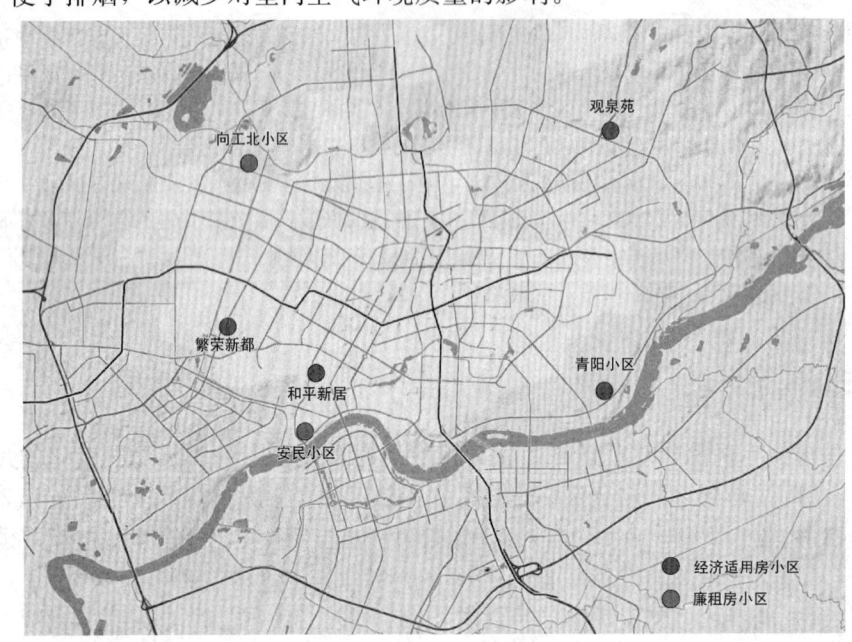

图 1　调研项目在沈阳市的分布图

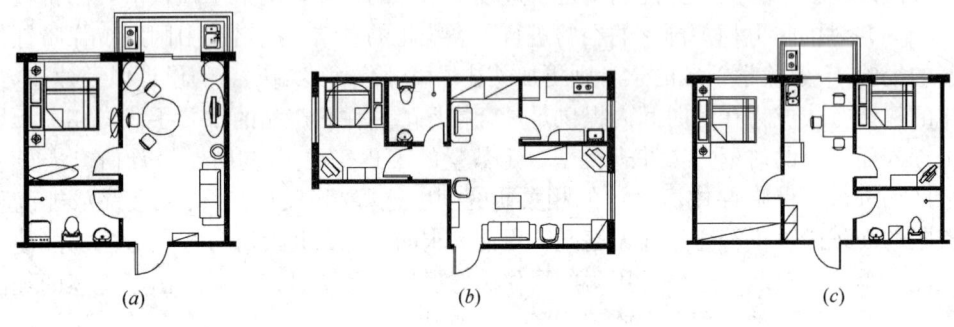

图 2　典型户型平面及室内空间利用

(a) 典型一室户平面；(b) 典型 L 形一室户平面；(c) 典型两室户平面

3　调研结果

调研发现，共有 101 户（27.4%）居民对室内平面布局进行了不同程度的改造以满足其居住需求。因此，改造行为存在一定的普遍性。以改造的目的作为划分依据，改造行为主要可以分为三种（图 3）：（1）通过增加隔断等措施分隔出独立的空间（n＝31）；（2）通过拆除现有隔墙合并空间（n＝41）；（3）通过改造扩大室内某一空间（n＝22）。三种改造行为从量上看并没有决定性差异，表明居民需求与现状的矛盾点并没有明显的倾向性。剩余样本的改造方式多根据家庭特殊需求进行改造，样本容量有限且没有明显的共性特征，因此本文只针对此三种改造方式进行论述。

通过增加隔断等措施分隔空间的改造活动目的在于增加室内的独立使用空间数量，增加的房间通常用作卧室或者餐厨空间。进行此类改造的家庭多数家庭成员较多，一室户型无法满足其需求，

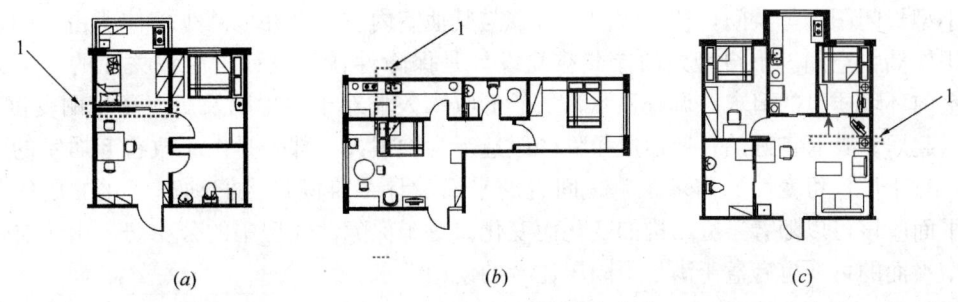

图 3　典型改造方式示例

（a）增加隔断；（b）拆除隔墙；（c）移动内墙位置

注：1 为改动位置示意。

因此选择通过增加隔断的方式来增加室内的独立空间作为卧室（图 3a）。隔断的出现会极大影响室内环境的采光，因此在隔断材料的选择上，住户通常会选用毛玻璃等透光材料，在保证房间隐私的前提下，尽可能减少对室内采光的影响。拆除室内隔墙合并空间的方法多存在于含有较小室内空间的户型中，如果存在阳台与厨房相连的情况，大多数居民选择将阳台与厨房合并以增加厨房的面积，增加的面积则用作储物空间。部分居民通过拆除隔墙将厨房与客厅相连，进行此种类型改造多发生于室内空间极度有限的家庭中。第三种改造方式多由于增加起居厅的面积。对于部分大家庭，家庭成员较多，需要一定的家庭活动空间。同时，改造后起居厅和南向房间的分隔材料也多采用透光材料以增加起居室的光照条件，创造相对舒适的环境。

4　原因与讨论

通过访问调查，这种普遍存在的保障性住房室内环境改造行为的主要原因可以归纳为两方面：制度性原因及设计性原因。制度性原因主要指保障性住房的分配方式为摇号配租的形式，虽然在一定程度上保证了分配方式的公平性，同时由于完全随机分配，并没有考虑申请人的家庭构成，容易造成入住之后的使用问题。设计性原因主要指设计人员对使用人群的家庭结构以及居住模式习惯的无视。由于对使用人群的居住需求不了解，容易造成设计产品与实际需求错位脱节，继而造成使用者的自发改造行为。目前的保障性住房设计基本沿用了商业住宅设计的模式，很多户型并没有经过推敲，只是简单地将现有户型进行整体缩小以满足现有规定对于户型面积的要求。然而，保障性住房由于其特殊的属性，和商品住宅存在较大的差异。这些差异主要表现在以下几个方面。首先，作为政策性住房，保障性住房具有面积限定。按照沈阳市规定，公租房的建筑面积应控制在 $60m^2$ 以内。虽然经济适用房和廉租房已经逐步被公租房取代①，其在建设初期也同样面临面积的限制。按照沈阳市以往的规定，廉租房的建筑面积不得超过 $50m^2$，经济适用房不得超过 $60m^2$。在有限的面积中实现完整的功能要求，需要设计人员对使用者的使用需求有全面深入的了解。其次，使用者的差异。总体来看，保障性住房的居住人群为中低收入人群，其中廉租房住户的收入水平更低。相对于商品住宅对于品质的追求，保障性住房侧重于满足基本的生活需求。但这并不等于不追求品质。通过对中低收入人群的需求进行了解，同样可以实现有限面积内的高品质生活。

由于保障性住房与商品住宅的差异性存在，保障性住房设计同样应与商品住宅有所区别。周燕珉等的研究[9,10]已经揭示了低收入人群的部分居住需求，结合此次调研我们在进行保障性住房设计时还应关注：第一，低收入人群关于储藏空间的需求。调查显示，低收入人群有不同程度的保存有用物品的倾向，例如旧家具、生活用品等。这些旧物需要有一定空间进行储藏。此次调研也可以看

————————————

①　经济适用房由于存在一定的管理问题以及制度设计漏洞已经逐步退出保障性住房供应，而廉租房与公租房的并轨也正在进行中。

出，对于小型封闭阳台等空间，住户倾向于将其与其他室内空间合并以减少墙体所占空间，同时增加的面积用作储物空间。小户型内的储藏空间设计是保障性住房设计中应该关注的一个方面。第二，对于室内环境质量的追求。调查显示，虽然低收入人群对于卫生间及厨房环境耐受度较高[12]，但依然希望起居室具有良好的日照通风条件，改造行为中很大一部分是出于改善起居室的环境做出的。第三，对于设计可变性的需求。单一固定的平面设计很难满足人们动态变化的居住需求，因此，户型平面应该可以随着家庭结构的变化而变化。对于保障性住房中的公租房，由于居住者流动性强，户型平面的可变也有益于满足不同居住者的使用需求。

现有保障性住房的改造受制于建筑结构等诸多方面的原因，不容易进行改造。可以预见，当现有的保障性住房居民在搬离现有住房后，新居民同样可能面临居住空间不符合需求的情况。重复改造将产生大量的建筑垃圾以及能源消耗，不符合可持续发展的原则。因此，革新保障性住房的生产建造方式从技术上给予可变性设计以支持是必须要解决的问题。目前，国家正在推行保障性住房向工业化生产方式转变。希望通过工业化的方式解决保障性住房生产建设中存在的工期长，质量低下等问题。目前，中国的工业化住宅发展规划很大程度上参考了日本 SI 住宅体系，即将住宅分为支撑体（S）与填充体（I）。填充体如何设计才能满足居住者的需求是工业化住宅发展过程中的一个重要的问题。以上对于居民室内环境改造行为的分类研究，对于未来中国的工业化住宅设计也具有很重要的参考意义。

5 总结

保障性住房作为解决中低收入人群住房问题的重要手段，随着建设量的不断增加，已经满足了部分低收入人群对于拥有一个住所的需求。然而，居住改造行为的存在也反映出居住者对于居住环境更高的要求。设计研究者应该着重了解居民的实际需求，通过设计手段尽可能满足居民多样化的居住环境需求。同时，随着时代和社会的进步，人们的居住习惯及需求也会随之发生改变，对于居住需求的持续关注有利于形成系统化的居住需求理论，为未来的住宅设计提供连续的经验积累。本文从调查研究出发，总结了居民自发室内环境改造行为的类型及其对设计的启示，作为研究的前期积累，希望对今后保障性住房的设计提供有益的参考。

致谢

作者感谢住房和城乡建设部软科学研究项目（2013-R4-18）以及中央高校基本科研业务费专项 DUT14RC（3）138 对本研究的资金支持。

Research on Internal Layout Adaptation in Security Housing of Northeastern China: Case Studies from Shenyang City

Li Zhubin[1], Fan Yue [1], Liu Wenzhao[2]

（1. School of Architecture and Fine Art, Dalian University of Technology;
2. Liaoning Urban & Rural Construction & Planning Design Institute）

Abstract: This study takes internal layout adaptation of security housing as a focus, explodes the reasons of mismatch between built environment and the actual needs of occupants. The six cases in this study were selected from Shenyang city. A total of 369 families in the case projects accepted our interview, and their internal layout was sketched by the interviewers. The results show 101 families remodeled the original internal layouts. The occupants remodeled based on three purposes, which have close relationship with their family composition and living mode. The remodeling behaviors also reflect occupants' diverse needs for a better environment. Current researches have discussed the diverse needs to a certain extent. How to fulfill occupants' needs on living environment should be an important issue on security housing design in China.

Keywords：Security housing, Internal, Environment improvement, Northeastern China

参考文献：

[1]   中华人民共和国住房和城乡建设部. 让老百姓都能早日实现住有所居[EB/OL]. [2015-3-19]. http://www.mohurd.gov.cn/zxydt/201503/t20150317_220494.html.

[2]   马光红，李宪立. 建立健全保障性住房规划建设管理体制研究——基于廉租房的视角[J]. 城市发展研究，2010，04：64-68.

[3]   杨赞，沈彦皓. 保障性住房融资的国际经验借鉴：政府作用[J]. 现代城市研究，2010，09：8-12.

[4]   刘东卫，开彦，张宏，等. "保障性住房工业化设计与建造"主题沙龙[J]. 城市建筑，2012，01：6-19.

[5]   宋毅. 深圳市龙华保障性住房工业化建设实践[J]. 住宅产业，2011，12：65-67.

[6]   李振宇，张玲玲，姚栋. 关于保障性住房设计的思考——以上海地区为例[J]. 建筑学报，2011（08）：60-64.

[7]   李钊，郭淳，刘吉臣，等. 保障性住房的发展与设计实践[J]. 建筑学报，2011，08：65-69.

[8]   李培. 经济适用房住户满意度及其影响因素分析——基于北京市1184位住户的调查[J]. 南方经济，2010，04：15-25；36.

[9]   周燕珉，王富青. 北京低收入者居住需求研究及对廉租房建筑设计的启示[J]. 建筑学报，2009，08：6-9.

[10] 周晓红，龙婷. 上海市低收入住房困难家庭居住生活行为的研究[J]. 建筑学报，2009，08：10-13.

[11] 祝峥，刘恋. 从天颂雅苑和阅景花园的设计说开去——深圳保障性住房设计初探[J]. 住区，2012，01：94-99.

[12] 李翥彬，（日）濑户口刚，霍克. 廉租房室内空间使用调查及其对保障性住房设计的启示[J]. 建筑学报学术论文专刊，2013，9：180-185.

东北地区保障性住房户外环境现状探析：以大连泉水小区为例

王 翔 范 悦 董 丽

（大连理工大学建筑与艺术学院）

摘要：保障性住房因兼具经济性与适用性的特点，为国家大力推广的居民住房形式，保障性住房的建设也逐渐开始规范化、标准化，极大程度上解决了中低收入者的住房问题。然而，由于地产商从中获得利益颇少、空间资源有限等诸多客观因素，保障性居住小区与其他商品房住区之间出现明显的断层，尤其是户外环境方面的设计手法简单且粗糙，使许多保障性住区的居民不能对此产生归属感，大片的公共空间被遗弃，小区失去活力。本文先从相关概念和理论入手，以东北地区保障性住房的实地研究为基础，通过走访与问卷调查对东北地区已建成的保障性住房户外环境与居民进行调查。在分析保障性住房小区特征、居民行为特征与现状户外环境及公共配套设施的基础上，总结现阶段东北地区保障性住房的特征及其环境景观存在的问题，从活力营造的设计角度，对保障性住房户外环境建设提出一些建议，希望能对以后的保障性住房的景观建设提供更多的参考及思路。

关键词：保障性住房，活力，户外环境，公共空间

1 研究背景和调研对象概述

1.1 相关概念

保障性住房指政府在对以中低收入家庭为主要对象实行分类保障过程中所提供的限定供应对象、建设标准、销售价格或租金标准，具有社会保障性质的住房。由廉租住房、经济适用住房和政策性租赁住房构成。保障性住房小区就是由这三种住宅形式组成的居住小区。[1]

1.2 调研对象

截至 2013 年底，大连市安排建设保障性住房 9 万套，竣工 5 万套，保障性住房的覆盖面积达 17.3%，并计划到 2015 年底全市城镇家庭保障性住房覆盖率达到 20% 以上，安排解决保障性住房 12 万套。本文调研对象泉水小区位于甘井子区泉水振兴路，作为大连保障性住房示范工程，内含经济适用房和公租房，有 A、B、C 三区（其中 A、B 区为公租房，C 区为经济适用房），是大连最大的保障性住房项目（表 1）。

调研对象概况   表 1

项目名称	责任部门	占地面积（hm²）	建筑面积（10⁴m²）	建设套数	建设方式	建设单位	开工时间	竣工时间
泉水 A 区	住房保障中心	7.03	26.17	5200	集中新建	大连市住房保障中心	2011.4	2012.10
泉水 B 区	公积金管理中心	9.79	40.14	7802	集中新建	大连市公共租赁住房投资管理有限公司	2011.4	2012.10

资料来源：作者自绘。

2 保障性住区居民行为类型和心理需求

2.1 居民的行为类型及特征

环境心理学中关于人的行为可以看作是处在环境中的人的内在生理和心理变化的外在反应，既是环境作用于人而产生的外显反应和活动，又是人作用于环境的活动。心理学中一般把活动视为身体有意识的运动，强调"有意识"是为了与"条件反射"相区别[2]。在扬·盖尔总结的三种户外活动基础上，我们对调研对象的空间活动进行细化分类，基本分为以下八类活动，如图1所示：

（1）交往：一类是没有特定的安排，如居民自主的闲谈、倾听、结交等活动；另一类是有一定的组织和安排，如社区公益活动、居民相约跳舞等。

（2）休憩：休憩是住区活动的基本形式之一，一般指在户外环境空间进行低强度运动或放松精神的活动，主要有步憩和坐憩行为等，如闲坐、散步、乘凉以及遛狗等。

（3）康体：户外环境空间内进行的康体活动一般是以健康为目的，如网球、羽毛球、跑步等。

（4）文娱：这类活动带有明显的文化性和娱乐性，如阅读书刊报纸、下棋、社区影视欣赏等。

（5）游戏：以儿童为活动主体的行为，游戏的过程多包含儿童探索和学习的因素，比如戏水池、室外器材游戏等。在这一活动中往往会有家长的陪同，所以儿童活动会引起成人间的交往活动。

（6）餐饮购物：在不少户外环境空间内，餐饮设施和日常购物环境比较快捷方便，居民往往以轻松愉快的心态参与进来，从而使餐饮购物等活动也带有了休闲色彩。

（7）晾晒衣物：实地调研发现居民借助植物景观进而晾晒衣物的情况较普遍，在户外环境设计中应该考虑居民晾晒衣物的行为。

（8）饲养宠物：实地调查发现不少居民有饲养宠物，在户外环境设计中也应该考虑宠物饲养的安全性以及排泄物的处理方式，有效的保持户外环境的整洁。

图1 居民活动类型
（资料来源：作者自绘）

2.2 景观环境对居民心理的影响

空间尺度的大小具有相对性，不同的人会有不同的心理感受。[4]通过心理学的研究表明，高大的空间一般给人以气派、庄严的心理感受，矮小的空间给人以简朴、亲切等心理感受。但从另一个角度讲，大而无挡的空间可能会让人觉得无所适从或不近人情，而过于闭塞的空间则有可能让人感觉封闭压抑。调研的泉水小区13处户外广场，大部分缺乏合理的活动分区和相应设施，给人感觉整个区域比较大，就产生空旷的感觉，空间比较离散，不具备生气，人们在这样的空间中缺乏一定的控制感，走访的部分居民也表示不愿停留在这样的空间中，相对会选择建筑一层的庭院中休憩交流。

（1）观赏距离与实体高度的比例关系：在居住区空间中，由于居民所处的观赏距离和建筑实体的远近不同，会使人产生不同的空间感受。如图2、表2所示观赏距离为 D，实体高度为 H。

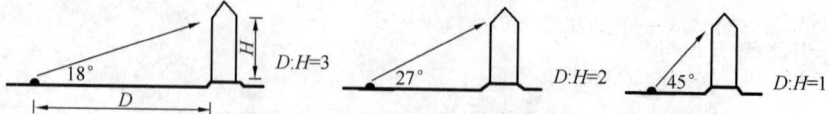

图2 视角与空间尺度关系示意图

（资料来源：〔美〕道格拉斯·凯尔博．共享空间——关于
邻里与区域设计．吕斌等译．北京：中国建筑工业出版社，2006）

实体高度与观赏距离关系表　　　　表2

$D:H$	垂直视角	视觉效果
3:1	18°	看清实体整体和背景
2:1	27°	看清实体整体
1:1	45°	看清实体细部

资料来源：作者自绘。

（2）空间比例与空间感的关系：空间本身长宽高的比例关系对于在其中活动的人会产生内聚或空旷的感觉，从而影响人对空间的感受（图3、表3）。调研小区的建筑物体量过大，给居民垂直维度带来知觉心理的压抑感（图4）。

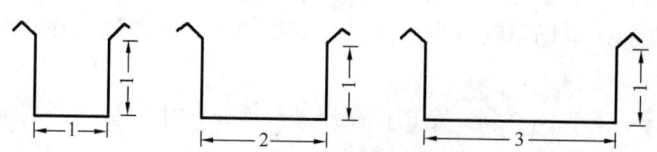 

图3　空间比例与空间感的关系　　　　图4　泉水小区建筑群

（资料来源：〔美〕道格拉斯·凯尔博．共享空间——关于邻里与区域设计．吕斌等译．北京：中国建筑工业出版社，2006.）

实体高度与空间距离关系　　　　表3

$D:H$	封闭与开敞	空间感受内聚感	空间类型
1:1	封闭	内聚感	"街型空间"
2:1	临界状态	安定感	"院落空间"
3:1	开敞	开放感	"庭式空间"

资料来源：作者自绘。

3 保障性住房户外环境设计中的活力营造

3.1 景观环境尺度和空间体量

户外环境空间的尺度要与住区用地条件、住区规模等相适应，但也并非是简单的用地比例关系，而是要有一个适宜的范围[7]。根据人类学家霍尔的研究，0～0.45m 为密切距离，0.45～1.20m 为个人距离，1.2～3.6m 为社会距离，3.6～7.6m 为公共距离（图5）。空间形状不同可以给人不同的心理感受和丰富的空间体验。在住区环境设计中我们主要研究的是立体形状对人的心理及行为的影响。立体形状主要分为球形、锥形和方形三种，球形空间给人一种聚合感和向心感，锥形空间给人以方向感和上升感，正方形空间给人一种静态感和庄重感，长方形空间则给人以动态感和方向感（图6）。

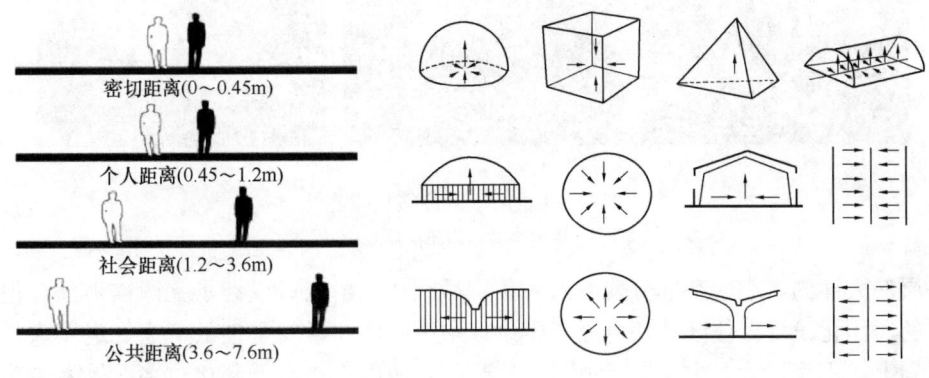

| 图5 人际距离示意图 | 图6 空间体量与心理感受 |

（资料来源：〔美〕保罗·贝尔，托马斯·格林等. 环境心理学. 朱建军，吴建平等译. 北京：中国人民大学出版社，2009.）

3.2 景观环境的限定和围合

户外环境中最常见的空间限定手法有地面铺装、高差变化、水面或绿化、柱廊隔断等。调研的多数户外环境空间的尺度较小，容纳的活动人数有限，所以空间的趣味性变得更加重要。户外环境要成为一个有活力的空间，其前提就是空间的可达性和便利性，如果能根据主要人行通道来布置户外空间，做到两者既相互独立又融为一体，就可以满足户外环境设计的初衷，如图7和图8所示。

实体围合形成空间　　实体占领形成空间　　占领物之间张力形成空间

图7 空间的基本限定方式

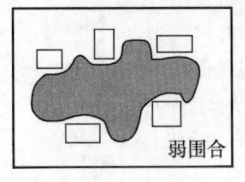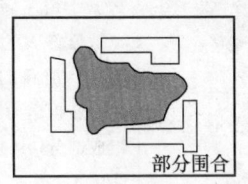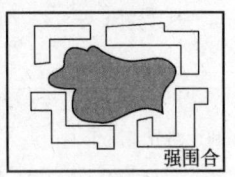

弱围合　　　　部分围合　　　　强围合

图8 空间的围合程度

（资料来源：作者自绘）

3.3 指向性户外空间的活力营造

（1）儿童游戏场地

如图9所示，在对泉水小区实地调研中发现，户外活动场地设计有儿童游乐活动设施，并且地面采用软质铺装，较好地考虑到了儿童活动安全问题。但由于户外设施在小区中的布局和组合关系缺乏推敲，使部分住区户外虽有一定的游戏区域和游戏设施，儿童的使用率却不高。其次，影响儿童游戏的主要原因是游戏场的规模和距离，是指活动空间和范围的大小以及游戏设施的丰富程度。

（2）老年人活动空间

调研案例中缺乏老年人的户外健身器械和无障碍活动场地（图10）。实地调查发现老年人群集

图 9 儿童游乐区设施与铺装
（资料来源：调研照片）

中在住宅一层的大厅内，小区有部分残疾人入住，虽在住宅出入口设计了无障碍坡道，但整体缺乏对弱势群体的通用化设计。住区外环境无障碍设计中更应该注意安全性的考虑，老年人活动空间在小区空间规划上，不宜设置在主交通干道附近；整个区域内不要高低起伏过多。针对老年人的特殊情况，要尽量满足老年人在休闲和社交等方面的需求，注重宅间庭院和绿地等方便到达的空间设计，步行空间每隔 50m 应设置休憩空间，其最小尺度应满足使用轮椅老年人的需求，应设置一些带有顶棚的座椅，以适合身体虚弱的老人在户外的停留[8]，表 4 对于休憩空间的设计要点作了总结。

图 10 老年人聚集在建筑内部
（资料来源：调研照片）

道路节点—休憩空间的设计要点　　　　　　　　　表 4

道路节点的位置关系事宜			
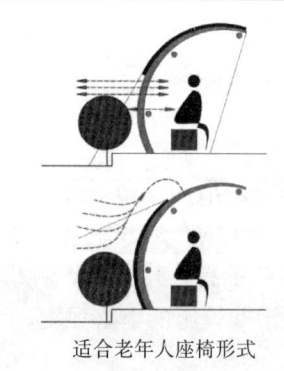 作为较长道路转折点的过渡空间		位于道路转折处，保持道路从直角过渡到主要道路的联系。整个转折角为道路的组成部分。下图的方式优于上图	该种形式既不能很好独立也不是道路的组成部分，使用效果一般
和道路分离属于独立式空间形式，可以兼做别的用途			位于道路顶端视野清晰，功能与道路转角处的前两种形式类似
休憩空间的座椅			
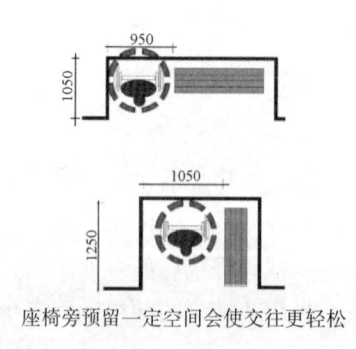 适合老年人座椅形式	座椅旁预留一定空间会使交往更轻松	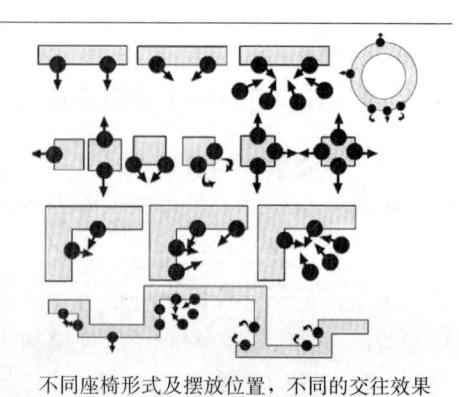 不同座椅形式及摆放位置，不同的交往效果	

资料来源：作者自绘。

4　结论

（1）根据笔者走访，泉水小区调研居民中 60 岁以上的占 22％，50～59 岁之间占 16％，40～49 岁之间的占 13％，步入老龄的人数比例较高且将快速增加。所以在户外环境设计中不仅要考虑其实际需要达到的功能属性，也要考虑设计客体的其他潜在功能，以防止在后期实际使用中造成不良的后果。

（2）居民倾向于在户外环境空间边缘活动，多数情况下不愿处于空间中的"焦点"位置，因此从一定意义上说，目前保障性住房户外普遍采取的单纯扩大户外空间尺度的做法并不一定可以吸引更多的居民，反而有可能使户外环境空间显得冷清，失去原有活力。

（3）保障性住房的供应对象为城市中低收入家庭。建筑面积和建筑造价受到严格控制，但保障性住房作为人类居住生活的物质载体这一根本属性没有改变，因此，如何在建设金额受较大限制的情况下为居民创造良好的居住环境，是提高居民整体的生活质量中亟待解决的矛盾之一。

Analysis on the Current Situation of the Outdoor Environment of Affordable Housing in Northeast Area：Case in Quanshui Community

Wang Xiang，Fan Yue，Dong Li

(School of Architecture & Fine Arts，Dalian University of Technology)

Abstract：Affordable housing is highly promoted by China as it balances economical efficiency and applicability. The construction of affordable housing in China is becoming normalized and standardized，which greatly solve the housing problem of mid-low class residents. However，developers benefit less from affordable housing and the space resource is also limited. Obvious gap occurs between the protection of residential quarters and other real estate settlements. Especially in the outdoor environment，design approach is simple and rough，which make many residents of the settlements can't feel sense of belonging. A large public space is abandoned and the district has lost its vitality. This paper begins with the concepts and theories，on the basis of Northeast affordable housing，visits and questionnaire survey have been undertaken in the Northeast region of affordable housing regarding the outdoor environment and residents. In the analysis of affordable housing complex characteristics，behavioral characteristics and current situation of basic resident outdoor environment and public facilities，this paper summarized the problems at this stage on the characteristics of affordable housing and environmental landscape in Northeast China. From a designing point of view on vitality creation，the paper gave some suggestions to the protection of proposed construction of housing outdoor environment to provide more information and ideas to the landscape construction of affordable housing in the future.

Keywords：Affordable housing；Vitality；Outdoor environment；Public space

参考文献：

[1]　中华人民共和国建设部. 城市居住区规划设计规范(GB 50180—93)[S]. 北京：住房城乡建设部标准定额研究所组织出版，2002.

[2]　杨德昭. 新社区与新城市：住宅小区的消逝与新社区的崛起[M]. 北京：中国电力出版

社，2006.

[3] 建设部课题组. 多层次住房保障体系研究[M]. 北京：中国建筑工业出版社，2007，12.

[4] Housing Development Board. HDB Annual Report2005/2006：Key Statistics[R]. Singapore：HDB，2006.

[5] 张文英. 对城市居住区环境设计现状的反思[J]. 中国园林，2005，1：62-63.

[6] ［日］伊達美徳. 初めて学ぶ都市計画. 市ヶ谷出版社，2008，3.

[7] ［美］保罗·贝尔，托马斯·格林等. 环境心理学[M]. 朱建军，吴建平等译. 北京：中国人民大学出版社，2009.

[8] 王江萍. 老年人居住外环境规划与设计[M]. 北京：中国电力出版社，2009.

[9] ［美］道格拉斯·凯尔博. 共享空间——关于邻里与区域设计[M]. 吕斌等译. 北京：中国建筑工业出版社，2006.

[10] 马建平. 中国保障性住房制度建设研究[D]. 吉林：吉林大学，2011.

城市空余地产转变为公租房的路径探讨

高永波

（华中科技大学建筑与城市规划学院）

摘要： 我国内地的房地产市场经过 10 余年的高速发展，房地产存量过剩问题越来越严重，而另一方面低收入群体"买房难"已成为当下最重大的民生问题之一。本文总结了国内外成功的公租房建设经验，辨析公租房与经济适用房之间的差异。然后结合国内城市房地产发展的现状和国家的政策背景，探讨城市空余地产转变为公租房的可能性，并研究空余房地产转为公租房在促进农民工市民化过程中可能发挥的作用。政府通过房屋统一租赁和住房补贴将商品房转化为公租房，可以降低以农民工市民化的成本，进而提高中国城镇化的质量。因此，由政府牵头将城市空余房地产转变为公租房，可以为公租房建设开辟一条新路径，并为降低中国城镇化成本提供一个新的方法。

关键词： 空余地产，公租房，可行性，农民工，城镇化

1 引言

2015 年伊始，国内的经济形势就不容乐观，第一季度的经济增速降到了 7%。回首过去十几年，中国高速发展的一个重要因素就是房地产业的兴盛。自 2013 年以来，房地产市场逐渐降温，存量过剩成为房地产市场一个严重的问题。政府对于房地产的调控政策主要集中两方面：一是防止存量进一步增加，提高行业效率；二是全力推动保障房建设，维护社会公平。李克强总理在十八届三中全会的政府工作报告中提到"住房保障将逐步实行实物保障与货币补贴并举，把一些存量房转为公租房和安置房"[1]。将城市空余地产转变为公租房，不仅有利于消化房地产存量，而且能够完善保障房体系，为广大购房困难的中低层收入群体提供应有的福利。

2 中国大陆以外地区保障房建设成功经验

公租房制度在世界上的许多发达国家和地区都已经非常成熟。中国香港和新加坡的公租房覆盖面比较广，基本上解决了大部分中低收入人群的居住问题。由于这两个城市人多地少，房价高企，中低收入阶层根本买不起房，如果不利用政府财力进行二次分配，平衡收入差距，将严重影响社会稳定和经济发展。当然，由于这两地与大陆在体量和收入水平上差异太大，不能完全照搬，但经济发达的一二线城市可以向其学习。美国的公租房建设对缓解社会矛盾，促进社会公平起到很大的推动作用，但由于美国 20 世纪 70 年代以后削减政府福利，仍有很大一部分中低收入阶层的住房问题没有解决。英国运用政府和社会力量共同推动租赁性保障房建设，基本解决了低收入阶层的住房问题，并致力于提高公租房租户的生活质量，值得我们学习和借鉴。

国外及中国香港地区保障房建设成功经验一览表 表 1

国家和地区	保障房制度	主要特征
中国香港	公租房	1. 覆盖面广，有超过 30% 的香港公民居住其中； 2. 专门立法，1973 年颁布《香港房屋条例》； 3. 机构专设，高效管理，公租房一切事宜由香港房屋委员会负责[2]
新加坡	公共组屋	政府征用土地，动用中央公积金储蓄建设公共组屋；政府、住宅合作社组织和个人共同出资，推进住房改进计划，解决经济弱势者的住房问题[3]

国家和地区	保障房制度	主要特征
美国	公租房	美国公租房源于富兰克林·罗斯福政府的"新政";依靠政府财政建设,进度和质量都达不到计划目标;二战后,大型公租房项目沦为贫民区;1974 年出台《住房法》规定政府应向接纳贫困租户的私营房企与房东提供相应补贴,直接向受助家庭发放房屋租赁券。虽然已有数百万家庭受益,但供给数量仍然不足[4]
英国	租赁性保障房	现有市政住房和住房协会住房两种供给模式,市政住房由政府直接出资建设,住房协会住房主要经营私营住房,但接受政府资金资助,具有公共租赁性质。20 世纪 90 年代实施"体面住房标准"计划,提高公租房质量;租户参与公租房的政策制定等事务[5]

3 国内保障性住房建设现状

截至 2007 年,我国城市常住人口中有一千万以上的低收入人群存在住房问题。[6] "由于国内城市居民社会分异加剧,低收入群体与高收入群体也出现空间分化,中国现有的城市低收入居民主要居住在老城棚户区、城中村和城郊低水平住宅之中,居住条件较差。虽然经过 20 年左右的保障房建设和棚户区改造,城市低收入阶层的居住情况已经得到很大改善,但由于房价较高、低租金小户型住房紧缺,许多大城市中低收入群体通过市场租赁或购买住房还是比较困难的。[7]"表 2 列举了国内几个具有代表性的一二线城市的保障房建设现状。

从表 2 可以看出,用地较为紧张、地价较高的上海、北京和深圳的公租房目标人群以本地户籍为主。而房价相对较低的广州、重庆和常州公租房则对本地户籍人口和外来务工人员一视同仁。其中常州的保障性住房体系以公租房为主,不仅实现了全覆盖,而且租金低,基本解决了中低收入人群的住房问题。值得一提的是,常州还推出的实物配租和租金补贴相结合的保障方式,从 2012 年就已经开始尝试租赁社会房源给保障家庭居住,一轮租赁期限为 3～5 年,房源到期后房主可以自由退出,由保障房收储管理中心收储新的社会住房。至今近 2900 户公租房保障家庭住在政府收储的这些房子里,2015 年第一期房源到期后,近八成房东愿意将房子继续租给政府。[8]

相对于经济适用房,公租房对于解决城市新就业职工、农民工的住房问题具有优势。这两类人的住房支付较低,买不起经济适用房,职能负担租金低廉的公租房。内地的公租房建设还迎合了新一代农民工扎根城市的新诉求。"80 后"、"90 后"农民工大多没有从事过农业生产,他们向往城市生活,希望能留在城镇,但大城市的购房和生活成本超过了他们的能力范畴。城市的发展又需要这些年轻的劳动者,因此为农民工提供公租房等居住福利是城市政府必须要承担的职责。

国内主要城市保障房建设经验一览表[9]　　　　　　　　　表 2

城市名称	目标人群	租金	建设途径	建设资金来源
上海	在上海工作,没有住房或人均住房建筑面积低于 15m² 的常住人口,包括户籍人口和外来务工人员	公租房的租金按略低于市场租赁水平确定,由各运营机构综合考虑房型、面积、区位等因素自主确定	结合旧城区改造、大型市政建设、大型居住社区等集中建设;新商品住房的建设项目中要有不低于 5%的比例配建经济适用住房;部分经济适用住房经批准转化为公租房	区、市各级政府出资,从银行贷款购买房屋出租,用租金来付息还本;或者运用非财政预算资金,例如保险资金、年金等低成本资金(年息 1.7%～1.9%),把高租金用于资金回报

城市名称	目标人群	租金	建设途径	建设资金来源
深圳	主要针对户籍人口，有条件地将非户籍专才纳入保障范围	公共租赁房租金以廉价为最高原则，每平方米租金10元以下，或以目前城中村房租价为标再下调50%	"十一五"规划有11.4万套公租房；采用公开招标、选择性招标和限制性招标多种方式建设公租房	由于公租房建设，建设资金由开发商提供，公租房所有权也归开发商，但房租由政府财政补贴
广州	既不符合廉租房申请条件，又无力购买经济适用房的外来就业人员，包括留在广州工作的大学生	将公租房租金计划分为三个档次，分别为同地段市场价的60%、48%和30%，将按住户收入水平高低分类收取	全市10万套直管公房可以转化为公租房；通过国企出地建保障房；从未被纳入改造的城中村中租下大批房源	自2006~2010年，广州市财政共筹集住房保障资金41.47亿元，有充足的资金保障
北京	市区内的公租房面向轮候的本地户籍家庭；村建公租房则针对外来务工人员	控制村建公租房的租金，让普通农民工也能住得起	政府组织建设和收购；国有企业、社会单位利用自有土地建公租房；鼓励城中村利用集体建设用地按规划建设公租房；在商品房小区中配建一定数量的公租房	通过政府公共土地和公共财政的投放支持公租房建设；公租房土地供应享受税收优惠；通过政策性贷款，引入信托资金等多种方式，多渠道筹集资金
重庆	"3+1"的公租房申请入住模式："3"是城市中低收入群体、有稳定收入的农民工和刚毕业留在重庆工作的大学生；"1"是特殊照顾人群	租赁价格控制在市场租金的60%以内；公租房承租人在租赁5年期满后可选择申请购买居住的公租房	先期试点以市地产集团为建设主体，以后会扩展至重庆市城投集团。投资建设主体拥有所建租赁房的完全产权，享有升值收益，但无房屋的定价权和转让权	发行12亿元地方政府债券专用于公租房建设；利用国有企业的国资预算以及融资能力，通过住房公积金贷款、政策性和商业性银行贷款筹措资金
常州	城市中低收入住房困难家庭、新就业人员和外来务工人员等	低保、特困家庭按使用面积1元/m²收，其他中低收入家庭按建筑面积3.5元/m²收，差额部分由政府补贴	政府组织建设，把经济适用房和公共廉租房转化为公租房；由保障房收储管理中心租赁社会房源给保障家庭居住	政府通过财政支出提供实物配租和租金补贴

4 城市空余房住宅转化为公租房的优点

4.1 提高租户的责任意识，保护房屋所有者的利益

从法律角度来看，产权不在政府手中，就意味着房屋产权所有者可以作为一个法律主体维护自己的权益，提高租户的责任意识，防止租户损坏房屋。如果公租房归政府所有，那么租户损坏住宅和社区的行为就只能予以行政处罚，甚至因为法不责众而不了了之。明确权责主体不仅能够保护房屋所有者的权益，还有利于保障公租房社区的公共利益。另外，利用已有的空余房屋为公众提供公租房还可以减少对房地产租赁市场的冲击，维持市场房租价格稳定，避免拥有大量空余房屋者大量破产，维护社会稳定。

4.2 利用"木桶效应"，提高城市居民整体居住水平

由于许多大城市的房屋租赁价格受到房价的影响依然较高，低收入群体通过市场租赁住房比较困难。如果将整个城市居民的居住水平视为一个水桶，那么低收入群体就是这只水桶的短板，因此，政府通过补贴等形式将市场房源转化为公租房，可以降低低收入群体租房难度，整体提高城市居民的居住水平。

4.3 保持农民工应对风险的能力，推进新型城镇化建设

由于农民工阶层具有乡村—城市双重身份，工作收入低且不稳定，因而在定居城市方面具有很大的不确定性和不稳定性；平时他们是租住在城中村的陋室或工厂宿舍，将来即使要定居城市，仍然难以负担经济适用房的费用。因此，入住政府提供的公租房可以让农民工保持较为灵活的居住形式，随时可以退出，很方便地就可以入住，有助于推动半城镇化渐进式地向新型城镇化转变。

4.4 提高房屋入住率，保持社区活力，增加税收

由于前几年的房地产投资热潮，相当一部分城市居民拥有两套及以上的住宅，许多城市居住小区房屋空置率很高。而随着最近房地产市场的降温，许多楼盘又有大量住宅销售不出去，加剧了房屋空置率。在这类社区，十分缺乏人气和商机。2013 年我国城镇住宅市场的整体空置率达 22.4％。共计约 4898 万套。IMF 驻中国代表在 2015 年 4 月的研究报告中也提到："中国住房供应过剩遍及全国，在较小城市和中国东北部尤其明显[10]。"如果能够通过政府补贴将这些空置住宅转化为公租房，则有利于提高其社区活力，支撑公共服务设施，既让租户获益，又让原来居住在这里的居民获益。由此创造的商机和公租房租赁者收入的提高也可以提高政府税收，弥补部分财政补贴的缺口。

4.5 拯救房地产市场，优化二次分配

将多余的房屋出租是多套住宅所有者保护资产价值的重要手段。民间自发的房屋出租分散、租期参差不齐，房租较贵，农民工一般是租不起的，导致大量房源空置。如果政府能够设立统一的交易平台，收储民间住房，通过政府补贴的形式统一出租给符合条件的中低收入群体，就可以激活房租租赁市场，并为房地产市场消化存量。政府的住房补贴也是缩小收入差距的重要手段。当然，这种住房福利是建立在政府具有雄厚财力的基础上，如长三角、珠三角等发达地区的城市可以将财政支出的重心转移到民生上，提高对低收入群体的房屋补贴。从西方发达国家的经验来看，欧洲自第二次世界大战以来就建立了完善的福利制度，民生支出占政府财政支出的比重很大，虽然经历了数次削减福利，但政府对于低收入群体的住房补贴仍然保留下来了，因为这项福利对于社会稳定和城市发展有着重要意义。

4.6 限制城市蔓延，保护耕地及生态环境

国内城市经过十几年的高速发展，在空间上已经出现过度蔓延的情况，建设用地占用了大量优质耕地和具有重要生态功能的山川林地。国内现有的公租房模式主要是政府投资建设新的公租房，仍需扩张城市用地。通过对现有空余房地产的二次开发，可以在不增加城市建设用地的前提下增加公租房的供应，有利于保护基本农田和生态环境。

5　城市空余住宅转化为公租房的阻力

5.1　法律缺失

现在国内还没有支持商品房转变为公租房的法律法规，导致国内此类公租房建设缺乏法律支持和统一管理，虽然一些地方政府已经开始积极尝试收储社会住宅作为公租房房源，但是缺乏更高层面的指导，难以进行推广。

5.2　市场惯性

因为中国的城镇化仍处于快速发展阶段，导致住宅的刚性需求居高不下，对公租房的需求很大，而一些大中城市的商品住房多为大户型，价格较高，不太适合作为公租房房源。供不应求的市场局面会提高商品房转化为公租房的成本。

5.3　路径依赖

原有的"城中村＋经济适用房"的保障房建设思路在许多城市仍然被沿用。现阶段农民工和城市贫民的居住需求在城中村里就得到了满足，对高质量的公租房需求较弱，即形成一种低端居住的路径依赖。相信随着农民工收入和对生活质量要求的提高，社会对于公租房的需求将不断提升。

5.4　资金问题

现在国内的地方政府大多负债累累，税收增速不断降低，而房价的泡沫还未被排除。如果地方政府按照市场价格补贴公租房，会承受巨大的财政压力。就现阶段来看，只能循序渐进，以新建为主，存量转化为辅。因为政府建设公租房的成本不必考虑地价，而且近期建材产能过剩，楼房建设成本较低，政府直接投资建设公租房的成本较低，且不受房地产市场泡沫的影响。

6　对城市空余住宅转化为公租房的几点建议

6.1　完善法律法规，为空余住房转化为公租房提供保障

国家应该出台专门的保障性住房的法律法规，对国内的保障房建设进行统一指导和规范管理，并为空余住房转化为公租房提供法律依据，避免一些不必要的纠纷。

6.2　政府提供财政补贴，保护房屋所有者的利益

由于产权不在政府手中，因此政府除了要补贴租户，还必须要保障房屋所有者的合法权益。政府收储社会空余住宅时必须按市场价支付房租，租户可按支付能力缴纳租金，差价由政府承担。政府也可以用其他优惠政策（例如容积率优惠等）换取房地产开发商低于市场价的房租。

6.3　循序渐进，量体裁衣，不可急于求成，造成过度负债

地方政府应根据自身财力进行城市空余住宅的吸纳和转化，由于国内一二线城市房屋租金普遍偏高，因此大规模进行转化会给地方政府造成较大财政负担。可以仿效常州，建立一套完善的保障

房收储管理机制，根据申请数量确定吸纳保障房的数量，避免公租房的空置和财政的过度开支。

6.4 开展多种形式的保障房建设，建立多梯度、全覆盖的住房保障体系

应建设公租房为主，经济适用法和廉租房为辅的多梯度、全覆盖的住房保障体系，根据地方实际情况，搭配三者的比例。仅仅依靠社会房屋资源，近期内也无法满足所有租房者的需求，还需要将政府投资建设与房屋补贴相结合，以扩大公租房供应数量。

7 总结

在保障房建设方面，我们可以向发达国家和地区学习，从国内成功案例吸取经验，但最终还是要落实到地方的实际情况。政府提出的存量转化为公租房的保障房发展方针，为我国的新型城镇化建设提供了一条可行的路径。我们有理由相信，随着保障房制度的不断完善，内地的"住房难"问题终将变为历史。杜甫诗云："安得广厦千万间，大庇天下寒士俱欢颜，风雨不动安如山。"解决住房问题将为维护社会稳定、推动中华民族的复兴作出极大贡献。

Study of Paths for the Transformation from City Surplus Realty to Public Rental Housing

Gao Yongbo

(School of architecture and planning ，Huazhong University of Science and Technology)

Abstract：After ten years of rapid development，the real estate market of China mainland is deeping in the problem of excess which is more and more serious. On the other hand，the low income group is hard to buy houses. That has become one of the most important problems of people's livelihood. This paper summarizes the successful experience of the construction of public rental housing in the world，analysis the difference between public rental housing and affordable housing. According to the present situation and the national real estate development of domestic city policy background，the paper explores the feasibility of the transformation from city surplus real estate to the public rental housing，and how the transformation promote migrant workers become residents of cities. If the government transfers city surplus real estate to public rental housing through the unified housing rental and housing subsidies，they can reduce the cost of the citizenization of migrant workers，and then improve the quality of urbanization China. Therefore，the transformation from the city surplus realty to public rental housing leading by the government，can open up a new path for the construction of public rental housing，and provide a new method to reduce the cost of Chinese urbanization.

Keywords：Surplus realty，Public rental housing，Feasibility，Migrant workers，Urbanization

参考文献：

[1] 李克强. 将一些存量房转为公租房和安置房 [N/OL]. 凤凰网. 2015 [2015-5-12] http：// house. ifeng. com.

[2] 陈林，董登新. 香港公租房模式浅析 [J]. 上海房地，2011，4：34-35.

[3] 崔晨. 新加坡住房保障 [J]. 北京观察，2010，8：16-17.

[4]　杨雁．美国公租房发展历程解读［J］．人民论坛，2012，11：247-249.

[5]　汪建强．浅析英国公租房租金制度及其对我国的启示［J］．价格理论与实践，2012，12：40-41.

[6]　杨曦．重庆与香港公租房制度的对比研究及启示［C］．规划创新：2010 中国城市规划年会论文集，2010，10.

[7]　陶承洁，吴立伟．对当前公租房规划建设问题的思考［J］．现代城市研究，2011，9：34-35.

[8]　常州部分公租房即将到期，八成愿把房子租给政府［N/OL］．新华网．2015［2015-4-29］.

[9]　袁业飞．公共租赁房：准备好了吗？［J］．中华建设，2010，8：18-23.

[10]　　IMF 关注中国楼市空置率：住房供应过剩遍及全国［OL］．珠海新闻网，2015［2015-5-11］．http：//www.zhnews.net/yaowen/149015.jhtml.

广州保障性住房的困境与出路——基于生活质量的视角

陈婷婷[1]　魏宗财[2]

（1. 香港理工大学建筑与房地产系；2. 香港大学城市规划及设计系）

摘要：我国保障性住房正处于大规模建设时期，已初步解决了部分低收入家庭的住房难题，但在建设和管理方面存在很多困境和不足，这导致保障房住区居民的生活质量并不高。广州作为我国最早实施保障性住房政策的城市之一，在提升居民生活质量方面已取得了初步的成效，但仍存在一些问题。通过长期跟踪研究广州市金沙洲新社区、大塘聚德花苑、天河广氮花园及荔湾芳和花园等典型保障房小区的发展，并于 2013 年对上述保障房小区的居民、政府管理人员及社区综合服务中心的工作进行了问卷调研和深入访谈，对其保障性住房的建设现状及存在的生活质量问题进行研究，并进一步从组织管理架构、资金供应和土地来源等深层次机制进行探讨，这对完善全国正如火如荼开展的保障性住房建设及相应的城市住房保障政策体系的完善具有重要意义。

关键词：保障房住区，生活质量，广州

1　引言

当前，解决中低收入群体的住房困难已成为国家和地方政府工作议程的"重中之重"。2014 年 3 月国家颁布的《国家新型城镇化规划（2014～2020 年）》将城镇化上升为国家战略，该规划提出稳步推进保障性住房等城镇基本公共服务覆盖全部常住人口，完善基础设施和公共服务设施，打造宜人、舒适的城市环境。

实际上，中国保障性住房正处于大规模建设时期，已初步建立了针对不同收入人群的保障房管理办法，解决了部分低收入家庭的住房难题。但在保障房政策实施的过程中，全国许多城市由于过度重视短期内保障房的建设数量，致使多数保障房住区都布局在偏远的郊区，公共服务设施配套严重滞后，建设后的管理方面仍存在"空白"，职住不平衡，生活成本提升等[1]，进而导致保障房住区居民的生活质量并不高。

广州作为我国最早实施保障性住房政策的先锋城市之一，在提升居民生活质量方面已取得了初步的成效，但仍存在一些上述的类似问题。笔者从 2010 年起就长期跟踪研究广州市保障房小区的发展，并于 2013 年对金沙洲新社区、大塘聚德花苑、天河广氮花园及荔湾芳和花园四个典型保障房小区的居民、政府管理人员及社区综合服务中心的工作进行了问卷调研和深入访谈，以深入了解保障房小区的建设现状及存在的居民生活质量问题，并进一步从组织管理架构、资金供应和土地来源等深层次机制进行探讨，这对完善全国正如火如荼开展的保障性住房建设及相应的城市住房保障政策体系具有重要意义。

2　保障性住区居民的生活质量分析框架与研究设计

2.1　保障性住区居民生活质量分析框架

城市生活质量是当前国际城市研究的一个热点，也是目前城市政府和居民密切关注的焦点之一。在 20 世纪 60 年代国际学者开始着手研究"生活质量"，并在随后几十年中蓬勃发展，这对居民及其生活的社区的长远福祉有着深远的影响[2]。当前，生活质量概念涵盖的范围包括：环境质量、安全、卫生、经济承受能力、睦邻友好、便捷性，以及邻里设施的情况，如公园、广场、人行

道、商店和餐馆等[3]。但需要提出的是,虽然"生活质量"这一词汇被广泛地运用到城市研究领域[3~6],但至今仍未形成既定的理论框架和统一的定义[7]。但一个广为采用的生活质量的分析框架包括客观环境及居民在生活中通过自身的居住体验感知居住环境和评价社区品质。

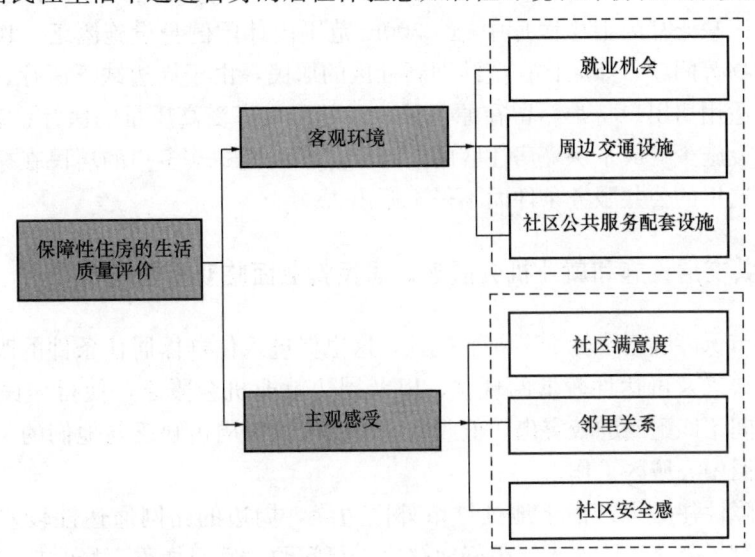

图1 城市生活质量评价的概念框架

本研究是面向居住在保障房住区的低收入群体。与其他社会群体不同,低收入群体更加需要公共服务设施、公共交通设施等等[8],故生活质量的概念框架偏重公共产品的供给及居民的主观感受,具体通过两方面的指标评价:一是客观环境方面,主要包括周边公共交通设施、公共服务设施、就业机会等;二在主观感受方面,主要的方面包括生活满意度及安全感。

2.2 研究设计

笔者通过长期跟踪研究广州市金沙洲新社区、大塘聚德花苑、天河广氮花园及荔湾芳和花园等典型保障房小区的发展,并基于上述构建的保障房居民生活质量分析框架,于2013年对上述保障房小区的居民、政府管理人员及社区综合服务中心的工作进行了问卷调研和深度访谈,共计入户调查和随遇调查636户家庭,有效问卷580份,并采用滚雪球抽样法每个小区选取20位居民进行深度访谈,以期了解保障房小区建设、管理以及评价居民入住小区后的生活质量现状等。

3 广州保障房住区建设存在的困境——基于生活质量的视角

3.1 区位偏僻,公共服务设施建设严重滞后

从全市尺度上看,广州市已建成和正在建设的保障性住区分散布局在广州中心城区的外围地区;但从小尺度来看,保障性住区在大塘、同德围、花地大道、棠下等局部地区又呈"集聚"的态势。实际上,随着广州市建成区地快速扩张蔓延,广州新建保障房住区的空间分布也随之向外围蔓延,特别是2007年后的保障房住区主要在更加远离中心城区的外围布局。据与相关负责部门的访谈,保障住房区逐步外移的态势主要受现状"土地财政"制度的影响,即政府通常将中心城区地价较高的地块拍卖出让,以获取巨大的土地收益,而将大多数的保障性住房项目布局于地价便宜的外围地带。

较为偏远的区位致使交通和生活不便一直是广州保障房住区居民所面临的最大"瓶颈"。由于广州市现有和正在建设的保障房社区主要位于中心城区的外围,周边严重缺乏公共服务设施,居民

必须返回中心城区去享受城市的公共服务。尽管近年来广州市在保障房住区的硬件配套设施方面不断完善和提高，但仍未能很好地满足日常需求。据调查发现，中小学、幼儿园、医院、体育健身等基本的公共服务设施较为匮乏。以广氮花园为例，截至 2013 年调研时，存在社区内缺乏幼儿园等教育设施，周边地区缺乏社区卫生医疗中心、500m 范围内休闲健身设施匮乏、1000m 范围内只有一处肉菜市场可购物等问题。如居住在金沙洲新社区的居民，由于周边缺乏医疗、教育等公共服务设施，80％的经济适用房用户将户籍留在原住址，以便回城享受高质量的医疗、教育服务。"上学难、就医难、休闲设施少"成了保障房住区的典型特点。大概 200 多户的居民在搬进来金沙洲新社区后因为难以适应这里的公共服务条件而不得不搬出去。

3.2　住区周边公共交通设施和就业机会匮乏，居民就业面临双重困境

近年来，广州市保障区建设标准不断地提升，这也促进入住群体居住条件的改善，但入住后周边公共交通设施的缺乏及可达性较低的现状，以及周边就业机会匮乏，使得居民的生活满意度较低。居住与就业空间不匹配问题较突出，低收入家庭由于社区周边缺乏与他们的工作技能相匹配的工作岗位，不得不回中心城区工作。

四个调研的保障性住房小区由于地处城市郊区边缘，周边的路网通达性较差，以广氮花园为例，即使其周边增设了公交线路亦未能很好地解决出行问题，反而加重高峰时期出城和进城的交通压力。根据问卷调查发现，居民认为搬进保障房社区后，对交通条件最不满意，仅有 5％的居民对现状交通较为满意。其中以金沙洲新社区最为最突出，居民的平均单程通勤时间由搬入前的 36 分钟上升至 90 分钟。实地调研发现，虽然仅有 20％的居民入住保障房后就业状态发生了改变，但居民在就业方面面临双重困境，以金沙洲新社区为例，一方面该社区 500m 范围内只有一个公交站，居民前往市中心至少要换乘 2 次公交或地铁，每天通勤时间在 3 小时及以上，故高额的通勤成本严重影响居民的生活质量；另一方面，金沙洲新社区周边的地区以居住楼盘为主，适合居民的劳动密集型就业机会缺乏，居民的再就业率很低，这也是当前住区居民失业率较高的主要原因。

3.3　住区邻里关系比较薄弱

当前，广州的保障房住区的居民主要包括拆迁安置户、经济适用房居民及廉租房居民等。但他们之间存在的隔阂，特别是业主（拆迁安置户、经济适用房居民）与廉租住户之间。虽然经济适用房居民对同区的廉租房住户有些同情和理解，但由于廉租房住户的日常生活中的一些不良习惯（如高空掷物、破坏公共桌椅、乱扔垃圾及社区时常发生的盗窃等），对他们持有一定的戒备心理。在平时，经适房的住户与廉租房住户来往不密切。如何促进不同社会阶层人群的良性互动，是保障房住区社区可持续发展和融入其他广州市社区急待解决的问题。

另外，根据金沙洲新社区金沙街家庭综合服务中心一位工作人员反映，住区的居民对周边孤寡老人缺乏关怀，在金沙洲社区至今出现了几例孤寡老人病死在家中无人知晓的情况，孤寡老人行动不便，很少与周围人群互动交往。像孤寡老人和残疾人这样的群体，大多采用集中模式独立安置在廉租房片区中，是使得他们与其他群体缺乏互动交流的主要原因。

3.4　居民安全感和满意度有待提升

除了住房室内环境的改善，住区公共空间的物质条件也是居民较为关注的方面。在公共空间的使用方面，据调研发现，居民对公共空间的使用率较高，在下午和周末的闲暇时间，常常可见到居民聚集在社区的公共空间交流或者进行娱乐休闲活动。但居民缺乏对公共空间的环境维护意识，随处可见烟头及其他垃圾；部分居民素质差，经常有高空掷物等破坏社区公共环境的行为，这也是居民抱怨较多的地方。

在保障房住区内部，经济适用房居民与廉租房居民对社区环境的满意度存在较大的差异。约86％的居住在经济适用房的调查样本对社区环境和社区建设持有较高的满意度，这很大程度上要归因于自有产权所带来的稳定感和安全感。而许多廉租房居民的满意度相对较低，这主要由于保障房住区主要采用了商品房小区的物业管理模式，管理费、垃圾费等新增的条目令住房开支陡然上升。95％的廉租房调查样本认为自身面临着管理费比租金还要昂贵的境况。

4 广州保障房住区生活质量较低的深层次原因分析

实际上，造成上述保障房住区生活质量较低的表层原因之下，隐藏着各级政府在住房保障责任、事权划分、财政支出分担、土地资源支撑等方面的深层问题，故需要从深层次的制度因素上去挖掘。Chiu也认为影响住房保障政策实施结果的关键因素主要包括三项：其一，政府的管治结构；其二，提供住房保障所需的资金；其三，保障性住房建设所需的土地。笔者以此为分析框架对保障房住区生活质量存在的问题进行深入研究。[9]

4.1 组织管理架构有待完善

对于保障性住房的管理架构，广州市的管理主体包括：广州保障性住房办公室（以下简称"市住保办"），是局级事业单位，它由之前的住房解困办转变而来，主要职责是制定和执行保障房土地和年度计划，监督和管理保障房的发展等；以及稍后成立的由市长担任组长的广州市保障性住房建设管理领导小组，主要负责监督保障房的建设进度和及时解决重大问题，市住保办成为其执行机构，这提升了住房保障管理机构的行政管理层次。但在住房保障的实施运作中，广州住保办主要负责保障性住房的选址、建设、管理和监督方面，需要和规划局、国土局、发改委、民政局等其他部门一起讨论制定保障性住房的选址、相关规划、周边公共服务设施及公共交通设施的建设等。[1]

虽然市层面的组织管理力量很强，但当前广州住房保障在基层管理上力量十分薄弱，应对上级政府安排的任务"捉见肘襟"。当前保障性住房住户申请资格的审核需要依托当地的街道办、居委会协助。另外，广州市保障性住房建设管理领导小组的组成成员相对单一，主要是政府各部门的负责人，在保障性住房规划、相关政策制定方面公众参与程度较低，而公众也缺乏表达自己"话语权"的渠道。[1]这部分归因于广州市住保办从业人员偏少，有正式编制的人员不足60人，与香港房屋署约8000人的日常工作人员数量相比，难以针对庞大的保障性住房的需求实施有效的管理。[1]尤其在中央政府"十二五"规划阶段，为了短时间内尽快满足低收入群体的住房需求，中央政府采取了计划经济时代的指标分摊式的安排，自上而下给各省份安排了年度需完成的任务，并与之签订了保障房建设目标责任书，以监督任务的完成情况，这实际上是保障性住房被纳入政绩考核体系；随后省政府与各城市政府也签订了住房保障目标责任书，将保障房建设任务进一步分配。但面对以数量为导向的保障房的大规模建设，保障性住区的质量得不到保障，其建成后管理方面存在"真空"，导致居民存在上述生活质量方面的诸多问题，特别是残疾人群体和低保困难户家庭。

4.2 缺乏稳定的资金来源

住房保障本质上属于国民收入再分配，目标在于调节社会公平和扶助弱势群体，由政府对社会财政的转移支付来实现[10]，这通常由中央政府在全国层面进行，而不是由地方政府承担。但在中国，依据国家在2007年后陆续颁布实施的《廉租住房保障办法》、《经济适用住房管理办法》、《公共租赁住房管理办法》等，中央政府将住房保障认定为"地方事权"，由地方政府承担住房保障的主要责任，故住房保障的财政支出以地方政府为绝对主导[10]，但与此同时，国家并未赋予相应的财权，即在财政预算并未考虑保障房建设的需要，致使地方政府在上级政府安排的大规模保障性住房建设任务面前存在较大困难。地方政府投入大量资金用于住房保障的建设,直接导致用于地方公共服务资金的减少,进而带来的公共服务水平降低,可能导致高收入、专业人员等对公共服务较为敏感的群体的逃离。故地方政府对住房保障实施的主动性很低。

当前,广州市保障性住房建设的主要资金来源是公积金增值收益、土地出让金净收益等。而这些来源均存在一定的变数,无法保证资金来源的长期性和稳定性。[1]另外,长期以来,各地方政府(包括广州市)对廉租房和经济适用房的建设缺乏足够的重视,一直未按国家政策要求足额提供土地出让金的 5% 用作保障房建设。[11]

4.3 缺乏稳定的土地供应支撑

在当前的制度环境下,土地出让的资金占地方政府财政收入的很大部分,而由于保障性住房的建设所需的土地都由政府无偿或低价供应。在地方政府对土地财政较为依赖的情况下,地方政府缺乏足够的积极性来推动保障性住房的建设。[1]为贯彻落实国家相关政策,加快保障房的建设进度,广州市于 2009 年颁布了《广州市保障性住房土地储备办法》,在国内建立了首个"双轨制"土地储备机制,明确保障性住房用地由市住保办独立储备,建立了"市区联动、以区为主"的住房保障土地储备制度,这些举措虽从一定程度上缓解了保障房用地的供应不足,但实际上,由于上述土地储备办法出台较晚,加上广州市的空间模式发展已从重视"增量"发展向注重"存量"规划转变,中心城区范围内已基本没有能用于保障房建设的闲置用地,只能在城市外围地区(如刚建成的龙归城等)储备用地。[1]

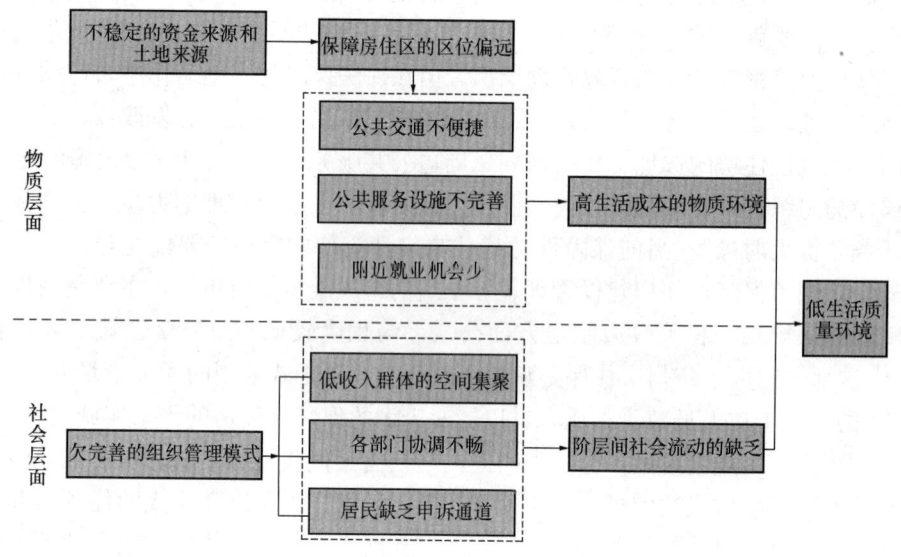

图 2　保障房居民低生活质量环境的形成机制

5　结论与讨论

同全国其他城市类似,当前广州保障性住房正在大规模建设时期,已取得了许多成绩。但研究发现,当前广州市住房保障停留在简单改善居民的居住条件的层面,只能有限度地提供低水平、最基本的保障,而且仍存在公共服务设施建设滞后、公交设施和就业机会匮乏等诸多问题。[1]笔者从组织管理架构、资金来源、土地支撑等深层次的制度层面对当前保障房住区存在的生活质量问题进行了深入挖掘,并建议广州在组织管理架构、资金投入模式、人居环境建设等方面改进完善,以进一步提高保障房住区居民的生活质量,具体来说:

在组织管理架构方面,进一步强化既有的住房保障部门的职能,将国土、规划、发改、财政等相关部门关于保障性住房的职能纳入，以确保广州市住房保障部门拥有更多的独立决策的权力，以减少部门协调间的"内耗"，及时响应保障性住房发展中遇到的挑战[1]。同时为满足日益增加的管理需求，应进一步增加人员编制以专责管理保障性住房社区，主要负责审核住户申请材料，执行有关指令、后期监督、收集居民意见、违规巡查和社区管理等工作。[12]

配备专项资金，探索"政企合建"模式。除国家要求的土地出让金的5%外，政府另外设置专项公共财政支出，专门用于保障性住房项目兴建和维护。为弥补政府投入的不足，建议进一步探索、规范、完善政府与企业合建保障性住房的制度，引导更多的社会资金参与建设[1]；另外，基于上述的分析，当前仅有廉租住房是基本保障公民住房权的住房救济，属于国民收入再分配范畴。而公共租赁住房、限价商品住房等都属于地方政府提供的公共服务范畴。因此，廉租住房的保障责任与财政支出应由中央政府承担。[10]

公共参与，营造"以人为本"的居住环境。保障房的建设不仅是提供给市民一个居所，更重要的是要提供一个舒服的居住环境。新建的保障房社区在选址上，充分尊重市民的需求，尽可能布局在交通和生活便捷的中心城区，建议将"三旧改造"的土地优先用于保障性住房建设；另外，在社区管理和社区文化的营造方面，建议设立"社区管理委员会"，让居民参与社区管理工作，增强居民的责任感和提高居民的归属感。[1]

当然，需要指出的是，任何国家或城市的住房政策都不可能是完美无缺的。而广州保障性住房的发展尚不足30年，若以2006年广州开始建设真正意义的"经济适用房"、"廉租房"算起，仅仅有9年的发展时间，故当前存在的问题和不足在所难免。下一步需立足于立身的实际，借鉴国内外保障性住房建设的成功经验，探索出一条具有较强可操作性的保障性住房建设道路。

Difficulties and Strategies of Affordable Housing in Guangzhou: the Perspective of Livability

Chen Tingting[1]　Wei Zongcai[2]

(1. Department of Building and Real Estate, The Hong Kong Polytechnic University;
2. Department of Urban Planning & Design, University of Hong Kong)

Abstract: The dramatic changes and rapid development of social housing in China have been widely advocated. Although the development process has been pushed very fast and the great efforts have been made to assist the urban household with housing difficulties, some practical issues in terms of quality of life have emerged in the implementation phrase. Imperfect management organization, limited financial support and rare land resources of Guangzhou still need to be improved in the long run. Through conducting investigation in Jinshazhou Garden, Jude Garden, Guangdan Garden and Fanghe Garden, and also interviewing the residents inside, government staffs, the paper argues that the establishment of exclusive management institution, the ownership of specific financial assets and "People Oriented" living environment are some feasible solutions for coping with current housing issues in Guangzhou, which may provide some reference for social housing development in other domestic cities.

Keyword: Social housing, Quality of life, Guangzhou

参考文献：

[1] 魏宗财，陈婷婷，孟兆敏等. 广州保障性住房的困境与出路——与香港的比较研究[J]. 国际城

市规划，2015，3(待刊).

[2] Myers D. Community-relevant measurement of quality of life：A focus on local trends [J]. Urban Affairs Quarterly，1987，23：108-125.

[3] Wheeler S. Planning sustainable and livable cities[M]. In：Gates R L. & Stout F. (eds.) The City Reader. London and New York，2001：487-495.

[4] Howley P，Scott M，Redmond D，et al. Sustainability versus liveability：an investigation of neighbourhood satisfaction[J]. Journal of Environmental Planning and Management，2009，52，847-864.

[5] Kaido K. Urban densities, quality of life and local facility accessibility in principal Japanese Cities[M]. In：Jenks M, Dempsey N. (eds.) Future Forms and Designs for Sustainable Cities. Oxford：Elsevior，2005：311-337.

[6] Smith T，Nelischer M，Perkrins N，et al. Quality of an urban community：a framework for understanding the relationship between quality and physical form[J]. Landscape and Urban Planning，1997，39，229-241.

[7] VCEC. Department of Sustainability and Environment，Inquiry into Enhancing Victoria's Liveability[M]. Melbourne：Victorian Competition and Efficiency Commission，2008.

[8] Knox P，Pinch S. Urban Social Geography：An Introduction[M]. Routledge，2014.

[9] Chiu R L H. Planning, land and affordable housing in Hong Kong[J]. Housing Studies，2007，22(1)：63-81.

[10] 齐慧峰，王伟强. 基于人口流动的住房保障制度改善. 城市规划，2015，(2)：31-37.

[11] 文林峰. 住房保障问题的再考察[R]/中国市长协会. 中国城市发展报告(2007). 北京：中国城市出版社，2007：253-263.

[12] Chen T T，Wong K W，Hui C M. The Development of Social Housing and Its Planning Implications in Guangzhou，China[M]. 2012 Yearbook of The Hong Kong Institute of Housing，2012. 146-153.

香港现有公共屋邨迈进可持续发展之路

陈少德　钟国存　区立基　卢颖妍　吴子杰　黄　盛

（香港房屋委员会）

摘要： 香港房屋委员会（房委会）是负责香港公共房屋的主要政府机构，其辖下租住公屋单位达 74 万个，为逾二百万居民提供居所。房委会配合时代变迁，应对社会不断转变的需求，致力令现有公共租住屋邨可持续发展。为此，房委会制定了全面的可持续发展策略，透过三个主要保养及改善计划：全方位维修计划、全面结构勘察计划，以及屋邨改善计划，达致可持续发展的目标。按此全面策略，房委会因应租户主要的关注和需求，主动进行维修、提升设施，妥善维修保养现有屋邨。要达到真正可持续发展，社区的支持故为重要，因此，房委会举办一系列推广活动及奖励计划，力求不断增进租户对这方面的认同及支持，以迈进可持续发展的生活模式。

关键词： 香港房屋委员会，公共租住屋邨，全方位维修计划，全面结构勘察计划，屋邨改善计划

1 引言

过去十年，有关可持续发展建筑物的研究不断，受惠于此，环保的设计概念、建筑方法及能源效益都取得长足进展。建筑业界把其中许多研究成果应用实践，使建筑物更加环保，不仅令碳足印减少，更可增加可持续发展的元素。香港房屋委员会（房委会）属于法定组织，负责规划、建造、管理及保养香港各类型公共房屋，在采用环保科技兴建新厦方面不逊于人。然而，要真正达到可持续发展，我们必须着重现有公共屋邨的生命周期。为维持 74 万个租住公屋单位的质素，同时兼顾可持续发展的原则，房委会制订全面维修保养和改善策略，内容涵盖全方位维修计划、全面结构勘察计划及屋邨改善计划。事实证明，这些计划能够延长现有公共屋邨的寿命，成效显著，更配合可持续发展的原则。不过，由于与可持续发展有关的因素，大多并非房委会能够直接控制，要真正达到可持续发展，单靠全面维修保养和改善策略，只收半功之效，余者须靠市民转变思想和生活模式。为此，房委会举办一系列讲座及推广活动，期望租户从中得到启发，实践可持续的生活方式。香港有二百万人住在公屋，房委会的日常运作及推广，不断促进香港社区的可持续发展。

2 为可持续发展制订全面维修保养和改善策略

可持续发展，是指当前的需要获得配合之余，日后的需要也不至于受影响。房委会矢志为低收入家庭提供优质房屋，贯彻可持续发展的理念，遂于现有公共租住屋邨实施全面的维修保养和改善策略，实践可持续发展的三大原则（图 1）。

2.1 全方位维修计划

房委会于 2006 年展开以客为本的全方位维修计划，主动为租户提供全面的服务，避免小维修问题变大。视乎其楼龄，全方位维修计划以五或十年为周期，三管齐下，为租户提供维修服务：（1）主动查找维修问题；（2）迅速响应租户提出的维修要求；（3）加强推广和教育方面的工作。全方位维修计划培训出一批家居维修大使，亲身前住公屋单位勘察室内状况，不用等到接获投诉或维修要求才回应。家居维修大使把勘察结果记录在电子记事本，再存放于房委特别为全方位维修计划研发的电脑系统内。小型维修工程会即场进行，至于较复杂的问题，家居维修大使会透过电子记事本发出施工通知单予维修承办商，以便迅速维修。为加强与租户沟通，房委会设立查询热线，由电

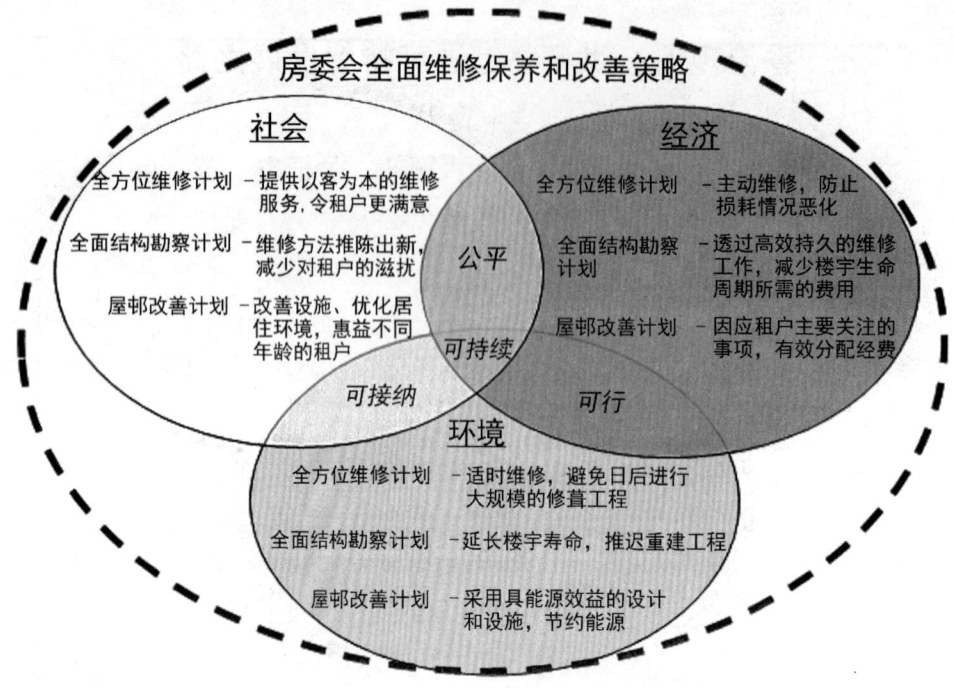

图 1　公共租住屋邨全面维修保养和改善策略

话查询中心提供服务支持，专责处理关于勘察预约、投诉及查询的来电。由电脑系统定期编制的报告，有助监察预约时间及维修服务。勘察结果和维修记录由电脑系统贮存，而房委会建立的综合资料库，有助翻查记录、进行深入分析，制订日后的维修保养策略。

家居维修大使勘察单位期间，会把握机会向租户讲解如何正确使用单位提供的装置和设施。为培养以客为本的文化，房委会为维修保养承办商举办研讨会和工作坊交流经验，并与屋邨管理咨询委员会（邨管咨委会）、区议会议员及租户定期开会，汇报进展、收集意见。为增加市民对全方位维修计划的认识，了解计划的意义，房委会设立维修保养教育中心和多个流动维修保养教育柜位，设置录像角，又摆放展板和建筑组件样办。此外，房委会在屋邨当眼位置播放由社会知名人士拍摄的宣传片，讲解如何妥善维修保养家居。

房委会全方位维修计划的维修策略成效卓著，能够从环境、经济及社会方面实践可持续发展的目标。环境方面，大规模修葺减少、公屋寿命延长，各方都受惠。经济方面，主动查找及解决小问题，能够避免小维修问题变大，借此节省生命周期的维修成本。社会方面，公屋损坏的地方及时维修，租户的居住环境更胜维修前，这点从租户的满意度可见一斑，自从全方位维修计划实施以来，超过80％租户感到满意。

2.2　全面结构勘察计划

全面结构勘察计划在 2005 年实施，为楼龄接近 40 年的屋邨进行全面结构勘察，勘察工作其后每 15 年进行一次。全面结构勘察计划，有系统及详细地勘察旧屋邨的结构状况，评估结构是否安全可予保留；及其保留的经济效益。房委会根据全面结构勘察的结果，特别制订修葺方案，使旧楼的楼龄最少延长 15 年。全面结构勘察一般包括以下六个步骤：

（1）桌面研究

全面结构勘察的资料研究范围包括维修历史及图则记录、设计的计算、以往的结构评核，以及过往的改善或加固工程记录，作出研究。而以往曾经大幅或多次修葺的地方将成为日后研究重点之一。

（2）目视勘测

目视勘测的范围包括所有公用及室外的地方。充裕的检测样本会对已租住单位的租户造成滋扰,为确保检测结果准确但又不扰民,实须制订具代表性的抽样方法(例如只对 5% 已有租户居住的单位进行检测)。若损耗情况因应工程质量、使用情况及效能表现不同而大有差异,检测的次数需增加来深入了解损耗的范围及严重性。我们会翻查维修记录并与租户会面,务求掌握损毁的由来及过往的问题和维修工作。除了把目视的结构损毁记录在案,目测工作有助探究导致结构损耗的症结和问题所在。

(3)测试

我们根据桌面研究及目视勘测所得,以确定测试项目来深入探究结构构件的状况,确定造成损毁的根本成因。破坏性测试包括钢筋锈蚀量度、混凝土芯抗压测试、碳化深度测量及氯化物含量分析。为对租户的影响减至最小,破坏性测试集中在公用地方及空置单位进行。无损测试则会在公用地方、空置及非空置单位进行。这些测试包括混凝土含水量测试以厘定渗漏程度、确定离层及剥落位置的空心混凝土检测、评估锈蚀风险的半电池电位法测试,以及了解钢筋锈蚀速度的锈蚀电流测量。

(4)楼宇使用年期的评估

按照欧洲规范 1990:2002[1](EN 1990:2002[1])对"可逆极限状态"所下的定义,结构性损坏如能在采取适当合理价值的行动后可逆转,该项损坏则可视为可接受的损坏。反之,当楼宇的结构性损坏未能在合乎经济效益的情况下恢复或维修,该项损坏已超出"可逆极限状态",即已是使用年期的终结。根据一个设计良好的测试计划所取得的足够数据,便可进行楼宇使用年期评估,从而制订出可持续性的维修方案,延长高楼龄楼宇使用年期的工序如下:

- 根据目前的结构状况,评核各个结构构件的剩余承载力及结构稳定性;
- 评核损耗的严重程度、幅度及性质。找出损耗的原因及机制,并评估影响损坏速度的元素,例如混凝土保护层、砂浆层厚度,以及物料强度;
- 根据目测的数据、现有氯化物含量、碳化深度及目前的锈蚀速度,估算各组结构构件日后的损耗速度,并考虑不同维修方案对日后损耗速度的影响;
- 评估将来结构的稳定性及结构构件在适当保养一下的剩余承载力。

(5)延长楼宇使用年期

结构损耗的过程复杂,涉及的元素众多,彼此间又互相牵扯。了解个中因由,对症下药,对延长高楼龄楼宇的使用年期,至为关键。房委会着重服务为本的文化,明白维修工作成功与否,大大取决于租户满意程度。租户虽然享用有关服务,却不一定理解维修工作须顾及长期质素或成本问题,他们更为关注处理维修的手法如何、维修工作是否造成不便(如尘埃、噪声、维修所需时间、维修次数多寡等问题),以及工人是否准时及有礼。因应这些挑战,房委会在全面结构勘察计划中,开发及实践多个可持续及以客为本的维修方法,如使用水力清刮技术来减低拆卸混凝土造成的噪声,又运用电渗透防水系统处理渗水问题。受惠于全面结构勘察计划及其他定期维修及改善项目,高楼龄公屋楼宇的结构得以保持,使用年期得以如图 2 般延长:

(6)监察效能表现

全面结构勘察计划致力通过搜集数据、积累知识和经验,使维修工作更具成效。为此,房委会长期监察维修工作的成效,借以完善日后的维修策略。监察方式包括目视勘测、混凝土含水量测试、无损测试及与访问租户。房委会根据监察结果调整并完善既定的维修方法,适当考虑到环境、成效、生命周期成本,以及对租户造成滋扰因素。

2.3 屋邨改善计划

全面结构勘察计划针对高楼龄公屋楼宇的结构可用年期,屋邨改善计划则致力提升高楼龄公屋楼宇的设备及设施,配合居民目前的需要,为他们提供安全舒适的居住环境。为加强社区的凝聚

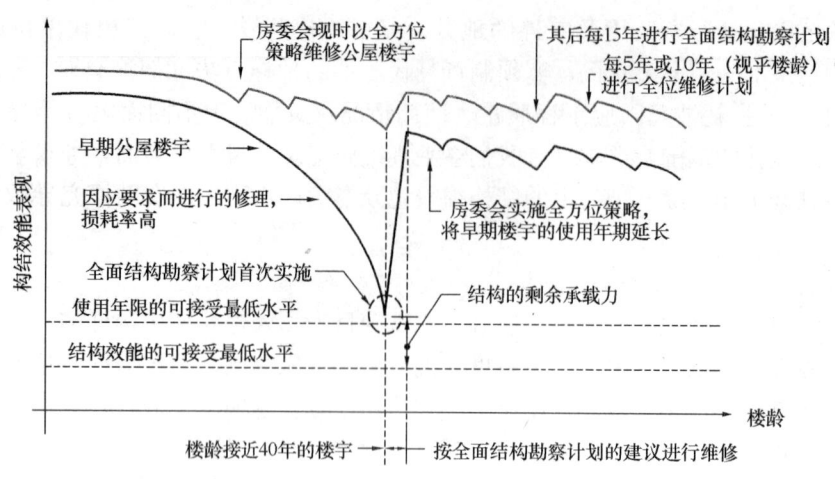

图 2　延长公屋楼宇的使用年期

力，屋邨改善计划不以设施为本，而奉行"以人为先"及"活动为本"的原则。在概念设计阶段，房委会透过租户意见调查及屋邨管理咨询委员会咨询工作，了解市民对某屋邨的主要关注事项。为制订以人为本的可持续改善计划，房委会研究及分析屋邨人口特征及独有环境。屋邨人口日渐老化，有见及此，房委会特别设计公用地方和非住宅处所来配合租户新需要。康乐设施（如长者健身器材）愈趋多元化以配合不同年龄群组所需。为使居民有更多机会聚首谈天，屋邨的公共空间重新设计。我们明白长者及残疾人士有特殊需要，遂于综合行人网络提供全天候通道，加建全新升降机及斜道等无障碍通道，便利租户出入。为缔造舒适的居住环境，我们翻新楼宇外墙及公共地方，又在单位内加设浴室安全扶手等设施，方便长者租户。此外，公屋楼宇的设计更加环保节能。举例来说，我们在低层机房大楼及非住宅处所的顶层建设绿化天台，除减低室内热能吸收，同时亦可美化周边环境。我们又推出节能措施，在大厦走廊装设具能源效益的照明装置。透过综合计划，老化的屋宇装备装置逐步更换及现代化，减低楼宇生命周期的总成本。在升降机现代化计划下，新安装的节能升降机与现有的升降机相比，能源成本节省逾 30%。屋邨改善计划奉行"以人为先"和"活动为本"的原则，不单使社区添上新姿，更使邻里关系更为紧密，居民不分年龄背景，人人安居乐业。

3　可持续发展的生活方式

为达到可持续发展的目标，房委会推出各项环保措施，竭力在日常运作中推动环保，又为住户制订并落实可持续发展的生活方式。社区的参与不可或缺，因此，房委会举办不同环保活动、教育推广及不同类型的比赛，向住户推广可持续发展的生活，加强他们在这方面的认识，又鼓励全民响应，减少浪费，循环再用物品，身体力行，保护环境。

（1）绿乐无穷在屋邨

为提高屋邨租户的环保意识，房委会推行"绿乐无穷在屋邨"长期社区环保计划，举办植树日和回收比赛等一系列教育暨社区活动。这些活动由房委会与区内环保团体合办，每年为约 30 个屋邨设计环保措施在邨内推行，不仅切实推动环保，更能促进社区联系。

（2）厨余回收

要减少厨余，公众教育和参与不可或缺。2011 年 12 月，房委会在两个屋邨内设置厨余处理机，推行厨余回收试点计划。计划逐步扩展至 14 个屋邨，其中有些在邨外把厨余循环再造，转化为鱼粮，亦有些在邨内进行微生物循环再造处理。截至 2014 年 3 月底，登记参与该计划的租户逾 3 000 人。为鼓励租户响应，房委会在全港屋邨举办连串减少浪费食物的活动，例如厨余有"宝"创意食谱比赛、光"碟"行动，又在全港屋邨的房屋资讯频道广播名为《一人一个惜食行动》和《轻食煮意》的短片。

（3）屋邨树木大使和社区植树

房委会招募逾 650 名住户出任屋邨树木大使，负责推广树艺。为增加这批大使的知识，培养他们对树艺的兴趣，房委会特别举办树木管理培训课程。借着社区植树运动，租户可一尝社区植树的乐趣，在邨内特设的花圃共享收成。租户的归属感大大增加，邻里关系亦见紧密。

（4）可回收废物交换奖励计划

为吸引更多租户加入废物回收的行列，房委会在全港屋邨设置收集柜台，鼓励租户捐出可回收的家居废物，换取一些小礼品。

（5）家居废物源头分类计划

房委会积极响应废物回收的工作，全力推行家居废物源头分类计划。2013～2014 年度，房委会共收集了 33618t 废纸、胶樽、铝罐和衣物，又积极参与环境保护署推行的各项计划，回收充电池、悭电胆、电脑等。

（6）绿化研究

我们推出多项先导计划，务求多管齐下，推动可持续发展的工作。例如，我们推出绿化先导计划，收集多余的年橘在年内循环再植。计划推出以来，回收的年橘逾千盆。

4　结语

房委会多管齐下，致力为公共屋邨迈进可持续发展之路。租户年纪渐大，现有公屋单位亦逐渐老化，有见及此，房委会透过三大主要措施：全方位维修计划、全面结构勘察计划和屋邨改善计划，将辖下的高楼龄屋邨打造得可持续发展。房委会心系 200 万租户，正因如此，所有维修方案及改进工程采取"以客为本"的原则，回应租户的关注和需要。房委会肩负重任，全力推动及促进可持续发展的生活方式，通过教育和推广活动，改变租户固有的看法及做法，采纳可持续发展的生活模式。尽管前路挑战重重，但房委会坚持不懈，致力使公共租住屋邨在环保、社会和经济三方面续创佳绩，带动全港迈进可持续发展的生活方式。

Rallying to Sustainability of Existing Public Housing Estates in Hong Kong

Chan S. T. , Chung K. C. Dauny, Au L. K. Bosco
Lo W. Y. Winnie, Ng T. K. Stanley, wouf S. Alan
(Hong Kong Housing Authority)

Abstract: The Hong Kong Housing Authority (HKHA) is the major government institution in Hong Kong for public housing with a stock of 740,000 public rental housing (PRH) units accommodating over two million people. To sustain the aging PRH estates while coping with the changing needs of the community over time, the HKHA has established a holistic strategy rallying to sustainability through three major maintenance and improvement programmes: the Total Maintenance Scheme (TMS), the Comprehensive Structural Investigation Programme (CSIP) and the Estate Improvement Programme (EIP). Through this holistic strategy, the aged estates are well maintained and rejuvenated through proactive repairs and upgrades of facilities addressing tenants' key concerns and needs. As the community support is crucial in achieving true sustainability, the HKHA, through a series of education programmes, promotional campaigns and incentive schemes，is constantly driving fundamental changes in tenants' attitudes and behaviours towards a more sustainable living style.

Keywords：Hong Kong Housing Authority，Public rental housing，TMS，CSIP，EIP

参考文献：

[1]　BSI．BS EN 1990：2002 Eurocode – Basis of structural design. British Standards Institute，2002.

The Changing Occupancy Profile of GSIS Metro Homes

Jocelyn Rivera-Lutap

(Department of Architecture and Interior Design, College of
Architecture and Fine Arts, Polytechnic University of the Philippines)

Abstract: The GSIS Metro Homes a 4-storey walk-up condominium buildings were built with the primary intention of providing affordable housing for the government employees. The primary intention of providing housing for one household was also altered since there are a number of units that are being leased to students as bed spacers. Some of the units are used entirely for bed spacers where the unit owners live in a different house or sometimes the homeowners would be living with the student lessees. The homeowners lease space in their units to augment for their amortization in the bank or the house rentals. In whatever case what is often not met in this kind of living condition are the necessary facilities that would make the units conducive to the studies of the student. The change of the occupancy profile would take a toll on the intended use of the building and an in-depth study of the performance-in-use of the project needs to be investigated.

Keywords: Occupancy rate, Student housing, Performance-in-use

1 Introduction

GSIS Metro homes housing project was a partnership between Government Security Insurance System (GSIS) and New San Jose Builders Inc. (NSJBI). The medium-rise walk up housing project was forged to address the housing backlog in the City of Manila. GSIS which is the registered owner of several parcels of land with an area of more or less 57,642. 26m² covered by separate titles entered into an agreement with NSJBI a duly licensed general engineering and building contractor with the technical, financial capacity to develop the subject property and constructed as a turn-key project, 4-storey walk-up condominium buildings. The project was aptly named as GSIS Metro homes consisting of fifty (50) buildings with 3,400 units. Through the GSIS Board Resolution No. 87 dated March 5, 1992 it has provided NSJBI authorization to undertake the development and construction of the project with no cost and no expenses whatsoever to GSIS except to undertake the financing needs to qualified buyers for the acquisition of the completed condominium. The priority of owning a unit was given to the Philippine government employees and were automatically members of GSIS. The project will be done in three (3) phases Phase I eight (8) buildings, Phases II, III-A and III-B forty two (42).

2 The Study Area-GSIS Metro homes

In 2004, a study on the occupancy rate of the medium-rise housing project in the District 6 of the City of Manila provided a clearer insight on the depth and breadth of the occupancy rate as a measure of performance-in-use of the housing project[1]. Phase 1 was completed with 8 buildings - buildings 1-4 and 6 having 72 units each while building 5 with 77 units and buildings 7 and 8 with 76 units each with a sub-total of 589 units. Phase II was converted into a Hostel which eventually closed in 2002 to re-open again in 2013 as a school building for the Polytechnic University of the

Philippines. For the third phase only III-A was realized with 7 buildings units varying from 76,77 to 78 with a sub-total of 542 units.

Figure 1. GSIS Metrohomes and its immediate vicinity. Within the 200 meter radius around GSIS Metro Homes are the Colleges of Architecture and Fine Arts, Engineering, Communications and the Institute of Technology of the Polytechnic University of the Philippines (PUP). There are approximately more than 6,000 students in these colleges. 400 meter radius from the housing project on the western part is the College of Communication and the Graduate School of PUP near another public higher education institution – Eulogio Amang Rodriguez Institute of Science and Technology "EARIST" which has a population of around 5,000 students from secondary, tertiary, technical vocational and graduate students. On the eastern side of GSIS Metro Homes is the main campus of the PUP with a population of 20,000 at any time which is comprised of students, staff and faculty. The means of transportation in the area would vary from the tribikes (manually operated bicycle with a carriage that can hold 3 passengers at a time), tricycles (motorcycle with carriage the can accommodate at least 4 in the carriage and a back rider of the driver), taxis, and other public transportation such as the jeepneys, buses, train and the elevated light railway transit. Which make the housing development accessible.

The primary intention of housing development is to provide a single unit for one household. A usual household for a Filipino family would have 5 members. The average area per unit is 43.87m². which is an acceptable in terms of the habitable house based on the World Health Organization standard of 18m². house with 4 occupants. The project was planned with a total of 50 buildings and 3,400 units but only 15 building were actually built with 1137 units. Shown on Figure 2. The 3 phases of GSIS Metro Homes From total units of 589 for Phase I, in 2003 the total occupancy rate is 463 or 78.96%, 23 or 3.90% unoccupied and 11 or

Figure1　GSIS mertohomes and
its immediate vicinity[1]

14.47% unsold. While in Phase III-A of the total 452 units the occupancy rate is 80.90%, 20 units or 3.69% unoccupied and 50 units unsold.

3　Polytechnic University of the Philippines as a Catalyst of Change

The Polytechnic University of the Philippines is one of the biggest public higher education institutions in the country with a total of more than 60,000 students in Manila campus alone to date. Since 2008 the university has expanded adding the Institute of Technology housing vocational technology courses and the population of non-traditional education and graduate student population has grown over the period of 10 years. The surge in number brought about the changing landscape of the areas around the university. Hasmin Hostel is a 7 story building operated by the university. 3 floors are dedicated for students and employees occupy the 4th to 6th floors. The ground floor is rented out to a 24/7 convenience store and review centers and the rest of the floors are utilized as classrooms for the College of Tourism, Hospitality and Transportation Management and the top, 7th floor has a multi-purpose room and VIP air-conditioned rooms. There are 25 rooms, each room accommodates 4 students with ensuite bathroom.

4　Literature Review

4. 1　Medium-Rise Housing

Residential use is the largest single category of land use embracing perhaps 80 percent of the total built-up area of the metropolis [2]. The function of a residential area is to support the needs of the residents in a way that also further such community goals as environmental quality and efficiency in the government services. Neighborhoods serve the following functions [3]. a) shelter, which encompasses the traditional concern of housing and basic services, such as water, sewer and electricity; b) security, providing a safe and stable , and ordered setting free of danger from traffic, violence, criminal actions, and other physical and psychological hazards; c) child-rearing, facilitating transmission of values through family, neighbors, peer group, churches, community organizations, schools and play space; d) symbolic identification, providing a sense of place, belonging, pride and satisfaction to the resident; e) social interaction, providing personal associations through social networks, organization, and physical facilities; f) leisure, providing recreation, entertainment, cultural and educational facilities and program and open space.

Homeownership provides a feeling of security and personal achievement, and therefore contributes higher self-esteem[4]. Several studies also show a relationship between homeownership and housing satisfaction which provides explicit information on whether the expectations of the owners are met. The primary considerations of the occupants in their decision to purchase/lease/rent unit were given a ranking on the basis of the following considerations, to wit: 1st - *economics* (e. g. acquisition cost per unit, costly rental , transport cost to work place and the like), 2nd-*resource/amenities* [e. g. ventilation, water, lighting and power, circulatory space (roads, hallways, stairs)]; 3rd *accessibility* (e. g. work place, school, market/ malls, places of worship, parks / recreation, health facilities, transport facilities); 4th *physical properties* [e. g. Aesthetics of the building, availability of living space, provision of open spaces, service area (laundry/ drying area)], and 5th *social properties* [e. g. Equity (ownership, distribution), Health, Safety/ Security, Family Solidarity, Life Support place, Planning and Management of housing and the like][1]. In the quotation of Gunnar Myrdal, "it becomes expensive if you do not have it" and economics ranking as one number consideration when the housing units were either purchased or rented cannot be overemphasized.

The "performance concept" as espoused by Gibson stands in sharp contrast to a view of architecture simply based on a philosophical, stylistic or aesthetic pursuit by designers[5]. The performance of the building can be evaluated through a series of assessments. Most homeowners consider the use of space in terms of the immediate needs of the first occupants. There are two prevailing performance assessments that are being used at the moment. The Post-Occupancy Evaluation (POE) which focuses on the requirements of the building occupants, including: health, safety, and security; functionality and efficiency of work flow; social, psychological and cultural performance and fitness, which includes visual-aesthetic quality and satisfaction and Building Performance Evaluation (BPE) a systematic and rigorous approach encompassing a number of activities including research, measurement, comparison, evaluation, and feedback that take place through every phase of a building's lifecycle including planning, briefing/programming, design, construction, occupancy and recycling [5].

Socio-economic and demographic profile of the households also play an important role in the evaluation of the level of satisfaction of homeowners. Several empirical studies pointed out important demographic determinants, such as age, gender, nationality, religion, source of income and gross monthly income of either the individual or family. Another important information is whether the unit is owned by the initial buyer of the property or they are second and third owner. Although the change of ownership can also be attributed to the owner purchasing a better property or it can also be an indication on low satisfaction level.

4.2 Architectural Determinants of Student Housing

The school environment and the living quarters of the student play a significant role in determining the success of the student. To be able to maximize the learning process it is imperative that the surroundings are conducive to studying both in school and their homes or living quarters. There are six factors in creating a perfect study environment: a) location, b) atmosphere (includes noise level, lighting and temperature), c) private vs group studying, d) resources, e) distractions, f) location[6]. The architectural determinants of student satisfaction in college residence is explicitly shown in the study conducted by Davis. In the study, there are several areas where the students have very strong opinions and these were: a) quiet, b) comfort control, c) study ability, d) aesthetic appeal, e) flexibility, f) size, g) privacy, h) individuality, i) relaxation, j) hominess, k) freedom to alter room, l) sociability, m) opportunity to develop friends. Ultimately the findings suggested that there is a need for the use of behavioral science in an architectural context. The combination of architectural behavior science allows architectural forms to respond to behavior[7].

The satisfaction and perception of students on rented apartments is relatively low due to the lack of facilities[8]. The needs of the student is very different from the needs of a family more specifically for technical courses that still use drafting equipment for manual drawings. The students living in private residences show that by living off-campus, the daily cost of living increases and students prefer to save by cooking at home [9]. It also becomes inevitable that support services would eventually proliferate when there is an increase in student population such as food, school supplies, computer rentals and laundry shops.

5 Methodology

The study utilized descriptive research. Observation of the activities and the development of housing units is usually an activity of the researcher since the study area is across the work place. Pictures collected over a period of time also provide a clear story on changes in the GSIS Metro homes. Several interviews were conducted in order to establish the depth and breadth on how the occupancy developed and change over time. It was also necessary to visit the results of the previous research on the occupancy rate of the area under study. Data on student population of the Polytechnic University of the Philippines was also studied in order to see the pattern of increase of enrollment.

6 Discussion

The GSIS Metro Homes was built with the primary intention of providing affordable housing for the government employees. The New San Jose Builders was commissioned to the design and construction of the housing complex while the GSIS provides as the principal financing entity for the buyers. The units at the lower ground is intended for commercial areas that would supplement and complement the needs of the occupants. The upper 3 levels are dwellings units, designed with a loft and a bathroom at the lower level.

Phase 1 has a total of 589 units the floors from 2 to 4 which are residential units are 100% occupied. However, in the commercial phase not fronting the main thoroughfare there are 12 units or 2% of the total units that are yet to be purchased. The roof tops of all 8 buildings in Phase I which were intended as a common drying area for the occupants have now been partially roofed and occupied as living units. Phase III-A has a total of 542 units for the 7 buildings and both the commercial and residential are fully occupied. Out of the 542, 20% or 108 units are occupied by multi-household. Multi-household units are currently occupied by students as bed spacers sometimes with the owner's family or the whole unit is occupied for lease. From an average of 5 people per unit, it has increased to 7 to 8 persons. This is realized through the conversion of loft to a full floor. The National Building Code of the Philippines through Republic Act 1092 states that for an area to be considered as loft it should have an area less than 50% of the its lower floor. The minimum height ceiling of the loft is 1.80. However, lower and the upper floor level is of the same area then it cannot be considered as a loft or mezzanine therefore a floor to ceiling clearance of 2.70 for naturally ventilated room and 2.40 for actively cooled room is required. Since most if not all of the units have extended the loft into full floor consequently it is not compliant with the NBC. None compliance with the code would mean closure of the establishment.

Both ground floors of Phase I and Phase III-A utilized the lower areas as commercial spaces. However, in Phase I (Figure3. Commercial established specific to students needs) the majority of the commercial spaces are engaged with fast food, computer shop and school supplies while in Phase III-A (Figure 4. Commercial spaces focusing on family requirements) most of the commercial units address the needs of the family. The shops in Phase III-A include a hardware, vulcanizing shop, car wash shop, health spa, bakeshop, laundry shop and a mini grocery. These establishments more so in Phase I have already encroached on the sidewalks making it difficult and dangerous to the people walking on this side. Sanitation facilities are also questionable since very few of the stalls would have their own kitchen and toilet facilities. There are no policies on how the waste from these food establishments are handled in terms of segregation and disposal. Ventilation poses as another problem that has to be addressed since there are no smoke vents on the stalls that cook food.

Figure 2   Commercial established specific
to student's needs (photos taken by JRLutap, 2015)

Currently there are no engineering and architecture students residing in the PUP Hasmin Hostel. One reason is the distance because the College of Engineering and Architecture building is 300 mts. away from the hostel. Most of the students would prefer to live in Phase I rather than Phase

Figure 3   Commercial spaces focusing on family (photos taken by JRLutap, 2015)

Ⅲ-A. Phase Ⅲ-A facilities have better condition as compared to Phase I which is 30 meters away from the main gate of the Colleges of Engineering，Architecture and Fine Arts. Figure 5 Phase I Students Living Quarters shows the insufficiency of decent living space for the students. Architecture students squat on the floor to work on their drafting assignments. Figure 6. Phase Ⅲ-A Students Living Quarters shows a well-lighted and well ventilated living units. However，orderliness，proper fixtures and furniture are very much desired.

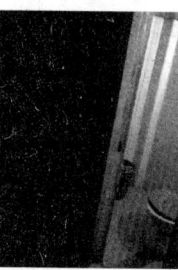

Figure 4   Phase I students living quarters (photos taken by JRLutap, 2015)

Figure 5 Phase Ⅲ-a students living quarters (photos taken by JRLutap, 2015)

7   Conclusion

The occupancy rate of a housing development is a critical indicator of the acceptability of the project. Although studies from private and public agencies unanimously agree that there is a backlog in decent housing provisions yet in the case of GSIS Metrohomes it has only reached the 80% occupancy on its 11th year after it was completed in 1993. As of year 2015 while Phase Ⅲ-A is already 100% occupied there are still units in Phase I with a total of 12 units that need to be sold. In the Philippine law，the liability of design and construction has a prescriptive period of 15 years. The primary intention of providing housing for one household was also altered since there are a number of units that are being leased to students as bed spacers. Some of the units are used entirely for bed spacers where the unit owners live in a different house or sometimes the homeowners would be living with the student lessees. The homeowners lease space in their units to augment either their amortization or the house rentals. In whatever case what is often not met in this kind of living conditions is the necessary facilities that would make the units conducive to the studies of the student and the privacy of both the families and students. The change of the occupancy profile would take a toll on the intended use of the building and an in-depth study of the performance-in-use of the project needs to be investigated.

GSIS 新城公寓的入住率变化简介

Jocelyn Rivera-Lutap

（菲律宾理工大学建筑与美术学院建筑与室内设计系）

摘要：GSIS 新城公寓是由 4 层楼高的步行式公寓组成的，这种公寓的原本意图是为政府雇员提供保障性住房。但是，因为有一些公寓被改造成了向学生出租的床，这种为政府雇员提供保障性住房的初衷已经变质了。某些业主甚至把整个公寓都改装成这种床出租，业主则有时候住在另一处，有时候和学生承租人住在一起。业主如此出租他们的公寓，是为了增加他们在银行或单位租金的摊销。但是，这种改造往往不能提供必要的设施和居住环境来帮助学生学习或为学生提供有利的学习环境。这种居住形式的改变对建筑用途产生了负面影响，对这种改造项目的使用性能的讨论还需更深入的研究。

关键词：入住率，学生公寓，使用效果

References：

[1] Rivera-Lutap, J. A.. A Study on the Occupancy Rate of a Medium Rise Housing Project：GSIS Metro Homes[D]. University of Santo Tomas，2004.

[2] Serote. E. M.. The Urban Land Nexus Theory and the Spatial Structuring of Metropolitan Manila[J]. Philippine Planning Journal，Vol. XXIV，No. 1，October，1992.

[3] Richman，A, Chapin, A Review of the Social and Physical Concepts of the Neighborhood as a Basis for Planning Residential Environments. Mimeographed manuscript[M]. Chapel Hill：Department of City and Regional Planning，University of North Carolina，1977.

[4] Teck-Hong，T. Housing Satisfaction in medium-and high-cost housing：The case of Greater Kuala Lumpur，Malaysia[OL]. [2015-5-6] https：//uhl4012ismailammar. wikispaces. com/ file/view/Social＋Stratification＋in＋Malaysia＋3. pdf .

[5] Mallory-Hill，S. ，Preiser，W. E. Watson，C. (editors). Enhancing Building Performance [M]. John Wiley and Sons，Ltd，2012.

[6] Ramsey，C. and Witter，A.. Ideal Study Environments and Factors that Influence Studying [OL]. [2015-5-6] http：//www. wcu. edu/academic-resources/writing-and-learning-commons-walc/course-tutoring-and-academic-strategies/ideal-study-environment-and-factors-that-influ-ence-studying. asp.

[7] Davis，G and Roizen，R.. Architectural Determinants of Student Satisfaction in College Resi-

denceHalls［OL］.［2015-5-6］. http：//www. edra. org/sites/default/files/publications/EDRA02-DavisG-28-44 _ 0. pdf.

[8] Akinyode，B. F.. Students' Satisfaction and Perception on Rented Apartment in Nigeria：Experiment of lautech Students［J/OL］. 2014，4（7）［2015-5-6］. http：//thejournalofbusiness. org/index. php/site/article/view/567.

[9] Abdullah，I. C.，Muslim，M. H.，ad Karim，H. A.. An Assesment on Variable Reliability in Investigating Students' Living Satisfaction in Private Housing Environment[M].［2015-5-6］. http：//www. sciencedirect. com/science/article/pii/S1877042813021058.

[10] Clements-Croome，D. Natural Ventilated Buildings-Buildings for the senses，economy and society[M]. United Kingdom，University of Reading，1997

[11] Reyes，M. C. L. Spatial Structure of Metro Manila：Genesis，Growth and Development［J］. Philippine Planning Journal，1998，XXIX(2)，XXX(1).

北京市住宅设计专项评议会机制和评审要点的试行推广

王鹏[1]　侯晓明[2]　刘晓钟[1]　高羚耀[1]　张龙[1]

王超[1]　王腾[1]　赵泽宏[1]　丁倩[1]　孟宇[2]

（1. 北京市建筑设计研究院有限公司；

2. 北京市勘察设计与测绘地理信息管理办公室）

摘要： 2013 年，为提高北京市保障性住房的设计水平和品质，由北京市规划委员会和市勘察设计与测绘地理信息管理办公室组织多家单位开展了"北京市提高住宅设计水平专项工作"；共同研究编制出包括"北京市住宅外部城市设计导则"和"住宅设计专项评审要点"等多项子课题成果；主要成果发布、宣贯和通过设计专项评议会试行。专项评议会机制和评审要点的试行推广，促进了保障性住房规划设计水平的提高。

关键词： 北京市，住宅设计，专项评议会，评审要点

1 引言

"十二五"期间，北京市要新建和改建几百万套保障性住房。本市保障性住房主要建设在城近郊区，有些分布在城际铁路沿线的"城市门户区域"。保障性住房的设计和建设水平直接影响到城市的外部形象和品质。2013 年，由北京市规划委员会和市勘察设计与测绘地理信息管理办公室（以下简称"市勘办"）牵头组织多家单位成立课题组并开展"提高居住建筑设计水平专项工作"；目标是切实提高居住建筑（特别是保障性住房）的规划设计水平和进一步提升首都住宅建设品质。

1.1 首先，课题组多次调研区县规划分局、实地踏勘，并完成了八项课题研究。

课题组承担子课题明细表　　　　表1

序号	课题研究	承担单位
1	北京城市居住建筑历史沿革与发展展望	北京市建筑设计研究院有限公司
2	北京市住宅外部设计导则（试行）（以下简称"导则"）	北京市城市规划设计研究院（弘都城市规划建筑设计院）
3	住宅设计专项评议会评审要点和流程（简称"要点"）	北京市建筑设计研究院有限公司
4	北京住宅现状调研和分析	中国建筑标准设计院
5	高容积率的住宅形态研究	北京市建筑设计研究院有限公司
6	提高住宅品质技术措施：景观、绿建和经营	北京住宅建筑设计研究院
7	北京市居住建筑规划管理技术要求研究	北京维拓时代建筑设计有限公司
8	住宅与城市的形态一体化建议	中国建筑设计研究院

资料来源：北京市勘办关于北京市提高住宅设计水平专项工作的汇报。

1.2 课题组配合市规划委编制了八项措施，作为加强行业专项管理、进行制度创新的举措。

八项措施明细表 表2

序号	措施	主要内容
1	加强精细化设计	依据《导则》要求，进行深入的精细化设计
2	建立联席会议制度	定期召开"行业总建筑师联席会议"，会商住宅设计问题
3	建立"责任建筑师"制度	建立"总建筑师制度负责制"和项目"责任建筑师"制度
4	建立行业评议制度	定期组织行业评议，以纪要形式向设计单位反馈评议意见
5	优化设计招投标	执行住宅项目招标文件新范本，建立相关招投标专家库
6	加大行业管理力度	曝光公示评议较差的设计单位和个人，纳入资质资格管理
7	树立社会责任、精品意识	对精品住宅和优秀建筑师加强宣传，建立奖惩制度
8	加强教育培训	开展建筑师业务培训、论坛交流和互评，提高公众参与度

资料来源：北京市勘办关于北京市提高住宅设计水平专项工作的汇报。

1.3 课题组工作采取"课题研究先行、规划分局实施"的模式，由市勘办进行协调组织，行业专家领衔，设计单位参与；具体研究成果和评议机制在区县规划分局审批项目中进行试点实施

2 北京市保障性住房小区的现状调研和分析

2.1 影响保障性住房外部形象品质的主要问题体现在：高度、体量、界面、色彩、风格等几方面

高度问题：中大规模小区缺少高度分区和标志性建筑物的设计；高度过于齐整，缺乏空间变化。

体量问题：小区规划设计常出现长板式高层建筑，破坏城市轮廓，阻挡城市"视廊"。

界面问题：小区规划设计缺少建筑沿城市道路开敞面比例的控制，造成沿街界面过于封闭。

色彩问题：小区建筑缺少色彩分区设计；使用过多高彩度色彩；相邻地块色彩差异大。

建筑风格问题：保障性住房外立面设计过于简单粗陋；相邻地块的建筑风格缺乏协调。

2.2 现状问题的原因分析

规划管理问题体现在：现行规划管理规定制定较早，规划指标比较粗放不科学。规划设计管理有盲点，重经济技术指标，轻城市设计引导。设计行业管理问题体现在：行业管理方面对保障性住房设计水平的监管乏力。少数设计师缺少责任心或者设计水平有限。

2.3 主要对策和措施

针对问题，课题组从设计行业管理的角度寻找对策，与规划管理措施并行、相辅相成。八项课题研究成果和八项措施的编制是为加强行业管理的举措；通过试点评议，逐步建立专项评议会制度。

3 住宅设计专项评议会机制

3.1 建立住宅设计专项评议会的例会制度

3.1.1 建立"行业总建筑师联席会"制度

住宅设计推行专基评审制度，定位为技术服务层次；是一个定位为不干涉传统的审查流程基础上，强化专家会专业指导的技术服务。

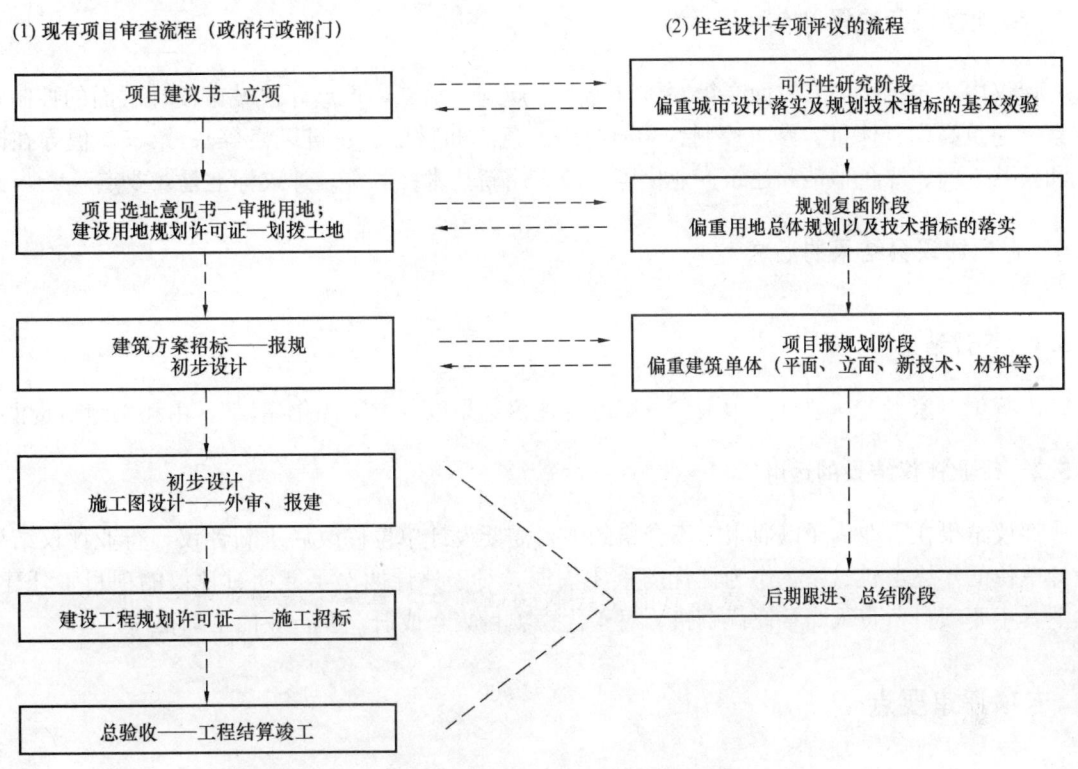

(1) 现有项目审查流程（政府行政部门）　　　　　　　　　(2) 住宅设计专项评议的流程

| 项目建议书一立项 | | 可行性研究阶段
偏重城市设计落实及规划技术指标的基本效验 |

| 项目选址意见书一审批用地；
建设用地规划许可证—划拨土地 | | 规划复函阶段
偏重用地总体规划以及技术指标的落实 |

| 建筑方案招标——报规
初步设计 | | 项目报规划阶段
偏重建筑单体（平面、立面、新技术、材料等） |

| 初步设计
施工图设计——外审、报建 | | |

| 建设工程规划许可证——施工招标 | | 后期跟进、总结阶段 |

| 总验收——工程结算竣工 | | |

图 1　专项评议流程与现有项目审查流程的关系图
（资料来源：北京市建筑设计研究院有限公司"住宅设计专项评审要点"）

3.1.2 定期举行市、区两级住宅设计专项评议会例会

3.2 评议对象

规划分局辖区内的居住建筑（以保障性住房为评议重点）项目，按照项目基本建设程序，从概念性设计阶段到施工阶段均可报送项目参加评议。

3.3 评议办法

3.3.1 评议的组织分工

各规划分局向市勘办申报项目，并负责统筹项目的设计单位、建设单位，提交设计成果。市勘办负责安排评议会时间、地点，遴选聘请专家，主持会议，撰写会议纪要及下发专家意见工作等。

3.3.2 建立专家库和成果数据库

专家库人员涉及住宅设计、管理方面的专家、学者和设计师骨干。成果库是指根据建设规模、设计水平高低、修改完善程度等对评议项目的成果进行分类整理入库，以便后续对比研究参考。

3.3.3 建立平台运作机构及秘书组

平台运行支持机构对平台日常运作进行管理调配。其中，秘书组主要工作包括：收件、组织会议、撰写会议纪要、记录评审结果并形成数据库。

3.4 专项评议会的评议内容及标准

评议内容包括以下几方面：第一，符合上位规划；第二，重点评议城市设计层面的控制和引导要素（建筑高度、体量、界面控制、交通组织、色彩和材质、建筑风格等）；第三，倡导在园林景观和公共空间、绿色节能和建筑产业化等方面应用新技术；等等。评议标准是《要点》。

3.5 专项评议会结果的汇总

3.5.1 评议结果

由每位专家参考《要点》填写"方案综合评议结果以及方案优化建议"，由秘书组负责汇总。

3.5.2 行业评议结果的运用

评议结果在行业内予以通报。不合格的项目需要设计单位修改后重新评议。行业评议结果纳入设计单位的年终考核体系，作为评优的重要依据。对于累计两次不能通过评议的项目责任建筑师，取消其主要项目负责人当年评优资格。对于优秀项目集合成册，在行业内培训推广。

4 专项评审要点

4.1 规划把控包括：要求项目提供所在街区的立体图，从三维角度进行场地分析和总体布局。

4.2 高度控制主要包括：高度分区设计。

占地面积 $10hm^2$ 及以上或建筑规模 10 万 m^2 及以上的居住区需进行建筑高度及建筑空间的设计，应明确标志性建筑的位置和高度。原则上要求同一居住地块内有不少于地上住宅建筑面积 10% 的住宅建筑，其建筑高度比控高下降至少一档（建筑高度 18m 以下的居住区规划方案不强求）。

4.3 体型控制主要包括：明确塔式、板式建筑的最大面宽；力争高层建筑挺拔，多层建筑舒缓。

塔式住宅：建筑的长高比不宜大于 1：1.5，其各个朝向的最大面宽不宜超过 40m。板式住宅：建筑高度在 18m 及以下时，不对其面宽进行控制；高度在 18m 以上、30m 以下时，沿城市道路连续展开面的宽度不应大于 120m；高度在 30m 及以上、60m 以下时，沿城市道路连续展开面宽度不宜大于 75m，特殊情况不应大于 80m；高度在 60m 以上时，其沿城市道路连续展开面的宽度不宜大于 55m，特殊情况不应大于 60m。

4.4 界面控制

通透率指贴临城市界面的建筑之间（高度在18m以上）开敞部分的宽度和与同一方向规划用地宽度的比例。沿城市主要通道的通透率宜大于40％，特殊情况下不应小于35％；临城市主、次干道的通透率宜大于25％，特殊情况下不应小于20％。

4.5 建筑风格

住宅建筑应与相邻地块的建筑在整体风格上取得协调。建筑风格应与类型、建筑高度相匹配。

4.6 色彩和材质选择

色彩分区：用地规模超过10hm²以上的居住区需进行色彩分区规划。色彩搭配：建议住宅建筑选择"暖浅低艳"的色彩作为基调色；建议基调色、辅助色、强调色的搭配比例为70％、25％、5％。立面材质：建筑宜选用安全、耐久、易维护的立面材料；避免大量使用玻璃幕墙和金属构件。

5 专项评议会机制和评审要点的试行和推广，促使相关设计单位提高设计水平

5.1 在2013～2014年，对重点区域的数十项保障性住房项目完成了十多次专项评议会。

其中，门头沟区主要有十多个棚改工程项目。案例分析：小园08地块棚改安置房：

图2 项目规划布局鸟瞰图评议前后比较（左图为之前）
（资料来源：北京市勘办关于北京市提高住宅设计水平专项工作的汇报）

图3 项目立面图评议前后比较（左图为之前）
（资料来源：北京市勘办关于北京市提高住宅设计水平专项工作的汇报）

5.2 专项评议会还进行了在建工程项目实地调研和现场服务。

市勘办组织对门头沟区主要棚改安置在建项目进行现场指导。案例分析：曹各庄 A 地块安置房：

图 4 项目现场评议服务

（资料来源：北京市勘办关于北京市提高住宅设计水平专项工作的汇报）

5.3 课题组对区县规划分局现场调研和宣贯交流，交流了规划管理中存在的问题和解决措施。包括：落实城市色彩规划、提高住宅设计水平的举措；城市设计在规划管理中的应用；等等。

5.4 总结与展望

评议会宜早不宜晚，在时间上应平行于规划分局对项目的技术审查，早于区县组织的委办局联席会议，这样，评议会的成果可以作为领导决策的基础依据。评议会的流程和制度逐渐标准化，体现在：评议会的专家遴选和聘请应该形成制度；评议会的过程和结果应该保证公开、公正、透明；会前的项目评议资料、决议模板等应准备充分；专项评议会应提倡加强实地调研和现场服务功能。

致谢

感谢北京市规划委员会叶大华和市勘办叶嘉同志！感谢课题组的合作团队和专家们！感谢各规划分局的领导和同事！感谢参加评议会的工程项目的设计和开发单位！

The Promotion of Expert Evaluation System and Review Points for Residential Design in Beijing

Wang Peng[1], Hou Xiaoming[2], Liu Xiaozhong[1],
Gao Lingyao[1], Zhang Long[1], Wang Chao[1],
Wang Teng[1], Zhao Zehong[1], Ding Qian[1], Meng Yu[2]
(1. Beijing Institute of Architectural Design;   2. Beijing Survey
Design and Mapping Geographic Information Management Office)

Abstract：In 2013, in order to improve the design level and quality of affordable housing in Beijing, Beijing Municipal Planning Commission and Survey Design and Mapping Geographic Information Management Office organized several planning & architectural design institutes to carry out the "special work to increase the level of residential design" in Beijing; developing joint research results including "Beijing city residential design guidelines" and "The review points for the residential design". Subsequently, "Guidelines" posted on the website of the Beijing Municipal Planning Commission; "The review points" were tested by the Municipal Planning Commission. The expert evaluation system and the review points of trial and promotion improved the affordable housing planning and design level.

Keywords：Beijing, Residential design, Expert evaluation system, The review points

参考文献：

[1]   北京市规划委员会和市勘察设计与测绘地理信息管理办公室．关于北京市提高住宅设计水平专项工作的汇报．

[2]   北京市城市规划设计研究院（弘都城市规划建筑设计院），北京市建筑设计研究院有限公司，中国建筑标准设计院，北京住宅建筑设计研究院，北京维拓时代建筑设计有限公司，中国建筑设计研究院等．北京市提高居住建筑设计水平专项工作课题研究系列成果．

[3]   天津市规划委员会．天津市规划建筑导则汇编［G］.

Sustainable Affordable Housing as A Call for Worldwide Urbanization

Dyan Arcel M. Coronacion

(University of Santo Tomas College of Architecture)

Abstract: Affordable Housing has become one of the most important programs of a government unit but becomes the weakest form of social benefit especially in Asia. Every generation, real estate market tends to increase but salary rate remains, which makes "affordability" hard to attain for the low-income earners. This paper provides a brief introduction about Affordable Housing and Sustainability and why these two must be incorporated. A basic comprehension of these two topics can develop into successful provision of housing development. It aims to identify affordable and environmentally stable housing solutions. Applicable policies will also be discussed to implement housing development programs in the country of China.

Keywords: Sustainable, Affordable housing, Urbanization

1 Introduction

1.1 Affordable Housing

A house basically provides shelter, comfort and security to people. Affordable housing is a unit provided, by the local government, exclusively for households with low income budgets. Its affordability is unstably increasing after the World War II thus making it more expensive since the 21st century (Haffner and Boumeester, 2010). Today, it is the task of the local government, together with private parties, to manage marketability and affordability of housing units especially the low income group.

Housing development mainly started in the United States and Europe. Asian countries then followed in the mid-20th century. Through the history, western and eastern countries are far different in affordable housing concerns and therefore have different policies when it comes to applying for a single unit.

1.2 Sustainability

Sustainable housing discourse and practice is largely focused on the physical application of well-grounded principles in the design of homes and the methods and materials used in construction. (Randolph et al, 2008) The usual but very effective strategies of Sustainability are natural ventilation, the use of solar panels and porous concrete blocks, and a universal design of spaces which makes it adaptable to change depending on current events or situations.

1.3 Affordable Housing in China

China has been increasingly populating for the last 30 years. More people move to the city where the money is thus creating congestive cities. Suitable and affordable housing environments in China are provided by the real estate department of province government. The 'Approach for Affordable Housing Management' document of 2007 carefully defines the affordable housing policies of financial supports from the local government. This consists of dwelling size, selling price, and application policies.

2 Summary

Affordable housing begins to be a main priority for all governments in the call of urbanization. But today, the concept of housing is no longer easily defined as providing a simple roof over one's head but it must effectively address issues in attaining sustainability, social and human development; also known as Sustainable Housing. It enables improved economic prosperity and social development through sustainable solutions such as access to neighborhood utilities and services, energy, and environmental awareness. It offers vast opportunities in seeking economic development, life equity, and unconditional care for the environment.

Provision of sustainable housing however fails to meet with the social, cultural, environmental and economic benefits of migrants because of poor relocation site with no considerations for the residents' main lifestyle and livelihood opportunities resulting to relocations on remote areas which contribute to amplified carbon footprint and other negative impacts on the environment.

With the arising and rapid growth of Urbanization, there is a need to increase the demand for affordable housing, urban infrastructure and services particularly in the populated areas in the world. Since government units try to resolve the problem; it resulted in emerging slums and informal settlements in such areas due to urban development in Asia, Africa and Latin America [2].

3 Review of Related Literature

3.1 China's Path to Urbanization

According to the China Program Director for the Natural Resources Defense Council (NRDC), Qian Jingjing, China is in the developing stage of a meeting the path to green urbanization which specifically addresses to the climate and life equity. China today is addressing global climate change in its urbanization path to recognize its efforts in producing low-carbon urbanization experiences and develop innovative technological practices [3].

At the United Nation's COP 20 Climate Conference' side event with the theme of "City's Green Low-Carbon Future" in Lima, Peru in 2014, from a literary work entitled the "Climate Change and Urbanization: Challenges and Progress in China", three urbanization factors for the Chinese community have been evaluated to seek climate-friendly solutions in 1) land use, 2) transportation and 3) energy. According to the Chairman of NDRC, Minister Xie Zhenhua, China has to grow from past experiences and study local and international green solutions which then developed the country's new urbanization path which is to promote green cities and low-carbon environment. The NDRC China Program created case studies of ideal cities in China and were also presented featuring Efficient land use in "landless investment", transit-oriented mixed land use, and planning integration; Green Transportation Development (Asia's first Bus Rapid Transit in Guangzhou), Hangzhou (Public Bicycle Rental System), and community carpooling; and Urban Energy Use Efficiency merely focusing on national low-carbon, net-zero energy and retrofits in Northern China's existing buildings [6].

The rapid growth of urbanization in China over three decades grew into having more opportunities in architecture and construction, employment, tourism and value of the country. Though the country created poverty as well, it is ranked as one of the world's largest economies. To further comply with the present and future situations, the country developed strategies in generating and consuming higher energy and water supply thus to bring about the increase the nation's emissions of greenhouse gases, and deteriorating natural resources which is a big challenge for China [6].

3.2　Affordable Housing Development Setbacks

Housing is a "human right"; no government can ignore this important right to the citizens. (Shen and Mehta, 2008) The local government itself must implement policies in providing housing to everyone and also develop more housing projects for the future generations.

Due to rapid growth of population and economy, demand in human essentials like food, shelter, and necessities tend to become available in the city resulting to more people moving to the city which causes over population and congestion. The competition in availing shelter increases as well as the demand to provide affordable housing developments.

Urbanization creates a wide array of human activities and infrastructures which contributes to improved environmental quality and survival. Development of Housing Projects creates a tool for Urbanization because these projects show economic growth of a nation. Among other tangible and intangible actions, policies will eventually take effect in providing equal rights to providing housing rights to low-income earners.

3.3　Affordable Housing Programs and Policies

3.3.1　United States

The American government has the ability to develop large-scale housing developments because of its fast pace boosting economy. "American Housing Act" was declared by the American government which supported low-income household resulted to an extended scale of public and affordable housing market and development in 1937. The government is tasked to make practical strategies in solving housing problems (e. g. low-rent housing, slum clearance) to promote a healthy environment and quality of life of an American household [5].

3.3.2　Hong Kong, China

As a former part of the British colony, its political and cultural process is fairly different from other parts of China. During the sixth annual policy address of Donald Tsang, former Chief executive of Hong kong special Administrative Region, the government will focus on subsidizing middle-income household in having their own housing units by constructing 5000 units under the scheme. Other than that, the government will also provide community care services for the needy like a monthly transport subsidy [5].

Today, Hong Kong uses the "Home Ownership Scheme" (HOS) which offers saleable and rentable houses at a low cost with about 30 to 40 percent price discount to the poor for a better quality of life.

3.3.3 Philippines

The "National Assembly No. 220" (*Batas Pambansa blg*. 220) in the Philippines was declared by the government as a policy for allowing private sectors to create socialized housing units to be sold to target beneficiaries which are the average and low-income earners. Each unit is to be sold at an affordability level of thirty percent (30%) of the gross family income. At the same time, BP 220 refers to government economic housing projects in depressed areas.

In order to avail housing units, the government offer loan packages with annual interest rates to interested citizens. Strong partnerships between private sectors and the Local Government Units (LGU) can generate more housing projects which will then promote more affordable socialized housing projects. Added to this, disaster resiliency, green technology and solutions must be incorporated in each housing unit not only to supply sheltering needs of families but to protect them from danger as well.

4   Research Methodology

This paper aims to find concrete issues, evidences, and solutions to further proceed with the economical and feasibility studies. The following methodologies enumerated were used to gather factual information, data and statistics of the researcher to supply the needs of this paper:

4.1   Archival Research

The purpose is to collect and synthesize evidences to verify facts that defend the hypothesis. It uses primary sources, secondary sources, and lots of qualitative data sources such as logs, diaries, official records, reports, etc. The limitation is that the sources must be both authentic and valid. An up-to-date resource that features current trends, concepts, and technology is a support to design the needs of the users and the environment today [10]. The researcher gathered significant information on historical overviews, backgrounds, statistics and a general idea related to affordable housing, sustainability and urbanization, community development, policies, programs, and case studies for the topic.

4.2   Case Study Research

A case study is an empirical inquiry that investigates a contemporary phenomenon within its real life context when the boundaries between phenomenon and context are not clearly evident and in which multiple source of evidence are used (Yin, 1989). It concerns with exploring, describing, and explaining a phenomenon [10]. This method allowed the researcher to study related case studies and to identify, compare, and analyze relationships between them and the proposed project to further use them as guidelines, references, or inspirations in designing effective facilities of the project.

4.3   Correlational Research

Correlation studies are designed to analyze the relationships between two or more variables, ordinarily through the use of correlation coefficients [10]. This method allowed the researcher to study and determine statistically significant relationships between two or more factors related to sustainability and affordable housing (e. g. Domestic Living, Green Technology).

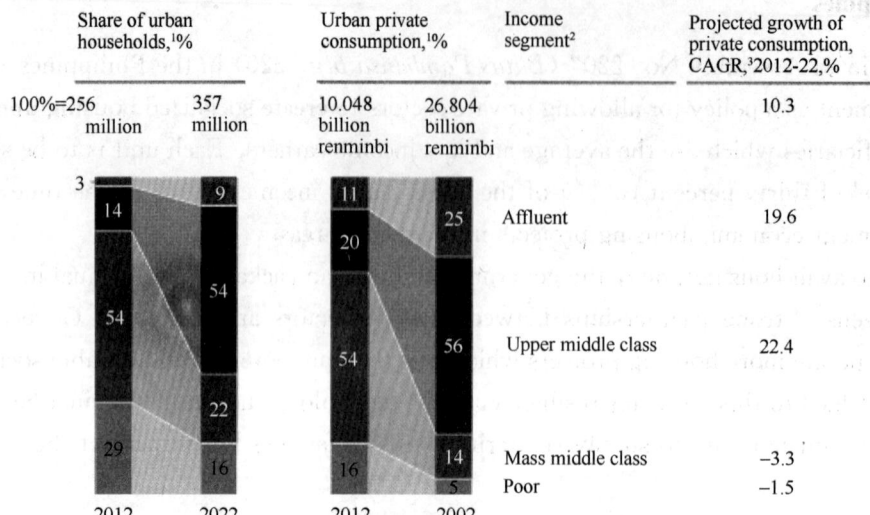

¹Figures may not sum to 100%,because of rounding;data for 2022 are projected.
²Defined by annual disposable income per urban household,in 2010 real terms;affluent,>229, 000
renminbi(equivalent to> $ 34,000);upper middle class,106,000 to 229, 000 renminbi(equivalent
to $ 16, 000 to $ 34, 000);mass middle class,60, 000 to 106, 000 renminbi(equivalent to $ 9, 000 to
$ 16, 000);poor,<60, 000 renminbi (equivalent to < $ 9, 000).
¹Compound annual growth rate.

Figure 1   The magnitude of China's middle class growth [7,8]

5   Hypothesis

As the socio-economic classes of people in China continue to increase the middle class income families (by 2022, there will be around 271 million people living in urban areas who will be part of it), it is still notable that there are still families that belong to the low income class (there will be around 57 million people living in urban areas). The purpose of this study is to determine the proper policies to be implemented which will greatly benefit those belonging to the low income class. Even though the low income class are small in numbers compared to the middle class, they are still plenty and should not be put aside. One must consider two things in this aspect. First, the low income class accounts for 57 million people in the population in urban areas. There will be long lines of people waiting for their houses to be built and be liveable. Last, awarding those houses will be very challenging for the government because there are still a lot of things to be discovered in the lives of those people such as their personal information and whereabouts to name a few.

6   Argument

Affordable housing can be viewed as a double-edged sword. First, the low-income households will have a better way of life. Since it is funded by the government, it will be quite easy for them to own their own homes. On the other hand, the government is a strong force to reckon with. It is the body who has the final say on commercial housing (whether in price, location, design, materials and etc.). Thus, the competition in the market will be steeper for most since transferring houses will be extremely difficult.

In order to truly achieve affordable housing, the local government must create strategies for the poor to eagerly possess their own housing units such as rentable housing units, housing incentives in personal savings, employment opportunities, and the like.

7　Conclusion

Affordable housing creates opportunities from artists and professionals, specializing in building design, worldwide to create new technologies and trends. Prototypes of affordable housing have been introduced to particularly help the people living on less than a dollar per day. On the other hand, the general approach to sustainable housing is to achieve benefits from sustainability dimensions of improving lifestyle and livelihood programs, economical contribution, and environmental enhancement. The strategic visions then come from supportive beneficiaries.

Not only through providing housing for the deeply needed households, but also taking care of the people under the local government unit through health care services, communal livelihood and recreational activities, can help a nation boost its economic growth and quality of life thus moving forward to global urbanization. Through this, China will attract more internal and external opportunities.

可持续的经济适用房为呼吁全球城市化

Dyan Arcel M. Coronacion

（圣托马斯大学建筑学院）

摘要：经济适用房已经成为一个政府单位中最重要的项目之一，但也成为特别是在亚洲社会效益最弱的形式。每一代人，房地产市场趋于增加，但工资率仍然存在，这使得低收入者的"承受能力"难以实现。本文介绍了经济适用房和可持续发展，以及为什么两者必须结合。对这两个主题的基本理解可以发展成为成功的提供住房的发展。其目的是确定经济实惠和环境稳定的住房解决方案。适用的政策也将讨论在中国实施的全国住房发展规划。

关键词：可持续的，负担得起的住房，城市化

References:

[1]　Mckinsey & Company. China's Green Revolution: Prioritizing Technologies To Achieve Energy And Environmental Sustainability [M]. Australia: Mckinsey & Company. 2009.

[2]　United Nations Human Settlements Program. Sustainable Housing For Sustainable Cities: A Policy Framework For Developing Countries [M]. Nairobi: Un-Habitat, 2012.

[3]　Natural Resources Defense Council. REPORT: China's Rapid Urbanization to Play Key Role in Curbing Country's Climate Pollution [R/OL], 2014. [2015-3-28] http://www.nrdc.org/media/2014/141210.asp.

[4]　Falcon, Ramon. Towards An Affordable Housing Program [M]. 1st ed. Manila: National Development and Economic Authority, 2015, 4.

[5]   Pullen, S. , Zillante, G. , Arman, M. , Lou, W. , Zuo, J. , Chileshe, N. (n. d.) . A Case Study Analysis of Sustainable and Affordable Housing [OL]. [2015-4-24], http: // www. academia. edu/791528/A _ CASE _ STUDY _ ANALYSIS _ OF _ SUSTAINABLE _ AND _ AFFORDABLE _ HOUSING.

[6]   Lin, J. The Development of Affordable Housing—A Case Study in Guangzhou City, China [OL]. 2011. [2015-4-24] http: //www. diva-portal. org/smash/get/diva2: 503601/FULL-TEXT02.

[7]   Barton, D. Mapping China's middle class [R/OL], 2013. http: //www. mckinsey. com/ insights/consumer _ and _ retail/mapping _ chinas _ middle _ class.

[8]   Image retrieved from: http: //www. mckinsey. com/~/media/McKinsey/dotcom/Insights/ Consumer And Retail/Mapping Chinas middle class/svg _ Q3 MiddleClassMainstream ex _ 1. ashx? mw=510.

[9]   Image retrieved from: http: //www. mckinsey. com/~/media/McKinsey/dotcom/Insights/ Consumer And Retail/Mapping Chinas middle class/svgz _ Web _ MiddleClassMainstream _ scrolling _ ex3 _ v2. ashx? mw=510.

[10]   University of Southern California. USC Libraries. In Organizing Your Social Sciences Research Paper [D/OL] . 2014-8-8 [2014-8-12]. http: //libguides. usc. edu/writingguide.

社会经济活动对城市低租金住区形态的影响：以深圳为例

刘一玮　贾倍思

（香港大学建筑学院）

摘要： 1978 年后的快速城市化造就了一批中国大都市，其中深圳是速度和生命力的代表。然而，推动城市发展的大量外来务工者和城市低收入群体长久以来依靠着遍布在城市中的民间低租金社区立足于这个城市，他们主动参与住区建设合作互惠。相比之下，新建成的政策性住房在社会生活的方面存在很多问题，解决这些问题需要深入研究住房形态和社会经济的关系，而民间低租金社区的发展和演变为这一关系的探讨提供了参考。本文以深圳为例，基于自发性城市化和开放建筑的空间层级理论，观察民间低租金住区中领域结构的演变规律，并进一步揭示社会经济活动在邻里和家庭两个层级上对住区形态的影响。文中针对三种不同类型的四个城市低租金社区进行深入调查，讨论了个体和群体在实体空间层级和领域结构体系中的参与和变化，以及住区形态对这些变化的回应。

关键词： 住房形态，保障性住房，民间低租金社区，领域结构

1　前言

　　大规模的保障性住房建设在改革开放将近 40 年后的今天登上舞台，与已步入平稳发展期的商品住房相互配合一同推动中国经济的稳定增长和持续的城市化。然而，面对不断膨胀的城市人口和高居不下的房价，政府提供有限的保障房在解决外来人口和低收入居民住房问题上始终是杯水车薪。在过去 30 年里，深圳近半数的人口居住在低租金住区中，这些民间性质的低租金住区为大量的"新深圳人"提供了便利的生活环境，为这座城市的发展贡献了巨大力量。面对已经投入使用的政策性保障房在社会经济方面出现的各种问题，如何在设计和建造过程中回应低收入居民独特的社会经济需求值得关注。本文以深圳的民间低租金社区为研究对象，首先在理论层面探讨了社会经济活动与住区形态的关系，基于 Habraken 等学者提出的层级理论，在邻里和家庭两个层级上对四个典型案例进行调查分析。最终我们发现城市低租金住区中社交包容性带来了丰富的模糊领域，同时，经济活动的渗入导致了领域层次的增加。在公共领域和私有领域之间存在动态的领域界限，而决定这一界限的群体和个体之间的关系在实体空间上的体现会影响到住区的价值和生活品质。

2　社会经济活动和住房形态的关系以及基于空间层级的认知方法

　　住房形态是一种物化的日常生活。Amos Rapoport 早在《住房形态与文化》一书中就提出，既定的文化背景和生活方式会产生复杂的居住需求，住房形态为了回应这些复杂需求而生，同时具有稳定而多变的特征。Rapoport 将住房的这一特征解释为对人类自身特征的一种延续，是固定的身体结构和生理构造与多变的意识及行为的结合（Rapoport，1969）。John Habraken 则认为人类行为和建构环境之间存在一种"本质关系"，即稳定的实体结构中发生着多变而无法预判的人类行为。他进而将对应这两种状态的建构要素分为两类，支撑结构和填充单元（Habraken，1972）。Aldo Rossi 也指出城市结构的复杂性和住房形态的双重特征使不同的价值体系可以共存，使不变的运行机制和多变的需求可以调和（Aldo，1984）。自此，人们对于住房的认识突破了实体形式的限定而进入空间形态的层面。

　　一旦我们意识到稳定的建筑实体和多变的生活需求之间的矛盾通过住房形态得以协调，并长久共存，另一个问题随即浮出水面，在居住的空间实体为了能够适应生活需求的变化而不断进行调整的过程中，住房形态也在逐渐演变。因此，住房设计的对象并不只是一组静态的空间结构，而是一

种能够应对某一特定生活方式中各种可变条件的动态体系，通过观察住房形态的变化来识别这些易变因素，是针对某种特定生活方式展开住房设计的前提。住房实体产生于某一时间点，荒废于某一时间点（可以是住房结构的物理寿命时间，也可以是住房不再满足使用需求而被废弃的时间），在这一过程中，人对空间的日常使用会形成一个弹性变化范围，在日常使用中的各种影响力的作用下，变化中的住房形态能够一直适应生活方式的发展。时间越久，影响力的产生越频繁，作用力越大，当日常使用的弹性极限被打破，就需要创造出新的住房。从可持续发展的角度来说，尽可能的增大日常生活对住房实体结构的影响区间，延长住房形态的变化时间，才能够有效地节约资源。我们需要发现和探究不同的影响力对住房形态的作用，考虑到低租金住区的特殊性，本文侧重两个方面：社会生活和经济活动。

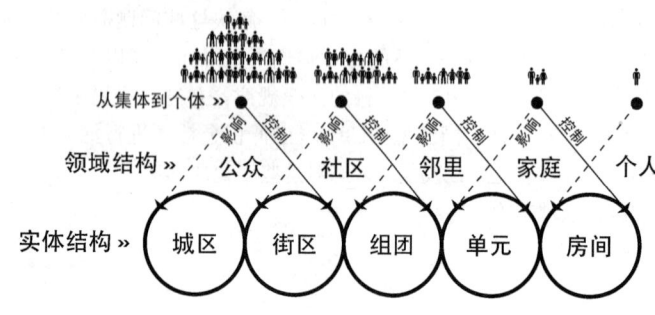

图1　实体层级和领域层级的相互关系
（图示内容源自开放建筑理论中的层级概念）

人对空间的控制和影响形成了领域的概念（Habraken，1998）。Sidey Brower用"领域感"这一概念来描述个人或群体对实体空间的占有、控制和使用（Brower，1980）。从可观察的角度来说，我们可以把住区形态理解为两套体系的叠加，稳定的实体结构和不断变化着的领域结构。空间层级的概念为我们提供了一个观察、认知和分析这两种结构关系的方法（Habraken，2002）。针对不同的研究，学者们设计了多种空间层级模型用于研究城市和建筑形态，比如 Kropf 的七层级模型（Kropf，1996），Kendall 的五层级模型（Kendall and Teicher，2010）。本文采用 Habraken 提出的能够反映人对空间控制影响的五层级模型来分析实体结构和领域结构的变化。如图1所示，领域层次由不同规模的人群对实体空间的控制和影响而产生。个体关系的基本单位是家庭，若干家庭共同生活的领域形成邻里，在更大的范围内邻里组成了社区，最终共同形成了城市公众。家庭可以直接决定房间的实体特征（如面积、布局），同时也影响着建筑单元的形式（如交通空间、交流空间的配置）。同理，邻里控制着建筑单元的形式并影响着组团，社区决定了住区组团关系并影响着街区公共空间的设计。本研究中，我们着眼于邻里和家庭两个领域层次，通过对住区建筑实体空间的观察和对居民的访谈，发现低租金住区形态的变化和居民社会经济活动的相互关系。

3　案例研究：深圳低租金住区的形态变化

中国的低租金社区通常有三类：外来人口聚居社区、旧城老住区以及缺乏维护的工人村（Liu and Wu，2006）。深圳市城市总体规划（2010~2020）中提到三类低租金住区，城中村、旧工业区以及旧居住区，政府考虑用适当的方式有选择地将这些住房改造成为政策性住房（邹兵，2013）。因此，我们在前期调研的基础上选择出这三类中的四个案例展开调研（图2）。

深圳的城中村是高速的城市化进程中衍生出的一种特殊的城市形态。相对宽敞的住房，低廉的租金，自生的经济机制让城中村成了深圳民间低租金住区的代表。大芬村位于深圳龙岗区，20世纪90年代初开始，大批的画家开始租住于此，他们和村民一起共同经营和改造着自己的住区，在短短的20年中从一个杂乱拥挤的城中村变成了一个充满特色和活力的低租金住区。

图3示意了大芬村从2003年到2015年在社区、邻里和家庭层级上发生的变化。虽然村民和住户的关系是租赁关系，附加在房租之上的绘画产业额外收入让村民愿意和租户一起商议和改造居住环境。高性价比的居住和商业环境吸引到越来越多的绘画行业工作者，商住相互促进的良性循环使

图 2 四个案例

（1）大芬村；（2）港莲小区；（3）工业住区 D；（4）富文宿舍

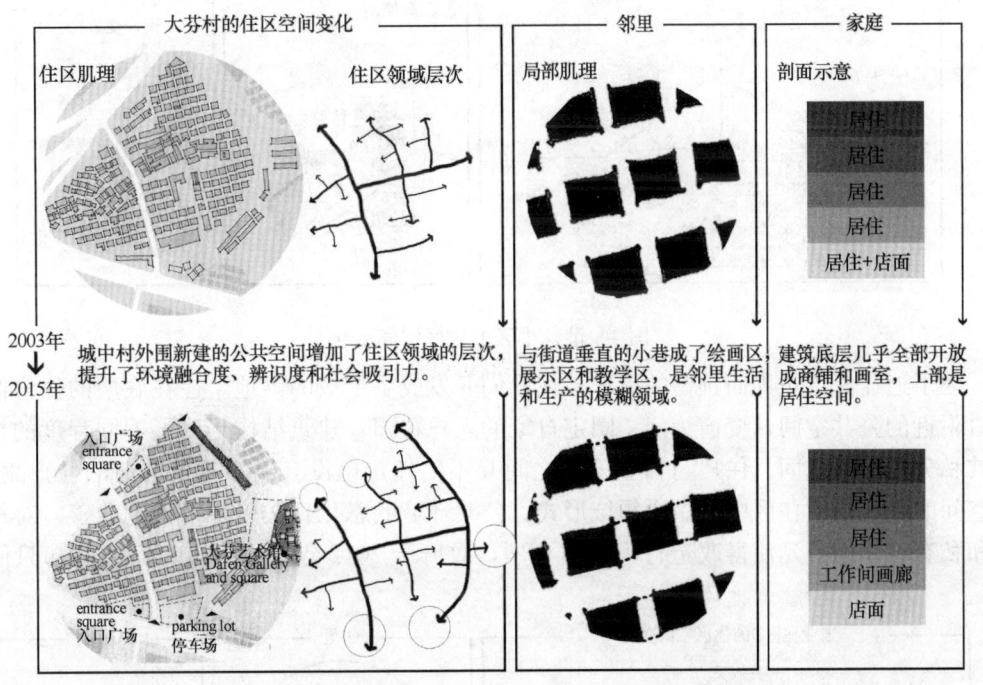

图 3 大芬村的住区空间变化和模糊领域的形成

得大芬村油画产业的影响力迅速扩大。在社区领域上的直接体现是，以大芬美术馆为代表的大量公共空间出现在住区周边，专业的规划设计逐渐渗入，但决策权依然在村民手中。村民和租客牺牲部分的私有领域来扩大住区的公共领域，带来了两个方面的明显变化：显著提升的住区文化影响力和更便利的生活环境，以及由此而产生的经济增量。建筑层面，由于受到集体土地宅基地要求的限制，大芬村以 4 至 6 层的单栋建筑格网布局为主，底层和二层几乎全部变成了商铺、画室和工作间，上部为居住。底层的四个立面被充分利用，侧边的小巷被改造成了绘画区域，人们在其间穿行可以随时欣赏现场绘画，有的店铺也会在小巷里开门以吸引人流。一个普通的画师在这里的月收入将近一万元，画室租金每间大约 700 元/月①，为了完成来自网络的大量绘画订单，画师们就地招揽学徒，一边教学一边生产，学生们学习绘画并以此创造收益，而这些领域性模糊的小巷就变成了他们在大芬村的临时工作空间。越来越多的人慕名而来，住区居民的身份认同感明显提升。

港莲小区是一个建于 1988 年的商品房小区，与香港一河之隔，今天除了部分户主家庭之外居住着大量的低收入人群，住区环境发生了很大变化。为了增加经济活动，沿街一侧的住房底层几乎全部被改造成了商铺或餐厅，入口广场变成了社会停车场，原有的两个入口也都被封死，人行入口和停车场入口设在一处，造成了很大不方便（图4）。住区内原有的公共空间被随处堆放着垃圾和废

---

① 信息来自于大芬村调研时对画家、住户和学生的随机访谈。

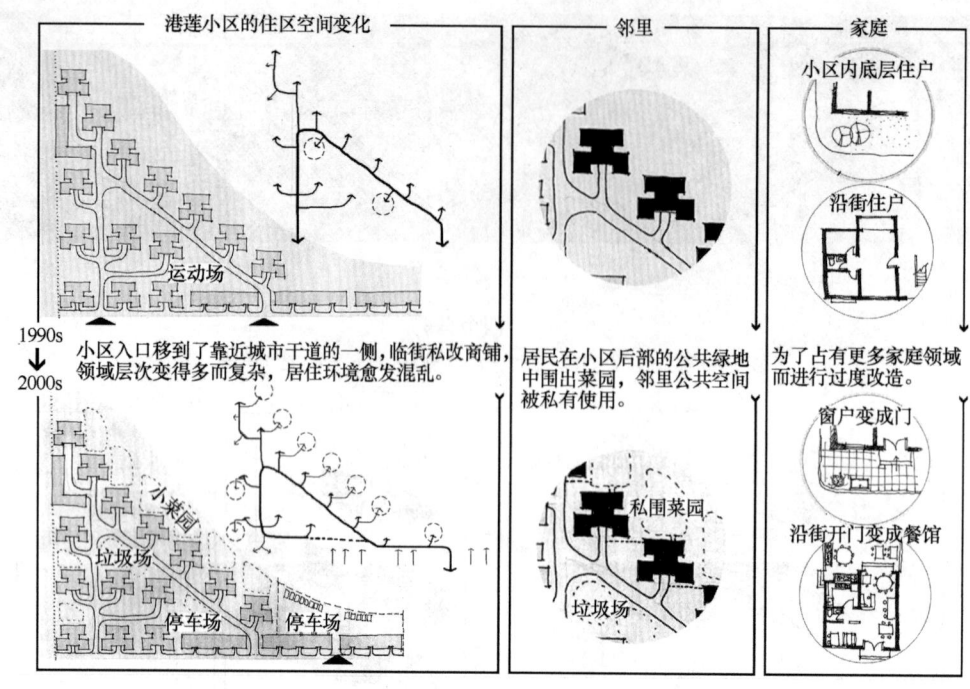

图 4　港莲小区的住区空间变化

旧家具，为了退让深港边界而预留的绿地被住户们开发成了零散的菜地。住在底层的住户们多数占用了入口附近的公共空间，变窗为门，圈定自家的入户花园。建筑结构受到了不同程度的损坏，公共空间被私分为私有空间。住户与物业公司之间互不信任，也没有能够有效沟通的住户集体组织，个体对空间的支配成了住区中的主要领域形式。公共环境的恶化长久以来得不到改善，对经济利益的追求和私有空间的蔓延使得改造行为愈演愈烈，政府于 2012 年提出拆改，而住区却只使用了不到 40 年。

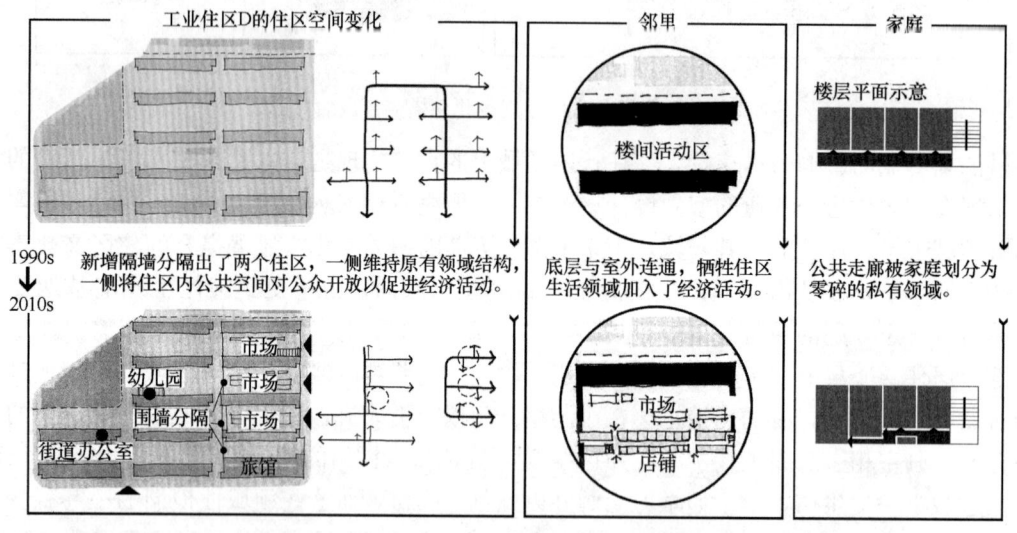

图 5　工业住区 D 的住区空间变化

　　工业住区 D 最初是单位合建的一个工人住宿区，今天由于复杂的产权关系分化成了两个独立的低租金住区。图 5 中可以看出，一道隔墙沿着建筑边界将底层公共空间分成了两个部分，一个是包括了部分政府办公楼、改建幼儿园的低租金住区，另一个是在原有住房基础上改建而成的综合市场。住户们用低廉的材料将建筑底层和公共空间完全连通，将独立的住房改造成了底商上住的综合体，底层是商铺，院子里是临时摊位区，并建有公共洗手间和休闲座椅。经济活动的介入使得住区和附近城中村的消费环境融为一体，住区的特征和区域影响力有了明显的提升，在这个案例中，提供更多社会经济活动的公共领域补偿了缩小的邻里生活领域，在家庭层面，公共领域被二次划分来弥补家庭领域的相对不足，家庭之间的合作协调最大限度提高了空间利用率。

美国某轮胎企业于 20 世纪 80 年代在深圳建厂，由于生产过程中会产生大量的污染被深圳政府要求搬离，留下的厂房及相关附属设施被另一家物业公司购买。工厂的闲置宿舍区于 2010 年左右被个人承包翻新重新投入使用。由于资金有限，一个生活区被分成了两个独立部分承包给不同的个人，富文宿舍是其中之一。承包人花了约 100 万人民币和四个月的时间在同乡的协作下完成了翻新和改造，如图 6 所示，原本的公用洗手间被改造，每个单位的

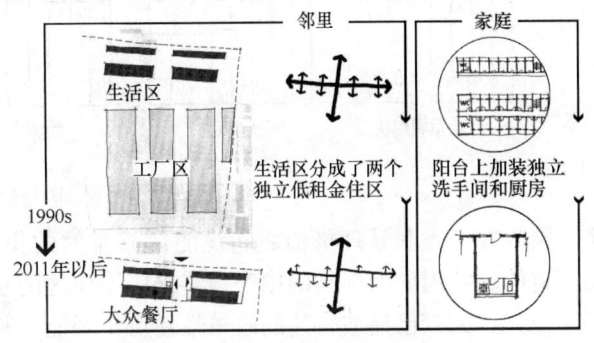

图 6　富文宿舍的住区空间变化

阳台上加装了独立的洗手间和厨房。相比多数城中村里的嘈杂拥挤，翻新后的房屋由于良好的通风采光和相对宽敞的居住环境很受欢迎，每月租金在 500 到 700 元之间，由于规模不大，承包人会不定期地组织集体活动，住户之间很快彼此熟识，承包人作为管理者负责住区里的所有事务。住区逐步加建了便宜的大众食堂，承包人响应住户需要在底层加了一间活动室作为麻将馆。租户的流动性很强，最长的会居住 6 个月左右，但由于老乡之间的相互介绍和张贴广告，有很多人排队等待入住，住区的收益虽然微薄但是稳定[①]。除了定期向工厂物业公司支付宿舍的租用费，房租收益多数用于聘请保洁人员，以及住区的日常更新维护和管理工作。然而，居民和承包人都表示会担心在这本期租约期满之后被停止续约，因为承包人的前期投入还需要更长的时间来收回成本，而居民也不想失去这一可以落脚的城市住区。

4　讨论与结论

将以上四个案例相比较，我们可以看出低租金住区中社交包容性的增强和经济活动的趋向性产生了大量的模糊领域，从而导致了住区内领域层次的增加。图 7 中示意了四个案例在邻里和家庭层级中领域层次的变化，大芬村和工业住区 D 中住户牺牲了部分的家庭私有空间形成发展经济活动的公共空间，附着在空间中的集体利益在专业设计的参与下被激发出来。大芬村中邻里领域让出空间给更大范围的城市公众，因此住区的领域层次增大到了四个层次。相比之下，港莲小区中部分居民占用公共空间为私有用途，局部形成了次级邻里领域，虽然改善了部分居民的生活条件和经济收入，但对整个住区的公共环境造成了破坏。富文宿舍是一个自治的小规模住区，人们以一种集体商议的方式应对空间的使用，两个独立的住区依然共同使用一个公共广场，充分保证家庭可支配空间独立完整，又出于对经济利益的保护，邻里领域的质量与活力得以维持。

仔细观察不难发现，住区公共领域和私有领域之间存在着一条动态界限，公共领域的增加会带来更多的经济机会和社交活动，当私有领域开始侵占公共领域时，有效的集体协商或专业知识的引导就显得尤为重要。如果说领域层次的增加反映出居民主动干预住区结构的愿望和能力，那在这一过程中集体和个人的关系便成了住区形态发展的导向。比如大芬村中，代表原村民利益的村委会与代表租客利益的画家协会，以及政府机构管理办公室之间可以有效沟通，以经济发展和提高生活环境质量为目标共同协商决策，引导和支持个人对居住环境进行干预，并有选择的接纳专业的规划设计意见，逐渐发展形成了富有特色的城市低租金住区。而然，以港莲小区为例的部分旧商品房小

---

① 富文宿舍的相关信息来自于对承租人进行的访谈。

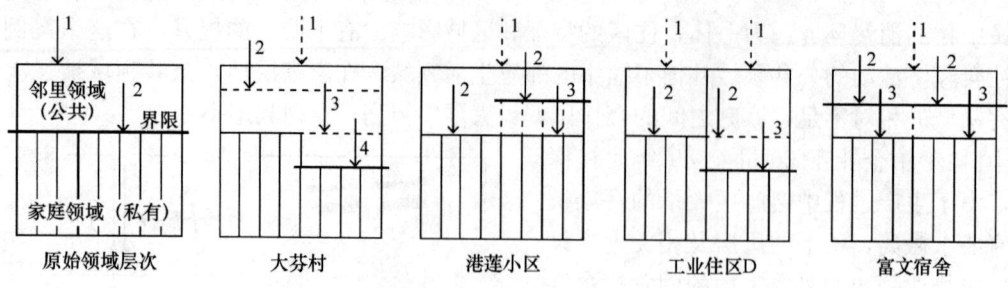

图7 四个低收入住区案例中领域层次的增加

区，因为在个人和管理机构之间没能形成有效的集体组织，沟通失效，个人行为得不到指导和反馈，集体利益因此而受到的损失最终加剧了住区的衰败。

今天，大量已建或待建的政策性住房是否能够长久的为民众提供可负担的、高质量居住环境需要更多的时间和耐心来检验。城市中为了适应居民生活而逐渐演变形成的低租金社区，在回应社会生活和经济活动的需求方面相较于普通住区有着明显的特征。在不同的社会组织模式和经济模式的作用下，有的住区产生了明显的价值增量而有些却愈发凋敝。如果我们把能够持久使用的、不断增值城市住区作为目标，对社会组织和经济发展模式的研究设计就应当先行于建筑实体的规划设计。好的住区环境能够在住户集体的干预和影响下适应不断变化的社会经济需求，这是我们面对大规模的政策性住房建设时应当明确的一个前提。

致谢

感谢香港大学研究生院、建筑学院、香港大学图书馆、深圳市莲塘街道办、明磊物业港莲小区管理处、大芬富文宿舍管理处以及调研过程中所有提供帮助和支持的单位及个人。

Influence of Socio-Economic Activity on Informal Low-Rent Community in Shenzhen, China

Liu Yiwei, Jia Beisi

(Faculty of Architecture, University of Hong Kong)

Abstract: China's urbanization in post-1978 gave birth to the first rapidly developing modern mega-cities, among which Shenzhen is the youngest and fastest-growing one. With limited resources and ample opportunities, a large number of migrant workers and low-income citizens dwelled in widely scattered urban informal settlements rely on various participation and collaboration. Newly built high-rise public housing in Shenzhen are problematic in the social aspects, while the residential morphology of informal low-rent settlements could provide reference for the future public housing plan and design. With Shenzhen as a notable example, this paper aims to reveal and interpret the transformation of territorial structure in urban low-rent housing, which are shaped by unique socio-economical requirements. The significance of this study is to explicate the importance of territorial self-regulation in urban low-rent settlements. Drawing on the concept of bottom-up urbanization and open building hierarchy theory, by looking closely into the intervention on level of neighborhood and family, this paper examines and compares four selected cases from three categories of informal public housing in Shenzhen: villages in the city, obsolete industrial living quarters, degraded commercial housing.

Keywords: House form, Public housing, Informal low-rent community, Territorial structure

参考文献：

［1］ Aldo，Rossi. The Architecture of the City［M］. Cambridge：MIT Press，1984.

［2］ Brower，Sidney N. Territory in urban settings［J］. Environment and culture，Springer，1980：179-207.

［3］ Habraken，Nicolaas John. Supports：an alternative to mass housing［M］. Translated by B. Valkenburg. London：Architectural Press，1972.

［4］ Habraken，Nicolaas John. The structure of the ordinary：form and control in the built environment［M］. Cambridge：MIT Press. 1998.

［5］ Habraken，Nicolaas John. The Uses of Levels［J］. Open House International，2002，27（2）：9-20.

［6］ Kendall，Stephen H，Jonathan Teicher. Residential open building：Routledge［Z］. 2010.

［7］ Kropf，Karl. Urban tissue and the character of towns［J］. Urban Design International，1996，1（3）：247-263.

［8］ Liu，Yuting，Fulong Wu. Urban poverty neighbourhoods：typology and spatial concentration under China's market transition，a case study of Nanjing［J］. Geoforum，2006，37（4）：610-626.

［9］ Rapoport，Amos. House form and culture［M］. Englewood Cllifs，New Jersey：prentice-hall，1969.

［10］ 邹兵. 由"增量扩张"转向"存量优化"——深圳市城市总体规划转型的动因与路径［J］. 规划师，2013，29（5）：5-10.

城市与建筑：设计、更新及改造
City and Building:
Design，Renew and Reconstruction

专题一：城市更新与建筑改造
Special Topic 1：Urban Renew and Building Reconstruction

An Investigation into the Use of Virtual and Augmented Reality in Space Utilisation and Efficiency in Small Scale Housing Design

Wolfgang Dokonal[1], Ernst Alexander Dengg[1], Michael William Knight[2]
(1. Graz University of Technology, 2. University of Liverpool)

Abstract: The rapid development of new VR devices such as the Oculus Rift and Google Cardboard together with applications such as 3D plus (by the Finnish company advice), Unity3D and Unreal Engine raises the question of how we can use these new applications and interfaces to improve the design and communication process. The question will be if there is any added value-besides the novelty factor-in using these new devices compared to conventional less immersive models or a traditional design process. To give an extra dimension or even several dimensions to the standard 3D model would allow users to immerse more deeply into the virtual project and to get more realistic insights of the design prototype.

Keywords: 3D modelling, Augmented reality, Virtual reality, Space optimisation

1 Introduction

There are already successful implementations of VR and augmented reality applications using 3D city models to visualise the impact of new projects in existing cities. There is also a long tradition to visualise interiors using these systems. Since the development of the first VR Caves, experts could use these expensive infrastructures to access models interactively and sometimes they were used to present final designs to the client or the general public. The new devices will allow a much cheaper and much more immersive interactive experience in exploring these models at a much earlier stage in the design process. By making it more accessible for the client or the general public it opens opportunities for a much more participatory design process where the client can take a more active part in the process at an early stage. Because of the positive market trend, VR and AR will also affect areas, in which designers and clients until now did not have the means to make use of it because there is an impressive amount of new developments and devices in the field. Referring to the "3D plus App", a relatively simple, but in terms of communication, very powerful Augmented Reality app, we can see that the trend is already there. VR apps for smartphones and tablets, allowing to walk through virtual environments and buildings are as well emerging, even though some issues e. g. how to physically walk through virtual space to avoid nausea, are not completely resolved.

2 Work in Progress

This research was mainly based on a course for architectural students at Graz University of Technology, Austria and teachers from Graz and the School of Architecture at the University of Liverpool, UK. Due to some postponement in the scheduling of the course major parts of the research will now happen after the deadline for this paper submission. Therefore, we can mainly present the layout of the research in this paper and will have to wait for our presentation at the conference to be able to present the results.

483

3　First Concepts

As mentioned above, conventional 3D models work fairly well in presenting static ideas and impressions of an architectural or urban design. The new devices raise the questions of if we can look more deeply into the optimisation of space or processes. There is a great potential for better and quicker communication between the client and the designers and inside a design team, due to its indisputable potential of immersive and fast knowledge transfer. Furthermore, it allows everyone involved in the process to get an earlier impression of the spatial qualities even before final, detailed materials and lighting effects are added.

As a first concept to check the usability of these devices, we use students to build their own flats as VR models using SketchUp and Unreal Engine. The idea behind that is that they should know their own environment out of their first hand personal experience quite well and therefore have a good basis for the evaluation of their "Virtual Flats". These "Virtual Flats" are then explored from the students who are living in the "Real Flats" by using Google Cardboard and Oculus Rift devices. Additionally we will also use some of the expensive Caves to explore the virtual flats. All students are required to document the experience in a questionnaire that we prepared for them where they have to address several issues concerning aspects like Perception, Immersion and technical issues (see detailed questionnaire in the appendix).

Another strand of investigation is the case study of an efficient small-scale living unit (see Figure 1). We use one of the very common floor plans used by MTRC (Mass Transit Railway Corporation) in Hong Kong, "LOHAS Park" -formally known as "Dream city" -where LOHAS stands for "Lifestyle of Health and Sustainability" to explore that. Naturally, in Hong Kong all these aspects have to be fulfilled using very small flats (app. 400 square feet/38 square meter). Most of the people living in these flats are quite satisfied with them-we were interested what western students would experience when they explore a virtual model of these floor plans.

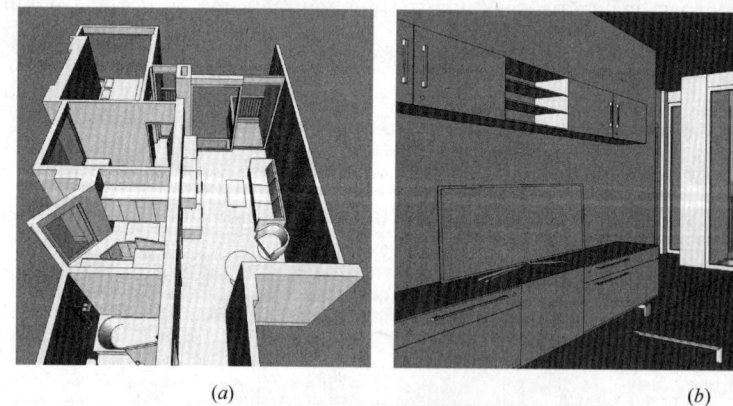

(a)　　　　　　　　　　　　　　(b)

Figure 1　3D-views of apartment B, Beaumont Tower 2, LOHAS park

(a) Top view of apartment B, Beaumont Tower 2, LOHAS park;

(b) Internal perspective of apartment B, Beaumont Tower 2, LOHAS park

[Source: Ernst Alexander Dengg (originator); designed according to an existing and furnished apartment, 2015]

484

4 Low Cost vs. High End

In addition to these personal experiences using low cost mobile VR devices we also try to find out if there is a big difference in the quality of the VR experience by using the very expensive VR labs that have been established before the development of the mobile VR solutions. Within our workshops we will have access to two different "conventional" VR Labs-The DAVE lab at Graz University of Technology in Austria-where DAVE stands for the "Definitely Affordable Virtual Environment" which is a "low cost" four sided CAVE. "Low Cost" in this case compared to the second "conventional" lab we could use which is the 1. 5 million pound VR lab at Liverpool University in the United Kingdom.

5 From SketchUp to Unreal and Beyond

For getting the 3D model into Unreal Engine, we exported the file from SketchUp as a FBX file (Google Earth file) . Naturally, we had to solve several issues in bringing the different SketchUp files into Unreal. Depending on how the students worked in SketchUp we experienced different problems. One of the issues is the way the collision detection feature works in Unreal, which makes it necessary to build the model in a different way to make it possible to walk through doors. Then we exported the virtual environment as an application coming from Unreal Engine to the mobile devices. One of the next problems was the preparation of the Unreal scene for the VR systems-the interface for the Oculus Rift is straightforward-the interface for cardboard is at this moment not fully implemented. The challenge is to create a workflow that can be easily used by students even if they have no special programming skills. At the moment we are preparing this workflow for cardboard and the results look promising.

6 Conclusion

As mentioned above most of our final results and the evaluation of the results of the questionnaire will only be available at the conference and we will present it in detail there. Our research will try to give new insights into some aspects e. g. the necessary levels of detail to make the best possible use of these new devices and the impact that these findings have on the design of efficient small-scale living spaces. We will draw conclusions on the ability of VR and AR to successfully communicate a spatial experience that is useful for the designer in creating efficient small-scale housing and contrast this with a traditional design method. With an easy to use Workflow, there is a great potential for Low-cost Virtual Reality and Augmented Reality devices. Because of the increased interest of the gaming industry this field is developing rapidly, there is an abundance of new devices, and improved systems are developed almost every month. If architects make intelligent use of these developments, they have a whole range of new possibilities for accessing the data at very low cost and comparatively little additional effort. Less "Augmented Reality", more "Augmented Information" .

App. 1　The Questionnaire

Explanation：

The questionnaire consists of two parts which are targeting on gaining different insights. In the first part, we will evaluate student's findings after immerging virtually into their own apartment. In the second part we look into the spatial perception of the LOHAS project.

For all statements below please answer with 1-5

(Legend：1. strongly agree, 2. agree, 3. neutral, 4. disagree, 5. strongly disagree)

1. Perception of planners

Please open the app of your self-provided floor plan with your VR device-Smartphone and VR HMD mount (virtual reality head-mounted display mount) -and put it on. Walk around freely and observe your apartment carefully. Please walk into every room and look around.

You have created a 3D model of it and you are living in the real apartment. Would you agree to the following statements：

　• Spatial perception is much clearer and closer to reality in the VR model-compared to the 3D CAD model.

　• Observing the design via VR-device helps to understand the design better.

　• The VR observation of space is no help at all.

　• I can easily orient myself like in the real apartment.

　• I get a good notion of the real apartment and about its atmosphere.

2. LOHAS apartment

Please open the file/app of the LOHAS floor plan with your VR device-Smartphone and VR HMD mount (virtual reality head-mounted display mount) -and put it on. Walk around freely and try to observe and to internalise the whole apartment for maximum 5 minutes. Please walk into every room and look around. We request to use the whole 5 minutes to get comparable results.

After the virtual walk through please answer following questions in chronological order：

A. Testing of perception (to get an idea how close we can come to reality)

For those questions you should know the size of one apartment/house you used to live in/spent much time in it. (don't answer if you do not have a quite precise idea of the living space size.)

　• What is the size of your reference apartment?

　• How much bigger/smaller is your reference apartment? (allowed are factors such as "1.5 times bigger" or percentage e. g. 150%)

Further estimations

Please try always to estimate as good as possible the room size/requested dimension. If you do not remember e. g. the requested room or get confused with them please do not answer the question.

　• What is the room height? (Remark：the whole apartment has the same room height)

- What is the size of the living room?
- What is the size of the bathroom?
- What is the size of the kitchen?
- What is the size of the bedroom? (consider, that the cabinet belongs to the apartment and has a depth of 58 cm)
- What is the total size of the living area in square metre/square feet.

B. Immersion and Benefits

- It was easy to immerse/grasp the layout of the apartment.
- After the walk through, I have a good imagination of the apartment.
- I have a good spatial perception.
- I think the virtual walk through the apartment makes it easier for me to understand/grasp the floor plan?
- Scenario: You are looking for an apartment to live in, and the building is not yet built. Normally that would mean you rely on renderings (visualisations) and floor plans for interpreting potential space.
- In this Scenario the VR model can facilitate better understanding of the potential built space and can also add value in decision making.
- The VR model can help me to understand the internal order, daily routine and circulation.

C. Improvements

What helped you to scale the dimensions in perceiving the spaces?

For the examples below, please comment them with 1-5

(Legend: 1. strongly agree, 2. agree, 3. neutral, 4. disagree, 5. strongly disagree)

- Proportions of room heights and width.
- Furniture.
- Doors.
- I would need more details (e. g. furniture and fixtures) to grasp the size of the apartment.
- I would need to see colours and materials of the interior to grasp the size of the apartment.
- I would need a more realistic visual information to grasp the size of the apartment.
- I would need to physically walk through the virtual reality to get a better understanding of the apartment size.
- I would need a better display resolution to immerse deeper (Please name the device).
- I would need a device with less lag (Please name the device).

探讨使用虚拟实境及扩增实境如何可充分有效地
利用小型房屋设计的空间

Wolfgang Dokonal[1]，Ernst Alexander Dengg[1]，Michael William Knight[2]

（1. 格拉茨技术大学；2. 利物浦大学）

摘要：Oculus Rift 和 Google Cardboard 等新的 VR 设备，3D plus（由芬兰公司咨询建议），Unity3D 和 Unreal Engine 等应用程序的快速发展，引发了如何通过使用这些新的应用程序和接口来提高外观设计和沟通过程的问题。这个问题是除了新奇的因素外，相比传统没有身临其境感的模型或传统的设计过程，这些新设备的使用是否有附加的价值。提供一个甚至几个额外的维度给标准的 3D 模型，能允许用户更深入地体验虚拟的项目，并对设计原型有真实的感知。

关键词：立体建模，扩增实境，虚拟实境，空间优化

References：

［1］ William R. Sherman, Alan B. Craig-Understanding Virtual Reality ［P/OL］. Elsevier 2003 IS-BN 1-55860-353-0 ［12.05.2015］. http：//www. cgv. tugraz. at/dave.

［2］ Jennifer Whyte. Virtual Reality and the build Environment ［P］. Architectural Press 2002 IS-BN 0 7506 5372 8 ［12.05.2015］.

城市建设中的历史街区保护模式研究

曾 皓 赵 祥

（西南科技大学土木工程与建筑学院）

摘要：在城市中，历史街区是展示传统文化和生活方式的物质载体，但却正在被快速的城市化蚕食破坏，如何合理保护和利用历史街区已成为城市建设中公众关注的焦点。本文阐述了历史街区的概念及国内外对其保护和发展的现状，分析了国外的保护理念和成功的案例，以国内众多的历史街区保护案例分析为基础，提出了历史街区的多元化保护模式分类，对不同模式的优劣进行了研究，并阐述了各自的适用范围。

关键词：历史街区，保护模式，城市建设

1 引言

在城市建设的热潮中，一方面众多自称"明清老街"、"唐宫宋城"的仿古街道层出不穷；而另一方面，很多货真价实的历史街区却没有得到应有重视，最终走向破败或消失。怎样保护历史街区的真实状态并使之具备长久的活力，是中国城市建设进程中不能回避的问题。

2 历史街区的概念及其保护

历史街区概念首次出现于 1933 年国际现代建筑学会通过的《雅典宪章》，它是指在城市中由传统街道、居住建筑群和文物建筑组成的较完整的，能体现传统风貌、民族或地方特色的区域[1]。因此，历史街区有别于历史遗址和历史建筑。历史遗迹是场景时间的停留，只具有展示性并没有生活内容，如圆明园；历史建筑的空间没有现实的使用价值，保护重点在于物质实体部分，如北京故宫、西安大雁塔等；而历史街区在现实中依然是承担了一定城市功能的生活空间。因此，功能性的维持是历史街区保护的最基本原则，需要在保存街区真实的历史遗存和建筑风貌的同时，维持并发展它的使用功能，适应城市发展的需要。

中国目前历史街区的保护情况并不乐观。一方面，我国许多城市建设一味追求速度和规模，粗放的开发模式使得历史文化风貌破坏严重；另一方面，物质生活高度发展后，人们更加渴望精神生活的丰富体验，亲身经历生活场景比在博物馆看文物更能理解传统。历史街区是联系城市历史活的线索，提供了一个连接传统的场所，具有独特的艺术价值、历史价值。如果历史街区被破坏，一些传统的生活方式及其相应的文化现象将失去合适的生存空间，那些独特的人文活动就难免快速消失。

3 历史街区保护遇到的困难

3.1 建筑失修，生活条件差

一些历史街区地处城市经济不发达区域，缺少资金投入来改善基础设施，房屋老化失修严重，影响了其功能运转。对于历史文化保护区内的建筑物，法律规定不得擅自改扩建，限制了有能力的住户自行改善居住条件，使得有经济实力的人基本搬出，导致街区内人口老龄化和低收入人群比重较大，许多历史街区几乎沦为了贫民窟，如重庆十八梯历史街区。留下的居民也并非因为历史街区

的深厚文化氛围，而是由于经济等原因被迫留下，如南京南捕厅历史街区曾经做过居民未搬迁原因的调研，其中 34％的居民认为搬迁补偿过低，23％认为安置房地点不合理[2]。因此，虽然在旁人眼中历史街区有厚重文化，但其原始住民则困于其中，由于居住条件较差，整体呈现出衰落、消极的特征。

3.2 注重短期利益，保护模式单一

许多历史街区处于城市老旧区域的核心地段，地价昂贵。相比起保护历史街区这种回报率低的项目，一些地方政府更倾向于土地开发一些能短期内产生高收益的项目，因此这些历史街区多被高档的办公楼和住宅所取代。城市管理者把旅游业作为重塑历史街区的有效手段，但过度开发旅游功能，导致街区原有性质的改变和传统风貌的消退。在经济效益的简单导向下，对历史街区保护的重点不明，手法简单粗糙，于是便出现了拆掉真古董，新建假古董的现象。

如何平衡商业营利和文化传承是历史街区保护的难点。解决这一难题需要准确理解历史街区保护的内涵采取与之相适应的保护模式，在这方面国外的理论与实践值得中国的城市管理者和设计人员借鉴。

4 国外历史街区保护理论与实践

1979 年，在澳大利亚的巴拉发表了《保护具有文化意义地方的宪章》，简称《巴拉宪章》，其中明确提出了"改造性再利用"的理念，即对某一具有文化价值的场所进行调整使其容纳新功能，并对建筑制定相应的维护、保存、修复、改建、重建等措施。这种做法没有在实际上削弱场所的文化意义，保持了历史的延续性，但为历史建筑或地段再度具有活力创造了条件。这种方法为西方所普遍认同并实践，其中意大利和日本的实践最为成功。

4.1 意大利

意大利在旧城保护方面有着很多严格的规定和管理，在历史街区改造过程中意大利政府对历史街区不是采取破旧立新的做法，而是通过功能置换努力挖掘其现实生活价值，区内的改造项目都有着严格的要求，除了聘请专业的设计、施工团队，一般还会组建一个由各界人士组成的评估小组，对修复和改造的可行性和修复后的效果进行客观和公正的评估。如果发生分歧，政府和设计师会主导协调工作重新设计改造方案，待评估通过后方能进行实施。[3]严格的保护、经营和管理不仅保护了历史的延续，也带来了良好的经济回报，如威尼斯每年都吸引 1200 万观光客，在城市经济上来看可算是取得了巨大成功。

图 1 京都街道

（资料来源：https://www.pinterest.com/robvanham/japan/）

4.2 日本

日本传统街区多以木构低层建筑为主，例如京都和奈良。因此其历史街区的更新主要以传统房屋的结构保护和功能改造为主，并注意历史街景的营造。在改造过程中采用小规模的渐进式改造，建筑立面恢复过去的原貌，内部空间通过新材料、新技术完善配套设施，是一种建筑表皮与内部功能脱开的做法，虽然功能与形式没有太多的联系，但街区的整体风貌得到了统一延续（图 1），为

具有活力的现实生活功能提供了一个具有传统风貌的容器。古都风景保存完好的京都每年吸引 5000 万人次的游客到访，市内 10% 以上的就业人口都与旅游业相关。

5 国内历史街区保护模式探析

5.1 国内历史街区保护的理念

中国正式提出历史街区的保护是在 1986 年，但至今未形成国家层面的法规。对于历史街区这种仍旧需要承载现代生活的城市区域，历史真实性的延续只能是部分和相对的，因此不同的保护观念只有合适与否而没有绝对的好坏之分，应该针对保护对象的不同特点采取不同的保护方法。每个城市的历史街区情况不同，应当综合考虑到现状条件、历史价值、实际利用价值和区域发展目标等因素，根据具体情况不同，一部分历史街区可能适用于采取西方注重物质形态的保护方式，另一些则适用于采取注重传统场所连续性的保护方式。

5.2 历史街区保护模式分类

近 30 年来中国实施了许多历史街区保护项目，其中不乏成功的案例。仔细分析这些案例，可发现其成功之处在于很少进行大拆大建式的整修，而是依据街区的实际情况，因地制宜地实施保护措施。为简化分析，在此抛开其他因素，只研究历史街区的实体空间（Space）和生活功能（Function）两者间的关系。依据这两者的关系，按照"X Space＋X Function"公式分为五类保护模式（表 1），以下将针对这五类模式与实际案例相结合进行说明。

保护模式分类   表 1

"OSOF" 模式	Original Space ＋ Original Function
"NSOF" 模式	New Space ＋ Original Function
"OSNF" 模式	Original Space ＋ New Function
"NSNF" 模式	New Space ＋ New Function
"SFM" 模式	Space and Function Mixing

5.2.1 "OSOF"模式——街区整体保存修缮

这种模式的特征是街区空间和活动内容在历史发展进程中没有过多的变化，只需要对街区做适当修缮维护，保护难度小，资金投入少，组成历史街区的所有元素也得到了原汁原味的保留。

代表案例：重庆磁器口、台州北新椒街、温州五马街。

磁器口是重庆市沙坪坝区的一个重要历史街区。这里地靠嘉陵江码头，一直是重庆重要的商业活动区。作为民俗文化的载体，磁器口具有历史延续性，从古至今的活动内容并没有太大变化。在地方政府的宣传推动下，磁器口"重庆小吃街"的形象带动了当地旅游业的发展，在经济上良性循环。磁器口街区的保护主要是进行损坏构件的修复和替换，而不做全面整修，这也使得古街建筑传统风貌能够最大限

图 2 磁器口街道

（资料来源：www. tour. cqnews. net）

491

度地完整保留（图2）。例如磁器口的街面铺地是粗平的毛石，这使得在街道上行走的舒适度不高，但人们能够真正体味到传统的生活气氛。

5.2.2 "NSOF"模式——强调场所功能的原始性

这种模式的特征在于街区内的城市生活成为保护的重点内容，通过对街区进行全面翻新或原址重建古建筑的方式以提高历史街区的环境质量，同时尽可能保留传统生活模式。

代表案例：北京前门大街、舟山定海古城、杭州河坊街。

前门大街一直是北京的一个主要的商业街，由于历史悠久，这里许多建筑出现了不同程度的损坏，影响了商业活动开展。为了保持前门大街的传统商业街地位，北京市进行了前门大街复兴项目，保留了9个20世纪20~30年代的老建筑，其余老店全部整改成明清时期的样式。修缮后的前门大街以传统商业、历史文化的集聚为特色，体现传统与时尚的交汇融合。

这种将原有建筑推倒重建的更新方式，表面上保留了居民的生活环境，但一定要准确把握好"拆"与"建"的尺度，否则失去了历史建筑的原真性，只能由新建筑来填补，极容易导致为人诟病的"仿古街"现象。

5.2.3 "OSNF"模式——实体保留与功能置换

这种模式侧重于保持历史街区内部建筑的完整性，将不适合该空间的功能内容置换掉。通过在原有街区内注入新的活动重新激发街区活力。

代表案例：成都宽窄巷子、上海外滩。

现存"宽窄巷子"是当年成都少城遗留的唯一部分，它是老成都"千年少城"城市格局和百年原真建筑格局的最后遗存，也是北方胡同文化和建筑风格在南方的"孤本"。2003年成都市政府遵循"修旧如旧、保护为主"的原则重新规划了街区。街区的建筑本身保持了原真性，改建或者改造的部分相对较少。可以让人从建筑围合的空间感受到原汁原味的古建筑氛围。在生活内容上注重传统氛围营造，小吃、茶馆、传统手工艺都在这里汇聚。改造后的宽窄巷子经济效益突出，仅2010年的产值就高达2亿，解决了3000人的就业。这里本是一个以居住为主的街区，但随着城市扩张，今天已变成闹市区，居住功能与其城市区位的冲突较大，不能满足现代社会的生活需求，所以对功能作了较大改造。通常的住宅功能转变私人会所或展览功能，外围沿街的建筑基本上也变为商业和饮食用途。

在这类改造中街区只起到了一个场所作用，历史街区原住居民的迁出使得原生文化失去了生存的土壤。在其间发生的社会活动与建筑原本存在的历史缘由没有太多联系，因此传统活动的内容应选择性保留，提取出能够反应传统并顺应场所发展的活动。

5.2.4 "NSNF"模式——提取传统元素，实体全面更新

这类模式的特征是由内而外从空间到内容的全面改造，为了适应新的功能需求，功能的变化也伴随着历史街区在城市中角色的转变。

代表案例：上海新天地。

"上海新天地"是以上海近代建筑的标志形象——石库门建筑聚集区为基础改造而成，改造于1999年动工，2001年大体建成。对历史建筑进行"存表去里"的改造，被保留的只是空间格局和外墙体，从屋架、地面到内部空间，都经过了改头换面的二次设计（图3）。通过全面的改造和商业运营，经典的石库门建筑群变成了一个有海派文化混搭特色的商圈，成了上海著名的高端消费场所。这种模式虽然在外观上保留了原有建筑的肌理形态，但是由于将原住民全体外迁，在如今的新天地已经无法再感受到过去里弄生活的场景，原住民被川流不息的消费者与游客所代替，不同于成

都宽窄巷子的"以旧换旧"模式，空间中发生的活动也与老上海的历史没有任何关系。

(a)　　　　　　　　　　　　　　　　　　　　(b)

图3　石库门改造后与改造前对比

(a) 改造后；(b) 改造前

(资料来源：a：www. suncolor. tuchong. com

b：www. news. china. com. cn)

5.2.5　"SFM"模式——渐进式改造

这种模式的特征是历史街区部分修缮改造、部分保留维护，新旧风格杂陈也表现了街区内部活动内容的多元化，原有居民生活模式和新注入的生活模式相互交织在一起产生了蒙太奇的时空拼贴效果。

代表案例：上海田子坊、杭州南宋御街、北京南锣鼓巷。

田子坊街区形成于20世纪20年代，处于原法租界和华人居住区，是上海保存历史文化遗存类型最丰富的街区之一。田子坊的"软改造"方案，即在尽可能维持城市街坊原貌原性质的情况下完成旧城面貌改造，不必伤筋动骨。这一改造过程全部由民众自发，政府并没有过多的干预，居民自行出租自有住房给艺术家作为工作室或改造为创意时尚的消费场所。一方面弄堂里不加修饰地呈现着日常生活杂乱、粗粝的面貌呈现出老上海最真实的生活面貌；另一方面商业和艺术并存，激发了街区活力。但一些住房难以商业化的居民被迫滞留在嘈杂的环境中生活，被改善的空间往往不服务于原住居民。

6　结论

不同城市的历史街区在各自城市的经济、社会背景下表现出多样的现实价值。因此对历史街区保护和利用时，必须从实际出发，既不能一拆了之，也不能过于乐观估计历史遗产所带来的经济效益。选择了错误的保护模式不但起不到促进经济增长、提高城市文化品位的作用，反而会对街区环境和历史建筑带来负面影响。前述的保护模式类别只是理论分析，具体的项目应该因地制宜结合城市的历史文化背景和发展方向，同时考虑街区内居民的需求，将历史街区的建筑实体空间和居民的生活功能相结合统筹考虑，探索一种既能保护历史遗迹的真实，也有利于历史街区活力长久延续的保护模式。

The Analysis of Protection Mode of Historic Blocks in City Construction

Zeng Hao，Zhao Xiang

(School of Civil Engineering and Architecture South
West University of Science and Technology)

Abstract：The historic blocks，which are material carriers that demonstrate the traditional culture and lifestyle，are being destructed by rapid urbanization in cities．How to protect and utilize the historic blocks properly has become the focus of public concern in urban construction．This paper describes the concept of historic block and the status quo at home and abroad for its protection and development，and analyzes the protection ideas and cases abroad．Based on the study on many historic block protection cases in our country，it classifies the protection modes and explains the pros and cons of different modes，then expounds their respective scope of application．

Keywords：Historic block，Protection mode，Urban construction

参考文献：

[1]　杨雪伦，贾馥冬．探讨我国城市历史街区的更新与保护[J]．河北：河北建筑工程学院学报，2011(04)：36-38．

[2]　谢文兴．城市跟新中的历史街区[D]．江苏：南京人学，2011．

[3]　张明欣．经营城市历史街区[D]．上海：同济大学，2007．

以科学风水为思维的旧建筑改造设计的探索与实践：以福建省平潭县白青乡白青卫生院为例

李彦颐[1]　李子耀[2]　邱克豪[3]

（1. 台湾树德科技大学建筑研究所；2. 勃翔股份有限公司；
3. 勃翔股份有限公司/台湾淡江大学土木工程学系）

摘要： 面对全球气候变迁的风险与自然资源与能源的逐渐短缺，近年来各先进国家的新建筑的比例已逐步减少，取而代之的则是对旧建筑的改造与再利用，以延长其使用年限、降低其总体的能耗，并有效减轻环境污染，进而推动整体生态环境的可持续发展。相较于新建建筑的营缮行为，旧建筑的改造与更新，更加着重于如何对既成建筑与其周边环境进行科学的评价与分析，并以数据与可视化的方式对设计产生支撑作用，以作为规划设计前的基础指导方针。但是，以科学风水作为旧建筑改造和再利用的分析方法目前仍未有一套较为完整的论述方法。故本研究目的在于尝试建立以科学风水为思维的研究机制，以福建省平潭县白青乡白青卫生院之转型再生为操作对象，同时也为两岸绿色建筑与科学风水之实践交流平台。科学风水的重点不仅只是建筑单体，更关注于既成空间所生成的环境特征与气候趋势，包含了风、光、热、气、水等气候因子，并依据尺度的不同而有其探讨的重点，并将以反馈回旧建筑之修改建的手法，以提出经济与永续的就建筑的环境治理的对策。本次研究探索与操作中，团队试图提出不同于传统旧有建筑设计的思维，强调科学风水应用于不同尺度的环境分析，并据此分析出空间的环境特征，在科学风水下之空间与环境间之连续尺度反馈整体连续空间的元素改造设计为做法；分别从地理信息系统（Geographic Information System, GIS）建立区域的人文、景观、地理特征的区域空间格局为区域尺度架构，导入 GIS3D 信息化模型建置科学风水的环境模拟基础，透过环境模拟与计算软件（区域气候分析、气流与温热环境分析）进行区域与街廓尺度的环境与气候特征之数据化与可视化的工作，作为导入建置标准建筑信息模型（Building Information Modeling, BIM）之 3D 建筑信息模型之环境边界条件，并尝试建置于区域环境的 3D 模型中，以评测该环境因子对单体建筑之影响，最后则提出旧建筑再利用之修缮对策与方法并以验证其效果。有别于传统的旧建筑再利用重于单体建筑空间的设计，未能从区域的角度来探讨环境与气候因素可能带来的影响。团队透过此一案例操作，将同时建议旧建筑再利用之设计前端，应由区域的环境特征先行进行数据与可视化的模拟与分析，再逐步缩小范围至建筑单体，以全面掌握整体连续性空间的环境特质，更进一步的透过当地食材之生态共生设计，试图结合绿色建筑与"可食接口"间的共荣关系，建议出"可持续可食"的建筑对策；后续将针对建筑单体之环境特征进行设计实践，以创造一经济、省能、健康的永续性旧建筑再利用的治理对策与方法。

关键词： 科学风水，食物设计，3D 建筑信息模型，可持续生态建筑，绿色建筑信息模型

1 引言与思路

随着绿色环境维持与排放减量的环保意识不断上升与人类文化资产关注的力道逐渐显现，这些因素都对既有建筑与城区的开发模式构成诸多的影响，其中又以改造再利用为主的开发思想不断得到加强，在如此氛围下旧建筑再利用即成为世界对建筑开发首要考虑的方法之一，而这结构性调整对于建筑设计与环境分析的思路也产生新的冲击。

1.1 思路1：应建构从区域环境到建筑单体流动空间的科学风水分析方法

旧建筑再利用的环境分析，不仅只掌握场地内部环境的条件状况，将建筑与其所处环境看作是连续性的流动性空间，更需针对所处的区域周边进行调查分析与模拟，以趋近于真实的空间数据以作为环境分析的科学依据，亦即为一跨尺度的三维绿色信息模型（GREEN BIM）的建立与分析的过程。以此方式才能全面掌握旧建筑自身与所处环境的立命条件，建构科学风水的分析方法。

1.2　思路 2：旧建筑再利用的设计应立基于改善室内外环境为目标

旧建筑的再利用设计，应依循建筑与所在区域环境的模拟分析与可视化的科学化数据所提供的设计线索，进行反复验证，而其设计效果不仅应对建筑自身的性能有所提升，更重要的是能借助设计上的优化，有益于改善既成环境的微小气候。

1.3　思路 3：旧建筑设计后应成为区域循环系统的一环

从城市到建筑不仅是流动的空间体系，建筑更是整个城市循环系统紧密相连的一个关键的环节。因此，旧建筑再利用的设计，应考虑与城市有系统地相链接，借助水、绿、能源、食物等资源的共享，促使建筑作为供给与接收环境资源的载体。

基于上述的旧建筑规划设计思路，我们以福建省平潭县白青乡白青卫生院作为研究对象，尝试建构起以科学风水为思维的规划设计与研究的方法。

2　从区域到建筑：建构连续性空间尺度的模拟分析方法

建筑规划与设计不可忽视所在地环境对建筑本身或者建筑对既成环境的影响。如何全面掌握建筑场地与及其周边的环境状态，系为旧建筑再利用规划前期相当重要的工作之一。因此，本研究将尝试应用各种不同的软件，企图建立完整的旧建筑再利用的模拟与分析方法。

2.1　以 GIS 作为流动性空间的分析工具

在进行规划设计前，地理信息系统（GIS）作为首要涉入环境基础分析的科学方法之一，而其首要工作便在于如何框选适宜的地理范围。适宜范围的划定主要依据当地所在区域的地形、地貌、建筑量体、坐向与可能影响区域环境的元素进行综合的分析与判读，并采用实测地形图与卫星图像作为辅助工具，以选定一对区域环境最适切的影响范围。

选定范围后，应用 GIS 的数据分析与归纳的功能，从区域到空间连续尺度，借助 GIS 的可视化功能，理解周边地形地貌状态、建筑类型坐向、公共与开放空间、潮汐退缩等各种信息，而这些特征显现的不单仅表达旧建筑位处环境的平面分析，关键的在于如何转换成 3D 的信息模型，以作为后续绿色环境分析使用。

本研究应用 Esri ArcGIS 作为 GIS 分析软件，并配合 Data Interoperability 插件，将 GIS 数据转换成 3D 信息模型，包含地形、建筑物、地面设施物等，大大扩展了 GIS 作为三维分析、区域尺度的信息模型软件应用。

2.2　以 REVIT 建构单体的建筑信息模型

进入建筑尺度的可视化模拟，为求建筑更细致的环境影响因素的正确性，建筑信息模型（BIM）的建构为必要的工作。本研究依据现场调研所取得的数据信息，白青卫生院建筑单体部分直接采用 REVIT 建置三维建筑信息模型，并依据建筑材料进行三维模型的组件分类，以确实反映建筑之真实样态。

2.3　以 Ecotect Analysis 进行三维信息模型的统合

三维信息模型的建构位于计算机中提供拟真的可视化环境，以作为连续尺度环境模拟的基础。一般的做法大多于绿色建筑模拟软件中建置简化模型进行分析，因此无法与 BIM 与 GIS 所生成的信息模型有良好的交换兼容性与使用性，另外因建置简化模型则可能忽略许多影响分析判读的关键因素，使得模拟成果失真。基于上述分析方法的局限，本研究则尝试应用 Ecotect Analysis 作为模拟分析统合的软件，结合 GIS 生成大区域尺度的地形与建筑量体模型以及 REVIT BIM 所建置的细致三维建筑模型进行全面性的绿色环境分析。

本研究成功地将 GIS 与 REVIT 所制作的三维信息模型整合于单一绿色分析软件中，体现了三维信息模型共享的机制，一来不仅可缩短重新建模的工作时程；二来更可借助整合模型丰富的环境信息，提高环境模拟的可靠性。

2.4 应用 Ecotect Analysis 与 Phoenics 进行不同连续尺度的环境模拟与分析

科学风水体现于大地气候中风、光、热、气、水的表征现象。本研究首先由旧建筑所在地区域之环境进行分项的绿色环境模拟，气候信息来源系采用中国气象站提供之数据信息，另辅以 Autodesk 所提供的场地地理位置模拟气象站数据进行交叉比对修正以作为环境气候之基础数据源。接着检讨区域环境的各种可能影响建筑的各种现象，包含地表特征、周边建筑量体型态、物质表面的粗糙度等，重新检讨环境参数并加以修正，以符合真实的环境状态。

进入建筑场地的分析时，则以修正后之区域环境分析的环境参数进行模拟分析。此时的环境参数因已经修正，无论于日照遮挡分析、太阳辐射分析、风环境模拟分析等，皆能更准确地反映建筑自身与环境的真实状态。

本研究将环境分析模拟以流动性空间的思路看待，以 GREEN BIM 的概念建置环境区域与建筑三维讯息模型，并从区域至建筑的各种关键的影响因子进行评价，实践了一体化绿色环境模拟分析的方法。本研究以此方式进行分析模拟确实有其独特性与全面性。

3 三维信息化的环境模拟成果与分析

依据上述的 GREEN BIM 的绿色环境分析方法与思路，落实于本研究进行务实操作，其成果如下。

3.1 区域至街廓尺度的绿色环境模拟分析成果

平潭岛白青卫生院位于福建东部福州市，属于平潭县的平潭综合实验区，从卫星图与实测的 CAD 图的相叠合显示白青卫生院周边系以自然山丘地形、海岸为界，有明显的发展边缘，而聚落的样态也多依循着道路与地形而筑，另外从环境分析的角度来看，明显特征的地形起伏会影响区域的气候环境，因此大致上系以地形边界作为分析的范围。

从大的角度来看，白青卫生院周边区域的风环境，主导风向冬季以北北东季风为主；夏季则以南南西季风为主，虽西侧临海，但海陆风对季节主导风象的影响不明显，唯因地形上受北至西侧的山势所围，并向南缓降的态势与北侧聚落群密集的关系，风速略有增速的状况；另外，因北侧周边建筑量体的排列大致顺地形线平行，且建筑之间具有南北纵向的通道，经区域的 CFD 分析发现卫生院之北侧之聚落通道有缩口效应，增加了冬季东北风集中灌入而产生涡流的现象。另卫生院东侧因临海相对空旷，造成建筑东侧风速有加速的现象，易造成该区域的建筑壁面的损坏。

光环境方面，整体区域受到太阳光角度的影响，聚落建筑西侧于四季皆有永久阴影产生的现象，尤其是冬季永久阴影的范围最广，应避免于建筑的北侧种植好光性植栽。另于卫生院西侧受相邻建筑量体的影响，日照时数稍有减低。而整体来说本区域整体自然光照相当充足，具有潜力发展光辐发电或热的应用。

日照辐射部分，本区域夏季与冬季辐射量大约相差约一倍左右，另建筑北侧也受光照的影响，北侧的辐射量也相对较低。

3.2　建筑尺度的绿色环境模拟分析成果

由风环境来看，卫生院受冬季北北东风的影响甚巨，北面缩口加速后，于建筑北壁面造成强烈的风冲击，建筑南侧则有一滞留的风阴影区，因此对于北侧开口部挡风部分需一有效策略；而东侧区域因临空旷海滩，直接面临东侧高速风的吹袭，则易造成建筑壁面的损坏。而夏季吹南南西风，又卫生院南侧多为空地，因此对于气流的导引产生的不错的风环境。但进入到建筑内部，卫生院系为东西横向中央走廊的配置方式，夏季风无法由南侧房间穿越中央走廊进入北侧房间，因此势必针对室内风环境进行改善。

光环境上，经环境分析的结果，建筑设计采用中央走廊的方式规划，虽南北两侧的自然漫射光能够符合自然采光需求，但走廊却无法取得自然光。需仰赖人工照明，室内自然采光的部分应进行修正。

热环境方面，屋顶受热状况最高，一年累积量高达 $1200kWh/m^2$，之后依序为南侧与西侧次之、北侧与东侧再次之，屋顶与北侧立面辐射量差达 5 倍。而卫生院采用石砌构造，经实际探勘内部的保温与隔热性能相当优良，但因屋顶采用 RC 浇筑，应注意屋顶的隔热性能，需进行处理。

3.3　SWOT 综合分析

经综合上述之分析结果，再进一步借 SWOT 之分析，可更清楚了解本区域之科学化风水之态势：

3.3.1　机会与威胁分析

白青卫生院所在地的环境拥有良好的日照与风力，有机会应用光辐发电与风力发电，但相对也需注意建筑屋顶的隔热保暖的策略。另外在冬季北北东风的强力吹袭下，更须关注北侧的挡风策略与东侧可能造成的壁面损害。而近年极端气候出现的频率已日趋频繁，于规划设计时应谨慎考虑气候异变所造成的影响。

3.3.2　优势与劣势分析

白青卫生院受海岛型气候影响，气候大致良好，但是受到极端气候的影响，夏季极端高温高达 35.3℃，冬季虽无降雪纪录，但气温可低至 0.9℃，另外冬季的强烈季风也易产生冷击的现象。

建筑坐北朝南，开放空间配置于南侧，使得该空间拥有良好的户外使用的优势，也因为日照上相当充足，室内居室的自然采光大致良好，不过因为建筑采用中央走廊方式规划，其走廊空间几乎无自然采光，另外场地北侧四季皆会产生永久阴影，应预防潮湿与避免种植好光的植栽或作物。

4　依据科学风水所导引出旧建筑再利用的设计对策

回应既有的环境纹理与特征，我们依据这些环境线索建构主要的修缮设计对策。

4.1　被动式的环境调适系统的建构

为了促使现实气候环境得以借助被动式的方式进行调节，以达到最佳的气候调适效果。本研究以被动式系统循环的思维进行旧建筑之治理。

4.2　屋顶降温与建筑系统之串联

卫生院的屋顶为受热最高之区域，本研究以屋顶花园作为主要的隔热降温策略，另配合光辐发电与热之面板，以有效应用本区域之日照优势，来提供建筑所需之热水与电力，又可达到屋顶降温之效用。而屋顶的植栽绿化系统也采用回收之储集雨水进行浇灌，在喷洒过程中也有降温效果。

4.3　面对风环境特性的调适机制

冬季挡风、夏季导风为顺应自然环境气候的策略机制。冬季挡风部分，为避免冲击气流直对北向壁面吹袭并造成涡流，于平行三楼天花的位置设置了水平的导风板，将部分的风力向上扬升，以此渐少该处之正面风压。

东侧部分则以垂直之景观绿化方式，借助植栽通孔降低该处风速，以保护该处之壁面，降低可能的风力破坏。

夏天导风的策略主要以排热与通风效果为主。卫生院南侧夏季之受热状况较为明显，因此南侧居室应用管状的通风塔的形式借助自然南风的带动将内部热气排出；北侧居室则因中央走廊与南侧居室的阻隔，无法有效借助开窗产生风压对流，因此本研究于屋顶设置引风板，将夏季的南风导入室内，使北侧的居室能够有效达到通风的效果。

4.4　室内自然采光照度的增益

中央走廊式的建筑形态最易造成内部走廊自然采光不足的现象产生。为解决这个问题，于中央走廊的两侧楼板应用切割的方式，裁切出引光的洞口，借助屋顶天光的导入，以增加中央走廊的明亮度。

4.5　以农业为基底的建筑整体循环系统的建置

对于建筑的诊断与维护，不仅只从局部的修改，更应考虑建筑作为整个循环系统的载体下，对于健康的环境有更全面的提升。农业的栽培即是可能运用的一种方式。

本研究尝试将农业作为一种媒介，将建筑的整体循环系统借助农业培植的过程中进一步强化建筑的绿色与健康的体质。

主要的手法为应用回收的雨水作为串联的介质，借助重力的流动由上而下于壁面、管线、地面进行农业的栽培，并以鱼菜共生的理念进行系统的建置。

以此理念进行规划，建筑便不再是资源的消耗者，而因此转换为资源的提供者，借助具有创意的农业结合食材景观设计，不仅达到调适环境气候的功效，更创造出未来建筑生产资源的可能性（图1）。

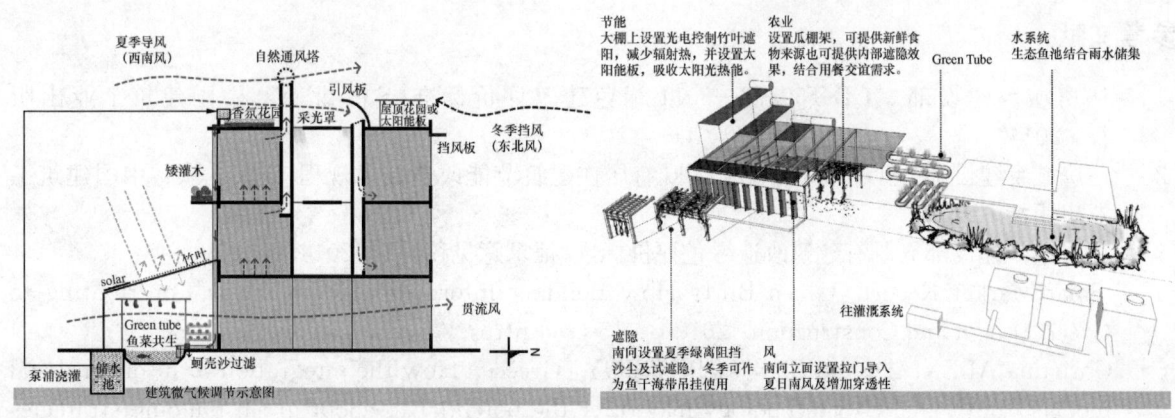

图1　微气候调节示意图

5　结论与建议

本研究以流动性连续尺度的空间形态的认知进行绿色环境的模拟与分析，应用单一三维信息模型建构连续性的空间环境，不仅可降低重复建模的工作，更可于模拟分析中全面的掌握区域与改造建筑间的交互影响。

经由绿色环境模拟分析后的结论，作为建筑改造论证的依据，更有其改造方法与造型的凭据，而这样的建筑规划设计的操作流程，也可作为未来操作各种规划设计方法的参考。

对于极端气候与食物逐渐短缺的问题将是未来我们所必须面对的重要课题之一。本研究应用被动式的设计方法以强化建筑的性能，并以农业的栽培的方式架构整体的建筑循环系统，不仅达到了节能减碳的效益，更重要的是以此能够创造出更健康的居住环境。

The Exploration and Practice on Old Building Renovation in the Spirit of Scientific Feng Shui-a Case Study of Bai Qing Health Center in Pingtan County, Fujian Province.

Li Yen-Yi[1], Lee Tzu-Yao [2], Chiu Ke-Hao[3]

(1. Department of Interior Design, Shu-Te University 2. Artsome Eco-Tech Trade Co. ,)

3. Department of Civil Engincering, Tankang University

Abstract：This research tends to propose a new method of ecological urban planning and designing-which differs from the traditional top-down method in Taiwan. Three main steps are included：1) to create environmental basemap through GIS tools；2) to analyze the basemap based on landscape ecology theory and landscape metrics；and 3) to estimate living environment through urban climate diagnosis. The method is eventually advised as a new angle to transform those traditional planning methods.

Keywords：Scientific feng shui, Food design, BIM, Ecological architecture, Green BIM

参考文献：

[1]　住房城乡建设部．GB-T50378—2014 绿色建筑评价标准[S]．北京：中国建筑工业出版社，2014.

[2]　住房城乡建设部．JGJ/T 129—2012 既有居住建筑节能改造技术规程[S]．北京：中国建筑工业出版社，2012.

[3]　住房城乡建设部．既有建筑改造绿色评价标准（征求意见稿）[S]．2014.

[4]　SmartMarket Report. Green BIM：How Building Information Modeling is Contributing to Green Design and Construction. 2010 [2015-5-8] http：//www. aia. org/.

[5]　Christina ALEXIADI and Chryssy POTSIOY, Greece. How the integration of n- dimensional models（BIM）and GIS technology may offer the potential to adopt green building strategies and to achieve low cost constructions. 2012 [2015-5-8] https：//www. fig. net/

[6]　黄旭．城市旧建筑小区盖造设计与实践探索[J]．城市建设理论研究，2012.36.

以当地性人才培训工作坊推动高雄厝深耕研究与制度

李彦颐[1]　苏志勋[2]　张博硕[3]　林嘉雄[4]　冯慧心[5]

（1. 台湾树德科技大学建筑研究所；2. 台湾高雄市政府工务局；
3. 台湾弘宪联合建筑师事务所/ 树德科技大学室内设计系；
4. 台湾树德科技大学室内设计系；5. 台湾树德科技大学建筑研究所）

摘要：全球温室效应与过度城市化造成的热岛效应同时影响着当下人们的生活起居与生活质量，因此暴烈化的气候造成许多生命、财产的损害。高雄市政府亟思改变转型，思考除期望由重工业外移改善"区域生活质量"长期发展之缓慢移转外，反思更因考虑根本性的问题解决方式，亦即从检视既有住宅法令与社会共识，让具有当地环境对应特色以及呼应日常生活之扎根性改变，将会是最直接有效改变并同时调适气候冲击的对应的方式。为响应国际减碳义务，降低地球环境负荷，未来的高雄市计划由工业城市的意象转型为健康、永续的南台湾都会区，并积极推动历史及生活环境营造，期望结合地域环境需求与当地人文特色，发展高雄地区当地建筑特色及生活文化—整体上称之为"高雄厝"计划。

高雄厝计划目的不仅仅是盖几栋当地形式的房子，更推崇在规划设计时段，需要考虑高雄厝五大核心价值："生态、经济、宜居、创意、国际"，以丰富的当地建筑与历史文化搭配前瞻的绿色建筑技术。而在整合性推动上，包含当地政策法令之改变制定有"高雄市绿色建筑自治条例"外，借助营建产业的法令依循度建立新建建筑之规范，并同时整合学术界领袖意见，同步推动由下而上透过地方小区营造参与之模式，建立城乡发展不同之推动模式，从而发展属于当地建筑之认同性、识别性、自明性与未来性，兼具国际观视野亦有本土化坚持的高雄厝。

关键词：人才培训，小区参与，地方发展，宜居发展

1 计划缘起

高雄厝计划乃是一当地改造引导计划，主要为辅导以及培育当地设计师与相关科系学生积极参与乡村风貌再造，透过前期研究将以当地化、区域化、标准化的方式进行培训课程的安排。同时结合"高雄厝当地设计者培训工作坊计划"前期推动成果为基础发展，并进一步响应国际减碳设计，降低地球环境负荷，未来高雄市必须由工业城市的意象转型为健康、永续的南台湾都会区，并积极推动历史及生活环境营造，期望结合地域环境需求与当地人文特色，发展高雄地区在地建筑特色及生活文化——"高雄厝"。而地方型高雄厝计划目的不只是盖几栋当地形式的房子，更要融入高雄厝五大核心价值："生态、经济、宜居、创意、国际"，以丰富当地建筑与历史文化、前瞻的绿色建筑技术、由下而上的小区营造参与，找到属于当地建筑之认同性、识别性、自明性与未来性，兼具国际观视野亦有本土化的坚持。

建置当地型高雄厝当地建筑期望寻求小区民众与设计施工团队共同营造，找到属于当地建筑之认同性、识别性、自明性与未来性，兼具国际观视野亦有本土化的坚持。为因应全球各先进国家对于环境"永续"、"绿"、"健康"发展的潮流趋势，已配合上级机关所颁"生态城市绿色建筑推动方案"进行一系列相关绿色建筑技术，包括：生态环境、能源利用与生活健康三大面向之改善与应用、落实，提供高雄市在新建与既有建筑物办理"绿色建筑改善"之绿色建筑技术研究与推广，并引导高雄市公有建物配合推动绿色建筑改善，迄今于公有建筑有许多具代表性的绿色建筑改善案例（图1）。

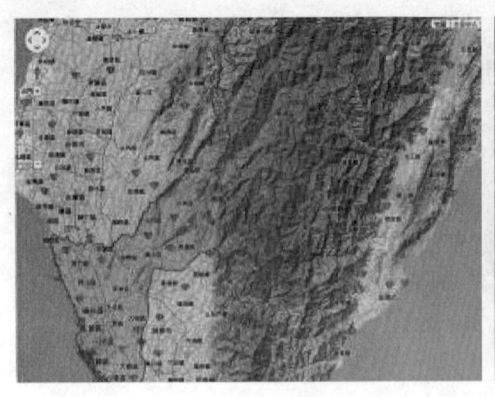

图 1　本文研究目标——高雄市美浓区航拍

2　计划目标

地方型"高雄厝"计划之执行核心，主要为高雄地区开启宜居建筑及环境之契机，借以加强推广高雄地区当地建筑特色及生活文化之概念与重要性，并形成南台湾新居住文化的运动。美浓区域内寻找适宜的建筑物进行整修，同时征求有理念的学生或优秀的建筑工作者与当地民众共同参与贡献想法与提供需求条件，以凝聚设计工作者对高雄地区建筑及生活环境操作的经验、汇集各方的创意构思、普查当地人文景观资料及集结（图 2），进而突破过去现代主义建筑思维之限制、机能主义的捆绑，整并实务与理想共构之设计作品或环境规划提案，期望为高雄培养当地具有人文思考、生态关怀之设计人才。

图 2　普查美浓区内古厝与烟楼形态

2.1　使用当地建筑形态

扩大建筑应用的可能性，由美浓既有特色建筑抽取元素，转为调和外部气候环境与建筑室内环境之间重要的建筑接口。例如：太子楼营造室内热流、伙房营造排除寒冷气流造成室内温度。

2.2　当地建筑材料应用

收集环境气象数据分析及生活文化的数据普查，集结作为日后设计的数据库，文化创意的基本材料，利用分析四季环境特色进行建筑设计建议，并大量使用当地既有建材或邻近地区之建筑材料（图 3）。

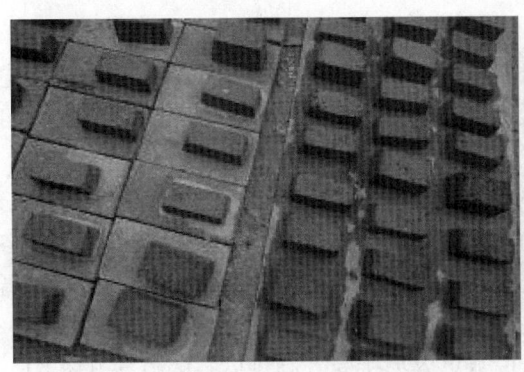

图3　运用在地旧建材与实验型建材共构修缮烟楼

2.3　新建筑概念纳入旧建筑更新使用

当地人士是最了解这城市的历史及风情，借助个人的生活经验，抽取前人旧建筑应用概念，运用现代新建筑概念手法融入既有旧建筑，企图借助日常生活起居改善，传达运用新建筑工法能有效改善居住环境质量，更达到节能减碳、冬暖夏凉的愿景（图4）。

图4　旧建筑更新再利用

2.4　人文生态城市景观的种子

高雄厝是一连串的人本居住运动，透过系统的课程培育当地化的种子，并以纪录片思维找寻高雄人生活文化的代表案例或内涵（图5）。

图5　依循文化脉络发展地方特色

3　执行计划

成立工作坊目标锁定当地的既有或旧有建筑为主且与小区活动能进行紧密结合，借此吸引当地建筑与设计的年轻伙伴或学子，以协同工作坊以及公民咖啡馆配合选定的讨论的驻点办公室进行深耕。包含潜力目标与当地工作者合作，地域环境与人文需求深入探讨与归纳，居民真正需求面向以及当地材料与材质及色彩，可能的新绿色建筑以及环境对应改造的做法及技术改良转换讨论等，并以此讨论归纳出潜在改造对象。

计划执行重点除了高雄厝核心十项设计准则外，预计赋予计划其他构成元素，如太阳光电、信息、地方文化、节能应用、环境科技等新课程元素。提升小区民众对于高雄厝的明了，共同打造一个专属地方特色的"高雄厝"。

本年度推广阶段期望能有效拉近与地方民众的距离，采用轻松简单方式在当地选择空间开阔、景色优美区域设置当地工作坊。积极增进与地方的对话交流意见，达到当地营造与提供设计咨询和当地居民大谈"埕"的场域建置。借助工作坊的成立，除了以驻点方式在美浓地区提供高雄厝的主要核心技术与价值应用，工作坊驻点计划以最有效率、零距离的与当地民众交换意见并提供一个场域给予民众能在工作坊内广泛使用，以环境教育让民众更容易接受"高雄厝"的概念（图6）。

图6 推动高雄厝工作坊与小区民众及设计师共同讨论

高雄位处全台日照时数高的范围，气候条件与地理环境条件可说是多样化，此外面对未来高龄社会的到来与永续环境的思维，故对高雄厝设计原则，将朝向三大核心理念：环境永续、反映当地自明性及居住健康；并设定两大方向：一是通则设计：以符合高雄厝内涵特性为出发点，从全面性的规划思维，制定指标性设计原则。二是地区性设计原则：大高雄地理特色为区隔，由环境特色与文化脉络来导入，经由操作设计手法来制定设计原则。

4 主要工作项目

高雄厝美浓屋的设计发想，借助设计讨论工作坊的研讨过程中，透过高雄厝第三届学员：张七斗建筑师、李长腾建筑师、冯慧心设计师、钟博任设计师、黄韵恩设计师、黄怡文设计师等参与设计讨论以及施工建议。同时邀请当地之美浓小学杨瑞霞校长、古椿宏主任、美浓田野学会温仲良老师以及多位共同参与培训老师李允斐教授、杨博渊教授等一起参与设计（图7）。

图7 共同参与讨论烟楼改造设计

针对高雄厝美浓屋规划改善计划，大致上可分为3～5年的整修期，第1～2年主要工作项目为环境清洁与废弃建材清运，优先整合公共空间与景观环境，希望打造可供民众与学童休憩空间，并利用树荫与建筑设计手法营造遮阴空间吸引附近民众前往驻留讨论体验改善后空间氛围。第二期、三期主要针对内部空间进行整修，包含第一期后段进行艺术创作与展示空间的规划、保存旧美浓记忆空间（烟楼空间）、地方讨论工作坊（半开放空间）、办公室空间（驻地工作室），同时针对建筑物坐落主要面向为东西向，易造成西晒面过热与南向空间温度过高等疑虑，以及思考相关隔热设计手法已调整舒适室内环境（图8）。

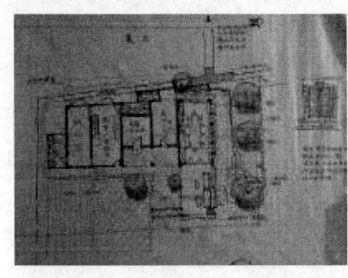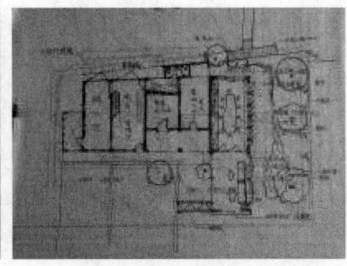

图8 计划各阶段修缮高雄厝美浓屋计划范围

主要保留旧美浓建筑材料的运用，运用红砖、红瓦、木料等方式进行遮阳与隔热设计，并保留既有开口部确保室内空气流通顺畅，并利用太阳光电板架设于西南向，营造出低碳建筑的概念同时运用 BIPV 概念，导入部分自然光源缩短室内使用日光灯管的时间。运用大木角料与细角料搭建工作棚架，可借助攀爬植栽营造遮阴效果，使民众能在遮阴下进行农作加工的作业，同时运用此做法保留了下舍与偏舍的空间使用机能。

5 计划成果与制度

"高雄厝"计划之执行，主要针对高雄地方乡镇已破损毁坏之建筑物进行整修与设计，但有别于一般旧建筑改造仅止于硬设备上的修整，本计划更着重于当地民众的参与和认同地方文化，因此在本计划推动的过程中不断寻找地方有志人士与地方社团机构进行讨论与邀请参与工作坊，在其中执行团队落实和地方人士与居住居民能有效沟通与讨论（图9）。

图9 当地人才培训与参与式营造成果

（1）针对不同地形、地貌、气候特色与居住族群，进行前期研究，并召开居民说明会以凝聚共识，邀请有志之士或屋主进行设计讨论工作坊。

（2）借助设计工作房的讨论过程中，能让设计团队与屋主以及地方文史团体能进行充分沟通，且能依照屋主的空间需求进行设计调配，对于计划的当地深耕有显著帮助。

（3）当地方建筑风气已形成后，可向主管单位申请制定相关法令与制度，透过地方参与式营造技术深化成熟，协助地方政府制定"地方建筑自治条例"。

The Driving Mechanism of Local Design Training Workshop to Promote the Transformation of the Kaohsiung LOHAS House

Li Yen-Yi[1]，Su Chih-Shun[2]，Chang Po-Shuo[3]，Lin Chia-Hsiung[4]，Feng Hui-Hsin[5]

（1. Shu-Te university architecture and interior design Dept；2. Public Works Bureau of Kaohsiung City Govemment；3. Shu-Te university architecture and interior design Dept；4. Shu-Te university Department of Interior Design / Lecturer；5. Shu-Te university Architecture and Interior Design Dept）

Abstract：Global warming and excessive urbanization heat island effect cause living influence and quality of life. Violent climate cause many lives and property damage. Kaohsiung City Government has striven to change，thinking to expect heavy industry move to "quality of life". From considering long-term development examine the existing housing laws and social consensus. With environmental correspondence characteristics and echo rooted change of daily life，it would be the most direct and effective change and corresponding ways of adaptation to climatic impacts. In response to the international carbon reduction obligations and reducing the environmental load will plan from industrial city transform into healthy city，sustainable South Taiwan city，and actively promotes the history and living environment. Expectations are combined with regional environmental needs and cultural characteristics. Development of the Kaohsiung area in architectural culture is called "houses in Kaohsiung" program. Kaohsiung CUO plans not only to cover several types of houses but also to consider five core values of the houses in Kaohsiung，"ecology, economy and livable, creative, international"，combing rich in architecture and green building techniques. In the integration promotion , included in policies，laws and changed to develop a "Kaohsiung City green building regulations"，followed the construction industry decree establishing the new building standards , integration, academic leaders and opinions , synchronize push from the bottom up through the involvement of local community building model , establishing different drive modes of urban and rural development , developing the belongs to the building of identity，identification, self-evident , the future, and both the localization of the houses in Kaohsiung and international view.

Keywords：Training, Community involvement，Local development，Livable development

参考文献：

［1］　李彦颐、杨博渊等 ."高雄厝在地设计者培训工作坊计划委托技术服务案"项目计划［R］. 高雄市政府工务局，2012～2014.

［2］　李彦颐 ."高雄市推动乡村绿建筑暨屋顶绿化改善工程"项目计划［R］. 高雄市政府工务局，2011.

［3］　李彦颐、杨冠雄等 ."高雄市低碳小区实作示范计划"项目计划［R］. 高雄市政府环境保护局，2010.

［4］　刘柏森 . 美浓油纸伞产业观光化与小区营造之研究［D］. 台湾：台湾师范大学，2014.

The Territories of Priority Development in Russian Far East as the Way of Urban Area Rehabilitation

Ekaterina Glatolenkova, Natalia Kozyrenko

(Pacific National University, Khabarovsk)

Abstract: The special attention is paid to the problems of the Far East and its sustainable development in Russia. Russian Far East has its own features and it's take a special place among the countries of the Asia-Pacific region. There are development history, the current status and problems identified in this article. The region was actively developed in the Soviet period because of the official resettlement programs and rapidly growing industry. In the post-perestroika period, the pace of economic growth had slowed, and the population who had lost their jobs and had found themselves in difficult financial conditions had left their cities and settlements. The existing system of large cities has changed little over the last 30 years. However, the network of small settlements with a population of less than 5 thousand people actively destroyed. On today the government is working on the sustainable territories development program. One of these territories is the Nadezhda district of Primorsky Krai. The concept of this program and its effect on the urban structure is researched in the article

Keywords: The territories of priority development, Monocities, Sustainable economical development, Transport infrastructure, Urban infrastructure

1 Introduction

In recent years, special attention is paid to the problems of the Russian Far East. In the age of geopolitical changes the issue of "eastern turn of Russia[1]" gets the most pressing. The Russian Far East throughout its history has played the role of the resource reserve with rich potential but with extremely poor transport and social infrastructure. The population of the Far East today is 6.2 million people. The population density is about 1 person per square kilometer.

2 Historical features of the development and establishment of the Far East

Far Eastern region is characterized by the wave-like behavior of the economic, demographic, infrastructural growth rate. This is due to the fact that at different stages of the development attention to the Far East was determined by the degree of its involvement in the economic activities of the country and strategic military situation.

Researches identify three main stages of town-planning in the region: pre-revolutionary, Soviet and modern Russian[2].

Pre-revolutionary period is divided into the period of tribute in furs (1632-1729), the expedition period (1730-1850), the south settlement (1851-1929). The main goal of the first explorers in the XVII century was the territory study for further deriving profit, shifting boundaries to the Pacific Ocean and paving the way to America. In XVIII-early XIX centuries an industrial image of the region began to form. Extractive industries were primarily developed[3]. From the middle of the 19 century a targeted settlement of the region began[2].

The Soviet period is divided into the period of industrial development (1930-1979) and the period of rapid development and structural reorganization (1980-1991)[4].

During the Soviet period the region grew rapidly thanks to mass resettlement programs and a rapidly growing industry. From 1926 to 1989 the population of the Far East increased from 1. 6 to 8. 1 million people[5].

In the period of post-perestroika (after 1991) economic growth has slowed down. People lost their jobs and found themselves in difficult financial situation. They began to leave the Far East, its towns and villages. The existing system of big towns and cities has not changed much over the past 20 years but the network of small towns and villages with the population less than 5000 people is actively destroyed. The decline in the population has been continued and in the period 1991~2015 amounted to 1. 9 million people [6].

3　Current situation of south settlements of the Far East: recovery is possible

A process of de-industrialization occurs all over the world today. In our region with predominant amount of industrial settlements this process reveals all the shortcomings of the previous times-extensive nature of territory development, export orientation and central funding. There are many changes occurred after the period of perestroika in the country: economic, demographic, environmental, town-planning and foreign policy. They all had a serious negative impact on the Far East development. This situation led to mass exodus (migration outflow over the period of 1991~2004 amounted to 70% of the total reduction in the number of residents[5]) . Today, a number of measures are taken to improve the situation in the Far East. These are both regional and federal development programs and also individual solutions for particular settlements.

3. 1　Programs and Development Strategies.

In the framework of the "Program of socio-economic development of the Far East and the Baikal Region" developed by the Government (adopted in 2014) the Far East is considered as the center of Russian economic partnership with neighboring countries such as China, Mongolia and the countries of Northeast Asia. "The aim of the Program is to accelerate socio-economic development of the Far East and the Baikal Region, focused on the implementation of export potential"[7]. The Program provides for the development of urban agglomerations and big cities. Khabarovsk Territory is considered to have two agglomerations-Komsomolsk and Khabarovsk, as well as areas of priority developments-Urgal zone in Verkhnebureinsky area and the coastal zone in the south-east. The coastal area will be formed on the basis of the transport and industrial hub of Vanino, Sovetskaya Gavan and De-Kastri ports. It is planned to expand the network of land transport by building of new highway and railway branch lines. The priority development of Khabarovsk agglomeration should be the development of the western and south-eastern suburban areas along the Russian Federation state border. Strengthening the role of Komsomolsk agglomeration is planned by complex integration of its constituent parts-Solnechnii, Amursk and Komsomolsk[8]. Local programs of socio-economic development are being carried out in all particular areas.

3. 2　Free economic zones and special economic zones

Free economic zones in Russia is a territory with a special tax and legal regime to attract investors in top-priority Russian industries[9]. The first free economic zone was established in 1991 in Nakhodka (Primorsky Krai) . Nakhodka is the largest port on the Pacific coast of Russia. According to the decree, the free economic zone was established in order to promote economic cooperation with foreign countries, attract foreign investments, increase regional export opportunities, develop new forms of management in the transition to a market economy providing preferential tax and customs regimes. However, after the economic crisis of 1998, free economic zones in Russia have been declared unprofitable and their funding was stopped. In 2006 the Decree on the establishment of free economic zone "Nakhodka" ceased to be in force and is no longer existed.

Special economic zones "replaced" free economic zones in 2005 when the Federal law No. 116 《On special economic zones in the Russian Federation》 was adopted[9,10]. In 2010 special economic zones were established on the island Russky in Vladivostok (the development of potential tourism) but at the beginning of 2015 it has been recognized non-demanded. Now there is only one special economic zone in the Far East. It is in Sovetskaya Gavan on the Tatar Strait coast.

4 Territories of priority socio-economic development

4.1 General provisions and implementation in the Far East

The Federal Law No. 473 "On the territories of priority socio-economic development in the Russian Federation" was adopted on December 29, 2014. It provides for state support through the territories of priority socio-economic development establishment as well as a special legal regime for entrepreneurial and other activity on these territories.

The enactment of the territories of priority socio-economic development corresponds to the "Program of socio-economic development of the Far East and the Baikal Region" . According to the official definition the territory of priority socio-economic development is "a part of the territory of the Russian Federation including administrative-territorial entity where in accordance with the decision of the Russian Federation Government a special legal regime is established for entrepreneurial and other activities in order to create favorable conditions for attracting foreign investments, ensuring accelerated socio-economic development and the creation of comfortable conditions for the population"[11].

The main purpose of the enactment is to create the most favorable conditions for attracting investors, creating a competitive environment in comparison with the Pacific Rim countries and the territories development. Some essential changes were made in certain legislative acts. A special legal regime was established to conduct entrepreneurial activity (favorable rents on real estate, tax incentives). A number of simplifications were made in various procedures (e. g. approval of the area planning documents without pre-trial hearing or cancellation of permits for the hiring migrant workers). In town-planning activity timeline for the documents preparation is reduced to 255 days [12].

4.2 The first territory of priority development: Nadezhdinsky district

Initially, more than 400 territories were considered. But eventually three prior territories were selected: two in Khabarovsk Territory and one in Primorsky Krai. It was decided that first three years the territories of priority development will be established in the Far East and then in other region of Russia.

The main difference between the territory of priority development and special economic zone will be creating conditions for a particular investor with an emphasis on foreign capital.

The law came into force on March 30, 2015. One of the first territories of priority development became Nadezhdinsky. The settlement Volno-Nadezhdinskoe is the center of Nadezhdinsky district. It is situated in the south of Primorsky Krai and has an access to the sea. There is a federal highway Khabarovsk-Vladivostok and Trans-Siberian Railway. The population is 38. 2 thousand people. Economy of the territory is defined by geographical location (agriculture, fishery, coal mining and production of construction materials). There has been a steady growth in production of consumer goods, increasing amount of investments and housing construction in recent years[13].

The project is conducted by the Government of Primorsky Krai together with Ministry for Development of Russian Far East. The territory of priority development Nadezhdinsky is seen as "dry port" ——a production and trading platform with major transport and logistics complex[12]. The area of the territory is 807 hectares. The volume of attracted investments in the first phase will amount to 6. 73 billion rubles in the budget financing of 3. 6 billion rubles. 1. 630 people will be employed.

As part of the second and third phases it is planned to attract private investments of about 30 billion rubles and providing employment for 7, 000 people. Total proceeds from taxes and fees in the Russian Federation budgets will amount to more than 33. 6 billion rubles[14].

5　Conclusion

It is necessary for Russia to consolidate its position in the rapidly growing Asia-Pacific Region and to pay greater attention to the problem of forming the resident population in the Far East. The Government has developed a number of programs and regulations to improve the social and economic conditions in the region. The territories of priority development are the most promising in the present context.　Special attention is paid to the development of production and investments in these areas and this will create many new vacancies. Along with the primary task of providing people with jobs another task is to ensure people's housing.

To neutralize the negative impact of the general crisis occurred in the period of change in the Russian Far East and for the sustainable development of the region it is necessary to create so-called "points of growth" which will contribute to the development of adjacent territories including urban, social and transport infrastructure, creating new economic bonds.

超前发展区域是俄罗斯远东地区市区重建项目

叶卡捷琳娜·格拉托连科娃　娜塔莉娅·科济连科
（哈巴罗夫斯克市，国立太平洋大学）

摘要：近年来，对俄罗斯远东地区及其发展问题给予了特别的关注。如今，在地缘政治变化的条件下，"俄罗斯向东转移"问题变得更加现实。文章探讨了远东地区发展和形成的历史特征，研究了其现在亚太地区国家中占有什么地位。本区域的恢复重建和吸引居民的倾向之一是以发展某一特定行业为目的的城市及居民点的联合。文章提出了对在俄罗斯远东地区形成超前发展区域起到的影响，考虑到该地区经济地理地位特点的因素，比较详细地研究了滨海边疆区娜杰日金斯基区域。

    关键词：超前发展区域，单一城镇，可持续发展，交通基础设施，城市基础设施

References：

［1］ Бляхер Л. Е. Восточный поворот России：возникновение и выживание естественного порядка в малых городах Дальнего Востока России. Изд-во Тихоокеан. гос. ун-та，2014：97.

［2］ Рыбаковский Л. Л. Население Дальнего Востока за 150 лет. -М.：Наука，1990.

［3］ Ковалева З. А. ，Плохих С. В. История Дальнего Востока России：Учебное пособие.- Владивосток：ТИДОТ ДВГУ，2002：244 с.

［4］ Козыренко Н. Е. Эволюция градостроительных систем на Дальнем Востоке. Дис... канд. архитектуры：18. 00. 04. -М.：МАРХИ. 1988.

［5］ Центр миграционных исследований（ЦМИ）. Миграция как фактор развития Дальнего Востока［DB/OL］.［2015-5-10］. http：//migrocenter. ru/publ/konfer/ekaterinburg/m_ekaterinburg07. php.

［6］ Федеральная служба государственной статистики［DB/OL］.［2015-5-10］. http：//habstat. gks. ru/.

［7］ Министерство Российской Федерации по развитию Дальнего Востока，2013-2015 гг［DB/OL］.［2015-5-10］. http：//www. minvostokrazvitia. ru/activities/theprogram/index. php.

［8］ Официальный информационный интернет-портал Хабаровского края. 2014-2015［DB/OL］.［2015-5-10］. http：//www. khabkrai. ru/.

［9］ Циклопедия［DB/OL］.［2015-5-10］. http：//cyclowiki. org/wiki/Особые_экономические_зоны_в_России.

［10］ Официальный сайт компании. КонсультантПлюс［DB/OL］.［2015-5-10］. http：//www. consultant. ru/document/cons_doc_LAW_173553/.

［11］ Официальный сайт компании. КонсультантПлюс［DB/OL］.［2015-5-10］. http：//www. consultant. ru/document/cons_doc_LAW_172962/.

［12］ Инвестиционный Портал Приморского края.［DB/OL］.［2015-5-10］. http：//invest. primorsky. ru/images/textdoc/zor/tor. pdf.

［13］ Официальный сайт администрации Надеждинского муниципального района［DB/OL］.［2015-5-10］. http：//www. nadezhdinsky. ru/about/ekonomika-rayona. htm.

［14］ Официальный сайт информационного агентства《Дейта》2001-2015［DB/OL］.［2015-5-10］. http：//deita. ru/news/economy/03. 04. 2015/4870980-tor-nadezhdinskiy-807-gektar-chistogo-polya-i-nikakikh-obyazatelstv/.

冬冷夏热地区既有住宅建筑产品化改造初探：以立面改造为例

张李瑞　张　宏

（东南大学建筑学院）

摘要：建筑一旦建成即变成既有建筑。从它建成那一刻开始就逃脱不了改造或拆除的命运。2005 年，中国现有建筑面积达到 440～450 亿 m²，其中居住建筑面积大概在 270 亿 m²，全社会每年建筑竣工面积超过 20 亿 m²，到 2014 年约 580 亿 m² 既有建筑。在建筑全生命周期中，既有住宅建筑改造至关重要。反思当前设计思潮过度追求效率，忽视老建筑的更新，一味地拆旧建新，片面追求 GDP，给社会资源带来极大浪费，给社会及环境带来更多问题。既有建筑改造节约资金，延长其使用寿命，使其能更好地被利用，创造良好的建筑品质和环境，对可持续发展与节能有着非常重大的意义。本文基于工业化建造思路，摒弃传统手工模式，以建筑构件产品化为设计前提，提供一整套可供选择的建筑构件产品库，即可在库中选择现成产品，快速出方案，快速落实既有建筑改造所需资金，人员，时间，工具等，在理论与实践中，建立以建筑构件产品化为中心的既有住宅建筑改造的指导方法，为建筑改造提供一个全新的视角。

关键词：既有住宅建筑改造，建筑工业化，产品化改造，构件产品库，夏热冬冷地区

1　引言

伴随着中国 GDP 的突飞猛进，许多城市现在的拆迁已成为社会热点问题，这其中负面信息居多，更有甚者会伴随拆迁户或拆迁队的死亡事件。许多建筑在其"青壮年"时期就被拆除，例如武汉外滩花园小区仅仅建成 4 年；更夸张的是合肥维也纳森林花园小区在建设到 16 层还没完工，却惨遭爆破"牺牲"……中国是世界上每年新建建筑量最大的国家，但不相称的是建筑平均寿命仅 25～30 年。在经济利益和 GDP 崇拜的背后，许多尚好的建筑草率被拆除。

在这场"大拆大建"的运动中，中国创造了两项世界第一：消耗了全球最多的水泥和钢材，也产出了全球最多的建筑垃圾。我国建筑垃圾的数量已占到城市垃圾总量的 30%～40%。在每万平方米建筑的施工过程中，仅建筑垃圾就会产生 500～600t；而每万平方米拆除的旧建筑，将产生 7000～12000t 建筑垃圾。建设"节约型"社会、建设"和谐"社会等发展观的提出，坚持可持续发展等国家政策的贯彻实施，使既有住宅建筑改造在新世纪登上了新的台阶。但当下改造依然得不到及时引导与技术支持，特别是在既有住宅建筑的改造中，体现得较为突出。这些改造由于长期处于混乱中，在改造风格和设计思路上随意随性，经常伴随着一些质量安全隐患。政策法规方面依然是采用定性制约的方式，对改造过程的监管不够完善，造成大量"遗憾且无法弥补"的改造建筑问世。

来自于西方建筑思潮与改造实例大量引入后，我国改造思潮开始慢慢发展，海归派学者带来了西方观念及作品并积极在本土实施，期间有对中国特色的探寻，也有支离异化的学步。改造技术长期以来不被重视，鲜有从学术角度挖掘并探究其深层价值及意义。当前，在大多数情况下，城市建设管理部门对更新改造的理解从操作层面上依然是"再造"，这导致大批项目打着"更新改造"的旗号大拆大建。

既有住宅建筑改造在中国发展方兴未艾，越来越多的人意识到既有建筑改造的重要性，但在中国当下建筑界，关于既有建筑改造更多是混乱，希望通过本文的研究，对建筑改造提供一个全新的视角，引入一套更加贴合实际，更加有实际应用价值的既有住宅建筑改造模式，从而在理论与实践中，建立以建筑构件产品化为中心的既有住宅建筑改造的指导方法。建筑构件产品化的重要性：将建筑拆分成建筑构件，从而使构件可以产品化，符合建筑工业化的建造逻辑，指导既有建筑改造中，保留不变的，多是结构构件，剩下建筑构件用产品化构件代替，例如外围护构件、性能构件、

装饰构件等。这样可以加快建筑改造速度，并且全程可控。构件产品库的重要性：提供一整套可供选择的建筑构件产品库，即可在库中选择现成产品，快速出方案，快速落实既有建筑改造所需资金、人员、时间、工具等。原本复杂的既有建筑改造问题变得简单可控。

总之，要把当前停留在图纸和文字中的建筑改造真实地落实到建筑改造实践中去，要让建筑设计从业者及甲方清清楚楚要怎么改造、改造什么、改造的费用以及改造可以带来什么好处，使既有建筑改造图表化，清晰可控，是本文试图达到的最终目的，后续研究中将继续下去。

2 冬冷夏热地区既有住宅建筑改造特点

既有住宅建筑改造必须是在满足建筑热工性能基础上，其中气候因素、运行状况以及各种建筑改造措施等都会对建筑热工性能产生影响。由于中国南北气候差异较大，在具体的措施方面也有着很大的不同。笔者所在的南京就位于冬冷夏热地区，该地区夏季闷热潮湿，冬季寒冷干燥。随着经济发展和人民生活水平快速提高，空调设备也得到普及使用。如何通过改善建筑围护构件热工性能，使建筑物具有良好的室内热舒适性，降低建筑耗能成为急需研究的课题。20世纪80年代以来的既有建筑仍占有相当大比重，在研究对冬冷夏热地区既有住宅建筑的节能改造时需注意以下几个方面：

(1) 增强外围护的保温性能，降低外围护的传热系数。

(2) 增强外窗的保温性能，注意窗型材与玻璃材料的选择。

(3) 改善遮阳设施，会大大降低建筑的冷热负荷。

(4) 应积极处理屋顶，增加空气间层或绿化，能有效改善建筑物理性能。

3 既有住宅建筑屋顶改造工业化技术

屋顶被称为建筑的第五立面，是建筑外观改造中的重要组成部分。

3.1 传统屋顶改造

传统屋顶改造主要是平改坡，屋顶绿化及附加表皮三个方面。

平改坡，多是20世纪70~80年代的平屋顶老小区，屋顶漏水等现象严重。加之随着城市高层越来越多，领导更加关注城市第五立面而突然兴起的。由于缺乏相应技术及认真论证，第一轮平改坡现多已沦为"平改破"问题非常严峻。

自20世纪50年代后，西方发达国家开始重视屋顶绿化技术。在我国，屋顶绿化更多是景观专业人员在设计，多为草本和地被类景观化处理，因缺乏建筑师及结构师的参与，大量屋顶绿化不涉及灌木及乔木。随着这些年的实践也暴露出了非常多的问题：例如绿植的搭配不合理、水土流失严重、破坏屋顶结构、漏水渗水及霉斑、排水管径偏小、结构余量不足等。

所谓屋顶附加表皮，不是常规意义上指的加建，这是创造一个介于平屋顶与新附加屋顶之间的空气间层，这个空间某种程度上能够实现一定的功能使用效果，同时又能满足建筑防水保温隔热，却不危及原建筑结构系统。

3.2 既有住宅建筑屋顶产品化改造

用建筑工业化中的建筑构件产品化思维来进行思考，可以附加一层建筑屋顶构件，可以是木的，也可以是轻钢结构或者轻铝结构，极少增加屋顶的荷载，这层屋顶构件产品可以是平的或坡的，可以附加在原平屋顶上或原坡屋顶上，上面可以做绿化也可以做太阳能光电光热等，当然也可以仅仅是一层有良好物理性能的屋顶表皮层。

在工厂生产好成品构件，利用大型车辆一次运输到位，利用垂直运输装备，运输到屋顶上，与屋顶进行简单的连接，即可完成，现场干作业，一栋楼的改造时间可以控制在一天内完成，后续的屋顶绿化、光电光热或表皮层也可以做成构件产品，再进行二次安装。整个过程对本栋楼的居民生活几乎没有影响，同时不会带来屋顶施工坠物而引发的建筑事故。建筑构件产品均是在工厂生产，时间、人员、财务等均可做到全程可控，不会像传统那样施工现场混乱不堪，伴随居民生活的各种不便。

利用构件产品化原理做屋顶绿化改造，在绿化产品构件设计生产中，与智能滴灌系统相连接，可以合理利用水资源。将土壤也做成绿化构件产品中的一部分，与原屋顶是脱离开的，这样可以解决屋顶灌溉与渗漏问题，利用最少的土解决屋顶绿化问题，又不增加太多负荷。同时等于增加一层空气层，对屋内的物理环境能起到良好的影响。当选择太阳能产品，可以积极产能，产生的电能可以自用也可以上国家电网，实现产能住宅概念，即每栋建筑就是一个小型的太阳能发电站。

既有住宅建筑屋顶产品化改造的现实性。比传统技术手段来得更加巧妙，不受原建筑屋顶的结构及形式限制，衔接处理简单可靠，材料均来自于工厂，施工操作省时省力省人，并更加精确。

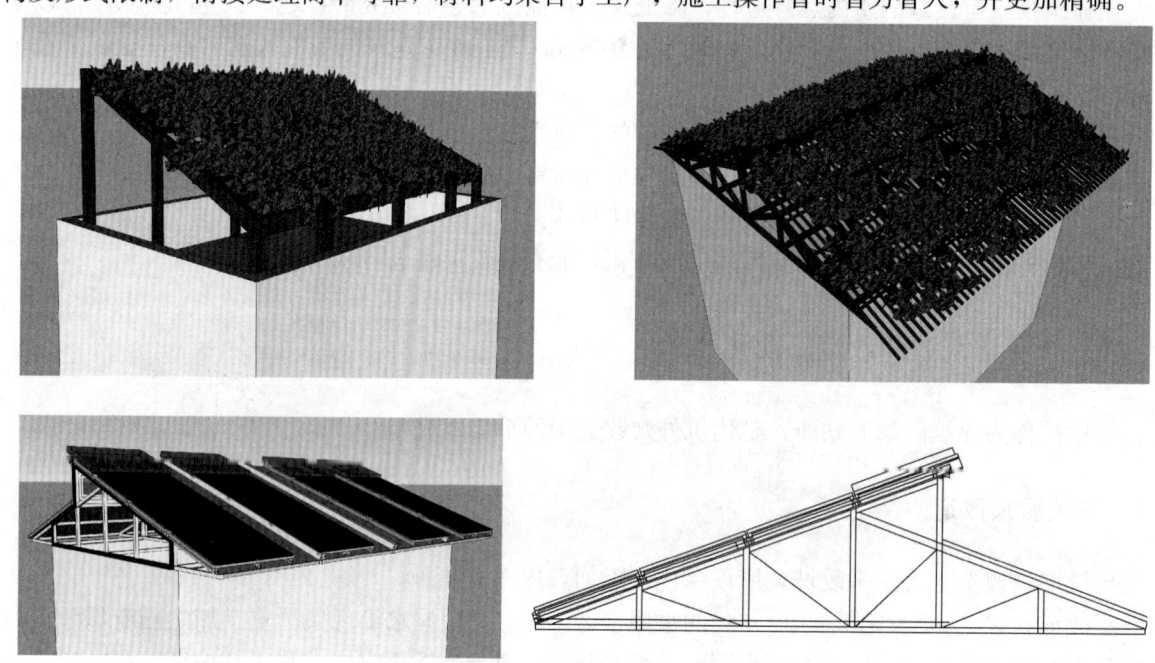

图 1　轻铝结构屋顶改造示意图

（资料来源：东南大学张宏工作室）

4　既有住宅建筑立面改造工业化技术

4.1　传统立面改造

传统立面改造包含表皮更新、外置表皮、内置表皮等。

对于建筑的表皮更新来说，包括更换饰面材料及更换表皮。更换饰面材料较为简单，不涉及原建筑外观及体量的变化，不影响原建筑的立面造型。但这仅是对原建筑的表皮外观进行适当优化，基本不涉及性能提升。例如利用涂料、真石漆等进行重新喷涂。耗时耗力，虽然花的钱不多，但考虑到没有本质变化及提升，某种程度上也是一种资源的浪费。更换表皮是另外一种方式，需要建筑的结构围护相互独立，例如框架结构的公寓式住宅，可在保留结构体系的前提下对围护体表皮进行更换。外观变化了同时可能带来性能的提升。所花的时间更长，对内部住户造成的影响更加深远，需要全程撤离甚至是搬空，所需资金难以估计，甚至超出新建。

外置表皮即在原建筑立面外侧增加一层新的表皮，强调附加性，例如幕墙表皮系统。但是也是受到原建筑的限制，例如原建筑开窗位置需要留好开孔开洞，才不会影响采光通风。内置表皮多用于历史文化建筑，在内部进行表皮更新，不会破坏建筑的主体结构和外观体系，同时兼顾保护遗迹留存记忆而又不牺牲内部使用人员的安全舒适。

4.2 既有住宅建筑立面产品化改造

利用产品化逻辑，在立面改造中，东南大学张宏工作室已成功开发若干种产品原型。这里介绍其中两种，一种是轻型结构构件产品，一种是现浇无机双层保温墙体。

轻型建筑构件产品，附加在原来既有住宅建筑表皮的外部，有一定的间隔，受力直接传到地面，与原住宅产品的连接仅起稳定作用，在这层附加的骨架中可以产生新的空间以及新的使用功能，例如空调机位。当然也会更新立面及外观。相对而言，其在表皮的选择和设计上有更多的余地，受约束较少。而且，可以通过绿化，或增加玻璃幕墙，穿孔板等一系列方法，使其视觉效果上突破原住宅建筑的限制。层次感更加明显，特点鲜明给人耳目一新的感受。

这个设计的核心在于内部的架子，采用不锈钢方管，方管与方管之间利用螺栓连接固定，辅以市场即可买到的拉锁，形成稳定的一套架子系统，每个架子系统高 3m 左右，宽与长可以根据实际需要进行定制，架子系统在工厂组装完成，运到现场后即是一个个完整的模块，将最下面一层与地面预先定位并预埋的金属件进行连接，上部的模块再利用起重设备进行吊装，类似搭积木样的拼接方式，模块与模块之间的连接也是利用螺栓，可以大大提高工作效率同时降低工作强度，架子系统同时也是施工的脚手架与安全架，无需再添加其他设备即可形成最终的骨架形态，骨架形态全部完工后，再根据造型或功能需要辅以其他造型元素，这些元素只与架子发生关系，与建筑主体相脱离开，互不影响。当需要做绿化时，爬藤植物顺着不锈钢方钢管或拉锁逐渐爬升，根系在地面上，为以后的植物养管带来极大便捷，无需架设滴灌系统。顶部甚至可以利用架子系统做成太阳能广场。

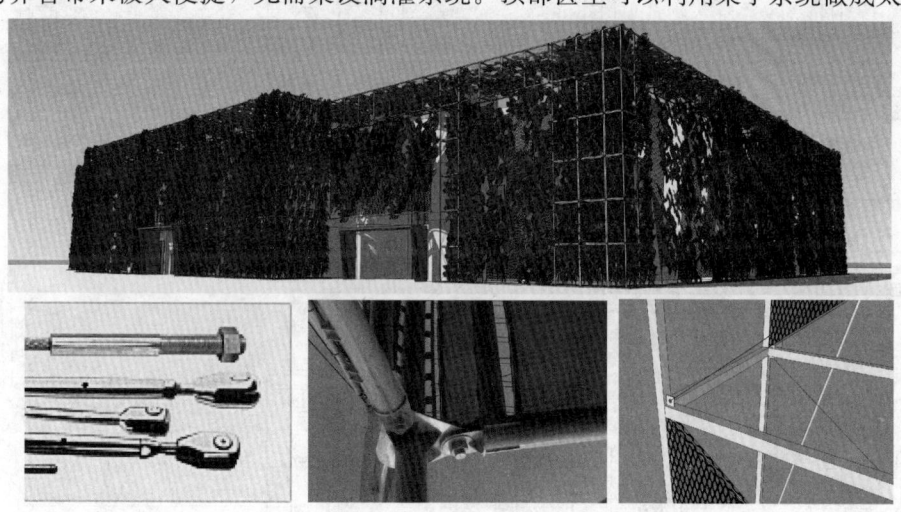

图 2　轻型既有住宅建筑改造示意图
（资料来源：东南大学张宏工作室）

现浇无机双层保温墙体及其施工方法（ZL 2011 2 0242934.2）由高强度预制墙件、无机保温层、内墙板或内结构形成三组复合构造，形成外强、内中、里弱的复合层墙体；既满足外部建筑外环境对墙体高强度要求，又满足建筑内环境对墙体柔和要求，同时实现高强度、中强度的墙体对柔弱保温层的夹固，综合利用自然原理，包括热传导、热对流、热辐射原理、空气对流原理、温室效应原理、蒸发效应原理，实现外围护墙体的集保温、反热、隔热、密封、散热、降热于一体的复合节能墙体。无机双层保温墙体，前后两面为 50mm 厚预制混凝土板，整个板作为一种建筑构件部件，两边各翻折出来一个肋，肋与肋接，形成的空腔填充 100mm 厚无机保温材料增加其刚性。

现浇无机双层保温墙体可以更换原建筑外围护，这是一种高效生产运输安装的产品。可以在工厂中定制生产含窗户部件、纯墙板部件、含空调机位部件的产品，用运输设备运到现场后，在现场利用起重设备拼装。在定制含窗户部件的产品时可定制含有三玻两空气层，内含铝合金卷帘一体化的窗户产品，同时带来外墙与外窗热工性能的一致提高，遮阳的问题也在玻璃间层巧妙解决了。现浇无机双层保温墙板两侧翻折出来的肋同时也是立面上的造型元素，可以采用对缝、错缝等多种处理手法。立面造型更加丰富多彩。在提升性能的同时，美观问题也得到了极大的提升。墙板系统与主体结构之间连接，可以利用图 3 中所示连接构造图。在等待改造的既有住宅建筑中，去除原外围

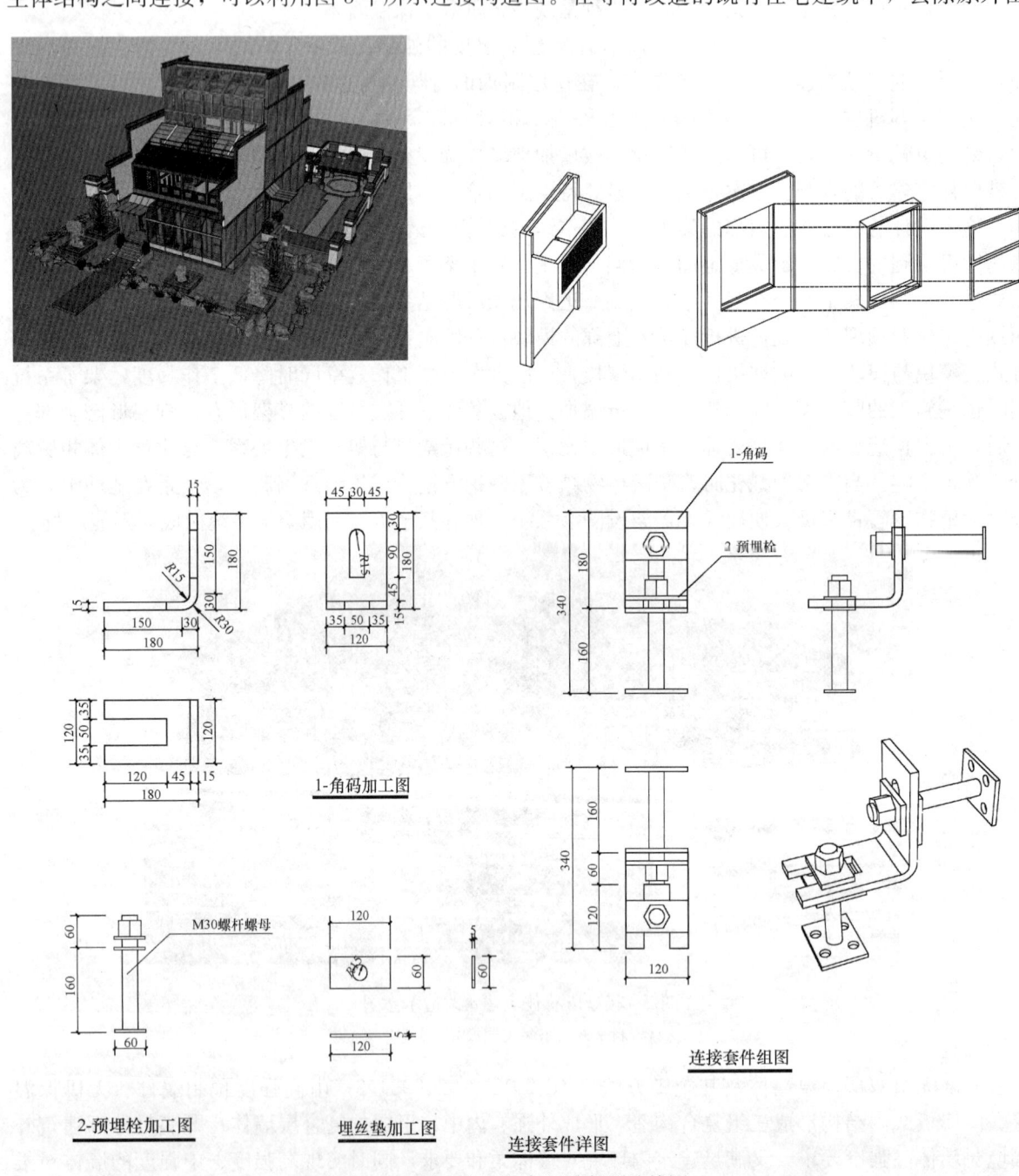

图 3　现浇无机双层保温墙板图连接图
（资料来源：东南大学张宏工作室）

护，将连接构件通过膨胀螺栓或其他手段连接到主体结构上，然后将现浇无机双层保温墙板安装到连接件上。统一预留好缝，最后将缝做好防水及保温措施。如此一个既有住宅建筑立面产品化改造就算是完成了。

5 总结

从此次对既有住宅建筑改造的研究中我们可以得出，中国现有大量既有住宅建筑急于改造，虽然越来越多的人意识到既有住宅建筑改造的急迫性，但在中国当下建筑界，更多的是混乱。基于工业化建造思路，摒弃传统手工模式，以建筑构件产品化为设计前提，以利于生产、运输、施工、维护，以及再次更新，可节省既有建筑改造的时间和成本，提高效率，并且全程利用图表系统，清晰可控。最重要的是全部部件产品在工厂中生产，现场仅是运输及吊装，极大地缩短工期，并且对内部人员造成干扰极小。采用产品化逻辑进行改造，所有产品可以回收，不会产生新的垃圾，并出现问题方便及时维修，乃至建筑构件产品因某种原因需要拆除时亦可迅速整体拆除，不造成二次建筑污染与浪费，方便未来进行的再次改造。既有建筑产品化改造必然成为未来的趋势之一。

The Productization Renovation of Existing Residential Architecture in Hot Summer and Cold Wind Zone: Take the Facade Reconstruction as An Example

Zhang Lirui, Zhang Hong

(School of Architecture, Southeast University)

Abstract: Building will become existing building upon completion, and can't escape the fate of reconstruction or demolition. In the year 2005, the existing building area of China is 44-45 billion square meters, of which the residential construction area is 27 billion square meters. The annual new construction area is 2 billion square meters, while the areas of existing buildings in 2014 reach 58 billion square meters. In the building's life cycle, the renovation of existing residential buildings is essential. Reflecting on the current design trend that excessive pursuit of efficiency, neglecting the old building's updated, demolition the old buildings while building new to blind-sided pursuit of GDP, all of which bring the tremendous waste and many social and environmental problems. Existing buildings' renovation can save money and prolong building's life, so that it can be used to create the building's quality and environment better, which has a very important significance on sustainable development and energy efficiency. The paper try to make the productization library of building components, select the shelf products in the library to implement the project design, the necessary funds, personnel, time and tools quickly. Hope that this study can provide a new perspective, and make a new existing residential buildings renovation mode which is more valuable and closer to the reality.

Keywords: Existing residential building renovation, Building industrialization, Product renovation, Components product library, Hot summer and cold winter area

参考文献：

[1] 马兴能，郭汉丁，尚伶. 国内外既有建筑节能改造市场培育实践研究分析[J]. 建筑节能，

2012(02).

[2]　张琦. 既有建筑节能改造管理研究[D]. 天津：天津大学，2010.

[3]　(美)亚历山大·纽曼. 建筑物的结构修复——方法·细部·设计实例[M]. 惠云玲，郝挺宇，等译. 北京：中国建筑工业出版社，2008.

[4]　贺静. 整体生态观下既存建筑的适应性再利用[D]. 天津：天津大学，2004.

[5]　Sorrel S. The economics of energy service contracts[J]. Energy Policy，2007.

城市设计视角下中国住宅本土化设计的三种方法

李振宇　李　垣

（同济大学建筑与城市规划学院）

摘要： 中国当代住宅在高速增长和高效建设之时，也面临着多样性缺失的挑战。不少中国建筑师因此思考建筑和住宅设计的本土化方法，以对抗住宅建设的整体趋同倾向，其中包括社区在城市设计视角下的形态探索。我们选取当代中国住宅本土化设计实践的典型案例：菊儿胡同（1987）、土楼公社（2008）、拙政别墅（2012），比较不同样本的设计差异，寻找其地方原型，推演从原型到类型的变型过程，分析本土化设计的具体方法：适应原有城市肌理，塑造区域城市氛围，重现地方居住原景。本土化探索是住宅设计对抗趋同与外来冲击的表现，目前正处在模仿民居原型与当代设计变型共存的阶段，向着批判的地域主义方向发展。

关键词： 中国，住宅，本土化，城市设计

1　引言

在复杂的政治和经济环境影响下，伴随不断发展的全球化和城市化进程，中国城市在改革开放以后经历的成长是空前的：一方面依据城市规划的引导寻求合理目标，另一方面，在经济增长的支持下实现持续扩张。道路交通等基础设施的完善，更为城市建筑的大规模建设提供了基本保障。在这些城市建筑中，住宅建筑的比例占到一半以上。

20世纪80年代后期，住宅商品化改革促进了住宅商品市场的建立，也开启了中国商品房发展的"黄金时代"，随着90年代初社会主义市场经济理论的建立，房地产市场更是蓬勃发展，增量空前。在看似庞大的需求面前，效率成为住宅建设的首要目标。成功的市场推广案例和逐渐严格的规范要求，令住宅设计受到越来越多的约束。而以大型地产与设计集团为代表的投资方，也在住宅产业化不断成熟的今天，一再推出各式各样的"标准化设计"。

在这样的发展背景下，中国建筑师面临的，既是纷至沓来的信息、前所未有的挑战，也是千载难逢的机遇。大批优秀建筑师在这里获得了许多锻炼和思考的机会，一部分人对住宅设计整体趋同的设计形势，提出了质疑，并从自身出发，作出新的尝试。从吴良镛"广义建筑学"、"人居环境学"理论的提出，北京菊儿胡同（1987）的试验开始，到"本土"建筑师王澍对住宅设计差异性的强调（2006），中国建筑师，始终没有忘记中国建筑的地缘文化意义。作为设计者，他们对千篇一律"国际式"的对抗，主要体现在"地域性"、"本土化"的设计方法上。这类方法牵涉城市设计、空间关系、形式材料等多个方面，其中，从城市设计视角展开的解读，是一种对住宅建筑较为宏观的概括。

2　本土化设计的三种方法

就总体而言，城市设计视角下的中国当代城市住宅，可以从三个方面尝试本土化设计的突破：（1）适应原有城市肌理；（2）塑造区域城市氛围；（3）重现地方居住原景。这三类方法，是对已有尝试的概括，代表了中国住宅建筑从设计"困局"中走出去的第一步。

2.1　适应原有城市肌理

城市从聚落发展而来，也因为最初的居住形态形成了基本的城市肌理。城市肌理作为城市组织

形态的表现，反映了城市格局的尺度、城市建筑的密度、城市景观的精度等多个层面的要素。除了记录客观的发展情况，城市肌理所代表的生活方式，也是城市居民的集体记忆。

对于中国这样历史深远的国家来说，城市的肌理形态是积数千年之功形成的。在类似北京、西安这样的古都里，城市生活的悠久印记，更为明晰；城市肌理与建筑形态的关系，也易于辨认。街坊、巷弄、广场等社区空间，都与城市的道路系统息息相关。

当今中国城市面对大量的新建工程，城市原有肌理遭遇不同程度的破坏。对于已有的整体或地区形态，在住宅行列式布局盛行的今天，建筑师将住宅的本土化设计探索，指向城市肌理的层面，以实现城市空间的延续、综合或变异。这对于平衡本土建筑文化来说，不失为一种有效的方法。

以北京菊儿胡同为例。20世纪80年代，吴良镛在审慎的"有机更新"理论指导下，开始整治北京的旧城，创造了"类四合院"的新"街坊体系"，是为菊儿胡同。吴良镛曾称赞北京的规划格局"逻辑性、艺术性是世界城市史上罕见的巨大创造"（1991），他反对那种不假思索地推光重建，提倡用一种顺应城市肌理的方式，进行可持续的更新与改造。

北京旧城的基本格局来自13世纪的元大都，经过明清两朝的发展，如今具有三个基本特点：（1）大干路、大街坊、小胡同的街巷体系；（2）交通、商业、居住功能混合；（3）胡同与四合院紧密结合，形成系统。对比北京基本道路布局，不难发现，对于北京城的圈层—格网系统，菊儿胡同采取了顺应了肌理的小网格系统——用建筑塑造合院，再以合院为单位，形成生活组团，胡同串接在组团之间，整体结构严谨、均匀。北京的"大街坊"结构促成了里巷外多是大街的情况，具体到菊儿胡同：北临鼓楼东大街，东面交道口南大街，均为繁华街道。从大街，到胡同，到里巷，到庭院的层级推进，反映了菊儿胡同面对外部城市环境的温和态度。

菊儿胡同城市肌理　　　　　　　　　　　　　　　　　　　　　　　表1

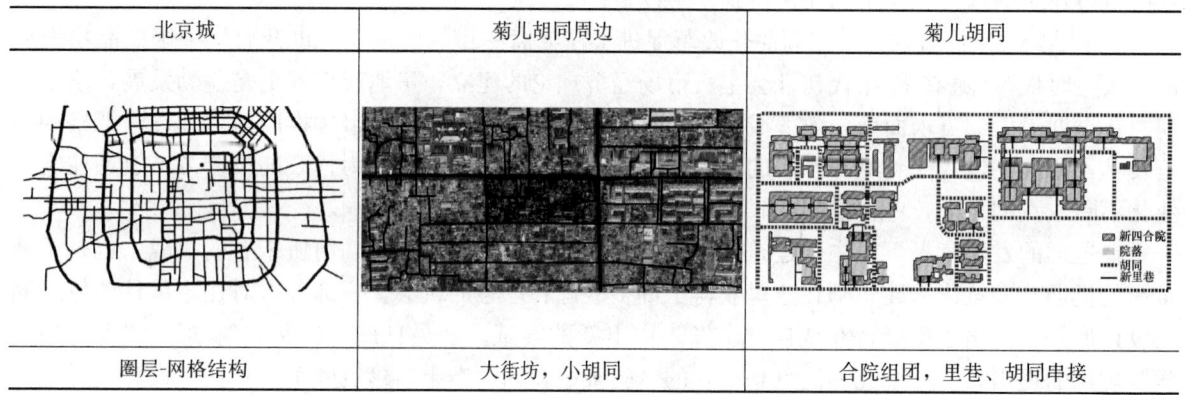

北京城	菊儿胡同周边	菊儿胡同
圈层-网格结构	大街坊，小胡同	合院组团，里巷、胡同串接

在这样的城市形态里，合院起了连接建筑单体、形成区域环境的重要作用。作为最早的一类建筑形式，合院体系是中国很多种建筑类型的源头。西周时期，陕西岐山凤雏村就出现了四合院，此后漫长的历史过程中，这种基本的围合方式以各种形式得到广泛使用。菊儿胡同的设计便是以一种典型的合院形式——北京四合院为原型。低层住宅围合的"基本院落"构成主要的生活空间；联系院落的里巷则源于合院原型中的服务性交通道——南方称之为"备弄"或"壁弄"。以居住原型为基础，菊儿胡同在回应和联系城市的层面，进行了一定的变型。与四合院的完全封闭不同，菊儿胡同中的合院在至少一面是设出入口的，这些开口与里巷以及胡同相连，构成了"合院—里巷—胡同"的区域格局；另一方面，由于围合实体的高度达二到三层，较原型有所提高，因此合院与胡同的尺度也有所扩大。

在适应北京旧城原有肌理的前提下，菊儿胡同改造工程提取四合院原型中的部分元素进行适应性、可持续的更新，建筑从总体布局到屋顶形态，都体现了对北京城的大格局和对南锣鼓巷小区域的肌理性认同。这里的本土化设计方法体现了对原型的复合性传承，从城市角度来说，形成了一种新的、半开放式的合院体系，是对四合院这个传统围合方式的现代改造。

图1 菊儿胡同实景

（资料来源：吴良镛. 北京旧城与菊儿胡同［M］. 北京：中国建筑工业出版社，1994.2. 作者摄）

菊儿胡同所代表的，是适应城市肌理的住宅本土化设计方法，在当代中国城市的应用。正如北京宪章所说，"建筑是地区的建筑"，住宅也是城市的住宅。菊儿胡同的实践，印证了当今行列式布局以外的其他可能性：融入城市肌理，回归历史记忆和有交往的生活。

2.2 塑造区域城市氛围

以居住区为主体的城市区域，既是城市整体的一部分，本身又构成一个个相对独立的个体。区域是人们在城市中行走时的一个重要外部参照，而区域本身的主题和特点是其能够被识别的关键因素。建筑在城市区域中所起的作用，是纹理、空间、形式等多方面的，它们都有可能充当这个区域的主题。在中国大量的居住原型中，很多情况下住宅并非以单体的方式出现，而是通过群体组合产生地区性的城市氛围。当新建筑以这一类本土居住形式为原型时，往往可以提炼区域性城市和社区模式，将其应用在本土化设计的重新探索上。

图2 土楼公社实景

（资料来源：都市实践提供）

中国民居的典型代表之一，客家土楼，就是这样一类原型。作为一种适应大家族聚居的巨型建筑，土楼采用夯土墙和木梁柱共同承重，通常具有外圈高、内圈低、墙体厚实的特点——对外部环境呈现很强的隔绝性与对抗性。从外向内的功能分布依次是居住楼房、辅助用房、祖堂，空间布局中轴对称，生活以祠堂为核心展开。

通过对土楼的形态演绎，都市实践在广东南海进行了一项低收入集合住宅尝试：土楼公社（2008）。建筑师试图通过环形的总体布局，创造既适合邻里交往又隔绝外部不利影响的社区空间。具有亲和力的环形布置方式，为社区内部营建了柔滑的视觉边界，圆形所产生的向心力，又给人们创造一种温馨安逸的居住氛围；另一方面，外凸的形状和密集格网式辅助木百叶的立面，将城市的喧嚣排除在这个独立社区之外，为内部的居民形成一道心理屏障。

从总平面上看，土楼群落是一个个独立内向的封闭个体自由组合的结果；而土楼公社在新的城市环境中并不具有这样的居住氛围，因此它所呈现的继承自土楼的相对内向特征，令其在区域内成为城市空间的焦点。平面上，土楼公社的布局继承了客家圆楼的外环布置方式，对周边城市环境形成向心性的空间主导。但是不同于原型中高度由外至内逐渐降低、城市影响在各个方向完全一致的特点，土楼公社的围合高度是变化的，因此对环境的导向不尽相同；另外，土楼公社的平面是一个连续的整体，住宅与城市的边界有敞开的入口，而非原型中的同心圆设计——只在立面上设有狭窄的门洞，几乎与外界隔绝。客家圆楼的城市特性，在这个设计中既得到了继承，又实现了变化：城市形态和区域边界的处理方式有所不同。因此，土楼公社可以说是具有土楼特性的新型集合住宅。

客家土楼与土楼公社平面比较

表 2

特　点	客家土楼群平面	土楼公社周边环境	特　点
封闭个体的群体组合，关注内部空间			城市空间不完善，周边较松散，缺乏区域中心
特　点	客家土楼平剖面	土楼公社平剖面	特　点
同心圆设计，出入口狭小，比较封闭			连续的线性整体，入口开放，朝向城市的流动空间

这类住宅表现出的对区域氛围的主导力，是城市设计视角下住宅设计的又一种方式。当住宅处于城市环境相对不完善的情况中时，引入土楼这样的本土民居原型，通过形式的分解和重塑，实现塑造区域城市氛围的目标，既为城市形态增添多样性，又是对传统居住文化的重新演绎。

2.3　重现地方居住原景

中国的不同地方都有各自的居住形态，这些居住形态体现出不同地域的自然地理以及文化特征。在民居从产生到成形的漫长的历史过程中，它们的总体布局、空间形式都逐渐形成一种有明显地域标识的模式，同时跟特定地区的生活习惯、居住方式息息相关。

与上面提到的两种融合城市、转译民居的方法不同，在当代的一些住区中，建筑师将地方的特征性住宅形态引入设计，为使用者提供一种具有明显区域标签的生活方式，借此作为设计的主要出发点。在城市设计视角下，住宅能够通过整体布局重现这种居住原景。

位于苏州古城百家巷中，与拙政园仅一街之隔的拙政别墅（2012），是这种设计方法下的典型产物。似乎是为了表示对中国古典园林的敬意，拙政别墅意在"仿古"，对拙政园所代表的江南私家园林的居住氛围进行了原景重现。这样的出发点虽然直白，但是不得不说是有深刻的地域人文基础的。对于有着"园林梦"的苏州人来说，苏州园林是他们为之自豪的文化遗产，也是他们魂牵梦萦的居住理想。而在最负盛名的拙政园对面，重新建立这样一种生活氛围，是对地域文化最直接的解说。

由于靠近拙政园，这个项目在规划时受到"容积率小于0.4"，"檐口高度小于6.5m"的严格限制。显然这个地区需要的，就是一个能让当代人便捷居住的"古典"园林。然而，对于一个有现代居住要求——比如行车的小区来说，用古典园林的方式布置，最大的问题就在于调和"今"与"古"的矛盾。在现代化的小区中加入园林的景观、屋顶等，是一种常用方式，可这种拼贴法不符合这个项目想要达到的、构建本质意义上园林生活的目的；而怎样还原园林气质，又不折损使用的便捷度，也是一个需要解决的问题。

对比该项目布局与拙政园总平面示意图，可以读出：拙政别墅尽力保留了园林中水面的自由形态和建筑布置的拓扑关系。对于园林来说，宅与景的关系是居住氛围的关键因素，因此拙政别墅的设计者在总平面中采取了将宅放入园中的做法，同时宅内也留有小院。这种大园—中宅—小院的做法，一方面保证景的重要地位，另一方面在容积率、日照等多种现实因素的要求下尽可能实现形态上与园林的接近。为了在不破坏宅园景致的前提下保证行车，设计者将车行出入口设于小区外沿，停车位全部放在地下，实现彻底的人车分流，将地面全部留给行人，这种处理方式，也是为了保证一种中国园林的纯粹感。

当然，尽管有强烈的园林精神，拙政别墅的实际使用要求决定了它的水域面积不可能像真正的园林那么大，建筑布置也不如原型中疏朗别致，毕竟拙政园只属于一个家庭，而拙政别墅却是多户共享的社区，属性的差异决定了它们在总体布局时侧重点的不同。但是从墙内有园，园中有景，景里有水，水边有宅的角度来说，拙政别墅已经基本实现了园林居住的重演。从应对城市的意义上来说，它相当成功地描摹了园林本来应对城市环境的态度：古城文化与水城格局下的私人天地，既内向封闭，又因地制宜。

特　点	拙政园总体布局	拙政别墅总体布局	特　点
形态自由，建筑与水面的拓扑关系			园中有宅，宅中有院，建筑组团环绕小块水面
特　点	拙政园实景	拙政别墅实景	特　点
回廊曲折，步移景异，建筑形态开放			模仿园林景象，建筑相对独立封闭

拙政园与拙政别墅比较　　　　　　　　　　　　表 3

资料来源：1. http://www.szzzy.cn
2. 洪杰，殷新. 苏州拙政东园园林别墅区设计探索 [J]. 建筑学报. 2009 (5)：31-33.

城市生活景象千变万化，在住宅设计中将原本的历史的居住图景提取出来，放到新设计中重新洗印，再现出具有地方特征的生活氛围，是本土化在城市设计层面的又一种方法。这种方法体现出的，主要是本土化设计的传承性特点；比较适应肌理的方法对周边城市环境的充分考虑，原景重现的方式更侧重于区域性的主题和特点，力求原汁原味地铺陈原型中的居住环境，而只在一些功能上应当代人的生活要求作出调整。

3　小结

在城市设计视角下，住宅中经常采用的本土化设计方法，包括适应原有城市肌理、塑造区域城市氛围、重现地方居住原景三种。具体来说，适应原有城市肌理以一种融合的态度应对环境，通过对城市总体肌理形态的适应，表现对城市历史的尊重，继承和发展原有的社区生活；塑造区域城市氛围，以主导者的姿态凌驾于环境之上，通过内向性或突出性的形式特征，取得对所在区域的控制权，这种方式适合于居住原型指向性较强、同时周边环境整体氛围不统一的设计；而重现地方居住的原景，则是一种修正性的方法，它取材于具有明显地域特征，并形成了浓厚生活氛围的民居原型，态度介于前二者之间：一方面希望适应于当地的城市文化环境，另一方面又想要营建具有自身色彩的居住情境，尽管这类情境带有较明显的标签感。

三种本土化设计方法图示　　　　　　　　　　　　　　　表4

适应原有城市肌理	塑造区域城市氛围	地方居住原景重现
融合环境，尊重历史	主导环境，统领区域标识	模仿原型，有标签色彩

　　中国住宅自改革开放以来始终受到外来力量的冲击，"中国文化与西方文化的交织与融合已经成为中国城市空间和建筑的重要特征"（郑时龄，2014）。对住宅设计的本土化方法探索，既是对"千城一面"的反思，也是中国建筑师对外部冲击作出的顽强反抗，意在寻找中国文化和建筑的固有特征。从菊儿胡同、土楼公社、拙政别墅等实践中可以看出，本土化设计的发展阶段正处在一个模仿民居原型与当代设计变型共存的阶段，未来会逐渐摆脱原型的束缚，朝着批判的地域主义方向发展。

致谢

　　本文为国家自然科学基金面上项目资助（项目名称：当代中国住宅建筑的类型学特征研究；编号：51278337）。

Three Localized Design Methods on Chinese Residential in Urban Design

Li Zhenyu，Li Yuan

(College of Architecture and Urban Planning，Tongji University)

Abstract：Chinese residential is facing the challenge from diversity loss，in the meantime of high-speed growth and high-efficiency construction. Some architects therefore started to think of localized methods to fight against the overall convergence trends of residential design，including the form exploration in urban design. Three typical samples [Ju'er Hutong (1987)，Tulou Commune (2008) and Zhuozheng Villas (2012)] were chosen and analyzed：comparing different samples，seeking local prototypes，deducting from prototypes to neo-types. Three specific methods were summarized：matching original urban texture，leading regional atmosphere，and rebuilding local life. Localized design in residential is to fight against convergence and external shock，and now in the stage of imitating prototypes and translating contemporary types at the same time，advancing towards critical regionalism.

Keywords：China，Residential，Localization，Urban design

参考文献：

[1]　Aldo Rossi. The Architecture of the City[M]. The MIT Press，1984.

［2］ Dong Yijia，Li Zhenyu. The Values of Low-coverage High-rise Housing for the Urban Development of Shanghai［C］. UIA，Durban. 2014：533-539.

［3］ To Kien. "Tube House" and "Neo Tube House" in Hanoi：A Comparative Study on Identity and Typology［J］. Journal of Asian Architecture and Building Engineering. 2008（11）：255-262.

［4］ 洪杰，殷新. 苏州拙政东园园林别墅区设计探索［J］. 建筑学报. 2009，5：31-33.

［5］ 李振宇，李垣. 本土材料的当代表述——中国住宅地域性实验的三个案例［J］. 时代建筑. 2014(3)：72-76.

［6］ 刘晓都，孟岩. 土楼公社［J］. 中国建筑装饰装修. 2010，6.

［7］ 吴良镛. 从"有机更新"走向新的"有机秩序"——北京旧城居住区整治途径(二)［J］. 建筑学报. 1991，2：7-13.

［8］ 郑时龄. 当代中国建筑的基本状况思考［J］. 建筑学报. 2014，03：96-98.

Open Design in the Control of Urban Regeneration

Li Guopeng, Fan Yue
(Dalian University of Technology)

Abstract: As stated by Open Building theory, the built environment can be seen as having a hierarchical structure in which higher levels serve as the setting and context in which lower levels operate. The hierarchies consist of "Tissue, Support, and Infill", thus, the implications of Open Building thinking into urban regeneration shapes the urban traditions and memories. This paper, taking a design work "Sustainable Change" from Sino-UK Higher Education Collaboration on Architectural Design as an example, introduces the possible procedure to achieve the control of urban regeneration. The design work took the existing road system, infrastructure, and historical buildings as the fundamental concept to determine the "Tissue" and left the "plot" in between the Tissue open for future development. The Tissue controls the development and regeneration of each plot of Infill and at the same time introduces light, movements, and landscape evaluations into the urban site. This method using Open Building theory into urban regeneration concerns the dimension of time and the interaction between the development and the built environment.

Keywords: Open building, Control, Urban regeneration, Design work

1 Introduction

Currently, the surge of construction, particularly the residential section, has been slowed down; however, the issues from the large-scale and disordered developments in the urban area from the past decades are getting increasingly serious. Traffics have been blocked by the huge residential districts; public facilities are barely reachable; environmental issues, such as noise, pollution, and micro-climate destruction, emerge. This situation is even worse in big cities with more vehicles. It is unrealistic to put down the whole city and then build another fancy one. Thus, to make a good use of the opportunity during urban regeneration to rebuild the city traffic system, to relieve the environmental issues become one of the key strategies in the control of city development. It would be better if the urban traditions and memories can be recalled through the regeneration process. This paper, taking a design work "Sustainable Change" from Sino-UK Higher Education Collaboration on Architectural Design as an example, introduces the possible procedure using Open Building Theory to achieve the control of urban regeneration in the central area of Harbin City.

2 Open Building Theory in Urban Planning

Habraken first articulated the principles of Open Building in his book Supports: an Alternative to Mass Housing, first published in Dutch in 1962and in English in 1972 and 1999. In his book, Habarken analysed the effects of mass housing construction in the Netherlands, such as monotony, the lack of occupant participation and the failure to benefit from industrialisation. He formulated a radical alternative: the concept of separation of "support" or base building from "infill" or interior fit-out in residential construction and design. Open Building, then, was based on the belief that variety and diversity may produce better mass housing, both productively and efficiently.

Later, in 1964, the Foundation for Architects Research (the SAR) was founded in the Netherlands, and Habraken was appointed as director of the new research office and was given carte blanche to explore the possibilities of his support theory. From 1965 to 1973, in an effort to alleviate the monotony, both for the individual occupants and for the benefit of urban fabric, SAR's research was developed into different levels of decision-making (tissue, support and infill) in the building process, which respectively refer to the urban fabric, base buildings and fit-outs. In this type of urban predicament, architects proposed redirecting the housing effort towards the large-scale building of generalised infrastructures sensitised to the urban context, the industrialised production of an infill system to acknowledge and accommodate the diverse needs of the occupants, and adding the critical degree of adaptability long-removed from mass housing. The individual dweller was thus considered to be an active participant in housing processes.

The concept of levels is the central idea of Open Building. Three levels of hierarchy are distinguished, these being tissue, support and infill. They are separated, yet coordinate. Higher levels serve as the setting and context in which lower levels operate. As such, higher levels exercise dominance over lower levels, while lower levels are dependent on higher-level structures. Figure 1 indicates the principle of levels developed by the Open Building Research Group, Delft University of Technology.

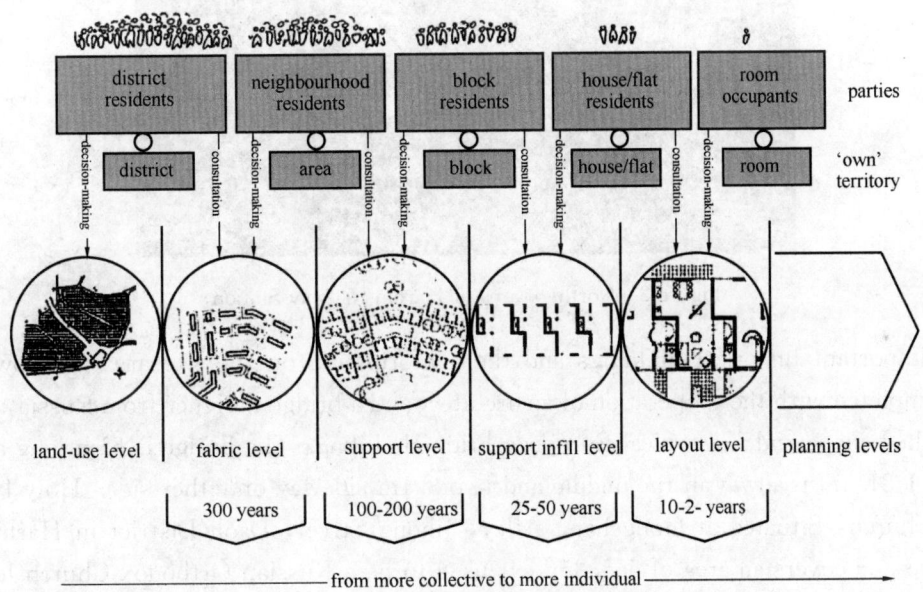

Figure 1　Principle of levels, from OBOM, TU Delft, 1990
(Source: Kendall, 2004, p. 91)

The design professions, for their part, have evolved naturally in correspondence to the behaviour of levels (urban planners, urban designers, architects and interior architects), each operating according to a certain level of intervention.

3　Urban Regeneration of Northern Area of Harbin Railway Station

3.1　Project background

The Harbin railway station located in the center of the city, is both an important hinge of the railway passenger transport and the biggest transport hub of inter-city rail and railway in Heilongjiang province. It's multiple functions consist variety of transport, including railway, highway, bus, taxi, etc, as well as the transport hub of internal and external traffic.

Due to the historical and geographical factor, the railway divides and restricts the traffic channels on both sides of the station, the transit traffic and local traffic here are mixed seriously, which makes a slow development in the Northern area of the station.

The site of the design work is located to the northern area of Harbin Railway Station, which covers an area of 14 hectares (Figure 2). It is surrounded by Haicheng Bridge, Tielu Street (to Jihong Bridge) and Jihong Street. Except for the Railway Station, most of the buildings on the site were multi-storey dwellings built in the early 1990s. They are in high density, with little intervals between each other. The building layout is closed in form and buildings are poor in quality. These make them quite different from buildings in Daoli District, both in function and shape.

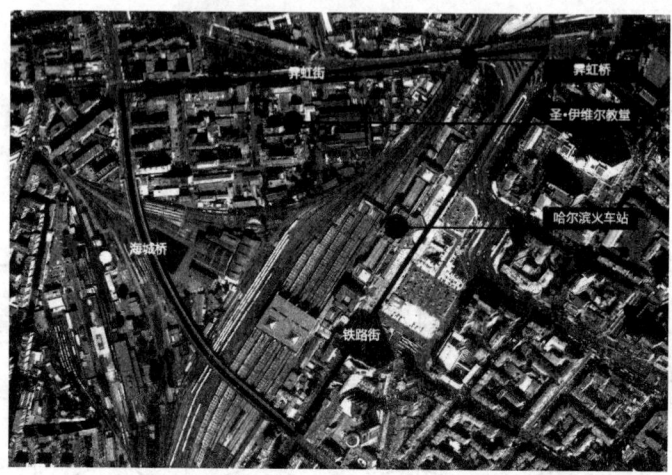

Figure 2　Northern area of Harbin Railway Station

Some important historical buildings and their information on the site are as follows: Jihong Bridge: Completed with the cooperation of an architect and a bridge designer from Russia, the bridge is in an arched shape and is a typical European bridge building. The bridge is 51m long and 27.6m wide, with a 21.4m roadway in the middle and two 3.1m sideway on either side. Holy Iveron Icon Orthodox Church: Situated at Gongchang Alley, Jihong Street, Daoli District in Harbin, it was built in 1908 and covers an area of 555.8m^2. It used to be a Russian Orthodox Church for military use. It is an Eclecticism building and in brick-wood structure. Gongchang Alley: It used to be a part of Jihong Street and was separated from the street in 1931. Jingxiao Alley: It was formed in 1931 and was named after a Japanese puppet police training school situated there.

The aim of the design project is to improve transport environment, to promote the central area of Harbin City and to awaken the historical memories.

3.2　Open design procedure

The Open Building Theory has been brought into consideration for the design and control of urban zoning. As stated by Open Building Theory, the built environment can be seen as having a hierarchical structure in which higher levels serve as the setting and context in which lower levels operate; the hierarchies consist of "Tissue, Support, and Infill", the implications of Open Building thinking into urban regeneration shape the urban zones and territories, as well as traditions and memories.

Therefore, firstly, this design work took the existing road system, infrastructure, and conserved buildings (Figure 3) as the fundamental concept to determine the "Tissue" and left the "plot" (Figure 4) in between the Tissue under control.

Holy Iveron Church   Jingxiao Alley   Railway Factory   Heating Chimneys

Figure 3   Historical elements from the northern area of Harbin Railway Station

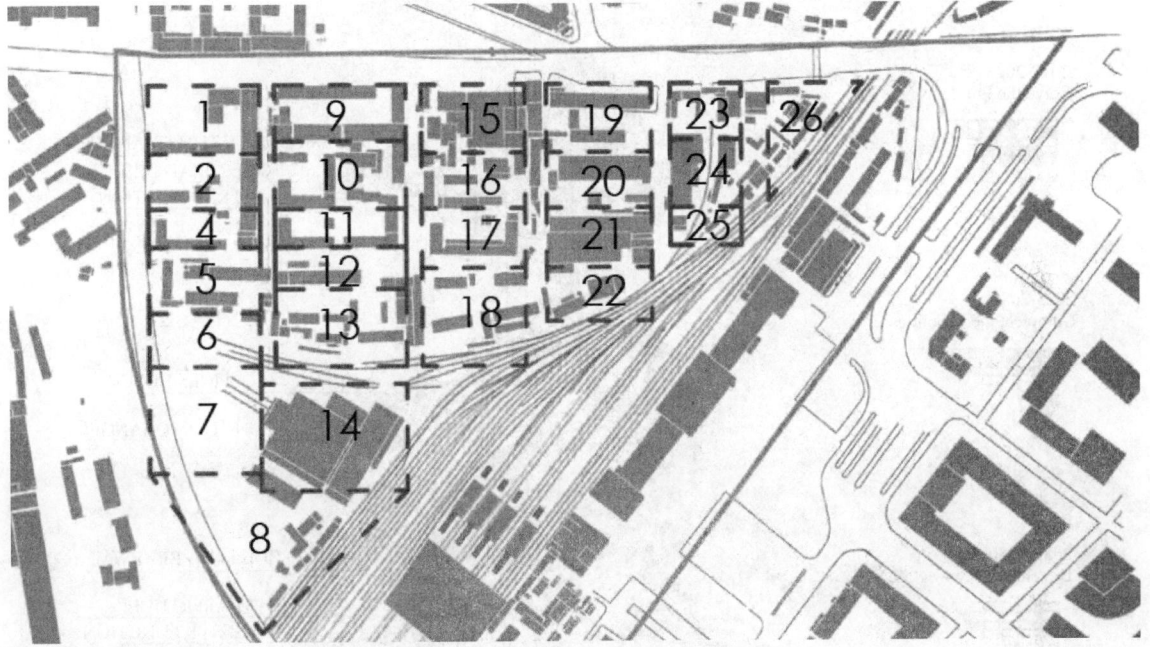

Figure 4   The plots within the urban tissue

Secondly, the "Tissue" horizontally and vertically controls the development and regeneration of each infill zone and at the same time introduces light, movements, and landscape evaluations into the urban site(Figure 5).

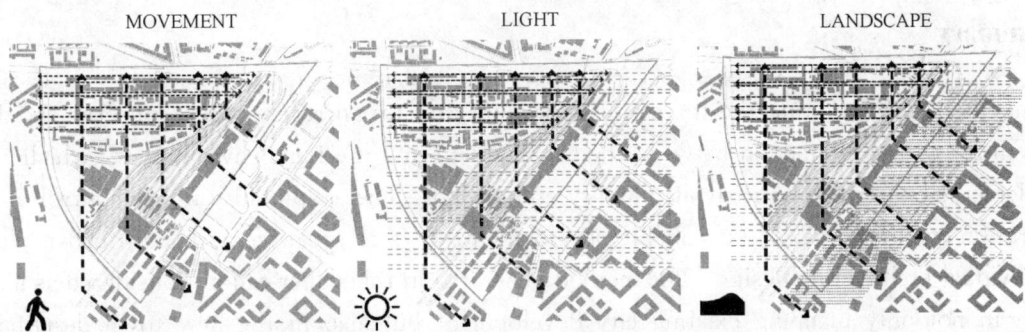

MOVEMENT   LIGHT   LANDSCAPE

Figure 5   Movement, light and landscape within the urban tissue

And thirdly, the concept of adaptability is introduced to add the flexibility of each infill zone and territory for both a short-term time adaptation and possible future development, based on the survey of building conditions and possible plot utilise(Figure 6).

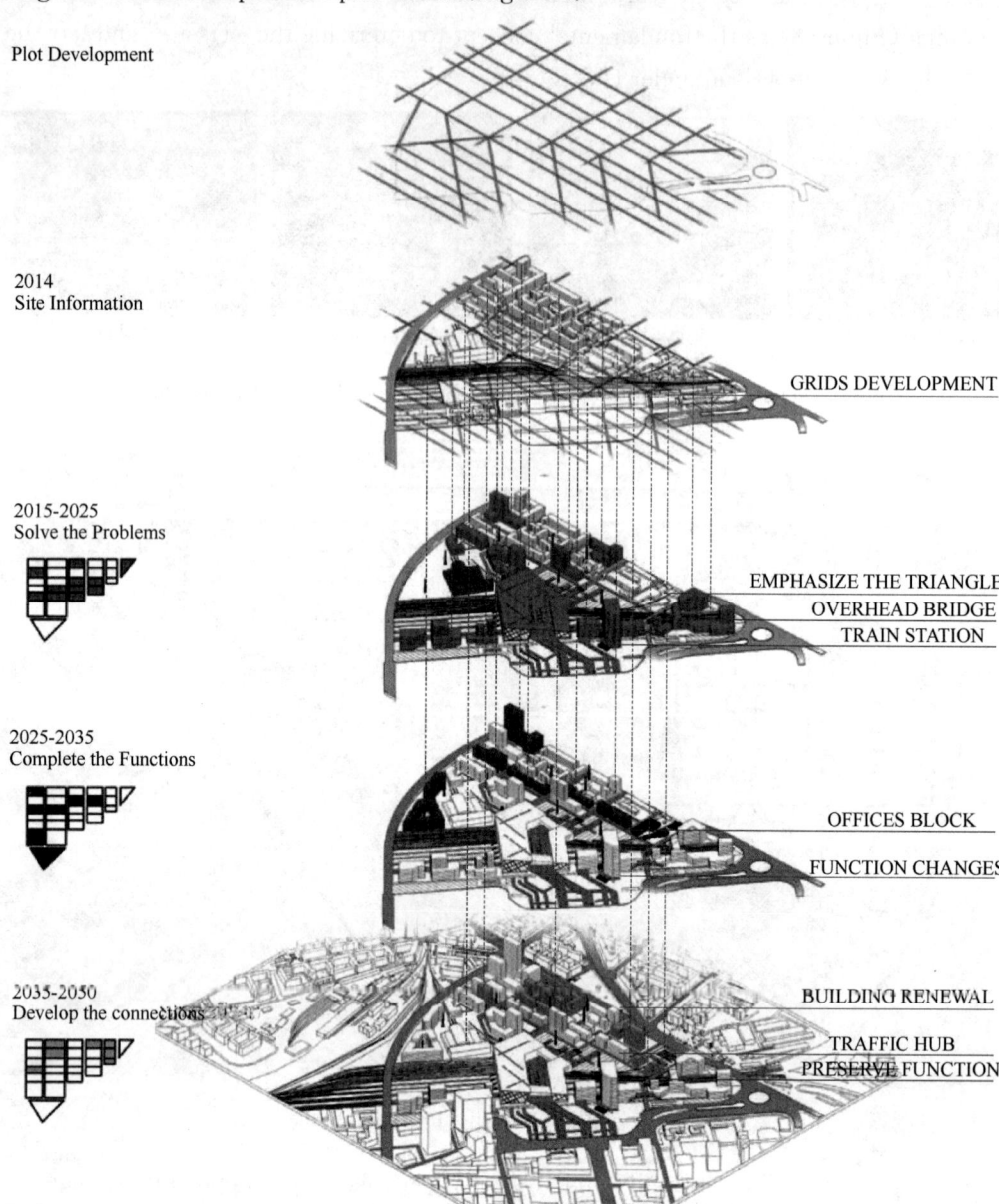

Figure 6　Plot change with time

4　Summary

This method integrating the three-step procedure into urban regeneration concerns the dimension of time and the interaction between the development and the built environment，which are the basic elements constructing urban adaptability and control. The adaptability in the control of urban regeneration ensures a way of sustainable development. It is of great value in both urban planning and individual architecture design. The method generated in this paper can be considered as a design strategy in not only planning existing city development but also in the new town design in the process of the rapid urbanisation in China.

Acknowledgements

This work was supported by the Dalian University of Technology [DUT15RC(3)013]. Also great acknowledgement is made to the design contributors: Michaela Mallia, Huo Ran, Matryn Webb, Zhalagenbaier, Guo Ziyi, and Ulysses Sengupta.

城市再生控制的适应性设计

李国鹏　范　悦

（大连理工大学）

　　摘要： 开放建筑思想认为建成环境是一个层级的系统：在这个层级系统中高层级代表着环境和背景，低层级则根据高层级的控制来发展。这个层级系统是由城市肌理、支撑建筑和内装体系构成；因此在城市再生中应用开放建筑的思想可以有效地塑造城市传统和记忆。这篇文章以中英高校建筑工作坊的一个设计"可持续改变"为例，介绍一种有效的城市再生控制的设计手法。设计中以现有道路系统、基础设施、历史建筑为基础来设计并保留城市肌理关系，使得在肌理体系中的独立地块具有对未来发展的灵活性。在城市肌理体系控制地块发展的同时，阳光、交通与景观体系也被引入到地块中。这种运用开放建筑思想来设计城市更新的方法注重时间的维度以及城市发展和建成环境之间的互动。

　　关键词： 开放建筑，控制，城市更新，设计作品

References：

[1] Bosma, K., D. van Hoogstraten, et al. Housing for the millions: John Habraken and the SAR (1960-2000)[M]. Rotterdam: NAI Publishers, 2000.

[2] Cuperus, Y. An Introduction to Open Building[OL]. [2015-1-23]. http://cic. vtt. fi/lean/singapore/CuperusFinal. pdf.

[3] Dekker, K. Research information: Open Building Systems: a case study[J]. Building Research & Information, 1998, 26(5): 311-318.

[4] Friedman, A. The adaptable house : designing homes for change[M]. New York, London, McGraw-Hill, 2002.

[5] Habraken, N. J., J. T. Boekholt, et al. Variations : the systematic design of supports [M]. Cambridge, Mass. : Laboratory of Architecture and Planning at MIT, 1976.

[6] Habraken, N. J. CONTROL HIERARCHIES IN COMPLEX ARTIFACTS in the Proceedings of the 1987 Conference on Planning and Design in Architecture at the International Congress on Planning and Design Theory [C]. Boston, Massachusetts: The American Society of Mechanical Engineers, 1987.

[7] Habraken, N. J. THE USES OF LEVELS Open House International[J], 2002, 27(2).

[8] OBOM, Delft University of Technology, The Netherlands. Open Building Strategic Studies[OL]. 2013 [2015-1-23]. http://www. obom. org/.

[9] Walker D. The architecture and planning of Milton Keynes[M]. London: Architectural Press, 1981.

从美浓屋建筑更新改造探讨高雄厝设计准则之当地转化

冯慧心　李彦颐　杨博渊

（树德科技大学建筑与室内设计研究所）

摘要： 高雄近年来积极推动"宜居城市"的计划，转化原本重工业城的印象，将传统工业区高污染的刻板印象逐渐以新能源、创意产业和永续科技的都会区取代传统工业城，因此高雄市府规划推动高雄厝执行计划，制定兴建高雄厝设计准则、高雄厝指标及认证机制，针对因地制宜的方式打造地方型高雄厝，提供当地居民参与讨论和计划，对于未来居住有更新的认知与体会。本研究以高雄市农村形态之美浓区旧有烟楼建筑为目标，集结当地美浓居民与建筑设计之专业人士，依循高雄厝十大设计准则，分别针对五大主轴进行高雄厝美浓屋的建筑更新，其中依循：环境对应、TYPOLOGY、材料使用、建筑语汇和原生植物的主轴进行发展与研究讨论，结果归纳出高雄厝当地转化实行之要点：地方自主意识的唤起、文化历史与地域背景定位及具完善、永续、健康之生活机能的经济实践模式。

关键词： 高雄厝，美浓屋，高雄厝设计准则，当地转化，宜居城市

1 研究目的

历经出口贸易海港和传统炼钢、造船和石化工业的岁月，高雄近年来积极推动"宜居城市"的计划，转化原本重工业城的印象，将传统工业区高污染的刻板印象逐渐以新能源、创意产业和永续的科技都会区取代传统工业城。联合国人类住居规划署（UN habitat）指出，至2009年以来世界上大多数的人口皆居住于城市中，以现今社会来说，所居住的城市区域中融合了当地历史、文明、多样性和当地文化。因此高雄市府规划推动高雄厝执行计划，制定兴建高雄厝设计准则、高雄厝指标及认证机制，目前针对因地制宜的方式打造地方型高雄厝，提供当地居民参与讨论和计划，对于未来居住有更新的认知与体会，符合联合国人类住居规划署建议，笃力推行"改变城市的当地者"，让城市变成更适合当地居住者（A city changer）。

目前高雄厝计划主要针对乡村地区之住宅设计为主，宗旨不单只是盖几栋当地形式的房子，同时辅以周边环境对于居住质量影响多寡为主要考虑依据，更须融入高雄厝五大核心价值："生态、经济、宜居、创意、国际"和高雄厝之设计准则，以当地建筑与历史文化、绿色建筑技术和小区营造参与讨论，找到属于当地建筑之认同性、识别性、自明性与未来性，兼具国际观视野。此研究以高雄市农村形态之美浓区旧有烟楼建筑为目标，探讨以目前所制定之高雄厝设计准则结合当地人文景观，成为富含本土化内涵之美浓屋建筑。

2 研究目标

2.1 美浓区之环境现况

美浓位于高雄市，东邻高雄县六龟区、东南邻屏东县高树区、南邻屏东县里港乡、西邻旗山乡、北邻杉林乡，乡镇据民以客家人为最多。面积约为120.0316km²，共计19个村里数。美浓区的平原部分大半为荖浓溪与美浓河之行水区，其地形包含丘陵、坡地与平原面积，受到地形影响属于热带型气候，气温由西南冲积平原向东北山区递减，形成垂直气候带。每年的5～10月属雨季，其余为干季，雨量分布不均。因地处北回归线之南，夏季阳光直射，夏季气温偏高，6～9月平均温度在27℃以上，全年平均22～25℃之间，夏半年雨量十分丰沛为湿季，降雨量全年约在2000～

2500mm 之间。美浓区整体属于以农为主之传统产业区，主要经济农作物为稻米、香蕉、烟草等，传统客家聚落文化依山傍水的特殊景致，因远离城市尘嚣完整保存了优美的生态景观和河洛，休闲农业与特色农产品为美浓区近年来的发展重点（图1）。

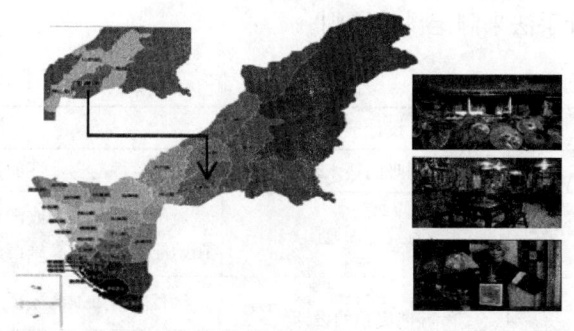

图 1　美浓区行政区域图
（来源：高雄市政府全球信息网）

2.2　美浓屋建筑场地条件

美浓地区于日据时代因烟业产业兴盛，根据美浓志的记载：1976 年，美浓镇种烟人家有1791 户，面积高达 $2235hm^2$，种烟面积占全镇可耕种面积四千余公顷的六成左右，写下美浓种烟史上最高纪录。中国台湾加入世界贸易组织（WTO）后，专卖制度的烟作事业，由高收入的行业面临台湾烟酒公司不再收购的烟叶，而烟楼成为美浓区的闲置空间。因此本研究在美浓区域内寻找适宜的建筑物进行整修时，针对烟叶文化之当地形态的烟楼建筑，进行美浓屋建筑的改造。

图 2　美浓屋建筑改建外观现况

图 3　美浓屋建筑改建背面现况

3　研究方法

3.1　当地工作坊扎根计划

借助美浓区当地工作坊和公民咖啡馆的成立，访谈地方耆老与士绅，汇集当地居民与建筑设计之专业人士，就其当地生活经验和建筑设计背景进行讨论，探讨旧有或既有建筑之当地材料、色彩和当地居民之需求，结合建筑与设计之技术，以环境对应的方式转换成为贴近当地化之美浓屋建筑。

3.2　高雄厝十大设计准则

高雄市全境在北回归线以南，各行政中包含热带型气候和温带型气候，并且对于未来全球高龄化的社会变迁和永续环境的思维，高雄厝十大设计准则之制定（表1），朝向环境永续、反映当地自明性及居住健康之核心理念而行，并由两大方向而制立：

（1）通则设计：以符合高雄厝内涵特性为出发点，从全面性的规划思维，制定指标性设计原则。

（2）地区性设计原则：由大高雄地理特色为区隔，由环境特色与文化脉络来导入，经由操作设计手法来制定设计原则。

高雄厝十大设计准则　　　　　　　　　　　　　　　　　　　　　　　　表1

项　次	设计准则	内　容
1	会呼吸的透水基盘	透过草坪与透水性的设计，让建筑物与土地联结与触动
2	有效的深遮阳	经由挑檐或遮阳或阳台等设计，对应出四个区域不同的方位与特性，能带来凉爽的遮阳，使其凸显出高雄市气候环境的性格
3	绿能屋顶的设计	将目前高雄地区屋顶层的现况，重新整合为具有自然生态风貌的特色，并搭配间接减低直达热负荷，与塑造出开放性的逃生平台
4	当地材料与技术的导入	高雄市的历史与地域特色，最直接的叙事方式，便是经由材料与技术手法，来呈现设计元素上，让用户更贴近建筑物
5	融入场域的意象设计	不同地理场域，可产生不同的对话，而要传递出独有的关系与地域性味道，需由场地内外的调和，来展现出意象的环境自明性
6	埕空间的创造	多元的族群文化建构了高雄市不同的聚落风貌，而河洛、客家、原住民族等所共通的集会场所氛围，更是当地文化中不可或缺的象征，故由天井、露台、阳台等小空间来重新诠释
7	人性化的空间通用设计	经由通用设计的观念，可让每个空间环境的使用性，提升至无论年龄、身心机能等差异，皆能享有舒适自在的使用
8	合宜的使用空间机能	由使用者的空间机能为出发点，寻找合宜的空间使用量，不仅可免除不必要的空间，更可创造更多舒适环境与生活多样和谐与互动性
9	环保健康建材的应用	一般民众在室内空间的时间约占每天的 90% 以上，因此居住空间的健康生活是必要的，故纳入环保健康的观念，来提升优质的环境
10	创造有效通风的开口	经由开口部之设计，使空气自然对流，达成室内自然通风之均匀性，降低室内二氧化碳，并改善室内空气温湿度

4　研究结果

经由美浓工作坊和公民咖啡馆的成立，集结当地美浓居民与建筑设计之专业人士，依循高雄厝十大设计准则，针对五大主轴进行高雄厝美浓屋的建筑更新。

4.1　"环境对应"及"材料使用"

根据当地美浓人与艺术家的画作所描述之客家建筑，留白的蓝天、绵延的山脉、槟榔树、烟楼与三合院所形成的天际线称为美浓之美，由此可知新建的美浓屋建筑势必离不开天、地、人之间的关系，因此美浓屋建筑控制在两层楼之高度，延续背山往水的风水习俗，使更新改造后美浓屋建筑，在视觉高度中依然看得到建筑物、槟榔树和美浓山脉所构成的天际线。高雄厝十大设计准则中"会呼吸的透水基盘"，目的为透过草坪与透水性设计，让建筑物与土地联结与触动。建筑材料之使用，保存红砖、红瓦、木料等当地建筑材料，并作为遮阳与隔热之设计，便于日后材料的取得、维修和保养。

4.2　"TYPOLOGY"

观察美浓区建筑形态上发现，美浓客家建筑以三合院为主，典型的三合院屋型在形态或是形式上皆具有防备性的象征，由建筑立面的观点来看，虽然客家人对于外人而言具有防备性，但对于自家人却非常宽阔，由传统的美浓客家三合院的"廊"与"埕"为主要往来动线和公共空间的意义可窥知一二。因此美浓屋建筑改造后将客家三合院的"廊"与"埕"的概念分布在第一层，另外开放式"埕"的场域，由天井、阳台和露台等空间来重新诠释，传承"埕"在客家文化中的好客，健谈和信任的精神。

4.3 "建筑语汇"及"原生植栽"

美浓区之烟楼并非传统建筑，而是大量标准化之建筑。烟楼具有经济财富的象征含义，借助空间性质之转换，将烟楼重新改造成符合现代化建筑的使用空间中。早期美浓三合院建筑是以黑砖黑瓦为主，但经过1977年塞尔达台风肆虐后，大部分的建筑物受损，使黑砖黑瓦的生产供不应求，因此现今美浓区所看到的红砖红瓦之材料皆为近代之建材。美浓区整体仍以农为主之传统产业，改造后的美浓屋建筑，在腹地旁保留了菜圃之耕地，保留当地居民对于环境的现况和生活习性，主建物旁营造棚架的氛围，以攀爬类蔬果或花卉营造遮阴效果，使农务者可于遮阴的环境下进行加工作业。过去建筑中下舍与偏舍的空间也由棚架或工作空间转化之手法，被运用和保留在美浓建筑中，对于移居的外地人士，此空间正好满足田园农耕之乐趣（图4、图5、图6、图7）。

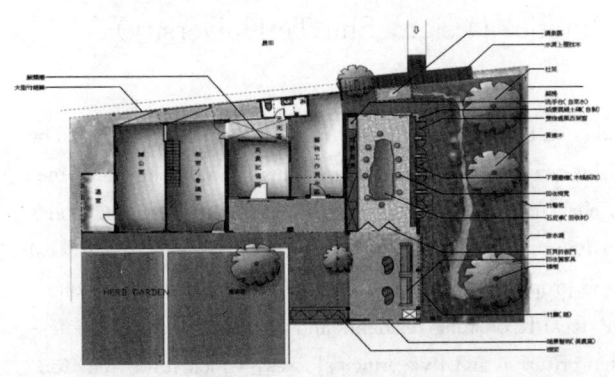

图4 设计愿景平面图

图5 当地材料为主之室内设计实景图

图6 "廊"与"埕"空间转换之实景图

图7 香草花卉植栽于居住空间中之实景图

5 结论与建议

借助地方自我主义的兴起，进而提高对于当地化的认同，延伸至当地文化历史和人文、产业的了解，重新诠释区域在城市中的定位和未来方向，将实质性之地方经济效益整合入规划中，使整个城市区域兴建或改造不单只是建筑物更新，而是为当地之居民提供更多的附加价值，借以吸引更多新的移居住民。由实务面来说，就笔者对于台湾房屋室内设计之专长，更新或改造之美浓屋建筑材料的转换和应用可由文化石、木纹砖或含石英成分的石材，取代传统木结构和地面铺面、立面或柱体结构；改造后美浓屋格局，可将西方住宅中开放式的空间设计融入公共空间的营造，与客家三合院的"廊"与"埕"的概念有异曲同工之妙；建筑语汇中烟楼的意义，以天窗或天井的形式导入居住空间中，将原本烟产业中财富的象征，同时融入新式的建筑里；原生植栽的概念，可由香草花园或是食用蔬菜圃取代，结合餐桌上日渐西化的佳肴中。由以上构思和建议，期望更新改造后的美浓屋建筑，成为更贴近现代人需求之建筑，依旧与天空、月光山形和槟榔树间形成美丽的天际线。

Exploring the Local Transformation of Design Criteria of Kaohsiung Lohas Building from Renovation and Modification of Architecture in Meinong

Feng Hui-Hsin，Li Yen-Yi，Yang Po-Yuan

(Graduate School of Architecture and Interior Design，Shu-Te University)

Abstract：Kaohsiung city has launched preferable city plan to turn over the image of healthy industrial city. The stereotype of highly-polluted industrial area will be replaced by new energy, innovation, industry and sustainable metropolis. Therefore, Kaohsiung City Government promote to enact plan; set the criteria of designing Kaohsiung Lohas Building, the landmark of Kaohsiung Lohas Building and verifying mechanism ; set in appropriate ways to build local Kaohsiung Lohas Building and offer local people to discuss and propose so that they have never recognition and experience . The research aims at studying Tobacco Barns, rallying local Kaohsiung residents and architecture design professsionals to renew Kaohsiung Lohas Building in Meinong by ten criterion and five principal axes, which follow environment correspondence, TYPOLOGY, material application, architecture terminology and protoplasmic plant. These five principal axes have been developed and discussed and have induced local conversion points. These five principal axes have been developed and discussed and have induced local conversion points：The rise of local autonomy, Background positioning of cultural history and area, It can provide complete sustainable and healthy living requirements in economic practice mode.

Keywords：Kaohsiung Lohas building, Meinong house, Ten criteria of Kaohsiung Lohas building designing, Local transformation, Livable city

参考文献：

[1]　台湾高雄市市政府工务局．2014 年高雄厝在地设计者培训工作坊计划[R]．委托技术服务案．2014.

[2]　钟万顺等人．2014 高雄厝在地设计者培训工作坊计划成果专辑[R]．高雄市政府工务局，2014.

[3]　采荷设计 Color-Lotus Design. [2015-3-27]. http：// http：//www. colorlotus-design. com//

[4]　Ecuador will host the United Nations Conference on Housing and Sustainable Urban Development in October 2016. 2014[2015-3-27]. http：//unhabitat. org/the-new-urban-agenda-will-be-decided-in-quito/

[5]　林芳怡（主编）．宁静的地景革命：第二期宜兰厝建筑图集．宜兰县政府，仰山文教基金会策

划[M].台湾：田园城市出版，2003.

[6] 李绿枝(总编辑).起造一个家：宜兰厝·居家质量提升指南(刘镇豪绘图美术编辑)[M].台湾：仰山文教基金会出版，1997.

[7] 吴凯蕙导演.建筑.台湾行[CD].台湾：台视文化出版，2009.

[8] 钟兆生.美浓地区烟楼空间营造之研究[D].台湾：树德科技大学，2006.

[9] 陈建堂，刘起孝.德国工业区域形态发展转型——鲁尔工业区为例[M].经济部工业局/经济部国营会.2002.

城市与建筑：设计、更新及改造
City and Building:
Design，Renew and Reconstruction

专题二：历史街区保护
Special Topic 2：Conservation of Historical Buildings and Streets

"一墙之隔"——长沙白果园地区城市社区空间结构变迁及优化策略研究

许昊皓[1,2]　刘江德[2]　陈翚[2]

（1. 东南大学建筑学院；2. 湖南大学建筑学院）

摘要：长沙作为中国中部地区非常重要的历史文化名城，其街巷空间基本保持了历史原貌，形象地记录着古城的民族和地域关系以及工程技术、环境变迁等信息，是珍贵的历史文化遗产。然而城市的发展是一个不断更新、改造和新陈代谢的过程，特别是在当前城市化进程加速的情况下，种种原因造成了目前历史文化名城社区公共空间以及街巷结构的发展与形成过程中，常常产生"一墙之隔"的空间碎片以及许多消极空间。本文试图以长沙市白果园地区为例，运用空间句法理论针对社区的公共空间进行分析和研究，通过探索型的方案提出激活城市历史区域公共空间的策略和改造的初步设想。

关键词：老城区，空间结构，空间句法，激活策略

1　引言

长沙作为中国中部地区非常重要的历史文化名城，其街巷空间基本保持了历史原貌，形象地记录着古城的民族和地域关系以及工程技术、环境变迁等信息，是珍贵的历史文化遗产。然而城市的发展是一个不断更新、改造和新陈代谢的过程，特别是在当前城市化进程加速的情况下，种种原因造成了目前历史文化名城社区公共空间以及街巷结构的发展与形成过程中，常常产生"一墙之隔"的空间碎片以及许多消极空间。

空间句法是一种关于空间和城市的理论[1]，已经被广泛地应用于城市空间形态与功能分析、城市规划之中[2,3]、历史街区再生研究[4~6]，社区邻里空间[7]，以及历史城区空间结构与演变[8~10]等诸多方面。空间句法的研究具有两个优势，它既能深入浅出的分析区域内公共空间的形态特征，同时作为一个可交互的界面，又可以直观地呈现结构特征和预期结果。本文试图以长沙市白果园地区为例，结合空间句法理论，从城市认知的角度切入，对白果园的城市界面与场所、节点、标志物以及其他空间要素进行历史研究与分析，总结提炼其城市公共空间特性。本文即尝试将这一理论和方法运用于长沙市白果园地区的可持续再生方案设计和评价中，深入思考城市旧区保护与开发的可持续发展问题，结合激活城市历史区域公共空间的策略，提出探索型的改造初步方案。

2　白果园地区现状分析

2.1　历史沿革

白果园地区位于长沙市核心商圈，毗邻黄兴路步行街、化龙池、人民路、解放路等重要商业区域，是长沙市五个重点历史保护区域之一。白果园地区包含育英街、东茅街、登隆街、苏家巷、里仁巷、耕耘圃、白果园巷等主要街道（图1）。区域内重点保护白果园、化龙池、小古道巷、大古道巷、南倒拖靴、一步两搭桥、磨盘湾、《湘江评论》印刷处、程潜公馆、甘露井、予园公馆、八大公沟遗迹、善化县学宫照壁、善化县学宫围墙及拱门等18处历史文化资源（图2）。区域的核心街巷如登隆街、苏家巷、耕耘圃自20世纪初资料记载沿用至今，其空间位置基本未发生很大变动，区域道路分支也是随建筑形式的改变发生变化，街道空间的转变记录着该片区社区结构的变化。而在2007年左右进行的城市道路改造中，为了将人民路拉通，拆除了部分建筑，将此区域分割为南

北两块区域。从轴线的整合度数值分布我们可以很清晰地看到大尺度的城市干道的引入强烈地改变了此区域的整体空间结构（图3）。

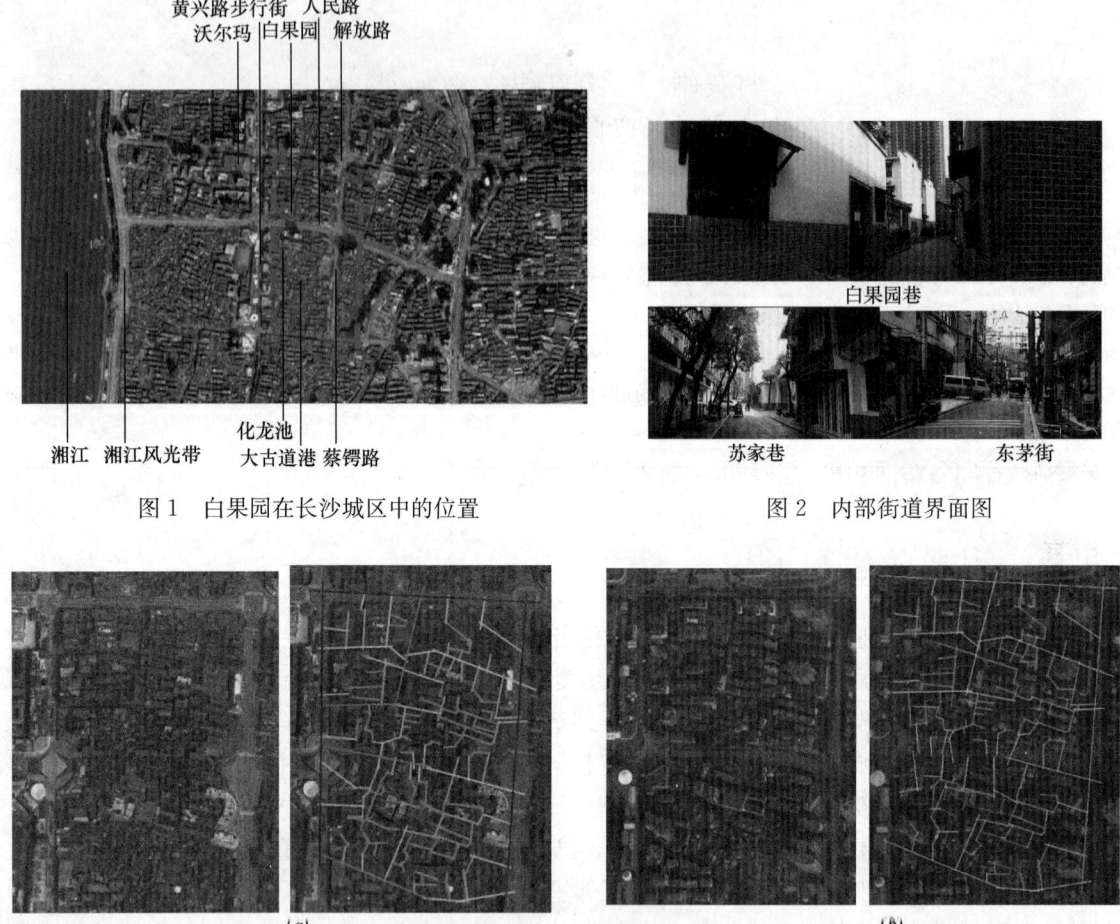

图1　白果园在长沙城区中的位置　　　　　　　图2　内部街道界面图

图3　白果园地区公共空间结构历史变迁图

（a）2000白果园地区空间肌理及整合度轴线；（b）2010年白果园地区空间肌理及整合度轴线

2.2　现状分析

在长沙城市发展过程中，以白果园为代表的老城区在周边区域高速现代化建设的包围下更新缓慢，积重难返而一度成为城市建设的痼疾。其中，以苏家巷为界限，南北两部分在建筑形态、基础设施等方面有很大差别。南部地区保留了近现代建筑的形式与社区的肌理，以2～3层近现代木结构建筑为主，每栋建筑独享前院；北部地区在20世纪80～90年代基本改做了现代砖混结构居民楼，供民主党派居住，多为6～8层，几栋居民楼间共享院落。整体基础设施在消防、卫生、排水及供气等方面存在破损严重、功能配套不全、设施不达标等情况。

2.3　区域公共空间的句法分析

句法分析的轴线图建立在清楚认知研究区域的图底关系（图3）基础上，从空间结构现状图底关系得到布局的肌理图，进而得到轴线分析图，并通过空间句法软件Depthmap计算相关量化数值得到相应的句法特征值，如整合度和选择度，并以色彩来区分不同的数值大小（图3）。

（1）片区形态和空能布局基本合理

从全局整合度状况我们可以看出，该区域四周的城市主要干道与步行街数值分布较高，该区域内的核心街道登隆街与苏家巷也有较高的数值,而内部的其他小巷则呈现比较均匀的内向的态势,这种数值上的反应符合社区建筑功能分区的现状,四周与区域核心街道商业空间集中,其他区域多为居住区域。白果园区域北部经过城市改造已经形成了一些商业性的街道(图4)。在片区中部的街道东茂街的选择度非常高,这也与我们区域内建筑功能分析中得到的这条街附近的商业比较繁华的特点非常吻合。

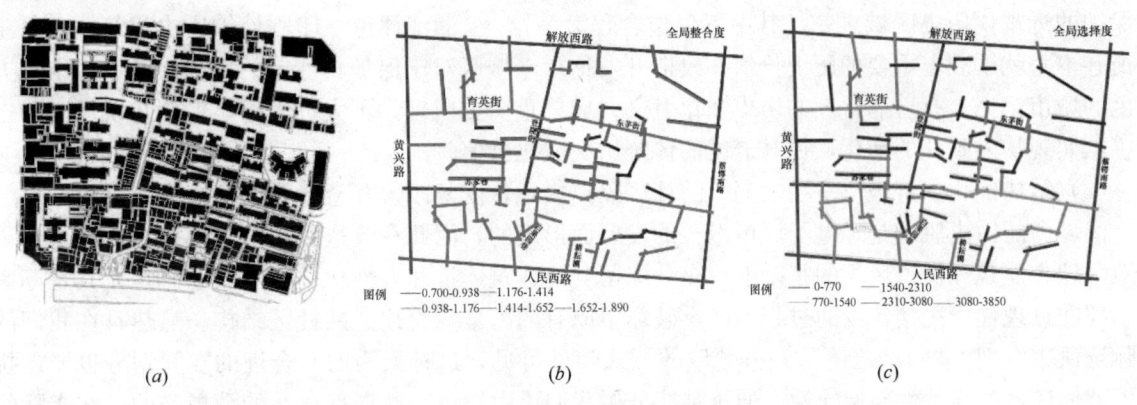

(a)   *(b)*   *(c)*

图 4   白果园区域公共空间的句法分析
(a) 白果园区域建筑图底关系;*(b)* 白果园区域轴线整合度图;*(c)* 轴线选择度图

(2)便捷性差,路网连接不合理,且公共意识薄弱。

白果园南部地区的区域内小巷的选择度明显低于主要的干道,这说明白果园地区内部的道路比较曲折,可达性与便捷性不高。造成这个问题的主要原因在于该区域特殊的尽端式的空间结构,这种空间结构在长沙很多历史街区中均能发现,是近现代长沙大户人家家族内向型关系的产物。调研发现,导致便捷性差的原因,除了路网连接和道路宽度不合理外,人们的社会活动和公共行为也是重要的影响因素。由于没有严格的建筑规范,白果园地区的房屋建设普遍存在私搭乱建现象,而且由于各建筑的年代不同,产权所述层数与类型不同,也导致各街巷道路更加曲折、沿边参差不齐,呈现许多封闭的无法打开的空间和界面(图6)。

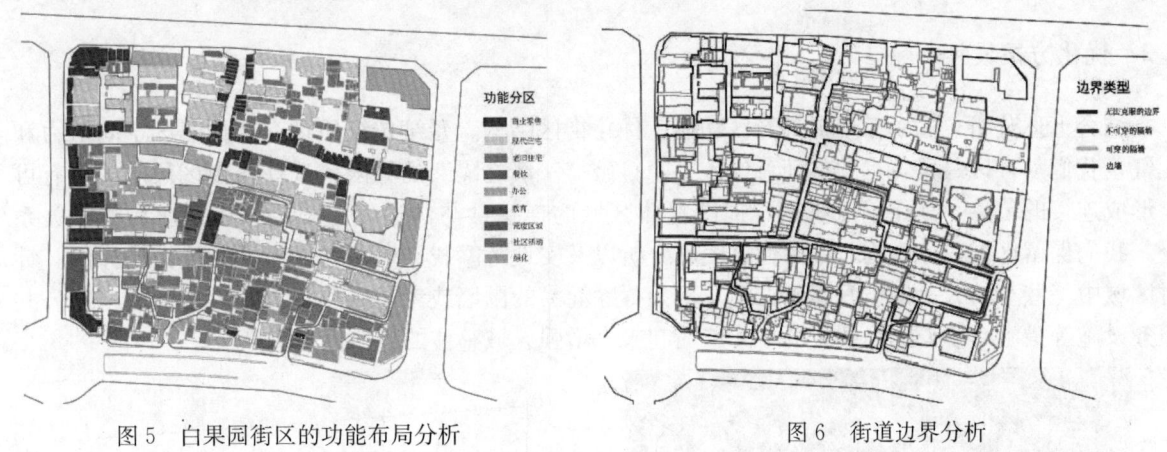

图 5   白果园街区的功能布局分析   图 6   街道边界分析

3   白果园地区的空间激活与优化

3.1   改造策略

在对白果园地区公共空间和功能结构存在问题和实地调研情况进行分析的基础上,在对老区路网结构进行调整的同时,充分利用登隆街、苏家巷、程潜公馆等自身物质空间资源,本文将白果园地区空间激活策略集中在功能提升、环境改善和社区营造三个方面。

（1）功能提升，挖掘老区的传统历史文化功能和产业服务功能。

在白果园地区苏家巷以南的区域，已经在进行对于历史建筑的保护及修复，而北部区域已经基本被改作现代商品式居民楼，其中登隆街上最具长沙特色的老剧院也在几年前被拆除，如今此区域已处在艰难的转型期，街区在保留历史特色基础上的功能转型已迫在眉睫。白果园地区是长沙市重点保护的近现代历史区域之一，其中不仅包含程潜公馆、《湘江评论》印刷处等历史建筑，几条主要街巷本身承载着重要的历史价值。改造开发这片老城区对于保护长沙市的历史文脉、传承地方特色的城市记忆，有着非常大的历史文化意义。应尊重历史肌理，不大拆大建，保留传统尺度和空间感，实现从内到外的活化，提升老区的传统历史文化价值。

（2）结构优化，打破"一墙之隔"的社区隔离模式，恢复改善登隆街周边结构。

区域内的历史肌理是经过了城市漫长的发展而形成的，因此在改造规划中应在分析历史上白果园地区地方建筑和街道风貌的基础上，充分保留当前建筑体量和人性化的空间尺度感，尤其是苏家巷北部在近现代居民楼建设的过程中严重破坏了原有的内聚与交往式的社区结构。热热且在我们的实际调研中发现，"一墙之隔"划分领域的方式随处可见，这种人为的不合理的空间划分也严重扰乱了整体区域的通达性与便捷性。通过轴线分析我们可以发现一些局部存在的消极空间，在实际的操作中，可考虑加强现有院落之间的沟通，打开这些空间界面，增加空间之间的联系，激活被人为划分出的消极空间。例如在现已建成的城市住宅间加入小型的社区活动中心建筑或景观小品，以活跃住宅区的气氛，在与主要街巷的连接处，适当恢复如老剧院等公共连接性较强的建筑。

（3）社区营造，增加节点空间，提升整体空间活力和人气。

老旧社的改造成功与否与社区的组织和公众的参与密不可分。丰泉古井社区构成了苏家巷以北现代居民社区的主要部分，这一社区内的居民以城市职工为主，在改造的过程中要重视弱势群体，关注维护原有的空间活力和人气，不能以拆代建，以另一居民阶层替代原有居民的阶层。因此，在白果园地区的激活和改造的过程中，一方面要充分考虑到原有居民的生活需求，另一方面也需要加强社区建设，鼓励社区主体充分表达自身利益诉求，形成一套以社区为核心的公众参与体系。居民、政府和规划师多方利益充分沟通，统一认识，公平协商，以找到各方都认可的平衡点。

3.2 优化方案设计

结合上述分析，为了实现提升老区功能、优化街区结构、延续传统肌理、增加老区空间活力和人气，我们从社区最具特点的空间意像入手，打破"一墙之隔"的界限，选择在街区尺度内最有可能形成连接的节点，期望以点带面，提高整体区域的连接性与沟通性（图7、图8）。在整体关系上，我们保留区域总体结构，试图通过图底分析以及实地考察找到一些可以打通和连接的界面。针对区域中一些小的人为的空间阻隔方式，例如拆除简易的围墙或者是围栏等，或者是增加一些公共服务设施等措施，使原本尽端式的空间连通起来，增强区域整体的连通性（图8）。

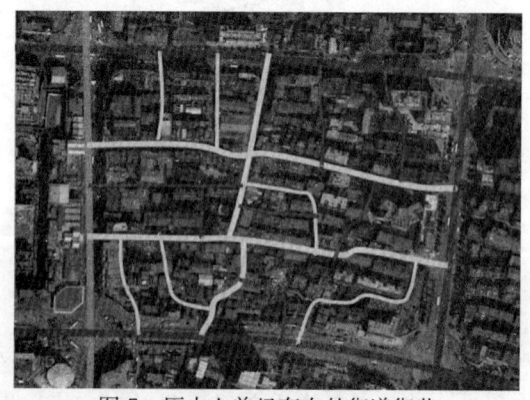

图7 历史上曾经存在的街道街巷

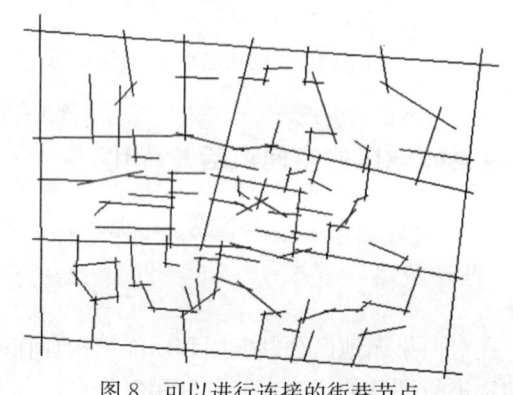

图8 可以进行连接的街巷节点

社区空间活力和人气也同样可以通过空间句法对轴线深度值的调整加以实现，同时，通过对路网的调整反映在整合度值上的变化，也能实现对人们在社区内部街道空间交往强度的空间分布引导（图9）。我们选择场地南部局部来进行局部性的整改（图10），一方面考虑到消防需求，必须在里仁巷内拆除一些建筑，开辟供消防车通行的机动车道（当前老区内没有任何的消防设施）。同时在基地内打通部分道路，拆除一些阻隔性的围墙，减少末端路，增强场地内的房屋可达性，反映在句法分析轴线图上是深度值降低，说明内部交往空间可达的便捷程度增加，反应在整体上就是可理解度（智能度）上升（图11）。

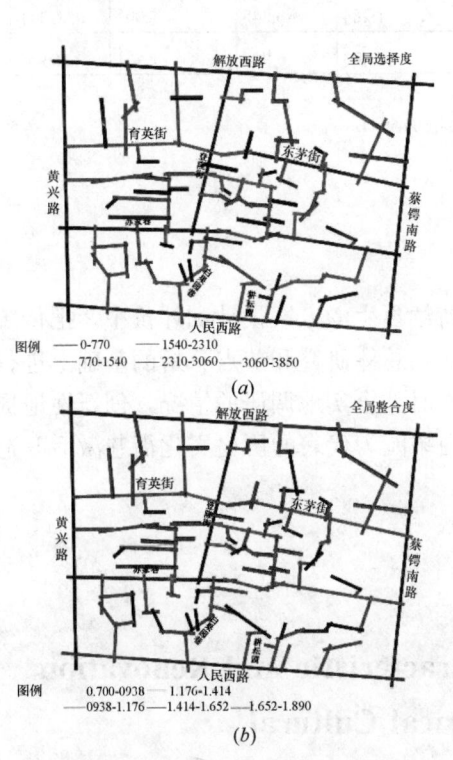

图9 改造方案的轴线分析图
(a) 选择度分析；(b) 整合度分析

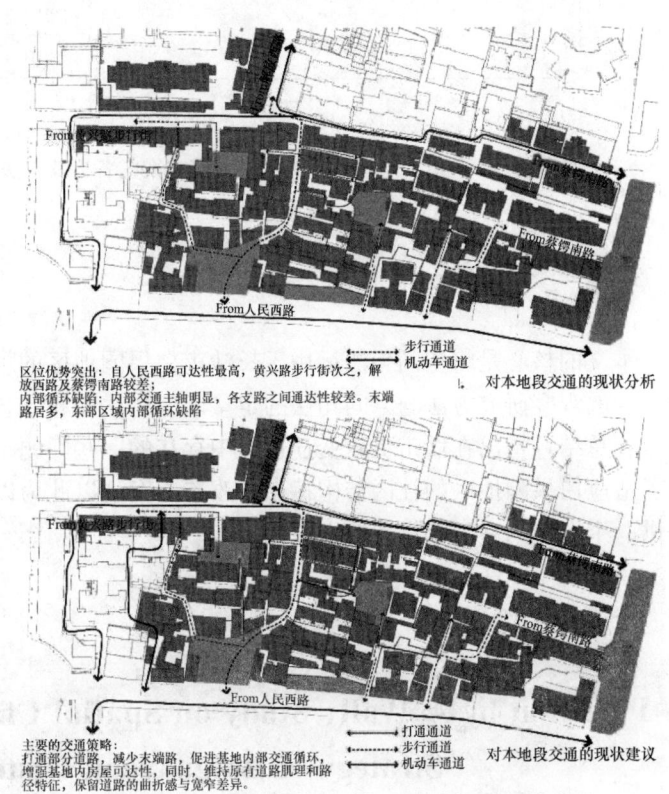

图10 局部区域的节点整改建议方案

3.3 保护与更新策略的句法评价

对比白果园区域内部路网调整的句法参量分析结果发现，在对社区中几个节点进行适当的改造后，社区的整体结构关系得到了保留，社区整体的整合度基本维持不变（表现为主要轴线的数值几乎没有变化）（图12），但是同时与现状对比后发现，社区的结构整体性也得到了较大提升，如可理解度从0.271提升到了0.286。部分街道的选择度得到明显提升，如育英街的选择度从6.791上升到了6.856，选择度的提高对改善社区目前形态和功能

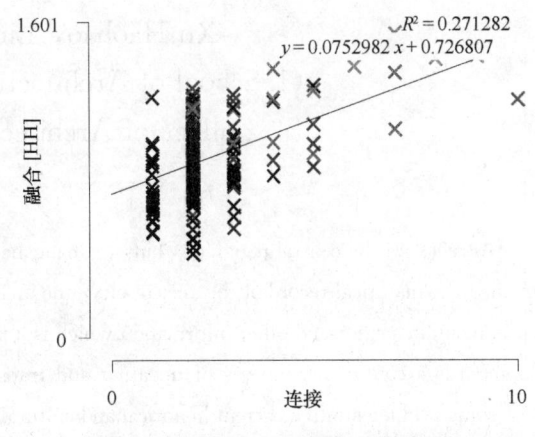

图11 改造前后的可理解度散点图

问题都是有利的。因为选择度代表了这一空间在整体系统中可被经过的概率，节点的打通，同时在每个分片区内部形成通路后，人们的出行更为便捷，既分担了主干道路的人流量，又可以促进该片区的商业过渡发展。

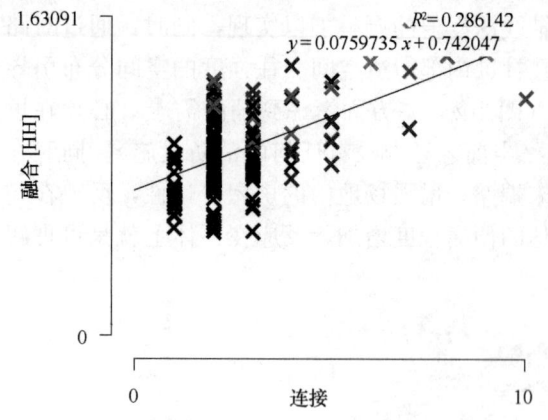

	现状		方案	
	全局整合度	选择度	全局整合度	选择度
育英街	1.506	6.791	1.505	6.856
东茅街	1.366	7.512	1.406	7.639
登隆街	1.862	7.954	1.877	8.169
苏家巷	1.888	8.256	1.869	8.221
白果园巷	1.265	6.669	1.259	6.724
耕耘圃	1.284	6.045	1.005	6.111
里仁巷	1.423	6.808	1.451	6.956

图 12　现状与方案的各街巷句法变量值对比

4　结语

本文的核心是将空间句法运用于长沙市白果园地区的可持续再生的方案设计和评价中，把传统的定性的观察研究方法与空间句法的定量研究方法互相结合，在总体研究和节点分析的基础上进行思考和总结，指出在城市更新变迁过程中存在的一些问题。同时结合实地调研的情况，创新性地提出了适应白果园地区的社区结构特点的改造方案，以此为以白果园为代表的历史文化街巷激活改造提供一个有益的参考和发展的方向。

Partition by A Wall, Study on Spatial Characteristic and Renovation Strategy of Baiguoyuan Historical Cultural District in Changsha

Xu Haohao，Liu Jiangde，Chen Hui

(1. School of Architecture，Southeast University；

2. College of Architecture，Hunan University)

Abstract：In the central region of China , Changsha is a very important historical and cultural city, its street space remained the historical record of the ancient city, the image of national and regional relations as well as the engineering, environmental changes and other information which is a precious historical and cultural heritage. However, the city development is a continuous process of updating and transformation, especially in the current situation. Some reasons cause some problems in the current historical and cultural city community public space and the development of the structure and forming process, where often have a "wall" space debris and many negative space. This paper attempts to take the BAIGUO area Changsha City as an example, using the space syntax theory to analyze and Research on community public space, discuss the impact of changes in the public space in the city development of land use and the activities of the people.

Keywords：Old city zone, Space structure, Space syntax, Activation strategy

参考文献:

[1] 段进,(英)比尔·希列尔.空间句法与城市规划[M].江苏:东南大学出版社,2007.

[2] 杨滔.数字城市与空间句法:一种数字化规划设计途径[J].规划师,2012,4:24-29.

[3] 伍敏,杨一帆,肖礼军.空间句法在大尺度城市设计中的运用[J].城市规划学刊,2014,2:94-104.

[4] 吕斌.转型期中国城市空间可持续再生的课题与途径[J].资源产业,2005,6:62-63.

[5] 陈圆圆,吕斌.基于空间句法的旧城区可持续再生空间设计方案评价[J].规划师,2014,02:79-84.

[6] 王西西.城市纹理断裂区的缝合[D].天津:天津大学,2012.

[7] 黄健文.旧城改造中公共空间的整合与营造[D].广东:华南理工大学,2011.

[8] 全水.基于空间句法的喀什历史文化街区空间特征研究[D].哈尔滨:哈尔滨工业大学,2012.

[9] 段兴平.基于空间句法的昆明老城区空间演变研究[D].云南:昆明理工大学,2011.

[10] 王涛.基于空间句法的青岛老城区空间结构研究[J].浙江建筑,2011,06:13-16.

上海中心城区既有围合式住宅调研及启示

卢 斌

（同济大学建筑与城市规划学院）

摘要： 通过对上海中心城区既有的共计 138 例围合式住宅的实地调研和相关文献资料的收集和查阅，作者对所有案例进行了系统性的研判和分析，从中挑选出三个典型案例并从历史发展、城市设计和建筑设计等三个维度进行了详细阐述，然后指出当下上海围合式住宅所面临的五大挑战，最后提出设计上的五点启示。

关键词： 围合式，住宅，上海，类型学

1 引言：围合式住宅作为一种有益的补充类型

改革开放三十多年以来，中国城镇住宅的建设发展突飞猛进，尤其是在以上海为代表的特大城市里，地价、房价和总建设量犹如三驾马车齐头并进、不断提升。然而，就是在这样如火如荼的发展背景之下，住宅的规划和建筑设计方法却日渐趋同，总的来说可以用"高层、行列式、低覆盖率、高绿化率"这样几个关键词来概括当下上海城市住宅的主要特点。由此，本文作者通过长期的博士论文课题研究，提出以围合式住宅作为高层行列式的对比类型，探索它的潜在优势，发现它的可能缺陷，并使之能够具备更好的适应性，成为未来上海城市住宅的一种有益的补充类型。

本篇会议论文是作者对上海中心城区（即以外环线为界定的约 860.2km² 的建成区）既有的共计 138 例（相关信息更新到 2014 年 12 月 31 日）各类围合式住宅的调研报告，旨在以类型学的方法对调研案例进行分析、归纳并总结，再指出它们所面临的主要挑战，最后提出相关启示。

1.1 上海中心城区既有围合式住宅统计数据概况（图 1）

首先从空间分布上来分，大多数围合式住宅案例位于上海的浦西一侧，共计 132 例（占比 97％）而仅有 6 例（占比 3％）位于浦东一侧，这与上海的城市住宅发展的脉络相吻合。再细分来看，88 例（占比 63.8％）位于上海市核心城区（即内环内）以内，而余下的 50 例比较均匀地分布在了内、中环间和中、外环间，这也与城市发展由中心向外延伸的趋势相一致。其次，从住宅高度来分析，共有 106 例的层数为 4F～6F，即所谓"多层"的概念，而 23 例为小高层（7F～11F），仅有 6 例中高层（12F～18F）和 3 例大高层（18F 以上）。最后，从住宅类型细分，87 例（占比 63％）是 1949 年新中国成立后至 20 世纪末（也就是商品房出现之前）所大量建造的"工人新村"或者说"老公房"，12 例 1949 年新中国成立前的老上海公寓，还有 7 个国际社区案例，而自 20 世纪末商品房开始迅速发展以来，却仅有 32 个围合式商品房，从此数据不难看出围合式类型在上海所遇到的尴尬境地！

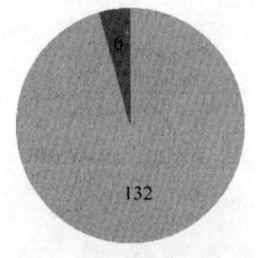
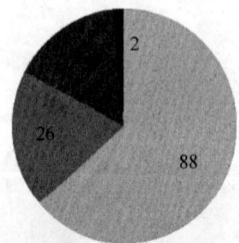
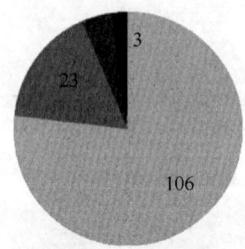
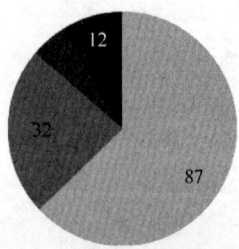

■ 浦西 ■ 浦东　　■ 内环内 ■ 内中环间　■ 多层(4-6F) ■ 小高层(7F~11F)　■ 老公房 ■ 商品房
■ 中外环间 ■ 外环外　■ 中高层(12F~18F) ■ 大高层(18F以上)　■ 国际社区 ■ 老上海公寓

图 1 上海中心城区既有围合式住宅统计数据概况

1.2 上海中心城区既有围合式住宅空间分布图（图2）

下图是上海中心城区地图、几条主要交通干道示意以及138例围合式住宅案例的空间分布情况。

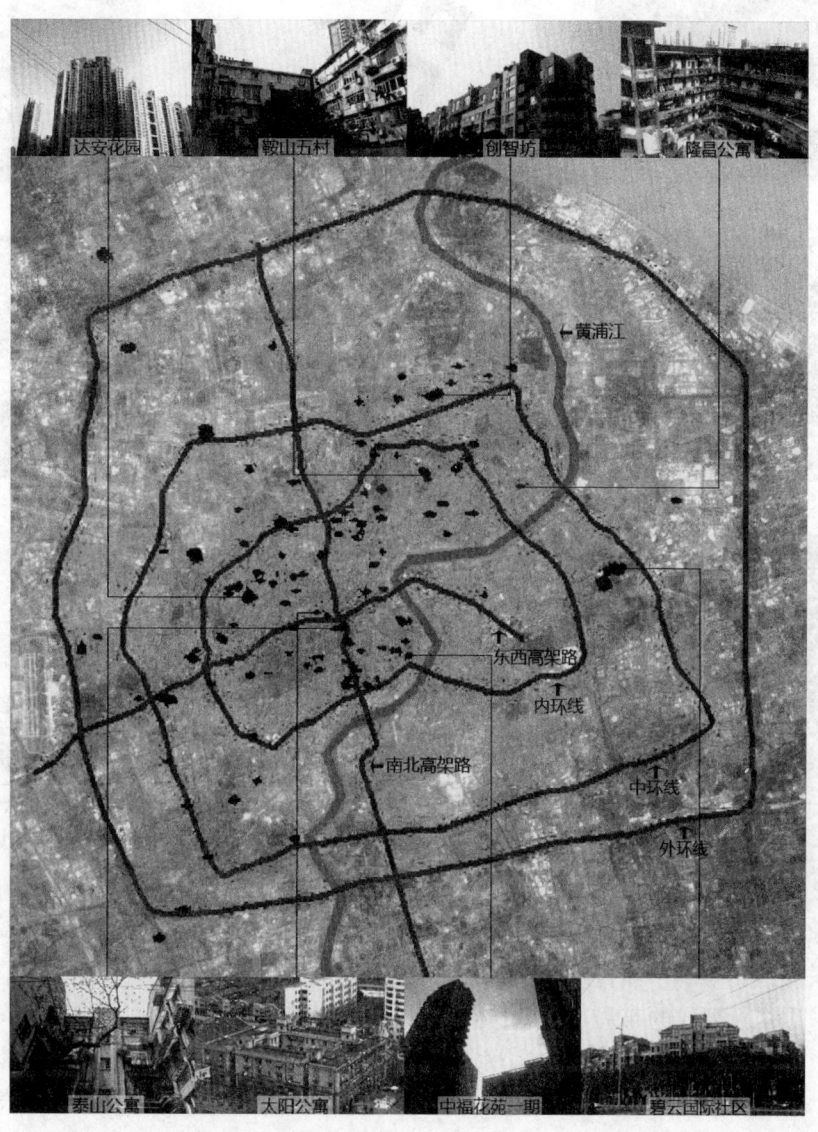

图2 上海中心城区既有围合式住宅空间分布图

2 上海中心城区既有围合式住宅调研分析

调研分析采用类型学的方法，从138个案例中挑选出来具有代表性的三个案例，它们分别是泰山公寓、控江四村和梧桐花园，然后在历史发展、城市设计和建筑设计三个维度上对它们进行分类阐述和比较研究，并分析各自特点和优势（表1）。

2.1 历史发展

首先，围合式住宅在今天的上海虽然属于较少数甚至是极少数案例，但其实这种类型早在20世纪的20～30年代就已经开始出现在老上海的街头。当时，以武康公寓、浦西公寓、培文公寓等为

三个代表性案例资料汇总　　　　　　　　　　　　　　　　　　　　　　表1

	历史发展	城市设计	建筑设计
泰山新村 （1930 年）			
控江四村 （1987 年）			
梧桐花园 （1997 年）			

代表的一批老上海公寓均采用了围合式的布局。其中，建成于 1930 年的泰山公寓就是一个很具代表性的案例，该公寓坐落在淮海中路 622 号，当年由建业地产公司投资，建成后的初期供出租使用。等到了 1949 年新中国成立之后至 20 世纪 90 年代的 40 多年里，以曹杨新村、鞍山新村等为代表的一批受苏联模式影响的"新村式"住宅小区陆续地登上了历史舞台，可以说它们中的绝大多数都步调一致地采用了行列式的布局，以求达到当时社会环境所优先考虑的效率性和均好性。但在这些海量的新村中，我们还能找到极少的采用围合式布局的个别案例，诸如建成于 1987 年的控江四村。从 20 世纪 90 年代至今的 20 多年里，上海的城市住宅得到了史无前例的高速发展，在如潮水般的商品房建设过程中，多、高层行列式住宅继续强化和巩固它的主导地位，成为政府、开发商和购房者三方面都喜闻乐见的商品房类型，即便如此我们也还是能够见到一批以安亭新城、创智坊、达安花园和梧桐花园等为代表的围合式商品房，它们正在给这个日渐单调的城市空间带来一丝变奏。

　　小结：通过粗略观察已过去的上海百年住宅发展历史，围合式住宅在这里始终没有能够得到人们的青睐，没有能够成规模地发展和建设。但是，事实上它却也不曾断代过，它始终在每个发展阶段都非常低调地扮演着陪衬者的角色，成为藏匿于这个城市空间里或隐或现的一分子。

2.2　城市设计

　　其次，从城市设计的维度来观察，被挑选出来的三个典型案例虽各自处于迥然不同的社会发展阶段，但它们却都各自带有鲜明的个性特征，而纵览 138 例上海中心城区既有围合式住宅，几乎所有案例都或多或少地从属于这三个城市设计方法。（1）泰山公寓是由沿着淮海路被分成三排两列布置的 6 幢三合院住宅所组成的，每个三合院的平面均为直角 C 形，开口朝南，均为四层高，并且幢与幢之间严格对齐，故形成很强的整体性，与周边较为随意的城市空间形成鲜明的对比。（2）控江四村的城市设计更加注重顺应周边的既有环境和限制，在不很规则的用地范围内，因地制宜地设计了尺度适宜、富于变化的层层围合院落，这种方法与泰山公寓更加强调自身的设计思路大相径庭。（3）梧桐花园的用地位于上海寸土寸金的徐汇区（原法租界）内，这里的城市道路具有非网格化和自由生长的特点，故而梧桐花园与前两者又各有所不同，它采用了较为自由、随意的平面形态以及高低错落的层数控制，其所形成的城市形态更加富于变化，不拘泥于规则。经过统计调查发现，位于黄浦（包含卢湾）、静安和徐汇等行政区内的围合式住宅案例比较多地都沿用了梧桐花园的城市设计方法。

小结：围合式住宅所采用的城市设计方法中，大致可以归纳为以泰山公寓为代表的"强调几何和突显自我"的第一种，以控江四村为代表的"因地制宜和尊重现状"的第二种和以梧桐花园为代表的"顺势而为和自由生长"的第三种。通过对上海中心城区内所有的 138 个案例进行观察发现，几乎每一个案例都能找到它所对应的一种城市设计方法。

2.3 建筑设计

第三，从建筑设计的维度来细究。这三个案例在尺度上有着非常明显的差别，泰山公寓每幢三合院的平面尺寸大约是 20m×20m，每层一梯两户，一共 4 层 8 户，其所围合出的庭院尺寸为 10m 见方，庭院剖面的高宽比大约为 1∶1，庭院尺度亲切宜人。相比之下，控江四村的尺度大了不少，它的庭院尺寸大约在 40～50m，住宅共计 6 层，庭院剖面的高宽比大约为 1∶2～1∶3，与泰山公寓形成截然不同的两种空间感受。如果说泰山公寓与控江四村代表了小型和中型两种围合式住宅的话，那么梧桐花园毫无疑问代表了大型围合式住宅，它的最高处为 18 层（不计 1 层沿街商业），所围合出来的内庭院尺寸为 50m 见方，庭院剖面的高宽比和泰山公寓一样，约为 1∶1，但是就人类的自身尺度而言，相同的高宽比所带来的空间感受是完全不同的。

小结：经过充分的调研和统计，在既有的 138 个围合式住宅案例中，共计有 106 例是 4～6 层高的多层式围合，而其中工人新村和老公房占多数，它们所围合出来的庭院使用效率普遍较低，有些甚至被用来做设备机房或是停车用房。另有 23 例 9～11 层高的小高层式围合，6 例 12～18 层高的中高层式围合，3 例 18 层高以上的大高层式围合。除第一类多层式围合之外，后三类高层式围合住宅中基本都是商品房发展过程的少数案例，其中含有 7 例国际社区（古北和碧云），这可能和外国人与本地人不同的居住习惯有关。总之，四种高度的围合带来的则是小、中、大和超大四种尺度的内部庭院，经过统计，庭院尺寸大约为 10～50m 不等，庭院剖面的高宽比大约在 1∶1～1∶3 区间内变化。

3 上海中心城区既有围合式住宅调研小结

作者通过实地探访和问卷调查等调研工作方式，在所有 138 个案例中发现和总结了关于上海围合式住宅的固有矛盾及其所面临的五大挑战，然后结合作者相关课题的长期研究提出了关于如何改善上海围合式住宅设计的五点启示，作为本篇论文的小结。

3.1 上海围合式住宅面临的五大挑战

上海围合式住宅在当下城市发展建设过程中之所以境遇尴尬，通常与其所面临的五大挑战息息相关。（1）由围合式布局的固有特性所致的住宅朝向上的挑战，显而易见，南北朝向与东西朝向在围合式布局中是必然并存的。但在位于中国第 3 气候区（即冬冷夏热区）的上海，当地人民却已经长期习惯于"坐北朝南"的居住模式；（2）由围合所带来的侧向日照遮挡上的挑战，除去行列式住宅需要解决的前后遮挡问题，围合式住宅还不得不考虑来自两个侧面的日照遮挡，这对于在严寒冬日里阳光本来就稀缺的上海来说无疑又是雪上加霜；（3）也是由围合所带来的通风遮挡上的挑战，尤其是对于面向庭院内的住宅而言，将会由于四面被堵而导致风流不畅；（4）来自视线与噪声干扰上的挑战，这种固有矛盾在围合式住宅的转角处表现得尤为明显，有时候噪声干扰也可以来自于底层的沿街商业；（5）由于围合式住宅的空间层次界定比较模糊而带来的居住安全上的挑战，公共空间和私密空间之间的混乱现状使得现在的许多围合式住宅存在诸多方面的安全隐患。

3.2　上海围合式住宅设计的五点启示

　　针对以上这些矛盾和挑战，结合作者的长期研究，可以提出关于上海围合式住宅设计的五点启示：（1）"转一转"，就是将围合式总平面转向，从正南正北的朝向转为南偏东和南偏西朝向，以此来平衡围合式住宅的每一边朝向，以期能够获得朝向均好性的目的，事实上根据《住宅设计标准》DGJ08-20-2013/J10090-2014（原：DGJ08-20-2007/J10090-2007）4.1.4 条款的规定，住宅的朝向限定已从原来的"应"字变为现在的"宜"字，据此可以推断上海城市规划管理部门已经开始有意识地放宽对于住宅建筑朝向的控制；（2）"断一断"，就是将原本 100％围合度的组团在局部位置断开，这样的开口既有利于减少部分的侧面日照遮挡，又能够为自然通风留出进出口，从而将有效地改善面向庭院内的住宅的自然气候条件，而且具体的开口位置可以结合上海地区夏季盛行南风（包含东南风和西南风）和冬季盛行北风及西北风的实际情况来考虑；（3）"拔一拔"，就是将组团的局部区域拔高，即增加住宅层数，从而既可补偿部分由于"断一断"所带来的容积率上的损失，又能以高低结合的活泼体量来打破一溜齐平的天际线；（4）"混一混"，这里指的是两种层面上的混合，第一种是"底商上住"式的混合，这样的混合模式已经在既有的案例中找到许多应用和实践，并收获了相当不错的实际效果，商业和住宅可谓各取所需。而第二种混合指的是在不同住宅类型上进行的混合，具体来说，设计时可以在日照和通风等条件较差的位置考虑布置临时性的周转用住宅，比如青年公寓或公共租赁房等，而将具备更好自然采光通风位置留给商品住宅以彰显社会公正性；（5）"错一错"，指的是详细的住宅建筑平面上的改善和优化设计，比如可以在不利朝向位置上将窗户的朝向错位来获得尽可能好的朝向，也可以通过平面挖槽的方式，人造出有利的朝向来（图 3）。

　　总而言之，只要上海城市住宅建设各方力量愿意承担更多的社会责任、投入更多的人文关怀、付出更多的辛勤劳作，围合式住宅作为一种有益的补充类型必将能在上海这片热土之上大有作为！

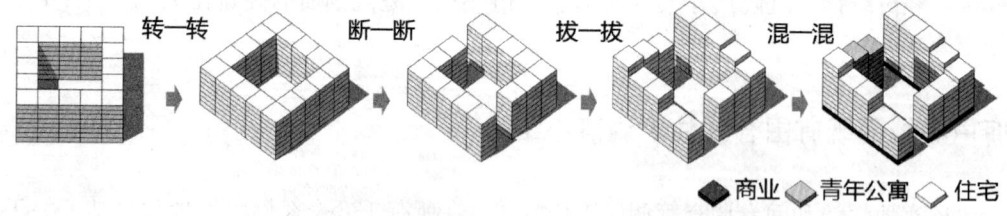

图 3　上海围合式住宅设计的五点启示

致谢

　　本篇论文的写作受到国家自然科学基金项目《当代中国住宅建筑的类型学特征研究》的资助（编号：51278337），在此谨向基金及基金项目负责人同济大学李振宇教授表示由衷的感谢和敬意！

Research and Revelation on the Existing Enclosed Housings in the Central City of Shanghai

Lu Bin

(College of Architecture and Urban Planning，Tongji University)

Abstract：After the site visit on all of the 138 enclosed housings in the central city of Shanghai and the collection and reading work of the cases' relevant material，the author makes systemic research and analysis on all the cases and elaborates on three typical examples in the following three aspects as historical development，urban planning and architectural design. Then the author points out the five challenges that the current Shanghai enclosed housing are facing. Last，five related revelations are put forward.

Keywords：Enclosed，Housing，Shanghai，Typology

参考文献：

[1] 卢斌，李振宇. 以上海临港新城 WNW-C1 限价房项目 6A 地块规划及建筑设计为例谈中国保障性住房类型创新设计 [J]. 城市建筑. 2013，1：34-37.

[2] 卢斌，李振宇. 上海保障性住房设计类型创新探索——以围合式为例 [C]. 第十届中国城市住宅研讨会，2013.

[3] 上海市测绘院. 上海市影像地图集（中心城区）[M]. 上海：上海科学技术出版社，2001.

[4] 上海市城市规划管理局. 上海市城市规划管理技术规定[Z]. 2003.

[5] 上海市建筑建材业市场管理总站. 上海市工程建设规范——住宅设计标准[Z]. 2007.

[6] （日）芦原义信. 街道的美学 [M]. 尹培桐译. 天津：百花文艺出版社，2006.

[7] 薛顺生，娄承浩. 老上海经典公寓[M]. 上海：同济大学出版社，2005.

[8] （美）雅各布斯. 伟大的街道 [M]. 王又佳，等译. 北京：中国建筑工业出版社，2009.

[9] Gill Grant. Planning the Good Community：New Urbanism in Theory and Practice [M]. [S. L.]. Taylor & Francis Group，2006.

[10] Michael Southworth，Eran Ben-Joseph. Streets and the Shaping of Towns and Cities [M]. [S. L.]：Island Press，2003.

[11] Li Zhenyu，Lu Bin. 4 Suitable Design Strategies on Enclosed Housing in China——Case of Shanghai [C]. [S. L.]：UIA World Congress of Architecture，2014.

[12] Rob Krier. Town Spaces [M]. [S. L.]：Birkhlauser，2007.

基于"都市聚落"理念的城市企业类单位大院更新规划研究

常 江 杨 帆

（中国矿业大学）

摘要：本文通过考察聚落的主要特征与发展演变过程，认为聚落除具有容纳居住、生产活动的容器功能以外，储存、延续并发展地域文脉的文化功能也是其重要功能之一。然而这一重要功能在现代城市聚落中正逐渐丧失。由此本文提出"都市聚落"理念，旨在通过对场地文脉要素的提取、梳理与筛选，延续并优化有较高保留价值的文脉要素，从而恢复现代城市的文化功能，构建现代"都市聚落"。

关键词：都市聚落，文脉，企业类单位大院，更新规划

1 聚落概述

1.1 聚落的内涵

"聚落"一词诞生于原始社会的人类聚居点，是人类各种相对集中、稳定的居住场所的总称，包含居住设施、生活服务设施、生产设施及开放空间等组成要素。依据聚落居民主要从事的经济活动类型、聚居规模与密度等特征，可将聚落划分为乡村聚落与城市聚落两类，以农业人口为主的乡村聚落是历史上占主导地位的传统聚落形式，以非农业人口为主的城市聚落则是现代社会人类聚居的主要形式。[1]

1.2 聚落的特征与功能

传统的乡村聚落在不同的地理位置与文化背景下产生了不同的建筑形态和空间景观，具有独特的地域景观特征；乡村聚落以小农经济模式为主，生产与生活用地紧密结合，具有自给自足的经济特征；宗族和血缘关系是维系乡村聚落居民的重要纽带，因而聚落具有社会网络紧密、居民归属感较强等社会特征。[2]这些特征在聚落稳定、连续的发展过程中不断累积，构成聚落各种外显的环境特征、空间符号与内隐的文化传统、思维方式，即显性文脉与隐性文脉。[3]地域文脉以聚落为载体集中呈现，亦随聚落的发展而不断传承与演变，正如芒福德所说，聚落"专门用来贮存并流传人类文明的成果"[4]。可见聚落除了具有容纳居住、生产活动的容器功能以外，储存、延续并发展地域文脉的文化功能也是其重要功能之一。

2 从乡村聚落到都市聚落

2.1 聚落的演化与文脉的断裂

随着商业手工业从农业中的分离，一种新的聚落形式开始脱胎于乡村聚落之中。聚落的内部功能走向多样化，聚居规模与密度逐渐提高，由此产生了城市聚落的雏形。古代城市多以自下而上的发展方式自然演进[5]，居民自发的建设行为多在尊重场地周边自然环境、城市街巷格局与建筑风貌的基础上进行，并不自觉地将世代沿袭而来的文化传统与价值观念渗透其中，由此在小规模、渐进式的改造中保证了由以上要素构成的显性文脉与隐性文脉在古代城市聚落中的传承。

然而，近代工业革命以来，生产力水平的大幅提高带来的是人类的建设活动愈发忽视环境要素

554

的限制与文化要素的发扬。在现代城市对旧城区的更新改造过程中,标准化、国际风的高楼大厦大规模地取代了地域文化特色浓厚的传统建筑,这在中国城市中尤为常见。大拆大建的改造方式片面追求经济利益的最大化而忽视城市文化功能的存续,随之而来的是城市面貌、聚居人群构成与活动方式的剧变。显性文脉要素的剧变也直接导致隐性文脉的传承失去了物质载体[6],无以为继,城市文脉由此产生了断层。文脉的传承这一聚落的重要功能在现代城市聚落中正逐渐丧失。[7]

2.2 都市聚落理念的衍生

"都市聚落"即针对城市内部地块更新提出的理念,旨在延伸传统聚落的内涵与功能特征,提倡渐进、融合式的改造更新方式,避免彻底摒弃场地原有文脉。理念注重对场地原有显性与隐性文脉要素的提取、梳理和筛选,以此延续并优化有较高保留价值的文脉要素,从而在地块层面上逐步恢复现代城市的文化功能,构建用地功能丰富、空间特色鲜明、社会关系和谐的新型"都市聚落"。

3 城市聚落中的企业类单位大院

3.1 企业类单位大院的文脉特征

企业类单位大院是计划经济时代背景下我国城市聚落发展的特殊产物之一,一般是由企业生产用地、职工居住用地及配套公共服务设施用地组成的城市综合性空间单元,是我国众多工业城市用地空间的重要组成部分。

从物质空间环境上看,企业类单位大院将工业文化、地域文化与时代特征等隐性文脉要素渗透于其建筑风貌与空间意象等显性要素之中,形成了大院独特的可识别性。[8]同时,大院内工业、居住、公共服务等各功能类型建筑混合布局,产生了职住一体、功能平衡的大院空间布局模式,这是企业类单位大院不同于普通居住小区的主要特征。从社会与文化角度看,单位大院中的居民职业联系、社会联系紧密,较强的居民构成同质性带来了更为密切的人际交往,构成了紧密的社会网络,促进了大院归属感与领域性的产生,这是凝聚单位大院众多居民的重要隐性文脉要素。

3.2 产业转型背景下企业类单位大院的现状解读

随着城市"退二进三"的产业结构转型调整,位于城市中心区的企业类单位大院与周边用地性质的矛盾凸显,大院用地迫切需要进行调整与更新。作为典型的老工业基地城市之一,众多工业企业类单位大院的建设对徐州的城市空间结构产生了深远影响。在徐州由传统资源型城市向综合型城市转型的过程中,此类单位大院首当其冲,本文即以徐州市第二机械厂单位大院更新规划作为主要研究对象。

如图1所示,徐州二机厂单位大院兴建于20世纪70年代,紧邻贾汪区西南的夏桥与韩桥两大矿区,占地面积约290000m²,南部为企业生产区,北部为职工居住区。2003年二机厂停产倒闭,在工业企业退出的背景

图1 场地区位图

下，大院原先的文脉特征发生了较为显著的变化。作为大院内居民重要经济来源的工业厂房空置，大院居住区出现失业人员增多、居民净流出状况加剧、社区归属感弱化等问题而亟待改造。目前，我国对于单位大院的改造更新普遍停留于物质层面的环境改善，忽视文化层面场地文脉要素的保留与延续。[9] 本更新规划将以该地块的改造为契机，融合都市聚落理念，旨在为现代城市中场地文脉的延续、城市文化功能的复兴做出初步探索。

通过对单位大院内部及周边的现状文脉要素进行梳理，可进而对各类文脉要素进行筛选，划分为需保留的要素、无需保留的要素、经优化后有较高保留价值的要素等类型，并进一步分析各要素的现存问题，以指导下一步针对性优化策略的提出。表1对二机厂单位大院的文脉要素进行了梳理，分析场地文现有脉要素特征可知其主要存在以下问题。

徐州市第二机械厂地块文脉构成要素表　　　　　　　　　　　　　　　　表1

分 类			要 素 梳 理
显性文脉要素	自然环境	地景	农田
		水景	采煤塌陷地（池）、南湖
	人工环境	交通设施	贾韩路、贾汪煤炭运输铁路
		居住建筑	低层、多层行列式住宅，一梯四户点式住宅
		公共服务建筑	粮站、商店、职工活动中心、学校、卫生所
		工业建筑	厂房、仓库
		景观建筑	凉亭、长廊
		开敞空间	场地内部：篮球场、健身广场、小花园 场地外部：夏桥矿区（煤炭主题公园）、夏桥公园、南湖湿地公园
隐性文脉要素	文化传统		日常作息时间、企业单位归属感
	社会网络		居民构成、人际关系

3.2.1 功能混合的用地布局特征逐渐弱化

图2　场地周边用地功能分析图

在生产功能抽离之后，企业类单位大院内的生产—生活功能平衡体系被打破，场地转变为以生活类建筑为主导的用地功能较为单一的地块，这不利于其内部活动的集聚与活力的激发。因此，单位大院的更新规划宜延续并修复场地原有的生产—生活功能混合布局特征。另外，地块周边的建筑功能布局亦会与场地内部产生联系与互动。由图2对二机厂地块周边的用地功能布局特征分析可知，场地北邻贾汪城区，周边混合了居住、商办、工业、教育、医疗等多样化的用地功能，而场地东、西、南三面主要为农田、鱼塘、公园等自然开敞空间，该场地处于城市边缘人工要素与自然要素的融合节点之上。而场地内部较单一的用地功能未能与周边相协调，其复合程度相对于周边处于较低水平状态，从而形成了城市空间的断层，需通过规划进行融合与修补。

3.2.2 先天不足的空间意象要素体系亟待完善

单位大院中的典型空间意象是形成场地标识性的载体与构成场地显性文脉的主要要素。通过对二机厂工人居住区居民空间认知意象调查可知，城市意象五要素在场地内并未构成完整的空间意象体系，社区的主要节点要素为南北两个入口大门以及位于社区中心的商店，区域要素为球场和健身广场。由此可见场地内节点和区域要素相对单调、缺乏活力，而边界和标志要素缺失，存在公共空间界定模糊、使用率低下、领域感薄弱等问题，亟须通过规划改进以构建完善的空间意象体系。

3.2.3 发展动力缺失的居住空间环境逐渐滞后

大院住区建筑及空间环境在工业企业退出之后往往进入发展停滞期，这一时期大院空间面貌的相对稳定只是对于其各类显性文脉要素的被动式、机械式保存，不但会因疏于管理导致品质恶化，亦会由于其物质环境的变化逐渐滞后于社会环境的发展与居民需求的提高而遭受诟病，需借助改造契机完善提升其空间品质。

二机厂地块目前拥有 20 世纪 70 年代至 21 世纪初不同时期建设的各类住宅及厂房建筑，其空间风貌较好地体现了苏北建筑文化与时代特征。如 80 年代建设的二层住宅单元采用清水砖墙面与粘土瓦坡屋顶，红砖灰瓦加之装饰精细的屋脊、檐口、铁艺门窗，展现了 80 年代的建筑技艺与特色。然而早期建设的住宅由于缺乏管理与维护现已立面残破、内部空间狭小、房间布局不合理，已无法适应当前居民的居住需求，可在保留其外部形式要素的基础上进行内部结构的优化，从而在尊重场地历史记忆的前提下改善场地的居住空间环境。

3.2.4 紧密稳固的社会关系网络逐渐解体

单位大院中长久以来形成的紧密的社会关系网络与强烈的归属感是"都市聚落"维持向心力的重要力量。而场地内居住人群的稳定性是维护其紧密社会网络的前提，也是场地文化传统与生活方式稳定延续的保障。对于二机厂地块居民来说，其原有的作为二机厂职工的共同身份认同随着工厂的倒闭已不复存在，同时部分居民对大院未来的发展逐渐失去信心，为寻找更稳定的经济来源、更好的生活环境而选择搬离大院。居民的流失带来的是场地内原有的社会关系网络走向解体，大院归属感不断弱化，这些值得留存的要素急需在规划中得到关注。

4 基于都市聚落理念的企业类单位大院更新策略

基于上述对场地要素现状的分析，本文针对建筑功能布局、空间景观特色以及社会关系网络等亟待保留与优化的要素作为规划设计的切入点，提出以下更新策略。

4.1 新产业功能的植入

生产性功能的缺失、低强度的功能混合模式是单位大院失去活力的主要原因。作为承载一定范围内人类有机集聚的场所，都市聚落不仅应容纳最基本的居住功能，还应在小尺度空间范围内实现城市多样化功能的合理混合与平衡。通过将都市聚落理念融入大院改造，可将大院分解为由居住、商业办公、公共服务等多个具有不同主导功能的单元组成的聚合体，形成丰富、灵活而开放的城市空间单元，重新构建大院内平衡的职住关系。

在二机厂改造规划过程中，大院原有的职住平衡的功能布局模式应得到延续，而该场地周边自然要素与人工要素的交汇特征也应在场地内部得到回应。如图 3 所示，规划首先从功能布局入手，提出功能混合的布局原则，通过对大院内与工人社区相毗邻的闲置工业用地的功能置换，植入服务于城市的商业办公、文化娱乐功能，构建大院内部功能与居民就业的就地平衡。同时在社区内部增加公共服务设施，促进社区功能的完善。由此重新建立单位大院内部的职住平衡体系，将其改造为功能混合、协调发展的城市单元。

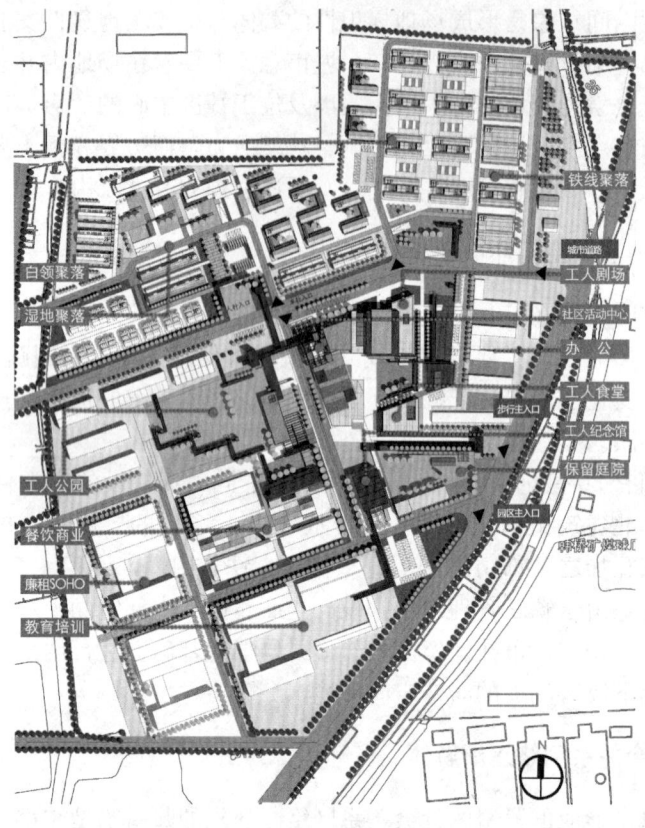

图 3　规划总平面图

4.2　新场地标志的创造

规划因地制宜，完善单位大院的空间意象要素体系，从而保证场地文脉的延续性，加强场地的可识别性与领域感。通过居民认知意象调查，规划中对大院的主要空间意象加以合理利用，保留并改造了大院居民使用率较高的球场与楼间空地等公共空间，提升其铺地、植被、景观小品设置等方面的品质，使其与居民生活需求相适应。此外，规划在工人社区南侧设置了工人剧院、社区活动中心、工人食堂、工业博物馆等一系列大中型公共建筑，结合城市广场组成场地内的新标志。标志性建筑的设计还融入了以工业特色为代表的城市文化特征，通过冷峻刚硬的立面材质与外露的复杂结构形态等要素突显场地特色，提升了场地的可识别性。

4.3　原有社会网络的延续与发展

最后，规划对于单位大院中的老旧住宅采取原地改造的方式。如对于地块西片 20 世纪 70 年代建设的 1 层平房，规划通过室外院落部分的加建将分立于院落两端的客厅、卧室等居住空间与厨房、卫生间等服务空间连为一体，在扩大居住面积、提升其居住品质的同时保留了住区原有的社会关系网络，促进和谐居住氛围的形成。规划期望在物质环境改善的基础上，辅以一定的经济、政策手段鼓励原住民回迁并吸引新居民入驻，从而延续并发展其紧密的社会关系网络。同时，在大院改造中新职住平衡体系的构建对于大院居民重新获得稳定经济来源，加强社区稳定性与场地归属感亦有着举足轻重的作用。

5　结语

本文提出的"都市聚落"理念旨在恢复在现代城市中逐渐失落的文化功能，这是发展到城市阶段的聚落愈发不可或缺的重要功能。基于这一理念的城市更新主要通过对场地各种文脉构成要素的梳理、筛选与改造使地块更新在满足现代城市需求的同时可延续原有的场所特征，以减少城市聚落空间断点与历史断层的出现。

The Research on Renovation Planning of Enterprise Unit Community Based on "Urban Settlement" Concept

Chang Jiang，Yang Fan

(China University of Mining and Technology，221116 Xuzhou，Jiangsu)

Abstract：By reviewing main characteristics and evolution process of human settlements，this paper puts forward that in addition to the function of accommodating living and productive activities，settlements also contain the important cultural function of storing，inheriting and developing of urban context. However，this important function is gradually on the decline in modern urban settlements. Thus，this paper proposes "Urban Settlement" concept，which is intended for the restoration of cultural function in urban settlement by extracting，combing and screening the contextual elements in the site，and optimizing those contextual elements with high conservation value.

Keywords：Urban settlements，Context，Enterprise unit community，Renovation planning

参考文献：

[1]　樊杰，等. 地理(七年级上)[M]. 北京：人民教育出版社，2012.

[2]　马航. 中国传统村落的延续与演变——传统聚落规划的再思考[J]. 城市规划学刊，2006.1：161.102-107.

[3]　常江，顾爱东，邓元媛. 显性文脉"织补"与隐性文脉"渗透"[J]. 城市发展研究，2014，21：1～7.

[4]　(美)刘易斯·芒福德著. 城市发展史——起源、演变和前景[M]. 倪文彦译. 北京：中国建筑工业出版社，2005.

[5]　董鉴泓. 中国城市建设史[M]. 北京：中国建筑工业出版社，2004.

[6]　周详. 地域文化时空观下的古村落保护与创新——以湖州荻港古村为例[J]. 广东园林，2014，36(6)：38-41.

[7]　刘士林. 芒福德的城市功能理论及其当代启示[J]. 河北学刊，2008，28(2)：191-194.

[8]　常江，陈华，袁媛. 作为产业类历史地段的工人村保护更新研究[J]. 现代城市研究，2008(9)：28～34.

[9]　陈眉舞. 中国城市居住区更新：问题综述与未来策略[J]. 城市问题，2002，108(4)：43-47.

遗产视角下的单位社区大院居住与保护矛盾分析
——以西安顺城北巷单位社区大院为例

齐一聪[1]　马　卉[2]

（1. 重庆大学建筑城规学院；2. 宁夏大学土木与水利工程学院）

摘要：单位社区大院在保护活化中不同于普通历史遗产的一大特征便是其与居住者特殊的关系，其大都伴随着正在使用中的居住者。从保护角度，单位社区大院具有很高的延续价值，然而对于大多数居住者而言，其生活条件又需要迫切改变。我国对于建筑及区域保护的讨论多集中于历史文化及产业文化建筑进行讨论，对于现实中占大多数的具有很高价值普通建筑尤其是居住建筑鲜有提及。本文以西安北顺城巷区域集体式社区大院为例讨论其保护与使用的矛盾，具有一定的普适性。

关键词：单位社区，大院，保护与居住，矛盾

1 前言

单位社区大院作为我国独特时期与经济体系的独特产物，其具有体现本国文化特色的多方面价值。然而某些价值极高的单位社区大院却处于极其尴尬的位置。从价值角度而言其具有很高的保护价值，从历史遗产角度而言其不属于历史遗产的范畴。因为建成年代的关系，许多单位社区大院往往在迫切保护改造之时仍然在被使用者使用着，因此对其保护处理中会出现许多不同于历史遗产保护的情况，其保护不仅牵扯到物质的延续，还往往伴随着居住者与保育工作间产生的各类矛盾，如基础设施落后、业态单一、交通堵塞、居住人口混杂，以及产权、经济等问题。因而讨论居住者与保护之间的辩证关系及处理方式，就显得尤其重要。本文以西安北顺城巷为例。

西安现存的明城墙于明洪武七年到十一年所建，其历史可以追溯到隋唐皇城。顺城巷即围绕城墙形成，古时为跑马道，新中国成立后在其周围兴建各单位集体大院。改革开放后，西安各地大兴土木，然而顺城巷却因其独特的地理位置，以及依托城墙悠久的历史文化与极具敏感性的地位，在近四五十年避开了房地产开发的风潮，现代发展及经济的侵蚀并没有过多影响到这里，使其在古城面貌日新月异的时候形成了自己独特的社区集体住宅文化氛围。单位集体社区大院是中国特殊时期的特殊产物，具有民族性、独特性与历史性，以业缘为主的社区关系使得社区居民相互熟悉，良好的社区氛围具有很高的人文价值，如图1。然而现今除了需求单一的老人，其他的居住者却对这里有着难以言说的复杂情绪。一方面，这里承载了其过往的城市记忆和既有的社会关系网络；另一方面，落后的交通与基础服务设施、破败的街巷面貌与日渐变差的区域治安在其生活上造成了各种不便。继续选择居住在这里对于大多数住民而言更多是迫于经济的无奈。

单位社区大院价值：（1）社会价值。单位社区大院是计划经济时的单位福利具有不可复制性。（2）人文价值。单位大院独特的院落式平面形制提供了公共活动空间，单位统一的集体组织形式提供的集体公共活动等，形成衣食住行集体化的居民活动形式，更加加强居民之间交往频率，使得居民间关系更加密切。其和睦的邻里关系，相比较现代社会"各顾各"现象更加难得，其人文价值越发珍贵。[2]（3）建筑价值。单位社区大院往往

图1　街边的象棋集会

（图片来源：作者自摄）

由于其独特的建成年代，多种限制下，形成了具有时代气息的独特建筑风格风貌与小尺度的街巷空间特征。（4）历史价值。单位社区大院作为我国特殊时代的特殊产物，其作为许多时代制度、形式等的承载物，反映、承载着历史，也承载着我国独特时期的社会生产模式、经济制度、社会制度、经济状况等等。（5）经济价值。单位社区大院因为其建成年代久远，且往往位于城市中心区，其土地的经济价值与城市的基础设施资源配置往往远远优异于城市的其他区位。

2 主要矛盾

然而国内大多单位社区大院都为解放初期所建，建国初期的中国正处于百废待兴的历史阶段，城市构筑物的建设技术以及所用材料的生产状况与综合考究都处于起步阶段，其质量普遍较低，因而在现代背景下给居民带来了诸多不便，成为政府甚至原住民心中迫切改变的对象，许多人文精神良好的社区因此在城市化的进程中陷入尴尬困境。

2.1 建筑及其设施落后

就基础设施而言，其社区内部污水横流、电线搭接混乱，少量居民还在使用煤炭，做饭则主要依赖于灌装煤气。社区内部未通天然气，墙体多为实心黏土砖，保温、隔声效果差，供暖设备老化，远远达不到热舒适性要求，条件稍好的居民则采用空调、电暖炉等方式辅助取暖，条件较差则只能以煤炭燃炉供热。排水设施不足且老化，设计落后，导致污水排放存在问题。社区内部巷道走向随意，宽度窄且存在死胡同现象，建筑多为砖木结构，防火设施缺失使得区域存在严重的消防隐患。建筑结构质量也不足以达到抗震要求，并且有些已成危房，若遇强震，不堪设想。多数户型内部无独立卫生间与完整的厨房设施，许多社区都是多栋住户共同使用两三间公共厕所，几个公共厨房，在居民日常生活中造成了极大地不便（图2）。

图2 房屋结构落后
（来源：作者自摄）

2.2 区域功能落后

单位社区大院及其相应街区因为其建成年代久远、规划形态落后，与迅猛发展中的城市环境逐渐脱节，导致其已无法为居民提供更便捷的生活条件，亦无法满足现今城市发展中对于区域功能定位中的新需求，进而产生了居民生活与历史街区固有的多种形态的矛盾，主要表现在：（1）街道占道严重；（2）交通出行不便；（3）区域功能落后三个方面。

街道占道：许多单位社区大院建成年代久远，西安顺城北巷现有社区所属区域建成于新中国成立之初，街道过窄，停车场缺少，导致许多路边停车的行为发生，使得本身狭窄的巷子更加拥堵。

交通出行不便：其区位离地铁换乘点距离过大，区域内交通相对封闭，公共汽车站点也不多，私家车无法停靠，不利于居民日常出行。

区域功能落后：以顺城北巷为例，其集市、茶摊、"麻将馆"等出现具有自发性与随意性，一般聚集在路边以及某些稍为宽敞的空地，往往会导致道路拥堵。自发性的公共交流空间的形成反映了单位社区的具有年代积累的区域活力与人文精神浓厚的社区环境，但其缺乏一定的规范性，在活动空间的环境上也较脏乱，过多的随意性对居住环境产生了不良影响，导致人情味浓厚的居民活动妨碍了他人交通、生活，甚至上升为街道占道行为（图3）。

图3 居民在院内打麻将
（来源：作者自摄）

自发的非规范性交流空间也反映了另外一个问题，即规范性公共交流空间的缺失。居民想要散步、运动、喝茶，甚至打麻将等都只能走到较远的地方才能进行，这就在很大程度上限制了居民公共休闲活动。

从商业角度上讲，单一的业态无法满足居住者多样的需求，使原住民在区域内的生活品质下降。对外来者而言，缺乏特色且形式单一的业态，降低了区域的文化魅力，从而降低了区域内经济优势。

2.3　居民自身对历史建筑的破坏

2.3.1　居民因为经济利益迫切希望拆迁

在许多单位社区大院地处旧街区中，因属市中心地带具有很高的商业价值。地方政府需要"旧城改造"以刺激城市地产经济，地方官员希望在其中获得政绩与权益，开发商为了地块的高经济利益，当地居民则需要以此获得高额的经济补偿以寻求更好的居住环境，在这样的利益的环境背景下，许多具有优良价值的历史街区都面临"推倒重建"。

2.3.2　居民自身对建筑进行违规加改建

居民自身对单位社区大院的建筑价值意识不够，在自身需求的驱动下对旧建筑进行违规加建或改建，其行为往往不具备规范性与专业性，操作过程随意，大都具有一定的破坏性，对旧建筑产生了严重的风格破坏、结构破坏，风貌破坏等，进而影响了整个区域，破坏了建筑的多方价值。

2.4　人口结构

单位社区大院所属街区人口普遍年龄偏大（图4），多数家庭只剩老人。一方面，年轻人与经济条件较好的原住民大都搬离到居住条件更好的城墙外，区域内养老设计规划尚不完善，中产阶级流失使得片区产业结构失衡，致使区域活力减弱。另一方面，旧街区因为廉价的生活成本吸引了一定比例的外来人口居住，其居住情况往往伴随居住户数的改变，导致居住密度增加，许多楼见缝插针，私自违规加建，居住环境日渐拥挤。在西安顺城北巷中这一情况日趋严重，外来人口

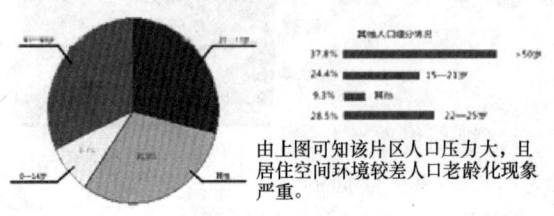

由上图可知该片区人口压力大，且居住空间环境较差人口老龄化现象严重。

图4　顺城巷人口结构分析图
（来源：作者自绘）

比例与日俱增，顺城巷的传统社区良好的居住形态与传统文化特色、社区非物质文化遗产的流失与改变已经初见端倪。原住民、外来人口、新增住户逐渐成为历史街区新的人口构成，其社会网络交集甚贫乏，导致本身良好的社区监督机制弱化甚至缺失，低收入者聚集同时导致区域治安变差。

怎么安排低收入者、弱势群体，甚至流浪者的生活，将标示城市文化的人文态度。"历史街区保护在改善街区环境面貌，提高居住质量的同时，往往会伴随出现街区及周边地段房价的大幅攀升、中产阶级等新居民到来和原住居民大量迁出等'绅士化'（gentrification）[3]问题"。

2.5　改造工作难以进行

改造工作难以进行包括原住民、政府、开发商之间关于改造的矛盾与产权、经济等问题。

原住民希望自身生活环境得到改善，对经济补偿抱有过多期望，其"拖延"等行为与开发商、政府展开博弈，或因为开发商利益至上任意剥削原住民房屋价值，使居民难以接受。在此过程中如果没有照顾大多数公众的利益，强行推倒重建，显然是一种错误行为。

单位社区大院是基于中国计划经济体制的特殊产物,其物权产权的处理方式在现代法规中并无规范可执行,然而我国对于土地的特殊定义使得单位社区大院相关产权更新、经济补偿等问题无章可循。基于这种现状,改造问题便趋于复杂,或涉及部门与个人利益,亟须进行有效沟通。

3 解决方案

3.1 优化人口结构

包括优化现有人口结构和控制改造后人口结构。

现有人口结构的优化除了保存合适比例的原住民外,还应顾及单位社区大院时代变迁所产生的新人口结构。低收入者的聚集产生其赖以生存的非规范街头行为、低技术含量的生产技艺及传统技艺的聚集,形成旧社区的文化特色。由流浪汉、低收入者及弱势群体聚集产生的社会形态也应被重视,而非粗暴驱逐与禁止。引导其街头文化的规范化,对弱势群体及流浪者关心及合理安置或许会使历史街区散发出时代发展的新魅力。

改造后人口结构的重要性不可小觑,在遗产的保护改造中,各项研究大都讨论其物质价值。以顺城北巷为例,其非物质价值远远超越其物质价值。保护物质遗产的价值在一定程度上是为了非物质文化遗产的良好的延续。非物质文化遗产在社区中包括社会结构、社区网络、传统交往方式等人文形态,在保护执行过程中没有固定形式可依,必须经过详尽的价值评定、社会调查,在评定基础上根据价值情况有针对性进行保育与改建,而后因为其非物质文化的可变性还需通过相应可控手段对改建后社区非物质文化维持情况进行控制。菊儿胡同在建成初期因其良好的物质空间与非物质文化得以延续受到了一致好评,但却因为物质文化延续的不可控因素导致改造后社区"缙绅化",非物质文化随着原住民的流失与社会网络的破裂消逝,因而对人员回迁的后期控制就显得尤为重要。

3.2 建筑角度改造方式

3.2.1 成套率改造

单位社区大院大多建成于新中国成立建国初期,当时经济落后,居住空间的标准也普遍较低,其功能户型多方面要求已无法满足现今居民居住要求,增加大户型比例,降低小户型比例,综合整治小区环境,进行成套率改造,通过夹层,局部加建等方式改变空间状况,以在一定程度上提高居民生活环境水平,也可以在一定程度上保证改建后足够的居民回迁率。[4]

3.2.2 建筑改造前评价及利用当地技艺进行改建

许多旧建筑也投入过人力物力进行翻修加固,但往往很快就又会产生裂缝等问题。产生问题的根本原因是对建筑改造前各方面分析缺失。对旧建筑的修缮要注重已有数据分析,综合考虑旧建筑核心价值、结构及设备、基础设施情况对其进行评估,制订最佳改造方案,以求最大化利用旧建筑价值,最少化投入改造资源,最优化居民居住体验,进而最大化其"再生"价值,如图5所示。

对于旧建筑的改造可以采用小规模渐进的方式,规模小,施工使用传统小规模技艺进行改造,有很强的针对性。不仅可以提高改造后质量,还延续了传统与地方技艺,增加了就业机会。以西安北顺城巷为例,因原承重结构与设备落后,所以只

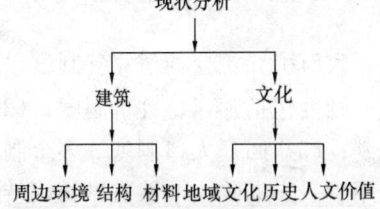

图5 空间重构分析图
(来源:作者自绘)

留外皮，换内部结构。然而对于某些结构设备质量良好的建筑，则内部结构可以适当保留，具体情况具体对待。美观上应尊重旧建筑本身建筑风貌特色，且注重地域文化特色的延续。同时进行设备隐藏等工作，以免破坏旧建筑良好的传统风貌。

3.3　区域角度

3.3.1　空间重构

旧物新用应从城市角度考虑历史建筑的辩证地位，有些错误的规划方式使得许多区域与城市整体割裂，既有结构被破坏，区域与城市得不到良好的对接，变为"异质"空间。"在中国，当前最为突出的城市空间重构特征是快速的城市化与城市经济和社会结构重构并存，城市在迅速向外扩张的同时也通过旧城改造创造更多的空间以满足社会经济发展的需求。"[6] 当旧的空间形态及经济结构无法满足现代需求时，改变区域对于整个城市功能定位，在此基础上进行改造，区域融合进整体城市，与周边区域协同发展，使区域在经济、功能结构上合理化，使居民生活便捷化，如图6所示。从宏观上进行整体调整，使人、建筑、街区、城市的关系更加协调一致。

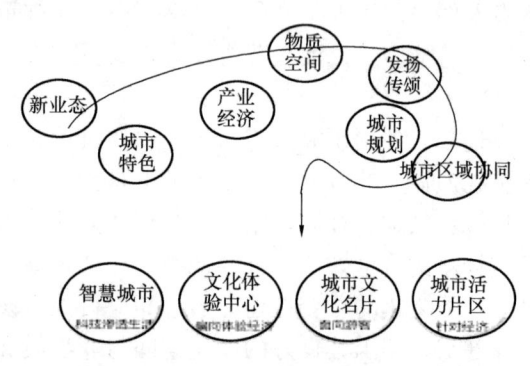

图6　现状分析层次图

（资料来源：作者自绘）

3.3.2　改建中对于某种"特色"的保留

旧建筑在区域规划中与现代城市脱节，甚至引起与现代城市生活不融洽的现象。然而正是这种脱离，使得设计在一定程度上摆脱了城市规划的各种规定与限制。沈福煦认为"改造设计摆脱了环境、区位的束缚，避开了导致城市千篇一律的'民族样式'、'时代特征'这些没有答案的争论，纯粹思考为人服务的建筑本体的塑造。建筑改造才能更加自由，区域才能更具独特性与文化性。"[7] 这种脱离已然成为城市记忆的一部分，是城市生活文化的精华。因而对于单位社区大院的更新改造，应综合各方仔细权衡，切勿简单粗暴。发掘其自身区域特色，强调对已有环境的更新升华。

3.3.3　公共空间的规划与营造

单位社区大院等老旧社区随着时间的推进人与人之间的邻里关系与社会网络已经相当熟络与融洽，许多原住民会自发性形成一些公共交流场所，然而其场所却缺乏规范性，易给周围其他居民带来交通、居住等不便。改造过程应该仔细研究公共交流场所的发生机制，使用可利用地块建立公共场所，将公共活动空间规范化，以求满足居民社会交往需求的同时不对整个区域造成不良影响。

3.4　宏观：政策制定及教育等

政府引导主要通过完善制度以及通过教育使得居民了解制度及单位社区大院的价值。

制度包括：（1）评价制度；（2）范围确定；（3）公众参与制度；（4）社会监督制度；（5）补偿机制；（6）回迁人口制度等多个制度的制定与完善，从改造初期、改造中到改造后投入使用，以及使用后一定期限内改造成果的保持都进行详细量化的规定，全方位规范改造中会面对的各种矛盾，进行规范性的标度。

民众对于价值极高的单位社区大院保护知识的缺失往往是产生各种不可调和矛盾的关键，公众对于旧建筑文化价值的意识淡薄不仅会导致单位社区的社区形态及建筑形态受到居民的破坏，还会致使居民产生对改造工作的不理解及不配合。公众对于各种法规制度的了解性不够也导致其利益容易在旧区改造中受到剥削和影响。改善这种情况应通过教育、媒体传播、舆论培养等方式提高居民文化自豪感，使其全方位意识到单位社区大院的综合文化价值，了解旧建筑保育活化中的各种制度，创造居民共同的顶层利益，维护居民的各方面利益，使得单位社区大院的保护更加有效。

4 总结

对于单位社区大院的保护，全社会普遍缺少关注与正确的价值认识，其与常规的历史遗产很大的不同点即为单位社区大院尴尬的无价值归属地位，并且往往还伴随着使用权与产权利益等复杂的问题，然而现代法制法规对其却没有详尽规范，导致许多优秀的单位社区大院被破坏或彻底摧毁，其所承载着物质或精神文明价值消逝。因而讨论单位社区大院与居住者的矛盾及其解决方法，对其保护具有重要的意义。

Analysis on the Contradiction between Community Residence and Protection in the Community of Units from the Perspective of Heritage-In Xi'an City Bei Xiang Unit Community Compound as An Example

Qi Yicong[1] Ma Hui[2]

(1. Chongqing University；2. Ningxia University)

Abstract：A major feature of modern heritage is different from the common historical heritage is its relationship with live special, most modern heritage are accompanied by the occupants are in use. From the perspective of the historical block protection, with the continuation of high value, but for the majority of the occupants, their living conditions and the urgent need to change. Discussion on modern architecture in China focuses more on the historical culture and industrial culture construction are discussed, for the reality of the majority of ordinary residential building construction especially rarely mentioned. Taking Xi'an north Shuncheng Lane area collective style community courtyard as example to discuss its protection contradiction and use, has a certain degree of universality.

Keywords：Unit community, courtyard, Protection and living, Contradiction

参考文献：

[1] 路风. 单位：一种特殊的社会组织形式[J]. 中国社会科学, 1989, 01：71-88.

[2] 张丽梅. 社会调控体系下单位社区发展研究[J]. 规划师, 2005, 10：88-91.

[3] 张松, 赵明. 历史保护过程中的"绅士化"现象及其对策探讨[J]. 中国名城, 2010, 09：4-10.

[4] 凌颖松. 上海近现代历史建筑保护的历程与思考[D]. 上海：同济大学, 2007.

[5] 马超. 旧建筑内部空间改造再利用研究[D]. 天津：天津大学, 2003.

[6] 廖玉娟. 多主体伙伴治理的旧城再生研究[D]. 重庆：重庆大学, 2013.

[7] 马超. 旧建筑内部空间改造再利用研究[D]. 天津：天津大学, 2003.

中国居住模式在异国条件下的适应性转变：
以中国驻外居住建筑为例

唐可清

[同济大学建筑设计研究院（集团）有限公司]

摘要： 驻外居住建筑是我国政府和企业驻外机构的核心组成部分，是驻外工作人员的居所。它既需要符合使用者源自国内的居住文化，又需对异国环境作出回应。它既反映了国内最新的城市化成果，如社区邻里规划、生活标准和国内商品房潮流等，又根据特殊的语境批判地形成不同于两地的变型，使国内的居住方式得以在异国沿用。本文以当前驻外居住建筑在技术体系和居住文化两方面的适应性转变为例，结合参与若干驻外建筑实践项目的经验，试图从另一角度观察当前中国城市化和居住建筑特征在国际语境下的适应性和可持续性。

关键词： 中国，驻外，居住建筑，适应性，转变

1 引言

新中国成立以来，尤其以改革开放之后，我国政府部门、各类大中型企业在世界范围内根据不断拓展的业务需求设置了众多驻外分支机构，如大使馆、总领馆、国际组织代表团处、经商处、中国文化中心、孔子学院、各类企业办事处等。近年来，驻外机构的建设获得了更大力度的支持，工程数量持续增加。例如国家财政每年用于政府型海外馆舍的建设费用超过 10 亿元，涉及 150 余个项目，其中大中型项目约 80 余个，处于施工阶段的项目约 40 个。[1]驻外建筑在探索中获得宝贵经验，形成一定规模的同时，大量驻外工作人员的居住和生活问题也随之而来。

驻外居住建筑与驻外机构的相对关系 表 1

	1. 与办公合并设置	2. 在馆区内独立设置	3. 在馆区外设置
布局方式	居住 / 办公 / 驻外机构	居住 / 办公 / 驻外机构	居住 / 办公 / 驻外机构
特点	1. 驻外居住建筑位于相应的驻外机构馆舍内部。 2. 居住建筑和办公建筑合并为一栋建筑，利于内部联系和统一管理。 3. 适合中小型的驻外机构	1. 驻外居住建筑位于相应的驻外机构馆舍内部。 2. 居住建筑独立设置，便于分区管理和必要的联系。 3. 适合场地条件宽松的中大型驻外机构	1. 驻外居住建筑位于相应的驻外机构馆舍之外。 2. 和驻外机构的主体分离，自成一体，单独设置后勤管理设施。 3. 适合规模较大且场地条件有限的驻外机构

注：资料来源：作者制。

驻外机构为驻外人员提供的居所在此称为驻外居住建筑。它被赋予了"驻外"和"居住"两层含义。一方面，驻外居住建筑与单纯的住宅不同，它是众多驻外馆舍中的关键组成部分，根据不同的建设条件，在馆舍布局中扮演着多种角色，见表 1。它的设计与建造方式也必然受到驻外机构自身性质的影响。几乎所有驻外机构对中国文化在建筑上的识别性都有着不同程度的关注；同时，一些特殊性质的建筑，如驻各国使领馆，对场地领域有着严格的准入限制，对设计和施工过程中的安

全性也有着较高的标准。受此影响，驻外居住建筑也同时获得了特殊的建筑身份。它构成了一个特殊的场所，它"打破了准现代的连续空间模式，取而代之的是一种后现代的不连续的空间。"[2]它既是中国的，又是当地的。在设计和施工过程中，不可避免存在中外两地技术和文化的碰撞。另一方面，由于使用者是国内派驻的工作人员，驻外居住建筑需要解决的一个重要问题是：以什么样的空间组织方式使带有国内生活方式的工作人员在有限任期内适应国外的生活。因此，驻外居住建筑在其实践过程带来了国内的居住标准，反映出一种将已知范式向未知环境的适应性的拓展。作为一种对地理特征尤为敏感的建筑类型，如不对既有范式进行调整，则很难在世界范围内沿用。在这一过程中可以观察到国内一系列业已沉淀下来的建筑特征和城市化成果是如何经过适应性转变从而走向国际化的。[3]这一过程使我国驻外居住建筑在若干方面上不可避免地表现出对国内既有居住建筑特征的发展、输出和批判。本文将着重围绕技术体系和居住文化两方面的问题进行展开。

2 技术体系对接中的"逆差"与"顺差"

驻外居住建筑虽然获得了较大发展，但总体数量仍然较少，尚未形成固定的操作模式；许多涉外工程出于自身的特殊性，相关信息不易被广泛获得和研究。因此，在较长的时期内都缺乏规范的建设流程和可供遵循的先例与研究样本。每一个项目都需要作为独特的事件在探索中推进。

由于涉及中外两地设计部门的协作，驻外居住建筑项目也往往面临着国内外两套技术体系，主要表现在结构和构造体系、设计和施工种的工业化运用程度、设计标准、制图语言和习惯、操作流程、依据和规范、报批环节、权责分配等方面的差异。

中方公司以什么样的角色和程度参与到驻外居住项目的建设过程中，是两地技术体系对接的直接结果。在一些技术体系成熟先进的国家，这一对接过程表现出"逆差"现象，驻在国的技术体系成为项目的主导。而在一些相对不发达的地区，技术体系的对接又表现为"顺差"现象，国内成型的设计和建造流程可较为顺畅地沿用，但同时还可能面对当地工艺和材料可能无法达到标准等另一方面的问题。

2.1 "逆差"现象

驻在国严格且复杂的建造报批程序、设计规范、特殊的地理气候因素、必要而独特的技术和工艺等都是造成"逆差"现象的原因。例如欧洲国家对历史建筑保护或在历史街区内的建造活动有着严格的技术要求和程序规定，日本对于抗震设计规范在每一次地震后都会进行大幅修编，无法在短期内被国内工程公司所掌握。因此在建设过程中需要以当地建筑公司为主。除此之外，许多国家对境外建筑材料设置严苛的准入制度。例如欧盟对于引进的建材产品均需通过 CE 认证，特殊环境下的产品还需获得 ATEX 认证等。

当地设计机构在设计过程中与国内决策者或未来的使用者缺乏有效沟通，较难掌握国内的居住习惯和文化。因此一些驻外馆舍项目逐步形成了由国内设计单位编制可行性研究报告和概念设计方案，确定基本的居住标准，而后转由当地公司完成施工图设计和报批工作的合作模式。

这一模式也存在着一些不足和不确定性。例如在驻外机构数量中占有较大比重的外交馆舍往往倾向由本国团队施工建造。中方团队不得不对外方设计文件进行翻译和再修改，使之在各个技术层面上适应中方团队的标准。中外两地重复的文件编制工作不可避免地增加了误差和错误概率。在部分驻外项目实践中，居住建筑也可能被剥离出来，进行单独的施工委托，减少了对接环节。但在有限的场地范围内划分出两个独立的施工区域，无疑增加了现场操作和管理的难度。

2.2 "顺差"现象

驻外居住建筑在一定的情况下也可由国内的设计单位承担。在大使馆、领事馆等有特殊要求的建筑项目中，这一方式较为普遍。在当地缺乏相应工业技术条件，或驻在地区有成熟的中资建筑公司时，都可以由中方为主进行驻外项目的设计和建造。当地单位协助完成图纸报批和相关流程。在这方面工作中，国内的许多大型设计院已积累了较为丰富的经验，如北京建筑设计研究院、中国建筑设计研究院、同济大学建筑设计研究院等。

这种"顺差"现象使国内的居住建筑特征和相应的技术特点可以连续地在异国实现。但由于在大部分技术体系上和当地有着较大的差异，在项目推进中，需要和当地各个部门进行协调的环节显著增多。甚至在个别地区为了引进国内工程队伍和建筑材料而需要通过政府渠道签订专门的双边协议，工程的复杂性因此而大为增加。将国内范式引出国门的过程中所遇到的许多问题，也折射出在快速城市化和城市重构背景下，国内住宅在住宅规范化、标准化、国际化方面所存在的不足。

3　居住文化批判的转译

驻外居住建筑将国内的居住文化带到世界语境中时所体现的延续和变化是同时存在的。这些对既有居住文化的质疑往往蕴含着驻外居住建筑设计的动力，可概括为社区（驻外居住建筑与所在地城市的关系）、布局（驻外居住建筑各居住单元之间的关系）、套型（驻外居住建筑居住单元内部空间的关系）三个层面上对现有中国居住特征的批判的转译。

3.1　社区安全的必要性与矛盾性

许多驻外项目都表现出对馆舍领域安全性的重视和门禁系统的坚持，并因此和当地城市文脉产生了一定的隔阂。当这种在国内城市中司空见惯的现象，出现在异国环境中时，却异常引人注意。

目前，许多地区的国际安全局势并不稳定，我国驻外机构的建设也需要将遭受直接或间接安全威胁的风险纳入设计中。欠佳的社会安全状况和恐怖袭击成了安全威胁的两大来源，而这些安全威胁都明显带有随机、业余和难以侦测的特点。因此驻外居住建筑在设计中需要考虑来自各个方向上可能的威胁事件。在一些外交馆舍项目中，建筑外墙至场地边界的距离也受到严格控制，使建筑到城市之间出现了一个空旷的用于预警的控制区域。在驻外居住建筑项目中，社区安全设计正从一个附属的设计环节转而成为需要充分研究的重要专题的趋势。[4]

对于驻外机构而言，在国内被广泛采用的门禁社区成了切实有效的选择，并且也早已为派驻的国内工作人员所熟悉。这一做法在对当地城市的态度上无疑是消极的。驻外建筑自身担负着传递开放友好信息的责任。这种责任在驻外建筑中受到了相比国内住区而言更高的重视。而目前设计师们所做的更多的是在于如何将相比国内更加严格的门禁社区设计得看上去更为亲切。随着中国驻外居住建筑的持续增加，相比用花园或广场来填充安全区域的做法，仍然需要得到更多创新设计。

3.2　布局思路的解放与拓展

国内以单元式为基础的集合住宅组织方式仍然是许多驻外居住建筑的设计起点。特殊的地理气候因素却为这一传统布局思路提供了最有效的拓展，促成了驻外居住建筑多样化的布局方式，见图1。在设计过程中主要表现为密度和朝向两方面的多样化。

一方面，集中与分散成了影响驻外居住建筑布局的重要考虑因素。驻外居住建筑属于集合住宅的范畴。出于安全、纪律、管理等方面的考虑，驻外人员需进行一定程度的集中，并限定在明确的领域或楼栋内。而一些人员较多的驻外机构，不能一次性获得足够规模的土地，馆员住宅只能分散在城市不同的区域中。但每一个驻外居住建筑项目也总是倾向于形成自成一体的微型社区。而在另一些国家，通过互惠等方式获得的土地面积较大，在同一场地内的分散式布置可以更有效地提高居住品质。因此在不超出规定的驻外居住标准的情况下，需要寻求既分散布置又便于进行集中管理的

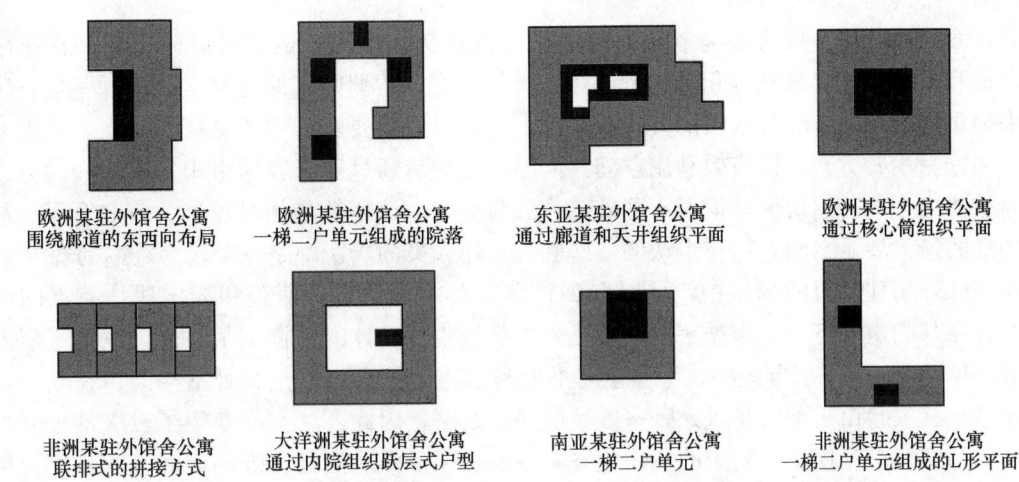

欧洲某驻外馆舍公寓　　　　　欧洲某驻外馆舍公寓　　　　　东亚某驻外馆舍公寓　　　　　欧洲某驻外馆舍公寓
围绕廊道的东西向布局　　一梯二户单元组成的院落　　通过廊道和天井组织平面　　通过核心筒组织平面

非洲某驻外馆舍公寓　　　　　大洋洲某驻外馆舍公寓　　　　南亚某驻外馆舍公寓　　　　　非洲某驻外馆舍公寓
联排式的拼接方式　　　　通过内院组织跃层式户型　　　一梯二户单元　　　　一梯二户单元组成的L形平面

图 1　　多样化的驻外居住建筑布局
（资料来源：作者制）

方案。崔恺院士在驻南非大使馆中进行了这方面的探索，并尝试了类似的低层集合住宅形式，通过引入组合型的微型合院形成分散居住单元之间的效组织。[5]

　　另一方面，不同于国内对住宅朝向的严格限定，一些国家的气候条件使驻外居住建筑的朝向获得了更大的灵活性。例如在德奥地区，南朝向并非是居住空间的首选朝向，而东西向则更受欢迎。在欧洲的许多新建驻外居住建筑项目中，虽然保留了单元式的格局，但已经见不到南北朝向的布局了，例如驻慕尼黑总领事、驻维也纳联合国和其他国际组织代表团的馆员公寓均优先采取了东西向的布局方式。在赤道地区，如南亚和非洲等地，不同朝向的差别较小，其控制建筑朝向的目的甚至从获取日照转为回避日照的手段。而在日本或韩国等与我国地理特征相似的地区，在场地条件允许的情况下仍然延续了南北向的布局原则。

　　这些转变，也使建筑师反思以行列式和南向为主的国内住宅设计思路是否是不变的定律。随着国内居住条件大幅改善，窗墙体系逐渐成熟，一些特殊的布局所带来的优点也许是值得尝试的。

3.3　套型设计中对既有价值的反思

　　驻外居住建筑的套型既反映了国内住宅市场中的既有价值，也存在多方面的改变。

　　虽然驻外居住建筑的对象是驻外人员个人，但仍反映出 20 世纪 90 年代后国内家庭式空间格局的特征。随着近年来驻外人员生活标准的日趋人性化、家属随行政策的放宽，驻外人员也逐渐具有完整的家庭生活。在走访中发现，一个套型内同时住着妻子、孩子和老人已成为较普遍的现象。由于各驻外机构对驻外人员的居住标准有严格的规定，因此小面积多居室户型更加受到欢迎。这也和目前国内房地产市场兴起的对小户型的研究潮流相契合。他们的共同特点在于，在有限总价和指标的基础上提高空间使用效率，以牺牲一部分室内舒适性换来了多代居的可能。

　　同时，国内套型设计的价值观中普遍存在的将公共交通空间压缩至最经济的倾向，在驻外居住建筑中发生了变化，空间组织呈现宿舍化和家庭化结合的现象。由于住房产权并非属于居住者，因此在驻外项目中淡化了"公摊"面积的概念，使得节省公摊面积不再成为设计中的首要衡量标准。一些部门甚至将低层驻外居住建筑的得房率控制在 70% 左右。而驻外生活的特点使邻里会面和集中成为更为可贵的需要。因此，驻外居住建筑体现出了明显的宿舍化的倾向。廊式或合院式成为常用的组织方式，既在最大限度上使一个主要出入口和门厅服务于尽量多的住户，又兼顾了不同住户间的均好性。例如驻东亚某驻外公寓，带有露天中庭和围廊的廊式空间串联起了不同套型，每套都具有一室一厅或两室一厅格局。在驻大洋洲某驻外公寓中，跃层式户型更具有家庭式的私密性，但同时围合成为一个内向的公共庭院。

此外，套型中的诸多要素都有着不同程度的转变。例如中国式的户外晾晒习惯，在东南亚国家，如印尼和马来西亚等地同为积极的价值标准，但在许多欧洲国家的居住文化中并不被肯定，甚至会招来邻里的非议。在驻外人员的日常生活中，餐厨设计需要考虑中式烹饪的特点，又需要有效兼顾单身和家庭用餐方式，以有效利用空间。同时，入户后通过宽大客厅组织居室空间的方式也成为国内商品住宅中的普遍价值，但对于驻外工作人员而言，访客数量相对较小，宽敞客厅往往成为无序和杂乱的最大展示空间，这在走访的一些驻外工作人员的居所中是一个较为普遍的现象。

从这些驻外居住建筑的套型中，可以看到许多兼具国内住宅价值观和异域居住特点的创新设计。如作者参与的由同济大学李振宇教授、王志军教授主持设计的驻德国某驻外公寓的平层方案和错层方案，见图2。在平层方案中，客厅空间不再是套内的核心，而是和卧室空间、独立的餐厨空间一起连接至玄关。由于不再是进入卧室区域的必经之路，因此客厅空间获得了较大的独立性，在必要时可作为临时卧室使用。封闭的一体化餐厨空间在保证中式烹饪特点的同时，既降低了用餐空间的仪式性，便于单身驻外生活，增加空间使用率；又利于在有家人随行时促进家人交流。在跃层方案中，在有限面积下，通过错层的空间布局方式，提高了各个空间的独立性和私密性，并预留了可供拓展的屋顶花园空间。在驻外居住建筑的套型设计中，既可以看到国内住宅设计潮流的影响，又发生着不同于国内的改变，从而激活了一些独特的品质。

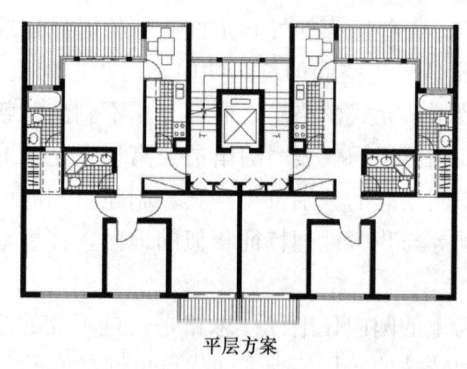
平层方案

错层方案

图2　驻德国某驻外公寓
（资料来源：作者绘，设计者：李振宇，王志军）

4　结论

驻外居住建筑因其"驻外"和"居住"的双重性，为国内建筑师对中国建筑的识别性的思考提供了多样且多元的视角和样本。[6]虽然驻外居住建筑仅服务于特定的人群，其规模和复杂程度也无法和国内住宅实践相提并论。但也许正因为其局限、少量和单纯赋予了它更多的试验性。它以实用为首要目的，沿用了国内住宅的发展成果，而在不经意间又形成了对国内城市化浪潮下的快速低成本复制的批判。[7]驻外居住建筑所呈现的一系列现象，为国内住宅设计提出了两方面的问题：

第一，什么是中国住宅的特征，以及这些特征通过什么样的标准与异国对话？中国的城市化和住宅发展历经改革开放以来三十余年的积淀，逐渐展现出自身的技术特点和居住文化。而新常态下的国内经济形式也为这些积淀走向世界提供了机遇和动力。对国内住宅特征的理解、定义甚至一定程度的量化因而显得更为重要。

第二，中国住宅的特征在世界范围内可以走多远？在一定之"法"的基础上是否可以有更多的创新的"式"？[8]这一问题取决于国内研究者们在多大的尺度上来"规定"中国住宅的范式，并且避免类似带着商业动机的标准化走向教条。

"中国建筑的现代性必然不同于欧洲或美国式的现代性"，"也不是单纯靠移植外国或境外建筑师的设计能够实现的。"[9]当我们试图从国外案例中寻找答案，并希望将它们改造引入国内实践的时候，我们是否也可以尝试从另一个方向进行思考：我们将以什么样的方式向外输出中国居住特征，以及它可以具有多大的适应性？

The Adaptive Transformation of the Chinese Residential Model in the Foreign Context: A Study on the China's Overseas Residential Architecture

Tang Keqing

［Tongji Architectural Design（Group）Co., Ltd］

Abstract: China's overseas residential building is one of the most significant constitutions of China's overseas premises, which has experienced a big development in recent years. It is the basic territory in which most Chinese staffs from the overseas branches of the government and enterprises live. Therefore, it should be built based on the Chinese living culture, while it has to respond an entirely different circumstance. It reflects the latest domestic urbanization achievement, such as the trend of community planning, new-fashioned living standard and housing forms. Meanwhile, the international context transforms the existing domestic paradigm into something new and unique, and further expands the definition of Chinese housing to match a broader context. This paper takes the phenomenon of the adaptive transformation of China's overseas residential buildings as an example, to observe the flexibility and sustainability of today's Chinese housing and urbanization.

Keywords: China, Overseas, Residential architecture, Adaptive, Transformation

参考文献：

[1] 田建伟. 驻外使领馆馆舍建设项目业主方风险管理[D]. 天津大学，2010.

[2] 阿尔贝托－阿莱西. 建筑的身份？[J]. 世界建筑，2006，8：17-20.

[3] 崔彤. 重构平衡——外交使馆作为一种建筑类型[J]. 世界建筑，2006，8：100-103.

[4] 唐可清，李振宇. Terrorist Attack Prevention through Environmental Design: Four Levels of the Adaptive Security Design for the Overseas Diplomatic Premises. 第十一届环境行为研究国际学术研讨会（EBRA）论文集，2014.

[5] 崔恺，康凯，喻弢. 国家的门脸儿：南非使领馆设计[J]. 建筑学报，2013，6：22-25.

[6] 李振宇，唐可清. 从多样到多元：中国驻外外交馆舍的文化价值与设计手法刍议. 建筑师，2014，4：82-89.

[7] Li, Xiangning. Towards a "Critical Pragmatism": Contemporary Architecture in China. Area, (137): 8-16.

[8] 李振宇，张萌. 走向"有法无式"的可持续发展之路：2007Holcim 可持续建筑论坛评述[J]. 建筑学报，2007，8：39-41.

[9] 郑时龄. 当代中国建筑的基本状况思考[J]. 建筑学报，2014，3：96-98.

什么是好宅：台北十三号整宅之社区
文化保存与城市更新试验

吕　行

（台湾大学，建筑与城乡研究所）

摘要： 台北市万华区十三号整宅由于屋龄老旧，不敷使用，里长积极推动自办更新，但台北市现行的城市更新制度尚不成熟。面对城市更新，十三号整宅这样相对弱势的社区，居民的利益如何保障？社区内良好的邻里情感、特有的文化资产如何延续？面对自办更新的种种困境，本文以十三号整宅为例，透过文献回顾、案例分析、田野调查和参与式的设计试验四种研究方法，探究文化再现对老旧社区的保存力量，并试验性编写老旧弱势住宅城市更新的设计准则。

关键词： 老旧住宅，居住权利，文化保存，城市更新，参与式规划

1　前言

建于 1974 年的台北市"十三号"整建住宅（以下简称整宅）社区内有很多珍贵而古早的独立店铺，同时邻里感情良好，这些在现代化的门禁社区很少看到，是宝贵的社区资产。与此对立，社区内部建筑老旧、空间狭小，因此里长积极推动自办更新，但台北市现行的自办更新机制尚不成熟。

面对城市更新，十三号整宅这样相对弱势的社区，居民的利益如何保障？社区的邻里情感、独特的文化资产如何延续？新兴社区如何避免造成绅士化的社会排除？这些是探讨城市更新不可回避的课题。本文以十三号整宅作为试验性规划设计的场地，探讨城市更新的过程中，社区文化资产将以何种形式延续？文化保存对于城市更新产生的化学效应为何？如何透过参与式规划，让居民积极参与自办更新，从而享受到真正意义的"好宅"？

2　文献回顾

2.1　弱势住宅城市更新的挑战

城市更新以促进城市土地有计划之再开发利用，复苏城市机能，改善居住环境，增进公共利益为主要目的。台湾在历经 50 年快速经济发展与城市成长后，自 20 世纪 80 年代，随着后福特主义与新自由主义的影响，为了回应全球经济挑战，政府将城市更新作为振兴经济的策略（周素卿，2009）。自 1998 年通过城市更新条例，台北市的城市更新在台湾就占据重要地位。目前，台北的城市更新案件除灾害案件外，多由建商主导，集中于房价高、区段佳，尤其是容积低利用之地区。屋龄 30 年以上之四五层老旧公寓虽因使用防灾机能不足而亟须更新，但往往因容积奖励诱因不足而不受市场青睐。

即便建商乐于投资，民众也认为建商不透明、隐匿利益，造成民众怀疑。因应高龄化社会来临，政府力推市场八成左右的四五层老旧公寓自办更新，可见自办更新将成为未来城市更新主流。不过，至 2011 年，除 921 灾害重建案，台北市办理的 540 个城市更新案件中，自办更新的案件仅有 8 件，且一半案件不是未见后续作业就是筹组失效或撤销，更无完工案例可循（苏瑛敏，2011：76）。数据显示，自办更新之推动未如预期。在自办更新极不成熟之时，十三号整宅如何开创先河呢？

根据 Carmon 对世界各国城市更新的研究，推行成功需同时具备下列五项：（1）防止弱势团体

被隔离；（2）兼顾经济发展与社会公平；（3）渐进与软性的解决方式；（4）促进公私合作关系；（5）不同的地区需采取差别的处理方法。整宅因其特殊性，与一般民间办理城市更新有所差异，未来更新重建后，须满足居民对社会面财产权的保障、经济面财产价值的提升及环境面实质属性的改善（方定安，2008：238）。在此之外，我们也必须意识到对于老旧社区，其累积的文化资产对居民生活的重要性，在更新后，无形的文化资产如何延续？

2.2　城市更新后的文化保存

Ha 针对低收入社区的住宅更新提出，更新后除了提升低收入户的财产价值外，须保留原来社区的结构与文化。即在整宅更新后，保证他们的生活圈不被隔离，所以保留现有的生活文化是至关重要的。在十三号整宅，有很多拥有几十年历史的传统独立店铺。像整宅中的一家杂货铺，不论是店铺的布置，还是售卖的产品都有着古早的台湾风味。其他传统店铺还有：理发店、成衣店、干洗店、馒头店、旧书店等。十三号整宅因楼与楼的间距大，公共空间充裕，因此在一楼有很多店铺，特别是临近西藏路、万大路部分。这些店铺是整宅内最具特色的空间符号。不同店家串联出特有的空间文本，是在城市更新中值得被保留的文化。

以往文献对于老旧社区城市更新的讨论，关于社区文化与资产的保留之讨论甚少。简·雅格布斯提出，城市的活力来源于不同年代的建筑并存。然而没有社区意识的城市更新加速了既有地方生活脉络的瓦解，地方的多元性在拆除重建后可能产生绅士化的现象，形成高层门禁社区（张维修，2011）。即便老旧社区的建筑不能保存，但既有的生活形式、邻里情感等可以用文字、影像等方式被记录。

香港的公营房屋系统世界闻名。1953 年圣诞夜，石硖尾邨的大火令近 6 万人痛失家园。为安置灾民，政府于 1954 年兴建首批六层高的徙置大厦，这是香港政府兴建的首个公营大型屋邨。石硖尾徙置区的兴建、发展、转化和拆卸，见证了过去 50 年来香港的社会变迁。《我住石硖尾》一书，以照片、文字和复制历史档案的形式，展示行将消失的石硖尾徙置区的故事与生活面貌，再现战后香港公营房屋的发展史。虽然石硖尾公屋没能全部保留，但通过书的再现，让香港的公屋文化得以记录与延续。《美荷楼记》也是对于石硖尾公屋历史记录的书。书中用十五位旧居民在徙置大厦中度过难忘的岁月，展示了石硖尾特有的社区文化。石硖尾盛载许多人的故事，在经历社会变迁后，最终美荷楼作为唯一一栋被保留下来的"H 型"大厦，被改建成青年旅社和社区文化展示馆。

虽然十三号整宅未来城市更新势在必行，但作为台北市整宅的代表之一，十三号整宅可以但借鉴以上两本书的成功经验，将其四十余年的生命史和它独有的整宅建筑形式，通过文字、照片、影像等方式记录。那么，通过文化再现的方式，是否对未来城市更新的规划设计能产生积极的影响呢？

3　研究方法

面对自办更新的种种困境，本文以十三号整宅为研究对象，采用文献回顾、案例分析、田野调查与参与式规划设计试验四种研究方法。首先，分析世界各地老旧住宅城市更新成功案例，找出面对城市更新，既有的社区资产和邻里情感以何种方式延续。此部分重点分析香港石硖尾公屋的保存案例。其次，爬梳台北市城市更新条例，找出老旧住宅更新政策不完善之处，分析弱势住宅自办更新的困境。再次，进入社区与居民互动，进行问卷、访谈和工作坊，以深入了解社区情况和居民对于城市更新的想象。然后，根据前期积累的资料，探讨文化保存对老旧社区的重要性，用社区志的方式记录整宅文化史。同时通过居民的参与，加强他们的社区意识，鼓励他们积极参与城市更新。最终，通过家屋测绘，利用空间剧本、拼贴等方式让居民和专业者共同设计未来的家屋，提出从使用者角度出发的建筑设计准则，作为未来城市更新的设计指导，以保障居民在城市更新中的利益，让居民享受真正意义的"好宅"。

4　台北市整宅发展与城市更新制度

4.1　整宅兴建的历史

1949 年国民党政府迁至台湾，导致大量外省军民移入，台北人口激增。大多数市区内的摊贩亟须解决生计，无法获得土地，更无力兴建符合标准的房屋，于是市内充斥着违章建筑。20 世纪 60 年代，农业社会开始向工商业社会转变，第二波城乡移民潮随之出现。为配合升格直辖市，市政府开始把城市建设列为施政重点项目。其中为了公共安全及修建淡水河沿岸堤防，市府开始推行拆除违建并以"整建住宅"来安置拆迁户的政策。1962～1975 年间，整宅兴建总计 23 处，共 11012 户。南机场十三号场地便在第二期四年计划之"万大计划"中（徐韵涵，2011）。

1972 年，台北房价上涨，城市土地变得昂贵，原住宅贷款条件无法适应社会变迁，台北市府至此结束了"四年整宅计划"，重新拟订"国民住宅五年计划"。1982 年，政府将兴建国宅的责任推向民间（徐韵涵，2011）。1990 年后，由于住宅环境老旧、简陋，城市更新策略逐渐开启。

4.2　整宅城市更新的原因

台北市整宅住户大多为低收入户，整宅兴建之初为减轻住户的负担采用小坪数单元规划。居住空间原已不足，加之住户人口逐年增多，造成居民搭盖违建、违规使用等情形严重。又因早年整宅并未重视管理问题，公共设施及公共空间长期缺乏维护和管理更加速了居住环境的衰败与生活质量的低落。随着城市社经环境变迁，现在的整宅表现为：高密度小空间、环境窳陋脏乱、土地产权复杂、社经背景属低阶层，已然成为台北市的"新贫民窟"（方定安，2008：239）。

面临居住环境恶劣及边缘化的社会后果等问题，整宅亟须更新。台北市政府为提升整宅居住环境，针对整宅之城市更新政策均以拆除重建为优先政策。但相对于其他城市更新区域，整宅难以吸引建商进入，拆除重建的实质进展很有限。台北市政府自 1994 年颁布《台北市城市更新实施办法》以来，仅一处整宅（水源一期）重建的案例，且该案的更新改建成功却是因为捷运施工导致建筑物倒塌，不得不重建。实质采取最多的还是整宅的修整维护，并多注重外墙清洗、立面改善拉皮等项目。就目前台北市整宅城市更新的情势，十三号整宅的自办城市更新之路充满艰辛和挑战。

4.3　台北市的城市更新制度

谈到城市更新，必然涉及"容积奖励"。容积奖励是公共部门在城市治理时，将原本专属于公共部门权力的容积制度释放至市场，期待引来更多资金进入城市治理（杨少瑜，2007）。目前，容积奖励在城市更新中扮演财务可行的最佳角色，对十三号整宅的自办更新，容积奖励是很关键的。政府一直以优厚的容积奖励刺激整宅自办更新。《台北市城市更新自治条例》第 20 条，整宅得享有无条件给予至法定容积 1.5 倍的奖励。2009 年政府针对 30 年以上之中低层老旧公寓更新，给予最高 2 倍法定容积，以增加城市更新诱因。政府虽已放宽容积，但容积奖励不是万灵丹，由于整宅各户持分面积过小，以至更新后大部分住户仍无能力取得较大面积之持分，造成实际推动的困难（方定安，2008：239）。

根据《台北市城市更新自治条例》容积奖励第 4 项，十三号整宅周边缺乏属于居民的公共设施，现有公共空间多为非正式场域，如三太子宫前空地、婆婆自行搭建之棚架，故更新中可透过增加社区公共设施争取更多容积。及第 6 项，帮助既有违建户在更新中被列入考虑，也是争取容积的机会。

城市更新的游戏规则非常复杂，居民需仰赖专业者的解释与整合，也考验居民与实施者间的互信关系。就政策而言，政府极力推行老旧社区城市更新的目的是提升城市质量。而老旧社区住宅担负了台北市廉价住宅的供给作用，政府拆掉这些住宅，理当增加新的廉价住宅，以至市场平衡。所以应重点考虑，十三号整宅城市更新后，弱势租户能否顺利搬回社区？弱势居民是否会被排除？原有的社区网络能否保留？所以，如何让更新过程透明化，保障弱势居民基本的居住权益，维持现有的社区网络，成为老旧弱势社区更新的重要议题。

5 十三号整宅之规划设计实践

5.1 十三号整宅现况

南机场十三号整宅建于 1974 年，至今已有 40 余年，坐落于万大路与西藏路的交叉口，东邻莒光新城。场地总占地面积为 19653.38m²，共容纳 15 栋整建住宅。整宅内分甲、乙、丙三种户型，面积为 9、12、15 坪（1 坪＝3.3m²）。由于建筑老旧，社区存在诸多问题亟待改善（图 1～图 3）。

（1）管道老旧、漏水：邻长王先生家的厨房、厕所的管道严重漏水，导致墙面被水浸湿，出现掉皮现象。这种情况发生了很长时间，且很难维修，在很多家户都有出现。

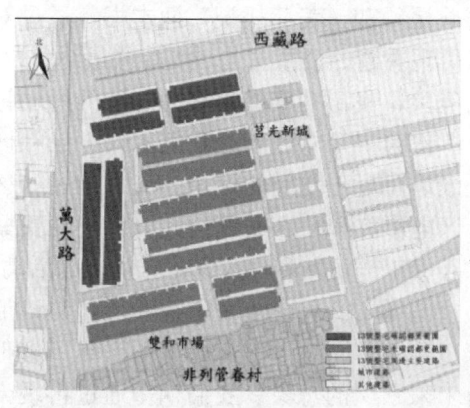

图 1　十三号整宅区位图　　　　　　　　图 2　十三号整宅街景图

（2）居住空间狭小：多数家户内摆满家具，甚至很多物品置于公共空间。室内活动空间狭小，常于室外活动。一层家户，大多占用骑楼空间。二楼及以上家户，将阳台向外推出，或占据原本就不宽裕的走道空间。顶楼家户，违章加盖现象严重。

（3）人口组成：十三号整宅原始居民以违建拆迁户、受灾户、眷村军人、受政府安置的低收入户为主。整宅内部弱势群体较多，高龄化的现象显著。社区内单亲家庭、独居老人、精神疾病患者、新移民居多，大多经济状况不良，有些没有自己的房屋，只能靠租屋暂时解决居住问题。

虽然有种种问题，但十三号整宅的建筑形态颇具特色，受到现代主义的影响。建筑物虽然内部空间狭小，但随处可见住户的巧思及创意，将空间效用发挥到极致。因久居于此，邻里熟悉，妇人聚集在旧书摊前聊天；老奶奶在自行搭建的棚架下，边看孙子，边讨论盆栽种植；充满历史与故事的三太子宫在袅袅烟雾中安详地伫立在社区中央，邻长就坐在桌前与居民泡茶，准备祭拜的供品；巷弄里传统的、自营式的小型店铺：理发厅、西服行、国术馆、馒头摊等，不但丰富了社区活力，也支撑着社区的小型经济网络。这种和睦的邻里情感和社区文化是宝贵的社区资产。

图 3　骑楼空间占用情况

虽然社区饱含浓厚的地方感，我们也必须看到屋龄老旧、室内狭小、卫生及排水问题，严重影响居民基本的生活机能。由于整宅位于交通要道的交会处，即将兴建的地铁万大线也在附近，地理位置优越。既为城市区域的发展，又为解决社区的居住问题，十三号整宅进行城市更新是势在必行的。

面对即将城市更新的整宅，居民们似乎还未察觉这样的变动可能会巨大地改变现有的生活。一次次的公听会与抽签日，居民们满心期待的倒数着搬进高楼大厦的新家中，看着华丽壮观的建筑示意图：大坪数、家家户户相同的设计——看似完美、现代、整洁，却好像忘了想象中对于家的样貌：可以打篮球的空地、种花草的阳台、自然采光的客厅、与孩子共寝的卧房、独立的厨房、可看见马路的落地窗——这些隐藏在居民们心中，对于"好生活"的空间想象。而婆婆自搭的棚架、施阿伯的三太子宫、古早味的馒头店、休憩聊天的小公园，以及热闹的双和市场，这些地方都将变成什么样子？

5.2　社区文化保存实践——社区志

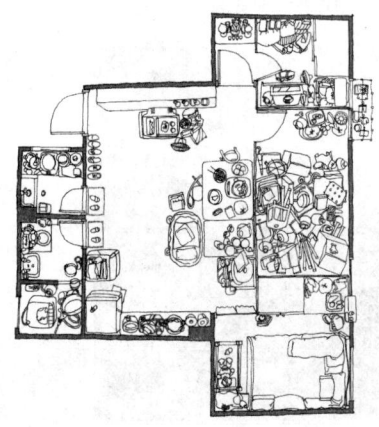

图4　小家工作坊：戴家测绘

面对社区未来的改变，我们"四菜一汤"工作室花费一年的时间，最开始借由十分钟短片的拍摄，进入社区，了解到十三号整宅面临的城市更新议题。同时间看到《我住石硖尾》和《美荷楼记》两本书，通过对社区生命故事的记录来再现香港的公屋文化，美荷楼最终争取到保留。借鉴这样的成功经验，我们期望借由"写志"的行动记录十三号整宅社区文化。作为空间专业者，我们不仅记录社区的生命故事，同时也记录居民对于空间的使用。我们透过社区活动的举办，比如：社区电影院和社区居民彼此熟悉建立更紧密的联系。随后展开"小家工作坊"和"大家工作坊"的活动。

小家工作坊（图4）以家户或店家为单位，访谈他们的生命故事、进行家屋测绘，同时借由专业者的引导了解他们的空间使用情况和对未来家屋的想象。我们期望通过再现人与空间的互动让居民重新思考什么是好的空间？

大家工作坊（图5）是处理社区公共空间的议题。我们通过举办社区活动，带动居民参与，观察居民对公共空间的使用。同时透过访谈了解在整宅的历史脉

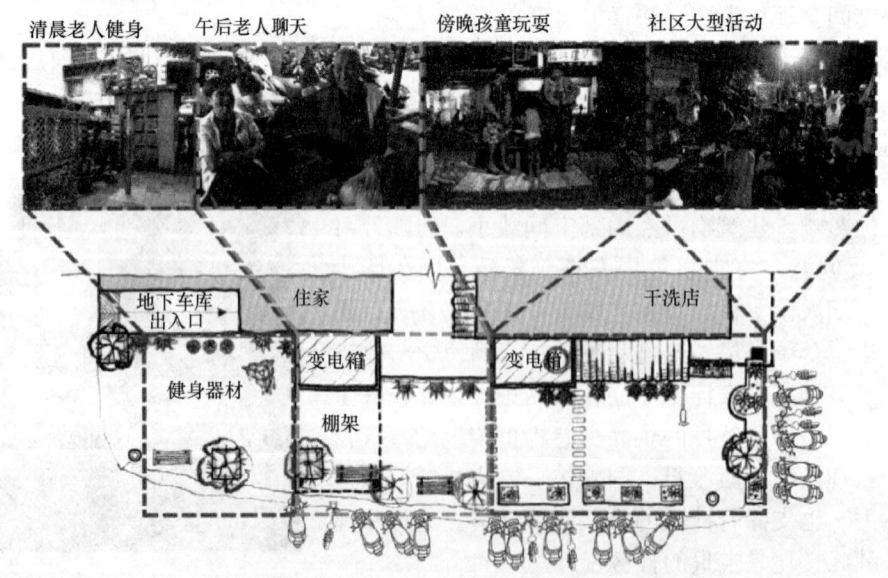

图5　大家工作坊：小花园使用情况时间切片

络中，公共空间有什么样的改变？什么人在什么时间使用了社区的公共空间？对于他们哪些空间有独特的意义？

最后，通过一系列的工作坊累积十三号整宅的生命故事，透过写志记录社区文化。通过居民讲述自己的生命故事，来再现他们日常的生活脉络，借由这种再现来让居民重新思考自己与社区之间紧密的联结与邻里情感的珍贵，从而加强他们对于地方认同和地方感的形成。当他们对于自己居住的地方形成一种认同时，他们开始渐渐形成社区意识，这样在未来自办更新中，他们才会主动去为自己争取权利，为自己争取未来真正的好家，而不只是接受一个大坪数的新房子。同时，我们希望借助这本社区志，让人们对于整宅社区的地方意象有所改变，不只看到房屋老旧、弱势标签，也能感受到这种特殊而珍贵的地方情感。同时，当有更多人看到关于十三号整宅的社区志时，会吸引专业的规划者注意到，十三号整宅作为台北市整宅建筑形式的代表是值得被保留下来的。

5.3 编写建筑设计准则

在为社区写志的过程中，我们透过深入的家户访谈、平面测绘，结合有关现有空间使用的问卷调查，了解居民现在的空间使用状况，随后编写出属于特定家户的空间使用剧本。借由空间剧本的写作，探讨家户现有居住空间的问题与未来的需求，最终编写出特定家户在未来新的居住空间中合理的使用需求。最后再将相似使用情况的家户归类整理，统整出符合使用者需求的空间设计准则，从而期望作为未来都更时，新的空间设计指导性的纲领。

6 结论

十三号整宅未来城市更新势在必行。作为相对弱势的社区，在利益巨大的城市更新过程中，他们的利益如何被保护？我想只有居民自己站出来才是保护自己最好的方式。同时，在城市更新过程中，社区既有的文化资产和邻里情感如何延续？面对这些议题，我们团队试图通过书写社区志的文化记录方式来应对。透过再现的力量，争取最大限度的社区网络保存，同时加强社区居民对地方的认同，形成共同的社区意识，在未来可以自主的面对城市更新。同时借由专业者的介入，在写志的过程中，通过深入了解家户的空间使用情况，为居民编写一套从使用者角度出发的设计准则，作为居民与设计师沟通的桥梁，指导未来的城市更新设计更符合居民的生活需求。

城市更新是一个漫长的过程，本实践只进行短短一年，未来还有很长的路要走，所以只是一个试验性的实践初探，希望借由文化再现的力量对城市更新产生积极的化学效应。同时希望作者在台湾的试验可以为中国内地老旧住宅更新，特别是北京胡同的文化保存与更新议题提供借鉴性的参考，期待作为空间专业者的我们从使用者的角度出发做设计。

致谢

感谢十三号整宅里长、居民的配合与支持。感谢一同编写社区志的"四菜一汤工作室"所有成员。感谢整个规划试验中给予指导的赖仕尧老师、邱启新老师、余映娴助教。感谢本论文的指导王志弘老师。

What is A Good Accommodation：the Experiment about Cultural Preservation and Urban Renewal of the No. 13 Community in Taipei

Lyu Hang

(Taiwan University，Graduate Institute of Building and Planning)

Abstract：The No. 13 Community is located in Wanhua District Taipei City，which is built in 1974. The community leader is promoting urban renewal actively，because those buildings are too old to live comfortably. However，the current politics of urban renewal in Taipei is not mature，which still have some loopholes. Faced with urban renewal，how to protect the interests of residents in those relatively weak community，like the No. 13 Community? How to continue the good relationship between neighborhoods? How to protect the community's cultural asset? In order to answer those questions，this paper will use four methods (literature review，case study，field study，and the experimental participatory planning) to study the effect of cultural record for the old community，and try to write design guidelines of urban renewal for old and weak community.

Keywords：Old residential，Living right，Cultural preservation，Urban renewal，Participatory planning

参考文献：

[1]　方定安．弱势小区更新政策取向之研究-以台北市整建住宅社区为例[J]．建筑与规划学报，2008，9.(3)：235-52.

[2]　吴圣洪．台北市整建住宅更新改建对策研究：以南机场整宅(忠勤小区)为例[D]．台湾：台北科技大学，2005.

[3]　周素卿．再造老台北：台北市都市更新政策的分析[J]．地理学报，1999，25：15-44.

[4]　胡皓玮．都市居住的社会排除与包容：以台北市南机场整建住宅社区为例[J]．台湾大学，2013.

[5]　徐韵涵．台湾可负担住宅政策与执行方法初探—以台北市为例[D]．台湾：成功大学，2011.

[6]　许德和．整建住宅住户社会网络结构与影响更新因素之研究—以台北市整建住宅社区个案为例[D]．政治大学，2010.

[7]　张维修．都市更新不曾发生：台北市的上流化政策分析[J]．台湾大学建筑与城乡研究学报，2012，20：63-92.

[8]　杨少瑜．从公私部门角度探讨容积奖励机制之目标与效益—以台北市违例[D]．台湾：成功大学，2007.

[9]　苏瑛敏．浅谈民众自力更新公私协力之议题与策略[J]．中华工程，2011，90：72-9.

城市动态历史空间的特征与保护
——以广州"老字号"电车为例

沈　欣[1]　余亦奇[2]　王楚涵[2]　卢　芳[3]
（1. 香港中文大学；2. 伦敦大学学院；3. 中山大学）

摘要：当前，在新型城镇化的背景下，城市历史空间的保护日益受到重视。长期以来，历史建筑、街道等静态历史空间备受关注，而对于电车这类基于长期运行而产生的动态历史空间的保护却往往被人们所忽视。当代城市社会研究正从静态转向动态，本文选取历史电车线路这一动态历史空间作为研究对象，基于实地调研、问卷与访谈，对广州历史电车线路进行研究。研究表明，电车作为动态历史空间的代表，其意象要素包括电车外观、路线、线路名称、站点名称、沿线景观以及沿线用地功能，其中最重要的要素都与城市发展密切相关，且承载着老城居民的时代记忆，因此该类动态历史空间与老城区有着密不可分的关系。与在未来的动态历史空间保护中，我们必须认识到旧城保护与动态历史空间的相互依存关系，并重视对功能的延续；在保护的机制上，必须在电车线路的规划、变更中更多引入"公众参与"。

关键词：动态历史空间，电车，老城区，历史保护，公众参与

1　引言

1.1　研究背景

当前，随着国内城市化水平的不断提高，旧城改造已经成为许多城市发展所要应对的一项巨大挑战。国家新型城镇化的发展目标中明确提出"注重人文城市建设，文化特色得到有效保护，城市发展个性化，城市管理人性化"，其中，历史空间的保护是十分重要的一环。广州是一个历史悠久的城市，同时也是国内城市化水平最高的城市之一，其旧城改造与城市更新等问题一直备受关注。在全国多个城市接连淘汰运营多年的电车这种公共交通工具的背景下，2012 年 3 月 25 日，广州市电车公司被授予"老字号"称号，成为老广州一个新的历史符号。

1.2　研究意义

在历史空间的保护中，长期以来，历史建筑、街道等静态历史空间备受关注，而对于类似电车这类基于运行而产生的动态历史空间的保护却往往被人们所忽视，此方面的研究较少。当代城市社会研究正从静态转向动态，因此本文选取历史电车线路这一动态历史空间作为研究对象。

旧城保护一直面临着完善城市功能与保留历史文脉的两难处境，引入对动态历史空间的保护为更好地保护旧城历史文化提出了一种新思路。与此同时，现今的城市规划工作往往偏离人的生活，对生活方式的保留关注不够，历史电车线路承载着城市生活文化的基因，对它的保护也体现了对人居生活方式的关注。

动态历史空间是展现城市文化的鲜活窗口，是一个城市的记忆载体，对它进行保护和传承，为打造城市个性、感受城市魅力提供了新途径，也为发展城市旅游提供了新模式。

1.3　研究目的

本研究选取历史电车线路这一动态历史空间代表为研究对象，通过对广州历史电车线路的研

究，旨在探索动态历史空间具体包含哪些意向要素，动态历史空间的保护价值，以及应如何对动态历史空间进行保护等问题。

2　研究方法

本次调研于广州荔湾区、越秀区、天河区及海珠区进行，主要采用问卷调查、访谈、文献资料整理与分析、实地观察与体验等方法。其中，问卷调查的对象是乘客、司机、市民，以实地发放问卷为主，并引入网络问卷的方式，共发放问卷 260 份，回收 233 份，有效问卷 217 份；同时，对政府、电车公司、乘客、市民等进行访谈，录音并整理记录，提炼有价值的信息。

2.1　调研线路的选取

广州电车于 1960 年通车运营，在 20 世纪 80 年代之前只有 4 条线路，现存线路共 14 条。101、102、103、104 路电车线路从最初的 4 条线路演变而来，其中 102 路电车线路完全保留原始线路，未作改动，因此选取其为主要调研线路。

2.2　调研技术路线（图 1）

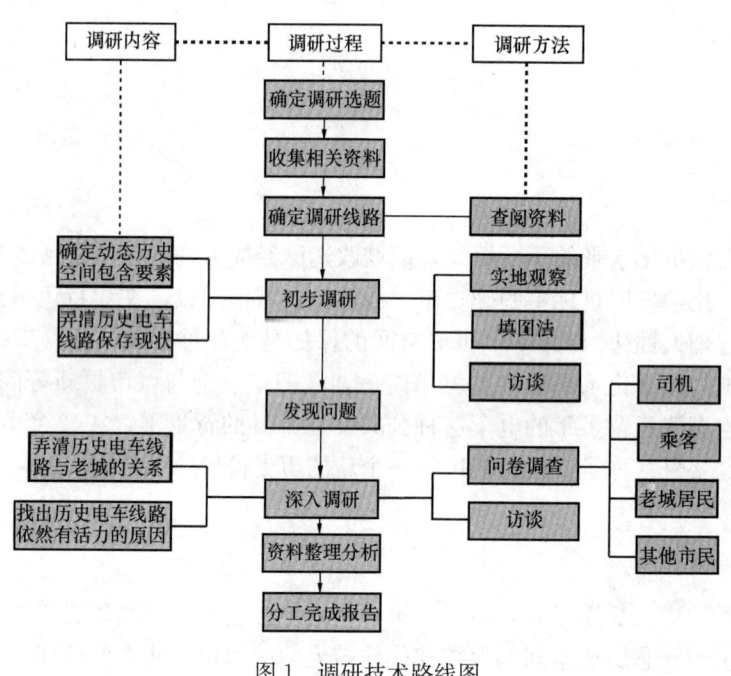

图 1　调研技术路线图

（图片来源：作者自绘）

3　动态历史空间的构成

3.1　文献查阅：空间三要素

整理相关领域部分学者研究（John Urry，孙施文，柴彦威）发现：电车沿着线路的运行形成的是一个穿梭在老城中的动态空间，人们从电车内观察电车外的老城，获取了连续的、不断流动的景观变化（图 2）。因此动态历史空间的构成要素不仅有电车的行驶线路，还有电车主体以及线路周围的空间标志及功能（图 3）。

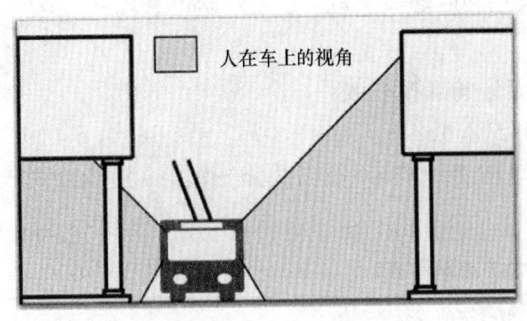

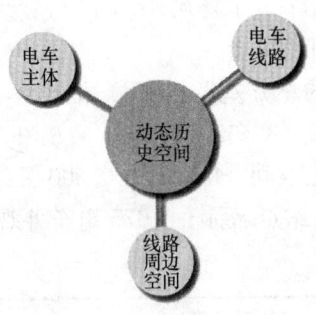

图 2　动态历史空间示意图

（图片来源：作者自绘）

图 3　动态历史空间三要素

（图片来源：作者自绘）

3.2　人群访谈：意向六要素

对访谈者关于问题"提及电车，您第一个想到的是什么？"的答案进行整理，提取关键词得到表 1。

电车"关键词"表　　　　　　　　　　　　　　表 1

选　　项	小计	比　　例
电车的两条辫子	29	69.05%
马路上的电线	15	35.71%
长长的中间带通道的车	10	23.81%
东山口总站，西门口等站名	25	59.52%
南方大厦、烈士陵园、农讲所、中山医	20	47.62%
骑楼	20	47.62%
去某地的常用交通	17	40.48%
去某地干什么事	23	54.76%
自己常坐的某辆车	13	30.95%
本题有效填写人次	42	

数据来源：作者调研及整理。

对访谈者用词进行归纳整理，发现电车作为动态历史空间的六个主要意象要素为电车外观、行驶路线、线路名称、站点名称、沿线景观和沿线用地功能。对此六要素的重要性进行检验发现，无论是市民、乘客、还是司机对于这六要素重要程度的判断，选择"非常重要"和"比较重要"选项的都达到 50% 以上，因此将这六个要点作为电车的意象要素是合理的。

3.3　定量分析：三大核心载点

历史电车线路在老城区诞生并与之共同成长，因此我们猜想，在上述六要素中最为核心的要素应该与城市相关，即沿线用地功能、沿线景观和行驶路线。通过 SPSS 软件计算主成分系数验证上述猜想。

由成分得分系数表得到两个主成分的具体表达式：

$F_1 = -0.168$ 电车外观 $+0.382$ 行驶线路 $+0.057$ 线路名称 -0.048 站点名称 $+0.399$ 沿线景观 $+0.432$ 沿线用地功能；

$F_2=0.517$ 电车外观－0.016 行驶线路＋0.395 线路名称＋0.430 站点名称－0.107 沿线景观－0.059 沿线用地功能。

由解释的总方差表（表2）得到两个主成分的加权系数：

$$F = 2.452/(2.452+1.348) \times F_1 + 1.348/(2.452+1.348) \times F_2 = 0.645 \times F_1 + 0.355 \times F_2$$

动态历史空间（电车）＝0.300 沿线用地功能＋0.241 行驶线路＋0.219 沿线景观＋0.177 线路名称＋0.122 站点名称＋0.075 电车外观

总方差解释表 表2

成分	特征值			被提取的载荷平方和			正交旋转平方和		
	总数	%方差	累积值%	总数	%方差	累积值%	总数	%方差	累积值%
1	2.452	40.870	40.870	2.452	40.870	40.870	2.060	34.339	34.339
2	1.348	22.473	63.342	1.348	22.473	63.342	1.740	29.003	63.342
3	0.695	11.583	74.926						
4	0.599	9.978	84.903						
5	0.532	8.867	93.770						
6	0.374	6.230	100.00						

抽取法：主成分分析

数据来源：作者调研及整理。

由上式可知，在动态历史空间的六个构成要素中，最主要的是沿线景观、沿线用地功能和行驶线路，与我们的猜想一致。

4　动态历史空间的保护价值

4.1　电车本身保存了老城的时代风貌

从1960年第一辆电车开通至今，电车车型为了顺应时代发展的需求做出了一定改变，但其最重要的标志——"长辫子"、架在空中的电线、集电杆——依旧保留，这些元素保存了20世纪后半叶老广州一个时代的城市风貌（图4）。

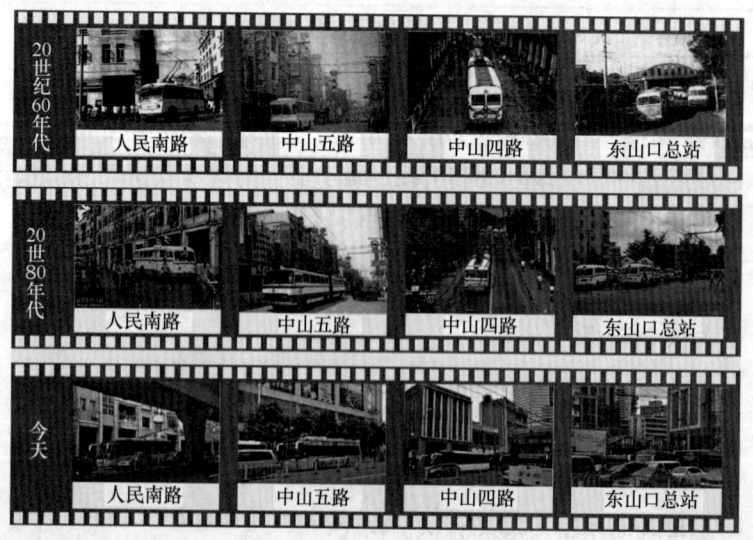

图4　广州电车今昔对比图
（图片来源：作者自绘）

4.2 沿线城市景观具有广州历史特色

102路沿线遍布广州的历史建筑（图5），以传统骑楼为代表（图6），与南方大厦、北京路口等标志性建筑共同还原了广州老城区的历史风貌，而电车为人们提供了一个绝佳的视角来感受广州，随着电车的前进，近代广州发展历程中各时期的城市景观渐次展现，有如一次时光隧道之旅。

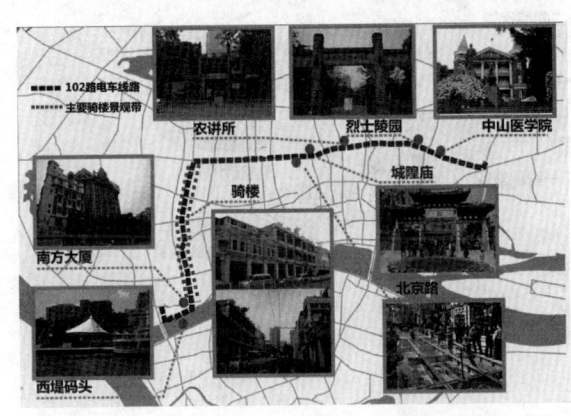

图5　102路电车沿线景观
（图片来源：作者自绘）

图6　广州骑楼分布图
（图片来源：作者自绘）

4.3 站名饱含广州千年历史

部分站名从古沿用至今，饱含一个地方的历史文化，见证了城市历史的发展。同时人们对老城区的认识和空间分布的感知，有很大一部分是靠站名来记忆的，即地名三个属性中的指位性，如到达农讲所，人们会很明确地知道东边是大东门，西边是财厅，加强了人们对老城的认知。

4.4 沿线空间节点构成了广州近代发展的缩影

102路沿线分布着近代历史上对广州繁荣起到里程碑作用的空间节点：十三行商圈、北京路商圈、东山口地区历史名校、人民路传统居住区等。这些空间节点如广州近代历史的缩影，述说着广州的发展。

4.5 电车站点分布密度合理、尺度宜人

在调查中，选择"线路站点与出发点距离较近"和"线路站点与目的地距离较近"的总和达到84.44%。另外，15.56%的人选择"没有进出地铁站的麻烦"，可见电车站点具有相对方便的特点。

分析站点周边用地功能发现，102路线路的站点位于各主要用地功能节点位置，与老城主要也是最好的就医、上学、购物、休闲等功能区契合度极高（图7）。

4.6 行驶线路延伸以满足老城居民出行

20世纪60年代启动的第一批线路以两纵两横的形式遍及当时的城区，并以城市主要轴线中山路为主要行驶路线。随着城市南北向的扩展，线路也随之向北向南延伸，扩大了两纵两横的覆盖范围，满足了老城区居民的出行需求，并且使老城与新城紧密联系起来。

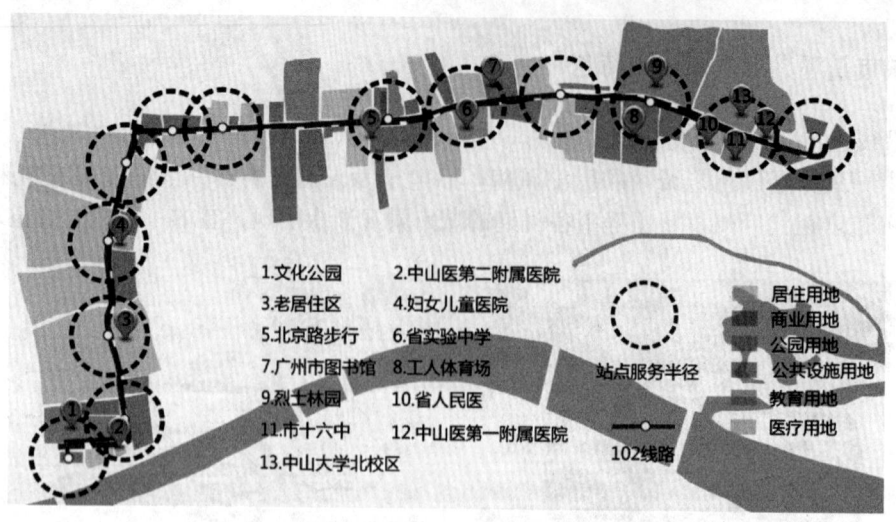

图7　102路电车沿线用地功能分布图

（图片来源：作者自绘）

5　结论

　　动态历史空间与城市中的其他历史空间一样，具有保护价值。在保护中，要同时从外观、线路、线路名称、站点名称、沿线景观、沿线用地功能六个方面考虑如何保护。

　　以电车为代表的动态历史空间符合老城的空间格局，满足老城发展以及市民的需求。它如同基因一样嵌入老城中，成为老城不可分割的一部分。所以我们在保护旧城时要认识到保护动态历史空间其实是保护老城十分重要的部分。

　　功能的延续是电车能够保留下来的深层原因，只有维持动态历史空间的功能性，才能让它在这个飞速发展的时代被保留下来。在今后动态历史空间的保护工作上，需要从它的功能入手，在旧城的保护上，同样要以此入手。

　　在考虑对动态历史空间的保护时，要考虑不同利益群体的诉求。在强调历史价值保护的同时，不能忽视电车对社会的服务职能以及电车公司的生存问题。

　　广州电车的发展是与城市的发展步调一致的，电车线路与老城格局契合度极高。而电车与老城历来具有互为特色、互相依赖的关系，二者的结合即为一种动态历史空间。因此，政府与规划者在进行旧城改造、城市更新时，一定要将电车与老城的关系纳入考虑范围，从而更好地对动态历史空间进行保护。

The Characteristics and Preservation of the Urban Dynamic Historic Space-Take the Old Trolleybus of Guangzhou as An Example

Shen Xin[1], Yu Yiqi[2], Wang Chuhan[2], Lu Fang[3]

（1. The Chinese University of Hong Kong；2. University College London；

3. Sun Yat-sen University）

Abstract：At present, under the background of New Urbanization, the protection of urban historic space is receiving increasingly more concern. For a long time, the static historic space, like historical buildings and streets, has been given great attention, while the dynamic historic space has always been neglected. In this research, the dynamic historic space refers to the space that is created by the trolleybus based on its long-term running following a constant route. Nowadays, the urban and social study is transforming from static to dynamic, and this paper studies the historical trolleybus and its route, based on field investigation, questionnaire and interview. Study shows that the trolleybus, as the representative of the dynamic historic space, its image element includes appearance, route, route name, station name, the landscape and land use function along the route. We find that the most important factors are closely related with the urban development, and carry the old-city residents' collective memory of the old times, so the dynamic historic space has an inseparable relationship with the old city. As a result, to preserve the dynamic historic space in the future, we must be aware of the interdependence between the old city and dynamic historic space, and attach great importance to the continuation of function. On the protection mechanism, we should encourage the "public participation" in the process of trolleybus line planning and adjustment.

Keywords: Dynamic historic space, Trolleybus, Old city, Historic preservation, Public participation

参考文献：

[1] 孙施文. 城市规划哲学[M]. 北京：中国建筑工业出版社，1997.

[2] Ferentzy A. John Urry, Mobilities[J]. Sandbox Journal for CanJSoc, 2009, 34(1)：188-190.

[3] 张剑. 保存广州城市记忆工程的思考[J]. 广东档案，2007，5：22-24.

[4] 杨俊宴，吴明伟. 城市历史文化保护模式探索——以南京南捕厅街区为例[J]. 规划师，2005，20(4)：45-48.

[5] 沈丽珍，顾朝林，甄峰. 流动空间结构模式研究[J]. 城市规划学刊，2010，5：26-32.

[6] 王茂军，柴彦威，高宜程. 认知地图空间分析的地理学研究进展[J]. 人文地理，2007，22(5)：10-18.

[7] 冯骥才. 城市为什么要有记忆？[J]. 重庆建筑，2006，11：5-5.

绿色建筑与建筑技术
Green Building and Building Technologies

专题一：绿色建筑与建筑节能
Special Topic 1：Green Building and Energy Conservation

纵向分割法建立绿色建筑全生命周期评估模型

赵春晴

（上海市建筑科学研究院）

摘要： 本文介绍了采用纵向分割法建立绿色建筑全生命周期评估模型的分析思路，即以时间为纵轴，将建筑所涉及的物质组成、技术组成等分割成子系统，对子系统进行完整的全生命周期评估分析后，再建立建筑全生命周期评估模型。本方法可在一定程度上避免常规方法中易出现的问题，而且最终的分析数据库既可以为建筑行业所用，也可为建筑相关的其他产业提供数据参考，从而有助于带动全社会各行业进行全生命周期评估。

关键词： 纵向分割法，全生命周期，绿色建筑

1 概述

绿色建筑是指"在建筑的全生命周期内，最大限度节约资源（节能、节地、节水、节材）、保护环境和减少污染，为人们提供健康、实用和高效的使用空间，与自然和谐共生的建筑"。定义中强调是在建筑的"全生命周期"内实现节约资源，因此有必要利用全生命周期评估理论对绿色建筑的环境效益进行评价。全生命周期评估理论起源于国际标准 ISO 14040，该标准提出了全生命周期评估研究的总体框架、原则和要求，评价结果关注的是评价对象的环境影响值。绿色建筑作为建筑业改善环境的主要措施和手段，通过全生命周期评估理论对其进行剖析，是评价其环境效益最直接有效的方式。

近年来，随着全生命周期评估理论应用的逐渐广泛化，对于绿色建筑的全生命周期评估研究也逐渐增多。最初比较多的应用是对绿色建筑全生命周期的经济性分析：张仕廉等提出了一套基于全社会视角的 LCC 分析研究方法，对绿色建筑的全生命周期成本进行了重新界定[1]；张倩影通过全生命周期评价从经济学角度对绿色建筑进行分析研究，并借助标杆管理分阶段对绿色建筑进行评价[2]；曹申等按成本发生时间对绿色建筑全生命周期内产生的各项成本进行分类分析，对绿色建筑的增量成本及回收期进行了研究[3]；吕赛男基于全生命周期成本提出绿色建筑节能技术优化方法，为设计人员在设计中实现节能减排提供了一定的选择依据。[4]后来随着对环境关注程度的日益增高，全生命周期评估理论有了更加深入的应用：郑立红等以天津某办公建筑为例，对绿色建筑全生命周期碳排放进行了核算并分析节能减排效益[5]；彭渤通过对大量建筑全生命周期能耗和二氧化碳排放计算的典型案例进行比较分析，总结绿色建筑的碳排放特点，分析了不同因素的影响敏感性。[6]

上述研究在建立绿色建筑全生命周期分析模型时，皆将建筑作为整体进行子系统分割，通常一级子系统分为：建筑材料生产阶段、建筑施工阶段、建筑运营阶段和建筑拆除回收阶段。表面看来，这样的分析模型很合理，也相对比较容易理解。但是，建筑作为一个很复杂的"系统"，包含的各种材料、技术、过程等分析对象数量繁多，而且各个对象本身的生命周期并不一致，如果将建筑整体进行分割来进行全生命周期分析，容易出现一些问题，比如分析过程出现缺项漏项、建筑组成部分全生命周期分析的不连续性、难以考虑建材使用寿命不一致情况等。因此本文提出了采用纵向分割法进行绿色建筑全生命周期评估，用一种全新的思路建立绿色建筑全生命周期评估模型，从而在一定程度上避免分析过程中出现的上述问题。

2　纵向分割法建立绿色建筑全生命周期评估模型

2.1　纵向分割法定义及特点

2.1.1　定义

本文提出的纵向分割法是相对于常见的建筑全生命周期评估模型建立方法而言，常见方法通常是以时间轴为纵轴，对建筑系统进行横向分割，可用图1概括。而纵向分割法是以时间轴为纵轴，对建筑系统先进行纵向分割，然后子系统再按各自的生命阶段进行横向分割，可用图2概括。

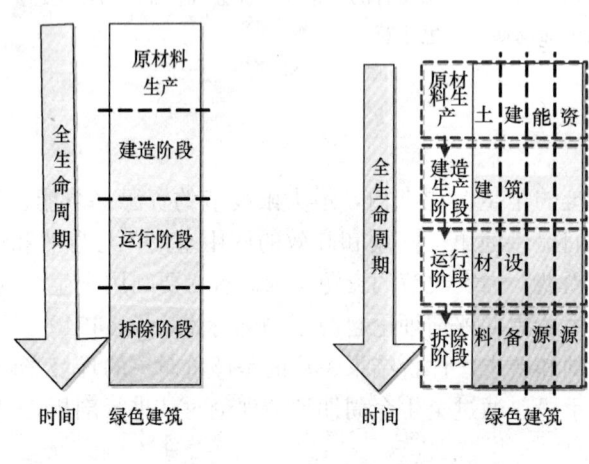

图1　横向分割法模型　　　　图2　纵向分割法模型

2.1.2　特点

纵向分割法的特点是先建立建筑各部品的全生命周期评估模型，然后建立建筑全生命周期评估模型时直接调用完整的部品全生命周期评估模型，部品的生命阶段不必按建筑整体的各生命阶段进行分解，保持其完整性和独立性。而横向分割法的特点是保持建筑在不同阶段的完整性，例如原材料生产阶段包括了建筑所有部品的生产分析，其使用、运行、拆除及回收利用等将被分解到其他建筑生命阶段进行分析。通过比较两种方法的分析过程，纵向分割法的优势主要体现在：

（1）便于考虑设备与建筑生命周期不一致情况。例如全热交换器设备平均使用寿命为10年，而建筑一般生命周期为50年，如果采用横向分割法建立模型，需要在建筑的各个生命阶段将设备或材料生命周期较短的情况考虑进去，增加更新换代产品全生命周期分析过程，并将其分解到建筑生命周期的各阶段中。如果采用纵向分割法进行分析，则可以直接增加或调用相关产品的全生命周期评估，不必再进行分解，分析过程相对简化。

（2）假设条件较少，提高分析结果的可靠性。例如在建筑建造阶段需要考虑各部品的运输过程，通常为了简化分析过程，会将建筑材料、设备和部品等运输的相关数据进行统一设定，因为再重新对逐个部品进行单项统计分析，工作量较大。但是这种假设条件对于绿色建筑而言难以分析建筑材料本地化的优势以及所带来的社会、经济和环境效益。如果采用纵向分割法，可在建筑部品的生命周期评估中进行相对完整且真实的数据分析，在一定程度上减少工作量，同时也避免了过多的假设条件。

（3）模型建立过程更具条理性，避免缺项漏项情况。纵向分割法建立的评估模型中子系统的分析具有连贯性和完整性，而横向分割法的分析过程对于建筑材料、设备、部品等组成部分而言，其生命阶段是被分解到建筑各生命阶段中进行分析，子系统并无完整的全生命周期分析过程。由于建筑组成部分非常繁多复杂，如果分析过程中梳理思路不清晰，比较容易出现缺项漏项情况。采用纵向分割法建立建筑全生命周期评估模型可以将子系统的完整分析作为基础，将庞大的建筑模型模块化，在一定程度上保证了分析过程的全面性。

（4）调整灵活。建筑全生命周期模型的建立是相对复杂的过程，建立思路和方法对后期模型调整有很大的影响。纵向分割法中子系统是相对独立的分析过程，后期调整很灵活方便，不仅可以较快地进行局部调整，也方便进行整体更改或替换，对于不同建筑方案的对比分析、绿色建筑方案的建立以及后期改造方案的确定都有较大的益处。

（5）数据库在各行业之间可以相互调用。建筑所涉及的生产行业很广泛，相关行业提供的数据质量也是保证建筑全生命周期分析结果质量的重要因素。如果采用纵向分割法建立全生命周期模型，可以同时建立相关生产行业的全生命周期分析数据库，如果相关行业已建立了全生命周期分析数据库，建筑模型可直接调用相关分析模型，同时各建筑模型之间也可以进行方便的子系统调用，从而在建筑行业及相关产业之间形成良性互动，相互补充和协助，为全生命周期在各行业的推广及应用提供帮助。

2.2 纵向分割法建立绿色建筑全生命周期评估模型具体流程

2.2.1 建立绿色建筑全生命周期评估基础模型

绿色建筑全生命周期评估基础模型即未采用绿色技术的建筑分析模型。在确定评估目标和范围后，首先需要对分析建筑所有组成部分进行分析和分类，建立各组成部分的全生命周期评估模型，然后再组建建筑的评估模型，基本思路如图3。

2.2.2 建立绿色建筑全生命周期评估模型

建立未采用绿色技术的建筑基础模型后，即可在此基础上建立绿色建筑的评估模型，通过分析绿色建筑所增加的技术内容，对基础模型进行更改，建立绿色建筑全生命周期评估模型。以公共建筑二星级常用技术为例，绿色建筑全生命周期评估模型建立过程中需更改的内容如表1。

绿色建筑全生命周期评估模型建立方案　　　表1

公共建筑二星级采用技术	基础建筑模型需增加分析过程	基础建筑模型对应调整分析过程
被动技术-自然通风	分析因改善建筑自然通风效果的设计所引起的建筑材料变动，并对增加的建筑材料进行全生命周期分析	调整自然通风效果优化后为通风系统节约的能耗
可再生能源应用	可再生能源设备的全生命周期评估	删减可再生能源所替代的能源系统的全生命周期评估
节水灌溉	节水灌溉设备的全生命周期评估	删减节水灌溉所替代的灌溉系统的全生命周期评估
分项计量	分项计量设备的全生命周期评估	—
高效照明	高效照明灯具的全生命周期评估	删减普通照明灯具的全生命周期评估
室内空气质量监控	监控设备的全生命周期评估	调整空调通风系统因采用室内空气质量监控系统所节约的能耗
导光管系统应用	导光管系统的全生命周期评估	调整照明系统因采用导光管所节约的能耗

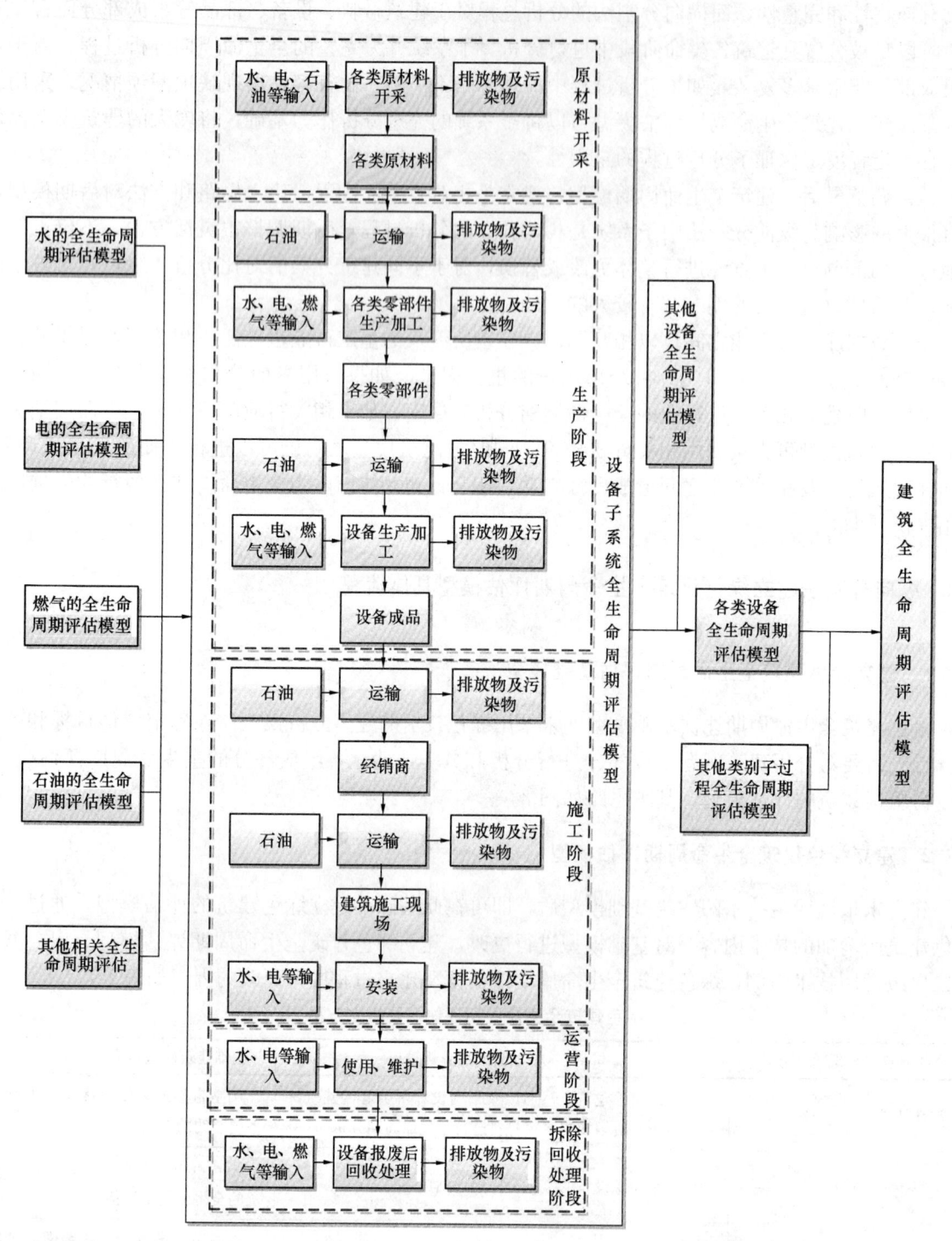

图 3 绿色建筑全生命周期基础模型简化建立流程

3 结论

绿色建筑全生命周期评估的实现是一个复杂且长期缓慢的过程，其所涉及的领域相当广泛，可延伸到全社会的各个行业。欧洲、美国等发达国家的全生命周期评估发展经历了近半个世纪，很多成功的研究方法和实践经验值得我们的学习和思考。本文提出的绿色建筑全生命周期评估思路与以往的思路不同，仍需应用到实际项目进行深入的思考和探讨，但在一定程度上可为全生命周期评估理论在绿色建筑行业及其相关产业的应用起到参考作用。

Establish LCA Model of Green Building with Longitudinal Segmentation Method

Zhao Chunqing

(Shanghai Research Institute of Building Sciences)

Abstract：This article introduces the longitudinal segmentation method to establish the life cycle assessment (LCA) model of green building，which is dividing the building model into subsystem with construction materials，technical composition etc. In the vertical axis of time. At first，the LCA models of subsystems are established，then complete LCA model of the whole building. This method may avoid some problems in conventional methods，and the final analysis database can be used in the construction industry，also can provide reference data for other construction-related industries，which help drive the society to conduct a life cycle assessment in various activities.

Keywords：Longitudinal segmentation method，Life cycle assessment，Green building

参考文献：

[1] 张仕廉，刘伟. 基于全社会视角的绿色建筑 LCC 分析方法研究[J]. 资源环境与发展. 2006，2.

[2] 张倩影. 绿色建筑全生命周期评价研究[D]. 天津：天津理工大学，2008.

[3] 曹申，董聪. 绿色建筑全生命周期成本效益评价[J]. 清华大学学报(自然科学版)，2012，6.

[4] 吕赛男. 基于全生命周期成本的绿色建筑节能设计优化研究[D]. 江苏：南京林业大学，2012.

[5] 郑立红，冯春善. 绿色建筑全生命周期碳排放核算及节能减排效益分析-以天津某办公建筑为例[J]. 动感(生态城市与绿色建筑). 2014，3.

[6] 彭渤. 绿色建筑全生命周期能耗及二氧化碳排放案例研究[D]. 北京：清华大学，2012.

[7] 朱嬿，陈莹. 住宅建筑生命周期能耗及环境排放案例[J]. 清华大学学报(自然科学版)，2010，3.

[8] 李骁. 绿色 BIM 在国内建筑全生命周期应用前景分析[J]. 土木建筑工程信息技术. 2012，2.

[9] 赵华，张峰等. 绿色建筑部品全生命周期成本与效益评价方法研究[J]. 施工技术，2011，23.

[10] 任国强，张倩影等. 全生命周期评价在我国绿色建筑中的应用[J]. 沈阳农业大学学报(社会科学版)，2007，5.

[11] 樊兴斌，赵飞. 绿色建筑全生命周期造价管理[J]. 合作经济与科技，2008，8.

[12] 王宇. 基于设计方案的公共建筑全生命周期能耗分析与评价[D]. 北京：清华大学，2012.

[13] 王上. 典型住宅建筑全生命周期碳排放计算模型及案例研究[D]. 四川：西南交通大学，2014.

Indicator Model Based Energy Efficiency Retrofit of Residential Buildings for Sustainable Urbanization

Rolf Katzenbach, Frithj of Clauss, Zheng Jie

(TU Darmstadt Energy Center, Darmstadt, Germany)

Abstract: As the center of life residential buildings provide us the most important living shelters. The design and technical standards of buildings, the energy performance and the interactive operation between buildings and inhabitants have a significant impact not only on effective energy conservation, sustainable resource exploitation and environmental protection, also on living comfort and well-being of building occupants as well as energy economics like financial worries of residentiary and governments. Domestic energy consumption connects the individual behaviors with the development of whole community, global climate and energy crisis.

This paper issupposed to figure out, how to achieve a sustainable living environment against the background of swift residential building demands, of energy shortage and environmental pollution driven by goals for adapting to a rapid urbanization process. The core of this paper is about how energy efficiency indicators can be defined and developed that can provide guidelines and standards to residential buildings during the retrofitting process or new constructing procedure. The general thread of this paper starts from background and current situation analysis which refers to the energy efficiency in European residential sectors especially in Germany, followed by concrete methodologies and Information and Communications Technology (ICT) based approaches for covering the improvement of building operation and maintenance with low cost investments, and then analyzing the impact of the energy technics and the user behavior also consciousness on energy and resource conservation with reasonable judgement. Based on them the energy-saving and environment-protective measures will be introduced by stating the purposes and significance of these efforts. The concluding part of this paper will be focused on results and impacts assessment through its primary coverage of reference value and social interaction for a sustainable urbanization with smart living style in green buildings.

Keywords: Energy efficiency indicators, Sustainable urbanization, Green building, Smart living

1　Introduction

With the rapid economic development and increasinginformation and communication technology the energy allocation has changed observably from the main part in infrastructure and industry decades ago to more energy consumption falling upon domestic sector, especially in habitable area which is gradually expanded and complicated during the continuous urbanization. The residential building sector impacts upon not only economic and social life, but also upon the environmental and climate compatibility. Besides a cutting-edge and tangible technical investigation for building energy equipment or system as a whole, pursuing an optimal energy conservation and CO_2 emissions reduction from our living units needs be considered and supported by many other aspects including the government and construction departments, the enterprises that work as energy providers and also the public participation namely energy users or households themselves, because their energy using behavior and energy saving awareness are vital for the total energy efficiency systems. From other point of view, it reflects if the urbanization has been developed in a sustainable and healthy way.

The average share of final energy for residential sector worldwide was reported nearly 20% until 2011 and yet a obviously higher household energy consumption in EU countries with an average share of 28.6%. From 2008 to 2011 this proportion in Germany was floating between 25% and

30%. In China this value was smaller than average with a share of 11%, because the government still gives the priority to infrastructure and industry for keeping a rapid economy growth, and the both belong to high energy intensity sectors. However, through long term investigation on energy consumption in residential building sector it was found that the consumed household energy was much more than we really needed for our living and production, which has brought out on one hand a serious finance pressure for government and also each household itself, on the other hand a fearful environmental pollution which is particularly concerned in most developing countries. How to manage energy consumption and establish an effective assessment mechanism to test the energy efficiency in residential buildings base on their practical local situation about energy supply systems, energy using patterns and behaviors, as well as financial support and energy policies etc., and it has become a research focus by all the stakeholders. As the precondition of the assessment mechanism the energy efficiency indicators acting as standards of measurement shall be defined and introduced to judge which energy consumption model is supposed to be more effective than others. Energy efficiency indicators are intensities, presented as a ratio between energy consumption (measured in energy units) and activity data (measured in physical units)[1]. In compliance with a series of indicators and local energy policies as well as available technical and economic conditions, a methodological approach for energy and resource management can be developed to serve for energy efficiency performance in residential building system. Our research work aims to figure out how to combine these indicators in a building unit generated by one or more different energy systems and how can the benefits and responsibilities of all stakeholders be balanced and coordinated.

2 Energy Involvement in residential Building Sector

Generally final energy consumption in residential buildings is allocated into many different parts such as space heating, water heating, lighting, cooking and application. The difference of energy allocation results from not only the climate conditions of regional areas, but also from energy using patterns and energy consumption models in each household, that would explain the noticeable energy using difference in urban and rural areas especially. With a fast urbanization how to achieve a sustainable urbanization and ensure a stable household energy supply and also reduce environmental pollution therefrom has been followed with much more interest than ever before.

In Germany, according to the statistics approximately 70% of final energy supply in residential buildings was consumed for room heating in 2011, behind followed the energy consumption for hot water supply with a share of 13%. The rest were allocated by cooking (and clothes drying and ironing) 6%, lighting 2%, 9% for information and communication technology (ICT) and other electric applications[2]. This energy distribution situation decides the optimization emphasis on heating energy system of residential buildings in Germany. At this rate, a few of energy conservation concepts and measures have been proposed to optimize its energy efficiency, particularly for existing housing construction.

2.1 Energetic Modernization

Energetic modernization was advanced in Germany as a strategy initially to meet the climate protection goals in residential sector, but with the implementation of different modernized measures for energy system in housing constructions the stakeholders have benefitted from them much more than expected. For real estate developers or building owners, the value of the buildings has risen and the attractiveness and rent ability of the real estate have been largely improved for a long term, which provided a great favor to them. For inhabitants more comfortable living environment were guaranteed with an increase of energy efficiency in their living space, at the same time for households they have more independence on the continuous rise in energy prices which could raise the disposable income of households and individuals obviously. Besides, the greatest achievement in environmental aspects was CO_2 emissions were proved as declined[3]. From another standpoint a successful energetic modernization in existing residential buildings is worth being further developed as a standard for new residential building construction.

Energetic modernization is in a sense a general definition aiming to recover the energy efficiency of a building system to its primarylevel or make it better and it involves the two main measures: refurbishment of building components, retrofit of the building construction and its energy equipment as a whole. Depending on the diversity of residential building constructions there are different modernization programs with separate energy efficiency standards that defined in German Energy Saving Ordinance 2009 (*EnEV-Energieeinsparverordnung* 2009). Table 1 illustrates the energy saving of the residential building construction built between 1958 and 1968 with 1.778m² reference area for 24 dwellings through three different modernization standards[3].

Residential building modernization[3]   **Table 1**

Option 1: Energetic modernization based on EnEV 2009	
Modernized Building Component	Descriptions of individual Measures
Exterior wall	Thermal insulation system on the old rendering, New fabric-reinforced rendering
Basement ceiling	Insulation on the underside, glued or dowelled
Top-floor ceiling	Insulation with walkable floor coating
Windows	Two-panes window with insulated glazing, Plastic window frame
Modernized Installation Equipment	Descriptions of individual Measures
Ventilation	Demand based exhaust air installation with regulated DC-ventilator: Air exchange at 50 Pa pressure difference (Blower-Door Test). 1/h
Heating	Combined heat and power generation (fossil fuel), new long-distance heating compact station with reduced power rating including buffer tank, control equipment and pumps Transfer station outside the thermal envelope
Water heating	Hot water supply with combined heat and power generation
Expected results about final energy demand	About 54% energy demand reduced

Option2: Energetic modernization based on kfW70-standard ①	
Modernized Building Component	Descriptions of individual Measures
Exterior wall; Basement ceiling; Top-floor ceiling; windows	The same modernization for building components like option 1
Planning performance	Additional planning-and construction services for high quality in details, Thermal bridge loss coefficient＝0.02W/ (m² · K)
Modernized Installation Equipment	Descriptions of individual Measures
Ventilation	Demand-based exhaust air installation with heat recovery and regulated DC-ventilator: Air exchange at 50 Pa pressure difference (Blower-Door-Test): 1/h
Heating; water heating	The same modernization for building components like option 1
Expected results about final energy demand	About 69% energy demand reduced

① kfW: Kreditanstalt für Wiederaufbau (*Reconstruction Credit Institute*), a German government-owned development bank. "kfW 70" identifies that 30% less primary energy consumption than which in a comparable new building.

continued

Option 3: Energetic modernization based on kfW55-standard①

Modernized Building Component	Descriptions of individual Measures
Exterior wall; Basement ceiling; Top-floor ceiling	The same modernization for building components like option 1
Windows	Three-panes window with insulated glazing, Plastic window frame (suitable for passive houses)
Planning performance	Additional planning- and construction services for high quality in details, Thermal bridge loss coefficient = 0.04 W/ (m² · K)
Modernized Installation Equipment	Descriptions of individual Measures
Ventilation	The same modernization for building components like option 2
Heating; water heating	The same modernization for building components like option 1
Expected results about final energy demand	About 75% energy demand reduced

2.2 Low-Energy Building

New residential building with low-energy consumption as a type of building construction was developed to use less energy from any source than a traditional building by a same or better living condition. New low-energy residential building is especially worthy for new developed towns or cities that aim to relieve the acute housing shortage caused by a fast urbanization. The building structure requires energy conserved concept running through from design, construction to operation and maintenance. In Germany, a proved primary energy balance in the entire year is the basic requirement for new (residential) building construction. In 1990 the first passive house in the world was built in Darmstadt Germany (see Figure 1), which as an effective energy-saving building standard was widely used with its fundamental principles: super insulation, windows with particularly high thermal insulation value, stringent levels of airtightness, air-to-air heat exchanger, minimal thermal bridging and total primary energy use (including domestic hot water (DHW), room heating and cooling, auxiliary and household electricity) shall be less than 120kW · h/ (m² · a)[4]. According to the measured heating energy consumption the first passive house showed a significant decline of more than 90% less heating energy consumption (just 9.2kW · h/ (m² · a)) by comparison with average consumption in traditional house 160kW · h/ (m² · a) .

Figure 1　Passive House in Darmstadt-Kranichstein, Germany[5]

① kfW: Kreditanstalt für Wiederaufbau (*Reconstruction Credit Institute*), a German government-owned development bank. "kfW 55" identifies that 45% less primary energy consumption than which in a comparable new building.

From the view point of profitability, utilization of renewable energy in new residential buildings is more cost-efficient than it is used to modernize the existing building. The German Renewable Energy Heat Act (*EEWärmeG*) prescribes that at least 15% heating and cooling energy demand can be covered by using solar panel, or at least 30% can be covered by using gaseous biomass and even 50% energy produced by liquid biomass can be fed for space heating and cooling.

3　Methodologies

3.1　Retro-commissioning

Retro-commissioning (RCx) is defined as "a systematic investigation process for improving or optimization an existing building's performance"[6]. The goals of RCx are proposed to assure the building and energy system to function well as a whole and make all stakeholders benefit from it. For building owners, RCx reduces the costs of building operations and maintain a well-performed building systems and related equipment; for energy providers or managers, a platform is created for achieve more effective information and energy saving measures by caring for building system, at the same the work capabilities of staff to cope with complicated household energy management can be improved; for inhabitants or energy users, energy consumption and costs are saved as possible as expected and their living comfort like indoor environmental quality is supposed to be optimized[7]. According to authors' work experiences with RCx figure 2 shows how RCx methodology is applied in the field about energy efficiency in residential buildings.

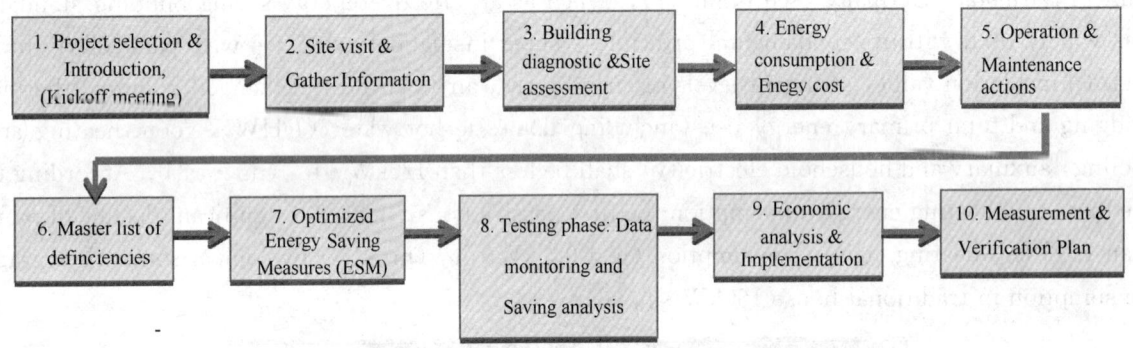

Figure 2　Retro-commissioning work process

(Source: edited by authors based on work projects)

3.2　IPMVP

International Performance Measurement and Verification Protocol (*IPMVP*) helps to tackle inefficient energy consumption issues through defining standard terms and suggesting best practices for quantifying the results of energy efficiency, water efficiency and renewable energy utilization in measurement and verification (M&V) plan to report a saving of the investigated projects[8]. Energy savings are determined in IPMVP:

$$Energy\ Savings = (Base\_year\ Energy\ Use) - (Post\_Retrofit\ Energy\ Use) + Adjustments^{[9]}$$

(1)

In our research projects two time quantum for M&V are planned: baseline period and reporting period for energy saving measurement according to the structure of IPMVP.

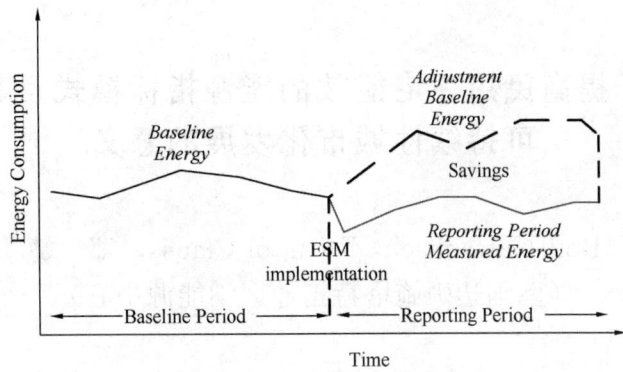

Figure 3   Timeline for implementation of M&V plan based on IPMVP[9]

3. 3   ICT-based solutions

A systematic energy management in residential buildings can be reachedthrough a good combination of two processes: energy output system and energy using system. The energy output system requires a strictly energy management by providers who is responsible to control or avoid the peak consumption of heating energy and water, and to manage the production and distribution of renewable energy and optimize the domestic energy consumption in line with supplier requirements and tariffs. For the energy using system, inhabitants play the leading role for reasonable and convenient energy consumption which depends on the energy conservation awareness of each user. It has been proved that a multi-level and multi-form energy coaching are effective ways to convey more energy saving information to inhabitants that have different educational background and income levels.

In order to verify the success of any energy efficiency optimization measure, a cost-benefit-analysis is applied to analyze all input and output of energy and costs which come about during the whole optimization process from human and material costs to energy saving in consumption and money as well as CO_2 reduction.

4   Conclusion

Urbanization is an inevitable development trend resulting from the fast economicgrowth. Pro and con of urbanization depends on how it can be rationally promoted with the request that any damage or negative effect is not allowed to fall on the existing cities' economic and environmental development. How to keep an energy stability and balance in residential building sector with increasing urbanization process has become a decisive factor for a sustainable and orderly urbanization, and will be achieved through a broad range of missions in all involved sectors, such as well-proved political regulation, reasonable and strong financial support, rational energy allocation, environmental protection and other social effects. Residential buildings as the fundamental living center of human beings have to be guaranteed with a high effective energy and resource models and their energy system shall be endowed with a well self-regulating function to deal with any problem or difficulty caused by excessive urbanization, which will be a challenge for a harmonious development of the whole community.

基于提高民用住宅能效的能源指标模式及其对
可持续性城市化发展的意义

Rolf Katzenbach，Frithj of Clauss，郑　婕

（德国达姆施塔特工业大学能源中心）

摘要： 民用住宅为人类生活提供了最重要的庇护所，其设计理念和建造标准，能源配备模式和运行方式以及住宅与住户之间的相互作用对整个民用建筑的能源开发使用和由其而导致的环境变化产生了很大的影响，同时也影响着居住者的生活舒适度。低效的能源使用模式会引发一系列的后续矛盾，比如能源经济状况恶化，政府和居民自身的财政压力增大等。民用能源将个人能耗习惯与方式和由此而引发的区域或全球气候变化以及能源危机问题紧密地联系起来，这就促成对该领域的持续关注和研究，目的是为了寻求在住房需求不断扩大化的同时实现其与环境生态的持续健康的发展，使得城镇化进程避免受到能源危机和环境的影响。本文将明确对于民用住宅的能效指标的理解与正确运用，由此根据作者的实践与科研经验提出方法策略去指导民用住宅的能源系统改造更新。文章将首先介绍欧洲民用建筑领域里目前的能源消耗情况（以德国为例），然后引入具体的方法论和以信息交流技术为基础的将能源有效利用的建议，其宗旨是保证民用住宅的能源系统能以一种低成本的模式高效地运行。本文的研究目的是提出一种模式，一方面能对民用住宅的能源利用效率进行分析和评估，另一方面也反映绿色建筑和智慧居住概念对城镇化的可持续发展发挥的社会效应。

关键词： 能效指标，城镇化的可持续发展，绿色建筑，智慧居住概念

References：

[1] International Energy Agency. Energy Efficiency Indicators：Fundamentals on Statistics[R]. May 2014.

[2] Private household energy consumption for living in Germany by the areas of application from 2005 to 2013（in TWh）. Data source：BDEW；Statistisches Bundesamt；RWI Essen；AGEB，http：//de. statista. com.

[3] H. Discher, E. Hinz, A. Enseling, N. Pillen. Dena-renovation study（*Dena-Sanierungsstudie*）[M]// The German Federal Ministry of Transport, Construction and Urban Development. Berlin，8 December 2010.

[4] Passivhaus Institut. Quality standard of passive houses[OL]. http：//passiv. de/.

[5] Dr. Wolfgang Feist. 15 Anniversary of the Darmstadt-Kranichstein Passive House-Factor 10 is a reality[M]. Passivhaus Institut，September 2006.

[6] Portland Energy Conservation，Inc.（PECI）. Retrocommissioning Handbook for Facility Managers[M]. Oregon Office of Energy，March 2001.

[7] RetroCom Energy Strategies，Inc. Retro-Commissioning Process Manual[M]. Office of Construction and Facilities Management，Washington，DC. June 1，2014.

[8] www. evo-world. com.

[9] IPMVP Committee. International Performance Measurement and Verification Protocol-Volume I（2002）[OL]，www. ipmvp. org.

辽南小城镇住居建筑节能一体化研究：
以大连金州区青岛村为例

丁晓博　赵嘉依　李世芬

（大连理工大学）

摘要：针对经济转型时期小城镇郊区土地置换后的农民生产生活方式的转变，以大连金州区三十里堡街道青岛村新农村住居设计为例，综合不同类型家庭模式和传统住居空间特色，在规划布局、建筑功能组织、单体构造等方面将建筑设计与节能措施相结合，探讨具有地域特色的住居建筑与节能一体化设计方法。

关键词：辽南小城镇，居住模式，节能，一体化设计

1　引言

在城市化进程快速发展的今天，小城镇建设越发成为政府和社会关注的重点。转型时期小城镇，城郊聚落居民的生产生活模式发生了剧烈转变，由传统的农业生产向农业生产加外出务工，房屋出租多重组合方式发展与转变。同时，随着国家相关可持续建筑与节能政策法律法规的更新与颁布，以及居民环保与可持续发展意识的提高，节能一体化设计也成为小城镇住居发展的大趋势。

辽南地区即中国辽宁省的南部辽东半岛地区，作为一个历史悠久的地域，这里处渤海、黄海之间，与山东半岛遥遥相对，地理位置优越。特殊的地貌造就出独特的文化氛围以及鲜明的气候条件：温带季风气候即冬季温暖干燥，夏季凉爽多雨。

本文以辽宁省大连市金州区三十里堡街道青岛村（图1）为研究对象，对村民进行巡访调查，总结了村镇住居设计面临的问题，如：村落无明确的共享交流空间、卫生环境较差、储物空间不足、停车空间稀缺、宅基地利用率低、缺乏满足基本日常生活的院落空间、私密性差、

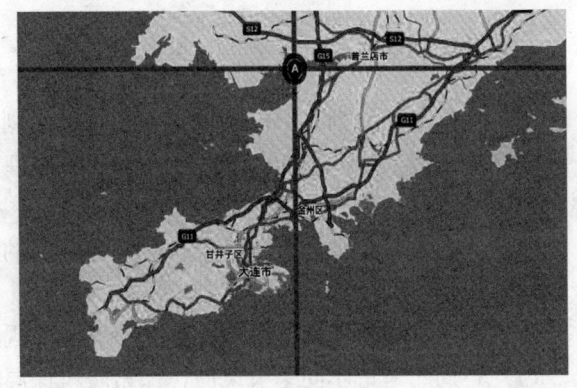

图1　青岛村位置
（资料来源：课题组自绘）

室内隔热保温性差、室内空间混乱分区不明确、能源利用率低等；同时也了解到村民对于节能技术应用于自家自户从而达到节能节财的意愿与需求。

2　多维视角下的规划布局

2.1　组合形式

为了更好地达到节能节地的目的，规划设计在传统的住居原型，即"户户相邻相对，独院独户"的基础上，采用双拼，镜像以及多联方式，创造更多的空间可能性（图2）。在"横平竖直"的平行街道规划的基础上，在局部采用独户或几户错动的手法，在平面组合上变化，形成围合空间，也同时作为住民休憩交流共享的交流和聚集人气的场所。

图 2　单元排列方式

（a）双拼；（b）镜像；（c）多联

（资料来源：课题组设计绘制）

2.2　规划与节能措施

在村落规划设计时，节能措施一并考虑在规划设计中，主要反映在：

（1）考虑设置集中雨水收集装置和中水处理系统，收集的雨水可并入各户院内进行种植的浇灌；

（2）考虑设置地源热泵、地下换热站等空间的可能性，结合共享空间规划出预留场地，方便后续更新与改造；

（3）考虑以不同组团为单位的集中沼气池的规划设置，考虑风向及能源提供路线等问题；

（4）布局时考虑不同季节风向，探索防风保温与组团规划结合以及风能利用的可能性；

（5）公共服务设施尽量考虑节能设备，如路灯考虑使用利用太阳能发电的产品。

3　建筑设计与节能一体化布局

针对辽南小城镇的住居研究与分析，对建筑单体设计进行了深入探讨。本方案建筑面积208.82m²，占地面积226.8m²。设计理念中包含了"人性化生长"的概念，即从小城镇住户的切身利益出发，以其需求为主线，以最大限度和最多变化可能性为出发点，以节地节能为最终目标，使住居从需求中"自然生长"出来。

3.1　院落布局设计

小城镇住居的探索不同于城市的别墅设计，除满足基本的居住要求外，通过调查与研究，辽南小城镇居民各户需拥有独立的南北院，而且室外空间中还要具有种植、饲养、停车、晾晒、纳凉、聊天等多重功能，并且有足够的储物空间。综合辽南小城镇传统住居院落形态和调研结果，在青岛村的农民住居建筑和院落关系上采取建筑坐北朝南，设南北一大一小两个院落，明确院落分工的方式：南院作为主要院落，院落大门偏向一侧布置，南院西侧为晾晒场地，南端靠院墙处设鸡舍狗舍，满足居民日常饲养需求，狗舍面向院门。南院东侧影壁后为种植区，闲置时为活动场地。院门外部设有门牌标识、信报箱等功能空间，满足住户多重需求。院墙开竖条冰裂纹饰条窗，内有院内绿植，既隐秘又通透，取自传统民居形态。北院为生活辅助院落，车库门亦在北侧。除作为辅助出入口外，具有设置化粪池出料口，加建扩展储藏空间的可能性，满足储藏需求（图3）。

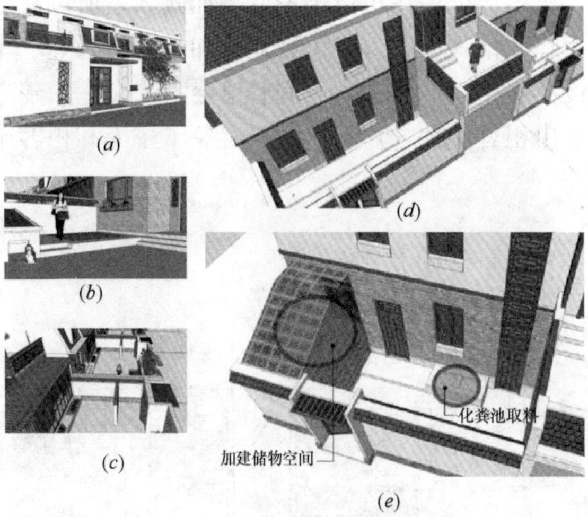

3.2 空间可变性

依据居民生活生产，家庭组织模式的不同，住居空间具有可变性，可根据模式的不同转换房间的功能满足不同的需要。

（1）三代居：子孙与老人共住，形成一个大家庭，儿女与父母各自经济独立但共同生活在一个家中，各自既有私密空间又有共同的活动场所，即一个家庭中存在两个核心。此模式下，住居入户一楼东边设有阳光间，入户西边为客厅，东边依次为餐厅和带有火炕的卧室为老人房，尊重老年人传统的生活习惯；同时厨房和餐厅都设在老人卧室一侧，方便老人使用，且一楼方便老人行动。二楼南侧卧室作主卧及儿童间，北侧为书房使用。二层面对楼梯同时设有家庭起居室，供娱乐休闲使用。二层室外露台于此开门，方便全家人休闲、晾晒使用（图4）。

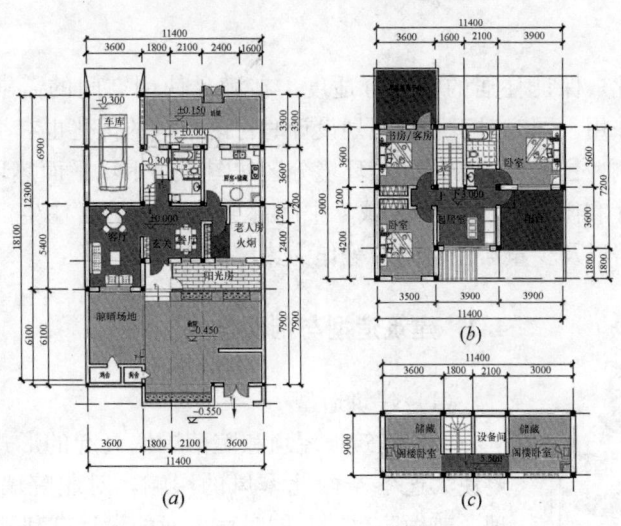

图3 院落空间
(a) 院门；(b) 狗舍；(c) 种植场地；
(d) 北院；(e) 改造后北院
（资料来源：课题组设计绘制）

图4 三代居
(a) 三代居；(b) 三代居二层平面；(c) 三代居阁楼平面

（2）两代居：此模式下主要为夫妇与尚未经济独立的子女共同居住，农村家庭有两个孩子的比例较高，考虑到可能出现一个子女已婚与父母同住，另一个子女尚未独立等多种情况，这样的家庭空间中需要的卧室较多。所以此模式下一楼仍然保留带有火炕的卧室为起居空间，兼做会客餐厅功能。二楼南侧卧室作主卧及儿童间，北侧为书房使用。北侧卧室和儿童房均可根据具体要求改为卧室或其他功能空间（图5）。

（3）小规模家庭居住＋出租：小城镇多位于城市周边，存在产业工人或外地农民工租住的需求，出租部分房屋可以为家庭增加收入，所以在设计中考虑到将部分房间进行出租的可行性。

在此模式中，方案可在北院加室外楼梯登上车库的屋顶平台，直接由此进入房间。同时房间内加设小卫生间，考虑卫生间管道会落入车库，建造时预留管道直接通到化粪池最佳。这种设计既满足了出租者单独入户的需求又避免了主人和租客南北流线的交叉（图6）。

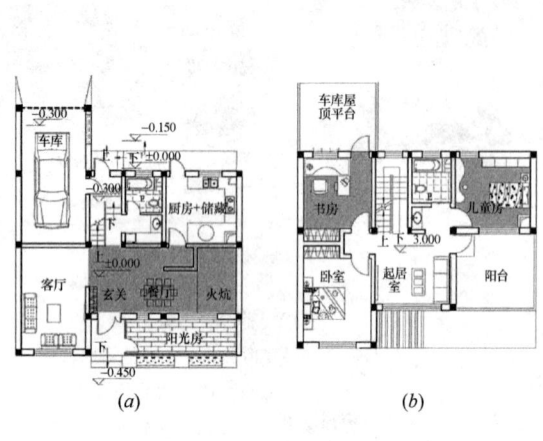

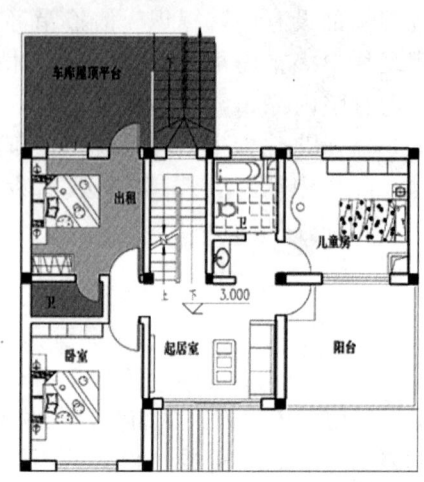

图5　两代居

（a）两代居一层平面；（b）两代居二层平面

图6　出租模式

（资料来源：课题组设计绘制）

4　节能一体化设计

4.1　平面功能

合理的开间和进深比，保证住居的室内舒适度。在满足使用空间的需求的基础上适当增加进深，起到了节约用地的作用，同时对于后续规划设计时村落结构的优化也有举足轻重的作用。

以本方案两代居为例，住居方案的平面热环境分区如图7所示：平面热环境设计大体分为三个区域，建筑的南部的客厅和阳光间为得热区域，中间部分为舒适的居住生活区，北侧主要为为车库、楼梯、卫生间和厨房以及少量居住空间的等作为热量传递的缓存区。

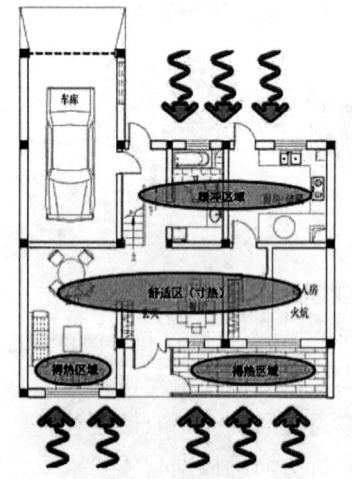

图7　平面热环境分区

（资料来源：课题组设计绘制）

4.2　建筑造型与剖面设计

（1）建筑造型

（a）建筑坡屋顶和院落围墙高起的形式有利于抗风，同时为避免大连冬季西北季风的影响，对北院墙进行了加厚加高的处理，兼做防风墙，同时坡屋面的设计有利于雨水收集（图8）。

（b）建筑北立较少凹凸变化，减少了热损失面面积，且北向窗户尺寸适当减小。为了获得较多的日照南立面开窗相对较开敞。南北立面的处理充分考虑了保温节能的设计理念（图9）。

（c）南立面坡屋顶角度设计时符合大连市光伏板最佳铺设角度范围，有利于最大限度的收集太阳能。

（2）剖面设计

方案剖面设计上，在屋顶处理上采用双坡屋顶，设计有阁楼和百叶窗，进行了通风设计（图10）。建筑通风设计主要采取自然通风，前面提到，为减少热损失，北向立面开窗小；同时为了获得较多的日照南向开窗较大，且设计了阳光房进行热量的储存。于是夏季温度较高时建筑内部将会形成热压和风压差自然形成穿堂风，达到自然通风的效果。同时，阁楼向南设计有高 550mm 的可推拉的通风百叶窗，有助于整个住居通风系统的循环。

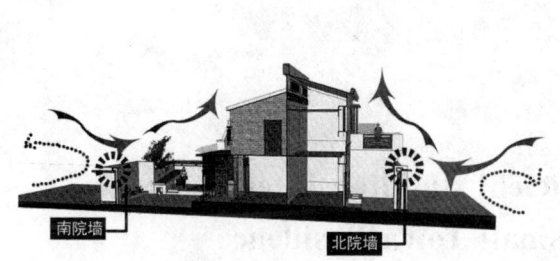

图 8 建筑防风设计
（资料来源：课题组设计绘制）

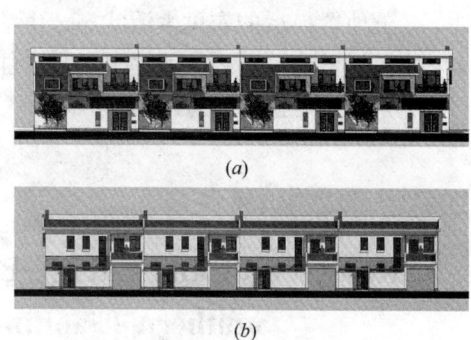

图 9 立面造型
（a）南立面；（b）北立面

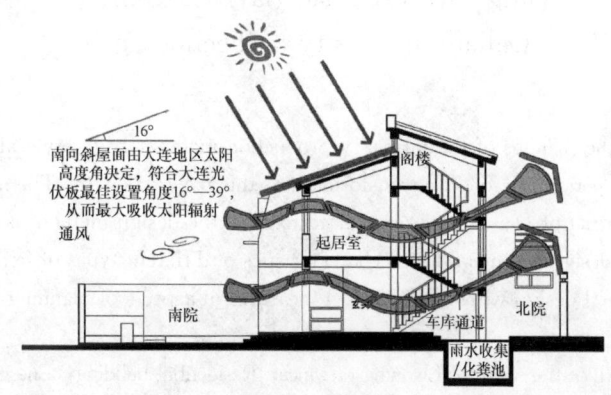

图 10 通风设计

4.3 其他节能措施

（1）太阳能：方案采用太阳能热水器，热水器设备置于阁楼上，集热设备支撑于南向坡屋顶上。同时，南向坡屋顶处铺设光伏电板，用于太阳能的收集，可用于太阳灶、太阳炕的使用。

（2）雨水收集与利用：方案利用南北两个方向的坡屋顶进行雨水收集，雨水汇集后经过落水管进入过滤系统，最终储存在蓄水系统中用于灌溉植被或生活洁厕用水。

（3）沼气池、化粪池的预设计：方案设计师考虑沼气池、化粪池设置于建筑下方或被原地下的可能性，留出了预留场地供其后期建设（图11）。

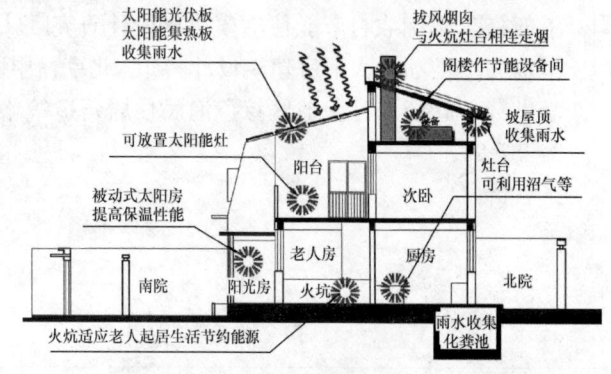

图 11 节能措施
（资料来源：课题组设计绘制）

5　总结

　　我国正处于社会和经济的转型期，位于城市郊区的城乡接合部的区域体现出城市和乡村生活模式的混合，土地置换后的农民生活状态、生活需求存在较大差异性，对建筑节能的认识也处于较低水平，如何在保留地域基因的前提下提高居住空间的适应性，将节能措施与建筑设计更加有机结合起来，是进一步需要探讨的课题。

Research on the Energy-Efficient Building Integration for
Southern Liaoning Small Town Residence
——A Case Study of Qingdao Village in Dalian

Ding Xiaobo，Zhao Jiayi，Li Shifen

（Dalian University of Technology）

Abstract：According to the changes of the farmer's production mode and life style after the land replacement of small suburb town during the period of economic transformation，this paper takes the The new rural residence design of Qingdao village in Jinzhou district of Dalian for example, to explore the design method of regional residential building and energy saving integrated design we integrate the characteristics of different types of family mode and traditional living space，combine architectural design with energy saving measures in aspects of planning，functional organization and construction of functional monomer．

Keywords：The small town of the south of Liaoning province，Residential building，Energy saving，Integrated design

参考文献：

[1]　李崴．辽南海岛旅游型村镇住居模式探讨[D]．辽宁：大连理工大学，2008．

[2]　宋盟官．辽南地区绿色乡村住居建构研究[D]．辽宁：大连理工大学，2009．

[3]　王新焱．冀南农村节能住宅模块化设计研究[D]．辽宁：大连理工大学，2011．

[4]　渠箐亮．被动式太阳房建筑设计[M]．北京：中国建筑工业出版社，1987：40-45．

[5]　李世芬，赵琰．辽南地区绿色渔民住居营造策略探讨[J]．大连理工大学学报（社科版），2008，3：87-91．

辽南地区农村住宅节能设计研究：
以大连市七顶山村镇社区为例

胡文荟　赵欣悦　高　瑞　黄小芙
（大连理工大学建筑与艺术学院）

摘要：本文通过对大连城市周边农村住宅的调研，分析辽南地区农村住宅建筑节能现状及节能方面存在的问题，并提出符合农村住宅实际的节能改造建议，为辽南地区农村住宅的节能建设提供有价值的参考。

关键词：新型城镇化，农村住宅，节能，调研

1　引言

随着新型城镇化的发展，城市的范围在不断扩大，许多城市周边的村庄在不断地被括进城市的范围，同时村庄自身也在不断地翻新改建，这种建设量是惊人的，也是值得我们关注的。

农村住宅的建设在保持高增长的同时，建筑能耗占全国建筑总能耗的比例也在不断增加，尤其北方寒冷地区，冬季采暖能耗偏高，建筑节能任务十分艰巨。农村住宅有其不同于城市住宅的特点，农村住宅节能问题的解决应当深入农村，通过调研发现实际问题，探索解决途径。本文选取了大连市七顶山地区作为研究范围，重点研究辽南地区农村住宅的建筑特点和节能现状等，从建筑布局，功能排布，围护材料和能源利用等方面进行调研并提出自己的一些建议。

2　调研地点选取

七顶山乡位于辽宁省大连市金州区，地处辽东半岛南端，物产丰富，历史悠久，村民普遍依靠种植果蔬发家致富，人均年收入2万元以上。七顶山乡由于其优越的地理位置始终处于城镇化建设的最前端，它紧邻渤海海湾，自然风光秀丽，已引进旅游开发项目，首批300户居民在2008年完成动迁，搬迁到集中建设的多层集合住宅中。本文主要列举两户建于20世纪80年代的和90年代中后期的农村住宅，分析他们的异同，探索新型城镇化背景下农村住宅节能发展进程与方向。

3　调研内容

3.1　村落的形态及建筑布局形态

七顶山乡采用了行列式的规整布局方式（图1），摆脱了原始的自由式的布局，住宅的朝向为南偏东25度左右，西侧大片农田，东侧为樱桃园种植山区。在城镇化的建设背景下，村中五六十年代老宅比较少，现存的住宅多为20

图1　七顶山村镇社区整体朝向示意图

世纪80～90年代后翻建，还有许多2000年之后兴建的二三层小楼。

3.2　建筑院落的组成

建于 20 世纪 80 年代住宅：院落由正房，厢房（杂物间），厕所，院墙围合而成。院落面积 114m² ，呈矩形，开间尺寸 9.7m，进深 12m，以储藏生产工具和农产品为主，布局紧凑，院落中没有绿化和树木，缺少公共空间（图 2a）。

建于 20 世纪 90 年代中后期的住宅：由二层的农宅和院墙围合而成，院落宽敞，由于住宅一层作为储藏空间，节省出了院落空间作为绿化和养殖区域。院落空间也为规整矩形，开间 20m，进深 11.8m，面积 236m² 。中间为水泥铺地，两侧栽种了经济果树，美化了空间。有利于夏季空气调节（图 2b）。

(a)　*(b)*

图 2　住宅院落内景
（图片来源：作者自摄）

3.3　建筑的功能划分

建于 20 世纪 80 年代住宅：平面采取对称的形制，形式简单，布局紧凑。中间一条走廊连接了各个功能房间，两进深合计五间房。虽然保留了堂屋的形式，但功能也被削弱，多作为饭厅使用，会客等功能一般被南侧居室的"炕"所替代。南北分区明确，南侧作为居室部分，北侧作为储藏间和厨房，北侧的辅助用房成为居室的冷空气缓冲区，增加了南面房间的保温性能。缺点是南北之间有墙直接划分成两部分，不利于主卧室的通风，容易造成夏季过热，这种布局在七顶山农村中较为普遍，它功能的分区十分简洁明了（图 3a）。

建于 20 世纪 90 年代中后期的住宅：随着农民生活的富足，大连地区开始进入楼房时期，此处农宅改建为两层，一层作为仓储空间，二层为主要生活空间，功能划分自由灵活，接近现代集合住宅的形式。堂屋在形式上的中心性已基本瓦解，南面中间区域设置宽敞的客厅，卧室的功能更加多样性，住宅内增加了独立卫生间和洗澡间，与采暖炉共同布置。较之前建筑功能更加丰富，布局更加合理。建筑最东侧留出面宽 1.2m 的长条形储藏空间，其作用相当于双层墙体，增强了建筑外墙的保温性能（图 3b）。

3.4　建筑的围护结构

建于 20 世纪 80 年代住宅：室内热环境和舒适度比较差，墙体材料为黏土砖和木材，砖木结构，外墙为 370mm 厚，内墙 240mm 厚。南北居室之间有墙阻隔，通风效果较好，南向窗子面积大，门窗框为木构架，开启方式为外开，因为木质受温度影响较明显所以木窗框容易变形，密闭性

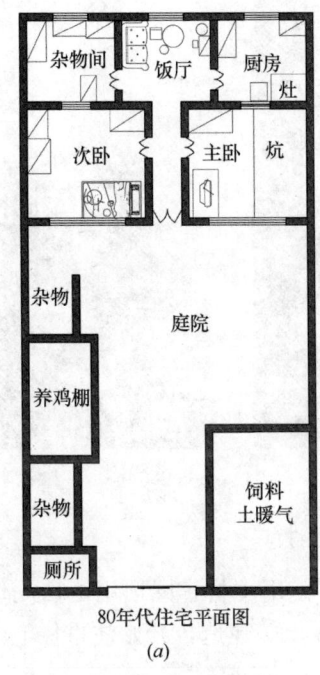
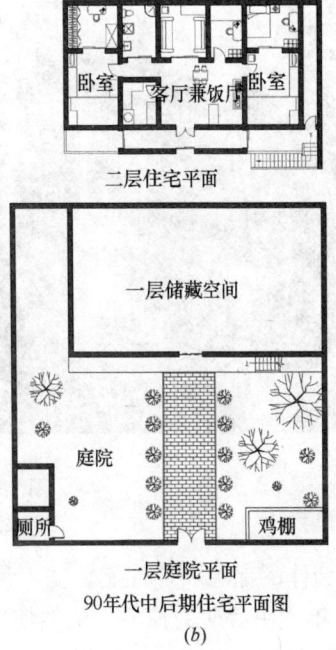

80年代住宅平面图
(a)

二层住宅平面

一层储藏空间

庭院

厕所   鸡棚

一层庭院平面
90年代中后期住宅平面图
(b)

图3 住宅及庭院平面图
（图片来源：作者自绘）

不好。冬季户主会在窗户外糊上一层塑料防止漏风。

建于20世纪90年代中后期的住宅：室内热环境有很大改观。墙体材料主要为黏土砖和钢筋混凝土，结构为砖混结构，墙370mm厚，室内外瓷砖贴面装饰，保温隔热效果较80年代增强。建筑造价增加。南向大面积开窗，北向开小窗，采光通风效果较好，窗框为铝合金，单层玻璃，密闭性比木窗要好。

3.5　冬季采暖夏季降温方式

由于大连地区属季风性大陆性气候，三面环海同时具有海洋性气候特征，夏季温暖无酷暑，冬季寒冷但是没有严寒，节能方面大连地区主要解决冬季取暖问题。

建于20世纪80年代住宅：主要的取暖方式是传统的火炕，同时以煤、秸秆为燃烧材料。住宅南北开窗，夏季以风扇为主要的降温方式。建于90年代中后期的住宅居民冬季有两种取暖方式，一是购买千元左右的"土暖气"，以煤为主要原料，用管道连接，采用"土暖气"进行采暖，这是主要的取暖方式，另外，房间中安防了空调，不过独自在家的老人称用不习惯，不经常使用。村民在二层入口处屋檐下加建了简易的附加阳光间，作为建筑入口前的缓冲空间，大大减少了入口处门窗的冷风渗透，同时也可以储存热量，有利于冬季室内的保暖（图4）。

4　调研结果分析

4.1　大连市七顶山农村住宅发展历程

七顶山农村住宅主要的建设年代大致能划分为3个阶段，其采用的建筑材料和建造方式都不一样。从结构形式来看，主要经历了土坯房—砖木—砖混这样的演变过程。20世纪50～60年代保留完好的住宅在七顶山乡比较少，且多已经残破不能居住。70～80年代的住宅约占60%，结果为砖

图4　冬季取暖

（图片来源：作者自摄）

混或者砖木结构，墙体的保温隔热性能较差，且门窗多使用木材，屋顶用麦秸泥作为保温层，墙体没有保温措施。90年代中后期的住宅，依然使用实心黏土砖建造，开始注重住宅的外观的美化，但是还没有意识到建筑节能的重要性。

4.2　农村住宅在节能方面存在的问题

4.2.1　建筑外围护结构保温性能差

在冬季房屋向外散失的总热量中，约有70％～80％是通过围护结构的传热向外散失的，约有20％～30％是通过门窗缝隙的空气渗透向外散失的。调研的住宅都没有做外墙的保温，且施工工艺差，极易产生热桥。所以在农村地区的建筑节能的薄弱环节首先是在外墙，外墙是围护结构中面积最大的，也是散热最多的。现在大连地区现农村住宅中广泛采用的普通黏土砖墙，这种材料的传热系数大，保温效果差，其保温性能还不如土坯房。其次是窗、门和屋顶的气密闭性较差，会出现空气渗透，造成大量的热量损失尤其是20世纪70～80年代修建的住宅，门窗多为木制，耐久性差，容易出现不易察觉的变形，造成漏风。铝合金或塑钢窗框，不易变形，但导热系数也大。这些方面都直接导致农宅冬季的室内的热舒适度降低。此外，南面的开窗面积过大，也影响冬季保温。

4.2.2　冬季采暖的能耗高

冬季的取暖方式是农村住宅节能的关键环节，经过笔者的调查，该地区农村住宅大部分家庭冬季依靠"烧炕"取暖，主要燃烧物为煤，同时还会大量燃烧植物秸秆，能源的利用率较低，燃烧所产生的浓烟直接影响环境，同时也对农宅室内卫生的清洁不利。

4.2.3　能源利用的问题

笔者在调研中发现，对于太阳能等清洁能源的使用比较少见，太阳能设计和技术的普及率不高，很少有家庭采用一些特殊的被动式技术来利用太阳能，太阳能热水器的使用率也不高，村民普遍对这方面没有了解，虽然询问时农户很有意愿安装，但是还缺少一个普及推广的契机。

5 农村住宅节能设计建议

5.1 建筑布局的整合

院落空间的整合：为增加院落空间的使用率，解决院落空间局促的问题，建议丰富院落的空间层次，在入口处制造高差，将入口抬高，空出台阶下的空间和叠盖的屋顶产生双层的储藏空间和晾晒空间，调研中发现许多实例，可以在新建住宅中推荐。

住宅平面：在满足功能使用要求的前提下应进行热环境分区设计，将储藏空间厨房等次要功能房间置于北面，形成热缓冲区，将起居室和卧室等主要功能房间置于南侧，保证获得充足的阳光。这一点在依然遵从传统住宅形式的 20 世纪 80 年代老房子中反而做得比较好，新建住宅中却往往被忽略。最后建议在住宅入口设计门斗，冬季入口是住宅的唯一开口部位，增加一个门斗可以有效地防止冷风吹入室内，也减少室内热空气的流失。

5.2 传统建筑材料的再利用

对于加强围护结构的保温措施，普通住宅最好的方式应当是采用最常用的节能复合式墙体，增加保温层，但是会大大增加住宅的造价，施工工艺也更复杂，农村住宅多为自建，难以统一的要求和规范，农民更倾向于选择低成本低造价的材料。20 世纪 90 年代后的住宅基本都是砖混结构，而例如夯土，草砖等传统建筑材料已经不被看好。事实上，与黏土比较，砖砌体和混凝土结构的运用使建筑更加牢固，但是他们导热系数也更大，所以保温性能反而是传统的土坯房更优越。现在通过对传统材料特性和构造上的改进，这些材料的强度和耐久性也得到明显改善，所以这些传统乡土材料在农村地区推广是非常适合的，既可以减少造价，对于环境没有任何污染，而且在使用寿命结束后不会产生建筑垃圾，施工方便，非常适合农村层数低，规模小的住宅。但深究根本，村民的观念中普遍认为砖混结构更坚固，所以传统材料通过改进后，即使各项性能已经有了明显改善，也应该通过实验房等展示，让村民有直观的感受，才能慢慢地接收，从而得到推广。

5.3 推进被动式太阳能采暖

被动式太阳能取暖是在不增加机械设备的条件下，通过对建筑布局、构造和材料等的处理，使建筑本身能够吸收、储藏太阳能，从而达到采暖目的，辽南地区的太阳能资源十分丰富，地区最冷月的年平均气温 -4.5 至 $-6℃$，没有严酷的寒冬，气候温和，比较适合应用太阳能采暖，而且很早就开始了被动式太阳房的建设。被动式太阳能房按照收集太阳能的方式分为直接受益式，集热蓄热墙式和附加阳光间式，根据农宅气候条件经济条件等不同因素可以选择不同的方式，或者将这三者组合一起应用。比如增加南面开窗面积，同时将窗间墙变为集热蓄热墙，或者将檐下空间改造成为附加阳光间，冬季加玻璃或塑料薄膜，夏季可以做花架或者种植空间，不占用院落面积。与传统的农村住宅相比，被动式太阳能住宅虽然因加强了保温和采取了特殊的墙体结构，建设期的投资会增加约 $10\%\sim15\%$，但建成后每年每户可节约 50% 左右的冬季用煤或柴草。农村被动式太阳房的采暖方式还可结合农村传统与灶炕取暖系统结合，弥补太阳能不稳定的因素，在阴雨天或者一年中最冷的日子作为补充。此外，调研中发现村民普遍对太阳能的使用有比较高的热情，乐于接受和尝试这种新型清洁能源，因为相比起燃煤，使用太阳能取暖的会使室内环境的更加干净整洁。

6 结语

农村住宅的节能设计，需要对当地进行实地调研，并根据当地实际条件，应用适宜的材料和技术，不能盲目跟随城市住宅建设，这是普遍认可的提高农村住宅节能技术水平的原则。不论是既有农宅的改造还是新型农村社区的建设都应当把节能作为一个指导因素，尽量从建筑自身的优化与改进入手，提倡太阳能等清洁能源的应用，创造"绿色宜居"的农村住宅生活。

The Research on Energy-Saving Design of Rural Residence in the Southern Area of Liaoning: Cite Qiding Mountain Village in the City of Dalian As Example

Hu Wenhui，Zhao Xinyue，Gao Rui，Huang Xiaofu

(School of Architecture and Fine Art，Dalian University of Technology)

Abstract：By investigating the countryside around Dalian，I analyze the present energy saving situation of the rural residence and energy saving problems existing in the countryside of southern area of Liaoning province，then I take some energy saving suggestions that fit with the reality of the rural residence，to provide valuable reference information for the construction of energy saving rural residence in China.

Keywords：New type of urbanization，Rural residence，Energy saving，Investigation

参考文献：

[1] 金虹，赵华. 关于严寒地区乡村住宅节能设计的思考[J]. 哈尔滨建筑大学学报. 2001，06：96-100.

[2] 朱兰玺. 山东寿光农村住宅建筑节能研究[D]. 山东：山东大学，2010.

[3] 程强. 北京延庆地区农村住宅节能设计研究[D]. 北京：清华大学，2008.

[4] 卢艳. 德国住宅设计中的太阳能利用系统[J]. 建筑学报，2003，03：61-63.

[5] 杨雪. 旅顺地区农村住居模式探索[D]. 辽宁：大连理工大学，2007.

[6] 宋晔皓. 关注地域特点——利用适宜技术进行生态农宅设计[M]. 北京：中国建筑工业出版社，2001.

日本资源循环型住宅全生命周期评价（LCA）工具研究及启示

王 云 苏 媛 范 悦

（大连理工大学建筑与艺术学院）

摘要：日本在发展资源循环型住宅的背景下，以全生命周期为视角构建了 LCA（Life Cycle Assessment）工具，比较全面地反映了住宅在长寿命、可再生和资源的高效利用这三方面所需达到的基本目标，推动了传统住宅向资源循环型住宅的转变。在发展绿色、可持续住宅，探索适合中国住宅现状的绿色住宅评价标准的过程中，对日本 LCA 工具的研究具有一定的借鉴意义。基于上述初衷，本文首先对日本 LCA 工具的产生、发展、构成及特点进行了阐述和总结；其次对中国绿色住宅评价标准的现状进行了梳理和归纳；最后，从相互比较中获得启示。

关键词：资源循环，住宅，评价工具，LCA，绿色标准

1 引言

资源循环型住宅，始于 2000 年日本经济产业省开发的同名项目，指以全生命周期为考虑对象，从规划设计到建造、使用（居住、装修）、拆除、处理以及再生（再次利用、再生利用）的各个阶段都要满足：①长寿命；②可再生；③高效利用资源这三项目标的住宅。[1]其产生从实践上对住宅的资源循环意义进行了技术解读，随之而来的技术开发与评价体系的建立则促使了概念的普及及理论向实践的转变。

在进行相应的评价体系的建构过程中，日本进行了较为深入的探索，开发了全生命周期评价（Life Cycle Assessment，英文缩写 LCA）工具，因其在综合评定建筑物的资源循环性能方面所表现出的优越性，成为现今主流的资源循环住宅评价工具。[2]

2 日本的 LCA 工具

2.1 产生和发展

LCA 的概念源自 1963 年的世界能源大会[3]，2002 年，国际标准化组织为其制定了 ISO 140140 标准，才使得它的方法论得以规范化。[4]日本对 LCA 较为深入的研究始于 20 世纪 90 年代末（1995～1997 年），研究展开于日本建立资源循环型社会的大背景下，得到了日本通商产业省和 250 个国家性质的产业及学术组织的支持，旨在为日本全社会建立完善的 LCA 工具及全套数据库，制定 LCA 的应用规程，最终促使了 LCA 工具在日本的推广。[5]

这项遍及日本全社会的研究项目在建筑领域便体现为 2003 年由日本建筑学会（AIJ）颁布的《建筑物的 LCA 指标》，随即开发的 AIJ-LCA 工具，成为适用于建筑可持续性能的评价工具。[6]相比于以往的建筑标准，它是完全针对建筑资源循环性能的评价工具。适逢以全生命周期为考虑对象的资源循环型住宅项目在日本的推广，住宅的 LCA 工具成为官方实施激励机制时的判断工具和住宅普及过程中的启蒙工具。[1]

2.2 体系构成

2.2.1 体系内涵

传统的 LCA 工具包含诸多评价指标，有 LCE（Life Cycle Energy）、$LCCO_2$（Life Cycle CO_2）、

LCSO$_X$（Life Cycle SO$_x$）和 LCNO$_X$（Life Cycle NOx），最常用的 LCE 和 LCCO$_2$ 以降低能耗和防止地球变暖为目的。在考虑了建筑的全生命周期过程的资源投入量和废弃物的发生量等因素后，又导入 LCR（Life Cycle Resource）和 LCW（Life Cycle Waste），LCA 的内容得到了进一步的扩充（图1）[7]。

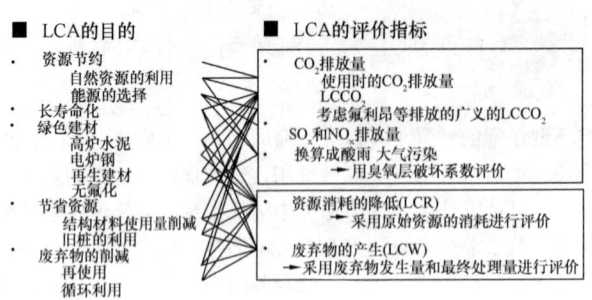

图1　LCA 工具的组成

［资料来源：资源循環性の評価機能を持つLCAツールの概要：
建物の資源循環性評価手法の開発その1（環境工学）］

2.2.2　指标内容

评价指标由大、中、小三个层级构成，分别对应了 5 个大项目，11 个中项目和若干小项目。5 个大项目依次为：（1）原始资源投入量的削减；（2）建设废弃物的最终处理量的削减；（3）耐用年数的提高（长寿命化）；（4-1）能源消耗量和 CO$_2$ 排放量的削减；（4-2）降低运行阶段的能源消耗。大项目的设定围绕着资源循环型住宅的三个目标——长寿命目标、可再生目标和资源的高效利用目标对住宅进行全面评价（图2）。[8]

2.2.3　评分方法及评价等级

评价实施过程分为评分和等级评定两大步骤。

评分是对各大项目中所包含的各子项目逐条计分的过程。日本建筑学会对各个大项目所包含的子项目的分值有所设定，对各大项目在评价体系的总体中所占的权重亦有所考虑（图3）。[8]

在评分结束后，依据最终总得分来评定一个住宅项目所处的等级。日本建筑学会对 LCA 评价体系内的项目等级做了相关规定，共分五级，随着等级的降低，所考虑和采用的技术也以此降低：最高级别 4 级为理想的资源循环型住宅等级，在日本，至今还没有住宅能够达到该等级，可以说它是资源循环型住宅未来的目标；3 级为采用现有技术实现的最高水平的资源循环等级；2 级为考虑了一定程度的资源循环的等级；1 级为考虑了最低限度的资源循环的等级；最低等级 0 级则为完全没有考虑资源循环的等级（图3）[4]。在具体的评价实施过程中，依靠开发相应的软件来进行评分测算。上述的评分方法和等级判断方法作为软件编写的逻辑，最终的评价过程仅需对各项数据进行录入，即生成相应的各个项目所对应的分值及等级。[1]

2.3　体系特点

作为具有可持续性质的住宅评价工具，与其他类似的评价体系相比，LCA 工具紧紧围绕着资源循环型住宅的实现目标，具有诸多自身的特点，具体体现在：

（1）关注住宅的全生命周期。以往的评价标准多关注规划与设计阶段的内容，而 LCA 工具则关注住宅的全生命周期，其评价内容涵盖了住宅的建造、使用（居住、装修）、拆除、处理以及再生等各个阶段。如对于能耗方面的评价，从指标内容可知，不仅考虑了对建造时能耗的评价，亦考虑了对运输、材料生产和使用时的能耗的评价。

LCA工具评价表(集合住宅)

大项目	中项目	小项目		
1.原始资源投入量的削减	1-1再利用、再生材料的使用	1-1-1地基、桩采用再利用、再生材料		
		1-1-2墙体采用再利用、再生材料		
		1-1-3外装修材料采用再利用、再生材料		
		1-1-4内装材料采用再利用、再生材料		
		1-1-5设备材料采用再利用、再生材料		
		1-1-6其他外部设施采用再利用、再生材料		
2.建设废弃物的最终处理量的削减	2-1促进废弃物的减排量(reduce)	2-1-1减少新建、改造时的建筑废弃物		
	2-2促进再利用和再生处理(recycle)	2-2-1各阶段recycle的促进	地基、桩	
			墙体构成材料	
			外装材料	
			内装材料	
			设备材料	
			其他外部设施	
			利于各部分再生的构造方法的采用	
			利于拆除的结合方式的选用	
		2-2-2 cascade recycle的促进	材料recycle的促进	地基、桩
				墙体构成材料
				外装材料
				内装材料
				设备材料
				其他外部设施
				利于再生的构造方法的应用
				分离解体的容易性
			保温recycle的促进	地基、桩
				墙体构成材料
				外装材料
				内装材料
				设备材料
				其他外部设施
				分离解体的容易性
3.耐用年数的提高(长寿命化)	3-1提高物理耐久性	3-1-1基础、桩/墙体的高耐久性		
		3-1-2外装的高耐久性		
		3-1-3内装的高耐久性		
		3-1-4设备材料的高耐久性		
		3-1-5基础、桩/墙体的延命化		
		3-1-6外装的延命化		
		3-1-7内装的延命化		
		3-1-8设备材料的延命化		
	3-2提高功能耐久性	3-2-1大跨度构造		
		3-2-2 高层高		
		3-2-3 易于变更的内装		
		3-2-4 易于变更的设备		
	3-3援助机制的确立	3-3-1 运营维护体制的完善		
		3-3-2 改造体制的完善		
		3-3-3 维护管理、保证制度的有无		
		3-3-4 信息管理系统的完善		
4-1能源消费量和CO$_2$排放量的削减	4-1-1建筑建造过程中能源消费量、CO$_2$排放量的削减	4-1-1-1设备材料制造时	Recycle材料制造时能源消费量	
			原始材料制造时能源消费量	
			Recycle材料制造时CO$_2$排放量	
			原始材料制造时CO$_2$排放量	
		4-1-1-2建造施工时	低燃费卡车的使用	
			卡车运载能力的提升	
			输送形式的变更	
			当地建材的使用	
			当地建材的使用	
	4-1-2拆除时能源	4-1-2-1废弃物处理过程中能源消费和CO$_2$的排放量	节能处理技术的采用	
		4-1-2-2拆除过程中能源消费量和CO$_2$的排放量	低燃费卡车的使用	
			卡车运载能力的提升	
			输送形式的变更	
			低燃费重型机械的使用	
4-2降低运行阶段的能源消耗	4-2-1建筑物的热负荷抑制	高气密性		
		高隔热性		
	4-2-2自然能源的利用	自然能源的直接利用		
		自然能源的间接利用		
	4-2-3设备系统的高效化	空调设备		
		换气设备		
		照明设备		
		热水供给设备		
		电梯设备		
		能源利用一体化设备		

图 2　日本集合住宅的 LCA 工具评价表

[资料来源：1.（日）茂呂隆，丸山則義，木戸一成，資源循環型住宅のラベリングツールの開発（その1）（環境性能評価，環境工学 I），学術講演梗概集．D-1，環境工学 I，1077-1078，2004-07-31

2.（日）清家刚，（日）秋元孝之主编，日本资源循环型住宅技术开发项目组编辑．可持续性住宅建设［M］．北京：机械工业出版社，2005]

（2）关注住宅的长寿命性能。长寿命作为资源循环型住宅的三项目标之一，对其评价包含了多重内容。项目 3-耐用年数的提高是专门针对住宅的长寿命化方面的内容进行的评价。其中不仅包含了传统评价体系中常见的对于物理耐久性的评价，还包含了对住宅的功能耐久性和援助机制的评价

大项目	分数
1.原始资源投入量的削减	30
2.建设废弃物的最终处理量的削减	30
3.耐用年数的提高（长寿命化）	20
4.能源消费量和CO_2排放量的削减	20

等级	评价内容
4	理想的资源循型住宅等级（目前还未实现）
3	采用现有技术实现的最高水平的资源循环等级
2	考虑了一定程度的资源循环的等级
1	考虑了最低限度的资源循环的等级
0	完全没有考虑资源循环的等级

图 3　评价等级和评分方法

［资料来源：（日）清家刚，（日）秋元孝之主编，日本资源循环型住宅技术开发项目组编辑.
可持续性住宅建设［M］. 北京：机械工业出版社，2005.］

内容。

（3）关注住宅的可再生性能。大项目 1-原始资源投入量的削减和大项目 2-建设废弃物的最终处理量的削减是对住宅可再生目标的评价。通过对其下具体的中项目和小项目的解读可知可再生部分主要涵盖了减量化（Reduce）、再利用（Reuse）和再生利用（Recycle）三方面的内容，即通常所说的 3R 技术。可见 LCA 工具的体系设定内容比较全面地反映了住宅的可再生性能——不仅从资源的来路和去路两个方向进行了评测，还对可再生的三种具体技术形式进行了分类评价。

（4）关注住宅高效利用资源的性能。资源循环型住宅的第三个重要目标为资源的高效利用。在这里，资源的高效利用意味着住宅的低能耗。LCA 工具中的大项目 4-1-能源消费量和 CO_2 排放量的削减和大项目 4-2-降低运行阶段的能源消耗为对高效利用资源目标的评价。

3　启示

日本在建立资源循环型住宅的背景下发展了 LCA 工具，在当前中国发展可持续住宅的背景下，研究其体系的构成与特点颇有启发和借鉴意义。

中国现行的与可持续建筑相关的标准有《绿色建筑评价标准》，它以"四节一环保"目标作指导，为绿色建筑的等级认证的提供了依据。其指标体系包含了七大项：节地与室外环境、节能与能源利用、节水与水资源利用、节材与材料资源利用、室内环境质量、运行管理和施工管理。现行的新版"绿标"从 2015 年 1 月 1 日起实施，是对旧版内容的更新的结果。如现行的"绿标"中增加了"施工管理"这一大项的内容，将评价分为设计评价和运行评价两部分，这些更新内容都从一定程度上体现了评价内容由以往的只关注单一环节向关注建筑生命周期各环节评价的转变趋势。[9]

另外，中国针对住宅性能方面的评价标准还有《住宅性能评定技术标准》，它是专门针对住宅的综合性能评定而编写的标准。它将住宅的性能划分为适用性能、环境性能、经济性能、安全性能和耐久性五个方面，其中所涉及的环境性能和耐久性能方面的内容与 LCA 工具的评价内容相近。[10]

具体到高效利用资源这一方面的标准，中国有《民用建筑热工设计规范》，这是对包括住宅在内的各类民用建筑进行能耗计算的依据，与性能评定类的标准有所不同，它属于强制性的规范。[11] 在它的基础上制定了不同热工分区的节能规范，如《严寒和寒冷地区居住建筑节能设计标准》，使得对节能设计的规范过程具体到特定的热工分区，还具体到了住宅——这种特定的建筑类型。[12] 另外，各城市有相应的节能标准作实践的补充，如《大连市居住建筑节能设计（节能 65%）规定》，使新建住宅的能耗控制在较为理想的范围内[13]（图 4）。

由中国与绿色、可持续住宅相关的标准的现状可得到以下事实：中国的标准已在不断地发展和完善，但尚需精细化、专门化；中国有专门的绿色建筑评价标准，但仍缺乏专门的绿色住宅评价标准；中国的绿色标准在全生命周期方面尚属起步阶段；中国关于能耗方面的标准相对完善，而关于可再生和长寿命方面的内容还较为匮乏；中国标准所关注的长寿命方面的内容更侧重于建筑的物理耐久性，而对于功能的可变性方面的内容仅作了少量关注。

标准名称	类型	性质	内容	与LCA工具比较			
				长寿命相关项	可再生相关项	资源的高效利用相关项	备注
绿色建筑评价标准	国家标准	等级认定	节地与室外环境、节能与能源利用、节水与水资源利用、节材与材料资源利用、室内环境质量、运行管理和施工管理	■合理采用高强建筑结构材料 ■合理采用耐久性好、易维护的装饰装修建筑材料 ■室内空间采用可重复使用的隔断 ■采用整体化定型设计的厨房、卫浴间	■再生水利用技术 ■建筑材料的循环利用——建筑中采用可再循环材料和可再利用建筑材料 ■使用以废弃物为原料生产的建筑材料 ■采用工业化生产的预制构件	■冷热源、输配系统和照明等各部分能耗应分项计量 ■围护结构 ■供暖、通风与空调 ■照明与电气 ■节水系统/器具与设备 ■节材优化设计/土建工程与装修工程一体化 ■指定并实施施工节能和能方案，检查并记录施工能耗 ■指定施工节水和用水方案，检测并记录施工水耗 ■减少预拌混凝土的损耗 ■采取措施降低钢筋损耗 ■使用工式定制模板，增加模板周转数	评价对象涵盖各类建筑，评价内容广
住宅性能评定技术标准	国家标准	等级认定	适用性能的评定、环境性能的评定、经济性能的评定、安全性能的评定、耐久性能的评定	■结构设计的耐久性 ■外墙装修（含外墙外保温）的耐久性 ■防水工程与防潮措施的耐久性 ■管线工程的耐久性 ■设备的耐久性 ■门窗的耐久性	■再生能源利用 ■可再生材料利用 ■建材回收率	■围护结构节能要求/综合节能要求 ■节水器具/中水利用/雨水利用 ■新型墙体材料取代黏土砖	针对住宅的性能进行的综合性评价，包含但不强调住宅的绿色节能部分
民用建筑热工设计规范	国家标准	强制性	热工分区、建筑热工设计要求、围护结构保温设计、围护结构隔热设计、采暖建筑围护结构防潮设计	■围护结构的防潮设计	□	■建筑热工设计分区规定 ■冬季保温设计 ■夏季防热设计 ■空调建筑热工设计 ■不同热工分区围护结构保温类型的选择 ■窗户保温性能和气密性和面积的规定	主要提供建筑热工分区及设计依据，适用对象为民用建筑（不只针对住宅），与资源的高效利用方面相关
严寒和寒冷地区居住建筑节能设计标准	行业标准	部分强制性	严寒和寒冷地区气候子区与室内热环境计算参数、采暖通风与空气调节能设计	□	□	■体形系数控制 ■窗墙比控制 ■门窗密闭性 ■围护结构传热系数限定 ■围护结构热工性能的权衡判断 ■采暖、通风和空调技能设计	主要提供住宅节能的量化依据，与资源的高效利用方面相关

图 4 中国绿色住宅相关标准与 LCA 工具的比较分析
（资料来源：作者自绘）

中国与日本的住宅发展阶段不同。资源循环住宅在中国尚属全新的概念，在日本却已积累了相对成熟的经验，并逐渐演化为其他更为深入的住宅实践。在中国发展可持续住宅的背景下，对其既有经验作研究和总结当然是必要的，但在此之前须认识到中日住宅本身在类型、结构体系和平面布局等方面的差异所在。若知 LCA 工具所面向的资源循环型住宅是以日本各项本已完备的住宅技术为依托的，如其中最为关键的 SI（Skeleton-Infill）体系。正是基于这些技术，才使得日本的住宅实现了清晰的结构和建造逻辑，正是基于此，LCA 工具中所指向的各类目标才可以轻松实现。因此，在我国绿色住宅标准的探索过程中，所应看到的不仅仅是日本评价标准的具体内容，而是评价项目与具体实践目标的对应关系和这背后所体现出的对住宅现状的尊重。

致谢

感谢新世纪人才基金项目（NCET-11-0049）、住房和城乡建设部软科学研究项目（2013-R4-18）对本论文写作过程的基金支持。

The Study on Life Cycle Assessment Tool of Japanese Resource Recycling Oriented Housing and Its Enlightenment

Wang Yun，Su Yuan，Fan Yue

(School of Architecture & Fine Arts，Dalian University of Technology)

Abstract：Under the backgrounds of developing the Resource Recycling Oriented Housing，Japan has developed LCA Tool based on the concept of *life-cycle*，which reflects the three key points of it-long life，ability of recycle and resource effective utilization of resources，promoting the transformation of traditional house to resource -recycling ones. In the process of improving the evaluation norms for Chinese green house，to study Japanese's LCA tool can provide some reference. Aiming at such reasons，firstly in the paper，the development，composition and features of LCA tool are elaborated；secondly，China's relevant evaluation norms for green house are generalized；finally the enlightenments are gained from the comparisons and summaries.

Keywords：Resource recycle，Housing，Evaluation tool，LCA，Green norm

参考文献：

[1]　（日）清家刚，（日）秋元孝之主编，日本资源循环型住宅技术开发项目组编辑．可持续性住宅建设[M]．北京：机械工业出版社，2005．

[2]　陈滨，范悦译．21世纪型住宅模式[M]．北京：机械工业出版社，2006．

[3]　Roger Bacon DriveReston，LIFE CYCLE ASSESSMENT：PRINCIPLES AND PRACTICE，Scientific Applications International Corporation（SAIC）11251，VA 20190．

[4]　ISO，http：//www. iso. org/iso/home/store/catalogue _ tc/catalogue _ detail. htm? csnumber=37456．

[5]　Life Cycle Assessment Society of Japan，http：//lca-forum. org/english/project02/，2014-12-14．

[6]　丸善（発売），建物のLCA指針（案）：地球温暖化防止のためのLCCO[2]を中心として，日本建築学会，1999．

[7]　資源循環性の評価機能を持つLCAツールの概要：建物の資源循環性評価手法の開発 その1（環境工学），日本建築学会技術報告集（22），341-346，2005[2005-12-20]．

[8]　（日）茂呂隆，丸山則義，木戸一成，資源循環型住宅のラベリングツールの開発（その1）（環境性能評価，環境工学I），学術講演梗概集．D-1，環境工学I，室内音響・音環境，騒音・固体音，環境振動，光・色，給排水・水環境，都市設備・環境管理，環境心理生理，環境設計，電磁環境 2004，1077-1078，2004-07-31

[9]　中华人民共和国住房与城乡建设部、中华人民共和国国家质量监督检验检疫总局，绿色建筑评价标准[S]．北京：中国建筑工业出版社，2014．

[10]　中华人民共和国建设部、中华人民共和国国家质量监督检验检疫总局，住宅性能评定技术标准[S]．北京：中国建筑工业出版社，2005．

[11]　国家技术监督局、中华人民共和国建设部，民用建筑热工设计规范[S]．北京：中国建筑工

业出版社，1993.

[12] 中华人民共和国住房和城乡建设部，严寒和寒冷地区居住建筑节能设计标准[S]. 北京：中国建筑工业出版社，2010-03-18.

[13] 大连市城乡建设委员会，大连市居住建筑节能设计（节能 65％）规定[S]. 北京：中国建筑工业出版社，2006.

Research of New Energy Integration Design of Residential Sustainable Building in Japan

Su Yuan, Zhu Qidong, Fan Yue

(School of Architecture & Fine Arts, Dalian University of Technology)

Abstract: This paper has carried on the preliminary exploration of new energy integration design based on energy-saving technique of the residential sustainable building. The introduced SI residential design mode separated the structure and infill part in the architectural design. The insulation structure as infill body parts in the maintenance structure is easy to replace and recycle, new energy equipment as the additional artifacts connects the main body part and architecture. At the same time the natural condition was used and the building layout was improved using simple form design; insulation energy saving maintenance structure was adopted; furthermore renewable energy sources were introduced under the right conditions.

Keywords: Sustainable building in Japan, Energy efficiency improvement, New energy integration

1 Introduction

With the development of society, the increased consumption of energy and resources and the mass production of pollutants caused a series of environmental problems. It is a pressing matter of moment that transforms the society from a mass production, mass consumption one to the "sustainable economy society". The consumption of residential building in the energy and resources occupies a large proportion. Construction and housing industry must change the mode of development. In the past, lots of countries have begun to study residential house and explore the mode of the low-carbon sustainable building. The consumption of buildings resources takes up a large proportion. In Japan, construction waste accounts twenty percent in the construction management. In the 20th century, Japan changed the "demolish rebuild" construction mode to the sustainable building mode, put forward the notice the "excellent long-term residence" proposal. In fact, as early as in 1966, the Japanese government has formulated the first five-year plan period house construction (a family, a house). In 2000, in the eighth five-year plan period house construction (2000-2004), the Japanese government has carried out "residential development project to create life value", putting forward to provide with comfort and low cost housing for a long time. Sustainable building has been put forward in the "residential development project to create life value"[1, 2].

In China, Baoxing Qiu, the minister of the Ministry of Housing at the Sixth Conference of the International Energy Green Building introduced that the new building was the most in the world in 2010. We build over two billion square meters per year by consuming the 40% of cements and steels in the world, but only maintaining for 25 to 30 years. We need to consider why building's quality will be different and why Chinese residential is short life. According to the Japan sustainable building analysis and combining with the current situation of China's development of residential construction, we should promote the reasonable strategy to develop a recycling society.

2 Concept of Residential Sustainable Building in Japan

Resource recycling residence is a kind of sustainable development. It uses the durability technology and renewable technology to save resources and protects the environment. Sustainable building has stages of building cycle, the different technology in different stages of the work content as follows: 1) Planning and designing. Before we design a house, we should think of the problem about dismantling, processing and regeneration. 2) The circulation of materials, the production of equipment. This stage includes circulation of materials, the production of equipment. 3) Building stage. It requires for minimized energy consumption. Main jobs are new construction technology and the utilization of waste. 4) Running (live and transform) stage. It wants to consider of energy saving and the maintenance in full life-cycle. 5) Demolition stage. Pay attention to the classification of recycling and reducing the waste. 6) Recycling stage. Consider to promote recycling and recycling. 7) Assessment of the whole management.

3 The characteristics of Residential Sustainable Building in Japan

Figure 1shows resource recycling in whole life cycle of residential building in Japan. Figure 2 shows SI building concept of sustainable building in Japan. Sustainable building considers the full life-cycle of building. It includes: 1) durability. 2) resources circulation. 3) reducing energy consumption. Residential structures (frame) have excellent durability. It includes using of interior decoration and equipment (with everyday life) and modification of the equipment. In the demolition or renovation of homes, it is easy that construction materials, structural components and equipment are removed. Residential uses a certain number of reuse or recycling materials. It brings new energy saving effect between housing supply and demand. In the whole building life, "plan and design - build - use (living, decoration, the transformation) -remove-process, recycle" of the entire process, durability, resource recycling and reducing energy consumption should be the goal. As much as possible for new housing, the houses should be high durable and easy to change materials. For old residential, after the process of its transformation or dismantling, the building materials and garbage recycling will be used in new construction.

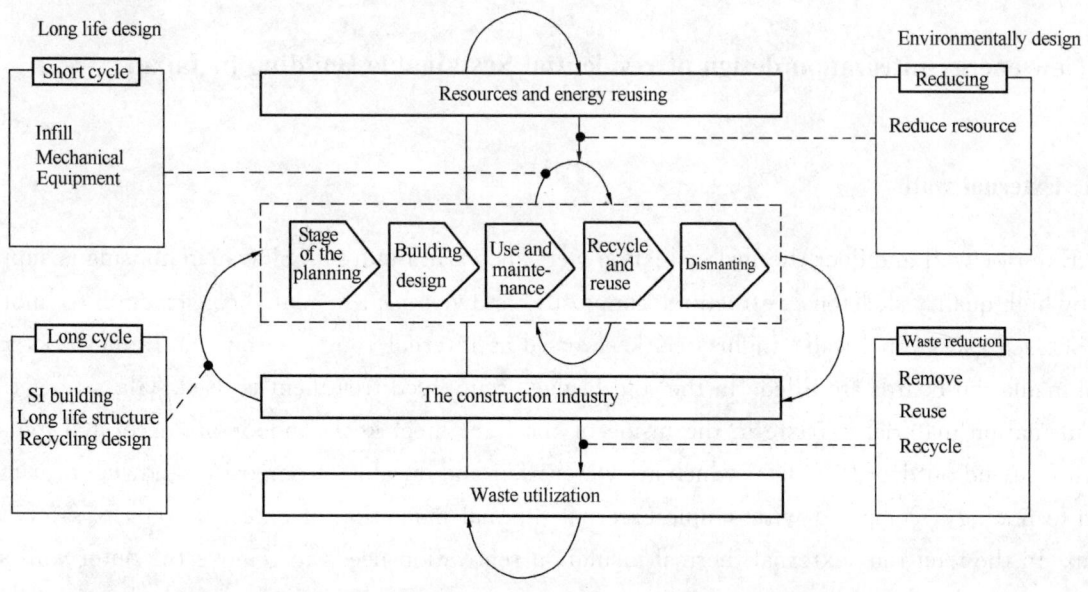

Figure 1   Resource recycling in whole life cycle of residential building

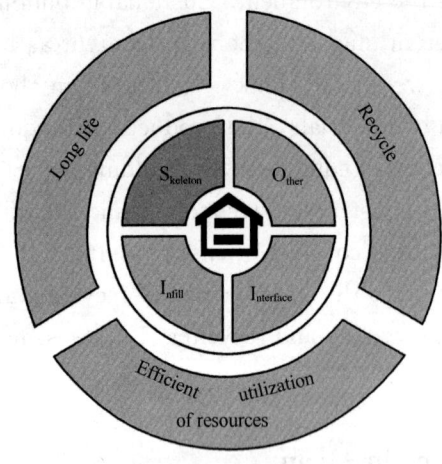

Figure 2　SI building concept of sustainable building in Japan

(Source：Figure 1 and Figure 2 are drawn by author according to the data sorting)

4　Residential Sustainable Building technologies

Sustainable building development had learned many excellent residential design experiences. All of the technology run through the full life-cycle residential. It should classify the stages. In different stages, sustainable building is classified as the block, building, building structure (palisade structure, timber), roof, inside and outside decoration materials, equipment, etc. According to the architectural surroundings, parts, such as classification, we combine them to form a system. Technology development project can be divided into 3R (recycle, reuse, reduce) technology, evaluation of the residence management technology and low energy consumption technology. Residential construction needs to use a lot of materials. The volume of these materials is very big. In the construction process, using and removing of these materials can bring big problem to the environment. Therefore, the first thing is to reduce the generation of waste (Reduce), in order to ensure that various performance of residential, reducing the usage of materials is very difficult. It is necessary to consider using reusing and recycling technology. Waste of the production of residential in use process is amazing. It has brought a lot of load on the environment, so reducing emissions should be considered in the design of building. At the same time, to extend the life of housing, it needs to update and reform that the old building and replace for some materials and building components. In order to make these abandoned building materials and components not becoming environmental garbage, we need the materials to be used or recycled again. 3R is actually the integrated technology.

5　New energy integration design of residential Sustainable Building in Japan

5.1　External wall

Exterior wall and floor thermal insulation were shown in Figure 3. SI system housing is supported by high quality skeleton as structure. composite sandwich heat-insulated construction technology can be used as external wall. Light steel keels used as internal stent, within the framework, rock wool insulation boards are filled. In the cold bridge, reinforced treatment is used. Glass fiber thermal insulation material is paste in the inside of the light steel keel. Indoor pre-decorated gypsum board face and outdoor PVC bar, which are waterproof and durable. Composite sandwich heat-insulated technology, compared with simple external thermal insulation of external wall, is safety and cheap. In the long run, external thermal insulation renovation needs to remove the outer wall surface part, which is costly and time consuming. Composite sandwich heat-insulated construction can renovate together with the interior trim, most part are prefabricated, therefore, time cost is short and repair can be done at any time.

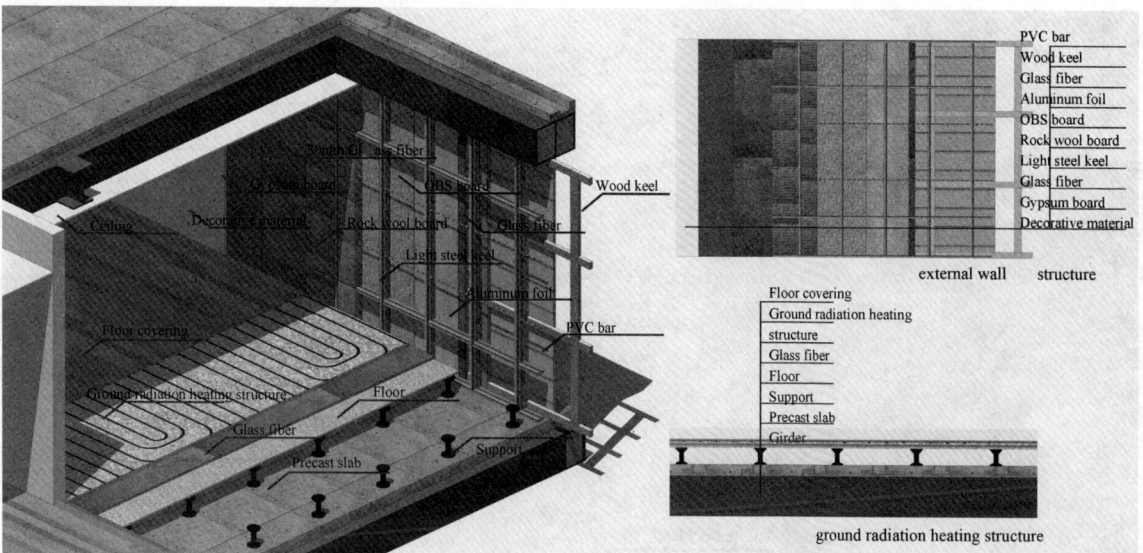

Figure 3   Exterior wall and floor thermal insulation
(Source: Figure 3 is drawn by author according to the data sorting)

5. 2   Building heating

The indoors ground radiation heating structure is usually used in the sustainable buildings in Japan; heating efficiency can be measured in single-family. Users can change the indoor temperature according to the outside condition. Because of the good heat insulation effect of the composite sandwich heat-insulated technology, the ground radiation heating equipment can rapidly improve the indoor temperature in a short time, thus traditional energy has been effectively saved.

5. 3   Heat insulation of window

The windows of sustainable buildings acting as the indoor and outdoor ventilation components usually become cold bridge which affects the indoor heat preservation effect. Figure 4 shows super insulated broken bridge aluminum alloy material window. Residential Sustainable Building in Japan using light steel keel exterior wall, outside the window assembled with the exterior wall, which can improve the accuracy of the construction, and the heat preservation effect.

5. 4   Wall and Solar Integrated Design

SI system housing of the sustainable buildings in Japan can promote solar collector component design and improve the utilization of solar energy. Detachable solar panel interface has reserved at external wall, according to the location sites, the construction technology (roof, brick wall facade, other facades, indoor space, underground, etc.) and seasonal (summer and winter) in matching designs. Thus, in the installation, replacement and removal of solar panels, the main structure has no damage, and maintain of pipelines is easy, which achieve sustainable energy development. Meanwhile, the solar equipment combined with the building ornament to form a unique architectural style.

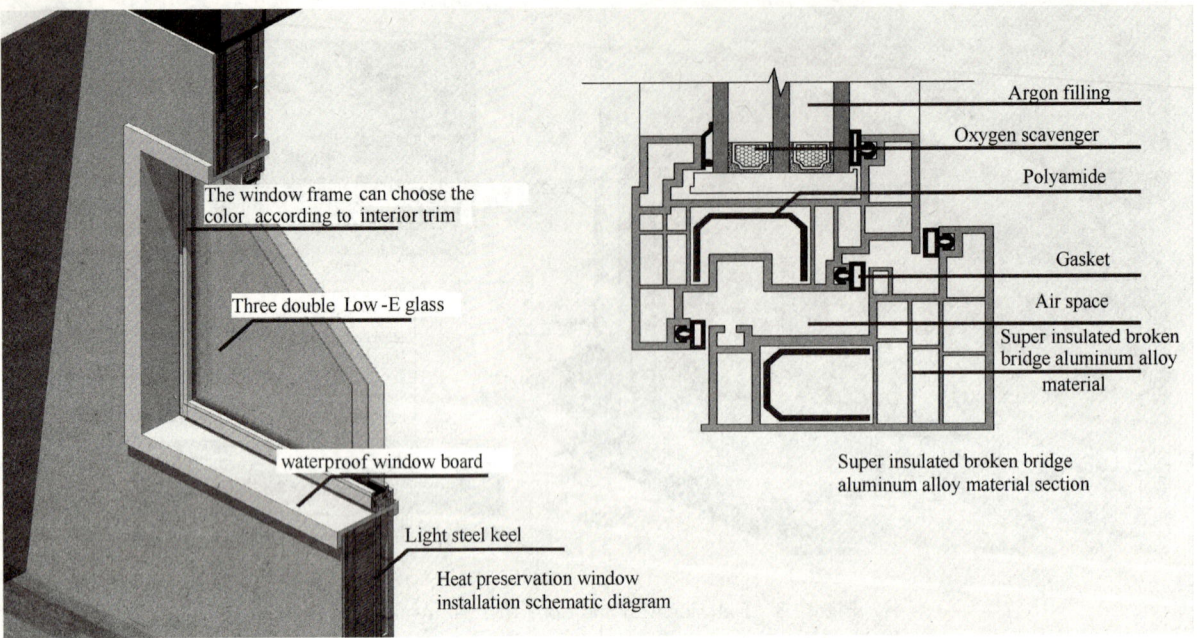

Figure 4　Super insulated broken bridge aluminum alloy material window

（Source：Figure 4 is drawn by author according to the data sorting）

5.5　Use of geothermal energy

Since solar energy is affected by time and weather largely，dense residential area is difficult to ensure adequate sunshine. The "geothermal" is a kind of reliable utilization energy. The feature of "geothermal" will remain at close to the average annual temperature in the area throughout the year，the temperature is constant，lower than the outdoor air temperature in summer，and higher in winter，which can be effectively used for heating cooling and hot water supply.

Ground source heat pump does not require complex design，do not need the room and cooling towers and other facilities，all needed is only a well，extraction of groundwater. It is possible to obtain geothermal. The water pumped from the extraction of geothermal heat pumps as electricity water pumped from extraction of geothermal power heat pump，and serve as a heat source for air conditioning and hot water supply. Within the same system（building）the users can freely choose the refrigeration or heating，and can realize the individual independent measurement fee. Due to groundwater temperature never below zero，in the north area can steadily run continuously.

6　Conclusion

This paper has carried on the preliminary exploration of new energy integration design based on energy-saving technique of the residential sustainable building. The introduced SI residential design mode separated the structure and infill part in the architectural design. The insulation structure as infill body parts in the maintenance structure is easy to replace and recycle，new energy equipment as the additional artifacts connects the main body part and architecture. At the same time the natural condition was used and the building layout was improved using simple form design；insulation energy saving maintenance structure was adopted；furthermore renewable energy sources were introduced under the right conditions.

Acknowledgement

We express our deepest gratitude to the "Pro-gram for New Century Excellent Talents in University" (NCET-11-0049), "General Project of Science Research from Department of Education of Liaoning Province" (L2013017), "Scientific Research Foundation for Doctors from Liaoning Province" (20141021), for the financial assistance provided to support this research.

日本资源循环型住宅的新能源一体化设计探索

苏 媛 朱启东 范 悦

（大连理工大学建筑与艺术学院）

摘要： 我国住房建设正进入转型时期，大规模住房建设存在着诸多问题：住房建设模式粗放，能源资源消耗高、利用率低、重规模轻效率、重外观轻品质、重建设轻管理，这些对于建设资源循环型社会及市民的舒适居住极为不利。同时，老旧住宅结构设计不合理，再加上家庭结构及生活方式变化，住宅建筑寿命普遍难以达到预期的设计年限。过早地拆除不可回收的构件、建材给环境带来了很大的压力。日本早年就在资源循环住宅建设中引入 SI 住宅设计模式，将住宅的承重结构与填充部分分开设计。维护结构保温构造作为填充体部分易于更换回收，新能源设备作为附加构件与建筑主体部分相联接。在建筑设计中利用自然条件，改善建筑布局，采用简单的形体设计；采取保温节能维护构造；并在适当的条件下引入可再生能源。最终提高住宅耐久性，增加资源循环利用，降低能耗，减少对环境的依赖。本文通过介绍日本的资源循环性住宅体系中的节能手法研究，对新能源一体化设计进行了初步探索。首先在建筑设计中引入 SI 住宅设计模式，将住宅的承重结构与填充部分分开设计。维护结构保温构造作为填充体部分易于更换回收，新能源设备作为附加构件与建筑主体部分相联接。同时利用自然条件的朝向、体型，改善建筑布局，采用简单的形体设计；在围护结构的保温隔热策略方面研究采取保温节能维护构造的优点和外窗保温的具体做法；并在适当的条件下引入可再生能源，如利用太阳能和利用地热能源等。节能型设计成本最低，也最容易实现，最应该提倡；其次是构件设计，新能源设备是锦上添花的辅助。提高能源效率、降低能源消耗、积极开发利用新能源是未来建筑的发展方向，是应对全球气候问题的有效手段，也是实现可持续发展的必然要求。从经济性角度讲，高质量的保温隔热材料与技术以及新能源利用设备等的初始投资比较高。但其能够真正减少住宅使用中对传统能源的消耗，减少建筑周期中的废物产生量，从长远来看将会形成良好的社会与经济效益。

关键词： 日本资源循环型住宅，高能效，新能源一体化

Reference：

[1] Matsumura Shuuichi, Tanabe Shinichi. Sustainable building in the 21st century [M]. The translator: Chen Bin, Fan Yue. Beijing: Beijing mechanical industry published , 2006.

[2] Qingjiagang, Qiuyuanxiaozhi editor. Sustainable building [M]. The translator: Chen Bin. Beijing: Beijing mechanical industry published , 2005.

[3] Qin Shan. Based on the SI system of sustainable housing theory research and design practice [D]. Design and research institute of China, 2014, 06.

[4] Li Zhengquan. The resource recycling of residential construction based on circular economy research [D]. Huazhong university of science and technology, 2006, 11.

［5］ Cui Guangxun ． Japanese housing system evolution and design strategy ［D］. Dalian university of technology.

［6］ Cheng Jiawei，Xia Haishan，Liu Chunmei. China's "short-lived residential" gene analysis and improvement measures study ［J］. Journal of housing industry，2014，04.

［7］ Guo Shu wen. Analyses the resource recycling residential construction，Wuhan university of science and technology school of management ［J］. Industrial construction，Vol. 2009 supplement.

"地域主义建筑"与"绿色建筑"
——以第二届（2014）中国梦绿色建筑创意设计大赛为例

张建新　马　鑫　刘　雁

（扬州大学建筑科学与工程学院）

摘要："地域主义建筑"和"绿色建筑"无疑是目前中国城市住宅设计创作中面临两个新型问题。本文以参加第二届（2014）中国梦绿色建筑创意设计大赛的研究性教学活动为例，从"地域主义建筑"出发，探讨具有地域特色的"绿色建筑"的可能性和有效性。在教学过程中，作者以研究性教学理念为基础，努力引导学生从建筑的三个基本问题研究出发，着力研究"地域主义建筑"与"绿色建筑"的个性问题及其相互关系，探讨具有地域特色的现代绿色住宅建筑创作之路，并由此得出了在未来具有中国特色的现代建筑创作的"大树"中，"地域主义建筑"是"根"、"绿色建筑"是"花"的结论。

关键词：研究性教学，建筑基本问题，地域主义建筑，绿色建筑，域性绿色建筑

1　引言

21世纪的中国正在从工业化社会跨入后工业化社会。以信息技术为代表的新技术革命的迅速发展，给中国社会经济结构、人们的价值观念、生活方式、文化习俗等带来了十分巨大的变化，全球化的趋势对中国各地富有地域特色的城镇及建筑造成了严重的威胁。与此同时，随着世界经济进入高速增长时期，环境污染在世界范围内蔓延，全球气候变暖对人类的生存环境和发展带来了严峻的挑战。在这样的社会环境背景下，绿色建筑设计思潮应运而生。因此，"地域主义建筑"和"绿色建筑"无疑是目前中国包括城市住宅在内的建筑设计创作中面临两个新型问题。

为了让学生进一步深入了解当今地域主义建筑观和绿色建筑的内涵、特点，熟悉和掌握地域主义建筑观和绿色建筑设计相结合的具体操作方法，扬州大学建筑科学与工程学院建筑系2014年特别选择"面向未来的可持续实验性住宅设计"为题开展毕业设计教学。该题目来源于设计网承办的第二届（2014）中国梦绿色建筑创意设计大赛。竞赛项目所在地为广州海珠生态城，方案设计需结合"广府文化"、市民低碳科技文化和生活方式的体验需求，探索地域文化特征，研究适合本土特色的低碳环保可持续使用城市小住宅。对学生而言，这样的选题具有一定的难度和挑战性。对于毕业设计指导老师来说，首先所要面对的问题是，如何有效引导广大学生启动和高质量地完成本次绿色建筑设计任务。于是，结合"广府地域主义"建筑观来创新岭南绿色建筑设计教学抓手的确定就成为当务之急。

2　思考与尝试

2.1　研究性教学及其内涵

研究性教学，是20世纪80年代以来面对知识经济的挑战，国际社会比较普遍认同和实施的一种新的教学模式。研究性教学的内涵包括：（1）开放性。研究性教学强调以学生为主体，教师为学生创造一个问题的情境，引导学生将兴趣转化为问题，使学生主动投入到研究性学习中。（2）问题性。研究性教学是以问题为中心的教学方法，教师进行教学设计的核心是设计问题情境，教师作为开放式探究学习环境的创设者，应该尽量引导学生从多角度思考问题，使问题成为激发学生学习的

动力，学生在学习过程中，通过分析问题，寻求解决问题的办法，以此培养和提高学生的自主学习能力和创造能力。（3）过程性。研究就是研讨问题，追根求源多方寻求答案。所以，研究性学习注重的是学生学习的过程，强调学生的主动探究和亲身体验。学生在探究式学习中不断发现问题、提出问题、分析问题和解决问题，从而获取知识、发展自身的能力。（4）自主性。在研究性学习中，从资料的收集、分析，问题的质疑、讨论，报告的撰写、修改，成果的整理、展示等一系列活动，教师只起指导和控制作用，可以通过与学生的讨论或组织小组探讨，引导学生向创新的方向发展。（5）参与性。研究性教学中鼓励学生通过个人、小组、集体等多种学习形式，尝试解决疑难问题，将自己所学知识应用于解决实际问题，有助于培养学生的责任感和协作精神。[1]

综上所述，研究性教学内涵的核心是其问题性。那么本次城市住宅的绿色建筑设计问题又该如何有效的提出、分析和解决的呢？

2.2　建筑的基本问题与个性问题

从辩证法的观念来看，建筑设计问题可分为个性问题和共性问题两种。个性问题是指与不同建筑类型有关的问题，往往表现为具体的、细节的问题，如绿色建筑与非绿色建筑之间本质性区别的问题。而共性问题则是指和建筑类型变化无关的问题，往往表现为抽象的、一般的问题，这就是建筑设计的基本问题，它对每一种类型的建筑设计过程都具有普遍的指导意义，如绿色建筑与非绿色建筑之间的共有问题，因此，我们认为建筑的基本问题和个性问题无疑都是可以用来启动研究性建筑设计的有效抓手，通过一系列的富有内在逻辑性的绿色建筑设计基本问题和个性问题的发现、分析和解决，可以基本架构建筑设计的全过程，从而有效地引导学生开展绿色建筑设计的研究性学习。

2.3　绿色建筑研究性教学的尝试

绿色建筑是指在建筑的全生命周期内，最大限度节约资源（节能、节地、节水、节材）、保护环境和减少污染，为人们提供健康、适用和高效的使用空间，与自然和谐共生的建筑。绿色建筑主要具有以下几方面的特点：第一，有应对气候、适应气候、利用气候的基本能力（功能），最大限度利用自然气候改善建筑室内外热环境；第二，有发展性地继承地方传统建筑营造技术与现代技术相结合的特征；第三，绿色建筑具有高水平的节能效率；第四，绿色建筑要在建筑的全生命周期内综合评价；第五，具有合理的成本增量等。[2]因此，本次绿色建筑设计面临的主要问题有以下三个方面：一是如何有发展性地继承地方传统建筑营造技术，并与现代技术相结合？二是如何应对气候、适应气候、利用气候，最大限度利用自然气候改善建筑室内外热环境？三是如何具有高水平的节能效率？面对上述问题，我们认为本次绿色建筑设计要从以下三个方面建立研究性教学的问题。

2.3.1　基本问题

对于广大学生来说，任何时候都要牢记学习建筑设计一定要回归建筑的基本问题，学会从建筑学的基本原理和形式规则出发，围绕建筑设计的各种基本问题来探讨设计方案的推动和完善，再好的创意也离不开场地总体布局、功能空间组织和材料、技术设计等问题的解决。哪些是建筑的基本问题呢？建筑的基本问题就是环境与场所、功能与空间、材料与技术之间的关系和互动问题。[3]因此基本问题包括以下几种：

第一种是环境与场所关系问题：首先是历史文化环境，这就要求我们去研究广府建筑、岭南建筑的地域特色，其特殊的气候应对策略、百姓生活轨迹的礼仪空间、宅加园的总体空间布局特色等；其次是具体的场地环境设计条件分析，如场地的周围出行道路和相邻建筑形成的限制条件，考虑场地地形地貌、边界退让要求、场地尺度、保留要素（如树木、建筑等）等；第三是初步考虑生态环境设计，包括建筑最佳朝向、场地通风分析、场地日照分析等；第四是在以上分析的基础上提出初步的总体布局方案和建筑形体；最后根据总体功能布局和建筑肌理研究细化场地总体设计和初步的建筑形体等（图1）。

第二种是功能与空间关系问题：首先要研究功能关系；其次是结合总体布局细化功能分区；再次是空间组织和布局，空间布局也要关注传统空间文脉的继承和延续，特别是地域特色明显的空间布局方式和空间形态肌理要得到重视，如门厅、神楼、天井、花园等；第四是基本空间设计与布局，基本空间设计要规整：一是便于框架结构支撑，二是易于满足空间适应性的要求，三是传统空间的设计经验等（图2）。

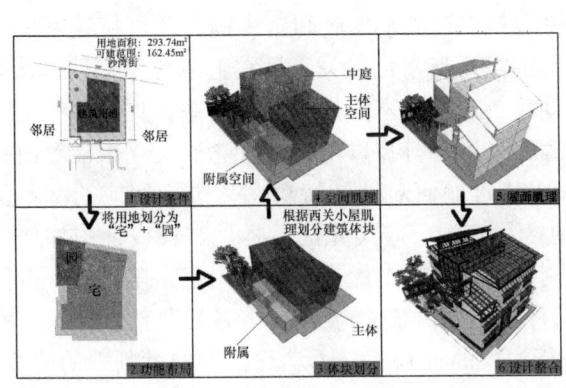

图1　形体生成分析

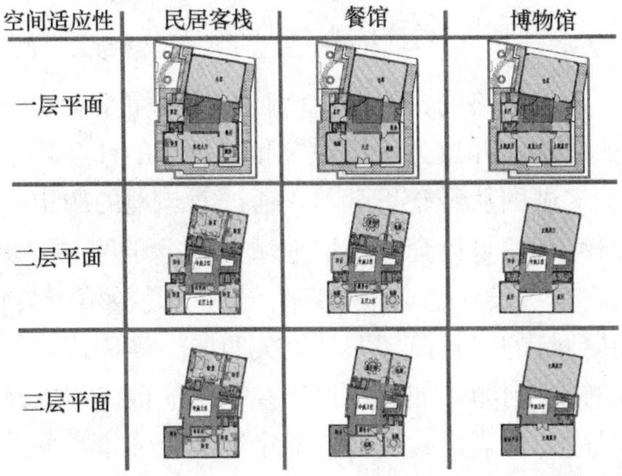

图2　空间适应性分析

第三种是材料与技术问题：首先是传统的木结构或者砖木结构已经不符合现代抗震规范要求，砖、木材料都已不是易得材料，也不再是严格意义上的绿色材料，而钢结构易得、可回收，也可工业化生产、现场安装，是目前比较绿色的材料和建造技术；其次，技术除了结构技术外，还包括绿色低碳技术的综合应用。项目地处广州，属于第四气候区，其基本节能设计重点在通风、遮阳，因此岭南建筑中的水平遮阳、天井热压通风、屋面绿化和架空设计、冷巷设置等传统的节能技术首先应该被优先采用，先进的太阳能光热、光电技术应该被有比较的选用，雨水收集、人工湿地技术也应该结合现代造园技术综合应用，尽量避免大批绿色低碳技术的堆砌（图3）。

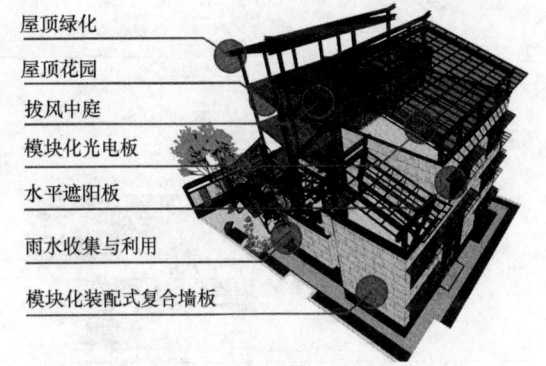

图3　绿色技术策略分析

2.3.2　建筑的核心问题

在这里我们补充一个建筑的核心问题的概念，核心问题就是建筑形式与美学问题，核心问题是基本问题的中心，但又高于建筑的基本问题。一切的基本问题的互动研究都要以围绕着核心问题的有效解决为标准。

建筑形式与美学问题又包括以下几个方面的问题：首先形式设计的基础首先是场地设计中的形体研究；其次是功能、空间设计中的立体功能空间模块；最后是结构框架式形式的支撑骨架。但前期的综合场地设计、功能设计和结构设计的设计成果只能是一个未来建筑形式的"裸体"，美学设计的任务就是为"裸体"建筑穿上一件符合美学标准的"表皮"外套。因此表皮设计就要满足以下

图4　传统和现代相结合的造型

几点要求：一是真实反映材料特性，二是反映材料建构细节，三是反映绿色材料和技术，四是呼应地域特色和传统的传承，五是要符合基本的美学法则——如整体性、对比、比例和尺度等（图4）。

2.3.3　建筑的个性问题

个性问题是指绿色建筑设计所特有的个性问题。

第一种是关注地域历史、文化和特色等方面的批判地域主义建筑问题。批判地域主义建筑是中国未来建筑设计创新发展和走中国特色可持续发展的建筑设计之路的一个必由之路。地域主义着眼于特定的场所与文化，关心日常生活与真实且熟悉的生活轨迹，并致力于将建筑和其所处的社会环境之间维持一个紧密与持续性的关系。更重要的是地域主义试图从经验里学习，通过对当地的历史、地理、经济、科技以及价值观念、文化生活等内容的研究和切身体会，获取地域性理念的来源，并形成建筑如何对地域特色文化进行回应的基本认知。[4]本次设计地点位于广州，这里是根植于岭南地区特有的广府文化的发祥地，在设计中如何传承其独特的"竹筒楼"、"大关西屋"等传统建筑形制必然是研究中优先考虑的内容。摆在设计者面前的首要问题是如何认识这些陌生的传统，以及如何传承它们？这需要设计者跳出具体的形象，跳出习用的词语，对当地传统建筑文化和审美意识进行深入的批判性（哲学意义上的批判）的研究，要作抽象的思辨和精神的凝炼，探索能和现代审美意识契合的、在精神层面上表达中国的建筑创作之路。做到，"不是"——形象上、技术上不是；"就是"——精神上、意境上就是。也就是要从一般的"形似"走向"神似"（图5）[5]。

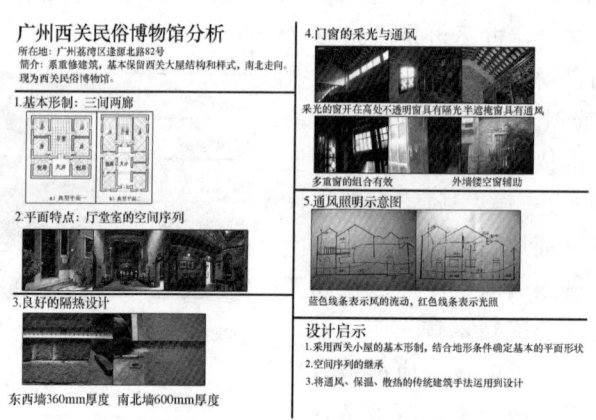

图5　岭南建筑地域特色分析

第二种是侧重可持续建筑观的绿色建筑问题。可持续发展是未来人类发展的必经之路，可持续建筑和城市发展是人类可持续发展战略的重要内容，要实现未来建筑和城市发展的可持续发展，就必须推广和使用绿色、生态、低碳的建筑技术。问题是绿色、生态、低碳的建筑技术是否一定是高端、昂贵的高技术呢？答案显然是否定的。以本次设计为例，广东地区传统的天井热压通风、窗户水平遮阳以及冷巷空间设计就是富有地域特色的成熟的低技术，大家在设计中应该优先选择使用，至于当前成熟的一些绿色、生态、低碳高技术，如钢结构技术、太阳能光热、光电技术、雨水收集利用、地源热泵空调技术等，设计者应该综合考虑各方面因素，进行有比较的选择和系统集成设计，避免高技术的堆砌（图6）。

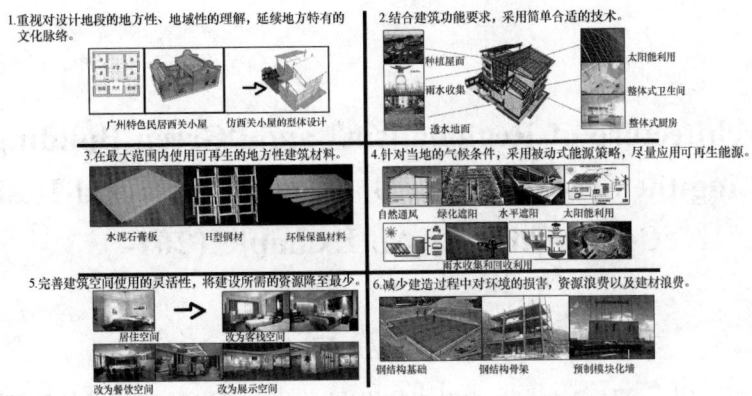

图6 建筑可持续性分析图

3 研究结论

通过本次"面向未来的可持续实验性住宅设计"的研究性教学研究和实践尝试我们得出如下几方面的结论：首先是通过绿色建筑设计的共性问题和个性问题帮助学生启动设计，为学生快速和有效发现、分析和解决绿色建筑设计过程中的各种问题提供了有效的抓手，从而有力地推动绿色建筑设计教学的开展；其次是通过建筑的基本问题进行设计启动，有助于建立绿色建筑的基本设计框架，并借以拓展绿色建筑设计的广度；再次是用建筑的核心问题组织设计综合研究，有助于抓住绿色建筑设计的本源，并借以挖掘绿色建筑设计的内涵；最后是用绿色建筑的特有问题组织教学中的绿色深入研究，有助于拓展绿色建筑设计研究的深度和高度。批判地域主义建筑观是绿色建筑的"树根"，有利于拓展绿色建筑设计的深度；可持续发展建筑观是绿色建筑的"树冠"，有利于拓展绿色建筑设计的高度。

总之，"地域性绿色建筑"是以可持续发展为核心思想，以绿色技术为手段，充分考虑地域环境与文化因素，营造出既符合当地自然环境与人文环境，又符合时代精神的建筑形态，是把"地域主义建筑"与"绿色建筑"相结合的、有良知和可持续发展的建筑观。因此，中国未来城市住宅的绿色建筑创作之路，不应该是简单的住宅设计外加绿色表皮，而是一定要结合中国各地的地域特色，自觉地走地域特色和绿色技术相融合的"地域性绿色建筑"的城市住宅创作之路。

致谢

本文受到扬州大学教改课题研究项目资助，课题编号：yzujx2013-190B。

"Architecture of Regionalism" and "Green Building": Taking the Second China Dream Architectural Design Competition as An Example (2014)

Zhang Jianxin，Ma Xin，Liu Yan

(College of Civil Science and Engineering，Yangzhou University)

Abstract："Architecture of Regionalism" and "Green Building" are undoubtedly two new issues in the design of urban residence in contemporary China. This paper takes the teaching of China Dream Architectural Design Competition as an example，explores the possibility and effectiveness of "Green Building" with regional features from the standpoint of "Architecture of Regionalism". During the process of teaching，based on the idea of discovery teaching，authors of this paper attempt to inspire students to start from three fundamental issues of architecture，study with special efforts the respective characteristics of "Architecture of Regionalism" and "Green Building"，and also the interrelationship between them，and explore the road to the design of modern green residence with regional features. Such practice leads to the conclusion that in the tree of modern architectural design in China，"Regionalism" is the "root"，and "Green Building" is the "flower".

Keywords：Creative teaching，Fundamental issues of architecture，Architecture of regionalism，Green building，Regional green building

参考文献：

[1] 刘健．实施研究性教学 培养大学生的创新能力[J]．北京市财贸管理干部学院学报，2006，2：42～45．

[2] 王辉，张原萍，杨柳青．论绿色建筑[J]．科技信息，2013，7：336．

[3] 陈秋光．"整体中片段"-关于建筑设计入门教学课程设置的研究与实践[J]．新建筑，2009，5：103．

[4] 凯瑟琳·斯莱塞．地域风格建筑[M]．江苏：东南大学出版社，2001．

[5] 秦佑国．中国现代建筑的中国表达[J]．建筑学报，2004，5：23．

建筑碳排放审计方法国际比较分析与经验借鉴

万诗羽

（香港中文大学）

摘要： 全球气候变暖，建筑作为重要的碳排放源头已成为碳审计所需要重点关注的问题。在《联合国气候变化框架公约》缔约第五次会议上中国承诺到 2020 年单位国内生产总值二氧化碳排放量比 2005 年下降 40%～45%。在中国快速工业化和城镇化的大背景下，要在短时间内实现如此规模的碳减排目标，需要巨大的努力，因此探索系统的建筑碳审计方法并辅助相关碳审计政策迫在眉睫。本文通过梳理发达国家和地区的建筑碳核算方法，通过从核算边界、核算清单，到具体的核算方法，分析在实际情况下各国所面临的问题及挑战，并借鉴其先进经验，确定与我国国情相适应的碳审计方法以及参考依据。

关键词： 碳审计，建筑全生命周期，碳排放清单，碳核算方法

1 建筑碳审计的概述

1.1 建筑碳审计的提出背景及发展

随着全球气候变暖，建筑物作为重要的能源消耗产品和碳排放的主要源头之一已经成为国际社会普遍关注的焦点问题。从 1992 年联合国环境与发展大会通过的《联合国气候变化框架公约》（UNFCCC）到 1997 年《京都议定书》的签订，世界各国为了应对气候变化和控制碳排放出台了一系列的政策和措施。[1] 为了更进一步推动全球的碳减排行动，并且更进一步落实减排政策，2000 年，政府间气候变化专门委员会（IPCC）编制的《国家温室气体清单指南》让各国开始投入到温室气体核算的队伍中来。关于建筑的碳排放核算，目前国际上的审计与报告都是基于 2004 年，世界资源研究所（WRI）及世界可持续发展工商理事会（WBCSD）制定的《温室气体议定书：企业核算与报告准则》和国际标准化组织制定的 ISO14064-67 温室气体排放量标准以及管理标准等系列文件[1]。毫无疑问，各国组织相关低碳标准与认证的制定已成为了碳审计开展的有力保障。然而关于如何恰当的划分建筑碳审计的边界，制定符合审计标准的清单条目，从而通过碳审计使得建筑能耗管理政策、程序与国家相关规定相符，达到预定减排目标是各国共同的目的，所以如何进行合理的建筑碳审计是特别值得探索的问题。

1.2 我国建筑碳审计的现状

中国正在进行大规模的工业化和城镇化，建筑业飞速发展，建筑物的碳排放已经成为温室气体排放的重要源头。[2] 在《联合国气候变化框架公约》缔约方第五次会议上，中国政府承诺到 2020 年单位国内生产总值二氧化碳排放量比 2005 年下降 40%～45%。关于建筑的低碳化控制，国务院在"十二五"节能减排综合性工作方案中提出"推动建筑节能，制定并实施绿色建筑行动方案"，并在《"十二五"建筑节能专项规划》中提到"实施绿色建筑规模化推进"和"试下绿色建筑普及化"。2007 年，《国家机关办公建筑和大型公共建筑能源审计导则》在一定程度上对我国的能源审计起到了指导作用。2010 年，国家发改委公布了《关于看展低碳省区和低碳城市试点工作的通知》，明确提出了要建立温室气体排放数据统计与管理体系。[3,4] 但对于已建建筑物以及有待开发的建筑项目在特定的时间段到底排放了多少碳，应该将低碳控制在怎样的水平等问题，以及采用怎样的碳审计清单和划分合理的审计边界已有的研究均没有具体涉及。因此，我国亟须借鉴国际上先进的建筑碳审

计经验，探索与我国国情相适应的碳审计方法和保障措施，从而在一定程度上控制我国建筑碳排放，实现低碳发展的目标。

2 国外建筑碳审计方法

2.1 美国建筑碳审计方法

美国在进行建筑碳排放核算时，对建筑碳排放的过程进行了分段，将碳排放的来源划分为直接排放和间接排放两个方面，同时结合碳审计公布的数据归纳分类。根据统计数据显示，美国约一半以上的建筑碳排放来自于家庭和个人的使用，因此民众的生活方式成了美国建筑碳审计的重点内容，并引用 LEED 等辅助标识来从民众的建筑使用方式上来控制碳排放量。关于建筑具体排放了多少碳，美国采用的比较普遍的方法是碳足迹核算，特别是将碳足迹的计算覆盖于建筑碳排放的整个生命周期，尽管全生命周期的碳足迹计算因为划定边界、范围以及在计算温室气体方法选择上存在一定困难和差异。美国大规模采用国际范围内普遍认可的，由世界资源研究所（WRI）及世界可持续发展工商理事会（WBCSD）所制定的《温室气体议定书》作为建筑碳审计的清单条目。在此条目范围内潜在的间接碳排放源将会被考虑在内。关于建筑全生命周期碳核算的具体操作方法，美国有两大主流方法：基于过程的计算和投入产出的计算。基于过程的碳核算即是对可以分析和可检测的每个过程阶段进行碳核算，从而确定整个生命周期的碳核算量。投入产出的碳核算方法则是针对于整条供应链上的碳排放情况，从而避免过程分段所造成的错误。但是在美国，投入产出的碳核算方法多是基于一个区域内的建筑碳核算，对于单体建筑通常是使用基于过程的计算。

2.2 英国建筑碳审计方法

英国作为最早提出"低碳经济"和"低碳审计"概念的国家，已经形成了较为详尽的建筑碳审计的体系，并在努力实现"零碳"目标。2009 年，在英国的政府工作报告中，隶属于英国下议院的环境审计委员明确了低碳审计的目标和内容，形成了一个完整的低碳审计的框架。[5] 通过建筑碳排放核算，详细的计算出每个社区建筑以及运营各阶段的全生命周期建筑碳排放量，并且综合考虑对各个阶段碳排放量的控制和减少的可行性措施，从而达到其"零碳社区"的目标。对于全生命周期内各个阶段的碳核算操作方法，2010 年英国政府低碳建设革新政策出台了新的核算标准，并在2011 年到 2012 年由欧洲标准科技委员会出台政策 CEN TC350 作为英国定义建筑或产品在基于过程的全生命周期的核算标准。该标准定义了全生命周期的四个过程 A1-3 产品、A4-5 建造过程，B1-7 使用过程、C1-4 拆除过程，以及生命周期结束之后的重利用阶段 D。英国政府致力于将整个社区的建筑碳排放控制在一个平衡的范围内，因此传统的碳审计则是使用投入与产出的碳核算方法。近几年为了避免投入产出所造成的高造价环保材料的使用限制，一些专家学者开始探索将基于过程的碳核算方法与投入产出的方法结合起来，并增加了碳核算边界的替换系统。

2.3 澳大利亚建筑碳审计方法

澳大利亚的建筑碳审计是根据澳大利亚绿色基建协会（AGIC）协会制定的方法理论，根据建筑全生命周期的能耗链条所进行碳足迹的核算和监测。这种方法和国际上普遍的基于过程的建筑全生命周期的碳审计方法基本一致，不过其碳审计边界不涉及建筑寿命结束之后建筑材料的重新回收和废弃掩埋处理等相关过程。澳大利亚的建筑碳审计所参照的清单是根据 ISO 14040-44 条目所涉及的建筑全生命周期建筑所排放的温室气体和能耗情况来确定。

2.4 香港建筑碳审计方法

香港是我国率先实行建筑碳审计的地区。香港作为以服务业为主导的经济体系，其建筑物的用电量占全香港的用电量的89%。据统计，由于发电所造成的香港温室气体排放占其总排放量的13%，其中由建筑物所导致的温室气体排放占总量的79%。[6]2008年，香港政府推出了香港首部建筑碳审计指引的文件，其所涉及的范围不仅涵盖商业和住宅用途的建筑物，同时也覆盖了大部分公共用途的建筑物。香港的建筑碳核算，是根据建筑在其使用过程所涉及的温室气体排放情况进行审计，并通过乘以与其相对应的全球变暖潜能值，将其转化为二氧化碳当量，从而确定出建筑碳核算的结果。香港政府在整个建筑碳审计的过程中起到了至关重要的作用。据统计，在2010年香港政府产业署管理的楼宇中，参与碳审计的建筑增加了44幢大型建筑，并将结果反馈于建筑使用用户和管理者，在一定程度上提高了其关于温室气体排放的认识，也在很大程度上降低了建筑碳排放。

3 国外建筑碳审计方法比较与分析

3.1 国际建筑碳审计方法的相似性分析

近20年，各国在进行建筑碳排放核算时都逐渐从原始的环境承载力计算转变为量化和通报温室气体排放数据的标准和指南的基于建筑全生命周期的建筑碳排放。就目前看来，关于建筑产品的碳排放评估最完整和全面的标准是英国的PSA 2050。核算所涉及的边界也都是基于全生命周期所涵盖的材料获取、制作、建造、营运、废除和重新利用六个方面来进行调整的。碳审计清单都是基于IPCC（全球政间气候管理委员会）、《京都议定书》中的清洁发展机制（CDM），世界资源研究所（WRI）和世界可持续发展工商理事会（WBCSD）制定的"项目核算GHG协议"，以及全生命周期下ISO 14040等系列文件[7]，并结合当地的政策背景以及能耗使用情况编制核算工具。均以二氧化碳当量作为衡量标准。对于核算数据的收集，即与IPCC的指南相类似，收集活动数据和排放系。碳核算的具体方法也普遍运用于三类：基于过程的全生命周期碳核算，投入产出的全生命周期核算以及两者的结合使用。与此同时，为了更好地配合各国实现低碳的目标，各国在进行建筑碳审计的同时还出台相应的政策进行辅助支持，例如利用IPCC的国际温室气体清单设置碳排放额度，将碳交易、碳信息披露、碳标识计划以及碳补偿计划共同配合作为补充。各国也形成了许多发展成熟的建筑评估体系作为辅助，例如美国的LEED评价标识、加拿大的ATHENA评价方法、荷兰的SimaPro、英国的Beam评价体系以及日本的CASBEE。

3.2 国际建筑碳审计方法之间的差异性分析

各国在进行建筑碳审计时重点不尽相同，因此在进行审计边界设定、碳核算清单条目以及具体的核算方法也存在一定的差异。美国将重点放在居民的生活方式上，因此侧重于建筑营运阶段的碳核算。然而有些项目为了特别针对运营期间的能耗以及碳排放进行研究，利用CDM项目中的减排量计算，然而运营期较低的碳排放在某些情况下是由于建设期采用了更高碳的技术或者材料，因此需要通过全生命周期的碳排放进行计算。英国侧重于建立零碳社区，即考虑各个阶段的减排可行性，并通过适当增加碳汇的方法达到碳中和，因此英国的建筑碳审计尺度多以社区为单位，由下至上收集数据，并形成了较为完整的碳审计框架。不同于英国利用PAS2050将建筑物作为产品进行建筑碳足迹的核算，日本作为亚洲地区较为先进的碳审计国家正在尝试并建立了不同的建筑碳审计标准，根据建筑形态的差异以及建筑功能的差别，通过利用其产业平衡表计算出结构、形态的差异性住宅建筑的碳排放情况以及系统能耗。针对全生命周期的建筑碳核算，其差异性可以总体概括为系统边界的界定、生命周期阶段的划分、清单的详细度以及考虑建筑物料回收及绿地碳汇等几个方面，根据各国国情、地区政策以及项目本身而存在差异。

3.3　国际建筑碳审计方法所面临的问题和挑战

各国在进行建筑碳审计时由于数据获取复杂，不仅涉及建筑本身等各方面诸多参数，以及能源、材料、机械等多种碳排放系数，所以国际碳审计方法所面临的问题和挑战可以概括为以下几个方面：

（1）各国不同地区不同建筑项目对于全生命周期的假设与限定条件不完全相同，从而导致建筑全生命周期较难划分，建筑碳排放系统边界难以界定，以及碳排放清单差别较大难以统一。因此国际上缺乏统一、规范的评价模式与方法。

（2）在建筑全生命周期的碳核算评价中，对于建筑材料、施工方式、运营模式以及拆除阶段的各类碳排放数据都极为缺乏，没有专门的机构和部门对相关数据进行整理和建立相关联的数据库。

（3）由于各国各项目之间进行建筑全生命周期碳核算时操作不统一，方法不尽相同，基本数据获取困难，导致各类项目与研究之间的碳审计结果不具有可比性，从而难以建立符合所有标准的碳排放定量评价工具。

（4）各国在对全生命周期建筑碳核算结果进行评价时，由于周期之间的相互联系及影响，以及当地环境与项目的差异性，会导致评价结果有误差，从而造成分析结果不够准确，影响审计结果和政策落实。

（5）建筑碳审计是各国实现低碳目标的手段之一，因此如何落实相应低碳政策在其审计手段上是各国普遍面对的难题。

4　国际建筑碳审计方法对我国建筑碳审计的经验借鉴及建议

通过前文对各国建筑碳排放核算方法的梳理，以及对各国在进行建筑碳审计时所面临的问题和挑战的分析，不难发现要进行合理并建立符合低碳目标的建筑碳核算方法需要把握全生命周期的各个阶段，综合考虑建筑碳核算的边界设定、碳核算清单的制定、碳核算方法的合理选择以及相辅助的碳审计政策等几个方面。根据我国目前的碳审计背景，可以归纳出以下几个方面以供未来建筑碳核算借鉴和参考。

抓住建筑碳审计的重点内容，对建筑的全生命周期进行恰当划分，使得周期中的每个阶段过渡自然，避免因边界的划分而产生较难收集及统计的碳排放。与此同时，尽量选择一组建筑作为碳审计的对象，在一定工地范围内进行核算，从而可以适当增加碳汇促进低碳目标。

为更好地确定所审计建筑物的碳排放源，应根据当地环境和项目自身的能源使用情况进行核算工具的建立，确定具体的直接或者间接碳排放因子。目前我国现有的碳排放因子主要由 IPCC 国家温室气体清单指南获得，是基于国际能源使用情况进行编制的，不适用于我国的情况。各省应该结合各自情况利用中国生命周期基础数据库（CLCD）来编制符合当地情况的温室气体建筑碳核算清单和消耗定额排放因子。同时应根据建筑形态、施工方式及功能划分进行核算，在一定程度上构成核算体系，便于归类，从而总结归纳出可比较和嵌套的碳审计模式。

结合我国工程管理对建筑建造和营运的管理，建筑碳审计模型的建立应该设立在建设相关主管部门进行工程项目活动开展之前，利用工程前期的工程设计和施工方案，从材料消耗、机械使用两个方面考虑，同时利用建筑工程量清单对分部分项工程进行分段审计，建立碳审计报告，也可引入 BIM 等相关建筑资讯模型，对建筑全生命周期进行监督控制，同时对温室气体排放进行核算。

建筑碳审计是与建筑碳交易相辅相成的，因此建立全国范围内的碳补偿制度，通过经济补偿的形式完善建筑碳审计，从而达到低碳减排的目标。与此同时，通过政府政策、各地规范制度，以及相关法律制度对整个建筑审计活动进行全面保障。相比较于其他发达国家，中国还没有建立详细的碳信息披露标准，对建筑物的碳审计也主要集中于碳排放核算和减排管理两个部分，然而对减排效果的测算仍然缺少验证措施。因此中国亟须建立与建筑审计过程相适应的减排效果测算，并将减排目标具体落实在碳审计和建筑碳减排的过程中。

致谢

此篇论文是基于本人在香港中文大学高级环境规划技术理学硕士专业的毕业论文进行组织和撰写的。在此特别感谢指导老师叶祖达教授的指导和中国城市住宅研究中心邹经宇教授的启发和帮助。

The International Comparative Analysis of Methodology for Building Carbon Emission Audit

Wan Shiyu
(Chinese University of Hong Kong)

Abstract：Nowadays，with global warming，buildings have become the most important source of carbon emission，in which people should pay more attention to. In the fifth contracting meeting of United Nations Framework Convention on Climate Change，China made the commitment that it would decrease the amount of carbon dioxide emission about 40%- 45% in 2020. What's more，in the background of fast industrialization and urbanization，and in order to realize the target of carbon reduction in such big scale，it is emergency to explore the systematic carbon audit method and some related carbon accounting policy. This paper makes an analysis on the carbon accounting for building in the developed countries and districts，from three aspects of accounting boundary，accounting list to the concrete method choose，in order to analyze the international problems and challenges based on their own situation and learn from their advanced experience，and finally find and adapt a more suitable building carbon accounting method for our country.

Keywords：Carbon audit，Life cycle of buildings，Carbon emission list，Carbon accounting method

参考文献：

[1] 陈红敏. 国际碳核算体系发展及其评价[J]. 中国人口、资源与环境，2011：09.

[2] 刘念雄，汪静，李嵘. 中国城市住区 CO_2 排放量计算方法[J/OL]. 清华大学学报（自然科学版）网络. 预览，2009：09.

[3] 谷立静. 基于生命周期评价的中国建筑行业环境影响研究[R]. 2009.

[4] 郑立红，冯春善. 绿色建筑全生命周期碳排放核算及节能减排效益分析——以天津某办公建筑为例[J]. 动感（生态城市与绿色建筑），2014：03.

[5] 杨应杰. 碳审计应用的国际比较与经验借鉴[J]. 现代企业，2013：06.

[6] 刘少瑜，苟中华，巴哈鲁丁. 建筑物温室气体排放审计——香港建筑物碳审计指引介绍[J]. 中国能源，2009：06.

[7] Downie, A., Lau, D., Cowie, A., & Munroe, P. Approaches to greenhouse gas accounting

methods for biomass carbon. Biomass and Bioenergy，2014：60(0)，18-31.

[8] Chen，G. Q.，Chen，H.，Chen，Z. M.，Zhang，B.，Shao，L.，Guo，S.，. . . Jiang，M. M. Low-carbon building assessment and multi-scale input-output analysis. Communications in Nonlinear Science and Numerical Simulation，2011：16(1)，583-595.

[9] Chau，C. K.，Leung，T. M.，& Ng，W. Y. A review on life cycle assessment，life cycle energy assessment and life cycle carbon emissions assessment on buildings. Applied Energy，2015：143(0)，395-413.

[10] Jiang，P.，Chen，Y.，Dong，W.，& Huang，B. Promoting low carbon sustainability through benchmarking the energy performance in public buildings in china. Urban Climate，2014：10，Part 1 (0)，92-104.

[11] Li，J.，& Colombier，M. Managing carbon emissions in china through building energy efficiency. Journal of Environmental Management，2009：90(8)，2436-2447.

[12] Shao，L.，Chen，G. Q.，Chen，Z. M.，Guo，S.，Han，M. Y.，Zhang，B.，. . . Ahmad，B. Systems accounting for energy consumption and carbon emission by building. Communications in Nonlinear Science and Numerical Simulation，2014：19(6)，1859-1873.

Motivation in Construction Waste Reduction

Li Yiman Rita

(Sustainable Real Estate Research Center/Department of Economics and
Finance，Hong Kong Shue Yan University)

Abstract：Construction waste has often been regarded as one of the major source of waste which dump to landfill. As many countries do not have sufficient space to construct new landfill. They are looking for solutions to deal with the issues. We illustrate that regulations and government guidelines provide some useful means to reduce waste. They provide the directions on waste disposals.

Keywords：Construction waste，Motivation

1 Introduction

Many years ago, the major problem that we face was insufficient resources. Our human society does not have sufficient food and clothes. Most of the activities were environmental friendly. Many were reused and reused until it could no longer be reused again. In the modern society, however, we face another problem. We want to use something new. Many of the construction materials are new product. In some circumstances, when there are excess steel, throwing away the steel may cost less than recycle. This economic incentive motivates some contractors to throw the construction materials than looking for means to manage it. As many countries are running out of landfill sites, the idea of win-win-win economic, social and environment development is on the lips of politicians, practitioners and environmentalists [6,7,9]. Many of the construction companies are looking for useful means to achieve it.

When we consider the abovementioned reasons, however, shall offer us some insights on how to manage waste. To certain extend, the costs of dumping waste to landfill is one of the reasons. Corporate image is another reason. Hence, some of the contractors think of some ways to reduce waste is due to the corporate social responsibility [8] which can be considered as an economic incentive as well. Companies with better social responsibility may attract more business, improve economy, achieve the goal of environmental protection.

2 Construction waste minimization program and architects' roles in reducing dump to landfill

Since construction waste becomes a serious issue for society and may reduce contractors' profit, different reduction plan existed to help waste producers to lessen the construction waste. In the worldwide, there have two major ways to reduce the construction waste, one is implementing the waste management system also called as waste minimization program [2] from the building construction process and the other way is to reuse, recycling and disposal those construction waste [1]. Another common way is to reduce construction waste via better design where architect play a very important role [10]. There are a number of ways they can do to reduce waste.

1) They should provide advice to their clients by briefing the contractors about the impact of

waste production and notice the benefits of cost savings.

2）Architects can initiate the waste reduction in the project level. It implies that the architects should estimate the construction waste and reviews it at different key design stages and provide any chances for waste reduction.

3）Architects should try to use reclaimed material, standardized components, prefabricated and off-site preparation of materials [3].

3　Motivation to reduce waste: a psychological perspective

The idea of motivation is often referred to the various means to propel somebody to do something. For example, theory X assumes human are lazy. They have to be propelled by various punishments. Hence, if there is some staff who do not work well, he or she will be punished. This theory share some common values with the incentive theory which suggests that negative incentive such as punishment shall offer useful insights in motivating human being to do something. On the other hand, theory Y suggests that human are self-motivated. So long as a good environment is provided, we shall be directed to do something as intended.

4　Construction waste reduction in the UK

The role of government can be a motivation to reducing waste[4]. In the UK, there is an action plan with regards to the suggestions on how to reduce construction, demolition and excavation waste dump to the landfill. It aims to reduce half of the construction, demolition and excavation waste. It also mentioned that overcoming the challenges or constraints require support from suppliers, product manufacturers, contractors etc. Apart from that the role of Government in implementing regulations and establishing waste institution are of equal importance [5].

5　Construction waste reduction in Japan

In Japan, incinerationis the primary disposal system for solid waste disposal. Landfill is only considered as the second most important way to dispose waste. Nevertheless, as there is an increasing concern about the environment and there are a lot of hurdles to construct new landfills, government has to introduce some laws to reduce waste. The first solid waste management law was enacted in 1971. However, this was a nominal standard without technical practice. 5 years later, the technical standard of operation and construction was implemented. It defined the needs and structures of waste management and control. Nevertheless, it only concerned landfills which were larger than 2000m². Later, in 1979, guidelines for the design, construction and operation of landfills were implemented to provide the minimum requirement to obtain government's subsidy which cover one-forth of construction costs. It also stated that Landfill is a process where waste is assimilated to the ecosystem. It stabilizes waste through a natural metabolic mechanism without any adverse impact on the environment. To contain waste and leachate, and to treat waste, leachate, and landfill gas. The followings are required [11]:

（1）A liner system, drainage system, leachate collection as well as a leachate treatment plant are required despite there is no detailed design criteria.

（2）Daily cover of 30cm should be applied after the compaction of refuse. Intermediate soil cover of 50cm or more final cover has to be applied.

Later，the standards were revised in 1998 to increase the standard. A vertical impervious wall structure had to be included for the leachate containment system in any area with natural liner or an impermeable sub-base. Under the social pressure against the uncontrolled landfills of environmental pollution and industrial solid waste，the "standard of landfill disposal" was extended in 1997 to apply to every landfill，regardless of size. In 2000，the "guidelines for the performance of Municipal solid waste landfills" was implemented. Starting from that time，any landfill has to be subsidized if it meets the criteria. The landfills surface area dropped. Hence，we can see the significant impact on waste management with regards to environmental protection [11].

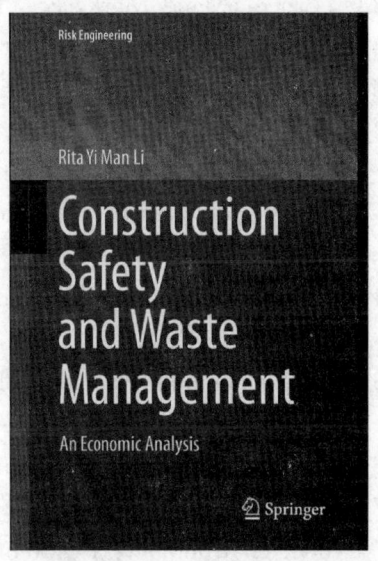

Figure 1　Construction Safety and Waste Management：An Economic Analysis（Springer，2015）

6　Conclusion

The study in the UK and Japan suggests that the major source of motivations come from government regulations. They are often the best ways to solve the waste problems as those who act against them will face penalty such as fines and jails. Therefore，theory X is one of the good way to explain human actions in construction waste reduction.

If you wish to know more about construction waste management，you may refer to my new book：Rita Yi Man Li（2015）Construction Safety and Waste Management，Springer，Switzerland.

7　Acknowledgement

The author would like to thank the assistance of Chan，C. P.，Cheung，W. Y. Chan，C. K.，Wong，Y. L.，Lai，Y. T. Wong H. Y.

减少建筑废物的动机

李绮雯

（可持续房地产研究中心/经济与金融的香港树仁大学系）

摘要：建筑废物常常被视为倾倒在垃圾填埋场的废弃物的主要来源之一。由于许多国家没有足够的空间来构建新的垃圾填埋区。他们正在寻找解决方案来处理这些问题。我们认为法规和政府的指导方针提供了一些有用的减少浪费的方法。同时提供了废物处置的重要方向。

关键词：建筑废物，动机

References：

［1］ Begum，R.，Siwar C.，Pereira J.，Jaafar A. H.. A benefit-cost analysis on the economic feasibility of construction waste minimisation：The case of Malaysia［J］. Resource，Conservation and Recycling 2006.

［2］ Bruce，Mand Mark，S.. Implementing a waste management plan during the construction phase of a project：a case study［J］. Construction Management and Economics，1998，16：1，71-78，DOI：10. 1080/014461998372600.

［3］ Coventry，S.，Guthrie，P.. Waste Minimisation and Recycling in Construction：Design Manual［M］. In：Construction Industry Research and Information Association Speeial publication 134. London，United Kingdom：Construction Industry Research and Information Association (CIRIA)，1998.

［4］ Hakan，A. Nilay，C，Burcu，S.. Construction and Demolition Waste Management in Turkey［M］. INTECH Open Auess Publisher 2012.

［5］ Katherine Adams，Peter Johnson，Jane Thornback，Charlie Law. WASTE：An Action Plan for halving construction，demolition and excavation waste to landfill［R］. 2011.

［6］ Li，Rita Yi Man. Building our sustainable cities［M］. US：Common Ground Publishing，2011.

［7］ Li，Rita Yi Man. The usage of automation system in smart home to provide a sustainable indoor environment：a content analysis in Web 1. 0［J］. International Journal of Smart Home，2013，7(4)：47-59.

［8］ Li，Rita Yi Man (2015) Construction Safety and Waste Management：an Economic Analysis. Switzerland：Springer

［9］ Li，Rita Yi Man，Ah Pak，Don Henry (2010) Resistance and motivation to share sustainable development knowledge by Web 2. 0，Journal of Information and Knowledge Management，9 (3)，251.

［10］ M. Osmani，J. Glass，A. D. F. Price. Architects' perspectives on construction waste reduction by design［J］. Waste Management，2008，28(7)：1147-1158.

［11］ Springer. Construction Safety and Waste Management［OL］http：//link. springer. com/book/10. 1007/978-3-319-12430-8.

［12］ Tanaka，N.，Tojo，Y.，Matsuto，T.. Past，present，and future of MSW landfills in japan［J］. The Journal of Material Cycles and Waste Management，2005，7(2)：104-111.

绿色建筑与建筑技术
Green Building and Building Technologies

专题二：建筑技术与信息科技
Special Topic 2：Building and Information Technologies

建筑信息模型基础的效能分析程序：以建筑日照分析为例

陈上元[1]　张淑芬[2]　陈正晏[1]

（1. 逢甲大学；2. 明志科技大学）

摘要： "建筑信息模型基础的效能分析程序"（BIM based BPA procedure）是指文本与数据在建筑信息模型（Building information modeling，BIM）与建筑效能分析（Building performance analysis，BPA）之间传输与交互应用的过程，应用该程序能够大幅提升"设计与分析"的决策效率，是计算机辅助建筑可持续性设计的有效途径。本研究采用"绿色建筑可延伸标记式语言"（Green Building XML，gbXML）标准，应用 Autodesk 公司产品 Revit 作为BIM 建模工具、Ecotect 作为建筑效能分析工具，以"建筑日照分析"为例，实证其构想，并且建立实务应用的工作流程。

关键词： 建筑信息模型，建筑效能分析，绿色建筑可延伸标记式语言，冬至日照时数，全天空照度

1 动机与目的

借着实务上要求进行"建筑日照分析"项目的委托，本文探索文本与数据在建筑信息模型（Building information modeling，BIM）和建筑效能分析（Building performance analysis，BPA）之间传输与交互应用的过程，即"建筑信息模型基础的效能分析程序"（BIM based BPA procedure），其研究目的在于应用该程序能够大幅提升"设计与分析"的决策效率，是计算机辅助建筑可持续性设计的有效途径。

2 文献回顾

建筑设计的过程，是"设计与分析"的决策循环[1~4]如果透过一致的交换格式（exchange format），使得模型与信息能够在 BIM（设计）与 BPA（分析）间有效的传递，则可以节省大量的重复建模、重复设置参数的时间。BIM 包含了几何、物理和拓扑信息，BPA 包括了：建筑日照、遮阳优化、热辐射、空调耗能、音效设计、通风环境、视觉影响、生命周期的能耗与碳排等建筑效能可视化与数值化的分析。据统计，目前世界上主要的效能分析软件约有 350 多种，但是因为缺乏统一的传输标准，几乎使用每一种软件，都需重新建模，耗费了大量工作时间。[5]这个困扰也存在于BIM 软件与 BPA 软件间的传输与交换。Bentley Systems 在 2000 年制定了绿色建筑可延伸标记式语言（Green Building XML，gbXML），开发用于传输建筑外壳、分区、机械设备模拟的初步能源分析所需要的信息，可作为 BIM 软件与 BPA 软件的传输平台，逐渐获得 BIM 大厂们的采用。[6]

3 理论与方法

本研究拟以 Autodesk 公司产品 Revit 作为 BIM 建模工具，它与同公司的建筑效能分析软件 Ecotect 和 Vasari 有很好的兼容性，并且透过 gbXML 格式作为 BIM 与 BPA 之间的传输标准。Ecotect 发展历史较早，Vasari 可视为 Autodesk 公司将 Ecotect 与 Revit 建模工具整合的软件，应用虚拟气象站的大数据演算，它改善了过去 Ecotect 受限于有限地点气象资料的限制，可推估出任一地点的气象数据进行环境仿真评估。目前 Vasari 仅为测试的 Beta 版本，尚无可供商业使用的软件，且就日照而言，较 Ecotect 分析工具少，目前无法就室内做照度分析。因此，如果需要分析的基地，其分析图具有商业用途，且已有 Ecotect 可以使用的气象资料（例如：台北、台中、台南），则建议

采用 Ecotect。本项目 Ecotect 在建筑日照分析上的项目包括：（1）冬至日照时数检讨；（2）室内照度分析。

4　实作案例

建筑信息模型基础的效能分析程序主要是指从项目需求的设定、BIM 建模、BPA 分析、分析说明到项目结束的一段过程，然而，考虑实务的条件，修正的流程如图 1 所示。

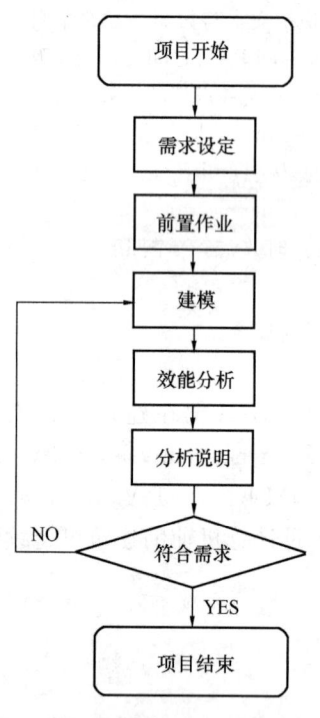

图 1　"建筑信息模型基础的
效能分析程序"实务应用
工作流程

4.1　项目开始

登录项目的信息，包括：（1）案名；（2）地址；（3）参与人员；（4）时程与进度。

4.2　需求设定

主要是描述与条列业主对于项目的要求和目的。针对本项目华厦的三楼对象，业主要求进行"建筑日照分析"，主要包括：（1）冬至日照时数检讨；（2）室内照度分析，两个作业要项，分析结果将作为分析对象符合法规的依据，以及未来室内照明设计的参考。

4.3　前置作业

根据需求设定，本项目将针对对象与周遭建筑体量进行"建模"与"效能分析"的工作，工作的前置作业，包括：

（1）现地会勘：就对象所在位置，观察与记录可能影响该对象日照环境的建筑物，并划定体量建模的范围，记录该范围内的建筑物门牌，以便日后查询楼高等基本数据（图 2）。

（2）现场测量：测量重点包括：（a）现况平面与座向；（b）隔墙；（c）地板至天花板高度；（d）楼层高度；（e）窗台高度与开口尺寸；（f）遮阳宽度、深度（图 3）。

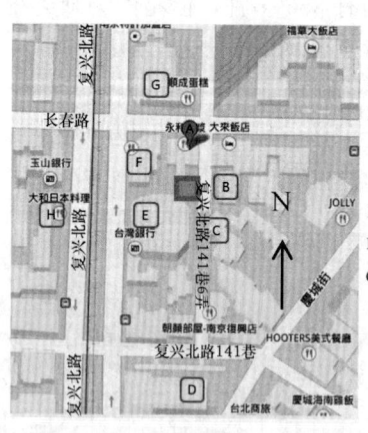

图 2　划定与记录体量建模的范围

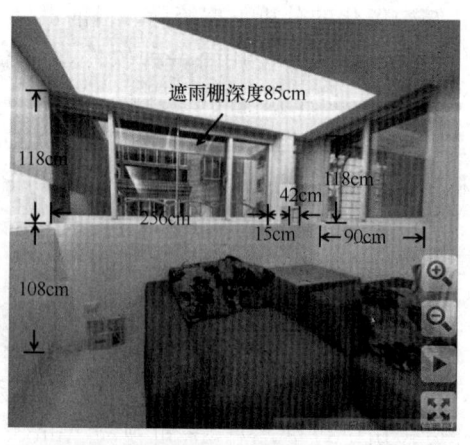

图 3　现场测量

（3）图资查询：查询地理信息数据库，例如：台北市都市计划整合查询系统[7]，应用数值地形图资以分析环境周遭体量轮廓、计算量体楼高与高度。查询时，首先必须输入门牌地址、地段地号。

4.4 建模

根据前置作业的轮廓与测绘资料建模。在 Revit 中，需要：（1）建立华厦与环境周遭体量的 BIM 建筑信息模型（图 4），并"汇出"成 DXF 格式档；（2）建立项目对象的"分析模型"（Analytical model），该分析模型是由 Revit 的 BIM 模型，透过"房间"（rooms）定义的（图 5），具备了体积（volumetric）与区划的（zonal）信息。当"分析模型"建成后，则汇出成 gbXML 格式档（图 7）。

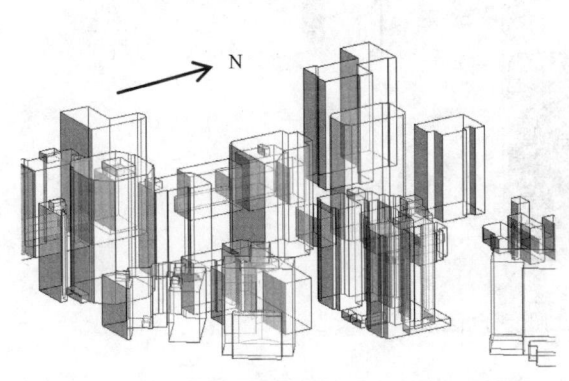

图 4　建立体量几何模型

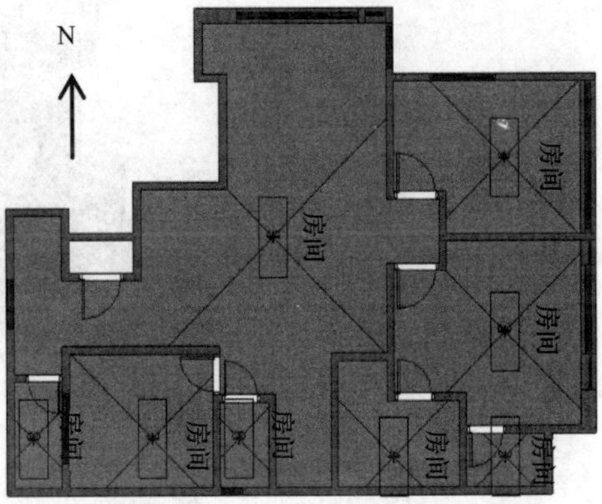

图 5　定义"房间"

4.5 效能分析

（1）冬至日照时数检讨

计算项目对象周遭的建筑体量在冬至日所造成的日照阴影，保证项目对象主要采光面的有效日照时数。

（a）在 Ecotect 中"汇入"先于 Revit 建立的 DXF 格式的几何模型。

（b）在 Ecotect 开启阴影，将太阳在冬至日的日轨上缓缓移动，观察与记录日照阴影投射在对象主要采光面的状况。本案对象的主要采光面为东面，其不受周遭阴影影响的时段为 10：00～12：00，故有 2h 的冬至日照（图 6）。

（2）室内作业面照度分析

（a）在 Ecotect 中"汇入"先于 Revit 建立的 gbXML 格式的文件分析模型（图 7）。

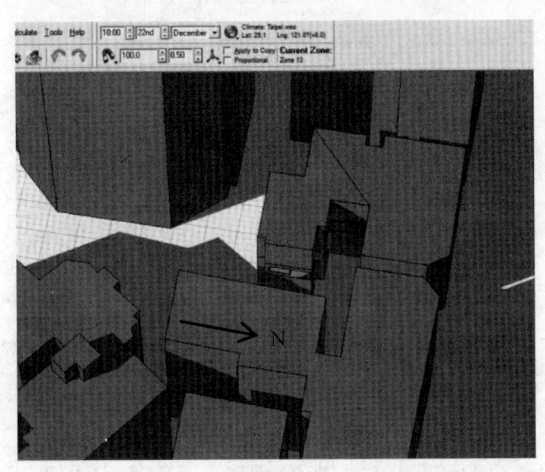

图 6　分析冬至日照时数

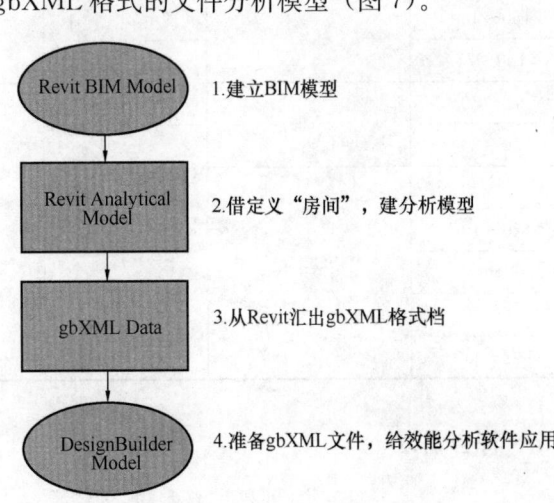

图 7　从 BIM 模型转成效能分析模型[8]

（b）设定分析网格至"分析模型"，并将分析网格设定在 80cm 的作业面高度。

（c）全天空照度设定：Ecotect 依照台北纬度，算出昏暗天候全天空照度是 11000lx。

（d）室内照度分析：将室内照度分析的最大数值可以设定在 600～1000lx 之间，而最小值设为 0lx，以便于通过网格中色块的分布，判读作业面照度现况，以作为照明设计的建议（图 8）。

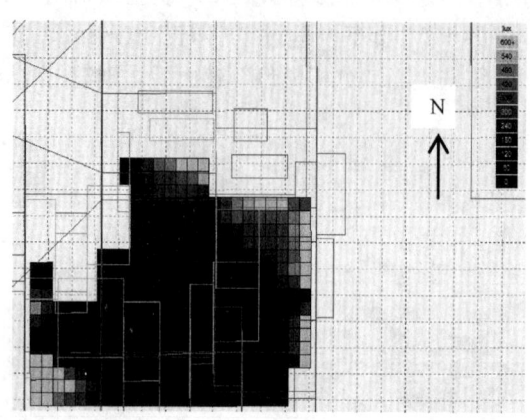

图 8　Ecotect 照度分析结果

4.6　分析说明

本项目对象的主要采光面向东，具有 2h 的冬至日照，已经满足且超过法规 1h 日照的要求。针对住宅内不同作业与活动，有不同作业面照度标准（表 1）。根据室内日照分析，本项目有 60％以上是照度不足 180lx，不符合于娱乐、阅读、调理等的作业面照度需求，需做重点的照明辅助。

CNS 室内照度标准[9]　　　　　　　　　　　　　　　　　　　　　　表 1

照度（lx）	起居间	书房	儿童房	客厅	厨房餐厅	卧房
2000～1000	◎手艺◎缝纫	—	—			—
1000～750		◎写作◎阅读	◎作业◎阅读	—	—	
750～500	◎阅读◎化妆（10）					◎看书◎化妆
500～300	◎电话（14）		—		◎餐桌◎调理	
300～200	◎团聚◎娱乐（13）	—	◎游玩	◎桌面（13）		
200～150				◎沙发	—	
150～100	—		◎游玩 全般	—		
100～75		全般	全般	—	全般	
75～50	全般			全般		
50～30						
30～20						全般
20～10						
10～5	—					—
5～2						
2～1						深夜

4.7　符合需求

检验分析结果是否已达到业主的要求，如果否，则回到建模程序、效能分析……，若达到业主要求则项目结束。本项目所提供的效能分析的结果已足够作为符合法规的依据以及室内照明设计的参考。若达到业主对作业的要求，则项目结束，否则重新建模。

5　讨论与建议

实作发现，BIM 模型具备三个特质：（1）为 3D 的几何模型；（2）为数据库；（3）是可在建筑生命周期持续使用的模型。BIM 软件是有别于一般专注在 3D 的几何模型与彩现的建模软件。建筑信息模型基础的效能分析程序（BIM based BPA procedure）是计算机辅助建筑可持续性设计的有效途径，应用"gbXML"标准的 Bim-based 效能分析程序，避免了过去在设计软件与分析软件间重复建模，提升"设计与分析"的决策效率。讨论与建议如下：

（1）后续的应用

根据 Ecotect 照度分析结果，检讨白天作业面照度不足之处，就 CNS 室内照度标准，进行重点的人工照明辅助设计。

（2）应用 BIM-based BPA 重新检视法规的限制、迈向效能基础的法规

建筑是立体的，法规的限制却经常是平面思考的，以冬至日照检讨为例，可以证明在法规检讨下所示的效能不良区域，却能够在立体的向度，拥有极佳的效能。按照台湾地区的建筑技术规则规定[10]，计算方式是依太阳 7：00～8：00am 及 16：00～17：00pm 时刻，建筑体量产生的四条阴影相交，取其全日无一小时日照区的两个交点的连接，成为临栋间距的界线（图 9）。然而如图 10 所示，建筑是立体的，即使是在全日无日照区立起来的体量，当超过某个高度后，便有终日不受临栋日照阴影影响的范围。

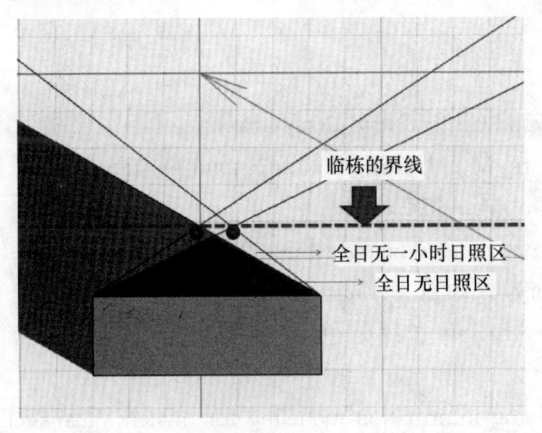
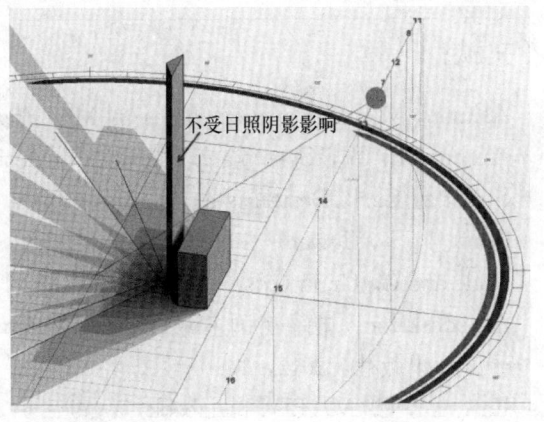

图 9　冬至日照与临栋界线检讨　　　　图 10　不受日照阴影影响的范围

致谢

建制智慧电网基础设施下的家庭能源觉察系统（MOST 103-2221-E-035-047-），2014 年度台湾 Green BIM 绿建筑信息模型应用架构研究（台湾建筑研究所）

Bim-Based Building Performance Analysis Procedure：Architectural Sunlight Analysis as An Example

Chen Shang-Yuan，Chang shu-Fen，Chan Zhang-Yan

（1 Feng Chia University；2 Ming Chi University of Technology）

Abstract："Building information modeling based performance analysis procedure（BIM based BPA procedure）" refers to the transmission and interactive applications of text and data between BIM and BPA. The application of the procedure can greatly enhance efficiency in decision making of the "Design and Analysis". It is an effective way that computer aids sustainable architectural design. This study adopts "Green building extensible markup language（green building XML, gbXML）" standard, and uses Autodesk Revit as BIM tool and Ecotect as BPA tool. It takes the "Architectural Sunlight Analysis" as an example, demonstrates ideas, and establishes practical application workflow.

Keywords：Building information modeling, Building performance analysis, Green building extensible markup language, Hours of winter sunshine, Illuminance from unobstructed sky

参考文献：

[1] Asimon, M.. Introduction to design[M]. Englewood Cliffs. New Jersey：Prentice-Hall，1962.

[2] Archer，L. B.. Systematic Method for designers[M]. Council of Industrial Design，1965.

[3] Steinitz, Carl. Design is a verb Design is a noun[M]. 1995：199.

[4] Gero, J. S.. Towards a model of designing which includes its situatedness[M]. H. Grabowski, S. Rude and G. Grein（eds）. Universal Design Theory, Shaker Verlag, Aachen, 1998：47-56.

[5] Autodesk Inc.，柏慕中国主编. Autodesk Ecotect Analysis 2011 绿色建筑分析应用[M]. 北京：电子工业出版社，2012，1.

[6] Eastman, C. M.. BIM handbook：a guide to building information modeling for owners, managers, designers, engineers, and contractors, 2008. Wiley.

[7] 台北市都市计划整合查询系统. ［2015-3-8］. http：//www. budwebgis. tcg. gov. tw/planMap/city-plan _ main. aspx.

[8] Design Builder Revit-gbXML Tutorial . ［2015-3-8］. http：//www. designbuilder. co. uk/downloads/db _ revit _ tutorial _ v1. pdf.

[9] CNS 室内照度标准. ［2015-3-8］. http：//www. chinaelectric. com. tw/cns _ 51. htm.

[10] 台湾营建署. 100. 07. 27 营署建管字第 1002912066 号函. ［2015-3-8］. http：//www. cpami. gov. tw/chinese/index. php? option=com _ content&view=article&id=14493&Itemid=114/.

街廓内巷道数量规划模式之研究

沈育生

（政治大学地政学系）

摘要： 街廓内巷道系统之规划是城市细部计划中重要的工作之一。因该道路系统功能迥异于一般干道系统，且目前缺乏客观规划方法，再加上过去的道路设计多以车优先角度出发，忽略行人之需要，因此，本研究针对街廓内道路系统规划中最为关键的"巷道数量"工作建构规划模式，用以决定街廓内巷道数量配置之多寡。本模式以多目标整数规划之方式进行设计，模式目标包括：可及性、易行性与交通安全，而限制条件则涵盖：旅运需求、紧急车辆通行效率、民众避难效率、噪声、空气质量、畸零地限制、道路建设面积上限、道路建设及维护成本限制、街廓设计风格。而本文以中心点法作为上述模式的求解方法，最后，透过高雄新市镇内住商混合街廓的实例应用，验证模式之可用性，并测试"交通稳静化"措施对规划结果的影响，以了解模式特性，而分析结果可提供应用模式时的进一步参考信息。

关键词： 道路规划设计，城市细部计划，巷道数量，街廓，多目标整数规划

1　前言

街廓内巷道系统之功能迥异于干道系统，其具有交通、防灾、生活、公共空间、城市型塑与社会活动等特殊之特征与功能。然过去研究多聚焦于干道系统之规划设计，忽视与居民息息相关之巷道系统，致使缺乏客观规划方法，只能依凭规划者个人经验来进行划设，而划设之合理性与可靠性常遭受质疑；再者，过去的道路设计多注重道路之交通功能，而忽略了其他功能，并因规划者多从车优先角度进行规划，忽略行人之需要，进而破坏地区环境的生活机能。

在街廓内之道路系统之规划元素中，巷道数量是重要的项目之一。当巷道数量规划不当时，在运输功能方面，会因此造成地区整体运输功能不佳，进而造成道路使用上的不便利，以及旅行时间的增加；在防灾与安全方面，会因此增加交通肇事的机会，以及救灾与避难的困难性；在生活环境方面，会因此造成噪声与空气的污染更严重，进而降低地区生活环境质量；在财政支出方面，会因此增加道路建设与维护成本，进而造成政府财政上的负担；在土地使用方面，会因此而产生畸零地，造成土地的闲置，以及降低房地产价值，故须特别重视。

过去关于巷道的研究多着重于分类、功能、特性以及考虑因素等原则性的讨论[1,9]，并不常见其量化分析之研究，而以规范性量化模式构建街廓内巷道数量之研究更是少见，虽有部分之研究[5,6]，但在因素完整性、因素间关系合理性、建模方式等仍具有相当的改善空间。为协助城市细部计划之规划者有系统及有效率地进行路网规划工作，本研究目的在因应街廓内活动之需求，建构适宜之街廓内巷道数量规划模式，并透过实例研究，验证模式的实用性，同时对实例提供具体的规划建议。本文内容分为五部分：在本段说明研究动机、目的、内容及过去研究成果后，第二、三段分别说明研究设计与模式建构，第四段则说明实例应用及敏感度分析之结果，最后提出结论与建议。

2　研究设计

2.1　决策情境

街廓内巷道数量之配置系为台湾城市计划中细部计划之决策事项。而本规划模式系适用于街廓

内道路路网为格子状路网之方整街廓；另外，本模式除可适用于新开发地区中的素地开发、新订城市计划等状况，亦可适用于已发展地区中的大规模重建开发、市地重划等状况。

2.2　模式构想及内涵

本模式系在交通运输（道路容量、道路宽度、道路使用者）、土地使用（土地使用分区、土地使用强度、建筑场地最小之宽度与深度、街廓之宽度与深度）、社会经济（人口组成、活动人口数）、生活环境（公害污染、宁适性）等条件已知情形下，决定街廓内巷道最适数量。综整相关研究，归纳出街廓内巷道数量配置须考虑的因素（包括：一是运输功能向度的可及性、易行性、旅运需求；二是防灾与安全向度的紧急车辆通行效率、民众避难效率、交通安全；三是生活环境向度的噪声、空气质量；四是设计向度的畸零地限制、道路建设面积上限、街廓设计风格；五是成本向度的道路建设及维护成本），并依据建模原则决定模式之目标式及限制式。

2.3　研究方法

街廓内巷道数量之配置决策中，常面临不同目标间的权衡，且巷道数量须为整数形态，故适合利用多目标整数规划方法，建构街廓内巷道数量规划模式，并透过敏感度分析，探讨不同参数条件下之变化情形。另外，本文所建构的规划模式，在求解上，采用中心点法[11]的求解方式。

3　模式建构

3.1　符号界定

本模式中之变量及参数界定如下：A：符号下标表示车辆；P：符号下标表示行人；e：自然数，约等于 2.718282；c：随路口数增加而使车行速度递减之参数，$c \geqslant 0$；d．随路口数增加而使行人步行速度递减之参数，$d \geqslant 0$；f：随紧急救难设施与灾害现场距离远近而调整之参数，$f \geqslant 0$；g：随避难设施与灾害现场距离远近而调整之参数，$g \geqslant 0$；B_A：建筑场地之最小面积规定（m^2）；C_{AK}：表示在道路服务水平 k 下，街廓内单一路段之平均车辆容量（辆/min）；C_{PK}：在道路服务水平 k 下，街廓内每一单位人行道面积可容纳之行人数（人/m^2）；D_A：街廓本身之车旅次发生数（辆/min）；F_A：平均单一路口之车辆流量（辆/min）；F_P：平均单一路口之行人流量（人/min）；F_N：地方政府在建设上之财政支出上限（千元）；$J_0^{(CO)}$：街廓内所允许之一氧化碳（CO）排放总量上限（ppm/h）；$J_0^{(HC)}$：街廓内所允许之碳氢化合物（HC）排放总量上限（ppm/h）；$J_0^{(NO_X)}$：街廓内所允许之氮氧化合物（NO_X）排放总量上限（ppm/h）；$J_A^{(CO)}$：每一辆车在路口启动时所排放一氧化碳（CO）之总量（ppm/辆）；$J_A^{(HC)}$：每一辆车在路口启动时所排放碳氢化合物（HC）之总量（ppm/辆）；$J_A^{(NO_X)}$：每一辆车在路口启动时所排放氮氧化合物（NO_X）之总量（ppm/辆）；M_r：每单位道路面积之平均建造及维护成本（千元/m^2）；m_A：小客车之质量（kg）；N_P：街廓内行人总数（人）；R：允许的噪声影响面积占街廓面积之比例；r：路口噪声之影响距离（m）；S_A^0：车辆自由流之平均车速（m/min）；S_P^0：行人自由流之平均步行速度（m/min）；T_A：紧急车辆到达灾害现场之时间上限（min）；T_P：民众由灾害现场逃至避难设施之时间上限（min）；V_P：街廓内平均之人行道宽度（m）；Z_X：街廓内纵向巷道 X 之虚拟变量（即是否将纵向巷道 X 与场地之距离纳入考虑）；Z_Y：街廓内横向巷道 Y 之虚拟变量（即是否将横向巷道 Y 与场地之距离纳入考虑）；L：街廓之横向宽度（m）；W：街廓之纵向长度（m）；l_0：建筑基地最小宽度之规定（m）；w_0：建筑场地最小深度之规定（m）；ϕ：街廓内巷道之路宽（m）；α：纵向道路数与横向道路数关系参数之下限，

$\alpha \geqslant 0$；β：纵向道路数与横向道路数关系参数之上限，$\beta \geqslant 0$；X：街廓内纵向之巷道总数（条）；Y：街廓内横向之巷道总数（条）。

3.2 规划模式

本文基于下述假设进行列式：（1）只考虑街廓本身所产生与吸引之行人与汽车旅次，且旅次均匀分布于街廓内，并忽略通过性旅次以及自行车与机车两种运具；（2）假设车辆之自由流旅行速度不超过道路之法定速限；（3）假设行人与驾驶者无交通违规行为发生；（4）小客车旅运需求皆均匀分布于街廓之中；（5）假设街廓内空气污染物质主要由行驶的车辆所排放；（6）假设街廓内之空气污染与噪声污染不因地点不同而有所差异；（7）防救设施位置可位于街廓内或街廓外，若设施位于街廓外时，则假设防救车辆由街廓四个街角进入；（8）假设灾害发生时，所有道路皆可通行；（9）假设车辆于路口停等所产生之噪声污染较路段行驶中明显，而将路段中所产生之噪声忽略不计。

街廓内巷道数量规划模式〔P1〕如下所示。其中，式（1）、式（2）、式（3）分别是可及性、易行性与交通安全之目标式。而式（4）为车旅次之需求限制；式（5）为人旅次之需求限制；式（6）为紧急车辆通行效率限制；式（7）为民众避难效率限制；式（8）为噪声限制；式（9）、式（10）、式（11）为空气污染物质 HC、CO、NO_X 之限制，但因目前国内并无街廓内 HC、CO、NO_X 允许排放上限规范，以及车辆启动时之相关污染排放数据，故此三式于实例分析时，暂排除于限制条件之外；式（12）、式（13）、式（14）为畸零地面积限制；式（15）为道路建设面积上限；式（16）为道路建设及维护成本限制；式（17）为街廓设计风格限制（即纵向道路数与横向道路数之关系限制），式（18）为决策变量之值域限制。

$$\text{Max} \qquad X + Y \tag{1}$$

$$\text{Min} \qquad \frac{(L+W)}{S_A^0 \times e^{-c(X+Y+1)}} \tag{2}$$

$$\text{Min} \qquad F_A \times F_P \times [(X+2)(Y+2)] \times (S_A^0 \times e^{-c(\frac{X+Y+1}{2})})^2 \times m_A \tag{3}$$

$$\text{Subject to:} \qquad (X+Y) \times C_{Ak} \geqslant D_A \tag{4}$$

$$\frac{N_P}{(X \times W + Y \times L) \times V_P} \leqslant C_{Pk} \tag{5}$$

$$\frac{(L+W)/2}{S_A^0 \times e^{-c(\frac{X+Y+1}{2})}} \leqslant f \times T_A \tag{6}$$

$$\frac{(L+W)/2}{S_P^0 \times e^{-d(\frac{X+Y+1}{2})}} \leqslant g \times T_P \tag{7}$$

$$[1 + (X+Y) + (XY)]\pi r^2 \leqslant L \times W \times R \tag{8}$$

$$F_A \times J_A^{(CO)} \times [(X+2)(Y+2)] \leqslant J_0^{(CO)} \tag{9}$$

$$F_A \times J_A^{(HC)} \times [(X+2)(Y+2)] \leqslant J_0^{(HC)} \tag{10}$$

$$F_A \times J_A^{(NO_X)} \times [(X+2)(Y+2)] \leqslant J_0^{(NO_X)} \tag{11}$$

$$(L/X)(W/Y) \geqslant B_A \tag{12}$$

$$\frac{L}{X+1} \geqslant l_0 + \varphi \tag{13}$$

$$\frac{W}{Y+1} \geqslant w_0 + \varphi \tag{14}$$

$$(XW + YL)\varphi \leqslant LW \tag{15}$$

$$(XW + YL) \times \varphi \times M_r \leqslant F_N \tag{16}$$

$$\alpha \leqslant \frac{Y}{X} \leqslant \beta \tag{17}$$

$$X, Y \in \text{non-negative integers} \tag{18}$$

4 实例分析

4.1 实例说明

为确认模式于实务应用之可行性，针对高雄新市镇进行实例分析。高雄新市镇采用分期分区方式开发，目前仍有很多地区尚未开发，故基于资料取得的考虑，选择第一期发展区作为本文案例之研究范围，并选定由第四种住宅区与第三种商业区所组成的住商混合街廓，作为实例街廓，如图1所示。另外，基于所构建之规划模式为特定时间点之分析，属于"静态（static）"之规划，并使用横断面（cross-section）之分析数据，因此，实例分析将以2014年作为本研究所界定之基年时间点，而以高雄新市镇之计划年期2017年作为规划目标年。至于实例分析之参数部分，则如表1所示。

实例分析之参数值　　　　　　　表1

参数	参数值	单位	参数	参数值	单位
c	0.04	—	R	0.5	—
d	0.001	—	r	10	m
f	1	—	S_A^0	500	m/min
g	1.5	—	S_P^0	90	m/min
B_A	600	m^2	T_A	5	min
C_{AK}	25	辆/min	T_P	9	min
C_{PK}	0.3	人/m^2	V_P	2.5	m
D_A	275	辆/min	L	406	m
F_A	20	辆/min	W	276	m
F_P	15	人/min	l_0	20	m
F_N	789740	千元	w_0	15	m
M_r	1.827	千元/m^2	ϕ	10	m
m_A	2000	kg	α	0.2	—
N_P	1150	人	β	1	—

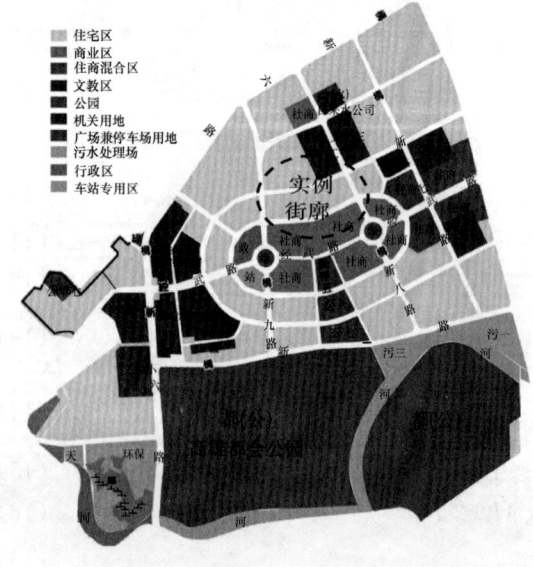

图1 模式规划实例地之示意图

（数据源：底图取自 http：//goo.gl/6ngjmo，并另行加工）

4.2 规划分析

本文依所建构之规划模式［P1］，利用 Center Method 求解后，分析结果显示，在案例街廓内之纵向巷道数为8条，横向巷道数为6条；而可及性、易行性及交通安全的目标值分别是14、2.48、6.58×10^{12}。另外，将模式规划结果与实际规划结果相比（如表2），可知模式规划道路数较实际规划道路数为高，显示实际规划采用大场地整体开发之理念，而调整模式［P1］中之 α 与 β，或是直接限制街廓内之纵向及横向巷道数之范围，可得到与实际规划接近之结果。

进一步比较三者在三个目标上的表现（如表2），与只考虑巷道（车道）的实际规划1相较，模式规划结果在可及性上表现最好，但在易行性与交通安全两个目标上较差，不过落后差距较在可及性的领先差距为小。若将实际规划之行人活动轴或绿地步道一并考虑而成为表2中的实际规划2，则对行人而言，模式规划与实际规划2的表现较接近。而比较三种规划结果在目标值的表现可知，三者之间为非劣关系，但大场地设计会有极差的可及性表现。若要平衡三个目标的达成度，大场设计宜搭配行人专用道或绿地步道来维持可及性，而小场地设计则需要搭配良好的交通管制措施来维持易行性与交通安全。

模式规划与实际规划比较 表2

项　　目	模式规划	实际规划1	实际规划2
纵向巷路数 X	8	1	10
横向巷路数 Y	6	1	9
可及性目标值	14	2	19
易行性目标值	2.48	1.54	3.04
交通安全目标值	6.58×10^{12}	1.2×10^{12}	8.89×10^{12}

注：实际规划1为实例街廓内巷道划设之结果。实际规划2为实例街廓内巷道与行人活动轴或绿地步道划设之结果。

4.3 敏感度分析

规划者常为维持街廓内的宁适性，而设计"交通稳静化"（traffic calming）相关措施，常见的做法为降低车流量与车速，当街廓有此设计需要时，巷道数目要如何因应规划？以下透过街廓内车旅次发生数 D_A 及街廓内车辆自由流平均车速 S_A^0 二参数之敏感度分析，进行探讨。

本文首先将车旅次发生数 D_A 逐次降低，发现在决策变量上（如表3），纵向与横向道路数随之减少；而减少的趋势是先明显减少纵向道路数，继而减少横向道路数。另外，在目标值方面（如表3），发现可及性随着车流量降低而变差，原因在于决策变量随车流量降低而降低，致使可及性变差；易行性会随着车流量降低而变好，其造成之原因有二，一是因为车流量减少后，会使得道路不再拥挤，进而促使车行旅行时间减少，二是因为决策变量随车流量降低而降低，进而使得路口数减少，降低车辆停等的时间，进而促使车行旅行时间降低；此外，交通安全亦随着车流量降低而变好，主因是车流量减少后，降低了交通肇事之几率，进而促使交通更安全。

本文继而将车辆自由流平均车速 S_A^0 逐次降低后，在决策变数上（如表4），发现决策变量并不跟随自由流车速而改变，显示巷道数目与自由流车速间较无关系。而在目标值方面（如表4），也发现可及性不随着车速降低而改变，原因在于道路数不随车流量降低而改变；但易行性随着车速降低而变差，原因是因为车速降低后，会进而促使车行旅行时间增加，使得易行性因而变差；同时交通安全随着车速降低而变好，主要是因为车速降低后，减低了交通事故之严重性，进而促使交通更安全。

不同车旅次数 D_A 下之分析结果整理表 表3

车旅次数 D_A	纵向巷路数	横向巷路数	可及性目标值	易行性目标值	交通安全目标值
275	8	6	14	2.48	6.58×10^{12}
200	7	5	12	2.29	5.61×10^{12}
150	6	5	11	2.20	5.19×10^{12}
100	6	4	10	2.11	4.63×10^{12}

不同车速 S_A^0 下之分析结果整理表 表4

车速 S_A^0	纵向巷路数	横向巷路数	可及性目标值	易行性目标值	交通安全目标值
500	8	6	14	2.48	6.58×10^{12}
417	8	6	14	2.98	4.58×10^{12}
333	8	6	14	3.73	2.92×10^{12}
250	8	6	14	4.97	1.64×10^{12}

5　结论与建议

　　细部计划中的巷道数规划虽为基础且重要之工作，但系统化的规划方法却未受重视，为改善上述问题，本文得到以下两项成果：一是以多目标整数规划方法建立街廓内巷道数量规划模式，规划者可应用此模式决定住商混合街廓内巷道最适数量，并据以进行后续细部设计工作，如微调道路网布设、道路几何线型设计等，以完成细部计划之道路系统规划。二是经由实例分析确认模式之实用性与特性，分析过程并可提供模式应用时参考。另外，在模式应用方面，一是建议须依当地之发展情况、目标以及限制进行调整，或可利用专家问卷与分析阶层程序法决定考虑因素与相对权重，以使模式之规划结果符合当地需求；二是模式规划结果可能造成相邻街廓道路不连续问题，规划者可将周围街廓特性纳入考虑来微调或修改模式，以维持道路之连续性；三是应用模式前须先依发展目标决定各项参数，例如若期望保留更多公共空间而要求大场地开发，则可设定较大的场地宽度与深度下限；而且部分参数需要进行实地调查与校估，以确保规划结果之可靠性；最后是本文所建构之模式具一定之复杂程度，于实际应用时恐有使用上的问题，未来可针对模式中相关联之参数予以简化其间关系，据此可减少参数与限制式数目，以及模式复杂度，有助对模式之了解与应用。

The Programming Model for Designing the Number of Lanes in the Block

Shen Yu-Sheng

（Department of Land Economics，Chengchi University）

Abstract：Designing the number of lanes in the block is the important work of city detail plan. This research aims at building the normative model to allocate the appropriate number of lanes in the block. The model is designed to a multi-objective integer programming, and its objectives include accessibility, mobility, and traffic safety. Moreover, the constraints include the travel demand, passing of emergency vehicles, escaping of refugees, noise, air quality, minimum area of building site, the upper limit of the area of road construction, the budget constraint of road construction and maintenance, design type of block. This research uses the Center Method to solve the developed model. A mixed-use block in Kaohsiung New Town is explored as a case study for verifying the applicability of model to practical works. The case study is also used to analyze the influences of traffic calming to identify model characteristics.

Keywords：Road design, City detail plan, The number of lanes, Block, Multi-objective integer programming

参考文献：

[1]　Mitchell D H，MacGregor S J. Topological network design of pedestrian networks. Transportation Research B，2001，35：107-135.

[2]　Girling L. The sustainable street：the environmental，human and economic aspects of street design and management. Landscape and Urban Planning，2003，62：117-118.

[3]　Wu Y L，Yeh K Y. Study on improvement alternative formulation and evaluation in local traffic planning process. Journal of Architecture，2000，34：57-85.（in Chinese）.

[4]　Hsu T P，Chen Y W. A comparative study on car and motorcycle traffic flow characteristics

on local streets. Journal of The Chinese Institute of Transportation，1999，11(4)：1-18.（in Chinese）.

[5] Ewing R. Sketch planning a street network. Transportation Research Record，1999，1722：75-79.

[6] Chen M H. Road network planning of an urban detailed plan master's thesis. Taipei：National Chiao Tung University，2002.（in Chinese）.

[7] 冯正民，曾平毅. 地区生活运输系统之规划[J]. 规划学报，1997，24(1)：79-97.

[8] Lillebye E. Architectural and functional relationships in street planning：an historical view. Landscape and Urban Planning，1996，35：85-105.

[9] 许添本. 小区化交通系统发展新理念[J]. 都市交通，1995，84：2-14.

[10] 林良泰，廖俊棠. 人车共存道路之理念与设计[J]. 都市交通，1994，76：21-28.

写字楼建筑物设置绿屋顶降温与舒适度之研究

苏瑛敏[1]　游素秋[2]

（1. 台北科技大学建筑与都市设计研究所；2. 台北科技大学建筑与都市设计研究所）

摘要： 全球环境急速变迁，如何降低城市热岛已成为国际关注议题；研究指出，透过屋顶绿化植物的蒸散作用可改善城市的热岛效应。2014 年台北市要求凡工程造价 5000 万新台币以上之公有及应取得绿色建筑达标之新建建筑物均要设置绿屋顶，绿屋顶的降温减碳效益成为重要政策议题。

过去对于绿屋顶之相关研究着重于降温及植栽种类、绿屋顶设置技术、法令之相关探讨，未能针对已设置绿屋顶之建筑物关注其后续管理维护状况。本研究针对两个实际设置绿屋顶之写字楼案例，以德国 Testo 175-H1 数位式温湿度记录器测量有无绿屋顶之屋顶面及直下方室内温度及湿度比较其差异，并以使用者问卷方式调查员工对绿屋顶降温及舒适度认知调查，从生理及心理层面探讨设置绿屋顶对写字楼建筑物之影响。

研究结果显示：（1）设置绿屋顶室外降温效果比室内降温效果好。（2）全面设置绿屋顶之降温效果比部分设置效果好。（3）设置绿屋顶可增加室外保湿效果及增加室内湿度。（4）受访者对绿屋顶之效益以"绿屋顶可以绿美化办公室屋顶环境"认同度最高。（5）全面设置绿屋顶且有开放的案例 B 比部分设置绿屋顶且不开放的案例 A，认同绿屋顶且较愿意去管理维护。（6）受访者支持设置绿屋顶认同度比例达 87.23%，而没有设置绿屋顶的主要原因以属于管委会管理需要全栋同意及会增加管理维护费用之支出为主要。在台北市积极推动绿屋顶之同时，希冀本研究结果可提供未来推动写字楼设置绿屋顶之参考。

关键词： 绿屋顶，屋顶降温，城市热岛，舒适度，写字楼建筑物

1　研究动机与目的

早在 1978 年起，台北市政府的建设局（目前的产业发展局），积极辅导台北市民设置绿屋顶花园，当时出版手册推广，并举办讲习观摩，但屋顶绿化效果不彰。直至 2014 年 11 月 10 日台北市通过"台北市绿建筑自治条例"，台北市政府为改善城市热岛效应推动绿屋顶。由公有及应取得绿建筑标章之新建建筑物开始实施，凡工程总造价 5000 万元新台币以上之公有及应取得绿建筑标章之新建建筑物均要设置绿屋顶，除了市有新建建筑物外，亦将持续推动既有所属建筑物的屋顶绿化改造，并逐步将绿屋顶政策纳入法令落实至私有建筑物。

本研究针对属于长时间使用及空调尖峰时间一致的高耗能写字楼建筑物做为研究建筑类型，考虑此类建筑物产权相对于住宅单纯，且在设置绿屋顶较易落实及节能效果显著动机下，对写字楼建筑物做绿屋顶降温效果及写字楼员工绿屋顶之认知调查。以案例 A（新北市板桥区）及案例 B（新北市新店区）为例，利用高精度 Testo 175-H1 温湿度监测仪器，每 15 分钟记录一笔数据连续 24 小时测量，分析研究案例 A、B 设置绿屋顶及未设置处之室内外温湿度差异，并以使用者问卷方式调查有设置绿屋顶写字楼案例员工及其他无设置绿屋顶写字楼员工之绿屋顶效益及管理维护认知，以作为未来推动写字楼建筑物设置绿屋顶之参考。

2　相关文献

"绿屋顶"（green roof）亦称为屋顶绿化或生态屋顶（eco-roof），意旨在屋顶上进行绿化达到建筑隔热降温、减缓暴雨径流、净化空气污染及生物跳岛等改善城市生态环境之目的。[1]针对绿屋顶整合其各项相关环境效益如下所述：（1）增加城市的绿化绿、美化环境及固定二氧化碳、达成减碳目标：依据 93—100"民间建筑物绿建筑设计及改善示范工作"90 件奖助案例为

数据库，分析各技术手法"成本—效益"，投入成本为该技术项目之合约发包金额（元），效益计算则以减碳量（kg）为主，搜集改善前后各一年内的电费、水费资料，并以比例分析法计算其成本—效益，其中屋顶绿化成本 1351000 元，减碳量可达 17779kg。[2]（2）都市降温、减少光辐射、消除热岛效应：夏季台北都市区域土地覆盖与地表辐射热平衡之关系[3]研究中指出在进行城市计划或造镇计划时，若能划设适当比例的蓝绿覆率，减少人造表面覆盖率，增加城市基地保水与土地蒸发散机制，将可有效抑制城市升温，舒缓城市热岛效应的强度。联合国环境署的研究也表示：如果一个城市的屋顶绿化率达到 70％以上，城市上空的 CO_2 含量将下降 80％，热岛效应现象可望纾解（Kolb and Schwarz，1999）。（3）屋顶保温隔热改善室内热环境、节约能源：在 Susana Saiz 等人（2006）之"比较与评估标准屋顶与绿屋顶的生命周期"（Comparative Life Cycle Assessment of Standard and Green Roofs）中，以生命周期评定（life cycle assessment，LCA）被使用来评定绿屋顶的效益，主要为降低能源耗损。关键是绿屋顶能附低太阳能吸收，导致较低的表面温度因而能透过屋顶降低热能。每年的能源使用能节省超过 1％，但夏天的冷却能节省超过 6％。借替换一般平面屋顶成绿屋顶，环境影响会降低介于 1.0％～5.3％。[4]（4）室内外温差变小，延长屋顶使用寿命：在不同屋顶绿化形式对屋顶隔热效果影响之研究，三种屋顶绿化形式可降低顶层室内温度约 2.4～2.6℃；降低室内顶棚表面温度约 5.7～8.7℃。草本及灌木屋顶绿化形式可降低室外屋顶表面温度约 9.4～13.4℃。其中草本及灌木屋顶绿化形式隔热效果较佳。[5]（5）减少径流量及尖峰流出率减轻城市排水系统之负担：施作屋顶绿化可使保水量提高约 17％，施做假俭草较虎尾兰有更高的保水量，平均提高 17％保水量，产生洪峰流量时间提前。此外，施作屋顶绿化使洪峰流量降低，且较厚介质有较高的减量效果，平均可推迟约 20min。[6]（6）隔绝噪声、净化空气：Currie and Bass（2005）曾利用其估算绿屋顶及绿墙对于多伦多地区的空污减量效益，在 Casey Trees Endowment Fund and Limno—Tech Incorporation（2005）的报告中也曾利用此模块，评估在华盛顿地区不同植物种植情境的减量效果，发现如全市皆为绿屋顶时，每年可达 58 metric tons 的空污减量。[7]（7）创造生物多样性：在地球生态系中活生物体从基因、个体、族群、物种、群集、生态系到景观等各种层次的生命形式均存在，水泥丛林中的屋顶绿化在城市生态系统中扮演相当重要之角色，而屋顶绿色空间创造出生物多样性并增加了城市生态系统之完整性。（8）提供休憩、疗愈、教育与园艺生产空间：在中小学及办公厅类建筑物设置绿屋顶除提供教育与参与植物种植蔬果绿化外，也提供了休憩园艺生产的绿化空间（环境效益项目数据源，张育森[8]）。

3 研究方法与研究设计

本研究以实地测量法针对有无设置绿屋顶之屋顶温湿度及直下方楼层室内温湿度每十五分钟记录一笔持续 24h 测量，统计分析其温度之变化趋势。本研究选择测量目标位于新北市板桥区（案例A），测量日期为 2014 年 8 月 8 日至 11 月 13 日。及新北市新店区（案例B）测量日期为 2014 年 7 月 11 日至 11 月 17 日。两个案例属于不同区位均为楼高十楼且实际大面积设置绿屋顶之既有写字楼建筑物，测量位置于研究绿屋顶之同一方位，并选择直下方室内有室内墙体区隔之完整空间，减少绿屋顶与非绿屋顶室内温度相互影响之可能性。测量日期以跨假日非空调时间持续 48h 测量。

3.1 实验测量仪器

本研究采用德国制高精度温湿度记录器 Testo 175 H1，仪器为陶瓷电容式湿度芯片，长期精准稳定可测量温度－20～＋55℃，湿度 0％～100％。以每十五分钟记录一笔持续 24h 自动测量。

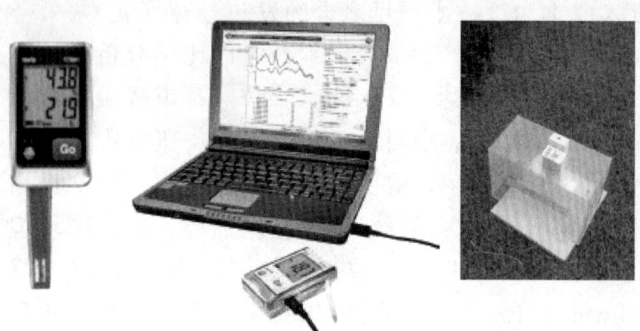

测量参数	温度(℃/°F)湿度(%Rf/%RH/℃ td/g/m³)
传感器类型	NTC温度传感器，电容式湿度传感器
精度	−20~+55℃，−40~+50℃ td,0~100%RH
分辨率	+−2% RH(2~98%RH),+−0.4℃ (−20~+50℃)

图1 高精度温湿度记录器 Testo 175 H1

3.2 研究对象分析与调查

（1）案例A——（台北板桥区），为地上10层写字楼建筑物。观察绿屋顶直下方为文康室且与其他室内空间隔墙区隔故将设定为绿屋顶测量实验组，另于一般屋顶直下方设定为测量对照。

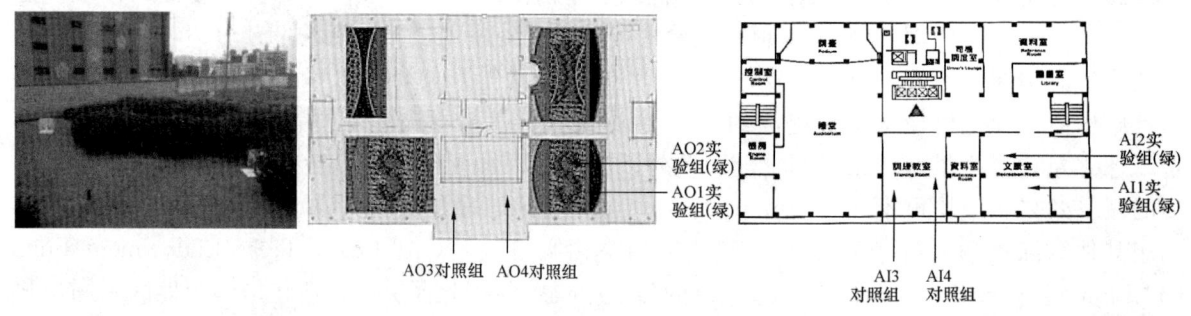

图2 案例A实景图及测站位置图

（2）案例B——（台北新店区），为地上10层写字楼建筑物。观察设置仪器测量之绿屋顶直下方为写字楼空间且与其他室内空间隔墙区隔，另于邻幢建筑物未设置绿屋顶之屋顶面及直下方之公共空间设定为测量对照组。本案例测量限制为B幢写字楼室内仅可测量电梯间附近之公共服务空间，但由于全幢建筑物均非设置绿屋顶，作为比较不同幢同高度之非空调日室内外温湿度变化。

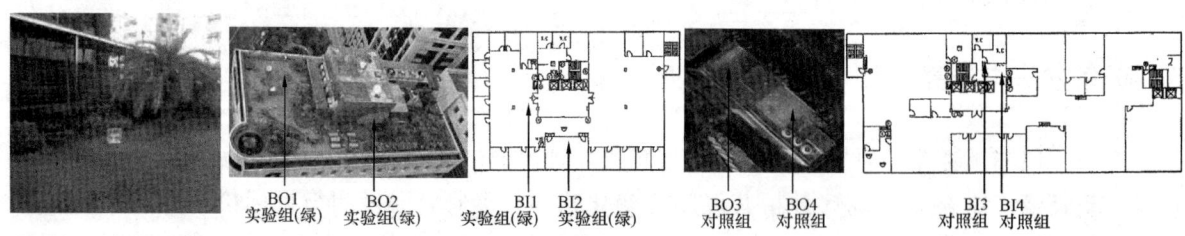

图3 案例B实景图及测站位置图

3.3 绿屋顶效益及认知问卷调查

本问卷调查之目的主要在于了解办公厅类建筑物有设置绿屋顶之写字楼员工，对绿屋顶之舒适度、环境效益、视觉心理、企业认同感及管理维护心理之认知；借以了解写字楼员工对绿屋顶之舒适度与效益认知心理。本研究分析数据样本所需之统计方法，主要采用的统计软件为 IBM SPSS22.0。共发放案例A问卷120份有效问卷回收108份，案例B发放问卷100份有效问卷回收90份，无绿屋顶发放100份有效问卷回收94份，总共发放320份有效回收问卷共292份，回收率91.25％。

根据统计得到下列结论：（1）比较受访者对绿屋顶之效益认知在生态方面绿屋顶效益认知的各题项中认知相同，以"绿屋顶可以绿美化办公室屋顶环境"得分最高。在视觉心理方面绿屋顶效益认知的各题项中，有绿屋顶以"接触绿屋顶让您心情放松舒压"得分较高而无绿屋顶以"绿屋顶会让您视觉感受愉悦"得分较高。（2）在企业附加效益方面绿屋顶效益认知的各题项中，有无绿屋顶均以"设置绿屋顶可以增加企业形象"得分最高。比较受访者对绿屋顶之管理维护认知各题项中，均以"支持办公室设置绿屋顶"得分最高。（3）无绿屋顶的受访者认为未设置绿屋顶原因各题项中，以"是因为屋顶属于管委会管理需要全栋同意"得分最高。（4）案例A、B常上绿屋顶的受访者会认为绿屋顶的效益较高，且较愿意去管理维护。而有参与绿屋顶管理维护的受访者会认为绿屋顶的效益较高。（5）另外案例B的受访者会认为绿屋顶的效益较高，且较愿意去管理维护。

4 实测结果分析

（1）全面设置绿屋顶的案例B（新店区）户外降温效果优于部分设置绿屋顶的案例A（板桥区）在炎热的7～9月均有降温2.68～5.11℃之效果。

案例A（板桥区）室外降温效果经实测8～11月有无绿屋顶之室外屋面温度（图4、图5），发现无绿屋顶之室外屋面温度8～11月均高于有绿屋顶屋面温度。

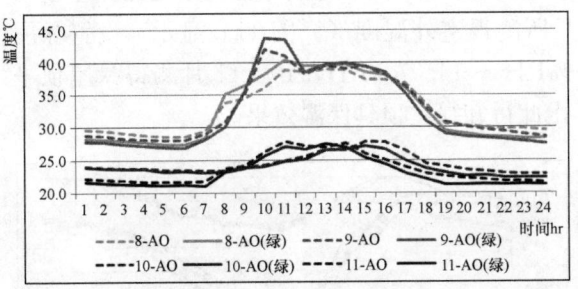

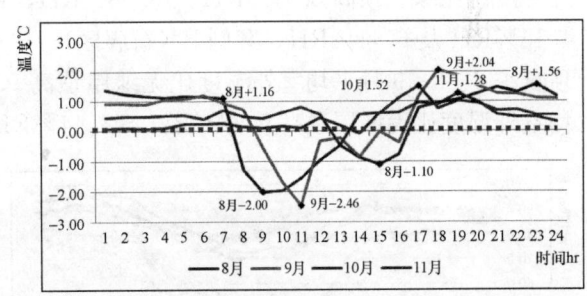

图4 案例A（板桥区）8～11月有无绿屋顶户外屋面月平均温度值折线图

图5 案例A（板桥区）8～11月有无绿屋顶户外屋面月平均温度差比较图

案例B（新店区）室外降温效果经实测案例B（新店区）7～11月有无绿屋顶之室外屋面温度（图6、图7），发现无绿屋顶之室外屋面温度均高于有绿屋顶屋面温度，依序为高2.68～5.11℃。但两案例在8、9月部分白天时段绿屋顶室外屋面温度有高于无绿屋顶之情形。

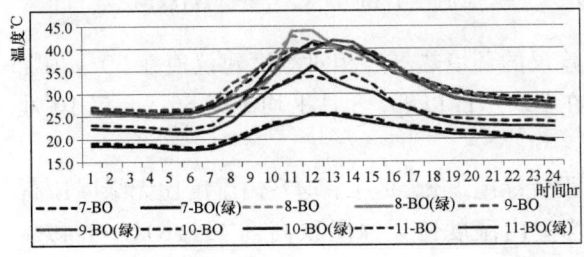

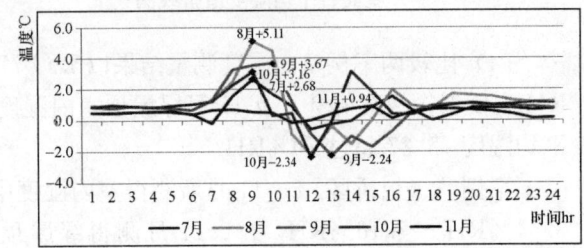

图6 案例B（新店区）7～11月有无绿屋顶户外屋面月平均温度值折线图

图7 案例B（新店区）7～11月有无绿屋顶户外屋面月平均温度差比较图

（2）全面设置绿屋顶案例B（新店区）比部分设置绿屋顶案例A（板桥区）室内降温效果好，降温效果温度中案例B最高可降温4.42℃。在室内降温中无论部分或全面设置绿屋顶均有降温效果。

案例A（板桥区）室内降温效果：经实测A（板桥区）8～11月有无绿屋顶之室内温度（图

8），发现无绿屋顶之室内温度8～11月均高于有绿屋顶室内温度高1.67℃、1.26℃、1.03℃、1.64℃。案例B（新店区）室内降温经实测结果（详图9）发现无绿屋顶之室内温度7～11月均高于有绿屋顶室内温度。

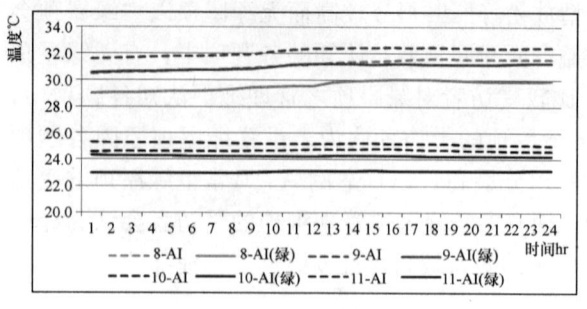
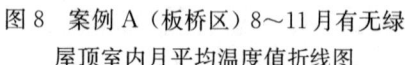
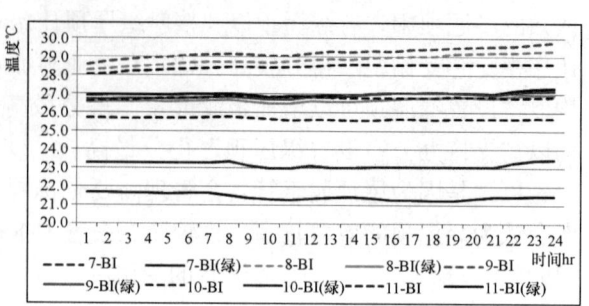

图8　案例A（板桥区）8～11月有无绿　　　　　图9　案例B（新店区）7～11月有无绿
　　屋顶室内月平均温度值折线图　　　　　　　　　屋顶室内月平均温度值折线图

（3）全面设置绿屋顶之案例B（新店区）比部分设置绿屋顶之案例A（板桥区）室外保湿效果好，在炎热的8月保湿效果湿度最高可达＋16.07％RH。

案例A（板桥区）8～11月所测得室外湿度（详图10）显示，设置绿屋顶夏季8、9月平均室外湿度比无绿屋顶高8.61％RH及8.98％RH，10、11月测得绿屋顶平均室外湿度亦比无绿屋顶高4.15％RH及6.41％RH。案例B（新店区）7～11月所测得室外湿度（详图11）显示，设置绿屋顶夏季7、8、9月平均室外湿度比无绿屋顶高9.75％RH～16.07％RH，10、11月测得绿屋顶平均室外湿度比无绿屋顶高9.76％RH～3.44％RH，由此得知绿屋顶具保湿效果。

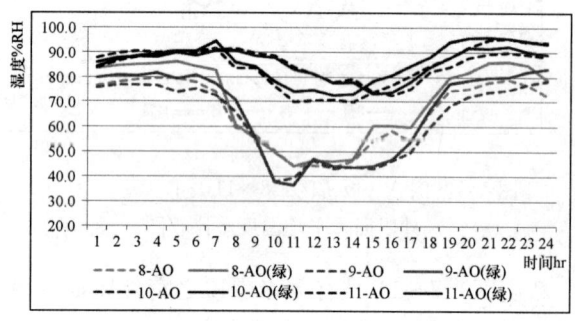
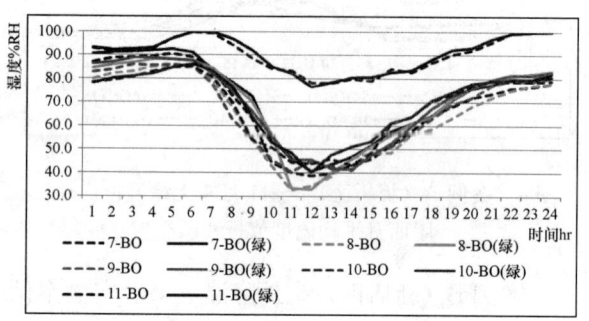

图10　案例A（板桥区）8～11月有无绿屋顶　　　　图11　案例B（新店区）7～11月有无绿
　　　户外屋面月平均湿度值折线图　　　　　　　　　屋顶户外屋面月平均湿度值折线图

（4）比较两案例室内湿度测量结果以ISO 7730建议的环境热舒适相对湿度建议值在30～70％RH为依据，两案例9月及11月绿屋顶室内湿度均在70％RH以下，8月平均湿度69.9％仅10月平均湿度75.87超过70％RH。

案例A（板桥区）8～11月所测得室内湿度中，设置绿屋顶8、9月平均室内湿度比无绿屋顶高8.54％RH～7.16％RH，10、11月测得绿屋顶平均室内湿度比无绿屋顶高8.46％RH～6.49％RH。两案例9月及11月绿屋顶室内湿度均在70％RH以下，8月平均湿度69.9％仅10月平均湿度75.87超过70％RH。测得室内湿度中设置绿屋顶会增加直下方室内空间之湿度。

5　结论与建议

本研究探讨的两个案例均为写字楼建筑设置的绿屋顶，除了提供写字楼屋顶休憩空间，并增加了城市的绿化及固定二氧化碳、达成城市减碳目标之功能。在实测绿屋顶室内外之温湿度差异比较及问卷调查分析后得到下列相关结论：

（1）设置绿屋顶室外降温效果比室内降温效果好有助于降低城市热岛。

综合案例 A 及案例 B 之 7～11 月测量结果，证实设置绿屋顶确实有助于降低城市热岛，全面设置绿屋顶的案例 B（新店区）降温效果优于部分设置绿屋顶的案例 A（板桥区）。

（2）全面设置绿屋顶之室内温度降温效果比部分设置绿屋顶降温效果好。

在室内降温中无论部分设置或全面设置绿屋顶均有降温效果。全面设置绿屋顶优于部分设置绿屋顶其降温效果可达 2.66℃。

（3）设置绿屋顶可增加室内外保湿效果。

全面设置绿屋顶之案例 B 比部分设置绿屋顶之案例 A 室外保湿效果好，在炎热的 8 月保湿效果湿度最高可达 16.07％RH。比较两案例室内湿度测量结果设置绿屋顶会加室内湿度。

（4）受访者对绿屋顶之效益以"绿屋顶可以绿美化办公室屋顶环境"认同度最高。

受访者在生态方面绿屋顶效益认知的各题项中认知相同，以"绿屋顶可以绿美化办公室屋顶环境"得分最高。在视觉心理方面，有绿屋顶以"接触绿屋顶让您心情放松舒压"得分较高而无绿屋顶以"绿屋顶会让您视觉感受愉悦"得分较高。在企业附加效益方面，有无绿屋顶均以"设置绿屋顶可以增加企业形象"得分最高。

（5）全面设置绿屋顶且有开放的案例 B 受访者，比部分设置绿屋顶且不开放的案例 A，认为绿屋顶的效益较高且较愿意去管理维护。

（6）无设置绿屋顶写字楼之支持设置绿屋顶认同度比例达 87.23％，没有设置绿屋顶的主要原因以屋顶属于管委会管理需要全栋同意及设置会增加管理维护费用为主要。

本研究测量案例 A 及案例 B 既有写字楼建筑物以上结论显示，大面积设置绿屋顶，对室内外温度降低效果显著，可减少写字楼空调耗能，并对户外湿度具有保水之功能，可减轻城市排水系统之负担，在台北市积极推动绿屋顶之同时，希冀提供未来推动私有写字楼建筑物设置绿屋顶之参考。

致谢

感谢科技部（计划案号：NSC101—2627—E—027—001—MY3）对本研究经费之补助。

Temperature Control & Comfort Level of Office Building with Green Roof

Su Ying-Ming，Yu Su-Chiu

（Department of Architecture，Taipei University of Technology）

Abstract：To reduce the urban heat island intensity in global sustainable environmental issues has become an international research focus. From international and Taiwan national report，through the roof greening，plant photosynthesis can effectively reduce the carbon dioxide in the air and the affection of the urban heat island effect. In 2014，Taipei City Government requires any public project costing more than 50 million and the new buildings obtaining Green Building Mark should build green roofs. Effectively reducing the temperature and carbon reduction of green roofs has become an important policy issue.

Most of the surveys from the past mainly focus on reducing temperature，plantation selection，green roof structure skills，and study of related policies. The past surveys have not shown and studied the management and maintenance of green roof buildings. This research shows actual report on high energy consumption office buildings with large area of green roofs and uses Banciao District and Xindian District in New Taipei City as two examples; collecting relevant literature and research as the study foundation for the implementation of policies national wide and overseas; organizing relevant literature and research for comparative analysis; plus using German Testo 175-H1 digital temperature and humidity recorder to record the temperature and humidity difference of roof surface and room temperature below between with and without green roofs. This research also uses survey questionnaire to investigate the office staffs' awareness of reducing temperature and sense of comfort of green roofs. In addition，the study of impact of how having green roofs on office building influences the perception of the architecture from physical and psychological level.

The results showed that：1. outdoor green roofswhich help reducing the urban heat island works more effectively than indoor green roofs. 2. full covering green roofs reduce room temperature more effectively than partially covered. 3. Green roofs help increasing the outdoor and indoor moisturizing level. 4. Most of interviewers who works in the office buildings without green roofs agreed "green roofs can create a more visually pleasant office environment". 5. Open and full covering green roofs in case B, the residents are more likely to support the benefit of green roofs and with higher interest to manage and maintain. 6. There are 87. 23% of office staffs of non-green roof support building green roofs. The main reason why the green roof is not set is because the roof is managed by the building management committee and any decision has to be agreed upon entire residents in the building. Secondly, green roofs will increase the maintenance cost. While Taipei City Government is actively promoting green roof policy, with high hope that this study will provide some helpful references of transformation of roof greening of office buildings.

Keywords：Green roof，Roof reducing temperature，Urban heat island，Degree of comfort，Office building architectures

参考文献：

[1] 蔡厚男. 绿屋顶技术手册[M]. 台湾：詹氏，2013.

[2] 台湾建筑研究所. 既有建筑物节能改善技术之研究[Z]. 2012.

[3] 吕罡铭，林宪德，张子莹，等. 夏季台北都市区域土地覆盖与地表辐射热平衡之关系[J]. 都市与计划，2013，40.

[4] 石佳玉. 台北市执绿屋顶政策之工具分析[D]. 台湾：东华大学，2009.

[5] 林姵均. 不同屋顶绿化型式对屋顶隔热效果影响之研究——以草本、灌木及棚架为例[D]. 台湾：朝阳科技大学建筑及都市设计研究所，2011.

[6] 台湾建筑研究所. 屋顶绿化建构技术之研究[Z]. 2009.

[7] 叶彦宏. 城市绿屋顶成本效益分析[D]. 台湾：交通大学，2012.

[8] 张育森. 绿屋顶的环境效益与相关技术探讨//节能减碳、永续270"都市新田园"绿屋顶、绿墙推广展示活动资料[Z]. 台湾，2010.

Ecological Urban Renewal Strategy Based on Technologies of GIS and CFD: Take Kwun Tong Industrial Area for Example

Zeng Ya[1]* , Wu Yaxin[2]* , Liang Yuqiao [3]*

(1. City Information Institute of Guangzhou; 2. Chengdu Tianfu New Area Institute of Urban Planning and Design; 3. Chinese University of Hong Kong; *. These authors contributed equally)

Abstract: With the application of GIS, considering three factors including waterfront, protection from industrial pollution and green environment, Land Suitability Evaluation of Kwun Tong industrial area was obtained. Combining with land use maps analyzed from the satellite images, a green system plan called "one central, two-belt, three-axis and multi-nodes" was proposed and used as a guide for urban ventilation improvement in this study. Through increasing green space and widening air corridors, CFD technology was applied in this ventilation improvement study by comparing the before and after-renovation models.

Keywords: Sustainable development, Ecology urban design, Urban transformation, Green space analysis, Wind environment

1　Introduction

In recent years, the combination of sustainable development and ecology theory in the field of urban design has become a heated topic. Especially in China, with high speed of urban development, old city centers and/or industrial areas need regeneration but severe environmental problems and energy issues still exist. It is critical to learn how to develop ecologically in sustainable urban transformation so in this study, with the application of GIS and CFD simulation, taking Kwun Tong, an industrial area in Hong Kong as an example, a feasible way in urban regeneration is discussed.

2　The Survey of Kwun Tong Industrial Area

Kwun Tong is located in Kowloon peninsula with a total area of about $1130hm^2$. It used to be a prosperous industrial center while until 1990s, with the decline of manufacturing industry, most of the factories or mills have been vacant. In recent years, with many large-scale development projects, Kwun Tong was supposed to be regenerated and evolved into another Central Business District in Hong Kong. The research area is a traditional industrial area of $72.6hm^2$, located in the southern part of Kwun Tong, with the boundary of Wai Yip Street, Hoi Bun Road, King Yip Street and Kwun Tong Road. The land use is mainly for industry, supplemented by commercial area, government area and some green space. See Figure 1.

Survey[1] was conducted in the vision of the renovation and improvement for this industrial ar-

Figure 1　Research area

(Source: Google map)

ea. The results show that air pollution and narrow pavements are the two primary problems. The green environment and recreation facilities also need improvement. Suggestions were given such as more space should be considered to create wider pavements or larger open space; coastal area can be developed into recreation area[1]. Therefore the study mainly focuses on the renovation of this old industrial area through the introduction of green space and the improvement of wind corridor.

3 Plan Guideline

3.1 Ecological Urban Design

In recent years, ecological environment become so important that the guidance of ecological theory has been applied to urban design or renewal, which provides a more scientific way for regeneration of traditional old industrial zone.

For example, "Zhongxin Tianjin Eco-City", a large-scale and far-reaching project, its "Ecological Urban Design Theory" can be used as a reference in urban design. With the understanding of ecological concept, it mainly uses 2 planning method: one is called "First land suitability, then construction land planning", mainly taking ecological structural integrity and land suitability into consideration before future designs and particularly, combining AHP and GIS to give ecological suitability evaluation to research area before defining the boundary of ecological green space[2]; the other is eco-oriented planning, including control guidelines, public policy and plane layout concept[2], which focuses aspects such as natural ecological patterns, cultural heritage, green transportation and water usage.

Based on the geographical areaand the characteristics of Kwun Tong, the "First land suitability, then construction" planning approach and ecosystem layout concept were applied.

3.2 Wind Environment Improvement

Street width, the prevailing wind, building height and orientation are elements can change wind direction and speed. Particularly, when the prevailing wind blowing over various heights of buildings, phenomena such as lift airflow, eddy current, flow around are produced, causing a more complex wind environment [3].

For Kwun Tong in this study, wind environment improvements mainly focus on analyzing wind environment status, broadening street, increasing green space and green corridor.

3.3 Case Study

To renovate the Kwun Tong industrial area, successful case studies on city renovation and ecological city design were used as reference. See Table 1.

List of case study   Table 1

City	Renovation Methods	Application
Stuttgart	Use Urban Climate Map for planning reference: "First green, then construction"; climate reports are included in every development plan; Stuttgart Congress designates high-rise (20m or above) non-construction zone and construction zone to ensure urban ventilation[4]	Eco-climate factors should be considered in renovation, especially improving green space and urban ventilation

continued

City	Renovation Methods	Application
Asahikawa	Connected the coastal area with green space: The concentrated large green space is "cold basis", connecting the separated green area and river to alleviate heat island effect[5]	Connect the coastal area with urban green space
Wuhan	Plan low density area to ensure urban air paths: Ensuring air path to extend to central districts, surrounding areas are planned in lower density with more open space[6]	Comply air paths with wind direction; low density design

4 Technology

GIS and the technology of CFD were applied in this study to make urban renewal more scientific.

4.1 Technology of GIS

4.1.1 Current Land Use Map

5 layers including the range of research area, green space, government use, commercial and other use were imported into GIS. Terrain Registration was done before drawing the current land use map. From Figure 2, the total area of 3 separated green spaces is 2.26hm². As the research area is 72.6hm² and the greening rate of urban renewal should be greater than 25%, at least 15.9hm² green space should be added.

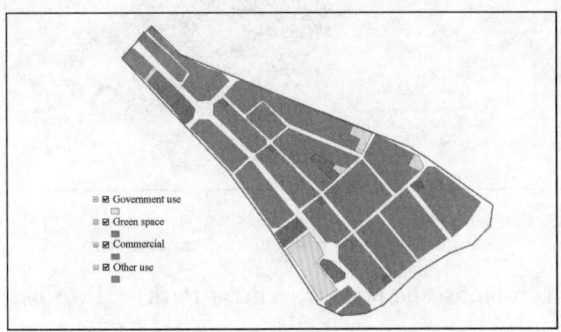

Figure 2   Current land use map
(Source: Town Planning Boad, Statutory Planning Porrtal 2)

4.1.2 Land Suitability Evaluation Map

3 evaluation indexes[7] including waterfront (sea between Kwun Tong industrial zone and Kai Tak Airport), protection from industrial pollution (two typical industrial zone based on existing situation investigation) and green space (three current green spaces) are considered. Then each index was weighted (weighting factors can be found in industrial land use suitability evaluation index system[8], respectively 0.28, 0.44 and 0.28) before overlaying and reclassification. The land suitability evaluation map is shown in Figure 3. Score of 5 represents places suitable for construction and specific classification is shown in Table 2.

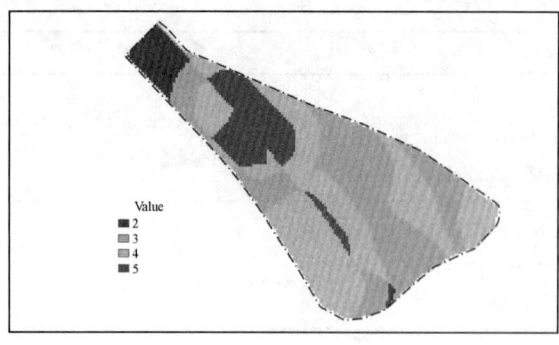

Figure 3　Land suitability evaluation map

Suitability rating standard[7]　　**Table 2**

Level	Evaluation scores	Suitability category
1	4. 5 – 5	Most suitable for construction
2	4 – 4. 5	Suitable
3	3. 5 – 4	Relatively Suitable
4	3 – 3. 5	Conditional construction
5	2 – 3	less Suitable
6	1 – 2	Least Suitable

Results are mainly in 2 – 5 levels so places of Suitable or Relatively Suitable are recommended to be Commercial or Creative Industry use while Conditional construction and less suitable place are considered to be green space. Based on scientific guidance of this land suitability evaluation map, a green system planning was proposed.

4. 1. 3　Green Space System Plan

Combining land use and land suitability evaluation, a green space system plan called "one central, two belts, three axes and several nodes" for Kwun Tong industrial area was obtained. See Figure 4.

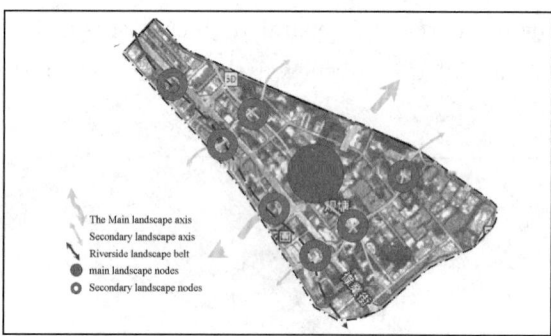

Figure 4　Green space system plan map

"One central" is the main landscape nodes, Central Park; "Two belts" are waterfront belt and the green walking trail paralleling to it; "Three axes" are mainly based on road grid and can be developed into greenways to strengthen the connection for green spaces; "Several nodes" are small green spaces in each neighborhoods. This map can be used as a guide in improving the wind environment in the study area.

4. 2　CFD Simulation

Wind tunnel and numerical simulation are commonly used in wind environment study[9]. Considering experimental difficulty, time and cost, CFD was used to simulate the wind environment in this study.

4. 2. 1　Performance Simulation

As wind direction showing in Figure 5(b), the predominant wind direction of Kwun Tong is from south-east. Fluent is applied in this study and the chosen mathematical model is k-epsilon. The simulation boundary, boundary condition and solution method are set as Figure 5(a), 5(c), 5(d), respectively.

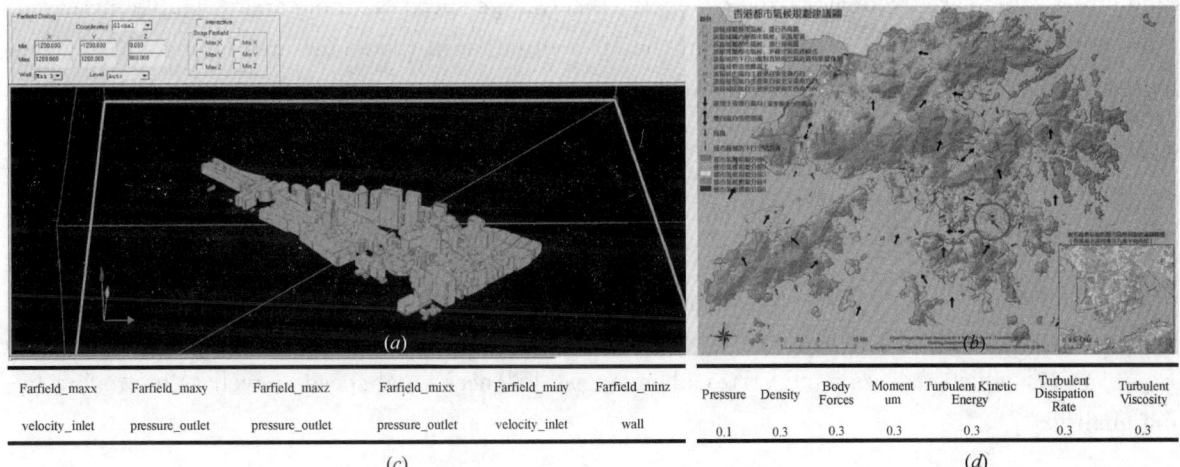

Farfield_maxx	Farfield_maxy	Farfield_maxz	Farfield_mixx	Farfield_miny	Farfield_minz
velocity_inlet	pressure_outlet	pressure_outlet	pressure_outlet	velocity_inlet	wall

(c)

Pressure	Density	Body Forces	Moment um	Turbulent Kinetic Energy	Turbulent Dissipation Rate	Turbulent Viscosity
0.1	0.3	0.3	0.3	0.3	0.3	0.3

(d)

Figure 5　Parameters setting

(a) Parameter setting of study site boundary; (b) Hong Kong Urban Climate Map and Standards for Wind Environment showing prevailing wind of Kwun Tong[10]; (c) Boundary condition; (d) Solution Method

Originalmodel performance shows in Figure 7(a). The construction orientation and dominant wind direction were found substantially parallel, but the wind speed declined dramatically due to the high building density and narrow streets. There are several stagnant wind areas and many serious vortex phenomena which are very detrimental to air circulation.

4.2.2　Proposed Scheme

Showing in Figure 6(b), 6(c), 6(d) and 6(e), Chapter 11 of "Hong Kong Planning Standards and Guidelines"[11] suggests: (1) The layout of an arrangement of buildings should be paralleled to prevailing wind direction; (2) The coastal land construction projects should avoid windshield design;

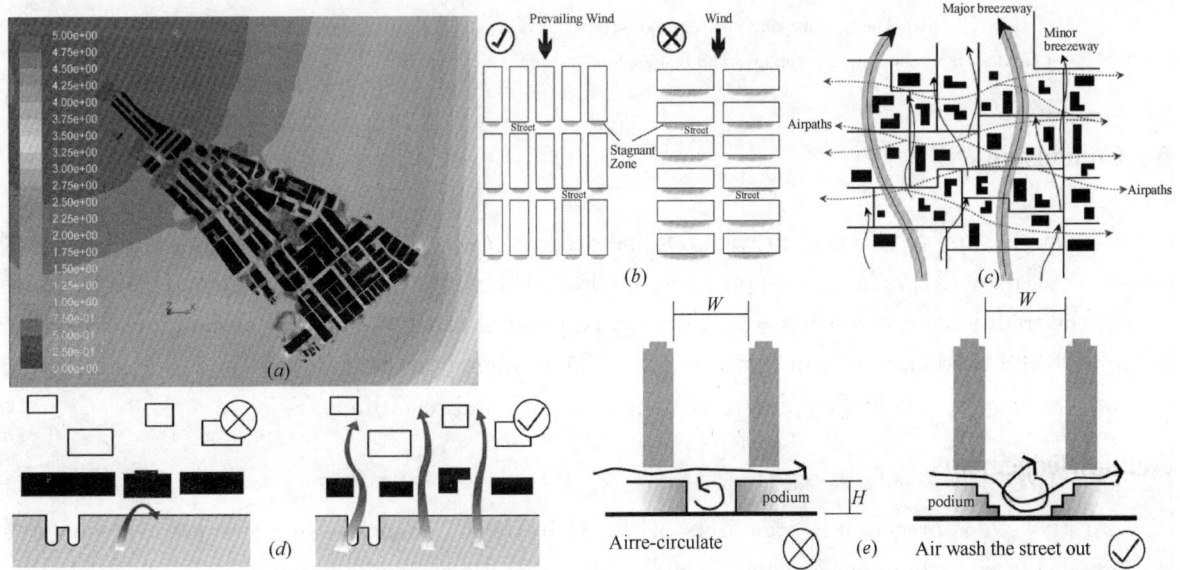

Figure 6　Guides for original project

(a) The velocity contour of the original project area in Z2 (5m/s max range); (b), (c), (d), (e)Guides for good air ventilation[11]

（3）Drive air flow with different height of buildings；（4）Green design for high-rise buildings；（5）Air ventilation of the skirt building can be promoted by step form.

By this guidance, a proposed scheme performance was obtained in Figure 8(*a*). After broadening street, there are two major wind channels, the average speed of whole area is highly increased. Some low wind speed space still exists but the air ventilation in the whole area is undoubtedly promoted.

4. 2. 3 Promoted Scheme by Green Space System

Proposed scheme improves wind environment while removing some buildings, therefore some buildings were added in the bay, which can not only improve wind environment but guarantee the gross floor area as well. Besides, green space system was taken into consideration. After combining wind channel and air pass with green space system, a promoted scheme was proposed, showing in Figure 7(*d*), which reduces wind vortex phenomena, balances wind speed as well as improving living quality.

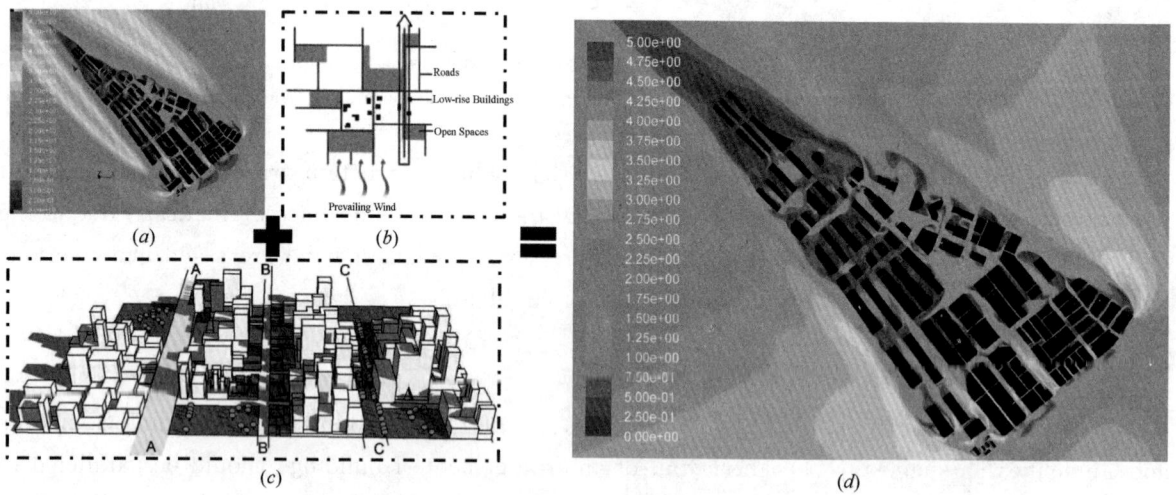

Figure 7　Improvement scheme

(*a*) The velocity contour of proposed scheme in Z2 (5m/s max range)；(*b*) and
(*c*) Guides about connecting green area and open space[11]；(*d*) The promoted scheme in Z2 (5m/s max range)

5　Conclusion

The application of GIS is to provide rational decision support for planning green space system of Kwun Tong industrial area. The application of CFD technology is to do numerical simulation, comparing the traditional urban renewal plan with the ecological urban design, which combines the green space with the wind environment improvement. The combination of technology and ecological urban renewal strategy make city planning more comprehensive and scientific.

Acknowledgements

Firstly, we appreciate the organizers of the 11th China Urban Housing Conference, who give us a chance to contribute our article. Secondly, we appreciate teachers who teach us advanced planning technology combining urban design. Finally, we show our great gratitude to experts and professors who contribute their valuable time in appraising all the articles!

基于 GIS 和 CFD 技术下的城市更新生态策略研究：以观塘工业区为例

曾　亚[1]*　吴亚芯[2]*　梁羽乔[3]*

（1. 广州城市信息研究所；2. 成都天府新区规划设计研究院；3. 香港中文大学）

摘要：利用 GIS 技术，主要从滨河、远离工业污染和绿地环境三个方面综合得出香港观塘工业区研究区域的用地适宜性评价，并结合卫星图片做出的土地利用现状图进行分析，在分析基础上，提出了"一心、两带、三轴、多节点"的绿地系统规划图。以绿地系统规划图为指引，我们拓宽了部分绿地及通风廊道，利用 CFD 技术对现状地块进行通风改造，将改造前后地块的通风进行对比，创造更好的城市环境。

关键词：可持续发展，生态城市设计，城市转型，绿地分析，风环境

References：

[1]　祁宜臻. 观塘工业区的活化和发展研究[M]. 香港：香港大学建筑学院小区项目工作坊，2013.

[2]　杨保军，董珂. 生态城市规划的理念与实践——以中新天津生态总体规划为例[J]. 城市规划，2008.

[3]　吴珍珍. 基于 CFD 模拟技术的深圳市城市风环境分析[A]. 工程质量 2009(11)：49-53.

[4]　李欣. 德国城市规划体系对我国城市建设的启示[J]. 山西建筑，2011(17)：19-21.

[5]　陈福妹. 绿道网络的生态环境功能及规划策略研究[D]. 武汉：华中科技大学，2011.

[6]　任超，袁超，何正军，吴恩融. 城市通风廊道研究及其规划应用[A]. 城市规划，2014(3)：52-60.

[7]　牛强. 城市规划 GIS 技术应用指南[M]. 北京：中国建筑工业出版社，2012，1.

[8]　王骎骎. 基于 GIS 用地适宜性评价方法及应用——新加坡怀化生态工业园概念规划[A]. 规划师，2011.

[9]　Edward Ng. Policies and technical guidelines for urban planning of high-density cities-air ventilation assessment (AVA) of Hong Kong[J]，2009.

[10]　香港规划署. 都市气候图及风环境评价标准——可行性研究[EB/OL]. 香港规划署网站. www. pland. gov. hk/pland_en/p_study/. 2010.

[11]　香港规划署. 城市设计指引第十一章. [EB/OL]. 香港规划署网站. www. pland. gov. hk/pland-tc/tech-doc/hkpsg/full/chll/chll_text. htm.

基于风环境的建筑形体优化方法研究——以太原市某项目为例

石郁萌[1]　陆　明[1]　王学楠[2]

（1. 哈尔滨工业大学建筑学院；2. 天津市建筑设计研究院）

摘要： 风环境与建筑形体轮廓关系紧密，在建筑形态生成中利用风环境对建筑形体进行优化是十分必要的。本文基于 STAR CCM＋的软件平台，以太原市某项目为例，研究对建筑形体生成过程中，如何利用风环境进行形体的逐步优化。从信息化的角度弥补了建筑创作长久以来"主观造型"缺乏环境因素考虑的缺陷。

关键词： 建筑形体，风环境，形体生产，优化

1. 引言

如今在中国，可持续设计理念已在世界范围内应用广泛。建筑的可持续化设计理念要体现在形体布局、室外环境、节能材料和节能设施的每个设计环节。合理的建筑形体设计，可以提高建筑自身效率，是建筑"主动节能"的主要途径；同时还可调节室外微环境，营造良好、舒适的室外环境。

风环境与建筑形体关系紧密，建筑体块关系与组织、立面形态都会影响气流的走向、强度等，关系到建筑自主节能与室外微环境。因此在建筑形体设计过程中，需要配合风环境对设计成果优化，使设计成果一次性满足绿色建筑与室外微环境的双目标。本文即探讨建筑形体的设计过程中，如何利用风环境进行形体优化。

2　风环境优化的作用与评价指标

2.1　风环境优化作用

（1）有害气体扩散

日常生活离不开开窗通风，建筑也是一样。建筑物形体、布局不合理导致的气流滞涩，阻碍了建筑与自然的"通风换气"，加剧空气中对危害物质的滋生和繁衍，影响人类健康。在我国爆发的 SARS 病毒就是严重的警告。建筑及周边良好的风环境能够加快有害气体的扩散，保证建筑及人类生活的健康。

（2）保证人们活动

建筑物形成的风场深深地影响了人们的生活，不合理的风场轻者会影响人们室外生活的舒适性，重者则会威胁人们的生命安全。1972 年，朴次茅斯市的一位老人，走到一座 10 多层建筑的拐弯处，突然一阵大风袭来，摔倒在地，造成该老人的头骨被摔破裂，最终死亡；同年，还有一个老太太在伯明翰一栋高楼外面被强风吹倒致其重伤不治。合理的建筑风场，不仅为使用者提供舒适感，更是对使用者生命安全的负责。

（3）有利于节能与生态

在资源短缺、环境问题严重的今天，节能成了必然要求。空调是当前城市居民尤其是炎热地区必不可少的降温工具。但是空调的大量使用对城市大气环境破坏严重，加剧城市资源浪费的同时使得城市环境愈加恶劣。

同时，北方的冬季，不合理的建筑风场形成的强风会增加建筑外墙的渗透压，带走建筑的大量

热量，增大了建筑供热的能耗。实现建筑的自然通风与冬季的保温保暖，是实现建筑节能的有效途径，有利于城市生态环境的可持续发展。

建筑形成的风场不仅仅影响了建筑自身的效率，同时更对人类生命安全、城市生态环境产生影响。因此，在建筑设计阶段就对建筑风环境作出模拟与测试，并结合评价优化建筑形体是十分必要的。

2.2 风环境优化评价指标

基于风环境对建筑形体进行优化主要有两个目标：

第一：为人们提供室外活动的良好微环境。不同性质建筑会发生不同形态活动，不同活动类别在各个季节的风感要求不同。因此，距离地面 1.5m 高度风速与舒适人感风速，是优化建筑室外风环境的主要评价指标。研究证明，当人行区域距地 1.5m 高度处风速为 $1m/s<v<5m/s$ 时，在夏季人们体感是舒适的，在过渡季室外舒适风速范围是 $0.6m/s<v<5m/s$，冬季室外舒适风速为低于 $3m/s$[2]。此外，室外活动场地风速舒适性区域所占比例大小也是优化评价的指标之一。

第二：兼顾自然通风与冬季保温。建筑单体迎背风面压力差值是评价建筑能否自然通风与冬季保温的重要指标，建筑物迎背风面压差在 1.5Pa 与 5Pa 之间可在夏季实现自然通风、冬季实现保暖。此外，建筑受风面风速也是实现建筑自然通风的重要因素。

在根据风环境的指标推敲建筑形体时，首先考虑建筑体块关系在距离地面 1.5m 处高度的风速场，依据人感舒适值评价并优化建筑形体；而后考虑建筑形体曲面是否能在不同季节形成合适的风压。整体实现从下至上、逐层优化的优化思路。

3 风环境在建筑形体的优化方法

3.1 风环境基础

本文结合太原市某项目，具体说明风环境在建筑形体优化方法与步骤。项目所在地太原全年风向受东南季风进退影响，冬季盛行西北风，夏季盛行西风。根据《中国建筑热环境分析专用气象数据集》提供的气象数据，将太原市典型气象年数据处理并取平均值（表1），作为风环境优化的参数基础。在根据设计理念形成建筑初步体块后，利用 STAR CCM＋对建筑形体进行不同季节风环境的模拟分析，根据模拟指标的评价对形体进行逐步优化。

风环境模拟的气象参数 表 1

季　节	主导风向	10m基准高度处平均风速（m·s⁻¹）
夏季	西风	2.1
冬季	西北偏北风	2.6

3.2 形体体块优化

根据设计理念，得到初步的建筑形体体块方案后，首先进行近地层形体优化。近地层形体优化指标是人行范围距地 1.5m 高度处风速。控制得当的建筑风环境可以为人室外活动提供舒适体验，同时使危害气体很快扩散。

方案初期形体体块是三个平行长方体（图1），利用软件模拟发现很大区域内出现了静风区，且形体两端出现涡流。因此进行形体优化，加入对向两个方形缓坡对气流进行缓冲与引导，形态优化后的气流组织图见图1。初次优化后可以看出，气流漩涡已大大减少，建筑风场整体分布均匀。为形成宜人的建筑室外风环境，此时需用人感风速值进行检验。

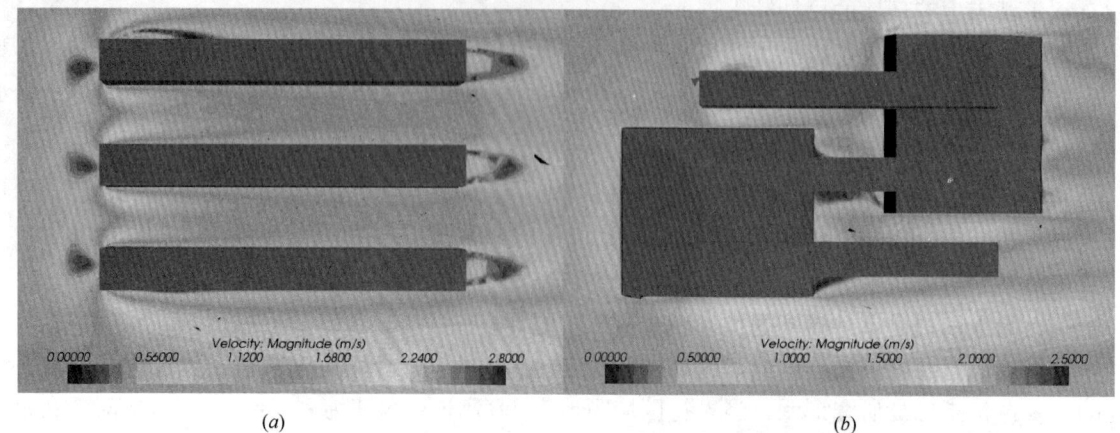

(*a*)　　　　　　　　　　　　　　　　(*b*)

图 1　优化形体风速标量图

(*a*) 方案初期建筑形体风速标量图；(*b*) 优化后建筑形体风速标量图

　　国际上对于风力等级的确定通常用蒲福风力等级表，根据蒲福风力等级表（表 2）[3]，在距地 1.5m 处高度风速小于 0.1m/s 时，人的感觉是闷促、憋闷的，体感不适。对比形体方案发现方形与条形交叉部分局部风速过小，可能会造成行人上述感受。因此进行二次优化，根据设计理念将条形形体进行扭转，并再次利用软件模拟检测。

蒲福风力等级表　　　　　　　　　　　　　　　　　　　　　　　　表 2

名　　称	1.5m 处风速	陆地地面物象	对人体的影响
无风	0.0～0.1	静，烟直上	无感，闷促
软风	0.1～1.0	烟示方向	不宜察觉
轻风	1.0～2.1	感觉有风	扑面的感觉
微风	2.1～3.4	旌旗展开	头发吹散
和风	3.4～5.0	吹起尘土	头发吹散、灰尘四扬
劲风	5.0～6.7	小树摇摆	感觉风力大，为陆上风容许的极限

　　将形体扭转优化后的气流组织图见图 2，可以看出，建筑室外场地风速过小的地方已基本消失，且条形形体间、条形与方形形体间的风场风速在 1.3～1.9m/s 范围内，是轻风级别，人感舒适；方形与方形之间区域风场风速主要分布在 0.3～0.9m/s 范围内，属于软风，人感不易察觉，适合人体静态活动。可确定此种建筑形体体块关系是可行的。

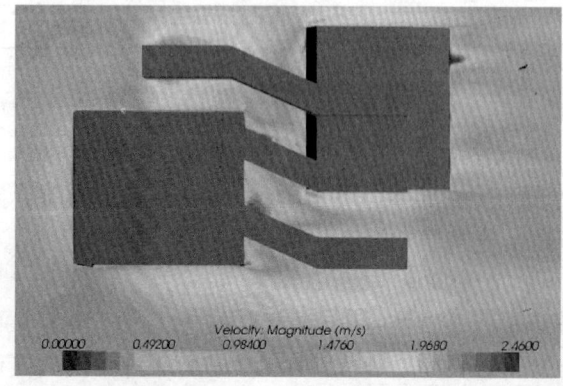

图 2　建筑形体扭转后风速标量图

3.3 形体曲面优化

3.3.1 高空层优化

在确定建筑形体基本体块关系后，在建筑曲面阶段进行形体的深化，与立面虚实关系的处理。在这个设计阶段中，形体优化目的是使建筑获得自然通风的能力，主要通过建筑高空层响应。建筑高空层空气流动速度会影响建筑受风面压差。根据研究结论，建筑迎背风面压差超过 1.5Pa 时，建筑可以获得自然通风。因此，距地 10m 高度处的风速值成为优化评价指标。当距地 10m 高度水平平均风速小于 1.3m/s 时，建筑正背面平均压差小于 2Pa，夏季不利于自然通风。而在冬季时，水平平均风速大于 2.2m/s 时，建筑迎背风面平均压差大于 5Pa，将会明显增大冬季冷风渗透量与渗入量，不利于冬季保暖[4]。因此本阶段的优化策略是，依据建筑距地 10m 高处风速值对建筑形体进行评价与优化，而后通过软件模拟建筑各个季节压强分布图进行检验，保证最终的形体方案实现自然通风与冬季保暖。

首先对建筑形体 10m 高度处进行风环境模拟（图 3a），发现条形体间风速在 2.4m/s～2.7m/s 内，局部更是出现了"狭管效应"，不利于冬季保暖；且东南角风速过慢，无法实现夏季自然通风。因此对建筑形体继续优化，将条形体错位并加入穿插条形体构成"之"字形。优化之后再次用软件模拟发现（图 3b），优化后的形体平均了之前过快、过慢的风速，风场整体强度适中，整体风速在 1.6m/s～2.3m/s 之间，满足建筑在夏季实现自然通风、冬季保暖的要求。

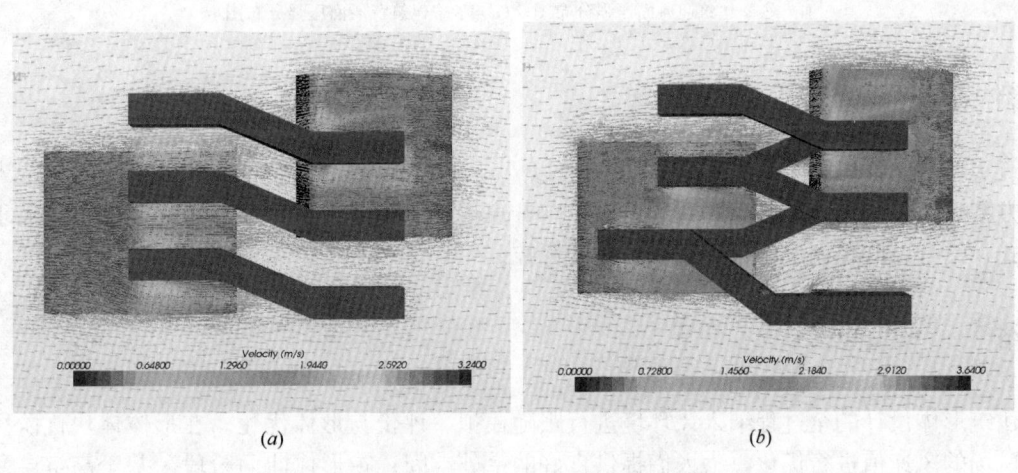

（a）　　　　　　　　　　　　　　　　（b）

图 3　建筑曲面阶段形体优化
（a）优化前建筑形体风速矢量图；（b）优化后建筑风速矢量图

3.3.2 曲面压强检验

在随后的设计过程中，基于立面形体考虑，将"之"字条形体与方形体间部分进行高度不一的局部挑空，并将最北面条形体整体升高。利用软件进行建筑迎背风面压强模拟与检测，分析结果如图 4 所示。

可以看出，夏季建筑约 80% 迎背风面压强差大于 1.5Pa，形成室内自然通风的压强差条件，为夏季开窗自然通风提供基础条件；冬季非迎风面的压强差在 1.2Pa 左右，可有效避免冬季建筑的冷风渗透，有利于建筑供热能耗的降低，实现建筑节能。

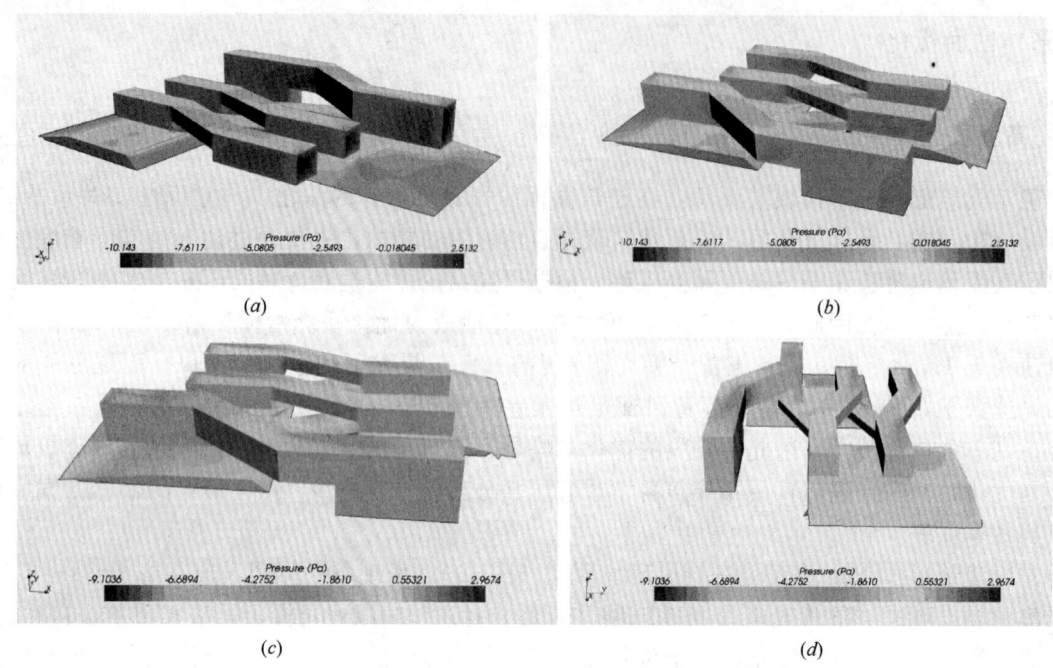

图 4　冬、夏季建筑迎背风面压强分布

(*a*) 夏季建筑迎风面压强分布图；(*b*) 夏季建筑背风面压强分布图
(*c*) 冬季建筑迎风面压强分布图；(*d*) 冬季建筑背风面压强分布图

3.4　形体表皮优化

建筑实现自然通风除了建筑迎背风面压差以外，还需要表皮上进风口与出风口存在适当的压差。本方案建筑采用玻璃幕墙，幕墙既可以正向开窗也可以侧向开窗，根据对通风的不同需求选择开启方式，结合百叶控制风量，实现风环境的可控。

4　总结

在建筑形体设计的全过程纳入风环境进行跟随模拟、评价与形体优化。在形体体块优阶段，基于室外风场的风速值进行优化，为人们提供良好的室外空间；在形体曲面阶段，基于高空层受风面风速与迎背风面风压差进行深度优化；在形体表皮阶段，根据通风需求确定开窗。最后完成形体设计，获得可持续、高效率的建筑方案。

在建筑创作中，基于风环境对建筑形体进行优化设计，从信息化的角度弥补了建筑创作长久以来"主观造型"缺乏环境因素考虑的缺陷，取得了建筑形体创作中主客观因素的平衡。将对环境影响的评价引入到建筑设计及优化的全过程，通过建筑形体对微气候的调节获得良好的建筑外部环境，是实现国家人居环境目标的重要一步。

5　致谢

本文的研究项目得到了哈尔滨工业大学重点项目创新培育计划——"基于微气候调节的严寒地区聚居区景观设计方法与评价研究"、"中央高校基本科研业务费专项资金资助（项目资助编号：HIT. KISTP. 201419)"资助。

Research on Method of Built Forms Optimization based on Wind Environment: A Study in Taiyuan, China

Shi Yumeng[1], Lu Ming[1], Wang Xuenan[2]

(1. Harbin Institute of Technology; 2. Tianjin Architecture Design Institute)

Abstract: Wind environment connects closely with building body contour. Using wind environment to optimize the shape of the building in architectural form generation is necessary. Based on STAR CCM + software platform, a project in Taiyuan as example, this study investigated how to optimize architectural form step by step taking the advantage of wind environment, in the progress of architectural form creation. It makes up for the defect that architectural creation has long been lace of environmental considerations in terms of the "subjective modeling", from the perspective of information technology.

Keywords: Architectural form, Wind environment, Shape generation, Optimization

参考文献：

[1] 韩昀松. 基于日照与风环境影响的建筑形态生成方法研究[D]. 黑龙江哈尔滨工业大学，2013.

[2] 李宝鑫，蒋益清，庄和锋，刘小芳，芦岩，吴坡. 基于室外风环境和室内自然通风模拟优化的建筑体形可持续设计方法研究[J]. 绿色建筑，2014，04：56-58.

[3] 王晶. 基于风环境的深圳市滨河街区建筑布局策略研究[D]. 黑龙江哈尔滨工业大学，2012.

[4] 钱杰. 建筑底部架空周围风环境特性研究[D]. 重庆大学，2010.

[5] C. W. Tsang, K. C. S. Kwok, P. A. Hitchcock. Wind tunnel study of pedestrian level wind environment around tall buildings: Effects of building dimensions, separation and podium[J]. Building and Environment, 2012, 49.

[6] Yafeng Gao, Runming Yao, Baizhan Li, Erdal Turkbeyler, Qing Luo, Alan Short. Field studies on the effect of built forms on urban wind environments[J]. Renewable Energy, 2012, 46.

[7] 杨丽. 绿色建筑设计：建筑风环境. 上海：同济大学出版社，2014.

[8] C. W. Tsang, K. C. S. Kwok, P. A. Hitchcock. Wind tunnel study of pedestrian level wind environment around tall buildings: Effects of building dimensions, separation and podium[J]. Building and Environment, 2012, 49.

[9] Zhixiang Yu, Hao Wu, Pengbo Zhang. Research on Wind Environment and Wind Load of Low Rise Buildings Based on QSMA Technique and Feature Geometry[J]. Energy Procedia, 2012, 16.

The Use of BIM and COBie on Utility Installation

Chau Saiwai[1], Leung Wingtai[1], Tam Siuming[1], Leung Chichung[1],

Chan Chunhong[2], Lee Tszhang[2], Gao Chaohengfeng[2]

[1. Water Supplies Department, Hong Kong; 2. Summit Technology (Hong Kong) Limited]

Abstract: Compared with other stages in the asset lifecycle (i. e. asset planning, acquisition, design and construction), asset operation and maintenance will require much more resources particularly for those assets whose operation will last for decades. The authors participated in a pilot project intending to locate a suitable successor to an existing A-MIS for utility installations. The authors also expected to make use of current BIM technology trend to integrate BIM model and AMIS via COBie into its development and deployment. It is also the authors' intention that the new system will help explore the potential use of COBie for integration of BIM and AMIS for asset management. From the results of pilot project, the application of BIM and COBie on asset management for utility installation is highly viable. This article discussed the results and the challenges encountered in the implementation of BIM and COBie under the pilot project.

Keywords: BIM, COBie, Utility installation, Asset management

1 Introduction

Usually, Asset Management (AM) is the last phase of a project lifecycle; yet it is most important. Asset Management differs from Facility Management in that the prime focus is on the level of services achieved by the asset and to ensure that the asset is sustainable and operated in a safe, environmental, reliable and efficient manner, while the conventional facility management concentrates on maintenance and repair of the facility's equipment.

For any given projects, its planning, design and construction phases only consist of a small fraction of its total asset lifecycle cost; operation and maintenance can take up to 80% of its total asset lifecycle cost. When we take total asset lifecycle cost into consideration, the importance of asset management would become more apparent. It has been estimated that operating and maintenance can cost up to 50% of total asset lifecycle cost for a standard office building[12]. The percentage of management cost of a utility installation is even greater as utility installation is built to last for decades as a minimum.

The authors would argue that asset management actually extends to entire project lifecycle. During planning, stakeholders are establishing a list of potential assets. During design, stakeholders are finalizing selection and processing asset acquisition. During construction, the assets are to be installed. After completion of installation, assets will eventually be put into operation and under maintenance during AM phase. The entire lifecycle is in reality, centered on asset management.

Regardless of how one views asset management, it is unequivocal that asset management has yet been given the attention it deserves. Information passed along to asset management teamis sometimes always in a chaotic state. Data are riddled with errors and fallacy[7]. Frequently, data are only provided in hard copies, and asset management team has to manually digitized data to be used in A-MIS[2].

The latest trend of asset management is the implementation of Asset Management Information

System (AMIS). Although AMIS is a momentous landmark, asset management as an industry has failed to keep up with the current technological trend. Henceforth, the authors reckoned the urgency of exploring more advanced alternatives to current AMIS. As part of the search for improvement, the authors experimented with BIM and COBie functions on their utilization on utility installations, and have documented the results in this paper.

2 Literature Review

Building Information Modelling can be defined as "an IT enabled approach that involves applying and maintaining an integral digital representation of all building information for different phases of the project lifecycle in the form of a data repository[5]". The benefits of BIM have long been recognized. Using BIM has been known to reduce design and construction cost, increase client satisfaction, and improve productivity[4]. Because of the benefits offered by BIM, the involvement of BIM in construction has progressively been made mandatory by governments across the globe[9]. Norway has gradually made it compulsory for all major infrastructure and public projects to include BIM in project specifications. The United Kingdom has established BIM as part of its procurement policy. France has announced its goal to include BIM as public procurement by 2017. Clearly, the benefits of using BIM during planning, design and construction are indisputable, and BIM will eventually be adopted on a global stratum.

The current challenge is the adoption of BIM in asset management. BIM is frequently argued to hold great potential in increasing efficiency for asset management[3]. Recent research includes BIM-based augmented reality for facility maintenance where users are provided with travel and repair direction through BIM models[6]. A second research includes utilizing BIM models to map failure location and frequency. Based on historical data, the BIM-based system can assess potential causes of failure and predict next incidence time and location[11]. The issue is that these are all research; practical application of BIM for asset management is rare, and one of reasons has been cited to be the difficulty on transferring data between BIM and asset management team[8]. Thus, there exists a need for a media for data transfer between BIM and AMIS.

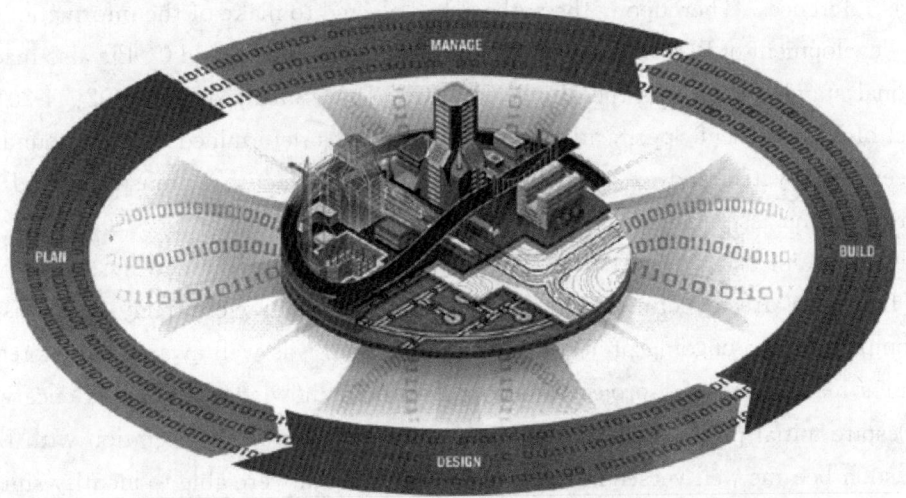

Figure 1   Ideally, BIM should extend to all project phases.
The reality is that BIM has progressively been adopted in the earlier
phases, but less so in asset management

Construction Operations Building Information Exchange (COBie) is a standard data storage format designed to facilitate information exchange between software programs[1]. For this paper, COBie was employed to transfer data from BIM model to AMIS. The intent of COBie is to collect and accumulate facility information throughout project lifecycles: planning, design, construction and asset management[8]. When transiting into asset management, AMIS can incorporate the COBie file and spare the asset management team of manually rekeying data based on handover material[6]. Not only does COBie would reduce the time of manual input by the asset management team, it would also put the responsible parties in charge of inputting their respective data; thus, lowering the chance of error.

3 Methodology

3.1 Background

As mentioned previously, the authors attempted to implement BIM and COBie-based AMIS on utility installation. The utility installation in question is a salt water pumping station built and commissioned nearly two decades ago. The O&M staff and asset management team have already implemented highly customized in-house Maintenance Works Management System (MWMS) for managing maintenance works in various installations. Although the current MWMS has executed its works order function competently, the asset owners desired to raise the asset performance of the installation and investigate potential successor before the current in-house MWMS becomes outdated and dysfunctional.

3.2 Research Framework

With that said, publication on the use of BIM and COBie in the water industry is scarce. Also, the current in-house MWMS was tailor-made for the needs of water industry, and its uniqueness rendered it considerably more challenging to locate an external project in comparable circumstances to be used as references. Thereupon, the authors had elected to make of the information available in MWMS for development of BIM and COBie. The development of BIM and COBie also made reference to international standards such as the Hong Kong CIC BIM Standards, BS1192: 4-2014 and BIM Forum Level of Development Specification. The decision was determined on the grounds that similarity between new system and existing system would allow smoother transition, and shorten the learning curve for the asset management team.

The advantages of using the existing MWMS as foundation for the new system are that the required data fields are already defined, and that years of legacy data were freely at the disposal of the authors. Compared to an ongoing project, development team was well aware of their requirements, and the team's main role at the project was to share their knowledge and experience with the authors[13]. Despite initial predicament at sharing their knowledge and expectation with the authors, the authors soon became well-versed in the current MWMS and were able to identify suitable area to store legacy data. Once the authors had transferred the legacy data into the BIM models, exporting such data into COBie format can be achieved by commercially available software.

The disadvantage of having abespoke system like MWMS was its vastly specialized nature. The system's exclusiveness was no doubt its merit and allowed the system to perform its duty for the past decades. Unfortunately, the architecture of BIM and COBie were created for general purposes. They were not designed to cater for utility installation, let alone, the water industry. Attempting to implement BIM and COBie over the existing MWMS proved greater challenges than expected.

3.3 Challenge

As indicated previously, BIM and COBie were not the quick-fix as the authors had envisioned originally. For instance, data hierarchy found in the MWMS was impossible to recreate in BIM by default. This data hierarchy consisted of parent asset and child asset relationships supporting the system in fulfilling its functions[10]. This data hierarchy structure can be found in the database of every utility installations managed by the MWMS, and, therefore it was crucial in the development of a successor maintenance system. Regrettably, parent and child relationships between assets were not

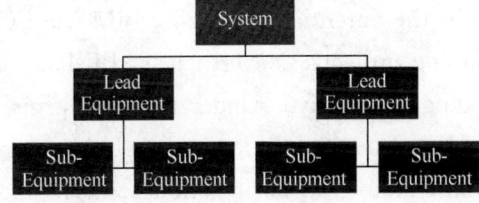

Figure 2　Asset hierarchy in the current MWMS

supported in BIM, and it thus complicated the data migration exercise of information into COBie. To resolve this issue, the authors and the asset management team had agreed to modify and improve the function of BIM and COBie. In consideration of this particular issue, the authors decided to utilize an uncommon component of COBie called "Assembly". Data for "Assembly" can be stored in BIM but cannot be extracted from BIM by standard commercially available software and the authors had to develop customized computer programs in order to overcome this challenge.

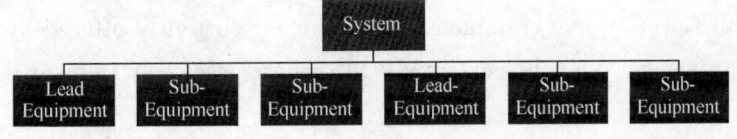

Figure 3　Asset hierarchy in BIM by default.
Such relatively simple level structure is inadequate to represent the
level structure essential in MWMS

The second challenge was the lack of publication and research on COBie for Asset Management and particularly in an asset intensive business like water industry. COBie had been coming into the sight of professionals, and COBie-related research has been on the rise. However, in-depth knowledge of COBie was still at a premium. This project was very much a pioneer in utilizing COBie in asset management, and even more so, in the water industry. The third challenge was the overwhelming amount of legacy data. The installation being studied in this project had been in-service for nearly two decades. Attempting to manually input all relevant data into BIM model proved to be extremely difficult, time consuming and prone to human error. Furthermore, the above mentioned problem was only the tip of an iceberg. The current MWMS is responsible for supporting hundreds of installations, some of which are more than ten times the size and complexity of the installation of this project. The authors had no choice but to develop a customized computer programs to overcome such tedious tasks in the future.

4 Discussion

To put it bluntly, this projectwas a first and an eye-opener for the authors. For better or worse, this project revealed to the authors that BIM and COBie on managing utility installations were very much in its infancy. This is not only because of the absence of related researches and publications, but also because of the lack of established standards for BIM and COBie for this type of utility installation. This incompatibility can be attributed to the generic nature of BIM and COBie. The use of BIM and COBie during design and construction is unquestioned, and the authors do not doubt the potential of utilizing BIM and COBie for facility management for residential or commercial building projects. Nevertheless, BIM and COBie for asset management of utility installation are exceedingly exclusive. Under the pilot project, the COBie for the pumping stations were specifically developed to suit the customized in-house system. Consequently, the solutions developed during this project likely will not be one size-fit-all and applicable to related services of the same locale without mentioning the global industry.

The authors are by no mean discouraging the use of BIM and COBie for utility installation. As a matter of fact, the authors agreed unanimously that the gain and potential offered by BIM and COBie far outweighed the expenses and limitation. BIM and COBie will undeniably present great services to the asset management team; for example, 4D simulation of maintenance tasks, interactive simulation of installations with live data update and convenient work ordering through tablets are all exciting new development for the field of asset management. As BIM and COBie for utility installation is in a very much embryonic state, these are only fractions of the possible future development. Disregarding the future prospect, the 3D interactive environment currently offered by BIM and COBie is already a major improvement over the currentMWMS where asset management team is not provided with 3D visualization.

5 Conclusion

This pilot projectaffirmed the feasibility of BIM and COBie on utility installation. There are without a doubt, numerous obstacles before widespread implementation. Amount of research on this area is inadequate. Professional interest in the subject is limited. The compatibility with existing systems is minimal. By all means, future research and modification are essential for asset management team of installations to come to an agreement with the benefits of BIM and COBie. Even so, the authors would argue that BIM and COBie are still promising candidate for the next technological breakthrough in asset management and utility installations, and assertions in this paper had demonstrated that BIM and COBie are undeniably viable options. The authors themselves will follow with additional research projects, and is confident that other researchers will follow suit.

Acknowledgements

The authors would like to express their gratitude to Water Supplies Department and its staff for their support in writing this paper. This project and this paper would not have been possible without their patronage and thrive for improvement. The authors would also like to acknowledge the staff of Summit Technology and Sino-iTech in their roles in developing the aforementioned project and providing the basis of this paper.

BIM 和 COBie 在公用设施上的应用

周世威[1]　梁颖泰[1]　谭少明[1]　梁志聪[1]　陈振康[2]　李子铿[2]　高超程丰[2]

（1. 香港水务署；2. 云峰科技香港有限公司）

摘要： 从建筑生命周期总资源消耗的角度统计，相对于规划、设计和建造，资产管理阶段的消耗会占有更多的比例。作者参与了一个先导项目。运营方希望更换原有的设施管理系统以改善当前的管理模式，同时希望新的设施管理系统可以利用 BIM 平台整合模型与信息，并以此项目来探索 BIM 在设施运营管理中的发展潜力。在实现项目目标的过程中，COBie 作为信息传递介质，被应用于 BIM 平台与最新的设施管理系统之间。最终，项目成果证明了 BIM 和 COBie 在资产管理领域应用的可行性。文中将讨论在项目实施中的研究结果和遇到的挑战。

关键词： BIM，COBie，公用设施，资产管理

References：

[1]　Anderson, Anne, C S Dossick, et al. Seeking new social norms: Facilities services organizational isolation in the University of Washington's digital transition[C]. Rheden: Proceedings of the Engineering Project Organizations Conference. 2012.

[2]　Becerik-Gerber B F J, Li N, Calis G. Application areas and data requirements for BIM-enabled facilities management[J]. Journal of Construction Engineering and Management, 2012, 138 (3): 431-42.

[3]　Bryde, David, Martí Broquetas, etal. The project benefits of Building Information Modelling (BIM)[J]. International Journal of Project Management, 2013, 31, (7): 971-80.

[4]　Eadie R, Browne M, Odeyinka H, et al. BIM implementation throughout the UK construction project lifecycle: an analysis[J]. Automation in Construction, 2013, 36: 145-151.

[5]　Gu, Ning, Kerry London. Understanding and facilitating BIM adoption in the AEC industry [J]. Automation in Construction, 2010, 19, (8): 988-990.

[6]　Koch, C, Neges M, König M, et al. Natural markers for augmented reality-based indoor navigation and facility maintenance[J]. Automation in Construction, 2014, 48: 18-30.

[7]　Love P E D, Matthews J, Simpson I, et al. A benefits realization management building information modeling framework for asset owners[J]. Automation in Construction, 2014, 37: 1-10.

[8]　Lucas J, Bulbul T, Thabet W. An object-oriented model to support healthcare facility information management[J]. Automation in Construction, 2013, 31: 281-291.

[9]　Masood R, M K N Kharal, A R Nasir. Is BIM adoption advantageous for construction industry of Pakistan? [J]. Procedia Engineering, 2014, 77: 229-238.

[10]　Michele D S, Daniela L. Decision-support tools for municipal infrastructure maintenance management[J]. Procedia Computer Science, 2011, 3: 36-41.

[11]　Motamedi A, Hammad A, Asen Y. Knowledge-assisted BIM-based visual analytics foe failure root cause detection in facilities management[J]. Automation in Construction, 2014, 43:

73－83.

［12］　Schade，Jutta. Life cycle cost calculation models for buildings［C］. In 4th Nordic Conference on Construction Economics and Organisation，2007：321.

［13］　Volk R，Stengel J，Schultmann F. Building Information Modeling（BIM）for existing buildings — literature review and future needs［J］. Automation in Construction，2014，38：109-127.

虚拟与真实空间中市场的层级结构：对北京三环内菜市场规模和网络点评的空间句法分析

盛　强　夏海山　刘　星
（北京交通大学建筑与艺术学院）

摘要：当代快速的城市发展普遍存在着对大型项目的重视，而忽略了对小尺度日常生活空间品质的关切和营造。菜市场是城市商业中较为稳定而传统的功能，反映着城市日常生活的活力，有重要的社会和经济意义。本文将基于 2009 年对北京三环路以内所有 183 个菜市场摊位数的实地调研，尝试应用空间句法模型来量化分析市场所在空间的拓扑连接参数与市场规模之间的关系。其结论显示影响这些菜市场规模的重要因素是城市街道空间体现出的层级结构。另外，随着网络点评平台的发展，菜市场这类满足基本日常生活的城市功能近年来也在大众点评网上出现。初步的研究显示这些市场的评论数量信息反映了它在网上的可见度，而其网上可见度则与其真实规模和使用状况存在一定的关联。

关键词：菜市场，层级运动网络，中心流，空间句法

1　市场与自组织的空间规律

当代快速的城市发展改变的不仅是物理空间形态，更是城市经济和社会发展的反映。然而，目前城市建设中普遍存在着对大型项目的重视，而忽略了对小尺度日常生活空间品质的关切和营造[1]。在单纯追求经济利益和形象工程的前提下，众多的城市更新和改造工程日趋"贵族化"和"场景化"。全球化的视野似乎进一步强化了我们意识中先进—落后、高级—低级的差异，而旧城中小摊贩的聚集和喧嚣杂乱的市场则无疑属于后者，需要被改造和升级。2003 年在全国范围内展开的"农改超"工作便是这个背景下的一个实例。城市更新的社会学意义本应在于为不同群体提供生存和发展的空间，而"农改超"目标的提出则忽视了各阶层生存发展状况的差异和与市民的多样化需求。该项目自施行之日起在国际学术界就不乏质疑的声音[2,3]，而实际效果的不理想也恰恰说明它在理论上的问题。本文以菜市场为切入点，目的并不在于对当年"农改超"工作的评价，而是试图从菜市场规模与分布的空间关系出发，作为一种自组织的经济行为发掘其背后的空间逻辑。

选择菜市场作为研究对象，主要是出于下述原因：

（1）菜市场作为一种最普通且基本的日常生活商业功能，在相当一段时间内仍然会是日常购物活动的一部分。从西方发达国家的情况来看，规律性的集市仍然长期存在，几乎是城市各个阶层都会光顾的购物场所。

（2）从日常生活活力的角度来看，根据已有的研究[4]，街区中最有活力，最集中的聚集了各类商店、摊贩及社会行为的区段往往是在菜市场出入口附近。菜市场是街区活力重要的标志及催化剂。

（3）作为一种基本功能，菜市场体现出较大的临时性和自组织特征，它的出现和发展很少是规划的结果，却往往是规划整饬的对象。整饬的结果也往往难以预期：一些被治理的街市迅速在周围复苏，而一些被升级为超市的市场则难以为继。四年的研究周期（2005～2009）可以体现出一定的规律性。

2　市场的层级与空间的层级

2.1　北京中心区菜市场情况简介

本文选取的研究对象为北京三环路以内所有的固定菜市场、临时性早市和食品店或摊贩的聚集

地（图 3）。其数据来源为笔者在 2005 年到 2009 年间对该地区进行的地毯式调研，调研的内容包括标注它们的类型、在地图上的位置和具体的摊位数。

图 1　不同种类的菜市场

（资料来源：作者自摄）

比较 2005 年和 2009 年的状况，尽管在这期间超市的数量有所增加，但菜市场和单体小菜店的数量同样有增无减。首先需在此说明的是，本文将大于等于 5 个经营个体（不论是菜店还是摊位）的实体定义为菜市场。按这种算法，2005 年三环路内全部 179 个菜市场中有 43 个消失了，但其中只有 3 个被成功升级为超市。大部分（23 个）消失的原因是在城市开发项目被拆除了，而其他的则转为它用。但在这四年间新开业的菜市场也有 46 个，在图 4 中我们可以看到各个菜市场的规模（摊位数）和四年来的变化。

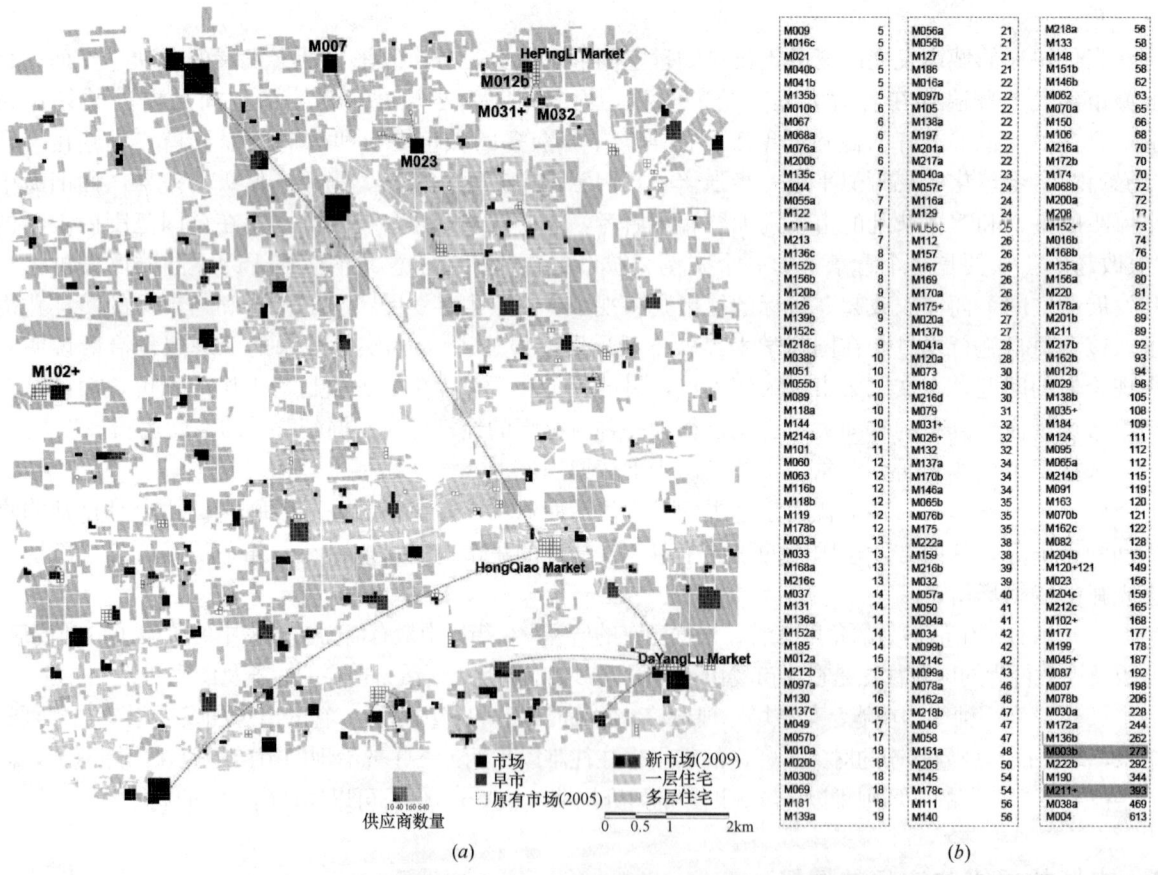

图 2　2005 年到 2009 年北京三环路内菜市场规模和位置的变化

（a）菜市场规模和位置的变化；（b）2009 年调研的数据

（资料来源：作者自绘）

从这个变化中我们可以看出以下几个趋势：首先，在最高级别的菜市场中，批发型的中心市场逐渐地从城市中心区外移。如天坛东门附近的红桥水产品市场在 2006 年被关闭，摊贩转向邻近三环路的四道口和玉泉营地区。相似的，左安门外的大洋路市场也由于轻轨的修建而大部被拆除，摊贩转向周围几公里内的新市场，原址只留下部分批发副食品的区域。中级别的菜市场（大于 150 小于 250 摊位）的变迁则体现了一种动态的稳定性。如和平里集贸市场在过去的 40 余年始终是该区域最重要的市场，而随着 5 号线建设的道路拓宽工程，原有的沿街市场已被几个相对集中的大型超市和菜市场取代。与之相似，四路通市场的拆除导致了周边几个已有菜市场的增容。小市场的变化趋势则比较复杂。一方面，随着中心城区商业的总体增加趋势，新的市场也不断涌现。其中大部分（28 个中的 20 个）直接位于城市级别的交通网络上，5 个位于更高级的大都市级道路，而仅有 3 家在街区内部开业。显然，即便菜市场的功能主要面向附近的居民，但对高层级的交通可见性仍是重要的因素。另一方面，除了前面提到过的由于城市开发而拆除的 23 个市场外，剩下的 20 个市场中的 13 个均为邻近中级市场的小市场。它们由于商品的趋同而缺乏与中级市场的竞争的能力而被自然淘汰。

总体来说，中小型菜市场尽管四年间在数量上变化并不小，但在位置上仍然保持着很大的稳定性。而大型市场特别是批发型市场的变迁空间规律明显表现出随城市扩张而外移且趋向于高层级的交通网络。分析对比菜市场本身的层级和城市空间中交通网络的层级之间的关联是这部分研究的重点。

2.2　菜市场的规模与等级：在统计学意义定义的层级关系

从图 3 针对北京三环路以内菜市场的分析中，我们也可以发现菜市场的规模（摊位数）大体上遵从幂律。在后面的研究中本文根据市场规模划分为如下几个等级：大型市场（大于 250 个摊位）、中型市场（150～250 个摊位）、小型市场（70～150 个摊位）和微型市场（5～70 个摊位）。需要说明的是，菜市场的分级方式对中心地研究来说本身是个复杂的课题，为了使数据较好离散的方法也很多[5,6]。本文采取的方式比较简单，目的在于在城市这个研究尺度上更客观的反映单体菜市场服务区的尺度。

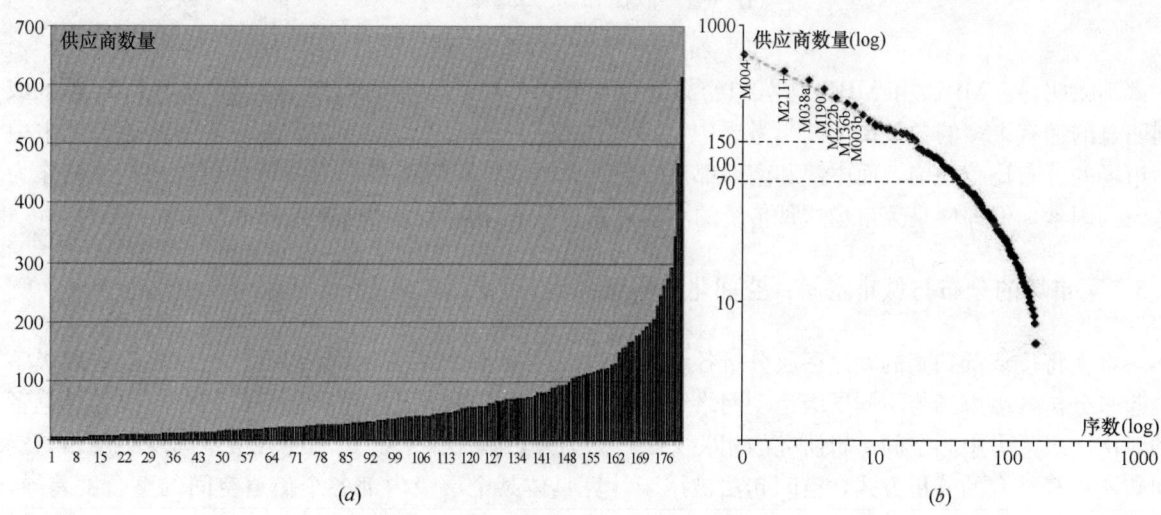

图 3　北京三环路内菜市场的规模（摊位数）所体现出的"幂律"。

（a）摊位数按小到大排序；（b）对摊位数和序数同时取对数

（资料来源：作者自绘）

基于各个规模级别的菜市场在北京三环路内的分布和间距，本文分析了各层级市场间的空间关系（图 4）。由于中型市场的服务范围大都超越了街区尺度，为了表述方便在底图中采用了根据大都市级交通网络划分的 31 个超级街区（Mega-block，编号 MB01 到 MB31）。

从结果上看，即便考虑到居住区的分布，无论是大、中型菜市场还是小型菜市场的分布的规律

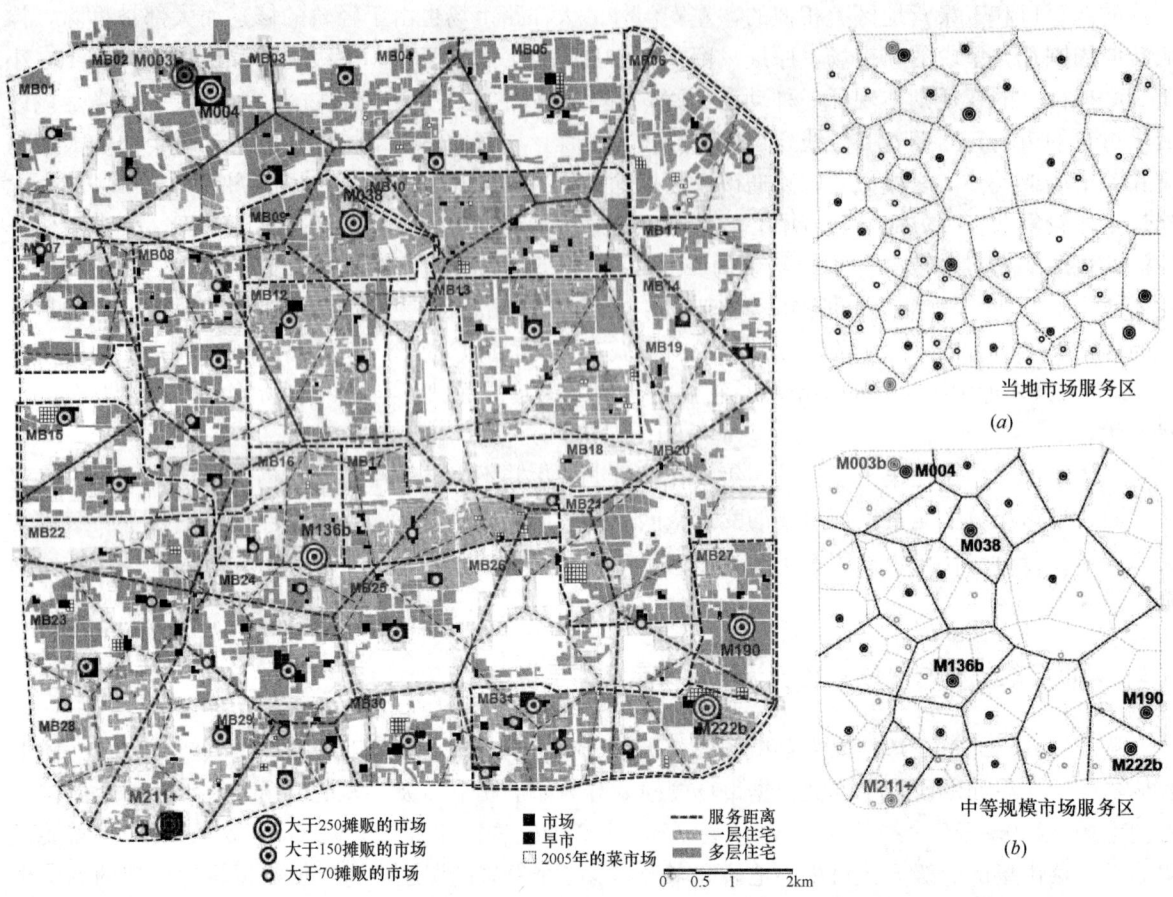

当地市场服务区

(a)

中等规模市场服务区

(b)

大于250摊贩的市场
大于150摊贩的市场
大于70摊贩的市场

■ 市场
■ 早市
□ 2005年的菜市场

--- 服务距离
一层住宅
多层住宅

0 0.5 1   2km

图4　对北京三环路内菜市场的中心地空间结构分析

(a) 小型菜市场；(b) 大、中型菜市场

（资料来源：作者自绘）

性都不太明显。MB10 和 MB13 等人口密集的区域很少有大于 70 摊贩的市场，而类似 MB31 等区域则明显的拥有更多的各级市场。当考虑中型市场的服务半径（平均 1.4～2km），北面的区域中中型市场的分布比较均匀，而中部和南部都比较混乱。因此，尽管大多数消费者会自觉地把距离作为考虑的因素，但即便是菜市场这种传统的功能分布也很难用简单的距离关系来把握。

2.3 菜市场的分布与城市空间：空间化的层级关系

本文将按从低到高的顺序逐层分析各级市场对该层级运动网络的依赖程度，然后将这些层级整合起来分析各级市场与不同层级运动网络组合的空间关系。对区域内路网层级的划分可以参见笔者的对街区级活力中心空间逻辑研究的相关文章[4]。另外，本文采取的是一种城市空间层级网络与空间句法计算结合的分析方式，空间句法被用于计算具体某个层级内部各个街道空间的整合度差异，而针对空间句法算法的介绍这里也不再赘述。

在街区级尺度分析中，全部 182 个市场中的 89 个在街区中局域整合度高（在该街区内整合度最高的 10％ 的街道段）的道路上设有入口。33 个市场位于几条内部街道与街区外部空间连接的必经之路上。这样算来，超过 2/3 的市场均有街区内主要道路的支持。另外 59 个缺乏街区级空间支持的市场大部分均直接面向城市或大都市级道路开口。如 M190、M127a 和 M222b 等较大的市场位于由大都市级道路限定的超级街区的中心。从这个意义上讲，相对于这些超级街区的空间结构而言，这些城市级的街道本身也可以算作"局域"整合度较好的街道了。另外一些比较小而直接面向城市或大都市级道路开口的市场（如 M218c、M144、M063 等）则发挥着类似超市的功能，并不完全依赖来自附近街区的客源。另外，M089 和 M130 为仅有的两个完全深藏于街区内部比较隐蔽的街道（整合度低）中的特例，它们所处的街区都正在或刚刚完成城市更新而展现出明显的临时性特征。

在城市级尺度（中尺度）分析中，全部 182 个市场中的 58 个在城市级道路上有入口。其中的 12 个在整合度好的城市级街道上，在右表中他们被单列出来，大部分为大、中型的市场。另外，89 个市场位于距离城市级道路一个拓扑步数的街道上，18 个市场直接位于区域级道路或与之距离一个拓扑学步数。由于区域级道路本身并不阻碍它被用作城市级别的交通，这些市场也可以被理解为与城市级运动网络有直接的空间联系。因此，总体算来共有 165 个市场与城市级空间相连，达到了三环路内市场总数的 90.1%，仅有 18 个市场没有城市或区域级别的空间支持。

而在大区域级尺度分析中，仅有 7 个市场直接面向区域级交通网络开口。毕竟菜市场是一种低端的城市功能，而区域级交通沿线的土地价值较高，往往为更高端的功能占据。69 个市场与区域级空间相距一个拓扑步数，他们中的大部分为大型菜市场。由于区域级空间多为高速路和环路，对步行交通多有阻断作用，这样的结果比较合理。另外，当考虑到这些市场与更高级的交通网络的关系时，M004，M003b 和 M211+这些批发型的高级菜市场都在铁路沿线。究其原因大概是一方面是便利的运输（但其实很多货运依赖公路），另一方面是铁路沿线相对较低廉的工业和仓储用地。

当综合考虑菜市场与各个层级的交通网络关系时，如图 5 所示，25 个市场同时与三个层级的交通网络相连。在右表中它们的代码以深灰色为背景，其中多数为大、中型菜市场：9 个市场超过 150 个摊位，8 个市场超过 70 个摊位。作为该区域中最大的菜市场的 M004 明光寺水果批发市场甚至与四个层级的交通网络相连。129 个市场至少与两个层级的交通网络相连，在右表中它们的代码以中灰色为背景，其中 24 个缺乏街区级空间的支持。仅有 26 个市场只与一个层级相连，在右表中它们的代码以浅灰色为背景，他们大多为微型的市场，其中仅有两个超过 50 个摊位。总体来说，街区级空间的支持（局域整合度高）为菜市场提供了一个基本的条件，而与城市或更高级空间的联

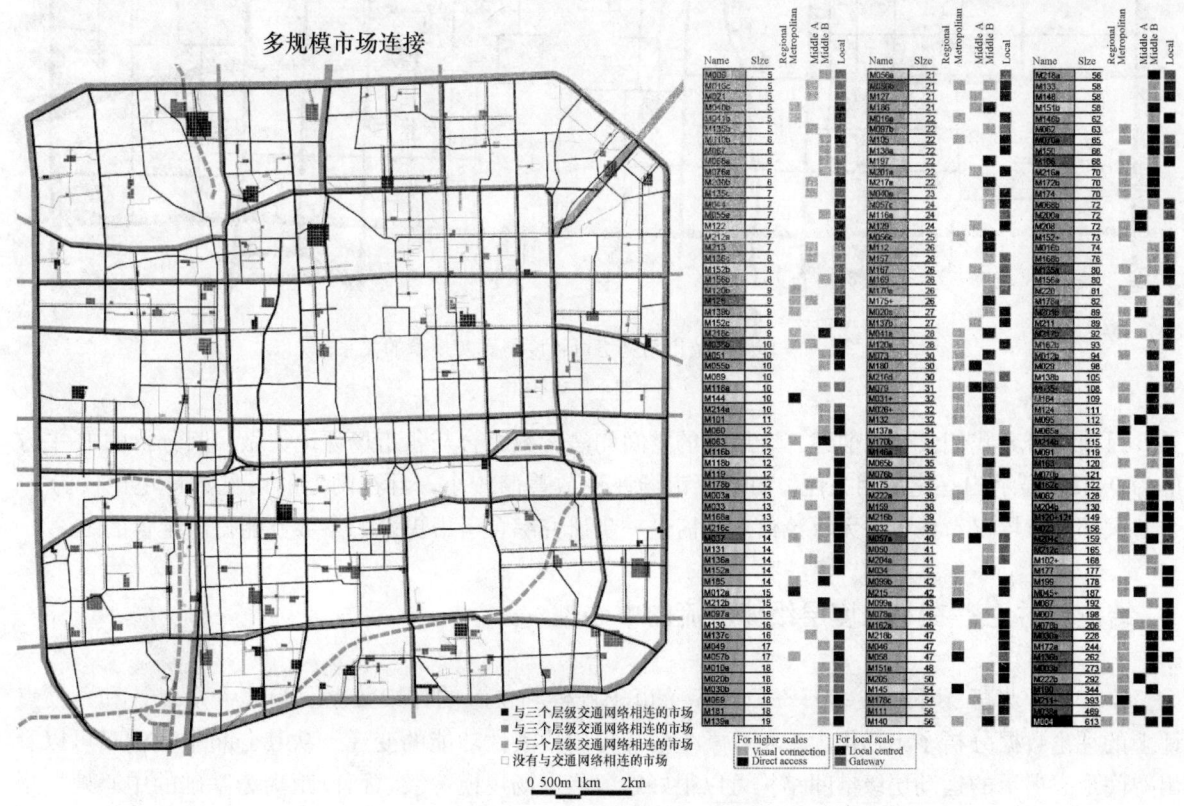

图 5　三环路内菜市场与各层级空间的关系

（资料来源：作者自绘）

系则为大多数较大市场的必要条件。

2.4　虚拟空间中的市场层级结构

随着近年来网络商业平台的迅速发展，大量实体商业的运营状况可以从网络平台中的可见度反映出来。具体对菜市场这种城市功能来说，大众点评网和百度点评网上都有对各个市场的相关信息。其中点评数信息是可供量化研究对比的重要开放信息源。从目前我们收集到三环路以内的点评信息来看，其分布有很大的不均衡性，而这在很大程度上反映出社群特征及功能特色的影响。例如，位于城市东南角三元桥地区的市场普遍有较高的评论数，而该地区临近使馆区和机场高速路，来此购物的有部分外国居民，而货品也相应地体现出异国特色，吸引了中国顾客的评价。同样，城市西北角的明光寺地区以水产和水果著名，也拥有较高的评论数。除此之外，占据空间优势的市场同样有较高的虚拟可视度，如前文提到过的 M012b（和平里地区的天丰利市场）等等。直观来看，评论数体现出远比摊位数更大的地区间的不均衡性（图6）。

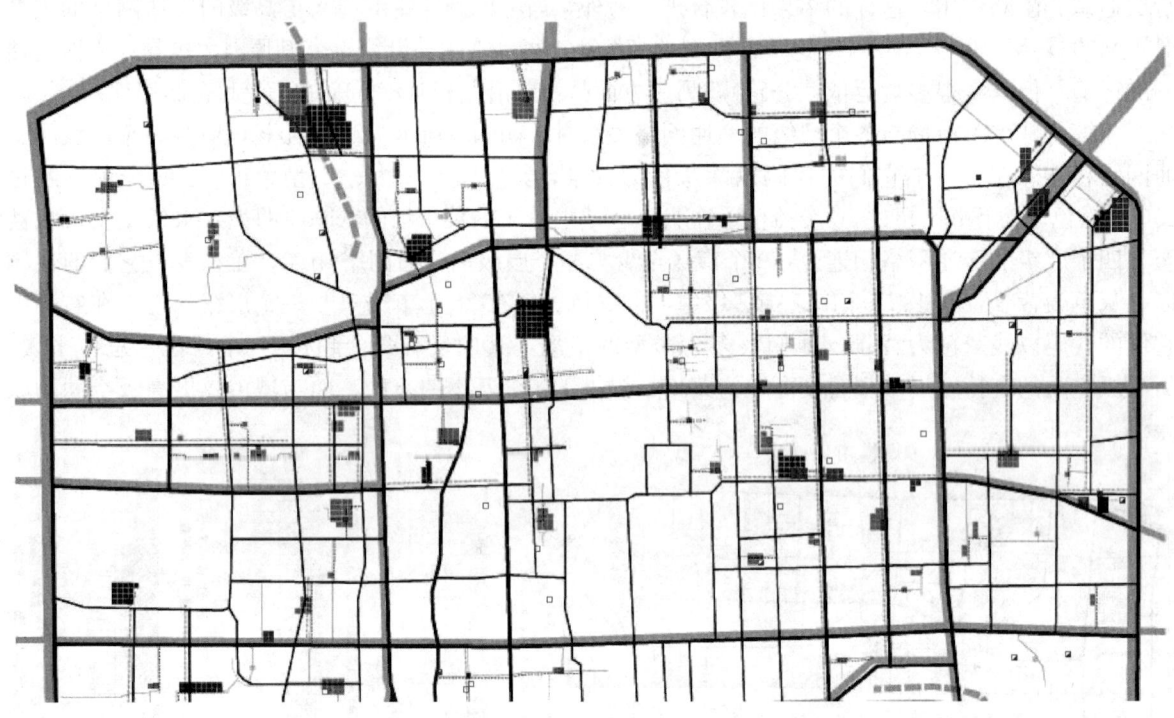

图6　三环路内菜市场网络可视度与真实规模的关系

（资料来源：作者自绘）

目前的研究我们尝试将前述三个层级的空间句法参数综合与各市场评论数做回归分析的 R 平方值为 0.32，显示出一定的相关性。由于菜市场评论数普遍较小，且在网上的可见数量也仅仅为 73个，大部分市场仅有位置并无评论信息，需进一步研究综合考虑更多的参数方能得出定量的结论。

3　结论与讨论：在小尺度层级体现流的中心性

本文基于北京三环路内 2005～2009 年菜市场规模和位置的详细数据及当代大众点评和百度点评上的评论数据分析了市场作为一种日常生活活力的代表性功能的变迁。从其分布中我们又可以看出空间形态揭示的运动层级空间结构可以很好地解释市场规模等级，而以距离为基础的中心地模型则有较大的困难。具体来说，路网密度较高、连接紧密的胡同地区更容易支持大量小型市场，而街道密集较低的大院地区则更容易支持少数较大的市场。进一步的，与多个尺度层级的运动网络均有较好连接的市场倾向于发展为更大的规模或功能特色，而这个空间优势也随着网络的使用被进一步强化。

Scale-Structure of Food Markets in Real and Virtual Space：A Space Syntax Analysis on Food Markets Inside 3rd Ring of Beijing

Sheng Qiang ，Xia Haishan, Liu Xing

（School of Architecture and Design，Beijing Jiaotong University）

Abstract：Current rapid urban development is mainly focusing on large-scale projects，but the local scale everyday life is often neglected. As a traditional service-based economy which can reflect the vitality of local life，food market is of great social and economic importance. Based on the survey of 183 food markets inside 3rd ring，this research use space syntax to analyze the location of these markets and their sizes. The result shows the size of these markets has clear relationship with the configuration of multiple layers of movement networks. Furthermore，based on the recent development of internet，some of the food markets are well-reviewed on web. Preliminary research indicates that their virtual visibility can provide additional information revealing their actual uses.

Keywords：Food market, Layered movement network, Central Flow, Space syntax

参考资料：

[1] 张杰，吕杰. 从大尺度城市设计到"日常生活空间"[J]. 城市设计，2003，27(9)：40-44.

[2] 朱李明. 演化与变迁：我国城市中的"农改超"问题[J]. 商业经济与管理，2004，148(2)：13-16.

[3] 皇甫梅风，郑光财，张琼，等. 居民消费习惯与"农改超"模式的思考[J]. 商业经济与管理. 2004，155(9)：17-20.

[4] 盛强. 社区级活力中心分布的空间逻辑——以北京三环内222个街区内小商业聚集为例[J]. 国际城市规划，2012，27(6)：69-76.

[5] 黄世祝. 台南市蔬菜集散的空间结构[D]. 台湾：台湾师范大学，1982.

[6] 樊铧. 民国年间北京城庙市与城市市场结构[J]. 经济地理，2001，21(1)：90-94.

应用 BIM 于城市水资源与植被系统整合的设计架构

郭瀚嵘　谢尚贤

（台湾大学土木工程学系）

摘要： 近数十年来，人类活动与城市化进展改变了地貌景观，造成自然植被的减少及地表条件的改变，进而影响城市的气候环境。在高楼林立的城市区域，由于房屋建材具有吸收与储存热的能力（heat capacity），因而使得区域气温增加。同时，因为地表粗糙度的改变，且建筑屋外壳总表面积较原始地貌增大许多，而造成城市区域强度更强的大气紊流作用。结合两者因素，则产生城市热岛效应（urban heat island）。由于城市热岛效应会影响微气候的变化，增加了城市暴雨的强度与发生几率。再伴随着城市化所造成的不透水面积的大幅增加，让强降雨造成的地表径流更容易造成市区水灾。为了因应上述问题，近年来欧洲有一群学者开始倡导 Blue-Green（BG）设计，尝试整合城市永续排水系统（属于 Blue 设计）及城市植被绿化（属于 Green 设计），来更有效率地使用城市的能源与水资源，并减少城市热岛效应与的水灾损失，提升城市景观及舒适度。近年来，BIM（Building Information Modeling）技术正以革命性的观念与先进技术引领建筑营建产业进步，走向 3D 对象化与系统化的生命周期产品信息与生产作业管理，来提升建筑工程之效能、质量、安全与永续性（sustainability）。在城市排水系统与植被绿化的设计上，可从单一建筑物的尺度到城市的尺度来考虑，过程也需要面临许多专业界面的沟通与合作，这些都是 BIM 技术应用可以发挥效用的地方。因此，本研究提出结合 BIM 技术与 Blue-Green 设计方法的实作框架，并针对建筑设计工作流程进行探讨。

关键词： 建筑信息模型，可持续城市发展，城市水资源与植被系统整合

1　引言

当自然土地环境被开发成为水泥丛林，其地貌与物理环境因而改变，再加上气候变迁与热岛效应因素，而造成极端气候所带来的降雨强度与几率不断上升[1,2]，常超过城市排水设计容量而造成洪灾，还有温度的不断上升也造成城市居住环境的恶化，且已有越来越多的证据显示人口集中在城市区域会加剧对环境的负面冲击[3~7]，发展新的城市设计规划方法来达成永续城市发展是迫在眉睫的议题。目前在欧洲正推行的 Blue-Green 城市设计理念，倡议整合所谓 Urban Blue 的城市水资源系统（包含废水回收再利用、雨水回收、暴雨管理作为新的水资源来源）及所谓 Urban Green 的植被系统（像是绿屋顶、绿化公园、街道、停车场、绿墙还有城市农业等）来达成更永续之城市发展。

由于在一般建筑物的实际使用过程当中，人类的活动会耗用大量的能源、自来水、食物等资源，且会产生建筑废热、垃圾与污水。因此，建筑环境的维持，本身是一件很耗费环境资源的事情。若建筑物能采用绿屋顶与绿墙，便可以储存及利用雨水与降低建筑室内温度，甚至绿屋顶若采用鱼菜共生技术且以绿墙作为垂直农场，则这些绿化也可以与食物生产结合，减少食物运送的碳足迹。若在水系统的方面可以针对雨水储存并搭配建筑污水回收系统，则可以节约建筑用水。而若是搭配再生能源技术如太阳能与风力发电，则可以提供浇灌维护与水系统的动力来源。整个永续设计还可从建筑本身联结到建筑外部的低冲击开发（Low Impact Development）设施，如透水铺面、雨水花园、湿地甚至到城市河流，如此不仅提高建筑环境的透水性，其蒸散冷却作用亦可以帮助应对城市热岛效应，在遇到过多的降雨时，也能够减缓径流的发生，即目前台湾正推行的海绵城市的概念。

近几年在国际上迅速窜起的 BIM（Building Information Modeling）技术[8]，是建筑信息建构与管理的过程，可运用在建筑与土建工程上，不仅可以减少传统作业上的失误与浪费，并能实现精实工程的内涵，进一步实践节能减碳的绿色建筑设计理念。[9] 而建筑工程项目在竣工交付后，BIM 更是建筑信息应用与整合的关键技术之一。过往用 BIM 技术与能源分析在绿色建筑设计上的应用，主要针对个别建筑物的能源或是建材使用进行优化。[10~14] 本研究应用 Blue Green 的设计概念，针对

692

城市水资源系统与植被系统进行考虑，不单只考虑建筑本体，并进一步整体考虑城市尺度应对热岛效应的议题，以 BIM 为实现 Blue-Green 设计之具体手法，进行城市环境整合之设计（图1）。

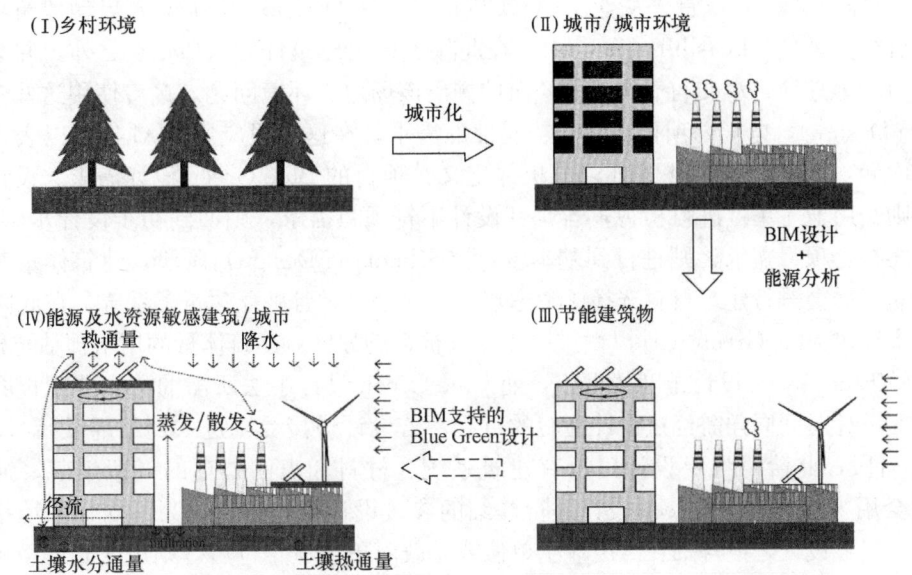

图 1　以 BIM-enabled Blue Green 设计来达成能源与水资源敏感城市之示意图
（资料来源：作者自绘）

2　城市水资源与植被系统整合的设计架构

水资源系统与植被系统的分类如图2，在建筑本身的水系统包括卫浴管线系统与中水回收系统，主要为机电管线厂商工程师负责。植被系统为绿屋顶、绿墙等系统，主要由绿屋顶厂商负责。若是考虑建筑物周围，水资源系统则会有雨水回收系统与下水道系统，这部分会衔接到水利工程公司的范畴，而植被系统则会有雨水花园等景观设计。由此可发现，在整合水资源与植被系统的永续设计手法，是需要不同权责划分的专业角色相互协调与沟通，再加上从建筑物规划设计到营运维护的建筑生命周期中，会有业主、建筑师、结构工程师、营造厂等不同角色需协调，

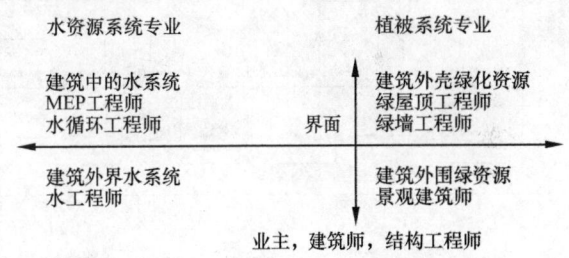

图 2　水资源系统专业与植被系统专业分类
（资料来源：作者自绘）

更何况要从单一建筑拉到城市尺度的规划情境，这当中非常需要 BIM 技术来协助整合与协调沟通。

以 BIM 为平台来模拟与整合水资源与植被系统的概念可见图 3。从建筑物本身的尺度来说，在建筑物进行绿化设计时，可依据气候数据，依据太阳辐射分析来辅助设计绿化区域，亦可同时考虑将绿屋顶连接雨水回收系统和中水系统结合，并以雨量数据作为绿屋顶储水空间和雨水桶容量设计的依据，硬件管线的配置则可供在三维空间中处理系统可能的冲突。而建筑场地范围内的雨水花园、植生沟、透水铺面与渗透侧沟等的低冲击开发设计，同样是被

图 3　以 BIM 架构水资源与植被系统整合之概念图
（资料来源：作者自绘）

整合于模型当中，并与单一建筑单元一同计算其整合设计手法对于城市环境的正向影响。

　　本研究针对建筑设计流程，提出一应用 BIM 进行 Blue-Green 设计的架构流程。以下流程采用 BPMN 流程[15]描述（图 4），首先从业主端（Client Staffs/Decision Makers）启动建筑项目，由设计团队进行可行性评估（Feasibility Study），在此除了提出建筑计划（Plan）之外，并会根据场地现况分析，由场地地质、水文与气候状况，而挖掘出该场地之环境问题。接着使用这些数据进行初步设计（Pre-Design），以规划项目空间与功能性的需求，在这阶段应用 BIM 技术以表达初步设计时间之设计内涵，而进一步应用 BIM 以分析并定义其项目的 Blue-Green 设计需求。设计团队将数据封装后，则交由业主单位进行检视，若是其设计不符项目需求，则回到初步设计步骤重新设计，若是设计方案符合项目需求，则进行到基本设计（Schematic Design）阶段，建筑体量基本上在此阶段会被确立，并会进行建筑材料选择、考虑建筑表面处理，且确立建筑子系统。在此阶段的 BIM 模型可被用来针对 Blue-Green 设计以做进一步的分析，例如针对建筑体量的用水预估与建筑外壳的辐射分析来做 Blue-Green 设计范畴的框定，而 Blue-Green 设计手法所需的空间分配也会在此初步分配。与基本设计时间同样需经过设计检验的过程，若设计被接受则进入到细部设计（Design Development）阶段，此阶段将要设计出所有建筑系统、材料和表面处理的一般细节。细部设计的 BIM 模型将会用来针对 Blue-Green 设计进行详细的参数设计，并会量化为不同的环境指标以进行交互式分析。细部设计之报告书在经由业主单位或是政府单位审查过后，则进入到准备申请绿色建筑报告文件的阶段，完成申请绿色建筑的流程后，则交由设计团队进行发包图说之制作，最后则进行发包。

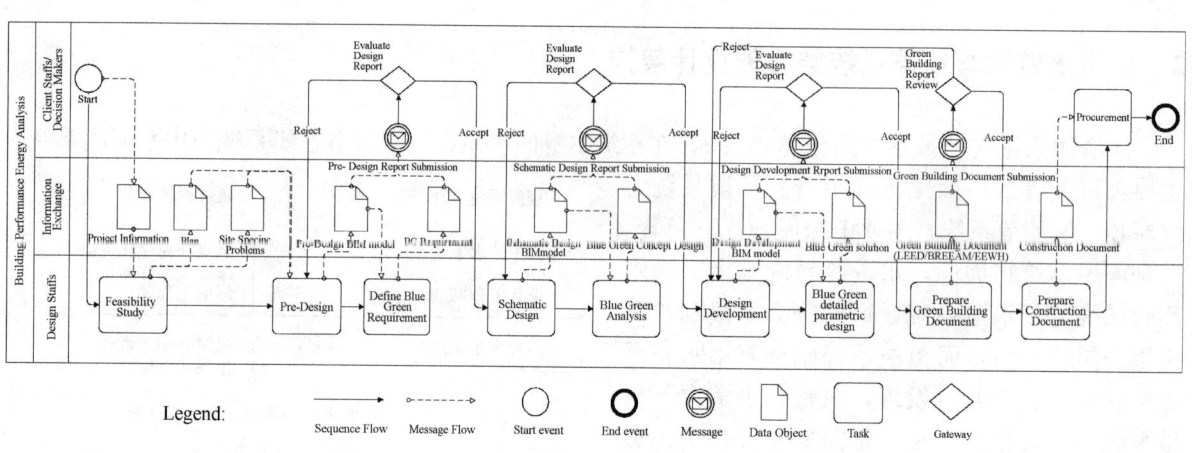

图 4　应用 BIM 进行 Blue-Green 整合设计流程图

（资料来源：作者自绘）

　　在使用 BIM 技术进行建筑设计当中，可以搭配应用既有的建筑性能分析工具以整合 Blue-Green 设计，但若要进行进一步的参数化分析，则是需要开发定制化①的功能。举绿屋顶设计为例，可以在前期基本设计时间，依据屋顶太阳辐射最大的部位进行初步配置，而集水量则可以根据气象数据以电子表格简单估算绿屋顶面积。在既有的分析工具方面，目前的建筑能源分析软件主要是将绿屋顶当作是一种材质做处理，将其传热系数设为定值，作为一种建材来执行分析，并无考虑含水量变化，因而往往在模拟上的误差相当大。市面上主要的 EnergyPlus 工具虽具备绿屋顶分析模块，但其分析所需要的参数过于繁复，不容易在建筑设计流程中使用。因此在进一步的参数分析设计上，可以进行既有的绿屋顶模块的 BIM 组件制作[16]，并针对其可能对应的水资源回收系统做一参数化设计，再搭配 BIM 软件 API 程序的开发，以针对绿屋顶性能做详细分析，亦能够在 BIM 模型中实时回馈详细的 Blue-Green 设计建议（图 5）。

---

① 定制化（customize），港台地区叫"客制化"，指个性化的一种服务，即根据客户需求而定制产品。——编者注

绿屋顶产品　　　　　　绿屋顶构件　　　　　　绿屋顶绩效分析工具

图 5　应用 BIM 进行 Blue-Green 定制化程序开发
（资料来源：作者自绘）

在应用 BIM 技术于单一建筑时，对于建筑物周围水资源系统与植被系统的描述与塑模亦需一并建立，并以此为基底来建立城市规划设计之数据库，而未来在进行新案例之设计，则取其周围场地案例进行背景参照，而新案例之水资源与植被系统亦需与周围案例相联结。从城市的尺度来说，热岛效应会影响整个城市的居住环境，而在 Blue-Green 设计中（图 6），由于建筑物之间会有传热效应，而自身的物理特性会随着含水量改变，因此可以用计算流体力学的工具

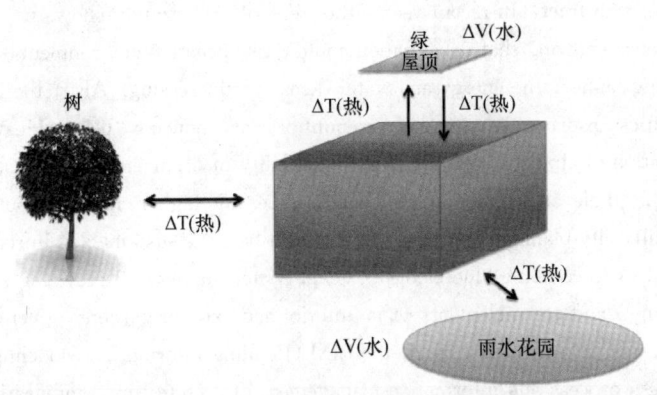

图 6　Blue-Green 设计中的建筑环境互动
（资料来源：作者自绘）

来针对城市环境进行模拟，以评估出需要多少的绿化面积，才能降低热岛效应的冲击。

3　结论

本研究提出应用 BIM 技术来支持 Blue-Green 建筑设计流程，界定 Blue-Green 概念于建筑设计流程中实际介入的切入点，并搭配定制化分析工具的开发，来实现城市水资源与植被系统之整合。设计流程从场地问题描述开始，进而界定 Blue-Green 设计的需求范围，再进行细部设计、搭配建立水资源与植被系统组件，并开发 Blue-Green 分析程序。接着延续此思路的架构，将建筑场地周围的低冲击开发设施一并建构。而在未来的新项目则将各既有项目之 BIM 模型作为参考背景模型，整合模型即可以作为城市尺度微气候模型之建置。目前针对建筑环境既有的量化指标，例如热舒适度、生物多样性、噪声减量、二氧化碳排放、河川水质、空气污染、洪灾风险等指标，可以在 Blue-Green 分析程序中扩充分析项目，将来这些现有的知识与相关的仿真工具，需要被整合并发展成为新一代的仿真系统，以利评估整个城市的生态系统，则整合量化后的指标将可以帮助城市规划者具体掌握 Blue-Green 设计的效益。

BIM Design Framework for City's Blue-Green Dream

Kuo Han-Jung, Hsieh Shang-Hsien

(Department of Civil Engineering, Taiwan University)

Abstract: In recent years, the trend of urbanization shows no stopping sign around the world. There is more evidence showing that urbanization could cause negative environmental impact. Since the urban population density is getting higher, the energy and water demand is increasing. Also, the building materials, e. g. concrete, commonly in the cities absorb and store a huge amount of heat, inducing "Urban Heat Island" which causes discomfort breezes, intensification of air pollution, increased probability of occurrence of intense convective storms, disruption of human activities due to elevated temperatures, health issues and higher energy consumption due to increased temperatures, etc. As a result, city planning and development must be more sustainable. In recent years, the Blue Green design methodology proposes to combine blue elements (e. g. water supply and recycling systems, waste water and rain water drainage systems) and green elements (e. g. interior and exterior gardens, green roofs, and green walls.) to achieve sustainable city design. On the other hand, the BIM (Building Information Modeling) technology has started to revolutionize the business process and information management of architecture, engineering and construction industry for better efficiency, quality, safety and sustainability. In this research, a BIM-enabled integrated design framework is proposed to facilitate the Blue Green design for city sustainability.

Keywords: Building information modeling, Sustainable city, Blue green dream

参考文献：

[1] Oke T R. The energetic basis of the urban heat island. Quarterly Journal of the Royal Meteorological Society, 1982, 108(455), 1-24.

[2] Masson V. Urban surface modeling and the meso-scale impact of cities. Theoretical and Applied Climatology, 2006, 84(1), 35-45.

[3] UN. World urbanization prospects: the 2005 revision. United Nations. Department of Economic and Social Affairs. Population Division, 2006.

[4] Arnfield A J. Two decades of urban climate research: a review of turbulence, exchanges of energy and water, and the urban heat island. International Journal of Climatology, 2003, 23(1): 1-26.

[5] Bornstein R, Lin Q. Urban heat islands and summertime convective thunderstorms in Atlanta: three case studies. Atmospheric Environment, 2000, 34(3): 507-516.

[6] Cox P M, Betts R A, Bunton C B, Essery R L H, Rowntree P R, Smith J. The impact of new land surface physics on the GCM simulation of climate and climate sensitivity. Climate Dynamics, 1999, 15(3): 183-203.

[7] Rozoff C M, Cotton W R, Adegoke J O. Simulation of St. Louis, Missouri, Land Use Impacts on Thunderstorms. Journal of Applied Meteorology, 2003, 42(6): 716-738.

[8] Eastman C, Teicholz P, Sacks R, Liston K. BIM Handbook: A guide to Building Information Modeling for owners, managers, designers, engineers and contractors. Second Edition, 2011.

[9] Krygiel E，Nies B，McDowell S. Green BIM：Successful Sustainable Design with Building Information Modeling，2008，188-200.

[10] Schlueter A，Thesseling F. Building information model based energy/exergy performance assessment in early. Automation in Construction，2009，18，153-163.

[11] Cho Y K，Alaskar S，Bode T A. BIM-integrated sustainable material and renewable energy simulation. Proceedings of the 2010 Construction Research Congress：Innovation for Reshaping Construction Practice，May 8-10，2010，Banff，AB，Canada，288-297.

[12] Kotwal T，Ponoum R，Brodrick J. BIM for energy saving. ASHRAE Journal，2011，53(9)：81-86.

[13] Zeng M. Future of green BIM designing and tools. Advanced Materials Research，2012，374-377，2557-2561.

[14] Kim H，Anderson K. Energy simulation system using BIM (Building Information Modeling). Proceedings of the 2011 ASCE International Workshop on Computing in Civil Engineering，June 19-22，2011，Miami，FL，USA，635-640.

[15] The Object Management Group. Business Process Model And Notation Version 2.0. 2011 [2015-3-20]. http：//www.omg.org/spec/BPMN/2.0/.

[16] NBS. NBS BIM Object Standard. 2014 [2015-3-20]. http://www.nationalbimlibrary.com/Content/BIMStandard/NBS-BIM-Object-Standard-v1_2_1114.pdf.

探讨迈向 IPD 流程之建筑设计优化

张益丰[1] 吴 楠[2] 施宣光[1]

（1. 台湾科技大学建筑系；2. 黎明职业大学土建系）

摘要： 迈向 IPD（Integrated project delivery）流程之建筑设计优化的关键是"跨专业知识整合"与"落实设计决策"。建筑信息建模（Building Information Modeling），是近年来在实务界逐渐形成趋势的建筑生命周期信息建构的概念与技术。该项技术搭配衍生式建模系统（Generative Modeling System）以参数式的技术进行建筑虚拟模型的建构，并链接各种有关建筑结构与物理环境的评估仿真系统，以协助知识整合与决策制定。建筑师必须在设计初期就将专业顾问的建议提前整合，发展设计方案。根据文献回顾与专家访谈，建筑设计的业务流程可以切割成配置（Site-plan）、基设（Permitting phase）与细设（Detailed design phase）三个阶段，每个阶段皆有工作循环，并设置里程碑以检视是否符合目标的要求。工作循环的内容由设计、建模与分析三个部分组成，经过反复讨论与修改，最后输出设计准则传递至下一阶段。根据建筑师的工作循环需求，本研究以衍生式建模作为整合策略的关键技术，发展辅助跨专业知识整合的衍生式建模工具，将建筑师与专业顾问所用的软件工具进行紧密串联，并将模拟分析的结果快速回馈给建筑师与专业顾问，加速建筑师、专业顾问与业主之间的决策，降低团队的沟通时间与成本。

关键词： IPD 流程，建筑信息建模（BIM），信息交付手册（IDM），衍生式建模系统

1 引言——研究背景与目的

从设计初期就导入 BIM[1]，辅助建筑师在建筑方案的发展过程中保持正确的发展方向，这有赖于跨专业知识整合与设计决策的传递。从 Eastman 引用自 Patrick Mac Leamy（2007）的设计资源投入及成效与时间关系图可知，在设计的初期进行设计决策变更所需付出的代价最小，而对整体造价与建筑物的效能的影响力却最大。本研究将针对跨专业知识整合与设计决策流程的议题，探讨 IPD 流程之建筑设计优化的信息作业内容，并结合绿色建筑设计，探讨如何在节能的目标上达到设计优化的实效。然而跨领域的专业知识与技术是否能与建筑生命周期各阶段的实务作业进行充分的跨领域整合，其整合的关键就是信息作业。

2 以 IPD 流程为基础的建筑设计

以 IPD 流程为基础的建筑设计，将专业顾问的意见与知识提前采纳[2]，让他们能在设计时间反映实务问题，透过有效的信息处理与传递，实时提供给建筑师以辅佐设计方案的进行。建筑师必须在设计时间就将节能顾问的建议提前整合，并分阶段处理建筑设计与能源之间的问题，提出各阶段的设计准则作为后续阶段的决策依据。设计初期所能掌握的信息少，因为缺少后期的工程信息，所以对于设计方案的评估不精确。但是初期设计与后期工程阶段的参与人员不同，因此会造成沟通合作上的断层。为了解决沟通断层的问题，本研究检讨现有的建筑业务流程，找出跨专业知识整合的可能性。根据文献回顾、专家访谈与案例分析的结果，本研究将建筑节能设计的业务流程分为配置、基设与细设三个阶段（图 1），每个阶段皆有工作循环与里程碑。其中里程碑的设置是为了检核该阶段的工作成果是否符合节能目标的要求，确保每一个阶段的节能设计准则能够传递至下一个阶段。业务流程的切割依据考虑各参与人员的工作内容、职务权责、团队合作模式，以及处理信息的最佳负荷量。

为了提升跨专业信息交换的效率，建筑团队必须确立信息交换的内容与交换格式的标准之制定。建筑信息量应该与建筑项目进度配合，针对特定阶段输出所需的信息项目。根据参与人员的需

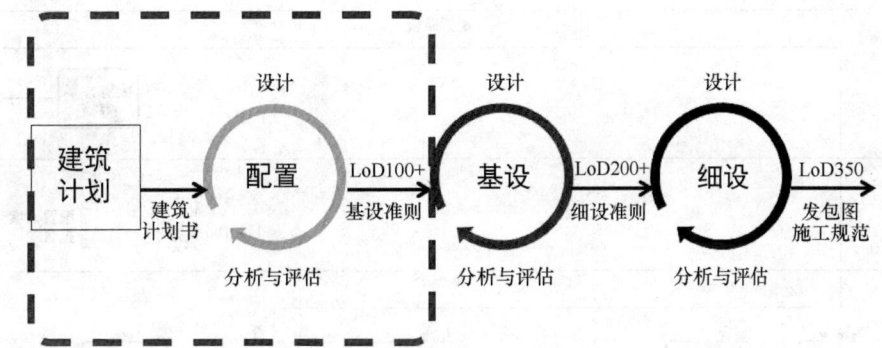

图 1　建筑节能设计的业务流程切割

求分析来制定交换资料的内容、定义、字段属性与关联，检讨业务流程来确定彼此的需求与工作职责。本研究整理配置阶段的工作项目，以 BPMN（Business Process Modeling Notation）绘制业务流程找出关键的作业时间点，确定不同对象的交换需求与项目文件。[3, 4, 5]在项目启动之后，业主将项目基本数据与建筑计划书交付给建筑师开始进行工作，并以访谈、电话或电子邮件等信息通路进行与业主以及节能顾问的非正式沟通。根据建筑计划阶段拟定的节能目标，进行配置方案的体量规划（小型循环）。建筑师将相关的项目数据，例如场地条件、使用需求与工程预算及时程交付给节能顾问进行可行性评估。节能顾问提出专业报告分析其达成节能建筑目标的可行性，以及相关配套之设计准则后整理成文件交付给建筑师。建筑师根据其可行性评估与节能目标进行评估。如果需要修改，则再与节能顾问重复上述的工作（中型循环）。此时可能以非正式沟通的方式反复修改，直到体量配置方案能够符合建筑计划书的目标。然后由建筑师整理成完整的配置计划向业主提出报告。业主接获配置计划书后进行审核，如果业主核可，则完成配置阶段的工作；如果业主未核可，则重新检视配置方案。这个工作过程是跨越业主、建筑师与节能顾问之间的大型工作循环。

3　衍生式建模的整合策略

衍生式建模是 BIM 的基础，也是信息整合的关键技术。透过衍生式建模技术将建筑节能相关的意见与知识提前采纳，让专业顾问能在概念设计时间反映实务问题，实时提供给建筑师以辅佐设计方案的进行。然而建筑师所需的专业信息若无法提前取得，将影响设计方案的进行与思考。在传统的建筑设计流程中，建筑师在前期扮演重要的决策角色，其他专业合作者都是被动等待，直到基本设计时间专业顾问才开始提供专业建议与初步设计，因此对于设计方案的辅助有限。为了改善这个问题，本研究设置工作循环，让各项目参与人员在业务流程中有整合的时间。以配置阶段为例，确定业务流程图之后，分析不同工作者与工作循环的关系。在每一个阶段，设计信息的沟通模式可以区分成三种工作循环（大、中与小），这三种循环会随着项目的进度与合作对象的不同而持续进行，并有反复修改的可能（图 2）。

本研究以衍生式建模进行跨领域专业知识整合[6]，将建筑师所用的设计工具与节能顾问所用的环境模拟分析软件进行紧密串联[7]，节省制作时间与降低模型编修成本。从微观的角度来看，每一个设计时间都有工作循环，由"设计"、"建模"与"分析"三个动作组成的。"设计"与"建模"之间是双向密集且工作分量大的作业，"建模"与"分析"之间仍是双向作业，不同软件之间数据的传递存在不同的数据格式，需要以通用格式作为数据交换接口如 IFC 或 gbXML 等，以串接设计信息、建模与分析软件。"分析"与"设计"之间是一种单向作业，工作量较小，以图像或数据表现数据分析结果，回馈给设计人员参考，进行设计方案的修正。

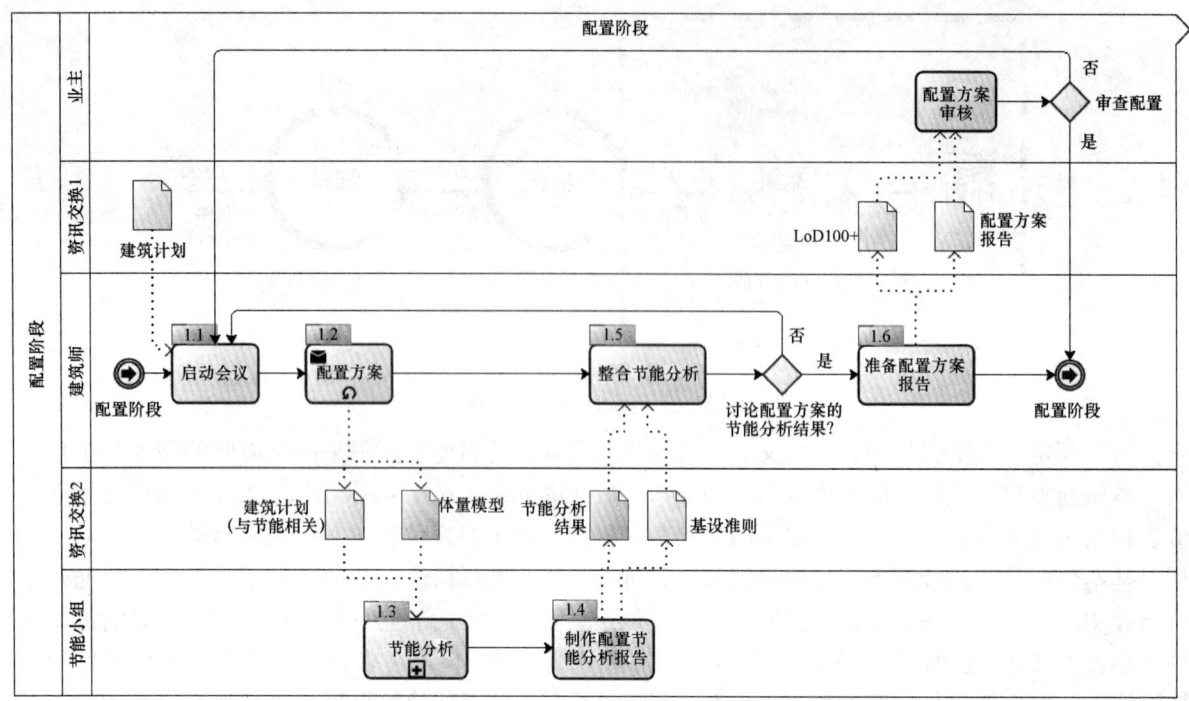

图 2　配置阶段的节能设计业务流程图

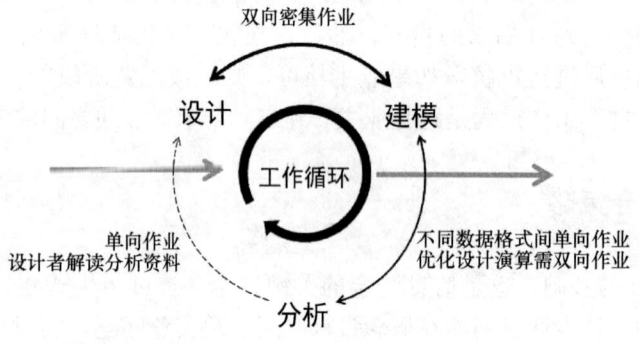

图 3　工作循环与信息整合策略

4　研究成果——衍生式建模工具

　　针对建筑师进行小型工作循环的需求，本研究根据衍生式建模的理论与方法，将节能设计的知识与方法整合到体量设计与建筑配置方案中，探讨 LoD 100[8]应包含的信息、节能分析的时间点、分析结果对设计方案的回馈，提供流畅的数据交换与及时回馈模拟结果。利用 Rhino 搭配 grasshopper 连接 excel 与 Ecotect 等软件，将设计时间考虑的因子参数化，作为建筑师在配置阶段的体量设计用工具。它可以视为是一种跨专业领域的桥梁，建筑师修改设计方案时能实时回馈能源分析的结果，让建筑师在设计与能源问题之间进行决策，而不用每次都请教专业顾问的意见，因此可以降低团队的沟通成本。其主要的目的：（1）体量方案的可行性评估；（2）找出设计准则，帮助设计决策的传递，避免在后续过程中违背前一个阶段的重要决定。本研究以一集合住宅为案例说明，验证其理论的可行。建筑师可以专注在设计方案的发展，复杂的楼地板面积、体积、外部表面积等计算皆可以快速得知，并可以直接将建筑模型与 Ecotect 连接，直接进行能源模拟的工作。

　　透过衍生式建模工具的开发，本研究整理出节能信息交换项目与可参数化的信息条列。根据文献

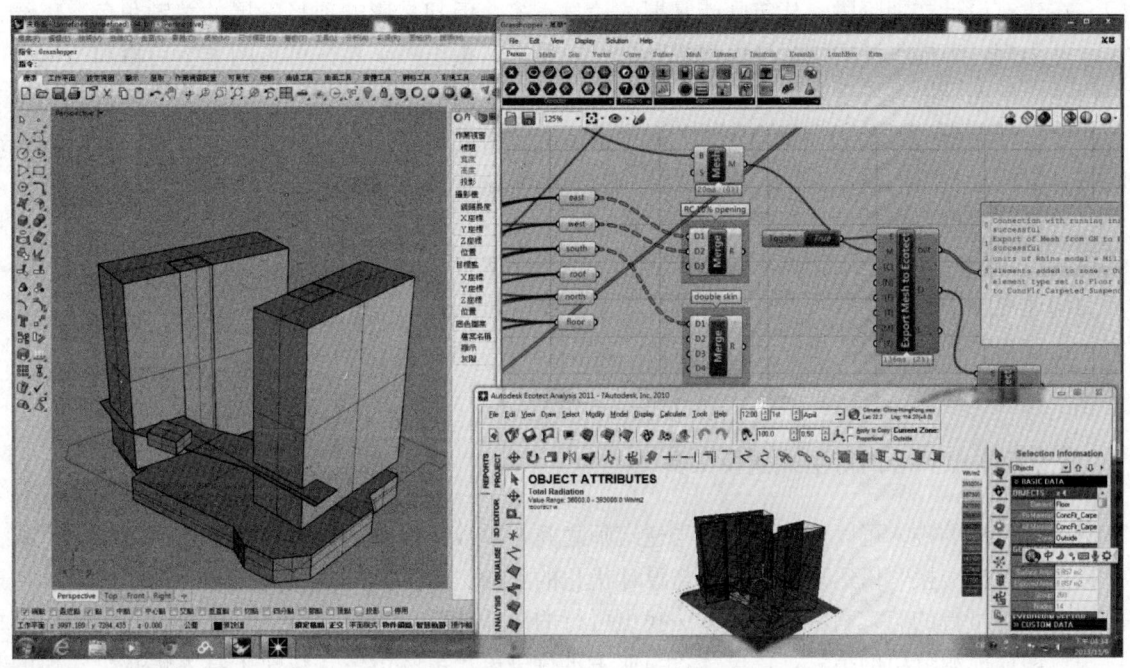

图 4　衍生式建模工具的操作成果

可知[9, 10]，在建筑物的能源使用上主要的耗能为空调与照明系统，这两者就占了整体能源使用的 60% 以上，因此在建筑体量配置阶段这两个因素可以作为内部能源模拟与机电设备的主要考虑。建筑师根据建筑类型找出相关的法规要求（开窗率、碳排放量或 EUI 值）作为后续配置方案的参考。在配置阶段所做的 BIM 模型应包含建筑体量、构造类型、外壳（皮层）与其他，其内容说明如表 1。

LoD 100＋ model　　　　　　　　　　　　　　　　　　　　　　　　　　　　表 1

项目	建筑环境	建筑体量 (building mass)	构造类型 (construction type)	外壳（皮层）	其他
内容	周边自然环境	几何形式（含垂直 与水平主要通道）	建筑物的使用性质 (building type)	各向表面 朝向方位	营运时间
	周边建筑物 体量	总楼地板面积、 各楼层面积	楼层数（building stories）	各向表面 构造类型	空间配置 (spatial configuration)
	外部空间	表面积、周长	地下室开挖 面积与周长	各向表面开 口比例	
	铺面、植栽与地形	体积	地下室层数		

　　配置阶段的节能分析的工作项目有：建筑表面太阳热辐射分析（thermal loads）、日照阴影分析、各向外壳热得热失、风场 CFD 模拟分析（室外风场，各向皮层外部风压）、内部主要气流（垂直与水平通道）、总耗能分析、空调与照明系统建议、工程预算与工期概估。最后输出基设准则，交付与下一阶段的参与者。基设准则的内容：各向外壳隔热系数、开口比例、空调与照明系统建议、预估耗能目标。

5　结论与建议

5.1　以 IPD 流程为基础的建筑设计优化

　　建筑设计最佳的效果发挥阶段是初期建筑设计时间，包含建筑计划、建筑配置阶段与外壳设计时间。在建筑设计初期阶段，建筑师能掌握的信息不多，但却是影响项目发展的关键角色。以绿色建筑设计为例，节能设计的概念经由建筑师的专业思考，提出一个具体可行的方案后再与节能顾问进行讨论。然而，事务所受限于时间压力必须在短时间之内完成它的工作。如果节能分析的结果来得太晚，设计者已经进入下一个设计时间，那么节能分析的结果无法回馈给设计方案，建筑师无法实时整合节能信息修改设计方案，将会无法有效发挥效益。这个时候小型工作循环就是非常关键的工作。建筑师掌握关键的设计策略，只要修改相关的参数，便能快速地调整设计方案。经过小循环优化演算，可以减少中型工作循环的错误尝试，加速团队合作的效率，快速整合顾问的意见，让大循环的沟通更加顺畅。各阶段的设计准则是一个重要的机制，提醒建筑师与专业顾问在发展设计方案时，不应违背前一阶段的决策。万一有重要的发现必须推翻之前的决定时，必须与专业顾问及业主讨论，修改目标。

5.2　跨专业知识整合的衍生式建模工具

衍生式建模的技术可以让专业顾问与建筑师之间，以数字技术建立适用性更广泛之定制化的建模工具进行数据交换，以达到知识整合与设计优化的目的。衍生式建模工具用来支持建筑设计初期的能源概估是可行的。它利用概估的方法找出可行的设计方案，有效地联结设计概念与能源仿真接口，快速回馈能源分析的结果，供设计者与业主进行决策。虽然衍生式建模工具大幅减少建模的时间，简化专业分析软件的操作，但是解读分析的结果与提出解决方案的跨领域知识仍然需要有专业顾问的支持。在后续发展上，可以考虑链接现有的营造工程数据库，提供实际的报价与单位信息，如建筑类型的用电密度、构造的单位成本价格、节能建材的材料信息等。透过这些数据，让建筑师可以对设计方案制定出更好的设计策略。观察实作测试的结果，本研究推论未来在建筑设计的初期阶段，建筑师与专业顾问之间的沟通将透过衍生式建模工具进行初步整合，建筑师将能发现更多跨专业领域的问题，避免错误的设计决策。

致谢

本研究感谢郭英钊与张清华建筑师、九典联合建筑师事务所、台湾建筑研究所人员陈建忠、刘青峰协助，以及科技专题补助，计划编号 NSC-103-2221-E-011-089。

Exploring the Integrated Project Delivery Approach for Architectural Design Heuristic

Chang Yi-Feng[1], Wu-Nan[2], Shih Shen-Guan[1]
（1. Department of Architecture，Taiwan University of Science and Technology；
2. Li Ming Vocational University）

Abstract：The key of integrated project delivery approach for architectural design heuristic is "multi-disciplinary knowledge integration" and "implement design decision-making". Building information modeling is a building life cycle information management concept and methods that has recently won growing acceptance among practical workers. This technology can be used in conjunction with a generative modeling system to construct virtual building models employed parametric methods. They can also be linked with various building structure and physical environment assessment and simulation systems to facilitate knowledge integration and decision-making. Architects must integrate the recommendations of energy conservation consultants during the preliminary design stage if they are to develop a correct design plan. According to a review of the literature and interviews with experts, architectural design processes can be divided into the site-plan, permitting, and detailed design stages. Each stage has its own work loops, and milestones are typically set to determine whether targets having reached. The content of each work loop includes the three actions of design, modeling, and analysis; after repeated discussion and revision, the final output design criteria are transmitted to the next stage. This study investigates operating processes and the drafting of a process flowchart during the site-plan stage, and seeks to confirm project documents and the information interchange needs of various project participants. In accordance with the needs of architects' work loops, this study employed parametric modeling as a key integration technology, and developed a one-parameter building mass design tool. By closely linking the design tools used by architects and the environmental simulation and analysis software used by energy conservation consultants, this tool can save design production time and reduce model revision costs. Furthermore, the results of simulation can be quickly returned to architects and energy conservation consultants, which can reduce team communication time and costs and accelerate decisions made by architects, consultants, and project clients.

Keywords: IPD (Integrated project delivery), Building information modeling, Information delivery manuals, Generative modeling

参考文献:

[1] Eastman, Charles M. Bim Handbook : A Guide to Building Information Modeling for Owners, Managers, Designers, Engineers and Contractors[M]. 2nd ed. ed. Hoboken, NJ: Wiley, 2011.

[2] buildingSMART. An Integrated Process for Delivering Ifc Based Data Exchange[Z]. 2012.

[3] Nawari N. Standardization of Structural Bim[J]. In Computing in Civil Engineering, 2011.

[4] Nawari, N. , and M. Sgambelluri. "The Role of National Bim Standard in Structural Design. " In Structures Congress 2010, 1660 - 1671, 2010.

[5] Nawari, Nawari O. Bim Standard in the Structural Domain[J]. Civil Engineering and Science 1, 2012(2): 42 - 51.

[6] Wu Nan, Shen-Guan Shih. A Bim Inspired Supporting Platform for Architectural Design. Computer-Aided Design and Applications[J]. 2014(3): 327-37.

[7] Shi, Xing, and Wenjie Yang. "Performance-Driven Architectural Design and Optimization Technique from a Perspective of Architects. " Automation in Construction 32, no. 0 (7// 2013): 125 - 35.

[8] AIA. G202—2013 Building Information Modeling Protocol Form[EB/OL]. [2013]. http: // www. aia. org/.

[9] Pérez-Lombard, Luis, José Ortiz, Christine Pout. A Review on Buildings Energy Consumption Information[J]. Energy and Buildings, 2008(3): 394 - 98.

[10] USDOE. 2011 Buildings Energy Data Book[EB/OL]. [2011]. http: //buildingsdatabook. eren. doe. gov/docs%5CDataBooks%5C2011 _ BEDB. pdf.

高温潮湿地区住宅研究：以日本熊本县熊本市古町地区
住宅与中国福建省泉州市蔡氏古建筑群为例

张 悦 田中智之

（日本熊本大学自然科学研究科）

摘要：本研究利用 Ecotect 软件，在假定材料相同的情况下，通过对日本熊本县熊本市古町地区住宅和中国福建省泉州市蔡氏住宅群两地的古建筑设计平面图进行分析，探究其各自的设计特点，并结合两方的特质，推导出适合现代住宅的、具有亚热带季风气候地区特征的、节能减排绿色低碳生态型的建筑设计范式，从而使设计过程更加简化，达到提升设计效率的目的。

关键词：高温潮湿地区，住宅研究，熊本古町地区住宅，蔡氏古建筑群，Ecotect

1 背景介绍

1.1 研究背景介绍

高温潮湿作为亚热带季风气候地区的主要气候特征，一直受到建筑设计师们的重点关注。为了适应高温潮湿的气候，中国与日本的设计师采用了各自不同的设计手法，并取得了一定成效。然而，20 世纪以来，随着近代文明与工业化的飞速发展，环境破坏愈演愈烈。现如今，亚热带季风气候地区的气候环境严重恶化，极端天气显著增加。

近年来，随着全球气候变暖的加剧，减少二氧化碳排放，降低能耗等问题越来越受到人们的关注。顺应节能减排的政策要求，人们对于低能源负荷型建筑的关注也大大增加。同时，随着全球环境保护意识的增强，"可持续发展的生态建筑设计"逐渐成为业内的热点课题。因此，设计出"适合亚热带季风气候地区特征的节能减排绿色低碳生态型建筑"已然迫在眉睫。

1.2 地域背景介绍

中国福建泉州市蔡氏古建筑群位于泉州市南安官桥漳里村，2001 年 6 月 25 日被列为第五批全国重点文物保护单位。由菲律宾归国华侨蔡启昌及其子蔡资深（1839～1911 年）兴建，始建于清同治四年（1865 年），于宣统三年（1911 年）竣工。[1]

日本熊本县熊本市古町地区是加藤清正于天正 19 年（1591 年）修建熊本城（日本三大名城之一）时，以熊本城为中心建立的城下町地区。城下町是日本的一种以领主居住的城堡为核心来建立的城市建设形式。世界大部分的城郭城市多是城墙包围整个城市，而日本的城下町则只有领主居住的城堡才有城墙保护，而平民居住的街道则没有城墙保护。[2]

1.3 软件背景介绍

Ecotect 生态建筑模拟软件是由英国 SQUARE ONE 公司开发的一款全面的技术性能分析辅助设计软件。该软件的设计理念来源于建筑气候设计系统的分析方法，是这种方法在计算机领域的再现。Ecotect 提供了一个交互式的分析方法，包含了热环境、光环境、声环境、日照、经济性及环境影响、可视度等综合技术分析功能，分析过程简单快捷、结果直观。[3]

2　研究方法

本研究利用 Ecotect 软件，在假定材料相同的情况下，通过对日本熊本县熊本市古町地区住宅和中国福建省泉州市蔡氏住宅群两地的古建筑的设计平面图进行分析，从其热度方面探究两地古建筑的设计手法，分别找出各自的设计特点，并结合两方的特质，从设计平面图上推测出适合现代住宅的、具有热带季风气候地区特征的、节能减排绿色低碳生态型建筑的设计特征。从而使得设计过程更加简化，以提升设计效率。

3　研究结果

3.1　平面形式

蔡氏古建筑群中的第一大住宅：蔡浅厝（图 1）的平面形式。其平面基本形式即中国古住宅的平面基本形式为——左右对称、正中天井（外部空间）的四合院或三合院。

日本熊本县熊本市古町地区住宅（图 2～图 5）[5] 的平面形式为——平面整体狭长、住宅最深处有庭院（外部空间）、从入口到最深处的庭院间由长廊联通并通过所有房间。

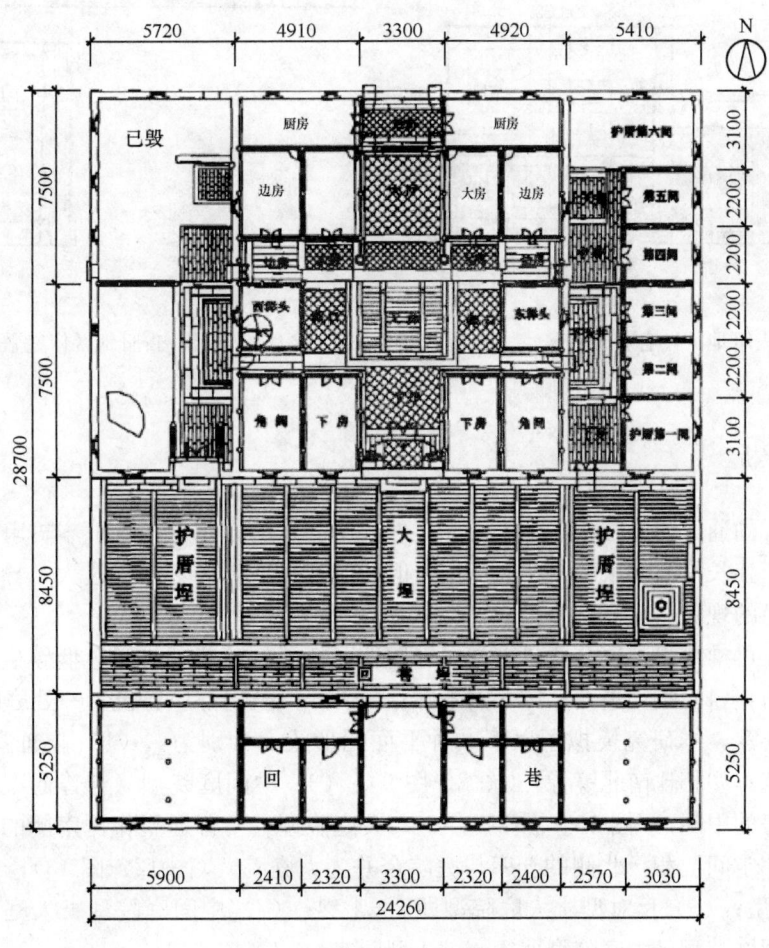

图 1　蔡浅厝平面图[4]

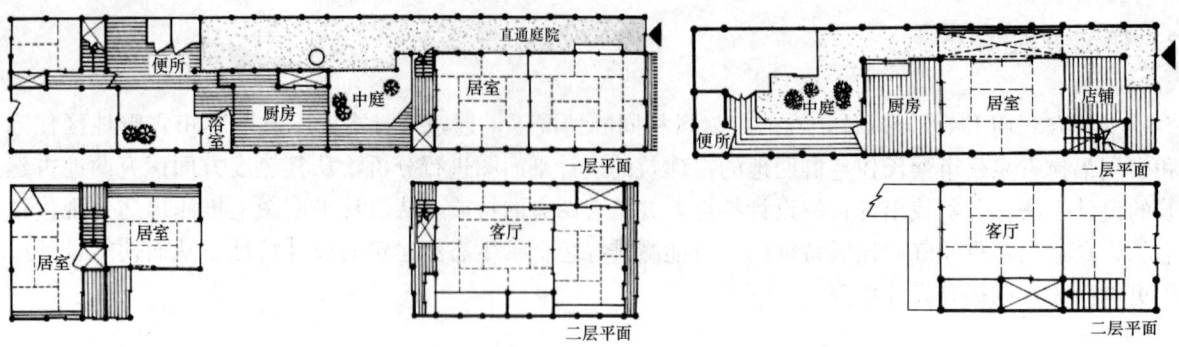

图 2　古町地区住宅平面之一　　　　　　　　图 3　古町地区住宅平面之二

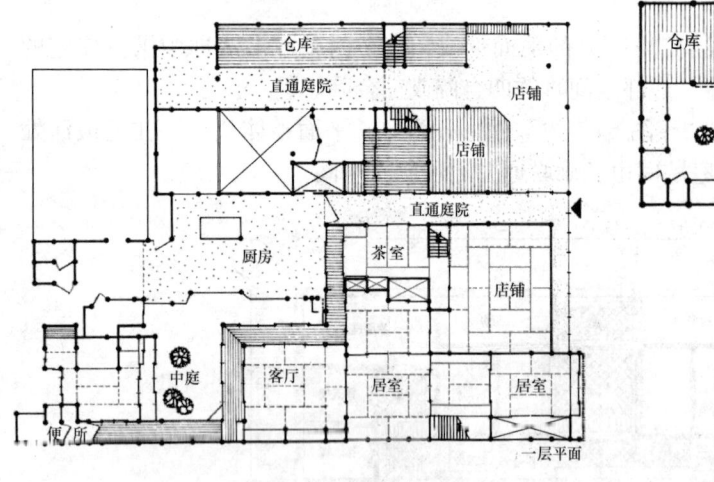
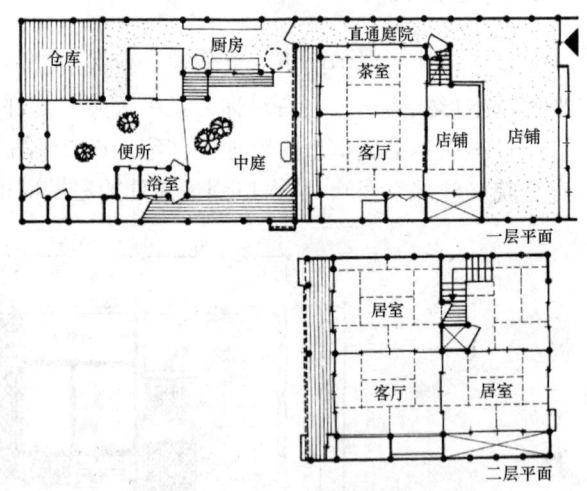

图 4　古町地区住宅平面之三　　　　　　　　图 5　古町地区住宅平面之四

3.2　平面特性分析

　　蔡氏古建筑群的通风降温方式多源于天井（外部空间）的作用。日本熊本古町地区住宅的通风降温方式则多源于狭长平面带来的自然风作用，但由于古町地区住宅进深过大，导致靠中间的部分房间出现采光不足的现象。

　　结合上述特征可推测出，适合亚热带季风气候地区特征的节能减排绿色低碳生态型的现代住宅的平面设计要素为：（1）狭长平面；（2）内走廊；（3）入口及内部应各设置一处庭院（外部空间）。

　　根据以上三要素，本研究模拟了以下 8 种平面图形式。分别为：（1）普通型（图 6、图 7）；（2）反对型（与基本型相比南北镜像）（图 8、图 9）；（3）中间庭院型（与普通型相比南侧的庭院改设为餐厅与厨房的中间）（图 10、图 11）；（4）大庭院型（与普通型相比南侧的餐厅和厨房合并为同一空间且缩小空间面积，北侧的仓库与庭院合并为大庭院）（图 12、图 13）；（5）反对型＋中间庭院型即 2＋3 型；（6）反对型＋大庭院型即 2＋4 型；（7）中间庭院型＋大庭院型即 3＋4 型；（8）反对型＋中间庭院型＋大庭院型即 2＋3＋4 型。

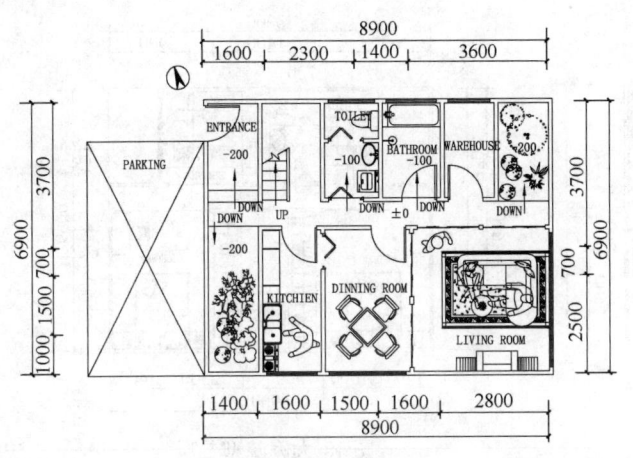

图 6　普通型一层

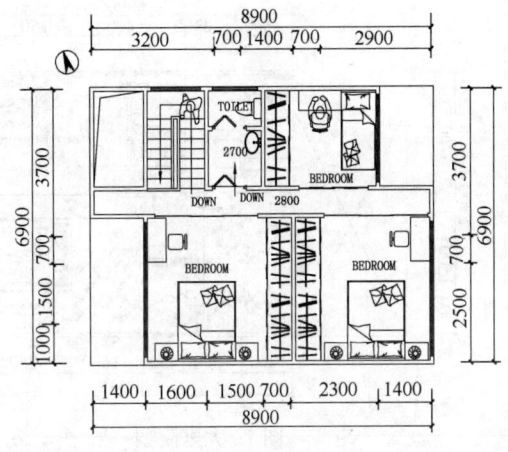

图 7　普通型二层

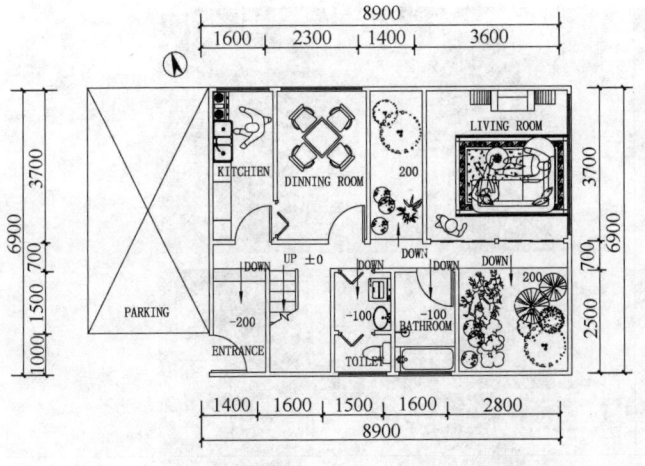

图 8　反对型一层

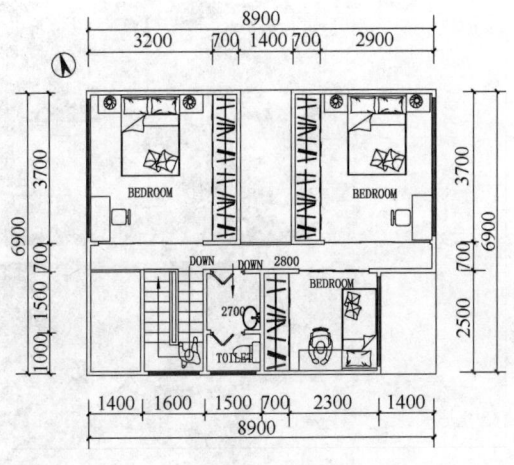

图 9　反对型二层

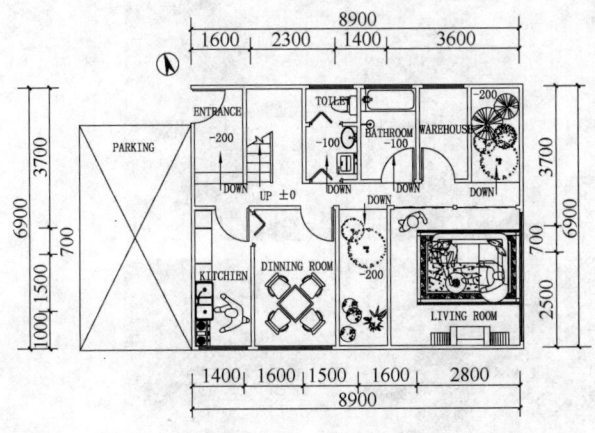

图 10　中间庭院型一层

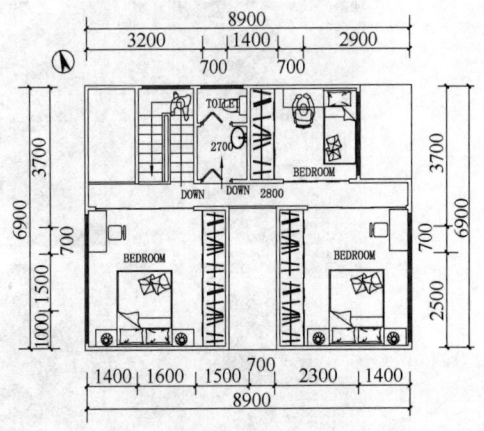

图 11　中间庭院型二层

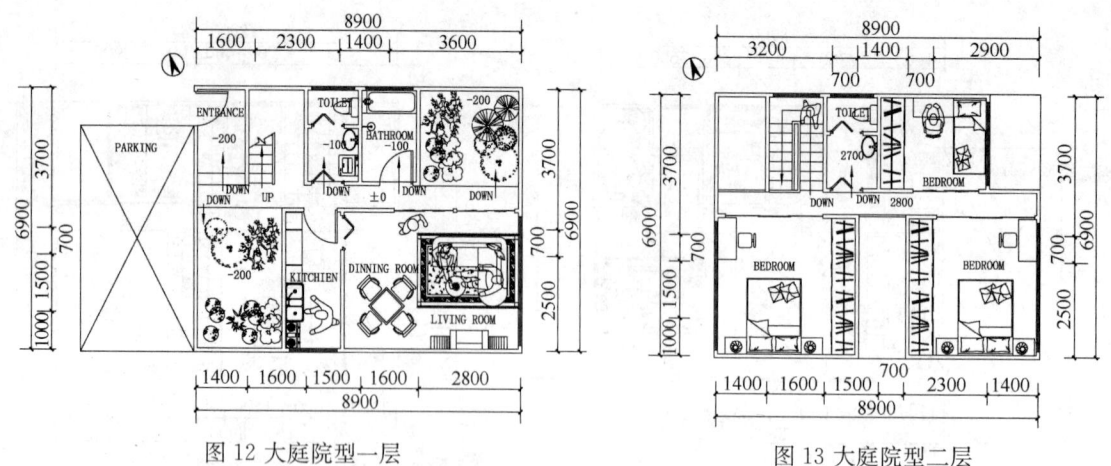

图 12 大庭院型一层　　　　　　　　图 13 大庭院型二层

3.3　Ecotect 分析结果

通过 Ecotect 软件分析图 6～图 13 的温度情况，得出以下结果，分别对应为图 14、图 15。

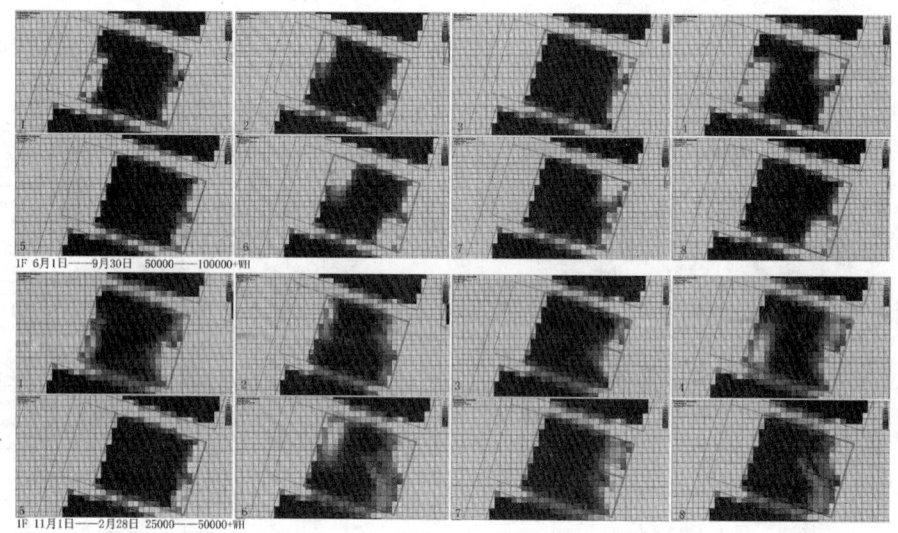

图 14　一层温度分析结果图（上：6 月 1 日～9 月 30 日；下：11 月 1 日～2 月 28 日）

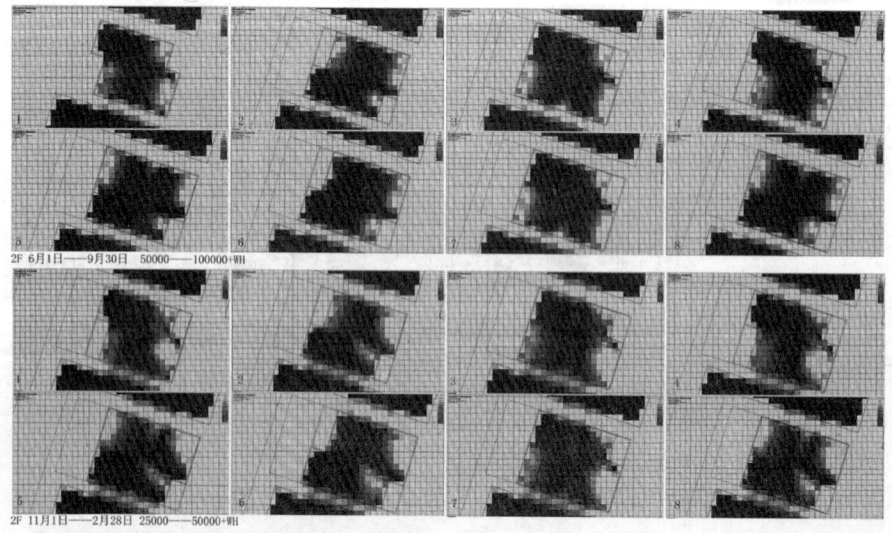

图 15　二层温度分析结果图（上：6 月 1 日～9 月 30 日；下：11 月 1 日～2 月 28 日）

4 结论

由 Ecotect 分析结果可知，一层夏季凉爽（深色覆盖面积多）的平面图形式为 3、5、7、8 型，冬季温暖（浅色覆盖面积多）的平面图形式为 4，6，8 型。二层夏季凉爽（深色覆盖面积多）的平面图形式为 3、5、7、8 型，冬季温暖（浅色覆盖面积多）的平面图形式为 1、4、5、8 型。

由分析结果可得知，反对型＋中间庭院型＋大庭院型即 2＋3＋4 型为最适合亚热带季风气候地区特征的、节能减排绿色低碳生态型的、现代住宅的平面图形式。

Comparative Study of Residential Design of Hot Humid Regions between China and Japan：A Case Study of the Furumachi Building Cluster in Kumamoto City，Japan and the Traditional Settlement of Cai-Clan in Quanzhou City

Zhang Yue，Tanaka Tomoyuki

(Graduate School of Science and Technology ，Kumamoto University，Kumamoto，Japan)

Abstract：This research assumes the same material situation to analyze the ancient architectural design plans between the Furumachi Building Cluster in Kumamoto City，Japan and the Traditional Settlement of Cai-Clan in Quanzhou City，by using the Ecotect software. Through exploring own design of these two areas and combining their characteristics，this paper deduces the examples of energy saving building design green carbon ecotype in modern residential in subtropical monsoon climate region，to make the design process more streamlined，and enhance the design more efficiently.

Keywords：Hot humid regions，Comparative study，Furumachi building cluster in Kumamoto，Traditional settlement of Cai-Clan，Ecotect

参考文献：

[1] 维基百科 . 蔡氏古民居建筑群[DB/OL]. http：//zh. wikipedia. org/wiki/蔡氏古民居建筑群 . 2015，1/2015，4.

[2] 维基百科 . 城下町[DB/OL]. http：//zh. wikipedia. org/wiki/城下町 . 2015，1/2015，4.

[3] Ecotect 建筑环境设计教程[M]. 云鹏译 . 北京：中国建筑工业出版社，1994：102.

[4] 王岚，罗奇 . 蔡氏古民居建筑群[J]. 北方交通大学学报，2003，1：90.

[5] 熊本開発研究センター . 熊本の街並み[M]. 熊本：熊本開発研究センター発行，1982：15－16.

住 宅 产 业 化
Housing Industrialization

ModRule: Sustainable Mass Housing System for the People

Lo Tiantian[1], Gao Yan[2]

(1. The Chinese University of Hong Kong ; 2. University of Hong Kong)

Abstract: This paper presents a novel design platform, ModRule, developed to promote and facilitate collaboration between architects and future occupants during the design stage of collective housing. Architects set the design-framework and the parameters of the platform, which allows the users to set their space requirements, budgets, and preferences etc. The platform employs gamification methodologies to promote incentives and user-friendliness to layperson who have no or little architectural background. By using the applications of Building Information Modeling (BIM), this platform, although simplified, still provides the basic information to generate a practical and flexible housing design. This enhanced integration of both bottom-up approach (user-centric) with the top-down approach (designer-centric) will greatly influence the architectural design for collective housing.

Keywords: Collective housing, Collaborative design platform, Open source design, BIM platform.

1 Background

"The strength of a nation derives from the integrity of the home. " ——Confucius.

The definition of home; is a house, apartment, or other shelter that is the usual residence of a person, a family, or a household. It could also be the place in which one's domestic affections are centered (www. dictionary. com) . Although the former is a physical product that many architects are trying to design, the latter is the intangible perception, which is hard to create.

One of the major challenges in urbanization is to provide city dwellers with housings [9]. There are many issues and problems with regards to the current housing design practice and they are identified as [8]:

(1) Issue 1: Financial risks in traditional housing supply chain

(2) Issue 2: Lost of individuality in the duplicated living environment

(3) Issue 3: The stringent statutory building code

(4) Issue 4: The problems of one-off planning methodologies in conventional housing design while addressing future uncertainties

(5) Issue 5: Main problems of bottom-up design approaches

(6) Issue 6: Collective housing evolution upon feedback of the occupants

Many cities currently are just focusing on providing housing, resulting in housing units becoming simple containers where families have to adapt instead of having their needs satisfied. Providing housing is just a start, providing one that fits the individual needs families is the one of the next challenges. Frei Otto did an experimental eco-house, Okohaus (1989 - 1991), inBerlin to demonstrate the possibility of a budget restricted resident able to house himself comfortably in a high dense urban environment without compromising the living quality. This eco-house is a collection of differentiated individual housing unit that suits the various needs of each family [5].

Another challenging aspect of collective housing is social sustainability. One of the possible solutions is to be flexible. Next21 (1994) is another experimental housing project inJapan designed by thirteen architects. The building system is designed in such a way that allows easy assembly and disassembly of some unit components. The experiment of replacing one unit in 1996 was a huge success[5]. La Meme, a student hostel (1970 – 1972), designed by Lucien Kroll also demonstrates the possibility of architectural adaptability to the unpredictable change of occupancy [6].

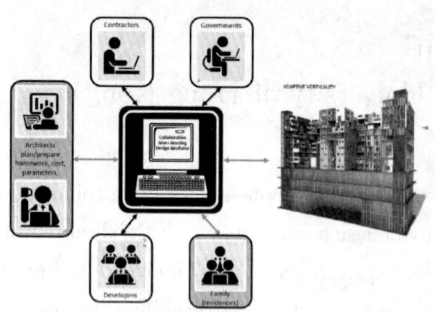

Figure 1　Focus of collaboration
between occupants and architects
(Source：Lo Tiantian)

However, with the advancement of technology in digital applications, there is a possibility for a user-centric design process [3]. 'Barcode housing system' [7] is such an example but the freedom of design provided for the occupant is limited. At present, most of the computational method addresses the possibilities of a fully parameterized design yet it is still mainly generated by a top-down approach of being controlled by solely architects. On the other hand, housing that highly engaged occupants closely are generated using primitive methods [1]. By adopting computational methods, the freedom of design can be developed further, yet maintaining the possibility of mass production for economical purpose [4].

Building Information Modelling (BIM) at present times is mostly focusing on the upfront stakeholders such as governments, developers and contractors. Occupants, who are actually the 'ultimate beneficiary', are usually not involved (Figure 1) . Therefore, this research will focus on the facilitation of the collaboration between occupants and architects. This paper also presents the extent of consistency versus individuality appearing in this design method, as well as the possibility of an integrated system of a bottom-up approach (user-involved) with a top-down approach where the housing design is automatically generated by computational processes.

2　Gamification

Gamification is the concept of applying game mechanics and game design techniques to engage and motivate people to achieve their goals[3]. The concept is not new, it is being used back in the 20th century by Cracker Jack to give toys as a gift in their boxes. Gamification is described as the use of game design elements in nongame contexts [2].

Before explaining how game design elements can be used in the proposed workflow in this paper, a reference to a game "Prison Architect" is necessary to paint a clearer picture.

"Prison Architects", a game designed for people to design their own prison. Although it is a game, the rules set, the parameters, the design components, and even the spatial relations are setup very comprehensively for the players to design their own prison (Figure 2) . This game relates to BIM to a great extent. For example, by telling the system what space it is, the players can only include certain furniture and require certain amounts of utilities, such as water and electricity. Although it is as complex as architectural design, the way that they provide guidance and requirements for each spatial type enables the players to design the prison without much difficulty. However, as simple as it may be, players still have to play a few times in order to truly grasp the whole gameplay.

Figure 2　A snapshot of the game
Prison Architect
(Source：Lo Tiantian)

3 ModRule

To attain an enhanced communication between architects and clients, 'ModRule', a collaborative design platform is developed. This takes reference with the 'Prison Architect' but tries to achieve the user-friendly professionalism.

By setting the best rules and parameters, the modular system is able to work diversely to generate a wide variety of design options for every individual occupant. It is a system that allows the architect to work more closely with potential inhabitants. The setup, therefore, is quite different from a normal design process. In ModRule, the housing design process is divided into four parts: (1) the overall form; (2) the spatial layout of units; (3) structure; (4) architectural components. The architect uses ModRule to plan a framework within which prospective users of the system are engaged (Figure 3).

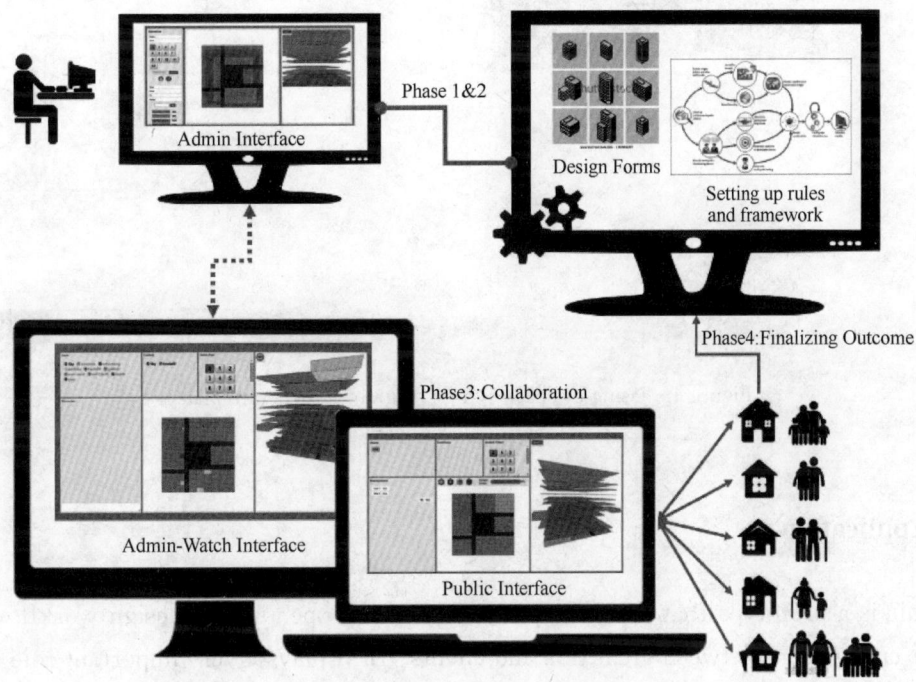

Figure 3　Workflow of ModRule
(Source: Lo Tiantian)

The ModRule platform (version 0.1), although it is divided into two main groups, i. e., the administrator for the architects and the public for the users, has three kinds of interfaces: (1) admin interface——in which the architect sets the initial design rules and parameters; (2) public interface——in which the public interacts with the model to 'design' its desired living space; and (3) admin-watch interface——in which the architect communicates with the public and oversees the whole collaboration process with data gathered from each individuals' movement [6].

After all of the prospective inhabitants fulfil their targets, the architect moves on to the next phase, in which every individual user plans his or her interior spatial layout (Figure 4). The process is simplified such that users with no knowledge of design will still be able to utilize it fully. The users will only need to drag the room types, make the connections, and the plan will appear immediately.

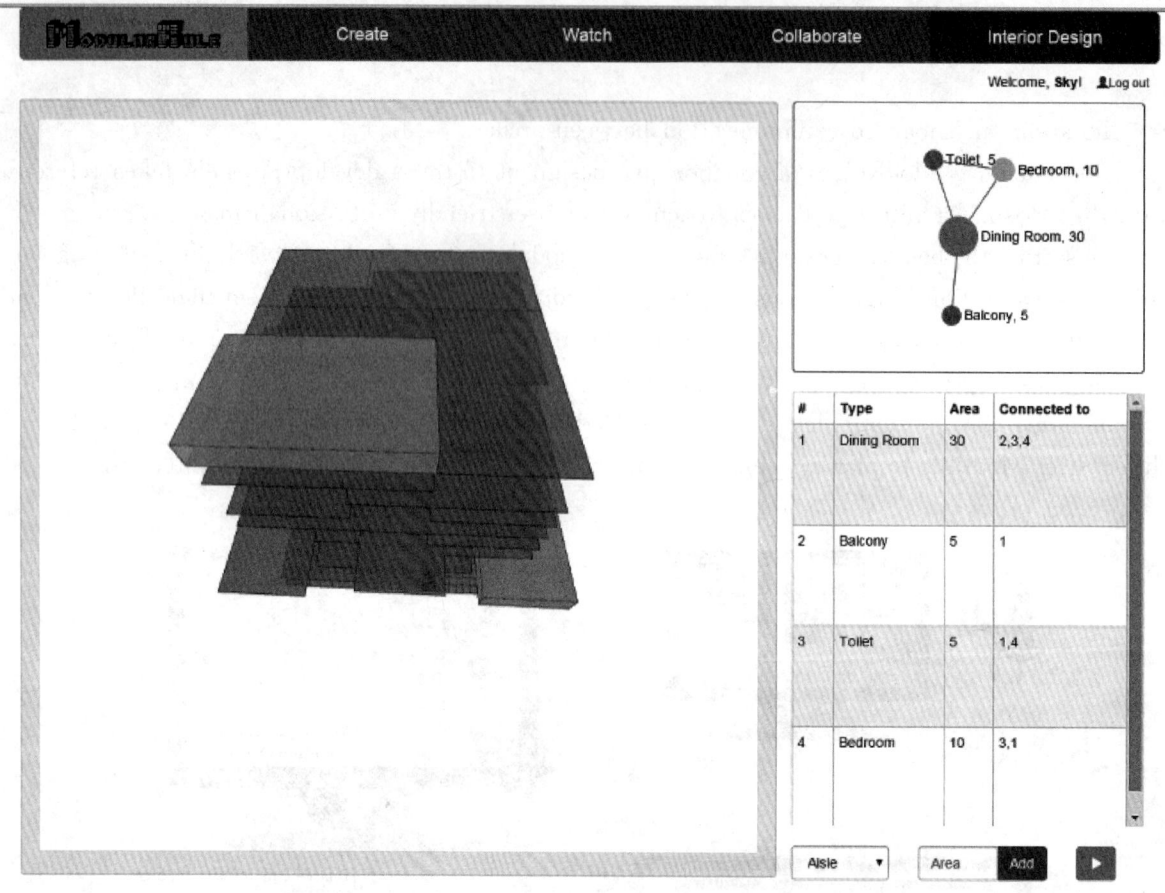

Figure 4   Using of space syntax diagram to generate plans

(Source: Lo Tiantian)

4   BIM Application

ModRule is a prototype that tests the possibility of the open-source design workflow that will allow direct engagement between architects and clients. BIM plays a very important role in the next stage of the design process. ModRule at present stage is still at the amateur level. The focus is in the formulation of design flows and the user-friendly interface. To push it to the next level, it will need to be integrated with BIM. For this research, Autodesk Revit is used as the medium to create example models.

In Revit architects create 3D models, but no longer 2D drawings in the first place. Instead, architects will be drawing walls, and inserting architectural components such as doors, windows and furniture. All components in Revit are known as "families" (Figure 5), and they include all the information that helps the system identify the model type. The families can be edited with the parameters. Advanced users can define a whole new family. This ensures an easy generation of the necessary building information after the design is done.

The creating and editing of families is very complex such that architects have to take course to ensure the families they defined are consistent with the appropriate standard, which will not disturb the post-design process. Nevertheless, inserting families is as easy as point and drop. This is where the users can come to play. All they need is the variations of families and the architectural framework pre-designed by the architects.

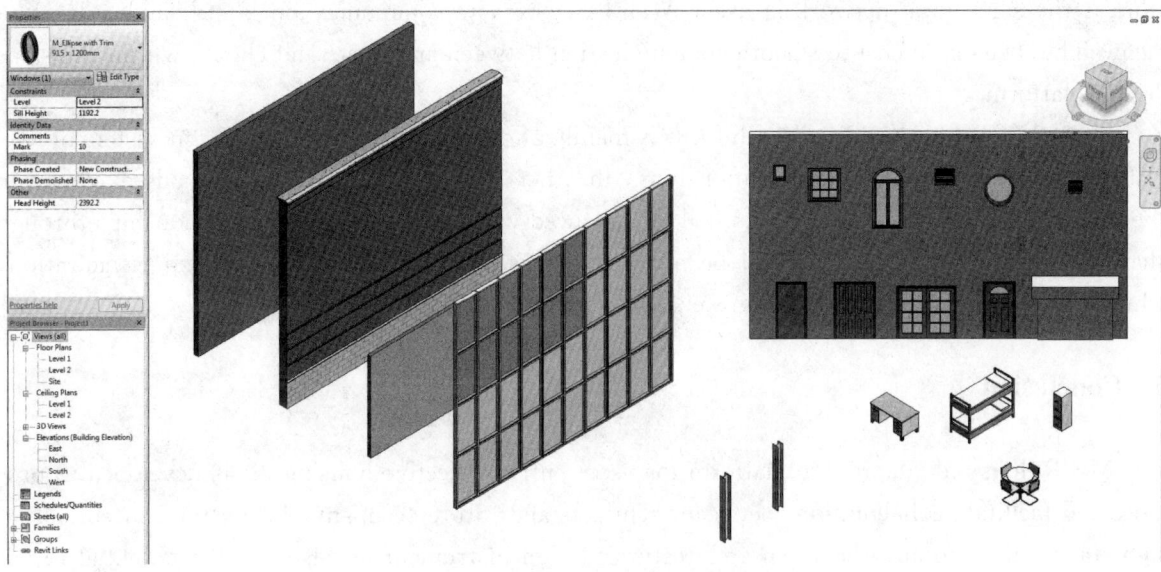

Figure 5   Library of revit families
(Source: Lo Tiantian)

The users can choose the families they want and insert them into the architectural framework that they have created in ModRule. In order to prevent the design becoming to open and chaotic, the architects will have to preselect and optimize the selection choices such that they can still be mass fabricated with cost efficiency.

5   Future Enhancement

ModRule 0. 1 is substantially lacking in visual capability and setting up the context of the design. The current studies are based upon the site scenarios. The availability of views, the amount of daylight, and orientation are arbitrary inputs in order to initiate the collaborative process. Even the designers who participate in the research studio find it difficult to imagine the visual outcomes. One development is to fuse the system with Fuzor (Figure 6) .

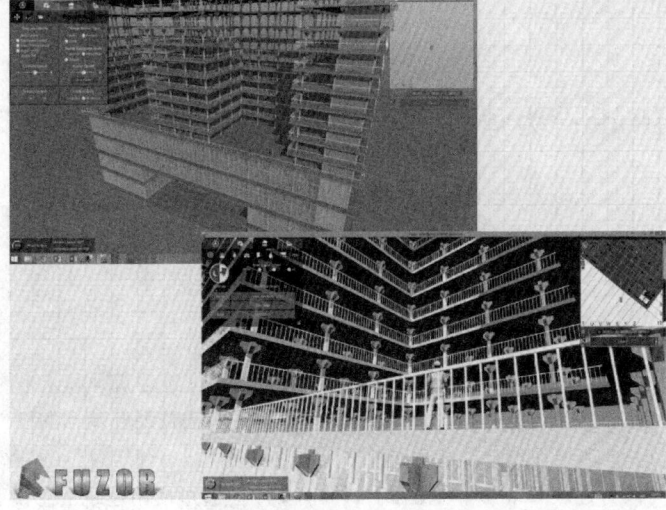

Figure 6   Screenshots of Fuzor
(Source: Lo Tiantian)

Communication is also limited to the local server network, i. e. the communication can only work if the same local network is used. Web-based remote communication is still under development. The focus is to ensure smooth communication between architects and clients within the same design platform.

Last, but not least, our research focus is mainly on turning the rule-based design system of ModRule 0. 1 into more parametric relationships. In other words, Space Syntax methods exploited in the previous two design studio works will be enhanced with parametric spatial relationships through shape grammars. ModRule 0. 2 will be primarily focused on remote discussion and visualization, which is expected to eventually integrate with the shape grammar in ModRule 0. 3.

6　Conclusion

ModRule is a digital design platform for user-centric collective housing. It is developed to promote and facilitate collaborations between architects and future occupants during the conceptual design stage. In addition to being an architectural design instrument, it also has the potential to address social, political, and economic criteria. Its aim is to open the decision-making process toward end-users. The system utilizes gamification methodologies as a reference to promote incentives and user-friendliness for laypersons. Thus, ModRule focuses on different aspects to translate a design environment into an interactive digital platform, while improving on remote control discussions, visualizations, and meaningful parametric design techniques. The collaborative tool instills a greater sense of belonging to the users, providing architects a better understanding of various individual needs and the computational response. The adopted open-source strategy and open-collaborative design approach of this research developed a design methodology that balances the bottom-up and top-down design processes. Such methodology guarantees mass-customization without sacrificing efficiency and cost-effectiveness. Future developments of ModRule will allow a better connection to BIM platform and a refinement of the algorithms that allow more sophisticated parametric control. The herein presented studies have shown that ModRule not only enables stakeholders to engage seamless in a collaborative conceptual design process, but also that the design results successfully exhibit the balance between desires of the users and the architectural novelty of the architects.

ModRule：为居住者而生的可持续大众住宅系统

卢添添[1]，高　岩[2]

（1. 香港中文大学；2. 香港大学）

摘要：本文介绍了一种新的设计平台——ModRule。该平台致力于促进建筑师和未来居住者的沟通，让两者在集合住宅的设计阶段更好地进行协作。利用这个平台，建筑师在其中只需规划好基本的设计框架与参数，具体的空间需求、预算、偏好等则交由未来居住者自己设定。考虑到缺乏或完全没有建筑背景的外行用户，该平台采用游戏化的方式来增强平台的用户友好性。ModRule 在操作上虽然简单，但通过使用建筑信息模型（BIM），为生成实用、灵活的住宅设计提供了基本的信息。这个平台整合了自下而上（以用户为中心）与自上而下（设计中心）两种方式，在未来将对集合住宅的建筑设计产生极大的影响。

关键词：群众住房，协同设计平台，开放源码设计，BIM 平台

References:

[1] Bech-Danielsen, C. "De-signed ecology" in T Oksala & GE Lasker (ed), Acta polytechnica scandinavica. Design. Evolution, cognition. Selected and edited papers from DEcon'94 symposium: Civil engineering and building construction series no. 105. Helsinki, s. 3 – 11, 1996.

[2] Deterding, S, Dixon, D, Khaled, R Nacke, L. From Game Design Elements to Gamefulness: Defining "Gamification"[C]. Tampere: Proceedings of the 15th International Academic Mind-Trek Conference (MindTrek'11), 2011: 9 – 15.

[3] Fabian, EH, Janssen, P Lo, T. T. Group Forming: Negotiating Design Via Web-Based Interaction and Collaboration[C]. Singapore: Proceedings of the 18th International Conference on Computer-Aided Architectural Design Research in Asia CAADRIA, 2013: 271 – 280.

[4] Gao, Y and Su, Y. 'Computational Design Research For High Density Social Housing in China', JET Vol. 2 No. 1. , Global Science and Technology Forum Journal of Engineering Technology, 2012.

[5] Lo, TT, Schnabel, MA, Gao, Y. Collaborative Mass Housing Design Practice with Smart Models[C]. Beijing: International Conference on Digital Architecture (DADA), 2013: 10.

[6] Lo, TT, Schnabel, MA, Gao, Y. ModRule: A User-Centric Mass Housing Design Platform', The Next City[C]. Sao Paulo: Computer-Aided Architectural Design Futures Foundation (CAADFUTURES), 2015: 20.

[7] Madrazo, L, Sicilia, Á, González, M, Cojo, AM. Barcode housing system: Integrating floor plan layout generation processes within an open and collaborative system to design and build customized housing' in T Tidafi and T Dorta (eds) Annual Joining Languages, Cultures and Visions: CAADFutures, PUM, 2009: 656 – 670.

[8] Gao, Y, Lo, TT, Chang, Q. Integrated Open Source Design for Architecture in High Density Housing Practice[J]. Journal of Civil Engineering 2014, 14.

[9] [DB/OL]. https://sustainabledevelopment.un.org/content/documents/3100statnote4.pdf.

[10] [DB/OL]. http://www.kalloctech.com/.

[11] [DB/OL]. https://badgeville.com/wiki/Gamification.

保障性住房中推广装配式混凝土住宅的可行性分析

殷惠君

（上海市房地产科学研究院）

摘要： 住宅产业化是实现保障性住房建设目标的关键举措，大规模的保障性住房建设也将为住宅产业化发展提供良机。从保障性住房与装配式住宅各自优劣势之间相互促进的角度探讨在保障性住房中推广装配式混凝土住宅的可行性，并结合国内某试点工程保障性住房项目，从建筑设计、质量、工期、节能等方面进行分析与总结，为我国保障性住房实现产业化提供参考。

关键词： 保障性住房，装配式混凝土住宅，住宅产业化，节能减排

1 引言

保障性住房建设是重要的民生工程。"十二五"期间我国城镇将建设保障性安居工程 3600 万套，覆盖面达 20％左右。随着资源环境约束进一步强化，我国住房发展的低碳转型势在必行。在保障性住房大规模建设的背景下，低碳建设保障性住房对于发展低碳经济有着极为重要的意义。

住宅产业化方式是建设低碳住宅的重要途径，有较为显著的低碳效益。与发达国家与地区的住宅工业化水平相比较，我国的住宅工业化仍处于初期阶段，尚未形成一个完善的住宅产业化机制。在国内，目前装配式住宅尚属新生事物，观望者多，实施者少，市场接受度小，阻碍了我国实现建筑产业化的进程。

鉴于装配式住宅推广初期成本较高，从发达国家和地区发展装配式住宅的经验来看，通常是从政府投资项目入手，如香港的公屋计划等。为此，不妨从保障性住房建设启动政府投资项目示范工程，通过政府投资项目的试点引领，让开发商切实感受到装配式住宅的优势，由此加快推进步伐。[1]

2 装配式住宅与保障性住房的相关概念

2.1 装配式住宅的概念

所谓装配式住宅，是指按照统一、标准的建筑部品规格制作房屋单元或构件，然后运至工地现场装配就位而建成的住宅。

就我国住宅装配化而言，关键是建立装配式住宅通用体系，这包含两方面的内容：（1）建立工业化住宅通用结构体系，即住宅主体结构实现工业化生产，达到施工工地现场拼装的要求，做到建筑和结构体系完善。（2）建立住宅部品体系，即以外围护、内装修、厨卫、设备、智能化等部品体系为重点，促进住宅部品体系向模数化、标准化、通用化、产业化方向发展，实现住宅部品的系列开发、集约化生产、配套化供应，发挥工业化生产的规模效应。[2]

2.2 保障性住房的概念及分类[1]

保障性住房是指政府在对中低收入家庭实行分类保障过程中所提供的限定供应对象、建设标准、销售价格或租金标准，具有社会保障性质的住房。包括两限商品住房、经济适用房、政策性租赁住房以及廉租房。

两限商品住房是指限制开发商拿地价格，同时限制其房价的一种面向城市中低收入者的商品房。限价房的套型建筑面积全部为 90m² 以下。

经济适用房是指政府在对中低收入家庭实行分类保障过程中所提供的具有社会保障性质的商品住宅。面积严格控制在中小套型，中套房面积控制在 80m² 左右，小套房面积控制在 60m² 左右。

政策性租赁房是指通过政府或政府委托的机构，按照市场租价向中低收入的住房困难家庭提供可租赁的住房，同时，政府对承租家庭按月支付相应标准的租房补贴。总体定位在廉租房与经济适用房之间，可以看作是可出租的经济适用房。

廉租房是指政府以租金补贴或实物配租方式，向符合城镇居民最低收入且住房困难的家庭提供的社会保障性质的住房。廉租房户型设定以一居室、两居室为主，建筑面积原则上按一居室套型建筑面积 35m²，两居室套型建筑面积 45m²，三居室套型建筑面积 55m²，是名副其实的"袖珍"户型。

2.3 适合保障性住房的工业化结构体系选择

装配式住宅在结构体系上可以分为三类，即预制混凝土结构体系，钢结构体系及木结构体系。预制混凝土结构体系又简称为 PC 结构。

装配式混凝土结构是在现浇混凝土结构基础上发展而来，其方式是将一些建筑构件从现场施工转移到工厂生产，仅是生产方式的转变。不会对住宅本身的居住属性造成不良影响，反而有利于提高住宅的综合质量，避免传统现浇混凝土住宅的诸多质量诟病。

在我国住宅建设中，钢筋混凝土结构依然占据着主导地位，与其他结构形式相比，其经过长时间的实践检验，技术成熟、耐久性好、结构刚度大而且造价相对较低，是我国现阶段发展住宅工业化的首选结构体系，也更适合保障性住房自身的基本属性。

3 装配式住宅与保障性住房的匹配性分析

保障性住房是为了满足弱势群体需求的特殊住宅，而装配式住宅作为产业化的代表，体现了一种全新的住宅施工理念，它们在定义上不存在联系，但从本质入手通过特点分析，发现二者的切合度很高、互补性很强，可互为依存、相互促进共同发展。

一方面，装配式住宅可为保障性住房的健康发展提供强有力的支撑，解决其造价低、质量高、工期紧、任务重的难题。另一方面，保障性住房满足装配式住宅标准化程度高、政策性依赖强等特点，二者的结合具有天然的技术优势、政策优势、成本优势及设计优势。以此为突破口发展住宅产业化能很好地规避商品房装配化过程中遇到的成本问题、政策问题和个性化问题，发展前景广阔。

3.1 满足设计标准化

装配式住宅发展的前提是设计标准化问题，没有严格的产业标准，装配式住宅很难全面发展。诚然全行业的标准化是个漫长过程，但保障性住房设计立面相对固定，户型单一变化少，结构形式简单等特点却能弥补装配式住宅的劣势。将装配式住宅引入保障性住房必将是一个双赢的局面。[3]

标准化问题是住宅产业化的核心和前提。如何实现保障性住房的标准化？一方面，可在国家制定的"保障性住房建设标准"框架下，针对各种小户型分别设计出若干个通用化户型，对开间、进深、层高、门窗等进行固化，形成标准化的住宅建筑体系。各地区可根据本地情况对设计进行一定修改，但要保证大部分的规格能够适应通用体系要求。然后按照工业化生产的要求分解成符合模数的部件，分类制定这些部件的通用化及规范化标准，通过合并同类项，尽量减少部品种类，使体系内的所有标准化构件能够相互协调、合理互换，逐步形成定型化的住宅构配件产品。[4]另一方面，为了避免单一化、模式化，设计应尽量成套系，保证各种户型可根据不同需求进行自由拆分和组合。

3.2 政策上的可行性

政府的缺位一直是造成装配式住宅止步不前的重要原因，长久以来我们的企业做了大量工作，也取得了许多卓有成效的技术成果，但面对诸如标准化问题、政策性问题等非技术问题时，企业行为往往无能为力，需要政府出面进行干预和引导。保障性住房这种"官方"背景很好地迎合了装配式住宅政策性依赖强的特点，因而在保障性住房中发展装配式住宅较商品房更具优势。

当一个产业处于新生阶段，投资者、消费者举棋不定的时候，政策的支持就显得尤为重要，"十二五"期间我国各地陆续出台了《保障性住房的实施细则》，《细则》对装配式住宅的开竣工面积均有硬性规定，这就为装配式结构住宅的推广提供了政策依据。

3.3 经济上的必要性

装配式住宅的工业化特性决定了其产品和成本之间存在一个盈亏平衡点，只有产品的产量达到一定的规模，成本才可降低，商家才可营利，以此类推，规模越大营利水平也就越高。"十二五"期间保障房的大量建设恰逢其时，为装配式住宅的发展带来了完美的契机。

预制装配式住宅造价比传统住宅高，主要有两方面原因：一是构件制作成本高，模具周转率低，摊销少；二是设计单位不熟悉，要求配套设计费用高。而保障性住房数量巨大，若引入预制装配式住宅，一则构件模具周转高，制作成本可降低，也可培育构件制作市场，成本还可再降低；二则随着设计标准颁布执行，设计单位有了技术支撑，将有更多设计单位参与，设计配套费就不存在了。[1]

3.4 工期上的合理性

保障性住房的施工特点通常是工期紧、体量大、任务重。为尽早实现对老百姓的承诺，大部分保障性住房都是由政府直接确定交房时间，开发商根据关键节点倒排工期，因而赶工现象往往不能避免，尤其是施工后期进入装修阶段，往往被安排在不利于施工的冬季、雨季进行，很容易出现为加快进度而忽略质量的现象。

装配式住宅的构件大多采用工厂预制加工：一方面大大减少现场支模及混凝土浇筑等湿作业环节，因而工期缩短，同时还能满足质量要求；另一方面，施工时间受季节性影响较少。

3.5 质量上的必然性

传统建造方式的住宅通常存在着开裂、渗漏等质量通病，作为民生工程的保障性住房，其工程质量尤其得到各方关注。房屋的质量很大程度上取决于构件的质量，以往现浇混凝土结构在施工现场条件的约束下，无法做到工业化生产的严格标准。预制装配式建筑构件在标准、严格的工业化生产模式下可做到每一个构件质量严格符合国家标准，只须现场组装即可投入使用。

4 产业化方式建造保障性住房的实例分析

4.1 项目概况

深圳龙华保障性住房项目是全国第一个按绿色建筑标准建设的保障性住房项目，其中

0008 地块共建 4002 套公共租赁房，总建筑面积达 21 万 m²，由 6 栋采用工业化技术建造的塔楼组成。

该项目建造的全过程贯彻了住宅产业化所倡导的标准化、模数化、机械化，其住宅产业化全过程设计理念是：套型设计标准化，模具数量最少化，连接节点简单化，构配件生产工厂化，施工机械化，建筑材料低碳环保化，组织管理科学化，实现生产制作易控，施工制作同步，运输方便高效，安装施工简单与维护保养经济。

4.2 建筑设计

作为住宅产业化示范项目，在建筑方案设计之初，就考虑了工业化生产方式的特点，结合住宅构件生产、运输、施工等方面做出了针对性方案设计规划。模块化的工业化设计理念贯穿了整个建筑设计过程，主要体现在以下三方面：

4.2.1 套型设计标准化

套型设计标准化是住宅产业化的基础。该项目套型单体设计从平面到装修全部采用标准化、模块化设计，4002 套保障房共分为 35、50、70m² 三种面积的标准化套型（图 1）。标准化套型设计均采用"模数化"的大空间外围墙体结构，套型内采用可灵活分隔的轻质墙体，提高了套型的可改造性与更新性，可以满足不同结构家庭的居住要求。

另外，由于套型在满足配比要求的基础上尽可能统一，从而实现了 PC 外墙种类最少化，模具使用最少化，有助于最大限度发挥住宅产业化的成本优势。

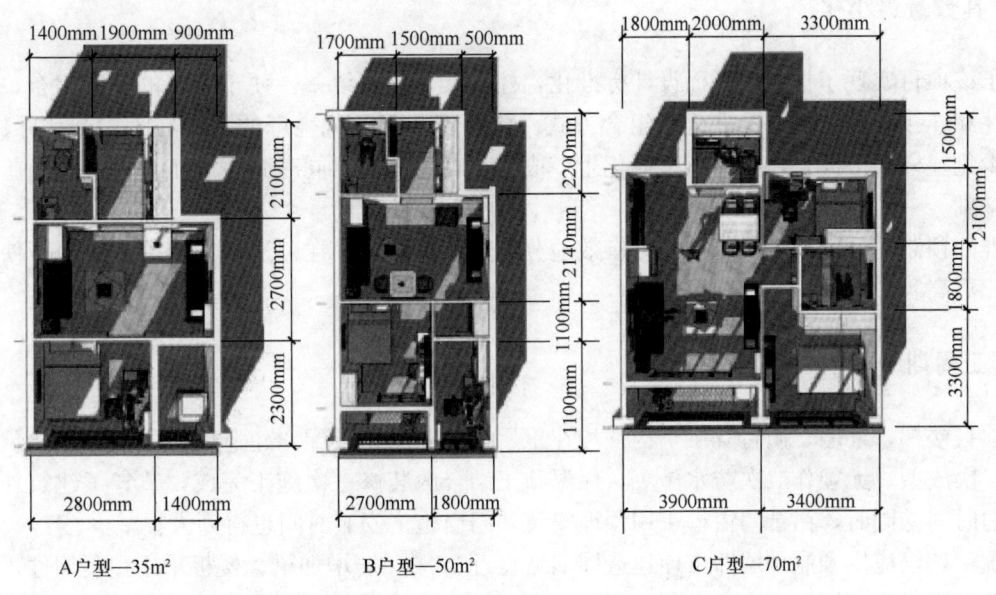

A 户型—35m²　　　　B 户型—50m²　　　　C 户型—70m²

图 1　深圳龙华 0008 地块保障性住房户型图

4.2.2 标准层设计标准化

标准层平面设计特点（图 2）：平面轮廓规整，外墙无明显凸凹，采用了外廊进行交通连接，标准开间采用模数化设计，总体布局采用了模块化组合的方式，最大限度满足工业化初期对建筑平面的要求。简单明了的套型设计满足了公租房的居住基本要求。

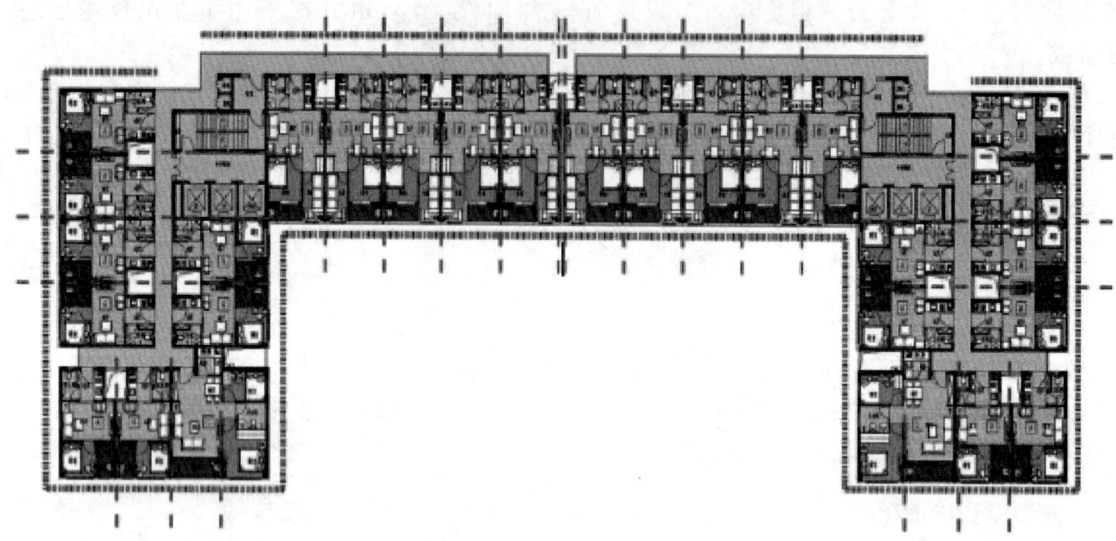

图 2 深圳龙华 0008 地块保障性住房标准层平面图

4.2.3 总体规划布局规模化

在满足规划设计要点的前提下，尽可能采用有利于工业化设计施工的规划布局，融入工业化模块设计理念的标准化单元，符合高效、集约的工业化生产要求。

4.3 模具数量最小化

由于该项目实现了标准层平面设计标准化，柱网尺寸规格统一，便于模块的安装组合，因此简化了构件和连接种类，形成标准化的组合方式。构件作为工业化生产的基本元素，其尺寸标准化、种类最少化、样式最简化，是降低工业化生产成本与时间周期，同时减少施工误差、提高施工效率的重要基础。

标准的预制构件大规模重复使用，有效地分解了模具成本，在建造成本等同的情况下使得建筑的性价比更高。

4.4 施工周期

该项目楼梯、外墙、阳台等维护构件均在工厂预制、现场装配，建造周期大幅缩短。预制外墙外立面一次成型，无须作二次防水施工，保温施工结合内装修一次施工完成，节省了建筑外立面装饰施工的时间。同时，由于门窗框采用预埋安装，门窗施工安装时间也得到大幅减少。

据统计，仅应用预制外墙即可使建造周期缩短近 20%，若增加梁、楼板采用预制构件，装配化建造工期将进一步缩短近 35%。在此基础上，若采用上部主体施工下部装修施工作业同步进行，则项目总工期可以节省将近 50%。

4.5 施工质量

该项目预制混凝土外墙构件在工厂生产，通过程序养护，具有强度高、密实度好、自防水性能优越等优点。门窗主框在工厂预制时就进行了埋设到位，现场施工时与墙体连接牢固。依据万科已建成的同类型工业化项目质量反馈统计，此类建筑外墙和门窗洞口的渗漏投诉率几乎为零，基本杜绝了传统工程项目外墙、门窗渗漏等通病，极大地提高了居住舒适度。

4.6 节能减排

该项目节能减排效益如下：一是预制构件在工厂采用循环水养护，减少了对水资源的使用和浪费；二是大钢模施工降低了对木模板的消耗；三是装配式建造方式在建造过程中的能耗较常规建造方式降低约 10%。该项目现场实施情况测算结果为节约施工用水约 30%，节约木模板用量约 27.5%，减少建筑垃圾用量约 20%。

4.7 全装修一体化

该项目采用了全装修一体化技术，使装修设计更为合理，便于大规模集中采购安全、环保的建材产品，通过标准化的装修和户内配置更好地保障装修质量。尽管没有完全实践 CSI 住宅建筑体系的要求，但是该项目体现了 CSI 的核心理念——主体结构与内装部品相分离的理念，使设计使用年限不同的结构与部品相分离，从而从设计源头上保证了装修品质。同时，装修部品选材上注重选用优质绿色的产品，采用工厂化生产、现场组装的方式，也杜绝了传统装修方式在噪声和空气上带来的污染。

5 结论

研究表明，我国发展装配式住宅的条件已经基本完备，应该从保障性住房建设入手，推进中适时出台有效的经济激励措施和相关技术措施，加强管理，大力推广装配式混凝土住宅，促进住宅产业化发展，提高住宅质量，改善居住环境，实现可持续发展战略，助力新型城镇化建设的发展。

致谢

本研究受上海市住房保障和房屋管理局 2015 年度科技计划项目《装配整体式混凝土住宅项目开发建设能力及标准化流程研究》资助（项目编号 FG2015-22）。

Feasibility of Popularizing the Precast Concrete Housing in Security Housing

Yin Huijun

(Shanghai Real Estate Science Research Institute)

Abstract：Housing industrialization is a key measure to support security housing construction. At the same time, the large scale of security housing construction will also provide an opportunity for the development of housing industrialization. This thesis probes into the feasibility of popularizing the precast concrete housing in security housing from the perspective of their mutual promotion. Then it analyzes and summarizes the security housing of a domestic pilot project, from graphic design, construction period and cost. This thesis provides reference for China's security housing to achieve housing industrialization.

Keywords：Security housing, Precast concrete housing, Housing industrialization, Energy saving and emission reduction

参考文献：

［1］ 沈定亮．保障性住房中推广预制装配式住宅的可行性［J］．上海建材，2010，4：8-10．

［2］ 黄灵，张德海，陶帅．预制装配式建筑在保障房中的应用［G］．沈阳科学学术年会，2012．

［3］ 张齐武，徐燕雯．经济适用房还是公共租赁房？——对住房保障政策改革的反思［J］．公共管理学报，2010，4．

［4］ 黄一如，周晓红，殷幼锐．装配式住宅内装做法的多样化和本土化［J］．中国建筑装饰装修，2011，2．

基于 DEMATEL 方法的住宅预制构件的供应商选择研究

詹　翌　潘雨红

（重庆交通大学管理学院）

摘要：结合建筑业的特点，针对装配式住宅预制构件的供应商有效选择的问题，建立住宅预制构件供应商的评价指标体系，并基于 DEMATEL 方法，以多利益相关者为主体，对供应商进行综合评价。再根据 DEMATEL 矩阵分析模型对指标进行权重划分，从而为利益相关者提供科学的选择依据。最后通过案例分析，论证该方法的可行性和有效性。

关键词：DEMATEL，住宅预制构件，供应商

1 引言

推广预制装配式住宅体系一直是国家"十二五"期间大力推广的政策之一。随着住宅产业化进程的不断推进，越来越多的建筑从业者开始意识到预制装配式住宅体系的重要性。同时，在预制装配式住宅体系产业链中，作为中间环节的预制构件生产供应商数量也呈增长态势。然而，与传统的现浇混凝土供应链体系相比，预制装配式住宅体系在预制构件供应商的选择上仍然存在诸多盲区与不足，传统建设模式下的供应链体系在国家法律法规的逐步完善下，有良好的约束条件和运作模式，具有自身的特点和优势。但过去的供需模式已然不能满足新型的住宅产业化对建筑部品的需求，对预制装配式建筑来说，工业化的生产装配方式必然促进新的供应模式，但目前针对住宅预制构件供应选择的研究还比较缺乏。

另一方面，对于一个大型预制装配式建筑项目来说，如何协调众多的利益相关者一直是一个难以解决的问题，沈岐平教授认为利益相关者管理是解决利益冲突，实现利益最大化和项目目标的重要途径和手段。[1]然而，不同利益相关者对供应商的选择存在着显著的差异，同时预制构件供应商选择的评价因素之间通常存在关联性，而忽略这种关联性必然会导致决策的结果产生误差。如何在众多利益相关者对供应商的不同需求中找到关键因素指标，结合各利益相关者的实际诉求，建立一套较为完善的选择评价体系，是一个迫切需要解决的问题。

基于以上问题，本文借鉴决策试验和评价实验室法（DEMATEL）的原理，以不同利益相关者为群体评价主体，分析影响住宅预制构件供应商选择的因素指标之间的关联性，对关键因素指标进行影响程度分析。同时结合案例分析验证 DMATEL 法在装配式预制构件供应商选择过程中的可行性，为利益相关者对装配式预制构件供应商的选择提供科学的评价方法和建议。

2 供应商评价指标体系的研究现状

早在 1966 年，美国学者 Dickson[2]根据问卷调查，总结出了质量、交货等 23 项供应商绩效评价的准则。Weber[3]根据 74 篇供应商选择研究的文献进行统计分析，发现价格、准时交货率和质量三个指标具有重要的影响。在国内，郭士正和卢震[4]认为对供应商进行评估的最基本的指标包括：技术水平、产品质量、供应能力、价格等其他指标。曹吉鸣[5]教授认为房地产合作伙伴评价因素可分为经营管理能力、员工能力、业务能力和财务成本四大体系。阮连法和陈佳玲[6]从绿色建筑供应商的角度总结出产品优势、运营能力等评价指标。可以看出，过去的供应商选择研究主要集中在工业、贸易经济等其他领域，而建筑领域的供应商选择研究大部分也是基于传统建设模式下的选择研究，针对住宅预制构件供应商的选择研究则较少。

虽然大部分领域对供应商评价指标的建立和划分都有一定程度的相似性，即对供应商的评价标准主要集中在产品质量、价格和交货期限上，但各行业仍具有各自显著的特点，倘若将现有的供应商选择评价模式直接应用在住宅预制构件供应商的选择上将会缺乏其适应性，不能很好地涵盖预制装配式住宅体系供需关系所反映的特点，无法对装配式预制构配件的适用性能、安全性能等方面进行评估，所以建立一套具有针对性的评价体系显得尤为必要。

3 构建住宅预制构件供应商评价指标体系

预制装配式住宅体系本质上是运用工业化的生产、安装方式建设住宅项目，使过去大量的现场施工工作在标准化的工业车间里完成，再经由运输至施工场地进行现场拼接安装，在满足时间、质量、成本以及客户需求的约束条件下实现项目目标，这种新的建设方式在一定程度上和制造业的生产运作方式类似，因此本文根据各自特点，在查阅关于制造业和建筑业供应商选择评价的相关文献基础之上[7,8]，结合我国《住宅性能评定技术标准》等行业标准文件[9,10]，建立了一套符合住宅预制构件供应商特点的评价指标体系，其中包括 7 个一级指标和 28 个二级指标，如图 1 所示。

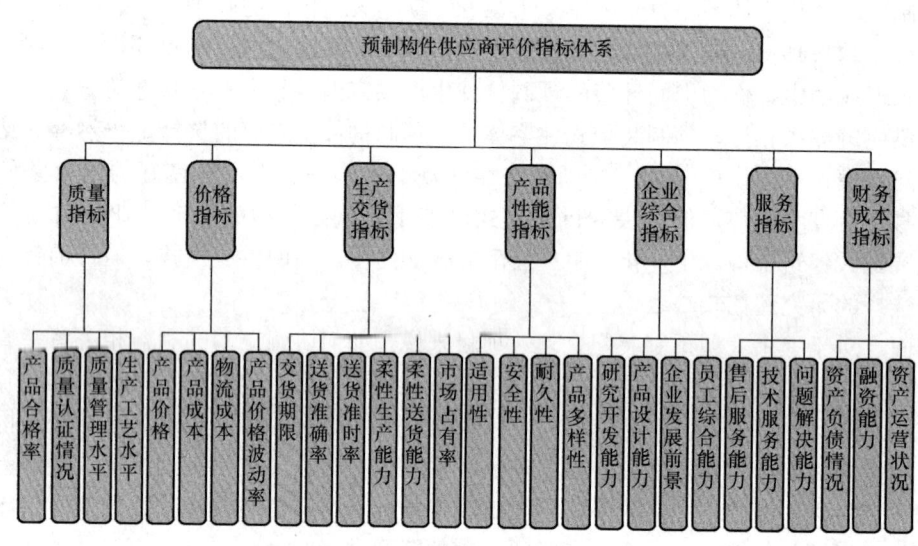

图 1　预制构件供应商评价指标体系

4. 建立基于 DEMATEL 模型的住宅预制构件供应商选择评价方法

4.1　建立利益相关者群体评价信息集合

首先应设二级评价指标集合为 C，C＝{C_1，C_2，…，C_n}(n＝28)，再根据评级指标体系建立语言评价集合 S，S＝{0（无影响/非常差），1（轻微影响/差），2（一般影响/中等），3（高度影响/好），4（重度影响/非常好）}，该语言评价集合 S 用来描述利益相关者群体对上述指标体系和预制构件供应商的评价。

4.2　基于 DEMATEL 法的规范化处理

DEMATEL 法又称之为决策实验与评价实验法，是美国学者 Gabus 和 Fontela 提出的一种基于矩阵与图论工具进行系统要素分析的方法[11,12]，该方法通过分析系统中各个因素间的逻辑关系以及影响强弱程度来对各因素进行定量评价，从而达到理想的评价效果。

目前，DEMATEL 在各领域都得到较为广泛的应用[13~15]，就预制装配式住宅体系的预制构件供应商的选择问题而言，同样可通过 DEMATEL 矩阵分析模型对各评价指标之间冗长复杂的关系进行分析处理，理清各评价指标因素内在和外在的联系，进而帮助利益相关者群体更客观精准地选择出相对较优的预制构件供应商。DEMATEL 法具体的计算步骤如下所示：

（1）设共 f 个利益相关者参与对指标体系进行评价，第 k 个利益相关者对指标体系的直接影响评价矩阵表示为 $X_k = [x_{kij}]_{n \times n}$，结果如式（1）所示。

$$X_k = [x_{kij}]_{n \times n} = \begin{array}{c} \\ C_1 \\ C_2 \\ \vdots \\ C_n \end{array} \begin{array}{cccc} C_1 & C_2 & \cdots & C_n \end{array} \\ \begin{bmatrix} - & x_{k12} & \cdots & x_{k1n} \\ x_{k21} & - & \cdots & x_{k2n} \\ \vdots & \vdots & \ddots & \vdots \\ x_{kn1} & x_{kn2} & \cdots & - \end{bmatrix} \tag{1}$$

$$x_{ij} \in S; \ i,j = 1,2,\cdots,n; \ k = 1,2,\cdots,f$$

（2）通过算数平均求出利益相关者群体给出的直接影响矩阵 $X = [x_{ij}]_{n \times n}$，计算如式（2）所示。

$$x_{ij} = \frac{1}{f} \left(\sum_{k=1}^{f} X_{kij} \right) \tag{2}$$

$$i,j = 1,2,\cdots,n; \ k = 1,2,\cdots f$$

（3）对直接影响矩阵 $X = [x_{ij}]_{n \times n}$ 进行规范化处理而得出规范化直接影响矩阵 $Y = [y_{ij}]_{n \times n}$，其中 $y_{ij} = x_{ij} / \max_{1 \leqslant i \leqslant n} \sum_{j=1}^{n} x_{ij}$。再利用公式 $T = \lim_{\lambda \to \infty} (Y^1 + Y^2 + \cdots + Y^\lambda) = Y(I - Y)^{-1}$ 求得综合影响矩阵 $T = [t_{ij}]_{n \times n}$，其中 t_{ij} 表示指标因素 i 给指标因素 j 带来的直接影响及间接影响程度。

（4）根据综合影响矩阵 T 计算出每个指标因素的影响度 R_i、被影响度 C_i、中心度 e_i 以及原因度 f_i，其计算公式分别为：

$$R_i = \sum_{j=1}^{n} t_{ij}, \ i = 1,2,\cdots,n$$

$$C_j = \sum_{i=1}^{n} t_{ij}, \ j = 1,2,\cdots,n \tag{3}$$

$$e_i = R_i + C_i$$

$$f_i = R_i - C_i$$

其中，影响度 R_i 表示该指标因素对其他指标因素的综合影响程度；被影响度 C_i 表示该指标因素受到其他指标因素的综合影响程度，中心度 e_i 表示该因素的影响程度和被影响程度之和，反映了该指标因素在指标体系中的相对重要程度；原因度 f_i 为该因素影响程度和被影响程度之差，侧面反映了该指标因素在评价体系中的作用和位置，即原因度大于 0 表明该指标因素总体在影响其他指标因素；原因度小于 0 表明该指标因素总体在受到其他指标因素的影响。

4.3 二级指标权重的分配

二级指标权重的分配反映了各指标因素的相对重要程度，其目的在于使整个指标体系在评价预制构件供应商时更加客观、准确。因此可根据原因度排序将指标体系中的二级指标因素进行权重重新分配。权重 z_i 的计算方法如式（4）所示。

$$z_i = \frac{e_i}{\sum\limits_{i=1}^{n} e_i}, \; i = 1, 2, \cdots, n; \; \sum\limits_{i=1}^{n} z_i = 1 \tag{4}$$

4.4 对供应商的选择评价

设待评价的预制构件供应商共 m 个，则可根据语言评价集合 S 建立群体评价矩阵 $H = [h_{iq}]_{n \times m}$，再将指标权重 z_i 分别与各供应商评价结果 h_{iq} 相乘，便可得出最终综合评价 h_q，计算公式如式（5）所示。

$$h_q = \sum_{i=1}^{n} (z_i \times h_{iq})$$
$$i = 1, 2, \cdots, n$$
$$q = 1, 2, \cdots, m \tag{5}$$

5 案例分析

某大型装配式住宅建设项目计划对预制外墙板、混凝土叠合板等多个建筑预制构配件进行采购，经多方调查筛选后决定对 A，B，C 共三家预制构件供应商进行选择评价。

5.1 评价指标体系的权重划分

为论证 DEMATEL 方法的可行性，同时保证指标权重的合理分配，文章通过访谈研究法对 5 位专家（利益相关者）进行访谈，访谈对象主要来自于建筑业从业者（项目经理、监理工程师、甲方派驻现场代表等）及该领域教授，通过电话或面谈的方式进行探讨，经过 2 周的采访和统计，得出了 5 份关于评价指标体系及针对供应商的评价结果，根据上述计算步骤便可求出各二级指标的中心度 e_i 和权重 z_i，评价结果如表 1 所示。

5.2 对住宅预制构件供应商的选择评价

根据访谈统计数据，结合公式（5）对供应商的初始评价结果进行修正，便可得出最终评价结果，即 $h_A = 2.84$，$h_B = 2.49$，$h_C = 1.81$。由此选择出最理想的预制构件供应商 A，综合排序结果为 A＞B＞C。

5.3 结果分析

根据上述表格，还可以从预制构件供应商的角度进行自我分析总结，通过中心度排序可以看出，以利益相关者为中心的客户群体关注度主要集中在质量管理水平、产品成本和安全性上，表明该类因素应是企业重点关注对象；影响程度较高的指标因素为柔性送货能力和问题解决能力，说明该指标因素对其他指标因素影响较大，侧面反映了综合、柔性的管理和处理能力能显著改善企业其他关键性指标。基于此，预制构件供应商可有效地抓住客户关注点，找出主要矛盾，不断深化改革，使得供需双方乃至预制装配式住宅产业链逐步走向绿色可持续发展的方向。

指标权重分配表　　　　　　　　　　　　　　　　　表 1

指标名称	R	C	e	f	z	指标名称	R	C	e	f	z
产品价格波动率	0.68	0.93	1.61	−0.24	3.62%	资产负债情况	0.45	0.82	1.27	−0.36	2.85%
售后服务能力	0.93	0.62	1.55	0.31	3.49%	员工综合能力	0.51	0.77	1.28	−0.27	2.88%
产品多样性	1.09	0.57	1.66	0.52	3.72%	产品设计能力	0.51	0.77	1.28	−0.27	2.88%
使用性能	1.05	0.73	1.77	0.32	3.98%	质量认证情况	0.48	0.47	0.95	0.02	2.13%
安全性	1.22	1.47	2.69	−0.25	6.06%	产品合格率	1.11	0.53	1.65	0.58	3.70%
耐久性	0.61	0.85	1.46	−0.23	3.28%	研究开发能力	1.00	0.53	1.54	0.47	3.45%
交货期限	0.97	0.43	1.39	0.54	3.13%	质量管理水平	1.12	1.64	2.77	−0.52	6.21%
技术服务能力	0.27	0.28	0.55	−0.02	1.24%	柔性送货能力	1.30	0.23	1.53	1.07	3.43%
物流成本	0.63	0.75	1.38	−0.12	3.09%	生产工艺水平	0.27	0.40	0.67	−0.13	1.51%
融资能力	0.62	0.80	1.43	−0.18	3.20%	资产运营状况	0.86	0.53	1.38	0.33	3.11%
送货准确率	0.62	0.82	1.44	−0.20	3.24%	问题解决能力	1.24	1.07	2.32	0.17	5.20%
柔性生产能力	0.56	0.88	1.43	−0.32	3.22%	产品价格	0.71	0.80	1.51	−0.09	3.40%
送货准时率	0.82	0.89	1.71	−0.07	3.85%	市场占有率	0.60	0.82	1.41	−0.22	3.17%
产品成本	0.90	1.80	2.71	−0.90	6.09%	企业发展前景	1.11	1.05	2.16	0.06	4.85%

6　结论

本文结合住宅预制装配式体系的特点，建立符合住宅产业化要求的预制构件供应商评价指标体系，以利益相关者群体为评价主体、借鉴 DEMATEL 矩阵分析模型计算出各评价指标权重，从而为决策群体提供客观科学的依据，有效避免因决策失误而可能带来的风险损失，降低了预制装配式住宅项目建设过程中的隐性成本。

基于 DEMATEL 法进行分析处理的优势在于：（1）考虑了指标因素之间的相互影响关系，而不是单向影响关系。（2）不仅反映出了各指标间的直接影响关系，也可通过矩阵分析出各指标间接影响关系，有效避免了语言信息在转化为数学模型过程中出现的信息丢失和曲解，使得评价结果更为全面、客观。（3）减少了系统要素构成，无须进行一致性检验等烦琐计算步骤，相对地简化了计算过程，便于决策者在实际选择评价中的应用。

综上所述，作为预制装配式住宅体系产业链的重要环节，预制构件供应商的选择评价是住宅产业化推进过程中不得不面临的问题之一，随着住宅产业化理念的不断深化和发展，新的生产工艺和方法必然会引发出许多亟待解决的问题，这也是人类社会和文明发展必然经历的路程。因此，构建良好的预制构件供应商评价指标体系，建立客观科学的评价方法，提高选择评价精度，减少决策中可能存在的失误，防患于未然，是确保整个建筑行业从粗放型转向集约型生产建设模式的必要手段。

致谢

感谢从事建筑工程项目管理工作的周清、涂颐林、李伦、潇洒为文章提供宝贵的数据资料，谨此致谢！

Research on the Suppliers Selection of Prefabricated Housing Components based on DEMATEL Method

Zhan Yi, Pan Yuhong

(Chongqing Jiaotong University)

Abstract：Combined with the characteristics of Construction Industry, it establishes an evaluation index system of the Suppliers of Prefabricated Housing Components in order to solve the problem of effective choice. It Uses the DEMATEL Method to evaluate the suppliers comprehensively by the multi-stakeholder. Then it divides the weight of index by the matrix analysis model of DEATEL, which provides scientific basis of selection for the stakeholders. Finally, it demonstrates the feasibility and effectiveness of this method through the case analysis.

Keywords：DEMATEL, Prefabricated housing components, suppliers

参考文献：

［1］ 沈岐平，杨静．建设项目利益相关者管理框架研究［J］．工程管理学报，2010，4(24)：412-419．

［2］ Dickson G. W. An analysis of vendor selection systems and decisions［J］. Journal of Purchasing, 1966, 2(1)：5-17.

［3］ Weber, Charles A., Current, et al. Vendor selection criteria and methods［J］. European Journal of Operational Research, 1991, 50(1)：2-18.

［4］ 郭士正，卢震．供应链与物流管理［M］．北京：机械工业出版社，2008：81-82．

［5］ 曹吉鸣，高翔．房地产供应链合作伙伴的模糊综合评价［J］．同济大学学报(自然科学版)，2005，33(6)：843-847．

［6］ 阮连法，陈佳玲．基于模糊 VIKOR 方法的绿色建筑供应商选择［J］．统计与决策，2011，21：62-64．

［7］ 徐兴，李仁旺，吴新丽等．面向供应链协同的供应商选择模型的研究［J］．浙江工业大学学报．2011，3(5)：550-554．

［8］ 郑晓云，贾玲．住宅产业化进程中建筑部品供应商的选择研究［J］．华东经济管理，2013，27(10)：93-97．

［9］ GB/T 50362—2005 住宅性能评定技术标准［S］．北京：中国建筑工业出版社，2006．

［10］ JGJ 1—2014 装配式混凝土结构技术规程［S］．北京：中国建筑工业出版社，2014．

［11］ Herrera F, Martinez L. A 2-tuple fuzzy linguistic representation model for computing with words［J］. IEE Transactions on Fuzzy Systems, 2000, 8(6)：746-752.

［12］ Fontela E, Gabus A. The DEMATEL observer, DEMATEL 1976 report［R］. Switzerland Geneva：Battelle Geneva Research Centre, 1976.

［13］ 索玮岚，樊治平，冯博．基于多因素关联分析的 IT 服务外包商选择方法［J］．工业工程与管理，2012，6(17)：1-6．

［14］ 李可柏，齐宝库，王欢．基于 DEMATEL 的装配式建筑发展制约因素分析［J］．住宅产业，2013，49-51．

［15］ 高沛然，卢新元．基于区间数的拓展 DEMATEL 方法及其应用研究［J］．运筹与管理，2014，23(1)：44-50．

装配式住宅的预制构件物流供应商的选择与优化

潘永飞　潘雨红

（重庆交通大学管理学院）

摘要：近些年，针对多个领域物流供应商选择的研究已经比较成熟，而针对装配式住宅预制构件的物流供应商的研究却很少。由于住宅预制构件所存在的特殊性，导致其物流供应商的选择具有独特性。本文基于数据包络分析法构建物流供应商的绩效评价模型，并以我国 10 家物流上市公司近年来的数据为样本进行实证研究，为相关决策部门提供参考。

关键词：住宅预制构件，数据包络分析法，物流供应商

1　引言

在 2014 年的国务院工作报告中，李克强总理多处提到了要推进住宅产业化。政协主席俞正声同志也专门召开会议讨论住宅的产业化问题，并指出住宅产业化非做不可，而且必须大力推进。随着我国住宅产业化政策的不断推广，各地政府也纷纷出台政策，鼓励和引导房地产企业建设装配式住宅。例如沈阳市建委颁布了《关于推动沈阳市现代建筑产业化工程建设的通知》（沈建发［2013］68 号），规定 2013 年起沈阳二环区域内、建筑面积 5 万 m² 以上的新开发建设的项目，必须采用装配式建筑技术开发建设，项目装配化率需达到 20％ 以上等[1]。装配式住宅是住宅产业化的重要标志，是以工业化的生产方式成批量地生产各种住宅构配件、部品，在施工现场装配而成的住宅建筑。工业化的生产方式极大地提高了企业生产的灵活性，也得到了广泛应用，但是生产方式的改变同时也对物流企业供应商提出了更为严格的要求。此外，特别是大型预制构件，如内、外墙板（PC板）、叠合楼板、阳台板、楼梯板等，运输过程中车辆的选择、沿线桥涵的限高、部品大小件的搭配[2]以及预制构件供应的及时性对产业化中物流供应商的选择都是一个严峻的考验。因此，科学地选择与优化预制构件物流供应商成为顺利推进住宅产业化进程的重要保障之一。

2　国内外研究现状

目前，国内外对装配式住宅预制构件的研究主要集中在构件的应用前景、成本分析、经济规模效应和构件供应商的选择等方面，对于装配式住宅中预制构件物流供应商选择与优化的研究还比较少。对于其他行业而言，物流供应商选择模型研究比较成熟。王道平、王旭等[3]采用数据包络法选取合理的评价指标，对钢铁企业的物流供应商进行有效选择，并提出了 DEA/AHP 模型的改进方法进一步优选供应商；史成东、陈菊红等[4]把交叉模型的评价结果设定为样本的期望值，将 BP 神经网络和交叉评价模型有机结合起来，构建了交通运输物流企业的供应商选择模型；刘天宇、王美强[5]结合 B2C 企业的现状，综合运用数据包络分析法（DEA）和德尔菲法（Delphi）对第三方物流供应商进行评价，具有很大的实用性和可操作性；Jackson J. D.、Boyd J. W.[6]通过 LRA（Logistic Regression Analysis）对影响物流供应商综合能力的多种因素进行分析，简单明了、易于操作；Chou S. Y.、Chang Y. H.[7]用模糊 SMART 方法表征专家意见，采取模糊理论来评价和选择物流供应商，在表达专家意见方面表现出一定优势。

基于不同领域物流供应商选择的研究成果，对于装配式住宅预制构件运输过程中供应商的选择研究具有一定的参考价值。但是预制构件因其尺寸较大，构件形状不一，对外观的完整性，如表面平整、无变形、无断裂、无缺边掉角等要求较高的特殊性[8]，加大了运输过程中预制构件管理的难

度，这正是有别于其他领域物流供应商选择研究的原因之一。因此做好预制构件物流供应商的选择与优化研究是经济新常态下推进我国住宅产业化快速发展的一个重要环节。现以住宅预制构件物流供应商为研究对象，选择合理的指标和模型进行评价，并提出相关的建议。

3 供应商评价指标体系的构建以及数据的搜集

3.1 指标的选取

目前国内外对装配式住宅中预制构件物流供应商选择优化的研究相对比较少，能够借鉴的经验并不多，但是装配式住宅中预制构件的采购、运输、仓储等管理方式兼具了建筑业和物流业的特点[9]。于是，本文对相关的参考文献[10~14]以及上市物流公司的财务报表进行了汇总，考虑可获得的评价信息及行业特点，从中筛选出装配式住宅预制构件物流供应商的选择指标体系，将财务指标分为成本型指标和效益型指标，再结合 DEA 方法的要求，将成本型指标作为 DEA 投入指标，包括销售费用、管理费用、研发支出和财务费用，效益型指标作为 DEA 产出指标，包括营业收入、基本每股收益、加权平均净资产收益率。

3.2 数据的收集及预处理

根据 2013 我国各大上市物流企业年报数据和 DEA 评价模型的特点，首先对上市物流企业的评价指标数据进行预处理，以消除峰值数据的影响。方式如下[14]：销售费用除以 10^3，管理费用除以 10^4，研发与支出除以 10^4，财务费用除以 10^3，营业收入除以 10^5。统计数据如下：

10 家上市物流公司重要投入产出指标预处理参数　　　　　表 1

物流公司	A	B	C	D	E	F	G	H	I	J
决策单元	DMU1	DMU2	DMU3	DMU4	DMU5	DMU6	DMU7	DMU8	DMU9	DMU10
销售费用	0.00	2.45	16.45	0.80	1.12	5.15	3.69	0.50	1.49	0.59
管理费用	13.13	0.73	2.87	1.48	0.97	5.58	1.79	2.27	1.07	21.51
研发支出	7.67	0.40	1.07	0.99	0.00	9.41	0.22	0.00	0.00	3.04
财务费用	1.86	0.06	0.77	0.96	0.73	0.44	12.97	0.62	1.88	8.57
营业收入	16.63	4.28	27.84	5.65	1.29	7.86	3.05	2.45	1.84	28.16
基本每股收益	0.64	0.32	0.48	0.03	0.12	0.32	0.18	0.62	0.10	0.23
加权平均资产收益率	8.67	10.01	6.12	2.21	4.01	9.80	5.73	11.36	3.73	10.76

4 模型的建立

数据包络分析方法（Data Envelopment Analysis），简称 DEA 是 1978 年由 A. Charnes, W. W. Cooper 及 E. Rhodes 提出的[15]。它是根据多指标投入和多指标产出对相同类型的单位（部门）进行相对有效性或效益评价的一种新的系统分析方法。在 DEA 方法中，有 N 家上市物流公司，即有 N 个决策单元（DMU），每个决策单元都有 m 种类型的"输入"以及 s 种类型的"输出"。其中 x_j 为第 j 个决策单元的投入量，y_j 是第 j 个决策单元的产出量，s^+、s^- 分别为投入和产出的松弛变量和剩余变量，通过对偶模型进一步引入松弛变量 s^+ 和剩余变量 s^-，得到如下模型：

$$\begin{cases} \min \theta \\ s.t. \sum_{j=1}^{n} \lambda_j x_j + s^- = \theta x_0 \\ \sum_{j=1}^{n} \lambda_j y_j - s^+ = y_0 \\ \lambda_j \geqslant o, j = 1,2,\ldots,n \\ \theta \text{ 无约束} \\ s^+ \geqslant 0, s^- \geqslant 0 \end{cases} \qquad (1)$$

设最优解为 λ^*，s^{*+}，s^{*-}，θ^*，则有如下结论：

若 $\theta^* = 1$，且 $s^{*-} = 0$，$s^{*+} = 0$。此时决策单元 j_0 为 DEA 有效。决策单元 j_0 的生产活动同时为技术有效和规模有效。

若 $\theta^* = 1$，此时决策单元 j_0 为弱 DEA 有效。

若 $\theta^* < 1$，此时决策单元 j_0 不是 DEA 有效。

5 实证分析

本文选取了 10 家上市物流企业作为研究对象，涉及的数据全部来自上市公司 2013 年的年报数据。运用 MATLAB 工具，运算结果如下：

```
lambda =

    1.0000    0.0000    0.0000    0.0000    0.0000    0.1124    0.0000    0.0000    0.0000    0.0000
    0.0000    1.0000    0.0000    0.0000    0.0000    1.3998    0.1672    0.0000    0.0000    0.0000
    0.0000    0.0000    1.0000    0.0000    0.0000    0.0000    0.0550    0.0000    0.0000    0.0000
    0.0000    0.0000    0.0000    1.0000    0.0000    0.0000    0.0000    0.0000    0.0000    0.0000
    0.0000    0.0000    0.0000    0.0000    1.0000    0.0000    0.0000    0.0000    0.0000    0.0000
    0.0000    0.0000    0.0000    0.0000    0.0000    0.0000    0.0000    0.0000    0.0000    0.0000
    0.0000    0.0000    0.0000    0.0000    0.0000    0.0000    0.3274    1.0000    0.0000    0.0000
    0.0000    0.0000    0.0000    0.0000    0.0000    0.0000    0.0000    0.0000    1.0000    0.0000
    0.0000    0.0000    0.0000    0.0000    0.0000    0.0000    0.0000    0.0000    0.0000    1.0000


s_minus =

    0.0000    0.0000    0.0000    0.0000    0.0000    0.0000    0.6307    0.0000    0.0000    0.0000
    0.0000    0.0000    0.0000    0.0000    0.0000    1.2185    0.0000    0.0000    0.0000    0.0000
    0.0000    0.0000    0.0000    0.0000    0.0000    4.8445    0.0000    0.0000    0.0000    0.0000
    0.0000    0.0000    0.0000    0.0000    0.0000    0.0000    7.1590    0.0000    0.0000    0.0000

s_plus =

    0.0000    0.0000    0.0000    0.0000    0.0000    0.0000    0.0000    0.0000    0.0000    0.0000
    0.0000    0.0000    0.0000    0.0000    0.0000    0.1999    0.1029    0.0000    0.0000    0.0000
    0.0000    0.0000    0.0000    0.0000    0.0000    5.1864    0.0000    0.0000    0.0000    0.0000


theta =

    1.0000    1.0000    1.0000    1.0000    1.0000    0.6659    0.5717    1.0000    1.0000    1.0000
```

图 1　基于 DEA 模型 MATLAB 运行结果

5.1 DEA 有效结果分析

由以上 MATLAB 分析的结果可以看出，$\theta^* = 1$，且 $s^{*-} = 0$，$s^{*+} = 0$，决策单元 1、2、3、4、5、8、9 和 10 是 DEA 有效的，这说明这 8 家物流上市公司在 2013 年的生产要素已经达到最佳组合，并取得了最佳的产出效果。

5.2 非 DEA 有效的投影分析

决策单元 6 和 7 为非 DEA 有效，说明 F 和 G 上市物流公司投入的资源没有得到充分利用，产出没有达到最优。

5.3 非 DEA 有效的调整及优化

对 F 和 G 两家上市物流公司的非 DEA 有效数据进行分析优化[15]。指标改进值汇总：

两个决策单元指标改进值汇总 表 2

一	成本型指标				效益型指标		
决策单元	销售费用	管理费用	研发支出	财务费用	营业收入	基本每股收益	加权平均净资产收益率
DMU6	3.43	2.49	1.42	0.29	7.86	0.52	14.99
DMU7	2.11	1.02	0.13	0.26	3.05	0.28	5.73

通过计算可知，若使决策单元 6 DEA 有效，则需降低销售费用，管理费用也要缩减为 2.49，研发支出也要有大幅度的降低，财务费用应减少到 0.29，对于输出变量，营业收入和加权平均净资产收益率不用作调整，基本每股收益需要提高，从而使 F 物流公司在成本（投入）和收益（产出）上资源能够得到最大的利用。对于决策单元 7 即 G 物流公司，其调整方法类似，不作赘述。

6 结论及建议

影响预制构件物流供应商选择的因素比较多，本文以 DEA 为基础，针对装配式住宅建立预制构件物流供应商选择指标体系，对投入产出指标进行评价，对非 DEA 有效物流供应商进行优化调整，从而实现物流上市公司的经营绩效评价。基于以上结论，提出相关建议。

第一，对于开发商而言，从上市物流公司的指标数据出发，充分考虑企业的经济运营状况，分析该公司对投入和产出资源的优化配置率，并对物流企业的信誉进行评估，同时兼顾物流公司所处的地理位置和服务点数量，从而选择合适的合作伙伴，形成一定程度的利益联合体，实现装配式住宅中产业链的整合。

第二，对于生产商而言，合适优质的物流供应商可以从源头上控制装配式住宅中的物资输入，保证预制构件的质量，使生产商为自己的产品赢得信誉，从而扩大收入来源。鉴于此，对于物流供应商的选择要考虑企业的管理模式、技术措施、客户满意度等因素，在彼此信任的基础上，建立长久的质量保证渠道，才能确保预制构件在装配式住宅中每一个环节得到合理的利用，从而推动住宅产业化的进程。

第三，对于施工方而言，正确地选择物流供应商可以保障预制构件及时、快速地到达目的地。因此在对上市物流企业的成本型和效益型指标深入研究的过程中，分析企业是否在选择运输工具以及堆放预制构件时，考虑产品的加固和保护，从而保证预制构件的完整性。它关系到工程质量、安全和进度，是装配式住宅推广进程中的一个决定性因素，本质上影响着施工方成本利益。

第四，对于上市物流企业而言，应当加强管理控制，提高企业的运作效率，需要不断地改进优化企业的经营方式和管理水平，在销售、管理、研发、财务等投入因素上总结经验，继续发挥优势，同时在收入、每股收益、净资产收益等产出因素上取得更大的进步，把握市场机遇，提高企业的核心竞争力。

致谢

在此论文完成之际，由衷地感谢导师对本人论文研究方向的悉心指导和文章内容的精心修改，同时也感谢培养我长大的父母和文章撰写过程中给过自己帮助的同学、朋友！

Research on Selection and Optimization of Logistics Supplier of Prefabricated Housing Components

Pan Yongfei，Pan Yuhong

(School of Management ，Chongqing Jiaotong University，Chongqing)

Abstract：In recent years，a variety of fields of manufacturing industry has been relatively mature，but the study of the logistics supplier of prefabricated housing components is very little. The choice of the logistics supplier is unique because of the particularity of existing residential prefabricated. Based on Data Envelopment Analysis，a logistics supplier performance evaluation model is presented in this paper. And with 10 listed logistics company's data as samples for empirical research in our country provides a reference for relevant decision-making departments.

Key words：Prefabricated housing components，Data envelopment analysis，Logistics supplier

参考文献：

［1］ http：//precast. com. cn/index. php/news _ detail-id-1177. html.

［2］ Venselaar M，Gruis V，Fenne V. Implementing supply chain partnering in the construction industry：Work floor experiences within a Dutch housing association［J］. Journal of purchasing and Supply Management，2015，(3)：1-8.

［3］ 王道平，王煦，王燕. 基于数据包络法的钢铁企业供应商选择模型研究［J］. 现代管理科学，2009(2).

［4］ 史成东，陈菊红，张雅琪. 基于 BP 神经网络和 DEA 的物流供应商选择［J］. 工业工程，2010，08(4)：112-116.

［5］ 刘天宇，王美强. 基于 DEA-Delphi 方法的 B2C 企业对第三方物流供应商的评价与选择［J］. 贵州大学学报(自然科学版)，2013，08(4).

［6］ Jackson J D，Boyd J W. A statistical approach to modeling the behavior of bond rates［J］. The Joumal of Behavioral Economics. 1988，17(3)：173-193.

［7］ Chou S Y，Chang Y H. A decision support system for supplier selection based on a strategy-aligned fuzzy SMART approach［J］. Expert systems with applications，2008，34(4)：2241-2253.

［8］ 李远成. 浅谈混凝土预制构件的施工［J］. 黑龙江交通科技，2011，11.

［9］ 郑晓云，贾玲. 住宅产业化进程中建筑部品供应商的选择研究［J］. 华东经济管理，2013(10).

［10］ Barros，C. P.，P. U. C. Dieke. Performance Evaluation of Italian Airports with Data Envelopment Analysis［J］. Journal of Air Transport Management，2007，13(4)：184-191.

［11］ Lam，S. W.，J. M. W. Low，etal. Operational Efficiencies across Asia Pacific Airports［J］. Transportation Research Part E，2009，45(4)：654-665.

［12］ 邓学平，王旭，Ada Suk Fung Ng. 我国物流企业全要素生产效率分析［J］. 系统工程，2008，26(6)：1-7.

［13］ 李友东，马占新. 改进的 DEA 模型及其在上市物流企业中的应用［J］. 北京交通大学学报，

2012，04.

[14] 周婷婷，刘名武，张旭. 我国上市物流企业绩效评价实证分析[J]. 铁道运输与经济，2014，(8)：10-14.

[15] CharnesA，CooperWW，Rhods E. Measuring the efficiency of decision making units[J]. European Journal of Operational Research，1978(2)：429-444.

The Role of Government and Foreign Investment in Hong Kong Real Estate Market After Financial Crisis

Li Yiman Rita

(Sustainable Real Estate Research Center / Department of Economics and Finance, Hong Kong Shue Yan University)

Abstract: The subprime crisis in the US spilled over worldwide. Its effect on Hong Kong property market, however, was not serious. The performance of Hong Kong housing market not only resisted the shock over from the crisis, but also experienced an upward trend after the crisis. This paper examines the reason behind via government policies analysis and FDI.

Keywords: Financial crisis, Government policies, FDI, Hong Kong

1 Introduction

The financial turmoil of the US and EU reduce investors' confidence in financial market. As the relationship between stock return, stock prices and rental rates are close [2], demand for property dropped during subprime crisis. Only 11046 units were bought in the first hand market (reduction by 45%) as compared with that in 2007. The new property supply shrank to about 10, 000 which was the lowest over the past 30 years [4]. Sometimes when the housing market collapses, the bank fastened the pace of decline, causing a drop in asset values [7]. Nevertheless, mortgage lenders loosened the criteria for borrowing after the crisis. Value of new mortgages rose by 34. 6% to HK $ 11. 4 billion in February 2009 as compared to HK $ 8. 5 billion in November 2008 [4]. The government avoided history repeats by regulations reforms[8].

2 Housing Market in Hong Kong (china) in Recent Years

The sales, purchases and consideration shared similar trend from 2000 in the first half of 2010. The domestic transaction reached the trough in February 2003, number of sale and purchase was 3,649and monthly consideration was HK $ 6405 million. At the-end of 2003, number of domestic transaction dropped from 72974 in 2002 to 71,576 in 2003, consideration dropped from HK $ 154252 million to HK $ 153,578 million. By the end of 2004, sale and purchase reached HK $ 276735 million. Domestic transaction stopped increasing until the second quarter in 2005. The sales and purchases, consideration declined and reached the trough in December 2005. It rose slowly from the trough in 2006. Yet, the rate of increase rose since the third quarter in 2007 to the peak in November 2007 during global financial crisis. The transaction was 15,759 with monthly consideration of HK $ 70116 million but domestic transaction reached the trough in November 2008. Monthly number of sale and purchase was 3264 with consideration of HK $ 9007 million. Domestic transaction and consideration declined from 123575 and HK $ 434033 million in 2007 to 95931 and HK $ 343827 million in 2008 and recovered in 2009. Number of sales and purchases was 115,092 with consideration of HK $ 425840 million. Transaction and consideration climbed in the first half of 2010 with 14,699 transactions.

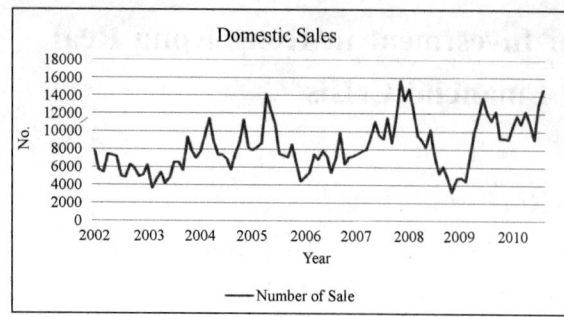

Figure 1　Domestic sales in Hong Kong[6]

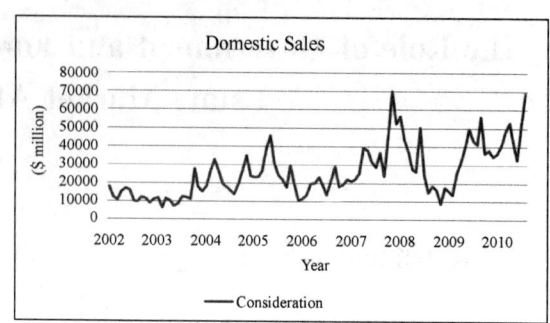

Figure 2　Domestic sales consideration [6]

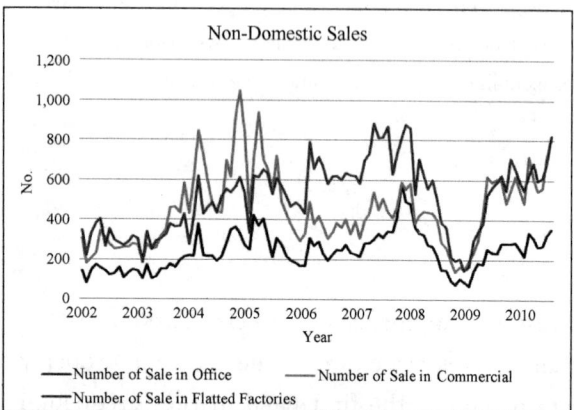

Figure 3　Number of non-domestic sales [6]

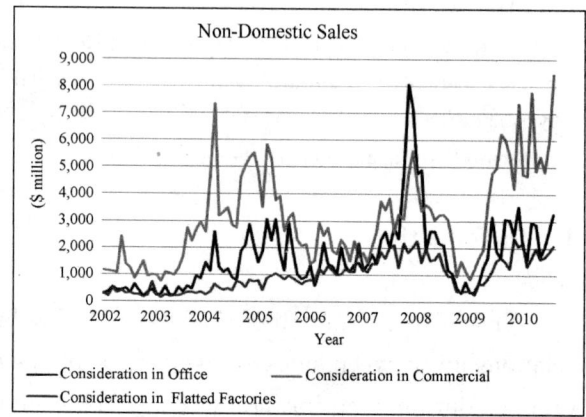

Figure 4　Consideration of non-domestic sales [6]

In 2002, factories had the highest sales of 3756 transactions, while office had the lowest sales with 1639 transactions. Commercial consideration was the highest among the three categories. Though factories had the highest sales and office had the lowest, consideration was about HK $4963 million and $4028 million respectively. In 2004, commercial grew from 4142 transactions to 7833, which was faster than office and factories. Office and commercial grew rapidly while factories grew gradually in 2004. They experienced a sharp cut in sales in 2005. Commercial sector had a dramatic decrease in sales from 7143 in 2004 – 4402. However, factories reached its peak at 9072 transactions in 2007. Besides, commercial and factories slumped in 2008 during crisis. Factories' sales declined significantly and recovered in 2009 – 2010.

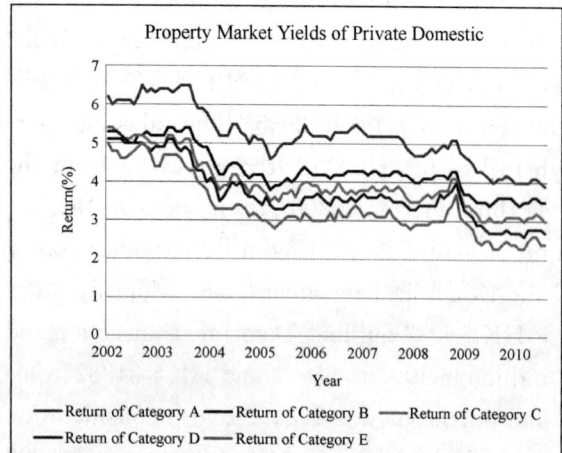

Figure 5　Private domestic market yield [6]

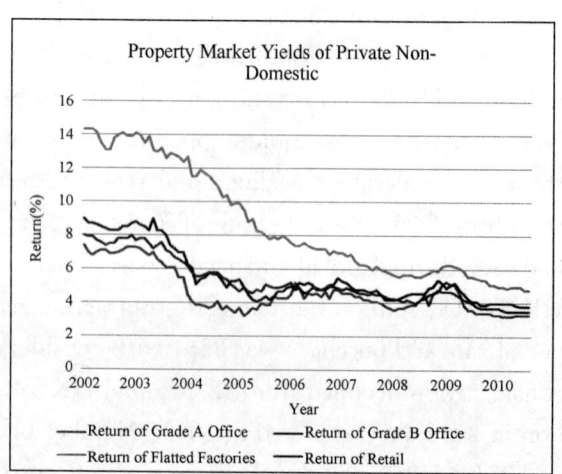

Figure 6　Non-domestic market yield [6]

The return of all domestic units shared similar trend. After 2008, the returns decreased rapidly till 2010. Grade A had the best performance in return at around 6 to 6.5%. In 2003, it dropped from 6.5% and stopped at 5% in 2005, kept rising in 2005 – 2008. In Jan uary 2007, the return was 5.3%. It kept decreasing and stopped at 3.9% in August 2010. In 2002 – 2003, the return of grade B was around 5%. In 2003, it dropped from 5% and stopped at 3.8% in 2005, kept rising in 2005 – 2008. In January 2007, the return was 4.3%. It dropped to 4% in Jan 2008. It rose to 4.3% in October 2008. It then decreased to 3.5% in August 2010. The return of grade C decreased in 2002 – 2010. In 2002 – 2008, it dropped from 5.4% and stopped at 3.5% in 2008. In January 2007, the return was 3.8%. It dropped to 3.5% in December 2007. It rose to 4.1% in October 2008. It kept decrease and stopped at 3% in August 2010. The return of grade D decreased in 2002 – 2010. In 2002 – 2008, it dropped from 5.3% to 3.3% in 2008. In January 2007, the return was 3.7%. It dropped to 3.3% in December 2007. It rose to 4% in November 2008. It kept decrease and stopped at 2.7% in August 2010. Grade E had the smallest return among all categories. The difference between grade A and E was almost 1%. The return of Grade E decreased 2002 – 2010. In 2002 – 2008, it dropped from 4.8% and to 2.9% in 2008. In January 2007, the return was 3.1%. It dropped to 2.8% in December 2007. It rose to 3.7% in November 2008. It kept decrease to 2.4% in August 2010 [6]. The return of factories decreased between 2002 and 2010. It dropped from 14.3% in 2002 to 5.8% in 2008. In January 2007, the return was 7%. It dropped to 5.6% in February 2008. It rose to 6.3% in February 2009. After that, it kept decrease and stopped at 4.8% in August 2010. The returns of the Grade A office, Grade B office and retail had similar trend. The returns dropped in 2002 – 2010. The returns dropped in the middle of 2003, stopped in 2005 and rose till 2009. After 2009, the returns decreased till 2010. Between 2002 and 2003, the return of grade A office was around 7%. In 2003, it dropped from 6.8% and stopped at 3.9% in 2005. It kept rising between 2005 and 2009. In January 2007, the return was 7%. It dropped to 5.6% in February 2008. It rose to 6.3% in February 2009. It kept decreased to 4.8% in August 2010. Between 2002 and 2003, the return of Grade B office was around 9%. In 2003, it dropped from 8.3% and stopped at 4.1% in 2005. It rose to 5.4% in November 2008 but decreased to 3.8% in August 2010. The global financial crisis caused significant slumps in domestic and non-domestic market. The sales volume and considerations declined during crisis. Nevertheless, recovery pace was fast.

3　HKSAR housing Policies, FDI and property market

In March 1999, the Mortgage Insurance Program was established to help home buyer to pay for lower down payments. It provided mortgage insurance to banks and banks can lend mortgage over 70% of the property prices. Some banks even lent mortgage up to 90% of the property prices. Housing price rose. In August 2010, the non-residential mortgage reduced to 60%. The property price over HK $ 6.8 million was not covered under the Mortgage Insurance Program [10]. The cost of home purchase rose and the demand of housing dropped. The price of presale is lowered to attract house purchase and developer benefits from earlier cash flow. In August 2010, home buyer could not resell the property before the completion of the Formal Sale and Purchase Agreement. Or else they would be forfeited 10% of property prices [1]. Transaction volume and price of the presale decreased. Buyers and sellers have to pay stamp duty according to the conveyance on sale, the agreement for sale of residential property and lease [9]. The HKSAR reduced the stamp duty for housing price below HK＄3 million after 28 February 2007，. e. g. before 28 February 2007，buying a house which was HK＄ million the seller and the buyer was required to pay HK＄2 million×0. 75％ ＝ HK＄15，000. After 28 February 2007，they need to pay HK＄100. The cost of buying house reduced. Housing demand rose. But the supply of houses could not follow the demand because of the restricted land supply. The excess demand caused the house price increase. The government raised the stamp duty of the housing prices over HK＄20 million after 1 st April 2010，e. g. buying a house of HK＄21 million，the seller and buyer shall pay HK＄21 million×3. 75％ ＝ HK＄0. 79 million as stamp duty before 1 st April 2010. After 1 st April 2010，they pay HK＄0. 75 million ＋（＄（21－ 20）million×10％）＝ HK＄0. 85 million. The cost of buying house rose，reduced the home purchase incentive，housing demand decreased and housing price decreased. Besides，the HKSAR used land-use planning system to impose constraints on land supply and development such as Town Planning and Buildings legislation to land lease conditions. It controls land supply by land auction and tender，lease modifications and exchange with affect housing price and market yield[3]. In land sale application，land is Listed in Sale by Application. Developers apply for land sale under the Land Sale by Application System. If it is approved，there will be tender. The developer submits application and the Lands Department offers to the highest bidder [11].

FDI mainly came from investment holding，real estate and business sector. Though the financial crisis lowered global investment by 40％，Hong Kong remains the world's fourth largest FDI recipient [5].

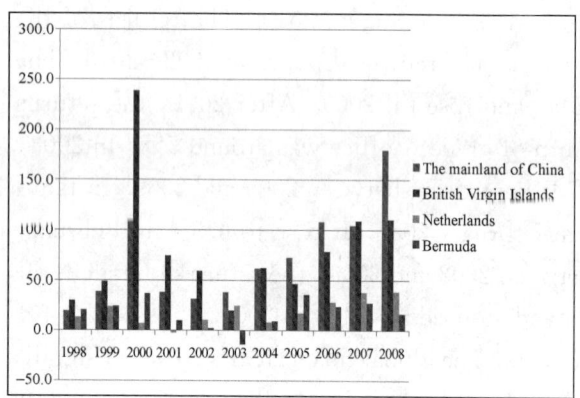

Figure 7　Major countries invests in HK [12]　　　　Figure 8　Major sectors received FDI in HK[12]

The information of the stamp duty from 01 April 1999 to now[9]　　　　　**Table 1**

From 1 April 1999 to 10：59：59a. m. on 28 February 2007			From 11 a. m. on 28 February 2007 to 31 March 2010			From 1 April 2010		
Amount or value of consideration			Amount or value of consideration			Amount or value of consideration		
Exceeds (million HK＄)	Does not exceed (million HK＄)	Rate	Exceeds (million HK＄)	Does not exceed (million HK＄)	Rate	Exceeds (million HK＄)	Does not exceed (million HK＄)	Rate
	1	＄100		2	＄100		2	＄100
1	1. 08	＄100＋10％ of excess over ＄1m	2	2. 352	＄100＋10％ of excess over ＄2m	2	2. 352	＄100＋10％ of excess over ＄2m

continued

From 1 April 1999 to 10: 59: 59a. m. on 28 February 2007			From 11 a. m. on 28 February 2007 to 31 March 2010			From 1 April 2010		
Amount or value of consideration			Amount or value of consideration			Amount or value of consideration		
Exceeds (million HK $)	Does not exceed (million HK $)	Rate	Exceeds (million HK $)	Does not exceed (million HK $)	Rate	Exceeds (million HK $)	Does not exceed (million HK $)	Rate
1.08	2	0.75%	2.352	3	1.5%	2.351	3	1.5%
2	2.176	$15,000+10% of excess over $2m	3	3.29	$45,000+10% of excess over $3m	3	3.29	$45,000+ 10% of excess over $3m
2.176	3	1.5%	3.29	4	2.25%	3.29	4	2.25%
3	3.29	$45,000+10% of excess over $3m	4	4.429	$90,000+10% of excess over $4m	4	4.429	$90,000+ 10% of excess over $4m
3.29	4	2.25%	4.429	6	3.00%	4.429	6	3.00%
4	4.428	$90,000+10% of excess over $4m	6	6.72	$180,000+10% of excess over $6,000,000	6	6.72	$180,000+10% of excess over $6m
4.429	6	3.00%	6.72		3.75%	6.72	20	3.75%
6	$6,720,000	$180,000+10% of excess over $6m				20	21.739	$750,000+10% of excess over $20m
6.72		3.75%				21.739		4.25%

FDI from major investor country 2004 - 2008 [13]   **Table 2**

Country	FDI inflow (HK $ billion)					% of investments
	2004	2005	2006	2007	2008	2008
The mainland of China	62.0	72.9	108.7	104.2	179.7	38.7%
British Virgin Islands	62.7	47.0	78.8	109.3	110.5	23.8%
Netherlands	8.8	17.0	28.1	38.0	38.6	8.3%
Bermuda	8.9	36.0	23.8	27.7	16.9	3.6%
United States of America	48.4	−29.7	51.3	35.8	14.1	3.0%
Japan	10.9	14.1	18.0	14.3	8.3	1.8%
United Kingdom	18.2	13.7	15.4	23.0	13.0	2.8%
Cayman Islands	6.5	12.0	18.4	10.9	3.8	0.8%
Singapore	3.2	11.0	8.1	16.4	9.4	2.0%
Cook Islands	*	2.3	0.9	0.8	7.5	1.6%
Other countries	35.4	65.3	−1.5	43.6	62.5	13.5%
All countries	265.1	261.5	350.0	423.9	464.3	100.0%

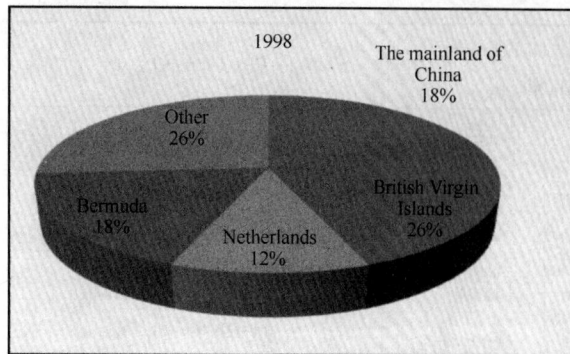
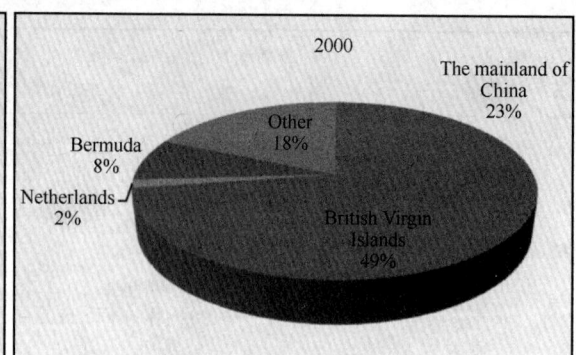
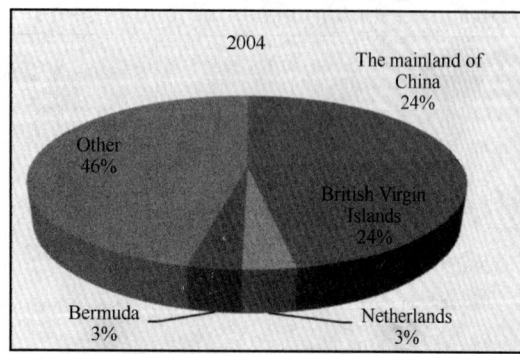
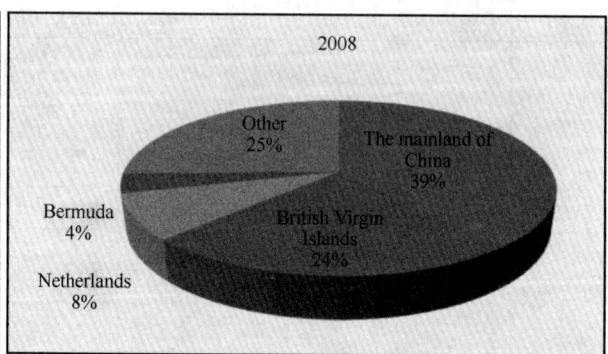

Figure 9   Major countries invests in Hong Kong[12]

Investment inflow to different economic activities in HK [12]   **Table 3**

Economic Activity	DI inflow during the year in HK $ billion					% of investments
	2004	2005	2006	2007	2008	2008
Investment，real estate and business services	105. 1	113. 9	145. 1	204. 7	232. 4	50. 1%
Wholesale，retail and import/export trades	49. 5	39. 7	73. 0	70. 8	70. 1	15. 1%
Banks and deposit-taking companies	34. 6	44. 5	45. 9	72. 3	81. 1	17. 5%
Financial institutions other than banks and deposit-taking companies	38. 6	14. 4	34. 9	28. 8	9. 4	2. 0%
Transport and related services	10. 7	13. 1	19. 8	17. 5	16. 2	3. 5%
Insurance	6. 5	9. 8	7. 3	1. 7	25. 2	5. 4%
Manufacturing	13. 6	7. 4	11. 0	6. 7	19. 1	4. 1%
Construction	−0. 6	1. 6	5. 0	10. 1	4. 9	1. 1%
Communications	2. 6	7. 5	2. 6	0. 5	−0. 5	−0. 1%
Restaurants and hotels	1. 4	0. 3	1. 5	2. 4	4. 5	1. 0%
Other activities	3. 3	9. 4	3. 9	8. 4	1. 8	0. 4%
All economic activities	265. 1	261. 5	350. 0	423. 9	464. 3	100. 0%

政府和外国投资在金融危机后香港房地产市场中扮演的角色

李绮雯

（可持续房地产研究中心/香港树仁大学经济与金融系）

摘要：美国次贷危机波及全球。但是它在香港房地产市场的影响并不严重。香港住房市场在经历了危机之后有上升趋势。本文探讨政府政策和外商直接投资对房地产的正面影响。

关键词：金融危机的影响，政府政策，外国直接投资，香港

References：

[1] Community Legal Information Centre. Sale and purchase of property under construction [OL]，2015. http：//www. hkclic. org/en/topics/saleAndPurchaseOfProperty/sale _ and _ purchase _ of _ property _ under _ construction/index. shtml.

[2] Daniel，C. Q. ，Sheridan，T. ，Commercial Estate Price and Stock Market Returns：An International Analysis[J]. Financial Analysts Journal，1997，53(3)：21.

[3] Eddie，C. M. Hui. ，Vivian，S. M. Ho. . Relationship between the Land-use Planning System，Land Supply and Housing Prices in Hong Kong[J]. International Journal of Strategic Property，2003.

[4] Irina，F. ，Joanne，Y. . Hong Kong's Residential Property：Nearing the Trough？[OL]. Hang Seng Bank，2009. http：//www. hangseng. com/ermt/eng/fxmv/pdf/ecof _ e _ 20090402. pdf.

[5] Li. T. ，Hong Kong favorite 4th for FDI[J/OL]. China Daily，2010. http：//www. china-daily. com. cn/hkedition/2010—07/24/content _ 11043903. htm.

[6] Rating and Valuation Department，2015. http：//www. rvd. gov. hk/en.

[7] Richard，J. H. ，Susan，W. . Real Estate Booms and Banking Busts：An International Perspective[J]. Center for Financial Institutions Working Papers，1999，99 - 27 (9)：75.

[8] Ruijue，P. ，William，C. W. . Effects of Restrictive Land Supply on Housing in Hong Kong：An Econometric Analysis. Journal of Housing Research，1994，5(2)：288.

[9] The Government of the Hong Kong Special Administrative Region，2015. http：//www. gov. hk.

[10] The Hong Kong Mortgage Corporation Limited. Mortgage Insurance Programme[OL]，2010. http：//www. hkmc. com. hk/eng/pcrm/ourbusiness/mip. html.

[11] The Lands Department，2010. http：//www. landsd. gov. hk/en/landsale.

[12] The Census and Statistics Department，2010. http：//www. censtatd. gov. hk/home. html.

The author would like to thank all the contribution of FIN433 students in this paper.